TWO INDUSTRY LEADERS. ONE SUPERIOR TEACHING TOOL. INFINITE LEARNING POSSIBILITIES.

Whether you want to supplement your classroom with customizable online content or deliver your class at a distance, Harcourt accommodates all your distance learning needs. Harcourt, a leader in providing lifelong learning solutions—in partnership with WebCT, a leading platform in electronic learning—brings you and your students the industry's most robust online courses.

WebCT facilitates the creation of sophisticated Web-based educational environments. It provides a set of course design tools to help you manage course content, a set of communication tools to facilitate online classroom collaboration, and a set of administrative tools for tracking and managing your students' progress.

Via the WebCT platform, Harcourt offers the following program choices:

1. **WebCT Testing Service**. If testing is all you want, we can upload the computerized test bank into a course that has no publisher content. If you like, we will even host it for you on our server.

2. **Free access to a blank WebCT template.** With a qualified adoption, Harcourt will host courses (without any Harcourt content) for you to input your original materials and use in your classroom.

3. **Customized course creation.** Harcourt will create an online course from your original content, your school's content, Harcourt's content, or any combination of these. Contact your local Harcourt representative for more details.

Harcourt WebCT Manuals
When you adopt a Harcourt Online Course, your students will receive Harcourt's

Guide to the World Wide Web and WebCT (packaged with the textbook).

(ISBN 0-03-045503-0)

To view a demo of any of our online courses, go to **webct.harcourtcollege.com**.

organizational behavior

organizational behavior

Richard L. Daft
Vanderbilt University
with the assistance of Pat Lane

Raymond A. Noe
The Ohio State University

Harcourt College Publishers

Fort Worth   Philadelphia   San Diego   New York   Orlando   Austin   San Antonio
Toronto   Montreal   London   Sydney   Tokyo

Publisher	Mike Roche
Marketing Strategist	Beverly Dunn
Developmental Editor	Tracy Morse
Project Manager	Angela Williams Urquhart

Cover and chapter opener illustrations © Steve Kropp/SIS. Author photos (p. xix) courtesy of Mitch Karam Studios (Richard L. Daft) and Jo McCulty (Raymond A. Noe)

ISBN: 0-03-031681-2
Library of Congress Catalog Card Number: 00-063427

Address for Domestic Orders
Harcourt College Publishers, 6277 Sea Harbor Drive, Orlando, FL 32887-6777
800-782-4479

Address for International Orders
International Customer Service
Harcourt College Publishers, 6277 Sea Harbor Drive, Orlando, FL 32887-6777
407-345-3800
(fax) 407-345-4060
(e-mail) hbintl@harcourtbrace.com

Address for Editorial Correspondence
Harcourt College Publishers, 301 Commerce Street, Suite 3700, Fort Worth, TX 76102

Web Site Address
http://www.harcourtcollege.com

Harcourt College Publishers will provide complimentary supplements or supplement packages to those adopters qualified under our adoption policy. Please contact your sales representative to learn how you may qualify. If as an adopter or potential user you receive supplements you do not need, please return them to your sales representative or send them to:
Attn: Returns Department, Troy Warehouse, 465 South Lincoln Drive, Troy, MO 63379.

Printed in the United States of America

0 1 2 3 4 5 6 7 8 9   048   9 8 7 6 5 4 3 2 1

Harcourt College Publishers

The **Harcourt** Series in management

To Dorothy, Roxanne, Solange, and Elizabeth
   —R. L. Daft

To Melissa, Tim, and Ray
   —R. A. Noe

preface

Organizations are undergoing unprecedented and revolutionary change. From the speed of decision making, to technological and global competitive pressures, to mergers and acquisitions, to the need to rethink business processes and alliances, organizations are constantly faced with shifting demands. And they must respond effectively, remaining flexible and transforming themselves for the new world of work. *Organizational Behavior* is written with these changes as a central focus—to explain through current, often high-tech examples what students need to know about organizations as they enter employment or continue their work lives. A major goal of this book is not just to explain the fundamental concepts of organizational behavior but to help students apply those concepts to their personal lives and work lives.

Applications and real-world focus

In today's information- and knowledge-based workplace, students need to think for themselves because they will be asked to do so often. In the early planning phase of this book, we sought advice from instructors who teach organizational behavior on what they wanted and needed in a textbook. The feedback was a resounding call for a book that took students beyond rote memorization to apply text concepts to their daily lives and the world around them. Instructors wanted a text that equipped students to think on their feet, and they also asked for examples that were deep as well as broad ranging. We took their advice to heart and have written a text filled with application exercises and current organization examples.

Application Exercises

Chapters contain a wealth of applications to get students involved with organizational behavior concepts from the start. At the end of each main text section are Apply It exercises—one to two per section. These features ask students to pause and reflect on what they have just learned to see how it applies to their experiences and day-to-day lives. Each chapter also includes a What Would You Do? box that discusses an organization's current experience with a topic related to organizational behavior. After reading background material, students are asked to put themselves in the shoes of a decision maker and propose a solution for the organization, whether in writing or discussion.

Self-Discovery Exercises are quizzes and self-tests that allow students to learn about their preferences or personal style or to gauge what their potential might be. Links to online personality tests are also included for students to explore further. An OB in Your Life exercise asks students to make observations, conduct interviews, or keep a log to track organizational behavior issues in their daily experiences and relationships. Two Web-based features, OB News Flash and Global Diversity Events, direct students to tap into the Internet for online research to see how chapter topics relate to current events. For those with limited Internet access, traditional research methods can also be used.

Each of these application features requires students to look around or within themselves to explore organizational behavior concepts in depth. This multipronged approach to applications helps students see the value of organizational behavior and provides them with a new lens through which to view the world.

Real-World Examples

Organizational Behavior is filled with examples, and they are drawn from a variety of organizational settings and people in the news to pique students' interest and provide the broadest applications. Opening vignettes, What Would You Do? boxes, extended in-text company examples, end-of-chapter Mini-cases, and end-of-part Video Cases and Integrative Cases all discuss current events in organizations and provide insight and quotations from the people who drive them. Here is a small sample of the organizations, people, and problems profiled in *Organizational Behavior*:

- Carly Fiorina of Hewlett-Packard and her strengths as a leader (Chapter 1 opening vignette) and Amazon.com's teamwork focus as it evolves and constantly reinvents itself (the Chapter 1 What Would You Do? box)

- The Massachusetts Institute of Technology's struggles with gender equity (Chapter 4 in-text example)

- How eBay's online community functions as a virtual group (Chapter 7 in-text example)

- Joe Boxer's creative organizational decision-making style (Chapter 10 in-text example)

- Phil Jackson's successful leadership of the Bulls and Lakers basketball teams (Chapter 11 opening vignette)

- Pat Means, publisher of *Turning Point* magazine, and her positive and powerful influence on the African-American population of Los Angeles (Chapter 12 opening vignette)

- The challenges Westinghouse employees face as they trade boredom for stress (Chapter 14 opening vignette)

- Cisco Systems—a "corporation of the future" (Chapter 18 in-text example)

Strengths of author team

As organizations today are finding out, teamwork can bring creativity and new ideas to a solitary task—in our case, authorship. We come from two different but complementary backgrounds ideally suited for organizational behavior. Richard Daft is a respected teacher, researcher, and author in the fields of management and leadership. Raymond Noe is an experienced teacher, researcher, and author in the fields of human resource management and training. Together we have more than 30 years of experience in teaching, researching, writing, and consulting in both larger organizational and smaller individual issues affecting today's businesses—from motivation and teamwork to knowledge workers and virtual organizations.

We both recognize the importance of readers and try to keep them foremost in our minds as we explain theory and applications. Throughout this text we have tried to use an approachable, inviting writing style to put students at ease and help them understand even the most complex concepts. And we both have tried to dig beyond the concepts to explain their significance, then bring them to life with current company examples and individual quotations. We hope that our efforts have succeeded.

Special features

Organizational Behavior contains a range of features to spark student interest and ground the text pedagogically.

- Chapter learning objectives are written in the form of a **Concept and Skill Preview,** which focuses students on both fundamental concepts and applications from the outset.

- **Opening vignettes** profile companies and individuals in today's news to provide a framework for upcoming chapter discussion. Vignettes highlight both successes and problems that organizations have faced to show students how organizations work through their challenges.

- Extended **in-text company examples** from a variety of work settings provide more detailed applications of concepts as the flow of the chapter continues. Typically a few paragraphs in length, these features engage students in the day-to-day events and activities of people and their organizations. These examples provide a focus for and bring immediacy to the chapter concepts. Web addresses for the companies profiled are listed on the text's Website. When you see the symbol ❦, go to the book's Website for the company's Web address.

- Full-color **photos** with their **essay captions** connect students with today's organizations visually and conceptually. Photos range from high-tech settings, to entrepreneurial startups, to traditional bricks-and-mortar businesses so that students can see the astounding variety of organizations today and explore their triumphs and challenges.

- **What Would You Do?** boxes help train students to become effective evaluators and decision makers. These boxes profile an organization's or person's situation and then require students to formulate a solution using text principles.

- **Apply It** exercises at the end of every main text section ask students to pause and apply text concepts to their lives—at work, at college, in volunteer organizations, and as members of groups. One to two questions are included.

- **Key terms and marginal definitions** highlight critical concepts and allow for quick review.

- The **Summary of Key Concepts** at the end of each chapter reviews the major concepts and groups them by main text headings.

- **Key Terms** lists provide page numbers where terms are defined and discussed.

- **Discussion Questions** provide critical thinking questions to involve students with chapter material.
- **Self-Discovery Exercises** help students explore their personal styles or learn about their future potential. Links to online personality tests are also provided for further exploration.
- **OB in Your Life** applications exercises are outside activities that ask students to apply text concepts to their lives. Students observe people, conduct interviews, or maintain logs to see how organizational behavior touches everyday life.
- Two Web-based exercises—**OB News Flash** and **Global Diversity Events**—explore current news from an organizational behavior and a global viewpoint. Students search the Web for late-breaking news on organizational behavior concepts, globalization, or workforce diversity issues to learn about their impact. For those with limited Internet access, exercises can be completed through traditional methods.
- **Minicases** dig deeper into text concepts to help students integrate what they have learned. Minicases highlight an issue, provide background discussion, and then ask students to answer three or four critical thinking questions. Minicases provide good material for class discussion or assignments, providing instructors flexibility in the format of their courses.
- End-of-part **Video Cases** provide written background on a company to accompany the videos. Four critical thinking questions focus students on issues in organizational behavior. The fourth question is related to a company's Website to allow students to check on a company's most current events.
- **Integrative Cases** at the end of each part focus on America Online and its amazing staying power in a volatile high-tech environment. Tracking the progress of this company and its CEO, Steve Case, gives students a flavor of the excitement and uncertainty involved in e-commerce organizations. Four critical thinking questions are provided, the last focused on AOL's Website.

Organization of the text

Organizational Behavior is divided into four parts and moves from a micro to a macro focus. Part 1, "The Scope and Context of Organizational Behavior," provides two chapters that serve to ground the remaining chapters. Chapter 1, "The Scope of Organizational Behavior," begins with a discussion of the importance of personal and interpersonal relationships in becoming an effective member of an organization. It defines organizational behavior, discusses the disciplines that have contributed to organizational behavior theory, and describes the objectives of organizational behavior. It also briefly discusses the roles and challenges of managers in today's organizations. Chapter 2, "Managing Diversity in the United States and Abroad," describes the increasing diversity of the workforce and the benefits organizations gain from diversity. The chapter also explores the different stages of globalization and the problems and challenges employees and organizations face as they open themselves to the global business environment.

Part 2, "Individuals in Organizations," focuses on the issues of individual employees and ways they relate to each other and the workplace. Chapter 3, "Individual Differences," discusses the changing psychological contract and the importance of person-job and person-organization fit. It then details the link between individual personalities, abilities, values, and attitudes and the work environment. The chapter also discusses concepts such as emotional intelligence, creativity, job performance, counterproductive behaviors, and organizational citizenship. Chapter 4, "Perception and Attribution," describes the perception process and how distortion, attribution, bias, and misperception can affect perceptions and ultimately judgments about the workplace.

Chapters 5 and 6 discuss content and process theories of motivation. Chapter 5, "Sources of Motivation," describes the content theories and the ways individual needs for affiliation, achievement, and power can motivate employees. The chapter also discusses intrinsic and extrinsic motivation, the links between job characteristics and design and motivation, and effects of current changes in the workplace on employees' higher order needs. Chapter 6, "Motivation Processes," explains the process theories of motivation and how the concepts of fairness and expectancy can influence behavior. The chapter also describes social learning and self-efficacy and explains how organizations can use reinforcement theory to change or maintain behavior. The chapter closes with a discussion of goal setting, incentives, and employee empowerment.

Part 3, "Interpersonal Processes in Organizations," broadens the focus to the interpersonal level and includes eight chapters. Chapter 7, "The Structure and Behavior of Groups," reviews the types of groups in organizations and discusses the synergy that can result from using groups to accomplish work. The chapter discusses the stages of group development; authority, status, and sources of conflict within groups; and factors that can contribute to or hinder group performance and interaction. Chapter 8, "Teams and Teamwork," describes the costs and benefits of teams, the types of teams found in organizations, and the factors that influence the success of teams, including selection, training, and organizational context. Also included are self-directed and virtual teamwork and the importance of trust and cohesiveness to team effectiveness.

Chapter 9, "Communication in Organizations," describes the components and purposes of communication and the importance of selecting a channel for communication in different situations. The chapter discusses the patterns of communications in organizations and the challenges that new technologies pose for effective communication. Chapter 10, "Decision Making in Organizations," describes the major processes and models of decision making in organizations, optimizing and satisficing, and group decision making and creativity.

"Leadership in Organizations," Chapter 11, discusses the meaning of leadership, strategies for effective leadership and followership, personal traits associated with leadership, and types of leaders and their effectiveness. Of particular note is the discussion of charismatic, visionary, transformational, and servant leadership. Chapter 12, "Power and Politics," discusses the sources of power and dependency in organizations and the ways power is acquired and shared. The chapter describes examples and effects of political behavior, as well as the ethical and unethical uses of power. The subject of Chapter 13 is "Conflict Management and Negotiation." This chapter explains the sources and stages of conflict in organizations and the pros and cons of different reactions to conflict. The chapter contains sections on the importance of conflict stimulation, strategies of conflict resolution, and negotiation strategies.

Part 3 concludes with Chapter 14 on "Stress and Stress Management." It describes the stress response and the benefits and drawbacks of stress. Current stressors in the workplace are described: change, job demands, effects of technology (including information overload and data smog), interpersonal relationships, and work-life conflict. The chapter discusses both physical and psychological consequences of stress and describes measures organizations are taking to help their employees manage stress, such as changing the organizational culture and creating a balance between work and life.

Part 4, "Impact of Organizations on Behavior," caps the organizational discussion by emphasizing the issues of organizational structure and design, job design, organizational culture, and organizational learning and change. Chapter 15, "Fundamentals of Organization Structure and Design," discusses the key elements of organizing—work specialization, chain of command, line and staff positions, and span of management. The chapter describes functional, divisional, and matrix organizations, as well as contemporary horizontal and network approaches to organization design. Also included are discussions of the use of structure to achieve strategic goals, the effects of technology on structure and design, and organic and mechanistic structures. Chapter 16, "Job Design," describes the relationship between job design and reengineering and organizational efforts of job simplification, rotation, enlargement, and enrichment. The chapter compares the job characteristics and social information processing models of job design and discusses the link between the sociotechnical systems model and increased satisfaction and empowerment. The chapter also details current influences on job design: job sharing and flextime, the impact of technology, flexible manufacturing, telecommuting, and alternative workspace design.

Chapter 17 discusses "Organizational Culture." The chapter explores the effects of organizational culture and the positive and negative effects of a strong organizational culture on employees. The chapter also describes the different types of cultures, the symbols and ceremonies associated with culture, and the creation of a high-performance organization. Symbolic leadership, selection and socialization, and cultural values are also discussed. The final chapter, "Organizational Learning and Change," brings the text full circle to describe the effects of today's changing environment on organizations and their employees. The chapter explains resistance to change, models for change, and the organizational development approach to change. The chapter concludes with a discussion of the adaptive learning cycle and ways to build a learning organization.

An end-of-book appendix titled "Methods for Researching Organizational Behavior" provides the basics of the scientific approach to research, research designs, data collection, evaluation of research, and ethical research design.

Superior support package

Daft and Noe's ancillary package is loaded with powerful resources for students and instructors alike. Combining the latest technology with proven teaching tools, the package enables students to put chapter concepts into action and gain valuable insight into real-world practices. In addition, an expansive collection of supplemental teaching materials offers support to instructors—from the novice to the most seasoned professor.

Daft and Noe Home Page

Organizational Behavior has crossed the line to online. Students and professors can tap into countless business and education resources with this leading-edge tool. This easy-to-navigate site contains a wealth of organizational behavior topics. After following the link to each topic, users will find topic-specific publication links, trends and forecasts, data, company profiles, general articles, tools, exercises, and much more. In addition, each topic site links instructors to teaching resources, bibliographies of articles related to text material, ideas on incorporating the Internet into the classroom, and more.

A **Self-Assessment** section makes many popular questionnaires available online to students. These questionnaires enable students to evaluate and learn about their own interests and skills and to receive broad guidance and practical advice on many areas related to organizational behavior.

In addition, the **Reading Room** links users to business journals, daily newspapers, magazines, and publications across the country and around the world.

A **Syllabus Generator** is available to help professors quickly customize a course syllabus.

In addition to these many features that benefit professors and students alike, students will find the following especially useful:

- An **Online Quizzing** section allows students to take multiple quizzes composed of approximately 15 to 20 questions each. Quizzes include true/false and multiple-choice questions covering the content in each chapter.

- A **Careers** section enables students to learn more about careers in organizations and to locate currently posted business job opportunities. Also, many sites include extensive career information and guidance, such as interviewing techniques and resume writing tips.

- A **Time Management** section features advice and guidelines on effectively managing your study, work, and leisure time as a college student, including how to set priorities and avoid procrastinating.

The *Organizational Behavior* Website is a reservoir of organizational behavior information. In fact, it includes so many resources for each chapter that it can be used as the foundation for a distance-learning course. Our interactive site helps students sharpen their surfing skills, while driving home key concepts. The site is located at

http://www.harcourtcollege.com/management

Instructor's Manual

Designed to provide support for instructors new to the course, as well as innovative materials for more experienced professors, the *Instructor's Manual (IM)* includes detailed "Lecture Outlines," annotated learning objectives, answers to chapter discussion questions, and teaching notes. The end-of-chapter exercises and cases offer additional support to instructors.

In addition, video notes are available to help instructors integrate video segments directly with classroom discussion. Support materials include a video outline, references to concepts within the chapter that are discussed in the video, answers to video case discussion questions, and individual and group exercises.

Computerized Instructor's Manual

The *IM* is available to instructors online via the *Organizational Behavior* Website in Windows format. This feature allows instructors to cut and paste custom lecture outlines electronically with ease.

Test Bank and Computerized Test Bank

Scrutinized for accuracy, the *Test Bank* includes more than 2,500 true/false, multiple-choice, short-answer, and essay questions, which have been rated for difficulty and designated as factual or application based. The *Test Bank* is available in printed or in Windows format. The newest computerized edition—ExaMaster99—is a cross-platform version available on CD-ROM that works with the latest versions of the Windows and Windows NT operating systems. ExaMaster99 includes online testing capabilities, a grade book, and much more.

RequesTest and Online Testing Service

Harcourt makes test planning quicker and easier than ever with this program. Instructors can order test masters by question number and criteria via a toll-free telephone number. Test masters will be mailed or faxed within 48 hours. Harcourt can provide instructors with software to install their own online testing program, allowing tests to be administered over networks or individual terminals. This program offers instructors greater flexibility and convenience in grading and scoring test results.

Study Guide/Workbook

Packed with additional applications, this learning supplement is an excellent resource for students. For each chapter of the text, the *Study Guide* includes a chapter outline; key term review; self-tests composed of multiple-choice, true/false, and short-answer questions; and more. In response to professor requests, the *Workbook* portion of this guide contains the Self-Discovery Exercises from the text as well as a wealth of other experiential exercises that can be assigned as homework or used in class.

Business Novel with Exercises: *Bottom Line*

This is a novel about the workplace, where the heroine, Lenore, is HR Director of Nelson Manufacturing, a small and well-run company suddenly taken over by a greedy and profit-driven conglomerate. Quickly the quality and profits plunge under the new regime. Along the way the various characters exhibit greed, ego, selfishness, sexual harassment, and gross insensitivity—as well as kindness, servant leadership, competence, and other organizational behavior topics your students will recognize from *Organizational Behavior*.

Dorothy Marcic of Vanderbilt University wrote *Bottom Line* for an audience that is fed up with the modern workplace—the same sort of people who love Dilbert. Ultimately, it is a morality tale of good versus evil in corporate America. It is a wonderful "case study" and is accompanied by a detailed study guide.

E-commerce Module: *E-commerce: Implications for Organizational Behavior in the New Economy*

The effects of the Internet and technology can be felt everywhere in organizations today. For those interested in exploring the impact of the new economy on organizational behavior, Daft and Noe offer *E-commerce: Implications for Organizational Behavior in the New Economy*. This standalone module follows the part outline of the main text, echoing the format of the text chapters, so adopters can easily fold the module into their teaching activities. The module highlights such issues as the ways in which e-commerce changes how organizations interact with their environments; implications of the global reach of e-commerce; the effects of technology on individuals within organizations; the many ways technology affects communication, teamwork, and decision making within organizations; and the impact of e-commerce on organizational culture.

Performance Module

In the real world, the bottom line is performance. Employees, managers, top-level executives, entire companies—everything—is evaluated on performance. This unique module takes an in-depth look at performance issues. It provides insightful material to reinforce class discussions and gives students practice with performance issues.

PowerPoint CD-ROM Presentation Software

This innovative presentation tool enables instructors to customize their own multimedia classroom presentations. The package includes figures and tables from the text, as well as outside materials to supplement chapter concepts. Material is organized by chapter. Instructors can use the material as is or expand and modify it for individual classes. The software is available in PowerPoint 97 format, which allows instructors simply to click on links to move from the PowerPoint presentation to Websites.

Overhead Transparencies with Teaching Notes

Created from artwork in the text as well as outside materials, the full-color acetates will enhance your lectures. They include detailed teaching notes.

Transparency Masters with Teaching Notes

Drawn from exhibits and tables in the text, these masters enable you to create even more visual illustrations to accompany your lectures. Additional detailed teaching notes are provided with this ancillary also.

Videos

A complete set of videos show students how organizations are dealing with issues such as diversity in the workforce, globalization, the importance of individuals in the larger organization, motivation, communication, leadership and teamwork, decision making, organizational structure, and organizational change. These videos support the written video case materials found at the end of each part in the textbook. Among the companies profiled are MultiGen-Paradigm software developers, Southwest Airlines, Hard Candy cosmetics, Centex home builders, JCPenney, and Fossil watches. Each video case write-up contains four critical thinking questions, with the last focused on the company's Website so that students and instructors can stay abreast of late-breaking company news. Teaching notes for the video package can be found in the *Instructor's Manual,* as well as on the *Organizational Behavior* home page.

WebCT Course: *Organizational Behavior Online Course*

Delivered via the WebCT platform, this integrated Web-based learning environment combines our innovative textbook and package with the vast resources of the Internet and the convenience of anytime learning. WebCT facilitates the creation of sophisticated Web-based educational environments. It provides a set of course design tools to help you manage course content, a set of communication tools to facilitate online classroom collaboration, and a set of administrative tools for tracking and managing your students' progress.

Extremely user friendly, the powerful customization features of the WebCT framework enable instructors to customize this online course to their own unique teaching styles and their students' individual needs.

Course features include content keyed to the textbook, self-tests and online exams, Internet activities and links to related resources, a suggested course syllabus, student and instructor materials, free technical support for instructors, and much more. The text's PowerPoint Presentation Software also is integrated into the WebCT course.

Additionally, with a qualified adoption, Harcourt offers free access to a blank WebCT template.

WebCT Testing Service   If testing is all you want, we will upload the computerized Test Bank into a course with no publisher content. If you like, we will even host it for you on our server.

Web CT Student Manual Included with the *Organizational Behavior On-line* course, this unique manual offers a wealth of information for Web users, from novices to the most advanced. The manual provides general instruction about the World Wide Web for Internet beginners, while more experienced users can skip to the step-by-step information on how to use WebCT's course tools.

Discovering Your Management Career CD-ROM

Available with *Organizational Behavior* is a CD-ROM titled "Discovering Your Management Career." It contains three programs, each of which may be used in conjunction with your course: Discovering Your Management Career, Career Design, and Management at Sea (commentary on actual footage from major sailing races illustrate how effective management can lead to better results).

Harcourt College Publishers will provide complimentary supplements or supplement packages to those adopters qualified under our adoption policy. Please contact your sales representative to learn how you may qualify. If, as an adopter or potential user, you receive supplements you do not need, please return them to your sales representative or send them to:

Attn: Returns Department
Troy Warehouse
465 South Lincoln Drive
Troy, MO 63379

Acknowledgments

Organizational Behavior would not have been possible without the guidance and constructive feedback of our focus group members and manuscript reviewers. We want to thank each of these experts for the time they spent providing insight and constructive criticism. Our text has benefited as a result.

Maryann Albrecht
University of Illinois, Chicago

Brett Andrews
LeTourneau University

Jodi Barnes Nelson
North Carolina State University

Regina Bento
University of Baltimore

Ray Coye
DePaul University

Robert Ledman
Morehead College

Sherry Moss
Florida International University

Rhonda Palladi
Georgia State University

R. J. Paul
Kansas State University

Joseph Rallo
University of Colorado at Colorado Springs

Elizabeth Ravlin
University of South Carolina

Raymond Read
Baylor University

Jessica Simmons
University of Texas

Kenneth Thompson
DePaul University

Randall Sleeth
Virginia Commonwealth University

Ellen Whitener
University of Virginia

Peter Sorensen
Benedictine University

Cheryl Wyrick
California State Polytechnic University, Pomona

Also, we want to thank the dedicated team members who were involved throughout the process and were committed to producing the best organizational behavior text possible. At Harcourt College Publishers, we are grateful for the enthusiasm and expertise of John Weimeister, Senior Acquisitions Editor, who brought us together for this effort. John's patient encouragement and coaching kept us on track and tuned to the vision as we worked through each chapter. Tracy Morse, Senior Developmental Editor, saw to it that we received focus group feedback and timely manuscript reviews and analysis, as well as coordinated each element of our extensive supplements package. Beverly Dunn, Marketing Strategist, provided market knowledge and suggestions throughout the project. Cathy Vahrenkamp, Editorial Assistant, skillfully pitched in to help whenever we needed it. At Elm Street Publishing Services, Karen Hill guided the text through the writing and development and coordinated the team's efforts. Phyllis Crittenden and Barb Lange stepped us through production, and Abby Westapher and Jan Huskisson provided permissions and photo research services. A special thank-you goes out to the entire team at Elm Street; their careful attention to detail contributed greatly to the quality of the final book. We are also very grateful for the dedication and skill of editorial associate Pat Lane, whose attention to detail in drafting a variety of materials, researching topics, and reviewing proofs carried the project through its many stages.

Richard L. Daft
Raymond A. Noe
June 2000

about the authors

Richard L. Daft
Vanderbilt University

Richard L. Daft, Ph.D., holds the Ralph Owen Chair of Management in the Owen School of Management at Vanderbilt University, where he specializes in the study of organization theory and leadership. Dr. Daft is a Fellow of the Academy of Management and has served on the editorial boards of *Academy of Management Journal, Administrative Science Quarterly,* and *Journal of Management Education.* He was associate editor-in-chief of *Organization Science* and served for three years as associate editor of *Administrative Science Quarterly.*

Professor Daft has authored or co-authored 11 books, including *Management* (Harcourt College Publishers, 2000), *Organization Theory and Design* (South-Western College Publishing, 2001), *Leadership: Theory and Practice* (Dryden, 1999), and *What to Study: Generating and Developing Research Questions* (Sage, 1982). He recently published *Fusion Leadership: Unlocking the Subtle Forces That Change People and Organizations* (Berrett-Koehler, 1998, with Robert Lengel). He has also authored dozens of scholarly articles, papers, and chapters. His work has been published in *Administrative Science Quarterly, Academy of Management Journal, Academy of Management Review, Strategic Management Journal, Journal of Management, Accounting Organizations and Society, Management Science, MIS Quarterly, California Management Review,* and *Organizational Behavior Teaching Review.* Professor Daft has been awarded several government research grants to pursue studies of organization design, organizational innovation and change, strategy implementation, and organizational information processing.

Dr. Daft also is an active teacher and consultant. He has taught management, leadership, organizational change, organizational theory, and organizational behavior. He has been involved in management development and consulting for many companies and government organizations, including American Banking Association, Bell Canada, National Transportation Research Board, NL Baroid, Nortel, TVA, Pratt & Whitney, State Farm Insurance, Tenneco, the United States Air Force, the United States Army, J.C. Bradford & Co., Central Parking System, Entergy Sales and Service, First American National Bank, and the Vanderbilt University Medical Center.

Raymond A. Noe
The Ohio State University

Raymond A. Noe is the Robert and Ann Hoyt Designated Professor of Management at The Ohio State University. He has taught for more than 15 years at Big Ten universities. Before joining the faculty at Ohio State he was a professor in the Department of Management at Michigan State University and the Industrial Relations Center of the Carlson School of Management, University of Minnesota. He received his B.S. in psychology from The Ohio State University and his M.A. and Ph.D. in psychology from Michigan State University. Professor Noe conducts research and teaches all levels of students from undergraduate to executives in human resource management, managerial skills, quantitative methods, human resource information systems, training and development, and organizational behavior. He has published articles in the *Academy of Management Journal, Academy of Management Review, Journal of Applied Psychology, Journal of Vocational*

Behavior, and *Personnel Psychology.* Professor Noe is currently on the editorial boards of several journals, including *Personnel Psychology, Journal of Business and Psychology, Journal of Training Research,* and *Journal of Organizational Behavior.* He has two widely adopted textbooks, *Human Resource Management: Gaining a Competitive Advantage* and *Employee Training and Development,* both published with Irwin McGraw-Hill. Professor Noe has received awards for his teaching and research excellence, including the Herbert G. Heneman Distinguished Teaching Award in 1991 and the Ernest J. McCormick Award for Distinguished Early Career Contribution from the Society for Industrial and Organizational Psychology in 1993. He is also a fellow of the Society for Industrial and Organizational Psychology.

brief contents

contents

what would YOU do?
Creating a Company for Today's High-Tech World, 28

what would YOU do?
DaimlerChrysler Employees at All Levels Resist Moves for Global Assignments, 71

part 2 | Individuals in Organizations

3   *Individual Differences, 88*

Smart People Mean Big Profits for Microsoft, 89

what would YOU do?
Rakesh Gangwal of US Airways, 119

what would YOU do?
Apparel Source Inc. Decides Going Green
Is Too Expensive, 135

what would YOU do?
Improving Motivation at Sandstrom
Products, 171

part 3|Interpersonal Processes in Organizations

what would **YOU** do?

what would YOU do?
Signicast Corporation's New Teamwork Strategy, 291

9 *Communication in Organizations, 302*

Canon Builds a Network of Communication, 303

what would YOU do?
Should Organizations Monitor Their Workers' E-mail?, 320

what would YOU do?
How Would You Avoid Singing the
Blues?, 348

what would YOU do?
The Follower, 383

12   *Power and Politics, 416*

what would YOU do?

what would YOU do?

13 *Conflict Management and Negotiation, 446*

14 *Stress and Stress Management, 478*

part 4 | Impact of Organizations on Behavior

16 *Job Design, 554*

GE/Durham's Teams Design Their Own Jobs, 555

what would YOU do?
A Company's Culture Keeps It in the
Danger Zone, 636

part 1

PART ONE

The Scope and Context of Organizational Behavior

Chapter 1
The Scope of Organizational Behavior

Chapter 2
Managing Diversity in the United States
and Abroad

one
CHAPTER

1

The Scope of Organizational Behavior

CONCEPT AND SKILL

preview

After studying this chapter, you should be able to:

- Identify the elements that interact to form organizational behavior in a given organization.

- Describe how applying the various management schools of thought might affect the behavior of individuals and groups, and ultimately the performance of organizations.

- Study a high-performance organization and identify aspects of organizational behavior that are well understood and managed in that organization.

- Give examples of the skills and functions required of a manager.

- Provide examples of organizations affected by trends that are shaping management.

- Identify principles of organizational behavior that might shed light on a given business problem.

Running a computer company involves a lot more than the click of a mouse. The new age of the Internet has made this high-tech industry so high speed that even the companies most respected for their products—like the venerable Hewlett-Packard—must stand ready to "aim, fire, re-aim, fire" to keep up, as consultant Vernon A. Altman describes it. Carly Fiorina, the new forty-something CEO of Hewlett-Packard, isn't afraid of the rapid-fire nature of the business. The former president of communications software giant Lucent Technologies' $19 billion Global Service Provider business is ready for the challenge. "It's not rocket science that we need to be innovating at a rapid rate," she says.

Fiorina already has a working knowledge of her organization and its place in the competitive high-tech industry. She also understands that her company's most valuable resource is its employees—knowledge workers who bring a high level of technical skill to the job. And she trusts them to help the company solve problems quickly and effectively. "Our people are very proud and smart," says Fiorina. "So, first you reinforce the things that work and then appeal to their brains to address what doesn't." Her management skills are admired throughout the industry. "I think the world of Carly," says Nina Aversano, president of North America for Lucent's Global Service Provider business. "She's a great leader." Fiorina has human skills that include a personal management style—she'll sit up all night with an employee who needs help on an important project; she'll shower employees who land major contracts with balloons and flowers. She is able to conceptualize and communicate major strategies across the company, and she has the technical skills not only to meet financial goals but also to provide input on specific projects. Thus, she's a well-rounded manager whose goal is to turn a company with a somewhat stodgy reputation into one that is synonymous with innovation. She values H-P's reputation for quality, but she's quick to quip, "We have to make sure [quality] represents the next century rather than the last one." And the next century is already here.[1]

> *"We have to make sure [quality] represents the next century rather than the last one."*
> —**Carly Fiorina**

Most students today have heard of such major computer and Internet companies as Hewlett-Packard, Microsoft, and Amazon.com. But you may not be aware of the range of issues those organizations face to remain competitive in their industries. Employees and executives need to make strategic plans, from the types of services they should offer to the number of countries into which they should expand to capture new opportunities. They also need to make routine, daily decisions quickly and well to keep customers happy and avoid wasting scarce resources such as money and time. And organizations need to maintain effective working relationships among employees who increasingly come from diverse backgrounds, in the United States and abroad. Because of the changing nature of the workplace and workers, it is important to learn about organizations and their environment.

Whether you want to become a CEO like Carly Fiorina of Hewlett-Packard or a salesperson, systems analyst, or production supervisor, your success depends not only on your own skills in a particular area but on other people and the relationships you develop with them. Specialized areas of knowledge are important, but they are not sufficient for success. A salesperson, for example, must cooperate with people who can provide information about an organization's products. Likewise, CEOs such as Fiorina draw on their knowledge and also enable and inspire the organization's people to carry out decisions. In fact, for any job in an organization, we can identify many ways in which success depends on relationships among people. This is especially true in today's workplace, where the rapid pace of change often requires a corresponding ability to transform to meet new challenges. Adoption of new technology, competition for scarce human resources, and the global scale of activity all demand that organizations remain flexible and open to change.

This textbook offers principles for understanding and managing human relationships and interdependencies, along with many examples of how organizations successfully (or unsuccessfully) position themselves for a new world of work. We begin in this chapter by defining *organizational behavior* as a discipline for studying people in organizations. We show why organizational behavior is important and how it affects an organization's managers. The chapter concludes by previewing the remainder of the book.

Organizational behavior describes how organizations and people interact

organizational behavior (OB)

The actions and interactions of individuals and groups in organizations.

Every day, organizations around the world bring individuals together. Each person in each organization contributes to meeting organizational goals. In addition, those individuals interact with one another and influence how well others in the organization achieve goals. This activity may be inspired or limited by the organization's values, structure, policies, and goals. Taken together, these activities and influences constitute organizational behavior. Thus, **organizational behavior (OB)** consists of the actions and interactions of individuals and groups in organizations. As a management discipline, OB is the study of human attitudes, behavior, and performance in organizations.

Organizations, Groups, and Individuals

Organizational behavior as we define it here studies three things: organizations, groups, and individuals. For example, if you were to study the organizational behavior of Hewlett-Packard, your study would include the characteristics of individual employees, the way they relate to each other in informal gatherings and formal relationships, the nature of these formal and informal groups, and the values, goals, and policies of H-P's departments and the company overall. A complete study would be an enormous undertaking, complicated by the fact that each of these elements of organizational behavior affects the others. To better express the scope of organizational behavior, let's look at each element.

organization

A social entity that is goal directed and deliberately structured.

Formally defined, an **organization** is a social entity that is goal directed and deliberately structured. To say that an organization is a *social entity* means it consists of two or more people. This entity is by definition *goal directed,* meaning people set it up to achieve a given outcome, such as making a profit, providing a service, or meeting a public need. The organization is also *deliberately structured;* tasks are divided up among the members, with each member of the organization responsible for certain activities. This definition covers many kinds of groups, from hospitals to government agencies to professional sports teams to manufacturing and service businesses.

At any of these organizations, much of the activity involves groups—people who routinely interact for some shared purpose. Departments, work teams, and social cliques are among the possible groups whose behavior affects the organization's success. The organization establishes groups when it believes a group effort is in the organization's best interests. Individuals establish groups as well to meet personal or professional needs. Some of the processes that occur in groups are leadership, decision making, conflict, and political behavior. Depending on how they are managed, these processes can benefit or hurt the organization.

The people who form an organization and its groups are, of course, individuals. Their uniqueness can sometimes make people challenging to organize and manage. Yet, it also makes them uniquely valuable to the organization. A dollar, in contrast, is pretty much like any other dollar; an iMac computer, except for color choice, is pretty much like any other iMac. But an organization cannot readily replace the leadership, knowledge, and personal skills that an employee such as Carly Fiorina brings to Hewlett-Packard. Organizations that can turn such assets to their advantage have, as we will show, an enormously valuable competitive strength.

Disciplines That Contribute to OB Theory

The study of organizational behavior is an interdisciplinary approach. It applies the behavioral and social sciences, including psychology, sociology, social psychology, and anthropology. Psychology contributes ideas about individuals, including the ways we perceive, learn, form attitudes, and make decisions, as well as what motivates us. Sociology studies how people relate to one another, including communications, conflict management, and the formation and behavior of groups. Social psychology blends elements of psychology and sociology to explore the ways people influence one another. Anthropology studies societies. It provides insights into organizational culture, including shared values and attitudes. Insights from anthropology have also helped organizations and their managers understand people from different national cultures.

Organizational behavior also draws on such business disciplines as industrial engineering, economics, and vocational counseling, as well as the study of ethics. Industrial engineering sheds light on the design of work processes. Economics explores the decisions we make about how to acquire and use resources. Vocational counseling relates skills and other individual characteristics to success in performing various kinds of work. And ethics explores the moral aspects of decision making and political behavior.

We all have experience as individuals and members of groups, so it's not surprising that many people view the principles of organizational behavior as merely common sense. However, ideas we call "common sense" sometimes turn out to be wrong. The ideal approach is to combine our own experience with an openness to continued learning. The field of organizational behavior can contribute to our learning process through theory,

Understanding organizational behavior is critical for managing workers on the Deepwater Pathfinder, *Conoco's new $265 million drill ship. The ship, which is half ship and half oil rig, leads the search for oil in the deep ocean and is home to a crew of 125 men and women who work 12-hour shifts, three weeks on and three weeks off. All crew members must work—and live—together for the organization to succeed, whether they work in the "doghouse" where drilling is controlled, on the bridge, or with drill crews manhandling pipe, as in the photo.*
(Source: © Greg Smith/SABA)

research, and practice. Theories provide a framework for explaining practical observations and conducting research to verify their validity. Researchers test and refine their theories through a variety of techniques:

- *Field studies* observe individual or group processes within actual organizations. Researchers do not have much control over the variables, but the natural setting can provide valuable insights to test more formally in other studies.
- *Laboratory studies* set up artificial situations so that researchers can manipulate certain variables and control for others. Although the setting is artificial, the results are more precise than in a field study.
- *Surveys* of a population sample specifically address people's attitudes and opinions. Unfortunately, what people say they think or intend to do can differ from what they really think or do.
- *Case studies* analyze a single group or individual in depth. This method can generate ideas to test with other forms of research.
- *Meta-analysis* involves collecting the results of several studies done on a single topic and using statistical techniques to pool the results. This approach can uncover a pattern in studies covering many subjects.

If research results or practical experience are inconsistent with a theory, this is a signal to look for problems in the theory or the way it was applied. Through this process, researchers develop and expand OB theory to increase its value for organizations.

As they carry out their work, employees and managers sometimes believe that practical experience is more relevant than theory and research. If managers read *Business Week* or *Fortune* to learn about what other companies are doing more than they read journals of behavioral science to learn what researchers are finding out, they may limit their effectiveness. Examples featured by business reporters may not apply to many readers' organizations, and those who try to apply the experiences of other organizations with no regard for theories and research can waste a good deal of time and resources. In contrast, those who learn basic principles of organizational behavior and then try to keep abreast of advances in the field equip themselves with an important tool—knowledge for sorting "commonsense" fallacies from "commonsense" realities.

The Foundations of OB Theory

The study of organizational behavior is a logical extension of the study of management. Theories about management started with the idea that managing is something that managers do to the people in organizations. Testing and exploring these ideas have shown that the influence also travels in other directions: The people in organizations influence managers and the organizations themselves. Furthermore, characteristics of an organization, such as its values and structure, influence the way managers and employees behave. Theories about management have therefore broadened to encompass theories of organizational behavior.

These foundations of OB theory, shown in Exhibit 1.1, are important because they continue to influence the assumptions people in organiza-

exhibit|**1.1**

Management Theories: Foundations of Organizational Behavior Theory

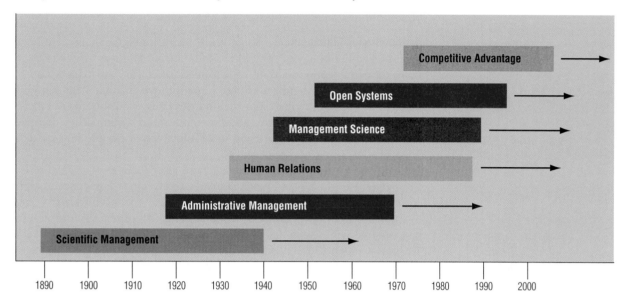

tions make. Even the earliest theories, which are no longer as influential today as they once were, continue to guide many managers. As you read the following description of management theory, think of managers you have encountered or worked for. Which of these theories do you think they subscribe to?

Scientific Management   Modern management theory began with the challenges of the Industrial Revolution. Unlike the tiny, family-owned businesses typical of earlier years, the manufacturing firms of the Industrial Revolution were larger and more impersonal, requiring decisions about how to set up plants and assign tasks efficiently. The new jobs and machines were unfamiliar to employees, as well as dangerous and demanding. Feeling exploited under these conditions, employees sometimes went on strike. Managers concluded their businesses were not receiving all the benefits they had expected from industrialization.

For help, they turned to a new way of studying work, pioneered by Frederick Winslow Taylor, an engineer.[2] Called **scientific management,** this school of management involves developing a standard method for performing each job, training workers in the method, eliminating interruptions, and offering wage incentives (pay linked to output). The principles of scientific management were applied very effectively in manufacturing settings, especially in assembly-line work. Taylor is well known for his time-and-motion studies, aimed at designing efficient jobs. He also considered workers' needs—for example, training and incentive pay. Thus, organizational behavior issues addressed by scientific management included motivation (discussed in Chapters 5 and 6), as well as work design (see Chapter 16).

The idea of studying work processes to make them more efficient continues today. It is the foundation of efforts to improve efficiency and quality.

scientific management

A school of management that involves developing a standard method for performing each job, training workers in the method, eliminating interruptions, and offering wage incentives.

However, the scientific management school was inadequate in other areas. Many workers thought that the approach dehumanized and exploited them, so the tension with management persisted and somtimes even increased in organizations that applied principles of scientific management.

Administrative Management   Some years after scientific management began to scrutinize the behavior of workers and their jobs, others turned to examining different components of organizational behavior: managers and the organization itself. Members of the administrative management school of thought investigated what organizational structure would be most efficient and advocated putting policies and procedures into writing. They theorized that organizations would function most effectively if people knew exactly what was expected of them.

The administrative management school also discussed the ideal role of a manager. Henri Fayol, a French manager and mining engineer, studied his own experience and generalized that a manager's job includes five basic functions: planning, organizing, commanding, coordinating, and controlling.[3] As we will discuss later in this chapter, the definition of a manager's job is not much different today, although the way a manager carries out those tasks is changing.

Other students of organizations applied the principles of social psychology. Mary Parker Follett used her training in philosophy and political science to conclude that organizations could reduce conflict by getting employees and managers focused on goals they share.[4] Chester I. Barnard's contributions include the observation that within an organization is an "informal organization" of cliques and social relationships that influences how the formal organization functions.[5] Today, researchers continue to look for ways that social psychology and other behavioral and social sciences can provide lessons in managing organizations.

The Human Relations School   Although organizations today accept the relevance of understanding human behavior, most managers gave much more credence to scientific management until about the 1930s. Then a series of experiments called the Hawthorne studies turned attention to such human factors as motivation. The Hawthorne studies, named after a test location at the Hawthorne Works of the Western Electric Company, involved adjusting job characteristics such as light levels to find factors that would influence worker productivity. The researchers were astonished to discover that productivity increased in the experimental group no matter what changes were made. People who heard these results concluded that the workers must have been motivated by the attention they were receiving. In fact, the research design adjusted so many variables and failed to control for so many others that the experiment did not conclusively link any factors to performance.

Despite the shortcomings of the Hawthorne studies, they benefited the study of management by persuading researchers that it is important to study the ways people relate to each other in organizations. The **human relations school** of management thus explores ways managers can influence productivity through positive human relations. It is based on the assumption that employees will work harder if they feel satisfied. Proponents of this approach, such as Abraham Maslow, investigated what will satisfy employees. (Maslow's theories and related ideas will be discussed in Chapter 5.)

human relations school

A school of management that explores ways managers can influence productivity by establishing positive relationships with employees.

Betsy Dickerson and Thom Havens, co-owners of Waterworks, a plumbing services company based in Columbus, Ohio, apply this line of thought to their treatment of employees. To give employees pride in the importance of their work, the partners redesigned employees' uniforms and provided them with spotless company trucks. Then they spent $2 million to renovate the company's offices. These physical changes are symbolic of the overall treatment of Waterworks employees, says Dickerson: "We're trying to get plumbing back to a profession rather than a trade. We like to think that we treat our employees the same as the employees downtown at IBM are treated . . . [including] the money they make." So far, the emphasis on positive relationships has paid off in fast growth; Waterworks recently made *Inc*. magazine's list of the top 100 inner-city businesses.[6]

Another theorist in the human relations school was Douglas McGregor, who focused on the ways managers think about employees. McGregor's experience as manager, consultant, and psychologist told him that managers make assumptions. Depending on whether managers are more attuned to scientific management or human relations, said McGregor,

By believing that managers can influence productivity through positive human relations, Paula Lawlor, cofounder and president of Medi-Health in Pennsylvania, has been able to grow her company to $7.5 million in revenues in just seven years. Medi-Health is a medical-records-outsourcing company, which helps hospitals and other health-care facilities sort through reams of patient records, organize them for accreditation processes, and abstract documents for inclusion in national health-care databases. Lawlor hires, motivates, and retains employees in this nonglamorous industry by creating an environment that's a magnet for talented, hardworking people. Managers run their divisions with maximum autonomy, hourly workers have the opportunity to become salaried consultants, and all employees have the freedom to move within the company until they find their niche. Employee training is a priority for Lawlor, and she also goes to great lengths to accommodate her employees' personal lives. For example, one top manager works out of her home in Cleveland, Ohio, and employees are allowed to bring their kids to work and arrange their schedules around family needs. (Source: © Nathaniel Welch/SABA)

exhibit | **1.2**

Theory X and Theory Y: Assumptions about Employees

Theory X	Theory Y
Employees dislike work; they will avoid it if possible.	Employees like work; working is as natural as resting and playing.
Because employees don't like work, the organization must coerce them to achieve its objectives.	Coercion is not the only way for the organization to achieve objectives; employees will exercise self-control to achieve objectives they are committed to.
Employees have relatively little ambition; they prefer to be directed and to avoid responsibility.	Many employees can use creativity to solve problems.
Employees mainly want security.	Most employees have the opportunity to use only part of their intellectual abilities on the job, but they want to use more.

these assumptions fall into one of two sets of beliefs, summarized in Exhibit 1.2:

1. Theory X assumes that workers dislike their work and must be coerced into doing it. McGregor associated scientific management with this set of beliefs.

2. Theory Y assumes that work is a natural part of employees' lives and that employees will be industrious and creative if they are committed to their work.

McGregor recommended Theory Y as a way to tap employees' full potential.

The superiority of Theory Y has never been scientifically tested, but McGregor's thinking appeals to many managers. More generally, researchers today continue to test aspects of the human relations assumption that satisfaction is related to performance. So far, as we will discuss in later chapters, the evidence has been mixed. Nevertheless, organizations continue to apply principles from the human relations school through initiatives that range from bringing humor and fun into the workplace to redesigning jobs and work processes so that they are more interesting.

The Management Science School Managers' attention shifted again in response to World War II and the development of computer technology. These changes created a need for logistics systems to move massive quantities of personnel, equipment, and supplies as needed around the world, as well as the tools for creating these systems. The military devised sophisticated mathematical models for making logistical decisions, and managers realized they could apply these efficiency tools to their businesses. The result was the **management science school,** which applies the scientific method of research and sophisticated mathematical techniques to management problems. Thus, as managers once studied the motions of individual workers, they began to study the activities of entire production and distribution systems.

Management science uses models to show how varying one factor, such as the addition of a machine, will affect cost and efficiency. These

management science school

A school of management that applies the scientific method of research and sophisticated mathematical techniques to management problems.

models typically employ many variables, so computers are used to perform the calculations. The development of computer technology therefore has enabled the widespread adoption of management science. Today, as computer systems grow increasingly sophisticated, more and more companies include such modeling capabilities within their information systems. Decision makers in modern organizations apply management science to help them locate facilities, schedule production, and plan their needs for personnel, equipment, and other resources. Whereas this school of thought was once the domain of specialists, it has become the basis for creating widely available tools to assist decision making at all levels of the organization. Some examples of these decision-making tools, will be discussed in Chapter 10.

The Open Systems School The early schools of thought focused on what occurs within an organization, but internal activities are also influenced by forces outside organizations: the actions of governments, suppliers, and customers. The **open systems school** describes organizations as systems that interact with their environment. As a system, an organization receives inputs from its environment and transforms them into outputs. Inputs include employees, money, raw materials, and technologies. Outputs include goods and services, pollution, and socially responsible activities. Organizations receive feedback from their environment, and this feedback influences future decisions.

The open systems school makes certain assumptions about organizations.[7] First, it assumes that organizations are influenced by the environment. Of these influences, most important is that an organization's success depends on whether it meets a need of its environment. Another assumption is that an organization is a social system, so its parts interact. If one part fails, the other parts must adjust, or the system cannot continue to function. For example, if a product must be recalled, the organization must respond to correct the problem with the product and the public's perception of it. This requires the cooperation of many functions within the organization. Similarly, the open systems model would have predicted the importance of cooperation between public relations and security personnel when someone breached security in an airport terminal serving United Airlines.

open systems school

A school of management that describes organizations as systems that interact with their environment, transforming inputs into outputs.

❦ United Airlines

One single passenger showed United Airlines the importance of outside forces to an organization's success. On a recent August afternoon, a young man carrying a briefcase climbed the stairs from a baggage claim area, then dashed past a security checkpoint at O'Hare Airport's Terminal 1. Was he frightened he would miss his flight? Or was he intent on planting a bomb that could end in tragedy?

United personnel couldn't know but had to act. When the man didn't respond to a security guard's shouts, airline officials called local police, security personnel from the Chicago Department of Aviation, and members of the Federal Aviation Administration's Civil Aviation Security Team. Now United's dependence extended to the help of these civil servants. However, they failed to locate the man, so they evacuated thousands of would-be passengers, along with employees and others who had been crowding the terminal minutes earlier.

As the terminal came to a standstill, flights from other cities were turned away, and passengers at other airports grew impatient when flights from Chicago failed to arrive. Eventually, United canceled over 200 flights and delayed many more, affecting 27,000 passengers nationwide and costing the company millions of dollars in overtime pay and lost revenue. Its flights were not back on schedule until the following day. In the meantime, United sent public relations employees to the airport to provide information about the evacuation to reporters and frustrated customers.

Months later, United still knew nothing about the man who had caused such a disruption to its system. Nor did anyone find any trace of an explosive. United's management and city officials maintained that the airline's people were correct to err on the side of safety. Others complained United had overreacted in its response to this apparent threat to the organization and its customers. Security agencies and United alike are conducting reviews of the incident.[8]

The open systems model of organizations would tell United to plan for unexpected problems and to set up systems to enable employees to make decisions in difficult circumstances. When problems occur, the airline should study what happened and rethink its plans. Today, when people think of their organization's role within the larger environment, they are applying ideas from the open systems school.

The Competitive Advantage School   For a business, it is not enough to think of the environment in general terms. Today's environment is simply too competitive. Long-term survival and success require that organizations identify ways they can create value better than their current and potential competitors. Doing this is called maintaining a **sustained competitive advantage.** The school of thought that addresses how to maintain such an advantage is the competitive advantage school. It studies how an organization can sustain a competitive advantage over the long term, and its conclusions have implications for how we view organizational behavior.

Researchers from the competitive advantage school have explored which types of resources are most likely to provide a sustainable competitive advantage. Resources can be considered to provide a relative advantage if they are

1. *Valuable*—The resource should benefit the organization in some way.
2. *Rare*—The resource should be in limited supply, or else it doesn't provide an advantage because all organizations would have it.
3. *Inimitable* (incapable of being imitated)—There must be no practical way to copy the resource.
4. *Nonsubstitutable*—If organizations can't substitute something else for a resource, the organization that has it has an advantage.[9]

These characteristics help organizations recognize where true sustainable competitive advantage comes from: not money or raw materials, which are available from many sources and can often be substituted; not technology or management techniques, which can be imitated; but the organization's human resources. People bring unique talents, knowledge, and experience to their work. If the organization knows how to acquire and use them wisely, it has the potential to sustain a competitive advantage for the long term. This knowledge, of course, comes largely from an understanding of organizational behavior.

Research backs up the theory of competitive advantage. One study measured organizational success by tracking companies' stock performance over a 20-year period, then identified the top five: Plenum Publishing, Circuit City, Tyson Foods, Wal-Mart, and Southwest Airlines.[10] Interestingly, these companies are not high-tech marvels or leaders in market share. They

sustained competitive advantage

A means by which an organization can create value better than current and potential competitors over the long term.

do not have the luck of being in the fastest-growing industries. Instead, they are known for creative leadership and highly motivated personnel. More recently, *Fortune* magazine conducted research to identify what it calls "the 100 best companies to work for in America," based on such criteria as generous employee benefits and positive employee attitudes toward management. Although this style of management might sound costly, *Fortune* discovered that the stock of the companies on the list has outperformed the Russell 3000, a broad stock index.[11]

Viewing human resources as a source of competitive advantage is essential for managing a new kind of worker. Throughout most of the twentieth century, organizations relied heavily on manual laborers. The techniques of scientific management and later schools of thought helped organizations increase efficiency, thereby dramatically improving the productivity of manual labor and enabling great prosperity in the developed nations.[12] However, modern organizations rely more and more on "knowledge workers," whose primary contribution to the organization is not manual labor, but what they know about customers or a specialized body of knowledge. Kristin Knight, a young entrepreneur who started a computerized graphics and Web design firm, learned the importance of knowledge workers the hard way. Her company, Creative Assets, was expanding from its Seattle base to a branch office in Portland, Oregon. Knight hadn't brought enough finance and technology staff on board to support the growth, and mistakes were costly. Knight says of her close call, "The only thing that sets you apart from your competitors is people. Find and keep the best employees you can possibly afford." Her lesson has paid off: earnings for a recent year were projected to be $9 million.[13] The lesson for organizations in general is that they must learn how to acquire, increase, and use knowledge—and thereby make productivity gains along the lines of past increases in manual productivity.

Ultimately, then, understanding organizational behavior is a practical need for managers. As a discipline, organizational behavior provides the theoretical basis for explaining such key interpersonal activities as leadership and motivation. Any organization can buy technology or merchandise. But the right combination of human behavior—in the form of organizational behavior—is what distinguishes organizations that use technology and sell merchandise better than their competitors do.

apply it

1. Think of an organization of which you are part. It can be a company that employs you or a campus organization or social group. What individuals and groups make up this organization?
2. From your experience with the organization, which research disciplines or management theories does the organization rely on? Think of characteristics of other people's behavior or activities that you perform and explain how the organization seems to fit the discipline you picked.

Studying organizational behavior can help shape successful organizations

The study of organizational behavior continues because it provides valuable information for organizations today. Every organization includes people and interpersonal behavior, and to understand them is to understand what gives life to an organization. More specifically, knowledge about organizational behavior helps organizations with key management activities: managing human resources, improving quality, and maintaining high-performance work systems.

Management of Human Resources

Like money, technology, and equipment, people are a resource of an organization. They have the potential to give an organization the benefits of their training, skills, experience, intelligence, judgment, and relationships. As we discussed under the topic of the competitive advantage school of management, these human resources are really an organization's only sustainable competitive advantage. Successful organizations therefore are good at managing human resources: acquiring them, keeping them, increasing their value, and deriving the benefits of their efforts.

Just as engineering teaches how to manage the organization's technology and processes effectively and finance teaches how to manage its money, organizational behavior offers principles for effectively managing human resources. As this field develops and matures, it increasingly provides organizations with insight into such important needs as leadership, motivation, hiring, training, and communication. Thus, the study of organizational behavior promotes organizational success through providing information on skillfully managing the organization's key resource, its people.

Total Quality Management

total quality management (TQM)

An organizationwide effort to continuously improve the quality of work processes.

Understanding organizational behavior not only helps with the process of managing human resources, it also contributes to the achievement of the organization's goals. In today's highly competitive work environment, organizations have realized that these goals must include providing outstanding quality. Thus, many organizations have committed themselves to **total quality management (TQM).** TQM is an organizationwide effort to continuously improve the quality of work processes—that is, the ways people, machines, and systems accomplish tasks.

TQM is based on the core values listed in Exhibit 1.3. To summarize, these values assume that if all the organization's employees continuously improve their work, the quality of the organization's goods and services will improve as well. In addition, productivity should increase, and costs should fall. To achieve such dramatic results, the organization supports TQM by enabling employees to take action and rewarding them when they do.

For managers, implementing TQM requires a sophisticated understanding of how people and organizations behave. A successful TQM effort depends on instilling the core values of the organization, empowering employees to make changes, motivating people to improve constantly, and

exhibit **1.3**

Core Values of Total Quality Management

Value	Description
Customer driven	Methods, processes, and procedures are designed to meet expectations of internal or external customers
Leadership	Top management fully supports and understands the quality process (possibly having received the same training as others in the organization)
Full participation	Everyone in the organization receives training in quality and has the perspective, goals, and necessary tools and techniques for improving quality
Reward system	Systems reward quality, ensuring continual support for the overall effort
Reduced cycle time	Strong effort is put forth to reduce cycle times in product or service output as well as support functions
Prevention, not detection	Quality is designed into the product so that errors are prevented from occurring, rather than being detected then corrected
Management by fact	Managers measure progress with feedback based on data, rather than relying on intuition
Long-range outlook	Managers constantly monitor the external environment, asking, "What level of quality or service must we provide to customers over the next one to three years, and how can we attain this goal?"
Partnership development	Organization promotes cooperation with vendors as well as customers, thus developing a network that helps drive up quality and hold down costs
Public responsibility	Organization fosters corporate citizenship and responsibility by sharing quality-related information with other organizations and working to reduce negative impact of waste generation and product defects or recalls

Source: Adapted from Richard M. Hodgetts, Fred Luthans, and Sang M. Lee, "New paradigm organizations: From total quality to learning to world-class." *Organizational Dynamics,* Winter 1994, pp. 5–19.

inspiring people to focus on customer needs. This focus may require employees to rethink their work and its place in the organization. Constant change can be tiring, so it takes a skilled leader to create and maintain such a dynamic environment. All of these skills are within the scope of organizational behavior.

Even an established leader can benefit from studying organizational behavior to continuously improve how he or she implements total quality management. For Charles J. Hickey, CEO of SurfSoft, the lessons began with reading about the management philosophy of an early TQM guru, W. Edwards Deming.

When Charles Hickey accepted the chief executive position at SurfSoft, a California software developer for high-tech companies, he was taking his second stab at running a software company. The first, Microport Systems, went bankrupt after several years because Hickey's technical background as a computer scientist did not prepare him to lead his employees. For a while, SurfSoft prospered under Hickey's direction. He hired salespeople and engineers and set up systems and departments. Revenues grew and

🐾 **SurfSoft Inc.**

eventually surpassed the million-dollar mark. Then the company took a familiar turn. Sales slowed even as Hickey pushed his salespeople to meet ambitious quotas, and employee turnover climbed.

It was about that time that Hickey read about Deming's management methods, and what he learned surprised him. Deming urged that managers should foster collaboration among employees and provide constant training and education. He also criticized Hickey's beloved tactic of motivating through sales quotas. From Hickey's perspective, Deming seemed to be telling him he was managing his company all wrong.

To get his company moving in the right direction, Hickey tried Deming's philosophy at SurfSoft. He ended sales quotas, immediately easing a major source of stress. He reorganized the company, eliminating layers of management and multiple divisions that had discouraged collaboration. He replaced the inflexible organizational structure with teams that crossed departmental lines. He also required the company's managers to read and discuss a business book every month as a way to foster learning and identify areas for improvement. SurfSoft's performance has improved: turnover has plummeted and revenues have soared. Even better, SurfSoft employees say they actually enjoy coming to work.[14] It is that type of constructive work environment that is the goal of TQM.

Creation and Maintenance of High-Performance Work Systems

performance

The attainment of organizational goals by using resources effectively and efficiently.

effectiveness

Accomplishment of the desired goal.

efficiency

The achievement of maximum results with minimal resources.

All employees are ultimately responsible for achieving high performance, and they can use a variety of methods such as TQM to obtain it. In this context, **performance** refers to the attainment of organizational goals by using resources effectively and efficiently. **Effectiveness** means accomplishment of the desired goal (rather than some other, unintended goal). **Efficiency** refers to the amount of resources used; efficient use of resources gets maximum results from minimal resources. A high-performance work system therefore attains its goals and does so in an efficient way. At one time, many organizations achieved efficiency and effectiveness primarily by keeping manufacturing and distribution costs to a minimum. Today, however, production technology and information systems are so widespread that organizations need other ways to achieve high performance. They are transforming themselves by emphasizing and fully using their human resources, such as employees' knowledge, commitment, and talents.

Creating and maintaining high-performance work systems therefore requires employees to understand and use the principles of organizational behavior. For these principles to be most effective, everyone must understand and care about the organization's goals. Efficiency can result only when the organization identifies and acquires human resources who are able to do the work necessary for achieving those goals without waste. Efficiency also requires clear communication and careful management of inevitable conflicts and stress. These people-oriented issues are essential, whether or not the company also invests in the latest machinery or information systems.

apply it

1. Current business news has been full of stories about successful start-ups—companies that go public and raise millions of dollars the first day the stock is traded. At a company enjoying such success, why should management care about organizational behavior?

Seated in this photo is Steve Jobs, CEO for Apple Computer in Cupertino, California. Jobs is a manager with a clear vision for Apple. He brought the company back from near-disaster by getting employees to focus on Apple's traditional strengths—innovation, excitement, and fun in computing. Jobs has a new mission: "to marry the iMac and the Internet with an easy-to-use new operating system and free Web services for everything from your photos to your home page." Known as the personal computer industry's chief aesthetic officer, Jobs has assembled a team of programmers, marketers, graphic designers, and Web experts to accomplish this goal. He turned Apple's boardroom into a designer's loft in the race to complete the OSX and Apple's new Internet iTools. (Source: © Oliver Laude)

2. Many observers worry that the new Internet businesses are not showing profits. Investors will eventually demand profitability as well as unique ideas. How can an understanding of organizational behavior help these companies achieve and maintain profitability?

Managers' skills, functions, and challenges have some common characteristics

We have said that the study of organizational behavior is critical for successfully managing organizations. To see why this is so, consider the skills and functions required of today's managers, as well as the challenges they face. A thread running through this description is that managers bring people together and get them working to achieve common goals. In fact, that is the definition of a **manager**—someone whose responsibility is to achieve goals by enabling and directing the activities of others in the organization.

manager

A person whose responsibility is to achieve goals by enabling and directing the activities of others in the organization.

Management Skills and Functions

Carly Fiorina of Hewlett-Packard and Charles Hickey of SurfSoft, described earlier in the chapter, are managers at different companies, yet they perform

<u>exhibit</u>|**1.4**

Basic Management Skills

Management Level

Top Managers

Middle Managers

First-Line Managers

Nonmanagers (Personnel)

Source: Excerpted from *Management,* 5th ed. p. 13, by Richard L. Daft, copyright © 2000 by Harcourt, Inc., reprinted by permission of the publisher.

similar activities. Whether an organization is large or small, whether it operates in the business, government, or nonprofit sector, it requires essentially similar skills and functions of its managers. We now explore those skills and functions to learn how they relate to the broader activities of an organization.

Management Skills   The skills that Carly Fiorina, Charles Hickey, and other managers need are of three basic types: conceptual, human, and technical, as illustrated in Exhibit 1.4.[15] The specific applications of these skills vary, of course. Nevertheless, we can observe some general patterns in what organizations require.

conceptual skills

The ability to see the organization as a whole and to see how its parts are related.

Conceptual skills are those that involve the ability to see the organization as a whole and to see how its parts are related. These skills include abilities related to thinking and planning. A manager with good conceptual skills appreciates how the team depends on and contributes to the division, how the division relates to others in the organization, and how the overall organization fits into its environment. Conceptual skills are necessary for appreciating how each member of an organization contributes to total quality, customer satisfaction, and organizational performance. These skills become increasingly important in moving to higher levels of the organization. At Cisco Systems, a major player in the telecommunications industry, Ammar Hanafi must use conceptual skills daily to carry out his work as mergers-and-acquisitions director. Hanafi is responsible for finding and acquiring companies that will enhance Cisco's existing strengths. He must be able to see Cisco's big picture—strengths, weaknesses, opportunities, and threats—and evaluate what a new acquisition can contribute. Besides the potential acquisition's product line, Hanafi also considers how well the company's employees can be integrated into Cisco and what Cisco must do to keep the employees (and their knowledge) from leaving after the acquisition takes place. Cisco considers it critical to retain the target companies' existing employees to benefit from their expertise, a testament to its recognition of their value.[16]

human skills

The ability to work with and through other people and to work effectively as a group member.

Human skills are abilities to work with and through other people and to work effectively as a group member. Examples of human skills are effectiveness in leading, motivating, communicating, and resolving conflicts. Because the essence of a manager's job is to get things done through others, human skills are an indispensable part of a manager's repertoire. They are equally important at all levels of management. Herb Kelleher of Southwest Airlines is a classic example of a manager with human skills. Kelleher, chief executive of Southwest since 1981, serves many roles at the airline—coach, quarterback, cheerleader, not to mention sometime Elvis impersonator—to bolster morale and make work fun. He "hires good people and gives them the freedom to do their job," says the company's marketing manager. But Kelleher is not above sitting down with employees to tackle problems together: "I give them a tremendous amount of latitude once they get started, but . . . when there is a problem, I make myself totally available for as long as it takes to get that problem solved." Under Kelleher's management, employees created the first airline industry Web site and set up the industry's first ticketless travel reservations, now a common service. In addition, Southwest is the only U.S. carrier to have turned a profit every year since 1973.[17]

Technical skills involve an understanding of and proficiency in performing specific tasks. A manager with technical skills has mastered the methods and equipment required for performing some function, whether it is selling services, designing a production or information system, or financing a capital project. Often an organization promotes someone to his or her first management job because that person has mastered a technical skill and can guide other employees to do the same. However, the person can succeed only by employing enough human and conceptual skills to manage. And as managers move up through the organization's hierarchy, technical skills may become less important. When JRL Enterprises, a small New Orleans–based educational software developer, was developing an interactive mathematics product for 21 schools, it relied on the technical expertise of software programmers and engineers. JRL's vice president of operations, Craig S. Lee, focused on ensuring that the company hired employees with the correct technical skills and that they could collaborate on a new network. Lee's technical background helped him provide guidance to his staff while they handled the details of setting up the network and developing the math software program. Lee helped the company succeed well enough to expand from 10 to 25 employees in one year, and together, they accomplished the mathematics program development.[18] In a small company such as JRL, managers may need to rely on their technical expertise more often than in larger organizations with more specialized departments and employee roles.

technical skills

The ability to understand specific tasks and to perform them well.

Management Functions   On the surface, a software development manager's job may seem to be far different from a telecommunications merger-and-acquisitions director's or an airline CEO's. However, as shown in Exhibit 1.5, the basic functions of any manager's job are similar:

* Planning
* Organizing
* Leading
* Controlling

A manager directs these activities to attain organizational goals efficiently and effectively, whether those goals are producing bug-free software,

exhibit **1.5**

Basic Management Functions

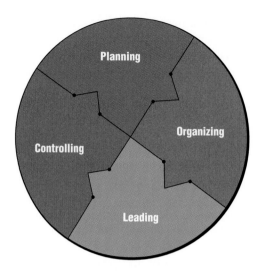

planning

The management function of defining goals and determining how to achieve them.

organizing

The management function of assigning tasks to departments, delegating responsibility, and allocating resources.

leading

The management function of using influence to inspire and empower others to work toward the organization's goals.

growing in a high-tech industry, or ensuring that planes arrive safely and on time.

Planning is the management function of defining goals and determining how to achieve them. Managers must clearly establish plans for where the organization is headed. Otherwise, they cannot share their vision of the organization's future with others. Planning activities may take many forms, from envisioning the organization's overall mission and establishing detailed objectives to asking employees to schedule work. The approach used may depend on the manager's individual characteristics, the scope of his or her responsibility, the experience and skills of employees, the organization's values, and the nature of the work to be done. Ammar Hanafi of Cisco Systems relies heavily on planning to make sure the company's acquisitions are selected well and carried out smoothly.

Through planning, managers decide what needs to be done; they also decide who will do that work and with what resources. **Organizing** is the management function of assigning tasks to departments, delegating responsibility, and allocating resources. Here are some examples of decisions that managers make in the course of organizing:

- How best to form a team to diagnose a problem
- Whether to make one sales manager responsible for selling to consumers and another responsible for business accounts
- Whether to contract with an outside firm to handle payroll and benefits administration
- How to cut out layers of management in an organization

As we will show in later chapters, the management function of organizing can influence organizational behavior—for example, how motivated employees are and whether they contribute ideas for improvement. Craig S. Lee of JRL Enterprises needed to master organizational skills to staff his organization and to set up a network to allow his fledgling company to grow.

Effective planning and organizing give managers a solid foundation on which to lead. The function of **leading** involves using influence to inspire and empower others to work toward the organization's goals. Herb Kelleher of Southwest Airlines is an effective leader, as shown not only in his company's high performance but in his employees' dedication to the airline. Just as planning establishes where to go and organizing provides the means for getting there, leading serves as a compelling invitation to embark on the trip. Chapter 11 explores the critical role of leadership in organizations.

Finally, **controlling** is the process of measuring performance, comparing it with objectives, and making any adjustments necessary for keeping the organization on track toward its goals. Controlling is an important check on the other management functions. If performance falls short of objectives, then the plans are unrealistic or improperly focused, the organization has not provided all the necessary resources (such as funding and qualified personnel), or leadership has been ineffective. So, controlling provides important feedback to managers—a performance problem uncovered through controlling signals a need for change in one or more of the other areas. Often, knowledge of organizational behavior can help employees identify and correct problems uncovered through controlling.

controlling

The management function of measuring performance, comparing it with objectives, and making any adjustments necessary for keeping the organization on track toward its goals.

In many organizations, employees at all levels help carry out the managerial functions. Recent trends have seen more delegation of authority and decision making to employees themselves, so it is important for all workers to understand and master these functions.

Management activities by definition cannot be isolated from an organization's people and environment. Rather, planning, organizing, leading, and controlling connect all employees with one another and with outside forces:

- Careful planning requires knowledge of an organization's strengths and weaknesses, including the knowledge of its human resources and their ability to work together. It also requires an appreciation of the threats and opportunities outside the organization. From salespeople to service technicians, employees have the potential to offer much information in this regard.
- Organizing sets up the systems that can foster or hinder cooperation and communication among an organization's human resources. It also can identify needs for hiring and training.
- Leading is a primary means by which an organization fully draws on the talents of its human resources.
- Controlling evaluates how well an organization and its people are interacting with the environment.

Challenges Facing Today's Managers

Changing expectations of how to carry out these functions, as well as changes in the global environment, have transformed modern organizations. The changes have in effect created a new world of work that demands even greater sensitivity to issues of organizational behavior than in the past. Some specific challenges facing today's managers are globalization, demographic changes, ethics, rapid change, and the need for continuous learning.

Globalization The environment of today's organizations is truly global. An organization may have offices, branches, or subsidiaries on different continents. Even the smallest organization may send people overseas or go on the Internet to arrange a deal. Employees may be local residents, often with varied ethnic backgrounds, or immigrants. Research by *Export Today* found that in the 20 U.S. states with the highest levels of foreign investment, a significant share of the population worked for foreign-owned firms—from 4.8 percent in Delaware and Illinois to 11.0 percent in Hawaii.[19] Customers, too, come from a global pool, especially for the growing number of organizations that have set up Web sites. And company ownership is also international, as stock purchasers make buy-and-sell decisions wherever the investments are most attractive, from exchanges in Japan and Malaysia to those in England and Germany. In sum, organizations' shareholders, suppliers, customers, managers, and employees may come from anywhere in the world. In the following example, a global perspective enabled Holiday Inn to find enough qualified employees in spite of a limited pool of local residents.

❧ Holiday Inn

Low unemployment rates in the United States have forced the Holiday Inn AquaDome and Resort Hotel in the Wisconsin Dells resort area to take a global approach to hiring. As Holiday Inn and other Wisconsin Dells businesses prepared for a recent summer tourist season, unemployment in Wisconsin was at just 3.1 percent, among the lowest rates in the nation. There wasn't much hope of attracting workers from local cities and towns.

So Holiday Inn joined other businesses in hiring candidates brought into the United States by Career Staffing, a local personnel agency. Career Staffing found qualified employees in Latvia, Lithuania, the Czech Republic, Poland, and South Korea.

Among the immigrant workers at Holiday Inn during a recent summer was Tatiana Luhova, on vacation from her studies as an international finance major at the University of Bratislava in Slovakia. She took a job as a housekeeper in order to earn the better U.S. wages and gain overseas experience. Her supervisor, Shandra Smith, was thrilled to see her. "A lot of workers just don't show up the next day," Smith told a reporter. "This is hard, repetitive work."[20]

From the example of the Holiday Inn staff, we can see that an organization may search worldwide to find good employees. But globalization presents both opportunities and challenges to an organization. The pool of employees, customers, and suppliers is larger than for an organization with a localized outlook. However, learning how to select and work with employees, customers, and suppliers from differing cultural backgrounds can be challenging. For instance, when Wal-Mart entered the German market, it had to develop strategies for motivating employees in a culture where business relationships are more formal than the exuberance and friendliness that Wal-Mart values. The company transferred some practices from the United States and adapted others. For example, its German employees join in the pep-rally-style Wal-Mart cheer, but in a bow to different cultural practices, they are not expected to adhere to the Ten-Foot Rule (U.S. employees must talk to any customer standing within a 10-foot radius). Instead, the company simply encourages employees to be friendly to customers.[21]

In addition to forcing companies to adapt to different cultures, the global marketplace stiffens competition by exposing each organization to a wider range of competitors than before. To keep up, organizations need knowledge about the values and expectations of their international customers and employees. They may acquire that knowledge through training, as well as through hiring people from diverse backgrounds—especially those able to communicate their knowledge effectively. Chapter 2 discusses these and other implications of the global environment.

Demographic Changes   Even within North America, the workplace is becoming more diverse than ever. The African-American, Hispanic, and Asian segments of the U.S. population are growing faster than the white population. The Census Bureau projects that the non-Hispanic white segment of the population will therefore fall from its 1995 level of 74 percent to 64 percent by 2020 and 53 percent by 2050.[22] This translates into more people of color in the workforce of most organizations. In addition, over recent decades the labor force participation of women has risen. Yet another source of workforce diversity is greater access to the workplace by people with disabilities. If the old image of a worker as a white, able-bodied, English-speaking male was ever adequate, it certainly is not today, nor will it be in the future.

To meet recruitment needs, organizations will obtain a growing share of human resources from immigrants, people of color, and other diverse populations. The resulting diversity in human resources can help organizations serve a diverse customer base and bring in a wider range of experiences. Diversity also poses challenges, however. In some cases, different segments of the labor force will expect and use different styles of leadership, communication, and decision making. Organizations therefore must be able to support a wider range of styles, or else they must equip their employees to understand and use the organization's chosen style. Employees need to be able to identify and correct situations in which misunderstandings may result from cultural differences. The next chapter explores diversity's potential benefits and challenges in greater detail.

Another equally significant demographic trend is that the overall population is aging. In other words, people are living longer, and the birthrate is slowing. So the proportion of the population over age 65 is growing, and the proportion of the population under age 25 is declining. Exhibit 1.6 shows the resulting rise in the projected median age of the U.S. population. By 2030, the Census Bureau forecasts that about one-fifth of the total U.S. population will be over 65.[23] If all of them were to retire at age 65, the Social Security burden on society would be enormous. However, because of increased health services and generally better nutrition, they will tend to be healthier and to have longer life expectancies than this age group has had in the past.

The aging population will also contribute to workforce diversity because organizations are likely to employ a growing share of older workers, many of them in their second or even third careers. Many qualified older workers may insist on working part time or for only a few months at a stretch, as a kind of semiretirement. Such arrangements demand greater flexibility from organizations. They also demand creativity. Individuals, organizations, and society may begin to redefine what it means to be "retired" to include second careers, part-time and temporary assignments, and other work arrangements.

Even more significantly, in the developed nations of the world, the birthrate has slowed dramatically. In some nations, it has slowed to the point where population growth comes largely from immigration, rather

exhibit **1.6**

Median Age of U.S. Population

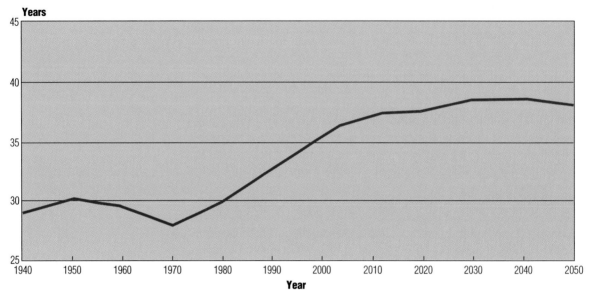

Note: Figures from 1995 to 2050 are projections from past data.
Source: Jennifer Cheeseman Day, *Population Projections of the United States by Age, Sex, Race, and Hispanic Origin: 1995 to 2050*, U.S. Bureau of the Census, Current Population Reports, P25-1130 (Washington, D.C.: U.S. Government Printing Office, 1996), p. 8.

than births. Census Bureau projections for the United States show the rate of population growth at a level below that of any period except the Great Depression. That rate is actually expected to decrease in the first half of the twenty-first century.[24] Similar trends are occurring in most parts of the world.[25] Noted business consultant Peter Drucker has observed that a population in which people older than a traditional retirement age outnumber young people, as is expected in the United States, Japan, and many European nations, is a condition that is unprecedented in recorded history.[26]

Because of the slowing birthrate, human resources will become even more scarce and, therefore, more valuable. Finding and keeping qualified human resources will become more and more challenging. Of particular concern is that as organizations' top leaders retire, there may be no large pool of replacements for these key positions. David Whitwam, chief executive of Whirlpool Corporation, once commented, "The thing that wakes me up in the middle of the night is not what may happen to the economy or what our competitors may do next. What wakes me up is worrying about whether we have the leadership capability and talent."[27] A survey of 150 *Fortune* 500 companies found that one-third expect some of their executives to leave within the next five years, yet as many firms report they are not confident of being able to find suitable people to replace them.[28] This problem is especially great in organizations that eliminated layers of management and, with them, a primary training ground for future executives. Such organizations need new ways of developing and attracting executive talent.

Ethics People have long been concerned about **ethics**—principles and values defining what conduct is morally acceptable. We encounter ethical issues whenever we are in a position to harm or benefit someone. Societies expect people in these situations to choose a course of action that meets ethical standards.

ethics

Principles and values defining what conduct is morally acceptable.

In organizations, the manager's role requires not only ethical behavior but also setting a standard for ethical behavior in others. Adding to this challenge, the public today scrutinizes managers' and organizations' behavior more closely than ever and evaluates their conduct. Furthermore, in a diverse workplace, employees are more likely than in the past to encounter differing definitions of what constitutes ethical behavior.

Although ethics is essential, there is no easy formula for defining ethical behavior in all situations. The law alone does not define ethical behavior; often, ethical standards for a particular situation are not spelled out anywhere. Instead, when faced with issues related to ethics, people are generally guided by one of the following views of ethics:

- *Utilitarian*—People evaluate a dilemma in terms of the potential harms and benefits of the available courses of action and consider who might be affected by the action. The ethical action is the one that results in the greatest good for the greatest number of people.
- *Golden Rule*—People evaluate possible actions by imagining how it would feel to be one of those affected by the action. The ethical course of action is the one that the decision maker would have preferred if he or she had been the affected party. This view of ethics is named after a teaching of Jesus that came to be known as the Golden Rule: "Do to others as you would have them do to you." Although the name comes from Christian tradition, similar precepts are part of other religions as well.
- *Kantian/rights*—People evaluate a situation based on the rights of the people involved. This view of ethics is based on the work of philosopher Immanuel Kant, who said that in a moral universe, each person has the rights of free consent, privacy, freedom of conscience, freedom of speech, and due process. An ethical choice would be one that avoids violating these rights.
- *Enlightened self-interest*—People pursue their self-interests on the assumption that as all members of society do this, society overall will benefit. Presumably, lying or hurting someone would not be in a person's own long-term self-interest. Such behavior would ultimately affect how other people treat you.
- *Justice approach*—People base decisions on what is fair, equitable, and impartial. Thus, you do not treat people differently based on arbitrary characteristics such as appearance. Furthermore, rules must be administered fairly so that everyone understands and is subject to them. Also, when someone causes a loss, that person should compensate the one who suffered the loss.

Depending on a person's or organization's views of ethics, the solution to an ethical dilemma may vary. The choice is especially difficult when any course of action hurts others or when individual or cultural differences support different approaches to ethics.

Given the challenges, skill in ethical decision making requires practice, as does any other complex skill. To create ethical organizations, top managers define, enable, and reward ethical behavior. Individuals, for their part, benefit from identifying and choosing to work in organizations that share their ethical standards. Future chapters provide guidance for many ethics-related issues, including understanding cultural differences (Chapter 2), motivating employees to behave ethically and in other desirable ways (Chapters 5 and 6), making ethical decisions (Chapter 10), leading employees (Chapter 11), resolving differences ethically (Chapter 13), and shaping an organization's culture, including its values (Chapter 17).

Technological and Organizational Change   We live in a time of extraordinary change. As the Industrial Age revolutionized the way people lived a century ago, moving them from agricultural work to factory work, today the Information Age is revolutionizing how we work. A key part of this change is the switch from organizations primarily relying on production workers to those relying on knowledge workers.

This change requires a redefinition of how the organization views the people who work there.[29] The traditional approach to management considers an organization's people to be *employees* who work full time and depend on the organization for their livelihood. Furthermore, these people are *subordinates;* that is, they take orders from their managers, who presumably know more than the employees do. This understanding overlooks some recent trends:

• A growing segment of the people who work for organizations are not employees but people providing services under contract—for example, people from an outsourcing contractor that provides data-processing services or independent contractors who handle engineering assignments for a fee. These people may work on temporary or part-time assignments.

• Knowledge workers function as *associates* more than as subordinates. In other words, they contribute specialized knowledge that their managers may not have. For example, they may know more about the organization's customers or about a specialized discipline. Managers depend on them to share information.

With knowledge workers the individual worker owns the "means of production"—that is, the knowledge for which he or she was hired. Managers cannot simply order these people to do tasks; they must share knowledge and collaborate on solutions. Furthermore, if a knowledge worker chooses, he or she can take that knowledge elsewhere. This makes skill at recruiting, retaining, and motivating talented people more important than ever.

Thus, to fully benefit from their workers' knowledge, organizations require a new style of management—one that focuses on developing and empowering employees. After all, if the manager knows less than the employees about information systems or lasers or medical diagnostics, the employees should be making decisions in the area of their expertise. And the manager's value? It lies less in knowing what employees know and more in the ability to empower and lead others. One organization that understands and appreciates the value of knowledge workers is Buckman Laboratories, a specialty chemical maker based in Memphis, Tennessee.

Buckman Laboratories

If any company requires knowledge workers, it is Buckman Laboratories, which develops and markets specialty chemicals requiring advanced research and development. Buckman's CEO, Robert Buckman, says he first began to appreciate the need to share knowledge in the 1980s: "We ran Ph.D.s around the world to exchange information about what worked in various situations. But we couldn't hire enough Ph.D.s and run them fast enough to meet the needs of our people on the front line or our customers." Further complicating the challenge, Buckman has customers in over 80 countries and people speaking over a dozen different languages.

Robert Buckman concluded that the solution was to develop an organizational culture, technology, and work processes that would encourage the sharing of knowledge. The company set up rewards for change by measuring performance in terms of the percentage of sales attributable to new products. It equipped personnel with laptop computers so that they can share information anywhere, anytime via the Internet. Buckman also shifted the focus of the company's information systems department, renaming it the "knowledge transfer department," reflecting its aim of focusing on the service it is supposed to provide. More broadly, as a leader, Buckman holds out the value of trust and empowerment. It's what he calls "building our rules for the 98 percent or 99 percent who do stuff right [instead of curtailing the few who do wrong]. If you make that mental shift, it's amazing what windows you . . . open for your people."[30]

In addition to knowledge workers such as those at Buckman Laboratories, today's organizations need flexible strategies to incorporate change as a source of opportunity for the organization. Change is a given in the current environment, with products, companies, and even industries experiencing shorter life cycles.[31] Furthermore, in the ethereal world of e-commerce, change happens faster than ever. In the words of JoMei Chang, who heads Vitria Technology, a software firm, "Because the Internet lowers barriers to entry, it amplifies weaknesses. There's no place to hide. It forces you to be on your toes, every minute, every second."[32]

Merely defending the organization against change in such an environment cannot be a source of competitive advantage. Successful organizations instead must anticipate change, look for the changes that they can benefit from, and plan how to incorporate those changes into their strategy.[33] Chapter 18 provides a more detailed discussion of change and how it affects organizations and their people.

Lifelong Learning In a related challenge, a changing environment demands that the acquisition of knowledge also be fast paced and relentless. For the manager, this requires constant learning plus the added challenge of enabling employees to learn. The solution at many organizations is to embrace a culture of lifelong learning—that is, to become a **learning organization.**

A learning organization recognizes that if the primary contribution of knowledge workers is knowledge, this defines how to increase and utilize the value of human resources. First, the organization's individuals and groups need the means to increase their knowledge. Second, they need to make their knowledge available to one another and to the organization. In the words of management consultant Peter Drucker, "Knowledge work requires continuous learning on the part of the knowledge worker, but equally continuous teaching on the part of the knowledge worker."[34]

learning organization

An organization that embraces a culture of lifelong learning, enabling its groups and individuals to continually acquire and share knowledge.

what would you do?

CREATING A COMPANY FOR TODAY'S HIGH-TECH WORLD

Amazon.com has been in existence less than a decade. But from its beginnings as the biggest online bookstore through its expansion to music and videos to its current incarnation as a seller of toys, home-improvement products, consumer electronics, and software, the company has been moving at lightning speed. Amazon's founder, Jeff Bezos, has been focused not only on selling products from the company's Web site but on providing its 13 million customers with personalized service, recommendations, and entertainment so they will keep coming back. Bezos relies on his employees to adapt to the many tasks the company needs to accomplish and to work together to help wherever they are needed at the moment.

From buildings scattered across Seattle, Amazon's 5,000-plus employees tackle their work and put in long days. Creativity is important for Amazon's editorial staff members, who bounce ideas off one another in meetings. They are responsible for guiding shoppers through the site by writing product reviews and interviews and offering gift ideas. Amazon's software developers must learn to write Web-coding programs on the fly to put documents online and to keep the site new and inviting. None of these knowledge workers seem to have current business cards to describe their positions—their jobs have changed by the time the company prints them up. Yet with all the high-tech work that goes on, nearly all Amazon employees spend half their time each December pitching in to wrap packages, man customer service lines, and help the "pickers" (warehouse order fillers) complete the mountain of customer orders for shipment. Nearly 40 percent of Amazon's employees work in the distribution and customer service centers, and speed and efficiency are critical skills for those workers.

Wherever Amazon's workers are located and whatever they do, their work ethic is strong. "You have to prove yourself. . . . But once [managers] notice that you're on time, hardworking, and consistent, good things happen. Some people are really motivated. Others aren't motivated at all. And they usually don't last long," says one employee who moved from the print shop to a distribution center. But for those who stay, there is teamwork and a feeling of belonging. "Everybody works really, really hard. It's that exhaustion-exhilaration feeling you had in college in finals week. But here, it's 24/7," says an Amazon manager.

Imagine that you are a manager working for an e-commerce business such as Amazon.com.

1. First, decide what products and services your company will offer, or pick a company that you're interested in. What type of employees do you need to accomplish your work?

2. What could you do to build a sense of common purpose among your employees? Ideas can range from on-the-job activities to social events.

3. How can you make your company stand out from its competition? That is, what types of resources do you need to build a strong company for a sustained competitive advantage?

Source: Michael Krantz, "Inside Amazon's culture: The inner workings and workers." Time.com: 1999 Person of the Year, December 27, 1999, accessed at www.pathfinder.com/time.

Effectively and efficiently managing knowledge workers therefore requires effective systems for communication, group decision making, and teamwork. In addition, organizations must value and reward training, collaboration, and other routes to learning. Managers will be charged with finding ways to set goals for learning and teaching. TQM will continue to be important, because the quality of knowledge is as essential as its quantity. Furthermore, knowledge workers themselves are often in the best position to define these standards.

Many observers of the business world have concluded that lifelong learning requires an entirely new way of looking at how organizations should be structured and how employees and managers should act.[35] Their combined vision of a learning organization is one in which teams of employees collaborate to meet customer needs in a fast-changing, diverse global environment. To foster learning, managers in this type of organization empower employees at all levels to share knowledge, identify prob-

exhibit 1.7
Traditional versus Learning Organizations

	Traditional Vertical Organization	**Learning Organization**
Forces on Organizations		
Markets	Local, domestic	Global
Workforce	Homogeneous	Diverse
Technology	Mechanical	Electronic
Values	Stability, efficiency	Change, chaos
Management Competencies		
Focus	Profits	Customers, employees
Leadership	Autocratic	Dispersed, empowering
Doing work	By individuals	By teams
Relationships	Conflict, competition	Collaboration

Source: Excerpted from *Management,* 5th ed. p. 24, by Richard L. Daft, copyright © 2000 by Harcourt, Inc. reprinted by permission of the publisher.

lems, and make decisions. This enables the organization to continuously experiment and improve its capabilities. Exhibit 1.7 contrasts this concept of a learning organization with the traditional vertical organization.

Understanding concepts of organizational behavior is especially important in a learning organization. That is because people skills like leadership and change management are essential when the environment is turbulent, employees are empowered to make decisions, and every response requires flexibility and change. Formal policies, procedures, and reports are simply too inflexible. Learning requires expanding what employees can do, rather than placing constraints on them.

apply it

1. Interview an older worker—one of your parents, your grandparents, or anyone who has been in the workforce a long time. Ask that person about his or her job—the types of skills needed, the amount of change encountered. Get a broad picture of the person's job. What type of skills did the person need day to day—conceptual, human, or technical? Could the person be considered a knowledge worker? Was learning and ensuring quality an important part of the job?

2. Now picture your ideal job. How does it differ from that of the person you interviewed? How is it the same?

This book shows how organizations, groups, and individuals interact

The remaining chapters of this book explore specific areas of organizational behavior. They are grouped into parts that detail ways in which individuals, groups, and organizations influence one another. This grouping is shown in Exhibit 1.8.

Chapter 2 concludes this introductory part by describing the context in which modern organizations operate. This context is increasingly global and diverse. The chapter therefore describes opportunities and challenges resulting from globalization and diversity.

Part II discusses the individuals who make up an organization, focusing on how organizations are affected by individual characteristics. Chapter 3 explores a variety of dimensions of individual differences: aptitude and ability, personality, attitudes, and values. Chapter 4 discusses the individual processes of perception and attribution (attributing causes to events). Chapters 5 and 6 explore motivation in terms of what motivates people and how the process of motivation works.

exhibit | **1.8**

Influences among Individuals, Groups, and Organizations

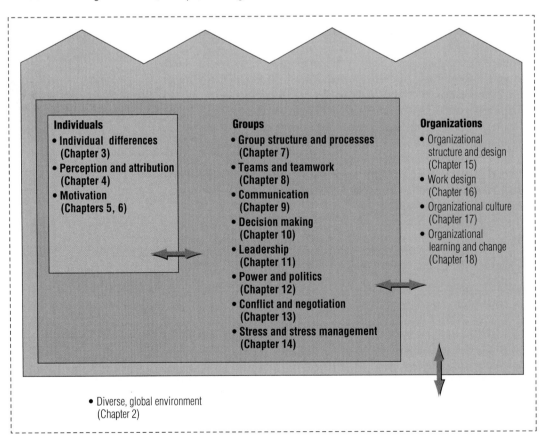

Individuals
- Individual differences (Chapter 3)
- Perception and attribution (Chapter 4)
- Motivation (Chapters 5, 6)

Groups
- Group structure and processes (Chapter 7)
- Teams and teamwork (Chapter 8)
- Communication (Chapter 9)
- Decision making (Chapter 10)
- Leadership (Chapter 11)
- Power and politics (Chapter 12)
- Conflict and negotiation (Chapter 13)
- Stress and stress management (Chapter 14)

Organizations
- Organizational structure and design (Chapter 15)
- Work design (Chapter 16)
- Organizational culture (Chapter 17)
- Organizational learning and change (Chapter 18)

- Diverse, global environment (Chapter 2)

The chapters in Part III cover interpersonal processes that take place in organizations. Chapter 7 defines *group* and discusses the structure and actions of groups. Chapter 8 examines a specific type of group that many organizations have formed: teams. It distinguishes teams from other types of groups and teamwork from other types of work. Chapter 9 discusses communication in organizations—what the processes are and how technology has influenced those processes. Chapter 10 explores decision making. We often think of decision making as something a person does independently, but many organizational decisions are made in group situations such as teams or meetings. Another interpersonal process that is sometimes considered an individual characteristic is leadership, the topic of Chapter 11. Today's organizations are increasingly recognizing leadership as a two-way process involving both followers and leaders. Next, Chapter 12 addresses issues of power and politics, including how people acquire and use power in organizations. Chapter 13 covers how conflict arises in organizations and how people manage conflict, including through negotiation. Chapter 14 concludes Part III with a discussion of stress in organizations and tactics for stress management.

Part IV covers topics related to the impact of organizations on individual and group behavior. Chapter 15 discusses organizational structure and design in terms of its impact on the organization's people. Chapter 16 explores ways in which organizations determine what work needs to be done and how it is allocated among employees. Chapter 17 defines *organizational culture* and examines how an organization's culture affects its people's behavior. Finally, Chapter 18 covers organizational processes that are especially critical in today's dynamic environment: continuous learning and change.

The wide range of topics presented in this book affect each member of an organization. We all perceive and communicate; we all make decisions and encounter stress; we all must understand the scope of our work assignments. Thus, any organization benefits when its people understand organizational behavior, and any employee can benefit personally from applying this understanding. The topics of organizational behavior are even more critical to organizations that apply them to transforming themselves so they can succeed in the modern workplace. Understanding and applying organizational behavior is the means by which managers and other leaders mobilize the organization's human resources to create a successful organization.

apply it

1. The topics of organizational behavior named in this section play a role in most organizational successes and challenges. To develop your appreciation of OB's relevance, find two or three news stories that describe an organizational success or problem. Was the success or problem related to the organization's people, its competitiveness, or its ability to change? Summarize your findings.

summary OF KEY CONCEPTS

- **Organizational behavior describes how organizations and people interact.** Organizational behavior (OB) consists of the actions and interactions of individuals and groups in organizations. An organization is a social entity that is goal directed and deliberately structured. The individuals in an organization may form groups, or the organization may structure them into work groups. The study of organizational behavior is an interdisciplinary approach that applies the behavioral and social sciences, various business disciplines, and the study of ethics. It builds on principles of the various management schools of thought.

- **Studying organizational behavior can help shape successful organizations.** Applying the principles of organizational behavior can help managers shape successful organizations. OB pro-

vides insight for the management of human resources, an organization's only sustainable competitive advantage. Organizational behavior also influences the success of management efforts such as total quality management and the creation of learning organizations.

- **Managers' skills, functions, and challenges have some common characteristics.** Managers need a combination of conceptual, human, and technical skills. They use those skills in carrying out the management functions of planning, organizing, leading, and controlling. These functions are especially important in today's fast-changing environment, as managers confront globalization, demographic shifts, ethical issues, new technology and organizational designs, and the need for lifelong learning.

KEY terms

organizational behavior (OB), p. 4

organization, p. 4

scientific management, p. 7

human relations school, p. 8

management science school, p. 10

open systems school, p. 11

sustained competitive advantage, p. 12

total quality management (TQM), p. 14

performance, p. 16

effectiveness, p. 16

efficiency, p. 16

manager, p. 17

conceptual skills, p. 18

human skills, p. 18

technical skills, p. 19

planning, p. 20

organizing, p. 20

leading, p. 20

controlling, p. 21

ethics, p. 25

learning organization, p. 27

DISCUSSION questions

1. Why is it so important for managers to support their commonsense ideas with an understanding of the research, theory, and practice in the field of organizational behavior? Can you think of a time when your own common sense turned out to be wrong? What were the consequences?

2. Think of an organization you have worked for or belonged to, and evaluate the way its managers fulfilled their responsibilities. What school(s) of management thought did the managers seem to follow? Explain your choice(s).

3. Return to the story of Carly Fiorina at the beginning of the chapter. What type of management skills does Fiorina possess? What type of workers does Hewlett-Packard employ? Why are they im-

portant to a company such as Hewlett-Packard? From the details provided, would you categorize H-P as a learning organization? Why or why not?

4. Why do today's organizations rely so heavily on the knowledge worker? Do you see yourself as a knowledge worker? Why or why not?

5. This is just the beginning of your course, but you can start thinking about ways that organizations can use knowledge of human behavior to manufacture and sell their products or offer services— and do it better than their competitors. Think of a store you have shopped in, a movie theater you've been to recently, or a product you've bought lately. In what ways do you think the organization that sold or manufactured what you

purchased can use human behavior to be the best at what it does?

6. In what ways do you think total quality management will be important for companies in the twenty-first century?

7. Think of a job you have had or a class project you have worked on with fellow classmates. Was collaboration a prominent part of the experience? If so, did collaboration increase the group's efficiency and effectiveness? If not, why not?

8. Again, think of a job you have had or a group project you have worked on, either in class or outside of class (such as a drama performance or community service project). In what ways might your employer or a group leader have used the controlling function of management to identify and correct problems?

9. What kinds of information might the employees of a beach or lake resort be able to offer manage-

ment to aid in planning? (Think in terms of the knowledge they may have.)

10. Through a knowledge of organizational behavior, what steps might the management of a casual-style restaurant chain take to stay competitive in light of an aging population?

11. How might the manufacturer of video games "redefine who its people are" in order to stay ahead of the competition?

12. Why will it be important for companies to become learning organizations as they meet the challenges of this century?

13. How does total quality management dovetail with the concept of the learning organization? Do you think it is possible to have one without the other? Why or why not?

S E L F - D I S C O V E R Y exercise

Rate each of the following questions according to this scale:

5 I always am like this.
4 I often am like this.
3 I sometimes am like this.
2 I rarely am like this.
1 I never am like this.

____ 1. When I have a number of tasks or homework to do, I set priorities and organize the work around the deadlines. **C**

____ 2. Most people would describe me as a good listener. **H**

____ 3. When I am deciding on a particular course of action for myself (such as hobbies to pursue, languages to study, which job to take, special projects to be involved in), I typically consider the long-term (three years or more) implications of what I would choose to do. **C**

____ 4. I prefer technical or quantitative courses rather than those involving literature, psychology, or sociology. **T**

____ 5. When I have a serious disagreement with someone, I hang in there and talk it out until it is completely resolved. **H**

____ 6. When I have a project or assignment, I really get into the details rather than the "big picture" issues.* **C**

____ 7. I would rather sit in front of my computer than spend a lot of time with people. **T**

____ 8. I try to include others in activities or when there are discussions. **H**

____ 9. When I take a course, I relate what I am learning to other courses I have taken or concepts I have learned elsewhere. **C**

____ 10. When somebody makes a mistake, I want to correct the person and let her or him know the proper answer or approach.* **H**

____ 11. I think it is better to be efficient with my time when talking with someone, rather than worry about the other person's needs, so that I can get on with my real work. **T**

____ 12. I know my long-term vision for career, family, and other activities and have thought it over carefully. **C**

____ 13. When solving problems, I would much rather analyze some data or statistics than meet with a group of people. **T**

___ **14.** When I am working on a group project and someone doesn't pull a full share of the load, I am more likely to complain to my friends rather than confront the slacker.* **H**

___ **15.** Talking about ideas or concepts can get me really enthused and excited. **C**

___ **16.** The type of management course for which this book is used is really a waste of time. **T**

___ **17.** I think it is better to be polite and not to hurt people's feelings.* **H**

___ **18.** Data or things interest me more than people. **T**

Scoring key

Add the total points for the following sections. Note that starred* items are reverse scored, as such:

1   I always am like this.
2   I often am like this.
3   I sometimes am like this.
4   I rarely am like this.
5   I never am like this.

1, 3, 6, 9, 12, 15   **C**onceptual skills total score ___
2, 5, 8, 10, 14, 17   **H**uman skills total score ___
4, 7, 11, 13, 16, 18   **T**echnical skills total score ___

The above skills are three abilities needed to be a good manager. Ideally, a manager should be strong (though not necessarily equal) in all three. Anyone noticeably weaker in any of the skills should take courses and read to build up that skill.

*reverse scoring item
Source: Excerpted from *Management,* 5th edition pp. 29–30, by Richard L. Daft, copyright © 2000 by Harcourt, Inc., reprinted by permission of the publisher.

ORGANIZATIONAL BEHAVIOR in your life

As you read in this chapter, researchers in the field of organizational behavior generate and test their ideas in a variety of ways, including surveys, laboratory studies, case studies, and field studies. To get yourself thinking like an organizational behavior researcher, conduct your own field study. Go to your local supermarket. While you are shopping for your groceries, look around at what's going on. Is the manager visible? How many check-out lines are open? How long are the lines? What day of the week are you shopping, and at what time? Roughly how many customers do you think are in the store? Is the courtesy desk open? How many people are staffing it? Is it easy to find a roving employee if you have a question? Do the employees wear name tags or uniforms? Overall, do the employees seem friendly and happy? Is there anyone available to help senior citizens or disabled customers? Are items easy to locate? Add your own questions to this list and jot down your observations.

When you get home, write down a summary of your observations and note whether, overall, the shopping experience was a positive one. Then recommend several ways in which the store manager could use his or her management skills—conceptual, human, and technical—to improve the way the supermarket serves its customers.

ORGANIZATIONAL BEHAVIOR news flash

@ The Women's National Basketball Association now makes sports headlines almost as frequently as the NBA. Teams such as the Houston Comets and stars such as Cynthia Cooper are household names to loyal fans. The fact that the media consider this organization newsworthy illustrates demographic changes—in the marketplace and in the workforce. The WNBA is an organization that is growing fast, and its managers and employees (not to mention the players) will have to acquire some knowledge of organizational behavior among changing demographics in order to survive in a fickle sports market.

Access the Web, and either use the "news of the day" listing on your search engine or type in the key name Women's National Basketball Association to locate information or articles on the organization. Print out whatever information you can and analyze the information from an organizational behavior perspective, focusing on how a diverse workforce and diverse marketplace will affect the way WNBA managers will need to develop and use their conceptual and human skills in the organization. Then imagine that you are a journalist for the business or sports section of the newspaper and write an article based on your analysis. You may be asked to discuss your article in class or submit it to your instructor via e-mail or printout.

global diversity EVENTS

Every day, the news is filled with stories about organizations—large and small companies, nonprofit organizations like the Red Cross and Sierra Club, as well as local, state, and federal government agencies. You can examine many of these stories from an organizational behavior perspective.

Access the Internet and look through any news page, even the one provided by your search engine, such as Yahoo! or Lycos. (If you don't have Web access, browse through a newspaper or news magazine.) Look for a story about a high-tech organization that is expanding globally into new marketplaces or on the Web. Some possible examples include Amazon. com, Dell Computer, or Oracle Corp. (Note that these are suggestions only; other companies or organizations are fine.) When you find an interesting story or stories, consider the following questions:

1. What special skills does the organization need in its employees? Its top managers?

2. Look for hints on how the company is organized. What departments does it have? How big is its workforce and where are they located? Who are its customers?

3. What types of change or trends are currently affecting the company?

minicase ISSUE

Controlling in a Chaotic Environment

Part of a manager's function is to control or measure performance based on an organization's goals. The control function uncovers problems to be corrected. But what if the top managers in an organization fail to take responsibility for the controlling function? That's what happened at Compaq Computer Corp., which, despite the high-profile acquisition of Digital Equipment Corp., has lost five of its eleven senior officers and posted first-quarter earnings in a recent year that were less than half of its Wall Street predictions. How could a formerly successful company perform so poorly?

Vision Lost. "We lost vision, we lost empowerment, we lost speed," concedes former chief strategist Robert W. Stearns. "We replaced it with bureaucracy and a team that has not jelled." But instead of monitoring performance and making corrections, Compaq's board of directors failed to take action when it became obvious that the company's strategy was not working. As the company tried to ward off low-cost competitor Dell and at the same time build itself into a full-service computer maker to take on IBM, Compaq became enmeshed in a tangled web of unrelated products and sales tactics, with no one emerging to identify the problems or to propose corrections.

After the departure of the company's top executives, Chairman Benjamin Rosen finally stepped in, promising to take immediate action. However, he diplomatically refuted those who criticized the board for inaction. "There has to be a line between not waiting forever . . . and acting capriciously," he said.

What's Next? What will Rosen do while the board searches for a new chief executive? Industry experts place the blame with Compaq's strategy and propose that Compaq should transfer most of its corporate business to direct sales (instead of relying on resellers) and should be wary of getting involved with consumer PCs because of stiff competition. Rosen has concluded that the problem lies elsewhere: "We believe our fundamental strategy is correct," he states.

Certainly, many challenges and decisions can influence the company's performance. One of these is determining how to integrate Digital's and Compaq's organizational cultures and technologies. Digital came to Compaq with some outdated businesses such as manufacturing computer boards, and someone needs to sort through all of Compaq's myriad technologies and products. Other challenges include the search for a new chief, a realignment of sales forces and outlets, initiatives into selling on the Internet, evaluation of products and technologies coming through acquisitions, decisions on staffing, and the growing trend of corporations buying directly from manufacturers. Compaq must decide which of these activities have business potential, which are already working well, and which need more (or less) resources. A strong dose of controlling activity at all levels of the company would probably help give back to managers the sense of vision they say they have lost.

1. If you were the interim CEO of Compaq, how would you use the management functions to begin turning the company around?

2. Imagine that you are on the board of directors at Compaq. Write a profile describing specific conceptual, human, and technical skills that you would look for in a candidate for the job of chief executive.

3. In what ways might Compaq benefit from a reliance on knowledge workers?

4. Look up some current news on Compaq and see whether any of your observations have been implemented. How is the company doing as a result?

Source: Gary McWilliams and Joann S. Lublin, "Compaq Could Have Averted Missteps," *The Wall Street Journal,* April 20, 1999, pp. A3, A6.

two
CHAPTER

2

Managing Diversity in the United States and Abroad

preview

After studying this chapter, you should be able to:

- Discuss the importance and dimensions of diversity as they apply to the workplace.

- Describe the benefits that organizations gain by managing diversity.

- Define *corporate culture* and its role in managing diversity.

- Suggest the characteristics of a program for effectively managing diversity.

- Explain how national cultures differ and how that affects organizational behavior.

- Identify different types of expatriates.

- Describe the various levels of global participation of an organization.

- Identify an effective cross-cultural preparation program.

Molex Is Everywhere

Molex makes more than 100,000 kinds of electronic and fiber-optic connectors and switches that are used in the electrical systems of cars, computers, medical equipment, and office electronics. Molex is a truly global company—both its products and employees are found worldwide. Although based in a suburb of Chicago, the $1.6 billion company operates 49 manufacturing facilities in 21 countries. Molex has nearly equal sales from North and South American and Far Eastern markets (approximately 40 percent each), with the remaining 20 percent of sales in Europe. Only one-third of Molex's 13,000 employees are located in the United States. Two-thirds of Molex's employees are local nationals; that is, Molex hires employees from the countries in which it has manufacturing facilities. These countries include Korea, Malaysia, Thailand, Japan, and Ireland. Because of its global reach, Molex can shift its business emphasis from one area of the world to another as economic conditions change. For example, during a recent economic downturn in Asia, Molex still invested in its operations for the future by remodeling warehouses and building inventory in Malaysia. At the same time, the company expanded its business by opening new factories in China and Puerto Rico. This global reach is emphasized in the company's corporate goals: excellent customer service, development of human resources, establishment of a truly global company, and meeting or exceeding financial targets.

To reach these goals, Molex realized that all employees have to understand the company goals and the needs of different global markets. The company goals have been translated into all the languages of its employees and displayed on posters in each of the company's facilities. Also, to encourage a wider corporate view, the company encourages relocation of employees to operations in different countries. Why? According to Molex's vice president of human resources for corporate training and development, "There's nothing like living and working with people outside your home country to make you understand you're really in something bigger than Molex Japan or Molex Germany." Molex has many different work arrangements, ranging from "regular expatriates," who live outside their home country for three- to five-year assignments, to "short termers," who visit a Molex facility in a different country for six to nine months.

Employees are also encouraged to communicate with each other through the company's global information system. This system connects all company operations with a single communications link. The global information system gives Molex a tool for integrating technology, manufacturing, and administrative systems around the world. Besides the information system, the company's chairperson, chief operating officer, and executive vice president personally spend a day at each location, touring the facility and meeting with employees. These meetings help to ensure that employees know the company's history, financial performance, and future plans. Molex's emphasis on global relocation and communication systems provides a corporate "glue" that holds together employees who have different backgrounds and perspectives.

> *"There's nothing like living and working with people outside your home country to make you understand you're really in something bigger than Molex Japan or Molex Germany."*
> —**Molex's vice president of human resources for corporate training and development**

The force of global business continues to dominate organizations and their employees. Look around you: It has brought Asian and European electronics, clothes, and cars to the United States, transported Hollywood movies, professional sports, and music to a global audience, and broadened the menus and tastes of diners around the world. Organizations continue to look for and find new opportunities across the globe. With today's use of technology, including the Internet, remote spots have become instantaneously accessible. Companies such as Coca-Cola, McDonald's, IKEA, DaimlerChrysler, Nokia, and Nike operate all over the world, employing thousands and bringing goods and services to a worldwide market. Like Molex, many of these companies operate in a climate of diversity because of their global operations. But the world's people are not homogeneous—they vary in many, often subtle, ways. So, it is critical for organizations to understand and manage their diversity.

Diversity refers to differences among people based on their identification with various groups.[2] The most recognizable group identification categories are gender and ethnicity. However, other types of group membership, including sexual orientation, physical ability, religion, or family status, may be "invisible." Companies such as Molex that operate globally also experience diversity in the different nationalities of their employees and customers. All types of group memberships can affect employees' attitudes and behaviors in an organization. They also affect their ability to work with other employees who identify with different groups.

diversity

Differences among people based on their identification with various groups.

Global reach and a diverse U.S. workforce increase the importance of managing diversity

Managing diversity is complex whether a company operates globally or within the United States. As we discussed in Chapter 1, technology is transforming the way work is conducted. Keep in mind that even if U.S. companies do not have a physical presence such as a plant or sales office in another country, Web technology gives companies access to international customers, vendors, and suppliers. Even without face-to-face interaction, employees need to understand other people's values, interests, and culture to successfully complete sales, provide information, and correctly interpret e-mail and other communications from around the globe. Managing diversity is relevant for every organization regardless of size or location because customers are also becoming more diverse. So, a company's profits and survival depend on its ability to manage diversity. The key is to understand and work with different employees and customers to maximize the benefits and reduce the drawbacks.

Global Business

More and more companies are entering international markets by exporting their products overseas, building manufacturing facilities in other countries, entering into alliances with foreign companies, and engaging in e-commerce (providing products and services using the Web). Some projections suggest that developing nations such as Taiwan, Indonesia, and China may account for over 60 percent of the world economy by 2020, while the share of economic activity of the United States and other industrialized countries' will drop from 50 percent to 38 percent.[3] The move to global markets is not unique to a particular sector of the economy or product market. For example, with the U.S. diaper market now flat, Kimberly-Clark and Procter & Gamble are targeting new markets such as China, India, Israel, Russia, and Brazil. The demand for steel in China, India, and Brazil together is expected to grow 10 percent annually in the coming years, three times the U.S. rate. Nucor Corp. is opening a minimill in Thailand and partnering with a Brazilian company for a $700 million steel mill in northeastern Brazil. Other steel companies, such as LTV Corp. and North Star Steel, are moving into Asia, Europe, and Australia.[4]

Consider also the business market in China. About 200 million of the 1.2 billion Chinese citizens live in cities where Western goods—from Hewlett-Packard computers to Combos salty snacks—are available. To capitalize on this new market, Starbucks coffee recently expanded into Beijing, China.[5] Because competition for local managers exceeds the available supply, companies have to take steps to attract and retain managerial talent. Prior to hiring new managers, Starbucks took time to research the motivation and needs of the potential local management workforce. The company found that the frequent movement of local managers from one Western company to another was caused by several factors. In the traditional Chinese state-owned companies, rules and regulations provide little room for creativity and autonomy. Also, Starbucks learned that in many joint U.S.–China ventures, local managers were not trusted. According to one managerial recruit, "People are looking for a good working environment where they can learn; they are looking for dignity." To avoid costly management turnover, Starbucks took steps in its recruiting efforts to emphasize the company's casual culture and opportunities for career and personal development. Starbucks has also decided to spend considerable time in training. New managers are sent to Tacoma, Washington, to learn the corporate culture and the secrets of brewing fancy coffees. This not only ensures Starbucks' reputation for high-quality coffee will be maintained in China, it also helps sell managerial recruits on staying with the company.

Diversity in the U.S. Workforce

Managing diversity is also important because the U.S. workforce is becoming increasingly diverse. By 2006, the workforce is projected to be 72 percent white, 11 percent African-American, 12 percent Hispanic, and 5 percent Asian and other ethnic or cultural groups.[6] The Asian and Hispanic labor force increases are due to immigration trends and higher-than-average birthrates. Women's participation in the labor force is expected to increase, while men's participation rates are expected to continue to decline for all age groups under 45 years. By the year 2020, it is estimated that women will comprise fully half of the total full-time U.S. workforce.[7] This change represents an enormous opportunity to organizations, but it also means that organizations must deal with issues such as work-family conflicts, dual-career couples, and sexual harassment. Since seven of ten women in the labor force have children, organizations should prepare to take more of the responsibility for child care. Another factor contributing to diversity is aging of the labor force, as discussed in Chapter 1. The labor force aged 45 to 64 will grow faster than any other age group as the baby-boom generation (those born from 1946 to 1964) continues to age.

Managing diversity involves a change in traditional beliefs and assumptions. Organizations have to take a broader view of the ideal employee and strive to operate bias-free. People of African, Asian, and Hispanic descent are expected to make up about 35 percent of the U.S. population by 2020. Already more than 30 percent of New York City's residents are foreign born. Miami is two-thirds Hispanic-American; Detroit is two-thirds African-American; and San Francisco is one-third Asian-American.[8] Whereas in previous generations most foreign-born immigrants came from Western Europe, 84 percent of recent immigrants come from Asia and Latin America.[9] These immigrants come to the United States with a wide range of backgrounds, and often without adequate English language skills. Organizations must not only face the issues of race, ethnicity, and nationality to provide a fair workplace but also develop sufficient educational programs to help immigrants acquire the technical and customer service skills required in a service economy.

Because of this diversity, it is unlikely that any one set of values will characterize all employees. However, research suggests that to maximize employees' motivation and commitment to company goals, employees should be given the opportunity to fully use and develop their skills, meet their interests, and live a desirable lifestyle, including a better balance of work and nonwork activities.[10] Fostering this type of work environment requires management practices that provide opportunities for individual contribution and entrepreneurship.[11]

Creating a diverse, inclusive workforce is a continuous process at Hewlett-Packard, where managers see diversity as an opportunity to tap a broad range of human potential and use it to keep learning, changing, and growing.[12]

Hewlett-Packard

Hewlett-Packard's commitment to diversity is an outgrowth of the company's founding values of treating each employee with dignity and respect. Hewlett-Packard recognizes many aspects of diversity, including race, gender, culture, age, economic status, sexual orientation, and physical ability. Employee involvement with others from different backgrounds is encouraged through participation in network groups that represent various minority groups in the organization. Workers also discuss diversity issues at coffee talks, task forces, diversity councils, conferences, and regular team meetings. Supporting diversity is ingrained in the culture at H-P. Managers and other workers are encouraged to challenge assumptions and biases and to challenge inappropriate language or behavior. Often, those who do so are rewarded for being "diversity champions."

Another key to H-P's successful diversity program is managers' leadership and involvement. Senior managers representing all of H-P's businesses develop and drive diversity initiatives worldwide. However, top managers then delegate responsibility and accountability to all managers and employees through performance plans and evaluation of their effectiveness. Diversity objectives are also stressed in hiring activities and decisions. For example, the company considers a diverse interviewing team as important as a diverse slate of candidates. This helps to ensure that minority candidates have equal opportunities to move into higher management positions. In addition, H-P sponsors a unique mentoring program to make sure that support for diversity is more than talk. The program matches minority employees with higher-level managers, who are then evaluated on their employee's progress. Many participants in the program have moved into higher-level jobs in the company. The company also supports and funds a number of other employee development and job enrichment opportunities for minority employees.

As you can see from reading about the experiences of Hewlett-Packard, Molex, and Starbucks, managing diversity is challenging. To help you gain a good understanding of how to manage diversity, we turn to the various dimensions of diversity and the ways attitudes toward diversity affect the degree to which companies are able to capitalize on the benefits of a diverse workforce. We examine the concept of company and national culture, especially how culture affects organizational behavior. We also examine what actions organizations can take to manage diversity in the United States, as well as to prepare employees to work in the global business environment.

apply it

1. Choose a company that you, a friend, or a relative work for. Find out what diversity challenges the company faces either in the United States or globally. Also, identify what the company is doing to manage diversity.

Diversity is more than race or color

As we mentioned earlier, diversity relates to differences based on people's identification with groups. Some differences are more visible than others. Several important dimensions of diversity are illustrated in Exhibit 2.1. This "diversity wheel" shows the combinations of traits that make up diversity.

exhibit **2.1**

Dimensions of Diversity

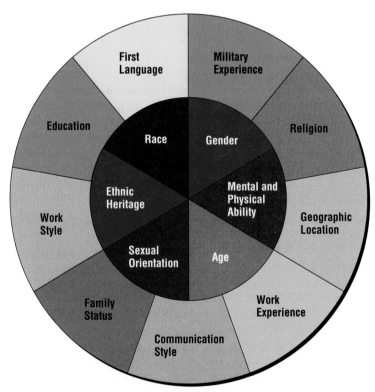

Source: Implementing Diversity by Marilyn Loden, Richard D. Irwin, copyright 1996. Reproduced with permission of The McGraw-Hill Companies.

The inner wheel represents primary dimensions of diversity, which include inborn differences or differences that have an impact throughout a person's life.[13] Primary dimensions are core elements through which people shape their self-image and world view. These dimensions include age, race, ethnicity, gender, mental and physical abilities, and sexual orientation. If you turned the wheel, these primary characteristics would match up with different secondary dimensions of diversity, shown in the outer wheel.

Secondary dimensions of diversity can be acquired or changed throughout a person's lifetime. These dimensions tend to have less impact than the primary dimensions, but they nevertheless affect a person's self-definition and world view and affect how a person is viewed by others. For example, veterans of the Gulf War may have been profoundly affected by their military experience and may be perceived differently from other people. An employee who has been a member of a college football team may be perceived differently from one who was active in theater or music. Secondary dimensions such as work style, communication style, education, and work experience are particularly relevant in the organizational setting.[14] The challenge for today's organizations is to recognize that each person can bring value and strengths to the workplace based on his or her own unique combination of diversity characteristics.

Benefits of Diversity

In the past organizations traditionally focused on a narrow model of business—that work is the most important part of an employee's life and increasing power and success in an organization were primary goals. Today, the importance placed on power and individual success has diminished. Many employees place greater importance on performing interesting work and finding happiness and balance in both their work and nonwork lives. They want to be responsible for making decisions regarding their work and the organization. Employees will work long hours in exchange for amenities that can help balance their work and nonwork activities. For example, at BMC Software in Houston, employees put in ten- to twelve-hour days. As one employee says, "This place isn't for wimps."[15] In return, the company provides the services of a bank, store, dry cleaner, hairdresser, nail salon, massage therapist, and sports facilities that help its employees meet a variety of personal and family needs. The range of amenities BMC Software provides is an example of one way that organizations manage diversity—by helping employees reduce stress and outside demands, the company can serve a variety of interests and lifestyles. As Roy Wilson, BMC's chief of human resources says, "Work/life balance? I know this is hard to believe, but you do feel like you can get away while you're here. It gives you a balanced life without having to leave."

Providing amenities also helps BMC retain top talent—one of the benefits of managing diversity. Exhibit 2.2 presents other benefits of managing diversity. Historically, in many companies managing diversity was seen as a way to reduce costs related to discrimination lawsuits rather than as a means to improve company performance. However, as Exhibit 2.2 shows, management of diversity definitely affects the bottom line by its influence on creativity, problem solving, employee retention, and creation of new

exhibit **2.2**   How Managing Diversity Can Provide a Competitive Advantage

Argument	Rationale
Cost	As organizations become more diverse, the cost of a poor job in integrating workers will increase. Those who handle integration well will thus create cost advantages over those who don't.
Resource acquisition	Companies develop reputations for favorability as prospective employers for women and ethnic minorities. Those with the best reputations in managing diversity will win the competition for the best personnel. As the labor pool shrinks and changes composition, this edge will become increasingly important.
Marketing	For multinational organizations, the insight and cultural sensitivity that members with roots in other countries bring to the marketing effort should improve these efforts in important ways. The same rationale applies to marketing to subpopulations within domestic operations.
Creativity	Diversity of perspectives and less emphasis on conformity to norms of the past (which characterize the modern approach to management of diversity) should improve the level of creativity.
Problem solving	Heterogeneity in decisions and problem-solving groups potentially produces better decisions through a wider range of perspectives and more thorough critical analysis of issues.
System flexibility	An implication of the multicultural model for managing diversity is that the system will become less determinant, less standardized, and therefore more fluid. The increased fluidity should create greater flexibility to react to environmental changes (i.e., reactions should be faster and less costly).

Source: T. H. Cox and S. Blake (1991), "Managing cultural diversity: Implications for organizational competitiveness." *Academy of Management Executive* 5: 47. Reprinted with permission.

markets for a company's products and services. Organizations that do not manage diversity will find that employees' talents are underutilized and their personal and professional needs are not being met. As a result, they can become dissatisfied and leave, resulting in a poorly performing, less competitive organization. Companies that are known for managing diversity also have an edge in recruiting talented employees. Managing diversity benefits employees as well. Employees are likely to experience feelings of accomplishment at work and feel they are valued.

Organizational Culture and Diversity

organizational culture

System of shared meaning held by employees that distinguishes the organization from other organizations.

The combined experiences of an organization's employees make up its culture. **Organizational culture** refers to a system of shared meaning held by employees that distinguishes the organization from other organizations.[16] Culture plays a number of different roles in an organization. It distinguishes one organization from another, providing a sense of identity for employees. Culture also provides standards, or norms, for how employees should act, what they should say, and what they should do. Thus, it guides and shapes the attitudes and behavior of employees. This system of shared meaning creates a "climate" or "feel" that is obvious to employees as well as company visitors.

Exhibit 2.3 shows the primary characteristics of an organizational culture. Evaluating an organization on these characteristics provides a picture of the organizational culture. For example, consider Southwest Airlines' unique culture.[17] Chairman Herb Kelleher believes that if you don't treat your own employees well, they won't treat customers well. Kelleher says,

exhibit **2.3** Characteristics of an Organizational Culture

Innovation and Risk Taking	Are employees encouraged to take risks?
Precision/Analysis/Attention to Detail	Are employees expected to exhibit precision, analysis, and attention to detail?
Outcome/Results Orientation	Does management focus on results or processes used to make the results?
People Orientation	Do management decisions take into account the effects on employees?
Team Orientation	Are work activities organized around teams?
Aggressiveness/Competitiveness	Are employees aggressive and competitive or laid back?
Stability/Maintenance of Status Quo	Do company activities emphasize growth or the status quo?

Source: Based on J. Chatman and D. F. Caldwell, "People and organizational culture: A profile comparison approach to assessing person-organization fit," *Academy of Management Journal* (September 1991): 487–516; J. A. Chatman and K. A. Jehn, "Assessing the relationship between industry characteristics and organizational culture: How different can you be?" *Academy of Management Journal* (June 1994): 522–553; M. Siegel, "The perils of culture conflict," *Fortune* (November 8, 1998): 257–262.

"Southwest's essential difference is not machines or things. Our essential difference is minds, hearts, spirits, and souls." How does this translate into day-to-day operations of the airline? Southwest Airlines is characterized by a fun atmosphere. For example, flight attendants have been known to pop out of overhead luggage bins. A large amount of time is devoted to employee recognition. The annual company chili cook-off, awards dinner, and Friday "Fun Day" where employees wear casual clothes or even costumes to work illustrate the company belief that relaxed employees with a sense of humor are productive employees. When Southwest won an award for customer service for the fifth year in a row, an airplane was dedicated to all employees; their names were engraved on the outside of overhead luggage bins. Employee involvement in decision making is also important. An active informal suggestion system and all types of incentives (cash, merchandise, travel passes) reinforce the idea that employees are expected to contribute to improving customer service and cost savings. The Southwest culture also places a high value on the flexibility of the workforce. Flight attendants, ramp agents, and even pilots prepare airplane cabins for the next flight by unloading baggage, cleaning bathrooms, and carrying out trash. As one employee stated, "We don't service an airplane, we attack it!" Kelleher trusts employees and gives them discretion in decision making because he believes that you cannot anticipate all of the situations that will occur on an aircraft or at the airport.

As the Southwest example illustrates, an organization's culture is heavily influenced by the personality and beliefs of the company's founders and top-level managers. Culture is also influenced by an organization's selection and training systems. For example, Southwest uses interviews and tests to determine whether job candidates will fit in with the culture. That is, do they have a sense of humor? Can they work effectively in a culture in which they are asked to use their own judgment and work beyond the job description? Organizations frequently emphasize their culture in advertisements and other recruiting tools to attract a certain type of person. Once employees join the organization, they learn the culture through stories, rituals, and symbols. For example, Southwest employees tell the story of a reservations clerk who flew with an elderly customer on the first leg of her flight to make sure she made her connecting flight safely. Rituals are activities that reinforce key organizational values. Southwest's "Fun Days" are an example of rituals. The airplane dedicated to all employees serves as a symbol of how Southwest values customer service and the employees who provide it.

Cultural Acceptance

Valuing diversity by welcoming, recognizing, and cultivating differences among people so they can develop their unique talents and be effective organizational members is difficult. Why? Organizations want employees to accept their culture, especially companies such as Southwest that have a very strong, clearly defined culture. At the same time, organizations have to be sure that they don't create a culture that is insensitive to people who are different or stifle the unique strengths that employees bring to work.

ethnocentrism

The belief that one's own group or subculture is inherently superior to other groups or cultures.

Ethnocentrism is the belief that one's own group or subculture are inherently superior to other groups and cultures. An ethnocentric view makes it difficult to value diversity, but viewing one's own culture as the best is a natural tendency among most people.[18] Moreover, the U.S. business world tends to reflect the values, behaviors, and assumptions of a rather homogeneous, white, middle-class, male workforce.[19] Indeed, most theories presume that workers share similar values, beliefs, motivations, and attitudes about work and life in general. These theories presume there is one set of behaviors that best helps an organization to be productive, and as such, should be adopted by all employees.[20] This one-best-way approach explains why a manager from one culture may cause a problem with an employee from another; for example, by touching employees from cultures that consider casual touching inappropriate, by not knowing how to handle a gift from an immigrant, or by requiring employees to work on weekends.

monoculture

A culture that accepts only one way of doing things and one set of values and beliefs.

Monoculture Ethnocentric viewpoints and a standard set of cultural practices produce a **monoculture,** a culture that accepts only one way of doing things and one set of values and beliefs. This can cause problems in a diverse workforce. People of color, women, gay people, people with disabilities, the elderly, and people with children or other family responsibilities may feel undue pressure to conform to a monoculture, may be victims of stereotyping attitudes, and may be presumed deficient because they are different. White, heterosexual men, many of whom themselves do not fit the notions of the "ideal" employee, may also feel uncomfortable with the monoculture and resent stereotypes that narrowly label all white males as racists and sexists. Valuing diversity means ensuring that all people are given equal opportunities in the workplace.[21]

For example, Johnathan Spiller, CEO of Armour Holdings, a company that makes protective gear for police officers, must travel extensively in his job. But the father of two believes commitments to attend his daughters' school events are also important. This runs counter to the traditional stereotype that white males are more involved with work than they are with family. He tries to attend his own daughters' events, and he also is committed to making sure no one at his 4,000-employee company has to make excuses for wanting to be involved with his or her family. Also, one of Armour's efforts to help employees balance work and family involves working with nine other companies to build a new child care center close to the worksite.[22]

Pluralism   The goal for organizations seeking cultural diversity is pluralism rather than a monoculture, and ethnorelativism rather than ethnocentrism. **Ethnorelativism** is the belief that groups and subcultures are inherently equal. **Pluralism** means that an organization accommodates several subcultures. Movement toward pluralism seeks to fully integrate into an organization employees who otherwise would feel isolated and ignored. As the workforce continues to change, organizations will come to resemble a global village.

Most organizations must consciously shift from a monoculture perspective to one of pluralism. Employees in a monoculture may not be aware of culture differences, or they may have acquired negative stereotypes toward other cultural values and assume that their own culture is superior. Through rigorous training to change both attitudes and behaviors, employees can be helped to accept different ways of thinking and behaving, the first step away from narrow, ethnocentric thinking. This type of training involves several steps: making stereotypes and values conscious, understanding the value of diversity and why negative stereotypes are limiting in organizations, working on business problems with people from different cultures, and improving communications and conflict skills. Changes at the organizational level are also necessary. For example, organizations should provide a system for women and members of ethnic groups to communicate their concerns and should reward managers for meeting diversity goals or creating a work environment that values diversity. Ultimately, through training, employees are able to take a broader cultural view, reducing or eliminating judgments of appropriateness, goodness, badness, and morality of differences. Cultural differences instead are experienced as essential, natural, and joyful, enabling an organization to enjoy true pluralism and take advantage of diverse human resources.[23]

UNUM Life Insurance Company of America has made a firm commitment to break out of monoculture thinking. Senior managers, most of whom were white males, began meeting regularly with representatives of minority groups and were shocked to hear how out of place many minorities felt in the workplace. Since then, UNUM has implemented a widespread diversity program, including a three-day diversity workshop to help employees develop "cultural competence," a newsletter covering diversity topics, and "Lunch and Learn" talks that help employees understand different cultures and perspectives. Most importantly, a diversity board made up of members from each minority group at the company meets monthly with UNUM's president to discuss systematic changes in policies and procedures to encourage and support diversity.[24] By helping all employees, beginning with senior managers, develop greater sensitivity toward and acceptance of cultural differences, UNUM is moving away from an ethnocentric attitude and is accepting and integrating people from diverse backgrounds.

ethnorelativism

The belief that groups and subcultures are inherently equal.

pluralism

An organization's accommodation of several subcultures, including employees who would otherwise feel isolated and ignored.

apply it

1. Think of an organization at school or at work. Does the organization have a distinct culture? Describe some of its stories, rituals, and symbols.

2. Does the organization have a monocultural or pluralistic viewpoint? That is, how accommodating is the organization of different subcultures? Provide examples of organizational policies, treatment of workers, or the work environment to support your answer.

Organizations struggle to provide fair, safe, and productive environments

Thirty years ago adult white males dominated the U.S. workforce, and economic conditions were fairly stable. This status quo did not allow all members of society to participate equally in business. Because of widespread prejudice and discrimination, legal and social coercion were necessary to allow women, people of color, and immigrants to become part of the economic system.[25] Today, the situation has changed. More than half the U.S. workforce consists of women and members of ethnic groups, and the economic picture is changing rapidly as a result of international competition. Let's look at some of the reasons for these dramatic changes and some remaining barriers to full participation.

Equal Employment Opportunity Laws

Federal laws prohibit discrimination based on race, religion, sex, or national origin. You may have studied equal employment opportunity laws such as the Civil Rights Act of 1964, amended in 1991, in other classes. Initially, equal employment opportunity laws were designed to assist businesses to recruit, retain, and promote members of ethnic and cultural groups and women in their workforces. The laws have since been expanded to cover persons with disabilities (The Americans with Disabilities Act of 1991) and older employees (Age Discrimination in Employment Act). Most research has focused on the progress of women and ethnic groups since these laws went into effect. To some extent, equal employment opportunity laws have been successful, opening organization doors to women and members of ethnic and cultural groups. However, despite the increased job opportunities, women and ethnic and cultural groups still encounter many barriers to top management posts.

To comply with equal employment opportunity laws, many companies actively recruited women and minorities or designated some job openings only for women or members of ethnic groups (a process known as *affirmative action*). Companies often succeeded in identifying a few select individuals who were recruited, trained, and given special consideration. These people carried great expectations and also were under great pressure to perform well. They were highly visible role models for the newly recruited groups and were generally expected to march right to the top of the corporate ladder.

Within a few years, it became clear that few of these pioneers would reach the top. Companies' top managers typically became frustrated and upset because the money poured into equal employment opportunity yielded few results. The individuals were disillusioned about how difficult it was to advance in organizations and felt frustrated and alienated. Managers were unhappy with the program failures and may have doubted the qualifications of people they recruited. Did they deserve the jobs at all? Were women and ethnic minorities to blame for the failure of the equal employment opportunity laws? Should companies be required to meet federally mandated minority-hiring targets?

In recent years, outspoken opponents of special recruitment and hiring of women and ethnic minorities have brought the debate into the public consciousness. National political leaders have made statements strongly opposing racial hiring preferences, and hiring and college admissions practices targeting minorities have been dismantled in several states. Women and ethnic minorities themselves often believe that special recruiting and hiring practices are harmful. One reason for this may be the stigma of incompetence that persons hired through these programs often experience. One study found that both working managers and students consistently rated women who were hired through a special affirmative action program as less competent and recommended lower salary increases than for men and women not hired through the special program.[26]

In the wake of such controversy, some companies are turning to different strategies to foster a bias-free workplace, such as employee training and special programs to increase appreciation of cultural differences, rather than strict head counts for hiring. Activists for social justice, on the other hand, argue that such efforts allow companies to put on a show of virtue without having to do anything concrete. Al Jackson, director of diversity and staff development at *Scholastic Magazine,* echoes the sentiments of many when he notes that most firms do not hire and promote women and minorities as readily as they do white males, no matter how much they talk about valuing diversity.[27]

Ultimately, the problem with special recruiting and hiring programs boils down to an unspoken and often unintended sexism and racism in organizations. Although it is rare to hear or see blatant expressions of racism and sexism in corporate America today, many minorities believe a more subtle but just as dangerous form has emerged. For instance, some whites believe racial discrimination is in the past and that African-Americans are pushing too hard and moving too fast. They often see the effort given to actively recruiting women and ethnic minority groups as unfair.[28] In addition, top managers often find it hard to understand just how white and male their corporate culture is and how forbidding it seems to those who are obviously different.[29] The special recruiting and hiring programs fail when women, people of color, and immigrants are brought into a monoculture system and when the burden of adaptation falls on the candidates coming through the system rather than on the organization itself. Part of the reason for the failure may be attributed to what is called the glass ceiling.

The Glass Ceiling

The **glass ceiling** is an invisible barrier that separates women and minorities from top management positions. They can look up through the ceiling and see top management, but prevailing attitudes are invisible obstacles to

glass ceiling

Invisible barrier that separates women and minorities from top management positions.

Barbara Hyder (left), photographed at the Vogue *Fashion Awards with model Roshumba, is a woman who has broken through that invisible obstacle, the glass ceiling, and moved into top management. She recently left her job as international regional president at Mary Kay Cosmetics in Dallas and joined the ranks of Internet executives as CEO of Gloss.com, an online beauty startup in San Francisco. Hyder gained executive experience at traditional beauty companies Maybelline and Mary Kay, where she launched international offices for both. She is an example of an increasingly common type of Internet executive: a seasoned member of the corporate managerial class who leaves a big, traditional, nontech company to try her hand as an Internet CEO. (Source: © Todd Chalfant)*

their own advancement. A recent study also suggested the existence of "glass walls," which serve as invisible barriers to important lateral movements within the organization. Glass walls bar women and minorities from gaining experience in areas such as line supervisor positions that would enable them to advance vertically.[30]

Evidence of the glass ceiling is the cluster of women and ethnic minorities at the bottom levels of the corporate hierarchy. A recent study shows that 97 percent of the top managers in the United States are white and at least 95 percent of them are male.[31] Women and ethnic minorities also earn substantially less. As shown in Exhibit 2.4, at all levels of education, women earn less than their male peers. As women move up the career ladder, the wage gap widens; at the level of vice president, a woman's average salary is 42 percent less than her male counterpart's.[32] Census data also show that African-American and Hispanic employees' average income is 60% or less of that earned by white employees.[33]

In particular, women who leave the corporate world to care for young children have a difficult time moving up the hierarchy when they return. One term used to describe this is the *mommy track,* which implies that women's commitment to their children limits their commitment to the company or their ability to handle the rigors of corporate management. These women risk being treated as beginners when they return, no matter how vast their skills and experience, and they continue to lag behind in salary, title, and responsibility.[34]

Another current issue related to the glass ceiling is homosexuals in the workplace. Many gay men and lesbians believe they will not be accepted as they are and risk losing their jobs or their chances for advancement. The director of human resources for a large Midwestern hospital would like to be honest about her lesbianism but says she knows of almost no one at her level of the corporate hierarchy who has taken that step—"It's just not done

exhibit | **2.4**

The Wage Gap

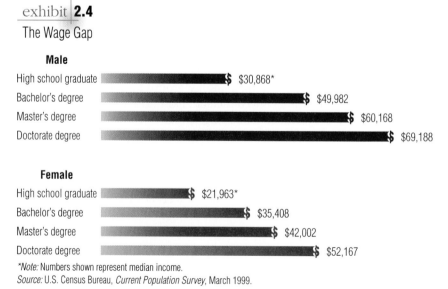

Male

High school graduate	$30,868*
Bachelor's degree	$49,982
Master's degree	$60,168
Doctorate degree	$69,188

Female

High school graduate	$21,963*
Bachelor's degree	$35,408
Master's degree	$42,002
Doctorate degree	$52,167

*Note: Numbers shown represent median income.
Source: U.S. Census Bureau, *Current Population Survey,* March 1999.

here."[35] Thus, gays and lesbians often fabricate heterosexual identities to keep their jobs or avoid running into the glass ceiling they see other employees encounter.

Why does the glass ceiling persist? The monoculture at top organizational levels is the most frequent explanation. Top-level executives tend to hire and promote people who look, act, and think like them. Compatibility in thought and behavior plays an important role at higher levels of organizations.[36] For example, in a survey of women who have managed to break through the glass ceiling, fully 96 percent said adapting to a predominantly white male culture was an important factor in their success.[37]

Another reason for the persistent glass ceiling is the relegation of women and ethnic minorities to less visible positions and projects so that their work fails to come to the attention of top executives. Stereotyping may lead to the assumption that a woman's family life will interfere with her work or that minorities lack competence for important assignments. Women and ethnic minorities often believe that they must work harder and perform at higher levels than their white male counterparts to be noticed, recognized, fully accepted, and promoted.

So how do such people break through the glass ceiling? Ability, motivation, versatility, self-confidence, and self-direction are key. Consider two women who are considered to be among the most powerful women in American business.[38] Carly Fiorina, the new CEO of Hewlett-Packard (profiled at the beginning of Chapter 1), won the job not because she was a woman but because she demonstrated an ability to pick up on what was important. She told the search committee, "I know what I don't know. And I know our strengths are complementary. You have deep engineering prowess. I bring a strategic vision which H-P needs." Nina DiSesa, chair of McCann-Erickson, the world's largest ad agency, says, "Competing in a man's world is what I want to do. I'm very much in touch with my male side. I'm really competitive, and I find confrontation stimulating. But I keep those qualities in check. I use my feminine traits—empathy, collaboration."

Emotional Intimacy

Close relationships between men and women often have been discouraged in companies for fear that they would disrupt the balance of power and threaten organizational stability.[39] This opinion grew out of the assumption that organizations are designed for rationality and efficiency, which were best achieved in a nonemotional environment. Close relationships between men and women were assumed to lead to romantic or sexual relationships, upsetting the stability of work.

A recent study of friendships in organizations sheds interesting light on this issue.[40] Managers and workers responded to a survey about emotionally intimate relationships with both male and female coworkers. Many men and women reported having close relationships with an opposite-sex coworker. The friendships resulted in trust, respect, constructive feedback, and support in achieving work goals. Called "nonromantic love relationships," these intimate friendships did not necessarily become romantic, and they affected each person's job and career in a positive way. Rather than causing problems, nonromantic love relationships, according to the study, affected work teams in a positive manner because conflict was reduced. In-deed, men reported somewhat greater benefit than women from these rela-tionships, perhaps because the men had fewer close relationships outside the workplace upon which to depend.

However, when such relationships do become romantic or sexual in nature, real problems can result. Office romance is on the rise, with more than 30 percent of employees reporting they have been involved with a coworker at some time in their careers. Although not all office romances lead to trouble, usually they create difficulties for managers. Such relation-ships disrupt productivity and distract coworkers. According to Dorothy Light, president of a human resource consulting business in Minneapolis, office romances are the biggest productivity disrupters next to mergers and downsizing. One of the most difficult dilemmas is how to deal with other staff members who may be jealous, intrigued, or embarrassed by the rela-tionship or may spend their time gossiping about the involvement of their coworkers.[41] There is a growing recognition that companies can't ban office romance, but it is an important issue that should be managed carefully.

Romances that require the most attention from managers are those that arise between a supervisor and a subordinate. These relationships often lead to morale problems among other staff members, complaints of fa-voritism, and questions about the supervisor's intentions or judgment. Al-though few companies have written policies about workplace romance in general, 70 percent of companies recently surveyed have policies prohibit-ing romantic relationships between a superior and a subordinate.[42] At IBM, training programs and written policies emphasize that a manager can be-come romantically involved with a subordinate only if he or she agrees to stop supervising the subordinate. If a manager wants to pursue a relation-ship with a subordinate, the company requests that he or she step forward and transfer to another job within or outside the company. The onus is on the manager rather than the subordinate to take action.[43] The most difficult part of an office romance often is when it comes to an end. At worst, such failed relationships can lead to claims of sexual harassment—one of the most troubling people issues managers face today.

Sexual Harassment

Although psychological closeness between men and women in the work-place may be positive, coercion into a sexual relationship by a person in power in an organization is not. Such behavior is called *sexual harassment,* and it is illegal. Unwelcome sexual advances, seeking of sexual favors, and other verbal or physical contact of a sexual nature are considered sexual harassment when they are demanded as a condition of employment, affect employment decisions (salary, working conditions, promotions), or create a hostile work environment. A hostile work environment is one that inter-feres with a person's work performance or that the person considers offen-sive.[44]

The number of sexual harassment claims filed annually in the United States has more than doubled in the last ten years. Nearly 16,000 claims were filed in 1997 alone.[45] For example, during that year, Mitsubishi Motor Corp. agreed to pay $9.5 million to settle with 27 female employees who claimed they were regularly groped and grabbed by male coworkers at the company's factory in Normal, Illinois. Some women said they had to agree to sex to win jobs. Mitsubishi has since sent the factory's 4,000 workers through an eight-hour course in sexual harassment awareness and has created a special unit to investigate all sexual harassment claims.[46]

A decision by the U.S. Supreme Court broadened the definition of sexual harassment to include same-sex harassment as well as harassment of men by female coworkers. In the suit that prompted the Court's decision, a male oil-rig worker claimed he was singled out by other members of the all-male crew for crude sex play, unwanted touching, and threats of rape.[47] Eight men, former employees of Jenny Craig Inc., sued the company charging that female bosses made lewd comments or that they were denied promotions because of their sex. A male worker at a hot tub manufacturer won a $1 million court decision after claiming that his female boss made sexual overtures to him almost daily. These are among a growing number of men urging recognition that sexual harassment is not just a woman's problem.[48]

Because the corporate world is dominated by a male culture, however, sexual harassment affects women to a much greater extent. Women who are moving up the corporate hierarchy in male-dominated industries report an especially high frequency of harassment. Surveys report an increase in organizations offering sexual harassment programs, but female employees also report a lack of prompt and just action by executives after incidents of sexual harassment. However, companies are discovering that an ounce of prevention really is worth a pound of cure. Top executives are seeking to address problems of harassment through company diversity programs, revised complaint systems and grievance procedures, written policy statements, workshops, lectures, and role-playing exercises to increase employee sensitivity to and awareness of the issue.[49]

apply it

1. Take a look at the college or university you attend or your workplace. How diverse is the organization? What efforts does the organization make to ensure equal employment opportunity?
2. Assume the role of a manager of a fast-food restaurant. What would you do to ensure that sexual harassment did not occur in your store? Would you develop a policy prohibiting dating or emotional relationships between employees? Why or why not?

Managing diversity is more than a training program

We have already discussed the importance of an organization's human resources in providing a competitive advantage. Since diversity is increasing in the workplace, organizations need to find ways to integrate people with a variety of backgrounds into their work processes to benefit from their knowledge and skills. So, how can diversity best be managed? Exhibit 2.5 shows some characteristics related to the long-term success of diversity programs.

exhibit | **2.5**

Characteristics Related to the Success of Managing Diversity

Top management provides resources, is personally involved, and publicly emphasizes diversity.

The program includes training and changes to company structure and policies.

Managing diversity is a business objective.

Milestones, goals, and objectives are identified and evaluated.

Manager involvement is mandatory.

Culture change is stressed.

Behaviors and skills needed to interact with others are taught.

Managers are rewarded for progress toward meeting diversity goals.

As shown in the exhibit, diversity needs to be defined as a business objective. For example, at Avon, understanding cultural differences is part of understanding the consumer. Cultural differences affect the type of skin-care cream consumers believe they need or the fragrance they may be attracted to. Serving its global customers is critical to Avon, and managing diversity is a company goal. To ensure that a diversity program is taken seriously by employees, a company's leaders and managers must come to terms with their own definitions of diversity. They should also be encouraged to think beyond race and gender issues to consider such factors as education, background, and personality differences.

Once a vision for a diverse workplace has been created and defined, the organization can analyze and assess the current culture and systems within the organization. This assessment must be followed by a willingness to change—to modify current systems and ways of thinking. Throughout this process, people need support in dealing with the many challenges and inevitable conflicts they face. Training and support are important for the people in pioneering roles.

Managers' Roles in Promoting Diversity

To promote positive change, executives must change their own assumptions and recognize that employee diversity is real, is good, and should be valued. Executives can lead the way in changing the organization to a culture in which differences among people are valued. Once managers accept the need to develop a truly diverse workplace, an organization can begin to plan for change. A program to implement such change involves three major steps: (1) building a corporate culture that values diversity; (2) changing structures, policies, and systems to support diversity; and (3) providing diversity awareness training. For each of these efforts to succeed, top management support is critical, and all managers must be accountable for increasing diversity.

Managers can start by actively encouraging and celebrating the new values, such as the promotion of minorities. In addition, managers can examine

Controlling In some countries, employees cannot be fired when things go wrong. Managers are often unable to get rid of employees who do not work out. In European countries, Mexico, and Indonesia, hiring and firing based on performance seems unnaturally brutal. Workers are protected by strong labor laws and union rules.

In other cultures, managers should also be careful not to control the wrong things. A Sears manager in Hong Kong insisted that employees come to work on time instead of 15 minutes late. The employees did exactly as they were told, but they also left on time instead of working into the evening as they had done previously. A lot of work was then left unfinished. The manager eventually told the employees to go back to their old ways since they were more productive.

Communication People from some cultures pay more attention to the social context (social setting, nonverbal behavior, social status) of their verbal communication than do Americans. In such *high-context cultures*, people

- use communication primarily to build personal social relationships
- derive meaning from context—setting, status, nonverbal behavior—more than from explicit words
- value relationships and trust more than business interests
- stress the welfare and harmony of the group.

In *low-context cultures*, people communicate primarily to exchange facts and information; derive meaning primarily from words; value business transactions more than building relationships and trust; and stress individual welfare and achievement more than group welfare.[66]

To understand how differences in cultural context affect communications, consider the U.S. expression "The squeaky wheel gets the grease." It means that the loudest person will get the most attention, and attention is assumed to be favorable. Equivalent sayings in China and Japan are "Quacking ducks get shot" and "The nail that sticks up gets hammered down." Standing out as an individual in these cultures clearly merits unfavorable attention.

High-context cultures include Asian and Arab countries. Low-context cultures tend to be American and Northern European. Even within North America, cultural subgroups vary in the extent to which context counts, explaining why differences among groups make successful communication difficult. White females, Native Americans, and African-Americans all tend to prefer higher context communication than do white males. A high-context interaction requires more time because a relationship has to be developed, and trust and friendship must be established. Furthermore, most male managers and most people doing the hiring in organizations are from low-context cultures, creating potential conflicts with people entering the organization from a higher context culture. Overcoming these differences in communication is a major goal of diversity awareness training.

Learning Managing across borders calls for organizations to learn across borders. One reason Japanese companies have been so successful internationally is that their culture encourages learning and adaptability. In Asia generally, teaching and learning are highly regarded, and the role of managers is seen as one of teaching or facilitating—of helping those around them to learn. It is partly this emphasis on continuous learning that has helped Matsushita Electric master markets and diverse cultures in 38 countries, from Malaysia to Brazil, from Austria to China, from Iran to Tanzania. One of Matsushita's top lessons for going global is to be a good corporate citizen in every country, respecting cultures, customs, and languages. In countries with Muslim religious practices, for example, Matsushita provides special prayer rooms and allows two prayer sessions per shift.[67]

Consider what AES Corporation, a U.S. producer of electrical power with headquarters in Arlington, Virginia, is doing to encourage continuous learning by giving freedom to front-line workers.[68] Lots of companies talk about pushing power and responsibility to lower levels, but few have pushed as far as AES. With nearly 6,000 employees (or more than 30,000, counting those working in joint ventures), AES has never established departments for human resources, operations, purchasing, or legal affairs. Fewer than 30 people work at headquarters. All functions are handled by decentralized teams, which include coal handlers and maintenance workers. For example, two control room operators led the team that raised $350 million to finance a joint venture in Northern Ireland. Teams seek advice from managers or anyone else who may have helpful ideas, but they make their own decisions.

AES disperses power and information so widely because its managers believe that's the only way to keep people thinking and learning. According to cofounder and CEO Dennie Bakke, if all information about financial matters comes to the finance department and all information about legal matters goes to the legal department, it is impossible to get well-rounded people who can think about the whole world. AES needs people to think about the whole world as it continues its rapid expansion internationally. The company opened its first plant in 1986. Today, it owns or has an interest in 82 power plants in the United States, Argentina, China, Brazil, Hungary, and other countries. The company has revenues of about $835 million and profits of $125 million. AES also believes in being a good corporate citizen in the countries in which it operates. It has planted 52 million trees in Guatemala, funded medical care in Kazakhstan, organized food banks in Argentina, and built schools in China. Although the company's social responsibility emphasis used to be on environmentalism, it has shifted gears to try to meet the needs of each specific country.

Bakke and cofounder and chairman Roger Sant believe AES has been able to expand so rapidly because giving people on the front lines the power to make decisions has made AES faster and nimbler than competitors. Oscar Prieto, a chemical engineer picked to lead AES's expansion into Brazil, agrees. He had worked at AES only two years when he was given the challenging assignment. He experienced the benefits of power in his own job and believed it could work cross-culturally. He chose Carlos Baldi, a 34-year-old engineer, to manage the plant in Santa Branca, a small facility near Sao Paulo that had previously been run as a top-heavy bureaucracy. After agreeing on shared goals and expectations, Prieto turned the plant over to Baldi and told him to run it as he saw fit. Now Baldi operates the same way with his people—he gives advice, not approval.

Power to the people doesn't always translate so well to other countries, however. For example, managers in Northern Ireland are having a hard time giving up control and operating the AES way. Yet, Bakke and Sant are committed to expanding AES's bottom-up system around the world. The company's mission statement declares that work should be fun, fulfilling, and exciting. At AES, that means giving workers freedom, challenge, and opportunities to think, learn, grow, and achieve.

Legal-Political Differences

In addition to national cultural differences, organizations must deal with unfamiliar political systems when they go international, as well as with different levels of government supervision and regulation. A country's legal system is an outgrowth of the culture in which it exists. The laws of a particular country often reflect societal norms about what constitutes legitimate behavior.[69] Following are some examples of what organizations and their employees may encounter.

Hu Mao Yuan is president and CEO of Shanghai Automotive Industry Corporation, the largest and most successful automotive manufacturer in China, and General Motors' joint-venture partner in China. Hu Mao is a pioneer among Chinese managers, working to modernize the economy.[70] Hu Mao admits that despite the modernization of the economy, there is still some risk in putting economic interests ahead of the interests of the Communist Party. Despite his successes (the company earned $164 million last year), Hu still has to work under constraints. Foreigners are not allowed to visit him at his office or at his home. So, he must work within these political barriers while trying to build a successful organization.

Governments can also mandate different work rules and regulations. The United States has a long history regarding fair pay and safe working conditions. For example, occupational health and safety laws help regulate safe working conditions. The Fair Labor Standards Act sets the minimum wage for jobs. In some countries, such as Germany, employees also have legal rights to form employee councils and give input into important decisions such as large investments or new competitive strategies. This type of employee "voice" is a legal right of German employees. In the United States, employees do not have this legal right, though they may obtain it through joining a union.

On the other side of the coin, Nike, the shoe manufacturer, has been charged with exploiting Taiwanese and Vietnamese workers.[71] However, the true picture of the situation is far from clear. Allegations against Nike that the pay is poor and employees work in unsafe conditions seem to vary from region to region. In the Sam Yang factory, employees say they are able to save as much as 40 percent of their salary. At the Pou Chen factory near Ho Chi Minh City, workers complain about low pay, poor food, and the fines levied on sewing machine operators when they break the needles in their equipment. Employees also complain they have wages deducted from their pay when they are sick. At the Pou Chen factory, fire-safety equipment is available, along with clean toilets, and ventilation systems clear the air of potentially deadly solvents that are used in shoe making. By contrast, an older state-owned factory in Hanoi that makes shoes for Western companies has a false bamboo ceiling that likely is a fire hazard.

To end the image problem Nike was facing in 1998, CEO Phillip Knight pledged to raise the minimum worker age requirement, adopt U.S.–style health and safety standards, and allow human rights groups to monitor working conditions in all international operations. Nike and other companies (including Reebok, Wal-Mart, and Levi Strauss) that manufacture products in low-wage countries are adopting codes of conduct and paying for independent outside reviews of their facilities by politicians and consultants to ensure exploitation is not occurring. Nike factories in Vietnam, Indonesia, and China were visited by Andrew Young, former U.S. ambassador to the United Nations. Young reported that the factories were physically as clean and modern as any manufacturing sites he had seen in the United States.

Human Capital and Education Differences

human capital

The knowledge, skills, and experiences of individuals, which have economic value.

Human capital refers to the knowledge, skills, and experiences of individuals that have economic value.[72] An organization's potential to find and keep qualified employees is an important consideration in any decision to expand globally. A country's human capital is affected by the educational opportunities available there. Third World countries such as Nicaragua and Haiti have low levels of human capital compared with other countries because of a lack of investment in education. Countries with high human capital are attractive sites for global investment. In Ireland, over 25 percent of 18-year-olds attend college, a rate much higher than that of other European countries. Ireland's high education level, strong work ethic, and high unemployment makes the country attractive for global operations. The Met Life Insurance company set up a facility for Irish workers to analyze insurance claims. The high human capital levels have prompted Met Life to determine whether other work can be shipped to Ireland.[73]

Economic Differences

A country's economic environment influences the development of human capital and the costs of potential employees. In socialist economic systems, the education level of the people is typically high because the education system is free. In the Netherlands, for example, government funding of school systems permits students to attend school through graduate school without paying.[74] However, under these systems there is little individual economic incentive because there are no monetary rewards for increasing human capital. In a capitalist system, such as in the United States, the opposite situation exists. There is less opportunity to develop without higher costs (for example, tuition increases at universities). However, those who invest in human capital, particularly through education, are able to gain more monetary rewards. For example, highly skilled workers receive higher rates of pay than lower skilled workers. In the United States, salaries usually reflect these human capital differences.

As the Starbucks Coffee example earlier in the chapter highlighted, most of Asia has a shortage of skilled workers. Retention of skilled employees is a major goal of organizations doing business in Asia.[75] Besides selling employees on the value of working for the company, companies also offer significant training opportunities as an employment benefit. For example, the Gillette Company offers an international training program where promising executives are sent to the corporate office in Boston for 18 months. The program costs range from $40,000 to $55,000 per employee. Also, McDonald's pays people differently depending on their skill and performance (known as *merit pay*). McDonald's has gradually implemented the merit pay system in Korea, a culture that emphasizes equality of treatment, so that people are paid differently, but the differences are minor in terms of overall compensation.

The health of the economic system also affects labor costs. In developed countries with high levels of wealth, labor costs tend to be quite high relative to those in developing countries. Also, a country's taxation system can affect a company's profits and pay levels for employees. International companies often have to pay foreign managers more than they would U.S. managers because of higher tax rates. For example, in France the highest personal income tax rate is 54 percent, compared with 40 percent in the United States.[76] Higher labor costs are one reason why a can of Coke in Frankfurt, Germany, costs 90 cents, compared with 53 cents in Madrid, Spain. In Denmark, government taxes account for about 25 percent of the cost of a Coke.[77]

Current Global Changes

Several recent social and political changes have increased organizations' involvement in the global marketplace. We now discuss some major developments that have made it necessary for organizations to better understand how to manage diversity abroad.

General Agreement on Tariffs and Trade   The General Agreement on Tariffs and Trade (GATT), signed by 23 nations in 1947, started as a set of rules to ensure nondiscrimination, clear procedures, the negotiation of disputes, and the participation of lesser developed countries in international trade. Today, more than 100 members abide by the rules of GATT. The primary tools GATT uses to increase trade are limits on the level of tariffs imposed on imports from other GATT members and most-favored-nation status, in which each member country grants every other member country the most favorable treatment with respect to imports and exports.[78]

GATT has sponsored various rounds of international trade negotiations aimed at reducing trade restrictions and encouraging closer relationships among member nations. The most recent round, the Uruguay Round, involved 125 countries and cut more tariffs than ever before. It also established the World Trade Organization (WTO). The WTO is a permanent global institution that can monitor international trade and has legal authority to arbitrate disputes on some 400 trade issues.[79]

While GATT and WTO make it easier for organizations to trade around the world, the violent protests at the WTO conference in Seattle suggest that some people believe that human rights, employee safety and health, jobs, family businesses, and the environment are not being protected, and may even be harmed by international trade agreements.[80]

European Union   Formed in 1958 to improve economic and social conditions among its members, the European Economic Community, now called the European Union (EU), has expanded to a 15-nation alliance including

Portugal, Spain, France, Austria, Italy, Greece, Belgium, Sweden, Luxembourg, the Netherlands, Denmark, the United Kingdom, Germany, and Ireland. Countries in Central and Eastern Europe hope economic and political conditions there will stabilize enough for them to begin joining soon.[81]

In the early 1980s, Europeans initiated steps to create a powerful single market system called Europe '92. The initiative called for creation of open markets for Europe's 340 million consumers. Europe '92 consisted of 282 directives proposing dramatic reform and deregulation in such areas as banking, insurance, health, safety standards, airlines, telecommunications, auto sales, social policy, and monetary union. Initially opposed and later embraced by European industry, the increased competition and economies of scale within Europe will enable companies to grow large and efficient, becoming more competitive in U.S. and other world markets.

euro

The single European currency that will replace up to 15 national currencies.

The most significant development of the EU is its monetary revolution and the introduction of the euro. The **euro** is the single European currency that has begun to replace up to 15 national currencies and unify a huge marketplace, creating a competitive $6.4 trillion economy second only to that of the United States. In 1999, 11 countries—Germany, France, Spain, Italy, Ireland, the Netherlands, Austria, Belgium, Finland, Portugal, and Luxembourg—formed the core group setting the exchange rates for adopting the single European currency, with the United Kingdom, Denmark, Greece, and Sweden expected to join later. The goal is to have the euro replace all national currencies of EU-member countries by mid-2002.[82] The implications of a single European currency are enormous within and outside Europe. As it replaces national currencies, the euro will affect legal contracts, financial management, sales and marketing tactics, manufacturing, distribution, payroll, pensions, training, taxes, and information management systems. Every corporation that does business in or with EU countries will feel the impact.[83] In addition, economic union is likely to speed deregulation, which has already reordered Europe's corporate and competitive landscape. Apple Computer is launching online software in six European countries to capitalize on the euro. Apple has priced all of its computers similarly across Europe and will allow customers to configure and buy their computers online in either euros or local currencies. Apple anticipates that the euro will stimulate an explosion in Internet shopping for computers and software.[84]

Although building alliances among countries is difficult, the benefits of doing so are overcoming divisions and disagreements. Canada, Mexico, and the United States have established what is expected to be an equally powerful alliance.

North American Free Trade Agreement (NAFTA)   The North American Free Trade Agreement, which went into effect on January 1, 1994, merged the United States, Canada, and Mexico into a megamarket with more than 360 million consumers. The agreement breaks down tariffs and trade restrictions on most agricultural and manufactured products over a 15-year period. The treaty builds on the 1989 U.S.–Canada agreement and is expected to spur growth and investment, increase exports, and expand jobs in all three nations.[85]

NAFTA has spurred the entry of small businesses into the global arena. Jeff Victor, general manager of Treatment Products, Ltd., which makes car cleaners and waxes, credits NAFTA for his surging export volume. Prior to the pact, Mexican tariffs as high as 20 percent made it impossible for the Chicago-based company to expand its presence south of the border. Similarly, StoneHeart, Inc., of Cheney, Washington, began selling its scooters for people with leg or foot injuries to a distributor in Canada.[86] Although many groups in the United States opposed the agreement, warning of job loss and the potential for industrial ghost towns, results so far have been positive. Ross Perot once warned of a giant sucking sound as Mexico inhaled jobs from America, but today that sound seems to be only an echo. Interviews with workers in various St. Louis–area companies found not a single person who knew of a colleague, friend, or relative out of work because of international trade.[87] Although criticism of NAFTA continues, many people believe there are important benefits. Experts stress that NAFTA will enable companies in all three countries to compete more effectively with rival Asian and European companies.[88]

The Growth of Asia   Countries such as Singapore, Hong Kong, and Malaysia have become significant world economic forces. In addition, China presents a tremendous potential market for goods. Despite an average annual income of only slightly more than $2,500 for urban Chinese (compared with $870 for rural citizens), according to the Gallup Organization's Third Survey of Consumer Attitudes and Lifestyles in China, more than 20 percent of Chinese intend to purchase a color television, washing machine, or refrigerator in the next two years.[89] At 16 percent of average household expenditures, the savings rate of Chinese families suggests that they may have the cash available to make these purchases despite their low annual income.

As we can see in the potential of China, despite the pitfalls of going global, organizations have huge incentives to compete in the global marketplace. With a broader range of markets to reach, organizations need to understand and manage diversity to perform well. We now turn to the different levels and forms of global participation that organizations can take to see how they can affect an organization and its employees.

apply it

1. Consider experiences you have had interacting with people from a different culture at work, school, or at home. How did their cultures differ from yours? Try to use Hofstede's five cultural dimensions in explaining the differences. How did the cultural differences contribute positively to your relationships? Negatively?

Organizations have different levels of global participation

As organizations move into the global marketplace, they frequently transfer employees from one country to another. These transfers bring people with organizational experience to new country operations. Also, organizations hire employees who have knowledge of a country and its business practices. Let's look at the different categories and terminology used in forging global business.

Global organizations that involve different national cultures aren't always easy to create or successful. Sina.com had been the odds-on favorite to become the leading Internet content provider for the Chinese-speaking world. Taiwanese entrepreneur David Chiang (photo) and his Chinese cofounder Wang Zhidong boasted that Sina.com was different from other Internet companies in greater China because they had installed experienced Silicon Valley professionals from companies such as Netscape and Oracle in most top executive posts. Drawing experienced high-tech employees enabled Sina to attract 1 million registered users and to line up $25 million from foreign investors, including U.S. banking firm Goldman, Sachs & Co. and Singapore's Economic Development Board. Chiang and Wang, however, clashed with their U.S. advisers about strategic decisions, a rift that sources say was caused by differences in personalities and management judgment—difficulties that arose from marrying the business cultures of Silicon Valley and Wall Street with those of China and Taiwan. Most of its American execs left within a one-month period, causing comments such as this one from a banker familiar with Sina, who said, "This is the absolute and utter meltdown of a company." (Source: © Chris Walton)

parent country

The country in which a company's corporate headquarters is located.

host country

The foreign country in which a parent-country organization is operating.

third country

A country other than the host country or parent country; a company may or may not have a facility there.

expatriates

Employees sent by a company in one country to work in operations in a different country.

parent-country nationals

Employees who were born and raised in the parent country.

host-country nationals

Employees who were born and raised in the host country.

third-country nationals

Employees born in a country other than the parent country or the host country but who work in the host country.

domestic organization

An organization that operates within a single country.

A **parent country** is the country in which a company's corporate headquarters is located. A **host country** is the country in which a parent-country organization is operating. A **third country** is a country other than the host country or parent country; a company may or may not have a facility there. **Expatriates** are employees sent by a company in one country to work in operations in a different country. There are three different types of expatriates. **Parent-country nationals** are employees who were born and raised in the parent country. **Host-country nationals** are employees who were born and raised in the host country. **Third-country nationals** are employees born in a country other than the parent country and the host country but who work in the host country.

Organizations also differ in the level at which they participate in the global market. Corporations can participate in the international arena on a variety of levels, and the process of globalization typically passes through four distinct levels. It is important to understand these levels because as a company becomes more involved in global markets, different types of challenges arise. As shown in Exhibit 2.8, these levels of global participation include the domestic, international, multinational, and global levels.[90]

Domestic Organizations

An organization that operates within a single country is a **domestic organization.** Most companies begin by manufacturing and marketing their product and service primarily within a single country. But few organizations today are truly domestic organizations. Even new businesses have a global reach because of the use of the Web to advertise and sell products and services. For example, an entrepreneur may develop a product that meets a market need within the United States. The product is manufactured and marketed primarily within the U.S. marketplace through sales representatives, suppliers, and the Web. However, customers in other countries

DAIMLERCHRYSLER EMPLOYEES AT ALL LEVELS RESIST MOVES FOR GLOBAL ASSIGNMENTS

Nearly a year after the former Daimler-Benz AG and Chrysler Corporation joined to form DaimlerChrysler, the new company remains essentially two separate companies, one German and one American. Chrysler was known for having a more progressive, open culture. The more traditional, top-down culture of Daimler-Benz was supposed to help both companies by improving Chrysler's quality while helping Daimler move beyond luxury cars and trucks. If DaimlerChrysler is to become an effective global company, it must convince employees at all levels that expatriate assignments are desirable.

Currently, the company wants to exchange 60 employees between Germany and the United States on expatriate assignments lasting between two and five years. Persuading Americans to move to Germany has been very difficult. Most Americans don't speak German and don't want to leave their homes for apartments or smaller houses in Germany, where real estate is more expensive than in the Midwest. Part of the problem is that Chrysler was a much less global company than Daimler, so it put less value on international assignments as experiences needed for employees to move into executive positions. Chrysler has roughly 300 employees living outside the United States, but Daimler has about 1,500 living outside Germany.

Cultural differences in formality are noticeable. One German expatriate believes that Americans characterize Germans as "running around in steel helmets and always saying, 'Yes, General.'" German employees are accused of seeing Americans as "cowboys who shoot from the hip."

One of the biggest issues, however, has been wages. Chrysler provides its expatriates with a generous package: a lump sum worth three months' salary to cover the expenses of setting up a house overseas, moving expenses including hotel stays and meals, and a salary bonus if the cost of living in the host country is higher than in the United States. Daimler offers a cost of living adjustment, but it provides only a small lump-sum relocation payment. Daimler pays only for hotel rooms—not for meals. In other areas, the Chrysler officials are less generous. Chrysler wants to provide employees with an elaborate brochure encouraging them to volunteer for expatriate positions and suggests that most of the information be posted on the company's intranet. The Germans object to posting the brochure on the intranet because all employees may not have access. They would like a paper version.

1. DaimlerChrysler has hired you as a consultant to help deal with this problem. What would you suggest they do to encourage employees to volunteer for expatriate assignments?

2. Should DaimlerChrysler have the same transfer package for German and U.S. employees? Explain.

3. Besides compensation and housing, what might be some other issues that cause employees to resist global assignments?

Source: J. Ball, "DaimlerChrysler's Transfer Woes," *The Wall Street Journal,* August 24, 1999, pp. B1 and B2; Associated Press, "DaimlerChrysler Moves Shift Power to Germans," *Columbus Dispatch,* September 25, 1999, pp. E1 and E2.

---

can also get the product directly by placing orders at the company Web site. As the product grows in popularity, the owner might decide to build additional facilities in different parts of the United States to reduce the costs of shipping the products long distances.

It is tempting to think that diversity issues do not apply to domestic companies. However, as we saw earlier in the chapter, diversity issues are still important because of the cultural differences within the United States. Domestic companies may also serve some foreign-born customers or hire foreign-born employees. At 3Com Corporation's factory near Chicago, 65 different national flags are displayed, each representing the national origin of at least one employee who works at the plant. The 1,200 employees at 3Com speak more than 20 different languages, including Tagalog and Chinese. At Rotoflow, a small southern California factory that manufactures giant turbines used in the natural gas industry, 30 nationalities are represented among only 200 employees.[91] Also, most companies face

exhibit **2.8**
Levels of Global Participation

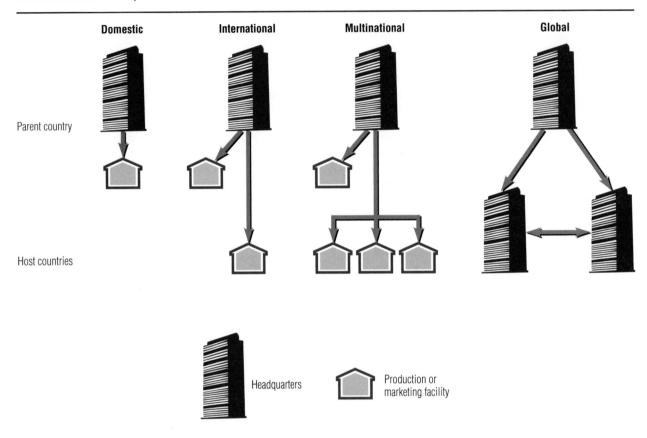

competition from other countries, and suppliers that can best meet their needs may be from other countries. For these reasons, it is important even for domestic organizations to be sensitive to diversity.

International Organizations

international organization

An organization that has one or a few facilities in another country.

An organization that has one or a few facilities in another country is an **international organization.** Organizations enter international markets by exporting their products, followed by building production or service facilities in other countries. Usually, the company enters one or a few select markets at a time. Such an organization typically creates an international division that is responsible for foreign operations. American Machinery Services, which makes spare parts for plastic-injection and blow-molding machinery, is an example of a company that is making the transition from a domestic to international organization. The company's goal is to have 10 percent of total revenue come from Mexico. The company intends to sell parts through independent Mexican sales representatives.[92]

Managers of international organizations need to pay careful attention to differences among countries. They need to understand customer needs and values in other countries as well as foreign employee needs and behaviors. Managers need to understand cultural differences and be flexible enough to adapt their management styles to those of the host country.

Multinational Organizations

Organizations with facilities in several different countries and a substantial proportion of sales in foreign countries are **multinational organizations.** Multinational companies are formed to take advantage of low production costs, to reduce product distribution costs, and to become more familiar with customer needs. A multinational company faces challenges similar to those of an international company, except that the complexity is greater because of involvement in more countries. Instead of having to consider only one or two countries' cultural, human capital, legal, and economic systems, the multinational company must address these differences for a large number of countries.

Multinational companies also employ managers from different countries, who become part of the corporate headquarters staff. So, managers from different countries must be integrated into the culture of the parent country. In addition, multinational companies move employees from countries other than the parent country to facilities in other countries. Cross-cultural training is critical to provide managerial skills for interaction with individuals from different cultures.

Multinational organizations create multinational families.[93] As more U.S. companies hire foreign-born employees and move them around the globe, the employees often have family members living in other countries. This places pressure on a company to provide more extensive travel budgets or risk losing valuable global employees who don't like the strain global assignments can place on family relationships. For example, Tupperware Corporation's senior vice president of product marketing flew to Belgium for a business meeting one spring. The following weekend, he attended a cousin's wedding in Scotland. The company gave the British executive time with his wife, who lives outside of Geneva, as well as with his college-aged son and daughter, who are students in England. Tupperware paid for the airfare.

multinational organization

An organization with facilities in several different countries and a substantial proportion of sales in foreign countries.

Global Organizations

A **global organization** has multiple headquarters spread across the world and relies on flexibility and customization of products and services to meet the needs of each global market. These corporations operate in true global fashion, making sales and acquiring resources in whatever country offers the best opportunities and lowest cost. At this stage, ownership, control, and top management tend to be dispersed among several nationalities.[94] Consider General Electric's global expansion as it creates a new oven and stove capital in Mexico.[95]

global organization

An organization with multiple headquarters spread across the world that relies on flexibility and customization of products and services to meet the needs of each global market.

General Electric (GE)

San Luis Potosi, a central Mexican desert town, once grew rich on silver. Now it's on its way to becoming North America's new oven and stove capital. GE is following the trail blazed by Detroit's Big Three automakers over the past 30 years. Like them, appliance makers first saw Mexico as a product market. Now they recognize that Mexico also makes sense as a low-cost manufacturing base to compete with Asian products in U.S. and world markets. Work is being completed on a plant expansion in San Luis Potosi by oven maker Mabe SA, which is 48 percent owned by General Electric. Mabe SA already makes almost one million gas ranges a year for U.S. markets. Mabe also plans to assemble 650,000 electric ranges to be sold in the United States under both the GE and Sears Kenmore brand. Expectations are for the factory to supply 40 percent of the GE ranges sold in the United States.

Employees at Mabe make stoves for about $15 per day, which is slightly more than GE workers earn per hour at a Georgia assembly plant. Besides labor cost savings, GE's expansion into Mexico is also attracting its suppliers. Although 70 percent of the components needed to build the gas ranges come from the United States, Mabe has attracted both large and small U.S. suppliers to the area. They include U.S. Steel, which provides the steel for the appliances, an Illinois-based glass manufacturer, which makes gas burners, and a Michigan firm, which manufactures gas pressure regulators.

Besides supplying the U.S. appliance market, GE is counting on growing local demand to support even larger operations (and, it hopes, profits). Although television sets are no longer a luxury in Mexican households, fewer than 70 percent have refrigerators, fewer than 50 percent have washing machines, and even fewer own dishwashers or clothes dryers. Compared with the more mature market in the United States, the potential in Mexico is huge.

Instead of distinguishing markets into "home" and "foreign" (as is the case for multinational firms), a global organization has headquarters in several locations. Also, in general, multinational organizations attempt to develop identical products and distribute them worldwide, and they are usually driven to locate facilities in a country to reach that country's market or benefit from its lower production costs. Global companies customize their products to meet customer needs and expect employee contributions from each country to create a more competitive position than if the countries' operations were separate units. That is, global companies try to achieve synergy from cultural differences.

Cross-Cultural Preparation for Global Employment

cross-cultural preparation

Activities for the employee and his or her family (or significant other) prior to departure, on-site, and in preparation for returning home (known as *repatriation*).

To prepare employees for global assignments, companies need to provide training in other cultures. **Cross-cultural preparation** includes activities for the employee and his or her family (or significant other) prior to departure, on site, and in preparation for returning home (known as *repatriation*). Most U.S. companies send employees on global assignments without any preparation. One estimate is that U.S. companies lose $2 billion a year as a result of failed overseas assignments! A "failed assignment" includes employees who return home early, as well as poor performance in the global location.[96] Failed assignments result in productivity reductions; damaged staff, customer, and supplier relations for the company; and interrupted careers and reduced self-images for the employees. So, it is in an organization's best interests to prevent failures whenever possible. Let's look at some predeparture, on-site, and repatriation assistance organizations can provide.

predeparture activities

Careful screening, selection, and training of employees to serve overseas.

Predeparture Phase **Predeparture activities** involve careful screening, selection, and training of employees to serve overseas. One reason many expatriates fail in global assignments is that companies choose employees who have the best technical skills, rather than those who have the personality and family support needed to be successful in global assignments. Exhibit 2.9 lists characteristics that employees need to be successful in global assignments. Organizations typically rely on interviews and tests to identify which employees are the best candidates for global assignments. Once selected, expatriates receive cross-cultural training to develop language skills and cultural and historical knowledge. Cross-cultural training methods range from lectures that expatriates and their families attend on customs and cultures in the host country to actual experiences in the home country in culturally diverse communities.[97]

Honest self-analysis by overseas candidates and their families may be more important than selection and training for ensuring the success of global assignments. Research suggests that the comfort of an expatriate's spouse and family, flexibility and adaptability, job knowledge and motivation, relational skills, and cultural openness are key predictors of successful assignments.[98] The greater an expatriate's family responsibility, the more attention should be paid to nonwork factors (e.g., housing, home leave, and personal security). Before seeking or accepting an assignment in another country, a candidate should ask himself or herself such questions as the following:

- Is your spouse interrupting his or her own career path to support your career? Is that acceptable to both of you?
- Is family separation for long periods involved?
- Can you initiate social contacts in a foreign culture?
- Can you adjust well to different environments and changes in personal comfort or quality of living, such as the lack of television, gasoline at $5 per gallon, limited hot water, varied cuisine, national phone strikes, and warm beer?
- Can you manage your future reentry into the job market by networking and maintaining contacts in your home country?[99]

On-Site Phase **On-site preparation** involves orientation to the host country and its customs and culture through training programs or a mentoring relationship. Expatriates and their families may be paired with a mentor

on-site preparation
Orientation to the host country and its customs and culture through training programs or a mentoring relationship.

exhibit | **2.9**

Characteristics Needed to be Successful in Global Assignments

- Competence in area of expertise
- Ability to communicate verbally and nonverbally in host country
- Flexibility, tolerance of ambiguity, sensitivity to cultural differences
- Motivation to succeed, enjoyment of the challenge of working in other countries, willingness to learn host-country culture, language, and customs
- Supportive family

from the host country who helps them understand the new and unfamiliar work environment and community.[100]

repatriation

Preparing employees to return to the parent company and country from the global assignment.

Repatriation Phase   **Repatriation** prepares employees to return to the parent company and country from the global assignment. Expatriates and their families often experience high levels of stress and anxiety, also known as *reentry shock,* when they return because of changes that occurred at home and at work since their departure. It is not uncommon for expatriates and their families to have to readjust to a lower standard of living in the United States than they had in another country, where they may have enjoyed maid service, a limousine, private schools, and clubs. This shock can be reduced by providing expatriates with personal and work-related mail and newspapers while they are on the global assignment. In addition to reentry shock, many expatriates decide to leave the company because the assignment they are given upon return has less responsibility, challenge, and status than the global assignment.[101] Managers need to discuss career plans before employees leave the United States to ensure that they understand the position they will be eligible for upon repatriation. For example, after eight years in Asia with Hill and Knowlton China, Diana Terry returned to job confusion and reentry shock.[102] In Asia, Terry had a car and personal driver. In Atlanta, she had to drive herself in traffic that had worsened while she was away. Terry felt totally out of sync with popular movies and music, but her most difficult problem was finding work. When she returned to the United States, the Asian economic crisis had hit, so companies were not interested in hiring someone with Asian experience. After months of consideration, her bosses could not find her a job that satisfied both her needs and theirs. Luckily, an affiliated company, Ogilvy Public Relations, needed someone to open an Atlanta office.

Monsanto's repatriation program deals with both career and personal transitions to meet employee needs at different phases.[103]

 Monsanto

Monsanto is a global agricultural, chemical, and pharmaceutical company located in 100 different countries. Preparation for repatriation begins before an employee leaves the United States. Employees and both their current manager and manager at the host location develop an agreement concerning the assignment and how it fits into the company's business objectives. How the knowledge gained during the assignment will be used when the expatriate returns is clearly specified. This includes having expatriates share their global experiences with U.S. peers, superiors, and subordinates.

The repatriation program also provides employees with a way to work through personal difficulties. After their return, expatriates meet with colleagues they have chosen for debriefing. The debriefing includes a trained counselor who discusses all the important aspects of repatriation and helps the employee understand what he or she is experiencing. The debriefing not only helps the returning expatriate but also helps educate peers and colleagues to better understand different cultural issues and the business environment.

apply it

1. Recall a time when you spent a long time away from home on vacation, for school, or for work. How did you feel when you returned home? How did your friends treat you? What were your immediate concerns? What types of things did you have to do to feel comfortable at home?
2. How could your "repatriation" have been made easier? Explain.

summary OF KEY CONCEPTS

- **Global reach and a diverse U.S. workforce increase the importance of managing diversity.** Companies are entering international markets by exporting their products overseas, building manufacturing facilities in other countries, and entering into foreign alliances. Because of immigration, an aging labor force, greater labor force participation of women and minorities in organizations, and an increased value on balancing work and nonwork, managing diversity is a key to success.

- **Diversity is more than race or color.** Diversity includes inborn differences, such as race, as well as secondary dimensions, such as work style, education, or skill level. Managing diversity benefits employees by creating a work environment in which they experience feelings of accomplishment and feel valued. For the organization, managing diversity facilitates creativity, better problem solving, and development of new markets for products and services. Organizations want employees to accept the organization's culture. At the same time, organizations need to be sure they create a culture that capitalizes on the unique strengths (skills, personalities, cultures) that employees bring to work.

- **Organizations struggle to provide fair, safe, and productive environments.** Special recruiting or hiring programs that organizations use to comply with laws written to ensure equal employment opportunity of women and ethnic minorities are often seen as unfair by white males and can give minorities a "stigma of incompetence." Women and ethnic minorities often face an invisible barrier—a glass ceiling—that keeps them from top management positions. Although close working relationships between men and women can be beneficial, when work relationships become romantic or sexual in nature, problems can result. Sexual harassment, whether it involves inappropriate or offensive remarks or solicitation of sexual acts, is illegal.

- **Managing diversity is more than a training program.** Managing diversity involves building a culture that values diversity, changing structures and policies to support diversity, and providing diversity awareness training.

- **Global factors affect organizations and their employees.** Five dimensions of national culture influence organizational behavior: power distance, uncertainty avoidance, individualism versus collectivism, masculinity/femininity, and time orientation. Decision making, leadership, motivation, and learning are influenced by these dimensions. The laws of a country highlight what constitutes legitimate behavior. Human capital refers to the knowledge, skills, and experiences of individuals that have economic value (e.g., education). The level of wealth and labor costs are economic characteristics that affect global organizations.

- **Organizations have different levels of global participation.** Employees who work globally can be expatriates, parent-country nationals, host-country nationals, or third-country nationals. The level of an organization's participation in the global economy can be domestic (operations within a single country), international (one or a few facilities in another country), multinational (facilities in several countries, with managers from different countries part of headquarters staff), or global (multiple headquarters spread across the globe, with customization of products to meet the needs of each market). For effective global assignments, employees need to be prepared. Cross-cultural preparation includes predeparture, on-site, and repatriation activities. Successful expatriates are supported by their families, have the technical and interpersonal skills necessary to work in another culture, understand the role of the global assignment in their career, and are prepared for the shock of reentry back to work and nonwork life in their parent country.

KEY terms

diversity, p. 39

organizational culture, p. 44

ethnocentrism, p. 46

monoculture, p. 46

ethnorelativism, p. 47

pluralism, p. 47

DISCUSSION questions

1. How can an organization benefit from diversity at home and abroad? What are the potential costs of diversity?

2. The United States is an example of a "masculine" culture. What "masculine" characteristics do you see exhibited by this culture? How might they be seen in the workplace?

3. Consider a time when you had to function in another culture, for example, on vacation or in a job. What were the major obstacles you faced? How did you deal with them?

4. If you were asked to help an expatriate from China working in the United States understand U.S. culture, what would you tell the person? What aspects of U.S. culture would be the most stressful for an expatriate from China? How would your answer differ if the expatriate were from England?

5. What questions might you ask in an interview to determine whether an employee is flexible enough to work successfully in a global assignment? What would you look for on his or her resume to suggest the assignment might be successful?

6. What factors might cause diversity programs to fail?

7. What trends are responsible for increased global participation by U.S. businesses?

8. Assume you are in charge of developing a diversity training program. Who would be involved? What would they do?

9. For an organization to effectively manage diversity, do you think changing the corporate culture is enough? Explain.

10. Do you think any organization can resist diversity today? Discuss.

SELF-DISCOVERY exercise

Test Your Global Potential

A global environment requires that American managers learn to deal effectively with people in other countries. The assumption that foreign business leaders behave and negotiate in the same manner as Americans is false. How well prepared are you to live with globalization? Consider the following.

Are You Guilty of:	Definitely No				Definitely Yes
1. Impatience? Do you think "Time is money" or "Let's get to the point"?	1	2	3	4	5
2. Having a short attention span, bad listening habits, or being uncomfortable with silence?	1	2	3	4	5
3. Being somewhat argumentative, sometimes to the point of belligerence?	1	2	3	4	5
4. Ignorance about the world beyond your borders?	1	2	3	4	5
5. Weakness in foreign languages?	1	2	3	4	5
6. Placing emphasis on short-term success?	1	2	3	4	5

	Definitely No				Definitely Yes

7. Believing that advance preparations are less important than negotiations themselves? 1 2 3 4 5

8. Being legalistic? Of believing "A deal is a deal," regardless of changing circumstances? 1 2 3 4 5

9. Having little interest in seminars on the subject of globalization, failing to browse through libraries or magazines on international topics, not interacting with foreign students or employees? 1 2 3 4 5

Total Score

If you scored less than 27, congratulations. You have the temperament and interest to do well in a global company. If you scored more than 27, it's time to consider a change. Regardless of your score, go back over each item and make a plan of action to correct deficiencies indicated by answers of 4 or 5 to any question.

Source: Reprinted from "Why Americans Fail at Overseas Negotiations" by Cynthia Barnum and Natasha Wolniansky, *Management Review* (October 1989), 55–57, Copyright © 1989 American Management Association International. Reprinted by permission of American Management Association International, New York, NY. All rights reserved. http://www.amanet.org

ORGANIZATIONAL BEHAVIOR in your life

The concept of culture is key to understanding and effectively managing organizational behavior in the United States and abroad. The purpose of this assignment is to help you identify a company's culture. Consider a company that you work for, one you want to work for, or a company that a relative or friend works for. Use interviews and/or personal observations to understand the organization's culture. To gain an understanding of the culture, answer the following questions:

What do the physical surroundings of the company look like?

What is the personal style of the employees you meet? Fun? Formal? Casual?

What symbols, rituals, and stories does the company have?

Does the company have a set of core values? What does it emphasize?

Does the company tolerate, accept, or actively encourage new ideas?

Does the company actively manage diversity? How? Through rules? Activities?

How are employees involved in decision making?

In addition to these questions, ask three of your own. Keep your answers to the questions in a "Culture Log."

Next, rate the organization's culture on each of the characteristics shown in Exhibit 2.3. Use a five point scale with 1 = Low, 3 = Average, and 5 = High.

ORGANIZATIONAL BEHAVIOR news flash

@ What are the largest global and multinational companies in the world? Check out the *Fortune Global 500* listing available at *http://pathfinder.com/fortune/global500/500list.html.* What countries are represented in the top ten? Which country has the most companies in the top ten? Select the industry of most interest to you and identify the top three companies and their home countries. Choose one of the companies within the industry you selected and, using any Web search engine, find a current news item related to the company.

global diversity EVENTS

The merger of Chrysler Corporation and Daimler-Benz AG has been rocky. The goal of the merger was to create one company striving to be the number one automotive transportation company in the world. The new name, DaimlerChrysler, symbolizes the ideal blend of the two companies.

Any merger is difficult, but it is particularly so for one involving two companies from different cultures. Access the Web and either use the "news of the day" listing on your search engine or type in the key name

"International Business" or "World Business" to locate information or articles dealing with global joint ventures or mergers. Identify the companies involved, their products and services, and their national cultures, and then suggest any potential problems that the companies might experience as a result of cultural differences. You may be asked to discuss your results in class or write a short paper or e-mail that you will give to your instructor.

minicase ISSUE

Culture Clash in a Global Environment

Background. Lincoln Electric Company was founded in 1895. It is one of the six major manufacturers of arc-welding products in the world. At the end of World War II, more than 50 manufacturers competed in the United States, so the industry is extremely competitive. Lincoln Electric also makes industrial electric motors, but arc-welding products account for more than 87 percent of its $853 million in total sales.

The Incentive System. Lincoln's incentive system—the practice of paying factory workers on the basis of how many units they produce instead of hourly wages or a salary with eligibility for a bonus—is a key component of the company's culture. The system has distinguished Lincoln from its competitors. Historically, bonuses have composed more than 50 percent of U.S employees' annual income. The incentive system has allowed their salaries to rank among the highest in the world. The incentive system was created in 1934, and bonuses have been paid every year since then.

Because of the bonus and piecework system, employees act like entrepreneurs. Absence and turnover rates historically are very low. Because the system motivates employees, they don't require much direct supervision. The supervisor-to-employee ratio at Lincoln's main U.S. plants is 1 to 100. In a typical U.S. factory, the ratio is 1 to 25. The savings from having few supervisors help the company pay the bonus.

Lincoln's International Expansion. Lincoln is primarily a U.S. company. Its two main plants are in the Cleveland, Ohio, area. Although Lincoln has had manufacturing and marketing operations in Canada,

Australia, and France for more than 40 years, all three were independent units. George E. "Ted" Willis, who became president of Lincoln Electric in 1987, dreamed of Lincoln becoming a global power. From 1987 to 1993, the company spent almost $325 million on expansion. Three new plants were built in Japan, Venezuela, and Brazil, and the company purchased eight plants in Germany, Norway, the United Kingdom, the Netherlands, Spain, and Mexico. Willis made the acquisition decisions and required all new foreign operations to report directly to him. None of the boards of directors had any international experience.

Resistance to the Incentive Program. Lincoln believed that because it had been so successful in the United States it could be successful around the globe. Examination of the manufacturing operations revealed that through applying Lincoln's manufacturing expertise, equipment, and incentive system to foreign operations, there were tremendous opportunities to reduce costs. However, without exploring the cultures in detail, Lincoln found that the European culture of labor was hostile to the incentive system. For example, even though German factory workers are highly skilled, they do not work the long hours that employees in the Cleveland factory do. In Germany, the average factory workweek is 35 hours. In the United States, the average workweek is between 43 and 58 hours, and the company can ask people to work longer hours on short notice. This type of flexibility is essential for the system to work. Because of these cultural differences, every European factory was operating at less than 50 percent of capacity.

Recovery from Mounting Financial Losses. The hostility toward the incentive system was one reason the company lost $12 million in 1992. The loss was primarily in the company's international operations; U.S. employees expected to receive a bonus. Lincoln faced a major problem. It could pay the bonus, but only by taking the company deeper into debt. Or the company could announce there would be no bonus and lose employees' trust, therefore sacrificing the company's competitive advantage. Also, if the company did not pay the bonus, it would have to hire more employees because productivity would decrease.

Lincoln Electric paid the bonus to its U.S. employees. The company's creditors allowed it to relax its immediate financial obligations. However, to save the company, two options were available. First, Lincoln could resort to massive layoffs of managers and employees; second, it could make efforts to increase revenues. Rather than risk the deterioration of morale, trust, and productivity that often accompanies downsizing, the company decided to raise cash through increased revenues and a public stock offering. The plan called for the U.S. factories to boost production and for the sales force to increase sales. The public stock offering meant that any bonus employees received would now come after shareholders received dividends. Essentially, the losses of the European op-

erations were being offset by U.S. employees. Managers and employees were asked to eliminate bottlenecks that were inhibiting production. The company used an all-out communication program to explain to employees how much money the U.S. operation needed to generate for the bonus to be paid in the future. The U.S. operations were able to save the company by making and exceeding sales goals and creating new welding products that are sold through Home Depot and Wal-Mart. The company has since closed unprofitable European operations, which has helped to reduce the debt.

1. Why were the European countries resistant to Lincoln's incentive plan? Aren't U.S. and European cultures similar enough?

2. What should Lincoln have done prior to opening global operations to ensure that the incentive system was appropriate?

3. Should Lincoln stop trying to implement the incentive system in future international operations? Explain.

Source: C. Wiley, "Incentive plans pushes production," *Personnel Journal* (August 1993): 86–91; D. F. Hastings, "Lincoln Electric's harsh lessons from international expansion," *Harvard Business Review* (May–June 1999): 3–11.

video CASE

JCPENNEY DOES DIVERSITY RIGHT

When James Cash Penney opened his first retail shop in Wyoming nearly a century ago, he named it The Golden Rule. His premise was that both customers and employees (whom he called "associates") should be treated according to the golden rule, with courtesy and respect. Although he couldn't have anticipated the tremendous change in global economics and demographics by the year 2000, somehow he had the wisdom to anticipate that the golden rule would still apply, no matter how much technology, the population, and the economy grew.

Today, with more than 200,000 associates worldwide, JCPenney operates more than 1,200 stores in all 50 states, Puerto Rico, Mexico, and Chile. In addition, Penney has acquired an interest in Lojas Renner S.A. of Brazil. To meet the needs of a diverse customer base, the company needs to reflect its customers' diversity within its own workforce. Recognizing that human capital is perhaps its greatest asset, "the JCPenney company does place a tremendous value on diversity . . . understanding diversity, valuing diversity, and certainly embracing it," notes Charles Brown, vice-president and director of credit.

Diversity training and a team of diversity advisors lie at the heart of Penney's commitment to equal opportunity and recognition throughout the company. The "Valuing Cultural Differences" program is a one-and-a-half day workshop designed to establish and enhance associates' awareness of each other. Two internal advisory teams—one on minorities and the other on women—helped developed Penney's official position on diversity, and they have since focused on three priorities: (1) mentoring young or new employees, (2) developing career paths, and (3) recruiting top minority candidates. JCPenney has received applause for its diversity training programs and its overall approach to diversity from such organizations as the Citizens Index, which profiles the social responsibility of 300 companies. "JCPenney considers the diversity of its workforce an important part of how it does business," states the index profile. It also notes, "JCPenney was named to *Hispanic* Magazine's 1997 list of the 75 companies providing the most opportunities for Hispanics. The company also publishes a report for its shareholders on the race and gender of its workforce."

What about the women of JCPenney's workforce? Have they been able to advance within the company? In the past, there was a glass ceiling. According to Cathy Mills, vice-president of corporate communications, although 60 percent of the JCPenney workforce was female, "they were at certain levels of the company, and the glass ceiling was very clearly defined in our company." Although the first level of management was predominantly female, the number diminished radically through upper levels of management. So W.R. Howell, chairman and CEO, "saw an opportunity to accelerate the representation of women at all levels of our company. The goal of the advisory team is 46 percent at all levels, all the way to the executive committee," says Mills.

For diversity policies to be effective throughout an organizational culture, they must begin at the top. CEO Howell fully supports the company's efforts, recognizing the importance of diversity as part of human capital. "Our diversity gives us a real competitive advantage," he remarks. "So we must use this tremendous resource to the fullest. We must make every effort to include the creative ideas and diverse viewpoints of all. This way, we will ensure our continued success."

Questions

1. In what ways does an organization like JCPenney benefit from encouraging a diverse workforce?

2. How do ethnorelativism and pluralism within an organization like JCPenney reflect the golden rule?

3. How will a strong diversity program prepare Penney employees who may someday transfer to one of the company's overseas operations?

4. Visit the JCPenney Web site at **www.jcpenney. net** and click on the "Career Opportunities" section. In what ways does the site reflect the company's commitment to diversity?

Source: JCPenney Web site, **www.jcpenney.net**, accessed May 15, 2000; Citizens Index, **www.citizensfunds.com,** accessed May 10, 2000; "Chamber Members Recognized Commitment to Women-Owned Firms Highlighted," *U.S. Chamber.com,* December 1999, **www.uschamber.com.**

video CASE

FOSSIL STANDS THE TEST OF TIME

Gone are the days when one watch will do—that is, if you want to be in fashion. Even though you only have two wrists, now you can choose a watch for every season, occasion, or outfit. The founders of Fossil, Inc., brothers Tom and Kosta Kartsotis, viewed watches as fashion pieces, not just functional timepieces. Consumers quickly took to the idea, and today the company manufactures and sells over 500 different watch styles around the world, in addition to a variety of other accessories, including sunglasses, handbags, and belts.

Within its first decade of operation, Fossil became an international organization, with its first foreign operation in Germany. But very rapidly Fossil increased its level of participation toward globalization. "That's where you really take time to become a partner, whether it be a distributor, a sales rep company, [or] our own wholly-owned subsidiaries," notes Gary Bolinger, Fossil's senior vice-president of international sales and marketing. Fossil products are now manufactured and sold in more than 70 countries.

Fossil managers developed a four-part strategy to achieve a worldwide presence. First, "it starts with product," explains Bolinger. Second is a marketing package that tells the company's story in a way that is "uniform and cohesive worldwide." Third is the business system and infrastructure within each country where Fossil plans to conduct business. Fourth is "finding the right partners that can execute this program and this plan in each of the various countries." Specifically, Fossil has formed joint ventures with organizations such as Seiko and Diesel. Fossil also owns its own companies in Japan, Italy, and Germany "where we can get the management in there that has our vision, shares the passion for the brand and can commit to the service that our customers demand in those markets," explains Richard Gundy, executive vice-president of Fossil. Naturally, trade issues arise in each of these countries, including the European Union, which now deals in the euro, the single European currency that will ultimately replace the currencies of individual European countries. But Fossil's strategic planning is designed to address these changes. "We talk with each of our distributors, if not daily, at least weekly with every country we're in around the world," says Bolinger. Thus, even though a currency may devalue by 30 percent one day and recover 50 percent the next day, Fossil's constant communication with distributors and others means that the company can make quick adjustments when necessary.

Another issue is Fossil's strong presence in Hong Kong, which was returned by Britain to China in 1997. Many experts speculated on how the change would affect businesses such as Fossil. Why would Fossil want to risk maintaining operations in an area of such political and economic uncertainty? According to the turnover agreement, "China will leave Hong Kong's political system intact for a period of fifty years and treat it as a special economic region," says Dermott Bland, senior vice-president of watch products at Fossil. In addition, says Gary Bolinger, Fossil chose Hong Kong for two reasons. "One is the infrastructure is there to carry out the needs that [we] have." The other reason is Hong Kong's human capital: "a mentality that the people of Hong Kong have that they can get anything done."

If Fossil already seems to be ahead of the clock in many parts of the world, the company's future goals are far from modest. "We want world domination," says Gary Bolinger. That means a Fossil watch on every person's wrist, a Fossil wallet in every man's pocket, and a Fossil handbag over every woman's shoulder. Even then, it's unlikely that Fossil's managers will take time out.

Questions

1. In terms of human capital, how might alliances with established foreign companies benefit Fossil overseas?

2. Do you think that Fossil's continued strong presence in Hong Kong is wise? Why or why not?

3. Visit the Fossil Web site at **www.fossil.com** to learn what you can about Fossil's global markets. What would Fossil's managers have to know about the culture, in say, Finland or Taiwan, to market products such as sunglasses, handbags, and watches in those countries?

Source: Fossil Web site, **www.fossil.com,** accessed May 10, 2000; "Diesel and Fossil Sign Worldwide License Agreement for Diesel Watches," press release, October 28, 1999, **www.fossil.com;** "Fossil Acquires Its Distributor in the U.K.," press release, September 21, 1999, **www.fossil.com;** and "Fossil and Seiko Complete Formation of Joint Venture Company, Announce License Agreements," press release, August 24, 1999, **www.fossil.com.**

integrative CASE

PART ONE

AOL: AMERICA'S ONLY LINE?

AMERICA ONLINE A few years ago, no one would have named AOL one of the most powerful media organizations in the United States. The Internet service provider had been besieged by its own weaknesses—poor performance brought about by ineffectiveness and inefficiency. In the mid-1990s, AOL failed to incorporate a good Web browser into its software; then the company found itself in trouble with investors because of accounting irregularities; finally, AOL alienated thousands of customers when it shifted to flat-rate pricing and failed to prepare for the huge increase in demand. Subscribers couldn't dial up, e-mails weren't delivered, and there was no one for customers to call for help. Eventually, cofounder and CEO Steve Case had to apologize in print advertisements, fix the problem, and offer refunds. For a while, it seemed that the damage was done. America Online was dubbed "America Onhold," and the unflattering epithet wouldn't go away. But making predictions in the volatile Internet industry is risky. Steve Case stubbornly refused to give up, and AOL has emerged stronger than ever as an organization. Experts who once laughed at Case's prediction that by the year 2005 AOL would be as intrepid a force on the Internet as Microsoft aren't laughing anymore. "When you see that 40 percent of all online traffic is coming through AOL, you've got to be there," says Larry Rosen, the founder of N2K, who recently made a deal to become the exclusive music retailer on AOL.

AOL's organizational culture reflects the managerial style of Steve Case. He's been described as "shy and unassuming, a worrier warrior," and a "quiet strategic thinker." Although he holds about $1 billion in AOL stock, Case usually eats in the company cafeteria and lives in a modest home outside Washington, D.C., with his wife and five children. He's the embodiment of "office casual" attire—jeans and a polo shirt, or sometimes a more flashy Hawaiian number. He seems like a normal guy, accessible to anyone, which is why people relate to him. In short, he has human skills. He also has the conceptual skills to run AOL; although he's not a "techie," he understands how technology affects the average person who is his customer.

In a criticism of his industry, he said, "Right now, there is too much focus on the technology and not enough on the consumer."

AOL's organizational culture reflected Case's entrepreneurial spirit even as the company mushroomed from a few employees to several thousand. Currently, about 9,500 people work for AOL. Yet Case began to lose control of the organization because it was growing without clear planning and controlling functions. "This place was entrepreneurial to the point of confusion," recalls Myer Berlow, an advertising executive who was hired in 1995. "Everyone got to do what they wanted." As management functions were sliding, so was the company's performance.

But Case never lost sight of his goal to make AOL a household name. Recognizing the importance of human capital, he hired new managers and at one point he even stepped aside as CEO. In an industry where brand name recognition and being first to market can mean the difference between success and failure, the company has been on the move. AOL invested in a number of strategic alliances, such as the one with Hughes Electronic Corp, which would send AOL over satellite TV, and another with 3Com and Motorola to put AOL on those companies' palm devices and smart phones. Still, Case had a hard time explaining to the public—investors and customers alike—exactly what AOL's resources were. "It was hard. People didn't quite get it," Case said in an interview for *U.S. News & World Report*. Once they did understand, they tended to brush AOL aside, believing that the reigning technology giants like Microsoft and AT&T would quickly grind AOL into the ground. But in a surprise move, even for an industry known for surprises, Case bid for Time Warner, creating what could be the largest merger in history.

In an environment that is constantly changing, and in which the rules seem to be rewritten every few months, it's difficult for a company like AOL to assess resources according to the traditional standards of how valuable and rare they are and whether they are inimitable and nonsubstitutable. But perhaps one of the company's most important resources will be managers who can recognize how and with whom to join forces, as in the deals with Motorola and Hughes. In addition, the company needs people who can anticipate new ways to be present in as many homes around the world as possible. Case wants AOL to be more than a household word; he wants his company to be a household necessity.

Questions

1. List several steps that AOL can take over the next five years to create a sustained competitive advantage in the marketplace.

2. In what ways might a merger with a large company change the organizational culture of AOL?

3. Do you think managers with conceptual skills or human skills will be more important to AOL's future? Why?

4. Visit AOL's Web sites at www.aol.com and corp.aol.com and look for ways that AOL as a system seems to interact with its environment. Discuss your findings in class.

Source: William J. Holstein and Fred Vogelstein, "You've Got a Deal!" *U.S. News & World Report,* January 24, 2000, pp. 34–40; Fred Vogelstein, "The Talented Mr. Case," *U.S. News & World Report,* January 24, 2000, pp. 41–42; Tim Jones and Gary Marx, "Weaned on Crisis, Landing on Top," *Chicago Tribune,* January 16, 2000, section 1, p. 1; "On the Case at AOL," *Businessweek Online,* January 10, 2000, **www.businessweek.com;** Om Malik, "Retail is the New AOL-MSN War Zone," *Forbes.com,* November 11, 1999, **www.forbes.com;** Marc Gunther, "Mr. Case's Neighborhood," *Fortune,* March 30, 1998, pp. 69–80.

part 2

PART TWO

Individuals in Organizations

three

CHAPTER

3

Individual Differences

preview

After studying this chapter, you should be able to:

- Discuss the role of the psychological contract in the workplace.

- Explain why person-job fit is important.

- Identify major personality traits and describe how personality can influence workplace attitudes and behaviors.

- Explain emotional intelligence and describe why it is important.

- Explain how individuals learn and how style differences influence learning.

- Define values and explain how they are important in the workplace.

- Define attitudes, including their major components, and explain their relationship to behavior.

- Discuss the importance of work-related attitudes.

- Discuss outcomes affected by individual differences: creativity, job performance, counterproductive behavior, withdrawal behaviors, and organizational citizenship.

T
he world of software development is constantly changing, so the ability to develop new products is the key to success. Microsoft's business strategy is to outsmart the competition by recognizing and quickly adapting to changing business conditions. To do this, Microsoft needs an organizational culture that fosters intellectual debate. Employees who lack skill and ability are not likely to be comfortable or successful in this climate.

General intelligence is the main characteristic that Microsoft evaluates in considering 120,000 job applicants yearly. The goal of its hiring is to find the smartest people and match them with the jobs that best suit their talents and abilities. General intelligence is valued even more than experience. Microsoft is known to have rejected job applicants with impressive experience in software development. Instead, Microsoft tries to hire academics from university math or physics departments—people who have "high horsepower" in terms of general intelligence but no experience in the software industry.

Employee selection and placement are so central to Microsoft that chairman Bill Gates often interviews prospective job candidates. Gates believes that intelligence and creativity are difficult to learn or teach, so Microsoft can't do much to develop people along these lines after they are hired. He also believes that smart people are a critical reason for Microsoft's success. According to Gates, "Take our 20 best people away, and I will tell you that Microsoft would become an unimportant company." Business experts who follow Microsoft agree. Their analysis of the company suggests that Microsoft's competitive advantage results from financial capital, good products, and an intelligent and motivated workforce. And as Microsoft positions itself to develop software for the new Web-based economy, its employees' talents will continue to be critical to its success.[1]

> *"Take our 20 best people away, and I will tell you that Microsoft would become an unimportant company."*
> —**Bill Gates,** chairman, Microsoft

People differ in many ways. General intelligence, which is so important to Microsoft as it shifts its focus to the potential of the World Wide Web, is only one of the many characteristics that vary among individuals. These differences affect day-to-day work processes and interactions, such as how employees interpret an assignment, whether they like to collaborate with others, and how they handle challenges. Productivity, innovativeness, creativity, and other organizational outcomes are influenced by how employees behave. People are an organization's most valuable resource—and the source of some of the most difficult problems. People problems can be particularly challenging due to the complex and unique qualities that people bring to the workplace.

Individual differences are characteristics that vary from one person to another. As the opening vignette illustrates, organizations such as Microsoft evaluate individual differences (in this case, general intelligence) to determine whom they will hire. Individual differences not only influence whether a person will be able to successfully perform a job but also affect how that person feels and learns in an organization. Your knowledge of individual differences can help you understand a behavioral situation or, more broadly, the way that employees tend to act in organizations.

individual differences

Characteristics that vary from one person to another.

This chapter introduces the role of individual differences among employees. We begin by describing the process of exchange through which an organization's relationship with each employee is developed. This process of exchange creates a unique psychological contract with each employee. Next we look at several important areas in which individuals differ: abilities, personality, values, and attitudes. The chapter concludes with a discussion of important outcomes influenced by individual differences: creativity, job performance, counterproductive behaviors, withdrawal, and organizational citizenship behaviors.

Individual-organization exchange influences organizational behavior

psychological contract

What an employee expects to contribute and what the organization will provide to the employee for these contributions.

Individuals act and react not only with each other but also with the organizations to which they belong. One way to understand the concept of individual-organization exchange is to think of it as a **psychological contract.** The psychological contract describes what an employee expects to contribute and what the organization will provide to the employee for these contributions.[2] The psychological contract represents the employee's and the organization's beliefs or perceptions of the terms of the employment relationship. Rarely are all of the terms of the employment relationship negotiated between the employee and the organization. Exhibit 3.1 shows the elements of a psychological contract. Unlike a sales or legal contract, a psychological contract is not written down. Organizations expect employees to contribute time, effort, skills, abilities, and loyalty. Employees expect organizations to provide inducements such as pay, status, and career opportunities.

For example, consider the psychological contract between LTV Corporation and its employees.[3] Through the efforts of employees such as Sam Kamins, Charles Pohl, and others, LTV Corporation managed to survive the collapse of the U.S. steel industry. Sam Kamins, a union representative, and Charles Pohl, an LTV manager, were key players when LTV entered the electrogalvanized steel market in a joint venture with Sumitomo (a Japanese organization). Steelworkers who were called back to work from a layoff needed to be retrained to strengthen their physical and cognitive abilities to fit the new job requirements. The new labor agreement, partially negotiated by Kamins, encouraged employees to learn a wide variety of skills. The new pay system introduced by LTV paid employees based on the skills they

exhibit | **3.1**   Elements of the Psychological Contract

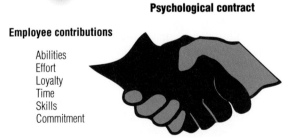

Psychological contract

Employee contributions	**Organizational inducements**
Abilities	Pay
Effort	Benefits
Loyalty	Job security
Time	Career opportunities
Skills	Status
Commitment	Praise
	Desirable organizational culture

learned. In addition to the written contract, LTV and its employees established a new psychological contract. LTV expected a higher level of skill and performance from its employees. In return, employees could expect to be trained properly, be given authority to make decisions related to their jobs, and be promoted for their efforts.

Changes in the Psychological Contract

Neither an employee nor an organization is likely to pay much attention to the psychological contract unless someone believes the contract is not being honored. Unfortunately, such instances are not rare; evidence suggests that psychological contracts are frequently violated.[4] Exhibit 3.2 shows the types of violations reported. If employees or organizations believe the contract is being violated, they may ask for a change in the contract or start behaving in a way that makes the contract seem fairer. Research shows that organizations' violations of the psychological contract are

exhibit **3.2**   Reported Organizational Violations of the Psychological Contract

Violation	Definition	Examples
Training/ development	Absence of training, or training experience not as promised	Sales training was promised as an integral part of marketing training. It never materialized.
Compensation	Discrepancies between promised and realized pay, benefits, bonuses	Specific compensation benefits were promised and were either not given to me, or I had to fight for them.
Promotion	Promotion or advancement schedule not as promised	I perceived a promise that I had a good chance of promotion to manager in one year. While I received excellent performance ratings, I was not promoted in my first year.
Nature of job	Employer perceived as having misrepresented the nature of the department or job	(My) employer promised I would be working on venture capital projects. I was mainly writing speeches for the CEO.
Job security	Promises regarding degree of job security one could expect were not met	The company promised that no one would be fired out of the training program—that all of us were "safe" until placement (in return for this security we accepted lower pay). The company subsequently fired four people from the training program.
Feedback	Feedback and reviews inadequate compared to what was promised	. . . (I did) not receive performance reviews as promised.
Management of change	Employees not asked for input or given notice of changes as they were promised	I was promised more knowledge and control over my future.
Responsibility	Employees given less responsibility and/or challenge than promised	(I was) promised greater responsibility, more strategic thinking/decision making.
People	Employer perceived as having misrepresented the type of people at the firm, such as their expertise, work style, or reputation	I was promised a dynamic and challenging environment . . . rubbing elbows with some of the brightest people in the business . . . a big lie. The true picture started to come out . . . after the initial hype . . . of working at one of the best 100 companies in the U.S. had worn off.
Other	Perceived promises not fulfilled by the employer that do not fit into above categories	Original representations of the company's financial and market strength became clearly fraudulent.

Source: Sandra L. Robinson and Denise M. Rousseau, "Violating the Psychological Contract: Not the Exception but the Norm," *Journal of Organizational Behavior* 15 (1994): 256. Copyright © 1994 John Wiley and Sons, Ltd. Reproduced with permission.

negatively related to employees' satisfaction, trust, and intentions to stay with the organization. Also, the more employees believe that the organization violated the psychological contract, the more likely they are to leave.

Review the list of contributions that employees make and the inducements that an organization provides under a psychological contract (Exhibit 3.1). Consider what may happen if either party believes the balance has been disturbed. If employees believe they have put forth great effort to help the organization reach its goals, they may ask for a promotion or pay increase. If employees do not believe that the company inducements fulfill the terms of the contract, they may put forth less effort at work or withdraw from work (take longer lunch breaks, refuse overtime, or show up late). If the organization believes that it is providing appropriate inducements but employees are not contributing to meet the contract, it may require employees to attend training programs or work longer hours or even threaten them with layoffs if their performance does not improve.

Traditionally, the psychological contract emphasized high performance, loyalty, and commitment from employees. In return, organizations would provide continued employment (job security) and opportunities for promotion. However, the terms of this traditional contract have been eroded.[5] The current competitive business environment demands frequent changes in the quality, innovation, creativity, and timeliness of employee contributions, the skills needed to provide them, and the amount of investment in human resources that organizations are willing to make. This has led to organizational restructuring, layoffs, and longer hours for many employees. In return for providing their services to organizations, many employees also want different inducements, such as flexible work schedules, comfortable working conditions, a say in how they accomplish tasks, training to prepare them for the future, and financial incentives based on how the organization performs.

The New Contract

In today's volatile work environment, traditional stability and long-term commitments have been discarded. The traditional psychological contract has been replaced with a new one. The new psychological contract emphasizes that it is an employee's responsibility to manage and develop his or her career.[6] The organization will not provide job security but will provide training and job experiences to help ensure that employees are able to find other employment opportunities. That is, the organization will provide employability but not employment security. For example, Ford Motor Company created the "Personal Development Roadmap" (PDR), a resource available on the company's intranet that gives marketing, sales, and service employees control over their personal and professional development.[7] The PDR helps employees determine what skills they have as well as how to enhance those skills or develop new ones. The PDR recommends education through Ford Motor Company classes and seminars, exploration of activities outside Ford, and new experiences such as job assignments, task forces, committee work, and volunteer work to help employees develop their skills. Although the Personal Development Roadmap uses new technology, the idea of employees taking charge of their personal and professional growth was a basic belief of Henry Ford, founder of Ford Motor Company. Ford was known to say, "Anyone who stops learning is old, whether at twenty or eighty. Anyone who keeps learning stays young."

Although the new psychological contract has many positive benefits, such as increased opportunities for personal growth and challenging jobs, it also has some potential drawbacks, including lack of identification with the organization, poor morale, increased cynicism, and increased employee turnover.[8] Despite the short-term focus of the new psychological contract, organizations and employees appear to benefit most when both parties emphasize a long-term commitment. Greater organizational performance and more positive employee attitudes are found in employment relationships in which the organization provides longer term career and financial commitments to employees compared with short-term rewards.[9] In return, employees work long hours, develop their skills, and perform beyond their expected job duties.

apply it

Think of a psychological contract in which you are involved. It might be a contract between you and an employer, coach, music instructor, professor, spouse, or other party.

1. What are the terms of the contract for you? For the other party?
2. Are you satisfied with the contract? Why or why not?
3. What changes might you try to make in the agreement?

Individuals' talents may suit them to particular jobs or organizations

Because of the wide variation among people's personalities and abilities and among jobs, it is important to match employees' skills and job characteristics so that people are well suited to the work they must perform. So, organizations need not only to determine what they need their employees to do but also to get a general sense of the type of people who would succeed at that type of work. The extent to which a person's ability and personality match the requirements of a job is called **person-job fit.** One of the most important parts of a manager's job is getting the right person-job fit. When hiring and leading employees, managers need to consider employees' strengths and the demands of a job, so that employees are more likely to contribute and be satisfied.[10] Bruce M. Hubby, chairman and founder of Professional Dynamic Programs, is a consultant who has designed surveys to help managers determine which candidates are right for which jobs. In the past two decades, he has helped more than 5,000 companies match people to jobs and jobs to people. In Exhibit 3.3 we present his tips for increasing the likelihood that there will be a good person-job fit.

Dennis Brozak, owner of Design Basics, was meticulous about person-job fit when it came time to pick his successor. The person he selected was Linda Reimer, whom Brozak had first hired as a part timer to photocopy

person-job fit

The extent to which a person's ability and personality match the requirements of a job.

exhibit | **3.3**   Suggestions for Getting the Right Person-Job Fit

1. People do best when they can use their natural strengths. Look for employees' strongest traits and create an environment that enhances them. When people act naturally, they are the most productive; when they are forced to act against their nature, they become stressed and less productive.

2. Learn which of the four basic traits is most prominent in a person. Dominance, extroversion, patience, and conformity are the four basic personality traits that describe most people. Dominant people are innovative and confident, and they like to be in control. Extroverted people are outgoing and social. Patient people know how to pace themselves; they are focused but adaptable. Conforming people have a strong sense of right and wrong; they are structured and quality oriented. Learning which basic trait is most prevalent (and how the other three factor in) will help managers determine who is right for a job.

3. Resist the urge to hire someone who is exactly like you. We naturally gravitate toward people who are like us, so a manager may hire someone who has the same natural strengths or personality traits, even if those strengths and traits are not right for the job.

4. Reshape the job, not the person. If an employee is struggling with a job because of poor person-job fit, it's much easier to reshape the job—or move the employee to another job—than it is to reshape the employee's personality. Usually, there's no need to let that worker go.

Source: David Beardsley, "These Tests Will Give You Fits," Reprinted from the November 1998 issue of *Fast Company* magazine, pp. 88, 90. All rights reserved. To subscribe, please call 800-688-1545.

blueprints. Over the years, Brozak added to her responsibilities as he discovered she was eager to learn the business, had financial acumen, cared about design and construction, and shared core values such as the idea that all work is honorable. To test her management skills, Brozak made Reimer human resources director, put her in charge of a product, made her an operations director, and then promoted her to vice president of product development. He says, "I wanted to find out a lot about her. Can she manage and motivate people? Can she delegate accurately and appropriately? And she had better be able to fire people when necessary. She has a big heart, but she passed that test, too." In each position, Reimer boosted the company's performance, so Brozak appointed her company president, a decision that has paid off in double-digit growth. Although a person toiling at the photocopier might not have seemed to be a candidate for company president just a few years later, Brozak's focus on abilities rather than job titles enabled him to achieve a good person-job fit for the company's top position.[11]

An understanding of personality also is important when considering changing the design of a job, because such changes may affect person-job fit. How flexible are employees? Will they be likely to voice their questions and concerns? Will the new work structure require a level of responsibility with which the employees will be comfortable? Personality does not easily lend itself to change. When person-job fit is poor, tasks need to be restructured or employees need to be replaced.

Besides considering the match between abilities, personality, and job requirements, many organizations, particularly those with a strong culture, are also evaluating job candidates on whether their personality, goals, and values fit the organization's culture. **Person-organization fit** refers to the match between an individual's personality, goals, and values and the organizational culture.[12] The changing nature of job requirements due to tech-

person-organization fit

The match between the individual's personality, goals, and values and the organizational culture.

nology improvements, customer needs, restructuring, globalization, and new product and service manufacturing and delivery mechanisms has forced organizations to de-emphasize person-job fit. Greater emphasis is instead being placed on identifying individuals who fit and support the organizational culture and have the ability to adapt and learn new skills as job requirements change. Consider the emphasis that AES Corporation places on person-organization fit.

❧ AES Corporation

AES Corporation is a global electricity company based in Arlington, Virginia. The company operates approximately 90 electricity plants in 13 countries, with 40,000 employees. CEO Dennis Bakke's goal is to ensure the company works according to four principles: fairness, integrity, social responsibility, and fun. At AES fun does not mean having parties. AES does celebrate achievements. But "fun" means that employees are totally engaged in their work, have complete responsibility for making decisions, and are accountable for results. What they do matters to the company and the communities it provides electricity to. The company gives employees the power and the responsibility to make important decisions and to feel like business partners, not machine parts. The company is organized around small teams. Teams take full responsibility for their work. AES has tried to eliminate all functional specialists. The company does not have corporate marketing, a finance group, or a human resource department.

Hiring the right employees is essential to making AES work. New employees need to be able to work in teams and fit in the company culture. In fact, AES rarely bases its hiring decisions on technical ability. Cultural fit is the primary criteria used for hiring; technical ability is second. Peer review is emphasized in hiring. Teams interview job candidates and focus on whether the person will be comfortable in the AES environment. Only after that is the candidate's technical expertise examined. The interview also tries to determine whether the candidate will accept decision-making responsibility and agree with the company's view that it is business's responsibility to improve the lives of people. In addition, candidates need to demonstrate their commitment to fairness. Finally, the interview tries to determine whether the candidate views "fun" as a full mind-body-soul engagement with work well done. Sample interview questions include, "What does 'fun on the job' mean to you?" "Recall a time when people around you were not being totally honest. What did you do?" and "What do you do when something needs to be done and no procedure exists?"[13] Through its careful selection of job candidates, AES equips itself to meet its challenges.

apply it

1. Think back about how you made the decision to enroll in your college or university. What personal characteristics (such as interests, values, goals, likes, or dislikes) and characteristics of the school (such as the student body, courses, campus, alumni, majors, housing) did you consider in determining whether you would fit in? What factors had the most important influence on your decision to enroll?

Individual differences can influence organizational behavior

To find and keep the right employees, organizations need to consider many different characteristics of individuals. Abilities, personality, and learning styles are all differences that people bring to an organization, and these differences can ultimately influence organizational behavior.

<u>exhibit</u> **3.4**   How Values, Attitudes, Ability, and Personality Influence Organizational Behavior

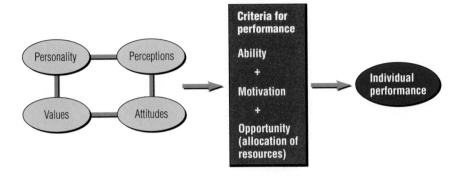

Individual differences affect both individual and organizational outcomes. That is, individual differences affect whether employees are satisfied, can perform effectively, and are creative and innovative. We will discuss these outcomes in more detail later in the chapter. Exhibit 3.4 shows how individual differences affect individual performance. Employees' attitudes are formed by their personality and values. These attitudes affect the development and use of abilities and motivation. For employees to be satisfied and perform well, they must have the right abilities and be motivated to use them. Employees need both ability and motivation to successfully perform.[14] A motivated but unskilled person cannot perform well, and a skilled employee who lacks the drive and energy to do a job likewise will not be successful. Also, as we will see later, personality affects performance and motivation.

As Exhibit 3.4 shows, ability and motivation occur in the context of opportunity. Opportunity affects the allocation of resources, including time, money, equipment, and the level of supervision needed to perform. If resources are scarce or the wrong resources are provided, it is unlikely that individuals will be able to perform regardless of their motivation, ability, or personality.

Ability

ability

What individuals know and can do if they choose.

aptitude

An individual's natural tendency to learn or understand.

physical abilities

Strength, endurance, flexibility, coordination, and balance.

psychomotor abilities

Muscle control and precise manipulations of fingers and limbs.

Ability refers to what individuals know and can do if they choose. Abilities are based on an individual's aptitude and learning experiences. **Aptitude** refers to an individual's natural tendency to learn or understand. Organizational behavior is influenced by two types of ability—physical ability and cognitive ability.

Physical and Psychomotor Ability   **Physical abilities** include strength, endurance, flexibility, coordination, and balance.[15] **Psychomotor abilities** include muscle control and precise manipulations of fingers and limbs. Different types of physical and psychomotor abilities are shown in Exhibit 3.5. Physical abilities are needed in physically demanding jobs such as those of professional athletes, construction workers, police officers, and firefighters. Psychomotor abilities are needed in jobs such as pipefitters, wood-

exhibit 3.5
Types of Physical Abilities

Type of Ability	Description	Example
Major Physical Abilities		
Static strength	Maximizes force that can be exerted against external objects	Lifting weights
Dynamic strength	Muscular endurance in exerting force continuously or repeatedly	Pull-ups
Explosive strength	Ability to mobilize energy effectively in bursts	Standing broad jump
Trunk strength	Dynamic strength limited to leg muscles	Leg lifts
Dynamic flexibility	Ability to stretch trunk and muscles	Twist-and-touch floor test
Gross body coordination	Ability to coordinate action of several parts of the body while the body is in motion	Jump rope test
Gross body equilibrium	Ability to maintain balance	Walking a balance beam
Stamina	Capacity to sustain maximum effort requiring cardiovascular exertion	One-mile run
Major Psychomotor Abilities		
Control precision	Tasks requiring finely controlled muscular adjustments	Moving a lever to a precise setting
Multilimb coordination	Ability to coordinate the movements of limbs simultaneously	Packing a box with both hands
Response orientation	Ability to make correct and accurate movements in relation to a stimulus under highly accelerated conditions	Reaching and flicking a switch as soon as a warning horn sounds
Reaction time	Speed of response when a stimulus appears	Pressing a key in response to a bell
Speed of arm movement	Speed of gross arm movements where accuracy is not required	Gathering trash and throwing it into a big pile
Rate control	Ability to make continuous motor adjustments relative to a moving target that changes in speed and direction	Holding a rod on a moving rotor
Manual dexterity	Skillful arm and hand movements in handling rather large objects under speeded conditions	Rapidly placing differently shaped blocks into the correct holes of a board
Finger dexterity	Skillful manipulations of small objects with the fingers	Attaching nuts and bolts
Arm-hand steadiness	Ability to make precise arm-hand positioning movements that do not require strength	Threading a needle

Source: Based on Edwin A. Fleishman, *The Structure and Measurement of Physical Fitness* (Englewood Cliffs, NJ: Prentice-Hall, 1964), pp. 31–42, 67–78.

crafters, and dentists. These jobs often require precise manipulations of objects and controlled muscle movements. Physical and psychomotor abilities may be needed not only to perform these jobs but also to ensure the safety of the individual employees or others.[16]

Organizations must ensure that physical and psychomotor abilities are essential for performing a job before refusing to hire or firing people who lack these abilities. According to the Americans with Disabilities Act, even if a job requires physical or psychomotor abilities, organizations may be required to provide additional equipment or help from coworkers for a person who does not meet the physical job requirements but may successfully perform the job with these accommodations.[17]

Cognitive Abilities **Cognitive abilities** refer to individuals' mental capacity to think and analyze information. There are several different types of cognitive abilities, one of which is known as general cognitive ability. **General cognitive ability** refers to an individual's capacity to acquire, store, retrieve, manipulate, and use information.[18] One way to think of general cognitive ability is that it is an overall measure of intelligence. General cognitive ability has been shown to be related to both performance on the job and success in training programs.[19] General cognitive ability appears to be

cognitive abilities

Individuals' mental capacity to think and analyze information.

general cognitive ability

An individual's capacity to acquire, store, retrieve, manipulate, and use information.

more related to successful performance of complex jobs (those requiring reasoning, new applications of skills) than jobs requiring physical abilities. Also, intelligence has been shown to be positively associated with job satisfaction.[20] This may be because more intelligent people work harder to get jobs that match their skills and interests.

Psychologists have debated for years whether the best measure of intelligence is a single overall measure of intelligence, such as general cognitive ability, or more specific abilities. Although it is easy to use general cognitive ability to categorize individuals, it is important to realize that individuals do vary on specific dimensions of cognitive ability. These dimensions include verbal comprehension, quantitative ability, and reasoning ability. **Verbal comprehension** refers to an individual's capacity to understand and use written and spoken language. **Quantitative ability** refers to an individual's speed and accuracy in solving math problems. **Reasoning ability** refers to an individual's capacity to solve different types of problems.

In organizations in which jobs are narrowly designed and repetitive, individuals typically need lower levels of these three dimensions. Although such jobs exist, their numbers are declining as customers insist on high-quality products and demand variety and customization to meet their needs.[21] Organizations are using new technologies and processes in a variety of ways to help meet customers' needs. In such organizations, machines may perform the repetitive physical, recording, and calculating tasks, while employees focus on using the machines' capabilities to produce customized products. Instituting this change in the workplace frees employees who have higher abilities to think quickly and creatively—to transfer knowledge and previous experiences to handle new customer needs. Such knowledge workers must be actively involved in setting work standards and take responsibility for the quality of products and services.

The literacy problem facing the United States underlies the lack of cognitive abilities among both current and new employees. As much as 20 percent of the U.S. workforce may be functionally illiterate; that is, have limited reading, writing, and math skills.[22] One estimate is that employees' lack of basic skills results in a $60 billion annual loss in productivity. Employees who can't understand warning signs or shipping instructions cause mistakes, accidents, and equipment damage, and companies may implement a new technology only to discover that employees don't have the abilities to use it. Companies ranging from Batesville Casket Company in Batesville, Indiana, to Motorola are spending money to train employees in basic skills. In many cases, the biggest challenge is getting employees to attend these training programs. Many employees are too embarrassed and self-conscious to admit to their employers (or friends and family) that they have reading or writing problems.

Personality

In everyday life—and so the workplace—we find people whose behavior is consistently pleasant, aggressive, or stubborn in a variety of situations. To explain that behavior, we may say, "He has a pleasant personality" or "She

---

verbal comprehension

An individual's capacity to understand and use written and spoken language.

quantitative ability

An individual's speed and accuracy in solving math problems.

reasoning ability

An individual's capacity to solve different types of problems.

Successful entrepreneurs such as Richard Branson, founder of Virgin Airways and other start-up businesses, require extensive cognitive abilities combined with a powerful drive for accomplishment. Business success brings such entrepreneurs extensive job satisfaction. Branson believes the kicks he gets from hot-air ballooning and starting a new business are similar. "It's about testing yourself. You're willing to go where most people won't dare."
Source: © Thierry Boccon-Gibod/Liaison Agency.

has an aggressive personality." An individual's **personality** is the set of characteristics that underlie a relatively stable pattern of behavior in response to ideas, objects, or people in the environment. Understanding an individual's personality can help you understand how that person will act in a particular situation. Often, two people with comparable abilities perform quite differently on the job due to their different personalities. Managers and coworkers who appreciate the ways employees' personalities differ have insight into what kinds of situations will help them achieve peak performance.

The Big Five In common usage, people think of personality in terms of traits, or relatively stable characteristics of a person. Researchers have investigated whether any traits stand up to scientific scrutiny. Although investigators have examined thousands of traits over the years, their findings have been distilled into five general dimensions that describe personality. These often are called the "Big Five" personality factors, as illustrated in Exhibit 3.6.[23] Each factor may contain a wide range of specific traits. We will discuss specific traits as they relate to motivation, leadership, and stress later in the text. The **Big Five personality factors** describe an individual's extroversion, agreeableness, conscientiousness, emotional stability, and openness to experience:

1. *Extroversion* the degree to which a person is sociable, talkative, assertive, and comfortable with interpersonal relationships.

2. *Agreeableness* the degree to which a person is able to get along with others by being good natured, cooperative, forgiving, understanding, and trusting.

3. *Conscientiousness* the degree to which a person is focused on a few goals, thus behaving in ways that are responsible, dependable, persistent, and achievement oriented.

personality

The set of characteristics that underlie a relatively stable pattern of behavior in response to ideas, objects, or people in the environment.

Big Five personality factors

An individual's extroversion, agreeableness, conscientiousness, emotional stability, and openness to experience.

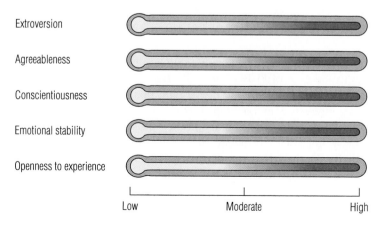

exhibit **3.6** The Big Five

A person may have a low, moderate, or high degree of each of these factors:

Extroversion

Agreeableness

Conscientiousness

Emotional stability

Openness to experience

Low   Moderate   High

4. *Emotional stability*   the degree to which a person is calm, enthusiastic, and secure, rather than tense, nervous, depressed, moody, or insecure.

5. *Openness to experience*   the degree to which a person has a broad range of interests and is imaginative, creative, artistically sensitive, and willing to consider new ideas.

As illustrated in the exhibit, these factors represent a continuum. That is, any individual may exhibit a low, moderate, or high degree of each quality. A person who has an extremely high degree of agreeableness would likely be described as warm, friendly, and good natured, while one at the opposite extreme might be described as cold, rude, or hard to get along with. In general, a moderate to high degree of conscientiousness is necessary for success in many jobs. Managers rate conscientiousness as one of the most important characteristics they look for in employees.[24] In addition, certain factors may be particularly important for specific kinds of work. Extroversion and agreeableness are important for success in sales and management jobs.[25] Successful entrepreneurs, such as Robert Steinberg and John Scharffenberger, display a high degree of creativity (openness to ideas) and conscientiousness.

❧ Scharffen Berger Chocolate Maker

Robert Steinberg and John Scharffenberger share a willingness to try new ideas—and a passion for chocolate, which they now manufacture and sell under the name Scharffen Berger. Chocolate has been around for centuries, but until these two came along, only a handful of chocolate makers actually imported, roasted, and ground their own cacao beans, and none of the other makers was independent.

Before venturing into candy making, Scharffenberger had already launched a successful sparkling wine business; his wine was used by Reagan and Gorbachev to toast the end of the Cold War. His goal was, as he put it, "to bring joy and innovation to the world of food." Steinberg, on the other hand, is a former physician who sold his practice to follow his interest in cooking when he was diagnosed with an incurable lymphoma. Both are creative men, willing to take chances on new experiences. "What they've done is really unusual," says Alice Medrich, a chocolate chef. "No one just starts a factory. It's too tricky." Steinberg puts it modestly: "Naiveté has worked well for me."

Scharffenberger and Steinberg also are extroverts who love to talk about their sweet passion. Most mass-market chocolates are mainly sugar, says Steinberg. "But chocolate really is a whole possibility of flavors." Scharffenberger claims, "People bite into our chocolate and go 'Wow'!" Both men are conscientious, dividing responsibilities according to their talents and interests. Steinberg has become a cacao expert, and Scharffenberger handles the marketing. They now have ten employees at their San Francisco factory, which produces 10,000 pounds of chocolate each month. In addition, Steinberg volunteers at a medical clinic, where he is fond of handing out free chocolate to patients.[26]

Another example of a personality trait common to entrepreneurs is persistence. In the case of FUBU The Collection, its four founders showed extraordinary conscientiousness. They sought financing at over 20 banks, but none was interested in backing a company selling urban fashions and owned by four young black men. Still they persisted, and one owner mortgaged his home. With publicity from rap artist LL Cool J, the company eventually began bringing in millions of dollars in revenues.[27]

Despite the logic and even the validity of the Big Five personality factors, they can be difficult to measure precisely. Furthermore, research has been mostly limited to subjects in the United States, so this theory is difficult to apply in an international context.

Cognitive Styles **Cognitive styles** refer to the different ways individuals perceive and process information. Carl Jung, a psychologist, believed that differences in behavior resulted from preferences in decision making, interpersonal communications, and information gathering. The Myers Briggs Type Indicator (MBTI) measures these preferences. The MBTI is the most widely used personality test in the United States. The MBTI classifies personalities on each of four dimensions:[28]

cognitive styles

The different ways individuals perceive and process information.

- *Energy (Introversion vs. Extroversion)* This dimension determines where individuals gain interpersonal strength and stimulation. Extroverts (E) gain energy through interpersonal relationships. Introverts (I) gain energy by focusing on personal thoughts and feelings.
- *Information Gathering (Sensing vs. Intuition)* This dimension relates to the action individuals take when making decisions. Individuals with a Sensing (S) preference tend to focus more on facts and details. Intuitives (N) tend to focus less on facts and more on possibilities and relationships between ideas.
- *Decision Making (Thinking vs. Feeling)* This dimension relates to how much consideration a person gives to others' feelings in making a decision. Individuals with a Thinking (T) preference are very objective in making decisions. Individuals with a Feeling (F) preference tend to be more concerned about the impact of their decisions on other people.
- *Life Style (Judging vs. Perceiving)* This dimension relates to an individual's tendency to be flexible and adaptive. Individuals who are Judging (J) focus on goals, establish deadlines, and like to reach closure on decisions. Individuals who are Perceiving (P) tend to dislike deadlines, prefer surprises, and often change their minds several times before making a decision.

Sixteen unique personality types result from the combination of the four MBTI preferences. Each individual has developed strengths and weaknesses as a result of the preferences. For example, individuals who are Extroverted, Sensing, Thinking, and Judging (known as ESTJs) tend to be practical and realistic. They have developed an extensive network of personal contacts. They like to organize and run activities. ESTJs also have several weaknesses because they tend not to use the opposite preferences: Introversion, Intuition, Feeling, and Perceiving. They may have trouble capitalizing on unexpected opportunities and may neglect important values because they tend to focus on the practical and logical. They may also be too task oriented and impersonal to their peers. Each of the 16 basic personality types has its own strengths and weaknesses.

The MBTI is useful for understanding communication styles and motivation and in career counseling, team building, and leadership. For example, it can be used to develop teams by matching team members with tasks that allow them to use their strengths. It can also be useful for the team members to understand how each of their preferences can be useful for problem solving. MBTI scores are related to a person's occupation and useful for career counseling. By taking the MBTI, employees can see to what occupations their preferences are most closely related. For example, managers tend to be ISTJs, INTJs, ESTJs, or ENTJs. Keep in mind that this generalization does not mean that individuals with these preferences will be successful managers.

One of the dangers of using the MBTI is the tendency to stereotype other people and develop unrealistic expectations for their behavior: "He is an ISTJ, so he is quiet and practical." The MBTI measures preferences, and the strengths of those preferences vary and may not always relate to an individual's behavior. Also, it is important to realize that MBTI types are not unchangeable personality patterns. People's awareness of their preferences, training, and life experiences can cause them to change their preferences.

Emotional Intelligence   New research suggests that in addition to cognitive skill and technical skills, emotional intelligence may be an important predictor of individual performance.[29] **Emotional intelligence** involves the ability to accurately perceive, evaluate, express, and regulate emotions and feelings.[30] Emotional intelligence includes self-awareness, self-regulation, motivation, empathy, and social skill. Exhibit 3.7 shows the five components of emotional intelligence. As you can see from the description of the components, they all affect interpersonal relationships.

emotional intelligence

The ability to accurately perceive, evaluate, express, and regulate emotions and feelings.

exhibit | **3.7**

Five Components of Emotional Intelligence

	Definition	**Hallmarks**
Self-Awareness	The ability to recognize and understand your moods, emotions, and drives, as well as their effects on others	Self-confidence Realistic self-assessment Self-deprecating sense of humor
Self-Regulation	The ability to control or redirect disruptive impulses and moods	Trustworthiness and integrity Comfort with ambiguity
	The propensity to suspend judgment —to think before acting	Openness to change
Motivation	A passion to work for reasons that go beyond money or status	Strong drive to achieve Optimism, even in the face of failure
	A propensity to pursue goals with energy and persistence	Organizational commitment
Empathy	The ability to understand the emotional makeup of other people	Expertise in building and retaining talent
	Skill in treating people according to their emotional reactions	Cross-cultural sensitivity Service to clients and customers
Social Skill	Proficiency in managing relationships and building networks	Effectiveness in leading change
	An ability to find common ground and build rapport	Persuasiveness Expertise in building and leading teams

Source: Based on D. Goleman, *Working with Emotional Intelligence* (New York: Bantam, 1988); D. Goleman, "What Makes a Leader?," *Harvard Business Review*, November–December 1998, pp. 93–102.

At video game developer THQ, managers have learned from their mistakes. In 1995, the company was on the verge of bankruptcy, and its shares were trading below $1. Enter CEO Brian Farrell, who integrated pop culture into the company and its products to boost sales. At the company's test facility (photo), executives learn from caffeine- and snack food-fueled crews of teenagers and twenty-somethings, who pull all nighters testing THQ's new video games. The three-year total return for THQ is up 99 percent, and Fortune *magazine recently rated it number 3 in its list of 100 fastest growing companies.*
(Source: © PabloSerrano)

Emotional intelligence may be most predictive of performance for employees in positions for which technical skills are less important for effective performance (e.g., management and sales positions). For example, at L'Oreal, sales agents hired on the basis of emotional intelligence sold approximately $91,000 more than salespeople hired using the company's traditional hiring method.[31] Salespeople selected on the basis of emotional intelligence also had a significantly lower turnover rate.

Given the increasing importance of interpersonal skills as employees work in teams and interact with people from different cultures, a key question is whether emotional intelligence can be learned. If emotional intelligence can be learned, an organization may be able to train current employees rather than replacing them with new employees who have higher levels of emotional intelligence. Emotional intelligence appears to be genetically based, as well as acquired through life experiences. To be effective, training to improve emotional intelligence should help employees break old habits and establish new ones.[32] This takes motivation, effort, time, support, and sustained practice. Training time is devoted to giving employees techniques to deal with negative emotions in the workplace. Also, emotional intelligence training needs to take an individualized approach—involving a personal coach, for example.

Learning

Closely linked to a person's abilities and personality is his or her capability for learning. We have already mentioned aptitude as an individual's natural tendency to learn or understand. The ability to learn can profoundly affect a person's success in an organization.

learning

A change in behavior or performance that occurs as the result of experience.

Years of schooling have conditioned many of us to think that learning is something students do in response to teachers in a classroom. However, today's employees need specific knowledge and skills as well as the ability to adapt to changes in the world around them. **Learning** is a change in behavior or performance that occurs as the result of experience. Experience may take the form of observing others, reading or listening to sources of information, or experiencing the consequences of our own behavior. This important way of adapting to events is linked to perception, because learning depends on the way a person perceives sensory data.

The Learning Process   Two individuals who undergo similar experiences—for example, employees who transfer to work in a foreign country—probably will differ in how they adapt their behaviors to (that is, learn from) the experience. In other words, there are individual differences in the learning process.

One model of the learning process, shown in Exhibit 3.8, depicts learning as a four-stage cycle.[33] First, a person encounters a concrete experience. This is followed by thinking and reflective observation, which leads to abstract conceptualization, and, in turn, to active experimentation. The results of the experimentation generate new experiences, and the cycle repeats.

The Best Buy chain of consumer electronics superstores owes its birth to the learning process of its founder, Richard M. Schulze. In the 1960s, Schulze built a stereo store called Sound of Music into a chain of nine stores in and near St. Paul, Minnesota. However, a tornado destroyed his largest and most profitable store, so he held a massive clearance sale in the parking lot. So many shoppers descended on the lot that they caused traffic to back up for two miles. Reflecting on this experience, Schulze decided there was great demand for a store featuring large selection and low prices, backed by heavy advertising. He tried out his idea by launching his first Best Buy superstore. Today there are more than 280 Best Buy outlets, and the chain's profits are in the billions of dollars.[34]

The arrows in the model of the learning process imply that it is a recurring cycle. People continually test their conceptualizations and adapt them as a result of their personal reflections and observations about their experiences.

Learning Styles   Individuals develop personal learning styles that vary in terms of how much they emphasize each stage of the learning cycle. These

exhibit **3.8**

Model of the Learning Process

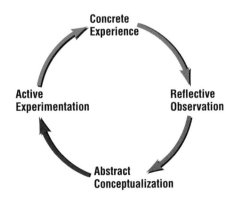

differences occur because the learning process is directed by individual needs and goals. For example, an engineer may place greater emphasis on abstract concepts, while a salesperson may emphasize concrete experiences. Because of these preferences, personal learning styles typically have strong and weak points.

To assess a person's strong and weak points as a learner in the learning cycle, researchers have developed questionnaires to measure the relative emphasis a person places on each of the four learning stages shown in Exhibit 3.8: concrete experience, reflective observation, abstract conceptualization, and active experimentation. Some people have a tendency to overemphasize one stage of the learning process, or to avoid some aspects of learning. Not many people have totally balanced profiles, but the key to effective learning is competence in each of the four stages when it is needed.

Each person's learning style is a combination of the emphasis placed on the four stages. Researchers have identified four fundamental learning styles that combine elements of the four stages.[35] Exhibit 3.9 summarizes the characteristics and dominant learning abilities of these four learning styles, labeled Diverger, Assimilator, Converger, and Accommodator. The exhibit also lists occupations that frequently attract individuals with each of the learning styles.

Divergers are particularly effective at generating ideas, seeing a situation from multiple perspectives, and being sensitive to other people's values. They tend to be in occupations that emphasize solving people problems such as human resource management or counseling. **Assimilators**

Divergers

A learning style in which persons are particularly effective at generating ideas, seeing a situation from multiple perspectives, and being sensitive to other people's values. They tend to be in occupations that emphasize solving people problems, such as human resource management or counseling.

Assimilators

A learning style in which persons are strong in planning, creating models, and developing theories. Assimilators are in occupations that emphasize ideas and abstract concepts, such as strategic planning or research.

exhibit **3.9**
Learning Styles

Learning Style Type	Dominant Learning Abilities	Learning Characteristics	Likely Occupations
Diverger	• Concrete experience • Reflective observation	• Is good at generating ideas, seeing a situation from multiple perspectives, and being aware of meaning and value • Tends to be interested in people, culture, and the arts	• Human resource management • Counseling • Organization development specialist
Assimilator	• Abstract conceptualization • Reflective observation	• Is good at inductive reasoning, creating theoretical models, and combining disparate observations into an integrated explanation • Tends to be less concerned with people than ideas and abstract concepts	• Research • Strategic planning
Converger	• Abstract conceptualization • Active experimentation	• Is good at decisiveness, practical application of ideas, and hypothetical deductive reasoning • Prefers dealing with technical tasks rather than interpersonal issues	• Engineering • Production
Accommodator	• Concrete experience • Active experimentation	• Is good at implementing decisions, carrying out plans, and getting involved in new experiences • Tends to be at ease with people but may be seen as impatient or pushy	• Marketing • Sales

Convergers

A learning style in which persons are good at making decisions, defining and solving problems, and applying ideas. Convergers are in occupations that involve technical problems, such as engineering or production.

Accommodators

A learning style in which persons' strengths include leadership, taking risks, getting things done, and adapting to new experiences. They are often drawn to occupations such as sales and marketing.

continuous learning

Looking for opportunities to learn from classes, reading, and talking to others, as well as looking for the lessons in life's experiences. Organizations promote continuous learning through processes and systems that enable employees to learn, share their growing knowledge, and apply it to their work.

are strong in planning, creating models, and developing theories. Assimilators are frequently found in occupations that emphasize ideas and abstract concepts, such as strategic planning or research. **Convergers** are good at making decisions, defining and solving problems, and applying ideas. Convergers may choose occupations that involve technical problems, such as engineering or production. **Accommodators'** learning style strengths include leadership, taking risks, getting things done, and adapting to new experiences. Because they like to influence others and like to interact with people, Accommodators often are drawn to sales and marketing.

An illustration of the Accommodator style is Steve Ballmer, who joined Microsoft to handle its sales and customer support. Now Microsoft's CEO, Ballmer is known for responsiveness to customer needs. When ABC, a Microsoft customer, asked Microsoft to make a change in its licensing agreement, Ballmer immediately called a meeting and resolved the concern by the next day. A former Microsoft executive describes Ballmer's approach to problem solving as "Don't have an elegant plan. Do the smart, obvious thing. Then fix it as you go." Ballmer even embodies some of the shortcomings of the Accommodator style. He is known for making statements that are more impulsive than diplomatic. For example, when the Justice Department launched its antitrust lawsuit against Microsoft, Ballmer publicly said, "To heck with [Attorney General] Janet Reno!"[36]

Jerry Hirshberg applies learning style principles to hiring practices at Nissan by hiring designers in pairs. When he hires a designer who is motivated by the freedom of pure color and rhythm, he next hires a very rational designer who focuses on analysis and function.[37] In this way, the company obtains balance.

Continuous Learning   To thrive or even to survive in today's fast-changing business climate, individuals and organizations must be continuous learners. For individuals, **continuous learning** entails looking for opportunities to learn from classes, reading, and talking to others, as well as looking for the lessons in life's experiences. For organizations, continuous learning involves the processes and systems through which the organization enables its people to learn, share their growing knowledge, and apply it to their work. In an organization in which continuous learning is taking place, employees actively apply comments from customers, news about competitors, training programs, and more to increase their knowledge and improve the organization's practices.

Someone who embodies the spirit of continuous learning is Dr. Ben Carson, a respected pediatric neurosurgeon. Carson notes that the medical community has learned more about the human brain in the past two decades than it knew in total before that. He expects that pattern to repeat itself, as researchers gain knowledge at an exponential rate. This humbling realization of what he has yet to learn inspires Carson to keep his mind open to new information. If a patient improved as a result of another doctor's surgery, Carson contacts that doctor to see if he can learn anything to apply when it is his turn to operate. He also builds on the knowledge gained from experience. For example, he found that patients were taking a long time to regain consciousness following a radical brain operation called a hemispherectomy. He evaluated the circumstances and revised how the procedure is performed so that a patient's brain stem would not be disturbed.[38]

As an employee, you can help yourself and set an example for others by being a continuous learner, listening to others, reading widely, and reflecting on what you observe. In a management position you can foster continuous learning by consciously stopping from time to time and asking, "What can we learn from this experience?" Organizations can allow employees time to attend training and reflect on their experiences. Recognizing that experience can be the best teacher, managers should focus on how they and their employees can learn from mistakes, rather than fostering a climate in which employees hide mistakes because they fear being punished for them. Managers also can encourage organizational learning by establishing information systems that enable employees to share knowledge and learn in new ways.

Managers at organizations such as Oracle, IBM, and Kodak are learning new approaches to business by attending "virtual reality school" at the U.S. Army's National Defense University (NDU).[39] At NDU's Decision Room Incorporating Virtual Reality, for example, people experience what it might be like to steer an open-air rig across the dangerous terrain of Mars, where the temperature falls 200 degrees below zero and dusty red soil swallows the truck tires. NDU is designed to help leaders think about national defense—and business competition—in a new way.

Students from companies across America regularly travel to NDU's Washington, D.C., campus to attend the Advanced Management Program (AMP), a three-and-a-half-month boot camp. During the program, they learn how digital technology is changing the nature of national defense, business, and even society itself. Every aspect of the AMP integrates the new realities of 21st-century combat with the new logic of business, and the students come from both worlds. Courses include Virtual Reality for Managers and Innovative Thinking for the Information Age.

Students at NDU learn in two different ways—they spend time in the classroom talking about big ideas such as strategy and the future of work, but they also venture into the real world, visiting innovative companies to see ideas in action. NDU encourages teamwork and group problem solving. Each student is issued a laptop stuffed with groupware and hooked up to a wireless communications network, so he or she can collaborate on projects and brainstorm solutions to case studies.

Jack North of GTE (the telecommunications giant) was one of the first nongovernmental students to graduate from the program, which he says "made me rethink much of what we do here [at GTE]." Inspired by what he learned, North returned to GTE and quickly installed groupware applications and desktop videoconferencing to promote collaboration and continuous learning at the health systems division he runs. "The program produces a whole group of managers who are ready to go back and become change agents," North says. "There's a lot of down-and-dirty practical reality."

How might you use information regarding your learning style to contribute to personal and organizational effectiveness?[40] First, through awareness of learning styles, you can understand how you approach problems and issues, and your learning strengths and weaknesses. Second, you can tailor one-on-one and team communications to different learning styles. Some people respond well to facts and figures. Others prefer anecdotes or graphic presentations. Information should be communicated in the preferred method to the receiver. If you are communicating to a team with diverse learning styles, try to include as many approaches as possible to match the learning styles of the team members. Third, try to include persons with different learning styles in your work team. Heterogeneity is important to generate creative ideas and innovative solutions. Fourth, you need to make sure that conflicts that arise between persons because of learning style differences are managed through emphasizing common goals, developing guidelines for how disagreements will be handled ("We are free to disagree, but the reason must be stated"), and allowing enough meeting time for both discovery of creative ideas as well as discussion to select an option and plan its implementation.

apply it

1. Identify a job that you or a friend have had either on a full- or part-time basis.
   - Write a paragraph describing the tasks, duties, and responsibilities of the job (also known as a job description).
   - Using the job description, identify the abilities and personality characteristics that a person needs to be successful in the job.
   - Discuss how you might determine whether a candidate for the job has the abilities and personality characteristics needed to successfully perform the job.
2. Consider the following comments of a friend: "I've always characterized creative visionary-type people as dreamers. When dreamers give me their vision, my gut reaction to these people is to say, "Well, if you want to do that, what you have to do is A, then B."
   - Do you think your friend can effectively relate to "visionary-type" people? Why or why not? What could he or she do to improve the relationship?
   - How would a "visionary person" react to your friend's comments about dreamers' vision?

Values are basic convictions that influence attitudes and behavior

In addition to ability, personality, and capability for learning, people differ in the values and attitudes they hold. Values and attitudes can affect behavior also, so they are important considerations for organizations.

Values

values

Beliefs that meet three criteria: they are stable, identify what a person considers important, and influence behavior.

Values are beliefs that meet three criteria: they are stable, identify what a person considers important, and influence behavior. Values are important because of their influence on attitudes and behavior.[41] One way to think

exhibit | **3.10**

Examples of Terminal and Instrumental Values

Terminal Values (Worthy Outcomes)	Instrumental Values (Appropriate Behavior)
A comfortable life	Ambition (being hardworking)
An exciting life	Open-mindedness
A world of beauty	Cleanness, neatness, tidiness
Inner harmony	Imagination
Social recognition	Politeness, courtesy, good manners
Wisdom	Self-control, self-discipline

Source: Based on M. Rokeach, *The Nature of Human Values* (New York: The Free Press, 1973).

about values is shown in Exhibit 3.10. **Instrumental values** are beliefs about the types of behavior that are appropriate for reaching goals. **Terminal values** are beliefs about what outcomes are worth trying to achieve. Individuals most value the instrumental values of concern for others, honesty, and fairness and the terminal value of achievement.[42]

Values and Environmental Influences   Values usually relate to those of the larger culture to which an individual belongs. Values are learned, not inherited. For example, in the United States independence is valued and is reinforced by many institutions, including schools, religious organizations, and families. As we noted in Chapter 2, to be successful in global assignments, employees need to understand the host country's culture. This is necessary because the culture shapes the values of the host country and affects the way that business is conducted.

Many organizations recognize that values are an important part of a strong organizational culture. For example, Gerald Levin, chairman of Time Warner, the entertainment company, is convinced that a company needs strong values to survive.[43] As a result, Time Warner is requiring its executives to attend a two-day program designed to define and communicate the company's core values and principles, including diversity, respect, creativity, teamwork, and integrity. He believes that his emphasis on defining and developing values isn't just so employees feel good. Rather, he believes that there is a link between company values and the value created for shareholders. Also, he recognizes that defining Time Warner's values is necessary to attract a new generation of employees, those who weigh a company's values in deciding whether they are interested in joining it. Indeed, research shows that the match between individual and organizational values is related to satisfaction and the decision to accept a job with a company.[44]

Value Differences and Changes   It is important to realize that values may differ by age, generation, and culture. For example, some argue that individuals who have entered the workforce since 1990 value flexibility, leisure time, job satisfaction, and family and work relationships more than previous generations.[45] Values also may change. For example, as many individuals age, they may place less value on accomplishments and more value on health and family relationships. At the societal level, we are experiencing a changing set of values (recall our discussion on managing diversity in

instrumental values

Beliefs about the types of behavior that are appropriate for reaching goals. Examples are ambition, imagination, and politeness.

terminal values

Beliefs about what outcomes are worth trying to achieve. Examples are family security, social recognition, and achievement.

Chapter 2). Managing diversity and valuing diversity would have seemed strange 20 years ago, when the United States saw itself as a "melting pot" where diverse immigrant and minority populations were blended into a homogeneous new culture. Realizing the value of capitalizing on diversity, the country has shifted from valuing a common identity to valuing individual and group differences. Consider how the values of Anita Roddick, founder and CEO of The Body Shop, influence organizational behavior.

🐾 The Body Shop

The Body Shop develops, manufactures, and sells more than 400 personal care products in 600 retail outlets worldwide and does over $200 million in sales. Anita Roddick calls her organization a "benevolent anarchy" in which there is a strong link between organizational values and success. What are the company values? The values include having fun, putting love where labor is, and going in the opposite direction of other companies in the personal care products industry. Employees are encouraged to question what they are doing and how they are doing it in order to find better working methods. There is even a Department of Damned Good Ideas! Because Roddick values creativity, franchisees and store managers receive intensive training at corporate headquarters in England. Managers also take seminars on how to encourage creativity among employees.

Each store has a "who's who" system that identifies each employee's responsibility within the store, so that individual accomplishments can be recognized. Roddick views each store as a "waterwell" where people come to gather information, much like members of tribal communities gather at a well. The Body Shop has also worked hard to identify itself as a socially responsible organization, including producing "natural goods" and committing money and time to social causes. Roddick travels the world not only looking for new ingredients for products but also looking for ways the company can change the lives of people. As a result, the company has been involved with Amnesty International, creating voter registration centers, and collecting toys for hospitals. How serious does The Body Shop take its commitment to values? The company publishes a yearly values report showing the progress the company has made toward social, environmental, and animal protection issues. Progress toward all three values is verified by external auditors.[46]

Attitudes

Some people show up at work eager to get started, whereas others appear to wish they were elsewhere. Some employees tackle problems with the expectation that they and their coworkers will cooperate to find a solution; others grumble or panic. These different kinds of behavior partly reflect variations in employee attitudes. Defined formally, an **attitude** is an evaluation that predisposes a person to act in a certain way. A person who has the attitude "I love my work; it's challenging and fun" probably will tackle work-related problems cheerfully, while one who comes to work with the attitude "I hate my job" is not likely to exhibit much enthusiasm or commitment to solving problems.

attitude

An evaluation that predisposes a person to act in a certain way and includes a cognitive, affective, and behavioral component.

Attitude Components   Behavioral scientists consider attitudes to have three components: cognitions (thoughts), affect (feelings), and behavior.[47] The cognitive component of an attitude includes the beliefs, opinions, and information a person has about the object of the attitude, such as knowledge of what a job entails and opinions about personal abilities. The affective component is the person's emotions or feelings about the object of the attitude, such as enjoying or hating a job. The behavioral component of an attitude is the person's intention to behave toward the object of the attitude in a certain way. Consider a positive attitude toward a job. The cognitive

*E*Trade chief executive officer Cristos Cotsakos values his employees and believes in shaping their attitudes to match the fast-paced, creative atmosphere of the World Wide Web. To encourage them to move faster, he organized a day of racing Formula One cars at nearly 150 miles an hour. To create a loose atmosphere, his employees carry rubber chickens and wear propeller beanies. And as shown in the photo, to bond as a team, managers attend cooking school, learning to depend on one another to whip up a gourmet dinner. Cotsakos's efforts to develop an employee culture with the right attitudes must be working. The company is experiencing rapid growth, with revenues up 112 percent, and it is forecasted to grow another 48 percent in one year.*
(Source: © Gerry Gropp)

element is the conscious thought that "my job is interesting and challenging." The affective element is the feeling that "I love this job." These, in turn, are related to the behavioral component—an employee might choose to arrive at work early because he or she is happy with the job.

Often, when we think about attitudes, we focus on the cognitive component; however, it is important to remember the other components as well. When people feel strongly about something, the affective component may predispose them to act, no matter what someone does to change their opinions. For example, if an employee is passionate about a new idea, that employee may go to great lengths to implement it. Likewise, an employee who is furious about being asked to work overtime on his birthday may act on that anger—by failing to cooperate, lashing out at coworkers, or even quitting—no matter what arguments the manager presents about the need to work. In cases such as these, effective leadership includes addressing the affect (emotions) associated with the attitude. Are employees so excited that their judgment may be clouded, or so discouraged that they have given up trying? If nothing else, the manager probably needs to be aware of situations that involve strong emotions and give employees a chance to vent their feelings safely.

Changing Attitudes Changing attitudes is difficult because, as shown in Exhibit 3.4, they are influenced by a person's values, personality, and perceptions. Changing one component of an attitude—cognitions, affect, or behavior—can help contribute to an overall change in attitude. Suppose a manager concludes that some employees have the attitude that the manager should make all the decisions affecting the department, but the manager prefers that employees assume more decision-making responsibility. To change the underlying attitude, the manager would consider whether to (1) educate employees about the areas in which they can make good decisions (change the cognitive component), (2) build enthusiasm with pep talks about the satisfaction of employee empowerment (change the affective component), or (3) simply insist that employees make their own decisions (change the behavioral component) with the expectation that, once they experience the advantages of decision-making authority, they will like it.

Conflicts among Attitudes Sometimes a person may discover that his or her attitudes conflict with one another or are not reflected in his or her behavior. For example, a person's high level of organizational commitment may conflict with that person's commitment to family members. If employees routinely work evenings and weekends, their long hours and dedication to the job may conflict with their belief that family ties are important. This can create a state of cognitive dissonance, a psychological discomfort that occurs when individuals recognize inconsistencies in their own attitudes and behaviors.[48] The theory of **cognitive dissonance,** developed by social psychologist Leon Festinger in the 1950s, says that people want to behave in accordance with their attitudes and usually will take corrective action to alleviate dissonance and achieve balance.

In the case of working overtime, a person who feels in control of her hours might restructure her responsibilities so that she has time for both work and family. In contrast, another individual who is unable to restructure his workload might change his attitude toward his employer, reducing his organizational commitment. He might resolve his dissonance by saying he loves his children but has to work long hours because his unreasonable employer demands it.

The attitudes of most interest to managers are those related to work, especially attitudes that influence how well employees perform. To lead employees effectively, managers logically seek to cultivate the kinds of attitudes that are associated with high performance. Two attitudes that may relate to high performance are satisfaction with a job and commitment to the organization.

Job Satisfaction A person's positive attitude toward his or her job is called **job satisfaction.** In general, people experience this attitude when their work matches their needs and interests, when working conditions and rewards (such as pay) are satisfactory, and when they like their coworkers. In the Emergent Solutions Group of accounting and consulting giant PricewaterhouseCoopers, a group of talented programmers and systems designers is developing an advanced computer system that models complex human behavior, such as the way people interact in stores. Employees often labor long hours because they are excited to be working on new technology. Their excitement and high motivation level suggest they are experiencing a high degree of job satisfaction.[49]

Job satisfaction level is related to many important outcomes, including psychological and physical withdrawal (for example, daydreaming or leaving the organization) and organizational citizenship behaviors (helping coworkers).[50] As we will see in Chapter 14, dissatisfaction resulting from having too much work to do or not having the resources to perform the work may cause harmful stress. Also, many people believe job satisfaction

cognitive dissonance

A theory that people want to behave in accordance with their attitudes and usually will take corrective action to alleviate dissonance and achieve balance.

job satisfaction

A person's positive attitude toward his or her job.

is important because they think satisfied employees will do better work. In fact, research shows that the link between satisfaction and performance is generally small and is affected by other factors.[51] The importance of satisfaction varies according to the amount of control the employee has; an employee doing routine tasks may produce about the same output no matter how he or she feels about the job. But, there are other reasons we should care about job satisfaction. When unemployment rates are low and workers can easily find jobs elsewhere, we want productive employees to be happy enough to stay with the organization. In addition, we may simply want employees to feel good about their work—and they may prefer to work with people who have a positive outlook.

Organizational Commitment   Another important attitude is **organizational commitment,** which is loyalty to and heavy involvement in the organization. An employee with a high degree of organizational commitment is likely to say "we" when talking about the organization. Such a person tries to contribute to the organization's success and wishes to remain with the organization. This attitude is common at the A. W. Chesterton Company, a Massachusetts company that produces mechanical seals and pumps. CEO James D. Chesterton takes a personal interest in his employees, and they in turn are very loyal to him and to the organization. When two Chesterton pumps that supply water on the Navy ship USS *John F. Kennedy* failed on a Saturday night just before the ship's scheduled departure, Todd Robinson, the leader of the team that produces the seals, swung into action. He and his fiancée, who also works for Chesterton, worked through the night to make new seals and deliver them to be installed before the ship left port.[52]

Most managers want to enjoy the benefits of loyal, committed employees, including low turnover and willingness to do more than the job's basic requirements. Organizational commitment has become especially important in recent years, because a tight labor market has forced employers to compete harder to attract and keep good workers in many fields. Adding to the challenge, past downsizing and restructuring have made many employees distrustful of their employers. A survey of 450,000 employees found that although most executives believe employees respect management, their employees' attitudes are in fact quite different.[53] The percentage of workers who say management is respected by employees has been steadily declining since 1991. In the most recent available year of the survey (1997), about 50 percent of employees reported that management generally is respected, compared with about 70 percent of top managers who believed that. Organizational commitment can be promoted by keeping employees informed, giving them a say in decisions, creating a sense of community, providing the necessary training and other resources that enable them to succeed, treating them fairly, and offering rewards they value.[54] Sears has made an effort to develop and measure positive employee attitudes.

organizational commitment

A person's loyalty to and heavy involvement in the organization.

In the early 1990s, Sears had the worst years in company history. For example, in 1992, Sears lost $3.9 billion on sales of $52.3 billion. Most of the loss was coming from the merchandising group. The merchandising group includes Sears's retail stores. Arthur Martinez took over as head of the merchandising group and tried to revitalize the business. First, Martinez sought to determine what was considered "world-class" standards for employee and customer treatment, financial performance, innovation, and

values. From this process came Sears's vision of becoming a "compelling place to work, shop, and invest," and its values of "passion for the customer, our people add value, and performance leadership."

Sears's vision and values were backed up with an important measurement system. Sears spent significant time trying to identify the link between employee attitudes and customer impressions (such as finding Sears a compelling place to shop). Ten questions on the annual employee attitude survey were related to employee behavior and customer satisfaction. Example items were "I like the kind of work I do," "My work gives me a sense of accomplishment," and "I understand our business strategy." Statisticians found that an increase in positive employee attitudes resulted in an improvement in customer impressions, which drove a .5 percent increase in revenue.

Building on the survey results, Sears has spent significant time trying to improve employee attitudes. The company has developed and communicated learning maps, which are visual representations that provide employees with information about Sears's business and its competitive industry. Sears also created a leadership model tied directly to the company's management development program. The leadership model emphasizes that to be successful at Sears, managers need to have a passion for the customer, lead performance, and develop employees and value their ideas. Although Sears still faces serious business competition, the company estimates that the employee-customer-profit model it developed resulted in an increase of $200 billion in revenues in 1997.[55] An increase in fourth-quarter 1999 earnings compared with 1998 earnings suggests that customers are recognizing and responding to Sears's vision and values.

Measuring Attitudes   How do we know what attitudes employees hold? Most attitudes are measured by asking employees to complete an attitude survey. Attitude surveys can be pencil-and-paper instruments or distributed via the Internet. Exhibit 3.11 shows examples of attitude survey items for measuring overall job satisfaction. There are many commercially available measures of job satisfaction, organizational commitment, and other attitudes. For example, *Fortune* magazine collects attitude survey data annually to help rate its "100 Best Companies to Work for in America."[56] The attitude survey contains items related to credibility ("Management keeps me informed about important issues and changes"), respect ("Management shows appreciation for good work and extra effort"), fairness ("People here are paid fairly for the work they do"), pride ("I feel I make a difference here"), and camaraderie ("This is a fun place to work").

Many organizations use attitude surveys as part of an ongoing process of measuring employee attitudes, presenting the results to employees, setting goals, making changes, and measuring goal attainment. This process is known as the **survey-feedback process.** The survey-feedback process allows an organization to monitor attitudes over time, measure the results of programs that are implemented to change attitudes, and compare employee attitudes with those of other organizations in the same industry. The survey-feedback process also allows the organization to compare departments, divisions, or units. Another benefit of survey feedback is that it gives employees an opportunity to voice their concerns and frustrations. This enhances their ability to handle dissatisfying work experiences.

For example, Baptist Hospital in Pensacola, Florida, uses a survey to measure employee satisfaction.[57] The survey revealed that the biggest concerns of employees were late performance evaluations, a lack of feedback, and lack of communications about issues that affected them. Based on the survey results, the hospital set goals for improving in these areas and rewarded and recognized managers who achieved the feedback and communications goals.

survey-feedback process

An ongoing process of measuring employee attitudes, presenting the results to employees, setting goals, making changes, and measuring goal attainment.

products. If they
doomed."[63]

Employees may
sonality characterist
ity needs to be stim
foster creativity.

Suzanne Merritt, senior cre
level managers, both for th
this by designing programs
agers drawing ideas on cor

Although this sounds
with clients to make sure th
ativity herself to design the
gies. She even keeps a "dr
solve problems.[64]

Job Performance

Job performance
havior or actions co
what organizations
following:

- *Job-specific task*
  ual performs the
- *Written and ora*
  uals write and s
- *Demonstration*
  extra effort
- *Personal discipl*
  senteeism or vic
- *Helping peers ar*
  ual helps and s
  work problems
- *Supervision/lead*
  of subordinates
- *Management* b
  goals for the wo
  and obtaining ac

As you can see fron
cording to the job.
concern to salespeo
mind that effective
ance of job tasks. H
are also key compor

Given the many
ability and personali

---

exhibit **3.11**

Sample Measure of Job Satisfaction

Instructions: Put a check beside the answer that you feel is most appropriate regarding your present job.

All in all, how satisfied are you with your job?
_____ Very satisfied
_____ Somewhat satisfied
_____ Not too satisfied
_____ Not at all satisfied

If a good friend of yours told you he or she was interested in working in a job like yours for your employer, would you recommend it to him or her?
_____ Strongly recommend this job
_____ Would have doubts about recommending this job
_____ Strongly advise against taking this job

Knowing what you know now, if you had to decide all over again to take the job you have now, what would you decide?
_____ Decide without hesitation to take the same job
_____ Would have some second thoughts about taking the same job
_____ Definitely decide not to take the same job

Source: R. P. Quinn and G. L. Staines, *The 1977 Quality of Employment Survey* (Ann Arbor: Survey Research Center, Institute for Social Research, University of Michigan, 1979). Reprinted with permission.

apply it

1. Many companies have value statements that define their beliefs about their products, services, treatment of employees, community contributions, and preservation of the natural environment. Go to your college or campus recruiting office and find brochures and pamphlets for companies that are recruiting at your school. Choose one brochure to analyze.
   - What values are stated in the brochure?
   - What values would you want a company that you work for to hold? Rank them in order of importance.
2. Consider jobs you have held or jobs friends and family members have had.
   - What job characteristics do you believe affect job satisfaction?
   - Write ten survey items designed to measure employees' job satisfaction.

Individual differences create positive and negative outcomes for organizations

We have discussed the effect that individual differences can have on people's performance. But they can also have positive and negative effects on an organization as a whole. Some of the most important outcomes related to individual differences include diversity, creativity, job performance, counterproductive behavior, withdrawal behavior, and organizational citizenship behavior. It is important to note that many of these outcomes are

is a relationship between cognitive ability and job performance; also, strength tests, which measure physical abilities, have been shown to relate to performance in physically demanding jobs.[66] Research into the Big Five personality dimensions found that conscientiousness was related to job performance for a variety of jobs.[67]

Organizations consider abilities and personality when selecting new employees or matching current employees with jobs. That is, organizations use abilities and personality to try to predict who will be successful in jobs. The key in trying to predict job performance is first to identify the relevant dimensions of performance for a job. Next, the organization needs to identify the abilities and personality characteristics that are most likely related to successful performance of these dimensions. Finally, it should consider how to measure the abilities or personality characteristics. Pencil-and-paper tests, interviews, and work samples are some of the ways used to measure abilities and personality.

Counterproductive Behavior

counterproductive behavior

Activities that damage the organization, such as drug use, theft, or violence.

Counterproductive behavior refers to activities that damage the organization, such as drug use, theft, or violence. It is estimated that organizations lose nearly $100 billion each year due to alcohol or drug use.[68] Employees' performance is impaired when they are working under the influence of drugs and alcohol, resulting in safety hazards for themselves, their peers, customers, and the general public.

Employee theft can involve theft of money or property or be more broadly defined to include wasting time. Organizations take two approaches to solving problems related to employee theft and drug use. One approach is to increase surveillance and security through searches or electronic monitoring. The other is to use preemployment tests to screen out potentially deviant employees.[69] Screening includes drug-testing programs (hair and blood analysis) and pencil-and-paper tests that ask job candidates about the degree to which they tolerate theft or drug use by others, have stolen or taken drugs themselves, or rationalize theft or drug use as a way for employees to "get even" with the organization.

Research suggests that counterproductive behavior may be affected by personality. For example, one study found that individuals who are low in agreeableness may be predisposed to hostile actions such as damaging equipment or taking supplies home without permission when they perceive that they are treated unfairly by an organization.[70] Another study found that individuals who dwell on their mistakes and shortcomings and focus on the negative aspects of their lives may also be more predisposed to theft.[71]

workplace violence

Physical assaults and threats of assault directed toward people at work.

Violence in the workplace has received considerable attention in the popular press. **Workplace violence** includes physical assaults and threats of assault directed toward people at work. Although the incidents of coworker violence remain low, they appear to be much more common because of the attention given them by the media.[72] An average of 20 employees are murdered each week in the United States. An estimated one million workers are assaulted annually in the workplace. Most of these as-

RAKESH GANGWAL OF US AIRWAYS

Running an airline isn't an easy job, as Rakesh Gangwal, CEO of US Airways, knows. Gangwal has had to make a number of quick, difficult decisions in his quest to turn the nearly bankrupt airline into a moneymaker. A quiet, disciplined man, Gangwal readily admits that he is "driven to succeed" but says he doesn't want his drive to become an issue of personal grandiosity. Others describe Gangwal as a quick thinker, a leader who is demanding and acts with authority. Gangwal spends his days poring over facts and figures, as well as talking to other people, to learn what he needs to know to solve tough problems fast. Gangwal has impressed the aviation industry with his role in the quick turnaround at US Airways. Now, he and his longtime mentor, Stephen M. Wolf (now chairman of the parent company US Airways Group), face new challenges. At one recent meeting, Gangwal pondered a potentially disastrous problem—a growing number of passengers have been complaining about rude

service, particularly at the airline's international terminal in Philadelphia, where part-time employees make up 42 percent of the workforce. A broader challenge is figuring out how to establish a strong global presence for US Airways, which is necessary for the airline to survive and grow. With customer service, global expansion, and overall profitability problems waiting to be solved, Gangwal must act quickly for the sake of the organization.

1. If you were Gangwal, what would you do to solve such diverse problems as unprofessional behavior by terminal staff and the need for global expansion?

2. What personality traits and problem-solving styles might be useful to a manager wrestling with these problems?

Source: L. Woellert and D. Leonhardt, "Pulling US Airways Out of a Dive," *Business Week,* September 14, 1998, pp. 131–132.

saults occur in service organizations including hospitals, nursing homes, and social service agencies. Factors that place workers at risk for violence include interacting with the public, exchanging money, delivering goods or services, working late at night or early in the morning, working alone, guarding valuables or property, and dealing with violent people or situations. Defensive security measures such as bulletproof glass, increased lighting, and video cameras are important deterrents to violence caused by customers or thieves.

What about violence caused by coworkers? Consider the case of Gian Luigi. Seeking revenge against his former employer, Luigi opened fire, killing eight people (including himself) and wounding six.[73] What can a company do to prevent this type of violence? Although we cannot guarantee that violence can be prevented, some suggest that we can be alert to certain personality characteristics that can make a person more susceptible to engaging in violent acts. For example, employees who are emotionally immature, have not learned to handle anger, or have untreated or diagnosed mental illnesses such as paranoid schizophrenia, bipolar disorder, or depression may potentially demonstrate violent behavior.[74] The U.S. Postal Service has trained more than 60,000 managers and union officials to identify unusual threatening or combative behavior and to refer workers for counseling. Warning signs include employees who talk about violence or scare coworkers, workers who express approval for violent solutions to problems, and employees who have explosive outbursts over minor disagreements. Violence can also be inhibited by providing employees with the means to vent their frustrations, including grievance processes, as well as security programs to screen out weapons from the workplace.

Withdrawal Behavior

withdrawal behaviors

Psychological or physical behaviors that individuals use to avoid dissatisfying work.

psychological withdrawal

Wasting time, daydreaming, and goofing off at work.

Withdrawal behaviors refer to psychological or physical behaviors that individuals use to avoid dissatisfying work.[75] **Psychological withdrawal** includes wasting time, daydreaming, and goofing off at work. These behaviors are not necessarily bad—they can be effective ways to reduce stress. However, when they occur too frequently, they are a problem. Psychological withdrawal occurs when individuals are dissatisfied or do not consider their job an important part of their life. Time-wasting behaviors indicate that the individual is not putting forth his or her best effort on the job. Results can be dissatisfied customers, poor product quality, and bad feelings among coworkers.

Psychological withdrawal often leads to an individual leaving the organization (or physically withdrawing).[76] Usually, individuals exhibit psychological withdrawal behaviors first, which signal to the organization that they are dissatisfied. If the dissatisfaction is not alleviated, individuals may begin to explore other job options and compare them with their current job. As a result, they may leave the organization.

physical withdrawal

Employee turnover, lateness, and absence from work.

Physical withdrawal includes employee turnover, lateness, and absence from work. *Turnover* means that the individual leaves the organization. *Absenteeism* refers to individuals temporarily missing work. Of course, there are legitimate reasons for missing work, including illness or death in the family. The type of absence that results from dissatisfaction with the work environment does not occur for legitimate reasons. Absence has been shown to be negatively related to both job satisfaction and organizational commitment.[77] Absenteeism is also costly for organizations. One estimate is that absenteeism costs U.S. industry $40 billion per year, with over half the absences due to stress (we discuss stress in greater detail in Chapter 14).[78]

What might an organization do to reduce absenteeism and turnover? The answer to this question is not as easy as it may seem. Absenteeism is affected both by personality and the individual's evaluation of the work environment. Individuals who find their work to be uninteresting and too routine are more likely to be absent. Also, introverted and conscientious employees are less likely to be absent.[79] Organizations cannot change employees' personalities. However, they can control absenteeism somewhat by selecting new employees who are introverted and conscientious.

To reduce turnover, the organization first needs to determine what type of turnover is occurring. That is, is turnover functional or dysfunctional for the organization?[80] Functional turnover can actually help an organization. If low-performing employees or employees with bad attitudes are leaving an organization, turnover allows the organization to replace these employees with higher performers. Yet, if valued employees are leaving the organization, this presents a problem. Second, the organization needs to consider whether the turnover is controllable. Turnover can be voluntary or involuntary. If individuals are leaving an organization for reasons beyond its control (such as moving to a new city because a spouse was relocated), then the organization cannot affect turnover rates. Organizations should focus instead on reducing voluntary, controllable turnover.

How can organizations reduce voluntary dysfunctional turnover? One way is to change the working conditions that are contributing to employee dissatisfaction and resulting in turnover. For example, consider the trucking industry. Truck driver turnover rates are high, ranging from 38 to 200 percent. Turnover is high for many reasons, including low pay, the long hours on the road, physical demands of unloading heavy freight on loading docks, the cramped working conditions (one trucker referred to his truck as a "kennel"), and close monitoring of their work using satellite tracking and on-board computers.[81] Increased pay, better benefits, reduced time required on the road, and limited electronic monitoring have been found to lower turnover rates of truck drivers.[82] Also, trucking companies have taken steps to improve the "kennel," including adjustable and comfortable driver's seats and easy-to-read controls, showers, cooking areas, and state-of-the-art color televisions and sophisticated sound systems.[83]

Organizational Citizenship Behaviors

At the opposite end of the spectrum from counterproductive behavior and withdrawal is organizational citizenship. **Organizational citizenship behaviors (OCBs)** refer to behaviors that individuals are not expected to perform as part of their jobs—that is, behaviors that go above and beyond expected duties, such as helping coworkers or helping achieve organization goals.[84] OCBs include behaviors that help others, make sure they are heard, protect others from harm, and promote cooperation and strengthen relationships. Examples of OCBs include encouraging others to speak up at meetings, helping orient new employees even though it is not required, or making yourself available to coworkers to discuss personal or professional problems they are facing.

Since these behaviors are not required, there is no formal organizational reward for demonstrating them or penalty for not doing so. When individuals think they are well treated by an organization, they are more likely to exceed the requirements of their jobs by helping others and the organization. That is, when individuals believe that the employment relationship is based on trust, shared values, and commitment, they are more likely to demonstrate OCBs. If employees believe that the organization views them as short-term, temporary, or dispensable workers, they are less likely to demonstrate OCBs.[85]

organizational citizenship behaviors (OCBs)

Behaviors that individuals are not expected to perform as part of their jobs. Examples of OCBs include encouraging others to speak up at meetings or helping orient new employees even though it is not required.

apply it

Think about a job you have had, your coworkers, and your boss.

1. What types of organizational citizenship behaviors have others exhibited toward you?
2. How did they make you feel about the job? About the company? About your coworkers?
3. What organizational citizenship behaviors have you demonstrated toward others?

summary OF KEY CONCEPTS

- **Individual-organization exchange influences organizational behavior.** Organizations expect employees to contribute time, effort, and loyalty. Employees expect organizations to provide rewards such as pay, status, training, and career opportunities. The psychological contract describes what the employee expects to contribute and what the organization will provide to the employee for these contributions.

- **Individuals' talents may suit them to particular jobs or organizations.** Because individuals are so different, it is important to match their skills and abilities to organizations. Person-job fit is the extent to which an individual's ability and personality match a job. Person-organization fit refers to the match between an individual's personality, goals, and values and the organization's culture.

- **Individual differences can influence organizational behavior.** Employees are unique individuals. Employee behavior is affected by ability, personality, and learning styles. Abilities refer to a person's skill in performing some activity. Abilities are physical and cognitive (ability to think intelligently). Personality is a relatively stable set of psychological characteristics and behavior patterns that distinguishes one person from another. Personality traits include the "Big Five" and emotional intelligence. Learning styles influence how individuals approach a problem and how they best learn.

- **Values are basic convictions that influence attitudes and behavior.** Values are beliefs that are stable, identify what the person considers to be important, and influence behavior. Organizations reinforce certain values as part of their culture. Individuals also hold sets of values. Values include beliefs about what kinds of behavior are appropriate for reaching goals (instrumental values) as well as beliefs about what ends are worth striving for (terminal values). Attitudes include a cognitive, affective, and behavioral component. Job satisfaction and organizational commitment are two important work attitudes. Many organizations measure employee attitudes using attitude surveys. Some organizations use attitude surveys as part of an ongoing process of measuring employee attitudes, presenting the results to employees, setting goals, making changes, and measuring goal attainment (known as the survey-feedback process).

- **Individual differences create positive and negative outcomes for organizations.** Why are individual differences important to organizations? Individual differences influence diversity, job performance, creativity, counterproductive work behaviors (such as workplace violence and theft), physical and psychological withdrawal (e.g., absenteeism), and organizational citizenship behaviors. These outcomes can greatly affect the success or failure of an organization.

KEY terms

individual differences, p. 89

psychological contract, p. 90

person-job fit, p. 93

person-organization fit, p 94

ability, p. 96

aptitude, p. 96

physical abilities, p. 96

psychomotor abilities, p. 96

cognitive abilities, p. 97

general cognitive ability, p. 97

verbal comprehension, p. 98

quantitative ability, p. 98

reasoning ability, p. 98

personality, p. 99

Big Five personality factors, p. 99

cognitive styles, p. 101

emotional intelligence, p. 102

learning, p. 104

Divergers, p. 105

Assimilators, p. 105

Convergers, p. 106

Accommodators, p. 106

continuous learning, p. 106

values, p. 108

instrumental values, p. 109

terminal values, p. 109

attitude, p. 110

cognitive dissonance, p. 112

job satisfaction, p. 112

organizational commitment, p. 113

survey-feedback process, p. 114

job performance, p. 117

counterproductive behavior, p. 118

workplace violence, p. 118

withdrawal behaviors, p. 120

psychological withdrawal, p. 120

physical withdrawal, p. 120

organizational citizenship behavior
 (OCBs), p. 121

DISCUSSION questions

1. Why is the concept of a psychological contract important?

2. Name and briefly describe the Big Five personality factors.

3. As a manager of a software company, what might you do to foster creativity in your staff?

4. Why is our understanding of organizational behavior enhanced by studying individual differences?

5. What are the potential results of a poor person-organization fit?

6. Describe a situation in which you learned how to do something—rollerblade, ski, play a musical instrument, play a sport. In your description, identify the four stages of the learning cycle.

7. What are some factors that relate to employees' levels of job satisfaction?

8. Why is organizational commitment important to organizations?

9. How can the cognitive and affective components of attitude influence the behavior of employees who need to learn how to work in teams in order to keep their jobs at an auto assembly plant?

10. When trying to choose new employees, do you believe that organizations should spend more time trying to determine a person's ability or personality? Explain.

11. Is absenteeism the only type of counterproductive behavior? Explain.

SELF-DISCOVERY exercise

High Five: How Many of the "Big Five" Personality Traits Are Yours?

Each individual's collection of personality traits is different; it's what makes us unique. But, although each collection of traits varies, we all share many common traits. To find out which are your most prominent traits, mark "yes" or "no" after each of the following statements. Then, for fun, compare your responses with those of classmates.

1. I love meeting and talking with new people at parties. _____

2. I try not to hold grudges against others. _____

3. I am focused on graduating from college and finding a good job in my field. _____

4. I enjoy performing under pressure—for example, in a big athletic event. _____

5. When I finish school, I want to travel around the world. _____

6. Final exams don't really bother me because I prepare well for them. _____

7. I like to take part in group projects. _____

8. I don't mind giving oral presentations in class. _____

9. Just for fun, I would sign up to take a course in a discipline completely outside my field. _____

10. I work summers in order to fund as much of my own education as I can. _____

Statements 1 and 8 deal with extroversion; statements 2 and 7 deal with agreeableness; statements 3, 6, and 10 deal with conscientiousness; statements 4 and 6 deal with emotional stability; statements 5 and 9 deal with openness to new experiences.

ORGANIZATIONAL BEHAVIOR in your life

Consider an organization or group to which you belong. It might be an employer, dorm, family, volunteer organization, music group, or sports team. Keep a log in which you identify the types of organizational citizenship behaviors displayed by you and other members of the group and why these behaviors are important. What other organizational citizenship behaviors could members display? How can the organization or group increase the level of organizational citizenship behaviors displayed by members?

ORGANIZATIONAL BEHAVIOR news flash

@ Search the Web using the key words "Learning Styles" and "Personality Tests." From the results of your search, choose and take an online learning styles instrument or personality test, print out the re-

sults, and submit a copy of the results and the instrument to the instructor (or give the instructor the Web site address for the instrument).

global diversity EVENTS

@ In the chapter, we have talked about how an individual's unique abilities and personality can affect his or her own performance, as well as the organization as a whole. Even large global organizations can be shaped profoundly by their employees. To see how a CEO's personality, abilities, and motivation can affect his or her organization, search the Web (or news articles in the library) for information on one of the following people:

*   Carly Fiorina of Hewlett-Packard
*   Ferdinand Piëch of Volkswagen

*   Dave Duffield of PeopleSoft
*   Steve Jobs of Apple Computer Corp.
*   Scott McNealy of Sun Microsystems

Write a one- to two-page paper on how this person's personality and abilities are reflected in the organization. What outcomes can be linked to those individual characteristics? How successful is the organization? Can any successes or failures be tied to the CEO? Be prepared to discuss your findings in class.

minicase ISSUE

Using Individual Differences to Find New Employees

Background. Maria Tray, owner and president of Columbus, Ohio–based Shared Resources, was having problems finding qualified new employees. Shared Resources builds and supports computer systems. The company includes branches in Cincinnati and Columbus, Ohio, and employs 53 people. The unemployment rate in Columbus was a mere 2.6 percent. To try to lure new employees, Tray tried but failed with incentives such as $50 gift certificates to any employee who submitted a qualified applicant in response to a job opening. She was turning away business due to the lack of employees.

Needed Skills. Tray notes that many of her employees and clients are women. She needs consultants who won't have a problem taking direction from women. They need engineering and consulting experience. Also, the new hires need to have good communications skills.

Finding Employees in India. To find qualified employees, Tray took a step that many large companies, let alone a company with only 53 employees, are reluc-

tant to take. She decided to recruit in India. Her recruiting costs in India were lower than her costs in the United States. The cost of recruiting in India, including her visit and airfare for the recruits, is about $6,800 per person. She typically pays an employee search firm about 30 percent of an employee's starting annual salary, which is approximately $15,000 per person.

She traveled 8,600 miles to Chennai, located in southern India, to recruit new employees. Chennai has a population of 6.3 million, making it India's fourth largest city. An Indian recruiter she had met in Columbus helped her place an ad in a local, English-language newspaper. The ad attracted 350 resumes. The Indian recruiter chose 117 for her to review. The 117 applicants were given tests covering both practical knowledge and technical skills. Fifty-one of the applicants who passed the test were interviewed. Some techniques that work in U.S. interviews didn't work in India. For example, to get candidates to talk about themselves, she asked them to name five words describing themselves. Many of the Indian prospects just stared at her or gave her politically correct answers such as "honest and hardworking."

Epilogue. Tray ultimately offered jobs to eight applicants, and six accepted. Four of the new hires are married and are bringing family members to the United States. She expects her six new employees to arrive soon.

1. How might you find out whether a potential employee had the ability to work with women?

2. What individual differences determine whether a person could be a successful computer consultant? What role (if any) does personality play?

3. Could an individual's development of the Big Five personality characteristics vary depending on the culture? Explain.

4. How would you determine whether the practical knowledge and technical skills tests were screening out job candidates who would be unsuccessful on the job?

Source: T. Aeppel, "A passage to India eases a worker scarcity in Ohio," *The Wall Street Journal,* October 10, 1999, pp. B1 and B18.

four

CHAPTER

4

Perception and Attribution

CONCEPT AND SKILL

preview

After studying this chapter, you should be able to:

- Describe, for a given event and observer of that event, the process by which the observer perceives the event.

- Identify examples of influences on your perceptions during the course of a day.

- Give examples of ways in which people's perception is subject to distortion.

- For a given instance in which a person made an attribution about the cause of an event, discuss how the person might have arrived at that attribution.

- Give an example of a manager or employee making a biased attribution.

- For a given manager or employee, suggest measures that the person can take to prevent and overcome misperceptions.

Comcast Passes from One Generation to the Next

Many young people go to work in the family business after graduating from college, and many families expect it. A daughter might take over a car dealership or a law practice; a son might take on the family restaurant or department store. But very few young adults have a father who is the founder and chairman of a giant cable company. That situation might seem enviable. Brian Roberts, now president of Comcast, would agree. But he would also say that following in his father's footsteps is difficult, not only because the industry itself is so fast paced and competitive, but because his success partly depends on the way people inside and outside the organization perceive him—as the boss's son.

The way people perceive each other in an organization has a lot to do with how smoothly the organization runs. If Comcast employees viewed Roberts as an insider, a youngster who did not have to work for his position or success, most likely he would have a hard time communicating with and delegating to others in the organization. If they perceived him to be just like his father, he would have difficulty stepping outside his father's shadow to make effective decisions on his own. Brian Roberts knew the potential problems of joining Comcast, but he did it anyway. "You are always the son of the boss," he now says. "You can either deal with that, or you shouldn't be there."

> *"You are always the son of the boss. You can either deal with that, or you shouldn't be there."*
> —**Brian Roberts,** president, Comcast

The younger Roberts has certainly dealt with the situation. As he recently completed a huge deal in which Microsoft Corporation invested $1 billion in Comcast, Roberts took time out to call his father. "I wanted to tell him we got it. But I also wanted to get his OK," explains Roberts.

How does Brian Roberts handle extra pressure in such an extraordinarily cutthroat business? He believes that he can achieve nearly anything, and he persuades others to go along, which turns into a self-fulfilling prophecy of high performance. "He questioned almost everything and tended to believe ideas he hatched himself," recalls Roberts's high school English teacher. Two decades later, Roberts still believes. Understanding that he needed both talent and hard work to improve Comcast's image, he lured Steve Burke, a highly successful marketer, away from Disney. "Most people thought I would never leave Disney," notes Burke. "I was even surprised myself. It was really Brian." By believing in his company's success and taking the right actions, Roberts achieves success.

Roberts also knows that by treating others with respect, he will be perceived with respect. When he first went to work at Comcast, "Brian spoke when spoken to and deferred to his elders," observes Steven Rattner, an investment banker for Comcast. Although Roberts gradually took over more authority, he has never missed an opportunity to learn from those with more knowledge or experience than he has, including his father. "I think they are mutual in their respect for each other," says an industry observer.

How do others view Brian Roberts? "I look at Brian as the next true leader in the industry," comments William T. Schleyer, former president of cable competitor MediaOne Group. It's a description that the boss's son probably wouldn't mind hearing.[1]

In today's fast-paced world, people are constantly bombarded with multiple images and messages. They often make quick judgments about what they have perceived and respond nearly instantaneously. Sorting through

perception

The process by which people notice and make sense of information from the environment.

all the different incoming information is something we may take for granted because it happens all the time. But consider a time when you and a friend talked to the same person or watched the same movie and came away with different impressions. Did you notice things your friend didn't, and did they lead to your different conclusions? Or did you and your friend's different backgrounds lead you to judge the situations distinctly? Often these different impressions and judgments result from differences in **perception**—that is, the process by which people notice and make sense of information from the environment. A person's view of the world is not a slice of objective reality, but that person's perception of it. We thus behave in response to the world *as we perceive it,* not necessarily the world as it really is. The more you know about the perception process, the better equipped you will be to diagnose and manage situations in which perception plays a role. Likewise, for organizations to operate successfully in a fast-changing environment, their people must be able to perceive opportunities and challenges accurately.

In this chapter we explain what perception is and how people perceive in organizations. We begin by describing the stages in the perception process. Then we identify factors that tend to distort people's perception, and describe a common application of the perception process: making attributions to explain behavior. Finally, we summarize some ways to prevent and overcome errors in perception.

Perception is a multistage process

So much of what we do and learn involves the experiences we have had. Those experiences are related to our perceptions of what we have seen, heard, touched, smelled, and felt. Other people have accumulated their sets of experiences and perceptions, some similar to and others radically different from ours. All of us bring these unique characteristics, experiences, and perceptions to our organizations. And with the continuing trend toward teamwork in organizations today, it is critical for team members to work together to reach goals. It can help you wherever you work to understand how people perceive their environment and make judgments about it. Some people pick up on sights more than sounds; others can grasp ideas in written words better than verbal descriptions. We may recall separate experiences and process those perceptions in distinct ways. You can be a better team member and employee if you understand and manage the basics of the perception process.

Stages in the Perception Process

The world is filled with sensory information: sights, sounds, smells, tastes, and physical sensations. Right now, without moving, notice the stimuli around you—perhaps other people in the room, music playing, the words on this page, the temperature of the room, the hum of a fan or air-conditioner's motor, the bottle of juice at your side, the hard or soft chair beneath you. You perceive these stimuli when you notice them and give meaning to them. For example, as liquid slips from your juice bottle into your mouth, you observe, "My juice is warm." You look at little black marks on paper, perceive words, and think, "This story is interesting."

exhibit **4.1** The Perception Process

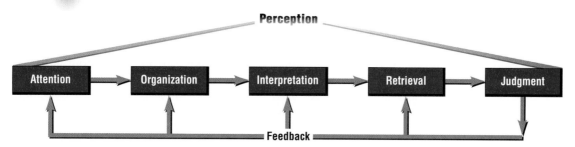

These responses may feel automatic. However, as pictured in Exhibit 4.1, the perception process actually involves five stages:

1. Attention
2. Organization
3. Interpretation
4. Retrieval
5. Judgment

When a person has paid attention to a stimulus, each step of the perception process provides feedback for the earlier steps. Based on this feedback, the person may adjust his or her perceptions.

Attention The perception process begins with **attention.** At this stage, people notice some of the information available and filter out the rest. For example, people listening to a speech might tune out most of it but pay attention when the speaker mentions something they are interested in. Or people in a meeting might not notice the fluorescent lights overhead—until the power goes out, leaving them in the dark.

> **attention**
>
> The stage in the perception process that involves noticing some of the information available and filtering out the rest.

It might seem obvious that a person can't perceive something without first paying attention to it. Nevertheless, people sometimes don't realize this fact. Consider the earlier example of Brian Roberts of Comcast. He stepped into a leadership role at the company and knew that people would have varied perceptions of the boss's son taking over. He already had most employees' attention at Comcast because of his visible top position. But once he had that attention, he had to prove himself as a capable individual to shape their perceptions of him. So, the context of a situation can affect the degree of interest in a stimulus.

Culture can also affect attention and perception. People in high-context cultures (defined in Chapter 2) expect that others will interpret the context of what they say, rather than paying attention only to their words. When people from such a culture interact with someone from a lower context culture, the other person may not pay attention to their subtle cues. Later we discuss factors that influence whether a person will pay attention to a particular stimulus.

Organization As a person pays attention to a stimulus, the person then begins to make sense of it. This begins with the stage in the perception process called *organization*. During organization, the perceiver sorts the information by using a frame of reference.

For example, Frank Tucker's frame of reference gave him an advantage in recruiting employees for Tucker Technology, the firm he founded to provide telecommunications installation and maintenance services. While Tucker was driving to work through an economically depressed part of Oakland, California, he noticed people standing around on street corners. Many observers would have seen these people as unmotivated or even as possible drug users or criminals. To Tucker, however, they were untapped human resources, so he organized the information he had in a unique way.

Many of the positions Tucker needed to fill required a little training coupled with a willingness to work in harsh conditions. So he began hiring unemployed people, training them, and paying them a good wage. He also participates on boards of directors for community organizations, which gives him access to the graduates of their training programs. Tucker's unique perception of people has thus given him an edge in competing for human resources.[2]

In the earlier example of Comcast, Brian Roberts wanted employees to organize their perceptions of him as more than just the boss's son—as a new leader. Let's look at the ways people typically organize stimuli they observe.

Mechanisms for organizing stimuli. To find a pattern in stimuli, people often use a mechanism such as one of the following:

- *Closure* People tend to perceive incomplete data in a whole, complete form. In part (a) of Exhibit 4.2, most people see the series of spots as a dog; the brain imagines the parts that are missing from the drawing. Likewise, a person who overhears one side of a phone conversation is likely to imagine the overall content of the conversation.

- *Continuity* People tend to perceive sensory data in continuous patterns, even if the data are not actually continuous. In part (b) of Exhibit 4.2, people tend to read the words as one complete sentence, even though the word *the* appears both at the end of the first line and the beginning of the second. Or, if you are trying to persuade someone to return your phone call, you might call once at 9:00, then again at 11:00 and 11:30, in the hope that the other person will interpret this as a pattern in which you will call more and more frequently until your call is returned.

exhibit |**4.2**
Visual Illusions

Read this sentence out loud.

**A BIRD IN THE
THE HAND IS WORTHLESS.**

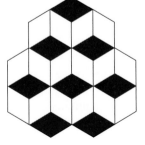

(a)   **(b)**   **(c)**

Source: Richard L. Daft, *Management,* 5th ed. (Fort Worth, Tx: Harcourt College Publishing, 2000), p. 483.

- *Proximity* When stimuli are near each other, people perceive them as being related. For example, if managers routinely review salaries and employee performance at the same time, employees are likely to perceive the two reviews as being related. Or when you give your boss the results of your work assignment, perhaps you will want to present them in person, so you will be associated with the success, rather than having your report in a pile of coworkers' weekly progress reports.

- *Similarity* When stimuli are alike in some way, people tend to group them. For example, in a meeting of ten people, if eight participants are white and two are black, some people may perceive the two black participants as a group—whether or not they are similar or related in any other way.

- *Figure-ground* People tend to perceive the sensory data they are most attentive to as standing out against the background of other sensory data. In part (c) of Exhibit 4.2, do you see six blocks that are purple on top or seven blocks that are purple on the bottom? The answer depends on your mental organization of the shapes drawn there. In terms of organizational behavior, a manager might perceive employees' activities as standing out against the background of their working conditions, or a group member's behavior as standing out against the background of the other group members' behavior. The way the manager organizes these observations will influence their perceived meaning.

Schemas Often when people organize stimuli, they use frames of reference called *schemas*. **Schemas** are cognitive (mental) structures in which related items of information are grouped together. Psychologists describe schemas in terms of scripts and stereotypes.

A **script** is a schema that describes a sequence of actions. Based on life experiences, people develop scripts in which they define the sequences involved in many activities, ranging from birthday parties to meetings to airplane travel. Exhibit 4.3 is a sample script for a job interview. How does your own script resemble or differ from this script? Scripts like these usually make a variety of activities easier to carry out. The script for a meeting, for example, tells you how to dress appropriately, follow an agenda, and take turns talking.

Because of differences in culture and experience, people sometimes come to a situation with different scripts. Especially within a diverse group, perceptions often differ as a result. When that happens, misunderstandings can occur. Conversely, people who understand the importance of scripts can present themselves in ways that will fit a script positively. That is essentially what Beth Thomas did when asked to prepare an ambitious training program for The Limited.

Beth Thomas was a training specialist with Victoria's Secret when she had an idea to make training more efficient and effective. She presented her idea to Jon Ricker, the chief information officer of The Limited, which owns eight store chains including Victoria's Secret, The Limited, Structure, and Bath & Body Works. Thomas offered to start a centralized training department that would teach basic skills to employees in all of the divisions, thereby ensuring that training would be consistent among the retail chains. Ricker not only approved the idea, he appointed Thomas director of training for the corporation's information technology department and requested that she broaden her plan to encompass training for all business processes.

schemas

Cognitive (mental) structures in which related items of information are grouped together.

script

A schema that describes a sequence of actions.

❦ **The Limited Inc.**

The responsibility was daunting, but Thomas charted a path to success. She started by defining an initial project she thought she could handle successfully, so company managers would perceive her as highly capable. However, she needed experts in the subject matter covered by the training, which would draw talented human resources away from other departments.

To get those valuable resources, Thomas framed her request as a script that company executives would readily recognize—a sophisticated business plan. She prepared a mission statement, needs analysis, billing structure, policies and standards, facilities requirements, a cost analysis, and a marketing plan. Using the language familiar to business executives, she presented her plan to The Limited's chief financial officer and chief administrative officer. She used it to shape their perception that training would not be just a cost to the corporation but an investment designed to benefit the company.

Thomas's presentation impressed the executives, and they granted their approval. She then presented her plan to the heads of the various retail chains, approaching them as potential customers. They, too, supported the program. Building on that initial success, Thomas now runs a 12-person group that trains up to 500 people a month—a service the departments are willing to pay for. And she even does it at a profit.[3]

prototype

A schema that summarizes a category of people or objects.

Other schemas, called **prototypes,** summarize what we have learned about categories of people or objects. Thus, we expect cars, offices, and managers to have certain features. Exhibit 4.4, for instance, is a prototype of an office. Suppose you were hired for an office job, and a team member showed you to an office without a chair or without lights. What would be your response? Or how would you react if your office included something outside of your prototype—say, a jackhammer or stove?

Like scripts, prototypes are helpful when they are accurate and everyone agrees on them. Also like scripts, they cause problems when they are inaccurate or when people have different prototypes for the same thing. For example, a group of leaders within the American School Food Service

exhibit | **4.3**
Script for a Job Interview

Setting: Office of prospective employer
Cast: Job candidate; human resources person (who will screen candidates and provide input into the hiring decision) or prospective supervisor (who makes ultimate hiring decision) or work team (for a self-directed work team that makes hiring decisions)
Attire: Job candidate wears suit or other conservative clothing. Other cast members dress according to their roles in the organization.

1. The job candidate arrives at the office five minutes before the scheduled interview and looks for a person seated at a desk outside an office (the receptionist).
2. The job candidate politely tells the receptionist his/her name and purpose of visit.
3. The job candidate sits quietly, when and where directed.
4. The person who will conduct the interview arrives at the reception area, introduces him- or herself to the job candidate, and they shake hands.
5. The interviewer ushers the job candidate to the office where the interview will take place.
6. The interviewer asks questions about the candidate's work history, skills, and personality, and the job candidate answers politely, emphasizing positives.
7. The interviewer invites questions, and the job candidate asks a few that are related to the job and the employer.
8. The interviewer makes a statement indicating they have arrived at the end of the interview. The participants stand up and shake hands.
9. The job candidate leaves the office and exits the building.

exhibit | **4.4**
Prototype of an Office

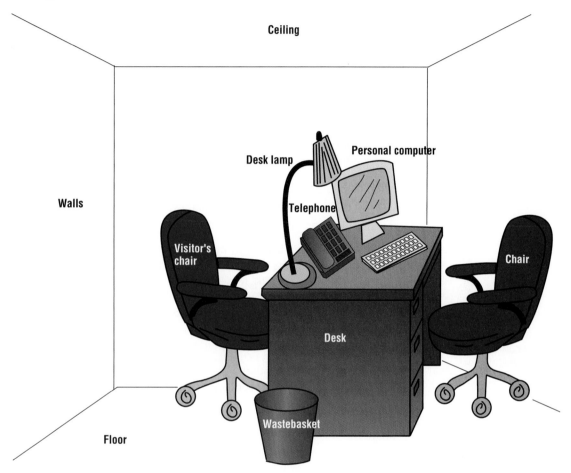

Association explored the ways employees categorized one another. They noticed that their members had different prototypes for cafeteria workers in elementary schools and those in high schools. The leaders perceived that members treated cafeteria workers in high schools with more respect, a difference that caused staffing problems in the elementary schools.[4] Later in this chapter, we will examine prototypes that lead to errors in perception.

Interpretation Fitting information into a schema begins the effort of giving meaning to the information. That effort continues with the next stage of the perception process, **interpretation.** In this stage, the perceiver looks for explanations for stimuli. For instance, if you walk into a room and see a digital clock flashing 12:00, you might interpret this to mean that power to the clock was interrupted. If an employee talks on the phone for three hours straight every morning, others in the office might interpret this behavior to mean his job involves a lot of phone contact or that he wastes a lot of time socializing on the job.

interpretation

The stage in the perception process that involves looking for explanations for stimuli that have been observed.

projection

Assigning one's own thoughts and feelings to a person being perceived.

attribution

Using observations and inferences to explain people's behavior.

retrieval

The stage of the perception process that involves recalling information about past events.

judgment

The stage of the perception process that involves aggregating and weighting information to arrive at an overall conclusion.

Psychologists who have studied the perception process have theorized that interpretation involves a combination of two processes, called *projection* and *attribution*. **Projection** involves assigning our own thoughts and feelings to the people we observe. Often, people do this unconsciously. For example, a manager whose primary interest is the company may expect others to share her enthusiasm for working long hours. Depending on how closely our own thoughts and feelings actually match those of other people, projection may introduce errors into the perception process. Correcting these errors requires a good dose of empathy coupled with awareness of our own attitudes and values.

Attribution involves using observations and inferences to explain people's behavior. In the case of Brian Roberts of Comcast, he wanted employees to attribute his successes to hard work, talent, and commitment, not to his family relationship. Like projection, attribution can be a source of errors. Later in this chapter, we examine the process of attribution, as well as sources of perceptual errors and methods for minimizing them.

Retrieval   After a perceiver has paid attention to a stimulus and made sense of it by organizing and interpreting it, the perceiver recalls information about past events. For example, during your performance review, you might want your boss to retrieve information about your past successes, your ability to share knowledge with others in your group, and all those nights you stayed late to work on a big assignment. This stage of the perception process is called **retrieval.** The retrieval stage provides information to use in the final stage of the perception process.

Judgment   The perception process ends with **judgment.** During this stage, the perceiver uses retrieved information to arrive at an overall conclusion. In the example of your successful project, you hope your boss concludes that your talent and hard work have significantly benefited the organization. To carry out the judgment stage, the perceiver aggregates and weights information.

Aggregating information means gathering pieces of information. A perceiver might, for example, aggregate information about the circumstances in which an event occurred or about the way others react to a behavior. In the airline industry, union and management groups have recently been engaged in a dispute that partly stems from a difference in how the two sides aggregate information. The unions observed a period of money-losing years for the industry, during which the employees accepted cuts in benefits and pay, followed by big profits for the major airlines. They aggregate this with the fact that the companies have rewarded their top executives with eight-figure salaries but have not granted generous wage increases to other employees. Their judgment is that the airlines are unwilling to distribute the wealth fairly. Airline executives aggregate different data to arrive at a different judgment. They notice that labor is an airline's only major unregulated cost, and that the other costs (fuel and interest rates) are likely to rise. Executives apparently do not incorporate information about their own compensation in arriving at their judgment that big wage increases would remove their company's ability to compete in a highly competitive, risk-filled environment.[5]

Weighting information means deciding how important information is relative to other information. People weight information differently accord-

what would you do?

APPAREL SOURCE INC. DECIDES GOING GREEN IS TOO EXPENSIVE

These days, environmentally sound business decisions are no longer perceived as extremist; in fact, they are part of the mainstream consciousness. "Going green" is often viewed by many managers as part of the cost of doing business, even if the gesture cuts into profits, because it is likely that potential customers will view the company positively. But one entrepreneur, who worked during his free time to save a 13.5-acre estuary on Vashon Island near Seattle, actually contradicted his personal beliefs when it came to an environmental decision involving his company, Apparel Source Inc.

Apparel Source Inc. isn't a tiny start-up. Although you may never have heard of it, the firm manufactures and sells $50 million of cotton knit shirts each year to moderately priced stores like Target. The company is privately held by Duncan Berry, who, while he was working to save the parcel of land now called Fern Cove Sanctuary, discovered that his own apparel manufacturing industry was pumping a huge number of toxic chemicals into the environment at its plants. He learned that 53 million pounds of pesticides and 1.6 billion pounds of synthetic fertilizers applied to U.S.–grown cotton each year are devastating farmland and seeping into food and cattle feed. Aggregating more information, Berry found that if his own company switched to a more environmentally sound organic blend of cotton, there would still be profits, although a bit slimmer than before. (Apparel Source

was making a gross profit of 5 percent to 18 percent on its shirts, depending on where they were manufactured, so there was some room to maneuver.) Berry didn't have shareholders to satisfy, and retailers who were concerned about their own image had already started to purchase blended-cotton items. Berry considered the information presented him, weighted the information, and decided he just couldn't take the cuts. Instead, he quit the board of Fern Cove.

In a competitive business environment, it's not surprising that an entrepreneur doesn't want to touch his bottom line—he's worked hard for every dime he's got. But it's possible that both retailers and consumers could perceive Berry's move negatively, causing a drop in sales. He decided he was willing to take that chance.

Imagine that you are one of Berry's top manager's at Apparel Source, and he values your opinion.

1. Would you aggregate different types of data from those that Berry aggregated? Why or why not?

2. How would you weight the information? What judgment would you come to?

3. Suppose you were also working on the Fern Cove board; would you quit the board to support your boss? Why or why not?

Source: Jeffrey L. Seglin, "It's not that easy going green," *Inc.,* May 1999, pp. 29, 32.

---

ing to their values, opinions, and other criteria. In the previous example, airline executives gave heavy weight to labor costs because these expenses have a major impact on whether the executives succeed and their companies survive. In contrast, they seem not to give much weight to their own high compensation as contributing to the airlines' expenses.

As another example, the process of aggregating and weighting information leads people to a fairly consistent pattern of judgments when they are driving during rush hour. Researchers at the University of Toronto studied that all-too-common frustration of rush-hour drivers: the feeling of being stuck in the slowest lane. The researchers found that most people arrive at this judgment by comparing the amount of time they spend passing other cars with the amount of time other cars spend passing them. But this process leads to a misperception. You pass a dozen cars much faster than those cars pass you when your lane is stuck, so when all lanes are traveling at the same average speed, each driver spends the majority of his or her time being passed by others. In the words of the study's sponsor, Dr. Donald Redelmeier, "You're going to have many more moments of frustration to balance the relatively few moments of pleasure." People worsen their

exhibit | **4.5**

Influences on Perception

Characteristics of the Perceiver

Sensitivity to stimuli
Learning
Moods, emotions
Recent experiences
Expectations, needs, values, interests

Characteristics of the Stimulus

Intensity
Contrast
Frequency
Novelty
Size
Motion

Characteristics of the Situation

Primacy effect
Recency effect
Schemas

discomfort with their patterns of attention: They study the adjoining lanes more when they are idle, and they tend to notice cars they have not yet passed more than the ones they have passed. Especially when people weight their frustration heavily, they reach the judgment that they are in the slowest lane. In fact, during rush hour, the average speed of all lanes tends to be the same. Yet research subjects typically judged that the adjoining lane was moving faster, even when data indicated its average speed was slower.[6]

Influences on Perception

Although people follow the same stages of perception, they differ in the way they perceive a given stimulus. If you want to deduce what someone else is perceiving, it is helpful to know what influences are likely to shape that person's perceptions. In general, our perceptions are influenced by characteristics of the stimulus and the situation, as well as by our own characteristics (see Exhibit 4.5).

Characteristics of the Perceiver   Some people simply appear to be more sensitive to stimuli than others; they notice every little thing.[7] These sensitive people perceive when a colleague has exciting news to deliver or needs some time to think. They may also be more prone to notice (and object to) a colleague smoking or playing a radio nearby; they just can't ignore the smoke or the radio.

Learning also influences perception. Your experience with stimuli provides you with information that helps you decide which stimuli are important and how you should respond. For example, you learn how to interpret facial expressions, loud noises, and classroom lectures. As people's learning experiences expand along different lines, so too do their perceptions. Thus, within any group—and especially within a diverse group—people's varied learning experiences will influence their perception process in different ways.

In addition, a person's state of mind at the time of the perception can influence how the person organizes and interprets the stimuli. Our moods and emotions tend to influence what we pay attention to and how we interpret it.[8] People who are optimistic and happy tend to interpret their surroundings more positively than do those who are pessimistic and depressed.[9] In addition, if you have recently used certain cognitive categories, you are likely to reapply them to what you perceive.[10] For example, if you have been wrestling with an ethical dilemma, you are more likely to see elements of ethics in the next decision that confronts you.

Finally, people share a tendency to perceive stimuli that match their expectations, needs, values, and interests. The link between needs and perception was tested 50 years ago with an experiment in which subjects looked at blurred pictures.[11] Some subjects had eaten an hour before the experiment, whereas others had not eaten for as long as 16 hours. Those who had not eaten for 16 hours were much more likely to see the images as pictures of food. In organizations, such influences on perception might play out in a variety of situations. For example, someone who is ambitious for a promotion might be inclined to notice and interpret colleagues' behavior as signaling they are competing for the job. Likewise, a salesperson might be keenly attuned to signals of people interested in the company's products. Later in this chapter, we explore how subjective factors such as these can bias perceptions.

Hershey Foods Corporation uses the bright color of its cherry-flavored Jolly Rancher candies to grab the attention of magazine readers. Being big, bright, and loud, this full-page ad is an example of the intensity characteristic of stimulus.

Characteristics of the Stimulus Some types of stimuli grab attention better than others. One important characteristic is *intensity*. People are most likely to pay attention to an intense stimulus, such as a bright light, a loud noise, or a strong odor. Advertisers take advantage of this knowledge about perception when they develop ads that are big, bright, and loud.

Another characteristic that makes a stimulus more attention getting is *contrast*. The source of the contrast may be a difference from surrounding stimuli—for example, being the only male participant in an otherwise all-female meeting. Or the contrast may arise from a change in the stimulus, as when a photocopier motor stops running after it has been on for a while. When you are unique in a group (the only male or female, the only person of a particular race, the only deaf person, the only person under 50), others in the group tend to scrutinize your behavior. They notice you more, by virtue of the way in which you contrast with the others in the group.

People also pay more attention to stimuli that occur with greater *frequency*. The frequency provides more opportunities for perception to occur. As advertisers know, if people hear or see the same message over and over, they are more likely to notice it than if they encounter the message just once.

Novelty also generates attention. Suppose you are on a team that is charged with improving quality. Various team members make the usual suggestions about measuring output and ensuring that suppliers meet high standards. Then a team member suggests something entirely new to the organization: spending one day a month at customer sites, working with customers and seeing how they use your product. Whether or not your team actually decides to implement this idea, everyone notices it because it is novel.

Two characteristics of visual stimuli also enhance the likelihood they will be noticed: *size* and *motion*. People are more likely to see something if it is big and if it is in motion. The banner ads on Web sites try to attract attention by using large, bold graphics and moving images.

Adapting these characteristics to our perceptions of other people, we can make some predictions about which people we are most likely to perceive. In general, a person is more likely to perceive someone who is novel (say, the only person with a beard), bright (wearing colorful clothing), behaving uncharacteristically for that individual or social position (being talkative when one is usually quiet), behaving unusually (making strange faces or laughing at inappropriate times during a meeting), extremely positive or negative (a basketball star or serial killer), and dominant in the perceiver's visual field (blocking the doorway or sitting in the center of a stage).[12]

Characteristics of the Situation   Perception also varies according to characteristics of the situation in which the stimuli occur. For example, people pay more attention to stimuli occurring near the beginning or end of a situation:

1. *Primacy effect*   Stimuli near the beginning of a situation receive attention. First impressions really do matter a lot.

2. *Recency effect*   Stimuli near the end of a situation receive attention. Your customer probably will remember the close of your sales presentation more than the points in the middle.

In addition, people evaluate a stimulus differently depending on whether it fits their schema for the context. For example, the people in a particular organization may consider shouting to be appropriate on the factory floor but not in the lunchroom. Or jeans may be considered appropriate for employees who work in the shipping department but not for those in the legal department. If a shipping department employee shows up in a jacket and tie, his coworkers will likely notice it and wonder whether he is headed for a job interview. In contrast, they might not pay much attention to whether he wears a blue shirt or green shirt with his jeans.

apply it

1. Suppose you want a long career with your current (or most recent) employer and want your supervisor to think of you as someone with management

potential. How could you use what you have learned about perception to influence the way your supervisor perceives you?

2. For one week, note some recent television, magazine, or Web site advertisements. Bring to class examples of ads that use intensity, contrast, frequency, novelty, size, and motion to gain attention. Also, during the week observe people in a crowd and note examples of each of the same characteristics. Who seems to be gaining attention with intensity, contrast, frequency, novelty, size, or motion? Explain why you think so.

Our perceptions are subject to distortion

Psychologists who have studied the perception process have determined that people simplify the work of perception by creating shortcuts for each stage of the process. These shortcuts make perception easier, but they also give people a distorted view of reality. In addition, people engage in **perceptual defense,** meaning they tend to protect themselves from ideas, objects, and people that are threatening in some way. This means people perceive things that are pleasant and ignore or disregard disturbing and unpleasant stimuli. Together, these sources of bias take the form of selective attention, simplification and stereotypes, selective retrieval, and the self-fulfilling prophecy.

perceptual defense

The tendency to protect ourselves from ideas, objects, and people that are threatening by selecting which stimuli to perceive and which to disregard.

Selective Attention

When you're sitting in a meeting, you need to pay attention to what is important—for example, what people are saying, the feelings they are expressing, the way they interact with one another. You aren't likely to benefit from paying attention to a fly buzzing around the room, the view out the window, or the air conditioning cycling on and off. They are distractions—they fill up your mind and keep you from more important demands on your attention. Since we can't possibly process all the stimuli around us, our minds select certain stimuli to perceive. In general, we tend to pay attention to the kinds of noticeable stimuli described in the preceding section, as well as to stimuli that match our expectations, needs, and interests.

A person's **expectations** are beliefs about future events. In the context of perception, an expectation describes what a person thinks he or she will perceive. If you expect that teamwork will be difficult and frustrating, you will take note of each conflict as it surfaces. If you expect that teamwork generates superior results, you will notice each accomplishment of your organization's teams.

expectations

Beliefs about future events.

Needs and interests shape perception in similar ways. People notice what they care about and what will help them. If your team is charged with setting up a computer network, chances are you will notice all the advertisements and news stories related to computer networking.

Simplification and Stereotypes

Distortions also occur in the way people organize and interpret information. People use prototypes that are oversimplified and hence make inaccurate perceptions. These biases include stereotypes, halo error, and contrasts.

stereotype

A rigid, widely held prototype about the general characteristics of a group of people.

Stereotypes A **stereotype** is a rigid, widely held prototype about the general characteristics of a group of people. Common stereotypes relate to age groups, religious groups, racial and ethnic groups, and both sexes. People also hold stereotypes about people from particular education levels, occupations, and economic classes. Especially in a diverse group where individuals are not familiar with the characteristics of the other members, the group members are likely to rely on stereotypes.

Like any prototype, stereotypes simplify reality. When we use a stereotype, we put a person into a category, then attribute to that individual all the characteristics we associate with that category. Simplification during stereotyping is especially problematic, because human beings are so complex. Reducing people to simple categories clouds their individual differences, ignoring ways individuals differ from the groups we associate them with. Consequently, stereotypes are unlikely to describe individuals accurately.

Furthermore, because people are the resources most essential to success, organizations cannot afford a simplistic understanding of their employees or of their customers. Stereotyping in terms of positive traits is harmful because it is a substitute for really learning about a person, so it can lead to hurt feelings and poor decisions. Potentially even more harmful is for organizations to let negative stereotypes prevent talented people from advancing and fully contributing. The same principles apply to employees' stereotypes about their customers—for example, guessing based on someone's clothes, speech, or skin color whether that person will be a big spender.

Jennifer Lawton, senior vice president of Interliant, a consulting and Internet hosting company, discusses the continual battles she has waged throughout her career as an entrepreneur and executive in a traditionally male-dominated field. She urges individuals to take an active role in dispelling stereotypes: "Society has a lot of control over what people perceive as the right job or the wrong job for anyone. This is especially true of women entrepreneurs. It's assumed that men will be in control positions and women will not. . . . What I've found works best is to understand who you are and how you work, and then to analyze how you fit or don't fit with current stereotypes. Figuring [this] out . . . enables you to set expectations for people in advance, so they don't have the opportunity to apply an inappropriate stereotype. In short, it allows you to manage the situation."[13]

Stereotypes exist for all occupations, including professional fishermen. Contrary to the "rugged individualist" image of brute strength, "You'd be surprised," says lobsterman Richard Cook, "how many guys you see in lobster boats reading the stock pages in the newspaper." Another widely held stereotype of men spending their days wearing yellow rain gear while battling foul weather and high seas is also broken, replaced by a casually dressed astute investor analyzing the investment prospects of his lobster fishing profits.
(Source: © Greg Miller)

Besides being a significant problem for individuals, stereotypes are a persistent challenge for organizations because they are, by definition, widely held beliefs. This can make stereotypes difficult to recognize. If "everyone knows" women are more interested in people's feelings than in solving a complex problem, women team members may not be called to use their technical expertise. And this situation can exist for stereotypes related to age and racial and ethnic groups, as well as gender. These assumptions prevent the group from exploring a person's true capabilities and tapping his or her true potential.

Because employment decisions involve perceptions about individuals, stereotypes can bias these crucial decisions. Inaccurate assessments of individuals harm both individuals and the organization. Employment decisions

Performance Areas	Excellent	Good	Average	Fair	Poor
1. Takes initiative in solving problems.	X	—	—	—	—
2. Arrives at work on time.	X	—	—	—	—
3. Works well with others on team.	X	—	—	—	—
4. Is knowledgeable about work area.	X	—	—	—	—
5. Encourages and supports others in common goals.	X	—	—	—	—
Overall rating:	X	—	—	—	—

exhibit **4.6**

Halo Effect in a Performance Appraisal

based on stereotypes fail to accurately identify the potential contributions people can make and also open the organization to charges of discrimination. Conversely, decisions that accurately reflect and develop each person's unique set of knowledge and skills enable organizations to tap this essential resource.

Halo Error   Another misuse of prototypes is the **halo error,** a perceptual bias that occurs in rating. The person making the rating has an overall opinion of someone, and that opinion shapes the perceiver's ratings of specific behaviors or characteristics. Thus, if you have a favorable opinion of someone, you tend to view the person's characteristics and behaviors more favorably than if your overall opinion is negative. Often, when applied to negative bias, this perceptual distortion is called the *horns effect.* Exhibit 4.6 provides an example of the halo effect in a performance appraisal.

Like stereotypes, the halo-or-horns bias oversimplifies our perceptions of other people. It therefore interferes with accurate employment decisions and, when negative, can prevent talented people from contributing to the organization.

Contrasts   People also organize information by contrasting it with other information. The other information serves as a reference point for the new information. In the process of making these contrasts, perceivers can make perceptual errors.

If the reference point is very high or low, the perceiver can make an error called a **contrast effect.** This error involves perceiving something as larger or smaller than it really is because it differs significantly from the reference point used to interpret it. Suppose an organization decides to institute a quality improvement program. In an effort to motivate employees by demonstrating how significant the program can be, the organization relates a story in which an employee's idea saved the company $23 million. Later, some employees have ideas that would each save the company tens of thousands of dollars each year. But although the company would value these ideas, the employees may not suggest them because, compared with the multimillion-dollar example, their ideas seem small and insignificant.

halo error

A perceptual bias in which the perceiver has an overall opinion of someone, and that opinion shapes the perceiver's ratings of specific behaviors or characteristics.

contrast effect

A perceptual error that involves perceiving something as larger or smaller than it really is because it differs significantly from the reference point used to interpret it.

Nike

In combatting some negative media attention, Nike has contended that people are, in effect, making contrast errors in their perceptions of the wages its subcontractors pay their workers.

Nike doesn't produce the shoes that bear its name. Rather, it contracts with factories, mostly in Asia, to make the shoes. Activists have repeatedly criticized Nike for allowing its contractors to pay extremely low wages. The company insists that the problem is in how the wages are perceived by observers in the West.

Kimberly Miyoshi of Global Exchange, a San Francisco–based organization, puts the complaint this way: "Americans pay $100 for a pair of shoes that a worker gets $3 a day to make. They pay Michael Jordan $40 million to endorse them." Thus, Miyoshi is contrasting the workers' wages with the cost of the shoes and the endorsement fees paid to Jordan. The $3 sum is paltry by either measure.

Nike and others insist that critics are not using the appropriate reference points. Rather, they say, it is more valid to compare Nike contractors' wages with other wages paid in the region and with the amounts necessary to provide an acceptable standard of living. Workers in Indonesian Nike factories earn a monthly equivalent of $37 to $45, which exceeds the minimum wage in Indonesia. Researchers at Dartmouth College determined that Nike contractors in Indonesia and Vietnam paid their workers enough for them to save some of their earnings after feeding and housing themselves. Thus, if the reference point is the local minimum wage or an amount that allows workers to save some of their earnings, the wages paid by Nike contractors look more generous.[14]

anchoring and adjustment effect

A perceptual error that involves making an insufficient adjustment from the anchor (reference point) used.

When people make contrasts, they also may make an error known as the **anchoring and adjustment effect.** This process involves making an insufficient adjustment from a reference point, called an "anchor." When people interpret an anchor they know is inappropriate, they correct it, but typically by less than enough to make it accurate. In the earlier example of a quality improvement program, employees are initially thinking of the story of the employee who saved $23 million, and this amount is their anchor. To encourage more participation and ideas, managers might ask employees to suggest a level of savings they think is worth pursuing through quality improvements. Employees might realize the anchor amount of $23 million is large for a typical improvement and adjust the worthwhile amount to $1 million ideas. But, as noted before, managers may actually expect the savings from each idea to be much less, and they could provide better leadership and guidance by using a target more typical of their expectations so that employees' perceptions would be more accurate.

Selective Retrieval

People further distort perception by being selective in the information they retrieve. Their memories fade, but not randomly. Psychologists have noticed patterns in the information people lose. Typically people forget (fail to retrieve) information that is inconsistent with their scripts and prototypes.[15] Thus, a person who holds a prototype that accountants are dull and unimaginative is unlikely to remember any interesting conversations with accountants. People do tend to retrieve information that matches their existing points of view, just as they are more likely to notice such information in the first place.

performance cues

Information from an external source that biases what people recall.

Another influence on retrieval is **performance cues.** These items of information come from an external source that biases what people recall. For example, in studies of performance cues, researchers grouped subjects and gave them tasks to perform. Afterward, although the groups' performances were similar, the researcher told half the groups that they performed well and the other half that they performed poorly. In groups that heard they performed well, subjects recalled more examples of effective leadership and group processes. People from groups told they performed poorly recalled more negative examples of group processes.[16]

Distortions in the Judgment Stage

Perceptual distortions can also lead to misjudgments. Errors in judgments can be categorized into two types: the assimilation effect and the self-fulfilling prophecy.

Assimilation Effect   The judgments a person has made in the past influence the way the person will perceive stimuli in the future. Through a tendency called the **assimilation effect,** people tend to bias future judgments in the direction of their past judgments, so they make new judgments that closely resemble previous ones. In other words, they assimilate their judgments. This assimilation occurs through a combination of phenomena, chiefly priming and the confirmation bias.

assimilation effect

The tendency to bias future judgments in the direction of past judgments.

Priming, in research, is a technique in which the researchers ask people to recall a set of events before asking them to make a judgment that may be related to those events. In such studies, people weight their judgments in terms of the events for which they were primed. In organizations, people use priming, too. For example, to introduce an idea about customer service, an employee of a store might begin, "Remember how thrilled those customers were that day we remembered their shoe size?" People will hear the employee's idea in terms of that past success. Priming influences judgment because people give more weight to freshly retrieved information than to information that is hard to recall.

priming

Asking people to recall a set of events before asking them to make a judgment that may be related to those events.

The **confirmation bias** is a tendency to heavily weight information that reaffirms past judgments, while discounting information that contradicts past judgments. Evidence suggests that this tendency is most pronounced when people's judgments are made public. One reason for this may be that people want others to think they are consistent.[17]

confirmation bias

The tendency to give heavy weight to information that reaffirms past judgments and to discount information that would contradict past judgments.

The Self-Fulfilling Prophecy   Misjudgments affect not only the perceiver's own behavior, but also the behavior of those being perceived. Suppose, for example, that a manager notices an employee hard at work every evening as the manager is leaving. She may perceive either that the employee is hardworking and committed to success or that the employee is struggling because of poor time-management skills. The manager's perception will affect how she treats the employee, and the manager's treatment will affect the employee's performance.

In general, evidence suggests that high expectations lead to high performance, and low expectations lead to inferior performance. In terms of perception, this means people try to keep their perceptions in line with what they expect. This relationship between perceptions and performance is the **self-fulfilling prophecy,** also called the *Pygmalion effect* (a reference to the Greek myth about the sculptor Pygmalion). Exhibit 4.7 is a

self-fulfilling prophecy

The effort to keep perceptions in line with expectations, resulting in high performance when expectations are high and low performance when expectations are low.

exhibit **4.7**
Self-Fulfilling Prophecy

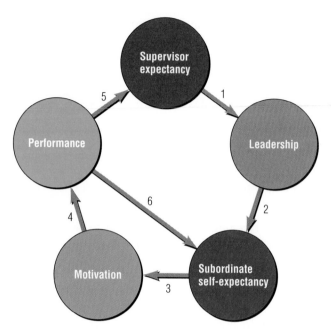

Source: Republished by permission of the Academy of Management from "Self-Fulfilling Prophecy as a Management Tool: Harnessing Pygmalion" by D. Eden, *Academy of Management Review,* January 1984, p. 67, copyright 1984. Permission conveyed through Copyright Clearance Center, Inc.

model of how the self-fulfilling prophecy links a leader's expectations to the group's performance. This model involves 6 linkages:

1. The leader's expectations influence his or her leadership actions.
2. Leadership helps the group members develop expectations for their performance.
3. The group members' expectations influence their motivation (see Chapter 6 for a discussion of this linkage).
4. Group members' motivation influences how hard they try and how well they perform (see Chapter 5).
5. Group members' performance provides feedback that reinforces the leader's expectations.
6. Performance also provides feedback to group members concerning their own expectations.

Thus, when group members try to succeed and perceive that they have done so, their success encourages them to continue this positive approach.

The self-fulfilling prophecy has been tested on many groups, starting with a study involving grade-school children. In that study, researchers assigned the children randomly to groups called "high potential" and "control." Based on the group assignments, the researchers told teachers that some students had "high potential" and others did not. Children assigned to the high-potential group later performed significantly better on IQ tests and tests of reading ability.[18] Other studies tested this effect in adults, including electronics assemblers, military trainees, and participants in job-training programs.[19] For example, in a study using trainees and instructors in the Israeli Defense Forces, the researchers told four course instructors that certain trainees had high potential, others had normal potential, and still others had unknown potential. Despite what the researchers said, the trainees were assigned to these categories at random. The trainees who were labeled as having high potential scored significantly higher on achievement tests, had more positive attitudes, and held their leaders in higher esteem.[20] Apparently, the leaders demonstrated that they expected a lot from these trainees, and the trainees responded positively.

The subjects in these studies were all men, which raises the question of whether women in organizations also are subject to the Pygmalion effect. This possibility was investigated with another study involving cadets in the Israeli Defense Forces.[21] The researchers found a Pygmalion effect for both male and female cadets—but only when the leader was a male. The cadets also tended to rate the women as better leaders than the men. Left to future research is the reason for the differences. Could it be that the female leaders were less able to inspire their cadets to achieve based on their perceptions of the cadets? Or did they perceive actual ability levels more accurately than their male counterparts did?

For leaders who can apply it, the self-fulfilling prophecy has the potential to help or hurt the organization's performance. An organization benefits when its leaders inspire people to meet high expectations. Therefore, organizations should reward those in leadership positions when they set high standards for their followers.

apply it

1. The sales manager of a software company returns from lunch to find many items on his desk: an internal report showing that quarterly profits have exceeded forecasts for the second quarter in a row, a newspaper article forecasting that growth in the software industry will plateau within the next 20 years, and phone messages from a supplier's salesperson and a newspaper reporter. In addition, his phone is ringing, a spider is building a web in the corner of his office, and two people down the hall are arguing loudly. What distortions in the manager's perception might occur in this situation?

2. How might the perceptual distortions you described in the preceding question affect how well the sales manager performs his job?

People make attributions to explain behavior

Suppose you are a production manager. Every month, you look at reports detailing the quantity produced and defect rate for each workstation. This month some production teams produced more than others, and some exceeded quality goals while others fell short. How do you interpret this information? Certainly, many variables may be relevant, from order volume and product complexity to staffing patterns and motivation levels. As you interpret production reports, part of your analysis involves *attribution,* defined earlier as using observations and inferences to explain the behavior of others. In this case, you apply your observations and powers of reasoning to explain why the production teams performed as they did. The resulting attributions will influence your approach to controlling production.

Attribution is a process people use in a variety of situations. People make attributions about the behavior of managers, coworkers, customers, and strangers. People make attributions when they perceive events ranging from a person shouting on an elevator to the results of their performance on a project and a customer making a major purchase. For example, if you get a test back and your grade isn't what you expected, would you assume that the test was unfair, that you didn't spend enough time studying although you are capable, or that you just aren't able to understand the subject? Those assumptions ("I messed up" or "It's not my fault") are attributions. People attribute success or failure to different causes.

Models of Causal Attribution

When people make attributions about the success or failure of a person's actions, they have just a few alternatives:

- They can credit the success or failure to the person's ability. ("She is so smart, I knew she could land that account.")
- They can credit the person's effort. ("She made the sale because she worked hard for it.")
- They can attribute it to luck or other outside forces such as karma or God's will. ("She's lucky she landed that contract.")
- They can attribute it to the relative difficulty of the task. ("Of course they signed the contract. It was an easy sale. They already knew they needed our services.")

To better understand these alternatives, we can group them according to the two criteria shown in Exhibit 4.8:

1. *Stability of the cause*   The extent to which the cause of the behavior is permanent (stable cause) or temporary (unstable cause).
2. *Locus of causality*   Whether the success or failure resulted from some characteristic of the person (internal locus) or factors other than the person (external locus).

exhibit | **4.8**

Attributions Interpreting Task Performance

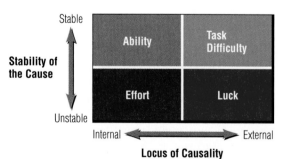

Source: Based on B. Weiner, I. Freize, A. Kukla, L. Reed, S. Rest, and R. M. Rosenbaum, "Perceiving the Causes of Success and Failure," in E. Jones, D. Kanouse, H. Kelley, R. Nesbitt, S. Valins, and B. Weiner (eds.), *Attribution: Perceiving the Causes of Behavior* (Morristown, NJ: General Learning Press, 1971), pp. 45–61.

Thus, when we attribute a success or failure to *ability,* we are saying that it resulted from some permanent (stable) characteristic of the person who succeeded or failed (internal locus). When we attribute success or failure to *effort,* we are saying the locus of causality is internal, but the cause is unstable (meaning a person might try hard sometimes but not others). Attributing an outcome to *task difficulty* means the cause is stable but the locus of causality is external (the task itself is what made success or failure likely). Attributing the outcome to *luck* means that the cause was unstable and the locus of causality was external (maybe the person will experience different luck next time).

In choosing from among these alternatives, people tend to follow predictable patterns. Do you tend to see your accomplishments as a result of your abilities, your effort, the difficulty of the task, or luck? What about other people—how do you tend to view their successes? Understanding these patterns can give you insight into how you perceive others and how they are likely to perceive you. According to psychologists, people base attributions on a combination of consensus, consistency, and distinctiveness (see Exhibit 4.9).[22]

Consensus describes the extent to which others, including the perceiver, engage in the same behavior or experience the same outcome. In other words, it compares different people performing the same kind of task. As shown in Exhibit 4.9, when consensus is high, the perceiver is more likely to attribute the cause of an outcome to external factors. In contrast, if different people tend to exhibit a variety of behaviors or experience mixed results, the perceiver is more likely to attribute the outcome to the person's ability or effort. For example, if you are being assessed on your performance on a project, your boss will likely take into account how well other people have performed similar assignments. If your boss views these other situations as equally challenging and sees that most people have succeeded as well as you did, he or she will more likely attribute your success to something about the project.

Consistency is the degree to which the person being observed behaves the same way or obtains the same outcome at different times. It compares the performance of the same person at similar tasks at different times. In situations with high consistency, the perceiver is more likely to attribute an outcome to internal factors—something about the person being perceived. Low consistency usually results in external attributions to task difficulty or luck. In the case of impressing your boss, he or she is more likely to attribute your success to you if he or she often sees you working hard or succeeding. People also make attributions about their customers. When Paul Bartko, CEO of an e-commerce specialist called MBC Group, observes

consensus

The extent to which people engage in the same behavior or experience the same outcome.

consistency

The degree to which a person being observed behaves in the same way or obtains the same outcome at different times.

	Perceiver's Attribution	
Criterion	**When High**	**When Low**
Consensus	Attribution to external factors	Attribution to internal factors
Consistency	Attribution to internal factors	Attribution to external factors
Distinctiveness	Attribution to internal factors	Attribution to task difficulty (external)

exhibit **4.9**
Criteria Used for Making Attributions

exhibit **4.10**
Biases in Attributions

Self-Serving Bias (our own performance)	Fundamental Attribution Error (performance of others)
Successes attributed to internal causes Failures attributed to external causes	Underestimates importance of external causes Overestimates importance of internal causes

a prospective customer rant about frustrations with a whole series of former vendors, Bartko attributes the dissatisfaction to the prospect, not to all the ex-vendors. Bartko concludes that the prospect must be impossible to please.[23]

distinctiveness

The extent to which a person being perceived achieves the same results on tasks that are much different.

Distinctiveness means the extent to which a person being perceived achieves the same results on tasks that are much different. In this case, the perceiver is comparing the same person's performance of different tasks. When a perceiver observes someone succeed at widely differing tasks, the perceiver is more likely to attribute the success to internal causes—the person's ability or effort. With success at only one type of activity, the perceiver is more likely to credit task difficulty. In the case of your successful project, your boss is most likely to give you the credit if you perform well at other, unrelated activities.

Biases in Attribution

The process of attribution involves judgment calls. It functions as a way to make sense of a world in which most situations are too complicated to analyze fully. Not surprisingly, psychologists have found that biases creep into this process. People tend to interpret information in a way that puts the perceiver in the best light. As shown in Exhibit 4.10, the form of these biases differs according to whether we are perceiving ourselves or others.

self-serving bias

The tendency to attribute our successes to internal causes and our failures to external causes.

In the case of a person evaluating his or her own performance, a **self-serving bias** creeps in. People tend to attribute their successes to internal causes—their own abilities and effort. They tend to attribute their failures to outside causes, either luck or the difficulty of the task. This bias may not always be a problem. For example, a study of sales representatives in the United Kingdom found a link between internal attributions for success and higher sales and performance ratings.[24] Other studies conclude that people who attribute their success to internal factors tend to have higher expectations about their future performance and a greater desire to achieve, and they set more challenging goals for themselves.[25]

fundamental attribution error

The tendency to overestimate the impact of internal factors and underestimate the impact of external factors on other people's behavior.

With regard to other people's performance, perceivers sometimes reach the opposite conclusions. Perceivers tend to apply the **fundamental attribution error,** which overestimates the impact of internal factors and underestimates the impact of external factors on other people's behavior. Thus, perceivers tend to give other people too much blame for their failures and too much credit for their successes. In the following example, consider whether Disney's chief executive or his critics may have made attribution errors.

Mickey Mouse is just about the most lovable rodent around, but investors no longer seem to love the company that created him. From 1998 to 1999, the price of Walt Disney stock dropped by more than one-third as sales and income declined. Recently, a *Fortune* magazine reporter spent a couple of hours interviewing Disney's CEO, Michael Eisner, to learn his perceptions of the company's situation. Eisner was adamant that the press was unfair to lay the company's difficulties at his feet: "The criticisms of me and Disney today are as shortsighted as were the praises of me and Disney in high economic times."

Of course, Eisner isn't just sitting back and waiting for better times. He has developed a strategy that emphasizes growth overseas, where the market for Disney's offerings is less saturated, as well as development of relatively new media such as a portal site on the World Wide Web. He is cutting costs and reorganizing the giant company. Nevertheless, he told the reporter that many of the company's recent problems have been beyond his control: "A lot of things happened together to make our earnings slide." For example, video sales have slumped industrywide, and a recession in Asia dampened global demand for Disney's licensed products. Others attribute some of the problems to management decisions, however. For example, on cable television, the Disney Channel lags behind Nickelodeon and the Cartoon Network in capturing young viewers aged 2 to 11, and critics say the reason is that Disney hasn't kept up with contemporary tastes.

Some company insiders have grumbled that Eisner insists on making too many decisions himself, rather than delegating them to the people who are closest to their audience. The company has grown from a cartoon studio to an entertainment conglomerate, and the chief executive's involvement in day-to-day decisions may be incompatible with the company's size. A former Disney executive told the *Fortune* reporter, "The company has changed and the world has changed, but Michael hasn't changed. Now he's got to change." Eisner's explanation: "If there's an area where I think I can add value, I dive in."[26]

Walt Disney

Can you see evidence of attribution errors in this example? What do you think may have contributed to them? One interesting finding is that cultural influences may shape people's use of the self-serving bias and attribution error. In a study of Korean managers, they tended not to exhibit the self-serving bias when accounting for group failure. Instead of attributing the failure to the group's members, they tended to accept responsibility for it.[27] Cultures, such as Korea, that place a high value on collectivism, as described in Chapter 2, may thus make different attributions than those that value individualism, such as the United States.

Managers' Uses of Attributions

Most organizations give their managers some responsibility for evaluating employees' work. In addition, the controlling function of managers requires that they routinely evaluate the performance of their group and identify areas where group performance is out of line with goals. Because of this, managers make attributions as part of their formal duties, and these attributions directly affect employees (for example, in determining whether a person will get a raise).

What we know of the attribution process tells us that when managers evaluate an individual's or group's performance, they will probably make comparisons. They will notice whether the persons or groups being evaluated have performed well in the past. They will consider whether they have noticed comparable performances from other individuals and groups. They will have opinions about whether the tasks at hand are comparable to tasks at which others have succeeded or failed. All of these comparisons are likely to shape whether the manager credits people for their successes and blames them for their failures. Furthermore, attribution biases may influence this process in favor of the manager's self-image.

Managers who recognize the weaknesses of this process can apply self-corrections. For instance, they can gather as much information as possible before reaching a conclusion and ask the people being evaluated to provide their own evaluations. In addition, they can reevaluate attributions that fall into a pattern of blaming the situation for their own failures but blaming other people for theirs.

These corrections are especially important in organizations today, where managers focus on teamwork and empowerment of employees. Managers need to lead their teams in making attributions about teamwork (for example, "Why did we do so much better this time?"). Not only will human biases creep into attributions about what the team did, but team members will make attributions about their individual contributions and those of their teammates. As team leaders, managers are responsible for ensuring that the teams perceive their performance accurately, so that they can accurately identify areas needing correction.

apply it

1. Think about the classes you took last term and the grades you received. Did you learn much? Were your grades good? To what do you attribute this success (or lack thereof)? Consider your talents and efforts, those of your instructors, and any external factors.

2. Do you think your instructors would make the same attributions as you made above? Explain.

We can prevent and overcome some of our misperceptions

Errors in attribution and other aspects of perception can make life more comfortable. They simplify our view of the world and protect us from having to adjust to new information. But that comfort can come at a high cost. People who are locked into their own view of the world will miss opportunities and problems that don't fit their existing ideas. Particularly in a diverse and changing organization, it is essential to expand our outlook and take into account other points of view. This challenge is especially important for managers, who must be able to identify and manage the contributions of diverse human resources.

There are ways to prevent and correct misperceptions at each stage of the perception process. At the attention stage, we can be aware of our expectations and make an extra effort to notice information that does not fit those expectations. One way to do this is to discuss situations with people who are likely to share a different perspective. They may raise additional possibilities to explore. Hearing those possibilities may make them an area of interest, and thus something we are likely to notice.

Similarly, in the organization stage of perception, it is helpful to be aware of your scripts and prototypes. Make a habit of checking the contents of these schemas to see if they fit other people's scripts and prototypes.

Also, ask yourself how well the scripts and prototypes apply to the situation at hand. You can become more sensitive to the use of schemas by learning about the ones a variety of other people use. The more people and situations you are familiar with, the better prepared you will be to adapt your scripts and prototypes when the situation calls for modification. For instance, the administrators of the Massachusetts Institute of Technology (MIT) tested their schemas when members of MIT's faculty accused the prestigious university of sex discrimination.

Several years ago, the Massachusetts Institute of Technology disappointed one of its professors, molecular biologist Nancy Hopkins, by dropping a popular course Hopkins had helped to establish. MIT then added insult to that injury. It also allowed the cofounder of the course, a man, to develop a book and CD-ROM package based on the course. Hopkins evaluated her two decades at MIT and decided the decisions were part of a pattern of sexual discrimination at MIT—and that she had suffered quietly long enough.

Professor Hopkins and several of her colleagues complained to MIT's administration that it wasn't treating faculty members evenhandedly. They requested permission to form a committee to research the problem. As scientists themselves, the administrators saw merit in this approach, and the faculty group began gathering data. They tallied the percentage of female undergraduates, graduate students, faculty, and department heads, noting a steady decline in the percentages as they moved from the bottom to the top of the hierarchy. (In fact, MIT had never had any female department heads.) They recorded membership of academic committees, and few women were on the important ones. They interviewed male and female colleagues about their experiences. Interview data showed women were more likely than men to feel like outsiders in departmental decision making and were less likely to receive generous counteroffers when other organizations sought to hire them away. They even measured office space, concluding that the amount of space allocated to women averaged half the amount granted to their male colleagues.

When the committee recently presented the data to MIT's administrators, the administrators agreed the institution had a problem. MIT issued a report calling sex discrimination a major challenge the institution would face. It committed to placing more women in faculty positions. The women already in such positions hope this step will be the first of many.[28] MIT's effort to become aware of its assumptions is at least a positive beginning toward change.

**Massachusetts
Institute of Technology**

Misperceptions in the interpretation stage may take the form of attribution or contrast errors. To correct errors of interpretation, spell out your interpretation and compare it with that of other people who observed the same stimuli. If you interpret the situation differently, ask how the other people arrived at a different interpretation. Perhaps they paid attention to different stimuli or organized information differently. Even if you cannot agree on whose perception was most accurate, at least you will identify areas of controversy and perhaps gain some understanding about why your perceptions differ.

In the retrieval stage, people can guard against biases by recording relevant information as they receive it so that recall will not be as selective. For example, if your job includes evaluating your own performance or that of others', you can keep an ongoing log of accomplishments and other performance data. When it is time to evaluate performance, you can review all the information in the log, not just the incidents you retrieve from memory.

People can also make retrieval more accurate by intentionally looking for different points of view. People will be likely to retrieve different elements of a situation, and together these viewpoints will draw a more complete picture. For example, Ron Pearson, the chief executive of the Hy-Vee supermarket chain, decided that managers at his company should not per-

Market share and profits for General Motors Corp. dropped during the 1980s and 1990s. At first, the corporation's management attributed the slump in profits to the need to tighten its belt—to use fewer workers and lower production costs. After reexamining relevant information and looking for different points of view, the world's largest carmaker has come up with a different judgment: Build cars people want. To capitalize on this new plan, the company is moving more aggressively and faster. "There were times when great ideas came through, but things weren't in place to get them done," states Ed Welburn (photo), director of GM's Corporate Brand Center. With new product ideas, GM stole the buzz at recent auto shows by uncloaking such concept cars as its Chevrolet SSR, a cross between a pickup and a roadster (Welburn was the lead designer). Concept cars measure public response to innovative product ideas. In a survey of 900 people attending the auto shows, the SSR ranked near the top, providing GM with more relevant information to store and retrieve to make future business decisions. (Source: © Donna Terek)

ceive the industry's standard employee turnover of 51 percent a year as a given. Rather, he instituted a survey of outgoing employees to find out why they were leaving. Over one-third complained that they weren't appreciated and that managers didn't pay much attention to them. Pearson was surprised: "That's something we thought we were good at." Of these employees, he learned further, half had left the company before receiving a performance review. So Pearson attributed part of the turnover to a need for more frequent performance reviews.[29] Even if you must evaluate a situation alone, you can try to minimize perceptual errors by thinking about the situation from different points of view.

In the judgment stage, remember that people tend to arrive at conclusions that support earlier judgments. If your judgment does not match that of others who are perceiving the same situation, explore the reasons for the difference. At what stage of the perception process did your perception differ from the other people's? Consider whether correcting an error you made at an earlier stage will produce a different judgment. Or do you and others weight the information differently? So many individual and cultural factors shape perception that you and the others may never arrive at the same judgment. Even so, the process of trying to prevent and correct perceptual errors can help you appreciate more varied ways of understanding a situation and perhaps lead you to more informed decisions and more creative solutions to problems.

Management consultant Peter Drucker recounts an example of a publishing company where managers examined their perceptions and developed a winning strategy as a result.[30] At a typical book publisher, the majority of sales and an even greater share of profits come from selling the "backlist," that is, the titles that are at least a year old. But most publishers invest most of their marketing dollars in selling the company's new titles. At the board of directors meeting of one large book publisher, a director asked the board to take a fresh look. She asked, "If we were to start now, knowing what we do about the source of our profits, would we handle the backlist the same way?" The board members, now perceiving the situation as one in which they could create a unique strategy, unanimously agreed they would *not* handle the backlist the same way. They abandoned their old prototypes about backlists and set up an entire unit devoted to the backlist, freeing others in the organization to concentrate on new titles. A couple of years later, the company's sales from the backlist had tripled, and its profits had doubled. As this example illustrates, an organization needs to manage its perceptions as well as its assets in order to carry out the kinds of transformation necessary for future success.

apply it

1. Think of a situation recently where you and a friend observed the same thing—a conversation with someone, someone's behavior—but drew different conclusions. Go back through the event from the two perspectives. Where do the two perceptions differ—at the attention, organization, interpretation, retrieval, or judgment stages? What are the possible causes of these differences? Could any misperceptions have been corrected? If so, how?

2. Remember a time when you had a first impression of someone who you got to know better later. Was your initial perception accurate or inaccurate? What helped confirm your impression or change your mind about the person?

summary OF KEY CONCEPTS

- **Perception is a multistage process.** Perception is the process by which people notice and make sense of information from the environment. It is a multistage process involving attention, organization, interpretation, retrieval, and judgment. The process is influenced by characteristics of the perceiver, stimulus, and situation.

- **Our perceptions are subject to distortion.** The process of perception is not entirely objective. Rather, people engage in perceptual defense, protecting themselves by perceiving things that are pleasant and fit existing views while ignoring or disregarding stimuli that would be disturbing or unpleasant. They pay attention selectively, and they simplify the way they organize and interpret information. For example, people use stereotypes, the halo error (or horns effect), and errors in contrasting stimuli. People also are selective about the information they retrieve, being influenced by their expectations, existing points of view, and performance cues. Perceptual biases

may compound themselves through the assimilation effect, and they may produce a self-fulfilling prophecy.

- **People make attributions to explain behavior.** Attributions may be internal (ascribing an outcome to ability or effort) or external (ascribing an outcome to luck or task difficulty). People base these attributions on their perceptions of consensus, consistency, and distinctiveness. Attributions are subject to biases. People tend to make internal attributions about their successes and external attributions about their failures. They tend to rely too much on internal attributions about other people's behavior. Cultural influences also may shape attributions.

- **We can prevent and overcome some of our misperceptions.** Basic methods include being aware of our biases and seeking information about other people's perceptions. In doing so, it is helpful to intentionally seek different points of view and to explore the reasons for differences.

KEY terms

perception, p. 128
attention, p. 129
schemas, p. 131
script, p. 131
prototype, p. 132
interpretation, p. 133
projection, p. 134
attribution, p. 134
retrieval, p. 134

judgment, p. 134
perceptual defense, p. 139
expectations, p. 139
stereotype, p. 140
halo error, p. 141
contrast effect, p. 141
anchoring and adjustment effect, p. 142
performance cues, p. 142

assimilation effect, p. 143
priming, p. 143
confirmation bias, p. 143
self-fulfilling prophecy, p. 143
consensus, p. 147
consistency, p. 147
distinctiveness, p. 148
self-serving bias, p. 148
fundamental attribution error, p. 148

DISCUSSION questions

1. As an employee, why is it important for you to understand the stages of your boss's perception process? As a manager, why is it important for you to understand the stages of your employees' perception processes?

2. Right now, pay attention for several minutes. Jot down all the stimuli that you notice around you. Then compare your list with those of your classmates. Which stimuli are noted by everyone? Which are only noted by one or two people?

3. Think of a time when you overheard one side of a conversation—on the phone, behind a door, or the like. What exactly did you hear? What did you imagine the other person said? Now, think of a possibility other than what you initially imagined. How might this possibility change the content or outcome of the conversation? How might this type of situation cause problems in the workplace?

4. Think of a brief script for one of the following scenarios:
   • asking your parents if you can borrow their car
   • asking your boss for a day off
   • breaking up with a boyfriend or girlfriend
   • inviting a friend over for dinner

   If possible, try your script out on a classmate. How effective is it? Why is it successful or unsuccessful?

5. Suppose you work for a firm where the design department is known as being creative and not worried about budgets; the accounting department is known as being conservative, unimaginative, and miserly. How might these prototypes be accurate or inaccurate? What types of problems might they cause among employees of the different departments?

6. Imagine you walked into your boss's supposedly empty office to leave a report on the desk, and found another employee there, closing a drawer to the desk. How would you interpret this information? Why? Discuss your interpretation with your classmates.

7. If you wanted to be noticed in a business meeting that you knew would be attended by middle-aged men wearing dark suits, what steps might you take to generate positive attention?

8. Suppose you are a manager for a company that has been going through tough times—sales have been down, there have been recent layoffs, and rumors are running wild that the firm may be sold to a company overseas. How might you actually make use of employees' perceptual defenses (without being untruthful) to motivate them to continue to work in the face of such upheaval and uncertainty?

9. Make a list of assumptions that you have made about a group of people—say, senior citizens, psychology majors, or tennis players. Do you have any friends or family that are members of the group? Do they fit your stereotype or not? Why is it important for a manager to be aware of any stereotypes that he or she holds about groups of people?

10. How might the organizer of a road-race fundraiser for a nonprofit organization use the self-fulfilling prophecy to motivate volunteers?

11. If everyone in your class scored an A on the final exam for this class, how would you explain the outcome? Why? If everyone *except you* scored an A, how would you explain the outcome? Why?

12. In what ways can people prevent and correct misperceptions at each stage of the perception process? Why is this an important goal for managers?

SELF-DISCOVERY exercise

Accuracy of Perceptions

PURPOSE: To understand how accurately we perceive our commonplace world.

PROCEDURE: This is a timed test (10 minutes). Place your answer to the left of the number; you are encouraged to guess.

_____ 1. On a standard traffic light, is the green on top or on bottom?

_____ 2. The stripes of a man's tie usually slant down in what direction from the wearer's view (left, right, both)?

_____ 3. In which hand is the Statue of Liberty's torch?

_____ 4. Name the six colors in the Campbell's soup label.

_____ 5. What two letters of the alphabet do not appear on a telephone dial?

____ **6.** What two digits on a telephone dial are not accompanied by letters?

____ **7.** When you walk, does your right arm swing with your right leg or your left leg?

____ **8.** How many matches are in a standard pack?

____ **9.** On the American flag, is the uppermost stripe red or white?

____ **10.** What is the lowest number on an FM radio dial?

____ **11.** On a standard typewriter, over which number is the "%" symbol?

____ **12.** Which way does the red diagonal slash go in the international "no parking" or "no smoking" signs?

____ **13.** How many channels are on a standard VHF television dial?

____ **14.** Which side of a woman's blouse has the buttonholes?

____ **15.** On the California license plate, is the state name at the top or the bottom?

____ **16.** In which direction do the blades on a fan rotate?

____ **17.** Whose face is on a dime?

____ **18.** How many sides does a stop sign have?

____ **19.** Do books have their even-numbered pages on the left or the right?

____ **20.** How many lug nuts are on a standard American car wheel?

____ **21.** How many sides are there on a standard pencil?

____ **22.** Sleepy, Happy, Sneezy, Grumpy, Dopey, and Doc. Name the seventh dwarf.

____ **23.** How many hot dog buns are in a standard package?

____ **24.** On which card in the deck is the cardmaker's trademark?

____ **25.** On the back of a $5 bill is the Lincoln Memorial. What's in the center of the back of a $1 bill?

____ **26.** There are 12 buttons on a touch-tone telephone. What symbols are on the two buttons that bear no digits?

____ **27.** How many curves are in a standard paper clip?

____ **28.** Does a merry-go-round turn clockwise or counterclockwise?

Scoring:
26–28 Excellent
23–25 Good
18–22 Okay
14–17 Fair

Discussion:
1. What are some reasons you may fail to perceive, or perceive incorrectly, your commonplace world?
2. How much of our perception comes from experiences stored in our subconscious (those items at which you guessed)?
3. Is it important to perceive our immediate environment/surroundings accurately? Objectively? Why? Why not?

Answers
1. Bottom
2. To the right
3. Right
4. Blue, red, white, black, gold, yellow
5. Q, Z
6. 1,0
7. Left
8. 20
9. Red
10. 88
11. 5
12. Top left to bottom right
13. 12 (no #1)
14. Right
15. Top
16. Clockwise as you look at it
17. Roosevelt
18. 8
19. Left
20. 5
21. 6
22. Bashful
23. 6
24. Ace of Spades
25. ONE
26. *, #
27. 3
28. Counterclockwise

ORGANIZATIONAL BEHAVIOR in your life

We hope this chapter has opened your eyes to the ways that you—and everyone else—perceive an event, from the attention stage through the judgment stage. To develop your awareness further, go to a public place where there are a lot of people—a mall, a quadrangle at your college or university, the cafeteria, a sporting event, or the like. Take a pad of paper with you. Find a place to sit or stand, and pay attention to the stimuli around you, including the actions of people. Jot down as many stimuli as you can in a 15-minute period.

When you get back to your study area, begin to organize the information, noting the method you use for finding a pattern to the stimuli. Now, begin to interpret what you experienced, looking for explanations for what you observed and why. Next, retrieve information about past events to support your interpretation. Finally, write a description of your 15-minute observation, concluding with a judgment about the events you observed. Share your experience with the class, discussing what you each learned about the way you gather and make sense of information around you.

ORGANIZATIONAL BEHAVIOR news flash

On Wall Street, perception is everything. Never is this more apparent than when earnings are different from expectations. Executives often try to manipulate investors' perceptions of their companies by releasing information on profits early to lower expectations or to explain their view of the company's performance.

Pick a company you are interested in and read some recent press releases on profits and performance. To find them, check the news listings on your search engine, such as Associated Press or Reuters, or type in the company's name and search its Web site. Some examples you might try are Apple Computer, Amazon.com, or Wal-Mart. When you've examined your articles, consider the following questions:

1. In what ways might the perceptions of certain sectors of the public as well as investors be subject to distortion?
2. What steps might managers take to prevent or overcome misperceptions?
3. Imagine that you are a spokesperson for one of the companies. Using specific concepts you've learned about perception (such as priming), write a brief press release announcing the company's recent performance, putting the event in a positive light.

global diversity EVENTS

It seems that hardly a week goes by when the Red Cross isn't in the news from somewhere around the world, providing relief to victims of natural disasters like hurricanes and tornadoes; finding shelter for refugees; offering food and medical care to people who have suffered from terrorism or war. All of this assistance requires millions of dollars, for the American Red Cross as well as for the different national branches of the International Red Cross around the world. It also requires an ability to communicate and operate across borders anywhere on the globe. Perception of the organization is key to the success of the Red Cross's fundraising efforts, and the perceptions of its employees and volunteers are also critical in their work.

Using news listings on your search engine, such as Reuters, AP, ZDNet News, and the like, look for stories about the Red Cross. You can also access the organization's different sites by typing in the keywords American Red Cross or International Red Cross. (Of course, if you find interesting stories about a similar nonprofit organization, you may use those.) When you find a good story or stories about the organization, consider the following questions:

1. What special skills do employees and top managers need in terms of understanding the perception process as they apply it to their work at this organization?

2. What types of attribution errors might organization workers make about the people they are serving? How about governments whose citizens need the organization's services?

3. What steps might a fundraising manager take in order to make a successful presentation about the organization to a potential corporate donor?

minicase **ISSUE**

Avoiding Misperceptions Based on Stereotypes

Background. The consequences of racial discrimination are damaging both to an organization and the individuals involved. However, this kind of behavior can be difficult to prevent and correct because it often involves misperceptions. These difficulties seem to have contributed to ongoing disputes at American Eagle, a commuter airline.

The dispute came to light when Tony Lee, an African-American former airplane mechanic, filed a racial discrimination lawsuit against the company. He complained that he was fired unfairly after years of harassment while working in American Eagle's Miami maintenance hangar. The facility was staffed with about 80 mechanics. Most were older, white maintenance workers, earning about half the amount they once brought home from jobs with Eastern Air Lines. The remaining few employees were primarily younger and African-American or Latino. The evidence suggests their older coworkers had little ability to perceive what it felt like to be in the minority.

What Happened? According to interviews with current and former American Eagle employees, as well as company documents and court depositions, racial slurs in many forms were common inside the airline's Miami hangar where Lee worked. Offensive graffiti reportedly adorned the facility's bulletin board and restroom walls. Cartoons and pictures depicted African-American people in terms of blatant and dehumanizing stereotypes—starving Somalians and even animals. After Lee was promoted to crew chief, the facility's decorations included a life-sized poster of a basketball player wearing a mop and carrying a watermelon, with Lee's name written across the chest. For people knowledgeable about the uglier aspects of American history, all these are familiar as symbols of racial hatred and oppression.

While some employees perceived these items as insulting and threatening, others saw them differently. Some employees saw the posting of cartoons and other paraphernalia as stress-relieving stunts in the

context of a high-stress environment. They noted that it was common for employees to engage in a variety of stunts, including playing around on the company's maintenance tractors. Employees also noted that jokes were told about many categories of people, on subjects ranging from ethnic background to weight to religion. In the context of the intentionally shocking radio shows popular on U.S. radio stations, they believed, racial slurs were just a form of humor. "Some people made fun of people, but mostly we were making fun of stereotypes," comments one white mechanic who was questioned in Lee's lawsuit. "I never meant to be offensive."

However, other workers, both African-American and white, claim they kept quiet about the problem because they were afraid to anger management and risk losing their jobs. "It was a very tough place for black people to work," recalls Christine Horne, a white mechanic.

Among the managers at American Eagle, some seem not to have perceived the potentially offensive activity at all. Edgar Cerezo, former maintenance base manager in Miami, tried to inform executives at American Eagle's regional headquarters in Nashville. Cerezo sent them a package containing cartoons and written slurs that had appeared in the hangar, but the company later said it had never received the package. Likewise, in a deposition related to Lee's lawsuit, Lee's supervisor denied noticing any racially based graffiti in the hangar. However, after a union official complained to the company, Cerezo received orders to paint over graffiti in the restroom.

American Eagle executives claim that they never saw any race-related problems at the Miami hangar. "You've got to know about it in order to deal with it," noted one spokesperson. This lack of knowledge could have involved a lack of attention or a failure to interpret the offensive items as offensive, rather than a lack of opportunities to see evidence of harassment. Several executives were reported to be in the maintenance hangar during the time when the life-size poster was on display, and many cartoons were posted in a

highly visible location near the time clock. Furthermore, executives expressed the judgment that employees should be able to feel in control of their environment—in particular, that the workers who had been
offended should have torn down the posters and cartoons. However, after a review triggered by a complaint to the Equal Employment Opportunity Commission, management did distribute a letter to employees
stating that "we will not tolerate continuation of this
conduct" and warning that anyone caught harassing
another employee would be fired. No one has yet
been fired for harassment.

Current Conditions. Recently, AMR (American
Eagle's parent) demolished the old Miami hangar and
moved all of its operations to the main American Airlines maintenance terminal. Although some workers
say that general working conditions have improved,
others perceive the situation differently: "Freedom of
expression is gone," laments a white mechanic. "The
good joking back and forth is gone."

1. Consider this case from the varying perspectives
   of the people involved. What causes "jokes" to be
   perceived differently by different groups? What
   characteristics of the perceiver are involved in this
   problem?
2. The hangar contained two fairly distinct groups of
   employees, older white male workers and
   younger racially and ethnically diverse workers. In
   addition to language and racial differences, do
   you think the different ages of the groups could
   have led to some of the problems? If so, how?
3. Why do you think upper management at the company did not make the same judgment about the
   problem that middle manager Edgar Cerezo did?
4. What perceptions would be most beneficial for
   the organization and its employees? How could
   they have used an understanding of the perception process to improve the situation at American
   Eagle?

Source: Scott McCartney, "What some call racist at American
Eagle, others say was in jest," *The Wall Street Journal,* April
20, 1999, pp. A1, A8.

five
CHAPTER

5

Sources of
Motivation

preview

After studying this chapter, you should be able to:

- Define *motivation* and discuss the differences between intrinsic and extrinsic motivation.

- Explain the differences between current approaches and traditional approaches to motivation.

- Explain the hierarchy of needs theory and its implications for motivation.

- Discuss the differences between the need for affiliation, need for achievement, and need for power.

- Explain how job characteristics influence employee motivation.

- Discuss the pros and cons of the job design approaches for need fulfillment.

- Give examples of how benefits help meet employees needs.

- Explain how the use of new manufacturing and communication technologies might adversely affect employees' higher order needs.

Sas Institute Meets Employees' Needs

James H. Goodnight is founder, chairman, and majority owner of SAS Institute, a highly profitable company whose main product is statistical software. The company's software helps customers quickly analyze large amounts of data. SAS Institute serves more than 30,000 customers in over 120 countries. Many employees see Goodnight as a benevolent dictator. Perks given to his 2,700 employees at the company's headquarters, located in a 200-acre campus in Raleigh, North Carolina, include private offices for all employees, a free clinic staffed with two doctors and six nurse practitioners, a 35,000-square- foot recreation facility, and a pianist who entertains daily in the lunchroom. Although the software industry is known for 60- to 80-hour weeks, SAS promotes a 35-hour weekly schedule and provides two company day-care centers. It is common practice for employees to receive an extra week of paid vacation between Christmas and New Year's, along with a bonus. Coffee break rooms are stocked with free soft drinks, fruit, candy, and pastries. SAS has an active eldercare program that helps locate nursing care facilities for employees who need to help an aging or ill parent. A full-time specialist helps employees select office furniture that is designed to alleviate stress and back and eye strain. An artist-in-residence helps them choose paintings for their office walls. SAS has funded housing subdivisions in the Cary, North Carolina, area. If employees purchase a home there, they get a 10 percent discount on the land. They also get discounts on country club memberships and are eligible for cheap airfare on Midway Airlines, in which Goodnight has a financial interest.

While providing a large range of unique perks, SAS Institute does not provide those that are fairly common in the software industry: The company doesn't offer stock options. SAS doesn't have commissions for its sales force because Goodnight believes they result in high-pressure sales tactics. SAS also doesn't have tuition reimbursement because Goodnight believes that this policy encourages employees to leave after they earn their degrees.

Meeting employee needs has had a positive effect for SAS Institute. As one management consultant commented, "Let's face it, the 'Big Brother' thing works. People are clamoring to get in there." Turnover has been close to 4 percent—that in an industry where turnover typically is greater than 20 percent. High performers seldom leave SAS to go to the competition, and the company receives a huge number of job applications each year.

Why do employees stay? It's not the salary. As one employee stated, "I could make more money somewhere else, and about twice a month headhunters call, but money isn't everything. You're treated as family here." One estimate is that SAS saves $50 million per year with its low turnover rate. This more than pays for the perks, which also buy loyalty and priceless levels of employee motivation.[1]

Organizations are focusing on the needs of their employees as never before, offering an array of benefits, reorganizing work processes to make them more interesting, giving employees more power to control their jobs. Why are they doing this? With today's reliance on knowledge workers and their unique abilities, it is important for organizations to ensure that their employees are committed and motivated to perform well. But what are the keys to employee motivation? Successful organizations are exploring that question and coming up with new answers to set themselves apart from their competitors, as SAS is doing.

The challenge for SAS Institute and other companies is to keep employee motivation consistent with organizational goals. Motivation is a challenge for organizations because motivation arises from within employees and typically differs for each employee. For example, Janice Rennie makes a staggering $350,000 a year selling residential real estate in Toronto; she attributes her success to the fact that she likes to listen carefully to clients and then find a house to meet their needs. Greg Storey is a skilled machinist who is challenged by writing programs for numerically controlled machines. After dropping out of college, he swept floors in a machine shop and was motivated to learn to run the machines. Frances Blais sells World Book Encyclopedia. She is a top salesperson, but she does not care about the $50,000-plus commissions: "I'm not even thinking money when I'm selling. I'm really on a crusade to help children read well." In stark contrast, Rob Michaels gets sick to his stomach before he goes to work. Rob is a telephone salesperson who spends all day trying to get people to buy products they do not need, and the rejections are painful. His motivation is money; he earned $120,000 in the past year and cannot make anywhere near that amount doing something else.[2]

Rob Michaels is motivated by money, Janice Rennie by her love of listening and problem solving, Frances Blais by the desire to help children read, and Greg Storey by the challenge of mastering numerically controlled machinery. Each person is motivated to perform, yet each has different reasons for doing so. With such diverse motivations, it is a challenge to motivate employees toward common organizational goals.

In this chapter we review several perspectives on motivation and cover the content theories that describe the employee needs and processes associated with motivation. **Content theories** emphasize the needs that motivate people. At any point in time, people have basic needs such as those for food, achievement, or monetary reward. These needs translate into an internal drive that motivates specific behaviors in an attempt to fulfill them. An individual's needs are like a hidden catalog of the things he or she wants and will work to get. The hierarchy of needs theory, the ERG theory, acquired needs theory, cognitive evaluation theory, two-factor theory, and the job design approaches all help you understand what motivates people. The second part of the chapter describes how a work environment can be created to meet employee needs and hence elicit appropriate and successful work behaviors. Tactics might include ensuring that the organization's benefits meet employees' needs and reward them for directing energy toward attainment of organizational goals. Or they might involve redesigning jobs using new technology so that employees' achievement or safety needs are fulfilled.

content theories

Motivation theories that emphasize the needs that motivate people.

Motivation energizes, directs, and maintains behavior

Most of us get up in the morning, go to school or work, and behave in ways that are uniquely our own. We respond to our environment and the people in it with little thought about why we work hard, enjoy certain classes, or

motivation

The forces either within or external to a person that energize, direct, and maintain behavior.

find some hobbies or sports so much fun. Yet all these behaviors are motivated by something. **Motivation** refers to the forces either within or external to a person that energize, direct, and maintain behavior.[3] An individual's motivation influences enthusiasm, directs energy toward an outcome, and maintains behavior even when the behavior does not immediately result in a reward or the work environment makes it difficult to perform the behavior. Employee motivation affects productivity, and part of a manager's job is to channel motivation toward the accomplishment of organizational goals. The study of motivation helps us understand what prompts people to initiate action, what influences their choice of action, and why they persist in that action over time.

A simple model of human motivation is illustrated in Exhibit 5.1. People have basic needs, such as food, achievement, or monetary gain, that translate into an internal tension. This tension motivates specific behaviors to fulfill the needs. The behaviors may be positive or negative from an organization's perspective. Positive behaviors include high quantity or quality of work performed or good customer service, and organizations want to enhance them. Negative behaviors from an organization's perspective include withdrawal behaviors such as absenteeism and counterproductive behaviors such as theft. Keep in mind that although absenteeism and theft are seen as negative by the organization, individuals may steal or fail to show up for work because it helps them fulfill a need. For example, a person may steal because he can sell the stolen property to a pawn shop and get money to buy groceries or drugs. People who steal may also do so because it meets their need to feel important or challenged. To the extent that the behavior is successful, the person is rewarded by satisfying the need. The reward also informs the person that the behavior was appropriate and can be used again in the future.

Intrinsic and Extrinsic Rewards

intrinsic rewards

The satisfaction a person receives while performing a particular action. Examples include feelings of accomplishment and challenge.

extrinsic rewards

Rewards given by another person as a result of a particular action, such as completion of a task, good performance, or positive behavior. Examples include promotions and pay increases.

Rewards are of two types: intrinsic and extrinsic. **Intrinsic rewards** are the satisfactions a person receives while performing a particular action. The completion of a complex task may give a pleasant feeling of accomplishment, or solving a problem that benefits others may fulfill a personal mission. For example, Frances Blais sells encyclopedias for the intrinsic reward of helping children read well. **Extrinsic rewards** are given by another person as a result of the employee's performing a particular action such as completion of a task, good performance, or positive behavior. For example, a manager may recommend promotions or pay increases for employees who perform well. Rob Michaels, who hates his sales job, nevertheless is motivated by the extrinsic reward of high pay.

The importance of motivation as illustrated in Exhibit 5.1 is that it can lead to high performance within organizations. One recent study found that high employee motivation goes hand in hand with high organizational performance and profits.[4] So, managers can use motivation theory to help satisfy employees' needs and simultaneously encourage high work performance. Particularly in today's era of low unemployment, with many companies scrambling to find and keep qualified workers, managers are searching for the right combination of techniques and rewards to keep

exhibit 5.1
Model of Motivation

NEED Creates desire to fulfill needs (food, friendship, recognition, achievement) → **BEHAVIOR** Results in actions to fulfill needs → **REWARDS** Satisfy needs; intrinsic or extrinsic rewards

FEEDBACK Reward informs person whether behavior was appropriate and should be used again

workers happy and productive. Workers at many of today's leading companies say they are motivated by factors such as a fun, challenging work environment; flexibility that provides a balance between work and personal life; and the potential to learn, grow, and be creative in their jobs.[5] However, it is important to emphasize that studies of successful companies suggest that helping employees meet both their basic and higher level needs is likely to result in the highest levels of motivation.[6] That is, organizations need to provide employment security and high wages along with a positive working environment.

Foundations of Motivation

Assumptions about motivation and use of rewards depend on your perspective. Three distinct perspectives of employee motivation are the traditional approach, the human relations approach, and the human resource approach.[7] Scientific management, the Hawthorne studies, and Theory X and Theory Y, described in Chapter 1, have important implications for motivation. The most recent theories about motivation represent a fourth perspective called *contemporary approaches*.

Traditional Approach Scientific management is an example of the traditional approach to motivation, which emphasized increasing the efficiency of an employee's job and providing economic rewards for high performance. This approach led to the development of systems in which people were paid strictly on the quantity and quality of their work outputs. The traditional approach emphasized external factors in motivation, those related to economic rewards for productivity.

Human Relations Approach The view of *economic man* was gradually replaced by a more sociable view of employees in managers' minds, partly in response to the Hawthorne studies. The human relations approach emphasized that noneconomic rewards—such as congenial work groups that met social needs—seemed more important than money as a motivator of work behavior.[8] For the first time, workers were studied as people, and the concept of *social man* was born.

Human Resource Approach The human resource approach carries the concepts of economic man and social man farther to introduce the concept of the *whole person*. Human resource theory suggests that employees are complex and motivated by many factors. For example, the work by McGregor on Theory X and Theory Y argued that people want to do a good job and

Luis Espinoza has two careers and loves them both. In his regular job, he is a process electrical systems technician for the Ispat Inland/Nippon steel-finishing plant in New Carlisle, Indiana. In his second job he is founder of Inca Quality Foods, which distributes and sells Hispanic food products in grocery stores, including such chains as Kroger. His job with Inca brings him intrinsic rewards because of its roots in one of his great passions: his Hispanic heritage. Espinoza's knowledge of the particular tastes of consumers who come from Mexico, the Caribbean, and Central America gives him an edge with supermarket customers. It is also making his entrepreneurial venture a great success. With approximately $500,000 in revenues last year, "Inca is growing faster than I can handle," Espinoza says.
(Source: © Jeff Sciortino)

that work is as natural and healthy as play. From a motivational perspective, assuming that employees are competent and able to make major contributions to an organization means that more attention should be placed on ensuring that job and work conditions spur greater motivation levels.

Contemporary Approaches   Contemporary approaches to employee motivation are dominated by three types of theories, each of which will be discussed in this chapter and in Chapter 6. In this chapter we discuss content theories, which stress the analysis of *underlying human needs*. Content theories provide insight into the needs of people in organizations and help managers understand how needs can be satisfied in the workplace. Process theories and reinforcement theories and applications are discussed in Chapter 6. Process theories concern the *thought processes that influence behavior*. They focus on how employees seek rewards in work circumstances. Reinforcement theories focus on how employees can be *encouraged to learn desired work behaviors*. In Exhibit 5.1, content theories focus on the concepts in the first box, process theories on those in the second, and reinforcement theories on those in the third.

apply it

1. Observe the behavior of a friend or fellow employee. What needs seem to be met by his or her behavior? What types of rewards does the person receive as a result of the behavior?

2. The news is filled with stories of computer hackers attacking companies' Web sites. Considering that hacking is criminal behavior and could be punished severely, what might be motivating these hackers? Consider both intrinsic and extrinsic rewards, and create a list.

Employees are motivated by different types of needs

Content theories of motivation recognize that motivation is based on needs and the extent to which they are satisfied either on or off the job. These needs range from basic human needs of food, water, and sex to higher level needs such as belongingness, esteem, achievement, and self-fulfillment.

Hierarchy of Needs

hierarchy of needs

Motivation theories that propose that humans are motivated by multiple needs and that these needs vary in importance.

Probably the most famous content theory was developed by Abraham Maslow.[9] Maslow's **hierarchy of needs** theory proposes that humans are motivated by multiple needs and that these needs vary in importance, as illustrated in Exhibit 5.2. Maslow identified five general types of motivating needs; in order of most basic to higher level, they are as follows:

1. *Physiological needs*   These are the most basic human physical needs, including food, water, and sex. In an organizational setting, these needs are reflected in the needs for adequate heat, air, and base salary to ensure survival.

2. *Safety needs*   These are needs for a safe and secure physical and emotional environment and freedom from threats—that is, for freedom

exhibit **5.2**

Maslow's Hierarchy of Needs

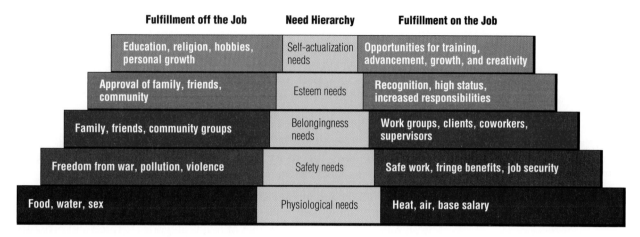

Fulfillment off the Job	Need Hierarchy	Fulfillment on the Job
Education, religion, hobbies, personal growth	Self-actualization needs	Opportunities for training, advancement, growth, and creativity
Approval of family, friends, community	Esteem needs	Recognition, high status, increased responsibilities
Family, friends, community groups	Belongingness needs	Work groups, clients, coworkers, supervisors
Freedom from war, pollution, violence	Safety needs	Safe work, fringe benefits, job security
Food, water, sex	Physiological needs	Heat, air, base salary

from violence and for an orderly society. In a workplace, safety needs reflect the needs for safe jobs, fringe benefits, and job security.

3. *Belongingness needs*   These needs reflect the desire to be accepted by our peers, have friendships, be part of a group, and be loved. In an organization, these needs influence the desire for good relationships with coworkers, participation in a work group, and a positive relationship with supervisors.

4. *Esteem needs*   These needs relate to the desire for a positive self-image and to receive attention, recognition, and appreciation from others. Within organizations, esteem needs reflect a motivation for recognition, an increase in responsibility, high status, and credit for contributions to the organization.

5. *Self-actualization needs*   These needs represent the desire for self-fulfillment, which is the highest need category. They concern developing our full potential, increasing our competence, and becoming a better person. Self-actualization needs can be met in an organization by providing people with opportunities to grow, be creative, and acquire training for challenging assignments and advancement.

According to Maslow's theory, low-order needs take priority—they must be satisfied before higher order needs are activated, so the needs are satisfied in sequence: Physiological needs come before safety needs, safety needs before social needs, and so on. A person concerned about physical safety will devote his or her efforts to securing a safer environment and will not be concerned with esteem needs or self-actualization needs. But once a need is satisfied, it decreases in importance and the next higher need is activated. At All Metro Health Care in Lynbrook, New York, CEO Irving Edwards set up a special "customer service" department for his home health aides to help meet their basic needs, such as applying for food stamps and finding transportation and child care. Three employees are available solely to help workers with these issues. Once these lower level needs are met, employees usually desire to have higher level needs met in the workplace, so Irving developed programs such as an award for caregiver of the year, essay contests with prizes, and special recognition for high scores on quarterly training exercises.[10]

ERG Theory

Clayton Alderfer proposed a modification of Maslow's theory in an effort to simplify it and respond to criticisms of its lack of verification.[11] His **ERG theory** identified three categories of needs:

1. *Existence needs*   needs for physical well-being
2. *Relatedness needs*   needs for satisfactory relationships with others
3. *Growth needs*   needs for development of human potential and the desire for personal growth and increased competence

The ERG model and Maslow's need hierarchy are similar because both presume that individuals move up the hierarchy one step at a time. However, Alderfer reduced the number of need categories to three and proposed that movement up the hierarchy is more complex, reflecting a frustration-regression principle, that is, failure to meet a high-order need may trigger regression to an already fulfilled lower order need. Thus, a worker who cannot fulfill a need for personal growth may revert to a lower order need and redirect his or her efforts toward making a lot of money, requesting a job transfer, or looking for a job outside the company. The ERG model is less rigid than Maslow's need hierarchy, suggesting that individuals may move down as well as up the hierarchy, depending on their ability to satisfy needs.

Need hierarchy theory helps explain why organizations find ways to recognize employees and encourage their participation in decision making. Fine Host Corp., a food service company in Greenwich, Connecticut, regularly gives quality awards and posts workers' names in company buildings to recognize their good work. Employees receive framed certificates when they complete training courses. According to president and CEO Richard Kerley, "Though there may be economic restraints on what we pay them, there are no restraints on the recognition we give them."[12] The importance of filling higher level belongingness and esteem needs on the job was illustrated by a young manager who said, "If I had to tell you in one sentence why I am motivated by my job, it is because when I know what is going on and how I fit into the overall picture, it makes me feel important."

Many companies are finding that having fun at work is also a great, high-level motivator, particularly for today's young, well-educated, computer-savvy workers who are in high demand and can command high salaries wherever they go. At Vantage One Communications Group, a marketing firm in Cleveland, Ohio, employees regularly take breaks by playing foosball in the company's rec room. Such diversions lighten up the daily routine and create a feeling of belongingness and community. An employee of GoldMine Software, a Pacific Palisades, California, company where the refrigerator is regularly stocked with Sierra Nevada and Pete's Wicked Ale, puts it this way: "It's like the coolest house I lived in at college; everyone has this weird, wacky thing about them—everyone's totally different—but we all get along so well."[13]

Some companies, including Time and Xerox, use sabbaticals to help employees rest, recharge, and meet a variety of needs.

Sabbaticals are leaves of absence that often include full pay and benefits. Many of Time's employees are creative people who use sabbaticals as an opportunity for rest, relaxation, and personal growth. The intent of the program was to give employees a chance to focus on personal priorities, which would allow them to be more productive and creative when they returned to work. The sabbaticals are available to employees with 15 or more years of service. Employees may take up to six months' leave or break the leave into two separate three-month leaves. Employees receive up to 50 percent of their normal pay.

Xerox's sabbatical program helps employees meet the needs they have to help others. Xerox's leave program allows employees to take up to one year off. Xerox pays the employees' full salaries while they work for the nonprofit group of their choosing (religious or political activities are excluded). Other organizations such as McDonald's and Hewitt Associates (a management consulting company) also use sabbaticals to help employees cope with job stress.[14]

Time Inc. and Xerox Corp.

Acquired Needs Theory

Another needs theory focuses on how individuals' needs can change over time. The **acquired needs theory** proposes that certain types of needs are acquired during an individual's lifetime. In other words, people are not born with these needs but may learn them through their life experiences.[15] The three needs most frequently studied are these:

1. *Need for achievement* the desire to accomplish something difficult, attain a high standard of success, master complex tasks, and surpass others.
2. *Need for affiliation* the desire to form close personal relationships, avoid conflict, and establish warm friendships.
3. *Need for power* the desire to influence or control others, be responsible for others, and have authority over others.

Early life experiences determine whether people acquire these needs. For example, if children are encouraged to do things for themselves and receive praise and other rewards, they will acquire a need to achieve. If they are rewarded for forming warm human relationships, they will develop a need for affiliation. If they get satisfaction from controlling others, they will acquire a need for power.

For more than 20 years, David McClelland studied human needs and their implications for management. People with a high need for achievement tend to be entrepreneurs. They like to do better than their competitors and take sensible business risks. On the other hand, people who have a high need for affiliation are successful "integrators," whose job is to coordinate the work of several departments in an organization.[16] Integrators typically include project managers, who must have excellent people skills. People high in need for affiliation are able to establish positive working relationships with others.

A high need for power often is associated with successful attainment of

acquired needs theory
A need theory that proposes that certain types of needs are acquired during an individual's lifetime.

need for achievement
The desire to accomplish something difficult, attain a high standard of success, master complex tasks, and surpass others.

need for affiliation
The desire to form close personal relationships, avoid conflict, and establish warm friendships.

need for power
The desire to influence or control others, be responsible for others, and have authority over others.

During her 15-year career as a renowned executive assistant for a high-powered Wall Street CEO, Melba Duncan excelled. Capitalizing on her experience and past success, Duncan then founded New York City–based Duncan Group Inc., the only executive-search firm in the country that deals exclusively with administrative-support professionals. Since 1985 Duncan has been placing cream-of-the crop executive assistants with companies such as IBM, Home Depot, and Bankers Trust. With over 1,500 employee-search companies in North America, Duncan's niche in the market has brought her success and power; in a recent year the company racked up close to $1 million in revenues. (Source: © Erica Freudenstein)

top levels in an organizational hierarchy. For example, McClelland studied managers at AT&T for 16 years and found that those with a high need for power were more likely to follow a path of continued promotion over time. More than half the employees at the top levels had a high need for power. In contrast, managers with a high need for achievement but a low need for power tended to peak earlier in their careers and at a lower level. The reason is that achievement needs can be met by accomplishing a task itself, but power needs can be met only when a person has reached a level where he or she can oversee and direct others. However, a high need for power can also be dysfunctional. If a person generates conflict that helps him or her meet personal needs, such as improving a personal reputation or increasing personal influence, it can hurt the organization's effectiveness.

apply it

1. Choose one of two roles: student or employee. Consider your needs in that role. Using Alderfer's ERG theory, list the existence needs, relatedness needs, and growth needs that your role satisfies. Note any experiences that frustrated your efforts at satisfying your needs. As a result of your frustration, did you refocus on lower level needs? Which needs? Did anything motivate you to strive again for meeting higher level needs? What motivated you?

Motivation may come from performing a behavior or job

Several of the need theories explicitly recognize that employee needs can be met and motivation influenced by simply performing a behavior or by holding a job with certain job characteristics. These theories include cognitive evaluation theory, two-factor theory, and job characteristics theory.

Cognitive Evaluation Theory

Cognitive evaluation theory helps to explain the role of intrinsic motivation in a person's performance. As discussed earlier, a person who is motivated by intrinsic rewards performs without the motivation of external rewards. **Cognitive evaluation theory** takes this idea one step further, suggesting that providing extrinsic rewards for behaviors that previously had been intrinsically rewarding tends to decrease motivation.

According to cognitive evaluation theory, there are two motivational systems—an intrinsic system and an extrinsic system.[17] Intrinsic motivators include achievement, responsibility, and competence—motivators that come from performing the task or job. Extrinsic motivators include pay, promotion, feedback, and positive working conditions—motivators that come from the environment. Intrinsically motivated individuals believe their behavior is caused by internal needs, that is, they perform for their own achievement and satisfaction. Cognitive evaluation theory suggests that certain aspects of a work situation (e.g., the company's pay system) may lead an individual to question why he is performing a behavior. If such people come to believe they are performing a behavior because of pay or

cognitive evaluation theory

The theory that there are two motivational systems—an intrinsic system and an extrinsic system. One of its major assumptions is that providing extrinsic rewards for behaviors that previously had been intrinsically rewarding tends to decrease motivation.

working conditions rather than an internal need to perform well, this will decrease their intrinsic motivation.[18] And intrinsic motivation is believed to be more desirable than extrinsic motivation. The reason? Intrinsic motivation does not depend on variations in the work environment, which may be difficult to change. For example, external rewards such as promotions and pay increases can be limited by an organization's competitive environment.

Consider Dennis Gentry and his intrinsic motivation.[19] The 35-year-old is a senior software engineer with a six-figure income at the interactive television company TiVo Inc. He and his friends (engineers, accountants, and marketers) have their pick of great jobs at companies with stock option packages that promise wealth before they turn 40. Even though they're all making good salaries now, what they prize most is personal freedom. Gentry's motivation flows from his aptitude for programming—work that is his idea of play and has been his chief passion for more than ten years. He doesn't have to look for work. He's always just walked into companies and told them he wanted to be there. A friend of his "is working for the money, not because it's fun," he says. But "he's making too much to stop," Gentry explains.

The detrimental effects of extrinsic rewards on interest in a task have been shown in a number of studies. However, research suggests that simply providing extrinsic rewards does not automatically decrease intrinsic motivation.[20] Cognitive evaluation theory emphasizes that situational factors will only decrease intrinsic motivation if they are perceived to be controlling by an individual. Situational factors can enhance intrinsic motivation if they provide information about our competence and a sense of personal control. For example, positive feedback from colleagues can increase desire to perform a job well even though that feedback comes from colleagues in the environment (a situational factor) rather than from the task itself.

Two-Factor Theory

Frederick Herzberg developed another popular theory of motivation called the *two-factor theory*.[21] Herzberg interviewed hundreds of workers about times when they were highly motivated to work and other times when they were dissatisfied and unmotivated. Based on these findings, he developed the two-factor theory. The **two-factor theory** suggests that the work characteristics associated with dissatisfaction are quite different from those pertaining to satisfaction, which prompted the notion that two factors influence work motivation.

The two-factor theory is illustrated in Exhibit 5.3. The center of the scale is neutral, meaning that workers are neither satisfied nor dissatisfied. Herzberg believed that two entirely separate dimensions contribute to an employee's behavior at work. The first, called **hygiene factors,** involves the presence or absence of job dissatisfiers, such as working conditions, pay, company policies, and interpersonal relationships. When hygiene factors are poor, work is dissatisfying. However, good hygiene factors simply remove the dissatisfaction; they do not in themselves cause people to become highly satisfied and motivated in their work.

The second set of factors does influence job satisfaction. **Motivators** relate to high-level needs and include achievement, recognition, responsibility,

two-factor theory

The theory that two factors influence motivation. The work characteristics associated with dissatisfaction (hygiene factors) are quite different from those pertaining to satisfaction (motivators).

hygiene factors

The presence or absence of job dissatisfiers, such as working conditions, pay, company policies, and interpersonal relationships. When hygiene factors are poor, work is dissatisfying.

motivators

Factors related to high-level needs, such as achievement, recognition, responsibility, and opportunity for growth. When motivators are present, work is satisfying.

exhibit **5.3**
Herzberg's Two-Factor Theory

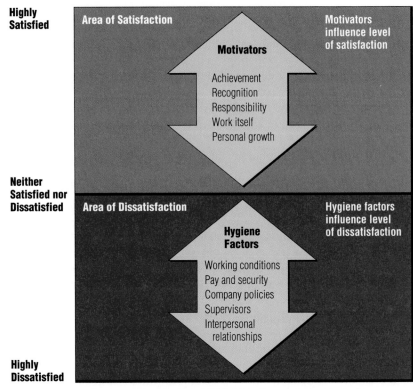

Source: Reprinted from *Organizational Dynamics,* Winter 1987 © 1987, with permission from Elsevier Science.

and opportunity for growth. Herzberg believed that when motivators are absent, workers are neutral toward work, but when they are present, workers are highly motivated and satisfied. Thus, hygiene factors and motivators represent two distinct factors that influence motivation. Hygiene factors work only in the area of dissatisfaction. Unsafe working conditions or a noisy work environment will cause people to be dissatisfied, but their correction will not lead to a high level of motivation and satisfaction. Motivators such as challenge, responsibility, and recognition must be in place before employees will be highly motivated to excel at their work.

The implications of the two-factor theory for organizations and their managers are clear. Providing hygiene factors will eliminate employee dissatisfaction but will not motivate workers to high achievement. On the other hand, recognition, challenge, and opportunities for personal growth are powerful motivators and can promote high satisfaction and performance. A manager's role is to remove dissatisfiers—that is, to provide hygiene factors sufficient to meet basic needs—and then use motivators to meet higher level needs and propel employees toward greater achievement and satisfaction.

Keep in mind, though, that Herzberg's theory has been criticized because researchers have often found that hygiene factors, as well as motivators, relate to job satisfaction.[22] However, his two-factor theory was the first to identify job-related factors that may be responsible for employee satisfaction and motivation. One of the major contributions of the two-factor theory was that it influenced further exploration into how job characteristics might meet employee needs. Managers at Outback Steakhouse have

IMPROVING MOTIVATION AT SANDSTROM PRODUCTS

After 13 years at Sandstrom Products, a manufacturer of paints and coatings, Leo Henkelman was thinking about quitting. He'd started as a paint runner, the lowest job in the plant, and worked his way up to a mill operator position. Henkelman spent his days mixing paints in a giant blender, following formulas supplied by the lab. As he gained knowledge and experience, he came up with a lot of good ideas for improving formulas; yet the guys in the lab continually ignored his suggestions. "It was like they hired me from the neck down," he said. "Warm body, strong back, weak mind." Increasing pressure from quality-conscious customers multiplied the frustration he shared with most of the operators, who felt powerless to change anything. Some workers, including Henkelman, just stopped caring. Finding no challenge at work, he

would show up with a hangover and just put in time until he could clock out and hit the bottle again. Top management knew the company had problems—for one thing, Sandstrom was hemorrhaging cash, losing money for the third year out of the last five. Things had to change, or Sandstrom would go broke.

1. If you were the president of Sandstrom Products, how would you motivate employees like Leo Henkelman to give their all to the company?
2. Is high motivation even possible in this kind of routine manufacturing operation?

Source: D. Whitford, "Before and After," *Inc.,* June 1995, pp. 44–50.

---

tried hard to ensure that employees experience positive hygiene factors at their restaurants.

Outback Steakhouse

With their years of experience in the restaurant business, Robert Basham, Timothy Gannon, and Chris Sullivan, founders of Outback Steakhouse, were acutely aware of the importance of hygiene factors in the food-service industry. The average restaurant is designed to maximize the number of customers that can be served in the dining room, often at the expense of the food preparation area. But Outback emphasizes the best possible spaces for servers and kitchen staff to do their jobs effectively, even at peak business times. Outback's dinner-only policy and maximum five-day workweek give managers and staff time for a life outside the restaurant, which cuts down on employee turnover. Each server handles only three tables at a time, ensuring first-class service to customers and higher tips for servers.

To motivate managers, Outback offers them ownership incentives and rewards. After making a $25,000 investment and signing a five-year contract, Outback managers receive 10 percent of the earnings of their restaurants each month. This cut of the profits provides the average manager with a total income of about $118,600 per year, far above the rest of the industry. In addition, managers receive about 4,000 shares of stock that are vested at the end of five years. Hourly staff also participate in a stock ownership plan. Managers are further motivated by the level of responsibility Outback bestows on them. Restaurant managers have the authority to make their own decisions, rather than merely implementing decisions dictated by headquarters.

Has Outback's motivational approach worked? The company grew to more than 200 stores in only six years and now operates 611 Outback Steakhouses and is approaching $2 billion in revenues. As Timothy Gannon put it, "We believe if you treat employees as if you were one of them and give them the right environment, they will blow you away with their performance."[23]

Job Characteristics Theory

Herzberg's two-factor theory laid the groundwork for researchers to investigate how job characteristics might meet employee needs. Research has identified four approaches that have been used to understand job characteristics and job design[24] These include the motivational approach, the mechanistic approach, the biological approach, and the perceptual-motor approach. Exhibit 5.4 shows the job characteristics that each of these

exhibit | **5.4**   Different Approaches for Designing Jobs

The Motivational Job Design Approach

1. *Autonomy*   Does the job allow freedom, independence, or discretion in work scheduling, sequence, methods, procedures, quality control, and other types of decisions?
2. *Intrinsic job feedback*   Do the work activities themselves provide direct, clear information about the effectiveness (in terms of quality and quantity) of job performance?
3. *Extrinsic job feedback*   Do other people in the organization (such as managers and coworkers) provide information about the effectiveness (in terms of quality and quantity) of job performance?
4. *Social interaction*   Does the job provide for positive social interaction (such as teamwork or coworker assistance)?
5. *Task/goal clarity*   Are the job duties, requirements, and goals clear and specific?
6. *Task variety*   Does the job have a variety of duties, tasks, and activities?
7. *Task identity*   Does the job require completion of a whole and identifiable piece of work? Does it give the incumbent a chance to do an entire piece of work from beginning to end?
8. *Ability/skill-level requirement*   Does the job require a high level of knowledge, skills, and abilities?
9. *Ability/skill variety*   Does the job require a variety of types of knowledge, skills, and abilities?
10. *Task significance*   Is the job significant and important compared with other jobs in the organization?
11. *Growth-learning*   Does the job allow opportunities for learning and growth in competence and proficiency?

The Mechanistic Job Design Approach

1. *Job specialization*   Is the job highly specialized in terms of purpose and/or activity?
2. *Specialization of tools and procedures*   Are the tools, procedures, materials, etc., used on this job highly specialized in terms of purpose?
3. *Task simplification*   Are the tasks simple and uncomplicated?
4. *Single activities*   Does the job require the incumbent to do only one task at a time? Does it not require the incumbent to do multiple activities at one time or in very close succession?
5. *Job simplification*   Does the job require relatively little skill and training time?
6. *Repetition*   Does the job require performing the same activity or activities repeatedly?
7. *Spare time*   Is there very little spare time between activities on this job?
8. *Automation*   Are many of the activities of this job automated or assisted by automation?

The Biological Job Design Approach

1. *Strength*   Does the job require fairly little muscular strength?
2. *Lifting*   Does the job require fairly little lifting, and/or the lifting of very light weights?
3. *Endurance*   Does the job require fairly little muscular endurance?
4. *Seating*   Are the seating arrangements on the job adequate (with ample opportunities to sit, comfortable chairs, good postural support, etc.)?
5. *Size difference*   Does the workplace allow for all size differences between people in terms of clearance, reach, eye height, leg room, etc.?
6. *Wrist movement*   Does the job allow the wrists to remain straight, without excessive movement?
7. *Noise*   Is the workplace free from excessive noise?
8. *Climate*   Is the climate at the workplace comfortable in terms of temperature and humidity, and is it free of excessive dust and fumes?
9. *Work breaks*   Is there adequate time for work breaks given the demands of the job?
10. *Shift work*   Does the job not require shift work or excessive overtime?

exhibit **5.4** *continued*

The Perceptual–Motor Job Design Approach

1. *Lighting*   Is the lighting in the workplace adequate and free from glare?
2. *Display*   Are the displays, gauges, meters, and computerized equipment used on this job easy to read and understand?
3. *Programs*   Are the programs in the computerized equipment for this job easy to learn and use?
4. *Other equipment*   Is the other equipment (all types) used on this job easy to learn and use?
5. *Printed job materials*   Are the printed materials used on this job easy to read and interpret?
6. *Workplace layout*   Is the workplace laid out so that the employee can see and hear well enough to perform the job?
7. *Information input requirements*   Is the amount of attention needed to perform this job fairly minimal?
8. *Information-output requirements*   Is the amount of information that the employee must output on this job, in terms of both action and communication, fairly minimal?
9. *Information-processing requirements*   Is the amount of information that must be processed, in terms of thinking and problem solving, fairly minimal?
10. *Memory requirements*   Is the amount of information that must be remembered on this job fairly minimal?
11. *Stress*   Is there relatively little stress on this job?
12. *Boredom*   Are the chances of boredom on this job fairly small?

Source: Reprinted from *Organizational Dynamics*, Winter 1987, © 1987, with permission from Elsevier Science.

---

approaches emphasize. *Job design* is the application of theories to the structure of work for improving motivation, productivity, and satisfaction. We will discuss job design in more detail in Chapter 16. Here we will focus on how job characteristics might affect employee need fulfillment.

The Motivational Approach   The motivational approach is based on studies by psychologists and management scholars. The motivational approach uses the job characteristics model developed by Richard Hackman and Greg Oldham.[25] Hackman and Oldham's research concerned **work redesign,** which is defined as altering jobs to increase both the quality of employees' work experience and their productivity. Their research into the design of hundreds of jobs yielded the job characteristics model, which is illustrated in Exhibit 5.5. The **job characteristics model** consists of three major parts: core job dimensions, critical psychological states, and employee growth-need strength.

Core job dimensions.   Hackman and Oldham identified five dimensions that determine a job's motivational potential:

1. **Skill variety** is the number of diverse activities that compose a job and the number of skills used to perform it. A routine, repetitive, assembly-line job is low in variety, whereas an applied research position that entails working on new problems every day is high in variety.
2. **Task identity** is the degree to which an employee performs a complete job with a recognizable beginning and ending. A chef who prepares an entire meal has more task identity than a worker on a cafeteria line who ladles mashed potatoes.
3. **Task significance** is the degree to which the job is perceived as important and having impact on the company or consumers. People who

work redesign

Altering jobs to increase both the quality of employees' work experience and their productivity.

job characteristics model

A model for designing motivating work consisting of three major parts: core job dimensions, critical psychological states, and employee growth-need strength.

skill variety

The number of diverse activities that compose a job and the number of skills used to perform it.

task identity

The degree to which an employee performs a complete job with a recognizable beginning and ending.

task significance

The degree to which the job is perceived as important and having impact on the company or consumers.

exhibit **5.5**

The Job Characteristics Model

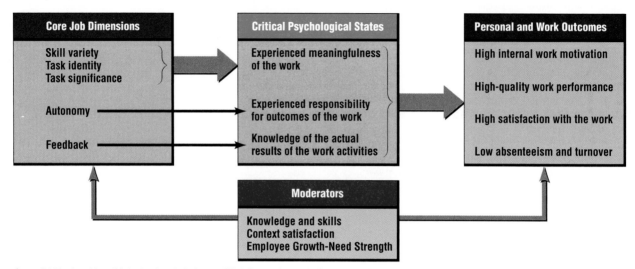

Source: Exhibit adapted from "Motivation through the Design of Work: Test of a Theory" in *Organizational Behavior and Human Performance*, volume 16, page, 256, © 1976 by Academic Press, reproduced by permission of the publisher.

distribute penicillin and other medical supplies during emergencies would feel they have significant jobs.

autonomy

The degree to which the worker has freedom, discretion, and self-determination in planning and carrying out tasks.

4. **Autonomy** is the degree to which the worker has freedom, discretion, and self-determination in planning and carrying out tasks. A house painter can determine how to paint the house; a paint sprayer on an assembly line has little autonomy.

5. *Feedback* is the extent to which doing the job provides information back to the employee about his or her performance. Jobs vary in their ability to let workers see the outcomes of their efforts. A football coach knows whether the team won or lost, but a research scientist may have to wait years to learn whether a project was successful.

The job characteristics model states that the five core job characteristics cause employees to experience critical psychological states, which can lead to high levels of motivation, satisfaction, and quantity and quality of performance. The relationship between core job dimensions and work outcomes varies depending on the employees' growth-need strength, knowledge and skill, and context satisfaction.

Critical psychological states. The model maintains that core job dimensions are more rewarding when individuals experience three psychological states in response to job design. The three **critical psychological states** influenced by job characteristics include meaningfulness of the work, responsibility, and knowledge of results. In Exhibit 5.5, skill variety, task identity, and task significance tend to influence the employee's psychological state of experienced meaningfulness of work—that the work itself is satisfying and provides intrinsic rewards for the worker. The job characteristic of autonomy influences the worker's experienced responsibility. Finally, feedback provides the worker with knowledge of actual results. The employee thus

critical psychological states

Psychological states influenced by job characteristics including meaningfulness of the work, responsibility, and knowledge of results.

knows how he or she is doing and can change work performance to increase desired outcomes.

Personal and work outcomes. The impact of the five core job dimensions on the psychological states of experienced meaningfulness, responsibility, and knowledge of actual results leads to the personal and work outcomes of high work motivation, high-quality work, high quantity of work, high satisfaction, and low absenteeism and turnover.

Moderating factors: employees' growth-need strength, knowledge and skill, and context satisfaction. The relationship between core job dimensions and work outcomes is moderated by employees' growth-need strength, knowledge and skill, and context satisfaction. This means that the relationship between the core job characteristics and the work outcomes can vary. **Growth-need strength** refers to the need for growth and development. If a person wants to satisfy low-level needs, such as safety and belongingness, the presence of the five core job dimensions will have less effect on satisfaction, motivation, or high quality or quantity of job performance. When a person has a high need for growth and development, including the desire for personal challenge, achievement, and challenging work, the presence of core job dimensions will be positively related to satisfaction, motivation, and performance. People with a high need to grow and expand their abilities respond very favorably to the application of the model and to improvements in core job dimensions.

growth-need strength

The need for growth and development.

Employees who do not have the knowledge and skills to perform their jobs will likely become frustrated, rather than motivated, as the presence of core job dimensions increases. Employees must have a certain level of knowledge and skills to perform their jobs successfully, to enjoy meaningful work, and to feel personally responsible for the work they perform.

Context satisfaction refers to an employee's satisfaction with work conditions, such as pay, supervision, coworkers, and job security. Employees who are satisfied with their work conditions are more likely to be motivated by a job that includes task and skill variety and high levels of responsibility. Employees who are dissatisfied are more likely to focus on how to reduce the dissatisfying aspects of their jobs (recall our discussion of hygiene factors earlier).

context satisfaction

An employee's satisfaction with work conditions such as pay, supervision, coworkers, and job security.

Research supports the job characteristics model's predictions of employee attitudes and behaviors, and the idea that the job characteristics directly affect the critical psychological states, which in turn lead to attitudes and behavior.[26] There is less support for the roles of growth-need strength, knowledge and skills, and context satisfaction.

The Mechanistic Approach The mechanistic approach of the job characteristics theory is based in industrial engineering. As you can see in Exhibit 5.4, the focus of the **mechanistic approach** is to identify the simplest way to perform a job to maximize efficiency. This approach can often make work so simple that anyone can perform the job with minimal training. Organizations might rely on the mechanistic approach if they have difficulty finding workers with high skill levels who want to perform interesting and meaningful work. You would be right to think that jobs designed this way lack meaningfulness. But keep in mind that some individuals view work as

mechanistic approach

A job-design approach that emphasizes identifying the simplest way to perform a job to maximize efficiency.

a way to fulfill lower level needs rather than as a means to meet belongingness, esteem, or self actualization needs. They might look to nonwork activities such as hobbies or friends to meet their higher level needs. So, these individuals might not react as negatively to jobs designed according to a mechanistic approach as you might.

The Biological Approach   The **biological approach** to job design focuses on individuals' physical capabilities and limitations. The biological approach is based on ergonomics. **Ergonomics** emphasizes the relationship between an individual's physiological characteristics and the physical work environment. The goal is to minimize the physical strain on the employee by structuring the work environment around the way the human body naturally moves. The biological approach emphasizes the design of technology and equipment (including chairs, desks, and height of computer keyboards) to minimize physical fatigue, aches, and pains. For example, in jobs that require a lot of typing at a keyboard, workers can suffer elbow and wrist injuries from the repetitive motion of the tasks. The City of Portland, Oregon, recently analyzed 1,500 computer-intensive jobs to improve their ergonomics.[27] Each employee's physical characteristics, such as height and arm reach, were measured. Based on these measurements, recommendations were made for each employee's work surface height, chair model, keyboard height and placement, pointing device, monitor height, and source document placement. Some of the modifications to the work environment included providing chairs that tilt forward for computer work, writing, and other work that involves forward reach, negative- (or reverse-) slope computer keyboards, and the use of trackballs instead of mice or other pointing devices.

Jobs designed according to the biological approach help employees meet lower level safety needs. Studies have found that ergonomic designs result in both benefits to employees (in reduced number and severity of injuries) and organizations (in fewer lost workdays).[28] Also, if employees do not have safe and comfortable working conditions, it is unlikely they will respond to jobs that have high levels of autonomy, skill variety, or other motivating job characteristics.

The Perceptual-Motor Approach   The **perceptual-motor approach** to job design focuses on an individual's mental capabilities and limitations. In this approach, jobs are designed so that they do not exceed humans' mental capabilities. The perceptual-motor approach focuses on making sure that an individual's information-processing capabilities are not overloaded. Jobs that require high levels of information processing include air traffic controller, nuclear power plant operator, and oil refinery operator. For example, investigations of recent accidents at nuclear power plants suggest that operators may have been unaware of potential problems in the nuclear reactors because they were unable to monitor hundreds of displays, gauges, and lights.[29]

While simplifying the information-processing requirements of a job can make it safer and easier to perform, it also can make it less interesting. For example, computer software programs called "expert systems" are available to assist managers in identifying solutions to performance problems and to help physicians diagnose patients' illnesses. These systems simplify the job,

---

biological approach

A job-design approach that focuses on individuals' physical capabilities and limitations. The goal is to minimize the physical strain on the employee by structuring the work environment around the way the human body naturally moves. The biological approach emphasizes the design of technology and equipment.

ergonomics

The science concerned with the relationship between an individual's physiological characteristics and the physical work environment.

perceptual-motor approach

A job design approach that focuses on an individual's mental capabilities and limitations. In this approach, jobs are designed so that they do not exceed humans' mental capabilities. The focus is on making sure that an individual's information-processing capabilities are not overloaded.

but they also might eliminate job characteristics that managers and physicians enjoy and that make their jobs challenging and rewarding.

Is One Approach the Best?   The answer is no. In considering how to design jobs to meet employee needs, it is important to use a combination of all four job characteristics approaches. Cost and benefits for the organization, as well as for employee needs, should be considered.

Exhibit 5.6 shows the positive and negative outcomes and met and unmet needs that result from the different job design approaches. Solely using the motivational approach may result in jobs that are performed inefficiently or place high physical or mental demands on employees. The motivational approach may also result in higher training costs, basic-skill requirements, and pay requirements for the organization.[30] Jobs designed to meet mental and physical demands may result in safer but more boring work because they don't provide opportunities for achievement, use of multiple skills, or a sense of significant accomplishment. For example, poultry-processing jobs require limited skills.[31] Job titles include "deboning," "scalding," and "dripping." These jobs are organized into an assembly line. Employees carry out tasks such as slaughtering chickens, gutting them, slicing off wings and legs, and peeling off skin. It is unlikely that the skill requirements of these tasks can be increased due to the nature of the job—poultry must be deboned to be sold. However, the repetitive nature of the tasks place the employees at risk for cumulative trauma injuries. Also, the work environment is foul smelling and messy. Improving poultry-processing

Job Design Approach	Positive Outcomes	Negative Outcomes	Needs Met
Motivational	Higher job satisfaction Higher motivation Greater job involvement Higher job performance Lower absenteeism	Increased training time Lower utilization levels Greater likelihood of error Greater chance of mental overload and stress	Belongingness Esteem Self-actualization
Mechanistic	Decreased training time Higher utilization levels Lower likelihood of error Less chance of mental overload and stress	Lower job satisfaction Lower motivation Higher absenteeism	Physiological Safety
Biological	Less physical effort Less physical fatigue Fewer health complaints Fewer medical incidents Lower absenteeism Higher job satisfaction	Higher financial costs because of changes in equipment or job environment	Physiological Safety
Perceptual–motor	Lower likelihood of error Lower likelihood of accidents Less chance of mental overload and stress Lower training time Higher utilization levels	Lower job satisfaction Lower motivation	Physiological Safety

exhibit | **5.6**

Outcomes and Needs Met from Different Job Design Approaches

plant jobs using a biological and motivational approach would most likely benefit both the organization and its employees greatly. Combining job tasks, automating others, and tidying up the workplace might increase the significance of the work and make it less physically demanding.

Consider how Sequins International Inc. used multiple job design approaches to meet employee needs and improve motivation.

❧ Sequins International Inc.

Sequins International Inc., based in Woodside, New York, faces tough global competition, particularly from factories in China and India, where women and children hand-sew sequins for meager wages, producing $100 million in wholesale goods annually. To compete, U.S. manufacturers use machines that were first developed in the 1940s. The machines save labor but create other problems: The repetitive motions used in the process produce an array of muscle pains, as well as mind-numbing boredom. With funding from the Ergonomics Project, administered by the International Ladies Garment Workers Union, Sequins International redesigned the machines to reduce the physical stresses experienced by sequin sewers. At the same time, skill variety was increased, as inspection jobs that were once performed separately were integrated into the manufacturing process. This gave workers increased task identity and a greater stake in quality control.

Because Sequins's workforce is 80 percent Hispanic and many workers have poor English skills, the company offers English lessons during lunch hours three times a week. Classes in mathematics and statistical process control (quality improvement methods) are also available to train workers for a variety of new tasks. Two teams, one for product satisfaction and the other for customer support, monitor quality control and machine maintenance as part of the production process, as well as provide operators with ongoing feedback and training.

These improvements in job design and motivation dramatically increased worker satisfaction. As a result, absenteeism is down two and one-half times in some areas. In addition, Sequins International has reduced the cost of producing a unit of goods by 30 percent and realized 30 percent cuts in cycle time, inventory, and overhead.[32]

apply it

1. Think of a time when you felt satisfied simply by performing an activity or task. What was the activity or task? Were you rewarded for it? How?

2. Consider a job that you currently hold or have held in the past (either a paid or volunteer position). Using the job characteristics model, evaluate the extent to which the job is high, medium, or low on each of the five core job dimensions (autonomy, skill variety, task identify, task significance, and feedback). Explain your rating. How would you recommend improving the job to increase its motivating potential?

Organizations meet employee needs through benefits, job experiences, and new technologies

Employees have a variety of needs, and organizations have a corresponding variety of ways to help meet them. One way for organizations to help employees meet safety and security needs is to provide benefits such as insurance, paid vacations and holidays, fitness centers, and day care for children. Organizations can also use new technology and job experiences to help stimulate employees' intrinsic motivation and fulfill growth needs.

Employee Benefits

Benefits are provided as part of employees' total compensation—that is, in addition to salary. They include social insurance (Social Security), medical and disability insurance, retirement plans, paid vacations and holidays, and family-friendly policies such as child care. Benefits are expensive for organizations. One estimate is that they add an average of 41 percent to every payroll dollar.[33] Although they are expensive, benefits are important because they can influence whether individuals want to join an organization, are satisfied with it, and stay. They help meet employees' basic safety and security needs. For example, employees with medical coverage do not have to worry about paying for all costs of treatment for illnesses. Retirement plans meet security needs by providing financial security for employees when they decide to quit working. Organizations typically have a choice in the types and amount of benefits they provide to employees. One exception is social insurance; organizations are legally required to contribute to Social Security. There are several ways that organizations use benefits to help meet employees' needs and therefore increase their motivation. They can expand the types of benefits offered, help employees balance work and life activities, and give employees choices and control over benefits.

Expanding Types of Benefits   Recognizing that employees have a variety of needs, many organizations are offering unusual benefits to meet them. Exhibit 5.7 shows some unusual benefits offered by organizations. Meeting these needs helps organizations attract and retain employees, especially when unemployment rates are low. Given some organizations' recent emphasis on the bottom line, which has resulted in downsizing, layoffs, and reduced long-term commitment to employees, people are often ready and willing to leave an organization if they can find another that better satisfies their needs or emphasizes the importance of its workforce. So, organizations look to benefits as one way to reduce costly employee turnover and to attract high performers.

Helping Employees Balance Work and Life   To help meet employees' security and safety needs, created by the stress resulting from conflicts between work and nonwork activities, many companies have developed policies and programs that give employees flexibility to choose where and when work is performed. For example, *job sharing* refers to a work arrangement

benefits

Social insurance (Social Security), private group insurance (medical and disability), retirement plans, pay for time not worked (vacations and holidays), and family-friendly policies (such as child care) are examples of benefits. They are usually provided to employees as part of their compensation.

Company	Benefit
MBNA	On-site dry cleaning, shoe repair, and hair salon
Qualcomm	Three recreational centers including tennis and sand volleyball
Born Information Systems	Access to lakefront homes in vacation spots in Minnesota
Timberland	Pet insurance to cover veterinarian bills
J. P. Morgan	Free lunch every day for all employees at 60 Wall Street
Xerox	Account of $10,000 to help employees buy a first house or pay tuition
CMP Media	$30,000 total benefit for infertility treatments and adoption aid
Adobe Systems	Three-week paid sabbatical every five years.

exhibit **5.7**
Unusual Benefits

Source: Based on R. Levering and M. Moskowitz, "The 100 Best Companies to Work for in America," *Fortune*, January 12, 1998, p. 87; K. Dobbs, "Winning the retention game," *Training*, September 1999, pp. 51–56.

in which employees divide the hours, responsibilities, and benefits of a full-time job. Flextime and compressed workweeks are examples of alternative work schedules that change the hours that employees perform work. Traditional U.S. work hours are five days and 40 hours per week. With a flextime schedule, employees still work 40 hours per week but have a choice when to start and end their workday. With a compressed work schedule, employees also work a 40-hour week, but instead of working Monday through Friday, they may work four 10-hour days. Both flextime and compressed workweeks help employees by giving them time to meet family demands such as paying bills, caring for infants and small children, and avoiding the stresses of commuting to and from work during rush hours.

Andersen Consulting provides employees with a unique benefit to help avoid time conflicts.[34] Andersen has established an on-site concierge service that runs employees' errands. The service was developed in response to employee complaints about not having enough time to handle personal business. Most Andersen employees are consultants who spend a large amount of time traveling and working overtime and odd hours, and they have little time to do routine chores. The concierge service does many personal errands for employees, including picking up a car from an auto repair shop, making dinner reservations, or overseeing painters or other repairpeople who are working on the employees' homes.

Many companies are beginning to provide child care and elder care to help employees meet their needs for safety and security of family members. Child care and elder care services are necessary to meet the needs of a diverse workforce. Almost two-thirds of women with children younger than 14 years of age are in the workforce. At least 20 percent of all employees now care for a parent. The care of the elderly is expected to increase in importance because the percentage of people over the age of 65 is expected to increase. Both child care and elder care needs result in absenteeism, work interruptions, negative attitudes toward work, and lack of energy.[35]

To meet these needs, organizations are providing on-site child care and elder care or referrals to reputable child care and elder care providers. First Tennessee Bank was losing 1,500 days of productivity a year because of child care problems, and it considered creating an on-site child care center. However, based on the results of a survey on child care issues, First Tennessee discovered that the real problem with child care occurred when children were sick and not allowed to attend their normal child care facility. As a result, the bank established a sick-child care center. The program paid for itself in the first nine months of operation as absentee levels quickly dropped.[36] Eddie Bauer is helping employees meet elder-care needs in several ways.[37] The company's resource and referral programs help employees deal with housing concerns. Counselors are available to provide advice on how to evaluate elder-care facilities and answer questions regarding the aging process, caregiving at home, and other issues. Eddie Bauer also provides videos, articles, and books on age-related issues.

flexible benefit plans

Also known as cafeteria-style plans, benefit plans that permit employees to choose the types and amounts of benefits that best meet their needs.

Giving Employees Choice and Control   **Flexible benefit plans** permit employees to choose the types and amounts of benefits that best meet their needs. These programs are also known as cafeteria-style plans because of employees' ability to pick and choose from a variety of benefits. Most plans require employees to have minimal levels of certain benefits such as health care coverage. In some plans, employees can receive money for choosing fewer benefits in some areas. They also can pay more to purchase extra benefits. For example, employees can give up vacation days for more salary, or they can use their salary dollars to purchase extra vacation days.

Motivation can be enhanced in several ways with flexible benefit plans.[38] These plans can create a better match between employee needs and benefits by permitting the employee to choose. Also, it is in an organization's best interests to ensure that employees understand what benefits are available to them and the value of these benefits. Because employees actively participate in choosing their benefits with flexible plans, they gain a better appreciation and awareness of what the organization is providing them to meet their work and nonwork needs.

Some organizations, such as the New Jersey Public Service Electric and Gas Company, are also helping employees choose benefits that best match their needs by using interactive computer technology to access benefit information, make changes, and review plans.[39] An advantage to computerized benefits is that employees can get information when they need it—their access is not restricted to certain times of the day when the benefits office is open. Also, employees can shift benefit allocations, get real-time information on savings or retirement plans, choose a health plan, or research choices. Ernst & Young is helping employees meet their needs by asking them *not* to use their computers or phones sometimes.

☙ Ernst & Young

Ernst & Young managers are trying to change the way the firm operates to improve female professionals' motivation and decrease turnover. To begin with, workers are told not to check their e-mail or voice mail on weekends and holidays. But what if a report is delayed or a client has to wait for an important piece of information? Top managers say, "So be it." It is one small step in a widespread effort to lessen the demands on Ernst & Young's professional employees. Although the intense work environment—with long hours and constant travel—affects men as well as women, top executives believe women generally feel a greater strain because of greater commitments outside work. They decided that only a complete overhaul of how people think about work could decrease the strain on female employees and root out systemic biases toward men at the company.

The company's efforts to rethink work grew out of a 1996 critique by Catalyst, a research group on corporate women, that underscored the firm's gender-related problems. Although Ernst & Young hired male and female entry-level professionals in equal numbers, only 8 percent of the firm's partners were women. In addition, only 27 percent of women staffers reported that becoming a partner was a "realistic goal," compared with 59 percent of their male counterparts. The company was losing 22 percent of its female professionals annually, costing around $150,000 per job to hire and train replacements.

Ernst & Young chairman Philip A. Laskaway created an "Office of Retention" and hired Deborah K. Holmes, the young lawyer who had headed the Catalyst study, to find ways to turn things around. One of the first problems Holmes and her team identified was that biases toward men served to demotivate female employees. One woman, for example, had her expense report rejected after she took a client for a manicure. If it had been a golf game or another traditionally male diversion, it would have readily been approved. To solve the problem, a task force worked on broadening the range of acceptable entertaining activities for clients, including family-friendly activities such as picnics and baseball games.

The firm also is developing ways to avoid forcing employees to compromise their personal lives in order to meet business expectations, including incorporating elements such as a casual-dress policy and flexible work schedules. In addition, there are efforts to hire more administrative staff who can assume some of the duties once handled by professionals. One unique program is called "client triage." Partners now routinely consider the demands on their employees in assessing a client's profitability to the firm.

They work with each client before a project begins to come to clear, mutual expectations about what will be required of staff members. A "utilization committee," made up of employees from all levels, meets regularly to reconcile client demands with employees' personal needs.

Most partners at Ernst & Young support the new ideas, but Holmes knows the company has a long way to go in changing attitudes and structures to provide greater motivation and job satisfaction for female professionals. "There's no silver bullet for work-life balance," she says. Maybe telecommunications-free weekends are a good place to start.[40]

Job Experiences

In addition to providing employee benefits, organizations also look at their range of job experiences for employee motivation. Job experiences can be used to motivate employees to learn and prepare them for the future. Using job experiences to motivate learning is a powerful force in a company's continued competitiveness. A *learning organization* is an organization that has an enhanced ability to learn, adapt, and change to meet environmental challenges such as new products, markets, competitors, or customer changes.[41] In a learning organization, employees continuously attempt to learn and apply what they have learned to develop, modify, and improve products and services. For an organization to be competitive and survive in today's turbulent environment, becoming a learning organization is a must.

job experiences

Relationships, problems, tasks, or other features that employees face in their jobs. Motivation can be enhanced by providing employees with challenging job experiences.

Job experiences refer to relationships, problems, tasks, or other features that employees face in their jobs.[42] Exhibit 5.8 lists some job experiences and the lessons learned from them. To be successful in their jobs, employees should "stretch" their skills. That is, they should be motivated to learn new skills, apply knowledge and skills in a new way, and demonstrate competence in new experiences. For example, General Electric has used job experiences to develop its managers' global skills.[43] The program begins with an assessment of a manager's leadership effectiveness. Managers receive feedback on how close their leadership behavior matches that needed to be successful in a global environment. Next, the managers receive a challenging assignment in an international location. These assignments require managers to visit a global location and gather information. For example, to consider how General Electric might market lighting products in Western Europe, managers interviewed customers, suppliers, and vendors. The managers shared the results of the research with other managers and then returned to the United States to present their recommendations to heads of business units and Jack Welch, CEO of General Electric.

The Container Store was recently named Fortune *magazine's best company to work for in America. The store stresses to its sales associates the need to stretch their skills to provide superb customer service. To recognize employee efforts, the store promotes a "being Gumby" program. Being Gumby is one of the highest compliments employees can receive. It means that they're being flexible—going outside their regular job to help another worker or a customer. By winning little Gumbys for office shelves and seeing a human-sized Gumby on display at corporate headquarters, employees are motivated to stretch their hospitality and sales skills to enable them to meet higher-level achievement and esteem needs. Being Gumby is one of the chief goals of Container Store workers.*
(Source: © 2000 Brian Coats)

Using job experiences to enhance employee motivation is not limited to management positions. For example, entry-level employees at Marriott are trained to handle a variety of positions and to move from one department to another.[44] One employee worked in maintenance, room service, and as a cook in Marriott's aggressive cross-training

exhibit **5.8**
Job Experiences and the Lessons Learned from Them

Making transitions	*Unfamiliar responsibilities* The manager must handle responsibilities that are new, very different, or much broader than previous ones.
	Proving yourself The manager has added pressure to show others she can handle the job.
Creating change	*Developing new directions* The manager is responsible for starting something new in the organization, making strategic changes in the business, carrying out a reorganization, or responding to rapid changes in the business environment.
	Inherited problems The manager has to fix problems created by a former incumbent or take over problem employees.
	Reduction decisions Decisions about shutting down operations or staff reductions have to be made.
	Problems with employees Employees lack adequate experience, are incompetent, or are resistant.
Having high level of responsibility	*High stakes* Clear deadlines, pressure from senior managers, high visibility, and responsibility for key decisions make success or failure in this job clearly evident.
	Managing business diversity The scope of the job is large with responsibilities for multiple functions, groups, products, customers, or markets.
	Job overload The sheer size of the job requires a large investment of time and energy.
	Handling external pressure External factors that affect the business (e.g., negotiating with unions or government agencies; working in a foreign culture; coping with serious community problems) must be dealt with.
Being involved in nonauthority relationships	*Influencing without authority* Getting the job done requires influencing peers, higher management, external parties, or other key people over whom the manager has no direct authority.
Facing obstacles	*Adverse business conditions* The business unit or product line faces financial problems or difficult economic conditions.
	Lack of top management support Senior management is reluctant to provide direction, support, or resources for current work or new projects.
	Lack of personal support The manager is excluded from key networks and gets little support and encouragement from others.
	Difficult boss The manager's opinions or management styles differ from those of the boss, or the boss has major shortcomings.

Source: C. D. McCauley, L. J. Eastman, and J. Ohlott (1995). "Linking Management Selection and Development through Stretch Assignments," *Human Resource Management* 84: 93–115. Copyright © 1995 John Wiley and Sons, Inc. Reprinted by permission of John Wiley and Sons, Inc.

program. The employee went on to school at the company's expense and completed more than 40 management courses. He became general manager of his own hotel, and now he is vice president for owner relations.

In Chapter 16, we will discuss in greater detail how the design of work can be used to motivate employees.

New Technologies

New manufacturing and communications technologies are constantly being introduced into the workplace, and they have revolutionized the types of tasks that individuals perform at work. These new technologies can affect motivation by changing the job characteristics and needs that can be met through work. Advanced computer technology reduces the time that individuals devote to actually performing a task and increases the time they have to spend in monitoring and maintenance activities. For example, consider the new breed of Airbus passenger jets. The planes can be flown from takeoff through landing without human intervention. The pilot's role is to correctly program the computer with data regarding weather, fuel, destination, and flight-path coordinates and monitor the controls to ensure the equipment is operating properly. In manufacturing settings, robots are used in auto assembly to perform dirty and dangerous welding and painting tasks previously completed by hand.

Although new technology can be used to make jobs safer and more efficient, it can also make jobs less interesting and decrease employee motivation. For example, consider two alternative advanced manufacturing technologies.[45] In the specialist control system, operators are responsible for loading, monitoring, and unloading the machine and alerting an engineer if the process malfunctions. In the operator control system, they perform these tasks and also are responsible for maintenance and programming. The operator control system increases the employees' skill variety, task significance, task identity, and autonomy. Employees working in the operator control system increased their performance, were more satisfied with their jobs, and felt less pressure than employees in the specialist control system.

Increasing use of videoconferencing, collaborative work software, and Internet technology for communications gives organizations the ability to locate employees across the globe and have them work together while decreasing travel time and cost. Communications technology can increase employee access to different perspectives and experts.[46] However, one potential drawback of this technology is that employees' levels of intrinsic motivation may be reduced if they enjoy meeting others face to face in their jobs. Also, social needs may not be met.[47] As a result, work may become dehumanized without personal relationships. To reduce the potential negative effects of communications technology on employees, organizations need to teach employees how to communicate with each other effectively and give them the opportunity to shape their forms of communication so they feel comfortable working with each other and don't feel that social aspects have been eliminated entirely.

Technology can also be used to motivate employees to generate and share knowledge (a process known as *knowledge management*).[48] Technology such as Lotus Notes, e-mail, or a company intranet can create a system that allows employees to store knowledge and share it with others. This is another important feature of a learning organization. For example, a Buckman Labs employee in Indonesia was able to obtain information stored in K'Netix, the company's Web-based database, and ask other employees for help through e-mail.[49] The K'Netix database contains information on a wide variety of business problems, solutions, and experiences of company employees. Employees at all levels have the chance to add information to the system and help other employees. The system helped one employee develop a proposal that won the company $6 million in business. Besides having the technology, Buckman Labs supports knowledge sharing by using it as one criteria for promotions and explicitly stating the value of knowledge contribution in job descriptions and performance evaluation forms.

apply it

1. The use of computers and the Web in the classroom has greatly increased in the last several years. How has new technology positively influenced your motivation as a student? Your learning? Has it had any negative effects on your learning or motivation?

summary OF KEY CONCEPTS

- **Motivation energizes, directs, and maintains behavior.** Motivation includes forces inside or external to an individual that create enthusiasm, provide direction, and generate persistence to pursue a course of action.

- **Employees are motivated by different types of needs.** Needs are internal drives that motivate individual behaviors. There are different types of needs according to the hierarchy of needs theory and ERG theory. They include needs for physical well-being, esteem, safety, security, belongingness, and self-actualization. Acquired needs theory argues that the need for achievement, need for affiliation, and need for power can be learned though life experiences.

- **Motivation may come from performing a job.** Cognitive evaluation theory argues that individuals are motivated simply by performing a job, and providing individuals with increased external rewards for job performance may *decrease* their motivation under certain conditions. Two-factor theory suggests that work characteristics related to dissatisfaction differ from those related to satisfaction. Motivators such as achievement, recognition, and responsibility can influence satisfaction. Hygiene factors such as working conditions and pay need to be present so that individuals are not

dissatisfied. The four methods of job design each emphasize meeting a different employee need. The motivational approach based on the job characteristics model allows employees to meet higher level needs for esteem and self-actualization. Biological, perceptual-motor, and mechanistic approaches ensure that employees' physiological and safety needs are met.

- **Organizations meet employee needs through benefits, job experiences, and new technologies.** Flexible benefits programs allow employees to choose the type and amount of benefits that best meet their needs. Companies are also providing flexible schedules and elder and child care to help employees balance work and life activities and avoid time and schedule conflicts. Job experiences that make employees use new skills or "stretch" their current skills can be used to motivate employees to learn and help them meet higher level achievement and esteem needs. New technologies such as e-mail and the Internet can help employees learn and contribute to a learning organization. A danger inherent in use of these technologies is that they may reduce employees' level of participation in the work and amount of personal contact with others, therefore creating unmet belongingness and esteem needs.

KEY terms

content theories, p. 161
motivation, p. 162
intrinsic rewards, p. 162
extrinsic rewards, p. 162
hierarchy of needs, p. 164
ERG theory, p. 166
acquired needs theory, p. 167

need for achievement, p. 167
need for affiliation, p. 167
need for power, p. 167
cognitive evaluation theory, p. 168
two-factor theory, p. 169
hygiene factors, p. 169
motivators, p. 169

work redesign, p. 173
job characteristics model, p. 173
skill variety, p. 173
task identity, p. 173
task significance, p. 173
autonomy, p. 174
critical psychological states, p. 174

DISCUSSION questions

1. Would you rather work for a manager high in need for achievement, need for affiliation, or need for power? Why? What are the advantages and disadvantages of each?

2. A survey of teachers found that two of the most important rewards were the belief that their work was important and a feeling of accomplishment. Is this consistent with Hackman and Oldham's job characteristics model? Why?

3. The teachers in question 3 also reported that pay and benefits were poor, yet they continued to teach. Use Herzberg's two-factor theory to explain this finding.

4. One small company recognizes an employee of the month who is given a parking spot next to the president's space near the front door. What need theories would explain the positive motivation associated with this policy?

5. What characteristics of individuals determine the extent to which work redesign will have a positive impact on work satisfaction and work effectiveness?

6. Why has Maslow's hierarchy of needs theory been criticized?

7. You overhear several of your employees commenting that use of e-mail and videoconferencing has made their jobs less satisfying. Why might this be the case?

8. How do flexible benefit plans contribute to employee motivation?

9. Your boss says, "I don't understand what job experiences have to do with motivation. To motivate employees, just make sure you reward them well." What do you tell her?

10. What do drive, energy, and maintenance have to do with motivation?

11. Can use of the motivational approach to job design *not* result in high levels of motivation? Explain.

SELF-DISCOVERY exercise

What Motivates You?
You are to indicate how important each characteristic is to you. Answer according to your feelings about the most recent job you had or about the job you currently hold. Circle the number on the scale that represents your feelings—1 (very unimportant) to 7 (very important).

When you have completed the questionnaire, score it as follows:

Rating for question 5: Divide by 1:   **security**
Rating for questions 9 and 13: Divide by 2:   **social**
Rating for questions 1, 3, and 7: Divide by 3:   **esteem**
Rating for questions 4, 10, 11, and 12: Divide by 4: **autonomy**
Rating for questions 2, 6, and 8: Divide by 3:   **self-actualization**

The instructor has national norm scores for presidents, vice presidents, and upper middle-level, lower middle-level, and lower-level managers with which you can compare your mean importance scores. How do your scores compare with the scores of managers working in organizations?

1. The feeling of self-esteem a person gets from being in that job	1	2	3	4	5	6	7
2. The opportunity for personal growth and development in that job	1	2	3	4	5	6	7
3. The prestige of the job inside the company (that is, regard received from others in the company)	1	2	3	4	5	6	7
4. The opportunity for independent thought and action in that job	1	2	3	4	5	6	7
5. The feeling of security in that job	1	2	3	4	5	6	7
6. The feeling of self-fulfillment a person gets from being in that position (that is, the feeling of being able to use one's own unique capabilities, realizing one's potential)	1	2	3	4	5	6	7
7. The prestige of the job outside the company (that is, the regard received from others not in the company)	1	2	3	4	5	6	7
8. The feeling of worthwhile accomplishment in that job	1	2	3	4	5	6	7
9. The opportunity in that job to give help to other people	1	2	3	4	5	6	7
10. The opportunity in that job for participation in the setting of goals	1	2	3	4	5	6	7
11. The opportunity in that job for participation in the determination of methods and procedures	1	2	3	4	5	6	7
12. The authority connected with the job	1	2	3	4	5	6	7
13. The opportunity to develop close friendships in the job	1	2	3	4	5	6	7

Source: Lyman W. Porter, *Organizational Patterns of Managerial Job Attitudes* (New York: American Foundation for Management Research, 1964), pp. 17, 19.

ORGANIZATIONAL BEHAVIOR in your life

We hope this chapter has given you a better understanding of how factors internal and external to individuals influence their motivation. To further develop your understanding of motivation, find three people in different careers to interview. Interview someone with a professional job, someone in a skilled or semiskilled trade, and someone who does volunteer work. Ask all of these people what they believe motivates them. Also, ask them what needs their work helps them meet and what needs they have met outside work. What similarities and differences occur in their responses? Share your interview results with the class and be prepared to discuss what you learned about motivation from the interviews.

ORGANIZATIONAL BEHAVIOR news flash

 Pick a company you are interested in learning more about (and maybe even working for). Visit its Web site. To find the Web site, type in the company's name on your search engine. At the company

Web site, research the company by reading about its history, policies, philosophy, objectives, and any other information provided. When you've completed your investigation, answer the following questions:

1. Why might you want to work for this company?
2. Which of your personal needs will be met by working for this company? Use specific examples from the Web site to justify your answer.

global diversity EVENTS

Using news listings on your search engine, such as Reuters, AP, ZDNet News, and the like, look for stories about Habitat for Humanity, Big Brothers-Big Sisters, The Peace Corps, Amnesty International, Doctors without Borders, Greenpeace, or other organizations that provide aid to those in need or protect the natural environment. When you find stories about the organization, consider the following questions:

1. What needs do individuals meet by working at these organizations?
2. Why would a for-profit company encourage employees to work for these organizations?

minicase ISSUE

Unmet Needs Cause Resentment within the Workforce

Background. United Parcel Service (UPS), the world's largest package distribution company, transports more than three billion parcels and documents annually. Using more than 500 aircraft, 157,000 vehicles, and 1,700 facilities to provide service in more than 200 countries and territories, the company employs more than 330,000 people and has continued to expand its global product and service offerings. Although UPS is known for its package distribution capabilities and global reach, the company has developed innovative technology that has positioned it to be the delivery service of choice for Web retailers. For example, UPS provides online tools that allow retailers to directly link online ordering with shipping, inventory, and billing systems. This technology is an important reason why UPS delivers more than 55 percent of all goods ordered online. Many leading business publications have recognized UPS for its success in e-commerce. For example, commenting on UPS's success in becoming the major delivery service for products purchased over the Web, *Forbes* magazine noted that "UPS used to be a trucking company with technology. Now it's a technology company with trucks."

Relationship with Employees. UPS believes that its most valuable asset is loyal and capable people. The commitment and motivation of UPS employees are achieved through two long-standing company policies: employee ownership and training. UPS was one of the first companies to use stock as part of employee compensation. Stock ownership promotes ex-

cellent service because every manager and employee stockholder is working for his or her own business. Until November 1999, UPS was a privately held company; UPS stock was available only to employees and managers and not traded on the stock exchange. In November 1999, UPS became a publicly traded company through a public offering of 109 million shares of stock. This was the largest initial public offering (IPO) ever by an American company.

Since its beginning, UPS has been committed to training. Training activities started by the founders continue, including the James E. Casey Scholarship program, the UPS Foundation, and the UPS Urban Internship program through which 40 UPS managers and supervisors are sent each year on month-long community internships.

The Teamsters Union represents UPS drivers and other nonmanagement employees. Despite the relatively good relationship that the Teamsters Union and UPS enjoyed, in 1997 a labor strike damaged relations, motivation, and employee morale—this despite the fact that UPS workers enjoy job security and are the highest paid in the industry. Under the new labor agreement, UPS agreed to increase salaries by $3.10 an hour for full-time employees and $4.10 per hour for part-time employees over the life of the contract. The company also agreed to convert part-time positions into 10,000 new full-time jobs. With the labor dispute settled, UPS moved quickly to rebuild business and make up for lost revenues. The company reported $352 million in profits in the first quarter of 1998, an increase of over $100 million from the first quarter in

1997. But financial success has not resulted in improvements in employee relations.

Pressure of Technology on Jobs. Technology use is not all positive at the company. Employees complain about unreachable productivity goals, and some drivers have had nervous breakdowns because of the pressure to produce. Productivity levels are set by computer analysis. For example, the computer says drivers have to do 20.2 stops per hour, but drivers claim they can do only 15. Supervisors track the productivity levels of the drivers and demand to know why deliveries took longer to complete than the computer projections predicted.

Many drivers think that customer service is slipping because of the time pressure they are under, although the company service index is currently at its highest levels. One driver notes, "They don't even care what drivers look like in the morning, from what I can tell. They just got away from all of those things that set us apart, and I think it is a huge mistake. But they're making so much money now that they're not going to change it. Eventually, it's going to hurt us." The senior vice president for human resources responds to such complaints by saying that drivers want the company to choose between increased productivity or better service. The company believes you can't be productive without giving good service.

Strained Relationships and Morale. UPS has not yet created the new jobs it promised in the labor agreement because of reduction in the volume of packages delivered due to the strike. Ten thousand workers were laid off during the strike, and the company argues that it needs to restore the old jobs before moving to create new ones. Also, cost-cutting measures implemented by the company, such as letting packages sit on trucks for an extra day, make it less likely that new full-time jobs will be created.

Despite attempts by management to reduce hard feelings resulting from the strike, relationships between first-line supervisors and workers are strained.

The supervisors kept the business running during the strike, and they were threatened by workers as they crossed picket lines. As a result, some supervisors have retaliated against workers by becoming more strict in enforcing work rules. UPS's annual survey of employees showed that employee satisfaction dropped 5% from previous years. Survey results also showed that employees believed improved communication was necessary. Employees are proud to work for UPS, but they want more feedback and information about the company. Employees also complain that some top-level executives are out of touch and that they are not interested in hearing the workers' ideas or reactions to policies.

Moving UPS Forward. The bitterness and anger continue. Some blame the Teamsters for spreading rumors and straying from the facts in their communications to workers. Others blame UPS's management. One Teamster spokesman says, "If you want cooperation, it doesn't come from taking away people's rights. It comes from treating people respectfully and solving problems with the union on the job, and we're willing to walk the extra mile to do that."

1. Explain the lack of employee satisfaction at UPS from the perspective of job design methods.

2. What employee needs are being met at UPS? What needs are unmet and may be responsible for poor morale?

3. Discuss the drop in employee morale from the perspective of the two-factor theory.

4. What can management do to improve morale and motivation?

Source: R. J. Grossman, "Trying to heal the wounds," *HR Magazine,* September 1998, pp. 85–92; "UPS at a glance," "The UPS Story," "UPS Public Offering Priced at $50 Per Share," and "UPS Recognized by *Forbes, Business Week,*" from the United Parcel Service Web site, www.ups.com, accessed January 2000.

Motivation Processes

CONCEPT AND SKILL

preview

After studying this chapter, you should be able to:

- Identify and explain the process theories of motivation.

- Discuss how the concept of fairness is used in understanding employee motivation.

- Describe the expectancy model.

- Discuss the role of social learning and self-efficacy on motivation.

- Describe reinforcement theory and ways it can be used to motivate employees.

- Discuss the characteristics of effective goals.

- Discuss how incentives can be effectively used to motivate employees.

- Describe the four elements of empowerment and ways they heighten employee motivation.

Jack Welch has been chairman and chief executive officer of General Electric Company (GE) for nearly 20 years. His lessons on motivation have been shaped from his work experience at GE as well as at other companies. According to Welch, the most important job he has—and the job he devotes more time to than any other—is motivating GE employees. Welch believes in rewarding employees who succeed and weeding out those who don't make their goals. This is in part based on an experience earlier in his career in which he was at a workplace where everyone got the same raise. That experience made him aware of what types of frustrations employees can experience. Welch says, "You drive into the big parking lot, put your car among rows and rows of other cars, go into the office, and some [idiot] tells you what to do and how to do it. If you don't get recognized and you have the wrong boss, it's awful." As a result, on every performance appraisal professional employees are told where they stand—from the top 10 percent down to the least effective 10 percent. Performance ratings directly affect employees' eligibility for stock options. Those at the low end get no options and are asked to leave the company. Welch advocates motivating average employees by telling them they are eligible for options but only if they improve their performance. He believes that employees need to be "graded" on a curve. For every ten employees, one is a star and one needs to be let go. Otherwise, all employees will be evaluated as above average.

Although he personally finds giving employees big raises rewarding, he also recognizes that employees need to receive other types of rewards—to "raise their hand, to be seen, to make a statement. You have to be rewarded in the soul and the wallet." He believes that goals are not as helpful for motivating employees as a work environment in which employees feel free to contribute their ideas. Welch says, "If I turn to you and say I want every growth idea you have in your body—and I ask, 'What do you need, do you need more people, do you need more research and development?'—you will come in with all kinds of things that I have never thought about. Then I can say, 'I don't like that idea, I don't want to do that one, but I would like to do that one.'"

Having the ability to take risks and make mistakes also influences employee motivation, according to Welch. His views on risk taking were influenced by an experience in his first job at GE, when there was an explosion at his plant. Instead of yelling at him or criticizing him, his bosses were supportive and encouraging. This experience helped form Welch's emphasis on risk taking at GE, which he believes is necessary to ensure the vitality of the company. According to Welch, "A small company can only make one or two bets before they go out of business. But we can afford to make lots more mistakes, and in fact we throw more things at the wall. The big companies that get into trouble are those that try to manage their size instead of experimenting with it."

Welch also acknowledges that managers and employees need to "be on the same page" to maximize motivation. Managers and employees need not dress the same or enjoy the same life activities. But business values, treatment of people, and important behavior must be clearly specified and agreed upon; otherwise, managers and employees will be working toward opposite goals. Welch's motivation lessons have helped to shape the company through more than 600 acquisitions and years of record earnings and made GE's management style one that many companies are trying to imitate.[1]

Jack Welch on Motivation

"You have to be rewarded in the soul and the wallet."
—**Jack Welch,** chairman and chief executive officer General Electric

In today's competitive environment, few organizations can survive without motivated employees. Organizations continually look for ways to encourage their workers and tap their potential. People are motivated not only by their individual needs, as we saw in the previous chapter, but by the way they are viewed and treated by others in an organization. Their successes are also based on how they view themselves and what they believe they can accomplish. Competitive organizations are reviewing and refining their internal processes and systems to ensure that they reward employees for achieving objectives related to organizational goals.

Jack Welch's secret for success at General Electric is motivated employees who are willing to take risks to help grow the business. The challenge for Jack Welch and other CEOs and managers is how to keep employees motivated. Motivation comes from within a person, and managers can affect motivation only by changing the environment or providing conditions that help employees meet their needs. Not only does Welch ensure that employees receive rewards for a job well done, but he also makes sure that the organizational culture allows employees to make a difference at GE. One assumption underlying Welch's motivation philosophy is that employees choose behaviors based on the outcomes or rewards they expect to receive and their perceptions of how they are treated at work. That is, Welch's motivation philosophy is based on a process theory of motivation.

process theories

A group of theories that explain how employees select behaviors with which to meet their needs and determine whether their choices were successful.

Process theories explain *how* employees are motivated—that is, how employees select behaviors to meet their needs and determine whether their choices were successful. In contrast, the content theories of motivation discussed in Chapter 5 emphasize *what* motivates employees—that is, motivation results from an individual trying to meet basic underlying needs (such as food, friendship, recognition, or achievement). Process theories suggest that motivation varies from situation to situation and is affected by changes in the environment. Welch's motivational philosophy also emphasizes that there is not one approach, or one right answer, for motivating employees.

Wal-Mart Stores Inc. is the country's largest private employer, with 885,000 U.S. workers. Wal-Mart discount stores are nonunion stores and in recent years, the company has entered the food business with giant supercenters and grocery-like Neighborhood Markets. Motivated by a perception of decreasing equity between the 1 million of its members who work in supermarkets and the nonunion Wal-Mart workers, the United Food and Commercial Workers union (UFCW) is striving to unionize Wal-Mart workers. Recently the UFCW won the first union election in a U.S. Wal-Mart store when the meat department workers (photo) in Jacksonville, Texas, voted to join the UFCW. Workers at 100 other Wal-Mart outlets, also concerned about fair treatment, are inquiring about holding their own union elections. (Source: © Reid Horn)

This chapter reviews process theories of employee motivation: equity theory, expectancy theory, goal setting, and two learning theories that emphasize how the consequences of behavior affect motivation—reinforcement theory and social learning theory. As you will see, these theories provide a different perspective on motivation, especially when we examine their applications in organizations. Organizations use all of the theories in designing programs related to employee motivation and managing employees. These programs include performance management and incentive systems, management by objectives, management of nontraditional employees, behavior modification, and empowerment.

Motivation Is Based on Perceptions of Fairness

Sometimes an individual's motivation can be increased or decreased when making comparisons with others' situations. **Equity theory** focuses on individuals' perceptions of how fairly they are treated compared with others. Equity theory proposes that people are motivated to seek social equity in the rewards they expect for performance.[2] Exhibit 6.1 provides an overview of equity theory. According to equity theory, if people perceive their rewards as equal to what others receive for similar contributions, they will believe that their treatment is fair and equitable, and they will be satisfied. As shown in Exhibit 6.1, people evaluate equity by comparing their inputs to and outcomes of a job (expressed as a ratio of outcomes to inputs). Inputs to a job are an individual's education, experience, effort, and ability. Outcomes from a job include pay, recognition, benefits, and promotions. Then people compare their inputs and outcomes to those of others, a process known as social comparison. The input-to-outcome ratio may be compared with another person in the work group or a perceived group average.

A perceived state of equity exists whenever the ratio of one person's outcomes to inputs equals the ratio of another's outcomes to inputs. Perceived inequity can occur in two ways. One way is underpayment in comparison with others. Perceived inequity occurs when the input/outcome ratios are out of balance, such as when a person with a high level of

equity theory

A process theory of motivation that focuses on individuals' perceptions of how fairly they are treated compared with others.

exhibit **6.1**
Overview of Equity Theory

	Person A	Social Comparison	Person B	Result
Inequity Underpayment for Person A; overpayment for Person B	Outcomes / Inputs	<	Outcomes / Inputs	Person A: Angry Person B: Guilty
Equity	Outcomes / Inputs	=	Outcomes / Inputs	Person A: Satisfied Person B: Satisfied
Inequity Overpayment for Person A; underpayment for Person B	Outcomes / Inputs	>	Outcomes / Inputs	Person A: Guilty Person B: Angry

education or experience receives the same salary as a new, less educated employee. Underpayment results in anger. Perceived inequity can also result from overpayment. Overpayment results from an employee discovering she is making more money than other people who contribute the same inputs to the company. For example, as shown in Exhibit 6.1, when Person A believes she is overpaid, she feels guilty. The feelings of guilt may make Person A try to correct the inequity by working harder, getting more education, or considering lower pay. Perceived inequity creates tension within individuals that motivates them to bring the inequity into balance.[3]

The most common methods for reducing a perceived inequity are the following:

- *Change inputs*   A person may choose to increase or decrease his or her inputs to the organization. For example, underpaid individuals may reduce their level of effort or increase their absences. Overpaid people may increase effort on the job.

- *Change outcomes*   A person may change his or her outcomes. An underpaid person may request a salary increase or a bigger office. Also, a union may try to improve its members' wages and working conditions to be consistent with a comparable union whose members make more money.

- *Distort perceptions*   Research suggests that people may distort perceptions of equity if they are unable to change inputs or outcomes. They may artificially increase the status attached to their jobs or distort others' perceived rewards to bring inequity into balance.

- *Leave the job*   People who feel inequitably treated may decide to leave their jobs rather than suffer the inequity of being under- or overpaid. In their new jobs, they expect to find a more favorable balance of rewards.

The implication of equity theory is that employees evaluate the equity of their rewards compared with others'. However, in most companies it is impossible to know the salary level of other employees accurately because the information is not publicly available or shared among employees. To find evidence of inequity, some employees are beginning to use the Web to find salary ranges for jobs.

In most cases equity theory relates to employees' perceptions within the workplace; an increase in salary or a promotion has no motivational effect if it is perceived to be inequitable relative to that of other employees. In the current tight labor market, there is a shortage of talented employees and intense competition between companies. Because of the intense competition, many organizations are paying new employees more than employees with more seniority.[4] This has resulted in frustration and poor morale among long-term employees. For example, Scott Sangster joined PricewaterhouseCoopers two years ago after earning his master's degree from Northwestern. Current applicants with similar education backgrounds are being offered salaries and signing bonuses that are nearly 30% higher than what Sangster received. "It can be a real morale buster," says Sangster.

Employees often leave a company because they are upset with the perceived inequities. So, organizations are attempting to combat this problem. Some employees receive counteroffers of pay increases from their companies once they have another job offer. Also, to retain more senior employees whose salaries are being overtaken by the rookies, some companies are bumping up their employees' pay every six months—or even four times a year. Others are giving more "perks," such as flexible schedules or stock options.

In practice, the usefulness of equity theory for understanding employee motivation has been criticized for two reasons. First, it is not clear how employees change their behaviors, or even whether they do, in response to overcompensation—that is, getting *more* than they deserve. Second, equity theory focuses on the perceived fairness of the *amount and allocation* of rewards among individuals. This is known as **distributive justice.** Distributive justice affects the level of satisfaction that a person has with the outcomes he or she receives. However, recent research has suggested that perceptions of fairness are also influenced by procedural justice. **Procedural justice** refers to perceptions of the *process used* to determine how rewards should be distributed.[5] That is, employees may consider how managers evaluate subordinates and determine pay increases or other rewards. Procedural justice affects trust and commitment.

As a result of these findings, the ideas of equity theory have been expanded to include consideration of both procedural and distributive justice, that is, to consider the process through which the outcome is determined, as well as the outcome itself. We will discuss the implications of equity theory for pay and performance management later in the chapter. But distributive and procedural justice have been shown to be related to a wide variety of employee perceptions and behaviors both negative and positive, including reactions to pay decisions, performance management systems, and disciplinary decisions; intentions to leave a company; and organizational citizenship behaviors.[6] When individuals experience an unfair process, they may seek retribution to punish those who are responsible for it. For example, employee theft has been found to increase when employee pay was reduced.[7] However, employee theft occurred only among employees who had not received adequate explanation from management for the pay reduction.

Organizations need to make many different decisions concerning employees, including what the rates of pay will be, what new technology to implement, and who will be laid off in a downturn. To help ensure that employees view the process used to reach a decision as fair, three conditions need to exist.[8] First, employees should be involved in decisions that affect them (called *engagement*). Engagement results in better decisions and greater commitment by those affected by the decision. Second, all employees who are involved need to understand the rationale behind the decision. An explanation allows employees to understand and trust managers' intentions even if the decision is not in the employees' best interest. Finally, managers need to clearly state the standards employees are judged by, including the rewards and penalties for not reaching the standards (called *expectation clarity*). Consider how international pharmaceutical company Rhône-Poulenc Rorer improved its performance management system to increase employees' perceptions of equity and fairness.

distributive justice

Part of equity theory that focuses on the *amount and allocation* of rewards among individuals.

procedural justice

Perceptions of the *process used* to determine how rewards should be distributed.

Rhône-Poulenc Rorer (RPR) is a pharmaceutical company that operates in more than 60 countries, including the United States. A new performance management system has been developed at the company to give managers a better way to communicate goals and expectations. Also, the system allows managers more flexibility in rewarding employees. To design the system, the company's human resource managers conducted interviews and held meetings with employees and their supervisors.

❦ **Rhône-Poulenc Rorer (RPR)**

They also looked at other companies and consulting firms to identify "best practices" in performance management.

The new appraisal system focuses on the company's key objectives, the day-to-day accountabilities of each position, and behaviors identified as important for all positions, including customer focus, teamwork, and people management skills. The new system permits managers to be more specific in setting and measuring performance objectives. Using the new system, managers are able to make more meaningful decisions and clearly distinguish the rewards given to high-performing, average, and marginal employees. Managers review the salary budget, historical and current compensation data, and salary surveys of other companies. Managers can draw from salary increase monies, bonuses tied to the company's financial performance, or stock options.[9]

apply it

1. Consider a time when you believe you were unfairly treated. Describe the experience. Explain your feelings of unfairness using equity theory or distributive and procedural justice.

Motivation is based on expectations and rewards

expectancy theory

A process theory of motivation that proposes that motivation depends on individuals' expectations about their ability to perform tasks and receive desired rewards.

As we've seen, employees can make judgments about their work situations based on the equity they perceive within the organization. Another factor they can consider is their own abilities and expectations for rewards as they review their work environment. **Expectancy theory** suggests that motivation depends on individuals' expectations about their ability to perform tasks and receive desired rewards. Expectancy theory is associated with the work of Victor Vroom, although a number of scholars have made contributions in this area.[10] Expectancy theory is concerned not with identifying types of needs, but with the thinking process that individuals use to achieve rewards. Consider Bill Bradley, a university student with a strong desire for a B in his accounting course. Bill has a C+ average and one more exam to take. Bill's motivation to study for that last exam will be influenced by (1) the expectation that hard study will lead to an A on the exam and (2) the expectation that an A on the exam will result in a B for the course. If Bill believes he cannot get an A on the exam or that receiving an A will not lead to a B for the course, he will not be motivated to study exceptionally hard.

Expectancy theory is based on the relationship among an individual's effort, the individual's performance, and the desirability of outcomes associated with high performance. These elements and the relationships among them are illustrated in Exhibit 6.2. The keys to expectancy theory are the expectancies for the relationships among effort, performance, and outcomes with the value of the outcomes to the individual.

E → P expectancy

A judgment as to whether putting effort into a given task will lead to high performance.

$E \to P$ **expectancy** involves a judgment as to whether putting effort into a task will lead to high performance. For expectancy to be high, the individual must have the ability, previous experience, and necessary machinery, tools, and opportunity to perform. For Bill Bradley to get a B in the accounting course, the $E \to P$ expectancy is high if Bill truly believes that with hard work he can get an A on the final exam. If Bill believes he has neither the ability nor the opportunity to achieve high performance, the $E \to P$ expectancy will be low and so will be his motivation.

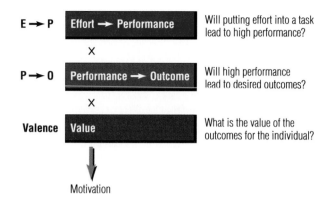

exhibit **6.2**
Major Elements of Expectancy Theory

P → O expectancy involves whether successful performance will lead to the desired outcome. When a person is motivated to win some job-related award, the expectancy is related to the belief that high performance will truly lead to the award. If the P → O expectancy is high, the individual will be more highly motivated. If the person expects that high performance will not produce the desired outcome, motivation will be lower. If an A on the final exam is likely to produce a B in the accounting course, Bill Bradley's P → O expectancy will be high. Bill may talk to the professor to see whether an A will be sufficient to earn him a B in the course. If not, he will be less motivated to study hard for the final exam.

Valence is the value of outcomes, or their attractiveness, for the individual. If the outcomes that are available from high effort and good performance are not valued by employees, motivation will be low. Likewise, if outcomes have a high value, motivation will be higher.

Expectancy theory attempts not to define specific types of needs or rewards, but only to establish that they exist and may be different for every individual. One employee may want to be promoted to a position of increased responsibility, and another may have high valence for good relationships with peers. Consequently, the first person will be motivated to work hard for a promotion and the second for the opportunity for a team position that will keep him or her associated with a group.

A simple sales department example will explain how the expectancy model in Exhibit 6.2 works. If Jane Anderson, a salesperson at the Diamond Gift Shop, believes that increased selling effort will lead to higher personal sales, we can say that she has a high E → P expectancy. Moreover, if Jane also believes that higher personal sales will lead to a promotion or pay raise, we can say that she has a high P → O expectancy. Finally, if Jane places a high value on the promotion or pay raise, valence is high and Jane will have a high motivational force. On the other hand, if either the E → P or P → O expectancy is low, or if the money or promotion has low valence for Jane, the overall motivational force will be low. For an employee to be highly motivated, all three factors in the expectancy model must be high.[11]

Exhibit 6.3 shows several questions that you might consider in trying to use expectancy theory to understand or change employees' motivation. You need to consider both the potential causes and consequences of performance. Potential causes of performance include the employee's ability level, self-confidence, and understanding of what level of performance is

P → O expectancy

Involves whether successful performance of a task will lead to the desired outcome.

valence

The value an individual places on an outcome.

exhibit | **6.3**

Evaluating Behavior Using
Expectancy Theory

Aspect of the Theory	Question to Ask
Effort-to-Performance Relationships	
Capability	Does the employee have the ability to perform well?
Confidence	Does the employee believe he or she can perform the job well?
Challenge	Does the employee have to work hard to perform the job well?
Criteria	Does the employee know the difference beween good and poor performance?
Performance-to-Outcome Relationships	
Credibility	Does the employee believe the manager will deliver on promises?
Consistency	Does the employee believe that all will receive similar rewards for good performance and similar negative outcomes for poor performance?
Outcome-to-Valence Relationships	
Compensation	Does the employee value the rewards associated with good performance?
Effort-to-Performance and Performance-to-Outcome Relationships	
Cost	What does it cost the employee—in effort and forgone outcomes—to perform well?
Effort-to-Performance-to-Valence Relationships	
Communication	Does the manager communicate with the employee verbally and nonverbally—receiving as well as sending messages?

Source: Based on Walter B. Newsom, "Motivate, Now!" *Personnel Journal*, February 1990, pp. 51–55.

expected. Important performance consequences include employees' beliefs that management will deliver promised performance outcomes and the value they place on those outcomes. Communication is also crucial. Managers must let employees know what level of performance is expected and what will be received for meeting performance expectations. Also, managers need to communicate that they believe employees can meet performance expectations. Consider how Trident Precision Manufacturing motivated employees to improve product quality.[12]

❦ Trident Precision Manufacturing

Trident Precision Manufacturing is a precision sheet metal fabricator and electromechanical assembly business. Trident's products include simple brackets for machines that sort X rays and other parts for larger machines such as lasers and photocopiers. Although Trident's customers were happy with its products, Trident was having difficulty meeting quality standards. Products often reached the end of assembly with major defects, and they had to be redone. The company's informal motto was "we make it nice because we make it twice."

Senior management and employee teams investigated the quality problems. First, they focused on the effort-to-performance relationship. They found that one motivational issue was that managers were not selective in hiring, meaning some employees did not have the capability to perform well. Employees who lacked the capability were not motivated to improve product quality and were more likely to leave the company—Trident had an astounding 41 percent turnover rate! Besides making sure that new employees had the appropriate skills, Trident also developed a 25-hour training course on quality for current employees. The course focuses on problem solving, quality improvement, just-in-time manufacturing, and interpersonal communications skills. To ensure that employees' capabilities remain high, each year they receive at least 15 additional hours of training. Besides improving their capabilities, the training has boosted their confidence and understanding of the difference between a high-quality and poor product.

The second important aspect of Trident's approach was its focus on improving managers' credibility. Even if employees have the capability and confidence to perform, their motivation will be reduced if managers do not give employees the opportunity to perform—to improve quality. At Trident, employees were told they could shut down the assembly line to correct quality problems. Trident managers tell employees: "You own it; fix it." Managers established credibility by allowing employees to halt production to fix flaws, inviting them to make suggestions for improving the assembly process, and implementing their suggestions. Over 98 percent of employees' process improvement suggestions have resulted in changes in daily work routines.

The third important aspect of Trident's program was linking outcomes with rewards that employees value. Employees can clearly see the link between good performance and rewards because they are provided often: On average, each employee receives special recognition over ten times a year. Managers have given employees many different types of thank-yous, ranging from hockey tickets to dinners for two. As one of Trident's human resource managers commented, "If you want to change your culture, start thanking people. Don't wait until the end of the year."

As a result of focusing on improving employee motivation, Trident's turnover rate dropped to 3.5 percent, the company has quadrupled its annual revenue, lowered its product defect rate from 3 percent to .007 percent (nearly perfect!), and won numerous quality awards.

As you try to apply expectancy theory in your work, keep in mind a few research findings.[13] First, there is support for the elements of expectancy theory. Second, people's *intentions* to behave a certain way have been found to be more strongly related to the expectancy model than their actual behaviors, such as performance, effort, or choice. Finally, expectancy theory is best suited for understanding individual behavior rather than for making comparisons between individuals.

apply it

1. Choose a behavior of a friend at work or at home that you would like to better understand (and maybe even change). Using the model of expectancy theory shown in Exhibit 6.2, analyze the person's behavior according to each aspect of expectancy theory—effort-to-performance relationship, performance-to-outcome relationship, and outcome-to-valence relationship. To change the behavior, which of these relationships would you try to influence? How?

Motivation is based on learned consequences of behavior

Learned consequences of behavior can also affect people's motivation. Learning the consequences of our behavior begins at birth. As people move through life, they perform certain acts and see the consequences of those acts. They also observe others and see that their actions end in certain results. Both types of observations involve learning. Two theories help explain how individuals are motivated based on the consequences of their behaviors: reinforcement theory and social learning theory.

Reinforcement Theory

Reinforcement theory explains motivation by looking at the relationship between behavior and the consequences an individual experiences. It focuses on modifying employees' on-the-job behavior through the use of

reinforcement theory

A motivation theory based on the relationship between a given behavior and its consequences.

exhibit **6.4**
Types of Reinforcement

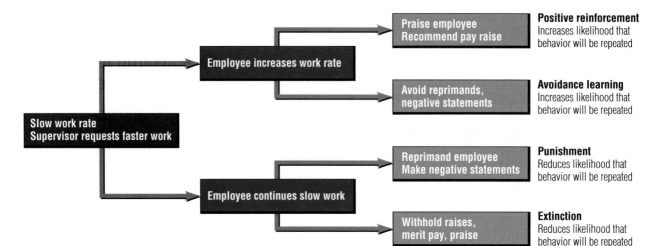

Source: Based on Richard L. Daft and Richard M. Steers, *Organizations: A Micro/Macro Approach* (Glenview, IL.: Scott, Foresman, 1986), p. 109.

organizational behavior modification (OB mod)

The set of techniques by which organizations use reinforcement theory to modify human behavior.

immediate rewards and punishments. **Organizational behavior modification (OB mod)** is the name given to the practical application of reinforcement theory to modify human behavior.[14] The basic assumption underlying behavior modification is the *law of effect,* which states that behavior that is positively reinforced tends to be repeated, and behavior that is not reinforced tends not to be repeated. Reinforcement is defined as anything that causes a certain behavior to be repeated or inhibited. The four reinforcement tools are positive reinforcement, avoidance learning, punishment, and extinction. Each type of reinforcement is a consequence of either a pleasant or unpleasant event being applied or withdrawn following a person's behavior. The four types of reinforcement are summarized in Exhibit 6.4.

positive reinforcement

The administration of a pleasant and rewarding consequence following a desired behavior.

Positive Reinforcement   **Positive reinforcement** is the administration of a pleasant and rewarding consequence following a desired behavior. A good example of positive reinforcement is immediate praise for an employee who arrives on time or does a little extra in his or her work. The pleasant consequence will increase the likelihood of the excellent work behavior occurring again. Frank Bohac, CEO of Computer Systems Development in Albuquerque, New Mexico, has rewarded his employees with computers, vacations, and even horses for meeting personal and organizational goals.[15] Studies have shown that positive reinforcement does help to improve organizational performance. In addition, nonfinancial rewards, such as positive feedback, often are as effective as financial incentives.[16]

avoidance learning

The removal of an unpleasant consequence following a desired behavior.

Avoidance Learning   **Avoidance learning** is the removal of an unpleasant consequence following a desired behavior. That is, employees learn to do the right thing by avoiding unpleasant situations. Avoidance learning is sometimes called *negative reinforcement.* Avoidance learning occurs when a manager stops criticizing or reprimanding an employee once an incorrect

Barry and Eliot Tatelman recently sold their furniture business, Jordan Furniture, to the nation's preeminent investor, Warren Buffett. Much of the success of their furniture business can be attributed to their fun-loving spirits. They liked to have fun and they wanted their customers to enjoy themselves, so they made sure that their employees also had fun. Recently, as positive reinforcement for jobs well done, they closed all four of their stores and flew all of their employees to Bermuda. The Tatelmans considered the extravagant holiday, which cost about $750,000, to be worth the cost as a motivational tool. "It's making the employees feel important, and they are," says Eliot.
(Source: © Webb Chappell)

behavior has stopped. Avoidance learning can also lead to employees learning to avoid interactions with their manager, so this approach should be used carefully. For most employees, it is better to change or "shape" their behavior using positive reinforcement than to use criticism.

For example, consider Bill Prince's use of avoidance learning.[17] Prince became a middle manager at BellSouth by turning around underperforming organizations in a dozen cities. But he said he did it in a "brusque and unfeeling manner." He fired many employees, and those that remained were treated coldly, praised infrequently, and publicly demeaned for mistakes. Employees complained that Prince pushed too hard and treated them rudely. His boss concluded, "He essentially saw people as instruments to get things done through, but didn't concern himself with their feelings." Now, after attending a leadership development program that his boss emphasized he attend or look for another job, Prince is careful to focus on fixing the problem, not condemning the person who made the mistake.

Punishment **Punishment** is the imposition of unpleasant outcomes on an employee. Punishment typically occurs following undesirable behavior. Punishment is usually explicitly stated in employment contracts and union agreements. For example, a construction employee can be suspended without pay for a day for not wearing a hard hat when required. The use of punishment in organizations is controversial and often criticized because it fails to indicate the correct behavior. However, almost all managers report finding it necessary occasionally to impose forms of punishment ranging from verbal reprimands to employee suspensions or firings.[18] For example, a supervisor may berate an employee for performing a task incorrectly. The supervisor expects that the negative outcome will serve as a punishment and reduce the likelihood that the behavior will recur.

punishment

The imposition of unpleasant outcomes on an employee. Punishment typically occurs following undesirable behavior.

extinction

The withdrawal of a positive reward, meaning that behavior is no longer reinforced and hence is less likely to occur in the future.

Extinction   **Extinction** is the withdrawal of a positive reward, meaning that behavior is no longer reinforced and hence is less likely to occur in the future. If a perpetually tardy employee fails to receive praise and pay raises, he or she will begin to realize that the behavior is not producing desired outcomes. The behavior will gradually disappear if it is continually nonreinforced.

Some executives use reinforcement theory very effectively to shape employees' behavior. Jack Welch, profiled at the beginning of the chapter, has always made it a point to reinforce behavior at General Electric. As an up-and-coming group executive, Welch reinforced purchasing agents by having someone telephone him whenever an agent got a price concession from a vendor. Welch would stop whatever he was doing and call the agent to say, "That's wonderful news; you just knocked a nickel a ton off the price of steel." He would also sit down and scribble out a congratulatory note to the agent. The effective use of positive reinforcement and the heightened motivation of purchasing employees marked Jack Welch as executive material in the organization.[19]

Reinforcement Schedules

schedule of reinforcement

The frequency with which and intervals over which reinforcement occurs.

A great deal of research into reinforcement theory suggests that the timing of reinforcement has an impact on the speed of employee learning and behavior. **Schedules of reinforcement** pertain to the frequency with which and intervals over which reinforcement occurs. A reinforcement schedule can be selected to have maximum impact on employees' job behavior. There are five basic types of reinforcement schedules: continuous reinforcement and four types of partial reinforcement.

continuous reinforcement schedule

A schedule in which every occurrence of the desired behavior is reinforced.

Continuous Reinforcement   With a **continuous reinforcement schedule,** every occurrence of the desired behavior is reinforced. This schedule can be very effective in the early stages of learning new behavior, because every occurrence of the desired behavior has a pleasant consequence.

partial reinforcement schedule

A schedule in which only some occurrences of the desired behavior are reinforced.

Partial Reinforcement   In the real world of organizations, it is often impossible to reinforce every correct behavior. With a **partial reinforcement schedule,** the reinforcement is administered only after some occurrences of the correct behavior. There are four types of partial reinforcement schedules: fixed interval, fixed ratio, variable interval, and variable ratio.

fixed-interval schedule

A reinforcement schedule that rewards employees at specified time intervals.

Fixed-interval schedule: The **fixed-interval schedule** rewards employees at specified time intervals. If an employee displays the correct behavior each day, reinforcement may occur every week. Regular paychecks or quarterly bonuses are examples of a fixed-interval reinforcement. At Leone Ackerly's Mini Maid franchise in Marietta, Georgia, workers are rewarded with an attendance bonus each pay period if they have come to work every day on time and in uniform.[20]

fixed-ratio schedule

A reinforcement schedule in which reinforcement occurs after a specified number of desired responses, say, after every fifth.

Fixed-ratio schedule: With a **fixed-ratio schedule,** reinforcement occurs after a specified number of desired responses, say, after every fifth. For example, paying a field hand $1.50 for picking ten pounds of peppers is a fixed-ratio schedule. Most piece-rate pay systems and sales contests are considered fixed-ratio schedules.

Variable-interval schedule: With a **variable-interval schedule,** reinforcement is administered at random times that cannot be predicted by the employee. An example would be a random inspection by the manufacturing superintendent of the production floor, at which time he or she commends employees on their good behavior.

Variable-ratio schedule: The **variable-ratio schedule** is based on a random number of desired behaviors rather than on variable time periods. Reinforcement may occur sometimes after 5, 12, 13, or 27 displays of behavior. One example is the attraction of slot machines for gamblers. People anticipate that the machine will pay a jackpot after a certain number of plays, but the exact number of plays is variable.

The schedules of reinforcement are illustrated in Exhibit 6.5. Reinforcement can be a very powerful motivator of behavior. For example, a car salesman in Columbus, Ohio, needed to sell one more car to win a trip to Jamaica and Mexico.[21] Although he started experiencing lower back pain, he ignored it because he had a potential customer. He says, "I thought I had kidney stones. I was stooped over a little bit from the pain, but I wanted to win." He sold the customer a truck, claimed the prize, and drove himself to the emergency room. An X ray showed that he had broken a major artery in his abdomen, a potentially deadly medical problem.

The effects of reinforcement on learning and motivation are different for each schedule of reinforcement. Continuous reinforcement is most effective for establishing new learning, but behavior is vulnerable to extinction. Partial reinforcement schedules are more effective for maintaining behavior over extended time periods. The most powerful is the variable-ratio schedule, because employee behavior will persist for a long time to gain the reinforcement.[22] One

variable-interval schedule

A reinforcement schedule in which reinforcement is administered at random times that cannot be predicted by the employee.

variable-ratio schedule

A reinforcement schedule based on a random number of desired behaviors rather than on variable time periods.

exhibit | **6.5**

Schedules of Reinforcement

Schedule of Reinforcement	Nature of Reinforcement	Effect on Behavior When Applied	Effect on Behavior When Withdrawn	Example
Continuous	Reward given after each desired behavior	Leads to fast learning of new behavior	Rapid extinction	Praise
Fixed-interval	Reward given at fixed time intervals	Leads to average and irregular performance	Rapid extinction	Weekly paycheck
Fixed-ratio	Reward given at fixed amounts of output	Quickly leads to very high and stable performance	Rapid extinction	Piece-rate pay system
Variable-interval	Reward given at variable times	Leads to moderately high and stable performance	Slow extinction	Performance appraisal and awards given at random times each month
Variable-ratio	Reward given at variable amounts of output	Leads to very high performance	Slow extinction	Sales bonus tied to number of sales calls, with random checks

small business that successfully uses reinforcement theory is Parson's Pine Products.

Parsons Pine Products

Parsons Pine Products has only 75 employees, but it is the world's largest manufacturer of slats for louvered doors and shutters. Managers have developed a positive reinforcement scheme for motivating and rewarding workers. The plan includes the following:

1. *Safety pay* Every employee who goes for a month without a lost-time accident receives a bonus equal to four hours' pay.
2. *Retro pay* If the company saves money when its workers' compensation premiums go down because of a lower accident rate, the savings are distributed among employees.
3. *Well pay* Employees receive monthly well pay equal to eight hours' wages if they have been neither absent nor tardy.
4. *Profit pay* All company earnings above 4 percent after taxes go into a bonus pool, which is shared among employees.

The plan for reinforcing correct behaviors has been extraordinarily effective. Parsons's previous accident rate had been 86 percent above the state average; today it is 32 percent below it. Turnover and tardiness are minimal, and absenteeism has dropped to almost nothing. The plan works because the reinforcement schedules are strictly applied, with no exceptions. Owner James Parsons has said, "One woman called to say that a tree had fallen, and she couldn't get her car out. She wanted me to make an exception. If I did that, I'd be doing it all the time."[23]

Reinforcement also works at such organizations as Campbell Soup Co., Emery Air Freight, Michigan Bell, and General Electric, because managers reward appropriate behavior. They tell employees what they can do to receive reinforcement, tell them what they are doing wrong, distribute rewards equitably, tailor rewards to behaviors, and keep in mind that failure to reward deserving behavior has an equally powerful impact on employees.

Reward and punishment motivational practices are used in many organizations, with as many as 94 percent of companies in the United States reporting that they reward performance or merit with pay.

Social Learning Theory

social learning theory

A learning and motivation theory that proposes that individuals learn to behave by observing others, or models.

Social learning theory proposes that individuals learn to behave by observing others, or models.[24] Individuals will be motivated to adopt the model's behavior that they see is reinforced or rewarded. According to social learning theory, motivation and learning are based on observing others, understanding their behaviors, and interpreting their actions. A key assumption is that through observing the activities and reward patterns of others, individuals make choices about future behaviors. Individuals are most likely to model individuals whom they are similar to, or attracted to, based on their trustworthiness, expertise, status, or ability.

Besides emphasizing that individuals may be motivated to engage in certain behaviors based on what behaviors they see others get reinforced for, social learning theory also emphasizes that motivation is influenced by an individual's judgment about whether he or she can successfully behave in a certain way, called **self-efficacy.** Self-efficacy affects one of the major components of expectancy theory—the effort → performance relationship described earlier. Research has demonstrated a strong relationship between self-efficacy and learning and performance.[25] An individual with high levels

self-efficacy

A person's judgment about whether he or she can successfully behave in a certain way.

of self-efficacy will exert more effort and is more likely to persist when encountering obstacles or barriers to performance. An individual with low self-efficacy is more likely to quit trying, believing that he or she cannot perform the behavior. For example, employees may not be motivated to use a new software package if they don't have confidence in their abilities to master the skills needed to use it.

apply it

1. Consider an activity at home or at work that you really want to do. It could be a hobby, sport, project, or even homework for this class. Using reinforcement or social learning theory, try to explain your motivation for performing this activity.

2. For a week, jot down examples you see of people's behavior related to reinforcement theory. Find at least one example each of positive reinforcement, avoidance learning, extinction, and punishment in action. Then, try out one of the strategies to see whether it can change someone's behavior (be careful about the situation that you try this on since you're new at this practice). How successful are these strategies? Bring your notes on what you observed and tried to class for discussion.

Motivation is based on a desired future state

Motivation can also be affected by a person's desire for the achievement of certain outcomes. **Goal-setting theory** suggests that an employee's behavior is influenced by a future state that the employee desires to reach. This desired future state is known as a **goal.** Goal-setting theory assumes that motivation comes from conscious goals and intentions.

goal-setting theory

A theory that suggests that employee behavior is influenced by a future state that the employee desires to reach.

goal

A desired future state.

Criteria for Effective Goals

To ensure goal-setting benefits for the organization, certain characteristics and guidelines should be adopted.[26] The characteristics of effective goals are listed in Exhibit 6.6 and meet the following criteria.

They Are Specific and Measurable When possible, goals should be expressed in quantitative terms, such as increasing profits by 2 percent, decreasing scrap by 1 percent, or increasing average teacher effectiveness ratings from 3.5 to 3.7. A team at Sealed Air Corporation, a manufacturer of packaging materials, was motivated by a goal to reduce by two hours the average time needed to change machine settings. The team was spurred to keep going when members could see that their earliest efforts reduced changeover time by a significant amount.[27] Not all goals can be expressed in numerical terms, but vague goals have little motivating power for employees. Goals should be precisely defined and allow for measurable progress. For example, Liisa Joronen, chairman of SOL Cleaning Service, believes in giving teams the right to set their own performance goals; however, she's a stickler for accountability. "The more we free our people from rules," she says, "the more we need good measurements." Every time SOL lands a contract, the salesperson works at the new customer's site along with the SOL team that will do the future cleaning. Together they establish

exhibit | **6.6**
Characteristics of Effective Goals

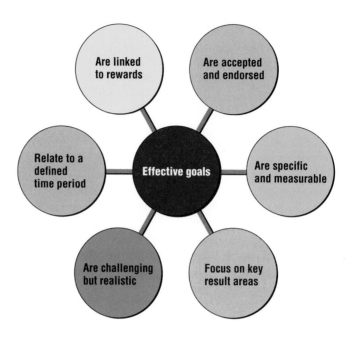

performance goals. Every month, customers rate the team's performance based on the goals.[28]

They Are Focused on Key Result Areas   Goals cannot be set for every aspect of employee behavior or organizational performance; if they were, their sheer number would render them meaningless. Instead, managers should identify a few key result areas—perhaps four or five for any organizational department or job. Key result areas are activities that contribute most to company performance.[29] Robert Hershey, partner in charge of KPMG Peat Marwick's World-Class Finance Practice, recommends that companies as a whole track no more than 20 key result areas in four distinct categories: financial indicators, customer-related indicators, process-related indicators, and future-value indicators (including human resources).[30]

They Are Challenging but Realistic   Goals should be challenging but not unreasonably difficult to reach. One newly hired manager discovered that his staff would have to work 100-hour weeks to accomplish everything expected of them. When goals are unrealistic, they set employees up for failure and lead to decreasing employee morale.[31] However, if goals are too easy, employees may not feel motivated. Tom Peters, coauthor of *In Search of Excellence,* believes that the best programs start with extremely ambitious goals, called *stretch goals,* that challenge employees to meet high standards. Companies such as 3M bring out the best in their employees by making goals ever more challenging. The CEO of 3M has decreed that 30 percent of sales must come from products introduced in the past four years; the old standard was 25 percent.[32] Managers should, however, make sure that goals are attainable within the existing resource base, not beyond a department's time, equipment, and financial resources.

They Are Related to a Defined Time Period   Goals should specify the time period over which they will be achieved and include a deadline on which goal attainment will be measured. A goal of setting up a customer database could have a deadline such as June 30, 2002. If a strategic goal involves a two- to three-year time horizon, specific dates for achieving parts of it can be set up. For example, strategic sales goals could be established on a three-year time horizon, with a $100 million target in year one, a $129 million target in year two, and a $165 million target in year three.

They Are Linked to Rewards   The ultimate impact of goals depends on the extent to which salary increases, promotions, and awards are based on goal achievement. People who attain goals should be rewarded. Rewards give meaning and significance to goals and help commit employees to achieving them. Failure to attain goals often is due to factors outside employees' control. For example, failure to achieve a financial goal may be associated with a drop in market demand due to industry recession; thus, an employee could not be expected to reach it. Nevertheless, a reward may be appropriate if the employee partially achieved goals under difficult circumstances.[33]

They Are Accepted and Endorsed   For goals to affect performance, individuals must accept a goal and endorse it—that is, be committed to it. One way to foster acceptance and commitment is through allowing individuals to participate in setting the goal rather than assigning them a goal. In fact, self-set goals are frequently more desirable than assigned goals because they automatically create higher levels of commitment to the goal.[34]

Potential Negative Consequences of Goals

While goal setting is one of the easiest motivation theories to understand and apply, it is important to understand the potential negative consequences of goals.[35] First, goals can narrow an individual's focus so that he or she performs only behaviors directly associated with meeting the goal, at the cost of other important behaviors. Second, individuals can experience conflict and sacrifice performance on one goal to meet another goal. Third, difficult goals do not always result in high performance on complex tasks; goal setting may cause individuals to adopt less effective work strategies.

For example, a Minneapolis-area department store established sales goals for all salespeople. Salespeople were rewarded for selling merchandise. As a result, it was in a salesperson's best interest to "upsell," or try to convince a customer that he needed additional apparel that he didn't necessarily come to the store to purchase. For example, a salesperson might suggest a tie to go with a dress shirt. Returned merchandise was counted against the salesperson's sales. Also, salespeople received no incentives for performing routine but important tasks such as stocking inventory. What happened? Stockrooms were a mess, and when customers wanted to return merchandise, they were told to take it to another branch of the department store in the same area. Clearly, the sales goals were effective in generating sales but thus created animosity between stores, customer dissatisfaction with "pushy" sales practices, and sloppy inventory control. As a result, the store discontinued the goal program.

Let's look at how Etec Systems uses goals to motivate employee performance.

🐝 Etec Systems

Etec Systems, Inc., practically owns the market for pattern generation equipment—expensive machines that use lasers and electron beams to print intricate patterns onto silicon wafers. However, when Stephen Cooper took over as Etec's new president, the company was generating red ink at the rate of $1 million a month. What's worse, politicians and the press were pointing to Etec as a symbol of the decline of U.S. industry. Everyone thought Cooper was crazy when he announced a goal to generate $500 million in revenues by the year 2000. Four years later, Etec was being hailed as one of the most remarkable comebacks in Silicon Valley. Revenues increased by 75 percent and keep going up, while profits also are steadily growing.

High-tech industries change so rapidly that many people think it's impossible to plan for the future. At Etec, managers spend most of their time dealing with short-term crises. Yet Cooper turned Etec around by getting back to the basics of planning: "When a company has a clear mission, and people know how their individual mission fits into the big picture, everyone paddles in the same direction," he says. The company is well on its way to reaching Cooper's audacious goal, thanks to a specific, step-by-step plan that helps employees maintain clarity in the face of rapid change. To be successful, Cooper says, people need to understand two fundamental issues: "What's expected of me and how do I accomplish it?"

At Etec Systems, all 800 employees are intimately involved in planning. Cooper wants everyone to understand the mission and to understand how his or her work fits into the big picture. He sets stretch goals that prompt employees to reach for the stars. Each employee develops a personal list of goals and plans that correlate with those of the department and organization. Each person in the company, from shop-floor workers to the CEO, identifies five to seven key goals, creates metrics to track progress, and ranks each goal's importance relative to the others. However, Etec realizes that plans cannot be static. Each week, every employee meets briefly with a direct supervisor to review plans and work together on modifications. The end result of Etec's simple system is that every person in the organization knows what he or she should be doing, how important it is relative to other assignments, and how it relates to the goals of other employees. Etec's system thus enables the company's 800 employees to manage themselves. In a company moving as fast as Etec, says manager Phil Arnold, the system helps you to "keep your eye on the ball."[36]

apply it

1. Pretend that you are a coach of a college sports team. Using goal-setting theory, what steps would you take to motivate your team? How would you decide which goals to choose?

Process theories of motivation are applied in many ways throughout organizations

Since process theories of motivation relate to the situations that employees face, organizations can vary those situations so that they are more rewarding for employees. And motivated employees can make the difference between success and failure. Process theories are applied to managing employee performance, providing incentives through compensation, empowering employees, managing nontraditional employees, and motivating across cultural barriers.

Performance Management

performance management

The process through which managers ensure that employees' activities are meeting organizational goals.

Performance management is the process through which managers ensure that employees' activities are meeting organizational goals.[37] Performance management systems are used to help identify what employee behaviors, results, and activities are necessary for meeting the organization's strategic plans. They are also used for many administrative decisions such as pay raises; determining incentives, promotions, and layoffs; and recognition of individual performance. In addition, performance management systems are used to develop employees by providing feedback on their strengths and weaknesses. Performance management systems have three parts—defining performance, measuring performance, and feeding back performance information to employees.

Several process theories of motivation can be used to increase the effectiveness of performance management systems. Goal setting is very important. As we mentioned earlier in the chapter, it is one of the most effective motivators of performance. For a performance management system to result in improvement, manager and employee should agree to a specific improvement goal and a follow-up date to review the employees' progress toward the goal.

Acceptability of feedback and decisions made using the performance management system is also important. Acceptability is affected by the extent to which employees believe the system is fair. Research suggests that performance management systems that are perceived as unfair are likely to be legally challenged, used incorrectly, and decrease employee motivation.[38] There are several implications of procedural and distributive justice for performance management systems.[39]

As Exhibit 6.7 shows, to enhance employees' perceptions of fairness, managers need to make sure employees understand the performance standards on which an incentive or pay plan is based. Managers need to ensure that consistent standards are used in evaluating employees, employees are

---

exhibit **6.7**
Fairness Perceptions

Indicate the extent to which your supervisor did each of the following:

1. Was honest and ethical in dealing with you.
2. Gave you an opportunity to express your side.
3. Used consistent standards in evaluating your performance.
4. Considered your views regarding your performance.
5. Gave you feedback that helped you learn how well you were doing.
6. Was completely candid and frank with you.
7. Showed a real interest in trying to be fair.
8. Became thoroughly familiar with your performance.
9. Took into account factors beyond your control.
10. Got input from you before a recommendation.
11. Made clear what was expected of you.

Indicate how much of an opportunity existed, after the last raise decision, for you to do each of the following things:

12. Make an appeal about the size of a raise.
13. Express your feelings to your supervisor about the salary decision.
14. Discuss, with your supervisor, how your performance was evaluated.
15. Develop, with your supervisor, an action plan for future performance.

Source: Republished by permission of the Academy of Management from R. Folger and M. A. Konovsky from "Effects of Procedural and Distributive Justice on Reactions to Raise Decisions," *Academy of Management Journal 32,* 1989, p. 115, copyright 1989 Academy of Management. Permission conveyed through Copyright Clearance Center.

allowed to challenge the evaluation, and timely and complete feedback is provided. Also, employees should be given an opportunity to provide their views regarding their performance and the ways it should be evaluated, as well as an opportunity to appeal any decision they feel is incorrect.

Organizational Behavior Modification

As we mentioned earlier, organizational behavior modification (OB mod) is a motivation technique based on reinforcement theory that provides managers with a behavior management framework to identify, analyze, and modify employees' behavior for performance improvement. OB mod involves five steps: identifying, measuring, analyzing, intervening in, and evaluating behavior.[40] The first step is to identify the behavior that needs to be changed. The behavior should be observable (e.g., coming to work on time, behaving safely). The second step is to measure how frequently the behavior occurs. The next step is to analyze the cues or antecedents and the consequences of the behavior. Next, an intervention strategy is applied, which may include any of the types of reinforcement shown earlier in Exhibit 6.4. The last step is to test the effectiveness of the intervention strategy to determine whether it led to observable behavior change.

For example, an organizational behavior modification program in a bakery focused on eliminating unsafe employee behaviors.[41] These behaviors included employees who climbed over conveyor belts (rather than walking around them) and stuck their hands into equipment to free jammed material without turning the equipment off. Employees were shown slides of safe and unsafe behavior. After watching the slide show, employees were shown a graph of the number of times safe behaviors were observed during the past several weeks. Employees were encouraged to increase the number of safe behaviors they demonstrated on the job. They were told that there were several reasons for increasing the number of safe behaviors: for their own protection, to decrease company costs, and to help the plant improve its safety ratings. Safety reminders were posted in employees' work areas. Also, data showing the number of safe behaviors performed by employees continued to be collected and displayed on a graph in the work area. Managers were trained to praise the employees whenever they saw them performing a safe work behavior. The data showing the number of safe behaviors and the managers' recognition of safe behavior were the positive reinforcers. As a result of the program, the incidence of safe behavior rose from 70 percent to close to 100 percent.

Is OB mod effective? A recent review of research on OB mod programs that focused on performance over the last 20 years found on average a 17 percent improvement in performance.[42]

Management by Objectives

management by objectives (MBO)

A method of management whereby managers and employees define goals for every department, project, and person and use them to monitor subsequent performance.

Management by objectives (MBO) is a method whereby managers and employees define goals for every department, project, and person and use them to monitor subsequent performance.[43] A model of the essential steps of the MBO process is presented in Exhibit 6.8. For MBO to be successful, the following four steps must be taken:[44]

exhibit | **6.8**

Model of the MBO Process

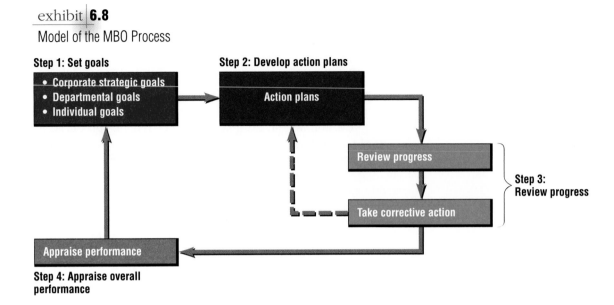

Step 1: Set goals

- Corporate strategic goals
- Departmental goals
- Individual goals

Step 2: Develop action plans

Action plans

Review progress

Take corrective action

**Step 3:
Review progress**

Appraise performance

**Step 4: Appraise overall
performance**

1. *Set goals* This is the most difficult step in MBO. Setting goals involves employees at all levels and looks beyond day-to-day activities to answer the question, What are we trying to accomplish? A good goal should be concrete and realistic, provide a specific target and time frame, and assign responsibility. Goals may be quantitative or qualitative, depending on whether outcomes are measurable. Quantitative goals are described in numerical terms, such as "Salesperson Jones will obtain 16 new accounts in December." Qualitative goals use statements, such as "Marketing will reduce complaints by improving customer service next year." Goals should be jointly derived. Mutual agreement between employee and supervisor creates the strongest commitment to achieving goals. In the case of teams, all team members may participate in setting goals.

2. *Develop action plans* An action plan defines the course of action needed to achieve the stated goals. Action plans are made for both individuals and departments.

3. *Review progress* A periodic progress review is important to ensure that action plans are working. These reviews can occur informally between managers and subordinates, and the organization may wish to conduct three-, six-, or nine-month reviews during the year. This periodic checkup allows managers and employees to see whether they are on target or whether corrective action is necessary. Managers and employees should not be locked into predefined behavior and must be willing to take whatever steps are necessary to produce meaningful results. The point of MBO is to achieve goals. The action plan can be changed whenever goals are not being met.

4. *Appraise overall performance* The final step in MBO is to carefully evaluate whether annual goals have been achieved for both individuals and departments. Success or failure to achieve goals can become part

of the performance appraisal system and the designation of salary increases and other rewards. The appraisal of departmental and overall corporate performance shapes goals for the next year. The MBO cycle repeats itself on an annual basis.

The specific application of MBO must fit the needs of each company. For example, Producers Gas and Transmission Company is a medium-sized refinery and distributor of gasoline and other refinery products. A major concern of top management was an unusually high employee accident rate during the previous year. Ten employees had minor injuries, four were severely injured, and one was killed. The company lost 112 employee days of work due to accidents. Top management discussed the accident rate with department heads and decided on a corporate goal of a 50 percent reduction in all accidents for the following year.

Middle managers developed an action plan that included (1) establishing an employee safety training program, (2) creating a companywide safety committee, and (3) setting up a new system of safety recognition. Also, (4) line supervisors were asked to develop safety training sessions for their departments within 60 days, and (5) middle managers were given 30 days to nominate supervisors to the safety committee. Finally, (6) the safety committee had 30 days in which to design a safety recognition program, including awards.

Progress was reviewed through the compilation of quarterly safety reports measuring the percentage of accidents compared with the previous year. The action plan could be revised if obstacles were discovered. The safety committee appraised the safety performance of each department every 90 days and posted the results for all employees to see. Letters of commendation were given to departments that met or exceeded the 50 percent reduction goal.

At the end of the year, an overall performance appraisal was held for individuals, departments, and the corporation as a whole. Departments that had successfully reduced accidents by 50 percent were given awards. Information about safety procedures and accident rates was used to set a new safety goal for the next year. Delinquent departments were given stringent goals. Most important, the company achieved its goal of reducing accidents by 50 percent. The MBO system energized employee actions companywide toward a goal deemed critical by top management. MBO got all employees working toward the same end.[45]

Many companies, including Intel, Tenneco, Black & Decker, and Du Pont, have adopted MBO, and most managers believe that MBO is an effective management tool.[46] Managers believe they are better oriented toward goal achievement when MBO is used. Like any system, MBO achieves benefits when used properly but results in problems when used improperly. Benefits and problems are summarized in Exhibit 6.9.

The benefits of the MBO process can be many. Corporate goals are more likely to be achieved when they focus manager and employee efforts. Performance is improved because employees are committed to attaining the goal, are motivated because they help decide what is expected, and are free to be resourceful. Goals at lower levels are aligned with and enable the attainment of goals at top management levels.

Benefits of MBO	Problems with MBO
1. Manager and employee efforts are focused on activities that will lead to goal attainment.	1. Constant change prevents MBO from taking hold.
2. Performance can be improved at all company levels.	2. An environment of poor employer-employee relations reduces MBO effectiveness.
3. Employees are motivated.	3. Strategic goals may be displaced by operational goals.
4. Departmental and individual goals are aligned with company goals.	4. Mechanistic organizations and values that discourage participation can harm the MBO process.
	5. Too much paperwork saps MBO energy.

exhibit 6.9

MBO Benefits and Problems

Problems with MBO occur when a company faces rapid change. The environment and internal activities must be somewhat stable for performance to be measured and compared against goals. When new goals must be set every few months, there is no time for action plans and appraisal to take effect. Also, poor employer-employee relations reduce effectiveness because there is an element of distrust between managers and workers. Sometimes goal displacement occurs if employees focus exclusively on their operational goals to the detriment of other teams or departments. Overemphasis on operational goals can harm the attainment of overall goals. Another problem arises in mechanistic organizations characterized by rigidly defined tasks and rules that may not be compatible with MBO's emphasis on mutual determination of goals by employee and supervisor. In addition, when participation is discouraged, employees will lack the training and values to jointly set goals with employers. Finally, if MBO becomes a process of filling out annual paperwork rather than energizing employees to achieve goals, it becomes an empty exercise. Once the paperwork is completed, employees forget about the goals, perhaps even resenting the paperwork in the first place.

Incentive Compensation

Many organizations use various types of incentive compensation as a way to motivate employees to higher levels of performance. **Incentive compensation** includes rewards employees receive, including stock or cash, for meeting individual, team, department, or organizational goals. However, keep in mind that effective organizations do not use incentive plans as the sole basis of motivation. Exhibit 6.10 summarizes several methods of incentive compensation.

The use of incentive compensation methods is a focus of some controversy. A review of research studies of the effects of rewards on performance found about half of the studies reporting a detrimental effect and half of the studies reporting no effect or a positive effect.[47] Studies focusing primarily on the relationship between financial incentives and performance have found that financial incentives are not related to the *quality* of performance but are related to the *quantity* of performance.[48] A growing number of critics say that financial rewards do not motivate the kind of behavior

incentive compensation

The use of such rewards as stock or cash when employees meet individual, team, department, or organizational goals.

exhibit 6.10

Incentive Methods

Program Name	Purpose
Pay for Performance	Rewards individual employees in proportion to their performance contributions. Also called *merit pay*.
Gain Sharing	Rewards all employees and managers within a business unit when predetermined performance targets are met. Encourages teamwork.
Employee Stock Ownership Plan (ESOP)	Gives employees part ownership of the organization, enabling them to share in improved profit performance.
Lump-Sum Bonuses	Rewards employees with a one-time cash payment based on performance.
Pay for Knowledge	Links employee salary with the number of task skills acquired. Workers are motivated to learn the skills for many jobs, thus increasing company flexibility and efficiency.
Team-based Compensation	Rewards employees for behavior and activities that benefit the team, such as cooperation, listening, and empowering others.

When Wall Street firm Goldman Sachs went public in 1999, after 130 years as a partnership, every employee received compensation in the form of a stock award. However, the company uses more than incentive compensation to reward its employees. Those working late into the night are ferried home by a free limo service, and others like Mark Diorio (photo), who helps manage Goldman Sachs's database team, can work flexible hours to meet their family needs. Diorio works at home Mondays and alternate Fridays to be there for his kids.
(Source: © Don Standing)

that organizations want and need, arguing that "carrot-and-stick" approaches are a holdover from the Industrial Age and are inappropriate and ineffective in today's economy. Today's workplace demands innovation and creativity from everyone—behaviors that rarely are inspired by money or other financial incentives. Reasons for criticism of carrot-and-stick approaches include the following:

1. *Extrinsic rewards diminish intrinsic rewards*   As discussed previously, when people are motivated to seek an extrinsic reward, whether it be a bonus, an award, or the approval of a supervisor, generally they focus on the reward rather than on the work they do to achieve it. Thus, the intrinsic satisfaction people receive from performing their jobs actually declines. When people lack intrinsic rewards in their work, their performance stays just adequate to achieve the reward offered. In the worst-case scenario, employees may cover up mistakes, such as hiding an on-the-job accident in order to win a safety award.

2. *Extrinsic rewards are temporary*   Offering outside incentives may ensure short-term success but not long-term high performance. When employees are focused only on a reward, they lose interest in their work. Without personal interest, the potential for exploration, creativity, and innovation disappears. Although the current deadline or goal may be met, better ways of working will not be discovered.

3. *Extrinsic rewards assume people are driven by lower level needs*   Rewards such as bonuses, pay increases, and even praise presume that the primary reason people initiate and persist in behavior is to satisfy lower level needs. However, particularly among today's knowledge workers, behavior also is based on yearnings for self-expression and on feelings of self-esteem and self-worth. Offers of an extrinsic reward do not encourage the myriad behaviors that are motivated by people's needs to express themselves and realize their higher needs for growth and fulfillment.

what would you do?

BLOOMINGDALE'S INCENTIVE PAY PLAN

Bloomingdale's is at the forefront of a quiet revolution sweeping department store retailing. Thousands of hourly sales employees are being converted to commission pay. Bloomingdale's hopes to use commissions to attract better salespeople, to motivate employees to work harder, and to enable them to earn more money. For example, under the old plan, a Bloomingdale's salesclerk in women's wear would earn about $16,000 a year, based on $7 per hour and a 0.5 percent commission on $500,000 in sales. Under the new plan, the annual pay would be $25,000, based on a 5 percent commission on $500,000 in sales.

John Palmerio, who works in the men's shoe salon, is enthusiastic about the changeover. His pay has increased an average of $175 per week. But in women's lingerie, employees are less enthusiastic. A target of $1,600 in sales per week is difficult to achieve but is necessary for salespeople to earn their previous salaries and even to keep their jobs. In previous years, the practice of commission pay was limited to big-ticket items such as furniture, appliances, and men's suits, where extra sales skill pays off. The move into small-item purchases may not work as well, but Bloomingdale's and other stores are trying it anyway.

One question is whether Bloomingdale's can create more customer-oriented salespeople when they work on commission. They may be reluctant to handle complaints, make returns, and clean shelves, preferring instead to chase customers. Moreover, it cost Bloomingdale's about $1 million per store to install the commission system because of training programs, computer changes, and increased pay in many departments. If the overall impact on service is negative, the increased sales may not seem worthwhile.

1. What theories of motivation underlie the switch from salary to commission pay?

2. Besides commissions, what other incentives might Bloomingdale's consider to motivate sales employees? Bob Nelson, author of two best-selling books on motivation, *1001 Ways to Reward Employees* and *1001 Ways to Energize Employees,* provides many excellent resources at his Web site (www.nelson-motivation.com). Check out the page titled "Bob Nelson's Guide to the Best Employee Rewards and Recognition Sites on the Web." Use the Web site in answering this question.

3. As a customer, would you prefer to shop where employees are motivated to make commissions?

Source: Based on Francine Schwadel, "Chain Finds Incentives a Hard Sell," *The Wall Street Journal,* July 5, 1990, p. B4; and Amy Dunkin, "Now Salespeople Really Must Sell for Their Supper," *Business Week,* July 31, 1989, pp. 50–52.

As Rob Rodin discovered at Marshall Industries, today's organizations need employees who are motivated to think, experiment, and continuously search for ways to solve new problems. Everybody thought Rodin was crazy when he decided to wipe out all individual incentives for his sales force at Marshall Industries, a large distributor of electronic components based in El Monte, California. He did away with all bonuses, commissions, vacations, and other awards and rewards. All salespeople would receive a base salary plus the opportunity for profit sharing, which would be the same percentage of salary for everyone, based on the entire company's performance. Six years later, Rodin says productivity per person has tripled at the company, but still he gets questions and criticism about his decision.[49]

Alfie Kohn, one of the most vocal critics of carrot-and-stick approaches, offers the following advice to managers regarding how to pay employees: "Pay well, pay fairly, and then do everything you can to get money off people's minds." Indeed, as discussed in Chapter 5 and in this chapter, there is some evidence that money is not primarily what people work for. Managers should understand the limits of extrinsic motivators and work to satisfy employees' higher, as well as lower, needs. To be

exhibit **6.11**

Principles for Effective Use
of Incentives

1. The organization should first identify what it wants to accomplish with an incentive program.
2. If an incentive is unavailable, don't use it.
3. Employees need to be eligible for a reward to be motivated to obtain it.
4. For incentives to be motivating, they must be visible.
5. A good incentive rewards for the past and motivates for the future.
6. Incentives need to be administered on a timely basis.
7. The best incentives are those the employee does not automatically receive.
8. Don't underestimate the importance of nonfinancial incentives.
9. Get peers, subordinates, and customers involved in determining incentives.
10. Employees need to understand how their behavior determines the incentives they receive.

Source: Based on S. Kerr, "Practical, cost-neutral alternatives that you know, but don't practice," *Organizational Dynamics,* 1999, pp. 61–70; S. Hays, "Pros and Cons of pay for performance," *Workforce,* February 1999, pp. 69–72; and J. Laabs, "Line Managers Can Make (or Break) Incentives Programs," *Workforce,* February 1999, pp. 80–83.

motivated, employees need jobs that offer self-satisfaction in addition to a yearly pay raise.[50]

It is unrealistic to assume that all incentive programs work or that, by taking away individual incentives, productivity will improve. These programs can be effective if they are used appropriately and combined with motivational ideas that provide employees with intrinsic rewards and meet higher level needs. Exhibit 6.11 lists principles for the effective use of incentives. As the exhibit shows, it is important to first identify the purpose of the incentive program. For example, is it better service, higher productivity, or a combination of the two? Employees need to understand how their work behavior affects the incentive. Also, everyone who contributes to reaching the desired outcomes should receive an incentive, with the amount based on the importance of their contribution. To effectively use incentives, this means you need to identify every employee's role in reaching the outcome. Compensation experts call this identifying the "line of sight." For example, in selling a piece of software, salespeople have a major role. However, administrative staff and product engineers may also support the sale. It is important to identify how you will measure whether employees are meeting the purpose of the program. Will you use objective data, such as sales, or more subjective data, such as performance ratings? You also need to evaluate employees using information from people who are in the best position to evaluate them—including customers and peers.

Incentives can be motivating only if they are visible and received as soon as possible. Consider the effects of a low quiz grade on your performance if you receive it the day after you take the quiz instead of two weeks later. You can change your behavior! Effective incentives can also be lost. That is, employees will not continue to receive the incentive if they (or the organization) do not meet their goals. Incentives are extra—employees should not begin to view them as a "right" or "entitlement." Nonfinancial incentives can also be used. Nonfinancial incentives include recognition, time off, or the opportunity to perform interesting and meaningful work.

Empowerment

The newest trend in motivation is **empowerment,** the delegation of power or authority to subordinates in an organization.[51] Increasing employee power heightens motivation for task accomplishment because people improve their own effectiveness, choosing how to do a task and using their creativity.[52] Most people come into an organization with the desire to do a good job, and empowerment releases the motivation that is already there.

Ralph Stayer, CEO of Johnsonville Foods, believes a manager's strongest power comes from committed and motivated employees: "Real power comes from giving it up to others who are in a better position to do things than you are."[53] The manager who shares power with employees receives motivation and creativity in return.

Empowering employees means giving them four elements that enable them to act more freely to accomplish their jobs: information, knowledge, power, and rewards.[54]

Information about Company Performance   In companies where employees are fully empowered, such as Com-Corp Industries, no information is secret. At Com-Corp, every employee has access to all financial information, including executive salaries.

Knowledge and Skills to Contribute to Company Goals   Companies can use training programs to help employees acquire the knowledge and skills they need to contribute to organizational performance. At Tellabs, Inc., a maker of sophisticated telephone equipment, CEO Grace Pastiak personally leads workshops for about a dozen factory workers each month, enabling them to solve problems and make quality improvements on their own.[55]

Power for Substantive Decisions   Workers must be given the authority to directly influence work procedures and organizational performance, often through quality circles or self-directed work teams. At Compaq Computer, salespeople now work out of their homes and set their own schedules. The company provides a fully equipped, networked computer so workers can share information with colleagues and access comprehensive databases. Under the new system, Compaq's sales force has set new records for productivity.[56]

Rewards Based on Company Performance   Organizations that empower workers often reward them based on the results shown in the company's bottom line. Johnsonville Foods instituted a "company performance share," a fixed percentage of pretax profits to be divided every six months among employees. Individual shares are based on a performance appraisal system designed and administered by a volunteer team of line workers.[57]

Many of today's organizations are implementing empowerment programs, but they are empowering workers to varying degrees. At some companies, empowerment means encouraging workers' ideas while managers retain final authority for decisions; at others it means giving employees almost complete freedom and power to make decisions and exercise initiative and imagination.[58] Current methods of empowerment fall along a continuum, as illustrated in Exhibit 6.12. The continuum runs from a situation

empowerment

The delegation of power or authority to subordinates in an organization.

exhibit | **6.12**

A Continuum of Empowerment

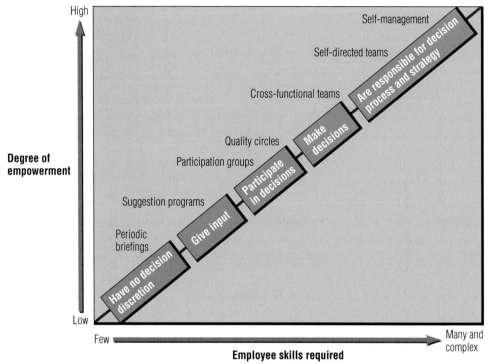

Source: Based on Robert C. Ford and Myron D. Fottler. (1995). "Empowerment: A matter of degree." *Academy of Management Executive 9,* no. 3: 21–31; Lawrence Holpp, "Applied Empowerment," *Training,* February 1994, pp. 39–44; and David P. McCaffrey, Sue R. Faerman, and David W. Hart. (1995, November–December). "The appeal and difficulties of participative systems." *Organization Science 6,* no. 6: 603–627.

in which front-line workers have almost no discretion, such as on a traditional assembly line, to full empowerment, where workers even participate in formulating organizational strategy. An example of full empowerment is when self-directed teams are given the authority to hire, discipline, and dismiss team members and to set compensation rates. Few companies have moved to this level of empowerment. One that has is W. L. Gore and Associates, which operates with no titles, hierarchy, or any of the conventional structures associated with a company of its size. Gore's culture emphasizes teamwork, mutual support, freedom, intrinsic motivation, independent effort, and commitment to the total organization rather than to narrow jobs or departments. With empowerment, workers are motivated because they are intellectually challenged, provided with opportunities to use their minds and imaginations, and given the power to make decisions that affect their work. Research indicates that most people have a need for self-efficacy, which is the capacity to produce results or outcomes, to feel that they are effective.[59] By meeting higher level needs, empowerment can provide powerful motivation.

Empowerment in Strategic Planning   One application of empowerment is employees' involvement in strategic planning. Today, some companies are involving workers at every level of the organization in the strategic planning process. Such organizations are called *learning organizations,* and we will cover them fully in Chapter 18. In this new paradigm, middle managers and planning staff work with line managers and front-line workers to develop dynamic plans that meet the organization's needs. In a complex and competitive business environment, traditional planning done by a select few no longer works. Strategic thinking and execution become the expectation of every employee.[60] Planning comes alive when employees are involved in setting goals and determining the means to reach them.

Becoming a Learning Organization and Empowering Employees

Start with a strong mission: Employee commitment and involvement are critical to helping companies compete in today's rapidly changing world. A compelling mission often serves to increase employee commitment and motivation as well as provide a guide for planning and decision making.[61] In a six-year study of exceptional companies that have stood the test of time, including Wal-Mart, 3M, General Electric, and Johnson & Johnson, James C. Collins and Jerry Porras identified a number of timeless fundamentals that helped make these companies great. They found one of the key factors to be that these companies were guided by a core ideology, values, and a sense of purpose that go beyond just making money and that provide a guide for behavior. For example, a lot of the faith Johnson & Johnson executives place in decentralized managers can be traced to the well-known Johnson & Johnson Credo, a code of ethics that tells managers what to care about and in what order. Interestingly, in this complex $15 billion organization that has never lost money since going public in 1944, the Credo puts profits dead last on the list of things managers should care about.[62]

Set stretch goals: Stretch goals are highly ambitious goals that are so clear, compelling, and imaginative that they fuel progress. When shifting to a learning organization format, top managers can set stretch goals to compel employees to think in new ways. Motorola used stretch goals to improve quality. Leaders first set a goal of a tenfold increase in quality over a two-year period. After this goal was met, they set a new stretch goal of a hundredfold improvement in quality over four years.[63]

Create an environment that encourages learning: A basic value in learning organizations is to question the status quo. Constant questioning opens the gates to creativity and learning. Companies such as Nucor Steel encourage and reward constant experimentation and risk taking. So much worker experimentation is going on that Larry Roos, manager of the Crawfordsville, Indiana, plant, says, "Half the time I don't know who's doing what out there." Although an environment of rampant experimentation can lead to failures, more importantly, it leads to flexibility, learning, and improving.[64]

Design new roles for planning staff: Learning companies transform the conventional planner's job.[65] Planning specialists serve as facilitators and supporters; they do not decide on the substance of goals and plans. Planning experts can be very helpful in gathering data, performing statistical analyses, and doing other specialized tasks. The key difference is that, rather than looking for the "right answers," they supply information to broaden the consideration of issues and support strategic thinking.

Make continuous improvement a way of life: Involving everyone in planning encourages employees to continuously learn and grow, thus helping the organization improve its capability. No plan is set in stone because people are constantly learning and improving. Highly successful companies such as 3M often make their best moves through constant experimentation and improvement. 3M encourages its employees to try just about anything and gives them 15 percent of their work time to do so.

Planning still starts and stops at the top: Top managers create a mission that is worthy of employees' best efforts and provide a framework for planning and goal setting. Even though planning is decentralized, top managers must show support and commitment to the planning process. Top managers also accept responsibility when planning and goal setting are ineffective, rather than blaming the failure on lower level managers or workers.

Springfield Remanufacturing Corporation is an example of a company that believes in empowering employees; it is even involving them in strategic planning.

❦ Springfield Remanufacturing Corporation

Jack Stack, chairman and CEO of Springfield Remanufacturing Corp. (SRC), believes companies can thrive by tapping into people's universal desire to win. SRC, which began as a division of International Harvester, is a business Stack calls tough, loud, and a dirty place where people work with plugs in their ears and leave the factory every day covered in grease. Stack has built a highly successful company based on the philosophy that the best, most efficient, most profitable way to operate a business is to give everybody a voice in how the company is run and a stake in the financial outcome, good or bad.

Stack involves every employee in the planning process and uses a bonus system based on hitting the plan's targets. SRC's planning officially kicks off when Stack and other top executives meet with the sales and marketing managers of SRC's 15 divisions in a formal two-day event. But before that meeting, the sales and marketing managers have done their homework by meeting with managers, supervisors, and front-line workers throughout their divisions. If a manager's plan is beyond the plant's capacity, the workers suggest workable alternatives. By the time managers present their plans to the top brass, everyone in the various divisions has had a say and has thus developed a sense of ownership in the plan.

All employees have access to the company's financial data and can compare performance to the plan. SRC has invested heavily in financial education for all workers—everyone learns what's at risk and what's to be gained, and everyone knows how to make a difference. Kevin Dotson, an ex-Marine who works in the Heavy Duty warehouse, says he learns something new about the financial statements every time he goes to a meeting. "It's not like you have just one meeting and learn everything. . . . But you do understand the lines on the statement that you actually affect. That's how you see how you can be more efficient or how we as a small team within a large team can improve so the next group can take the hand-off more smoothly. We all have different jobs, but we're all pulling for the same goals."[66]

Management of Nontraditional Employees

Many organizations are faced with the problem of finding new employees due to labor shortages and potential employees' lack of skills (recall our discussion of literacy problems in Chapter 3). As a result, organizations are starting to tap nontraditional labor markets, such as people on welfare, to fill job openings. For example, Marriott International operates a welfare-to-work program in several large cities.[67] Marriott is finding hotel employees in people who were previously on welfare because they had dropped out of high school, had problems with drug addiction, had arrest records, and had psychological problems from poor family relationships. Marriott developed the program because it was having difficulty attracting individuals to its lower paying jobs. Most of these people need extensive training in both job skills and life skills, such as how to balance a checkbook. Also, many have not had successful work experiences. As a result, they are likely to have low self-efficacy. Low self-efficacy can cause people to leave jobs, resulting in expensive turnover and training costs for the company.

To improve self-efficacy and motivation with nontraditional employees, organizations can take several steps.[68] First, these employees need to be shown the success of their peers who are now in similar jobs. Second, they need to be constantly reinforced by managers to build their self-confidence. Finally, managers need to help remove any obstacles that may decrease motivation to work or remain employed. In Marriott's case, it removed obstacles by helping to arrange child care, purchasing appropriate work clothes, providing transportation to work, and providing a toll-free telephone number where employees' questions could be answered by a trained counselor.

Cultural Differences in Motivational Processes

Although there are likely cultural differences in motivational processes, research is just starting to identify what those differences might be.[69] For example, a study of expectancy theory perceptions of Japanese, Korean, and American salespeople found significant differences between U.S. salespeople and Japanese and Korean salespeople, but few differences between Japanese and Korean salespeople.[70] U.S. salespeople reported higher expectancies and valued pay increases, job security, promotion, and personal growth and development more than Japanese and Korean salespeople.

Another study found that Dutch and French company executives were skeptical about the benefits of rewards based on performance.[71] Top management compensation practices in the United States, France, and the Netherlands differed. The length of time covered by top managers' compensation plans was much longer in the United States than in the other countries. Top managers' compensation plans in the United States put much more money "at risk" (meaning they would receive the money only if certain company financial goals were reached). However, U.S. managers also had larger bonuses than top managers from France and the Netherlands.

Reactions to pay plans are likely due to national cultural differences in uncertainty avoidance and individualism (recall our discussion of national cultural differences in Chapter 2). Stock options are regarded in France as unjust, shady, immoral, and excessive.[72] "In France everyone thinks it is OK to win several million dollars in a lottery or if you are a football player, but not if you are a successful entrepreneur or manager," says Pascal Brandys, founder of a French biotechnology company. U.S. managers are less resistant to uncertainty and more individualistic than their counterparts in France and the Netherlands. Continuing studies of cultural differences in motivation will no doubt uncover other factors that organizations will need to consider.

apply it

1. Assume that you are a manager of a fast-food restaurant. Your employees are teenagers who work part time. You have recently noticed that the seating area of the restaurant is dirty—tables are sticky, food is left on the tables, napkins are strewn all over, newspapers are not picked up. Using one of the process theories of motivation discussed previously, provide your ideas for motivating employees to clean up the seating area.

summary OF KEY CONCEPTS

- **Motivation is based on perceptions of fairness.** This chapter discusses the process theories of motivation. Process theories explain how individuals choose behaviors to meet their needs and determine whether their choices were successful. Each theory provides a different perspective about motivation. Equity theory emphasizes that motivation is based on how individuals perceive the fairness of outcomes they receive. Fairness is determined based on individuals' perceptions of their inputs and outcomes compared with the inputs and outcomes of others. While equity theory focuses on an individual's evaluation of outcomes, procedural justice suggests that motivation is also affected by perceptions of the fairness of the process through which decisions are made or outcomes are allocated.

- **Motivation is based on expectations and rewards.** Expectancy theory suggests that individuals' choices of behavior are based on the values placed on the outcomes received for the behavior, the amount of effort they believe it will take to demonstrate the behavior, and the likelihood that they will receive outcomes for demonstrating the behavior.

- **Motivation is based on learned consequences of behavior.** Both reinforcement theory and social learning theory suggest that individuals' motivation is based on learning to behave in certain ways based on the reinforcements received. Reinforcement theory emphasizes the reinforcements that an individual personally receives for behavior. Social learning theory suggests that motivation is based on the reinforcements that an individual sees other people receive.

- **Motivation is based on a desired future state.** Goal-setting theory suggests that motivation is based on individuals' conscious attempts to try to reach goals. The characteristics of effective goals include that they are specific and measurable, focused on key areas, challenging but realistic, related to a defined time period, linked to rewards, and accepted and endorsed.

- **Process theories of motivation are applied in many ways throughout organizations.** Process theories of motivation are applied in several motivational programs used by organizations. The recent trend toward empowerment motivates by giving employees more information and authority to make decisions in their work. Several different incentive plans are used, including pay for performance, gain sharing, lump sum bonuses, pay for knowledge, employee stock ownership plans (ESOPs), and team-based compensation. Performance management systems can be used to motivate individuals by providing reinforcement for effective work and providing specific feedback about performance areas that need improvement. Behavior change programs (OB modification) are often used to change behaviors such as accidents and absenteeism by modifying the reinforcements received for these behaviors. Self-efficacy, individuals' confidence that they can successfully perform a job, must be actively managed for nontraditional employees, who may have limited work experiences and success on the job. In addition, cultural differences should be considered to ensure that any motivation plan will suit employees.

KEY terms

process theories, p. 192

equity theory, p. 193

distributive justice, p. 195

procedural justice, p. 195

expectancy theory, p. 196

E → P expectancy, p. 196

P → O expectancy, p. 197

valence, p. 197

reinforcement theory, p. 199

organizational behavior modification (OB mod), p. 200

positive reinforcement, p. 200

avoidance learning, p. 200

punishment, p. 201

extinction, p. 202

schedule of reinforcement, p. 202

continuous reinforcement schedule, p. 202

partial reinforcement schedule, p. 202

fixed-interval schedule, p. 202

fixed-ratio schedule, p. 202

variable-interval schedule, p. 203

variable-ratio schedule, p. 203

social learning theory, p. 204

self-efficacy, p. 204

goal-setting theory, p. 205

goal, p. 205

performance management, p. 208

management by objectives (MBO), p. 210

incentive compensation, p. 213

empowerment, p. 217

DISCUSSION questions

1. Campbell Soup Company reduces accidents with a lottery. Each worker who works 30 days or more without losing a day for a job-related accident is eligible to win prizes in a raffle drawing. Why has this program been successful?

2. If an experienced secretary discovered that she made less money than a newly hired janitor, how would she react? What inputs and outcomes might she evaluate to make this comparison?

3. Take the role of a manager having to get an assistant to use a new software package that replaces one she likes and is comfortable using. What should you do to ensure that your assistant will believe the decision to use the new software package is "fair"?

4. What are the characteristics of effective goals? Would it be better to have no goals at all than to have goals that do not meet these criteria?

5. Many organizations use sales contests and motivational speakers to motivate salespeople to overcome frequent rejections and turndowns. How would these devices help motivate salespeople?

6. How might incentives actually demotivate employees?

7. Explain the relationship between self-efficacy and motivation.

8. What do reinforcement theory and social learning theory have in common? How are they different?

9. Do you think an empowerment program of increased employee authority and responsibility would succeed without being tied to a motivational compensation program, such as gain sharing or ESOPs? Discuss.

10. Integrate several of the process theories discussed in this chapter into a model of motivation. What did you include? Why?

SELF-DISCOVERY exercise

Expectancy Theory and You

Your assignment, your job, is to use expectancy theory to determine how much you are going to study for this course. The outcomes and performance alternatives that are relevant to this determination are listed below. You should draw the expectancy theory diagram and do the necessary calculations to identify the most motivating option. In particular, you will need to

1. assign valences to the outcomes
2. identify the instrumentalities for each performance-outcome relationship
3. calculate the values for each performance alternative
4. assign expectancies to each performance alternative
5. calculate the force for each performance alternative

Outcomes	Assign valences to outcomes
• Getting a good grade in the course • Socializing with friends • Money from part-time job	
	Identify instrumentalities for each performance-outcome relationship
Performance-outcome relationships • Study a lot —good grade 　　　　　—socializing 　　　　　—money • Study moderately—good grade 　　　　　—socializing 　　　　　—money • Don't study—good grade 　　　　　—socializing 　　　　　—money	
Performance alternatives	Calculate values, assign expectancies, calculate forces
• Study a lot 　Value of performance alternative 　Expectancy 　Force • Study a moderate amount 　Value of performance alternative 　Expectancy 　Force • Don't study at all 　Value of performance alternative 　Expectancy 　Force	

Source: Adapted from Courtney Hunt, Northern Illinois University, "Must see TV: The timelessness of television as a teaching tool," presented at Academy of Management, August 2000. Used with permission.

ORGANIZATIONAL BEHAVIOR in your life

Choose two persons you know pretty well (friends or relatives) who have a job. Meet with these people and interview them about their jobs. Take notes on their answers to the following questions.

1. How would you describe your job?
2. Do you have goals at work? If so, what are they?

3. Do you feel the goals motivate your behavior? Why or why not?

Using the criteria for effective goal setting discussed in this chapter, provide your own evaluation of the motivational impact of their goals. Be prepared to share your answers in class.

ORGANIZATIONAL BEHAVIOR news flash

@ Using your Web search engine, use the key words "employee ownership" to search for articles that discuss the pros and cons of employee own-ership of a company. Print out an article that discusses employee ownership. How might ownership improve employees' motivation? Result in less motivation?

global diversity EVENTS

@ We may personally experience unfairness or read newspaper stories or watch television reports in which a person claims he or she is being treated unfairly. Using news listings on your search engine, such as Reuters, AP, ZDNet News, and others, look for stories that deal with the topic of justice or fairness. These could be stories related to unfairness that occurs in the United States or abroad, at work or in society. When you find these stories, consider the following questions:

1. What issue is considered to be unfair in the story? Describe it.
2. Why are the circumstances or outcomes perceived as unfair? Use distributive and procedural justice theory to support your arguments.
3. What steps could be taken to make the circumstances or outcomes be perceived as fair or just?

minicase ISSUE

Motivating a Coach through Goals

Coaching Credentials. John Cooper, head football coach at Ohio State University, has an impressive record. In his twelfth year at Ohio State, he has a record of 97 wins and 33 losses. Only Woody Hayes (1951–1978) and John Wilce (1913–1928) have coached at OSU longer than Cooper. He is the first head coach ever to lead both a Big Ten and a Pac 10 team to Rose Bowl victories—Ohio State over Arizona State and Arizona State over Michigan. His OSU teams have produced a Heisman Trophy winner, 15 first-team All-Americans, and 12 first-round NFL draft picks. His overall record in 21 years as a head coach is 168 wins, 72 losses, and 6 ties.

Football Revenues Support Other Programs. Ohio State cannot afford for people to lose interest in its football team. During the 1997–1998 fiscal year, football generated more than one-third of the revenue for an athletic department that offers one of the most comprehensive intercollegiate sports programs in the country. In that year, football revenue after expenses totaled more than $14.8 million. Men's basketball showed a profit of nearly $3.9 million. All other sports combined—men's and women's—lost nearly $8.7 million.

The extent to which football enhances Ohio State University's national visibility on television and in other media had much to do with the five-year, $9.3 million contract the athletic department signed with Nike three years ago. One game in sold-out Ohio Stadium translates into more than $3 million in revenue for the athletic department. One great season means much more. It is commonplace for universities to see donations schoolwide multiply when their football team reaches a major bowl game such as the Rose Bowl, for example.

Cooper's New Contract. Cooper recently signed a new five-year contract worth $1.1 million annually, with incentives that could make the contract worth even more. He has joined a growing list of college football coaches who are now millionaires, including Steve Spurrier of Florida ($2.5 million per year), Joe Paterno of Penn State, and Bobby Bowden of Florida State (both $1.5 million per year). Cooper's previous contract was signed in 1995 and worth $700,000 per year; it still had four years remaining before it expired. Both Cooper and Ohio State agreed that the contract should be renegotiated. Athletic Director Andy Geiger explains the rationale behind the contract this way: "I want them focused on what they should be focused on. I want them to be well rewarded and secure in what they're doing. And I don't want to be in a situation of wondering every year whether I'm going to be able to keep my coach, if I've got a real good one." The terms of the contract are shown below.

1. What are the positive and negative features of putting academic incentive clauses in a football coach's contract?

2. Should any other incentives be included in the contract? Explain.

3. Why did the university feel that it needed to renegotiate Coach Cooper's contract?

4. Do you think the contract will have any effect on football players' motivation?

5. Using equity theory, explain how the football players may view the contract as "unfair."

Cooper's contract

Base salary	$200,000
Guaranteed yearly bonus	$100,000
Television appearance package	$450,000
Radio appearance package	$25,000
Nike endorsement package	$310,000
Summer camp	$5,000
Coca-Cola endorsement package	$10,000
TOTAL	**$1,100,000**

Academic Incentive Clauses—Up to $175,000 per year

• Graduation rate of players as measured by the NCAA:	• Pecent of players with cumulative GPA of 3.0 or better:	• Percent of athletes whose GPA rises from one year to the next:
50%—$20,000	25%—$20,000	70%—$10,000
60%—$50,000	40%—$35,000	80%—$15,000
70%—$100,000	60%—$50,000	90%—$125,000

Athletic Incentive Clauses—Up to $172,000 per year

• **Participation in the BCS* championship Game:** $70,000; victory in that game, an additional $30,000	• **Participation in any of the other three BCS bowls:** $60,000	• **Participation in any other bowl:** $40,000
• **Top-10 finish in either AP or ESPN-*USA Today* poll:** $40,000	• **Big Ten championship (or share):** one month of salary	• **Nine or more regular-season wins:** $15,000

*Bowl Championship Series

Source: Based on T. May, "OSU Signs Cooper to New Five Year Pact," *The Columbus Dispatch,* October 9, 1999, pp. 1A and 2A; B. Baptist, "Football is King (and It Had Better Stay That Way)," *The Columbus Dispatch,* December 6, 1998; and B. Baptist, "Paying to Be the Best," The Columbus Dispatch, December 7, 1998.

video | C A S E

SOUTHWEST AIRLINES: WHERE INDIVIDUALS MAKE A DIFFERENCE

If Southwest Airlines is known for anything, it's its people. From the company's unique CEO to its pilots, flight attendants, and ground crew, the individual personalities, energy, and talents of its employees have built a successful organization—and one that constantly surprises. Listen to Libby Sartain's description of Herb Kelleher, Southwest's CEO: "Where else would you find a CEO who dresses up as Elvis Presley, who's on a first name basis with 20,000 employees, and who has a heart as big as the state of Texas, or the whole country?" Sartain is vice-president of people at Southwest, and she, like everyone else who works for the airline, seems to love her job.

Kelleher's attitude toward his employees is that each individual makes a vital contribution to the organization. In a light-hearted rap performance, Kelleher sing-songs to his workers, "Without your help there'd be no love—on the ground below or in the air above. You're truly my source of strength and pride. And I sure am glad you're on my side." Kelleher himself scores high in the Big Five personality factors: he's an agreeable, conscientious, emotionally stable extrovert who is open to new experiences, even if it means making fun of himself by dressing as Elvis.

Kelleher's beliefs and attitudes toward work and people encourage organizational commitment, and Southwest has one of the most committed workforces in the industry, with a low percentage of turnover even though 85 percent of employees are union members. Kelleher also advises managers to pay attention to employees' personal needs, whether they are ill or celebrating a birthday. "We'd rather have a company bound together by love than motivated by fear," he says.

In selecting employees, Kelleher values attitude over ability and aptitude. "A good attitude is most important," he notes. "It's something you can't change, but you can teach people to do whatever job you want them to." Kelleher also focuses on individual creativity. "Southwest's culture is designed to promote high spirit and avoid complacency," says Libby Sartrain. "Our employees are encouraged to be creative and innovative, to break the rules when they need to, in order to provide good service to our customers." This philosophy has re-sulted in an unbeatable workforce that has won Southwest the airline industries' Triple Crown award five years in a row: first in on-time performance, first in customer satisfaction, and first in baggage handling from 1992 to 1996.

In sum, Kelleher believes that individuals count, whether they are pilots, baggage handlers, ticket agents, or passengers. "We've always done it differently. You know, we don't assign seats. Used to be, we only had about four people on the whole plane, so the idea of assigned seats just made people laugh. Now the reason is you can turn the airplanes quicker at the gate. And if you can turn an airplane quicker, you can have it fly more routes each day. That generates more revenue, so you can offer lower fares." Herb Kelleher has figured out the secret: individuals make a difference in profits.

Questions

1. How important is person-organization fit at Southwest? Why?

2. Based on what you've read and seen about Southwest Airlines, create a list of three instrumental values encouraged by Herb Kelleher. How do you think these values contribute to the success of Southwest as an organization?

3. Do you think that Herb Kelleher's popularity creates a potential halo effect? Why or why not? If so, how might this affect the organization's success?

4. Visit Southwest's Web site at **www.iflyswa.com** and click on the "Careers" section. Browse through the site, then write a brief description of what you believe the psychological contract is between Southwest and its employees.

Source: Southwest Airlines Web site, **www.iflyswa.com;** "Chief Executive of the Year," *Chief Executive Magazine,* 1999, **www.chiefexecutive.net;** Steve Salerno, "Laughing All the Way," *Worth Online,* 1999, **www.worth.com;** "Herb Kelleher," *News You Can Use,* December 21, 1998, **www.usnews.com;** Herb Kelleher, "A Culture of Commitment," *Leader to Leader,* No. 4, Spring 1977, **www.pfdf.org;** Monte Enbysk, "Southwest Airlines Succeeds by Sticking to the Basics," *Washington CEO,* July 1995, **www.waceo.com.**

video CASE

TREATING EMPLOYEES RIGHT

What gets employees moving? What attracts them to certain companies, makes them want to stay, and keeps them working toward their greatest potential? Sometimes it is extrinsic rewards—a good salary and a timely promotion. Sometimes it is intrinsic rewards—the satisfaction of a job well done or pride in learning a new skill. In many cases, empowerment plays a role—the delegation of decision-making authority to employees throughout an organization. The companies profiled in this video case may take different approaches to motivation, but they all share one basic philosophy: motivating employees means treating them right.

Recognition is also an important component of motivation at most of these companies. Harold Holigan, Chairman and CEO of Holigan Companies, says, "You motivate [employees] by being interested in the employee and making sure that they have a good job. Make sure that they're recognized, make sure that they get the benefits of being a company member." Dineh Mohajer, founder and president of Hard Candy cosmetics, agrees. "I think it's important to recognize when people do well. To recognize them with words and appreciation financially. You have to make them feel as though it's their company, too."

Today, organizations understand that benefits are an effective way to meet many employee needs. In addition to traditional benefits such as vacation and medical insurance, companies are finding imaginative ways to enhance the quality of their employees' lives, through such benefits as flexible work hours and fitness programs. "We look at how we can provide a really good environment for our employees and keep them motivated," says David Gatchel, president and CEO of Paradigm Entertainment, a software development company. "People can relax as far as their dress. The hours are flexible. We provide free soft drinks and snacks, and distractions for people when they want to take a break—foosball or pool or basketball—activities where the employees can relax a little bit . . . then refocus and get back to it." Beth Haba, human resources manager for Yahoo!, the Internet portal and search engine, describes her organization's focus on the flexible work environment. "This is truly a flexible environment in that . . . people can come into work anywhere

between 8:00 a.m. and 12:00 p.m. Some people choose to work a later hour because that's when they are creative."

The managers at these companies view creativity and participation through empowerment as their lifeblood. "We have a culture that we've developed and an environment where creative people can flourish," remarks Gary Bolinger, senior vice-president of international sales and marketing for Fossil Inc., marketer of fashion watches, sunglasses, and other accessories. Drew Pearson, founder and CEO of Drew Pearson Companies, an athletic apparel company, says, "We always encourage employee participation because we see our employees as customers."

Motivating employees is as complex as the range of approaches taken by all these companies, and as simple as JCPenney's adoption of the golden rule: treat others—employees and customers alike—with the same courtesy and respect as you would wish to be treated with yourself.

Questions

1. Why do you think these companies place such emphasis on creating benefits that will help employees balance their work and home lives?

2. In what ways might these organizations use Hackman and Oldham's five core job dimensions to motivate employees?

3. In what ways might managers at these companies use social learning theory to motivate employees?

4. Visit the Web site for any one of these companies and browse through it to learn what you can about its approach to motivating employees. Then create a chart showing ways in which the company meets Maslow's hierarchy of needs.

Source: Company Web sites, accessed May 2000; "Drew Pearson Marketing, Inc.," *Hoover's Online,* **www.hoovers.com** Steve Salerno, "Laughing All the Way," *Worth Online,* 1999, **www.worth.com;** "Chamber Members Recognized Commitment to Women-Owned Firms," The U.S. Chamber of Commerce, *USChamber.com,* December 1999, **www.uschamber.com;** "Diversity in the Workplace: A Statement of Principle," American Corporate Counsel Association, July 20, 1999, **www.acca.com.**

integrative CASE

PART TWO

AOL: A PLACE WHERE PEOPLE WANT TO WORK

AMERICA ONLINE "You never hear anybody from AOL say, 'I don't like my job . . . I'm looking for someplace else to work.' All my other friends say, 'Hey, get me a job at AOL—we want to work at AOL.'" An AOL employee named Makis is speaking, at the top of the company's "Careers" page on the company's Web site. AOL, like any other organization, is a collection of diverse individuals who all need to work together toward common goals. How do company managers determine the right person-job fit in each of AOL's different divisions? How do managers keep AOL employees enthusiastic and motivated to do their most creative and productive work?

AOL looks for employees who share the company's values, including leadership, creativity, diversity, education, and family life. They also look for people who share the attitude that the Internet is in the process of transforming "virtually every aspect of the economy and society." AOL wants individuals who can act like pioneers but work together in teams, developing strong organizational commitment. To attract talented people, AOL posts specific job listings on its Web site so that potential candidates can view them from anywhere in the world. "To build a global community, we need to recruit the best talent from every segment of our society," says Robert Pittman, president and COO. "To be successful, the employees of America Online have to reflect the community they serve."

One place that AOL recruiters actively seek employees is college campuses. The company schedules on-campus visits at colleges around the country, and students can log onto the "College Connection" section of the Web site to find out more about AOL's recruitment efforts. "AOL's recruiters look for varied skills and achievements supported by diverse work experience and excellence in education," notes the Web site. The company looks for graduates with a variety of abilities, including business and computer science, but stresses that "even if you don't see a position that matches your skill set, please apply anyway."

Motivating employees once they are hired—particularly in an environment with a strong economy and rapidly changing technology—requires flexible thinking on the part of management. AOL management views its workforce as the power behind its products, services, and vision for the future. Thus, it looks for new ways to energize employees with both intrinsic and extrinsic rewards. "See why AOL is one of the coolest teams in cyberspace!" boasts the Web site. The company offers challenging work in a casual-dress setting and a compensation program with an enticing array of professional perks like flexible hours and work-life benefits that respond to today's realities. An AOL benefits package includes everything from stock options and a 401(k) plan; medical, dental, and vision healthcare plans; education assistance; dependent care resources; and paid time off. If these benefits sound fairly standard, try a few others: the Mother and Me program, which provides lactation rooms for new mothers; $4,000 toward the adoption of a child; free concierge services; and ClubNet, which offers stress and time management classes as well as access to athletic facilities. Finally, AOL reinforces values and organizational commitment through fun outings such as picnics and holiday parties.

Strategies for successfully recruiting the right people and motivating them to do their best depend on public perception of the company as a whole. Who would want to work for a company that has suffered from financial failure or bad press? AOL has been through several public relations crises, perhaps the worst being when it changed its pricing policy without anticipating the increase in demand, and customers were left "on hold" for hours at a time, unable to access the Internet. But founder Steve Case turned the nightmare into an opportunity to change people's perceptions about the company. He apologized personally to his customers through widespread print advertisements, and he offered refunds for their trouble. Thus, he strengthened his image as a nice, average guy (who just happens to wear the same khakis and polo shirts that his employees and customers wear) in an extremely competitive industry. The public seemed to follow, possibly attributing the company's failure to bad luck—AOL couldn't control the number of people who would respond to the new pricing—or the difficulty of the task itself—once AOL was deluged with new subscribers, it was extremely difficult to meet their needs. In either case, customers came back; and AOL now has more than 22 million members. And that, according to AOL, is just the beginning.

Questions

1. Based on what you have read, describe in a sentence or two what you think the psychological contract between AOL and its employees could be.

2. In your opinion, what are the most important abilities for an AOL employee to have? Why?

3. How has public perception of Steve Case shaped the image of AOL?

4. Visit the AOL Web site at corp.aol.com and click on the "Careers" section. What techniques does AOL use on the site itself to motivate job candidates to apply to the company? Do you think you would make a good candidate for AOL? Why or why not?

Source: AOL Web site, accessed April 20, 2000; Fred Vogelstein, "The Talented Mr. Case," *U.S. News & World Report,* January 24, 2000, pp. 41-42; Tim Jones and Gary Marx, "Weaned on Crisis, Landing on Top," *Chicago Tribune,* January 16, 2000, pp. 1, 14; Marc Gunther, "The Internet Is Mr. Case's Neighborhood," *Fortune,* March 30, 1998, pp. 69-80.

part 3

Interpersonal Processes in Organizations

seven
CHAPTER

7

The Structure and Behavior of Groups

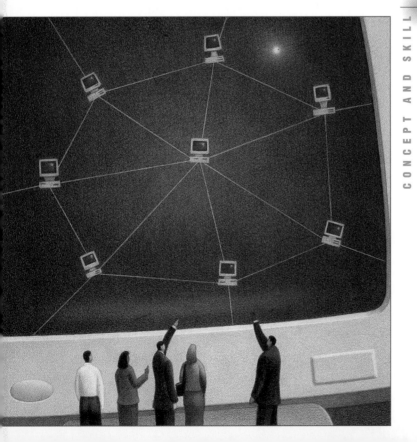

preview

After studying this chapter, you should be able to:

CONCEPT AND SKILL

- Recognize the kinds of groups you encounter, participate in, and read about, as well as their stage of development.

- Analyze the roles played by the members of a group, including the group's authority structure, the status of group members, and sources of conflict within and among roles.

- Give an example of (a) a group that does more than the organization requires, (b) one that accomplishes more than its members could as individuals, and (c) one that accomplishes less than its members could as individuals.

- For a given group, discuss factors that can or do contribute to its performance.

- List examples of interactions between groups in a given organization.

I t's not what you know, it's who you know. No one knows—and practices—this old adage better than Louis Dell'Ermo, founder and CEO of Gateway Security. His company is based in a town often known best for its toughness, crime, and poverty—Newark, New Jersey. "We were here when no one wanted to be," says Dell'Ermo of his company's beginnings. Dell'Ermo got his start in the security business when he was a cop. Prudential asked him to handle security for the Gateway Center, a huge office-and-hotel complex right in downtown Newark. Dell'Ermo believes that Prudential was drawn to him because of his involvement and membership in high-profile civic groups like the Police Athletic League and the Boys Club. Prudential managers believed—and rightly so—that his association with these groups meant that he understood the community. Dell'Ermo agreed to give it a try.

To get the job done, Dell'Ermo went to other groups where he had personal and professional connections—retired or off-duty police officers, firefighters, and teachers. Employees from these groups "gave us some credibility," notes Dell'Ermo. Then Dell'Ermo tapped his contacts on the Police Athletic League football team (which he had coached), and eventually went to some of the local security-training programs, where he found employable graduates. "When you hire people, you try to hire people from the community," he says. "They can tell by the noise of the traffic what's happening. They know what to expect."

From that first assignment, Gateway Security added more clients; the smaller firm tended to beat out national security companies for business because Gateway was operating in its own backyard, where its employees were locals who understood how different groups within the community operated. Gateway's customers appreciate the company's status. Dell'Ermo's connections have made Gateway a community-based organization. Gateway's people, in turn, link its clients to the community where they operate. "It boils down to a more nebulous thing, like being part of the neighborhood," explains Dennis Frost of Cogswell Realty Group, one of Gateway's customers. "That's what Gateway does for me; it makes me part of the neighborhood."[1]

Gateway Finds Security in Groups

> *"[It's a] more nebulous thing, like being part of the neighborhood."*
> —**Dennis Frost,** Cogswell Realty Group

Have you ever felt the power of a group? Perhaps you were uncertain about how to solve a problem, but as soon as you started talking it over with someone, the answer came to you. Or maybe you've left a meeting or rally all fired up about a cause or a project. Maybe you squeezed out an extra ounce of energy, thanks to the encouragement of your teammates. Or, like Louis Dell'Ermo of Gateway Security, maybe you have enjoyed the chance to help and be helped by the people you have met in groups.

Of course, other group activities are less positive. Some groups engage in destructive actions or bring out the worst in their members. Many people have had the unfortunate experience of sitting through a meeting in which participants rambled or bickered for hours, without ever reaching agreement or making constructive plans.

Your career and your organization alike will benefit if you take part in groups that work effectively toward positive goals. Sociologists, social psychologists, and observers of organizational behavior have much wisdom to contribute on this subject. Applying their insights, this chapter describes the behavior of groups in organizations, as well as the impact of groups on their individual members. We also discuss processes that are typical of groups and identify factors that influence groups' performance. Whereas most of this discussion emphasizes the activities that occur within groups, the final section of the chapter covers intergroup behavior—that is, the ways groups interact with one another.

Groups naturally form and develop in organizations

group

Two or more members of an organization who interact, share norms and goals, influence one another, and identify themselves as a group.

People are by nature social beings. Starting with our family, we rely on and interact with others throughout our lives. When we take jobs in organizations, we participate in various kinds of work groups. The University of North Texas's Center for the Study of Work Teams forecast that in 2000, 80 percent of *Fortune* 500 companies would have half of their employees working in teams, just one type of group.[2] Given that group participation is essential to organizational life, it is helpful to understand what groups are, why they are formed, and how they operate.

To study groups, social scientists start by defining the term. In the context of organizational behavior, a **group** is two or more members of an organization who interact, share norms and goals, influence one another, and identify themselves as a group. This definition distinguishes group behavior from occasional interactions, such as an employee handling a customer's order or complaint. It also distinguishes a "group" in an interpersonal sense from passive membership in an organization. Thus, belonging to the American Automobile Association (AAA) or the World Wildlife Federation is not participating in what organizational behavior means by a "group," assuming all you do is pay a membership fee in exchange for the occasional towing service or the satisfaction of protecting the environment. However, interactions need not be face to face; people might be part of a "virtual group" that interacts primarily or exclusively online.

Let's now consider why people in organizations form groups. Then we will consider the kinds of groups they form and the way they develop.

Reasons for Forming Groups

Group formation can meet both organizational and personal goals.[3] In general, the organization uses groups to improve efficiency and effectiveness in achieving its goals. Individual goals combine a desire for high performance with social and emotional needs. Exhibit 7.1 summarizes some typical reasons for forming groups.

Groups contribute to organizational goals by accomplishing what individuals cannot do alone. A group of employees may offer more diverse talents or more varied perspectives than can an individual alone. Each participant can contribute what he or she does best. When people cooperate and pool those talents or perspectives, they equip themselves to manage the complex environment in which modern organizations function.

Even when a situation is relatively simple, a group effort may contribute more stamina and enthusiasm than individuals could muster on their own.

Meeting Organizational Goals	Meeting Personal Goals
Greater effectiveness from the pooling of knowledge, talents, and perspectives.	Satisfaction of social needs through participation in the group's activities.
Greater efficiency because each member contributes his or her specialty, rather than handling all aspects of the group's task alone.	Professional and personal development as a result of observing group members with greater knowledge or skill.
Greater effectiveness and efficiency when group members lead and motivate one another.	Greater commitment to goals created by the group members.

exhibit | **7.1**

Reasons for Forming Groups

Group members can lead and motivate one another, so that people work harder toward their shared goals. Furthermore, when people arrive at a decision as a group, they are all committed to carrying out their decision successfully. The result is **synergy**—creation of total output that is greater than the sum of its parts. As we will describe in later sections of this chapter, good leadership can build an environment that fosters these group characteristics and directs them in support of the organization's objectives.

synergy

Creation of total output that is greater than the sum of its parts.

Organizations may also obtain the benefits of group membership by having employees participate in groups that link members of more than one organization. For example, employees from 14 companies participate in an organization called LearnShare. LearnShare members collaborate to create and share training materials. They also conduct research projects and invite experts to speak at the group's meetings. The group gives members access to knowledge and talents they might not have on their own.[4] Similarly, Karen Westerman, president of Country Maid Bakery in Northbrook, Illinois, gets advice for running her small business from a peer group of entrepreneurs. The group helped her evaluate an opportunity to acquire another company.[5] These examples illustrate a type of *networking*— that is, drawing on group relationships to ask for and provide advice and assistance. The story of Louis Dell'Ermo of Gateway Security at the beginning of this chapter also is an example of networking; Dell'Ermo drew from his personal and professional connections to help him build his security business.

Groups have the potential to meet their individuals' social needs. A well-functioning group also can provide its members with encouragement and education. Many people feel empowered when they tackle a problem as part of a group or team. A company that appreciates the importance of groups in meeting social needs is digitalNATION, which provides services that get its clients onto the Internet.

digitalNATION

Staying at the leading edge of the Internet requires intense commitment and hard work. To keep valuable employees in such an environment, digitalNATION knows it must look after their needs, including their social needs. Founder and CEO Bruce Waldack gets to the heart of the matter: "Employees want good salaries, but today, they also want more. They want to like their coworkers and hang out with them."

DigitalNATION responds to that need by providing plenty of opportunities for employees to have fun together. The Alexandria, Virginia, company's employees can participate in outings for bowling, paintball, sailing, and scuba classes. The company also arranges to have spur-of-the-moment Chinese buffets brought into the office. Waldack credits the bonding as an important reason for the company's impressively low turnover. Over a recent two-year period, just five employees quit, and two of those later returned.[6]

Of course, the benefits of forming groups are only the *potential* of groups in organizations. Groups do not always provide all the benefits mentioned. Furthermore, groups can have negative effects. For example, a group whose goals are inconsistent with the organization's may be disruptive. And an organization whose people form very tightly knit groups may consume so much of the individuals' lives that they have difficulty maintaining family and other nonwork relationships. However, people who are knowledgeable about groups and group processes can diagnose problems and help groups to function so that they do provide the desired benefits.

Types of Groups

The reasons for establishing a group influence the form the group takes. As shown in Exhibit 7.2, groups in organizations may be informal or formal. A person may also use others as a reference group.

Formal Groups   The management function of organizing involves grouping employees together to meet organizational goals. For example, an organization's managers might say that everyone who sells is in the Sales Department, that everyone developing the Alpha Computer is part of the Alpha Team, or that everyone providing services to universities is part of the Schools Division. Besides departments, teams, and divisions, organizations also form groups called committees, task forces, and quality circles.

People in these groups have interrelated tasks; that is, the success of one person in the group depends on the contributions of the others. Furthermore, when the group meets its goals, it also advances the objectives of the organization as a whole. In general, a group formed by the organization to contribute toward attaining organizational goals is called a **formal group.**

Managers can create formal groups along the lines of the organizational chart. The term **command group** describes a group that consists of a manager and the employees who report to that manager. When employees join an organization, they automatically become part of a command group with their manager and coworkers.

Managers also may form **task groups** by bringing together employees to work on a particular project or task. Examples of task groups include a committee to set up disaster plans to follow in the event of an emergency and a cross-functional team that meets weekly to review customer feedback. The first example is a closed-ended task group; when the committee has drawn up the procedures, it will disband. In contrast, the cross-functional team is an open-ended task group. As long as customers are providing feedback, the committee will continue to meet. In other words, the project has no specified end, so the group's life cycle has no specified end.

---

formal group

A group formed by the organization to contribute toward attaining organizational goals.

command group

A formal group that consists of a manager and the employees who report to that manager.

task group

A formal group that brings together employees to work on a particular project or task.

---

exhibit | **7.2**

Types of Groups

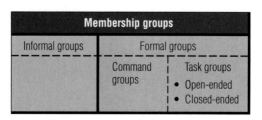
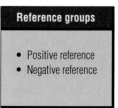

Membership groups			Reference groups
Informal groups	Formal groups		• Positive reference • Negative reference
	Command groups	Task groups • Open-ended • Closed-ended	

Informal Groups   Not all groups are created to meet the organization's objectives. People also form groups to meet their own needs. For example, they may build friendships in the organization, or they may look for opportunities to spend time with more experienced colleagues who have wisdom to share. Sometimes individuals strive to be part of groups that can be a source of power, such as the old boys' (or old girls') network, the executive committee, or employees who control access to resources, from the supply cabinet to capital expenditure decisions. These relationships, which do not correspond to lines on an organizational chart, are called **informal groups.**

Although informal groups are not formed expressly to achieve organizational objectives, their purpose can be consistent with them. For example, high-tech computer companies may encourage their employees to work together, play together, and socialize over meals. They can then begin to build relationships and enthusiasm that can help them when they need quick feedback or additional ideas. Similarly, when an individual who belongs to this informal group needs information from another part of the organization, he or she may have a ready source of information in another member of the group.

So, informal groups can smooth the interactions among an organization's employees. Many organizations therefore encourage informal groups by sponsoring opportunities for employees to socialize or engage in cooperative or developmental activities together. For instance, Agency.com, a Web site design agency, sponsors programs when at least five employees express an interest. It has paid the expenses of fishing trips, as well as classes in improvisational theater, Latin dancing, and specialized areas of programming. Employees participate after work or during their lunch break. Management believes these programs are a valuable way to foster cooperation, encourage employee development, and provide stress relief.[7]

However, informal groups also can interfere with the organization's performance. For example, a clique may shut out someone, even if that person needs to interact with its members. Likewise, socializing during work hours may interfere with productivity. In those situations, effective leadership requires limiting or discouraging the informal group's activities while the group is at work.

Reference Groups   Sometimes people are affected by a group even when they aren't a member of that group. People have **reference groups**—groups they use as examples to imitate. The expression "keeping up with the Joneses" describes the use of neighbors as a reference group. Whenever the fictitious Joneses acquire something, their neighbors try to acquire something of equal or greater value. Other groups may serve as a negative reference, meaning that people try to avoid being like them.

Reference groups in organizations might include high-level managers, successful colleagues, or any group the individual uses as a measure of his or her own behavior. In addition, members of organizations typically have reference groups outside the organization. For example, employees might compare their behaviors and values with those of a football team, religious leaders, and their families. The family is both a part of the organization and an important reference group for Heather Mirassou, who joined the family business, San Jose's Mirassou Winery. Mirassou, the company's marketing

informal group

A group formed to meet personal needs; membership does not correspond to lines on an organizational chart.

reference group

A group that people use as a source of examples to imitate (or avoid imitating).

director, says, "I just really looked up to these guys [her parents' generation of the family], and I wanted to be a part of that [organization]." She hopes to exert a similar influence on her two sons.[8]

Employees often use managers as a reference group. In that case, they emulate their managers' behavior, such as how the managers treat customers and how they dress. This gives managers an important opportunity for leadership. They can—and should—model the behaviors they want their employees to adopt.

Stages of Group Development

If you've ever belonged to a group for several months or years, you've probably noticed that the group changed over time. Perhaps participating in the group became more (or less) enjoyable, or maybe the group members learned to get along better than they once did. Sometimes the focus of a group's activities shifts over time.

Changes like these are common in groups. Researchers have looked for patterns in group behavior over time in an effort to create theories of group development. Ideally, if we know how groups change and develop, we can predict changes and influence group development in positive ways.

Many people who study groups believe that groups develop over a process that involves several stages. However, there is no full agreement about the number, sequence, duration, and content of the stages.[9] In the 1960s, educational psychologist Bruce W. Tuckman used his experience in conducting group therapy to develop a four-stage model of group development. He gave the stages easy-to-remember names: forming, storming, norming, and performing. Later, Tuckman and a doctoral student added a fifth stage, adjourning, to complete the model shown in Exhibit 7.3.[10] Because this model has become popular, we will use it as the framework for our discussion of group development.

Tuckman's model describes group development in terms of stages that happen in a particular order. However, the model does not specify the intensity or length of each stage. As you read about each of the stages, keep in mind that the stage may be long and significant for some groups but brief for others.

Forming   The group begins during the first stage, called *forming*. During this stage, the group's members experience some degree of uncertainty about the group and their participation in it. They may wonder who is in charge and what the group is supposed to be doing.

During the forming stage, leadership (described later in this chapter) is an important issue. The group may have a formal leader, such as the supervisor of a work group. If the group members do not perceive that this person is acting like a leader, someone else may take on the leader's role. When the members begin to think of themselves as a group, the group moves to the next stage of development.

Storming   Next, the group enters a difficult stage called *storming*. This stage features conflict among the members. Group members test their early assumptions about the group's leadership and goals. They may form subgroups and rebel against policies and procedures. They may argue and pro-

exhibit | **7.3**

A Model of Group Development

Forming
Uncertainty

Storming
Conflict

Norming
Conflict resolution
Generation of team spirit

Performing
Collaboration
Goal achievement

Adjourning
End of group
Transition

Source: This model is based on B. W. Tuckman and M. A. C. Jensen, "Stages of Small-Group Development Revisited," *Group and Organization Studies*, December 1977, pp. 419–427.

crastinate. Without skillful leadership, group development can stall at this stage, and the group is at risk for dissolving.

Norming   Groups that survive the storming stage enter the next stage, called *norming*. Typically, a group member who is not the leader but is respected by the others calls on the group to resolve its differences and focus on its goals. During the norming stage, the group talks about its conflicts and begins to resolve them. When this works, people define their roles more clearly and gain a feeling of team spirit.

At Boeing Company, human resource specialist Amy Gillespie observed the development of work teams to carry out production and support in the company's Airlift and Tanker Programs. She says that early on, there was confusion about roles. To many employees, teamwork primarily meant freedom to set their own hours and give themselves pay increases. They had to learn to make decisions that aligned with customer needs and company goals.[11]

Performing   Building on the team spirit of the norming stage, groups move into the stage called *performing*. During this stage, the group is considered mature. The emphasis is on carrying out the work for which the group was formed. The group's members collaborate, communicate effectively, and help each other. They use their cooperativeness to resolve conflicts as they arise. People are able to contribute to the group according to their individual strengths.

Boeing's Gillespie noticed when the Airlift and Tanker work teams entered this stage. Supervisors began to educate team members in how to interpret performance measures. With this understanding, the team members felt less intimidated about using statistics. The teams started to expand beyond interpersonal issues into evaluating how well they were performing. They began to take responsibility for making changes to enhance performance.[12]

Adjourning   Eventually, as with other kinds of life cycles, the life of the group comes to an end. When the group's work is done, it disbands. During this stage, called *adjourning,* the group members will probably feel a sense of loss. They grieve the end of their experiences as members of the group.

The significance of this stage is that group members are in a period of transition. When an organization ends a group—say, by disbanding a task force or relocating some employees from a group that had worked together—it can help group members make the transition by sponsoring ceremonies to mark the change. For example, the organization can hold going-away parties for employees leaving a location or "graduation ceremonies" for employees completing a training program. The transition can be especially constructive if the organization communicates and reinforces the lessons learned while the group was in its earlier stages.

apply it

1. Think of a time when you were new to an organization—for example, when you started a new job or when you started attending college. What kinds of formal or informal groups were you interested in being part of? (Consider,

for example, friendships, study groups, work teams, clubs.) What personal needs might your membership in these groups help to satisfy?

2. Of the groups you identified in question 1, which would help achieve the objectives of the organization (your employer or school)?

Group members play various roles

role

A set of behaviors that group members expect of someone in a certain position.

task roles

Roles that allow the group to define and pursue a group objective.

maintenance roles

Roles that involve building and sustaining positive relationships among group members.

In discussing the process of group development, we referred to the "role" of the leader. A leader is just one of the many roles possible in a group. In this sense, a **role** is a set of behaviors that group members expect of someone in a certain position. Thus, if you are a group's leader, people expect you to behave in a certain way. People expect followers to behave differently in some cases, because "leader" and "follower" are different roles. Other roles that are common in groups include those of the mediator, scapegoat, comic (who benefits the group by relieving tension), and devil's advocate.[13]

In general, groups need people to fill a combination of task and maintenance roles. **Task roles** are roles that allow the group to define and pursue a group objective. For example, someone in the group may routinely suggest ideas, remind the group to stay on task, or take notes of group discussions. **Maintenance roles** involve building and sustaining positive relationships among group members. People who take on maintenance roles include the ones who encourage participation by quiet group members or

Business development director Cindy C. W. Chiu is a group leader at Avery Dennison's Research Center in Pasadena, California. Her group's assigned developmental tasks are important to Avery Dennison. Known as the leader in the "sticky paper" business, the label manufacturer also is developing innovative new businesses. As stated in its annual report, "Sometimes what starts out as a label ends up as a whole new business. . . . Like proprietary film-coating technology. It allows us to develop all kinds of terrific new labeling products." With such new products on the horizon, Chiu is successful in her role as a group leader for product development.
(Source: Courtesy of Avery Dennison Corp.)

Task Roles	Maintenance Roles
Leader who inspires group members to carry out their tasks	Leader who inspires group members to cooperate
Spokesperson for the customer's point of view	Advocate for the quiet group members (ensures they participate)
Financial whiz	Stress reducer (injects humor at tense or boring times)
Note taker	Mediator (resolves conflicts among members)
Person who points out the manufacturing implications of the group's ideas	Cheerleader (makes sure the group celebrates each of its accomplishments)

exhibit **7.4**

Task Roles and Maintenance Roles for a Product Development Group

provide a humorous comment when a situation grows tense. When members of a group fill both kinds of roles, the group performs the right tasks to meet its objectives, and members interact in a way that fosters group development. Exhibit 7.4 gives examples of task and maintenance roles in a product development group. If a group does not function effectively, one possible source of the problem is that some of these roles may not be filled. (Chapter 8 addresses this issue in greater detail.)

Not only does a group require a variety of roles, but individuals play different roles in the various groups to which they belong. For example, one person might be chief of a work crew, first baseman on a community softball team, the unofficial organizer of an annual fishing trip with his college buddies, and the youngest among four brothers, who constantly remind him he is the only remaining bachelor. The members of his work crew treat him differently than his brothers do, and they expect different behaviors from him.

Role Expectations and Role Identity

As group members interact, people define their expectations and settle into roles. Group members' definitions of how a person with a given role should act in a particular situation constitute **role expectations.** For example, you probably can describe behavior you expect from a friend. You might say the role includes making himself or herself available when you have need of your friend. That behavior is one of your role expectations for friends. Likewise, an organization might expect that a good employee contributes suggestions and is not late for work. If everyone in the organization agrees on the role expectations for a "good employee," each employee knows how to fulfill that role.

Role expectations and group objectives define which attitudes and behaviors are consistent with a role. These attitudes and behaviors make up a **role identity.** When you take on a role effectively, not only do you carry out particular behaviors, but you tend to have certain attitudes that fit the role. For example, the role identity of a manager includes caring about the organization's success. That attitude helps the manager to lead, set goals, and manage time effectively.

role expectations

Group members' definitions of how a person with a given role should act in a particular situation.

role identity

The attitudes and behaviors defined as being consistent with a role.

Does it seem unlikely that a person assumes attitudes along with the other aspects of a role? If so, you may be surprised by the results of an experiment conducted by Stanford University psychologist Philip Zimbardo and colleagues.[14] They set up a mock prison in the basement of Stanford's psychology building and randomly assigned student volunteers to play the roles of prisoners and guards. Within days, the students had so fully taken on negative aspects of those roles (abusiveness on the part of "guards" and passivity on the part of "prisoners") that the psychologists halted the experiment to avoid further damaging the emotional health of the participants. In the realm of business, the following example describes how the founder of Kinko's had to adjust his attitudes to fit the role identity of a manager.

❦ Kinko's

When an *Inc.* reporter asked Paul Orfalea to describe his greatest mistake, the founder and chairman of Kinko's recounted a time when he was uncomfortable with some aspects of the manager's role. Orfalea said the managers reporting to him once included a man who was widely disliked in the organization. The man was quick to fire employees, and employees did not trust him.

The company's bookkeeper discovered that this manager was stealing. Orfalea confronted the man, who concocted a pitiful story about the stress he was under and said the stress had driven him to steal. Orfalea's role as company chairman required him to rid the company of someone who interfered with its success. However, he was more comfortable with the role of compassionate colleague. He decided to give the troublesome manager another chance.

The other employees were furious. They didn't see Orfalea as compassionate; they saw him as unjust. His role called on him to reward people according to their performance, and he had failed to do so. Orfalea has since come to share his employees' point of view. The manager stole again, and Orfalea fired him. He explains, "The hardest thing to do as the leader in this business is to hurt people's feelings, but sometimes you have to. . . . I'm still nice, but I don't tolerate lying and stealing."[15]

Taking on a role identity often involves a type of exchange. The organization or group sets forth its role expectations, and employees or prospective employees consider their own desires and expectations, then decide whether to accept the role identity. An example is the "psychological contract" discussed in Chapter 3. As the basis for this type of agreement, modern organizations often define employees' roles to include the responsibility for their own career development. Employees who accept this responsibility in exchange for employment incorporate it into their role identity as employees.

In some situations, the group has task roles that lay out precisely what is expected of each member, and group members quickly assume those role identities. For example, researchers studied the cockpit crew in an airliner. Even though the crew members started as strangers, they needed just ten minutes to begin operating as a high-performing group.[16] Fortunately for the safety of passengers, a cockpit crew is a rigidly defined group with a clearly designated leader. In other situations, group members define roles as the group develops.

Role Overload   As a person takes on tasks to fulfill a role, work becomes more challenging and time can sometimes become more precious. Occasionally, the demands of a role can exceed a person's abilities, which is called **role overload.** Steve Jobs is one person who understands role overload. Early in his career, when he was starting up Apple Computer, he worked extremely hard and long to fulfill his role as CEO. He says, "I worked really, really hard in my twenties. . . . Literally, you know, seven days a week, a lot of hours every day. . . . But you can't do it forever. . . . You have to come up with ways of figuring out what the most important things are and working with other people even more. Just working smarter to get things done." Now age 44 and running both Apple and Pixar, the movie animation company responsible for *Toy Story* and *A Bug's Life,* he has learned to focus his own activities and to delegate to avoid becoming overloaded. He says of his role at both successful companies, "My job is to recruit people and help create a situation where they can do the best work of their lives."[17]

Role overload also became an issue at Coldwater Machine Company when it began to delegate decision-making responsibility to teams of workers. Employees were taking on more responsibility, and some became nervous when they began to appreciate the scope of decision-making responsibility they were receiving. They wondered how they would manage the duties traditionally handled by a supervisor along with their other work responsibilities. Coldwater addressed this concern by allowing time for a transition to teamwork, assigning responsibilities gradually, and providing thorough training.[18]

Role Ambiguity   Sometimes group members experience **role ambiguity,** meaning they lack information needed for defining how to perform a role. A group member who thinks, "I don't know what these people want from me," is experiencing role ambiguity. Of course, this feeling is uncomfortable. A person experiencing role ambiguity will not enjoy participating in a group and may look for ways to avoid it. But, as in the case of role overload, groups can correct role ambiguity if they recognize and discuss such problems when they arise. Employees of high-tech start-up Versatile Systems of Seattle, a company that develops software for mobile computing devices, found themselves floundering with few guidelines and little idea of what owner Jim Lloyd wanted them to do. When they failed, Lloyd would assign them only the simplest tasks and would double-check everyone's work. Not surprisingly, turnover and firings escalated. Eventually, Lloyd learned that he was best at technical duties such as software programming and not good at all at managing people. He delegated recruitment and management duties to his brother, his "polar opposite." He says, "I know now that too much time with me is terrible for employees. So now I go into a department, exchange ideas, tell them where they fit into the vision, then I get out."[19]

Role Conflict

Another reason that people cannot always meet every expectation associated with their roles is that expectations are sometimes inconsistent. For example, an organization might expect its leaders to inspire both ethical behavior and an unrealistically high level of sales. In general, inconsistencies in the expectations associated with a person's roles are called **role conflict.**

role overload

The experience of having the demands of a role exceed a person's abilities.

role ambiguity

The condition of lacking information needed for defining how to perform a role.

role conflict

Inconsistencies in the expectations associated with a person's role.

what would you do?

ARE OFFICE ROMANCES APPROPRIATE?

Office romances develop all the time. Workers are human beings, and naturally there are times when two colleagues might be attracted to one another. But whether an office romance ends in marriage or tears, or just quietly proceeds for years, it is a prime example of role conflict in the workplace. Employees are members of a group of coworkers. They may be members of formal or informal subgroups within the company. As employees, their role is to perform and behave in ways that pursue the organization's objectives. In addition, the work group has norms that may not include dating—or may even discourage it. As members of a social couple, two employees may feel conflict if they discuss work issues with each other; if they take vacation at the same time; if they appear to favor each other in work-related decisions. Books and articles have been written about the topic, and talk shows have focused on it. *Fortune* columnist Anne Fisher addressed the topic in a recent column when a reader who was having an office romance wrote to describe how a human resources manager asked both parties to "sign a document stating that our relationship is mutually consensual," presumably to avoid complications from any possible charges of sexual harassment resulting from the relationship. The employee asked Fisher's advice on whether to sign the document.

Fisher consulted several experts on the matter. One recommended that the writer refuse to sign the document because there is no law against two people dating in the workplace. Another suggested signing the document with the proviso that only the legal department see it. You can explore this situation (or one like it) further by accessing Fisher's Web site at *Fortune,* **www.askannie.com.**

Imagine that you found yourself in a similar situation with a colleague, contemplating a dating relationship.

1. What is your role identity at work? How might this dating relationship change your role identity?

2. What role conflicts would you feel? Which role is more important to you?

3. Would you go ahead with a dating relationship? Why or why not?

4. Do you think that signing a document such as the one described would help resolve role conflict in this situation? Why or why not?

Source: Anne Fisher, "Ask Annie," *Fortune,* September 6, 1999, p. 296.

Role conflict may arise because of incompatibilities within roles or between roles (see Exhibit 7.5). A common source of role conflict is having multiple roles with conflicting requirements. For example, the role of spouse or parent requires quality time for a partner or children, and this may conflict with a demanding role at work. Because of his early overcontrol at Versatile Systems, Jim Lloyd experienced conflict between his role of CEO and that of husband and father of seven children. He became consumed with making his company a success and resented the time his wife wanted for family in the evenings and weekends. Lloyd had to learn to delegate tasks—such as financial management and accounting—to other people in the organization to regain control of his professional and family life.[20]

Likewise, the roles of family member and employee can conflict when a business owner or manager hires a relative. Such conflicts are tricky for both employee and employer to handle. According to consultant Leslie Dashew, kindness associated with the role of family member may dictate that an employee work at a discount to help out the employer, but economics associated with the role of being an employee call for less commitment from a low-paid employee. Furthermore, as a family member, the employer may feel uncomfortable about demanding better performance.[21]

Conflict within roles can result when a role requires a person to perform incompatible activities. The earlier example of expecting both ethics and

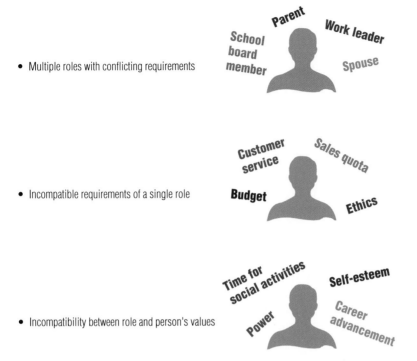

- Multiple roles with conflicting requirements

- Incompatible requirements of a single role

- Incompatibility between role and person's values

exhibit **7.5**

Types of Role Conflict

extremely high performance can cause this type of conflict within a role. For instance, a salesperson might be tempted to make unrealistic promises in order to close a sale. Or a person's role identity might include getting along with group members and offering fresh ideas. If a person has an idea that is likely to cause conflict, the person might hesitate to state the idea, even if it would be beneficial in the long run. This type of conflict can create a decision-making problem called "groupthink," discussed in Chapter 10.

Role conflict also arises when a person's role conflicts with his or her values. For example, Phyllis Jordan, founder of PJ's Coffee & Tea Company, realized that the responsibilities of being CEO of her company conflicted with her career interests. When her company's director of marketing left, Jordan found herself wanting that job, rather than her own top position, because marketing was the aspect of the business she really loved. So she hired someone else to be in charge of her company. Now PJ's Coffee & Tea is in the hands of someone Jordan trusts, and her role as marketing director fits her interests and abilities.[22]

Many of the conflict management principles we will discuss in Chapter 13 apply to managing role conflict. For example, when the organization determines that role conflict is a problem, it may try to minimize the sources of conflict. At the headquarters for Jamba Juice, a chain of fast-food outlets offering smoothies and other healthful treats, management determined that employees were under great pressure from the long hours they worked. Their work roles were in conflict with their personal roles. Jamba Juice responded by setting up opportunities to have fun at work: an on-site badminton court, as well as social occasions such as parties and picnics—all aimed at reducing the pressure and varying the routine of work. Explains Jamba Juice's vice president of human resources, Chris Baer, "Because we play here, too, employees think it's OK to spend the long hours here that they do."[23]

Authority Structure

Roles are often related to people's position in an organization. In particular, when organizations form work groups, they usually create an authority structure for the group. The **authority structure** defines a hierarchy of reporting relationships. It defines who is supposed to lead the group and how the group is supposed to fit into the overall organization. Exhibit 7.6 provides examples of authority structures for two types of work groups. In a traditional work group, employees report to a supervisor who in turn reports to the department manager. With a cross-functional work group, employees from different departments work with and report to a team leader, who is frequently a supervisor of one of the departments involved.

Leadership and Status

A group's authority structure may determine who leads a group, but not necessarily. As illustrated in Exhibit 7.7, leadership, status, and authority may be interrelated. However, a person can be a leader without necessarily having a position of high authority and status within the organization. As we describe in depth in Chapter 11, *leadership* is the process by which a leader influences followers. This influence process may be carried out by the person the organization places in charge of the group, but others may exert leadership as well as—or instead of—the person whom the organization assigns to be the leader. In general, group members seek leadership from someone who embodies the group's values, helps the group achieve its goals, and enables its members to satisfy their needs.

exhibit | **7.6**

Authority Structures for Two Work Groups

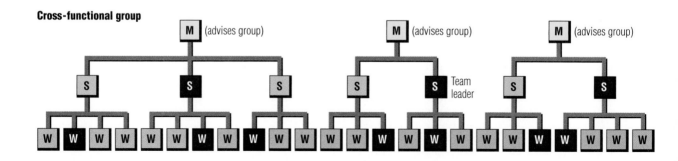

exhibit **7.7**

Authority, Leadership, and Status

Anne Zehren quickly took on the role of leader when she was tapped as publisher for a new magazine, *Teen People,* owned by Time Inc. Zehren's goal was, in her own words: "When I came here, I wanted to shake up the category and let advertisers and teenagers know that we're different, that we're going to take some risks and do things in a new way." She gave her ambition tangible form with eccentric touches: purple paint on the office walls and Gonging Ceremonies to signal employees' successes. Initially, the traditional managers of Time were aghast, but as Zehren began turning in impressive results, they became enthusiastic supporters of her leadership practices.[24]

Group Leaders   To identify who exerts leadership in a group, it is important to consider not only formal job titles and reporting relationships but also the behavior of the group members. Whose influence do group members follow? The answer to that question gets to the heart of who the group's leader really is.

Because a leader influences followers' behavior, the role of leader is especially significant. The leader may exert a small or large degree of influence, and that influence may encourage behavior that either supports the achievement of organizational goals, interferes with achievement of those goals, or is neutral from the organization's standpoint. Obviously, the organization benefits by appointing as group leader someone who is influential and who wants the group to support the organization's objectives.

Status.   Generally speaking, a person who exercises leadership has high status within the group; that is, people look up to the leader. **Status** is an agreed-upon rank that people give to groups or individuals within groups. The top-ranked members of a group have high status relative to the others. In addition, the group itself may have either high or low status within the organization as a whole. Groups assign high-status roles, such as leader or expert, to the high-status members and low-status roles, such as scapegoat or "go-fer," to the low-status members.

A high-status person may not always follow the group's standards for conduct. High-status people tend to be better able to resist pressure to conform. They don't care as much about the group's social rewards for conforming, so they can ignore pressure to do what everyone else is doing.[25] In addition, groups tend to give their high-status members more latitude, allowing them to do things their own way instead of according to the group's

status

An agreed-upon rank that people give to groups or individuals within groups.

standards.[26] The group permits high-status members to enjoy this freedom as long as they don't significantly detract from the group's achievement of its goals.[27] Thus, a group might let a high-status member get away with dressing unconventionally, showing up at meetings later than everyone else, or some other behavior that would be criticized if others did it.

Group members accept status and its privileges as long as they believe the hierarchy is fair. For example, a work group that meets regularly to generate new-product ideas might assign status according to group members' perceptions of each member's expertise and ability to contribute to the group. A senior member may have most status in this group because his advanced training and years with the company enable him to contribute much wisdom. The others respect him and accept his minor deviations from expected behavior—for example, eccentric clothes and bad jokes. This status hierarchy works because the senior employee has much to contribute, and the other group members recognize and admire what he knows. This situation is a kind of exchange, with the senior member providing the group with his wisdom, and the group returning the favor by ignoring his mismatched clothes and listening to his jokes.

However, if the organization were to use other criteria for assigning status in the group, conflict could arise. For example, the organization might ask a department manager to sit in on all the group's meetings. At first the manager, based on her rank in the company's hierarchy, sits at the head of the table, conducts the meeting, and schedules the next meeting. Chances are, the group will resist the manager's attempt to claim the privileges of a high-status position in this group. They may not protest openly, but they might resist her attempts to reorganize the meetings, thereby enabling the group leader to maintain his status with its attendant privileges.

As in this example, it is important to remember that a person's status in one context (for example, the manager's rank in the organization's hierarchy) does not necessarily match the person's status in another context (the manager's rank in the work group). In the early stages of a group's development, one of the activities that takes place is sorting out the status of the group members. Group members who simply assume that their status in another context will carry over may be surprised at how the other group members actually view them.

apply it

1. List a few roles you have. If you want, you can include roles you used to have or would like to have. For each role you listed, describe the role expectations.
2. For the roles you listed above, what potential or existing role conflicts do you see?

Groups can influence whether members meet expectations

So far, we have looked primarily at who belongs to groups and how group members relate to one another. But organizations rarely form groups as an exercise in relationship building. Usually, they want the groups to accom-

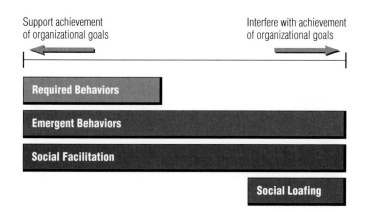

exhibit **7.8**
Types of Group Processes

plish something for the organization. Therefore, we need to consider what groups do—and compare those activities with what organizations *want* their groups to do. This is the study of group processes. The group processes that take place in an organization include those shown in Exhibit 7.8: required and emergent behaviors, social facilitation, and social loafing.

Required and Emergent Behaviors

When managers establish a work group, they have in mind what the group should do—the activities required for the group to achieve its objectives. But to fully understand group processes, we have to look at everything the group does. Group processes also include activities that may not be required for goal achievement. Thus, we describe a group's behaviors as including both required and emergent behaviors.[28]

Required behaviors are the activities that the organization defines as necessary conditions of group membership. Such behaviors include performing work assignments, treating coworkers and customers politely, and following policies and procedures. In exchange for performing the required behaviors, employees receive pay and benefits, continued access to the organization's resources, and continued group membership.

Defining required behaviors can set a group on course to success. For example, California's Office of Foreign Investment is charged with encouraging and helping foreign companies to set up businesses in the state. To get the job done, the agency sets up groups called Red Teams, which bring together representatives from all the organizations required to complete a foreign investment deal, such as city planning departments and zoning boards. Group members are required to study the investment plan, identifying areas where the plan needs to be adjusted to comply with local regulations. The group continues to meet until its members reach consensus on how to resolve all the differences.[29] Similarly, in the business sector, two pharmaceutical companies, Warner-Lambert and Pfizer, have formed groups that require—and inspire—behaviors that enable them to collaborate to an extraordinary degree.

required behaviors

Activities that the organization defines as necessary conditions of group membership.

❧ Warner-Lambert and Pfizer

Competition is a way of life in the pharmaceutical industry, so Warner-Lambert and Pfizer surprised observers when they decided to collaborate in marketing the cholesterol-reducing drug called Lipitor. The two companies teamed up because each had something impressive to offer: Warner-Lambert's scientists had developed the drug, and Pfizer had an awesome sales force, ranked first by doctors. Warner-Lambert

thought the product had great potential and wanted the selling power to gain market share at the expense of other companies' established products. Pfizer believed Lipitor was a superior product and wanted a piece of the action.

The two companies set up four teams, combining representatives of both companies, to make sales calls. The teams brought together researchers and marketing professionals from all levels in both organizations. That strategy was tested immediately. The Food and Drug Administration approved Lipitor faster than expected, and the teams had to scramble to get the product to doctors. Pfizer contributed sales training and a plan for reaching physicians. Warner-Lambert geared up to meet production and distribution needs. From the experience, the teams learned to value cooperation, open discussion, and sharing of resources, rather than focusing on the organizations' differences. Lynn Alexy, a vice president at Warner-Lambert, elaborates on these required behaviors: "[Team members from both companies] are committed to an atmosphere of mutual respect and trust, where conflicts are resolved in a constructive, open environment."

The approach has paid off dramatically. Lipitor set a record for first-year sales of a pharmaceutical product: $1 billion. Sales of Lipitor have more than doubled since then. It has become the best-selling drug for lowering cholesterol, with a 40 percent market share. Not surprisingly, the companies extended their agreement to collaborate on Lipitor for another decade—and then extended their collaboration to a planned merger of the two companies.[30]

emergent behaviors

Activities that group members perform instead of or in addition to required behaviors.

In contrast to required behaviors, **emergent behaviors** are the other activities that group members perform—what they do instead of or in addition to the required behaviors. Group members choose to do emergent behaviors because they enjoy them or expect that the behaviors will help them or the group to be more effective. For example, Anne Zehren of *Teen People,* mentioned earlier as an effective group leader, wasn't required by her organization to institute Gonging Ceremonies to celebrate her employees' successes—in fact, Time managers were surprised by the practice. But the gongings obviously worked for her group, as morale and achievement soared at the magazine.

Emergent behaviors can enhance a group's effectiveness, or they can interfere with work. Organizations try to specify enough required behaviors to prevent dysfunctional emergent behaviors. But, it is unrealistic to expect that an organization can predict and codify all behaviors, especially since some that are not task related are important for maintaining the group. Group members therefore should learn to identify and evaluate group behaviors as they develop. This enables the group to eliminate behaviors that are troublesome or unproductive.

Social Facilitation and Social Loafing

When people are in a group, they don't necessarily work the same way as they would when alone. For example, being in a group can influence how hard a person tries or how well he or she focuses on the task at hand. Two processes that influence the way people work in groups are social facilitation and social loafing.

social facilitation

The process by which the presence of a group causes performance to improve or decline.

Social Facilitation   In a group, by definition, people act in the presence of others. Sometimes having other people around causes a person to focus on the task at hand; at other times, it is a distraction. Thus, the presence of other people can cause performance either to improve or to decline. We call this influence **social facilitation.** Social facilitation can occur whether or not the observers and the person performing a task belong to a group. However, a group sets the stage for social facilitation. This is true of the Red Teams established by the California Office of Foreign Investment. Team members persist in making foreign investment deals over a period of hours, rather than sending reports and representatives from one agency to another. Using the teams has halved the time to complete a deal.[31]

The more managers know about how social facilitation works, the better able they are to define which tasks should be performed in a group situation. For example, research on social facilitation has found that when people perform simple, routine tasks in the presence of others, they tend to work faster and more accurately. In contrast, social facilitation tends to lessen performance of tasks that are more complex and require the worker to pay close attention.[32]

Social Loafing   A drawback of group work is that group members may not work as hard as if they were on their own. In a group process called **social loafing,** the effort of group members tends to decline as the size of the group increases. The individual members of the group "loaf," or do less than their best, apparently because they believe the group can achieve its objectives without all individuals' hardest work. As a result, the output of four people in a group is less than the sum of what each of the four could contribute as individuals.

social loafing

The tendency of group members to reduce their effort as the size of the group increases.

Social scientists have observed social loafing under the following circumstances:

* Group members perceived the task to be unimportant, boring, or simple.[33]
* Group members thought that their own output was not distinguishable from the overall output of the group.[34]
* Group members expected that the others in the group would loaf.[35]

In contrast, a laboratory study of social loafing found that when subjects expected their performance to be evaluated, social loafing did not occur.[36] This research suggests that social loafing is a real concern but that managers can limit its effects. Managers can help employees to define their tasks as significant, and they can establish measures of individual as well as group output.

Furthermore, the amount of social loafing that occurs may depend on the outlook of group members. A study that categorized subjects as "individualists" (focused on the self) or "collectivists" (group oriented) found that individualists were more likely to engage in social loafing. However, the effect was lessened when the group was small and each member was accountable for his or her individual results.[37]

These results are consistent with cultural differences. In general, people in the United States tend to have an individualistic outlook. They typically think of themselves more as individuals than as members of a society, and they highly value individual achievement. In Israel and the People's Republic of China, the culture is more "collectivist," meaning that people primarily define themselves as group members and value contributions to the group's well-being. Studies comparing the behavior of U.S. employees with that of Israeli and Chinese employees found that the employees in the latter two countries were less inclined to engage in social loafing. Instead, they performed better in groups than alone.[38]

apply it

1. Assume your professor has assigned you and two other students to prepare a research report as a group. You can deliver the report orally or in writing. From what you have learned so far about group processes, how might working in a group enhance the quality of your report? How might you encourage the group to gain those benefits of the group process?

2. What might contribute to social loafing by members of your group? How might your group prevent social loafing?

Group performance is influenced by certain factors

Because some kinds of group behavior are beneficial, and others interfere with organizational objectives, it is important for organizations to know how to set up groups so that they will behave beneficially. Research has investigated a number of group factors and identified several that are related to group performance. As shown in Exhibit 7.9, these factors include the size and composition of the group, the group's resources and tasks, its norms, its cohesiveness, and rewards for group (rather than individual) performance.

Size and Composition of the Group

Why does a baseball team have nine members on the field? Why does the U.S. Senate have 100 voting members? Why does Ford Motor Company have nearly 365,000 employees? Someone had to decide at some point what the optimal number of group members should be for each organization. In addition, someone had to decide what type of people would function best in those organizations—the types of skills and abilities the organization needed to perform well. The dynamics of groups change as the number of members increases or decreases. Also, each member's abilities affect the interactions and effectiveness of the overall group. Let's see how these factors affect group performance.

exhibit **7.9**

Factors Influencing Group
Performance

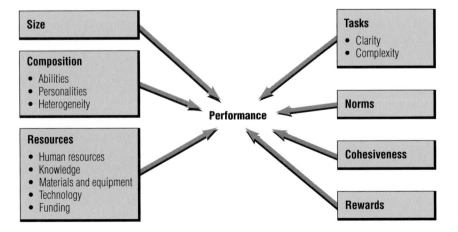

Group Size   Is there an optimal size for a group? And if so, what is that size? Suppose your job includes preparing a budget for next year, and you are expected to form a team from your organization's 150 employees to identify budget needs. Logically, you wouldn't try to sit in a circle with all 150 employees. You couldn't possibly have a real discussion. Rather, you'd want to bring together people representing as many viewpoints as possible, but few enough that everyone has time to speak and evaluate one another's ideas.

So far, research has not provided a firm rule for the number of people to put in a group. The definition of "group" suggests there is an upper limit: since group members must interact on an ongoing basis, the group must be small enough to permit such interaction. In a laboratory study where teams of two to six subjects made decisions about survival equipment required for a spaceship crew, decision quality did not improve as group size increased beyond five members.[39] However, when the objective of a group is to obtain ideas rather than reach a decision, groups with a dozen members or more can be more effective.[40] The greater number of people leads to a greater number and diversity of ideas.

Group Composition   Besides the number of group members, the person assembling a group must decide whom to include. Logically, the group should include people with needed abilities, whether computer knowledge, people skills, or organizational clout. A group that must carry out a complex task may combine people who have strong abilities in only some of the necessary areas, thereby giving the group as a whole all the necessary skills. However, the limits of individual abilities provide a boundary for how well the group will perform. Thus, if no member of the group has strong financial skills, it is unlikely that the group will make exceptional decisions about financial matters.

The personality of group members also influences group performance. Research into personality traits and group attitudes and behavior has found a positive link between certain personality traits and group productivity, morale, and cohesiveness. Those traits include sociability, self-reliance, and independence. In contrast, authoritarianism, unconventionality, and dominance have been negatively related to high group performance. However, no single characteristic alone was strongly related; instead, the personality traits when grouped together showed these relationships.[41]

Most group tasks require a variety of skills and knowledge. One way to introduce this variety is to make the group heterogeneous (composed of different kinds of individuals). Research supports the idea that heterogeneous groups that bring together people with different personalities, opinions, skills, perspectives, and genders are more likely to have the qualities needed by the group and to accomplish the group's tasks.[42] However, misunderstandings and conflict are more likely in such a group, so it will need skilled

General manager Robert Steele (center) is the leader of a diverse group of service staff employees at the Hyatt Hotel in Baltimore, Maryland. The group includes employees with varying skills and knowledge and also with diverse racial and ethnic backgrounds. Skilled management of its diverse groups has earned Hyatt the highest ranking for the hotel industry in Fortune *magazine's recent list of "The Diversity Elite."*
(Source: © Robert Wright)

leadership. In particular, when researchers have studied groups whose members differ in terms of race and ethnic background, they have found that group processes are more troubled in the early stages of group development. After several months, the differences in performance tend to disappear.[43]

Resources and Tasks of the Group

As we mentioned earlier in the discussion of group development, some groups have clearly defined roles and tasks, whereas others evolve more gradually. In a cockpit crew, people know precisely what is expected, and they quickly get to work. The clear structure and norms of a cockpit crew are essential for good functioning of a group in this situation. Other situations, however, may benefit from less structure. For example, a group that is supposed to generate ideas may ultimately fulfill this task better if roles are not overly rigid. Nevertheless, even an idea-generating group needs a clear concept of its goals and how to measure whether it has achieved them.

Groups, like individuals, need access to resources to be able to perform. At the top of the resource list are the talents and expertise of the group's members. Logically, the group will perform best if its members have great ability in carrying out the tasks that are relevant to the group's objectives.[44]

Thus, the nature of the group's tasks is important to success because it defines the group's needs. Those needs will vary depending on whether the group is charged with generating ideas, producing routine outputs, or solving complex problems. For example, we saw earlier that when the task is to generate ideas, the organization benefits by forming a larger group than it does when the task is to solve a complex problem. Similarly, a diverse group is especially beneficial when the task is to generate ideas. As in these examples, the type of the task influences group success indirectly by influencing the requirements for group effectiveness.

In addition, group members need to be clear about what tasks the group is supposed to perform. Goals should be clear and specific. The organization may want group members to establish the group's goals themselves so that they understand and are committed to those goals.

Group Norms

norms

Shared standards of behavior that define what kinds of behavior are acceptable and desirable.

What channels group members' abilities and efforts toward common goals? One force is leadership, discussed earlier in this chapter. In addition, group members' behavior is influenced by the group's **norms**—shared standards of behavior that define what kinds of behavior are acceptable and desirable. For example, a group's norms might include whether it is acceptable to disagree with the group's leader openly during meetings. Most work groups have norms that cover the following areas of behavior:[45]

- *Performance*   how hard to work, what procedures to follow, the importance of punctuality
- *Appearance*   how to dress, when to be busy, how to demonstrate loyalty to the group
- *Social arrangement*   whom to invite to lunch or after-hours social activities, which (if any) group members to befriend

- *Allocation of resources* how to distribute pay, job assignments, and resources needed to perform work

Some of these decisions may be subject to the organization's policies and procedures. However, even those guidelines are likely to be influenced by the organization's or managers' norms.

The Los Alamos National Laboratory, located in New Mexico, was established with the norm that people would exchange ideas freely and openly with each other, as in a university. The facility, which does defense-related research, also has the norm of protecting the nation's security by keeping secret information within the organization's walls. Recently, in a widely publicized incident, an employee was accused of spying and revealing nuclear secrets. The organization enforced the norm of protecting defense secrets by tightening security. Many of the scientists who were attracted to Los Alamos because of the norm of idea sharing were disheartened and thought the evolving relationships had been compromised, and some left the laboratory.[46]

Sometimes groups establish norms by discussing and agreeing on them. For example, at its first meeting, a group might decide that members should freely express their opinions in an informal process. Although most norms are unwritten, the group might decide to put some of these norms in writing so that group members can refer to them later. Other norms result from the group's experiences. For example, a high-status group member might state a norm and the others respond by adopting it. The group may also adopt norms because individual group members bring them to the group or because they happen to fit behavior patterns that the group used initially. When a certain behavior causes a problem for the group, the group members might agree to avoid it in the future. Conversely, when actions lead to positive results, the group may reinforce its success by creating norms to repeat similar behavior.

Groups reinforce norms by encouraging behavior that is consistent with the norms and punishing group members when they violate them. They might criticize nonconforming behavior, discuss the problem behavior with the nonconforming group member, or tease or ignore that person. If group members believe the situation is urgent, they might even intervene physically to induce the nonconforming group member to conform or leave.

Groups are most likely to establish and reinforce norms that help them function smoothly and survive. From the organization's perspective, a group should establish and enforce norms that support high performance—that is, achieve objectives consistent with the organization's goals. When the group has such norms, members tend to contribute to high performance even when the organization does not specifically require or reward such behavior. In this way, the organization's groups are productive without needing managers to monitor their every behavior.

Group Cohesiveness

To consider another variable that affects group performance, imagine that you want to start an e-commerce business. You have a product idea and marketing know-how, and you want to bring in two people to help you

group cohesiveness

Mutual attraction among group members and desire to remain part of the group.

All members of the Wild Type Band work in the laboratory at Johns Hopkins University. "Wild Type" is a term for a normal gene. According to a recent announcement by laboratory leader Dr. Bert Vogelstein, the group has developed an improved test for determining a person's cancer risk. Spending time together while performing, such as at a recent party for 400 science writers, helps enhance the cohesiveness of this high-performance group.
(Source: © Max Hirshfeld)

start the business—one to set up and maintain your Web site and another to handle the finances. You know that starting a business requires 80-hour workweeks, and you need partners who will commit themselves to maintaining this exhausting pace during periods of great uncertainty. For this level of commitment, the group consisting of you and your two partners must be highly cohesive. **Group cohesiveness** is mutual attraction among group members and desire to remain part of the group.

Eduardo Bedoya has built a successful business in a challenging industry by participating in a highly cohesive group of businesspeople. Bedoya's company, EBC Computers, sells computer parts and components to businesses and tech-savvy consumers that assemble their own PCs. As technology advances, prices of these items plunge, so EBC's very survival depends on getting the best price for just enough inventory to meet demand. Bedoya competes by participating in an informal network of about 50 brokers, all of them Chinese-American and based in California with Taiwanese suppliers. Bedoya, who immigrated from Peru, and the members of this network are in constant communication, trading gossip as well as making deals. The suppliers welcomed him into their network and gave him favorable payment terms because they found him to be trustworthy and he shares their enjoyment of strategy and negotiation.[47]

Cohesiveness is related to group performance, but as pictured in Exhibit 7.10, the type of relationship depends on the group's performance-related norms. Some groups have high-performance norms, meaning the group favors quality work and great output. Other groups have low-performance norms, as in an informal group that encourages conversation among group members even when it distracts them from working. In general, when cohesiveness is high, high-performance norms support high productivity, and low-performance norms support low productivity. In a group with low cohesiveness, the effect of norms is not as great.

Given the impact of cohesiveness, forming a cohesive group to start a business does indeed make sense. However, this is true only if the group members are all committed to the success of the business and therefore create high-performance norms. Assuming that you find two people with the necessary talents and commitment, how can you build a cohesive group? Sources of cohesiveness include time spent together, small group size (which encourages everyone to interact), the enjoyment of rewards arising from group participation, and the shared experience of threats from outside the group. These circumstances might seem to arise naturally in the cre-

exhibit **7.10**
Influence of Norms on Performance

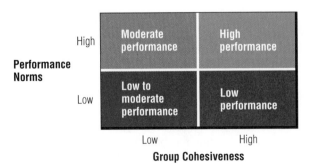

Performance Norms — High / Low

Group Cohesiveness — Low / High

	Low	High
High	Moderate performance	High performance
Low	Low to moderate performance	Low performance

ation of a new business, but you can enhance the opportunities to build cohesiveness by making sure you and your partners spend time with each other, not merely handling each aspect of the business independently. And as you face competition for customers and funding, you can define it as a challenge your team will face together as a unit. Furthermore, since cohesiveness is greater when group members are attracted to the group, you and your partners should inject both fun and concern for one another into your shared experiences and celebrate each success. A good example of building cohesiveness occurred in the early years of eBay, the online auction site.

When eBay launched its auction Web site, visitors to the site weren't just customers, they became part of an online community. Their interactions built cohesiveness, which in turn kept users, called eBayers, coming back again and again.

The cohesiveness resulted from eBay's practice of listening to eBayers. The company invited them to share ideas for improving the Web site, and it provided message boards at which they could help each other out. For example, as eBay grew, buyers had more difficulty determining whether sellers or their offerings were real. Some eBayers posted a solution on the message boards: eBay should set up a way for buyers and sellers to rate one another. So eBay created the Feedback Forum, where buyers and sellers post comments about each other. Company research indicated that buyers trusted these ratings; they were willing to pay extra for items sold by someone with a high rating in the Feedback Forum.

Another outcome of the message boards was that some highly committed participants began to play a significant role in those interactions. For instance, Jimmy Griffith spent hours coaching and lecturing users who violated the online community's norms. Before long, eBay hired Griffith, merging his online role with a full-time job as customer support representative. When eBayers checked the message boards, they could enjoy the folksy writings of this online mentor.

Recently, as traffic on eBay has increased and some embarrassing hoaxes have occurred, the company has substituted more formal policies for management by trust. Buyers can get insurance from Lloyd's of London, and sellers can pay to have their identity verified by Equifax. An escrow service holds the winning bidder's payment until a purchase is approved. Some eBayers expect that this spells the end of an era when the site linked a cohesive community of shoppers.[48]

Online, and in the real world, managers can use techniques that either increase or decrease cohesiveness. Given the relationship between group cohesiveness and performance, managers and group leaders should consider what is most beneficial to the organization. When a group has high-performance norms, leaders would enhance cohesiveness through such means as giving group members opportunities to spend time together on enjoyable activities. For a group with low-performance norms, leaders might limit group interactions or broaden interactions to increase group members' contact with people who have high-performance norms.

Rewards for Group Performance

If managers want group members to focus on group, rather than individual, performance, they logically should reward such behavior. However, recall from the earlier discussion of social loafing that individualistic employees will be inclined to engage in social loafing unless their individual performance also is monitored. Organizations can try to satisfy both principles by combining cooperative group rewards and competitive group rewards.

cooperative group rewards

Rewards based on the overall performance of a group.

competitive group rewards

Rewards allocated to individual group members according to their successful performance within the group.

Cooperative group rewards are rewards based on the overall performance of a group. For example, Continental Airlines pays all employees a bonus in every quarter when the airline meets objectives for on-time performance and customer satisfaction. Thus, everyone gets the same bonus based on the entire organization's performance. This type of reward is designed to encourage cooperation. Rather than saying, "Ticket agents don't do that," a ticket agent might perform the duties of another employee in order to improve a customer's satisfaction. Of course, if some employees notice that one employee is not trying very hard, they may be angry that the shirking employee receives the same reward. (This can ultimately be beneficial, however, if the employees apply peer pressure to improve their colleague's performance.)

Competitive group rewards allocate rewards among individual group members according to their successful performance within the group. The objective of such rewards is to be equitable by rewarding group members for their actual contributions to the group's success. Especially among individualistic employees, this reward structure may seem more fair than cooperative group rewards. However, measuring each employee's contributions to group performance can be difficult. Also, employees may cooperate less if they believe cooperation will lessen their relative contribution to the group.

apply it

1. Suppose you are the sales manager for a group of 12 salespeople. The four top performers in your department regularly leave work about an hour early on Fridays to socialize. You are concerned about whether this informal group has a positive or negative impact on the performance of your department. What would you want to know about the characteristics and behavior of this informal group?

2. As a manager trying to strengthen the overall performance of your department, how might you respond to the existence of this informal group? Would you respond differently if the informal group consisted of employees who were not your department's top performers?

Groups interact with other groups

In all but the smallest organizations, groups interact with one another. The organization is thus like a network of groups, such as departments, cross-functional teams, and informal groups. Not only does the organization depend on cooperation among each group's members, but groups must interact effectively with one another as well.

Interaction among groups is more difficult when members do not physically encounter one another, as in the case of workers on different shifts. Consultant William Sirois studies shift work and notes that employees on the night shift sometimes feel isolated from the rest of the company: "The cafeteria's closed and there are only leftovers in the vending machine; staff meetings are held during the day, and you have to interrupt your sleep to come in." According to Sirois, this sends a message that the organization

exhibit | 7.11
Intergroup Behavior: The Linking Pin Role

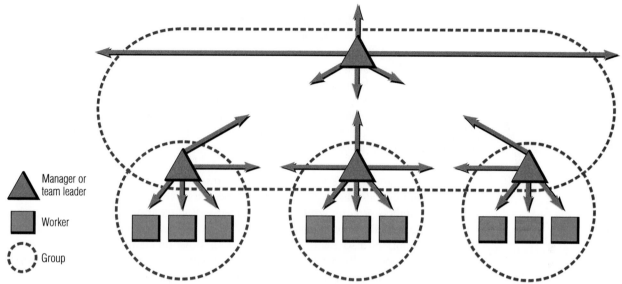

Manager or team leader

Worker

Group

Source: Rensis Likert, *New Patterns of Management* (New York: McGraw-Hill, 1961).

considers night workers to be unimportant.[49] Organizations that appreciate this challenge to intergroup behavior not only provide night-shift workers with pizza and fruit trays but also schedule meetings at times that minimize the disruption to members of all shifts. At Saturn Corporation, the human resource department encourages intergroup communication with production workers by scheduling some HR employees to rotate shifts along with the production crews. Doubletree Hotel schedules weekly staff meetings—which include shift managers, human resource managers, and representatives from care and safety committees—as early as 5:30 a.m. and as late as 9:30 p.m. to accommodate people working night shifts.[50]

Typically, group interactions involve a person from one group communicating with a person in another group. In terms of the organization's formal structure, the people who play this "linking pin" role are usually the group's managers.[51] As shown in Exhibit 7.11, the managers communicate with their employees, as well as with those above them in the organization's hierarchy, thus linking together various levels of the hierarchy. In addition, with traditional patterns of organizational communication, managers are the primary communicators between departments. In Chapter 9, however, we will see ways that modern organizations are fostering communication among employees at all levels. General Electric is an organization well known for taking the lead in this regard.

Jack Welch, the chief executive of General Electric since 1981, is widely known and respected for many of his innovations, including his declaration that GE would become "boundaryless." That mouthful of a term means that the company's employees are supposed to, in Welch's words, "look everywhere in the world for better ideas." In terms of organizational behavior, this includes communication and idea sharing among the various departments and levels of the hierarchy.

☜ General Electric (GE)

Boundaryless behavior has introduced a new style of selling to GE. Instead of thinking only about selling a particular product line, GE salespeople look for customer needs that someone at GE can satisfy. Gib Bosworth, an account manager for GE Capital Fleet Services, starts with discussing a client's fleet needs, but he doesn't stop there: "I may ask how they're financing their office equipment." If Bosworth detects a need that another GE division can satisfy, he contacts a colleague on his Boundaryless Sales Team. His teammate then serves the customer. In twice-yearly meetings, team members also share knowledge about selling practices.

Everyone wins, because everyone shares in the rewards according to his or her performance. Thousands of employees have stock options and are striving to improve performance so they can increase their ownership of the giant company. In the case of the Boundaryless Sales Teams, salespeople also receive $100 gift certificates for making referrals, as well as a chance to win trips. Furthermore, the top performers stand out because of GE's past efforts to become a lean organization. Social loafing is difficult, and high performance is valued.[52]

Part of GE's success may be attributed to effective interaction within and among its groups. Many of the issues that arise *within* groups have parallels *among and between* groups. For example, people in organizations define the status and roles of groups as well as individuals. Group members also make decisions about how much they will cooperate or compete with other groups in the organization. Sometimes organizations encourage intergroup conflict as a way to promote cohesiveness within groups and motivate groups to achieve (to outperform another group). At other times, organizations foster cooperation by forming cross-functional teams or other groups that bring together members of several groups. Another way to encourage cooperation is to establish organization-level goals and rewards, such as stock options at General Electric.

apply it

1. At a consumer electronics business, the research and development, manufacturing, and sales departments each have norms that include criticizing and joking about the other two departments. At budget time, the departments feel they are competing with each other for scarce resources. Each department tries to prepare a budget request that will grab a significant share of the company's resources. The company's executives believe the departments' intergroup relations are hurting company performance. What can the executives do to improve intergroup processes at the company?

summary OF KEY CONCEPTS

- **Groups naturally form and develop in organizations.** In the context of organizational behavior, a group is two or more members of an organization who interact, share norms and goals, influence one another, and identify themselves as a group. Group formation can meet both organizational and personal goals, including the synergy of a high-functioning group. Organizations create formal groups, including command groups and task groups. To meet personal needs, individuals also create informal and reference groups. Many people believe groups follow a process of development such as Tuckman's five-stage model: forming, storming, norming, performing, and adjourning.

- **Group members play various roles.** A role is a set of behaviors that group members expect of someone in a certain position. Group roles include task roles and maintenance roles. Group members define role expectations and create role identities. Problems occur when group members experience role overload, role ambiguity, or role conflict. In the case of work groups, the organization also defines an authority structure. People with high authority may have the role of leaders in the group, but leadership is also defined by group members. A related influence on behavior is the status of group members and of the groups themselves.

- **Groups can influence whether members meet expectations.** Organizations and group members have expectations for groups. Required behaviors are the activities necessary for accomplishing those expectations. Group members also may engage in emergent behaviors—activities they perform instead of or in addition to required behaviors. Being in a group may cause a person's

performance to improve or decline, through a process called the social facilitation effect. People may engage in social loafing, meaning that as the group increases in size, the individuals put forth less effort.

- **Group performance is influenced by certain factors.** A group should be small enough that its members can interact yet large enough to bring together all the necessary talents or viewpoints. The abilities and personalities of group members also influence success. Besides human resources, the group needs access to the other resources required for successfully carrying out group tasks. High-performing groups also have norms that are consistent with the group's objectives, coupled with a high level of cohesiveness. An appropriate reward structure supports high performance.

- **Groups interact with other groups.** Intergroup behavior includes communication among group members who perform a "linking pin" role. Organizations can encourage this type of communication to enhance cooperation among their groups. In addition, the principles of interpersonal conflict resolution apply to intergroup behavior.

KEY terms

group, p. 234
synergy, p. 235
formal group, p. 236
command group, p. 236
task group, p. 236
informal group, p. 237
reference group, p. 237
role, p. 240
task roles, p. 240

maintenance roles, p. 241
role expectations, p. 241
role identity, p. 241
role overload, p. 243
role ambiguity, p. 243
role conflict, p. 243
authority structure, p. 246
status, p. 247
required behaviors, p. 249

emergent behaviors, p. 250
social facilitation, p. 250
social loafing, p. 251
norms, p. 254
group cohesiveness, p. 256
cooperative group rewards, p. 258
competitive group rewards, p. 258

DISCUSSION questions

1. How is active membership in a group different from passive membership in an organization? How might a person turn a passive membership into an active one?

2. Suppose you didn't like the food served in the dining room at your college. Do you think it would be more effective for you to try to get the college to make a change by yourself or as a member or leader of a group? Why?

3. Describe an experience in which you were part of a command or task group, either at school or at work. (An example of a command group at school might be a teacher and students in your major, or a basketball coach and players; an example of a task group might include a theater production or a fund-raising effort.) How effective was the group in meeting its goals?

4. Why is it important for managers to recognize and understand the stages of group development? How might this understanding affect a group's performance?

5. Suppose a restaurant manager wants to create a group to identify ways to improve the restaurant's menu. What might some of the task roles of members be? What might some of the maintenance roles be?

6. Think of a time when you have experienced role conflict—as a student and a friend; as a sibling and a son or daughter; as a worker and a student; and so on. Describe the experience and what steps you took to resolve the role conflict. Would you take the same action again? Why or why not?

7. Suppose a small medical practice hired an office manager from one of the most prestigious hospitals in the area. How might this person's status change the way the office group functions?

8. Consider the leader of a group that is working overtime to launch a new product. What types of emergent behaviors might the leader use to enhance the group's effectiveness?

9. Think about a job you currently have or have had in the past. List the norms for performance, appearance, and social arrangement at the workplace. Now that you are consciously aware of these norms, how do you think they affected the performance of the work group?

10. Recently, Apple Computer changed its employee reward system from an individual bonus system to company stock options. Why do you think this change was made?

11. In today's work environment, it is common for groups in the same organization to be scattered all over the country, even all over the world, with much of their interaction taking place electronically. What steps might managers take to enhance interaction and cooperation among these groups?

SELF-DISCOVERY exercise

How Tolerant Are You?

To get an idea how well you would perform in a heterogeneous group, test your tolerance of others who are different than you. For each of the following questions, fill in the blank with the letter of the statement that best describes you.

_____ **1.** Most of your friends
  a. are very similar to you
  b. are very different from you and from each other
  c. are like you in some respects but different in others

_____ **2.** When someone does something you disapprove of, you
  a. break off the relationship
  b. tell how you feel but keep in touch
  c. tell yourself it matters little and behave as you always have

_____ **3.** Which virtue is most important to you?
  a. kindness
  b. objectivity
  c. obedience

_____ **4.** When it comes to beliefs, you
  a. do all you can to make others see things the same way you do
  b. actively advance your point of view but stop short of argument
  c. keep your feelings to yourself

_____ **5.** Would you hire a person who has had emotional problems?
  a. no
  b. yes, provided there is evidence of complete recovery
  c. yes, if the person is suitable for the job

_____ **6.** Do you voluntarily read material that supports views different from your own?
  a. never
  b. sometimes
  c. often

_____ **7.** You react to old people with
  a. patience
  b. annoyance
  c. sometimes **a,** sometimes **b**

_____ **8.** Do you agree with the statement, "What is right and wrong depends upon the time, place, and circumstance?"
   a. strongly agree
   b. agree to a point
   c. strongly disagree

_____ **9.** Would you marry someone from a different race?
   a. yes
   b. no
   c. probably not

_____ **10.** If someone in your family were homosexual, you would
   a. view this as a problem and try to change the person to a heterosexual orientation
   b. accept the person as a homosexual with no change in feelings or treatment
   c. avoid or reject the person

_____ **11.** You react to little children with
   a. patience
   b. annoyance
   c. sometimes **a**, sometimes **b**

_____ **12.** Other people's personal habits annoy you
   a. often
   b. not at all
   c. only if extreme

_____ **13.** If you stay in a household run differently from yours (cleanliness, manners, meals, and other customs), you
   a. adapt readily
   b. quickly become uncomfortable and irritated
   c. adjust for a while, but not for long

_____ **14.** Which statement do you agree with most?
   a. We should avoid judging others because no one can fully understand the motives of another person.
   b. People are responsible for their actions and have to accept the consequences.
   c. Both motives and actions are important when considering questions of right and wrong.

Circle your score for each of the answers and total the scores:

1.	a = 4;	b = 0;	c = 2
2.	a = 4;	b = 2;	c = 0
3.	a = 0;	b = 2;	c = 4
4.	a = 4	b = 2;	c = 0
5.	a = 4;	b = 2;	c = 0
6.	a = 4;	b = 2;	c = 0
7.	a = 0;	b = 4;	c = 2
8.	a = 0;	b = 2;	c = 4
9.	a = 0;	b = 4;	c = 2
10.	a = 2;	b = 0;	c = 4
11.	a = 0	b = 4;	c = 2
12.	a = 4;	b = 0;	c = 2
13.	a = 0;	b = 4;	c = 2
14.	a = 0;	b = 4;	c = 2

Total Score: ☐

0–14: If you score 14 or below, you are a very tolerant person and dealing with diversity comes easily to you.

15–28: You are basically a tolerant person and others think of you as tolerant. In general, diversity presents few problems for you, but you may be broad-minded in some areas and have less tolerant ideas in other areas of life, such as attitudes toward older people or male-female social roles.

29–42: You are less tolerant than most people and should work on developing greater tolerance of people different from you. Your low tolerance level could affect your business or personal relationships.

43–56: You have a very low tolerance for diversity. The only people you are likely to respect are those with beliefs similar to your own. You reflect a level of intolerance that could cause difficulties in today's multicultural business environment.

Source: Adapted from the Tolerance Scale by Maria Heiselman, Naomi Miller, and Bob Schlorman, Northern Kentucky University, 1982, in George Manning, Kent Curtis, and Steve McMillen, _Building Community: The Human Side of Work_ (Cincinnati, OH: Thomson Executive Press, 1996), pp. 272–277. Reprinted by permission of George Manning.

ORGANIZATIONAL BEHAVIOR in your life

As you've already figured out from reading this chapter, you are a member of several groups—your family, the dorm or special-interest house you live in, perhaps a sports team or musical group, a team of coworkers, and the like. Choose one of your groups and analyze it from the following standpoints:

- What was the reason for the group to form?
- What type of group is it?
- What is the size and composition of the group?

- What stage of development is the group currently in? How long has the group been in this stage?
- What role (or roles) do you play in the group? What roles do others play?
- What are some of the group's norms?

You can expand this exercise by interviewing other members of the group, asking them the same questions. Then, complete your analysis by describing ways you think the group is effective and ways you think the group's effectiveness could be improved.

ORGANIZATIONAL BEHAVIOR news flash

Unions are formal groups that may start informally—gossip at lunch, discussions during the commute, arguments over coffee. When a group of employees at a small company begins to consider unionizing, the results can include a change in norms, expectations, role identity—and lots of role conflict, especially for the company owner. This happened to Michael Powell, owner of Powell's Books of Portland, Oregon, a progressive place where customers could find dictionaries published in Apache and Zulu, where gay poets and Colombian dissidents were free to read aloud from their works. Powell, along with other progressive entrepreneurs, found himself stuck between his professed commitment to social responsibility and a group of employees who were dissatisfied with tiny pay increases and a recent reorganization. He was used to being a member of the group, and suddenly he found himself an outsider when his employees joined a union.

Other self-proclaimed progressive businesses have faced the same problem—in the past couple of years, Borders Books, Noah's Bagels, Starbucks, the Pacifica radio network, Whole Foods Markets, and even

Ben & Jerry's have all succumbed to union drives, leaving their formerly popular leaders on the outside. For these entrepreneurs, the change in their roles is unsettling at the very least. "You question everything," says Michael Powell. "There was a sense in my mind that we all made some sacrifices to be in the book business and that there was something special about this place. . . . Now I have to find the ground under my feet."

Using the news listings on your search engine, such as AP, Reuters, ZDNet News, and the like, look for stories about small companies such as those above whose workers have joined unions. When you find a story or stories that interest you, download it and study the situation from the perspective of groups. Then write a brief editorial analyzing the way unionization changed how groups functioned in the company, and discuss whether you think the change was positive or negative for the organization as a whole.

Source: Chris Lydgate, "Unionization Starts at Home," *Fortune,* June 7, 1999, p. 38.

global diversity EVENTS

Although the Japanese are well known for their development of electronic technology, the nation's business community so far lags behind the United States in building an Internet economy. So

Satoshi Koike, an entrepreneur based in California who runs a consultancy called Netyear Group, decided to do something about it. He used his Japanese contacts to start a business-networking group whose purpose is to help Japan's entrepreneurs launch and develop Web businesses. The group is now called Bit Valley, an abbreviated, translated version of *Shibuya,* or "Bitter Valley," the trendy Tokyo neighborhood where many of Japan's Internet entrepreneurs are located. Bit Valley has helped entrepreneurs start such companies as Indigo, Digital Garage, Netage, Cyber Agent, Horizon Digital Enterprise, and Rakuten, Japan's largest net shopping mall. When they aren't busy with net business, members gather socially in Shibuya bars to trade ideas and success stories. And although Bit Valley started as a tiny group, its membership—and influence—has swelled beyond the Shibuya neighborhood, now representing 1,200 members from over 400 businesses.

Bit Valley is just one global e-commerce group; there are many others. Using the news listings on your search engine, such as Reuters, AP, ZDNet News, and the like, look for stories about Japanese or other global e-commerce groups. (Or use the key words "global e-commerce groups" to find names of and stories about such groups.) When you find a good story or stories about such a group, consider the following questions:

1. Why was the group formed? What is the size and composition of the group? How cohesive does the group appear to be? What can you learn about the group's interaction with other groups?

2. In what ways might this group help its members overcome obstacles to global e-commerce that they might not be able to overcome on their own?

3. Imagine that you are an entrepreneur considering joining this group, or one like it. What role (or roles) would you expect to play as a group member?

Source: Irene M. Kunii, "Tokyo's Valley of the Netrepreneurs," *Business Week,* September 6, 1999, pp. 91–92.

minicase ISSUE

How to Train the Whole World (with Small Groups)

When Lynne McLaughlin, head of the Sun Software and Technology training group, gets a request for training in one of 40 products for which her group provides support, she sends out a group of professionals. She heads up a command group that, because of the level of expertise of its members, really functions like a task group, custom designing and implementing training for clients all around the world, including Antarctica.

The Challenge. The challenge is that the audience for these training sessions has only one common denominator, the fact that they use (or want to use) Sun software products. "There's no budget or bandwidth to deliver these courses in the audience's native language," explains McLaughlin, which means that the training group must find ways to present highly technical information in a format and language that the audience can understand, usually with English as a second language.

Group Size and Composition. The size and composition of the training group is key to its success: McLaughlin has only six key program managers on her staff, each of whom brings a particular expertise as well as contacts to the group. Each group member has a clear role identity, and expectations of all are well defined. Each member must act as a liaison with one or more of Sun's product groups, building relationships and learning the products proficiently enough to communicate with product developers; each must function as a liaison with vendors; and each must "own" a particular training project or method, such as the Web or classroom. Kavindra Patel specializes in the Web; Don Giberson specializes in Web-based training as well as project management products; Jane Fleming focuses on multimedia-based training; Bill Filler deals with authorization training and testing and classroom training; Adrian Kendrick handles new-hire training; and Barbara Dahl deals with product distribution.

"Because the department is small, and because of the large volume of products we have to train for, we had to work as a closed-loop group," comments Kavindra Patel. Patel is in charge of her own two training projects, maintains communication with eight product groups, and looks for new technologies that might assist in training. "Each of us has his own function, but we help each other out at the same time."

Norms. The group's norms include socializing with each other. Group members have parties together; they share the excitement of each other's successes and bolster someone who's down. They also joke around. If someone makes a "catty" remark during a staff meeting, a stuffed Sylvester the Cat is tossed to the person, who must wear the kitty on his or her head.

Outsiders are impressed with the Sun training group's success. "This group is able to produce different types of training, using a lot of delivery mechanisms, in a short amount of time. They assign the project, a team, a goal and—boom boom—it's done, tested, and out the door," says an admiring Dawn Zin-tel, president of the Training Alliance in Morgan Hill, California. The Sun group proves how much a few can achieve—while tossing a stuffed cat around a room.

1. What might happen to the Sun training group if it were increased in size to, say, 20 members?

2. Why is it important for Sun group members to have clear role identities? What might happen if one of the members sought to change his or her role?

3. Do you think this group would prefer cooperative group rewards or competitive group rewards? Why?

Source: Rochelle Garner, "Going Global with Sun," *Inside Technology Training,* March 1999, pp. 10–13.

eight
CHAPTER

8

Teams and Teamwork

CONCEPT AND SKILL

preview

After studying this chapter, you should be able to:

- Discuss the potential costs and benefits of organizational teams.

- Identify the types of teams in organizations.

- Explain the factors that influence the success of teams.

- Discuss the challenges of using self-directed teams and virtual teams.

- Explain what can be done to develop positive norms, trust, and cohesiveness within each stage of the group development process.

- Discuss the roles of selection, training, and the organizational context in creating effective teams.

Teams Pop the Rivets at Levi Strauss & Company

Levi Strauss is one of the world's greatest brands. No other company—including Tommy Hilfiger and Lee—comes close to it in jeans sales. One estimate is that 75% of American men own a pair of Levi's Dockers khakis. Bob Haas, Levi's chairman and CEO, has been intent on showing that a company driven by social values and that ensures that the factory worker's voice is just as likely to be heard as the top manager's can be successful. Levi's was one of the first companies to pull out of the lucrative Chinese market to protest human rights abuses. Because of his sincerity, Levi employees are loyal to Haas. But there is a downside: Haas's tendency to try to get everyone involved in decision making may result in the demise of the company.

Consider Levi's attempt to use teams in its plants that make blue jeans. The company directed its U.S. plants to abandon the traditional assembly system, in which a garment worker performed a single, specialized task like sewing zippers or attaching belt loops. Workers had been paid according to the total amount of work they completed themselves. In the new team system, teams made up of 10 to 35 workers would work together to assemble a completed pair of pants. The team would then be paid according to the total number of completed pants. Levi's believed that the teams would help alleviate the monotony of the old assembly system and reduce the number of injuries that workers received from repeating the same task over and over again. The use of teams was also expected to increase productivity.

> *"The reengineering changes had us confused. . . . One minute there was no customer service, the next minute they'd overdo it."*
>
> —Buyer at one major Levi's account

Unfortunately, teams at Levi's were a huge failure. Skilled employees found themselves arguing with slower colleagues, damaging morale, triggering insults and threats, and causing friendships to dissolve. Under the old assembly process, skilled workers could exceed their quota of belt loops or fly stitching by 20 percent. Under the team system, top performers' pay shrank, because team productivity was adversely affected by slower, inexperienced, or inefficient team members. The teams received limited supervision, and they were forced to resolve work pace and personality issues themselves. Productive team members were upset that they had to perform work for subpar workers. One seamstress even had to restrain an angry coworker who was going to throw a chair at a team member who constantly griped about her slow work!

Besides the anxiety and pain for team members, teams failed to reach many business objectives. The quantity of pants produced per hour (one of Levi's measures of efficiency) dropped 25 percent from preteam levels. Labor and overhead costs rose 25 percent. The teams did reduce the turnaround time from when an order was received to when the products were shipped by two weeks. However, the time saved was lost en route to retailers. Trucks loaded with pants sat outside warehouses because of problems installing new computers needed to track orders and communicate to retailers that orders were ready.

Why did this experiment to better workers' jobs fail? The organization was not prepared for the team concept. There were no set guidelines for managers on how to implement teams. As a result, managers created their own concept of teams, including pay plans and shop-floor designs. Worker preparation included brief team-building and problem-solving seminars. Workers were given time to master new machinery, but they thought they received inadequate training on how to balance work flow or identify quality problems. When such problems occurred, many managers simply told the teams that handling them was part of being "empowered." The teams also created negative peer pressure that did not fit with Levi's philosophy to promote teamwork, trust, diversity, and empowerment.

All of this turmoil took its toll on Levi's. One estimate is that Levi's share of the domestic jeans market fell from 48 percent to 26 percent due to competitors who were more responsive to customer needs and had lowered manufacturing costs by assembling jeans abroad. Levi's has lost market share to Millers Outpost, JNCO, Arizona, Fubu, and even JC Penney's and Sears, who were more responsive to young customer demands for jeans with wider legs and deeper pockets. As a result, Levi's closed 11 U.S. garment assembly plants and laid off approximately 7,000 workers. Unofficially, the teams are being scrapped at the remaining plants.

Aside from fixing its manufacturing problems, Levi's is also trying to be cool again. For example, the company launched Red Line jeans, distributing them to fewer than 25 cutting-edge shops. To try to tap the underground fashion market, there is nothing on the jeans mentioning Levi's. The response? Red Line is selling well. The plan is for Red Line's "hipness" to somehow seep into the company's other lines. The Docker's division is trying the same tactic to become something other than the "fat-man's khaki." It recently launched a line called K-1 Khakis, and some Dockers in Europe are made of high-tech fabrics like Gore-Tex to attract urban buyers. Although Levi's is down, the company is again trying to become synonymous with jeans. But teams are likely not going to be part of the company's revival.[1]

The problems facing Levi's also confront many other companies that are trying to use teams to become more flexible and responsive in an increasingly competitive environment. Although teams can result in many benefits, they can be a disaster if implemented incorrectly. But Levi's experience is not universal. Keep in mind that teams are being effectively used in organizations across the country and around the world. From the assembly line to the executive office, from large corporations such as British Petroleum and 3M to government agencies such as the United States Information Agency, teams are becoming the basic building block of organizations. One survey found that, within three years, the number of *Fortune* 1000 companies using work teams increased by almost 20 percent, and teamwork has become the most frequent topic taught in company training programs. Similarly, a study of 109 Canadian organizations found that 42 percent report "widespread team-based activity" and only 13 percent report little or no team activity.[2]

Teams are popping up in the most unexpected places. An electromechanical assembly plant found that both quality and productivity increased after it abandoned the traditional production line in favor of work teams.[3] At Mattel, a team of artists, toy designers, computer experts, and automobile designers slashed 13 months from the usual toy design process, creating Top Speed toy cars in only five months. Hecla Mining Company uses teams for company goal setting; a major telecommunications company uses teams of salespeople to deal with big customers with complex purchasing requirements; and Lassiter Middle School in Jefferson County,

Kentucky, uses teams of teachers to prepare daily schedules and handle student discipline problems. Multinational corporations are now using international teams composed of managers from different countries. Ford uses teams to spot quality problems and improve efficiency, and other manufacturers use teams to master sophisticated new production technologies.[4]

As we will see in this chapter, teams can be a powerful tool because they involve and empower employees. Teams can cut across organizations in unusual ways. Hence, workers are more satisfied, and higher productivity and product quality typically result. Moreover, teams create a more flexible organization in which workers are not stuck in narrow jobs.

This chapter focuses on teams and their new applications within organizations. We define various types of teams and explore ways to foster teamwork. We discuss how individuals can make contributions to teams and review the benefits and costs associated with teamwork. We also discuss steps that organizations can take to ensure that teams are effective.

Effective teams can result in personal satisfaction and increased productivity

In this section, we first define teams, discuss the potential costs and benefits of teams, and present a model of team effectiveness that summarizes the important concepts.

What Is a Team?

team

A unit of two or more people who interact and coordinate their work to accomplish a specific goal.

A **team** is a unit of two or more people who interact and coordinate their work to accomplish a specific goal.[5] This definition has three components. First, two or more people are required. Teams can be quite large, although most have fewer than 15 people. Second, people in a team interact regularly. People who do not interact, such as those standing in line at a lunch counter or riding in an elevator, do not compose a team. Third, people in a team share a performance goal, whether it is to design a new handheld computer, build a car, or write a textbook. Students often are assigned to teams to do classwork assignments, in which case the purpose is to perform the assignment and receive an acceptable grade.

Although a team is a group of people, the two terms are not interchangeable. An employer, a teacher, or a coach can put together a group of people and never build a team. The team concept implies a sense of shared mission and collective responsibility. "Teamwork and getting along with others is critical," says Pat Cook of Cook & Company, an executive recruiting firm in Bronxville, New York. "You can't afford to have a me-only employee who wants to be first in the boss's eyes and who alienates the rest of your staff," she says.[6] Exhibit 8.1 lists the primary differences between groups and teams. When the University of Kentucky Wildcats won the 1998 national basketball championship, coaches and commentators noted that the team had less individual talent and fewer stars than some other teams but achieved a high level of success through excellent teamwork—shared leadership, purpose, and responsibility by all members working toward a common goal.

Group	Team
Has a designated strong leader	Shares or rotates leadership roles
Individual accountability	Individual and mutual accountability (accountable to each other)
Identical purpose for group and organization	Specific team vision or purpose
Individual work products	Collective work products
Runs efficient meetings	Meetings encourage open-ended discussion and problem solving
Effectiveness measured indirectly by influence on business (such as financial performance)	Effectiveness measured directly by assessing collective work
Discusses, decides, delegates work to individuals	Discusses, decides, shares work

Source: Adapted from Jon R. Katzenbach and Douglas K. Smith, "The Discipline of Teams," *Harvard Business Review,* March–April 1995, pp. 111–120.

exhibit **8.1**
Differences between Groups and Teams

Model of Work Team Effectiveness

Some of the factors associated with team effectiveness are illustrated in Exhibit 8.2. Work team effectiveness is based on two outcomes—productive output and personal satisfaction.[7] Satisfaction pertains to the team's ability to meet the personal needs of its members and hence maintain their membership and commitment. Productive output pertains to the quality and quantity of task outputs as defined by team goals.

The factors that influence team effectiveness begin with the organizational context.[8] The organizational context in which the group operates includes such factors as accountabilities, culture, and reward systems. Within that context, teams are defined. Important team characteristics are the type of team, the team structure, and team composition. Factors such as the diversity of the team in terms of gender and race, as well as members' knowledge, skills, and attitudes, can have a tremendous impact on team processes and effectiveness.[9] The organization must decide when to create permanent teams within the formal structure and when to use a temporary

exhibit **8.2**   Work Team Effectiveness Model

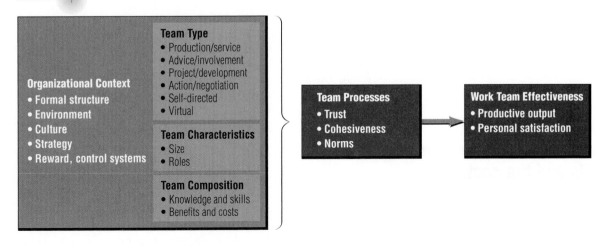

task team. Team size and roles also are important. Managers must also consider whether a team is the best way to do a task. If costs outweigh benefits, managers may wish to assign an individual employee to the task.

These team characteristics influence processes internal to the team, which in turn affect output and satisfaction. Leaders should understand and manage stages of development to create cohesiveness, positive norms, and trust in order to establish an effective team. These processes are influenced by team and organizational characteristics and by the ability of members and leaders to direct these processes in a positive manner. Roberts Express used teams to provide better customer service while increasing efficiency.

❦ Roberts Express

Roberts Express, the largest expedited freight carrier in North America, has moved it all—lighting equipment for Oprah Winfrey's show in the Texas town where she was battling cattle ranchers in a lawsuit, equipment to the *Titanic* set in Nova Scotia, Christmas cards to the White House. Roberts picks up most shipments within 90 minutes of receiving an order and delivers more than half of them on the same day. Most of Roberts's shipments have to get there fast—or else. Joe Greulich, manager of the company's management information systems, says Roberts is the "ambulance service for industrial freight."

Moving freight by truck more quickly and cheaply than air freight gave Roberts a competitive edge when the company started in the early 1980s. Roberts served customers in a limited regional area, so agents and dispatchers knew most of their customers and drivers by name. But the company rapidly expanded nationwide and was eventually making more than 200,000 deliveries a year. This success came at a price. Agents, unaware of which trucks or drivers were available, took orders and then passed them on to dispatchers, who scrambled to cover the deliveries. Service began to suffer. In addition, customers missed the intimacy of the old Roberts, where they could deal with an agent who knew their names and their company's needs. Roberts needed a way to serve each customer with the responsiveness and personal attention that the company had started out with.

Managers decided to reorganize into teams to help the growing company operate more quickly yet still serve customers as if it were a small, regional shipping service. Roberts shrank itself by dividing into several self-directed Customer Assistance Teams (CATs). Each CAT is assigned to a specific geographic region, and the company's phone system automatically routes calls accordingly. To regular customers, Roberts seems no bigger than a particular CAT—when calls come through from customers in New Jersey, they hear the same familiar voices and are usually rerouted to the dispatcher or agent they worked with the previous time. In addition, having agents, dispatchers, and other employees all working together to serve a particular region increases both the quality and speed of service. The team approach, combined with new information technology that helps Roberts employees always know where their drivers and trucks are located, guarantees that Roberts can continue its tradition of delivering hot, last-minute shipments right on time.[10]

apply it

1. Consider the teams you belong to at school or at work. Choose two. For each team, describe why you believe it is a team and not a group. Is the team effective? Why or why not?

To team or not to team: Consider the benefits and the costs

In deciding whether to use teams to perform specific tasks, organizations must consider both benefits and costs. Teams may have a positive impact on both the output productivity and satisfaction of members. On the other hand, they may also create a situation in which motivation and perform-ance actually decrease, as happened at Levi Strauss. As the opening vi-gnette illustrates, if organizations are not able or willing to take the steps to create effective teams, the costs of teams will likely outweigh the benefits.

Potential Benefits of Teams

Teams come closest to achieving their full potential when they enhance in-dividual productivity and build a sense of community and shared purpose among members of an organization. These benefits can be achieved through increased member effort, members' personal satisfaction, integra-tion of diverse abilities and skills, and increased organizational flexibility.

Level of Effort Employee teams can often unleash enormous energy and creativity from workers who like the idea of using their brains as well as their bodies on the job. Companies such as Kimberly-Clark have noticed this change in effort among employees as they switched to team ap-proaches. In the decade since Kimberly-Clark instituted teamwork at its mills, the company has been propelled into the top third of the most recent *Fortune* 500 list and, significantly, ranks 68th on *Fortune's* list of most ad-mired companies. In that survey, the company received its highest marks for quality of products, innovativeness, talent, and social responsibility.[11] The shift to a team approach is an important component of the evolution to a learning organization, as described in Chapter 1. To facilitate learning and problem solving, organizations are breaking down barriers, empowering workers, and encouraging employees to use their brains and creativity. Re-search has found that working in a team increases an individual's motiva-tion and performance. *Social facilitation* refers to the tendency for the pres-ence of others to enhance an individual's motivation and performance. Simply being in the presence of other people has an energizing effect.[12]

Satisfaction of Members As described in Chapter 5, employees have needs for belongingness and affiliation. Working in teams can help meet these needs. Participative teams reduce boredom and often increase employees' feeling of dignity and self-worth because the whole person is employed. People who have a satisfying team environment cope better with stress and enjoy their jobs more. At Kimberly-Clark, the company emphasizes these values in its work environment: "We expect our work environment to re-flect a sense of community while nurturing a commitment to innovation. [The K-C culture] encourages open dialogue and sharing of ideas."[13]

Expanded Job Knowledge and Skills The third major benefit of using teams is the empowerment of employees to bring greater knowledge and ability to the task. For one thing, multiskilled employees learn all of the jobs that the team performs. Teams gain the intellectual resources of several mem-bers who can suggest shortcuts and offer alternative points of view for team decisions.

Organizational Flexibility Traditional organizations are structured so that each worker does only one specific job. But when employee teams are used, from 5 to 15 people work next to one another and are able to exchange jobs. Work can be reorganized and workers reallocated as needed to produce products and services with great flexibility. The organization is thus able to be responsive to rapidly changing customer needs. Consider what Rohm & Haas Texas Inc., a Houston, Texas, chemical company, learned about trying to bring together people from different backgrounds and functions into teams.

❦ Rohm & Haas Texas Inc.

At Rohm & Haas, employees were organized into mandatory teams designed around natural work processes. For example, the company formed a team to monitor sulfuric-acid manufacturing. In the past, an employee was responsible for only three kettles (like cooking pots) out of a process that involved many different kettles. Employees were never really concerned about what happened before the chemical reached their kettle, nor did they care about what happened after the chemical substance left. By cross-training employees to understand the entire manufacturing process, management believed employees would care more about the end product and they would try to improve the process.

Rohm & Haas believed that a better company would result from increased involvement of employees in their work and from the diversity of team members. However, instead of accepting their new assignments, employees formed teams with members with whom they believed they had more in common. The movement to more homogeneous teams took place over three years because employees had to wait until team positions became available. The carefully designed mix of heterogeneous teams was eventually replaced with teams of similar members. The diversity of experience and perspectives that the company was hoping to achieve was lost as teams became increasingly all black or white. Managers realized that the team reorganization was a sign of a deeper diversity problem. They introduced diversity awareness training to help employees understand differences in others. Employees learned that there were social, moral, and business reasons to accept diversity. As a result, the movement to homogeneous teams was stopped. Employees are now more willing to work though their differences. And the process improvements that the company hoped to achieve are being reached now that employees are comfortable challenging each others' ideas.[14]

Potential Costs of Teams

When organizations decide whether to use teams, they must assess certain costs or liabilities associated with teamwork. Teamwork causes a fundamental shift in the relationships of managers and other employees. When teams do not work very well, the major reasons usually are power realignment, free riding, coordination costs, or legal hassles.

Power Realignment When companies form shop workers into teams, the major losers are low- and middle-level managers. These managers are often reluctant to give up power. Indeed, when teams are successful, fewer supervisors are typically needed. This is especially true for self-directed teams, in which workers take over supervisory responsibilities. The adjustment is difficult for managers who fear the loss of status or even of their jobs and who have to learn new, people-oriented skills to survive.[15]

free rider

A person who benefits from team membership but does not make a proportionate contribution to the team's work.

Free Riding The term **free rider** refers to a team member who attains benefits from team membership but does not do a proportionate share of the work.[16] As we discussed in Chapter 7, free riding sometimes is called social loafing, because members do not exert equal effort. In large teams, some people are likely to work less. For example, research found that the pull exerted on a rope was greater by individuals working alone than by individuals in a group. Similarly, people who were asked to clap and make noise made more noise on a per-person basis when working alone or in small groups than they did in a large group.[17] You have probably experienced the problem of free riding in student project groups. Some students put more effort into the group project than others, and often it seems that no members work as hard for the group as they do for their individual grades.

Coordination Costs The time and energy required to coordinate the activities of a group to enable it to perform its task are called **coordination costs.** Groups must spend time getting ready to do work and lose productive time in deciding who is to do what and when.[18] Once again, student project groups illustrate coordination costs. Members must meet after class just to decide when they can meet to perform the task. Schedules must be checked, telephone calls made, and meeting times arranged in order to get down to business. Hours may be devoted to the administration and coordination of the group. Students often feel they could do the same project by themselves in less time.

coordination costs

The time and energy needed to coordinate the activities of a group to enable it to perform its task.

Legal Hassles As more companies utilize teams, new questions of legality surface. A 1990 National Labor Relations Board judgment against management's use of union-member teams at Electromation, Inc., set a confusing precedent. The Wagner Act of 1935 was enacted to prevent companies from forming organizations or employee committees to undercut legitimate unions. At Electromation, the employee-management teams were formed to solve problems having to do with absenteeism and pay only after the union had begun an organizing effort.[19] Teams are legal, but not when they are used to undercut or replace a union.

Union leaders today generally support the formation of problem-solving teams but may balk when management takes an active role in the formation and direction of such teams. Increasingly vocal critics charge that the team concept is a management ploy to kill unions. Autoworkers especially are challenging team approaches because union jobs continue to disappear despite repeated concessions. Although few experts expect the courts to halt teams altogether, most believe that strict new guidelines will be implemented to control the formation and use of teams.[20]

apply it

1. Consider the sports, school, or work teams that you have been on. Give specific examples of what the team did to avoid free riding and minimize coordination costs.

Organizations rely on many different types of teams

We have seen that, although the potential benefits can be great, organizations can encounter several negative consequences in their efforts to form teams. Part of the success of implementing teamwork involves understanding the different types of teams that can exist within organizations. Exhibit 8.3 shows the different ways work teams are used in organizations. One of the easiest ways to classify teams is in terms of the work cycle (how quickly

exhibit | **8.3**

Types of Work Teams in Organizations

Types and Examples	Work-Team Differentiation	External Integration	Work Cycles	Typical Outputs
Production/service				
Assembly teams	Variable membership	Externally paced work	Work cycles	Food, chemicals
Manufacturing crews	requirements;	usually synchronized	typically	Components
Mining teams	sometimes high	with suppliers and	repeated or	Assemblies
Flight attendant crews	turnover; variable	customers inside	continuous	Retail sales
Data-processing groups	team life span;	and outside the	process; cycles	Customer service
Maintenance crews	often special	organization	often briefer than	Equipment repairs
	facilities required		team life span	
Advice/involvement				
Committees	Inclusive or	Few demands for	Work cycles can	Decisions
Review panels, boards	representative	synchronization with	be brief or	Selections
Quality circles	membership; often	other work-units;	long; one cycle	Suggestions
Employee involvement	short group life	external exchange can	may be team's	Proposals
groups	span and/or limited	be minimal	life span	Recommendations
Advisory councils	working time			
Project/development				
Research groups	Members usually	Often internally paced	Work cycles	Plans, designs
Planning teams	expert specialists;	project with deadline;	typically differ	Investigations
Architect teams	task may require	little synchronization	for each new	Presentations
Engineering teams	specialized	inside organization;	project; one	Prototypes
Development teams	facilities;	task can require much	cycle can be	Reports, findings
	sometimes	external	team life span	
	extended team life span	communication		
Action/negotiation				
Sports teams	Exclusive	Performance events	Brief performance	Combat missions
Entertainment groups	membership of	closely synchronized	events, often	Expeditions
Expeditions	expert specialists;	with counterparts and	repeated under	Contracts,
Negotiating teams	specialized training	support units inside	new conditions,	lawsuits
Surgery teams	and performance	the organization	requiring	Concerts
Cockpit crews	facilities; sometimes		extended	Surgical
	extended team life span		training and/or	operations
			preparation	Competitions

Source: Based on E. Sunstrom, K. De Meuse, and D. Futrell, "Work Teams: Applications and Effectiveness," _American Psychologist,_ February 1990, pp. 120–133. Copyright © 1990 by the American Psychological Association. Adapted with permission.

tasks are done and whether tasks are repeated), the amount of coordination required with others inside and outside the organization, the degree of autonomy or specialization of team members, and typical outputs expected from the team.[21]

Production or Service Teams

production or service team

A team directly involved in providing a product or service to customers, such as sales, food, chemicals, or repairs. Its work cycle is typically repeated many times, and it is integrated with customers and external suppliers.

Production or service teams are directly involved in providing a product or services to customers. Production or service teams include assembly teams, manufacturing crews, flight attendant teams, and maintenance crews.

The work of production and service teams is usually synchronized with vendors and suppliers and customers inside and outside an organization. The work cycle involved in building a product or providing a service is usually repeated. For example, consider an airline flight attendant crew. Although the arrival and departure locations and maybe even the type of aircraft changes, the flight attendants go through the same work cycle many times in a day. They greet and seat passengers, inform passengers of flight safety rules, serve meals, and help passengers leave the aircraft. When they perform their work depends on the flight schedule, air traffic, and weather. For example, during a turbulent flight, flight attendants may not serve meals or beverages. Effective flight attendant teams know when during the flight to serve meals or beverages so that passengers have time to enjoy them. If flight attendant teams were not synchronized with the flight time and weather, passengers would not be given enough time to safely and comfortably eat their meals or watch movies.

Production or service teams may include a single department in an organization. For example, the third-shift nursing team on the second floor of St. Luke's Hospital is a team that includes nurses and a supervisor. A customer order department, an accounting department, and a shipping department are all production or service teams. Each is created by the organization to attain specific goals through members' joint activities and interactions.

TEAM 500 at **Fortune** *magazine is a production team that provides readers with the ultimate scorecard for U.S. business—the* Fortune *500 list of the largest corporations in the United States. Team leader Mike Cacace (front, center) and his team members compile the data in a yearly statistical frenzy made more complicated by companies that delay reporting fiscal results and by the many recent mergers, acquisitions, and spinoffs. The team's hard work, however, has produced issues that are the biggest sellers in the magazine's history.*
(Source: © Robert Wright)

Advice or Involvement Teams

An **advice or involvement team** is composed of employees from about the same hierarchical level in an organization but from different areas of expertise. Team members may be drawn from several departments, are given a specific task, and may be disbanded after the task is completed. The life span of these teams can last from a few hours to a few years depending on the purpose of the team. Advice or involvement teams typically are asked to provide decisions, suggestions, proposals, or recommendations. They do not produce a product or provide a service. The most common types of advice or involvement teams are task forces, committees, and problem-solving teams.

A **task force** is a group of employees from different departments formed to deal with a specific activity and exists only until the task is completed. Sometimes called a cross-functional team, the task force might be used to create a new product in a manufacturing organization or a new history curriculum in a university. Several departments are involved, and many views have to be considered, so these tasks are best served with team members at approximately the same level in an organization. US Airways

advice or involvement team

A team that provides decisions, suggestions, proposals, and recommendations. Its work cycle may be brief and may not be repeated. It usually includes members with diverse skills who may come from different parts of the organization.

task force

A group of employees from different departments formed to deal with a specific activity; it exists only until the task is completed.

set up a task force made up of mechanics, flight attendants, dispatchers, aircraft cleaners, ramp workers, luggage attendants, reservations agents, and others to design and start a low-fare airline to compete with the expansion of Southwest Airlines into the East. The task force spent several months pricing peanuts, conducting focus groups, studying the competition, and developing a plan to present to senior management for a new low-fare airline, MetroJet.[22]

committee

A long-lasting, sometimes permanent team in the organization structure created to deal with tasks that recur regularly.

A **committee** generally is long lived and may be a permanent part of the organization's structure. Membership on a committee usually is decided by a person's title or position rather than by personal expertise. A committee often needs official representation, unlike a task force, for which selection is based on personal qualifications for solving a problem. Committees typically are formed to deal with tasks that recur regularly. For example, a grievance committee handles employee grievances; an advisory committee makes recommendations in the areas of employee compensation and work practices; a worker-management committee may be concerned with work rules, job design changes, and suggestions for work improvement.[23]

problem-solving team

Typically 5 to 12 hourly employees from the same department who meet to discuss ways of improving quality, efficiency, and the work environment.

Problem-solving teams typically consist of 5 to 12 hourly employees from the same department who voluntarily meet to discuss ways of improving quality, efficiency, and the work environment. Recommendations are proposed to management for approval. Problem-solving teams usually are the first step in a company's move toward greater employee participation. The most widely known application is quality circles, initiated by the Japanese, in which employees focus on ways to improve quality in the production process. USX has adopted this approach in several of its steel mills, recognizing that quality takes a team effort. Under the title All Product Excellence program (APEX), USX set up 40 APEX teams of up to 12 employees at its plant in West Mifflin, Pennsylvania. These teams meet several times a month to solve quality problems. The APEX teams have since spread to mills in Indiana, Ohio, and California.[24]

Advice and involvement teams are useful for several purposes: (1) They allow organization members to exchange information, (2) they generate suggestions for coordinating the organizational units that are represented, (3) they develop new ideas and solutions for existing organizational problems, (4) they assist in the development of new organizational practices and policies, and (5) they represent the first step in getting employees more involved in decision making and the conduct of their jobs, with the goal of improving performance.

Project or Development Teams

project or development team

A team that provides plans, designs, or prototypes of products or services. Its members may be specialists who are experts in their fields. Its work cycle differs for each project.

Project or development teams are created outside the formal organizational structure to undertake a project of special importance or creativity. Members of project or development teams usually have specialized areas of expertise, such as engineering. The output expected from these types of teams includes plans, designs, or prototypes of products or services. McDonald's created a special team to create the Chicken McNugget. E. J. (Bud) Sweeney was asked to head up a team to bring bits of batter-covered chicken to the marketplace. The McNugget team needed breathing room and was separated from the formal corporate structure to give it the autonomy to perform successfully. A project or development team still is part of the formal organization and has its own reporting structure, but members perceive themselves as a separate entity.[25] Often, organizations that are considering upgrading computer hardware and software systems will create a project or development team to investigate, develop or purchase, and integrate the new computer system throughout the organization. Such teams are usually cross-functional teams—composed of staff members from departments that will use the new system as well as information systems experts. For example, Aliant, a Canadian telecommunications company, used a project team to gather information from top executives to the final users of information to completely redesign its business processes and information system. Bon Benson, the company's chief financial officer, says, "We looked at every single business process that we would need to change. . . . Getting people to 'think outside the box' and learn to do their work differently was by far the most difficult task." But the company projects annual savings from operating costs to reach $8 million with the new system.[26]

Action or Negotiation Teams

Action or negotiation teams consist of members who are experts and work on specialized tasks. They are required to complete very complex tasks. The performance of the team members depends on their ability to work without distractions. Examples of action or negotiation teams include surgery teams, sports teams, airplane cockpit crews, and entertainment groups. These teams need continuous training to keep up with technology advances that affect how the task is completed. These types of teams are expected to be prepared to perform in many different conditions (e.g., bad weather, emergencies). As a result, team members have specialized skills that have been developed by extensive education and experience. Because action or negotiation team performance requires members to communicate with and help each other, team training is also important.

action or negotiation team

A team of experts who often perform in specialized facilities or need special equipment. The team performance is usually synchronized with that of other units in the organization.

Special Types of Teams

There are two types of teams that are unique. Self-directed teams are unique because the employees in the teams perform tasks usually reserved for managers, such as identifying and choosing new team members, meeting with customers and suppliers, ordering materials and supplies, and deciding what tasks each team member will complete and when. Virtual teams are unique because the team members may never meet face to face. They work as a team from different geographic locations, interacting using e-mail and the Internet.

Self-Directed Teams Employee involvement through teams is designed to increase the participation of low-level workers. Employee involvement represents a revolution in business prompted by the success of teamwork in Japanese companies. Hundreds of companies, large and small, are jumping aboard the bandwagon, including DaimlerChrysler, Cummins Engine, Wilson Golf Ball, and Edy's Grand Ice Cream. Employee involvement started out simply with techniques such as information sharing with employees or asking employees for suggestions about improving the work. Gradually, companies introduce problem-solving teams to encourage employees to make decisions and take responsibility for their work. The last step in the employee involvement process is to allow employees to be completely self-directed.[27]

As a company matures, problem-solving teams can gradually evolve into self-directed teams, which represent a fundamental change in how employee work is organized. Self-directed teams enable employees to feel challenged, find their work meaningful, and develop a strong sense of identity with the company.[28] **Self-directed teams** typically consist of 5 to 20 multiskilled workers who rotate jobs to produce an entire product or service or at least one complete aspect or portion of a product or service (e.g., engine assembly, insurance claim processing). The central idea is that the teams themselves, rather than managers or supervisors, take responsibility for their work, make decisions, monitor their own performance, and alter their work behavior as needed to solve problems, meet goals, and adapt to changing conditions.[29] Self-directed teams are permanent teams that typically include the following elements:

- The team includes employees with several skills and functions, and the combined skills are sufficient to perform a major organizational task. A team may include members from the foundry, machining, grinding, fabrication, and sales departments, with each member cross-trained to perform one another's jobs. The team eliminates barriers among departments, enabling excellent coordination to produce a product or service.

- The team is given access to resources such as information, equipment, machinery, and supplies needed to perform the complete task.

- The team is empowered with decision-making authority, which means that members have the freedom to select new members, solve problems, spend money, monitor results, and plan for the future.[30]

In a self-directed team, team members take over managerial duties such as scheduling work or vacations or ordering materials. They work with minimum supervision, perhaps electing one of their own as supervisor, who may change each year. Teams at Corning work without shift supervisors and work closely with other plant divisions to solve production-line problems and coordinate deadlines and deliveries. Teams have the authority to make and implement decisions, complete projects, and solve problems.[31]

Self-directed teams can be highly effective. Service companies such as Federal Express and IDS have boosted productivity up to 40 percent by adopting self-directed teams. Volvo uses self-directed teams of seven to ten hourly workers to assemble four cars per shift. However, there still is a reluctance among management to entrust workers with managerial responsibilities and duties. A survey conducted by the University of Southern California's Center for Effective Organizations found that, although 68 percent of *Fortune* 1000 companies report using self-directed teams, only 10 percent of workers are involved.[32]

Self-directed teams require certain conditions to be successful. Exhibit 8.4 presents these conditions. Work that is highly automated is unlikely to be improved by the flexibility and initiative that comes from teams. If employees do not have the motivation or physical or intellectual capacity to

---

self-directed team

A team of 5 to 20 multiskilled workers who rotate jobs to produce an entire product or service, often supervised by an elected member.

- The work processes can be improved by the increased initiative, flexibility, and cooperation of team members.
- Employees are willing and able to make self-management work.
- Managers can become "hands-off" leaders.
- The product or service market will support the improved productivity of teams without reducing the workforce.
- The organization's policy and culture support teams.
- The community supports teams.

Source: Based on J. Osburn, L. Moran, E. Musselwhite, and J. Zenger, *Self-Directed Work Teams* (Burr Ridge, IL: Irwin, 1990.)

exhibit **8.4**

Necessary Conditions for Self-Directed Teams to Be Effective

complete the tasks involved in self-management, such as record keeping, completing forms, or conducting quality analyses, self-managed teams will be ineffective. Managers need to allow employees autonomy to make decisions and give them access to information. With a shrinking product or service market, productive self-managed teams can exceed market demand for products and services and make it necessary to downsize. The organization's culture needs to support the transition to teams by being willing to communicate strategic plans to the team members—employees who affect whether goals and objectives will be reached. The community should also support a movement in the organization toward employee self-direction. Local and state political leaders can support self-directed teams by subsidizing training at local colleges and universities in interpersonal and technical skills employees need to work in self-directed teams. We will discuss in greater detail the types of training and changes in the organizational culture that are needed to support all types of teams later in the chapter.

Virtual Teams   A virtual team is a self-directed team that has resulted from globalization of business and advances in technology. **Virtual teams** use telecommunications and information technology to tie together geographically distant members working toward a common goal.[33] Virtual teams can be formed within an organization whose plants and offices are scattered across the nation or around the world. A company may also use virtual teams in partnership with suppliers or, in many cases, with competitors to pull together the best minds to complete a project or speed a new product to market. For example, Microsoft provides customers with developmental versions of its software prior to releasing them for sale to the general public. Virtual teams of customers evaluate the software and electronically give Microsoft feedback that it can use to modify the software. There is no face-to-face meeting between Microsoft and its customers. In a virtual team, leadership among team members is shared or altered, depending on the area of expertise needed at each point in the project. Team membership often changes fairly quickly depending on the task. Virtual teams have many benefits, including allowing people to work from anywhere at any time and reducing or eliminating expenses associated with travel and lodging. Virtual teams may also fail for several reasons: lack of purpose, poor leadership, communications problems, technical glitches, and cultural misunderstandings.

The success of virtual teams is dependent on several crucial elements, including careful selection of partners and team members, strong management

virtual team

A team that uses telecommunications and information technology so that geographically distant members can collaborate on projects and reach common goals.

support of the team and its goals, clear goals, utilization of the best communications tools and procedures, the development of trust among all members, and information sharing.[34] Glen Tines, a program manager with Hewlett-Packard, is a leader of a virtual team with the goal of designing a computer-training program for sales and support staff.[35] Trust grew out of weekly conference calls with team members who were located in different parts of the United States. As Tines says, "Everyone had assignments, but they had to have a commitment to each other to make deadlines and be there. That held us together." Trust was developed because team members went out of their way to take part in those meetings regardless of whether they were at home, at work, or on an airplane. The commitment to make deadlines and participate in the scheduled meetings held the virtual team together. Tines was trained in how to structure and manage virtual meetings, ensure all team members were contributing, and use the technology.

Consider also how VeriFone successfully uses virtual teams.

❦ VeriFone

VeriFone, an equipment supplier for credit card verification and automated payments, started out as a virtual company over 15 years ago and today uses virtual teams in every aspect of its business. Teams of facility managers work together to determine how to reduce toxins in their offices. Marketing and development groups brainstorm new products. Sales reps pool information and customer testimonials.

VeriFone's concept of virtual teams is highly flexible. Some teams may include only VeriFone employees, and others include outsiders, such as the employees of a customer or partner. Some are permanent, such as operational teams that run their companies virtually, while others are temporary. Any employee can organize a temporary virtual team to work on a specific problem. For example, one sales rep sent out an SOS when he saw a major sales prospect in Greece falling apart. Overnight, a team made up of sales, marketing, and technical support staff from around the world came together to provide data and testimonials that eventually helped the Greek representative make the sale.

Despite all this flexibility, VeriFone has some pretty strict "rules" to ensure that teams are not formed haphazardly. Employees complete a 40-hour training program in which they learn how to create a successful virtual team. In addition, leaders of virtual teams follow written procedures put together by the company's senior managers. VeriFone offers the following guidelines for successful virtual teams:

1. *Define the purpose*   A VeriFone team always starts by putting its purpose in writing. This keeps everyone on track and prevents misunderstandings.
2. *Recruit team members*   Most virtual teams should have between three and seven members. Also, the team should include people who represent a diversity of views and experiences. Selecting members in different time zones means productive work can occur around the clock.
3. *Determine the duration of the team*   Decide whether the purpose and goals call for a short-term task force or problem-solving team or for a long-term operational team.
4. *Select the communications technology*   All VeriFone staffers are well trained not only in how to use communications tools but also in when to use them. General guidelines are that for keeping in contact remotely, teams use beepers, cell phones, and voice mail; for disseminating information, they use faxes, e-mail, and application sharing over the network. For brainstorming, discussion, and decision making, teams use e-mail, conference calls, and videoconferencing. Selecting the right tool is critical to the success of the virtual team.

VeriFone employees also are trained to understand the psychological pitfalls of communicating virtually. Some subtleties of meaning are always lost and misunderstandings are more common than when teams work face to face. E-mail in particular can lead to misunderstandings, so team members communicate by phone or videoconference on sensitive or complicated issues.[36]

apply it

1. You likely belong to many teams at school or at work. List and briefly describe the types of teams you belong to. Classify them according to the types presented in this section.

Building effective team processes: Trust, cohesiveness, norms, and roles

As we mentioned in Chapter 7, after a group has been created, there are distinct stages through which it moves as it develops into a team. New teams are different from mature teams. Recall a time when you were a member of a new team, such as a fraternity or sorority pledge class, a committee, or a small team formed to do a class assignment. Over time the team changed. In the beginning, team members had to get to know one another, establish roles and norms, divide the labor, and clarify the team's task. In this way, members became parts of a smoothly operating team. The challenge for leaders is to understand the stage of the team's development and take actions that will help the team develop trust, cohesiveness, positive performance, and behavior norms and roles needed to be effective.

Let's examine how positive norms, cohesiveness, and trust can be built into teams by considering what organizations can do at each stage of the development process.

Forming

The forming stage of development is a period of orientation and getting acquainted. Members break the ice and test one another for friendship possibilities and task orientation. Team members find which behaviors are acceptable to others. Uncertainty is high during this stage, and members usually accept whatever power or authority is offered by either formal or informal leaders. Members are dependent on the team until they find out what the ground rules are and what is expected of them. During this initial stage, members are concerned about such things as "What is expected of me?" "What is acceptable?" and "Will I fit in?" As we mentioned in Chapter 7, the size of the team influences how easy it will be for members to get to know each other. The ideal size of teams is thought to be seven, although variations between 5 and 12 members are associated with good team performance.[37] Teams of this size are large enough to take advantage of diverse skills, enable members to express good and bad feelings, and aggressively solve problems. They are also small enough for team members to feel they are an important part of the team.

The development of cohesiveness is the major goal of the forming stage. As we discussed in Chapter 7, cohesiveness is defined as the extent to which members are attracted to the team and motivated to remain in it.[38] Members of highly cohesive teams are committed to team activities, attend meetings, and are happy when the team succeeds. Members of less cohesive teams are less concerned about the team's welfare. High cohesiveness is normally considered an attractive feature of teams. Cohesiveness can be developed through socialization, sharing goals, fostering competition, and rewarding team accomplishments.

socialization

A process by which team members get acquainted with one another and are encouraged to engage in informal social discussions.

Socialization is a process by which team members get acquainted with one another and are encouraged to engage in informal social discussions. Through frequent interactions, members get to know one another and become more devoted to the team.[39] The greater the amount of contact among team members and the more time spent together, the more cohesive the team. Socialization can also make other employees interested in working in teams. Typically, when teams are initially formed, employees resist. Employees may resist because they fear change or don't want to take on additional responsibilities. Warren Krompf, human resource director in the New York office of LeBoeuf, Lamb, Greene & McRae LLP, a law firm with 15 U.S. offices, recommends that an effective strategy is to "form teams with people you know—will have buy-in—get them working together and solving problems—and use them as an advertisement. Other employees can take a look and say, 'Those people are having a good time,' and the teamwork can spread."[40] Leaders also need to help the team develop operating ground rules that establish how the team is expected to behave.

adventure learning

Team training in which members participate in physically challenging, structured outdoor activities.

Organizations are using adventure learning to help socialize teams and help them develop cooperation, trust, and communications skills. **Adventure learning** involves teams participating in physically challenging, structured outdoor activities. For example, The Adventure Education Center in Worthington, Ohio, offers organizations rope courses and team challenges for employees to experience how to be better team members in a nonthreatening way. Climbing walls and rope courses up in the trees are designed to challenge individuals and teams. A trained observer watches the exercises and helps the teams understand how to use what they learned in their businesses. Evart Glass in Evart, Michigan, used adventure learning to prepare the company's 257-person staff to work in self-directed teams.[41] Employees experienced eight hours of cooperative and problem-solving activities such as a group juggle, trying to maneuver through a carpet-square maze with the pressure of a time limit, and having to complete a rope course. Following each activity, facilitators questioned the employees: What did you do? What did it mean? What are you going to do with it? To get through the activities, team members had to say when something didn't work and offer a way to fix it. As one of the trainers said, "This type of training seems to break down the personal walls that people build around themselves. It gets them into the open and contributing rather than just existing and doing their jobs."

A second way that cohesiveness can be developed is by establishing shared goals. If team members agree on goals, they will be more cohesive. Agreeing on purpose and direction binds the team together.

Two factors in the team's context also influence group cohesiveness. The first is the presence of competition. When a team is in moderate competition with other teams, its cohesiveness increases as it strives to win. Whether competition is among sales teams to attain the top sales volume or among manufacturing departments to reduce rejects, competition increases team solidarity and cohesiveness.[42] Finally, team success and the favorable evaluation of the team by outsiders add to cohesiveness. When a team succeeds in its task and others in the organization recognize the success, members feel good, and their commitment to the team will be high.

Chaparral Steel, a successful steel company in Midlothian, Texas, encourages team cohesiveness through promotion of the "Chaparral Process." The steelmaker strives to create super teams, in which each member sees his or her job in relation to the entire organization and its goals. Commitment to cohesiveness and efficiency enables Chaparral teams to perform amazing tasks. The purchase and installation of new mill equipment is a highly complicated task for any steel company, and calibrating and fine-tuning the steelmaking process can take years. However, a Chaparral team of four completed the worldwide search, purchase negotiations, shipment, and installation in only one year.[43]

Storming

During the storming stage, individual personalities emerge. People become more assertive in clarifying their roles and what is expected of them. This stage is marked by conflict and disagreement. People may disagree over their perceptions of the team's mission. Members may jockey for position, and coalitions or subgroups based on common interests may form. One subgroup may disagree with another over the total team's goals or methods to achieve them. The team is still trying to develop cohesiveness. During the storming stage, the team leader should encourage participation by each team member. Members should propose ideas, disagree with one another, and work through the uncertainties and conflicting perceptions about team tasks and goals. This stage is critical for the team to establish an identity based on blending the strengths and weaknesses of team members.

One of the causes of conflict during the storming stage is ineffective communications (we will discuss other causes of conflict and how to resolve them in Chapter 13). Communication can be facilitated by ensuring that conflicting parties hold accurate perceptions. Providing opportunities for the disputants to get together and exchange information reduces conflict. As they learn more about one another, suspicions diminish and improved teamwork becomes possible. Four guidelines can help facilitate communication and keep teams focused on substantive issues rather than interpersonal conflicts:[44]

- *Focus on facts* Keep team discussions focused on issues, not personalities. Working with more data and information rather than less can help keep team members focused on facts and prevent meetings from degenerating into pointless debates over opinions. At Star Electronics, the top management team meets daily, weekly, and monthly to examine a wide variety of specific operating measures. Looking at the details helps team members debate critical issues and avoid useless arguments.

- *Develop multiple alternatives* Teams that deliberately develop many alternatives, sometimes considering four or five options at once, have a lower incidence of interpersonal conflict. Having a multitude of options to consider concentrates team members' energy on solving problems. In addition, the process of generating multiple choices is fun and creative, which sets a positive tone for the meeting and reduces the chance for conflict.

- *Maintain a balance of power*   Managers and team leaders should accept the team's decision as fair, even if they do not agree with it. Fairness requires a balance of power within the team. When the team that designed a low-fare airline for US Airways first came together, everyone was asking about other team members' job titles to figure out the "pecking order." The team leader quickly made it clear that there was no hierarchy—everyone would have an equal voice and an equal vote.

- *Never force a consensus*   There will naturally be conflict over some issues, which managers find a way to resolve without forcing a consensus. When there are persistent differences of opinion, the team leader sometimes has to make a decision guided by input from other team members. At Andromeda Processing, the CEO insisted on consensus from his top management team, causing a debate to rage on for months. Eventually, most of the managers just wanted a decision, no matter whether it was the one they agreed with or not. Conflict and frustration mounted to the point where some top managers left the company. The group achieved consensus only at the price of losing several key managers.

Norming

As we discussed in Chapter 7, a norm is a standard of conduct that is shared by team members and guides their behavior.[45] During the norming stage, conflict is resolved, and team harmony and unity emerge. Consensus develops on who has the power, who is the leader, and what members' roles are. Members come to accept and understand one another. Differences are resolved, and members develop a sense of team cohesion. The main problem in this stage is that team members may not reveal good ideas because they fear causing conflict within the team. This stage typically is of short duration. During the norming stage, the team leader should emphasize oneness within the team and help clarify team norms and values. The team leader should also emphasize that it is fine to disagree and provide the team with conflict resolution strategies.

Develop Positive Norms   Because norms tell members what is acceptable and direct members' actions toward acceptable productivity or performance, organization and team leaders need to ensure that effective norms are developed. For example, four common ways in which norms can be developed for controlling and directing behavior are illustrated in Exhibit 8.5.[46]

Critical events: Often critical events in a team's history establish an important precedent. One example from history occurred when Arthur Schlesinger, despite his serious reservations about the Bay of Pigs invasion of Cuba, was pressured by Attorney General Robert Kennedy not to raise his objections to President Kennedy. This critical incident helped create a norm in which team members refrained from expressing disagreement with the president.

Any critical event can lead to the creation of a norm. Grace Cocoa Associates, a processor of more than 10% of the world's supply of cocoa beans, is composed of manufacturers representing five different continents

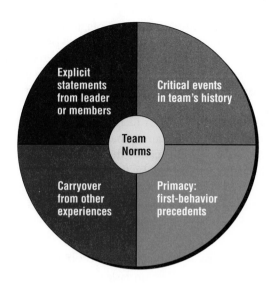

exhibit **8.5**
Four Ways Team Norms Develop

and more than 16 locations and countries as diverse as France, Germany, and Ecuador.[47] To be competitive, the company had to do a better job of encouraging managers to share best practices and new ideas. Early in the development of global teams, the company discovered that managers who called their counterparts in another part of the world to exchange ideas were criticized by their bosses. Managers had been trained and rewarded for maintaining tight local control. This was sabotaging the global team effort. As a result, most employees did not even try to think and act with a more global focus.

Primacy: Primacy means that the first behaviors that occur in a team often set a precedent for later team expectations. For example, at one company a team leader began his first meeting by raising an issue and then "leading" team members until he got the solution he wanted. The pattern became ingrained so quickly into an unproductive team norm that team members dubbed meetings the "Guess What I Think" game.[48]

Carryover behaviors: Carryover behaviors bring norms into the team from outside. The parks department in the City of Hampton, Virginia, is organized into self-directed teams.[49] The change to self-directed teams was not easy due to carryover behaviors. Supervisors who drove around in their pick-up trucks checking to see if the employees were cutting the grass as instructed had to give up control to the team. Team members had to take on more responsibility for whole projects such as maintaining the grounds around the public library, rather than just performing one piece of grounds maintenance (such as picking up trash). Carryover behavior also influences small teams of college students assigned by instructors to do work. Norms brought into the team from outside may suggest that students should participate equally and help members get a reasonable grade.

Explicit statements: With explicit statements, leaders or team members can initiate norms by articulating them to the team. Explicit statements symbolize what counts and thus have considerable impact. Making explicit statements is probably the most effective way for managers to change norms in an established team. For example, teams at Colgate-Palmolive Company have mission statements defining not only the team's goals but also how team members are expected to treat each other.[50] Each new team at Colgate conducts an exercise that gets team members to list their expectations for each other. This leads to discussion about respect for others' ideas, thoughts, and diversity.

Develop Member Roles   For a team to be successful over the long run, it must be structured to both maintain its members' social well-being and accomplish its task. In successful teams, the requirements for task performance and social satisfaction are met by the emergence of two types of roles: the task specialist and socioemotional roles.[51]

People who play the **task specialist role** spend personal time and energy helping the team reach its goal. They often display the following behaviors:

- *Initiate*   Propose new solutions to team problems.
- *Give opinions*   Offer opinions on task solutions; give candid feedback on others' suggestions.
- *Seek information*   Ask for task-relevant facts.
- *Summarize*   Relate various ideas to the problem at hand; pull ideas together into a summary perspective.
- *Energize*   Stimulate the team into action when interest drops.[52]

People who adopt a **socioemotional role** support team members' emotional needs and help strengthen the social entity. They display the following behaviors:

- *Encourage*   Are warm and receptive to others' ideas; praise and encourage others to draw forth their contributions.
- *Harmonize*   Reconcile group conflicts; help disagreeing parties reach agreement.
- *Reduce tension*   May tell jokes or in other ways diffuse emotions when group atmosphere is tense.
- *Follow*   Go along with the team; agree to other team members' ideas.
- *Compromise*   Will shift own opinions to maintain team harmony.[53]

Exhibit 8.6 illustrates task specialist and socioemotional roles in teams. When most individuals in a team play a social role, the team is socially oriented. Members do not criticize or disagree with one another and do not forcefully offer opinions or try to accomplish team tasks, because their primary interest is to keep the team happy. Teams with mostly socioemotional roles can be very satisfying, but they also can be unproductive. At the other extreme, a team made up primarily of task specialists will tend to have a singular concern for task accomplishment. This team will be effective for a short period of time but will not be satisfying for members over the long run. Task specialists convey little emotional concern for one another, are unsupportive, and ignore team members' social and emotional needs. The task-oriented team can be humorless and unsatisfying.

As Exhibit 8.6 illustrates, some team members may play a dual role. People with **dual roles** both contribute to the task and meet members' emotional needs. Such people may become team leaders because they sat-

task specialist role

A role in which an individual devotes personal time and energy to helping the team accomplish its task.

socioemotional role

A role in which the individual provides support for team members' emotional needs and helps strengthen the social entity.

dual role

A role in which the individual both contributes to the team's task and supports members' emotional needs.

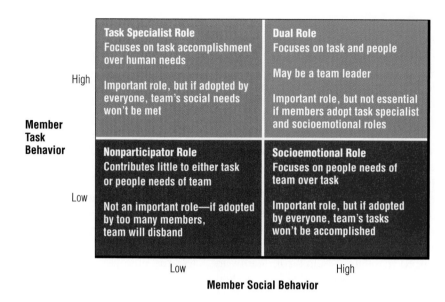

exhibit **8.6**
Team Member Roles

isfy both types of needs and are looked up to by other members. Exhibit 8.6 also shows the final type of role, called the nonparticipator role. People in the **nonparticipator role** contribute little to either the task or the socioemotional needs of team members. They typically are held in low esteem by the team.

The important thing to remember is that effective teams must have people in both task specialist and socioemotional roles. Humor and social concern are as important to team effectiveness as are facts and problem solving. Managers also should remember that some people perform better in one type of role; some are inclined toward social concerns and others toward task concerns. A well-balanced team will do best over the long term because it will be personally satisfying for team members and permit the accomplishment of team tasks.

nonparticipator role

A role in which the individual contributes little to either the task or members' socioemotional needs.

Performing

During the performing stage, the major emphasis in the team is on problem solving and accomplishing an assigned task. This stage is teamwork at its most productive—its peak performance. Members are committed to the team's mission. They coordinate their efforts with one another and handle disagreements in a mature way. They confront and resolve problems in the interest of task accomplishment. They interact frequently and direct discussion and exert influence toward achieving team goals. During this stage, the leader should concentrate on managing high task performance. Both socioemotional and task specialists should contribute to the functioning of the team.

Adjourning

The adjourning stage occurs in committees, task forces, and teams that have a limited task to perform and are disbanded afterward. During this stage, the emphasis is on wrapping up and gearing down. Task performance is no longer a top priority. Members may feel heightened emotionality, strong cohesiveness, and depression or even regret over the team's disbandment. They may feel happy about mission accomplishment and sad about the loss of friendship and associations. At this point, the leader may wish to signify the team's disbanding with a ritual or ceremony, perhaps giving out plaques and awards to signify closure and completeness.

Research suggests that teams need both time and training before they are productive. In one study of the implementation of teams in a plant that used the traditional assembly-line process, researchers found significant improvement in team effectiveness over a 20-month period.[54] Teams contributed to both improved productivity and quality. The company's management started with a trust-building phase that gradually increased the autonomy and responsibility of employees. This helped employees trust that management really was interested in their ideas. The company also introduced mandatory training in teamwork. Over the time period, employees became less concerned with individual issues such as the need for specific tools, and more concerned with team-oriented issues such as the need for training to reduce defects. Team members also began to rely less on managers or engineers to solve their problems and more on other team members.

Consider how Dreyer's Ice Cream creates effective teams in its accounting department.

❦ Dreyer's Grand Ice Cream

Dreyer's Grand Ice Cream's accounting department is organized into cross-functional work teams. The accounting department consists of four teams, each of which fulfills all of the accounting duties for a different geographic region of the country. These duties range from invoice creation to collections and accounts payable. It made sense to organize accounting into teams because accounting responsibilities are interrelated. "Finalizing invoices and collecting payment is a highly integrated process," explains Jeff Porter, corporate controller. "By integrating the accounting function, we've streamlined the process. People are now talking to each other about the whole process, not just the bits and pieces they know about." A credit analyst collecting on an account may discover a payment has been misapplied, for example. The analyst can easily talk to a team member who is a cash applications specialist and find out the reason for the mistake. Since both employees serve the same geographic region and have the same frame of reference, the problem is quickly resolved.

Dreyer's didn't immediately shove employees into cross-functional teams. First, the company got the employees used to the ideas of teamwork and empowerment. To facilitate the move to teams, each accounting subfunction, such as accounts payable, was reorganized into a single team and supervisors were made the team's "coach." The teams, which were initially functionally separate, were designed this way to get employees used to talking to each other, solving problems together, and reaching decisions without input from their supervisor. To ensure that employees had the interpersonal skills needed to work together, they received training in communications, negotiations, and conflict resolution. Also, employees were cross-trained to understand the tasks performed by their colleagues. After three years, when employees were comfortable and effective working in teams, the teams were shuffled and reorganized cross-functionally.

Working in teams, employees acquire a broader skill base, which makes them more marketable within the company. Employees also gain a sense of ownership of their jobs. "Our employees now derive the same job satisfaction that managers do," Porter explains. With happier employees, the efficiency of the entire department has improved. Since moving to teams, Dreyer's has experienced lower turnover and higher productivity, both of which translate into improving the company's bottom line.[55]

SIGNICAST CORPORATION'S NEW TEAMWORK STRATEGY

Signicast Corporation decided to build a new automated manufacturing facility. Management was interested in how Signicast could improve its casting service, which makes metal parts based on a customer's blueprints, such as a kickstand for a Harley-Davidson motorcycle or a part for a John Deere tractor. Customers were concerned with the long advance time that the company needed to make parts, unreliable deliveries, and cost. A new facility was proposed to address these concerns, and a team-based structure was suggested. A team consists of everyone on a 12-hour shift, and there are two day teams (6 a.m. to 6 p.m.) and two night teams (6 p.m. to 6 a.m.). Each team has its own supervisor. The plan is for manufacturing to be organized into four teams: wax, dip, melt/rough/

clean, and finishing. Each team will have a master technician, the expert for the team's operations. All other employees will have the same title of technician. The technicians operate equipment and inspection devices. Machines will perform the heavy labor. The master technicians will oversee how the plant is run. They will also train and evaluate the technicians' performance.

1. What steps should Signicast take to ensure that the teams are effective?

2. Signicast expects immediate results from the teams. Is this realistic? Explain.

Source: Based on B. Nagler, "Recasting Employees into Teams," *Workforce,* January 1998, pp. 101–106.

apply it

1. What types of roles have you played in the teams you are a member of—task specialist, socioemotional, dual, or nonparticipator?

2. Give an example, from your experience, of how team size has contributed or served as a barrier to team effectiveness.

Developing effective teams involves identifying team purpose, selection, training, and a positive organizational context

Since teamwork can improve employee commitment and productivity, it is critical for organizations to foster team development. There are a number of things that organizations can do to help ensure that teams are effective. We discuss them here.

Identifying Team Purpose

If team goals are unclear or poorly defined, team effectiveness will suffer. Unclear goals obscure a team's purpose, making it easy for team members to be indifferent to participation on the team and completion of the task. Clear, specific, and consistent goals provide a team with a sense of direction and an understanding of the importance of the team's outputs. A clearly defined purpose is the major reason teams have been successful at Ortho Biotech in Raritan, New Jersey.[56] The company drafted a mission statement designed to integrate business and diversity goals. As Andrea Zintz, vice president of human resources, explains: "We knew if we didn't build into the company vision a core value of respect for diversity, then our team endeavors wouldn't stand a chance." To gain commitment, every employee helped develop a one-page mission statement that includes a section recognizing the need to allow each member of the teams (regardless of race, gender, culture, or lifestyle) to contribute. The company also developed a list of norms and behaviors that were expected of employees in the teams. The list of norms and behaviors is displayed at every team meeting.

Selecting Team Members

One way to try to ensure that teams are effective is to choose individuals who have the "right stuff" needed to work in teams. This "right stuff" relates to the individual differences we discussed in Chapter 3, including abilities and personality. Exhibit 8.7 shows the knowledge, skill, and ability requirements for teamwork. Research shows that team members' general intelligence, specific skills, and personality characteristics—conscientiousness, agreeableness, extroversion, emotional stability—are related to team effectiveness.[57] Building teams with members who have the personality to develop positive social interactions with others (and therefore improve team cohesiveness) results in higher team performance. Pencil-and-paper tests

exhibit **8.7**

Knowledge, Skill, and Ability
Requirements for Teamwork

I. Interpersonal
  A. Conflict Resolution
  1. Recognize and encourage desirable, but discourage undesirable team conflict.
  2. Recognize the type and source of conflict confronting the team and implement an appropriate resolution strategy.
  3. Employ a win-win negotiation strategy, rather than the traditional win-lose stragegy.

  B. Collaborative Problem Solving
  4. Identify situations requiring participative group problem solving and utilize the proper degree and type of participation.
  5. Recognize the obstacles to collaborative group problem solving and implement appropriate corrective actions.

  C. Communication
  6. Understand communication networks, and utilize decentralized networks to enhance communication where possible.
  7. Communicate openly and supportively.
  8. Listen nonevaluatively and appropriately use active listening techniques.
  9. Maximize the agreement between nonverbal and verbal messages and recognize and interpret the nonverbal messages of others.
  10. Engage in small talk and ritual greetings and a recognition of their importance.

II. Self-Management
  D. Goal Setting and Performance Management
  11. Help establish specific, challenging, and accepted team goals.
  12. Monitor, evaluate, and provide feedback on both overall team performance and individual team member performance.

  E. Planning and Task Coordination
  13. Coordinate and synchronize activities, information, and tasks between team members.
  14. Help establish task and role assignments for individual team members and ensure proper balancing of workload.

Source: Reprinted from *Journal of Management 20,* 1994, "The Knowledge, Skills, and Abilities Requirements for Teamwork: Implications for Human Resource Management" by M. J. Stevens and M. A. Compton, p. 505, copyright 1994, with permission from Elsevier Science.

and interviews can be used to identify employees with the intelligence, personality, and other skills needed to work effectively in teams. For example, consider the Nucor Steel plant in Crawfordsville, Indiana.[58] To identify successful employees to work in its team-based environment, Nucor relies on basic math skills and mechanical tests as the first hurdle in its selection process. Then the company sends the job candidates to a psychologist, who determines whether they are interested in and capable of working in teams and whether they will be motivated by the team-based bonus system. This system allows employees to earn a weekly bonus of up to 150 percent of their base pay if quality and productivity goals are met by their team.

Training

Individual team members, as well as the team as a whole, need training to perform their tasks well. Also, because teams often take some of a manager's responsibilities, managers need training to be prepared for their new roles in a team environment. Training can occur before a team is formed or as a result of problems or issues a team is facing. If organizations cannot choose the employees who work in teams, they need to teach employees how to work effectively in a team environment. Even if organizations can select team members with desirable qualities, it is likely that at a minimum they will need to train managers and use team training techniques.

Team Member Training   Team members need to be trained in the technical aspects of their jobs. But it is critical that they receive training in interpersonal skills as well. Team members will need training in problem solving, listening, assertiveness, conflict management, and meeting dynamics.[59] Dettmers Industries, in Stuart, Florida, makes seating and table products for private aircraft.[60] Dettmers's teams were responsible for hiring, scheduling, customer service, quality, and their own cash flow. Dettmers's training program emphasized effective communications, team-building skills, and business processes. Employees were required to attend 13 hours of training every business quarter for a full year. One team leader said, "I was kind of skeptical about how this would work out. But now I don't think this would ever have worked if we didn't have the training." The training has paid off. Teams make products in one-third less time. Sales improved, and the new team-bonus system has helped employees earn 25 percent more than employees in comparable local industries.

In the early stages of development, teams tend to focus on people issues first as they develop norms, but once those issues are resolved, team members will need to understand how they can affect the processes for which they are responsible. For example, a team at Xerox Manufacturing Operations in Webster, New York, had to solve the high failure rate of a product with photo receptors that had to "rest" in the dark for 24 hours before being tested.[61] Using root cause analysis (which they learned in a quality skills class), the team reduced the rest time to 2 hours, generating a savings of $266,000.

Team Training   **Team training** involves coordinating the performance of individuals who work together to achieve a common goal. The three

team training

Coordination of the performance of individuals who work together to achieve a common goal. The three components of team training are knowledge, attitudes, and behavior.

components of team training are knowledge, attitudes, and behavior.[62] Team members must perform behaviors that allow them to communicate and coordinate activities. Team members need mental models (knowledge) that allow them to perform effectively in unanticipated problems or situations. Team members' beliefs about their goals and tasks and feelings toward each other relate to the attitude component. Research suggests that effectively trained teams develop procedures to identify and resolve errors, coordinate the gathering of information, and reinforce each other's behavior.[63] Often team training involves cross-training. **Cross-training** is training in which team members gain an understanding of and practice each other's skills. Cross-training is necessary so that team members are prepared to take another member's place should he or she be temporarily absent or permanently leave the team. Cross-training gives the organization the flexibility to reconfigure teams as needed to meet changing customer needs.

Effective team training involves simulated or real problems that the team will face. These problems allow the team members to see for themselves how their own individual skill strengths and weaknesses, as well as team processes, contribute to team effectiveness. Team members take responsibility for learning. Boeing used team training to improve the effectiveness of teams used to design the Boeing 777 airplane.[64] Training started with an extensive orientation that highlighted how team members were to work together. Team members then began their work assignments. Trainers were available to help the team members if they requested help. Trainers provided training in communications skills, conflict resolution, and leadership on an as-needed basis.

Teams also need to understand how their work affects the organization and how they can improve the quality of the product or service they are providing. Part of understanding how the team affects the organization is to clarify the team's values. Values help the team develop a shared sense of purpose. Team values can relate to communications, personal growth, integrity, or other principles that the team finds desirable. For example, an AT&T management team's value for teamwork was: "We foster an environment that supports team members cooperating to achieve our common goals. Our motto is we, not me."[65]

Manager Training   Managers are often frustrated by organizations' use of teams because they are used to commanding and controlling employees and solving employees' problems for them rather than waiting for a team to develop solutions. As a result, managers need to be trained in coaching and facilitation skills, skills that involve helping the team solve problems and identifying what resources the team needs and providing them. Michael Regan, president of The Journey to Teams Inc., a Raleigh, North Carolina, consulting firm, says, "Supervisors must stop acting like babysitters. It's a habit that when something goes wrong you find a manager, engineer, or staff member to fix the problem. Every pair of hands comes with a free brain, and the supervisor's job is to get access to that brain. They should not do the thinking and problem solving; their first job is to refuse to solve employees' problems for them and develop the employees' ability to think at work."[66] In the early stages of team development, managers may have to

---

cross-training

Training in which team members gain an understanding of and practice each other's skills.

play a more active role in helping keep the team on track and help with decision making. But after the team has matured, it is best for the manager to set a time period for team decision making and give the team the chance to make a decision within that time period. In this way, managers can foster independence.

Creating a Positive Organizational Context

As we noted earlier in the chapter and in Exhibit 8.2, the organizational context has a major influence on team effectiveness. We now address specific contextual issues, including accountability for work, defining appropriate boundaries for teams, team-based performance management and reward structures, and an organizational culture that supports teams.

Accountability for Work   Teams need to be able to measure their work and understand how it relates to organizational goals. Without measurement, teams tend to spend too much time on unimportant issues and lack clear focus. For example, at Coldwater Machine Co. LLC, an Ohio-based company, measures of scrap and rework, on-time delivery, and customer satisfaction are used to evaluate team effectiveness.

Appropriate Team Boundaries   The types of activities that teams can be involved in vary across organizations. Some employees hear the word "teams" and believe they can set their own schedules and give themselves a raise. Although this may be possible in certain circumstances, an organization needs to set clear expectations about what the teams can and cannot do. Otherwise, employees will be frustrated, and teams will be ineffective. For example, teams at Boeing Company's Airlift and Tanker Programs interview prospective employees and elect their own team leaders. But teams cannot fire poor-performing team members due to legal concerns.[67] At Unisys Corporation, teams are setting their own goals based on the company's business plan.

Team-Based Performance Management and Reward Structures   To be effectively rewarded and motivated, team members must receive a combination of individual and team rewards. If organizations do not add a team reward, there is no incentive for employees to work together. Recall our discussion of incentives in Chapter 6. Both monetary rewards (such as bonuses) and nonmonetary rewards (such as days off) need to be linked to team performance. To ensure that team members are cross-trained, members may receive incentives for learning new skills or other team roles. To reward teams, organizations must evaluate whether teams are successfully meeting objective team goals (such as reduced waste) as well as subjective measures (such as sharing information with other team members). Some teams use peer evaluations to measure the effectiveness of team member behaviors.

Organizational Culture That Supports Teams   Research suggests that there are specific characteristics that make teams more effective.[68] For teams to be effective, they must be autonomous and their members need to experience impact, meaningfulness, and potency. *Autonomy* means that teams experience freedom, independence, and discretion in their work. *Impact*

Members of the AMETEK Aerospace aircraft fuel-flow meter production team are winners of their company's Dr. John H. Lux Total Quality Accomplishment Award. Recently the team reduced the time to produce a fuel-flow meter from 13 weeks to eight days and improved on-time delivery to more than 95 percent. In the photo they raise their fingers in the air with pride in their accomplishments and signify recognition of their impact, meaningfulness, and potency for AMETEK.
Source: Courtesy of AMETEK, Inc.

means that the team believes it produces work that is significant for the organization. Team members experience impact by getting feedback from other organization members as well as directly interacting with customers. *Meaningfulness* means that the team believes that what it does is important in the larger community. *Potency* is the belief that the team can be effective. To create these characteristics, organizations may give teams more responsibility for meeting production or service requirements by allowing teams to make work schedules, job assignments, and quality improvements and to participate in setting productivity or service goals. Team leaders who energize, inspire, and set high performance expectations create teams who experience high levels of potency. As we discussed earlier in this section, allowing team members to cross-train, selecting new team members, and providing team incentives increase potency and meaningfulness of teamwork. Finally, legitimizing teams by providing them access to important resources (expertise, budgets) or strategic information will enhance feelings of autonomy, meaningfulness, potency, and impact. For example, Unisys Corporation teams saw the biggest improvement in exceeding product shipping schedules when the company changed its policy of enforcing set work hours. The company now allows each team to choose which of two work schedules it will use.[69] Also consider how Whole Foods Market, the largest natural foods grocer in the United States, has turned teamwork into a highly profitable business model.

🐾 Whole Foods Market

As recently as 1991, Whole Foods Market had barely a dozen stores in three states. Today, it has the clout of a nationwide chain, with stores in ten states and net profits that are typically double the national average. The Whole Foods culture is based on decentralized teamwork. Each store is an autonomous profit center made up of an average of ten self-directed teams—grocery, produce, and so forth. Teams—and only teams—have the power to approve new hires for full-time jobs. Store leaders screen candidates and recommend them for a job on a specific team, but it takes a two-thirds vote of the team to approve the hire. Team members determine their personal work goals together with their team leaders and are accountable to the company for meeting those goals. Everyone on the team works together to identify and work at accomplishing team goals. Team members are expected to hold each other accountable for their performance. Team members deal directly with products, customers, and vendors. Each team has a team leader who is expected to set high performance standards. Leaders serve as mentors, help team members set realistic goals, and give regular performance feedback.

The company believes the first prerequisite of teamwork is trust. That trust starts with the hiring vote. In addition, Whole Foods supports teamwork with wide-open information on financial and operations systems. Sensitive figures on store sales, salaries, and bonuses are available to any employee. Executive salaries are limited to no more than eight times the average wage. According to CEO John Mackey, open information keeps everyone "aligned to the vision of shared fate. . . . If you're trying to create a high-trust organization, an organization where people are all for one and one for all, you can't have secrets."[70]

apply it

1. Consider a team you have belonged to. It may have been a class team or a work team. Evaluate the team in terms of how the members were selected, what training they received (if any), and the organizational context (including accountability for the team, appropriate boundaries, and organizational culture). What could have been done in these areas to improve the team's effectiveness?

summary OF KEY CONCEPTS

- **Effective teams result in personal satisfaction and enhanced productivity.** Teams are two or more people with a shared mission and collective responsibility. Teams interact and coordinate their work to accomplish a specific goal. Team effectiveness is based on two outcomes—member satisfaction and productivity. Team effectiveness is influenced by internal team processes, which in turn are affected by team type and team characteristics. The larger organizational context—including reward and control systems, culture, and strategy—can help or hinder team development.

- **To team or not to team: consider the benefits and the costs.** Teamwork has both potential benefits and costs. Benefits of using teams include increased motivation, diverse knowledge and skills, satisfaction of team members, and organizational flexibility. Potential costs of using teams are power realignment, free riding, coordination costs, and legal hassles.

- **Organizations rely on many different types of teams.** Organizations use teams both to achieve coordination as part of the formal structure and to encourage employee involvement. The four different types of teams differ on the basis of the outputs, degree of specialization, integration with others inside and outside the organization, and work cycle. *Production or service teams* such as assembly teams or data-processing groups are directly involved in providing a good or service to customers, such as sales, food, chemicals, or repairs. Their work cycle is typically repeated many times. They are integrated with customers and external suppliers. *Advice or involvement teams* provide decisions, suggestions, proposals, and recommendations. Their work cycle may be brief and

may not be repeated. They usually include members with diverse skills who may come from different parts of the organization. *Project or development teams* provide plans and designs or develop prototype products or services. Their members may be specialists who are experts in their fields. Their work cycle differs for each project. *Action or negotiation teams* have specialized experts who often perform in specialized facilities or need special equipment. The team performance is usually synchronized with other units in the organization. Examples include sports, negotiations, and surgical teams.

Self-directed teams and *virtual teams* are two special types of teams. Self-directed teams perform tasks typically performed by managers, such as deciding how and when work is completed, selecting new team members, ordering materials and supplies, and meeting with suppliers and customers. Virtual team members are geographically dispersed from each other. They interact using technology such as the internet or e-mail. They may never have a face-to-face meeting.

- **Building effective team processes: trust, cohesiveness, norms, and roles.** Most teams go through systematic stages of development: forming, storming, norming, performing, and adjourning. Organizations can take several steps to ensure that team trust, cohesiveness, positive norms, and roles are developed. Socialization can be used to develop cohesive teams. Organizations can facilitate effective communications by having team leaders focus team discussions on facts, helping teams develop multiple alternative solutions, maintaining a balance of power in the team, and never forcing the team to reach consensus. Positive norms can be developed by ensuring that critical events, initial team behavior, and behavior carried over from other teams is supportive of positive performance norms. Explicit statements regarding team expectations are also useful for establishing positive team norms. Successful teams need members who take either task specialist or socioemotional roles. The task specialist helps the team reach its goal. Team members who adopt the socioemotional role provide support for team members' emotional needs and strengthen team unity.

- **Developing effective teams involves identifying team purpose, selection, training, and a positive organizational context.** What makes the difference between effective and ineffective teams? Team members need to be chosen based on intelligence, personality, and specific teamwork skills. Training is necessary for individual team members, the team as a unit, and managers. The training focuses on interpersonal skills, quality skills, team coordination and communication, and the manager's role to coach and facilitate teams. Performance management and reward systems need to be team based as well as individually based. Teams need to know their limitations as well as what level of products and services they are expected to deliver. Finally, it is important that team members believe their work is meaningful and important and that they have autonomy to make decisions. This can be done by giving team members responsibility for scheduling and assigning their work and interacting directly with the consumers of the product or service they deliver.

KEY terms

team, p. 270	problem-solving team, p. 278	task specialist role, p. 288
free rider, p. 274	project or development team, p. 278	socioemotional role, p. 288
coordination costs, p. 275	action or negotiation team, p. 279	dual role, p. 288
production or service team, p. 276	self-directed team, p. 280	nonparticipator role, p. 289
advice or involvement team, p. 277	virtual team, p. 281	team training, p. 293
task force, p. 277	socialization, p. 284	cross-training, p. 294
committee, p. 278	adventure learning, p. 284	

DISCUSSION questions

1. Volvo instituted self-directed teams to assemble cars because of the need to attract and keep workers in Sweden, where pay raises are not a motivator (because of high taxes) and many other jobs are available. Is this a good reason for using a team approach? Discuss.

2. During your own work experience, have you been part of a production or service team? A task force? A committee? A problem-solving team? An action or negotiation team? How did your work experience differ in each type of team?

3. What can organizations do during the forming stage of team development to ensure that team trust and cohesiveness are developed? During the norming stage?

4. How would you explain the emergence of problem-solving and self-directed teams in companies throughout North America? Do you think implementation of the team concept is difficult in these companies? Discuss.

5. Do you think that virtual teams are a good idea? Explain why or why not.

6. Assume that you are part of a student project team and one member is not doing his or her share. What would you do? Why?

7. What conditions do you think are necessary for adventure learning to socialize team members? Explain.

8. What is the relationship between team cohesiveness and team performance?

9. Describe the potential benefits and costs of teams. In what situations might the costs outweigh the benefits?

10. What is a team norm? What norms have developed in teams to which you have belonged?

11. One company had 40 percent of its workers and 20 percent of its managers resign during the first year after reorganizing into teams. What might account for this dramatic turnover? What should an organization do to ensure a smooth transition to teams?

SELF-DISCOVERY *exercise*

Is Your Group a Cohesive Team?

Think about a student group with which you have worked. Answer the questions below as they pertain to the functioning of that group.

	Disagree Strongly			Agree Strongly	

1. Group meetings were held regularly and everyone attended.   1   2   3   4   5

2. We talked about and shared the same goals for group work and our grade.   1   2   3   4   5

3. We spent most of our meeting time talking business, but discussions were open ended and active.   1   2   3   4   5

4. We talked through any conflicts and disagreements until they were resolved.   1   2   3   4   5

5. Group members listened carefully to one another.   1   2   3   4   5

6. We trusted each other, speaking personally about what we really felt.   1   2   3   4   5

7. Leadership roles were rotated and shared, with people taking initiative at appropriate times for the good of the group.   1   2   3   4   5

8. Each member found a way to contribute to the final work product.   1   2   3   4   5

9. I was really satisfied being a member of the group.   1   2   3   4   5

10. We freely gave each other credit for jobs well done.   1   2   3   4   5

11. Group members gave and received feedback to help the group do even better.   1   2   3   4   5

12. We held each other accountable; each member was accountable to the group.   1   2   3   4   5

13. Group members really liked and respected each other.   1   2   3   4   5

Total Score _____

The questions here are about team cohesion. If you scored 52 or greater, your team experienced authentic teamwork. Congratulations. If you scored between 39 and 51, there was a positive team identity that might have been developed even further. If you scored between 26 and 38, team identity was weak and probably not very satisfying. If you scored below 26, it was hardly a team at all, and resembled a loose collection of individuals.

Remember, teamwork doesn't happen by itself. Individuals like you have to understand what a team is and then work to make it happen. What can you do to make a student group more like a team? Do you have the courage to take the initiative?

ORGANIZATIONAL BEHAVIOR *in your life*

@ As we discussed in the chapter, teams mature as members build trust in each other. Find a sports team to observe. Watch the team perform personally or on television. As you observe the team, write down behaviors that you see that are related to building or detracting from teamwork, such as how team members react to success and failure, their emotions, and their actions. Find information from the team's Web site, game program, or team member interviews regarding the experience of individual team members and how long they have played together. Based on your analysis, write a short summary of whether you think the team is effective. Justify your answer with data from your behavior log and research regarding the team members.

ORGANIZATIONAL BEHAVIOR news flash

@ Use your search engine to find a site on team building such as **www.oeg.net/tmb.html**, which provides information on the team-building process. Another good site can be found at **http://users.ids. net/~brim/sdwth.html**, where you can click on "Sites on Team Basics" and read several of the linked features (most are fairly short). Select three ideas and apply them in a team to which you currently belong—an employee group, an athletic team, a campus or community organization, etc. Report to your class what ideas you implemented and what impact they had on your team's performance.

global diversity EVENTS

@ Using "news of the day" listings on Internet search engines such as Reuters, AP, or ZDNet News, find stories related to global teams. These could be work teams, peacekeeping teams, rescue teams, or other types of teams. Summarize one article. How might cultural differences affect whether the team described in your article is effective?

minicase ISSUE

Successfully Implementing Teams

Background. Several years ago, Acme Minerals Extraction Company introduced teams in an effort to solve morale and productivity problems at its Wichita plant. Acme used highly sophisticated technology, employing geologists, geophysicists, and engineers on what was referred to as the "brains" side of the business, as well as skilled and semiskilled labor on the "brawn" side to run the company's underground extracting operations. The two sides regularly clashed, and when some engineers locked several operations workers out of the office in 100-degree heat, the local press had a field day. Suzanne Howard was hired to develop a program that would improve productivity and morale at the Wichita plant, with the idea that it would then be implemented at other Acme sites.

Building Teamwork. Howard had a stroke of luck in the form of Donald Peterson, a longtime Acme employee who was highly respected at the Wichita plant and was looking for one final, challenging project before he retired. Peterson had served in just about every possible line and staff position at Acme over his 39-year career, and he understood the problems workers faced on both the "brains" and the "brawn" sides of the business. Howard was pleased when Peterson agreed to serve as leader for the Wichita pilot project. There were three functional groups at the Wichita plant: operations, made up primarily of hourly workers who operated and maintained the extracting equipment; the "below ground" group, consisting of engineers, geologists, and geophysicists who determined where and how to drill; and the "above ground" group of engineers in charge of refinement and transportation of the minerals. Howard and Peterson decided the first step was to get these different groups talking to one another and sharing ideas. They instituted a monthly "problem chat," an optional meeting to which all employees were invited to discuss unresolved problems. At the first meeting, Howard and Peterson were the only two people who showed up. However, people gradually began to attend the meetings, and after about six months, they had become lively problem-solving discussions that led to many improvements.

Next, Howard and Peterson introduced teams to "select a problem and implement a tailored solution," or SPITS. These were ad hoc groups made up of members from each of the three functional areas. They were formed to work on a specific problem identified in a chat meeting and were disbanded when the problem was solved. SPITS were given the authority to address problems without seeking management approval. There were some rocky moments, as engineers resented working with operations personnel and vice versa. However, over time, and with the strong leadership of Peterson, the groups began to come together and focus on the issues rather than spending most of their time arguing. Eventually, workers in Wichita were organized into permanent cross-functional teams that were empowered to make their own decisions and elect their own leaders.

After a year and a half, things were really humming. The different groups weren't just working together; they had also started socializing together. At one of the problem chats, an operations worker jokingly suggested that the brains and the brawn should duke it out once a week to get rid of the tensions so they could focus all their energy on the job to be done. Several others joined in the joking, and eventually, the group decided to square off in a weekly softball game. Peterson had T-shirts printed up that said BRAINS and BRAWN. The softball games were well attended, and both sides usually ended up having a few beers together at a local bar afterward. Productivity and morale soared at the Wichita plant, and costs continued to decline.

What Went Wrong? Top executives believed the lessons learned at Wichita should make implementing the program at other sites less costly and time consuming. However, when Howard and her team attempted to implement the program at the company's Lubbock plant, things didn't go well. They felt immense pressure from top management to get the team-based productivity project running smoothly at Lubbock. Because people weren't showing up for the problem chat meetings, attendance was made mandatory. However, the meetings still produced few valuable ideas or suggestions. Although a few of the SPITS teams solved important problems, none of them showed the kind of commitment and enthusiasm Howard had seen in Wichita. In addition, the Lubbock workers refused to participate in the softball games and other team-building exercises that Howard's team developed for them. Howard finally convinced some workers to join in the softball games by bribing them with free food and beer. "If I just had a Donald Peterson in Lubbock, things would go a lot more smoothly," Howard thought. "These workers don't trust us the way workers in Wichita trusted him." It seemed that no matter how hard Howard and her team tried to make the project work in Lubbock, morale continued to decline and conflicts between the different groups of workers actually seemed to increase.

1. What types of teams described in the chapter are represented in this case?
2. Why do you think the team project succeeded in Wichita but wasn't working in Lubbock?
3. What advice would you give Suzanne Howard and her team for improving the employee involvement climate at the Lubbock plant?

Source: Based on Michael C. Beers, "The Strategy That Wouldn't Travel," *Harvard Business Review,* November–December 1996, pp. 18–31.

nine
C H A P T E R

9

Communication in Organizations

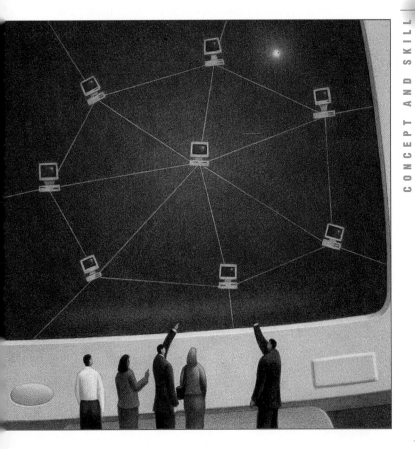

preview

After studying this chapter, you should be able to:

- Identify the components and purposes of a given communication.

- Suggest a variety of channels through which to communicate a message, and evaluate pros and cons for each possibility.

- Describe the patterns of communication that occur in an organization.

- Give examples of communication challenges that are common in modern organizations.

- Summarize several ways a person or organization can improve communications.

Canon Builds a Network of Communication

W hat if you had an idea for a new product you thought your company should produce, or a better way to distribute products, or a more streamlined design for existing products? Could you easily communicate your idea to the head of your company, or would it have to wend its way to the top, through layers and layers of management? Would anyone listen along the way? If you worked for Canon Inc., it would be easy to communicate, says Fujio Mitarai, Canon's president and CEO. "You just visit my page on our intranet. There's an e-mail link there, and the message would come straight to me."

In a world where many organizations focus primarily on communication that flows from the top of an organization to the bottom, Canon is unusual. The top definitely wants to hear from the bottom. Mitarai knows that some of the company's best ideas come from its employees, and employees need a way to communicate those ideas comfortably to someone who will listen and who has the authority to act on them. He also believes that research and development of new products (which come from those ideas) are the company's security in a sometimes uncertain Asian-Pacific economy. "R&D is our insurance policy," Mitarai explains. "It's our guarantee of future success." Without communication between workers and top management, there would be no R&D. R&D, of course, translates to new products, such as Canon's move toward technology that allows its machines to network with each other. "We are transforming ourselves from a company that is known for high-quality image processing into a company that is known for high-quality network technology," notes Mitarai. Even Canon's machines talk to each other.

Mitarai believes in and practices an open-door policy that coincides with the company's equal-opportunity philosophy of advancing employees based on merit. "It doesn't matter who you are or what your background is," he says. "If you pass an exam showing the right skills, you will move up the ladder." This recognition and reward of talent helps employees feel comfortable sharing their thoughts and ideas—they trust top management to be fair and truthful, and they know exactly what the rules are and how to get ahead at Canon. Communication at Canon flows freely in an atmosphere of trust. "Communication and accessibility are crucial parts of our corporate culture," notes Mitarai proudly. "My page gets more than 7,000 hits every month from our employees. It's an important way for me to stay in touch with everyone." Does communication translate to profits? It's hard to prove, but Canon has consistently posted record sales during times of economic difficulty throughout the Asia-Pacific region. With communication at the core, Canon is succeeding.[1]

> *Communication and accessibility are crucial parts of our corporate culture."*
> —**Fujio Mitarai,** president and CEO, Canon Inc.

"Communication is vital in today's information society, and an organization's competitiveness can often depend on getting information quickly and accurately, whether it relates to customer satisfaction, employee knowledge, or competitor strategy. Canon's managers obviously see the need for information to flow freely—in many different forms—throughout their organization.

The previous two chapters introduced groups and teams, describing in general how they behave. Group behaviors involve interactions among people, and this chapter is the first of several that look at the components of those interactions. In particular, we explore a fundamental way that people connect with one another: communication. We begin with a formal definition of the communication process. The chapter discusses how and why people communicate in organizations. It also addresses communication challenges that people face in today's organizations. We conclude the chapter by describing ways that individuals and organizations can improve communication.

Communication is an interpersonal process

communication

The process by which two or more people exchange information using a shared set of symbols.

The ancient meaning of *communication* is "to share," and that remains the essence of the word's meaning today. When people communicate, they are sharing messages and information with each other. When they communicate effectively, they are sharing the same message; that is, the listener or reader understands what the speaker or writer means. Thus, we can define **communication** as the process by which two or more people exchange information using a shared set of symbols. If you write a story on your computer but no one reads it, you have written but not communicated. Likewise, if you declare your career plans to an empty room, you have spoken but not communicated. For information to be exchanged or shared, other people must participate in the process with you.

To appreciate the role of communication in organizations, we first consider why it is important. Then we examine the elements of the communication process.

Purposes of Communication in Organizations

In successful organizations, communication is not just an afterthought—something that organizations cultivate after they have mastered product development and marketing. Communication is fundamental to the creation, maintenance, and survival of any organization. Organizations bring people together to work toward common objectives, and communication is the thread that binds them in their daily tasks. Communication enables them to define their objectives, share knowledge, and encourage one another. In addition, members of an organization communicate with people outside the organization to identify needs, learn skills, adhere to laws, obtain resources, sell products and services, and carry out many other tasks.

When communication is ineffective or absent, an organization cannot function properly. For example, during a blizzard in the Midwest, dozens of Northwest Airlines planes were stranded for hours on the runway at Detroit's airport. Why did Northwest allow planes to land on the snowy runways? Communication was lacking. Employees at its operations center, located miles away in Minnesota, didn't understand the seriousness of the conditions in Detroit, so they didn't divert the planes or cancel the flights there. The resulting bad publicity was disastrous for Northwest.[2]

Some organizations, excel in the practice of communication. At these organizations, people actively share ideas and urge one another to contribute their best effort. They exchange information about customers, work assignments, and new market opportunities. Skillful, goal-directed communication can drive the success of these organizations. At Domino's Pizza, executives conduct one-on-one job planning and review sessions with each of their managers every month. When one executive initially reacted to this policy by saying he couldn't possibly spend that much time meeting with each of his seven managers, he was told to track how much time he spent correcting problems. The executive discovered that in a single week he spent more time resolving problems and misunderstandings than he would have spent preventing them.[3]

When people communicate actively and in support of the organization's goals, they help one another learn about and fully participate in the life of the organization. For example, when Jerre Stead was head of AT&T's Global Information Solutions, he was charged with reorganizing what was then a money-losing operation. According to Stead, communicating with employees was essential to the success of the turnaround: "You can't change things unless people understand what's going on."[4] Similarly, Born Information Services, described in the following story, exemplifies an organization that appreciates the benefits of effective communication.

Companies are turning to technology to increase communication with customers, suppliers, and potential employees. The World Wide Web is just one additional way to increase communication. On the Domino's Pizza home page, the company invites prospective employees to "Join Our Team." It communicates with customers by helping online visitors order their pizza electronically. The combination of photos and words also helps sell the new Chicken Grill pizza.
(Source: Courtesy of Domino's Pizza LLC)

When Rick Born founded the company that bears his name, he wanted his employees to consider it the best place to work. Born reasoned that by keeping loyal and talented people on the payroll, he could build a good reputation with his customers while avoiding the costs associated with high turnover. To create an environment that is attractive to its staff of professional consultants, Born Information Services has focused on landing exciting cutting-edge assignments and has opened branch offices in lieu of requiring employees to travel.

When Born had grown to about 20 employees, the president, Dale Holmgren, initiated a new position: staff manager. This new level of manager is responsible for communicating with Born consultants who work at clients' workplaces. By calling these employees at least weekly and meeting with them monthly, the staff manager identifies areas where the employees need support from the home office. Often this help takes the form of directing the consultant to people in the organization who can provide support on the consultant's project. One staff manager also rescued a consultant being verbally attacked by a client and helped another consultant take a leave of absence to visit his native country. A consultant, Jon Jenkins, says the advice of his staff manager helps keep him from feeling "stranded" at the client site.

At a recent count, Born Information Systems had 45 staff managers, each providing support to 20 or fewer consultants. Their interactions have helped Born become a highly desirable employer. The company's chief financial officer says that although these paid communicators are a significant investment, the company enjoys above-average operating margins (operating revenues minus operating expenses) and half the industry's typical employee turnover. These measures signal that Born's commitment to communication is well placed.[5]

Born Information Services

Effective communication benefits organizations like Born, Domino's, and AT&T. Communication skill also benefits individuals. In a recent survey, human resource managers of large and small companies rated communication skills as the most important asset of a newly hired employee—

ranking even above education and experience.[6] Similarly, in a survey of 1,000 employees, 37 percent (the largest group) rated "communication skills or interpersonal relationship skills" as the most important skill set in a good boss; 42 percent said the most important cause of ineffectiveness was a lack of these skills.[7] Furthermore, there is evidence that high-performing managers outdo their less successful colleagues when it comes to selecting communications media (such as a letter, phone call, or face-to-face meeting).[8] People enhance their own status by letting others know about their contributions, and they help their coworkers by cooperating in achieving mutual goals. A person who engages in clear, helpful communications becomes trusted, liked, and respected. Thus, as effective communicators benefit the organization, they also benefit their own careers.

Elements of the Communication Process

Communication is a process that brings together three components and three actions, as illustrated in Exhibit 9.1. The first component is the sender. A sender is anyone who wants to convey an idea, get information, or signal an emotion. The sender initiates the communication process by **encoding** the idea, request for information, or emotion. This action entails selecting symbols, such as words or facial expressions, to create a message. The **message,** the second component of the communication process, is a tangible representation of the idea or other information to be sent. It may take the form of speech, written material (words and symbols), or nonverbal behavior. We will discuss these options later in the chapter.

Communication continues when someone receives the message. The receiver carries out the next activity in communication: **decoding.** This involves translating the symbols of the message in order to interpret its meaning. To do this, the receiver is expected to apply his or her experience, knowledge, and powers of perception. Suppose someone says to you, "How do you do?" If you interpret the person's speech as a request for an account of your medical history, you have decoded the speech literally but failed to take into account the custom of using these words as a polite greeting. Thus, decoding can be a complex activity.

In many situations, communication continues beyond decoding to a final activity, called **feedback.** This is a response from the receiver to the original sender. Examples of feedback include saying "OK," looking puz-

encoding

Selecting symbols, such as words or facial expressions, to create a message.

message

A tangible representation of the idea or other information to be sent in a communication.

decoding

Translating the symbols of a message in order to interpret its meaning.

feedback

A response from the receiver of a message to the original sender.

exhibit | **9.1**

The Communication Process

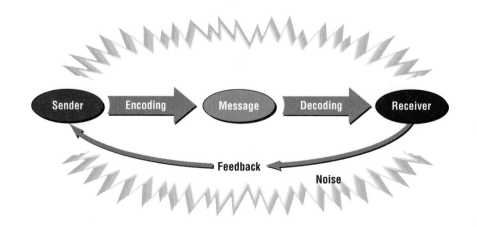

zled, or laughing. These reactions commonly signal agreement, lack of understanding, and a perception that the message was humorous.

Feedback is a useful part of communication because it provides information about whether the receiver correctly decoded the message. Successful salespeople are masters of decoding feedback, because it helps them understand their prospects and customers. For example, salespeople learn ways to interpret a prospect's statement that "I want to think it over." For Brad Long, national sales manager of Krystal Holographics, this statement is an opening to probe for the reasons behind the prospect's reluctance to make a decision. His experience is that when people need to think over a decision, they do not yet have enough information.[9] As in Long's case, interpreting feedback requires well-developed powers of perception.

Sources of Distortion in Communication

Identifying the elements of the communication process is useful because it helps us to diagnose communication problems when they occur. Much as a technician diagnoses problems in machinery by examining each part, would-be communicators can correct communication breakdowns by studying each element of the desired communication to look for sources of the problem. In general, **noise**—anything that distorts a message—can occur at any stage of the communication process.

noise

Anything that distorts a message.

Encoding by the Sender   Ideally, the sender of a message encodes it in a way that the receiver can interpret accurately. However, there are many reasons why the encoding may be less than ideal. A person could use words that have a different meaning to the receiver or are not in the receiver's vocabulary at all. Some messages are so full of jargon that receivers simply ignore them. For example, if someone told you that you "needed a T1 to have enough bandwidth to access files for Web content streaming," would you know what that person meant? If you didn't, would you be afraid to ask? Such problems can arise when the sender either lacks communication skills or does not evaluate whether the receiver is likely to understand the message. Also, sometimes the sender's emotional state makes it difficult for him or her to encode the message carefully. Thus, when you are angry, you might have difficulty expressing your position clearly and appropriately.

In encoding messages, the sender has to make some assumptions about what the receiver already knows. For example, the sender might assume the receiver speaks American English fluently and knows that "Give me a ballpark figure" means to give the message sender a rough cost estimate. When assumptions are incorrect, the receiver is apt to misinterpret the message. In this case, the receiver may think he has to obtain something—or someone—from a sports stadium. A dramatic case of mistaken assumptions occurred when employees at Lockheed Martin Astronautics provided the Jet Propulsion Laboratory (JPL) with data for guiding the Mars Climate Orbiter. Lockheed provided momentum data in pound-seconds, units from the English system of measurement. They assumed that JPL engineers would use the same units, but the government engineers, like most scientists, used the metric system and assumed the data were in newton-seconds, the metric unit for momentum. Guided by incorrect data, the $125 million spacecraft flew too far into the atmosphere of Mars and was destroyed.[10]

Another part of encoding involves selecting communication channels, such as writing a note or making a phone call. As we will discuss later in the chapter, some media are more effective in a given situation than are others. For instance, to convey an emotionally charged message, it may be most appropriate to discuss the message face to face. This enables the receiver to see and hear the sender's emotional cues, as well as to provide feedback that helps both parties understand the complexities of the emotional message. If the sender instead fires off an e-mail message, misunderstandings might result because of the lack of personal cues and the more static, one-way nature of e-mail. Conversely, if the sender delivers an oral message that involves many detailed pieces of information, the receiver may forget or fail to hear some important details. Written communication might be more effective for conveying this type of message.

Sometimes the sender delivers mixed messages—that is, some aspects of the message are inconsistent with other aspects. This often occurs when a person's words do not match his or her behavior. Or a sender who wants to deliver a message that conveys respect and sincerity might confuse the message by using terms that the receiver considers offensive. With a mixed message, the receiver must decide how to reconcile the conflicting parts of the message—and may not do so in the way the sender hopes.

Sending mixed messages can erode a person's credibility. If your coworker said one thing yesterday and the opposite today, will you believe your coworker tomorrow? Low credibility interferes with messages by causing the receiver to doubt the face value of the message. Other sources of low credibility include unethical behavior and lack of knowledge about or skill in the subject matter of the message.

In some cases the sender may obscure or distort a message intentionally. For example, the sender might believe that a blunt message will hurt the receiver's feelings, so the sender expresses the message indirectly to soften the blow. Also, people normally don't want others to see them in a bad light, so they try to present information in a way that enhances their strengths and minimizes their shortcomings. Manipulating information so that it appears more favorable is called **filtering.**

filtering

Manipulating information being communicated so that it appears more favorable.

The use of filtering gives rise to some ethical issues. In particular, is it ever right to distort or disguise the truth? A certain amount of filtering can smooth social interactions. Most people would agree that it's appropriate to say, "Great speech!" to your coworker, even if you thought the speech was dull (unless your coworker is really looking for your help in developing speaking skills). It doesn't hurt to help people gain confidence, and it often is beneficial. In more difficult situations, delivering an honest communication carries a potential cost to the communicator, whereas filtering would be harmful to others or to the organization itself. For example, when entrepreneur Norm Brodsky first decided to strike out on his own, he had to decide whether to tell his boss he was planning to start a competing courier business. Brodsky opted for total honesty, and his boss retaliated by calling all his customers to discourage them from taking their business to Brodsky. In this case, honesty triumphed. Brodsky was inundated with calls from those customers, asking when they could sign on with him.[11] Brodsky's experience suggests a moral: Never underestimate the desire of people to work with someone they respect and trust.

From the perspective of communication within an organization, when filtering is common, employees will have difficulty knowing what is really happening. Energy that could go toward collaboration and goal achievement may be directed toward uncovering the truth. Organizations therefore benefit from rewarding honesty, not just success.

Decoding by the Receiver   Miscommunications also occur because the receiver may decode the message inaccurately. Decoding a message is a type of perception, so mistakes often result from the kinds of perceptual errors described in Chapter 4. For example, the receiver may hold stereotypes about the sender or the content of the message, or the receiver may not notice aspects of the message that contradict his or her preexisting attitudes. People also are more likely to pay attention to a message when it applies to a subject that interests them and when the sender of the message has high status.[12] Besides paying more attention to some messages than others, people interpret them according to their perceptual biases, as described in Chapter 4.

Because of individual differences, it is not surprising that when a group of people receive a single message, they will decode it differently. This happened at Japan's largest securities brokerage, Nomura Securities Company. Nomura appointed Junichi Ujiie to be its president and lead the company out of a scandal that involved alleged payoffs to a corporate racketeer. Ujiie determined that the key to a more ethical culture was to shift the emphasis away from urging clients to invest in particular stocks. Instead of pressing salespeople to meet quotas, the company would emphasize selling mutual funds and offering investment advice. Some sales employees interpreted the directive as a request for totally new behavior and stopped recommending stocks altogether. Others concluded that the executives didn't understand what customers really wanted and continued with their prior methods. Amid the confusion, Nomura lost its bid to underwrite a public offering of stock in Nippon Telegraph & Telephone Corporation, and it wasn't even able to sell all the shares it was allotted by the issue's underwriter. CEO Ujiie later tried to explain that he had never meant to discourage employees from recommending individual stocks, but just to end the pushing of shares on investors who weren't interested.[13] To consider how your own individual differences affect how you listen, try the Self-Discovery Exercise on listening skills at the end of the chapter.

Besides perceptual errors, reasons for miscommunication at the receiving end include failure to fully employ a person's communication skills. Sometimes a receiver does not fully employ communication skills because he or she is upset, believes the message is unimportant, or believes the sender of the message is unimportant or unreliable.

Organizations sometimes add to the receiver's communication challenge by creating or permitting conditions in which it is more difficult to practice good communication skills. Such conditions as a noisy or poorly lit workplace interfere with effective communication. In addition, many employees experience information overload—they feel bombarded by so much information that they cannot effectively process it all. Organizations contribute to this when they expect employees to read unnecessary reports, attend unproductive meetings, or receive direction from several sources. For example, Herb Kelleher has described a report routinely generated in his company, Southwest Airlines. The report was one page long, and everyone on the distribution list studied it carefully. "And then," adds Kelleher, "we got real sophisticated and turned it into a 32-page report. Well, nobody ever asked a question about it again because nobody ever read it."[14]

apply it

Imagine that you accepted a new job last Thursday, and you are preparing to start work this coming Monday. But in the meantime, the organization you really want to work for just called to offer you a job.

1. What, if anything, will you tell the two organizations? Will you tell them everything about the situation, or will you try to shape your message to make it sound better or to be nice to one or both of the organizations?

2. Is the way you *want* to communicate also the most ethical approach? Why or why not? How will your communication shape your credibility?

Communication in organizations follows various patterns

channel

The carrier of a message.

Suppose a technical support representative is struggling to fulfill many responsibilities at work. How might she communicate her exhaustion to her colleagues? How might she renegotiate her workload with her supervisor? As the sender of these messages, the representative has some control over the communication channels she uses. A **channel** (or medium) is the carrier of the message. Examples include memos, phone calls, and facial expressions.

The various options for communication channels fall into the categories of written, oral, and nonverbal communication. Each has advantages and limitations. The selection of a channel depends in part on the direction of the communication. Thus, you might use different methods to communicate with higher levels of the organization's hierarchy (your supervisor) and with those at your level (your colleagues and your counterparts in other departments). Let's look at these patterns of communication in greater detail.

Written Communication

written communication

Any communication whose message is encoded in writing.

Much of the communication in organizations is written in some format. **Written communication,** as the name implies, encompasses any communication whose message is encoded in writing. These written messages may include not only words, but also agreed-upon symbols such as graphs and charts, the color yellow for a warning, red ink for numbers reporting a balance less than zero, or the sign of a crossed-out cigarette for no smoking.

Common channels for written communication include letters, memos, computer graphics and spreadsheet displays, e-mail messages, Web sites, newsletters, reports, online chat rooms and message boards, and handwritten notes. With this array of formats to choose from, people can decide whether a written communication will be formal or informal, personal or impersonal. In addition, the written message can be saved as a formal record of the communication. So, the sender can convey a long message without worrying that the receiver will forget part of it since the receiver can review and re-review the message. Written communication also gives the sender a great deal of control over the message. The sender can decide which parts of the message will be highlighted and usually has time to think carefully about how to phrase a message before sending it.

The major drawback of written communication is that it offers relatively low **channel richness**—the amount of information that a channel can transmit in one message.[15] A channel offers great richness if it has the following characteristics:

channel richness

The amount of information that a channel can transmit in one message.

- It can handle several cues at the same time.
- It allows for rapid feedback.
- It can be personal, that is, tailored to the individual receiver.

As shown in Exhibit 9.2, the various forms of written communication are all located near the low end of the spectrum of channel richness. The reason is that written communication provides little, if any, opportunity for observing the ways people communicate with their body and tone of voice, as described later in this section. In addition, feedback from written communication is relatively slow. By the time a sender realizes that the receiver misinterpreted a message, the receiver may already have acted on the message or formed an opinion about it or the sender.

If you want some of the advantages of written communication, you have some choice over the degree of channel richness. Some forms of written communication, notably e-mail, provide for quick feedback. In addition, many written communications can be personalized. When disseminating basic information to a wide audience, however, channel richness is not an important advantage. For example, to post safety warnings or job openings, the sender does not really need to communicate a mood.

exhibit **9.2**

Information Richness of Communication Channels

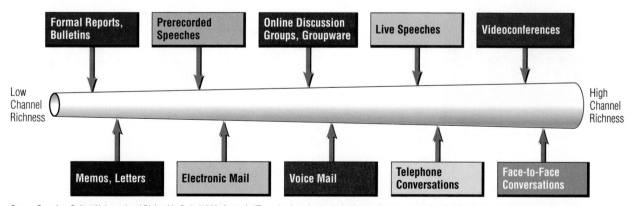

Source: Based on Robert H. Lengel and Richard L. Daft. (1988, August). "The selection of communication media as an executive skill." *Academy of Management Executive* 2:225–232; and Richard L. Daft and Richard H. Lengel. (1996, May). "Organizational information requirements, media richness, and structural design." *Managerial Science* 32:554–572.

Oral Communication

oral communication

All forms of communication using spoken words.

Before people learn to write, they are communicating. In organizations, much of the communication is also not written, but oral. **Oral communication** includes all forms of communication using spoken words. Channels for oral communication include face-to-face conversations, speeches, telephone conversations, and voice-mail messages.

A major advantage of oral, rather than written, communication is that it offers relatively great channel richness. With oral communication, the sender transmits tone of voice along with the words themselves. The sender's tone can convey a great deal of emotion, including the person's general mood and the intensity of his or her feelings about the message. Similarly, the receiver can convey level of interest, emotions, and understanding (or lack of it) through sounds like "uh-huh," "hmm," and "oh?" Furthermore, when oral communication occurs face to face, the receiver and sender can observe one another's posture and facial expressions.

Nonverbal Communication

nonverbal communication

Conveying messages without words; communication through channels such as body posture and facial expressions.

Some messages—perhaps most—are communicated without words. This **nonverbal communication** includes facial expressions, body posture and movements, and other behaviors that convey information. For example, when *Fortune* reporter Lauren Goldstein visited executive consultant Debra Benton, she learned that chief executives tend to use a set of nonverbal communication behaviors that help them maintain a position of leadership. CEOs stand up straight, use a calm tone of voice, keep their emotions under wraps, and put on a facial expression that signals "I'm interested."[16]

Often, the person sending nonverbal messages is not even aware of doing so. For example, cultures define the appropriate space between people who are strangers, friends, or family. Another person will interpret how close you stand to him or her to be a message about how emotionally close you want the relationship to be. If your culture defines an appropriate distance for business colleagues as one foot apart but a coworker's culture defines it as three feet, you may be surprised and uncomfortable when he keeps edging away from you, while he may be alarmed by your apparent effort at intimacy.

Decoding nonverbal communications may be difficult, because the meaning of a nonverbal message relies heavily on cultural norms and experiences. For example, if you are in a meeting and everyone is staring at you, what does their behavior mean? Did you do something to draw attention to yourself? If so, what was the action that had that effect? Is the group expecting a certain behavior from you? Does their silence signify respect, or are they signaling that your behavior was inappropriate? If you are not sure of the answers, you will certainly wish for some verbal communication to clarify the nonverbal messages. Perhaps you will initiate the verbal communication yourself.

People use nonverbal communication whenever they observe one another. Nonverbal communication sends messages and feedback in face-to-face encounters. In addition, people observe nonverbal messages when someone delivers a speech or leads a seminar. When these addresses are

Although we can't hear this woman's thoughts, we can certainly read her body language. Her facial expression and body posture communicate her displeasure. Such nonverbal communication is a critical channel for communication. (Source: © Christopher Bissell/Stone)

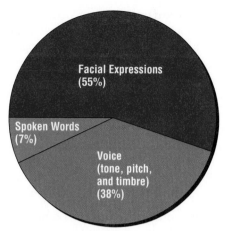

exhibit **9.3**
Importance of Channels Used in
Face-to-Face Communication

Source: Albert Mehrabian, *Silent Messages* (Belmont, CA: Wadsworth, 1971); and Albert Mehrabian," Communicating without words," *Psychology Today,* September 1968, pp. 53–55.

conducted before a live audience, the person delivering the speech or leading the seminar can (and should) also observe feedback from audience members. Nonverbal messages can signal whether the audience understands the message and is responding to it as desired.

In a study of face-to-face communication, Albert Mehrabian evaluated three channels used: the spoken words; the voice, including its tone, pitch, and timbre; and facial expressions.[17] Mehrabian identified how much impact each channel had on the way the receivers interpreted the message. As shown in Exhibit 9.3, facial expression had the greatest impact (55 percent of the total impact). The vocal impact was 38 percent, and the words accounted for just 7 percent of the total impact of the message.

The significance of Mehrabian's research is that communicators should devote at least as much care to their nonverbal messages as to their verbal ones. One manager who appreciates this principle is Quinton Studer, president of Baptist Hospital in Pensacola, Florida. To fulfill his objective of making Baptist "the best hospital in the country," Studer instituted a number of policies to enhance patient satisfaction. One of these is that employees are not to point. In other words, if someone asks for directions in the hospital, the employee is to take the person to the destination, rather than point to it. One of the vice presidents initially thought that was an inefficient use of his time. But by the second occasion on which he guided someone through the hospital corridors, he concluded that this effort was valuable because it signaled concern for patients and their visitors.[18]

Directions and Networks of Communication

Viewing the organization in terms of a hierarchy, we can map the directions of communication. Messages can travel downward, upward, or across levels of the organization's hierarchy and areas of task responsibility:

- **Downward communication** is communication from a sender to a receiver at a lower level in the organization's hierarchy. Managers use downward communication to inform employees about goals and expectations, to inspire and motivate employees, and to assign work.

downward communication

Organizational communication from a sender to a receiver at a lower level of the organization's hierarchy.

upward communication

Organizational communication from a sender to a receiver at a higher level of the organization's hierarchy.

horizontal communication

Organizational communication transmitted across a single level of the organization's hierarchy.

- **Upward communication** travels from a sender to a receiver at a higher level in the organization's hierarchy. Employees and managers use upward communication to keep others abreast of their progress and to request information or assistance. Many organizations also encourage upward communication that contributes to goal setting and knowledge sharing. Canon, the company profiled at the beginning of the chapter, uses an information network to ensure upward communication with its CEO.

- **Horizontal communication** involves messages that travel across one level of the hierarchy, from one employee to another, and from one group or department to another. Lateral communication is essential to knowledge sharing in a learning organization and in organizations where teams or other groups require employees to collaborate.

Studying the extent and effectiveness of communications in each direction can indicate whether the people in an organization are communicating enough that everyone has access to the information he or she needs. Sara Lee Corporation upset the local community as well as its employees because of insufficient downward communication. It failed to provide full information about plans to close its facility in New Hampton, Iowa. Mary Rosonke, the business agent for the union that represented Sara Lee's New Hampton employees, complained that the company gave them a month to come up with something to justify keeping the plant open but never disclosed what that "something" might be. Workers believed the factory was profitable, so they were confused as well as upset by the decision to close.[19] In contrast, civil engineering firm Anderson & Associates uses downward communication to support its philosophy that its employees are its owners (they participate in an employee stock ownership plan) and therefore are entitled to understand the business. The company posts all its financial records on its intranet and trains its employees to interpret the data.[20] Another example of a company that uses downward communication effectively is Ford.

🐦 Ford Motor Company

When Ford promoted Jacques Nasser to the job of president (and, later, chief executive officer), the company in effect committed itself to a global outlook. Born in Lebanon, Nasser grew up in Australia, where he took his first assignment with Ford as a financial analyst. From there, he moved to jobs in Latin America and Europe and eventually headed the division charged with marketing a global automobile. This background gave Nasser a breadth of experience and an exposure to the global economy that until then was unprecedented in the company. But how could Nasser communicate his global vision?

For Nasser, the answer includes a hefty dose of downward communication. Every week he sends all 89,000 Ford employees an e-mail about the company's operations. He routinely checks the company's intranet and has used it to host a series of online chats about the launch of Mercury Sable 2000. His commitment to employee learning includes doing some of the teaching himself. In one case, he delivered a three-hour talk, educating employees about the relationship between their work and the value of the company's stock. (Employees own one-fifth of the shares.) In another, he presented his corporate vision to a group of newly appointed executives undergoing training at headquarters.

Nasser also insists that his employees do plenty of communicating. For example, to improve the company's product development, he has designers, engineers, and marketers take a course in listening to consumers. This is followed by two months of "customer immersion," which involves spending time with targeted consumers outside the office.[21]

formal communication

Organizational communication along lines of responsibility and authority.

Formal and Informal Communication The messages that flow in any direction may be **formal communication**—that is, communication along the lines of responsibility and authority, as defined by the organization. A manager directing the work of his or her employees engages in formal communication. So do the employees when they report their progress to the manager or ask for information from the manager. And people who share work-related information across a level of the organization also are engaged in formal communication.

In addition, people communicate with one another for personal reasons unrelated to their work. This **informal communication** involves messages that are not strictly work related and do not necessarily travel along the lines of the organization's structure. Informal communication often travels through the **grapevine,** an unofficial network of employees who share information with one another. People participate in grapevines to obtain information the organization does not provide through formal channels. In a survey of workers in a variety of industries, 55 percent said they get most of their information through the grapevine.[22] In another survey, employees said they believe information they obtain through the grapevine more than what they learn through formal communication channels.[23] So, the grapevine is an important source of information for employees. People also participate in grapevines to meet social needs, reduce anxiety in the face of uncertainty, and enhance their status by signaling that they have access to valuable information.[24]

From the organization's perspective, the grapevine is a mixed blessing. It can help employees make sense of a situation and respond to problems quickly. It can give them a sense of certainty or control during times of stress and change. However, because managers do not control it, they cannot prevent the grapevine from spreading messages that are inaccurate or contrary to the organization's objectives.

Research provides more information about how—and how well—grapevines operate. Messages in a grapevine typically travel in one of two patterns (see Exhibit 9.4):[25]

1. ***Gossip chain*** One person conveys a message to many other people.
2. ***Cluster chain*** A few people convey a message to many other people. First, one person conveys a message to several people, then one of those people tells others, one of them tells still more people, and so on.

In both of these patterns, only a few people play an active role in spreading the message. This may increase the accuracy of grapevine messages. The fewer people who spread a message, the less likely that the message will become distorted by misunderstandings or noise along the way. In fact, evidence shows that 70 to 90 percent of the information that passes through the grapevine is accurate.[26]

Communication Networks If we observe who people communicate with in an organization, we find that their communications fall into defined patterns, which we call

informal communication

Organizational communication that is not strictly work related and may not follow lines of responsibility or authority.

grapevine

An unofficial network of employees who share information with one another.

gossip chain

A pattern of grapevine communication in which one person conveys a message to many other people.

cluster chain

A pattern of grapevine communication in which a few people convey a message to many other people; one person tells several others, then one of those people tells a few others, and so on.

As chairman of Ford Motor Company, Bill Ford Jr. routinely uses formal communication to address important issues regarding America's second largest industrial company. Ford, however, also enjoys communicating informally with workers, such as in this photo at Ford's Rouge plant complex, which is near his office in Michigan. He fraternizes with workers to improve relationships and communication between management and employees. "I always hated this us vs. them. We're one company," he says.
(Source: © George Lange)

exhibit **9.4**

Patterns of Communication in Grapevines

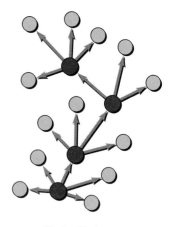

Gossip Chain
(One tells many)

Cluster Chain
(A few tell selected others)

Source: Based on Keith Davis and John W. Newstrom, *Human Behavior at Work: Organizational Behavior*, 7th ed. (New York: McGraw-Hill, 1985).

---

communication network

A pattern of organizational communication describing who people communicate with.

centralized network

A communication network in which most communications pass through a single individual.

communication networks. A group might, for example, have a member that everyone communicates with. When the group members have information, they share it with that person, and when they want information, they get it from that person. This pattern of communication is a **centralized network,** meaning most communications pass through a single individual. As shown in Exhibit 9.5, centralized networks may take the shape of a Y or a wheel (with lines of communication radiating out from the center like spokes).

In contrast, some groups feature communication in all directions. Group members might pass messages along from one to another, or everyone in the group might communicate with everyone else. Either way, a

exhibit **9.5**

Communication Networks

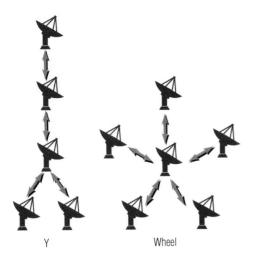

Y   Wheel

Centralized Networks

Circle   All Channel

Decentralized Networks

network where individuals share information equally is called a **decentralized network,** illustrated in Exhibit 9.5 as a circle or all-channel network.

decentralized network

A communication network in which individuals share information equally.

The nature of the communications network influences how well the group works. Experiments have found that people in centralized networks solve simple problems faster. But whereas decentralized networks were cumbersome for simple problems, they provided essential information sharing for tackling complex problems. Therefore, decentralized networks provided faster and more accurate solutions to complex problems.[27]

apply it

1. Imagine that you are a manager preparing for a performance appraisal of one of your employees. You want the employee to know that you are pleased with her performance in most areas but want her to develop better communication skills. In particular, you want the employee to be more active in keeping you informed about her activities and accomplishments. What would be the most effective way to communicate this information? Consider the content of the message and the channel(s) you would use.

2. At the end of your meeting with the employee, you observe that she seems very happy. You conclude that she understood her performance mostly met your standards, but you wonder if she understands the need to improve her communication. A month later, you notice her communication has not improved. You are still in the dark about what she is doing. How can you present the information again so that the employee is more likely to understand the need for change?

Communicating in today's organizations is challenging

Organizations today have some characteristics that make communication more challenging. Communication in modern organizations is more complex than in the past because it often involves new technology and a more diverse group of employees. In addition, the fast-changing, demanding environment favors learning organizations, and such organizations require a high degree of information sharing.

Effective Use of Communications Technology

Many of the most widely hailed advances in technology involve communications technology. Cellular phones, e-mail, videoconferencing, intranets, and extranets—these and other modern technologies enable people to share information with relative ease. People who have mastered these technologies can connect with one another anytime, anywhere via pager, cell phone, or computer. Ameritech's CEO is a heavy user of e-mail. He told a newspaper reporter that his one-day record was 864 messages received and that he corresponds with employees at all levels of his company. He added that he sends so many e-mail messages that on the rare occasions when he doesn't send any messages for a few days, people write to him to inquire whether he is okay.[28]

The communication capacity of these and other devices is expected to continue increasing. Here are just a few of the innovations announced around the time of this writing:

- Cellular phone maker Nokia predicted a new generation of phones with the ability to transmit multimedia files, enabling phone users to conduct videoconferences.[29]

- Several companies have been developing versions of a wearable personal computer useful for corporate trainers and service technicians, both of whom can benefit from the ready access to data while they are moving about.[30]

- Software such as TeleVantage enables personal computers to route calls to the phone of the user's choice and will also display a log of voice-mail messages on the user's computer screen.[31]

- Videoconferencing equipment, which until a few years ago required a special studio, has become available in increasingly affordable and powerful versions for personal computers.[32]

- Sprint has begun offering wireless Internet service in the United States. The service, which was already popular in Europe and some Asian countries, lets customers view Web pages on the screen of their wireless phone. They can also plug in a laptop computer to connect to the Internet via their wireless phone.[33]

Other technologies, such as voice-recognition e-mail that allows users to dictate messages to the computer, probably await us in the not-too-distant future. Thanks to such technology, many organizations have found practical ways to let each employee share information with anyone else in the organization who might need it. Production workers can submit ideas to executives, for example, and employees in different countries can collaborate on projects.

Problems of High-Tech Communication   Some people are so well connected through new technology that they feel too linked to their organizations and customers. They feel tethered to their work because someone can contact them about work at any time. They can tote a computer and pocket organizer on vacation, so they feel guilty if they don't. In these circumstances, the workplace expands to include wherever the employee happens to be. Don Wetmore, a consultant on time management issues, has found that most employees believe they should just work harder until they somehow start keeping up with all the information.[34] Of course, the easier it gets to send messages, the more messages are sent and the more elusive that goal becomes.

A related problem is that people feel overwhelmed by all the information streaming in over phone lines, via high-speed Internet connections, and through the mail. Consider the demands on the Ameritech CEO just mentioned, who received the 864 e-mail messages; in a ten-hour day, he would have had to handle over 80 messages an hour to keep up. Also, people have trouble knowing when they have enough information, given that a click of a mouse can deliver still more at little additional cost. More than one employee has squandered hours hunting up tidbits of information on the Internet and conversing with people in chat rooms. The topics may be work related, but the use of time may not be efficient.

Communications technology has another downside: it increasingly substitutes for face-to-face interaction. Personal relationships with colleagues, customers, or clients become more sterile as parties know each other only through electronic interactions. Facial expressions, gestures, and vocal inflections are more difficult to convey. Social events that served as the basis to develop trust, caring, mutual respect, expertise, and business contacts and contracts, such as dinners or meetings on the golf course or at the theater, are minimized.

Ethical Issues of High-Tech Communication Communications technology also adds to the ethical complexities surrounding communication in organizations. In particular, software enables organizations to gather detailed data about what employees are doing with their computers—who they are sending messages to, what Web sites they visit, and so on. For example, a company can buy a program like Message Inspector to search e-mail for key terms (such as offensive words or a competitor's e-mail address) that suggest possible problems. As shown in Exhibit 9.6, a 1997 study by the American Management Association found that almost 15 percent of the midsized to large companies surveyed said they review employees' e-mail messages, and almost 14 percent reviewed employees' computer files.[35] Just a year later, the AMA reported that 45 percent of employers were monitoring some combination of employees' e-mail, voice mail, computer files, phone calls, or other workplace activities (not including the use of security cameras).[36]

A case in point is Wolverton & Associates, a civil engineering firm, which uses software to track Internet usage and generate reports that rank the company's heaviest Internet users and most-visited Web sites. Douglas Dahlberg, the company's information technology manager and the only one with the authorization to access the whole system, not only can read these reports but also can investigate them by studying individual employees' usage and opening their files—even the ones they thought they had deleted. Despite this ability to pry, Dahlberg insists that he is focused only on the organization's needs—for example, the requirement that employees don't clutter the network lines and memory with personal matters. The company needs all the capacity it has for sending massive computer-aided design files to clients.[37]

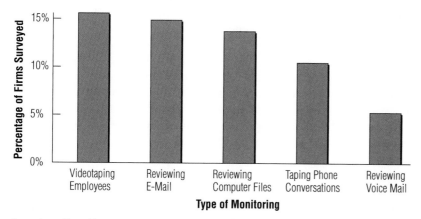

exhibit **9.6**
Midsized and Small Companies That Monitor Communications

Source: Laura Pincus Hartman, "The Rights and Wrongs of Workplace Snooping," *Journal of Business Strategy,* May–June 1998 (downloaded from the Northern Light Web site, http://library.northernlight.com, November 8, 1999), reporting data from a survey by the American Management Association.

what would you do?

SHOULD ORGANIZATIONS MONITOR THEIR WORKERS' E-MAIL?

With a computer at nearly every workplace (sometimes in every office or workstation), employees have a new way to socialize. They can send e-mail messages to friends and colleagues, they can check on their personal investments, they can order groceries, they can even listen to music. The big question is, Should they? The even bigger question is, Should their employers know about these activities?

Some people believe that organizations have a right to know. "When people get caught playing games or checking their stocks or buying cars online or setting up a date for the next night, and they're upset about it, I get wound up," says William Hubbartt, a computer-security consultant. "What's the question? You're on company time. You're supposed to be working. You got caught." Others disagree. David Krane, a marketing director for Certicom, an encryption company in California, believes that because workers often stay late or take work home on weekends, they should have at least a few minutes to conduct personal business online. "Work and personal life—it's all ubiquitous," he says.

The deeper question, of course, involves what constitutes an invasion of privacy. By law, employers are not required to notify employees that their computer communications are being monitored. But the idea of surveillance leaves many employees and managers feeling queasy. Some solve the problem with their choice of monitoring software—some programs are simply designed to ferret out e-mails containing off-color jokes or visits to online pornographic sites. Others are designed to detect potential industrial espionage. Programs like LittleBrother (from JSB Technologies) and MIMEsweeper (from Content Technologies) can monitor whatever customers want and run regular to intermittent checks. Investigator 2.0 keeps track of just about every keystroke a company's employees make. Companies vary greatly in their level of monitoring. Twentieth-Century Fox is interested only in keeping its movie ideas under cover, but Ameritech's policy states that its company's computers "are to be used only to provide service to customers and for other business purposes."

Imagine that you are a manager and your company requires you to use detection software to monitor your employees' online activities.

1. Would you notify your employees that they are being monitored? Why or why not?
2. How might this type of monitoring hamper other types of communication within the organization?
3. Do you think monitoring is appropriate? Why or why not?

Source: James Lardner, "Every Click You Make . . . ," *U.S. News and World Report,* November 8, 1999, p. 69.

The ethical issue of monitoring is whether organizations gather and use information in ways that violate employees' privacy. Some people are concerned that, especially when an organization has an employee use a secret password to log on, the employee expects communications to be private.[38] Furthermore, a reasonable employee might believe that it is acceptable to use the company computer to check a stock price or look up articles about aging parents during lunch hour, just as many employers would allow the employee to use a company phone to schedule a doctor's appointment.

For their part, some organizations say that monitoring employee computer use, including e-mail, is necessary—and not just to improve efficiency. Chevron lost a sexual harassment lawsuit in part based on evidence of harassment by an employee through messages saved in the company's e-mail server.[39] The company could logically conclude that if it had monitored e-mail messages it might have helped stop the harassment as well as avoided a lawsuit. Other reasons for monitoring computer activity might include ensuring that employees do not give away company strategies (say, by spending a lot of time in certain areas of competitors' Web sites) or that employees do not misuse copyrighted information. Illegal actions are not the only concern. Just as a letter going out on ABC Corp. letterhead reflects on ABC Corp., an e-mail message from jsmith@abccorp.com reflects on the company. Organizations naturally care about the reputation their employees create when they communicate with people outside the organization.

Organizations are developing guidelines for meeting these interests while respecting employees' privacy. Some approaches include disclosing the organization's use of monitoring and permitting employees to see information gathered about their activities.[40] When Wolverton & Associates gave its employees access to the Internet, the company informed them that it had "the ability to monitor *all* Internet usage" and that personal use was restricted to lunch breaks and time before and after work.[41] And at Nissan, employees see a message about the company's privacy policy every time they log on to the Internet from work.[42]

Communication across Culture and Language Differences

As we discussed in Chapter 2, today's organizations often bring together people from many different cultures. This diversity can make communication more difficult. Just as cultures provide norms and customs for other kinds of behavior, they provide guidelines for communication. When the sender and receiver are following different norms for communication, they may misunderstand one another. For example, suppose a manager from an egalitarian culture is speaking with an employee from a more authoritarian culture. The manager may assume that if the employee has ideas, the employee will volunteer them. However, the employee may actually view such behavior as rude and instead patiently wait for the manager to ask for his or her opinion. Meanwhile, the manager may conclude that the employee must not have any ideas to contribute. The result: The employee's ideas are lost to the organization, and the manager's group does not perform as well as it could with more effective communication. Similarly, Chapter 2 explained that cultures have a high-context or low-context style of communicating. People from low-context cultures may miss important nonverbal cues sent by people from high-context cultures.

Cultural differences also include values related to aspects of the organization's activities, such as how to treat customers or how to handle change. These, too, shape the way messages are encoded and decoded. According to Francis Meston, vice president of the European division of A. T. Kearney's Enterprise Information Practice, when people hear messages about change, what they are listening for depends on their culture. Germans, Meston says, are primarily interested in the details of how the change will take place, not in why it will occur. German workers appreciate a well-documented plan. In contrast, workers in the United States and United Kingdom expect a clear rationale for the change. Managers who successfully implement a change in these countries devote much more effort to messages that prove the change makes sense.[43]

The problems of cross-cultural communication are further complicated when people speak different languages. Either the sender of the message must determine how to encode it in the receiver's language, or the receiver must figure out how to decode it. The use of translators is an obvious solution, but it increases the likelihood that a message will be distorted (in this case, by errors in translation). The sender may also use nonverbal cues,

exhibit | 9.7
Tips for Cross-Cultural Communication

- Expect that a person from another culture is likely to have a different communication style.
- When people are unexpectedly loud or quiet, formal or informal, argumentative or conciliatory, consider that this may be a culturally based style.
- If the receiver does not seem to understand the message, explore whether it includes terms that are outside the receiver's frame of reference (for example, the Russian language does not have an exact term for *efficiency,* and Thais have no word for *no*).
- Use language that describes rather than interprets or evaluates. Description is less culturally based.
- Learn about the other people in the communication process.
- Use your knowledge about others to empathize with them.
- When you begin to interpret a situation, treat your interpretations as a hypothesis to explore together, rather than a definite conclusion.
- Seek and use feedback as much as possible.

Source: Based on ideas from M. Munter, "Cross-Cultural Communication for Managers," *Business Horizons,* May–June 1993, pp. 75–76; and N. Adler, *International Dimensions of Organizational Behavior,* 2nd ed. (Boston: PWS-Kent, 1991), pp. 83–84.

such as symbols and facial expressions, to convey meaning that does not depend on a shared language. (However, nonverbal cues, too, often vary among cultures.) In addition, the act of encoding a message into the receiver's language is itself a nonverbal message that the sender respects the receiver.

Because cross-cultural communication is so important in contemporary organizations, people enhance their value to the organization when they develop those skills. People can learn two or more languages. They also can learn about the communication practices of other cultures so that they correctly interpret such nonverbal cues as silences, nods, and smiles. Exhibit 9.7 provides suggestions for improving cross-cultural communication.

Communication in a Learning Organization

Learning organizations require all employees to make their knowledge available to others in the organization. Thomas Brailsford, manager of knowledge leadership at Hallmark Cards, puts the importance of sharing knowledge this way: "Knowledge has no value until it moves. . . . If I share what I know with you, I still own it. But now you own it, too, and it has grown in value."[44]

The sharing of knowledge is what enables the organization as a whole to learn. Consequently, learning organizations need a flow of communication unimpaired by distinctions of hierarchy, function, or department. They require **open communication,** or communication that involves sharing all types of information among all members of the organization. One organization that has fostered open communication is Bankers Trust (now part of Deutsche Bank), described in the following example.

open communication

Communication that involves sharing all types of information among all members of the organization.

Bankers Trust

Bankers Trust was one of the early companies to hop on the knowledge management bandwagon. The company's appreciation for sharing knowledge was a logical extension of its slogan, "Architects of Value." For a financial firm like Bankers Trust, the main source of value is its knowledge—about financial markets and about its customers' needs.

Bankers Trust set up systems and technologies that would make information sharing natural. Whenever a group of employees completes a project, the company brings together experts to assess the project. They answer a series of ten questions tailored to their particular area of expertise. The information from these sessions is entered into the company's intranet. Then, when another employee has a project with similar characteristics, the employee can use the intranet to learn from colleagues' experiences. All employees have access to this system.

Still, the company does not use technology as a substitute for face-to-face interactions. Leadership development, for example, is far more than a matter of reading data on a computer screen. For this challenge, Bankers Trust brings together its executives in a single location.

Some time after establishing its knowledge management practices, Bankers Trust was acquired by Deutsche Bank, a German banking giant. This change places its people squarely in an international environment. The experience in sharing information should equip Bankers Trust employees to make a smooth transition.[45]

Open communication, according to noted consultant Peter Drucker, is above all an interpersonal activity. That is, the sharing of information starts, not with information-processing equipment, but with the interaction of people. Information is "the key resource" of knowledge workers, and knowledge workers depend on one another to provide that essential information.[46] This places a dual responsibility on these people:

- They must determine what information they owe to others in the organization.
- They must determine what information they need from others in the organization.

Thus, a learning organization requires that its people communicate the information they owe, and this in turn requires that they communicate with others to learn their needs. Employees and managers also must be ready and willing to ask for what information they need. We will examine the topic of learning organizations in depth in Chapter 18.

apply it

1. What communications technology (e.g., word processor, telephone, pager) do you own or have access to? How does it help you communicate? How does it make effective communication more difficult for you?
2. If you were to take a business trip to Korea, what communication challenges would you expect to face? What skills and knowledge would help you? What would you want to learn before you go?

Individuals and organizations can improve communication

The principles of communication described in this chapter lay a foundation for improving communication in organizations. As with any other skill set, individuals can improve their ability to communicate. The key is to select specific improvements and to work on one or a few at a time. Organizations can also enhance communication by providing a favorable context for it.

Improving Personal Communication Skills

Organizations need employees with effective communication skills, especially since so much work is accomplished in teams. And team members often have different areas of expertise. E. Kelly Hansen, who heads Sun Tzu Security Ltd., a computer forensics company, appreciates the importance of communications skills, especially among technical people. Rather than believing technical expertise is a substitute for the ability to communicate, Hansen says organizations require technical people who can interact with nontechnical staff:

> It's imperative that employees regard [the technical expert] as a knowledgeable guide who's willing to show them the ins and outs of the network, and even to do some hand-holding when it's called for. If your employees are afraid to ask the scary techie a question, they may never learn how to properly use your computer system. In the end, mistakes will be made and data lost.[47]

Therefore, Sun Tzu and other organizations try to recruit and retain people who can communicate effectively.

Skills of Senders Effective communication combines many skills. Effective communicators see situations from the receiver's perspective so that they encode messages in ways that are both interesting and understandable. They speak and write clearly, and they match nonverbal cues to their words. At times when they are too emotional to do this, they give themselves time to calm down before communicating. In addition, effective communicators seek and pay attention to feedback. Exhibit 9.8 summarizes some tips for communicating clearly.

Effective communicators also choose the best channel for the message and receiver. They choose rich channels for nonroutine, complex, or sensitive messages.[48] They select more efficient channels for simple and routine messages. As president of Robin's Food Distribution, Robin Wold is frus-

exhibit | **9.8**

Tips for Clear Communication

- Think about who your audience is.
- Avoid jargon unless your audience uses the same terms.
- Use simple language (e.g., "before," not "in advance of").
- Avoid slang and metaphors (e.g., "hit a home run" for "succeed"), unless you are certain they are familiar to your audience.
- Use polite language.
- Watch for nonverbal and verbal cues that indicate the receiver understands the message.
- Invite questions to clarify your message.
- Match your nonverbal and verbal messages.
- State your feelings in terms of yourself ("I feel frustrated," not "You are frustrating").
- Be specific ("I would still like a chance to discuss my idea," not "Everyone always ignores my ideas").
- Send trustworthy messages; avoid filtering.

trated when people "hide behind" impersonal media like e-mail to deliver unpleasant news. Wold is quick to call the people affected when problems arise, so that they can collaborate on a solution.[49] When appropriate, effective communicators also try to add richness to the channels they select. For example, when giving a speech, they include visual aids or multimedia presentations and allow plenty of time for questions.

Effective communicators are also aware that some communication channels are public or create a permanent record, and they choose their words carefully when using such channels. As an illustration of what can happen in public channels, Mark McNutt responded to an *Inc.* article discussing the Web site for his company, Krystal Kleen Karpet Kare, with a posting on his Web site. Visitors to the site quickly took sides in the dispute, so it was no longer a disagreement between two parties but a kind of online warfare.[50] The lesson for communicators is, If you don't want the whole world to know you're angry, don't express your anger on the Internet.

Interpretation Skills   Both sender and receiver can enhance their communication skills by making a special effort to understand one another. They can observe implied as well as explicit messages and compare verbal and nonverbal cues. They can also check their assumptions with one another, to correct any misconceptions. And if the receiver does not automatically offer feedback, the sender can request it.

Especially in a diverse group (for example, both genders or people from more than one cultural background or even different regions of the United States), people should watch for indications that others have different ideas about appropriate ways to communicate. For example, do some members of a group always defer to the leader, or do some tend to speak louder and more assertively? These different behaviors may reflect differences of opinion, personality, or cultural norms. Understanding the source of the differences can improve the group's ability to communicate.

Listening Skills   In the case of oral communication, skillful receipt of messages means listening well. **Listening** is the process of hearing and interpreting the meaning of a spoken message. A listener interprets by decoding not only the words of a message but also nonverbal cues such as the speaker's behavior and tone of voice. Together, these cues provide information about facts and about the speaker's emotions and intentions.

Research supports the widely accepted opinion that most people do not listen very well. In a study that measured the amount of material people remembered and understood from a ten-minute message, subjects remembered an average of about 25 percent of the material 48 hours after hearing the message.[51] In the context of organizational behavior, imagine what an advantage it would be to an organization for its people to hear, not 25 percent, but 100 percent of what its customers want and for its managers to hear 100 percent of employees' ideas!

Fortunately, people can improve their listening skills. They can do so by concentrating on the message, rather than on formulating a response. They can provide feedback that tests whether they have received the message fully and accurately. Finally, asking questions or occasionally putting the message into your own words can determine whether you heard it correctly. If a coworker says, "We have to work late tonight!" you might say, "It

listening

The process of hearing and interpreting the meaning of a spoken message.

sounds like you're worried we won't be ready for tomorrow's presentation." This encourages your colleague to communicate not only about the presentation the two of you will do the next day but also about his feelings. Through this active approach to listening, you and your colleague can identify and resolve the challenges of preparing and delivering the presentation.

Lowering Organizational Barriers to Effective Communication

What seem to be "communication problems" sometimes have sources other than individuals' failure to speak, write, listen, or read well. Sometimes barriers arise at the organizational level—for example, the organization's structure, culture, or work design may discourage effective communication among people who could benefit from sharing knowledge. To overcome such barriers, organizations can encourage communication by providing formal communication channels. They can encourage communication through these channels in all directions and in an open manner.

Encouraging Communication in All Directions   Organizations crush barriers to communication by establishing adequate channels for communication in all directions: upward, downward, and horizontally. For example, Motley Fool, a popular online provider of investor education, set up a kind of electronic suggestion box for its employees to help encourage communication horizontally and up the hierarchy. The company invited employees to use the company's intranet to make anonymous suggestions for improving one another's job performance. Motley Fool was interested in honest but constructive criticism that was not tied to performance review. The goal is to help all employees improve performance before bonuses are awarded.[52] Of course, such a system works only if the company responds to the suggestions and enables its people to implement the desired changes.

Haworth, a manufacturer of office furniture, established an official policy to encourage employee suggestions. Employees submit ideas to a committee, which decides whether to accept each idea, reject it, or forward it to a specialist for further study. If the idea is rejected, the employee gets a thank-you note explaining why the idea was turned down. If the suggestion is accepted, the employee receives a monetary reward along with the satisfaction of seeing the idea put into practice. If employees choose to discuss their suggestions with their supervisors, the supervisors may offer comments but may not dismiss the idea. Haworth instituted this policy because it found that many employee suggestions had been rejected by supervisors.[53] Notice that this program provides for feedback to employees; they can see a response to their suggestion.

The Phelps Group establishes regular horizontal communication in weekly meetings that bring together the marketing agency's 50 employees. At each of these Monday morning meetings, teams present their current work, the employees hear announcements about important new business, and then every team has one minute to present a mini-lesson on topics ranging from a recent business article worth reading to how to unjam the photocopier. The company's CEO, Joe Phelps, views these meetings as an opportunity to build team spirit by getting employees to leave their computer screens and connect face to face.[54]

Enabling Communication through Appropriate Channels Organizations should regularly review the existing channels, looking for a mix of written, oral, and nonverbal communications. Do managers routinely discuss issues openly with employees, as well as provide performance appraisals and reports of the company's progress? Do employees contribute ideas and questions through reports, employee surveys, suggestion forms, and informal meetings? Does the organization simplify interdepartmental communication through intranets, cross-functional teams, and workplace layouts? If not, the organization can lower communication barriers by establishing these and other channels for communication.

For example, communication in an organization as large as General Electric can be difficult, so GE creates opportunities. Four times a year, GE's 40 top executives meet for two days to share what they have learned. The atmosphere is informal, to encourage openness. Similarly, Southwest Airlines fosters communication by encouraging its employees to call anyone in the organization if they have questions. In the words of CEO Herb Kelleher, "If you're a ramp aide in Los Angeles and you want to know something about Southwest Airlines, call the finance office, call the chief financial officer and ask him what you want to know."[55]

Smaller organizations can also apply these principles. As described in the following example, Quantum intentionally designed its work areas to encourage communication among employees.

If you have an appointment with an executive at Quantum in Milpitas, California, don't bother looking for a corner office with a great view. Quantum execs get assigned to offices in the middle of the floor, far from any windows. That's because Quantum, which boasts it has the world's highest volume in sales of hard disk drives for personal computers, has set up its work areas to foster creativity and collaboration among employees.

The design of Quantum's two headquarters buildings takes its inspiration from biology. Each building is shaped like an amoeba, wrapped in a membrane of floor-to-ceiling windows. At the center of each is a nucleus of executive offices. Around them are the employees, who work in low-walled cubicles, open to light from the windows. The objective of this design was to create a sense of open space to signal that the company values openness and informality, rather than hierarchical distinctions. The same principles apply to Quantum's facilities in Colorado, Massachusetts, Switzerland, and Ireland.

Quantum communicates its values through other nonverbal cues as well. The company has no dress code and no reserved parking spaces for managers. Everyone gets the same kind of furniture. Comfortable chairs are arranged to create seating areas near staircases and at the intersection of hallways: an invitation to sit down and swap ideas. Quantum's vice president of real estate, Norm Claus, calls the result "high-energy space."[56]

Managers can also open channels for communication through a practice called **management by wandering around (MBWA).** This is the practice of gathering information by visiting the workplace to observe and talk with employees. Managers who practice MBWA give their employees a chance to show what they are doing and to raise concerns and ideas. Their presence in the workplace sends a nonverbal message that managers are interested in employees' everyday activities and problems. In addition, the face-to-face communication provides a rich channel for managers to hear from employees.

management by wandering around (MBWA)

The practice of gathering information by visiting the workplace to observe and talk with employees.

Helping Employees Manage Information Overload   Besides encouraging communication in line with organizational goals, the organization can improve the quality of communications by helping employees manage information overload. For example, managers can evaluate whether they really need to encourage their employees to take a cell phone or computer on vacation to get "important" messages. Perhaps some of those messages can wait or be handled by someone who is not on vacation.

Sometimes technology provides solutions for managing a flood of information. For example, Wall Street on Demand, which compiles research reports for financial services companies, was flooded with so many e-mail messages that its customer service representatives were increasingly unable to provide quality service. The company bought a software package called the Internet Message Center, which identifies topics and routes messages to the appropriate employees. This relieves employees from sorting through all the messages to look for ones that are related to the area they serve.[57]

Facilitating Appropriate Networks   Organizations can also evaluate whether formal communications are expected to pass through networks suitable for the task at hand. As we saw earlier, centralized networks are most appropriate for simple, routine tasks. If the organization expects people to communicate about complex problems, it should not place many limits on who each person communicates with. Rather, the group will likely be more effective in a decentralized communication network.

As mentioned earlier, the grapevine can be a problem from an organization's perspective. When employees rely on the grapevine for information, rumors spread, and managers may not even know the content of those rumors. Organizations can gain more control over the communication process by providing plenty of information through formal channels. When employees believe they get enough information from downward communication, they are less apt to rely on the grapevine.

Cultivating Values That Support Open Communication   Perhaps most important, the organization can foster communication by cultivating a climate that values trust, openness, and learning. In contrast to the dysfunctional organization portrayed by the cartoon in Exhibit 9.9, organizations can state and reward values consistent with open communication. The resulting workplace atmosphere encourages employees to contribute their opinions and ideas. In addition, organizations can support employees who wish to learn communication skills through classes, seminars, and other training opportunities.

This kind of trust was essential to Mutual Group's decision to give employees access to the Internet. Some people worried that the access would cause employees to waste time, but the Canadian financial services company instead opted to trust employees with full use of this communication technology.[58] In Chapter 17, "Organizational Culture," we further explore how organizations cultivate desirable values.

apply it

1. Based on your self-knowledge coupled with what you have learned in this chapter, how might you improve your communication skills and practices? Which of these improvements will you work on first?

exhibit | **9.9**

An Organization with Low Trust and Poor Communication Practices

cathy®

by Cathy Guisewite

2. A software company has a reputation for failing to release new titles on the promised date. Its managers investigate and find a troubling pattern of communications: New-product schedules are developed at high levels of the organization and distributed to programmers and salespeople. When salespeople ask the programmers about products under development, the programmers say, "We're busy. Just read the schedule." The salespeople give their customers the dates from the official schedule, but the software is completed much later, and customers are unhappy. What problems in the organization might underlie the miscommunication? How might this organization encourage more constructive communication? Be as specific as you can.

summary OF KEY CONCEPTS

- **Communication is an interpersonal process.** Communication involves two or more people exchanging information using a shared set of symbols. In organizations people communicate to achieve organizational objectives and meet personal needs. The process involves several elements: A sender initiates communication by encoding a message, which the receiver then decodes, often providing feedback as well. Distortion, called noise, can obscure the meaning of the intended message.

- **Communication in organizations follows various patterns.** The sender selects from among communication channels, which fall into the categories of written, oral, and nonverbal communica-

tion. These vary in terms of their channel richness. In addition, organizational communication may travel downward, upward, or horizontally in terms of the organization's hierarchy. It may be formal or informal. Communication in organizations follows paths called communication networks, which may be centralized or decentralized.

- **Communication in today's organizations is challenging.** Technology provides many channels that enable communication anytime, anywhere. This provides opportunities but also can exhaust the communicators. In addition, technology sometimes enables people to choose impersonal channels even when they would benefit from more direct interaction. The increasing amount of messages sent across differing cultures and languages also complicates communication. Culturally based assumptions about a message's meaning may be incorrect. At the same time, the importance of learning in today's organizations creates a requirement for open communication.

- **Individuals and organizations can improve communication.** Individuals can learn to craft messages that take into account the receiver's point of view, and they can develop effective listening skills. Organizations can lower barriers to communication by establishing adequate and appropriate channels for communication in all directions. They also can help employees manage information overload, as well as create a climate of openness and trust.

KEY terms

communication, p. 304
encoding, p. 306
message, p. 306
decoding, p. 306
feedback, p. 306
noise, p. 307
filtering, p. 308
channel, p. 310
written communication, p. 310

channel richness, p. 311
oral communication, p. 312
nonverbal communication, p. 312
downward communication, p. 313
upward communication, p. 314
horizontal communication, p. 314
formal communication, p. 314
informal communication, p. 315
grapevine, p. 315

gossip chain, p. 315
cluster chain, p. 315
communication network, p. 316
centralized network, p. 316
decentralized network, p. 317
open communication, p. 322
listening, p. 325
management by wandering around (MBWA), p. 327

DISCUSSION questions

1. What might be some of the consequences to a design department if the manager of that department was not a good communicator?

2. How might a worker enhance his or her status in an organization through good communication?

3. Think of a conversation you recently had with someone. Try to list all the examples of feedback you gave that person while he or she was speaking; then list the feedback he or she gave you. Did the feedback enhance the communication? Why or why not?

4. Suppose you got a message from your boss that said, "See me ASAP." What assumptions has your boss made in encoding this message? In what ways might the message become distorted?

5. Suppose you had to deliver a message to a valued customer that a product he or she relied on was no longer available. Which medium would you choose to deliver this message? Why?

6. Do you think there is ever a business or work situation in which filtering information is ethical or appropriate? If so, describe the situation and why you think filtering is appropriate. If not, explain why not.

7. Suppose you arrived at your favorite store, ready to shop, only to find the windows dark and a handwritten sign hanging in the window that said "Closed." How would you decode this message? What factors might come into play as you formulate your interpretation? How might someone who had never been to the store before decode the message?

8. At many companies, employee performance reviews are given both in writing and in some type of personal conference. What are the advantages to using both of these types of communication?

9. The art director for a greeting card company is planning to give a presentation to staff members during which she will reveal some of her favorite designs from a new line of cards. Based on what you know about face-to-face communication from Albert Mehrabian's study, what considerations might she make as she prepares her presentation in order to give her message the greatest impact?

10. What types of formal communication take place at your current job (or a job you have recently had)? What types of informal communication take place? On which do you rely the most? Why?

11. Do you believe that a manager should take a computer and/or cell phone on vacation in order to stay in touch with the office? Why or why not?

12. The head of a chain of home improvement stores has decided that the organization must engage in open communication. What responsibilities are thus placed upon the managers of each of the stores?

13. As a worker, would you feel comfortable with your manager practicing MBWA? Why or why not?

S E L F – D I S C O V E R Y exercise

Listening Self-Assessment

Instructions: Choose one response for each of the items below. Base your choice on what you usually do, not on what you think a person should do.

___ 1. When you are going to lunch with a friend, you:
   a. focus your attention on the menu and then on the service provided.
   b. ask about events in your friend's life and pay attention to what's said.
   c. exchange summaries of what is happening to each of you while focusing attention on the meal.

___ 2. When someone talks nonstop, you:
   a. ask questions at an appropriate time in an attempt to help the person focus on the issue.
   b. make an excuse to end the conversation.
   c. try to be patient and understand what you are being told.

___ 3. If a group member complains about a fellow employee who, you believe, is disrupting the group, you:
   a. pay attention and withhold your opinions.
   b. share your own experiences and feelings about that employee.
   c. acknowledge the group member's feelings and ask the group member what options he or she has.

___ 4. If someone is critical of you, you:
   a. try not to react or get upset.
   b. automatically become curious and attempt to learn more.
   c. listen attentively and then back up your position.

___ 5. You are having a very busy day and someone tells you to change the way you are completing a task. You believe the person is wrong, so you:
   a. thank her or him for the input and keep doing what you were doing.
   b. try to find out why she or he thinks you should change.
   c. acknowledge that the other may be right, tell her or him you are very busy, and agree to follow up later.

___ 6. When you are ready to respond to someone else, you:
   a. sometimes will interrupt the person if you believe it is necessary.
   b. almost always speak before the other is completely finished talking.
   c. rarely offer your response until you believe the other has finished.

___ 7. After a big argument with someone you have to work with every day, you:
   a. settle yourself and then try to understand the other's point of view before stating your side again.
   b. just try to go forward and let bygones be bygones.
   c. continue to press your position.

___ 8. A colleague calls to tell you that he is upset about getting assigned to a new job. You decide to:
   a. ask him if he can think of options to help him deal with the situation.
   b. assure him that he is good at what he does and that these things have a way of working out for the best.
   c. let him know you have heard how badly he feels.

___ 9. If a friend always complains about her problems but never asks about yours, you:
   a. try to identify areas of common interest.
   b. remain understanding and attentive, even if it becomes tedious.
   c. support her complaints and mention your own complaints.

___ **10.** The best way to remain calm in an argument is to:

    a. continue to repeat your position in a firm but even manner.

    b. repeat what you believe is the other person's position.

    c. tell the other person that you are willing to discuss the matter again when you are both calmer.

Score each item of your Listening Self-Assessment

1. (a)	0	(b)	10	(c)	5
2. (a)	10	(b)	0	(c)	5
3. (a)	5	(b)	0	(c)	5
4. (a)	5	(b)	10	(c)	0
5. (a)	0	(b)	10	(c)	5
6. (a)	5	(b)	0	(c)	10
7. (a)	10	(b)	5	(c)	0
8. (a)	5	(b)	5	(c)	10
9. (a)	0	(b)	10	(c)	5
10. (a)	0	(b)	10	(c)	5

Add up your total score _____

80–100 You are an active, excellent listener. You achieve a good balance between listening and asking questions, and you strive to understand others.

50–75 You are an adequate-to-good listener. You listen well, although you may sometimes react too quickly to others before they are finished speaking.

25–45 You have some listening skills but need to improve them. You may often become impatient when trying to listen to others, hoping they will finish talking so you can talk.

0–20 You listen to others very infrequently. You may prefer to do all of the talking and experience extreme frustration while waiting for others to make their point.

Source: Reprinted with permission of the publisher. From *Managers As Facilitators,* pp. 134–136, copyright 1997 by Richard G. Weaver and John D. Farrell, Berrett–Koehler Publishers, Inc. San Francisco, CA. All rights reserved. 1-800-929-2929.

ORGANIZATIONAL BEHAVIOR in your life

In one day, you probably send and receive hundreds of messages. Keep a communication diary for a day: log in as many messages that you send and receive as you can. Note the channel of communication, any feedback that takes place, and whether or not you feel the communication was effective. Note also whether you feel overwhelmed by the amount of information and communication you receive in a day. Is this due to technology? Share the results of your communication diary with the class.

ORGANIZATIONAL BEHAVIOR news flash

@ It seems that Microsoft and its billionaire chief, Bill Gates, are hardly ever far from the news headlines, particularly since a court ruling that the company has engaged in monopolistic practices. Using either the listings on your Internet search engines—Reuters, AP, ZDNet News—or the key word Microsoft, see what you can find out about the way this organization communicates in light of so much controversy. (If you don't have Internet access, then head to the library for newspapers and news magazines.) When you find two or three good stories, download them and print them out. Then imagine that you are a spokesperson for Microsoft and write a brief outline for a plan of communication for (1) Microsoft workers and (2) the general public. Include your choice of channels for communication, the brief message itself, and your plan for handling feedback. (Note that the message is entirely up to you—you may decide to refute criticisms of the company, accept them, or deal with any other relevant matter.)

global diversity EVENTS

On October 31, 1999, a terrible human tragedy took place: Egypt Air Flight 990 plunged into the ocean off the island of Nantucket, Massachusetts, killing more than 200 people. Within a few days, it became apparent that this was not only a human tragedy, but also a tragedy of communication. American investigators interpreted statements made by the Egyptian copilot in a potentially incriminating way; members of the Egypt Air organization, as well as Egyptian citizens and journalists, interpreted the statements differently and accused Americans of jumping to conclusions based on stereotypes of Middle Eastern culture and religion. Thus, the U.S. National Transportation Safety Board, the FBI, Egypt Air, and various Egyptian government officials became embroiled in disagreements that were only intensified by the media on both sides.

Using the news listings on your search engine, such as Reuters, AP, ZDNet News, or the like, look for a story about an unfortunate event that involves more than one culture and the complications of communi-

cation in the situation. When you find a relevant story, consider the following:

1. Try to determine how the situation might have been avoided or improved if communication had been more effective.

2. Which communication channels might have been the best choice?

3. Imagine that you are a journalist covering the event or situation. Write an editorial on the subject, referring to communication as one of the factors either in the cause or the outcome of the situation.

Source: Farnaz Fassihi, "Egypt Recoils from Suicide Speculation," *The Providence Journal,* accessed on Yahoo! News, November 18, 1999; "Suicide Theory Takes Center Stage in Egypt Air Probe," (AFP), The Yahoo! Daily News, November 17, 1999; "Egypt Air Accuses U.S. of Jumping to Conclusions In Crash Probe," (AFP), Yahoo! Singapore-News, November 17, 1999.

minicase ISSUE

How an Entrepreneur Keeps in Touch with Everyone

Lely Barea seems to have it all—a great job at a successful company she helped start, three beautiful daughters, a Mercedes in which to zoom around Miami. She also seems to manage it all without a briefcase—instead, she relies on her cell phone. Understanding Barea's attachment to her phone is vital to understanding the way she operates her business, Ibiley Uniforms. Communication is her organization's lifeblood.

Staying in touch. Ibiley Uniforms, cofounded by Lely and Eddy Barea, supplies uniforms to public and private schoolchildren, to the tune of $7 million in sales a year. While the business is based in Miami (with six stores), the Bareas recently moved some of their manufacturing operations to Santo Domingo (capital city of the Dominican Republic in the Caribbean) and are planning to launch a nationwide wholesale business in the United States. Lely oversees design, manufacturing, and distribution, while Eddy handles marketing, sales, and finance. All of these ac-

tivities require staying in touch with employees, plant managers, distributors, and so forth. Lely values personal communication, regardless of the channel (although it's usually the phone). Whenever possible, she holds brief, daily meetings with Miami store managers before the stores open or after they close. She sends clear messages through her actions: She is never late for an appointment (she manages this by planning each day well in advance). Before attending a meeting with a store manager, Lely consults her electronic personnel file so that she can ask the manager pertinent questions without wasting time on background knowledge. She takes notes during the meetings and enters more information into the file. Finally, Lely has equipped all 24 managers who report directly to her with identical cell phones; she expects them to use the phones as vigorously as she uses her own.

Keeping Things Simple. Perhaps the secret to managing a complicated business and life is keeping things simple. Lely is highly organized and conducts her communication that way as well. She thrives on both upward and downward communication throughout her organization, but likes it to be as uniform as the clothes she manufactures. For instance, although the 24 identical cell phones cost about $200 apiece, when she has one message to deliver to several people at once, all she has to do is push a preprogrammed button, which connects her with her recipients, and broadcast the message once. Lely also prides herself on efficient delegation. Because she spends so much time traveling from store to store (and to Santo Domingo) in order to meet with managers and practice a bit of MBWA, she entrusts much of her paperwork to other employees. That way, the hours of her day are spent almost entirely on personal interaction with others, which she sees as crucial to the success of her organization. Finally, Lely keeps things simple by acting on issues immediately rather than saving them for later (her motto is "do it

now"). For instance, if she notices something is out of place in a store, she notifies the manager on the spot and expects the correction to take place right away. Thus, the message is sent, the issue is dealt with, and Lely is back in her Mercedes, racing toward her next destination.

1. Would you like to work for Lely Barea? Why or why not?

2. If Ibiley Uniforms became a larger organization, do you think that Lely's communication style would be as effective? Why or why not?

3. In what ways might you use some of Lely's communication methods at your own job?

Source: Emily Esterson, "A Wise Consistency," *Inc. Technology,* no. 3, 1998, pp. 37–38.

ten
C H A P T E R

10

Decision Making in Organizations

preview

After studying this chapter, you should be able to:

- Detail the process by which people make decisions in various situations.

- Distinguish between practices that result in optimal decisions and those that result in merely acceptable decisions.

- Identify influences on a person's or group's choice of a solution.

- Explain when and how to use group decision making.

- Describe ways to apply creativity to decision making.

- Summarize challenges that face decision makers in today's organizations.

Project Bark's Creator Makes Decisions to Shape His Organization

Few business activities involve more decisions than a start-up, particularly in the uncertain environment of high-tech Internet business. New entrepreneurs are forging ahead with creative ideas, trying to make good decisions with limited information, with few existing models to follow, and in a veil of secrecy to avoid giving competitors an edge. The mystery surrounding Project Bark (a code name for a start-up venture), cofounded by Pete Blackshaw and two partners, provides the perfect backdrop for examining the way organizations make decisions. Blackshaw wouldn't reveal much about the company before it opened its virtual doors on the Internet, but his decisions could affect not only his own company but an inner-city neighborhood as well.

Blackshaw (formerly with Procter & Gamble) and his partners decided to locate Project Bark in a loft in the middle of Cincinnati's bar and restaurant district, called Over-the-Rhine. Why not California or New York? Indeed, Blackshaw notes with humor, "Some of my California friends think I'm crazy, but I really think this is a wonderful place to start a business." Blackshaw based his location decision on certain criteria. First, rent for office space in downtown Cincinnati is cheap, so start-up capital wouldn't be swallowed by overhead expenses. Second, Cincinnati Bell's high-speed network is available and inexpensive. Third, the quirky neighborhood attracts the kind of young, innovative people Blackshaw would like to hire. "There's a lot of young people who work for these kinds of companies," notes real estate broker Larry Rytel of Colliers International. "They like the informal atmosphere." In fact, the neighborhood's pubs and restaurants became informal meeting places for Blackshaw and other Internet entrepreneurs, who ultimately formed the nonprofit group Main Street Ventures, which hopes to turn the neighborhood into a mecca for programmers, Web designers, and other high-tech professionals.

Blackshaw is not alone in his assessment of the potential of Cincinnati's Over-the-Rhine. He received venture funding from Blue Chip sources and others, who concurred with his decision. Shawn Reynolds of VisualNet agrees that the future of the area is bright, as do the founders of Ethos Interactive, Digital Bang, and Synchrony Communications, all of which are located there.

Blackshaw and other entrepreneurs like him chose their location from a number of alternatives, based on criteria that they believed were important or valuable. They were able to think creatively in making their decisions, and they were willing to accept a certain amount of risk. Perhaps these traits attracted investors to these high-tech companies in the first place. Regardless of what products each new Over-the-Rhine company decides to offer, the way they arrive at their decisions may predict their success better than any other factor. Ultimately, these decisions will not only affect the future of a Midwestern city but may change the way future Internet companies get their starts.[1]

People in organizations make decisions daily—from location decisions for a start-up company such as Project Bark to more routine decisions such as the amount of inventory to carry or reassignment of staff to handle a high-priority project. Regardless of the type of decision, the consequences affect an organization, its people, and its customers and suppliers. In today's fast-paced world, decisions need to be made as quickly and as accurately as possible, often without complete information at hand. And in today's lean organizations with their increasing emphasis on employee empowerment, decisions are also being pushed to lower levels so that the people most knowledgeable about an opportunity or problem can head off problems or respond effectively. It is critical that all members of an organization understand the concepts and processes of sound decision making.

This chapter begins by describing how an organization's people can and should carry out the process of making decisions. Next, we examine several influences on the choice of a solution. We then examine the use of groups to make decisions, including techniques for group problem solving. The next section covers the importance of creativity to organizational decisions and ways that organizations can foster creativity. Finally, we address several challenges that arise in organizational decision making.

Decision making is a multistep process

People make decisions all the time. You have decided to further your education by taking this course. Executives decide whether to hire a new employee or whether to conduct business on the Internet. In making decisions, people look at the alternatives and choose what seems to be the best option. Thus, a **decision** is a choice made from available alternatives. However, the process of decision making involves much more than a simple choice. Rather, **decision making** is the process of identifying problems and opportunities, then resolving them.[2] This process requires activity both before and after the choice itself. The decision maker recognizes the need for a decision, identifies one or more alternatives, weighs them, makes a choice, and follows up to implement the decision and evaluate the results.

This combination of activities is what Norm Brodsky did when he was running his 15-year-old messenger service and beginning to develop a records-storage business in a warehouse. Brodsky began the decision-making process when he noticed that problems at the warehouse were taking up an increasingly larger share of his time. He investigated and realized that the storage operations had a lot of business potential, assuming he spent even more time at the warehouse. As Brodsky explored further, he realized that if he moved all his business to the warehouse, he not only could develop the records storage business but would save money by operating only one location. Brodsky hated the thought of moving, however, so he considered every drawback of this alternative. His analysis showed that all the negatives could be overcome if he planned the move carefully, so Brodsky moved his messenger business to the warehouse. He later concluded that the change brought the company even more benefits than he had originally anticipated. In particular, starting fresh at a new location enabled the company to set up more modern information systems, which were critical to both the messenger service and records-storage businesses, as well as establish new procedures that built on the company's years of experience.[3]

Understanding decision making as a multistep process sheds light on how to make decisions effectively. A good decision maker does much more than select the best alternative from a known set of possibilities. He or she recognizes problems and opportunities when they arise, defines these

decision

A choice made from available alternatives.

decision making

The process of identifying problems and opportunities, then resolving them.

situations accurately, appropriately uses either predefined or creative criteria for evaluation, picks a good alternative, and follows through with the decision. As we will see later, an effective decision maker also knows when and how much to involve others in this process.

The specifics of the decision-making process vary, and people do not always use the same form of the process. Consequently, the theory of decision making includes more than one model. Let's look first at a "rational" and then at a "behavioral" model of decision making, keeping in mind that individual decision makers vary in how strictly they follow either process.

Rational Model of Decision Making

rational model

A model of decision making that applies principles of logic and economics to describe how a person would arrive at an optimal solution.

normative

Telling what people should do, not necessarily how they actually behave.

The **rational model** of decision making applies principles of logic and economics to describe how a person would arrive at an optimal solution.[4] Organizations benefit from solutions that are logically and economically optimal, so they presumably want decision makers to use the process described by the rational model. This model of decision making is **normative,** meaning it tells what people *should* do, not necessarily how they behave all the time in real life.

According to the rational model, decision making ideally involves the following steps, illustrated in Exhibit 10.1:

1. The decision maker establishes the scope of the decision situation (problem or opportunity) and the goal of the decision. This step assumes that it is possible to define the situation and desired solution accurately.[5] It also assumes the decision maker will do so logically.

exhibit **10.1**

Rational Model of Decision Making

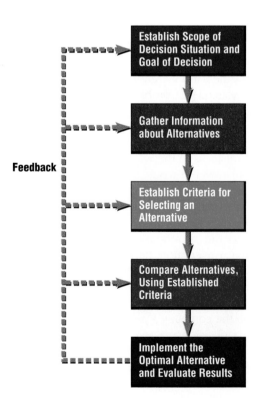

2. The decision maker gathers information about the alternative solutions, including their costs and probable outcomes. This step assumes that the decision maker can identify all the possible alternatives and estimate their costs and probability of success.

3. The decision maker establishes criteria for selecting an alternative, weighting the importance of each criterion. This involves recognizing relevant criteria and discarding irrelevant criteria, so that focusing on the selected criteria will actually address the decision maker's goals.

4. The decision maker compares the alternatives in terms of the criteria to be used and selects the one that is optimal. This step assumes the decision maker will assign values accurately and logically and will make the decision based strictly on these values.

5. The decision maker implements the decision and evaluates the results, gaining knowledge to apply to future decisions. This step assumes the decision maker can implement the alternative and can objectively measure its outcome.

Throughout this process, the rational model assumes that the decision maker is guided only by logical objectives, particularly the long-term performance of the organization. Other issues—such as fear, time pressure, political constraints, or shareholder demands for dramatic results—presumably do not shape the process, unless a rational decision maker determines they would affect the expected outcome. Of course, this leaves room for decision makers to decide what is rational and relevant. Many Internet retailers concluded that the fourth quarter of 1999 was the Christmas season that would determine which companies would gain enough market share to succeed in cyberspace. Therefore, they established attracting the largest number of customers as their desired objective, rather than profits, at least for the short term.[6] Time will tell whether they were correct, or even truly rational.

The goal of the rational model is **optimizing,** which means reaching the best possible decision. Decision-making techniques taught in finance and accounting courses are attempts to optimize in an economic sense. To optimize consistently, decision makers need complete knowledge about the alternatives and the criteria for comparing the alternatives. Complete knowledge is not a normal human condition, however; even when it is theoretically possible, acquiring it tends to be expensive and time consuming. So, people really apply the rational model only in an approximate way.

Although the rational model is an ideal, organizations do apply its principles. In highly complex, potentially costly situations, the risks are high, so decision makers strive to use the rational model. They try to define problems and goals precisely, to uncover all the alternatives, and to weigh them objectively. For example, in decisions about whether to expand into a new market or purchase expensive machinery, people often use mathematical models designed to compare the alternatives and select the one with the greatest expected payoff. Similarly, the following example describes how a decision maker at L. L. Bean uses elements of the rational model by trying to apply rational criteria when choosing the company's suppliers.

optimizing

Reaching the best possible decision.

🐾 L. L. Bean

As L. L. Bean's vice president of product acquisition, Rol Fessenden decides which manufacturers will provide the retailer's hunting boots and other rugged outdoor wear. He evaluates factories in dozens of countries and applies three criteria: product quality, delivery reliability, and price, in that order.

Putting price third in priority is rational, according to Fessenden. The reason is that price is only a portion of the total cost borne by L. L. Bean. The company, which stakes its reputation on its high-performance merchandise, also bears costs when products fall short of customers' expectations or fail to arrive when promised.

Fessenden's careful approach to evaluating alternatives prevents him from falling prey to stereotypes, such as the common opinion that foreign factories always offer the best deals. When he takes into account efficiency, quality, and reliability, he often finds the cost advantage of foreign factories to be small. A little more than half of the products sold by L. L. Bean are manufactured in the United States.

When Fessenden does approve a foreign supplier, he keeps an eye on working conditions at the overseas factories. This, too, is part of his rational approach. In his experience, companies that provide good working conditions are also careful about other aspects of running a business and therefore are more likely to meet Bean's criteria for quality and reliability. Comments Fessenden, "Where people mistreat employees, you tend to see reliability problems, too."[7]

As discussed later in this chapter, organizations also create policies and procedures to guide decision makers in evaluating general alternatives and provide standards for selecting an alternative. Then, when people make decisions in specific situations, they can complete the decision-making process. Finally, many organizations use decision-making software, and the software typically is based on the rational model. The software can help an organization's people adhere more closely to the rational model by speeding up the process. For example, it can show possible alternatives and apply the user's assumptions to forecast the expected payoff for each alternative.

Behavioral Model of Decision Making

Despite the help available from computers and other tools, people cannot always follow the rational model for decision making. Organizations are extremely complex, and managers do not always have time to follow a strictly rational approach. For example, Lillian Vernon, founder of the catalog company that bears her name, has said that her biggest mistake was failure to correctly define the problem and evaluate every alternative at a time when the prices of paper and postage unexpectedly rose. Faced with higher overhead costs, Vernon and her managers concluded the problem was shrinking profitability and that the solution was to raise the overall prices of the catalogs' product mix. Vernon cut out many of the catalogs' lower priced items, resulting in a higher end product mix, even though the lower priced items were the most popular among the company's customers. Fortunately, Vernon makes a practice of listening in on customer phone calls, and she quickly realized that the changes had alienated customers.[8] Like Vernon, many managers favor quick action over deliberate use of the rational decision-making model. They rely on easily recalled experiences and principles, often combining them in the form of "hunches" or "intuition."

Because the rational model does not describe a sizable share of the actual decision making in organizations, researchers have also explored the processes that people really use. Together, their observations form the basis of a **behavioral model** of decision making—that is, a model of how peo-

behavioral model

A model of decision making that describes how people actually behave throughout the decision-making process.

ple actually behave throughout the decision-making process. In contrast to the normative perspective of the rational model, the behavioral model is **descriptive.** In other words, it specifies what people *do,* not what they *should do.*

According to the behavioral model, people engage in **bounded rationality.**[9] This means they set limits on how rational they will be. People do this when they think, "I know flying is safer than driving, but I'm going to drive anyway because I prefer to feel more in control." Assuming that control versus safety are the only factors in the decision, it is based on emotions rather than logic. Similarly, the Institute of Medicine of the National Academy of Sciences found that fear may affect doctors' decisions on releasing information. Many decision-making errors occur in the U.S. medical system each year, resulting in tens of thousands of deaths annually. Establishing procedures and safeguards to correct sources of errors is difficult, not only because modern medical care is so complex, but also because many practitioners are reluctant to discuss their errors and near misses. According to surgeon and Yale professor Sherwin Nuland, this reluctance stems largely from the rise in malpractice claims and the greater likelihood that information will be made public. Doctors' fear then influences the process of analyzing the problems and making decisions that could lead to safeguards for patients.[10]

A major reason that people engage in bounded rationality is that considering all the alternatives can be impractical. The impact of a decision on the overall organization can affect the number of options considered. For example, it makes sense to evaluate all the possible suppliers of enterprise resource planning systems, information systems that are extremely expensive, available from only a few suppliers, complex, and can have a profound impact on the entire organization's performance and ultimate competitiveness. In contrast, researching all the possible suppliers of ballpoint pens would waste resources in most organizations. Likewise, most organizations will invest more time and money in considering alternative candidates for the job of CEO than they will in identifying one of a number of warehouse employees.

Especially for relatively low-risk decisions like buying pens or hiring warehouse employees, people engage in **satisficing**—choosing the first alternative they identify that meets minimal decision criteria.[11] For example, you might plan to buy any pens costing less than 90 cents apiece at the first store you pass on the way to work. Perhaps the store on the next block has the same pens for a nickel less, but the cost difference would not be worth the additional time. Thus, instead of optimizing (finding the absolutely lowest price), you satisfice.

A consequence of satisficing is that the order in which the decision maker considers the alternatives influences the choice of a solution. This differs from the rational model, where the decision maker ranks all the alternatives, so the order of evaluating them does not affect the decision. If a decision situation involves more than one acceptable alternative, the decision maker will select the first acceptable one, which may or may not be the best choice.

When more than one person is involved in making a decision, the process becomes more complex. The various decision makers contribute

descriptive
Specifying what people do, not necessarily what they should do.

bounded rationality
The practice of setting limits on how rational to be.

satisficing
Choosing the first alternative that meets minimal decision criteria.

different perceptions of the problem, the alternative solutions, and the criteria for selecting an alternative. For example, one member of the group may determine that a particular alternative will benefit both him and the organization, but that the personal benefit will be less important (or even negative) to others in the group. The alternative that he prefers may be influenced by his judgment of personal and group benefits. Thus, the behavioral model of decision making also includes the possibility that decisions will be more political—that is, shaped by compromises and alliances among decision makers. For example, Fed Chairman Alan Greenspan and Treasury Secretary Lawrence H. Summers are said to have similar approaches to decision making, as well as mutual respect. Because of their close relationship, each man's opinions have at times influenced the other's decisions.[12] For more on these topics, see Chapter 12, "Power and Politics," and Chapter 13, "Conflict Management and Negotiation."

Based on these observations about human behavior, we can sketch out a basic model of behavioral decision making that includes the steps shown in Exhibit 10.2:

1. Identify a decision situation (problem or opportunity) and try to achieve consensus on the nature of the situation and the type of solution required. In practice, people are most likely to identify decision situations when they are readily observable and affect a person's self-interests. This is consistent with the discussion of perception in Chapter 4.

2. Within the limits of time, energy, and expense available for making the decision, identify at least one alternative and seek agreement on the criteria to be used for evaluating the alternative(s). Try to choose criteria that support the decision maker's objectives.

exhibit | **10.2**

Behavioral Model of Decision Making

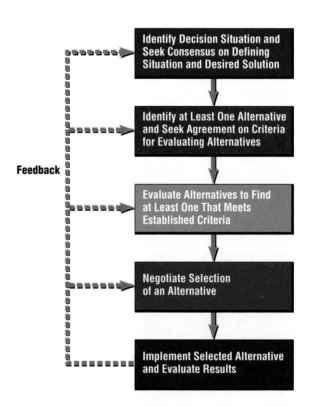

3. Evaluate alternatives until at least one meets the criteria. This tends to be an incremental process involving a series of comparisons.[13] Instead of objectively ranking all the options, decision makers compare a couple of similar alternatives in terms of limited criteria, looking for a basis to favor one alternative over another. The criteria for making these comparisons are often rules of thumb, discussed later under the topic of heuristics.

4. Negotiate the selection of an alternative to implement. This step recognizes that individual perceptions and personal objectives influence the choice of an alternative.

5. Implement the selected alternative and evaluate the results.

This process will not always generate the optimal decision. However, it may generate decisions that are at least minimally acceptable, take into account various points of view, and allocate resources to decision making in accordance with the importance of the decision.

Selection of a Decision-Making Process

Although bounded rationality and political behavior sometimes result in decisions that are less than optimal, the behavioral model of decision making may be desirable in some situations. Research has associated rational decision making with high performance in organizations whose environments are stable. In unstable environments requiring fast decisions, organizations performed best when decision makers used forms of the behavioral model.[14] Exhibit 10.3 compares these two approaches and lists conditions under which each is appropriate.

In practice, the rational model is the exception, rather than the rule, when people make decisions in organizations. People typically use the rational model only for decision situations that are simple, have few alternatives, and cost little to research.[15] For example, a company planning to invest in expensive equipment might solicit bids from the major suppliers and compare the bids based on quality, reliability, and cost. This approach approximates the rational model.

In contrast, when Aaron Fessler was an information systems administrator at a Washington, D.C., law firm, he was charged with connecting the firm's e-mail system to the Internet. He researched the project and concluded that doing it in-house would be very expensive. In 1995 when Fessler was investigating, the problem of how to proceed was open ended;

	Rational Model	**Behavioral Model**
Type of Model	Normative	Descriptive
Objective	Optimizing	Satisficing
Degree of Information	Complete	Partial
Appropriate Environment	Stable	Unstable
Level of Resources Required	High	Low to moderate

exhibit | **10.3**

Characteristics of the Decision-Making Models

there was no known set of alternatives for doing business in the age of the Internet. Fessler defined the problem from the standpoint of whether to complete his project as part of the law firm's staff or with a contractor specializing in this type of work—and then whether to become such a contractor himself. He decided to write up a business proposal and post it to an online newsgroup. In days he had received 200 replies from people interested in the proposed service. Based on that simple research, Fessler left the law firm to launch his new business, Allegro. In the unstable environment of the high-tech world, opportunities can be lost forever if decisions are not made quickly, so Fessler's choice worked out well for him.[16]

The rational and behavioral models do not have to be mutually exclusive, according to professors Howard Raiffa, John S. Hammond, and Ralph L. Keeney, who jointly authored the book *Smart Choices: A Practical Guide to Making Better Decisions*. They have instead described how people can use these processes together, with one informing the other. If, for example, a person attempts a formal analysis, but the conclusion conflicts with the person's intuition, the resulting discomfort can be a signal that further analysis is needed. Also, the systematic analysis can be used to test the assumptions that underlie the person's discomfort. In the same way, predetermined rational criteria can be useful for weighing the practicality of a proposed solution that matches a person's hopes and dreams. In an interview with *Inc.* magazine, Raiffa commented on the importance of including careful analysis in the decision-making process: "You may have a decision that was made by the seat of the pants and was not thought through clearly but that turned out miraculously well by luck. However, I think luck usually goes to the better decision maker."[17]

apply it

1. Describe a situation in which you made a decision consistent with the rational model of decision making and one in which your decision making resembled the behavioral model.
2. Which of these models does your decision making most often resemble? Why?

Situations shape the choice of a solution

The rational and behavioral models describe different ways of making decisions, but they do not explain why people use one approach or the other. By looking at various characteristics of the situation in which decision makers operate, we can see what shapes the choice of a solution, as well as the choice of a method for arriving at that solution.

Choice Processes

When making a choice, people can objectively evaluate as many alternatives as possible, or they can simplify the choice process in various ways. Exhibit 10.4 shows a contingency model that identifies criteria shaping the selection of a choice process. These criteria are characteristics of the task (the nature of the decision problem and the nature of the decision environ-

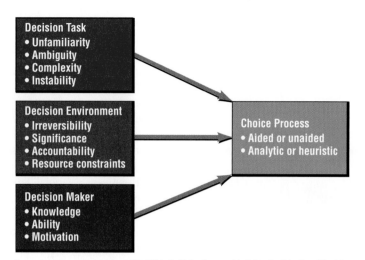

Source: Based on L. R. Beach and T. R. Mitchell, "A Contingency Model for the Selection of Decision Strategies," *Academy of Management Review*, July 1978, pp. 439–444.

exhibit | **10.4**
Criteria Shaping Selection of a Choice Process

ment) and characteristics of the decision maker. These criteria shape whether a choice will be aided or unaided, and whether it will be analytic or heuristic.

Aided and Unaided Choices An aided choice is one in which the decision maker uses tools to compare the alternatives. Decision-making tools include calculators, computer programs, and mathematical equations (for example, equations used in present-value analysis or cost minimization formulas). At Bluemount Nurseries, owner Nick Pindale uses an accounting technique called activity-based costing to identify which products are most profitable and which activities his company performs efficiently. Armed with this information, Pindale makes decisions about his product mix and work design.[18] Later in this chapter we discuss how information technology can aid in decision making. By providing access to more knowledge than most individuals or groups can easily recall on their own, information technology improves decision making in the turbulent, fast-paced environment of most modern organizations.

Another type of "tool" is to use additional human resources such as consultants to assist in analyzing the alternatives. For example, Ed Brookmyer, president of the Catalog Source, which supplies a variety of products to catalog retailers, uses a firm called Invent Resources to help him develop new product ideas. He approaches the company's scientists with ideas such as electronic luggage tags and an anti-ice spray for sidewalks, and they decide how the products can be manufactured to meet Brookmyer's general specifications.[19] Amazon.com gives its newer business partners, including Drugstore. com and Pets.com, a competitive advantage in the form of decision-making assistance. Every employee of these companies has a counterpart at Amazon.com who is available to serve as a kind of mentor. An employee at Pets.com can call his or her Amazon counterpart to get advice on business decisions.[20]

In contrast, to make unaided choices, decision makers rely on their own information and judgment. Albert W. Mandia used his judgment to

Health insurance coverage is one area in which decision makers must make rational decisions with as much information as possible. eHealthInsurance.com provides additional tools to help companies and individuals in their decision making. The company aids decision making by offering instant online quotes and price and benefit comparisons for a selection of health plans. It also offers live customer service agents at a toll free phone number to consult with potential applicants and answer their questions. Consumers can apply for health insurance through the eHealthInsurance.com site by taking the opportunity to "Click. Choose. Apply."
(Source: Courtesy of eHealthInsurance.com)

define the set of alternatives when he needed to find a new job. He was chief financial officer at Corestates Financial Corporation when it was acquired by First Union Corporation. Recognizing that the combined banks would not need two CFOs, Mandia reasoned that the banking industry was consolidating, so finding a new job as a bank CFO would be difficult. So, he broadened his search to consider any financial services company that offers services similar to a bank's. That approach helped Mandia find a position as CFO of American Business Financial Services, a smaller but rapidly growing business that specializes in consumer lending.[21]

Decision makers are most likely to make aided choices when the decision task is demanding and the consequences of the choice are great.[22] Pearce Jones, president of Design Edge, which provides product development services, relies heavily on financial reports to aid in decisions related to expanding his business. He tracks not only sales but profit margins—which are especially important since Design Edge attracts and keeps good employees by offering profit sharing. In a recent year, Jones observed that, although sales were growing rapidly, profit margins were significantly below his target rate of 30 percent. Jones temporarily halted expansion plans, such as adding office space and attracting new customers, concentrating instead on service to existing customers and expansion of cash reserves. That decision restored the company's profitability and positioned it for future growth.[23]

Analytic and Heuristic Decisions   Decision makers choose to make either analytic or heuristic decisions. An analytic decision is one that systematically compares alternatives according to a given set of criteria. This approach is consistent with the rational model. The following example tells how a business owner successfully applied an analytic approach to a decision about where to locate his business.

🐦 Archives Management

When A. J. Wasserstein earned his master's degree from New York University's Stern School of Business, he decided to start his own company. Called Archives Management, it would offer a variety of services related to file storage and retrieval. One of Wasserstein's early decisions involved where to locate the company. As he began the search, Wasserstein established two decision criteria: low cost and a location convenient to his customers.

Wasserstein spent six months looking at business properties near his Connecticut home. He visited a variety of towns and determined that the location that best fit his criteria was Waterbury, a blue-collar community with a history as a mill town. Not only did Waterbury have relatively low rents, but it is located at the intersection of two major highways, placing it within two hours' drive of all Wasserstein's business prospects. For the bargain price of $1,800 a month, Wasserstein bought and renovated a 50,000-square-foot brick warehouse.

Wasserstein knew that his space might have cost 30 percent more if he had insisted on a more up-scale address. What even his careful analysis didn't identify, however, was the support available to companies that locate in the inner city. His decision generated good publicity from the local newspaper, which helped him reap customers, investment dollars, and a flood of qualified job applicants.

Wasserstein continues to see positive feedback from that first location decision. Since launching Archives Management, Wasserstein has hired 30 employees and quadrupled his space. Today the company enjoys well over $2 million in annual revenues, along with a comfortable 23 percent profit margin.[24]

In contrast to the analytic approach, **heuristics** are shortcuts for making judgments about the alternatives identified, based on either the availability of information or assessments of likelihood. The **availability heuristic** is the tendency of decision makers to base judgments primarily on readily available information. This, as we discussed in Chapter 4, is an aspect of perception. People give more weight to information that is relevant to them, evokes emotions, is attention getting, or has occurred recently. Clearly, these are not objective criteria for weighting alternatives, but they certainly simplify the process.

The **representativeness heuristic** is the tendency to base the assessment of an event's likelihood on false analogies. For example, when Stanley Marcus was an executive with upscale retailer Neiman Marcus Group, he and his colleagues would base location decisions on cities' reputations among apparel makers. They would ask the makers of fashionable shoes and clothing where their sales growth came from, and they located Neiman Marcus stores in those cities. Boston did not have a reputation as fashionable, an opinion Marcus reinforced with his own impressions gathered as a Harvard student, so Neiman Marcus did not put a store in that city. However, when another company later bought Neiman Marcus, its management performed a demographic study and, based on the analysis, decided to open a store. The Boston store was very successful. Marcus concluded, "The word-of-mouth retail advice I had received was about Boston's near past, but the trends in the market showed that the city was becoming more contemporary. I wish I'd looked forward instead of back."[25]

In general, decision makers are most apt to use heuristics when a problem is familiar, straightforward, and stable. With unfamiliar, ambiguous, complex, and unstable problems, people more often use analytic choice processes. In addition, decision makers tend to make analytic choices when a choice is irreversible and significant, when the decision maker will be held accountable for the outcome, when the probability of a correct decision is low, and when time and money constraints do not prohibit the use of an analytic approach. Characteristics of the decision maker also influence the use of an analytic or heuristic approach. In particular, experienced and educated decision makers are more likely to use an analytic strategy, whereas decision makers who lack knowledge, ability, or motivation to make a good decision are more likely to rely on heuristics.[26]

heuristics

Shortcuts for making judgments about the alternatives identified.

availability heuristic

The tendency to base judgments primarily on readily available information.

representativeness heuristic

The tendency to base the assessment of an event's likelihood on false analogies.

Decision Environments

The way people make decisions also depends on how much information they have or can acquire. Your decisions about how to get to class are probably fairly straightforward. For most students, the available routes and available modes of transportation are the same for each class session.

what would you do?

HOW WOULD YOU AVOID SINGING THE BLUES?

Joe Fletcher had a good thing going. Formerly a writer of children's songs, he noticed that New England lacked a big-name rock and pop concert circuit and determined that this was his opportunity for fame and fortune. He founded Big World Productions and started conservatively with smaller shows in relatively well-populated areas such as Portsmouth, New Hampshire. He earned a reputation as a well-organized promoter, and his shows were successful. But he wanted more. He couldn't yet compete with the well-financed promoters in Boston, or even Portland, Maine, so he turned his sights to rural locations such as the Sugarbush ski area in Warren, Vermont, hoping that if he could attract top-name performers like Bill Cosby and Bob Dylan, the audience would come. People did attend these concerts, but not enough people. And, since top performers command top fees (up to $100,000 per event, with a 50 percent deposit up front), Fletcher's expenses increased. So he hired several employees and set out to book more shows. "To cover overhead, the tendency is to do more shows," he recalls.

In the end, Big World Productions could not keep up with its own expansion, and Fletcher folded his tent for good. Fletcher's decision-making process, which was far more heuristic than analytic, reflects a tendency to follow the representative heuristic. He based his assessment of the success of Big World's expansion into new markets on false analogies. For example, Fletcher reasoned that putting on more shows would naturally cover his costs; to accomplish this, he secured backing from several local investors. He also reasoned that loyal fans of top-name performers would travel to less-accessible, rural locations to see their idols. But in hindsight, one of Fletcher's backers says, "Logistically, [these shows] just didn't work. The types of crowds that go to see B.B. King and Ray Charles want to sit indoors in comfort, not climb a mountain and sit out with the mosquitoes." Finally, he assumed that because there were few big-name concerts in northern New England, the general public would agree that this was a cultural void and that audiences would flock to concerts if given the chance.

Other observers don't find fault with Fletcher's reasoning, except in hindsight. Tina Coulouras, director of events at the Lowell Memorial Auditorium in Lowell, Massachusetts, notes, "I would think people in Vermont would be starved for good entertainment and would have made the trip. Joe is a great marketer and really knows how to get the word out."

Fletcher's investor now says that he believes Big World would have continued to grow and profit if Fletcher had stayed with the product and the region he knew best. "The rule of thumb is that you stick near home," he observes. "You draw yourself a 25-mile radius." And Fletcher himself concedes that he should have "focused on doing the right show, not just a lot of shows. It's not about volume of sales . . . the days of Woodstock are over."

Imagine that you are in a financial position to back Fletcher or someone like him. To research further what you need to consider in order to make rational decisions about your investment and the direction you think the company should take, access a few relevant Web sites such as those for the business magazines *Inc.* and *Entrepreneur*. Also access Web sites for other concert promoters by using the key words "concert promoters" on your search engine. Then consider the following questions.

1. In assessing Fletcher's decisions, what alternatives might he have had to keep the company profitable? How would you assign value to each of these alternatives?

2. Do you think that the rational model and behavioral model should be mutually exclusive in making decisions such as this? Why or why not?

3. What types of tools might you use to aid your decision to invest in Big World or a company like it?

4. What risk factors and uncertainty factors would you consider in your decision to become financially involved with Big World Productions or a company like it? Would you be comfortable with these risks? Why or why not?

Source: Julie Carrick Dalton, "Concert Promoter Hits Rough Road in Vermont," *Inc.*, October 1999, p. 24.

Students quickly learn how long the alternatives take and which are most convenient. Deciding *whether* to go to class may be a little more complex for some students. Such a decision involves evaluating the likelihood you will learn something and the likely consequences of not attending. In other words, you have to decide the value of the alternatives and their likelihood. Your decision would be even more complicated if you had never really clarified why you decided to enroll in the class in the first place—that is, if you have no objectives for taking the course. In organizations, too, decisions vary according to the degree of certainty involved. As shown in Exhibit 10.5, people make decisions under either certainty, risk, uncertainty, or ambiguity.

Certainty   At one extreme in the range of possible decision environments, **certainty** describes a situation in which the decision maker fully knows all the relevant information. Suppose you need to prepare a report summarizing your group's accomplishments. You can prepare it on your computer, use the typewriter down the hall, or write it out on a tablet of paper. You opt for the computer. If this example seems simplistic, it is because real-world decisions rarely involve total certainty.

certainty

A condition in which the decision maker has full knowledge of all the relevant information.

Risk   Many decisions involve **risk**—a condition in which the decision maker has defined goals and knows possible outcomes, but the outcomes are subject to chance, which the decision maker can estimate. In other words, the decision maker has a certain amount of information: the desired outcome and the likelihood of the possible outcomes. However, the decision maker cannot be certain that a particular outcome will occur, only whether it is likely. For example, when Encyclopedia Britannica launched free Internet access to its 40-volume encyclopedia, the company based decisions on assumptions the site would get heavy traffic, but not so heavy as the 10 million attempts a day to log on to the site that actually occurred. The company quickly hired teams of consultants to expand the site's capabilities and fix software glitches. Jorge Cauz, who heads marketing for Encyclopedia Britannica, had this comment about the challenge of assessing risk: "Nobody in his right mind would have built an infrastructure capable of addressing the demand we had on the first day."[27] Of course, with this experience now a part of Internet history, future assessments will be much different.

risk

A condition in which the decision maker has defined goals and knows possible outcomes, but the outcomes are subject to chance, which the decision maker can estimate.

People differ in terms of their **risk propensity**—their willingness to assume risk in exchange for the opportunity of a possible return. Some people will accept a high degree of risk in exchange for the possibility of a large payoff. Others prefer to avoid risk, even if the potential payoff also is less. People who are willing to take chances (have a high risk propensity) are likely to make different decisions than people who prefer the tried-and-true, low-risk options. These differences, in turn, can determine whether an organization explores new products or new markets, hires creative people, or adopts leading-edge technology. In many organizations, attitudes toward

risk propensity

The degree of willingness to assume risk in exchange for the opportunity of a possible return.

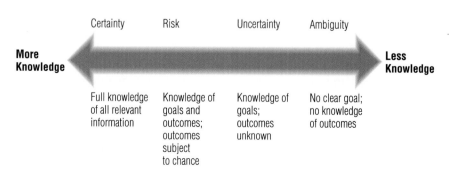

exhibit **10.5**
Decision Environments

risk drive decisions to outsource functions to organizations that offer expertise in the functional area. For example, John McGlone of the human resources consulting firm Buck Consultants has found that many small businesses prefer to have specialists handle human resource functions, because they are less likely to make mistakes—and more likely to accept the liability if they do.[28]

Uncertainty   Sometimes the decision situation is even more difficult. Under conditions of **uncertainty,** the decision maker knows the goal of the decision but has too little information to estimate the likelihood of the possible outcomes. Typically, uncertainty occurs because a situation is so complex that the decision maker has no practical way to estimate all the factors that would affect an outcome. International expansion of an organization involves decisions under uncertainty. Organizations have to consider each country's economy, laws, business opportunities, technology, and culture.

This complexity in global markets has influenced SpeechWorks to move slowly into foreign markets. The company, which offers computer speech recognition software, must develop products that handle local differences in conversational language, as well as carefully evaluate each market's opportunity, including its demand for the product and its technological sophistication. For help in handling the uncertainty, SpeechWorks forms partnerships with local companies that provide related products. Even with careful planning, SpeechWorks can't be certain of success. Steve Adams, the company's vice president of international operations, said that the company recently opened an office in Mexico City but still isn't sure the Mexican market for its services will be a strong one.[29]

Ambiguity   With **ambiguity,** the decision situation is even more difficult. Under this condition, not only does the decision maker lack information about possible alternatives and outcomes, but there is no clearly defined goal. For example, the preceding chapter mentioned that when Sara Lee announced it might close a bakery, the company said it might reconsider that decision if the union came up with "something." Not surprisingly, the quest to plan "something" was intensely frustrating for everyone who hoped to save the factory. As in this case, decisions made under ambiguity have a high likelihood of failure.

Organizational Constraints

Organizations can also affect the decision process. They influence decisions by limiting the resources available to decision makers, rewarding certain kinds of decisions, and establishing rules for making decisions.

Resource Constraints   Decision makers in organizations may operate within resource constraints. For example, a manager or team might have a budget, with the freedom to make choices as long as their costs remain within the limits of the budget. In this case, the financial constraints narrow the list of acceptable alternatives and may even dictate the only acceptable alternative. Michael Napoliello Jr. and Jason Moskowitz faced severe economic constraints when they started *The Wave,* a summer newspaper featuring announcements about arts and entertainment activities around the Jersey

---

uncertainty

A condition in which the decision maker knows the goal of the decision but has too little information to estimate the likelihood of the possible outcomes.

---

ambiguity

A condition in which the decision maker lacks information about possible alternatives and outcomes, and there is no clearly defined goal.

Shore. The two college students didn't have access to much capital, so they kept their enterprise alive by visiting advertisers and asking what they wanted in exchange for advertising in *The Wave*. The advertising agency for Anheuser-Busch wanted distribution at convenience stores, and the local 7-Eleven managers agreed to carry the paper in exchange for front-page advertising. The entrepreneurs even handed out Frisbees promoting Minute Maid in order to secure advertising from a Coca-Cola bottling company. (Coca-Cola owns the Minute Maid brand.)[30]

Other constraints limit the amount of time available for arriving at a decision. Time imposed a fearful constraint on the operator of McDonald's franchises in Yugoslavia. The golden arches are a symbol associated with American business, and when NATO began bombing Yugoslavia in 1999, local Serbs reacted by vandalizing the McDonald's restaurant in Belgrade. The managers closed for two weeks and quickly set about deciding how to distance the Yugoslavian restaurants from their American roots. They developed a marketing campaign that used symbols Serbians identified with their heritage, such as a traditional cap called the *sajkaca* perched on images of the McDonald's arches. The company also announced that it would donate a portion of revenues to the Yugoslav Red Cross.[31] There may have been better ways to handle the situation, but management could have lost its restaurants to local mobs if it had instead spent time analyzing every alternative.

Most people in organizations operate under less physically frightening conditions, but time constraints are severe nonetheless. In assessing his experience as CEO of Hewlett-Packard, Lewis Platt concluded that one of the biggest challenges of modern executives is the requirement to move quickly and deliver short-term results that satisfy shareholders:

> If you wanted to communicate with a partner 25 years ago, you'd send a letter, maybe make a trip. But because of the type of communications used, the pace of decision making was slow. With e-mail, you've compressed the time you're expected to deal with this problem. The world doesn't want you to slow down to make a good decision. Now you're lucky if you can sleep on it.[32]

As with financial constraints, time constraints may determine the outcome of decision making. Severe time constraints may require decision makers to choose the first acceptable alternative they can identify—thus favoring such easy-to-recall ideas as repeating whatever has been done in a similar situation in the recent past.

Besides money and time, other constraints may arise from the decision situation. For example, imagine that an airline passenger is upset with a flight delay. If the customer writes a letter to headquarters, the person who receives the letter has time to think over a response, but because the customer's trip is already over, the alternatives for how to correct the problem are limited. In contrast, if the customer complains noisily at the airport, the employee receiving the complaint has a different range of possible solutions, along with a great deal of urgency to resolve the problem quickly.

Evaluation Criteria   Organizations also influence decisions by establishing performance criteria. Decision makers want to arrive at decisions they will be rewarded for. If an organization bases performance evaluations strictly on financial criteria, these criteria will weigh heavily in employees'

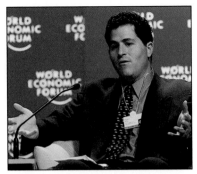

No other industry changes so quickly and requires such fast decisions as the high-tech field. Just as he encourages risk taking for his employees, Michael Dell, founder of Dell Computer, also makes some risky decisions to ensure innovation and the competitiveness of his company. Driven by the idea that consumers and businesses increasingly use PCs only to access the Web, where they find both software applications and data resources, Dell recently stated, "We're sending the message that it's not Dell the PC company, it's Dell the Internet infrastructure company." Basing his upcoming computers on a different operating system and chip technology reflects Dell's decision to initiate a new strategic focus for the future of the company. (Source: © AP/Wide World Photos/Michel Euler)

programmed decision

Routine decision made according to rules established for a particular situation.

decisions. Medicare recently established payment guidelines that specify higher payments to health plans for HMO patients deemed to have chronic illnesses. To qualify, patients must have been hospitalized with the illness for at least two days in the previous year. This guideline gives decision makers at health plans little incentive to make decisions that keep chronically ill patients out of the hospital.[33]

In contrast, if the organization highly values and rewards innovation (especially if it recognizes that mistakes are inevitable), decision makers will more often make innovative choices. Michael Dell, founder of Dell Computer, encourages risk taking if it "results in new information."[34] In other words, mistakes are acceptable if the person who took the risk gained knowledge to share with the organization to improve future decision making.

Similarly, organizations can encourage decisions that satisfy customers quickly and promote their image for customer satisfaction by empowering employees rather than penalizing them when they go out of their way. Journalist Jeffrey Seglin concluded that Dell empowers its customer support staff in this way, because of an experience Seglin had when traveling in Munich. Seglin was unable to power up his Dell notebook computer from his Munich hotel room, so he called Dell headquarters and asked for "customer support for small-business accounts." A Dell technician patiently helped Seglin solve his problem, even though he quickly realized that Seglin didn't actually have an account with Dell. A grateful Seglin credited the technician for putting customer needs first and Dell for providing an environment in which the technician did not fear getting into trouble for providing extra (i.e., unpaid-for) service.[35]

Programmed and Nonprogrammed Decisions Organizations determine in advance how much leeway to give employees to make particular kinds of decisions. They do this by programming certain decisions. A **programmed decision** is a routine decision made according to rules established for a particular situation.[36] For example, Taylor Group, which provides a type of computer consulting known as systems integration, has established an extensive multistep process for screening and interviewing job candidates, with each interview focusing on a different aspect of the candidate—from skills to compatibility with the organization's values. Taylor Group's management believes the formal process is worthwhile because candidates who survive the process are likely to stay with the organization for the long term.[37]

Programmed decisions do limit the development and selection of alternatives, which saves time and also may prevent errors. When situations routinely occur, organizations can improve efficiency by establishing programmed decisions. Programmed decisions are also helpful for emergencies. They enable employees to act quickly according to guidelines established earlier, when decision makers had the luxury to think through the alternatives carefully and rationally. Such guidelines might have prevented a disaster that recently occurred near Tokyo. At a factory built to supply fuel for nuclear reactors, workers improperly handled the uranium being processed, resulting in a nuclear reaction of the type that would normally occur in the controlled environment within a reactor. Radiation injured workers and escaped from the plant into the neighborhood. Within a mile of the plant, radiation levels were 15,000 times higher than normal for a city. Hours passed, and workers did not launch emergency backup procedures—because none had been prepared. It took almost 20 hours for the damage to be contained.[38]

In contrast, a **nonprogrammed decision** is one for which there are no predetermined decision rules. In the story about Project Bark at the beginning of this chapter, the company's partners had to arrive at their own criteria and set of alternatives for deciding where to locate. Especially in the realm of Internet enterprises, including Project Bark, there are no hard-and-fast rules to guide such decisions. Arriving at a nonprogrammed decision requires more effort and perhaps more time than making a programmed decision. Sometimes the consequences are not what the organization may have intended. For example, the U.S. Immigration and Naturalization Service (INS) operates under a law that allows it to permit immigration by individuals whose presence in the United States is in the national interest. The law does not define the specifics of the "national interest," leaving the decisions in the hands of the clerks in INS offices. Those admitted under the provision have included a Nigerian linguist, a Russian ballroom dancer, a Chinese nuclear physicist, a Russian acrobat, and a Korean golf course designer. According to Ed Skerrett, who leads the panel that hears appeals of individual cases, national interest "doesn't have to be national security. It can be just about anything. We've seen all sorts of things. Whatever. You name it."[39] This may not be what Congress had in mind when it passed the law.

On the positive side, a nonprogrammed decision leaves room for the decision maker to apply creative thinking to the particular characteristics of the situation. For example, when Lands' End began offering clothing and linens in Germany, it encountered a German law that prohibited unconditional money-back guarantees, on the grounds that such an offer is unfair (because it is "economically unfeasible"). Used to operating in the U.S. marketplace, Lands' End had no set procedure for what to do when its policies were considered too generous, so its marketers came up with a new advertising message to highlight the company's generosity—and its predicament. A Lands' End ad in Germany shows two images: a washing machine with the caption "guaranteed 6 months" and a Lands' End logo with the caption "Advertising banned in Germany."[40] The caption draws attention to the fact that Lands' End is offering something out of the ordinary, thereby generating publicity and word of mouth to communicate the details it may not advertise.

Given their advantages and disadvantages, nonprogrammed decisions are appropriate for situations that occur infrequently, are unstructured or poorly defined, and have important consequences.[41] In addition, many employees are motivated by the opportunity to think creatively and independently. Such employees will contribute most if the organization empowers them to make nonprogrammed decisions in areas where they have expertise.

Escalation of Commitment

Prior choices also can influence decision making. In a practice called **escalation of commitment,** people often increase their commitment to a previous decision in spite of evidence that it was wrong. Typically, this takes

nonprogrammed decision
Decision for which there are no predetermined decision rules.

escalation of commitment
An increased commitment to a previous decision in spite of evidence that it was wrong.

the form of people believing they have "invested" in the previous decision, so they will continue to contribute to that initial "investment." For example, a company might buy an expensive software system and then find that it doesn't provide the expected benefits. If the company's managers continue to pour money into fixing the system, even though it would be less costly to abandon it and use something else, the managers are guilty of escalation of commitment. (In the fields of accounting and finance, this is known as the error of basing investment decisions on "sunk costs.")

In contrast, decision makers at Hummer Windblad Venture Partners avoided escalation of commitment when they assessed their initial decision to invest in an early form of pen-based computing. Investors at the venture capital firm had been excited by the technology and invested $400,000 in its developer, which was called Slate. A few years later, Hummer invested another $700,000, but soon afterward realized that the market was far from ready to adopt the technology. Hummer sold its investment to Compaq at a loss, rather than pour more money into the failing enterprise.[42]

Besides financial investments, people also invest time in projects and emotions in relationships or ideas. In fact, research suggests that the amount of money invested in a project has less influence on escalation of commitment than does the nearness of the project to its completion.[43]

Because escalation of commitment is about more than money, it can apply not only to financial investments but to decisions about friendships, career choices, and prospective customers. If a person continues to pursue a course solely because of the prior decision error, the person is engaged in an illogical escalation of commitment. Recognizing and correcting for escalation of commitment are difficult because they require admitting the past mistake. Admitting a mistake is almost always uncomfortable, especially in organizations that have little tolerance for employee errors. Organizations that want to avoid the problems associated with escalation of commitment, therefore, need objective performance measures coupled with the recognition that mistakes are an inevitable part of learning and problem solving.

apply it

1. Assume the hard drive on your computer has crashed. You are deciding what to do. Which, if any, of the following circumstances would influence your decision?
   - During the past year, you added memory to your computer, replaced a defective disk drive, and upgraded to a faster modem.
   - Your school has just announced a special offer on the latest laptop computers.
   - You have a major paper due next week.
   - Last week your parents asked you to stop spending so much money.
2. For each of the circumstances in question 1 that you said would influence you, explain *how* it would affect your decision making. For each that you said would not influence you, explain *why* it would not.

Many of an organization's decisions are made by groups

In organizations, decision making is often a group process. This is especially true for decisions that have a significant impact on the organization's performance, as well as those that affect many of the organization's people. In keeping with that pattern, Kellogg uses group decision making for new product development, as described in the following example.

Executives at Kellogg agree that the company needs to grow faster. But in view of stiff competition and declining consumption of cereal for breakfast, they have long struggled to determine how. Kellogg's objective is to get consumers to buy more of the company's cold cereal and other food items. In part, this requires decisions about new products.

> **Kellogg Company**

At a company not known for its innovation, the executives decided they needed a new approach to decision making. Instead of leaving product development up to individual marketers, they set up cross-functional teams. In the team approach, marketing researchers, food technologists, engineers, and others collaborate on new ideas.

Donna Banks, who is in charge of research and development, maintains, "Creativity comes with diversity." With that attitude, she has diversified the decision makers in her own group by hiring people from nontraditional backgrounds. Her employees include scientists with nonscience college majors on their resumes, as well as employees from almost two dozen different countries. The teams have begun generating some successes for Kellogg, including Raisin Bran Crunch cereal and Rice Krispies Treats snacks. Other ideas that the decision-making groups have slated for the new product pipeline include Honey Frosted Mini-Wheats, 3-Point Pops, and Snack 'ums.[44]

Benefits and Drawbacks of Group Decision Making

Making decisions as a group can be beneficial. When people arrive at a decision together, they are more likely to support the decision and feel motivated to make "their" decision succeed. In addition, when problems are complex, different members of the group can improve the decision by contributing their experience and expertise to defining the problem, as well as identifying and evaluating alternatives. Evidence suggests that group decisions tend to be more creative than individual decisions.[45] James Biber, who gave up a successful solo career as an architect to join a 17-partner firm called Pentagram, would agree. Among the benefits of being with the larger firm, Biber appreciates the input from respected colleagues who can offer a fresh perspective. Besides offering day-to-day feedback, partners view and critique each other's work during twice-a-year partnership meetings. Biber believes his work is superior as a result of the collaboration.[46]

Many employees today expect organizations to value their opinions and knowledge and to let them have a voice in decision making. These employees will expect to play a role in making decisions, and they are likely to be dissatisfied if the organization prevents them from doing so. These expectations are appropriate in organizations that rely heavily on knowledge workers. The very role of knowledge workers demands that they contribute to decision making and share their knowledge for the organization's benefit. Thus, when K2 Design, a firm that provides design services to support electronic communications, needed new accounting software, founder

Matthew de Ganon brought together a team to pick the software. All those who would be affected by the new software met and identified their needs, observed demonstrations from vendors, and evaluated software and vendors according to a variety of decision criteria. The group selected software that supports better decision making and efficient operations.[47]

Not all employees want or expect to participate in decisions, however. Individual and cultural differences shape the degree to which employees want to participate in decision making. Also, for employees to have a positive attitude about their role as decision makers, they must have access to the information and authority required to fill that role.

As these qualifications indicate, group decision making is not beneficial for every employee or every situation. In the next section, we will examine how to identify which situations benefit from group decision making. Individual decision making is sometimes more appropriate because group decision making has drawbacks as well as benefits. In particular, groups tend to make decisions more slowly than individuals do. Group decisions also are more costly from the organization's perspective, because more people devote time to the process. For the sake of efficiency, organizations may rely on individual decisions when the benefits of group decisions are not important or when speed and cost containment are more important.

Another potential problem of group decision making is that group members may be biased in which viewpoints they air or support. They tend to state opinions only if they support the viewpoint of the group's high-status members,[48] and they tend to discount the views of people outside the group.[49] Expressing a viewpoint likely to evoke disapproval feels uncomfortable. An example of this problem occurred to newspaper columnist Leonard Pitts Jr. on an airline flight to Miami. Pitts suddenly heard a loud noise from somewhere near his seat at the back of the plane. Flight attendants and crew quietly investigated, then the pilot announced there was no danger. The noise was coming from air escaping around a faulty door seal. Since the noise was so loud, a flight attendant was asked to poll the passengers sitting near the source of the noise to determine whether they would land in Charlotte to have it fixed, or continue on to Miami. Only one passenger voted to land, not realizing that only one such vote was required. The captain announced the plane would land in Charlotte. Pitts relayed the woman passenger's reaction:

> When she realizes she is the only one who voted for this, the lady is mortified. The whole jetliner landing just on her say-so? . . . But truth is, nobody seems too distressed at her decision.
>
> Indeed, the senior attendant reassures her that she's not the only one who wanted to land—just the only one willing to say it.
>
> . . . I don't mind saying it: I was glad to land.[50]

In Pitts's experience, most passengers were unwilling to advocate an alternative that would inconvenience the group (the other passengers), even if they thought it was the optimal alternative.

Of particular concern is a behavior called **groupthink,** which occurs when commitment to group cohesiveness is so strong that group members are reluctant to express opinions contrary to the group consensus.[51] As we saw in Chapter 7, group cohesiveness can be beneficial. However, in the

groupthink

Reluctance of group members to express opinions contrary to the group consensus.

Pro	Con
People who arrive at a decision together are more likely to support it.	Depending on individual and cultural differences, some employees may not wish to participate in group decision making.
Group members can improve complex decisions by contributing experience and expertise in various areas.	Employees without enough information and authority will not contribute effectively.
Group decisions may be more creative than solo decisions.	Groups tend to make decisions more slowly than individuals do.
Many employees expect to have a role in decision making.	Group decision making is costly compared with individual decision making.
Group decision making fully employs the talents of knowledge workers.	Group members may bias their input in favor of what they perceive the group consensus to be. They may value group cohesiveness over finding the optimal solution.

exhibit | **10.6**

Pros and Cons of Group Decision Making

case of groupthink, the members value it so highly that they hold back knowledge or perspectives that would improve the quality of the group's decisions. Exhibit 10.6 summarizes the pros and cons of group decision making.

When to Use Groups

Considering that group decisions have both benefits and drawbacks, managers and other decision makers need to decide when a decision should be a group decision. Victor Vroom and Philip Yetton developed a model of decision making that provides some guidance in whether a decision should be made by a group, and Vroom and Arthur Jago later expanded the model.[52] Their model focuses on whether the leader (or manager) of a group should involve subordinates. Decisions to invite participation depend on the model's three components: leader participation styles, diagnostic questions, and decision rules. Research supports the usefulness of the Vroom-Yetton-Jago model.[53]

The Vroom-Yetton-Jago model assumes that decision makers have different styles for involving subordinates in decision making. As shown in Exhibit 10.7, these styles range from highly autocratic, with the leader preferring to make decisions alone, to highly democratic, with the manager letting subordinates identify alternatives and choose the solution to implement.

The manager selects a decision style by answering a set of diagnostic questions covering eight aspects of the decision situation:

1. *Quality Requirement (QR)* How important is the quality of this decision? (If a high-quality decision is important, the group leader should be actively involved in the decision.)

exhibit | **10.7**

exhibit | **10.7**

Styles for Involving Subordinates
in Decision Making

	Decision Style	Description
Highly Autocratic	AI	You solve the problem or make the decision yourself using information available to you at that time.
	AII	You obtain the necessary information from your subordinates and then decide on the solution to the problem yourself.
	CI	You share the problem with relevant subordinates individually, getting their ideas and suggestions without bringing them together as a group. Then you make the decision.
	CII	You share the problem with your subordinates as a group, collectively obtaining their ideas and suggestions. Then you make the decision.
Highly Democratic	G	You share a problem with your subordinates as a group. Your role is much like that of chairman. You do not try to influence the group to adopt "your" solution, and you are willing to accept and implement any solution that has the support of the entire group.

Note: A = autocratic; C = consultative; G = group

Source: The New Leadership: Managing Participation in Organizations by Victor H. Vroom and Arthur G. Jago, Eds. Copyright 1998. Reprinted by permission of Prentice-Hall, Inc., Upper Saddle River, NJ.

2. *Commitment Requirement (CR)*   How important is subordinate commitment to the decision? (If commitment is important, the leader should involve subordinates in the decision.)

3. *Leader's Information (LI)*   Do I have enough information to make a high-quality decision? (If the leader has too little information or expertise, the subordinates should help obtain information.)

4. *Problem Structure (ST)*   Is the decision problem well structured? (If the problem is ambiguous, the leader will have to work with subordinates to clarify the problem and identify possible solutions.)

5. *Commitment Probability (CP)*   If I were to make the decision by myself, is it reasonably certain that my subordinates would be committed to the decision? (If so, their involvement is less important.)

6. *Goal Congruence (GC)*   Do subordinates share the organizational goals to be attained in solving this problem? (If not, the group should not make the decision without the leader's involvement.)

7. *Subordinate Conflict (CO)*   Is conflict over preferred solutions likely to occur among the subordinates? (If so, they can resolve the conflict through participating in the decision process.)

8. *Subordinate Information (SI)*   Do subordinates have enough information to make a high-quality decision? (If so, they can take on more decision-making responsibility.)

The flowchart in Exhibit 10.8 illustrates how answering these questions leads to the choice of an appropriate decision style. It provides the third component of the Vroom-Yetton-Jago model, the decision rules. In fact, Vroom and Jago developed four sets of decision rules, each in the form of a decision tree that covers one of four different situations:

1. An individual-level problem under time constraints

2. An individual-level problem in a situation where developing employees' decision-making skill is important

3. A group-level problem in a situation where developing employees' decision-making skill is important

4. A group-level problem under time constraints

The decision tree in Exhibit 10.8 represents the four situations as an illustration of how managers can select the appropriate level of participation.

To use the decision tree, the decision maker starts at the left. The decision maker states the problem and then answers the first question: How important is the quality of this decision? Depending on the answer, the decision maker follows one of the branches of the decision tree to the next question, about subordinate commitment. The process continues until the decision maker reaches the end of a branch at the right of the chart. At the end of the branch is a label that identifies the appropriate decision style, using the codes from Exhibit 10.7. For example, if the quality requirement (QR) is high, the commitment requirement (CR) is low, and the leader's information (LI) is sufficient, a highly autocratic approach to decision making (AI) is most appropriate. In contrast, one situation calling for a high level of group participation (G) would be one with a low quality requirement (QR),

exhibit | **10.8**

Model for Choice of a Decision Style

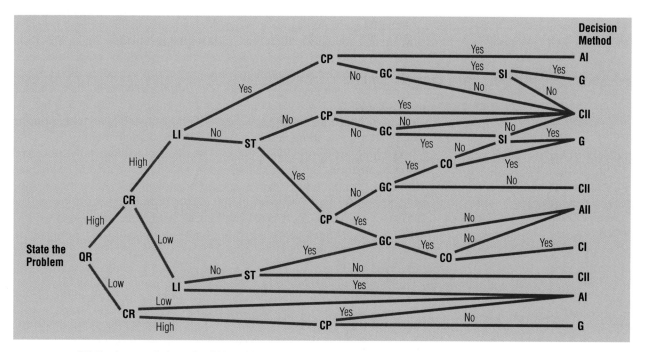

QR How important is the quality of this decision?
CR How important is subordinate commitment to the decision?
LI Do you have sufficient information to make a high-quality decision?
ST Is the problem well structured?
CP If you were to make the decision by yourself, is it reasonably certain that your subordinates would be committed to it?
GC Do subordinates share the organization goals to be attained in solving this problem?
CO Is conflict among subordinates over preferred solutions likely?
SI Do subordinates have sufficient information to make a high-quality decision?

Source: Adapted and reprinted from *Leadership and Decision Making* by Victor H. Vroom and Philip W. Yetton, by permission of Pittsburgh Press. ©1973 by University of Pittsburgh Press.

a high commitment requirement (CR), and a low commitment probability (CP) if the leader makes the decision alone. Because applying this model can be time consuming, it is most useful when time constraints are not severe and the outcome of the decision is significant.

Techniques for Group Problem Solving

As we noted earlier, a potential drawback of group problem solving is groupthink. Organizations can minimize groupthink by using techniques to ensure that contrary opinions are heard.[54] One approach is to formally assign to a group member the role of **devil's advocate.** This role involves challenging the statements and assumptions of the other group members. By assigning this role to a group member, the group signals that it values the airing of contrary opinions. An effective devil's advocate forces group members to think through their positions logically and thoroughly, thereby improving the ultimate decision.

A similar approach is to evaluate an issue with a technique called **multiple advocacy.** To apply this technique, the group assigns different points of view to different group members. Each group member is supposed to argue for the point of view assigned to him or her. This approach forces the group to carefully research and listen to different perspectives. As a result, the investigation of the alternatives is more complete and accurate.

When the emphasis is on building a consensus while airing all points of view, the group may decide to use the **Delphi method.**[55] To use this technique, the group uses questionnaires to gather anonymous judgments on an issue, then provides written feedback so that group members can compare the judgments. The process continues with additional rounds of surveys and feedback until the participants arrive at a consensus. This approach has the advantage of airing all viewpoints, but the lack of face-to-face discussion can lessen the understanding and commitment of the participants.

A technique that provides for face-to-face communication is the **nominal group technique.** This approach uses a structured group meeting with three parts. First, group members write down ideas individually. Then they discuss each idea as a group. Finally, the group votes on the ideas by secret ballot. The alternative with the highest overall ranking is the one the group selects.

devil's advocate

Group role that involves challenging the statements and assumptions of the other group members.

multiple advocacy

Group decision-making technique in which the group assigns different points of view to different group members, who must argue their assigned point of view.

Delphi method

Group decision-making technique in which the group uses questionnaires to gather anonymous judgments on an issue, then provides written feedback for comparing and refining judgments until the group reaches a consensus.

nominal group technique

Group decision-making technique using a structured meeting with three phases: (1) writing ideas individually; (2) discussing the ideas together; and (3) voting on the ideas by secret ballot.

apply it

1. Imagine that you have volunteered to coordinate the company picnic this year. Alone or with others, you will decide where and when it will be held, as well as the food and activities to be included. Which decisions will you want to make alone? For which decisions will you seek group participation? Explain.

Creativity can improve decision making

In the fast-changing, expanding global environment of modern organizations, many problems and opportunities are new and complex. Making good decisions about these problems and opportunities often requires creative thinking. Formally defined, **creativity** is the ability to combine or associate information in ways that generate new ideas. For example, when Mike Stephenson was enjoying a steak dinner in a Manhattan restaurant, he was captivated by the wine bottle on the table. It bore a personal message from the vineyard owner, along with the owner's signature. Stephenson, president of Great Lakes Hybrids, was inspired to put the same kind of personal communication on his own company's packaging of agricultural seed. The wine bottle inspired an alternative for a problem he had been trying to solve: how to differentiate his company as a high-quality supplier in what is largely a commodity market.[56] In solving problems, creative members of the organization are able to think beyond what has worked in the past, to find unique associations, and to craft solutions that the organization has never tried before.

Applications of Creative Thinking

When permitted to do so, creative individuals contribute fresh ideas to the organization. In theory, individuals provide creative ideas to the groups they take part in. When a group receives and applies these ideas, the organization as a whole implements more creative strategies.[57] As this theoretical perspective indicates, the benefits of creativity accrue only when the organization acts on ideas. Sitting around a table and throwing out ideas can be fun, but it is not beneficial by itself. For example, the Gardener's Supply catalog retailer enables implementation of new ideas as well as idea generation. The procedures came about after CEO Will Raap conducted a six-month trial in which half a dozen employees devoted eight hours a week to developing their ideas for new products, aided by mentors. Four of the employees performed so well that the company incorporated new product development into their jobs, and Raap expanded the program to include everyone. Not only is everyone encouraged to think up ideas, but the company educates them in the company's decision-making criteria, such as gross margins. For a recent holiday catalog, employees submitted 50 ideas, of which 10 qualified for the catalog, and 3 or 4 performed better than average.[58]

Some organizations are distinguished by their use of creative ideas. When people in leadership roles act creatively, members of the organization act on the ideas, and these organizations stand out for their creative behavior. A case in point is the creative leadership of Nick Graham, founder of Joe Boxer, an underwear company described in the following example.

Joe Boxer is not a person but a brand name for a line of men's undershirts. And as the name connotes, this is not a line to be taken seriously. The company's founder, Nick Graham, had the creative idea that a utilitarian product could be presented as a fun product. The high value Graham initially placed on innovation and fun has readily carried over to the company's marketing decisions ever since.

Joe Boxer's Web site says, "The company firmly believes in innovation and creativity above all else." These values are evident in the company's promotional activities, many of them initiated by Graham himself. For example, in the mid-1990s, Joe Boxer set up a billboard in New York's Times Square to display the world's largest e-mail messages. People write to timesquare@joeboxer.com, and after editing out inappropriate content, an employee transmits the messages to the billboard. Many are silly, but the technique draws publicity far beyond that of an ordinary billboard. A few years later, Graham tried something completely different: He arranged to fly 2,000 reporters from the New York Fashion Week to

creativity

The ability to combine or associate information in ways that generate new ideas.

❦ Joe Boxer

Iceland for the "Iceland Fashion Show" in Reykjavík. Graham called the stunt "co-branding with a small country." He has also started offering underwear in vending machines and in the past even launched some boxers into space—to a crew in the Mir space station.

Graham is confident that his creative approach to marketing gives his brand a positive and unforgettable image in consumers' minds. He told a writer for *Inc.* magazine, "As we get more and more confidence as a business, we get more and more crazy. Just imagine what we'll be like in five years."[59]

How Organizations Can Foster Creativity

To foster creativity, organizations can encourage individuals to develop their own creative potential and can provide situations that encourage groups to think creatively. Organizations that encourage creative thinking have been described as challenging, dynamic, and playful; as letting employees take risks, define their responsibilities, and devote time to developing ideas; and as supporting employees' ideas.[60]

Evidence suggests that the majority of people make creative decisions at least occasionally.[61] As with other kinds of thinking, it also makes sense that we can develop this ability through practice. Exhibit 10.9 describes some techniques for cultivating creative thinking: attribute listing, lateral thinking, and synectics. In addition, research indicates that people generate more creative solutions when they are simply told to think creatively and avoid obvious solutions.[62] Inviting others in the organization to think creatively therefore is an easy and logical way to promote creative decision

exhibit | **10.9**

Techniques for Cultivating Creative Thinking

Attribute Listing

- When generating alternatives, list the major attributes of the traditional alternatives.
- Explore each of the attributes listed, thinking of all the ways you can change it, and considering each change as a valid possibility.
- Eliminate alternatives only after considering all these possibilities.

Lateral Thinking

- Instead of following the decision-making steps in order, move to the next step only when the first is complete; rearrange the process.
- Start with a step where you have some ideas already, and make corrections as you see the need for them. For example, you could start with the desired solution, look for criteria that such a solution would require, then modify your criteria as you learn more about the problem and solution.
- This approach deliberately brings in random or seemingly irrelevant information if it might shed some light on the decision situation.

Synectics

- Proceeding on the assumption that most problems aren't totally new, use analogies and inverted logic to define the decision situation.
- Using each analogy, see if you can form a picture of your current problem in terms of something you are already familiar with.
- As you think about each analogy, look for principles you can apply to the new situation.

Source: M. Stein, *Stimulating Creativity,* vol. 1 (New York: Academic Press, 1974); E. deBono, *Lateral Thinking: Creativity Step by Step* (New York: Harper & Row, 1971); and W. J. J. Gordon, *Synectics* (New York: Harper & Row, 1961).

making. For example, during his daily workouts, Lonny Kocina, president of Media Relations, a public relations firm, wears a small tape recorder. As he jogs around a track, he daydreams. Whenever ideas come to mind, he dictates them into his tape recorder.[63]

Organizations can further encourage creativity by praising and otherwise rewarding creative decisions. This requires that organizations—and individuals themselves—allow time for thinking and encourage some degree of risk taking. Robert Lutz tried to accomplish this during his years as vice chairman of Chrysler Corporation. In his experience, product development decisions were often based primarily on analysis of marketing research data, excluding truly fresh thinking, and he encouraged his people to try innovations that made sense. For example, at one time, Ford and Chrysler were both considering whether minivans should have two rear sliding doors, rather than just one on the passenger side. According to Lutz, Ford analyzed its extensive marketing research and concluded that most people didn't care about a second sliding door—one was enough. In contrast, Chrysler decision makers started with an analogy: "We just said, 'Hey, all passenger cars, all station wagons, all sport utilities have four doors. Why should minivans be any different?' We just went ahead and did it, and it's now standard. When it became obvious that minivan buyers really wanted that fourth door, Ford had to scramble to catch up."[64]

The Tribune Company, publisher of the *Chicago Tribune,* has institutionalized creative thinking about the future. Through executive strategy sessions, partnerships with high-tech organizations, and assignments to monitor technological change, the company is attempting to be prepared for whatever changes technology may bring to the news business.[65]

One way organizations can foster creativity within groups is to provide opportunities for **brainstorming.** This decision-making technique brings together group members to present ideas freely and spontaneously as one of the participants creates a list of all the ideas. (The group tends to generate the most ideas if participants have time to list ideas silently before sharing them out loud.)[66] In a brainstorming session, participants can build on others' ideas, but they refrain from criticizing ideas. The purpose of this approach is to encourage idea sharing and flexible thinking. Later, when the brainstorming session is completed, the group evaluates the ideas. Ideally, the group will be able to identify ideas that are worth implementing, perhaps after some modification.

brainstorming

Decision-making technique that brings together group members to generate ideas freely and spontaneously, without criticism.

apply it

1. Apply your creativity. Imagine you work as a checkout clerk in a busy store. List 25 ways you can respond *constructively* when you encounter customers who are irritable and impatient. For help, try any of the techniques suggested for improving creative thinking.
2. Evaluate your list of ideas. Do any of them seem creative? Do you think you would have generated better ideas if you had worked with others on this activity? If you were the store manager, would you encourage your employees to try any of your ideas?

Organizational decision making is challenging

Creativity is important because decision making is such a challenging activity in today's organizations. Organizations expect their people to be skillful at choosing what problems to solve and who will make the decision. In addition, the decision makers in today's organizations are expected to make ethical decisions, consider cultural differences, and apply decision-making technology appropriately.

Choosing Problems to Solve

problem

Difference between a desired state and an actual state.

Decision making starts only when someone sees the need for a decision. Often the need takes the form of a **problem**—that is, a difference between a desired state and an actual state. If an organization has more orders than it can fill, its desired state of being able to fill all orders differs from its actual state. Conversely, Spencer Newman, founder of Adventurous Travel Bookstore, identified a problem when his online sales of travel and adventure books were no longer growing. The stagnant sales differed from his desired level of growth.[67]

These are examples of readily noticeable problems. Other problems are less noticeable. For example, an organization might have a goal that all employees should be highly satisfied and motivated, but it might not have the means to detect signs of dissatisfaction. Also, it is easier to respond to a change that is occurring than it is to notice the absence of a change you might benefit from making. Organizations need creative thinkers not only to identify creative solutions but also to ask creative questions. In the words of *Inc. Technology* editor Leigh Buchanan, "They might be questions that our competitors are already addressing, . . . questions that our customers have thought of but never expressed, . . . or . . . questions that have not yet occurred to anyone else, in which case . . . well, of such stuff are legends made."[68]

Thus, a significant challenge of organizational decision making is to detect problems. Whether organization members will detect a problem depends partly on what they consider important. Also, they will detect a problem only if they have a way to measure its existence. If competitors' activities are considered an important source of problems, the organization encourages people to watch competitors' activities. Similarly, organizations monitor financial and employee performance so that they can identify strengths and uncover problems. However, the more complex and changeable the organization and its environment, the harder it becomes to monitor every possible source of problems.

Besides simply detecting that a problem exists, successful decision making requires a problem to be defined accurately. Successful decision makers carefully define the underlying problem, rather than merely describing its symptoms. Thus, when Spencer Newman of Adventurous Travel Bookstore found that sales were stagnating, he did not simply define his problem as "flat sales." Rather, he looked for the reason for this trend. He studied the market and guessed that a growing number of shoppers were studying ATB's online catalog to identify books they wanted, then ordering online from a then-new market player called Amazon.com, which sold at a discount. Newman determined that his problem was a need for a strategy to differentiate his business from Amazon.com. He decided to do this by providing superior benefits. Newman's company offers in-depth knowledge from people who have actually traveled themselves, so he focused on the services available at his Web site, such as an online newsletter, maps, online book reviews by staff members, links to related Web sites, and the ability of customers to communicate with ATB staff via e-mail. He also featured hard-to-find titles, such as rare books and titles from foreign publishers. Newman concluded, "Amazon forced us to reevaluate the company, and that's probably good."[69]

Indeed, professors Raiffa, Hammond, and Keeney maintain that the most common problem with decision making is the failure to accurately define the problem. People tend not to analyze the situation, and often the situation changes even while the decision makers are analyzing alternatives. Nevertheless, Hammond has said, "A good solution to a well-posed problem is usually far superior to an outstanding solution to a poorly posed problem."[70] When people in an organization notice that a problem exists, they should therefore ask one another whether what they notice is merely a symptom of a deeper problem.

Choosing Decision Makers

Organizations control who makes decisions on behalf of the organization; this is part of the managerial function of organizing. To obtain high-quality decisions, organizations delegate decision-making authority to the people who have the most to contribute to that process. In the slower moving organizations of the past, the responsibility for complex, nonprogrammed decisions typically resided near the top of the hierarchy. The top managers were presumed to have the greatest ability to think strategically and direct the organization.

Today, organizations share decision-making authority more widely. Production workers make decisions about scheduling and product quality. Customer service representatives often have the authority to do whatever it takes to satisfy a customer. Teams of employees may decide how to predict and react to changes in the organization's environment. The objective of this approach is to apply all of the organization's human resources—including their knowledge and experience—to arrive at good decisions.

In a dramatic example of this approach, Staffing Solutions Group, which recruits staff for corporate clients, has a policy of letting employees decide how much the company will pay them. The company merely provides each employee with a worksheet accompanied by relevant financial data. Staffing Solutions has calculated the expenses it must cover, such as the costs of overhead and sales and marketing, along with a profit margin. Dividing this amount among the revenue-generating employees results in a number they can use to determine what they are worth to the company. If each employee costs Staffing Solutions $10,000 per year, an employee who wants to earn $35,000 must bring in $25,000 in revenues. The company lets employees set their own earning targets, and as long as they meet those targets, they have wide latitude in when, where, and how they work, as well as what they earn. So far, although employees give themselves raises every two years or so, they have consistently met their targets.[71]

A benefit of delegating decision making is that it provides an opportunity to develop employees' knowledge and skills. Jack Stack, chief executive of Springfield Remanufacturing Corporation, has used decision-making authority in this way. For example, a young Springfield manager responsible for a line of business once reported that although sales rose when he added some new product lines, profits were slipping. In response to questions from Stack, the manager said expenses might be too high on some of the new products. He was unable to say which products or which expenses, because his reports lumped the product lines together. Rather than lecturing the manager, Stack instructed him to study the problem until he could find its source. Eventually the manager traced the problem to the packaging for a single product line. In fact, the packaging was so expensive that the company was actually losing money on the product. This experience not only enabled the manager to correct the particular problem but trained him to make better decisions about product lines in the future[72]

Making Ethical Decisions

Decision making is the means by which people put ethics into practice. Conversely, ethics should be a consideration whenever people make decisions in organizations. Chapter 1 described several ways in which people apply ethical principles to their decisions.

In practice, experience shows that people do not always make ethical decisions. Sometimes this is because they have not developed the ability to do so. Ethical decisions require an awareness of how our decisions affect others, as well as a high value on protecting other people's well-being. People who have not practiced looking for the implications of their actions may not think to do so, and people who have not been taught ethical values may not be able to apply them.

In addition, people differ in their perceptions of how much power they have to choose the ethical course. Some people believe they must go along with what everybody else is doing. Others have what we defined in Chapter 3 as a strong internal *locus of control.* They believe they are responsible for their own actions and for the consequences of their behavior. Coupled with ethical values, the internal locus of control influences people to make ethical decisions.

Cultural differences with regard to ethics also complicate decision making. Cultures differ in their definitions of what constitutes ethical behavior. Exhibit 10.10 compares Russian and U.S. perspectives on business ethics. As shown in this matrix, some kinds of behavior are considered ethical (or unethical) in both cultures, whereas other kinds of behavior are defined as ethical by only one of the cultures. For example, U.S. managers view layoffs as an unfortunate but ethical choice when a company's profitability is at stake. When bicycle makers Huffy Corporation and Brunswick Corporation found they could not compete profitably with imported bicycles, they moved their production activities from North America to Asia, a decision both companies treated as a practical necessity.[73] In Russia, however, laying off employees would be considered unethical.

exhibit | **10.10**
Russian and U.S. Perspectives
on Business Ethics

Source: Adapted from S. M. Puffer and D. J. McCarthy, "Finding the Common Ground in the Russian and American Business Ethics," *California Management Review*, Winter 1995, p. 35.

Organizations can greatly influence the use of ethics in decision making. An organization's policies, procedures, and values shape employees' perceptions about the risks and rewards of making ethical choices. Similarly, professional and trade groups also may foster ethical behavior among their members. For example, the American Society of Magazine Editors recently released guidelines for ethical behavior regarding advertiser sponsorship of special issues and advertising sections in magazines. These guidelines are designed to distinguish advertiser-sponsored content from the magazine's own content, in an effort to uphold magazines' role as impartial reporters of information.[74] These kinds of guidelines are especially relevant because the current business climate for the news media is so fast changing and competitive that decision makers are tempted to cross ethical boundaries that were once more widely accepted. For example, *Los Angeles Times* publisher Kathryn Downing authorized a special issue of the newspaper's Sunday magazine covering the opening of the Staples Center sports arena. The decision generated $2 million in ad revenue, but at large cost to the newspaper's credibility, because it was a major partner in the arena and had failed to disclose that a share of the ad revenues would go to the arena.[75]

In contrast to this experience, if an organization highly values and rewards ethical behavior, even employees with little concern for ethics will favor the ethical course, because it is the one that gets rewarded. This is especially true when organizations spell out their expectations so clearly that even employees from different cultures recognize what the standards are. Furthermore, such an ethical organization will attract prospective employees who value an opportunity to apply high ethical standards at work.

Working with Cultural Differences

Different cultures teach different ways of making decisions. For example, people from different cultures vary in the ways they select problems and analyze alternatives, as well as whether they arrive at decisions democratically or autocratically.[76] Some cultures value logic and in-depth analysis; others place more emphasis on group harmony. Japanese decision makers, whose style emphasizes group harmony, typically collect a great deal of information and use it to arrive at a consensus.

As noted in the previous section, cultures sometimes differ in the way they evaluate the ethics of alternative actions. Most Westerners, for example, would disapprove of the way Pavel Borodin fulfills his role as head of Russia's Directorate of Presidential Affairs (DPA). The DPA manages assets it inherited from the Communist party, the former Soviet government, and other government institutions. It publishes no public accounts and uses its assets to provide personal benefits as needed to accomplish its political objectives. When former Russian President Boris Yeltsin was trying to persuade the Russian parliament to approve a prime minister, he announced on television that deputies' "problems with housing will be solved." It was Borodin who quietly arranged the solutions. Borodin sees his activity as appropriate management of the nation's property for the nation's benefit.[77] Those outside Russia might view his role as one of providing payoffs for a favorable vote.

Some cultures do not emphasize the importance of recognizing and solving problems. Indonesia and Thailand, for example, value acceptance of situations, rather than efforts to change them. In contrast, U.S. managers are relatively quick to seize on a problem and take action. If a U.S. manager working with people in Thailand wanted to initiate a decision, he or she would probably have to devote more effort to the early stages of the decision-making process before others would agree there was need for action. Conversely, if that manager waited passively for the Thai employees to report problems, the manager would probably not learn about situations he or she would view as significant.

Using Technology Appropriately

Decision makers also must decide when to use new technology to assist with decision making. Advances in information technology give organization members wide access to a variety of decision-making tools. As these tools become increasingly widespread, decision makers are expected to know when and how to use them. Decision technology falls into two general categories: tools for enabling group participation in decision making and tools for making aided choices.

Technology for Group Decision Making   Group decision-making tools include groupware and videoconferencing. These technologies, introduced in the preceding chapter, support decision making by enabling participants to communicate with one another and share images and documents without regard to their geographic location. They lower cost barriers to group participation, thereby enabling organizations to obtain the benefits of group

With today's need for fast-paced decision making and instant communication, it was bound to happen—the mobile office. Megacar, designed by German Kim Schmitz, is a complete mobile office containing technologically advanced systems. Megacar offers a flat-panel computer display that can be folded into the car's ceiling, Internet access, the power of 16 digital mobile phones, videoconferencing, and hefty encryption capabilities to protect the transmission of executive decisions. Schmitz has joined with auto-systems designer IVM Engineering Group to turn Megacar into a company to provide Internet access and portal services to mobile Internet users in their autos.
(Source: © Andreas Pohlman)

decision making without some of the costs. Such a system may also display anonymous comments, thereby preventing decision errors that result if group members defer to the high-status members' opinions.

An example currently being developed is CareInsite, which is intended to enable Internet communications among doctors, pharmacists, pharmacy benefits management companies, and insurance companies. CareInsite's developers hope that by using the system to look up medical records, order prescriptions, and submit insurance claims, doctors will improve their ability to make decisions that are both effective and cost efficient. One way the system can do this is by notifying doctors when they order an expensive drug for which there is a lower cost alternative.[78]

Technology for Making Choices Another application of technology is the **decision support system.** This type of computerized information system provides decision models created by experts. Decision makers answer questions about their goals and the situation, and the decision support system uses a decision model to analyze alternatives and recommend the alternative likely to provide the optimal outcome. New York University professor Steven J. Brams and Union College professor Alan D. Taylor have even developed decision software that incorporates subjective evaluations of fairness into decision models. The software does this by requesting that the participants assign values to whatever is to be allocated by the decision. It then makes allocation decisions that reflect these subjective valuations, resulting in decisions that seem fair to everyone concerned.[79]

Systems under development can help automate the whole decision-making process for routine decisions. For example, BusinessBots uses a kind of software called *bots* to search the Internet, looking for companies that offer a desired product at the desired price. The bots can even estimate quality, haggle for a better price, and close a sale, all within minutes.[80]

Besides automating analysis of alternatives, technology can help decision makers gather information about problems and alternatives. Invention Machine offers software that provides information to support product development decisions. The software is based on a database compiled from a wide range of cause-and-effect relationships reported in patent applications and scientific documents. Product developers with a general idea can enter their idea, and the system will search for related principles that can help them refine their idea. Or they can ask about a category of problem (such as how to reduce vibration or improve the flow of a liquid) and look at existing solutions applied in other situations. For example, Invention Machine showed engineers at an oil company an invention in the medical field that they could apply to delivering oil from refineries to tanker ships.[81] In the field of retailing, the following example shows how OfficeMax used information technology to help its managers make decisions about staffing.

> **decision support system**
>
> Computerized information system that uses decision models to analyze alternatives and recommend the alternative that will provide the optimal outcome, based on the user's information about the situation and goals.

In the mid-1990s, office supply superstore OfficeMax was growing so fast its people could hardly make decisions. Managers didn't have information readily available about whether stores were operating as profitably as they might. To gain control over its growth, company executives knew they needed help, so they turned to information technology.

As a result, the company installed an executive information system (EIS) to support decision making. The system gathers data about sales history and forecasts, as well as staffing levels at the company's

OfficeMax

stores. Unlike the company's previous information systems, the EIS flags trends so that managers can quickly identify and act on problems.

Soon after the EIS went to work, it pointed out a disturbing pattern: Customers in OfficeMax stores with relatively small staffs were buying less than customers in the other stores. Executives quickly diagnosed the problem. In the words of Scott Norris, manager of financial systems for OfficeMax, "We were losing sales because customers were walking out frustrated." OfficeMax's management decided that the stores with low sales needed to put more employees on the floor. In addition, the EIS provides decision support to store managers, who must make decisions related to staffing, merchandise display, and controlling theft.

According to Norris, the company's executives credit the EIS for helping them to achieve consistently strong sales growth over the last few years.[82]

As the Internet brings libraries of information to the fingertips of decision makers, organizations are likely to raise their expectations with regard to information gathering. For example, where once it was enough to analyze the competition in a home state, e-commerce now creates the expectation that decision makers will analyze competition globally and in cyberspace. Thus, as the decision-making tools proliferate, so do the expectations for decision quality.

apply it

1. Suppose you are setting up a joint venture with a team of Russian computer programmers. Your U.S.–based group is to handle the marketing of software to be developed by the Russian team. Given the differing views of business ethics illustrated in Exhibit 10.10, how can you and your Russian counterparts arrive at ethical decisions about employee compensation and product pricing?

2. In your answer to question 1, who do you assume will make the decisions about compensation? About pricing?

summary OF KEY CONCEPTS

- **Decision making is a multistep process.** The rational model of decision making is a normative model with the following steps (1) establish the scope of the decision situation and the goal of the decision, (2) gather complete information about the alternative solutions, (3) establish criteria for selecting an alternative, (4) compare the alternatives in terms of these criteria, and (5) select and implement the optimal alternative and evaluate the results. The behavioral model is a descriptive model that says people modify the rational model by engaging in bounded rationality, satisficing, and political behavior. In organizations, people generally use the rational model for decision situations that are simple, have few alternatives, and cost little to research.

- **Situation shapes the choice of a solution.** The choice process may be aided or unaided.

Aided choices are most likely when the decision task is demanding and the consequences of the decision are great. Decisions may be analytic or heuristic. Heuristics are most commonly used for situations that are familiar, straightforward, and stable. From simplest to most difficult, decision environments involve certainty, risk, uncertainty, or ambiguity. Organizations may impose constraints on decision makers, such as limiting their time, resources, or evaluation criteria. Escalation of commitment also influences decisions about committing further resources to a project.

- **Many of an organization's decisions are made by groups.** Group decisions can benefit from a diversity of experiences and viewpoints, and group members may be more committed to a decision they have made together. However, group decisions take longer and are subject to groupthink.

Vroom, Yetton, and Jago have developed a decision tree for use in determining when the benefits of group decisions outweigh the drawbacks. Groups can improve decision making by appointing a devil's advocate or using multiple advocacy, the Delphi method, or the nominal group technique.

• **Creativity can improve decision making.** Creative individuals contribute fresh ideas to groups; when groups receive and apply these ideas, the organization as a whole acts more creatively. Organizations can foster creativity by encouraging individuals to develop their creativity and by rewarding creative decisions. They can encourage creative ideas in groups by using brainstorming.

• **Organizational decision making is challenging.** Decision makers must carefully recognize and define problems to solve. They must choose the appropriate decision makers, recognizing that delegation of decision making can enable the organization to fully employ its human resources. Decisions should be ethical, which requires that organizations reward ethical decisions. Decisions in today's organizations often involve people with cultural differences that affect decision-making style, as well as the choice of alternatives. Technology can assist in decision making, but it also raises the organization's standards for the quality of decisions.

KEY terms

decision, p. 337

decision making, p. 337

rational model, p. 338

normative, p. 338

optimizing, p. 339

behavioral model, p. 340

descriptive, p. 341

bounded rationality, p. 341

satisficing, p. 341

heuristics, p. 347

availability heuristic, p. 347

representativeness heuristic, p. 347

certainty, p. 349

risk, p. 349

risk propensity, p. 349

uncertainty, p. 350

ambiguity, p. 350

programmed decision, p. 352

nonprogrammed decision, p. 353

escalation of commitment, p. 353

groupthink, p. 356

devil's advocate, p. 360

multiple advocacy, p. 360

Delphi method, p. 360

nominal group technique, p. 360

creativity, p. 361

brainstorming, p. 363

problem, p. 364

decision support system, p. 369

DISCUSSION questions

1. Identify briefly the five steps of decision making in the rational model. Why is it important for managers to know and understand these steps?

2. Think of a job that you currently have or have had in the past, and describe a situation at work in which you used bounded rationality to make a decision. Considering what you now know about decision making, was this the most effective way to make your decision? Why or why not?

3. If you were the manager of a discount store such as Wal-Mart, Target, or Kmart, how might you use the concept of satisficing on the part of customers to determine the layout of products in your store?

4. Would a stockbroker operating on the floor of the New York Stock Exchange during a heavy day of trading be more likely to engage in rational decision making or behavioral decision making? Is this the most effective method, given the environment? Why or why not?

5. What decision-making tools might an accountant use to determine whether a manufacturing company should build another plant?

6. Why is the availability heuristic not necessarily the best way to make judgments?

7. What steps could a manager take to reduce uncertainty in the process of making a decision to expand a company's operations overseas?

8. If a dining customer in an upscale restaurant sends a meal back to the kitchen, complaining that the meal is inadequate, what kinds of resource constraints might the wait staff face in making decisions about how to handle the situation? How might a waiter operate successfully within these constraints?

9. Deciding which college to attend (or whether to accept a job offer) is an example of a large, nonprogrammed decision in your life. Describe how you arrived at either decision. Do you feel

satisfied with your decision-making process? Why or why not?

10. Have you ever been part of a group decision with which you disagreed? Describe the incident, including the process through which the group reached its decision.

11. How might a manager prevent cohesiveness in group decision making from turning into groupthink?

12. Suppose your manager asked you to come up with some ideas for an afternoon outing for you and several coworkers that would be both relaxing and motivating. Asked to think creatively in this fashion, what would you come up with?

13. In what ways could a large health maintenance organization benefit from some delegation of decision making to customer service representatives?

SELF–DISCOVERY exercise

What's Your Personal Decision Style?
Read each of the following questions and fill in the blank with the letter of the answer that best describes you. Think about how you typically act in a work or school situation and mark the answer that first comes to your mind. There are no right or wrong answers.

1. In performing my job or classwork, I look for:
  a. practical results.
  b. the best solution.
  c. creative approaches or ideas.
  d. good working conditions.

2. I enjoy jobs that:
  a. are technical and well defined.
  b. have a lot of variety.
  c. allow me to be independent and creative.
  d. involve working closely with others.

3. The people I most enjoy working with are:
  a. energetic and ambitious.
  b. capable and organized.
  c. open to new ideas.
  d. agreeable and trusting.

4. When I have a problem, I usually:
  a. rely on what has worked in the past.
  b. apply careful analysis.
  c. consider a variety of creative approaches.
  d. seek consensus with others.

5. I am especially good at:
  a. remembering dates and facts.
  b. solving complex problems.
  c. seeing many possible solutions.
  d. getting along with others.

6. When I don't have much time, I:
  a. make decisions and act quickly.
  b. follow established plans or priorities.
  c. take my time and refuse to be pressured.
  d. ask others for guidance and support.

7. In social situations, I generally:
  a. talk to others.
  b. think about what's being discussed.
  c. observe.
  d. listen to the conversation.

8. Other people consider me:
  a. aggressive.
  b. disciplined.
  c. creative.
  d. supportive.

9. What I dislike most is:
  a. not being in control.
  b. doing boring work.
  c. following rules.
  d. being rejected by others.

10. The decisions I make are usually:
  a. direct and practical.
  b. systematic or abstract.
  c. broad and flexible
  d. sensitive to the needs of others.

Scoring: Count the number of **a** answers. This is your **directive** score: _____.

Count the number of **b** answers for your **analytical** score: _____.

The number of **c** answers is your **conceptual** score: ———.

The number of **d** answers is your **behavioral** score: ———.

What is your dominant decision style? Are you surprised? Is it what you expected?

Source: Adapted from Alan J. Rowe and Richard O. Mason, *Managing with Style: A Guide to Understanding, Assessing, and Improving Decision Making* (San Francisco: Jossey-Bass, 1987), pp. 40–41.

ORGANIZATIONAL BEHAVIOR in your life

Without even thinking about it, you make hundreds of decisions every day. Most of these are programmed decisions—which brand of milk to buy, which route to take to class. Others are nonprogrammed—say, if a friend calls and asks if you want to go off-campus for the weekend. Tomorrow, create a log of all the decisions you make during one day. First, make a two-columned chart that's easy to carry with you—one column for programmed decisions and one for nonprogrammed decisions. Record each decision as soon as you can after you make it. At the end of the day, count up how many of each type of decision you made. Share your findings with the class.

ORGANIZATIONAL BEHAVIOR news flash

@ The Internet has changed the way many company managers make decisions. In cases where they once made analytic, rational decisions, they now have to make quick, heuristic decisions based on hunches or intuition, engaging in forms of bounded rationality. Why? Because information flows through the Internet and transactions are made with great speed. If decisions are not made quickly, a company could lose out on huge business opportunities. Meg Whitman, the CEO of eBay, the successful online auction site, confirmed in an interview with Diane Sawyer that the high speed of Internet business requires her to make decisions "based on instinct." Of course, this type of decision making also reflects a willingness to accept a certain amount of risk.

Using the news listings on your search engine, such as AP, Reuters, ZDNeT News, and the like, look for stories about Internet-based companies such as eBay, Amazon.com, pets.com, and so forth to see what you can learn about the way managers of these companies make decisions. If you cannot find news stories that relate to decision making, access a company's site and browse through it carefully, noting features of the site that reflect certain decisions. Then, imagine that you are a consultant to the company of your choice, asked to assess the organization's decision-making processes. Write a memo to the CEO describing your findings.

Source: Televised interview, *Good Morning America*, ABC News, Thursday, December 9, 1999.

global diversity EVENTS

@ One of the biggest—and perhaps riskiest—decisions an organization can make is to expand overseas. This type of expansion is fraught with potential pitfalls in the decision environment, which range in severity from uncertainty to ambiguity. Yet the application of rational decision making can lead the organization to tremendous payoffs through expansion, whether it is a global movement or simply the transfer of certain operations to one or two foreign countries. Intel Corp., Amkor Technology Inc., Texas Instruments, and other semiconductor chip companies have made this decision, establishing plants in the Philippines to manufacture, assemble, and test chips. For example, Intel spent $500 million to build a plant there that will assemble its Pentium III chip as well as other products.

Why would these large companies invest millions of dollars in a country that has traditionally relied on agriculture to fuel its economy and is located halfway around the world? Their main answer is skilled labor. The Philippines has an English-speaking school system with a high rate of literacy and graduates 30,000 to 40,000 engineers a year. But wages for these workers hover as much as 30 percent lower than those of workers in Malaysia and other nearby countries, not to mention those of the United States. "The workforce is the main reason we came, and the main reason we're expanding," explains Desmond Wong, a spokesperson for Texas Instruments' Asian operations.

Intel and the other companies mentioned are just a few manufacturers who have decided to invest heavily in moving portions of their operations overseas. Using the news listings on your search engine, look for stories about organizations that are moving some or all of their operations overseas. (Or look for information on Intel, Texas Instruments, and Amkor Technology by typing those key words into your search engine.) When you find a story or stories that interest you, consider the following questions:

1. On what basis did the company (or companies) make the decision to expand overseas? Does it appear that managers used an analytical decision process or a heuristic decision process?

2. Is there a risk of escalation of commitment in any of these expansions? If so, describe how you think this might happen.

3. In what ways might cultural differences and ethics complicate decision making as organizations try to expand overseas?

Source: Robert Frank, "U.S. and Philippine Companies: Joined at the Chip," *The Wall Street Journal,* September 2, 1999, p. A9.

minicase | I S S U E

Learning the ABCs of Aided Decisions

Thanks to technology, more and more tools are available to help managers make rational decisions. But managers must be able to choose the right tools for the right situations. They must also be aware that the tool cannot make the decision for them; rather, they must use the information provided by the tool to make the decision for themselves. Nick Pindale, CFO of Bluemont Nurseries Inc., has found making aided decisions for his nursery much easier.

Choosing the Right Tool. Bluemont nurseries stocks about 1,500 plant varieties, but several years ago, Nick Pindale came to the realization that some were profitable and others were not. He needed to determine which were the winners and which were the losers in order to decide which to keep and which to drop. Clearly, he could not make this decision based completely on his own observation and judgment; if he tried to do that, he would likely fall into choices based on heuristics, which in this case would be no more accurate than good guesses. So Pindale turned to an accounting method called activity-based costing, or ABC. He divided Bluemont's nursery tasks into categories such as potting, planting, fertilizing, pruning, and so forth, assigning a cost to each task. Then he identified the ones his nursery could perform cost effectively and those it could not. The information he came up with helped pinpoint which plants were profitable and which were not. Based on the information, he could decide which species to keep and which to trim from the inventory.

Risks of Aided Decisions. The right tool does not guarantee the right decision. Gary Cokins, author of *Activity-Based Cost Management: Making It Work,* warns that managers who are new to the process of ABC tend to get bogged down in detail. For example, Nick Pindale could break planting down into several separate tasks, but this wouldn't help illuminate the overall process. So, it's important for managers to understand how to use the tool to get the best information, leading toward the optimal decision. And the decision maker still needs to apply his or her own expertise and judgment to the decision itself; a tool is not a substitute for the ability to make a rational decision.

Benefits of Aided Decisions. Used skillfully, aided choices can benefit a company in many ways. A good decision tool—whether it's a system like activity-based costing, a computer software program, or a procedures manual developed by an organization—can actually help delegate decision making so that more employees in an organization can make rational decisions. It can help decision makers avoid heuristics, and reduce risk and uncertainty as it did for Nick Pindale. Indeed, Bluemont blossomed with the use of its new accounting system. "Five years later, not one of our original greenhouses is still standing," notes Pindale. "We've added state-of-the-art machinery in our potting line. And we've doubled in size." Those are results to grow by.

1. What might be some of the resource constraints that Nick Pindale could face in making decisions based on the information given to him by his accounting system?

2. How might Pindale use his decision-making tools to evaluate existing programmed decisions or create new ones for his nursery?

3. Since Nick Pindale is now the third generation of a family business, in what ways might he successfully be able to rely on his own judgment and information to make decisions about his company?

Source: Mark Henricks, "Beneath the Surface," *Entrepreneur,* October 1999, pp. 108–113.

eleven
CHAPTER

11

Leadership in Organizations

preview

After studying this chapter, you should be able to:

- Define leadership and find ways to practice leadership in your daily life.

- Recognize leaders in your school, community, and workplace.

- Implement the strategies for effective followership at school and work.

- Identify and describe personal traits and characteristics in yourself or others that are associated with effective leadership.

- Distinguish between autocratic versus democratic leadership behavior and job-centered versus employee-centered behavior.

- Explain how leadership is often contingent on people and situations and name the characteristics that may substitute for or neutralize leadership behaviors.

- Create your personal leadership vision and describe the nature of visionary leadership.

- Define transformational leadership and explain its impact on people and organizations.

Phil Jackson led the Chicago Bulls to six NBA championships, but many critics dismissed his coaching ability. Anyone could win, they said, with basketball's greatest player, Michael Jordan, on the team. Now, people are taking a second look as Jackson smoothly guided the Los Angeles Lakers to their first NBA title in 12 years. Jackson's leadership has clearly made a difference. Before he took over as coach of the Lakers in June of 1999, the team was loaded with talent but couldn't get past the second round of the playoffs.

Jackson's leadership approach, based on Native American and Eastern spiritual principles, stresses awareness, compassion, and the importance of selfless team play to achieve victory. He directs his players to be focused and clear minded, to always respect the enemy, and to be aggressive without anger or violence. The key to a winning team, Jackson believes, is for every player—from the starters to the number 12 player on the bench—to let the "me" become the servant of the "we." By focusing everyone on the *we* rather than the *me,* Jackson enabled the Lakers to bond as a team and achieve the success that previously eluded them. His genius is not so much for devising strategy as for getting wealthy, pampered, and sometimes conceited young players to pull togehter mentally and spiritually to achieve a common goal. "It's been cool with Phil," Laker Kobe Bryant says. "He's opened our minds up, expanded the game of basketball beyond Xs and Os, to the point where it's really mental. It's about bonding, and about communication—a lot of it nonverbal—with one another. When we go into battle, we feel like we have a mental edge because of what Phil has taught us."

Although he is firm with his players, Jackson is never severe. When he's coaching, he says, "I try not to let myself get too rigid. My own personal tendency is to be fairly tight, precise, and dogmatic, but a dictatorial coach can frighten his team." Jackson meditates daily to help him stay loose and flexible, open to having fun and reacting to what is happening in the moment. Jackson also wants his players to stay loose and just enjoy playing the game, and he trusts them to be professionals on and off the court. He's never instituted a curfew on the road because he believes you can't treat players like little boys and expect them to behave like men. He believes each player has to come to the game with his own sense of professional responsibility and prepare for a game in his own way. As for the inevitable problems that arise among his players, Jackson deals with them on a one-on-one basis.

Even before he became a head coach, players recognized Jackson's leadership ability. In 1988, after Chicago's then-head coach Doug Collins was ejected early in a game, Jackson took over. As one Bulls player said about the experience: "It's like we were let out of a cage. We won the game because we were so relaxed—and we knew that Phil should become a head coach." Jackson's steady hand and calm leadership allows each player to develop to his fullest potential. Even more importantly, each player recognizes the power that comes when 12 individuals sublimate their own egos and desires to achieve a team goal.[1]

Phil Jackson Scores as a Leader by Inspiring Team Spirit

"He's opened our minds up, expanded the game of basketball. . . . It's about bonding, and about communication—a lot of it nonverbal—with one another."

—Kobe Bryant, Los Angeles Lakers

Leadership makes a difference—on the basketball court, in student organizations, and in the workplace. For example, Continental chairman Gordon Bethune turned the ailing airline around through his leadership. Previous leader Frank Lorenzo had conducted a "reign of terror" that left employees demoralized and distrustful of management. Bethune threw out the strict, intrusive employee rule book and began allowing workers to rely on their own experience and judgment. When the airline's on-time record improved, all workers received cash bonuses. Most importantly, Bethune began sharing financial information with employees and letting them participate in making the decisions that would directly affect their jobs and lives. "They were tired of broken promises and lies," he says. Bethune's leadership has been so effective that employees helped the company earn a spot on *Fortune* magazine's list of the 100 Best Companies to Work for in America.[2] There are leaders working in every organization, large and small. In fact, leadership is all around us every day, in all facets of our lives—our families, schools, communities, social clubs, and volunteer organizations.

Leaders use many different styles and behave in varied ways. Contrast the leadership style of Warnaco CEO Linda Wachner with that of Patricia Gallup, CEO of PC Connection. Wachner uses a tough, aggressive leadership style, which may include reprimanding or even humiliating employees in front of others. She frequently holds meetings until the wee hours of the morning and has been known to call employees at home on the weekends to ask questions. Her "Do It Now" philosophy energizes the entire workforce to strive toward her goal of becoming "the Coca-Cola of the intimate apparel business." Gallup, on the other hand, uses a friendly, open, and accessible style of leadership that encourages employees to talk with her about problems and concerns. She allows any worker to take a one-month leave of absence for any reason, provides full health insurance even for part timers, and rewards employees for their commitment with offbeat perks such as casino nights and hiking trips. Her philosophy is that "employees are customers too" and meeting their needs is an important part of running a business.[3] Both Gallup and Wachner are successful leaders, even though they use different styles and behave in different ways toward subordinates.

Important questions for organizational behavior are what makes a good leader and what impact leadership can have on the performance of others in the organization. This chapter will explore the topic of leadership in detail. We will define leadership, explore how leadership differs from management, and examine various theories of leadership effectiveness. The chapter will also discuss new styles of leadership, including servant leadership and charismatic and transformational approaches.

Leadership makes a difference in organizations

People have been fascinated by the topic of leadership for centuries, but the scientific study of leadership is fairly recent, beginning only in the early 20th century. Scholars and writers have offered hundreds of definitions of the term, and one authority on the subject has concluded that leadership "is one of the most observed and least understood phenomena on earth."[4]

Defining leadership has been a complex and elusive problem because the nature of leadership itself is complex. Some have even suggested that leadership is nothing more than a romantic myth, perhaps based on the hope that someone can come along and solve our problems as if by magic.[5] In recent years, however, there has been much progress in understanding the essential nature of leadership as a real and powerful influence in organizations. In a survey of 150 executives with the world's 1,000 largest corporations, nearly half of respondents rated leadership ability as the most important skill for managers in the 21st century.[6]

A Definition of Leadership

Leadership studies are an emerging discipline and the concept of leadership will continue to evolve. We define **leadership** here as an influence relationship among leaders and followers who intend real changes that reflect their shared purposes.[7] Leadership involves influence, it occurs among people, those people intentionally desire significant changes, and the changes reflect purposes shared by leaders and followers. *Influence* means that the relationship among people is not passive; however, also inherent in this definition is that leadership is multidirectional and noncoercive. Leadership is not something that is done *to* followers. In most organizations, superiors influence subordinates, but subordinates also influence superiors. The people involved in a leadership relationship want substantive *changes.* In addition, the changes are not dictated by the leader but reflect *purposes* that are shared by leaders and followers. Moreover, change is toward an outcome that leader and followers both want—a desired future or *shared purpose* that motivates them toward a more preferable outcome. Thus, leadership involves the influence of people to bring about change toward a desirable future.

One stereotype is that leaders are somehow different, that they are above others. In reality, the same qualities that make an effective leader make an effective follower.[8] Leaders and followers may sometimes be the same people, playing different roles at different times. In some modern team-based and learning organizations, many employees act as leaders at different times and in different circumstances. Half a century ago, management scholar Mary Parker Follett wrote that "it is of great importance to recognize that leadership is sometimes in one place and sometimes in another."[9] Her insight is increasingly relevant for today's organizations, in which leadership may be assumed by a team member with knowledge relevant to a particular problem and then relinquished to others as circumstances or problems change. Leaders can emerge from anywhere in the organization as well as through the formal appointment of authority to head a team or department.

Leadership versus Management

Some managers may be good leaders, but not all good leaders are managers. Leadership has little to do with the formal authority granted to managers in organizations. Much has been written in recent years about the difference between management and leadership. Good management and good leadership are both important to organizations—one cannot replace the other. One of the major differences between the leader and the man-

leadership

An influence relationship among leaders and followers who intend real changes that reflect their shared purposes.

ager relates to their sources of power. Since the manager's power comes from the formal authority granted within the organization structure, it promotes stability, order, and problem solving within the accepted structure and systems of the company. The power of a leader, on the other hand, comes from personal sources that are generally not invested in the organization, such as personal characteristics, goals, and values. Leadership promotes vision, creativity, and change rather than stability. In general, managers work with others to achieve organizational goals through planning, organizing, directing, and controlling employees and other resources. In contrast, leadership focuses on creating a shared vision and strategy and instilling the cultural values that can help others achieve it. Exhibit 11.1 illustrates the different qualities attributed to leaders and managers, although it is important to remember that some people may exhibit a combination of leader/manager qualities. Jack Welch, who is set to retire as head of General Electric at the end of 2000, is a good example of an executive who combines good management and effective leadership. Welch clearly understands and practices good management, such as controlling costs, establishing goals and plans, providing coordination, and monitoring company activities and performance. Yet he is also a master leader, actively promoting change, communicating a vision, providing a clear sense of direction, and energizing and inspiring employees.

The distinction between management and leadership is important because each produces different outcomes that are important for the organi-

exhibit | **11.1**
Leader versus Manager Qualities

Leader   **Manager**

Soul

Visionary
Passionate
Creative
Flexible
Inspiring
Innovative
Courageous
Imaginative
Experimental
Initiates change
Personal power

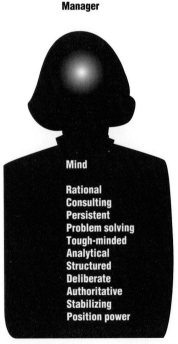

Mind

Rational
Consulting
Persistent
Problem solving
Tough-minded
Analytical
Structured
Deliberate
Authoritative
Stabilizing
Position power

Source: Based on Genevieve Capowski, "Anatomy of a Leader: Where Are the Leaders of Tomorrow?" *Management Review*, March 1994, p. 12.

zation. Because good management leads to a degree of stability, predictability, order, and efficiency, it helps organizations consistently achieve short-term results and meet the expectations of various stakeholders. Successful change, though, depends on effective leadership. Leadership means questioning and challenging the status quo so that outdated or unproductive norms can be replaced to meet new challenges. Good leadership can lead to highly valuable change, such as new products or services that gain new customers or expand markets. For example, Nina DeSesa, chairman and chief creative officer of McCann-Erickson New York, has used her leadership abilities to spark a creative and financial turnaround at the world's largest advertising agency. The changes DeSesa has brought to the company have attracted new high-profile clients such as Lucent Technologies, Motorola, Sprint, Hewlett-Packard's spinoff Agilent, and most recently, Microsoft. DeSesa used her softer, nurturing side to bring about change in what had been known as one of the roughest cultures on Madison Avenue. She believes a personal touch is important because she is constantly "dealing with big egos, big personalities."[10]

Thus, although good management is needed to help organizations meet current commitments, good leadership is essential to break out of unproductive patterns and move organizations into the future. The distinction between management and leadership also underlines the idea that leadership is not restricted to people in specific positions. Anyone in the organization may be a leader. In addition, all leaders are also sometimes followers.

Leadership and Followership

Many of us have heard the old saying, "You can lead a horse to water but you can't make him drink." A similar concept applies in organizations—leaders can successfully lead only when they have effective followers. Only in recent years have scholars begun to recognize the importance of followership in organizations.[11]

Followership is important to a discussion of organizational leadership for several reasons. Organizations generally have many more followers than leaders, so effective followers are critical to the success of organizations. Leadership and followership are fundamental roles that individuals shift into and out of under various conditions. Everyone, leaders included, is a follower at one time or another in their lives. Most people—even those who may have reached positions of high authority in hierarchical organizations—generally have some kind of boss or supervisor. In general, individuals are more often followers than leaders.[12]

Another reason followership is important is that a leader is influenced by the actions and attitudes of followers. For example, the contingency theories of leadership discussed further in this chapter are based on how leaders modify their behavior to fit situations, especially the needs and attitudes of followers. The nature of leader-follower relationships involves reciprocity, the mutual exchange of influence. Leaders and followers work together to achieve a shared vision, and followers' actions can either enhance the leader or underscore the leader's shortcomings.[13] In a performance study of U.S. Navy personnel, it was discovered that the outstanding ships were those staffed by followers who supported their leaders, took initiative, and did not avoid raising issues or concerns with their superiors.[14] The performance of followers, the performance of leaders, and the success of the organization are variables that depend on one another.

A third factor is that many of the qualities that are desirable in a leader are the same qualities possessed by an effective follower. The following qualities have been identified as characteristics of an **effective follower:**[15]

Effective followers are capable of self-management. They are able to think for themselves and work without close supervision. Effective followers understand their own strengths and weaknesses so that they can use their abilities to further the goals of the organization.

Effective followers are committed to something bigger than themselves. They care about more than their own personal goals and needs. Effective followers align themselves with a larger purpose and vision and commit to helping achieve them. Most of us have had the experience of working with people who are emotionally charged up about their work. These people see themselves as important to achieving a desirable goal, whether it be changing university policies regarding student housing, building a house for Habitat for Humanity, completing the design of a new product in record time, or helping an organization achieve a vision of being the best in its industry.

Effective followers work toward competency, solutions, and a positive impact. They generally hold higher performance standards for themselves than required by their boss or work group. These people discern the needs of the organization and work hard to develop skills that can help their team or organization excel.

Effective followers are courageous, honest, and credible. They do not try to avoid risk or conflict. Rather, effective followers have the courage to initiate change and put themselves at risk or in conflict with others, even their leaders, to serve the best interest of the organization. In addition, they establish themselves as independent, critical thinkers whose judgment can be trusted.

effective follower

A person who thinks independently, is capable of self-management, and plays an active role in the organization.

apply it

1. Think about a situation in which you have been involved (an athletic team, a class group project, a work activity) where some people emerged as "natural leaders" of the group. What caused you to identify these people as leaders? Consider your answer in terms of the definition of leadership and the qualities listed in Exhibit 11.1.

2. Identify a specific instance at school or work in which you think you were an effective follower. What caused you to be effective in this situation? How did your interaction with the leader affect your followership?

Do traits and behaviors define leadership?

The earliest definitions of leadership were based on the belief that leaders were born with certain personality traits. This belief eventually spurred researchers to try to identify these traits so that leaders could be predicted or

THE FOLLOWER

Claudia Danzler was thrilled when she was offered a job in the London division of Standard Products Ltd., a consumer products multinational. However, a few months later, she was miserable and told her friends she was considering quitting her job. The problem was Harold Davis, the general manager in charge of the London branch, to whom Danzler reported.

Davis had worked his way up to the general manager position by "keeping his nose clean" and not making mistakes, which he accomplished by avoiding controversial and risky decisions. As Danzler complained to her friends, "Any time I ask him to make a decision, he just wants us to dig deeper and provide 30 more pages of data, most of which are irrelevant. I can't get any improvements going because of his refusal to make a decision!" As one example, Danzler believed that a line of frozen breakfast and dinner foods she was in charge of would be more successful if prices were slightly lowered. She had worked for weeks with her product managers to prepare a detailed analysis, including charts and graphs, to justify a lower price. Davis had reviewed the data, but refused to make a decision. Now, he was asking for data on weather patterns that might affect shopping habits, a request Danzler considered absurd.

She knew Davis was terrified of departing from the status quo. For example, even though the frozen breakfast and dinner lines had been reformulated for the microwave ovens, they still had 1970s-style packaging. Danzler had heard that it took Davis more than two years of "convincing" to agree to a new line of toaster pastries. In another instance, Davis refused to approve a coupon program in March because in previous years coupons

had been run in April. Davis measured success not by new ideas or even sales results, but by hours spent in the office. He arrived early and stayed late and expected the same from everyone else. One of Danzler's product managers had already stopped putting forth any effort to come up with innovative ideas, and Danzler was struggling to keep the others motivated.

After two more months of frustration, Danzler made a final effort to reason with Davis. She argued that the biggest threat to the division was the failure to improve and innovate. She presented data showing that market share had continued to slip for the past four years, and urged new pricing and promotion strategies to help revive sales. Davis listened patiently, but then told Danzler that she and her product managers needed to build a more solid case before any changes could be made. Soon after, Danzler's two best product managers quit, burned out by the marathon sessions analyzing pointless data without results.

1. If you were Danzler, how would you improve your effectiveness as a follower? Would you support Davis even though you believe he is hurting the organization? Discuss.

2. What can you do as a leader to make the work situation better for your product managers?

3. Suppose you are Davis's supervisor and Danzler comes to see you. What would you say?

Source: Based on "General Products Britain," a case appearing in Richard L. Daft, *Leadership: Theory and Practice* (Fort Worth, TX: The Dryden Press, 1999), pp. 417–418.

perhaps even trained. As the limits of the trait approach came to light, researchers began to try to explain effective leadership in terms of a person's behaviors. In this section, we will examine the evolution of the trait and behavior approach to understanding leadership effectiveness.

The Trait Approach

Traits are the distinguishing personal characteristics of a leader, such as intelligence, self-confidence, and appearance. The earliest research focused on leaders (primarily men) who had achieved a level of greatness and, hence, was referred to as the *Great Man* approach. "Leader" was equated with "hero," a concept particularly ingrained in Western culture. For example, Homer's *Iliad* and *Odyssey* both portray strong leaders as heroes of their people. Fundamental to the Great Man approach was the idea that some people are born

traits

The distinguishing personal characteristics of a leader, such as intelligence, self-confidence, and appearance.

with traits that make them natural leaders. In general, research has found only a weak relationship between personal traits and leader success.[16] For example, rival football coaches Steve Spurrier at Florida and Phillip Fulmer at Tennessee have very different personality traits, but both are successful leaders of their football teams.

The diversity of traits that effective leaders possess indicates that leadership ability is not necessarily a genetic endowment. However, it is likely that some traits are associated with effective leadership. In addition to personality traits, researchers have looked at physical characteristics such as age and energy level, abilities such as knowledge and fluency of speech, social characteristics such as popularity and sociability, and work-related characteristics such as the desire to excel and persistence against obstacles. Exhibit 11.2 summarizes the physical, social, and personal leadership characteristics that have received the greatest research support. A recent study by Andersen Consulting, called "The Evolving Role of Executive Leadership," asked dozens of CEOs and hundreds of emerging leaders around the world to rate the importance of various traits to effective leadership in today's world. After analyzing patterns in the results, the team, with the assistance of leadership scholars including Warren Bennis and John O'Neil, found that people considered self-confidence, vision, and striving for personal excellence to be the top three characteristics of a leader. Ultimately, however, the total set of characteristics indicates that leaders in today's business world need the ability to build the organization's capabilities by developing partnerships, treating people with respect and dignity, and developing intellectual capital.[17]

exhibit | 11.2

Some Personal Characteristics of Leaders

Physical Characteristics	Intelligence and Ability
Activity Energy	Judgment, decisiveness Knowledge Fluency of speech

Social Background	Work-Related Characteristics
Mobility	Achievement drive, desire to excel Desire for responsibility Responsibility in pursuit of goals Task orientation

Social Characteristics	Personality
Ability to enlist cooperation Cooperativeness Popularity, prestige Sociability, interpersonal skills Social participation Tact, diplomacy	Alertness Originality, creativity Personal integrity, ethical conduct Self-confidence

Source: Adapted from Bernard M. Bass, *Stogdill's Handbook of Leadership*, rev. ed. (New York: The Free Press, 1981), pp. 75-76. This adaptation appeared in R. Albanese and D. D. Van Fleet, *Organizational Behavior: A Managerial Viewpoint* (The Dryden Press, 1983).

It is important to note that traits do not stand alone. The appropriateness of a trait or set of traits depends on the leadership situation. For example, a trait such as initiative may contribute greatly to the success of a leader in one situation but may be irrelevant to a leader in a different situation. Recent researchers still contend that some traits are important to successful leadership, but only in combination with other factors. Although some traits may have great value for leaders, they cannot provide a full understanding of effective leadership. Beginning as early as the 1940s, researchers began expanding our understanding beyond the personal traits of the leader to focus on behavior styles.

Autocratic versus Democratic Leader Behaviors

One study that served as a precursor to the behavior approach recognized autocratic versus democratic leadership styles. An **autocratic leader** is one who tends to centralize authority and derive power from formal position, control of rewards, and coercion of subordinates. A **democratic leader** delegates authority to others, encourages participation, relies on subordinates' knowledge for completion of tasks, and depends on subordinate appreciation and respect for influence.

The first studies of these leadership behaviors were conducted at the State University of Iowa by Kurt Lewin and his associates.[18] These experiments found that the groups with autocratic leaders performed well as long as the leader was present to supervise them. However, group members resented the close, autocratic style of leadership, and feelings of hostility frequently arose. The performance of groups assigned democratic leaders was almost as good, and these groups were characterized by positive emotions rather than hostility. Most interestingly, under the democratic style of leadership, group members performed well even when the leader was not present to directly supervise activities. The participative techniques and majority-rule decision making used by democratic leaders trained and involved group members to perform well on their own. These characteristics of democratic leadership may partly explain why the empowerment of employees is a popular trend in today's companies.

The early work at Iowa implied that leaders were either autocratic or democratic in their approaches. Further work by Tannenbaum and Schmidt indicated that leadership behavior could exist on a continuum, reflecting varying degrees of employee participation.[19] Thus, one leader might be boss centered (autocratic), another employee centered (democratic), and a third a mix of the two styles. The leadership continuum is illustrated in Exhibit 11.3. Tannenbaum and Schmidt suggested that leaders could adjust their style to fit the circumstances. For example, if there is time pressure on the leader or if it takes too long for subordinates to learn what they need to make effective decisions, the leader will use an autocratic style. When subordinates can readily gain the skills and knowledge needed to make decisions, a participative, democratic style can be used. Also, the greater the skill difference, the more autocratic the leader approach because it is difficult to bring subordinates up to the leader's expertise level.[20]

autocratic leader

A leader who tends to centralize authority and rely on formal position, use of rewards, and coercion to influence subordinates.

democratic leader

A leader who delegates authority to others, encourages participation, relies on subordinates' knowledge for completion of tasks, and depends on subordinate appreciation and respect for influence.

exhibit **11.3**

The Leadership Continuum

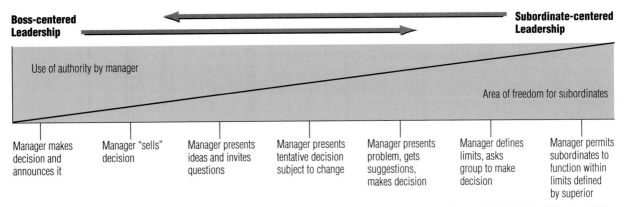

Source: Reprinted by permission of *Harvard Business Review.* An exhibit from Robert Tannenbaum and Warren Schmidt, "How to Choose a Leadership Pattern," May–June 1973. Copyright © 1973 by the president and Fellows of Havard College, all rights reserved.

John Peterman built the once highly successful J. Peterman Company using a democratic leadership style. For years, the J. Peterman catalog enticed customers with romantic ideas of living a new, adventurous life with a new pair of J. P. boots or an exotic-style shirt. Peterman instilled his vision for the company in the minds and hearts of all employees, and he prided himself on his participative leadership and flexible, easygoing corporate culture. However, when the company grew rapidly during the mid-1990s, problems began to occur. Eventually, the J. Peterman Company went into Chapter 11 bankruptcy and was purchased by Paul Harris Stores. Some critics suggested that Peterman needed a more autocratic leadership style to make the rapid, difficult decisions needed to deal with the company's growth. The freedom that had allowed employees to thrive in the early years became a liability during a period of rapid growth because new employees did not share the vision, philosophy, and knowledge that they needed to make good decisions.[21]

behavioral theories of leadership

A group of theories that suggest it is the behavior of the leader that determines leadership effectiveness.

The findings about autocratic and democratic styles provided a focus for subsequent research concerning leadership behaviors. **Behavioral theories of leadership** suggest that it is the behavior of the leader rather than specific personality traits that determine effectiveness. Important research on leadership behavior was conducted at Ohio State University, the University of Michigan, and the University of Texas.

Ohio State Studies

consideration

A type of leader behavior that describes the extent to which a leader is sensitive to subordinates, respects their ideas and feelings, and establishes mutual trust.

Researchers at Ohio State University surveyed leaders to establish the dimensions of leader behavior.[22] They ultimately identified two major behavior types, called *consideration* and *initiating structure.*

Consideration is the extent to which a leader is sensitive to subordinates, respects their ideas and feelings, and establishes mutual trust. Considerate leaders show appreciation for others, listen carefully to problems, seek input from subordinates, develop teamwork, and show concern for their subordinates' well-being.

Initiating structure describes the extent to which a leader is task oriented and directs subordinates' work toward achieving goals. This type of leader behavior includes directing tasks, giving instructions, planning, providing explicit schedules for work activities, emphasizing deadlines, and generally ruling with an iron hand.

Many leaders fall along a continuum comprising both consideration and initiating structure. However, the behavior categories are independent of one another. That is, a leader may display a high degree of both behavior types, or a low degree of both behavior types. Additionally, a leader might demonstrate high consideration and low initiating structure, or low consideration and high initiating structure. The Ohio State research found that the high consideration–high initiating structure style achieved better performance and greater satisfaction. However, more recent studies have found that all four of the leader behavior combinations can be effective depending on the circumstances.[23]

initiating structure

A leader behavior that describes the extent to which a leader is task oriented and directs subordinates' work toward goal achievement.

Michigan Studies

Around the same time as the Ohio State studies, a research study at the University of Michigan took a different approach by directly comparing the behaviors of effective and ineffective supervisors.[24] The Michigan researchers identified two types of leadership behaviors, *employee centered* and *job centered*. **Employee-centered leaders** focus on the human needs of their subordinates in order to build effective work groups and help them meet high performance goals. **Job-centered leaders,** on the other hand, direct activities toward efficiency, cost cutting, and scheduling. Job-centered leaders emphasize the technical and task aspects of the job rather than human needs and personal interaction.

In general, the Michigan group found that the most effective supervisors were employee centered in their behavior. These leaders were associated with higher group productivity as well as greater job satisfaction among subordinates.

employee-centered leader

A leader who focuses on the human needs of followers in order to build effective work groups and help them meet high performance goals.

job-centered leader

A leader who focuses on the technical and task aspects of the job and directs followers' activities toward efficiency, cost cutting, and scheduling.

The Leadership Grid

Blake and Mouton of the University of Texas proposed a two-dimensional leadership theory called the **leadership grid** that builds on the work of the Ohio State and Michigan studies.[25] The grid is based on rating leader behavior according to concern for people and concern for production, which are similar to the Ohio State dimensions of consideration and initiating structure and the Michigan dimensions of employee-centered versus job-centered leadership.

The leadership grid and five of its major management styles are illustrated in Exhibit 11.4. Each axis on the grid is a 9-point scale, with 1 meaning low concern and 9 high concern. *Team management* (9,9) is often considered the most effective leadership style and is recommended because organization members work together to accomplish tasks. *Country club*

leadership grid

A two-dimensional leadership theory that measures a leader's concern for people and concern for production.

exhibit | **11.4**

Leadership Grid Figure

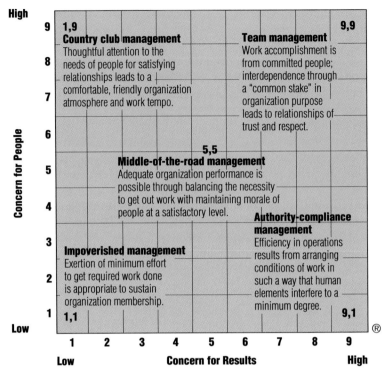

Source: The Leadership Grid Figure from Robert R. Blake and Anne Adams McCanse, *Leadership Dilemmas—Grid Solutions* (Houston, TX: Gulf, 1991), p. 29. Copyright 1991 by Scientific Methods, Inc. Reprinted with permission.

management (1,9) occurs when primary emphasis is given to people rather than to work outputs. *Authority-compliance management* (9,1) happens when efficiency in operations is the dominant orientation. *Middle-of-the-road management* (5,5) reflects a moderate degree of concern for both people and production. *Impoverished management* (1,1) means the absence of a management philosophy; managers exert little effort toward interpersonal relationships or work accomplishment. Consider the following examples of leader behavior in relation to the behavioral theories we have just discussed.

❦ Paychex Inc. and Team Tires Plus

Tom Golisano turned a seemingly obscure business into a gold mine by giving small businesses a place where they can outsource the routine tasks associated with producing paychecks. Paychex Inc. has made Golisano and his partners millionaires. Golisano holds his managers' noses to the grindstone. He insists that they keep the client base growing at 10 percent a year—to do so, every salesperson is required to make 50 calls per week, 8 personal presentations, and at least 3 sales. If they don't, they don't last long at Paychex. Golisano uses boot-camp discipline, requiring employees to observe a strict dress code and a clean desk policy. He prides himself on running a tight operation—no company cars or country club memberships at this company, even for top executives. Despite the grueling pace Golisano sets for managers, those who can meet the standards are handsomely rewarded with stock options, helping to keep turnover low.

Compare Golisano's style to that of Tom Gegax, who calls himself head coach of Team Tires Plus, a fast-growing firm with 150 retail tire stores in ten states. Gegax believes that you can't manage people like you manage fixed assets. His emphasis is on treating employees just as well as they are expected to treat their customers, or "guests," as they are called. Gegax personally leads classes at Tires Plus University, where employees learn not just about changing tires but about how to make their whole lives better. The company's wellness center offers monthly classes in health and nutrition. In addition, a course called "Balancing Your Personal Tire" is a favorite among workers seeking work-life balance. Shiatsu massage is available to employees at headquarters as well as in the retail stores. Gegax also makes sure stores are clean, bright, and airy, so that employees have a pleasant work environment. He believes all this translates into better service for guests. Employees, as well as customers, like the approach. Team Tires Plus welcomes more than 1.7 million guests a year and boasts an annual growth rate of 23 percent. "The last thing the world needs is another chain of stores," Gegax says. "What it does need is a company with a new business model—one that embraces customers and employees as whole people."[26]

The leadership behavior of Golisano is characterized by high concern for tasks and production and low concern for people. Tom Gegax, in contrast, is high on concern for people and moderate on concern for production. Even though these two leaders use very different styles, both are successful because of their different situations. The next group of theories builds on the leader-follower relationship of behavioral approaches to explore how organizational situations affect the leader's approach.

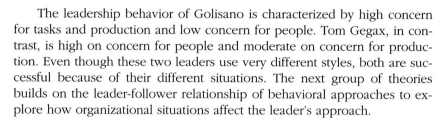

apply it

1. Think about a work supervisor you have or have had in the past. Which of the traits listed in Exhibit 11.2 did this person exhibit? Do you have the traits associated with effective leadership?

2. Imagine you are leading a team to develop a new approach to fall registration at your university (or choose another activity). Under what conditions do you think you might be more effective using a job-centered style of leadership? A people-centered style? Explain.

Contingency theories: Leadership style depends on the situation

The failure to find universal traits or behaviors that would always determine effective leadership led researchers in new directions. While leader behavior is still of concern, the central focus of this research was the situation in which leadership occurred. Several models of leadership that explain the relationship between leadership styles and specific situations have been developed. These are called **contingency approaches** and include the leadership model developed by Fiedler and his associates, the situational theory of Hersey and Blanchard, and the path-goal theory presented by Evans and House.

contingency approaches

Leadership models that describe the relationship between leader styles and specific organizational situations.

Fiedler's Contingency Theory

One early, extensive effort to combine leadership style and organizational situation into a comprehensive theory of leadership was made by Fiedler and his associates.[27] The basic idea is simple: Match the leader with the situation most favorable for his or her success. By diagnosing the leadership approach and the organizational situation, the correct fit can be arranged.

Leadership Approach   The cornerstone of Fiedler's contingency theory is the extent to which the leader is relationship oriented or task oriented. A relationship-oriented leader is concerned with people, as in the consideration style described earlier. A task-oriented leader is primarily motivated by task accomplishment, which is similar to the initiating structure style described earlier.

A leader's relationship versus task orientation was measured with a questionnaire known as the least preferred coworker (LPC) scale. The **LPC scale** has a set of 16 bipolar adjectives along an 8-point scale. If the leader describes the least preferred coworker using positive concepts, he or she is considered relationship oriented, that is, a leader who cares about and is sensitive to other people's feelings. Conversely, if a leader uses negative concepts to describe the least preferred coworker, he or she is considered task oriented, that is, a leader who sees other people in negative terms and places greater value on task activities than on people.

LPC scale

A questionnaire designed to measure relationship-oriented versus task-oriented leadership style according to the leader's choice of adjectives for describing the "least preferred coworker."

Situation   Leadership situations can be analyzed in terms of three elements: the quality of leader-member relationships, task structure, and position power.[28] Each of these elements can be described as either favorable or unfavorable for the leader.

1. *Leader-member relations* refers to group atmosphere and members' attitude toward and acceptance of the leader. When subordinates trust, respect, and have confidence in the leader, leader-member relations are considered good. When subordinates distrust, do not respect, and have little confidence in the leader, leader-member relations are poor.

2. *Task structure* refers to the extent to which tasks performed by the group are defined, involve specific procedures, and have clear, explicit goals. Routine, well-defined tasks, such as those of assembly-line workers, have a high degree of structure. Creative, ill-defined tasks, such as research and development or strategic planning, have a low degree of task structure. When task structure is high, the situation is considered favorable to the leader; when low, the situation is less favorable.

3. *Position power* is the extent to which the leader has formal authority over subordinates. Position power is high when the leader has the power to plan and direct the work of subordinates, evaluate it, and reward or punish them. Position power is low when the leader has little authority over subordinates and cannot evaluate their work or reward them. When position power is high, the situation is considered favorable for the leader; when low, the situation is unfavorable.

Combining the three situational characteristics yields a list of eight leadership situations, which are illustrated in Exhibit 11.5. Situation I is most favorable to the leader because leader-member relations are good, task structure is high, and leader position power is strong. Situation VIII is most unfavorable to the leader because leader-member relations are poor, task structure is low, and leader position power is weak. All other octants represent intermediate degrees of favorableness for the leader.

Contingency Theory   When Fiedler examined the relationships among leadership approach, situational favorability, and group task performance, he found the pattern shown in Exhibit 11.6. Task-oriented leaders are more ef-

exhibit | **11.5**

Fiedler's Classification of Situation Favorableness

	Very Favorable			Intermediate			Unfavorable	
Leader-Member Relations	Good	Good	Good	Good	Poor	Poor	Poor	Poor
Task Structure	High			Low	High		Low	
Leader Position Power	Strong	Weak	Strong	Weak	Strong	Weak	Strong	Weak
Situations	I	II	III	IV	V	VI	VII	VIII

Source: Fred E. Fiedler. (1972). "The effects of leadership training and experience: A contingency model interpretation." *Administrative Science Quarterly 17:* 455. Reprinted by permission of *Administrative Science Quarterly.*

fective when the situation is either highly favorable or highly unfavorable. Relationship-oriented leaders are more effective in situations of moderate favorability.

The task-oriented leader excels in the favorable situation because everyone gets along, the task is clear, and the leader has power; all that is needed is for someone to take charge and provide direction. Similarly, if the situation is highly unfavorable to the leader, a great deal of structure and task direction is needed. A strong leader defines task structure and can establish authority over subordinates. Because leader-member relations are poor anyway, a strong task orientation will make no difference in the leader's popularity.

exhibit | **11.6**

How Leader Style Fits the Situation

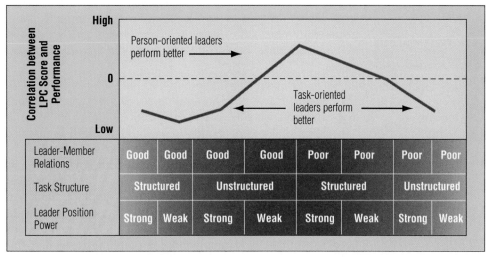

Source: Fred E. Fiedler. (1972). "The effects of leadership training and experience: A contingency model interpretation." *Administrative Science Quarterly 17:* 455. Reprinted by permission of *Administrative Science Quarterly.*

The relationship-oriented leader performs better in situations of intermediate favorability because human relations skills are important in achieving high group performance. In these situations, the leader may be moderately well liked, have some power, and supervise jobs that contain some ambiguity. A leader with good interpersonal skills can create a positive group atmosphere that will improve relationships, clarify task structure, and establish position power.

A leader, then, needs to know two things in order to use Fiedler's contingency theory. First, the leader should know whether he or she has a relationship-oriented style or task-oriented style. Second, the leader should diagnose the situation and determine whether leader-member relations, task structure, and position power are favorable or unfavorable. Fitting leader style to the situation can yield big dividends in profits and efficiency.[29] Maytag Corporation CEO Leonard A. Hadley has revitalized the company as a task-oriented leader.

❦ Maytag Corporation

When Maytag's No. 2 leader, Leonard A. Hadley, was halfheartedly promoted by the board to the chief executive position, few people expected him to bring any dramatic, positive changes to the struggling organization. Maytag's former leader, Daniel J. Krumm, had appointed Hadley as his successor, and the board simply went along for the sake of harmony. After Krumm died of cancer, Hadley found himself as lonely as the Maytag repairman. When the new CEO gave presentations at meetings of executives and analysts, few people attended. Participation in the company's quarterly conference calls was so dismal that they were eventually canceled.

However, Hadley rapidly emerged as a task-oriented leader determined to revive the company and prove his mettle. Within weeks, he fired a number of managers, including three top executives in Europe. He took a tough approach with new managers, pushing them to make the company's foreign operations profitable. As soon as they became profitable, though, Hadley sold them off, insisting that the company needed to focus its resources and energies. He invested heavily in technology and prodded researchers to break away from the long-held policy of never being first to market with a new technology.

The results of Hadley's leadership are impressive. Maytag is growing faster than rivals Whirlpool and GE's appliance division, and profits are soaring. A new front-loading washer, called Neptune, is one of the best-selling washers in the United States, despite its hefty price tag. In addition, the profits on Neptune are extraordinary. Maytag earns $4 for every dollar Whirlpool makes on its top-of-the-line washer. Maytag's stock price jumped from $14 when Hadley took over to $55 five years later. Hadley has gained new respect as a leader from subordinates, financial analysts, and the board. "Len Hadley has . . . done a spectacular job," one Maytag director said. "Obviously, we just lacked the ability to evaluate him."[30]

Leonard Hadley's experience at Maytag illustrates Fiedler's model. His task-oriented style was correct for a difficult, unfavorable situation.

An important contribution of Fiedler's research is that it goes beyond the notion of leadership styles to show how styles fit the situation to improve organizational effectiveness. On the other hand, the model has also been criticized.[31] Using the LPC score as a measure of relationship-oriented behavior or task-oriented behavior seems simplistic, and how the model works over time is unclear. For example, if a task-oriented leader is matched with an unfavorable situation and is successful, the organizational situation is likely to improve and become more favorable to the leader. Thus, the leader might have to adjust his or her style or go to a new situation.

Hersey and Blanchard's Situational Theory

The **situational theory** of leadership is an interesting extension of the behavioral theories described earlier and summarized in the leadership grid (Exhibit 11.4). More than previous theories, Hersey and Blanchard's approach focuses a great deal of attention on the characteristics of employees in determining appropriate leadership behavior. The point of Hersey and Blanchard's theory is that subordinates vary in readiness level. People low in task readiness, because of little ability or training or insecurity, need a different leadership style than those who are high in readiness and have good ability, skills, confidence, and willingness to work.[32]

The relationships between leader style and follower readiness are summarized in Exhibit 11.7. The upper part of the exhibit indicates style of leader, which is based on a combination of relationship behavior and task behavior. The bell-shaped curve is called a prescriptive curve, because it indicates when each leader style should be used. The four styles—telling (S1), selling (S2), participating (S3), and delegating (S4)—depend on the readiness of followers, indicated in the lower part of Exhibit 11.7. R1 is low

situational theory

A contingency approach that links the leader's behavioral style with the task readiness of subordinates.

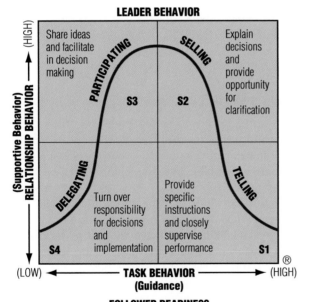

exhibit | **11.7**

Hersey and Blanchard's Situational Theory of Leadership

readiness and R4 represents high readiness. The telling style is for low-readiness subordinates, because people are unable and unwilling to take responsibility for their own task behavior. The selling and participating styles work for followers with moderate readiness, and delegating is appropriate for employees with high readiness.

To use this contingency model, the leader should evaluate subordinates and adopt whichever style is needed. If one or more followers are at low levels of readiness, the leader must be very specific, telling them exactly what to do, how to do it, and when. For followers high in readiness, the leader provides a general goal and sufficient authority to do the task as the followers see fit. Leaders must carefully diagnose the readiness level of followers and then tell, sell, participate, or delegate.

Kierstin Higgins, founder of Accommodations by Apple, a small company that handles corporate relocations, is a leader who understands how follower readiness determines leadership style. "Our employees are very young and energetic, but they're also very emotional, with major ups and major downs." She works closely with new employees and gives them more and more leeway as they mature in their readiness level. Higgins believes effective leadership in her organization means helping her young, relatively inexperienced workers "learn from the challenges they've experienced, as opposed to burning out."[33] A leader would need to use a different style with a part-time worker who was retired after 40 years in the business world.

Path-Goal Theory

path-goal theory

A contingency approach specifying that the leader's responsibility is to increase followers' motivation to attain organizational goals.

Another contingency approach to leadership is called the path-goal theory.[34] According to the **path-goal theory,** the leader's responsibility is to increase subordinates' motivation to attain personal and organizational goals. As illustrated in Exhibit 11.8, the leader increases their motivation by either (1) clarifying the subordinates' path to the rewards that are available or (2) increasing the rewards that the subordinates value and desire. Path clarification means that the leader works with subordinates to help them identify and learn the behaviors that will lead to successful task accomplishment and organizational rewards. Increasing rewards means that the leader talks with subordinates to learn which rewards are important to them—that is, whether they desire intrinsic rewards from the work itself or extrinsic rewards such as raises or promotions. The leader's job is to increase personal payoffs to subordinates for goal attainment and to make the paths to these payoffs clear and easy to travel.[35]

This model is called a contingency theory because it consists of three sets of contingencies—leader behavior and style, situational contingencies, and the use of rewards to meet subordinates' needs.[36] Whereas in the Fiedler theory described earlier the assumption would be to switch leaders as situations change, in the path-goal theory leaders switch their behaviors to match the situation.

Leader Behavior   The path-goal theory suggests a fourfold classification of leader behaviors.[37] The four behaviors the leader can adopt include supportive, directive, participative, and achievement-oriented styles.

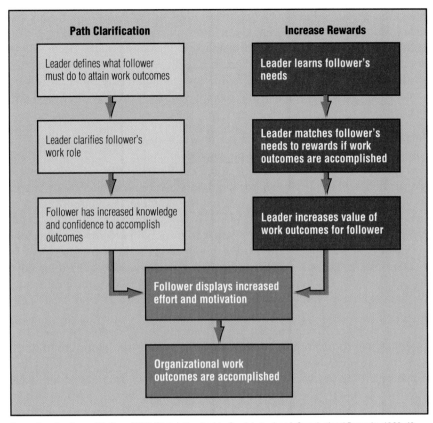

Source: Based on Bernard M. Bass. (1985, Winter). "Leadership: Good, better, best." *Organizational Dynamics 13:*26–40.

exhibit 11.8

Leader Roles in the Path-Goal Model

Supportive leadership involves leader behavior that shows concern for subordinates' well-being and personal needs. Leadership behavior is open, friendly, and approachable, and the leader creates a team climate and treats subordinates as equals. Supportive leadership is similar to the consideration leadership described earlier.

Directive leadership occurs when the leader tells subordinates exactly what they are supposed to do. Leader behavior includes planning, making schedules, setting performance goals and behavior standards, and stressing adherence to rules and regulations. Directive leadership behavior is similar to the initiating-structure leadership style described earlier.

Participative leadership means that the leader consults with his or her subordinates about decisions. Leader behavior includes asking for opinions and suggestions, encouraging participation in decision making, and meeting with subordinates in their workplaces. The participative leader encourages group discussion as well as written suggestions.

Achievement-oriented leadership occurs when the leader sets clear and challenging goals for subordinates. Leader behavior stresses high-quality performance and improvement over current performance. Achievement-oriented leaders also show confidence in subordinates and assist them in learning how to achieve high goals.

In the 1970s, Rick Inatome founded Ina-comp Computer Centers, and built the company into Inacom, a $7-billion busi-ness. Recognized as a leader in the "old" information-technology world, Inatome began as one of the twenty-something computer geeks jumping on a trampoline in Bill Gates's backyard during Microsoft's early days. Recently, Inatome was lured away from Inacom into leadership at ZapMe, an Internet media channel that offers speedy access to advertising-accom-panied content for 13- to 19-years olds. Inatome found that due to drastic changes in the new work environment, he had to change his leadership behavior. He dropped his role as a directive leader with established rules and practiced a more participative form of leadership. "All the old rules of hierarchy had been shattered," says Inatome, adding, "people were all working so hard around here, they didn't have time to figure out what was going on."
(Source: © Michael Grecco Photography, Inc./Icon)

The four types of leader behavior are not considered ingrained person-ality traits as in the Fiedler theory; rather, they reflect types of behavior that every leader is able to adopt, depending on the situation. Robert Galvin shifted to a participative style of leadership at Motorola. He became per-sonally involved in training workers in how their individual and team deci-sions affected the whole organization, and he significantly revised reward systems so that employees would directly benefit from their increased par-ticipation.[38]

Situational Contingencies   The two important situational contingencies in the path-goal theory are (1) the personal characteristics of group members and (2) the work environment. Personal characteristics of subordinates are similar to Hersey and Blanchard's readiness level and include such factors as ability, skills, needs, and motivations. For example, if an employee has a low level of ability or skill, the leader may need to provide additional train-ing or coaching in order for the worker to improve performance. If a sub-ordinate is self-centered, the leader must use rewards to motivate him or her. Subordinates who want clear direction and authority require a directive leader who will tell them exactly what to do. Craftworkers and profession-als, however, may want more freedom and autonomy and work best under a participative leadership style.

The work environment contingencies include the degree of task struc-ture, the nature of the formal authority system, and the work group itself. The task structure is similar to the same concept described in Fiedler's con-tingency theory; it includes the extent to which tasks are defined and have explicit job descriptions and work procedures. The formal authority system includes the amount of legitimate power used by managers and the extent to which policies and rules constrain employees' behavior. Work group characteristics are the educational level of subordinates and the quality of relationships among them.

Use of Rewards   Recall that the leader's responsibility is to clarify the path to rewards for subordinates or to increase the amount of rewards to en-hance satisfaction and job performance. In some situations, the leader works with subordinates to help them acquire the skills and confidence needed to perform tasks and achieve rewards already available. In others, the leader may develop new rewards to meet the specific needs of a sub-ordinate.

Exhibit 11.9 illustrates four examples of how leadership behavior is tai-lored to the situation. In the first situation, the subordinate lacks confi-dence; thus, the supportive leadership style provides the social support with which to encourage the subordinate to undertake the behavior needed to do the work and receive the rewards. In the second situation, the job is ambiguous, and the employee is not performing effectively. Directive lead-ership behavior is used to give instructions and clarify the task so that the follower will know how to accomplish it and receive rewards. In the third situation, the subordinate is unchallenged by the task; thus, an achieve-ment-oriented behavior is used to set higher goals. This clarifies the path to rewards for the employee. In the fourth situation, an incorrect reward is given to a subordinate, and the participative leadership style is used to change this. By discussing the subordinate's needs, the leader is able to

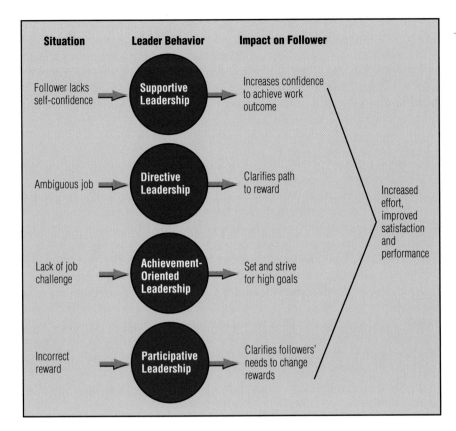

exhibit 11.9
Path-Goal Situations and Preferred Leader Behaviors

identify the correct reward for task accomplishment. In all four cases, the outcome of fitting the leadership behavior to the situation produces greater employee effort by either clarifying how subordinates can receive rewards or changing the rewards to fit their needs.

At Katzinger's Delicatessen, co-owners Steve and Diane Warren set higher goals for their workers and saw a sharp performance improvement.

When Steve and Diane Warren first instituted open-book management at Katzinger's Delicatessen in Columbus, Ohio, they hoped it would help them cut costs and save money. They trained workers in how to read the financials and told them Katzinger's would share the rewards with employees if financial performance improved. They were surprised when nothing happened, but soon realized that, even though workers wanted the rewards, they were not motivated by the vague goal. Most of the employees were young and mobile, not committed to a long-term career with the company, and they felt that they could do little to improve overall financial performance.

So, the Warren's proposed a specific, ambitious goal: if workers could reduce food costs to below 35 percent of sales without sacrificing food quality or service, they would be rewarded with half the savings. Employees immediately began proposing ideas to reduce waste, such as matching the delicatessen's perishable food orders more closely to expected sales. At the end of the first month, costs had fallen nearly 2 percent and employees took home about $40 each from the savings. Later monthly payouts were as high as $95. By the end of the year, food consistency and service had actually increased, even though Katzinger's had met its goal of reducing food costs to below 35 percent of total sales. The Warrens distributed a total of $15,000 to workers for helping to meet the goal.[39]

🍃 **Katzinger's Delicatessen**

An achievement-oriented style proved to be just right for leading the workers at Katzinger's Deli. Path-goal theorizing can be complex, but much of the research on it has been encouraging.[40] Using the model to specify precise relationships and make exact predictions about employee outcomes may be difficult, but the four types of leader behavior and the ideas for fitting them to situational contingencies provide a useful way for leaders to think about motivating subordinates.

Substitutes for Leadership

The contingency leadership approaches considered so far have focused on the leaders' style, the subordinates' nature, and the situation's characteristics. The final contingency approach suggests that situational variables can be so powerful that they actually substitute for or neutralize the need for leadership.[41] This approach outlines those organizational settings in which a leadership style is unimportant or unnecessary.

Exhibit 11.10 shows the situational variables that tend to substitute for or neutralize leadership characteristics. A **substitute** for leadership makes a leadership style unnecessary or redundant. For example, highly professional knowledge workers who know how to do their tasks do not need a leader who initiates structure for them and tells them what to do. A **neutralizer** counteracts a leadership style and prevents the leader from displaying certain behaviors. For example, if a leader has absolutely no position power or is physically removed from subordinates, the leader's ability to give directions to subordinates is greatly reduced.

substitute

A situational variable that makes a leadership style redundant or unnecessary.

neutralizer

A situational variable that counteracts a leadership style and prevents the leader from displaying certain behaviors.

exhibit | **11.10**

Substitues for and Neutralizers of Leadership

Organizational Variables	Task-Oriented Leadership	People-Oriented Leadership
Group cohesiveness	Substitutes for	Substitutes for
Formalization	Substitutes for	No effect on
Inflexibility	Neutralizes	No effect on
Low position power	Neutralizes	Neutralizes
Physical separation	Neutralizes	Neutralizes
Task Characteristics Variables		
Highly structured task	Substitutes for	No effect on
Automatic feedback	Substitutes for	No effect on
Intrinsic satisfaction	No effect on	Substitutes for
Follower Characteristics Variables		
Professionalism	Substitutes for	Substitutes for
Training/experience	Substitutes for	No effect on
Low value of rewards	Neutralizes	Neutralizes

Situational variables in Exhibit 11.10 include characteristics of the group, the task, and the organization itself. For example, when subordinates are highly professional and experienced, both leadership styles are less important. The employees do not need much direction or consideration. With respect to task characteristics, highly structured tasks substitute for a task-oriented style, and a satisfying task substitutes for a people-oriented style. With respect to the organization itself, group cohesiveness substitutes for both leader styles. Formalized rules and procedures substitute for leader task orientation. Physical separation of leader and subordinate neutralizes both leadership styles.

The value of the situations described in Exhibit 11.10 is that they help leaders avoid leadership overkill. Leaders should adopt a style with which to complement the organizational situation. For example, the work situation for bank tellers provides a high level of formalization, little flexibility, and a highly structured task. The head teller should not adopt a task-oriented style, because the organization already provides structure and direction. The head teller should concentrate on a people-oriented style. In other organizations, if group cohesiveness or previous training meets employees' social needs, the leader is free to concentrate on task-oriented behaviors. The leader can adopt a style complementary to the organizational situation to ensure that both task needs and people needs of the work group will be met.

apply it

1. You are the owner of a McDonald's franchise in a suburb of Houston. Finding good workers is difficult, but you have discovered that high school students and retired people often make excellent employees. Turnover is high, though, so you almost always have a mix of new workers and seasoned employees. Using Hersey and Blanchard's situational theory, discuss how you might behave as a leader in this environment.

2. Imagine that you have an extensive background in marketing, but you have just been hired to lead a team of engineers developing a new data storage system. You were picked by top managers for the job because of your excellent reputation for getting things done on time. Many of the team members resent the fact that you were chosen over one of their own and question how a marketing manager can lead the team to get the job done. Based on Fiedler's theory, what style of leadership would be best for this situation? Do you agree that this style would be most effective? Discuss.

3. Think back to teachers or supervisors you have had and try to identify one each who fits a supportive style, directive style, participative style, and achievement-oriented style according to the path-goal theory. Which style did you find most effective? Why?

Leadership is a process of interaction between leader and followers

In this section we will examine several additional approaches that focus more specifically on the process of interaction between leader and followers. These include the leader-member exchange model and the attribution theory of leadership, as well as charismatic, transformational, and visionary approaches to leadership.

Leader-Member Exchange Model

leader-member exchange (LMX) model

A leadership model that suggests that leaders develop unique one-on-one relationships with each subordinate, and that subordinates may exist in either an in-group or an out-group.

The **leader-member exchange (LMX) model,** developed by industrial psychologist George Graen and his associates, suggests that leaders develop unique one-on-one relationships with each subordinate. These relationships, called *vertical dyads,* are thought to result from the natural process of delegating and assigning work roles.[42]

Initial findings indicated that subordinates provided very different descriptions of the same leader. For example, some subordinates might report their relationship with a leader as having a high degree of mutual trust, respect, and obligation. Other subordinates might report a low-quality relationship with the same leader, such as having a low degree of trust, respect, and obligation. Based on these two extreme exchange patterns, subordinates were found to exist in either an "in-group" or an "out-group" in relation to the leader. Most of us who have had experiences with any kind of group recognize that leaders often spend a disproportionate amount of time with certain people, and that these "insiders" are often highly trusted and may obtain special privileges. In Graen's terms, these people would be considered to participate in an *in-group exchange* relationship with the leader, while other members of the group who did not experience a sense of trust, respect, and extra consideration would participate in an *out-group exchange.* In-group members typically receive more attention, more approval, and more status, but they are expected in return to be loyal, committed, and productive. Out-group members tend to be passive and do not have positions of influence or access to the leader. In addition, the leader is more likely to use formal authority and coercive behavior with out-group members.

Leaders typically tend to choose in-group members because they have personal characteristics similar to the leader, such as similarity in age, interests, and values, and because they often demonstrate a high level of competence and interest in the job. LMX theory proposes that these in-group members will have higher performance and greater job satisfaction than out-group members, and research in general supports this belief.[43]

In recent phases of LMX research, the focus has been on whether leaders can develop positive relationships with a large number of subordinates to encourage better performance and job satisfaction. The emphasis is on how the leader can develop beneficial relationships with everyone and provide all employees access to high-quality leader-member exchanges, thereby providing a more equitable environment and greater benefits to leaders, followers, and the organization. In this approach, the leader views each employee independently and may treat each person in a different but positive way. In what is sometimes called *individualized leadership,* leaders strive to develop a positive, trusting, and respectful relationship with each subordinate, even though the relationship will take a different form for each person, depending on the individual's needs. When he was coach of the Indiana Pacers basketball team, Larry Bird tended to use individualized leadership with his players. He tried to understand each players' unique personality and challenge or encourage each a little bit differently to help him achieve his best. In cases where leaders have been trained to improve leader-member relations with all workers, thus expanding in-group status to as many people as possible, performance and productivity have improved.

Attribution Theory of Leadership

Unlike other models of leadership we have discussed, attribution theory deals specifically with people's perceptions and subsequent behaviors. As described in Chapter 4, attribution involves using observations and inferences to explain events or people's behavior. When an event occurs, such as a colleague's promotion, people naturally attribute it to something, such as to the colleague's hard work and dedication or to favoritism on the part of the boss. The **attribution theory of leadership** suggests that the leader's judgment about and behavior toward subordinates is influenced by his or her interpretation of what causes an employee's behavior and performance.[44] This theory says that a leader's attributions, as much as the employees' behavior, determine how a leader relates to and interacts with employees. In turn, employees also attribute certain causes to their leader's behavior.

A leader will treat employees differently depending on whether the leader attributes an employee's successes or failures to the worker's personal skills, interest, and commitment or to factors over which the employee has little control. For example, when a leader believes a subordinate's poor performance is caused by the situation, the leader will provide additional resources, redesign job tasks, or attempt in other ways to change the situation. On the other hand, if the leader believes the employee's poor performance is caused by internal factors, she will attempt to motivate the employee to improve his skills, provide training and coaching, or perhaps reprimand the employee. Effective leaders carefully diagnose the causes of employee performance to provide the appropriate responses. Poor leaders often blame employees when they make mistakes or have difficulty completing tasks, rather than considering situational factors or the leader's own contribution to the problem. Joe Montana, the legendary quarterback of four Super Bowl-winning teams, points out that "when you're a leader, you've got to be willing to take the blame. People appreciate when you're not pointing fingers at them, because that just adds to their pressure. If you get past that, you can talk about fixing what went wrong."[45] Good leaders get beyond blame, learn to be careful and fair in their evaluations of employee performance, and select appropriate measures for dealing with performance problems.

As for employees' attributions, people often develop positive or negative attitudes about a leader based on their belief that the leader's behavior causes their own performance. When employees succeed, they tend to rate their leader as effective; when they fail, employees often rate their leader as ineffective and attribute their failure to the leader's actions rather than to their own.[46] At the organizational level, attribution theory partly explains the vulnerability of a CEO when the organization suffers a severe financial downturn, even though the situation may be caused by events completely beyond the top leader's control (such as poor economic conditions or a sudden, unforeseeable decline in the customer base). On the other hand, when an organization is highly successful, the CEO tends to be given credit, regardless of how much or little he or she contributed. Sometimes, improved performance is simply a result of better economic conditions, changes in the industry, or other factors that may have little to do with who is running the company.

attribution theory of leadership
A theory suggesting that the leader's judgment about and behavior toward subordinates is influenced by his or her interpretation of what causes an employee's behavior and performance.

Jerry Strahan is general manager for the approximately $3 million New Orleans-based hot-dog-vending company, Lucky Dogs. His sales force, men and women who propel Lucky Dog's 10-foot-long hot-dog-shaped carts through the French Quarter contains drifters, alcoholics, insubordinates, petty thieves, and brawlers. This unusual workforce greatly influences Strahan's leadership style. Strahan, who attributes his company's success to this nontraditional team of employees, appropriately responds to their unique behavior styles with flexibility. "Most of these guys are nonconformists. . . . They're not going to wear black pants and white shirts, even if we tell them to. So we have to be flexible. We make rules I know we're going to bend—I know we're going to break—because of the crew we have."
(Source: © Daniel Lincoln)

Her coworkers and friends say Saturn Corp. President Cynthia Trudell is "a car guy," perhaps the biggest compliment an auto executive can receive. In car parlance, that means somebody is as comfortable in an assembly plant as in a high-level corporate strategy meeting. Trudell's charismatic leadership style stems from her years in the engineering ranks, where she walked through a factory in work boots with union stewards as part of the job. Drawing on her earlier days as a plant manager, Trudell was key to inking an agreement that persuaded UAW leaders to support Saturn's long-standing policy for rewarding workers who meet productivity and quality targets. Remaining is the challenge of making Saturn just as popular with car buyers as she is with plant workers. (Source: © Bridget Barrett)

charismatic leader

A leader who has the ability to inspire and motivate followers to transcend their expected performance.

transformational leader

A leader who motivates followers to bring about change by focusing on a vision, shared values, and ideas.

Charismatic Leadership

People often make attributions of heroic or extraordinary leadership qualities regarding certain leaders. These charismatic leaders have long been of interest to researchers studying political leadership (Ronald Reagan), social movements (Martin Luther King Jr.), and religious cults (David Koresh). In recent years, attention has turned to the impact of charismatic leadership on organizations. Charisma has been called "a fire that ignites followers' energy and commitment, producing results above and beyond the call of duty."[47] **Charismatic leaders** have the ability to inspire and motivate people to do more than they would normally do, despite obstacles and personal sacrifice. They have a tremendous impact on followers because they appeal to people's hearts as well as minds. They may speak emotionally about putting themselves on the line for the sake of a mission. In addition, they have the ability to inspire others to do the same. Orit Gadiesh, chair of management consulting firm Bain & Co., is known as a charismatic leader who has the ability to fire people up. Her charisma, according to Bain's managing director, comes primarily from an intense passion about being true to herself and to the client. For Gadiesh, business success isn't systematic—it's about pulling emotional levers. Another charismatic leader is Herb Kelleher at Southwest Airlines, who is well-known for inspiring employees with his unconventional approach, what he calls "management by fooling around." Kelleher's charisma motivates employees to break the rules, maintain their individuality, and make their jobs fun.[48]

Although not everyone can develop the personal appeal of a leader like Orit Gadiesh or Herb Kelleher, charisma often comes from pursuing activities that you truly love. Leaders who love what they do often have a magical quality of charisma. Charismatic leaders are pursuing an idea, project, cause, or activity that they genuinely and deeply care about. They are engaging emotion in everyday work and life, which makes them energetic, enthusiastic, and attractive to others. People want to be around them and want to be like them.

Used appropriately, charisma can energize people and motivate them to extraordinary levels of performance. However, charisma isn't always used to benefit other people, the organization, or society. It can also be used for self-serving purposes, which leads to deception, manipulation, and exploitation of others.[49] Consider, for example, that while leaders such as Winston Churchill and Mohandas Gandhi exhibited tremendous charisma, so did Adolf Hitler and Charles Manson. Leaders use their charisma to achieve positive outcomes when they truly care about others, not just about themselves and their own needs and interests.

Transformational Leadership

Transformational leaders also possess charisma, but they are distinguished by their special ability to bring about significant change by paying attention to followers' needs and concerns, helping them look at old problems in new ways, and encouraging them to question the status quo. Transformational leadership is best understood in comparison to transactional leadership.[50]

The basis of transactional leadership is a transaction or exchange process between leaders and followers. The **transactional leader** recognizes followers' needs and desires and then clarifies how those needs and desires will be satisfied in exchange for meeting specified objectives or performing certain duties. Thus, followers receive rewards for job performance, while leaders benefit from the completion of tasks. Transactional leadership can be quite effective. By clarifying expectations, leaders help build followers' confidence. In addition, satisfying the needs of subordinates may improve productivity and morale. However, because transactional leadership involves a commitment to "follow the rules," transactional leaders generally maintain stability within the organization rather than promoting change. Transactional skills are important for all leaders, but when an organization needs change, a different type of leadership is needed.

Transformational leaders have the ability to lead changes in the organization's vision, strategy, and culture as well as promote innovation in products and technologies. Rather than analyzing and controlling specific transactions with followers using rules, directions, and incentives, transformational leaders focus on intangible qualities such as vision, shared values, and ideas in order to build relationships and engage followers in the change process. Transformational leadership is based on the personal values, beliefs, and qualities of the leader rather than on an exchange process between leaders and followers. Transformational leadership differs from transactional leadership in four significant areas.[51]

transactional leader

A leader who clarifies role and task requirements and indicates how subordinates' needs will be satisfied in exchange for the accomplishment of established goals.

1. *Transformational leadership develops followers into leaders.* Followers are given greater freedom to control their own behavior. Transformational leadership rallies people around a mission and defines the boundaries within which followers can operate in relative freedom to accomplish organizational goals.

2. *Transformational leadership elevates the concerns of followers from lower level physical needs (such as for safety and security) to higher level psychological needs (such as for self-esteem and self-actualization).* It is important that lower level needs are met through adequate wages, safe working conditions, and other considerations. However, the transformational leader also pays attention to each individual's need for growth and development. Therefore, the leader sets examples and assigns tasks not only to meet immediate needs but also to elevate followers' needs and abilities to a higher level and link them to the organization's mission.

3. *Transformational leadership inspires followers to go beyond their own self-interests for the good of the group.* Transformational leaders motivate people to do more than originally expected. They make followers aware of the importance of changing goals and outcomes and, in turn, enable them to transcend their own immediate interests for the sake of the organizational mission. Followers admire these leaders, identify with them, and have a high degree of trust in them. However, transformational leadership motivates people not just to follow the leader personally but to believe in the need for change and be willing to make personal sacrifices for the greater purpose.

4. *Transformational leadership paints a vision of a desired future state and communicates it in a way that makes the pain of change worth the effort.*[52] The most significant role of the transformational leader may be to find a vision for the organization that is significantly better than the old one and to enlist others in sharing the dream. It is the vision that launches people into action and provides the basis for the other aspects of transformational leadership we have just discussed. Change can occur only when people have a sense of purpose as well as a desirable picture of where the organization is going. Without vision, there can be no transformation.

Whereas transactional leaders promote stability, transformational leaders create significant change in followers as well as in organizations. Leaders can learn to be transformational as well as transactional. The most effective leaders exhibit both transactional and transformational leadership patterns, though in different amounts. One example of a leader who demonstrates both transactional skills and transformational qualities is Richard ("Dick") Kovacevich, CEO of Norwest Corp. Kovacevich has been called one of the best bankers in America because of his careful attention to the factors that keep banks stable and profitable. However, he's also known for spouting radical notions such as "Banking is necessary, banks are not." Kovacevich has inspired his followers with a vision of transformation—of becoming the Wal-Mart of financial services—and it looks as if the company is well on its way. At Norwest, for example, the average customer buys nearly four financial products, as opposed to the industry average of two, which translates into approximately triple the amount of profit for Norwest. Kovacevich leads with slogans such as "Mind share plus heart share equals market share." The company constantly tells employees that they are the heart and soul of Norwest, and that only through their efforts does the company succeed.[53]

Visionary Leadership

As you may already recognize, both charismatic and transformational leaders may be considered "visionary." In fact, throughout this chapter, we have used the term *vision* in referring to leaders. Creating and articulating a compelling vision is the primary job of a leader. Visionary leadership has been defined as a distinct category here because of the importance of vision to both leadership excellence and organizational success.

visionary leader

A leader who sees beyond current realities, creates a compelling vision of the future, and energizes followers to help achieve the vision.

vision

An attractive, ideal future for the organization that is credible yet not readily attainable.

Visionary leaders see beyond current realities; create and articulate a realistic, credible, and attractive vision of the future; and generate ideas about how to reach that future by building on the present.[54] This means more than planning and setting a direction for employees. A **vision** is an attractive, ideal future that is credible yet not readily attainable. Although it may be thought of as a dream for the future; it is also more than a dream. A vision is a highly ambitious view of the future that everyone can believe in, one that can realistically be achieved yet requires that employees put forth their best effort. In Exhibit 11.11, vision is shown as a guiding star, drawing everyone in the organization along the same path toward a future that is better in significant ways than what now exists.

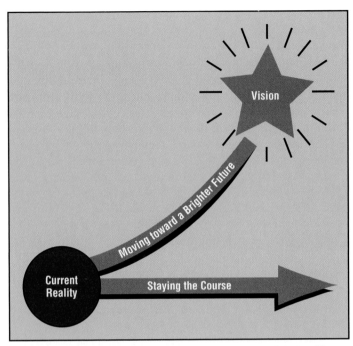

Source: Based on William D. Hitt, *The Leader-Manager: Guidelines for Action* (Columbus, OH: Battelle Press, 1988).

exhibit **11.11**
The Nature of the Vision

Visionary leaders guide followers along the path by linking the present to the future, energizing followers, helping people find meaning in their work, and establishing standards of excellence.[55]

Although a vision is always about the future, the leader connects the vision to the here and now. People working in organizations are under constant pressure to meet deadlines, complete projects, and solve immediate problems. Visionary leaders have *bifocal vision*. They help people aim toward dreams for the future while also enabling them to meet current obligations.[56]

In addition, visionary leaders find ways to *energize people and garner commitment*. People want to feel enthusiastic about their work. Many people voluntarily commit their time and energy to causes they believe in—a political campaign, the animal rights movement, environmental causes. Visionary leaders enable people to bring this same level of energy and enthusiasm to their work by giving them an inspiring vision to work toward; for example, something that makes life better for others, improves their communities, or enables their organization to succeed in important ways.[57] At Team Tires Plus, described earlier in the chapter, employee energy and enthusiasm are spurred by the vision of "changing the world one tire at a time."

Visionary leaders help people find meaning in their work. They understand that in today's world, the organization is the only "community" many people have. People love having a larger purpose for what they do, and they want to feel pride in their work.

Visionary leaders also give people a clear direction and provide a measure by which they can gauge their contributions to the organization. Most workers welcome images and lenses through which to see how their work fits into the whole. Think of how frustrating it is to watch a movie when the projector is out of focus. Today's complex, fast-changing business environment often seems just like that—out of focus.[58] Visionary leaders provide people with a focus button—the vision—that clarifies an image of the future and lets people see how they can contribute. They present a challenge and ask people to go where they haven't gone before.

A visionary leader speaks to the hearts of employees, letting them be a part of something bigger than themselves. Lorraine Monroe, who transformed Harlem's Frederick Douglass School from one of the worst to one of the best in New York City, refers to a leader as the drum major who keeps a vision in front of people. The following example illustrates how Monroe practices visionary leadership.

🐦 Lorraine Monroe and Frederick Douglass Academy

When Lorraine Monroe became principal of Harlem's Frederick Douglass School (which she renamed Frederick Douglass Academy), it was known for excessive violence, poor attendance, and low achievement. Only five years later, test scores of Frederick Douglass students ranked among the best in New York City, and 96 percent of the school's graduates went on to college.

Monroe came in with a vision of turning the school into one of New York City's finest. She inspired teachers and students to imagine greater possibilities for themselves and to believe they could achieve them. Her Twelve Non-Negotiable Rules and Regulations, based on respect for oneself, for one's associates, and for the school, formed a code by which everyone lived. Lorraine Monroe believes people are hungry for true leadership—for someone who believes in a dream and makes others believe in it too. Leaders, she says, "must do the hard work of never doubting [the vision's] importance" in order to keep others committed and fired up about their work. "People want to be about good things. . . .," she continues. "They want to believe that the work they do has meaning, some purpose beyond making a salary."

Monroe's philosophy makes her a true visionary leader. She believes a leader turns a workplace into a community by making sure people are nurtured and respected. She demands the best from people and helps them achieve it. She takes every opportunity to convey new ideas, hammer home the need for change, and give people the freedom to be "creatively crazy." Monroe has seen teachers do amazing things simply because someone asked them to and reminded them they had the capacity to do it. By freeing people from the mundane, giving their work meaning and purpose, and treating them with respect, Monroe has now rescued two troubled schools, Frederick Douglass and William Howard Taft High School in the Bronx. In 1997, she founded the School Leadership Academy at the Center for Educational Innovation, designed to foster creative educational leadership and pass on the leadership lessons Monroe has learned from more than 30 years as a teacher and principal. "I like to invent the future, to dream the next thing," she says. "That's the juice. And organizations suffer when a leader's juice is gone."[59]

apply it

1. Recall a situation in which you either assumed or were given a leadership role in a group, either at school, at work, or in a social setting. Try to remember your own behavior as leader. In what ways did your behavior illustrate transactional or transformational leadership?

2. Think about a job you have held (or, if you have never worked, the last class you completed). Do you believe the way your supervisor (or professor) treated you was based on attributions he or she made about your behavior? Explain. Did you make any attributions about the leader?

Leaders in learning organizations take new approaches

Visionary leadership is the only means by which a company can change into a learning organization. The view of leaders who set goals, make decisions, and direct people reflects an individualistic approach. In learning organizations, leaders think in terms of "control with" rather than "control over" others. To "control with," leaders build relationships based on a shared vision and shape the values and community that can help achieve it. In learning organizations, leaders help people see the whole system, facilitate teamwork, initiate change, and expand the capacity of people to shape the future,[60] as Lorraine Monroe did at William Howard Taft High School and Frederick Douglass Academy. Two new approaches to leadership, servant leadership and leading through empowerment, are particularly appropriate for today's learning organizations. In addition, people in learning organizations need to develop team leadership skills.

Servant Leadership

Servant leadership may be thought of as leadership upside-down. **Servant leaders** transcend self-interest to serve the needs of others, help others grow and develop, and provide opportunity for others to gain materially and emotionally while also achieving the organization's larger purpose. The fulfillment of others is the servant leader's principal aim.

servant leader

A leader who transcends self-interest to serve the needs of followers and help them learn and grow while also achieving the organization's larger purpose.

An extreme case of servant leadership was Mother Teresa, who spent a lifetime serving the desperately poor and afflicted. Her devotion to the cause inspired many people to follow her and helped to raise millions of dollars in financial support. Many people question whether leaders working in business organizations can ever achieve a similar level of selflessness. However, all leaders can operate from the basic precepts of servant leadership:[61]

Servant leaders put service before self-interest. They make a conscious choice to use their gifts in the cause of change and growth for other individuals and for the organization. The desire to help others takes precedence over the desire to achieve a formal leadership position or to attain power and control over others. The servant leader calls for doing what is good and right for others even if it doesn't "pay off." In addition, one of the servant leader's greatest gifts to others is listening, understanding fully the problems others face, and affirming his or her confidence in others. The servant leader tries to figure out the will of the group and then further it however he or she can. The leader doesn't impose his or her will on others. By understanding others, the leader can contribute to the best course of action.

Servant leaders build trust by doing what they say they will do, being totally honest with others, giving up control, and focusing on the well-being of others. They share all information, good and bad, and they make decisions to further the good of the group rather than their own interests. In addition, trust grows from trusting others and letting them make their own decisions. Servant leaders also help others move to higher levels of service and responsibility. Vaclev Havel, former playwright, dissident, and prisoner of the Soviet regime, who served as president of Czechoslovakia after the Soviet withdrawal, once said, "The salvation of this human world lies nowhere else than in the human heart, in the human power to reflect, in human meekness, and in human responsibility."[62] Servant leaders help others find the power of the human spirit and accept their responsibilities. This requires an openness and willingness to share in the pain and difficulties of others. Everyone has problems to deal with, and leaders bring out the best in people when they get close enough to have insight into their personal difficulties.

One example of servant leadership in the business world is Bob Thompson, who sold his road-building firm, Thompson-McCully Co., and then gave the money to his employees—the salespeople and secretaries, gravel pit workers and road crews, even some retirees and widows, as well as top managers. He also paid the taxes, so that workers who were given a million dollars would actually reach that magical milestone. "It's sharing good times, that's all it is," Thompson says. "We're dependent on people, so it would just not be fair not to do it." In addition, Thompson made sure the new owners would allow workers to keep their jobs; Thompson himself will stay to run the company. Thompson's workers describe him as a no-nonsense boss, who is very driven and very demanding, but always fair and always willing to listen.[63]

For leaders such as Bob Thompson, fully valuing and respecting others as human beings is an important aspect of leadership. To develop trust with others relies on the assumption that human beings have a moral duty to one another.[64] Servant leaders believe in a purpose higher than acquiring more money or material goods for themselves.

Leading through Empowerment

self-management leadership

A leadership style that relies on the empowerment of employees and helps followers lead themselves; sometimes called *participative leadership*.

Leaders in powerful positions once thought workers should be told what to do, how to do it, and when to do it. They believed strict control was needed to help everyone perform effectively. However, today's leaders, particularly in learning organizations, are learning to share rather than hoard power. Leading through empowerment, which may be called **self-management leadership,** participative leadership, or *superleadership,* relies on the empowerment of employees, an important trend that has had a tremendous impact on organizations and leadership. Self-management leadership essentially means leading others to lead themselves.[65] It calls for leaders to share power and responsibility with their subordinates in such a way that everyone becomes a leader. Leaders act as coaches and mentors, show trust in others, remove barriers to high performance, and offer encouragement and support.

Leaders who practice self-management leadership do not try to control employee behavior, but coach employees to think critically about their own performance and judge how well they are accomplishing tasks and achieving goals. Leaders also make sure employees have the information they need to perform effectively and an understanding of how their jobs are relevant to attaining the organization's vision. By linking individual jobs with the vision, employees have a framework within which to act. Self-management leadership hinges on providing employees with this directed autonomy.[66]

Although empowerment is a strong trend in organizations and there are more and more situations that call for self-management leadership, there has been little research to test the effectiveness of this new approach. As with other styles of leadership, it is likely that self-management leadership is effective for some, but not for all, situations.

Leading Teams

Learning organization leaders put in place an organization structure that supports the goal of engaging everyone in helping to increase the organization's capabilities. In many instances this involves self-directed teams focused on core processes, rather than people separated into functional departments. This raises the issue of team leadership. Successful teams begin with confident and effective team leaders. However, leading a team requires a significant shift in mindset and behavior for those who are accustomed to working in traditional hierarchical organizations where managers made all the decisions. Most people can learn the new skills and qualities needed for team leadership, but it isn't always easy. To be effective team leaders, people have to be willing to change themselves, to step outside their comfort zone and let go of many of the assumptions that have guided their behavior in the past. Five changes leaders can make to develop a foundation for effective team leadership are:

1. *Learn to relax and admit your ignorance.* Team leaders don't have to know everything, and they can't always be in control. To be effective, team leaders let go of the "If you don't know, don't ask" rule that is a legacy of the command-and-control system. Effective team leaders *do* ask—they aren't afraid to show that they don't know everything and they openly admit their mistakes. Although it is hard for many traditional managers to believe, admitting and learning from mistakes earns the respect of team members faster than almost any other behavior.[67]

2. *Take care of team members.* The leader sets the tone for how team members treat one another and their customers. Rather than always thinking about themselves and their chances for promotion or salary increases, effective team leaders spend their time taking care of team members. Two critically important needs shared by most team members are the needs for recognition and support.[68] Leaders frequently overlook how important it is for people to feel that their

contribution is valued, and they may especially forget to acknowledge the contributions of lower level support staff. Team members also need to feel that their leader will go to the wall for them and back them up. Top executives expect the team leader to represent the organization's needs to the team. However, the leader is also responsible for representing the team's needs to the organization, getting the team what it needs to effectively do the job, and being a champion for the team. Leaders take the heat so team members don't have to.

3. *Communicate.* Good communication skills are essential for team leadership, but this doesn't mean just learning how to express oneself clearly. It means, first and foremost, learning to listen. Effective team leaders ask more questions than they answer. By asking the right questions, leaders help team members solve problems and make decisions. In addition, leaders are responsible for helping team members focus on the issues, encouraging balanced participation in team meetings, summarizing differences and agreements, and brainstorming alternative ideas, all of which require careful listening.[69]

4. *Learn to truly share power.* Team leaders embrace the concept of teamwork in deeds as well as words. This means sharing power, information, and responsibility. It requires leaders to have faith that team members will make the best decisions they can, even though those decisions might not be the ones the leader would have made. It isn't always easy for a leader to let go and trust the team, as the leader of a sales team discovered. Having received a limited number of tickets to a much-coveted golf outing, he turned them over to the team, with the suggestion that they give one of the tickets to a manager from another department. When the team decided to give the tickets to exceptionally hardworking team members instead, the leader exploded. Only when he admitted his mistake and openly discussed it with the team did the sales team begin to function effectively again.[70] Effective team leaders recognize that it is example, not command, that holds a team together.[71]

5. *Recognize the importance of values.* Building a team means creating a community united by shared values and commitment. It is at heart a spiritual undertaking.[72] To promote teamwork, leaders use ritual, stories, ceremonies, and other symbolism to create meaning for team members and give them a sense of belonging to something important. Phil Fulmer, coach of the Tennessee Volunteers football team, recognizes the spiritual nature of building a team. During the season leading up to the Vols' winning of the 1998 National Championship, Fulmer used a walking cane as a symbol. At team meetings, Fulmer would arrange chairs in a circle. He would stand in the center—a coach walking softly but carrying a big stick—and talk about the energy of being a team, how everyone could pull together and be stronger. Team members then passed around the "Synergy Stick." "It was something different," one team member said. "It caught our attention and brought us together every time we saw that stick."[73]

apply it

1. Have you ever known anyone that you would consider a servant leader? What do you think motivated that person to service?

2. You have been designated leader of a class team project that will account for 50 percent of each person's grade for the class. Everyone has pitched in and worked extremely hard, and the project is completed three weeks ahead of time so that everyone can relax and enjoy homecoming weekend. Most others teams, however, have had various difficulties with their projects and have held meetings with the professor. Based on their influence, he has decided to cut the percentage back to 35 percent of the grade. How would you handle this situation? Why would you take the action you did?

summary OF KEY CONCEPTS

- **Leadership makes a difference in organizations.** Leadership is an influence relationship among leaders and followers who work together to bring about change toward a desirable future. Leadership and followership are different roles that people may shift into and out of. Leadership is distinct from management, although both are important to organizations. Management maintains stability and order, whereas leadership promotes vision, creativity, and change.

- **Do traits and behaviors define leadership?** Since the earliest studies of leadership, people have searched for specific traits or characteristics that contribute to effective leadership. Leadership is not a genetic endowment—that is, leaders are made, not born. There do seem to be certain traits, such as self-confidence, vision, and striving for personal excellence, that are associated with successful leaders. However, specific traits or sets of traits do not stand alone; their appropriateness depends on the leadership situation. Leadership behaviors have also been studied extensively. Autocratic leaders centralize authority and derive power from formal position, control of rewards, and coercion of subordinates. Democratic leaders delegate authority to others, encourage participation, and depend on trust and respect for power. Behavioral theories of leadership include those developed through the Ohio State and Michigan studies, and the leadership grid.

- **Contingency theories: leadership style depends on the situation.** Contingency theories explain the relationships among follower characteristics, the situation, and leadership style. These theories include Fiedler's contingency model, Hersey and Blanchard's situational theory, the path-goal theory, and substitutes for leadership. The substitutes for leadership approach suggests that there are some situational variables that are so powerful they make leadership unnecessary or irrelevant. The value of this understanding is that it helps leaders avoid leadership overkill.

- **Leadership is a process of interaction between leader and followers.** The leader-member exchange model suggests that leaders develop unique relationships with each individual subordinate, which may be either positive or negative. The most recent research has focused on how leaders can develop positive, mutually respectful relationships with each subordinate to provide greater benefits to the leader, the follower, and the organization. Attribution theory deals specifically with people's perceptions, as described in Chapter 4. A leader will treat an employee differently depending on whether the leader attributes the employee's successes or failures to personal issues or to situational factors over which the employee has little control. In recent years, leadership concepts have evolved from transactional to charismatic, transformational, and visionary approaches. Charismatic leadership is the ability to inspire and motivate people to go above and beyond the call of duty for a cause. Transformational leaders also may possess charisma, but they are distinguished by their ability to bring about change by focusing on followers' needs, helping them see old problems in new ways, and encouraging them to question the status quo. Vision is important to all leaders. Visionary leaders link the present to the future, energize people and garner commitment, create meaning in workers' lives, and bring out the best in employees by establishing standards of excellence.

- **Leaders in learning organizations take new approaches.** Visionary and transformational leadership are critical for companies shifting toward becoming learning organizations. In addition, leaders in learning organizations often become servant leaders who facilitate the growth and development of others in order to liberate followers' best qualities in pursuing the vision. Self-management leadership, or leading through empowerment, is also used in learning organizations, and people have to learn how to effectively lead teams.

KEY terms

leadership, p. 379

effective follower, p. 382

traits, p. 383

autocratic leader, p. 385

democratic leader, p. 385

behavioral theories of leadership, p. 386

consideration, p. 386

initiating structure, p. 387

employee-centered leader, p. 387

job-centered leader, p. 387

leadership grid, p. 387

contingency approaches, p. 389

LPC scale, p. 390

situational theory, p. 393

path-goal theory, p. 394

substitute, p. 398

neutralizer, p. 398

leader-member exchange (LMX) model, p. 400

attribution theory of leadership, p. 401

charismatic leader, p. 402

transformational leader, p. 402

transactional leader, p. 403

visionary leader, p. 404

vision, p. 404

servant leader, p. 407

self-management leadership, p. 408

DISCUSSION questions

1. Do you think it is possible to be both a good manager and an effective leader? Discuss.

2. Sarah Brewer became manager of an auto assembly plant and believed in participative leadership, even when one supervisor used Sarah's delegation to replace two competent line managers with his own friends. What would you say to Sarah about her leadership style in this situation?

3. Would you prefer working for a leader who has a "consideration" or an "initiating structure" leadership style? Why?

4. Does it make sense to you that a leader should develop an individualized relationship with each follower? Explain the advantages and disadvantages to such an approach.

5. Why would subordinates under a democratic leader perform better in the leader's absence than would subordinates under an autocratic leader?

6. Consider the leadership position of a managing partner in a consulting firm. What task, subordinate, and organizational factors might serve as substitutes for leadership in this situation?

7. Compare Fiedler's contingency model with the path-goal theory. What are the similarities and differences? Which do you prefer?

8. Why is visionary leadership considered essential to a learning organization? Do you think a person can be an effective leader without being visionary? Discuss.

9. Identify differences in how transactional versus transformational leaders relate to their followers.

10. Do you think self-management leadership should be considered a leadership style? Why or why not?

11. Why might a person need to go through significant personal changes to be a team leader? What are some of the changes required?

12. Discuss the role of follower. Why do you think so little emphasis is given to followership compared to leadership in organizations?

SELF-DISCOVERY exercise

Evaluate Your Leadership Potential

Questions 1–6 below are about you as you are right now. Questions 7–22 are about how you would like to be if you were the head of a major department at a corporation. Answer yes or no to indicate whether the item describes you accurately, or whether you would strive to perform each activity.

Now

____ **1.** When I have a number of tasks or homework to do, I set priorities and organize the work to meet deadlines.

____ **2.** When I am involved in a serious disagreement, I hang in there and talk it out until it is completely resolved.

____ **3.** I would rather sit in front of my computer than spend a lot of time with people.

____ **4.** I reach out to include other people in activities or when there are discussions.

____ **5.** I know my long-term vision for career, family, and other activities.

____ **6.** When solving problems, I prefer analyzing things to working with a group of people.

Head of Major Department

____ **7.** I would help subordinates clarify goals and how to reach them.

____ **8.** I would give people a sense of mission and higher purpose.

____ **9.** I would make sure jobs get out on time.

____ **10.** I would scout for new product and service opportunities.

____ **11.** I would use policies and procedures as guides for problem solving.

____ **12.** I would promote unconventional beliefs and values.

____ **13.** I would give monetary rewards in exchange for high performance from subordinates.

____ **14.** I would inspire trust from everyone in the department.

____ **15.** I would work alone to accomplish important tasks.

____ **16.** I would suggest new and unique ways of doing things.

____ **17.** I would give credit to people who do their jobs well.

____ **18.** I would verbalize the higher values that I and the organization stand for.

____ **19.** I would establish procedures to help the department operate smoothly.

____ **20.** I would question the "why" of things to motivate others.

____ **21.** I would set reasonable limits on new approaches.

____ **22.** I would demonstrate social nonconformity as a way to facilitate change.

Scoring: Count the number of yes answers to even-numbered questions: _____. Count the number of yes answers to odd-numbered questions: _____. Compare the two scores according to the following interpretation.

Interpretation: The even-numbered items represent behaviors and activities typical of leadership. Leaders are personally involved in shaping ideas, values, vision, and change. They often use an intuitive approach to develop fresh ideas and seek new directions for the department or organization. The odd-numbered items are considered more traditional management activities. Managers respond to problems in an impersonal way, make rational decisions, and work for stability and efficiency. If you answered yes to more even-numbered than odd-numbered items, you may have potential leadership qualities. If you answered yes to more odd-numbered than even-numbered items, you are stronger in management ability than in leadership. Remember that both are important, and both can be developed and improved with awareness and experience.

Source: Richard L. Daft, *Leadership* (Fort Worth, TX: The Dryden Press, 1999), pp. 55–56.

ORGANIZATIONAL BEHAVIOR in your life

Leaders need a personal vision before they can help others create a vision for the organization. A personal vision can give your life direction and purpose and provide a context within which to make day-to-day decisions. You may already have a vision for your future, but many people have a hard time letting go of the rational and the mundane in order to dream big dreams about the future.

Allow yourself at least an hour and find a quiet, private place where you feel comfortable to begin creating your own personal vision. You may want to play a favorite piece of music that you know helps you relax and get in touch with deep feelings, or you may prefer silence. Begin by thinking about an event or activity in your past where you felt totally "alive." Close your eyes and try to relive that feeling. Then, begin to think about what you want for your future. Imagine achieving something that you truly and deeply want—for example, living in the place where you most want to live, having the career you most desire, or establishing a personal relationship that you most wish to have. Push aside any thoughts about how possible or impossible it seems; just allow yourself to dream. Then, describe in writing the experience you have just imagined. Try to make it as real as possible, and write in the present tense, as if the dream has already come true.

Remember that vision comes from two sources: a foundation of personal experiences and your hopes and dreams for the future. No one else need ever see your description—this exercise is for you alone, so let yourself go and begin creating a personal vision.

Source: Based on "Drawing Forth Personal Vision," in Peter Senge, Art Kleiner, Charlotte Roberts, Richard Ross, George Roth, and Bryan Smith, *The Fifth Discipline Field Book* (New York: Doubleday/Currency, 1994), p. 201; and Joseph Boyett and Jimmie Boyett, *The Guru Circle: The Best Ideas of the Top Management Thinkers* (New York: John Wiley & Sons, 1998), pp. 27–29.

ORGANIZATIONAL BEHAVIOR news flash

@ Top leaders often get the credit when organizations succeed and the blame when their performance declines. Pick a company you are interested in and read some articles and press releases about the company's top leader or leaders. To find them, check news listings on your search engine or type in the company's name and search its Web site. You may also find articles in sources such as *The Wall Street Journal, Fortune, Business Week,* and *Fast Company.* You may want to consider well-known companies such as IBM, Microsoft, Cisco Systems, Coca-Cola, Home Depot, Hewlett-Packard, or Apple Computer because it should be fairly easy to locate information about their leaders. After reviewing the articles, consider the following questions:

1. Based on the information you have found, what have you learned about the leader's style? Select either the behavioral theories, one of the contingency theories, or transactional versus charismatic or transformational leadership and write a brief analysis of the leader's style.
2. What can you tell about the leader's vision from the articles you've read? Do you believe this is a vision that would inspire employees?
3. How has this leader made a difference (positive or negative) for his or her organization?

global diversity EVENTS

@ When a company goes through a merger, leaders face special leadership challenges. When the two companies that merge are from different countries, leadership is an even more difficult job. Using your search engine, look for news stories about the 1995 merger of Pharmacia of Sweden and U.S.–based Upjohn. Intended as a merger of equals, the combination of these two companies left people across three countries involved in bitter feuding. A new CEO has recently been trying to smooth things out.

1. What role has leadership played in the troubles and successes of the Pharmacia-Upjohn merger?
2. What characteristics and abilities do you think a leader would need to handle this situation? Discuss. Does the current leader demonstrate any of these characteristics and abilities?

minicase ISSUE

Leadership Change aboard the USS *Florida*

Background. The atmosphere in a Trident nuclear submarine is generally calm and quiet. Even pipe joints are cushioned to prevent noise that might tip off a pursuer. The Trident ranks among the world's most dangerous weapons—swift, silent, and armed with 24 long-range missiles carrying 192 nuclear warheads.

Trident crews are the cream of the Navy crop, and even the sailors who fix the plumbing exhibit a white-collar decorum. The culture aboard ship is a low-key, collegial one in which sailors learn to speak softly and peacefully share close quarters with an ever-changing roster of shipmates. Being subject to strict security restrictions enhances a sense of elitism and pride. To move up and take charge of a Trident submarine is an extraordinary feat in the Navy—fewer than half the officers qualified for such commands ever get them. When Michael Alfonso took charge of the USS *Florida,* the crew welcomed his arrival. They knew he was one of them—a career Navy man who had joined up as a teenager and moved up through the ranks. Past shipmates remembered him as basically a loner, who could be brusque but was generally pleasant enough. Neighbors on shore found Alfonso to be an unfailingly polite man who kept mostly to himself.

The Problems Begin. The crew's delight in their new captain was short lived. Commander Alfonso moved swiftly to assume command, admonishing his sailors that he would push them hard. He wasn't joking—soon after the *Florida* slipped into deep waters to begin a postoverhaul shakedown cruise, the new captain loudly and publicly reprimanded those whose performance he considered lacking. Chief Petty Officer Donald MacArthur, chief of the navigation division, was only one of those who suffered Alfonso's anger personally. During training exercises, MacArthur was having trouble keeping the boat at periscope depth because of rough seas. Alfonso announced loudly, "You're disqualified." He then relieved him of his diving duty until he could be recertified by extra practice. Word of the incident spread quickly. The crew, accustomed to the Navy's adage of "praise in public, penalize in private," were shocked. It didn't take long for this type of behavior to have an impact on the crew, according to Petty Officer Aaron Carmody: "People didn't tell him when something was wrong. You're not supposed to be afraid of your captain, to tell him stuff. But nobody wanted to."

Morale Suffers. The captain's outbursts weren't always connected with job performance, according to crew members. He bawled out the supply officer, the executive officer, and the chief of the boat because the soda dispenser he used to pour himself a glass of Coke one day contained Mr. Pibb instead. He exploded when he arrived unexpected at a late-night meal and found the fork at his place setting missing. Soon, a newsletter titled *The Underground* was being circulated by the boat's plumbers, who used sophomoric humor to spread the word about the captain's outbursts over such petty matters. By the time the sub reached Hawaii for its "Tactical Readiness Evaluation," an intense, weeklong series of inspections by staff officers, the crew was almost completely alienated. Although the ship tested well, inspectors sent word to Rear Admiral Paul Sullivan that something seemed to be wrong on board, with severely strained relations between captain and crew. On the *Florida's* last evening of patrol, much of the crew celebrated with a film night—they chose *The Caine Mutiny* and *Crimson Tide,* both movies about Navy skippers who face mutinies and are relieved of command at sea. When Humphrey Bogart, playing the captain of the fictional USS *Caine,* exploded over a missing quart of strawberries, someone shouted out, "Hey, sound familiar?"

Relieved of Command. When they reached home port, the sailors slumped ashore. "Physically and mentally, we were just beat into the ground," recalls one. Concerned about reports that the crew seemed "despondent," Admiral Sullivan launched an informal inquiry that eventually led him to relieve Alfonso of his command. It was the first-ever firing of a Trident submarine commander. "He had the chance of a lifetime to experience the magic of command, and he squandered it," Sullivan said. "Fear and intimidation lead to certain ruin." Alfonso himself seems dumbfounded by Admiral Sullivan's actions, pointing out that the *Florida* under his command posted "the best-ever grades assigned for certifications and inspections for a postoverhaul Trident submarine."

1. Discuss Commander Alfonso's leadership style in terms of the behavioral theories discussed in the chapter. Which do you think a leader should be more concerned about aboard a nuclear submarine—high certification grades or high-quality interpersonal relationships? Discuss.

2. Do you think Alfonso's attributions about the performance of those under his command affected his leadership effectiveness? Discuss.

3. Some officers believe Commander Alfonso got a bum rap. One said, "My opinion is, the man in command is in command." What do you think was meant by this statement? Do you agree with the decision to fire Alfonso? Why or why not?

Source: Based on Thomas E. Ricks, "A Skipper's Chance to Run a Trident Sub Hits Stormy Waters," *The Wall Street Journal,* November 20, 1997, pp. A1, A6.

twelve
CHAPTER

12

Power and Politics

preview

After studying this chapter, you should be able to:

- Identify, for a given person in an organization, sources of power and dependency relationships.

- Describe how people acquire and share power in an organization.

- Give examples of political behavior in organizations, including the impact on the user and the organization.

- Analyze ethical and unethical uses of power in organizations.

Some people encounter a bad situation and refuse to accept it. Where others may look at limitations, they focus instead on opportunities. Along the way, their drive and clear thinking can influence others to follow them in pursuit of their dream. Such a person is Pat Means, who not only built a business but helped a troubled community make a turnaround.

Means spent most of her early career in marketing. She started her own marketing and promotional services company in Dallas and continued in similar work when she later moved to Los Angeles. Then, in 1992, when it seemed that Los Angeles might sink beneath its racial troubles, Means had an idea: start a magazine that focused on the positive side of the city, "what was right with L.A.," she recalls. Although three out of four magazines fail, Means didn't care. She wanted to show African-American culture in a positive light. So, along with college friend Karen Hixson, she founded *Turning Point*.

From the outset, Means and Hixson saw *Turning Point* as an opportunity to have a positive influence on African-Americans. "We were [and still are] trying to play a positive role in the development of African-Americans," explains Means. Means uses her power as publisher to make ethical choices about where the magazine will be sold and what types of advertisements it will accept. *Turning Point* does not appear in liquor stores, nor does it accept advertisements from alcohol or tobacco companies. Decisions like these reflect the guiding principles of her leadership—to do what she thinks is right even if it isn't the easiest solution. Such principles can be infectious, extending to writers, designers, and photographers who work for the magazine. In the beginning, she convinced them to work for the magazine on speculation—for free, unless the magazine turned a profit. "Fortunately, we did make money on the first issue," Means recalls, "until we paid them." She and Hixson had just enough money left over to produce the second issue. From that small beginning, the magazine grew in influence—and copies sold. The magazine now makes roughly $1 million a year in revenues.

As *Turning Point* grew in size and stature in the community, Means and Hixson had access to prominent writers, professionals, and activists with stories to tell, gaining more power by attracting people with whom readers wanted to identify. Such celebrities now include actor/director/writer/producer Miguel A. Nuñez and Congressman John Lewis. Means has even had civil rights pioneer Rosa Parks to her home for dinner. "I get goose bumps when I think of [these people]," says Means.

Employees at *Turning Point* are empowered to make decisions and offer ideas. "I haven't done anything by myself," asserts Means. "Every time I turned around, there was someone there to give me a hand or advice, or to make some phone calls for me. The people who work here aren't employees; they're all partners. *Turning Point* is more than a magazine."[1]

Turning Point: A Magazine and Publisher with the Power to Influence

> "We were [and still are] trying to play a positive role in the development of African-Americans."
> —**Pat Means,** founder and publisher, *Turning Point*

Just as Pat Means of *Turning Point* used credibility and personal power to exert a positive influence on the African-American community in Los Angeles, power plays a role in people's day-to-day relationships within organizations. For their power, people rely not only on the authority that their positions give them but also on their personal characteristics and resources.

Organizations are currently experiencing a general shift in the way power is distributed—from a concentration at the highest levels to a move to push power lower in the organization. The reasons for this shift are varied, but in today's fast-paced environment, there is less time to run every decision by top managers. More than ever before, organizations are seeing the value of delegating power. Also, today's knowledge workers often have an immediate grasp of a situation and can make better and quicker decisions for their organizations. Within any organization, people have varying degrees of influence over one another, and their relationships are continually changing. In this chapter, we also explore how people add to, retain, and exert their influence.

The chapter begins by describing the general nature of power in organizations, including its sources and effects. Next, we look at the processes by which people acquire power for themselves or assign power to others. The next section explores organizational politics, through which the members of the organization use power to achieve objectives. These activities should be ethical, as described in the final section of the chapter.

Power influences what people can do in organizations

power

A person's potential to influence other people's behavior or to resist the influence of others.

Formally defined, **power** refers to a person's potential to influence other people's behavior or to resist the influence of others. It is by definition a *social* interaction because it involves the impact people have on one another. In organizations, people's behavior is partly shaped by their job descriptions, group memberships, and personal goals and abilities. In addition, people may use power to shape one another's behavior. For example, workers may comply with a supervisor's instructions because that person is "the boss," or team members might adopt an idea because it was submitted by a group member considered the most knowledgeable or persuasive.

As these examples suggest, power includes but is not limited to the scope of authority laid out in an organization's formal structure. To understand more clearly how people acquire and use power in organizations, let's begin by distinguishing power from leadership and looking at various aspects of power in organizations.

Power versus Leadership

If power, as we have discussed it so far, sounds like leadership, that is because the two concepts are closely related. As defined in the preceding chapter, *leadership* is an influence relationship among leaders and followers concerning the attainment of shared organizational goals. Whereas power is a general ability to influence, leadership influences in a specific direction, compatible with shared group objectives. A leader exercises power in a constructive way, guided by the leader's vision of where the organization needs to go and how to get there. Thus, power is an important resource of a leader. Pat Means of *Turning Point* is an example of a leader because she exerts her influence on followers to accomplish a common goal—being a positive force in the African-American community of Los Angeles.

Another way to understand the distinction is to say that a leader exercises power, but a person may exercise power without being a leader. For

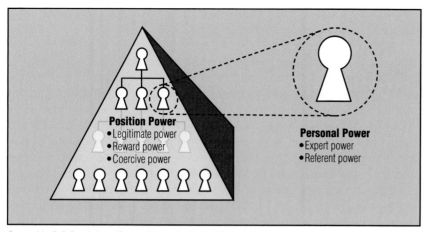

Source: John R. P. French Jr. and Bertram Raven, "The Bases of Social Power," in D. Cartwright and Alvin F. Zander (eds.), *Group Dynamics* (Evanston, IL: Row, Peterson, 1960), pp. 607–623.

exhibit **12.1**
Sources of Power

example, using power to attain personal goals is not leadership, but merely political behavior. We discuss political behavior later in the chapter.

Sources of Power

Some members of an organization have more power than others. That power comes from several sources. Some sources involve a person's position in the organization, and others arise from the characteristics of the individual. Exhibit 12.1 illustrates the five basic sources of power: legitimate, reward, and coercive power, which derive from a person's position in an organization, and expert and referent power, which flow from the individual's personal characteristics.[2]

Managers at Intel, the giant computer chipmaker in Santa Clara, California, recognize the power that arises from the ability to grant rewards to others. Every seven years an employee can take an eight-week paid sabbatical, and in a recent year, 1,803 employees did. Other rewards are given through special employee training. Pichet Mam, an Intel equipment technician born in Cambodia, has taken free company classes in Excel, PowerPoint, and English pronunciation. (Source: © Scott Baxter)

Position Power To establish a way of influencing people, organizations grant power according to various positions in the organization. People who hold certain positions have the authority to direct certain activities, as well as the ability to grant rewards for positive behavior and administer consequences for negative behavior. These abilities are sources of position power.

  Legitimate power is power that arises from the authority associated with a position in an organization. An organization's managers have some degree of authority over the activities they direct. Nonmanagement employees also may have legitimate power, such as the authority to immediately shut down manufacturing equipment that is not working properly or the authority to apply safe work standards. As long as people exercise power within their area of responsibility, other members of the organization accept this power as a part of organizational life, so they comply with it. The range of activities within which employees readily accept a person's use of legitimate power is called the employees' **zone of indifference.**[3] A

legitimate power

Power that arises from the authority associated with a position in an organization.

zone of indifference

The range of activities within which employees readily accept a person's use of legitimate power.

person who wants to exert influence in areas outside people's zone of indifference requires other sources of power.

reward power

Power that arises from the ability to grant rewards to others.

Reward power is power that arises from the ability to grant rewards to others. Most organizations provide their managers some control over rewards, ranging from pay raises to promotions. In addition, managers and others can give intangible rewards such as attention, praise, and recognition for accomplishments. Some positions offer other kinds of reward power, such as the ability to offer special deals, hand out desirable assignments or schedules, or control access to a high-status person by screening phone calls and making appointments. When people value these rewards, the person who can grant them has significant reward power. Gary Quick of Quick Solutions of Columbus, Ohio, an information technology consulting firm, uses his reward power to attract and retain talented employees. Among the rewards he gives to managers and their families are a welcome-to-the-company gift basket, a free week's vacation in a company condominium on Sanibel Island, Florida, and—for managers who stay with the firm for three years—professional house-cleaning services and $1,200 in vacation vouchers. Quick's former career as a professional headhunter led him to demonstrate his appreciation of his employees with these rewards. "I [interviewed] thousands of people and always asked them why they were leaving their current job. Most people said the same thing: 'My company doesn't care about me.'"[4]

coercive power

Power that arises from the ability to punish behavior.

The opposite of reward power is **coercive power**, the ability to punish behavior. Forms of coercive power include the authority to suspend, demote, or fire an employee or to give undesirable work assignments. Other ways to exert coercive power are criticism and denial of attention. If people want to avoid these punishments, the person who can administer them has significant coercive power.

compliance

Following the directions of a person with power, even if you do not agree with the directions.

When people successfully exercise position power arising from these three sources, the response is **compliance,** as illustrated in Exhibit 12.2.[5] This means people follow the directions of the person with power, whether or not they agree with those directions. Arriving at work on time to avoid a reprimand or out of a sense of duty is compliance, whether or not the employee is enthusiastic about working.

exhibit | **12.2**   Basic Responses to Power

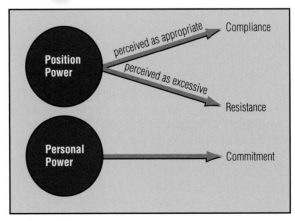

Source: Gary A. Yukl and T. Taber, "The Effective Use of Managerial Power," *Personnel,* March-April 1983, pp. 37–44.

what would YOU do?

WOULD YOU COMPLY OR RESIST?

People or organizations with power strive for compliance from employees or members, whether or not the power is legitimate. Sometimes resistance has huge consequences, as Hugh Thompson and Jack Rule—founders of Black Rock—learned.

The tiny start-up company was based on the idea for one product—a longer golf club. Hugh Thompson was a pro golfer who was plagued by too-short drives until he discovered that a simple shift to a longer club lengthened his drives. Immediately, he knew he had hit on an idea for a product that could sell. He and a partner, Jack Rule, raised the initial capital to produce their longer club—dubbed the Killer Bee—and decided to avoid direct competition in retail venues with giants like Callaway and Cobra by selling the club directly from an infomercial on the Golf Channel. Sales soared, and within a year the two took the company public. In another two years, Black Rock was producing a full line of clubs. Lasting success seemed like a short putt away.

But in their haste to win, Thompson and Rule had bypassed an important step—they had failed to have the club approved by the U.S. Golf Association (USGA). Although Black Rock was not legally required to obtain USGA certification, the association has such power in the golf world that certification (or lack thereof) has a strong influence on whether pros and amateurs will buy a product. Many golfers will only purchase clubs officially sanctioned by the organization. Worse, when the USGA finally did review Black Rock's clubs, it notified the company that three of its clubs—including the Killer Bee—did not meet USGA measurement specifications.

Sales plummeted, and Black Rock sent its clubs back to the factory to be retooled. When the USGA reversed its decision two months later, Thompson and Rule had already spent $500,000 for the design changes. A year later, unable to recover from its losses, Black Rock closed its doors.

The USGA has the legitimate power that its members confer upon it to make decisions about a variety of golf issues, including equipment specifications. Thompson and Rule resisted that power (or underestimated it) in their enthusiasm to get their product to market, and their compliance came too late to save their business.

Imagine that you are an entrepreneur seeking to enter an industry that is heavily influenced by the decisions of an organization such as the USGA. For instance, you might want to produce a new kind of tennis racket or a new line of uniforms. Choose an industry that interests you and research its related professional organizations to find out what kind of power they have—and whether you think compliance with their guidelines is necessary (in other words, what might be your zone of indifference). You can access relevant Web sites with key words—for sports, for example, USGA, NFL, NCAA, and the like. Then consider the following questions:

1. Does the organization combine effective leadership with power? How might this affect your business?

2. Does reward power or coercive power come into play? If so, in what ways?

3. Would you comply with or resist the organization's requirements in order to launch your business successfully? (Consider: If compliance caused you to compromise your ethics, would you do so anyway?)

Source: Joshua Macht, "Shortcut Derails Maker of Long Clubs," *Inc.*, August 1999, p. 25.

There are some limits to obtaining compliance. One is that people who do not share the values of the person in power are apt to limit their efforts. That is, they do whatever it takes to satisfy the person and to obtain rewards or avoid punishment, but they may not go beyond what is specifically asked of them and thus may not contribute their full potential. In addition, if use of position power exceeds a level people consider legitimate, they may resist. **Resistance** involves attempts to avoid following instructions. For example, a person may resist by saying, "That's not part of my job" or by hiding actions that might be punished if discovered. Because of these limitations, managers who rely solely on legitimate power for leadership may not lead as effectively as those who also have personal power.

resistance

Attempts to avoid following instructions.

Personal Power In contrast to legitimate power, personal power comes from the characteristics and qualities of the individual. It may arise from a

Expert power is power arising from the expertise and knowledge of people in organizations. Len Presta is a scientist for Genentech, a biotechnology firm. Using his scientific expertise, he patiently spent a year building a human antibody to fight breast cancer. Presta's bio-engineering successes are not only aiding women suffering from cancer but generating profits for his company. Products such as Herceptin, which had recent annual sales of $180 million, make biotech stocks highly noticed in the market.
(Source: © Michael Lewis)

expert power

Power that arises from important knowledge or skill.

referent power

Power that arises from personality characteristics that command admiration, respect, and identification.

commitment

Adopting a viewpoint and enthusiastically following directions.

person's knowledge and skills or from personality characteristics. One person who employs many facets of personal power is Melba J. Duncan, who transformed a career as an executive assistant into her own placement firm specializing in executive help. When Duncan was executive assistant to the chairman of the prestigious investment banking firm Lehman Brothers, she earned credibility and respect for her coolness under stress and her ability to bring order out of chaos. She also furthered her education in business and law. By the time Duncan started her own business, Duncan Group, she had developed a stellar list of acquaintances, including the chairs of large corporations, all of whom held Duncan in high esteem and many of whom were ready to provide guidance and referrals.[6]

Power that arises from important knowledge or skill is called **expert power.** People in organizations need certain kinds of knowledge, and their success depends on cooperation from the people who can provide that knowledge. For example, a person with great insight into what customers want or who understands the organization's technology commands expert power in the organization. Expert power is especially significant among professional and technical workers, who place a high value on expertise.[7] At Associated Builders and Contractors, young employees feel powerful enough individually to turn down overtime and insist on time to spend with family. According to the organization's vice president for education and workforce development, Dan Mosser, the fact that skilled tradespeople are difficult to replace gives them power to request control over their work hours.[8]

Referent power is power arising from personality characteristics that command admiration, respect, and identification. People try to be close to and resemble someone who has these characteristics. This is a form of influence over others, so it is a type of power. Some athletes can transcend the physical skills they demonstrate in their sport to become role models. Michael Jordan is one such athlete. Aside from his incredible basketball skills, Jordan became known for his hard work, determination, and will to succeed against all odds. The "I want to be like Mike" commercials capitalized on the admiration and respect of his fans—on his referent power.

Successful use of personal power produces **commitment.**[9] This means people respond to the power by adopting the powerful person's viewpoint and enthusiastically doing what the powerful person wants. When someone with personal power advocates the organization's objectives, that person is exercising leadership, as described in Chapter 11. A manager can lead effectively by combining personal power to generate enthusiasm with legitimate power to clarify what needs to be done.

Dependency: The Flip Side of Power

People in organizations are able to exert power because other people depend on them. So for power to exist, there must be dependency as well. Members of organizations depend on one another for cooperation, information, and rewards such as pay. Also, meeting social needs requires positive contributions from members of the organization.

The more people depend on someone, the greater that person's power.[10] Therefore, power is strongest under conditions that create dependency. Conversely, when people do not depend on someone, that person has little power over them. For example, an employer has great power when jobs are difficult to obtain, but for most organizations today, finding qualified talent is difficult. Derek Parnell felt powerful when he left his job as a computer technician with Productivity Point International to help start his own consulting business. Parnell had not felt much dependency on his employer, because he believes computer-related jobs are easy to find: "What's the worst that can happen if our company folds? Maybe I'll have to get a 'real' job."[11]

Dependency is related to a person's control over resources. As illustrated in Exhibit 12.3, it is greatest for resources with the following characteristics:[12]

- *Importance* People in the organization must perceive the resource to be important. Resources can be important for a variety of reasons. For example, they may be essential elements of a product offered by the company, they may directly generate sales, or they may reduce uncertainty for decision makers.

- *Scarcity* When a resource is difficult or expensive to obtain, it is more valuable than if it is widely available. Employees with specialized knowledge fall into this category. If an organization employs an inventor who has earned many patents and developed great knowledge of the organization's industry, that employee will possess unusual expertise. And since that employee is unique, the resource is scarce; the organization can thus have significant power because it employs this person.

- *Nonsubstitutability* Controlling resources without acceptable substitutes gives a person power. Such resources may include knowledge and

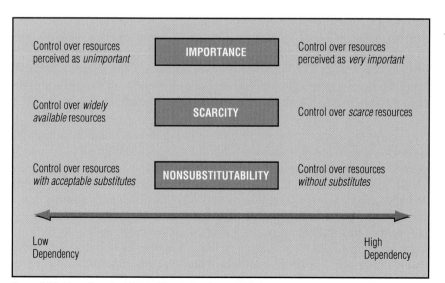

exhibit **12.3**
Conditions That Influence Dependency

Source: H. Mintzberg, *Power in and around Organizations* (Englewood Cliffs, NJ: Prentice-Hall, 1963).

experience, as well as access to people with referent power. In the past, when organizations' information systems were operated by specialists in chilly "computer rooms," these employees had power arising from their control over access to the company's computer power. Today, of course, employees can directly access much more computer power at their own desktops, so they are less dependent on any particular programmer, computer, or software.

In the following example, an executive has achieved significant power arising from his unique set of management qualifications. The uniqueness of these qualifications makes them scarce and nonsubstitutable, and his position as executive of a high-tech company makes his qualifications important.

🐾 Alteon WebSystems

Joe Booker, vice president of operations at Alteon WebSystems, has drawn on his exceptional determination and intelligence to build a successful career as a high-tech executive. In the course of his career, Booker has developed knowledge and experience that would make him extremely difficult for Alteon to replace.

After studying electronics at an Air Force school in Miami, Booker started his high-tech career with an assignment at Keeler Air Force base. He perceived that as an African-American in the 1960s, he was unlikely to be selected for one of the base's most desirable assignments, so he focused instead on building a good reputation as a top performer. Booker asked around and learned that the toughest job was working on Doppler radar. He landed the unwanted assignment and became skilled in the technology, thereby gaining expert power and obtaining additional career opportunities.

Booker's first civilian job was with IBM, and he again decided that he needed to take a job where he could readily demonstrate his value. So Booker took an assignment in manufacturing, where results could be measured quantitatively. It took him a while to develop expertise in manufacturing, but when he did, he became known as the one person who understood the technology well enough to help others with problems. Again, he had tackled difficult assignments that gave him power because of his unique knowledge.

Continuing this pattern of welcoming challenges, Booker ascended to management positions at Memorex Equipment Group and Shugart Associations. From there, he launched his own company, Vertex Peripherals. He later sold Vertex and handled a series of executive positions with other high-tech firms, finally landing at Alteon WebSystems in 1997.

Today, at Alteon, Booker can boast of more than two decades of operations and management experience. But Alteon needs more than Booker's demonstrated good judgment and his background in operations management. As a company that was just in its second year when it hired him, Alteon also needs his experience with start-ups. Furthermore, Booker's longtime willingness to learn and tackle the unknown makes him valuable at a company that offers an innovative product, Web switching to manage Internet traffic. In Silicon Valley, where Alteon is located, companies are desperately hungry for the combination of wisdom, experience, and technical expertise that only a few people such as Booker can offer.[13]

Although position power increases at higher levels of an organization's hierarchy, dependency often increases, too. Compared with an executive, a salesperson can work quite independently. The executive, however, depends on others to provide information and to carry out their work creatively and with a high level of commitment and skill. If the people reporting to the executive fall short, so will the executive. Arthur C. Martinez, chief executive of Sears during the 1990s, has a background in finance. In his role as CEO, he depended on a variety of managers with expertise in merchandising and marketing to help him turn around the chain's recent sluggish sales. According to retailing consultant Sid Doolittle, "It's impossible for the CEO to fix the stores, but he has to see that the stores get fixed."[14]

Obedience to Those with Power

Whereas dependency gives rise to power, the use of power can produce obedience. That is, a powerful person can issue a directive or make a request, and a dependent person will do as directed. When the person in power knows and cares about the organization's best interests, applies ethical principles, and knows what needs to be done, obedience is beneficial. Of course, in many situations, strict obedience is damaging because it causes people to engage in activities that are unethical, ineffective, or both. Thus, organizations benefit when employees obey directives but only within the limits of ethics and good judgment.

To test the limits of obedience, Stanley Milgram designed a series of experiments in which the researchers told subjects (falsely) that they were participating in research studying the effects of punishment on learning.[15] When subjects, representing a variety of ages and occupations, arrived at a university laboratory, they were all assigned the role of "teacher." The "learner" was actually an accomplice who pretended to be a subject. An experimenter in a lab coat instructed each subject to read a list of word pairs to the learner, who was strapped to a chair and had an electrode attached to his wrist. Then the subject "tested" the learner by rereading one word from each pair and asking for the associated word. Every time the learner made a mistake, the subject was to press a switch that supposedly (but not actually) administered a shock of 15 to 450 volts to the learner. The learner made many mistakes, and whenever a "shock" was administered, he reacted with a scripted response such as grunting, protesting, or screaming.

Even though many people expected that subjects would refuse to comply with a request that they administer intense shocks to an apparently helpless victim in a laboratory situation, most subjects actually did obey the instructions. In the initial series of experiments, 65 percent of subjects obeyed throughout the experiment, even to the point of pressing the switch that supposedly delivered a 450-volt shock. Although the remaining subjects did refuse to cooperate at some point, none quit before administering 300 volts. Apparently, administering shocks was within their zone of indifference for accepting the legitimate power of a researcher.

Surprised by these results, Milgram tried variations of the experiment to find conditions under which subjects would be less obedient. He found somewhat less compliance when the experiment took place in a run-down office, when the "learner" was seated closer to the subject, when the experimenter who issued orders was positioned farther away, and when subjects could observe one another. However, even in these situations, subjects did administer some shocks.

These experiments suggest that people with position power have an enormous resource in the form of their ability to influence others. People are inclined to do as instructed when the person issuing instructions seems to have the authority to do so. This is a potential that managers (or anyone else with position power) can use positively or negatively. If a manager issues an unethical directive, especially if it clearly lies within the scope of the manager's authority, the first instinct of many employees may be, "I'm just doing what I was told to do." Instead of taking responsibility for their actions, they shift responsibility to the manager, the one with the position power.

apply it

1. In your current job, what sources of power do you have access to? If you are not currently employed, consider your sources of power at your most recent job.

2. Whom do you depend on for resources at this job? What kinds of resources do these people control?

People acquire and share power to meet their objectives

Power relationships are dynamic. A person who joins an organization doesn't get a fixed amount of power. People acquire, use, and lose power in various ways. Thus, people's relative power over one another is constantly shifting. To meet their objectives, people try to shift the balance of power in their own favor.

The Process of Acquiring Power

People add to their power in an organization by extending their authority, gaining control over resources (such as funding or knowledge), and adding to their status, so that others value their respect and attention. Extending authority adds to a person's legitimate power and usually also increases power to deliver rewards and punishments. Gaining control over resources adds to reward and coercive power and, in the case of knowledge resources, expert power. Adding to personal status increases referent power.

For example, human resource specialists at many organizations have sought to add to their power in a positive way by presenting themselves as experts in enabling their organizations to implement strategic change.[16] In the past, people in organizations have sometimes viewed human resource professionals primarily as managers of specialized but routine decisions in areas such as compensation, benefits, and labor relations—all functions that many organizations are currently outsourcing. In contrast, some human resource professionals have positioned themselves as providing expertise in developing leaders and teams, building a learning organization, managing organizational change, and other key concerns of a modern organization. This control over knowledge resources gives human resource professionals greater position power as well as greater personal power.

There are many methods for acquiring power. Exhibit 12.4 summarizes some specific ways people can acquire and maintain power from each of the five sources identified earlier in this chapter. In general, people acquire reward power by consistently, fairly, and visibly delivering rewards that are valued. They acquire coercive power by using punishments that are seen as appropriate and by threatening only when they really can follow through. Ways to acquire legitimate power include adding to personal authority and demonstrating it. People acquire expert power by adding to and demonstrating their knowledge. Ways to acquire referent power include behaving in ways that others respect and appreciate. In each case, acquiring power

Source of Power	Methods for Building Power
Reward power	Discover what people want and need Gain more control over rewards Ensure people know you control rewards Promise only what you can deliver Don't use rewards in a manipulative way Avoid incentives that are complex or mechanical Don't use rewards for personal benefit
Coercive power	Identify credible penalties for unacceptable behavior Gain authority to use punishments Use only punishments that are legitimate Don't make rash threats Don't use coercion in a manipulative way Fit punishments to the type of behavior Don't use coercion for personal benefit
Legitimate power	Gain more formal authority Use symbols of authority Induce people to acknowledge authority Exercise authority regularly Follow proper channels when issuing directions Back up authority with reward and coercive power
Expert power	Add to relevant knowledge Keep informed about technical matters Develop exclusive sources of information Use symbols to verify expertise Demonstrate competency by solving difficult problems Don't make rash, careless statements Maintain a consistent position Don't lie or misrepresent facts
Referent power	Show acceptance of and positive regard for others Act supportive and helpful Don't manipulate and exploit others for personal advantage Defend people's interests when appropriate Keep promises Make sacrifices to show concern for others Use sincere forms of ingratiation

exhibit **12.4**

Building Each Source of Power

Source: Based on Gary A. Yukl, *Leadership in Organizations*, 3rd ed. (Upper Saddle River, NJ: Prentice-Hall, 1994), p. 243.

involves not only gaining control in some objective sense but also influencing other people's perceptions. Later in this chapter, we discuss a range of political behavior for carrying out these activities.

Coalitions

Acquiring power is sometimes a group effort. People may seek strength in numbers by forming a **coalition**, a group formed to achieve political objectives. A coalition may be a formal group such as a trade group, professional association, or labor union. In such a group, people share knowledge and increase their control over resources. Or a coalition may be informal, as in the case of **networking**—that is, cultivating a range of relationships with people interested in trading favors.

coalition

A group formed to achieve political objectives.

networking

Cultivating a range of relationships with people interested in trading favors.

In networking, people offer each other a kind of reward power. For example, the Massachusetts Institute of Technology (MIT) sponsors an annual entrepreneurship competition, launched with a "team-building dinner," a networking event at which business and technology students look for partners offering such desirable resources as funding or complementary areas of expertise. Winners of the competition have gone on to become real-world winners, including Akamal Technologies Inc. (recently valued at more than $1.5 billion) and Webline Communications Corporation (acquired for $325 million by Cisco Systems). That track record draws investors as well as students to MIT's networking dinner.[17]

In each case, a coalition involves creating a group that together holds more power by controlling more resources than an individual can acting alone. The group's members together have more knowledge, more relationships, and more work skills and potential than any of its members alone. In the following example, an entrepreneur used networking to create a coalition of people who contribute financial and knowledge resources to her company.

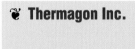

In a business environment where venture capitalists are pouring money into Silicon Valley's "dot.coms," a Cleveland manufacturing business is at a disadvantage, even if it is a high-tech manufacturer. To make matters worse for the company, called Thermagon, its founder, Carol Latham, was a chemist, not an experienced business owner. Latham therefore had to acquire resources by carefully extending her existing network of relationships.

After the usual lenders turned Thermagon down, Latham developed a plan for seeking funding from people she already knew. She determined that she would tap friends and relatives who would not seek control over business decisions, could contribute more than money, and who knew her personally. The last criterion was important because Latham is a person of integrity, and she wanted to work with people who could appreciate that. For example, a retired entrepreneur named Del Ingram said, "I brought in other investors because I had faith and trust in her integrity. After three companies, I've found that that's what business is all about."

Whenever Latham asked a person for financing, she also asked for the names of other potential investors. In this way, Latham obtained her first five investors, who brought in others. Networking gave Latham access to other resources as well. The people she met sent Thermagon highly qualified employees and consultants. Like the investors, they were eager to work with Latham because they appreciated her commitment and talent.[18]

Coalitions are especially important for individuals who do not see themselves as being able to acquire enough power alone to meet their objectives. The traditional example is that of a labor union. During the Industrial Revolution, individual production workers were seen as highly substitutable. In contrast, replacing an entire striking workforce would be difficult. Many workers therefore joined labor unions to increase their power and demand compensation, working conditions, and benefits that they could not get when acting alone. In a new twist on that model, many doctors today are considering collective bargaining through the American Medical Association. This is a means to preserve power as managed health care systems limit their professional autonomy and incomes by capping payments for patient visits, treatments, and tests.[19]

As with labor unions, the bigger a coalition is, the less substitutable and more important it becomes. Therefore, the builders of a coalition often try to make it as large as possible.[20] In South Korea, for example, the Korean

Confederation of Trade Unions has tried to convince the members of its nearly 2,000 unions to join together in a strike to protest government and business policies. Because recession has swelled the ranks of the unemployed in South Korea, the confederation's leaders believe that a strike can succeed only if all the workers participate.[21] In general, broad participation in a coalition can not only give the coalition influence in decision making, but help to ensure the successful implementation of a decision.

Empowerment

Organizations also put power to work by empowering employees to act on the organization's behalf. Empowerment of employees means transferring position power to lower levels of the organization. Empowered employees can make decisions about how to use the organization's resources to achieve organizational goals. Empowerment requires trust. Hubert Saint-Onge, a senior vice president at a Canadian financial services company called the Mutual Group, recalls that this issue arose when the company gave all its employees access to the Internet. Some Mutual Group managers worried that employees would use their Internet privileges to waste time. However, Saint-Onge pointed out that employees already were trustworthy users of an older communications technology, the telephone.[22]

The rationale for empowerment is to allocate power to the people who are best positioned to use it wisely. Often, people who are nearest to a situation, such as production activities or customer interactions, have the best information for making decisions. In the airline industry, air traffic controllers usually dictate the movements of aircraft because they have the most information about traffic on runways and in the surrounding airspace. However, federal regulations give pilots the ultimate authority to reject a controller instruction they consider unsafe. On a recent foggy night, a Providence, Rhode Island, controller directed a US Airways jet to take off, but the pilot refused. The pilot had heard an exchange between the control tower and a United Airlines crew in which the United crew was confused about its position on the runway. Knowing that the controllers at the Providence airport lacked radar to detect planes on the ground, the US Airways pilot decided to wait until he was positive the United crew was absolutely sure of its location. The decision was fortunate. The United plane was not where the controllers thought it was, but 4,000 feet down the runway directly in front of the US Airways jet.[23]

In an organization that empowers employees, managers reward effective decision making, rather than mere compliance with orders. They give up control over specific decisions but still provide leadership and rewards. Thus, empowerment changes the way power is distributed in organizations, but it does not necessarily remove position power from managers.

apply it

1. Suppose the owner of a catering business wants to empower employees to participate in expanding the business and scheduling work. What kinds of power should the owner grant to the employees?

2. How might these changes affect the owner's ability to acquire and maintain power? Do you think the overall amount of power in the organization will change? Explain.

People acquire and use power through political behavior

politics

The activities through which people acquire and use power.

Together, the activities through which people acquire and use power are called **politics.** Generally, political behavior describes activities outside a person's formal job responsibilities. For example, scheduling workers is a job responsibility, whereas persuading someone to work on New Year's Day involves political behavior, such as trading favors or convincing the person that it is a good idea.

Some people dislike organizational politics and wish they could work in an organization where people do not engage in such behavior. Political behavior can result in gains for some individuals at the expense of others and perhaps at the expense of the organization's objectives. However, an absence of political behavior is not possible and probably not even desirable. The decisions, conflicts, and perceptions that are part of organizational life create situations in which individual differences and nonrational criteria play a role. These factors cannot be handled purely through formal policies and position power.

Scope of Political Behavior

People engage in political behavior to further their objectives. Whether their political behavior is beneficial or harmful to the organization therefore depends partly on the nature of these objectives. Sometimes people try to enhance their power so they can perform their job better. In that case, politics may benefit the organization. At other times, people engage in political behavior to meet purely personal needs. If these needs are inconsistent with the organization's objectives, or if satisfying them through political means seems unfair to others, the political behavior may harm the organization.

Political behavior generally involves using one or more of the influence strategies shown in Exhibit 12.5: rational persuasion, inspirational appeal, consultation, ingratiation, exchange, personal appeal, coalition, legitimating, and pressure.[24] Not only are these strategies used to attempt to influence others, but people may use them to resist another's influence attempts. (Remember that resistance to influence is part of the definition of power.) For example, if a coworker uses ingratiation to convince you to help with a project, you might use rational persuasion to demonstrate that you are too busy. Through such attempts, the two of you will discover whether the colleague has enough power to influence your behavior—and whether you have enough power to resist.

Researchers have studied which of these strategies are most common in organizations and which are most successful. So far, research shows the most success with use of the three strategies listed at the top of the table—rational persuasion, inspirational appeal, and consultation—and the least success with the bottom three—coalition, legitimating, and pressure.[25] In

exhibit | **12.5**

Influence Strategies

Rational persuasion	Using logical arguments and factual evidence
Inspirational appeal	Appealing to ideals, values, aspirations
Consultation	Seeking participation in decisions
Ingratiation	Trying to put someone in a good mood before making a request
Exchange	Offering to trade favors, share benefits, or repay someone later
Personal appeal	Appealing to a person's loyalty or friendship
Coalition	Asking others to support a cause or activity
Legitimating	Claiming authority or associating a request with the organization's policies, norms, or procedures
Pressure	Making demands or threats; issuing persistent reminders

Source: Adapted from G. Yukl, P. J. Guinan, and D. Sottolano. (1995). "Influence tactics used for different objectives with subordinates, peers, and superiors." *Group and Organization Management 20:* 275.

light of that research, it is not surprising that Pat Farrah's career at Home Depot stalled out as he became known for making ruthless demands on his employees. He also had a reputation for brilliance in merchandising, which propelled him into Home Depot's executive ranks, but he became frustrated at his inability to control decisions at the growing number of Home Depot stores. Farrah left the company for ten years, returning after he reportedly mellowed and "learned . . . to . . . work more effectively with colleagues."[26] The research on political tactics also is consistent with the experience of Larry Ellison in setting a new direction for Oracle Corporation, as described in the following example.

℧ Oracle Corporation

Larry Ellison is the founder and chief executive of a Silicon Valley powerhouse called Oracle. The company established itself as a provider of database software, but Ellison feared it would lose its edge as the Internet began to dominate information technology.

Ellison had a vision: Oracle should apply Internet browsers to finding, analyzing, and reporting a company's data, rather than limiting these tasks to the traditional "client-server" tools (typically, a company's mainframe linked to PCs). As a leader, Ellison needed to use his powers to persuade others to act on that vision. He started by issuing orders: Employees were to convert all of Oracle's products so that they could work as an Internet application, usable by any computer with Internet access and a browser. Ellison added that all Oracle's client-server products would be phased out. Then Ellison went on summer vacation.

Upon his return in the fall, Ellison discovered that he had not achieved full compliance, much less commitment, from employees. Software developers were not seriously working on the Internet applications. In fact, employees were quietly telling customers that Oracle would continue to handle the old client-server products. Ellison realized he needed to exert power in other ways to demonstrate he was serious.

Ellison began personally directing software development, putting his physical presence behind his words. As Ellison's involvement grew, so did his excitement, and he began to inspire others at Oracle. Before long, software developers were creating the products Ellison had envisioned. Also, significantly, the company began applying the new software to managing Oracle itself—and so did hundreds of customers. Recently, a ZDNet online news story proclaimed, "Oracle is not your daddy's database company anymore."[27]

People cannot always use the three most effective political strategies, because these strategies are not always available or appropriate. For example, it would be difficult to create an inspirational appeal for every routine action, and some situations do not permit time for consultation. Also, individuals are more skilled at using some tactics than others, and they have access to different sources of power. For a person with access to coercive power, demands may be easier to express than logical arguments supported by evidence. Conversely, a person without much position power will not be able to rely as much on rewards or threats. The ability to use a variety of influence strategies can enhance a person's power. But some strategies may be unethical, especially when used deceptively or cruelly. For instance, engaging in apparently rational persuasion based on lies would be dishonest, forming a coalition to exclude someone because of his or her race would be unjust and potentially illegal, and pressuring someone who is frightened of your power is cruel.

Political strategies also differ according to a person's objectives. To convince others of an idea, people tend to appeal to reason. To obtain favors, people use more personal strategies, relying on friendliness. Research has shown that people are most successful at generating commitment when they base their attempt on a friendly relationship and when the influence attempt concerns something important and enjoyable.[28]

So far, the research on political behavior has a major shortcoming, however: it focuses only on North Americans. The influence strategies studied may not be equally effective in the context of other cultures. Depending on cultural norms, influence tactics that are effective among the dominant U.S. culture may be ineffective or even insulting to people of other cultures.[29] For example, in some cultures, people think of a hierarchy in terms of obligations rather than power. A high-status person in these cultures is seen as someone with a lot of responsibility. Thus, in Iran, a higher status person is responsible for protecting a lower status person, so a person interested in being protected might try to *lose* status.[30]

Reasons for Political Behavior

People use politics because they perceive that acquiring and using power will help them accomplish their goals. They are most likely to need this help under certain circumstances. People rely heavily on politics to resolve conflicts under the conditions shown in Exhibit 12.6. In general, political behavior prevails when tasks are complex and ambiguous and people who don't trust each other are competing for resources. Under these difficult—and common—circumstances, people use political behavior as a basis for making decisions and motivating others.

For example, a U.S.–based health maintenance organization set out to acquire a health care company in Argentina. The doctors at the Argentine company had heard horror stories about HMOs from their U.S. colleagues, so they were upset by the plan. The other Argentine employees handled the uncertainty by taking their cues from the doctors, and they became upset, too. The employees together held a controlling share of ownership. They would not approve the acquisition until the HMO's owners invested in a great deal of rational persuasion and other political tactics.[31]

exhibit | **12.6**
Conditions That Foster Political Behavior

Task Characteristics

- Goals are inconsistent.
- Performance criteria are ambiguous.
- Tasks are interdependent.

Situation Characteristics

- Communication is lacking.
- Rewards are uncertain.
- Employees are highly competitive.
- The consequences of failure are great.
- Power is spread out among many people.
- Resources are scarce.
- Trust among employees is low.
- People are working in groups in which no one has a position of authority over the others.
- The organization rewards political behavior.

Individual Characteristics

- People have a strong need for power.
- People score high in Machiavellianism.
- People have an internal locus of control.
- People are high self-monitors.

Sources: Don R. Beeman and Thomas W. Sharkey, "The Use and Abuse of Corporate Politics," *Business Horizons 30*, March-April 1987, p. 27; P. M. Fandt and G. R. Ferris, "The Management of Information and Impressions: When Employees Behave Opportunistically," *Organizational Behavior and Human Decision Processes*, February 1990, pp. 140–148; Larry E. Greiner and Virginia E. Schein, *Power and Organizational Development: Mobilizing Power to Implement Change* (Reading, MA: Addison-Wesley, 1988), pp. 18–23; R. W. Woodman, S. J. Wayne, and D. Rubinstein, "Personality Correlates of a Propensity to Engage in Political Behavior in Organizations," *Proceedings of the Southwest Academy of Management,* 1985, pp. 131–135; G. Biberman, "Personality and Characteristic Work Attitudes of Persons with High, Moderate, and Low Political Tendencies," *Psychological Reports,* October 1985, pp. 1303–1310; and G. R. Ferris, G. S. Russ, and P. M. Fandt, "Politics in Organizations," in R. A. Giacalone and P. Rosenfeld (eds.), *Impression Management in the Organization* (Hillsdale, NJ: Lawrence Erlbaum Associates, 1989), pp. 155–156.

Another reason that people engage in political behavior is that some organizations reward it. In an organization where the best-liked people get promoted, people will strive to be liked. Or an organization's executives might establish ambiguous tasks and performance criteria, expecting that if managers engage in power struggles, the most talented people will come out on top.

Furthermore, individual differences shape the extent to which people engage in political behavior. As discussed in Chapter 5, some people are motivated by a relatively strong need for power. These people are more likely to engage in political behavior because it is highly motivating for them. Along similar lines, some psychologists have noted that certain individuals engage in a behavior pattern called **Machiavellianism.** This style of behavior, named after a 16th century Italian philosopher famous for his advice to princes on how to gain power, involves the following behaviors:

- Using deceit in interpersonal relationships
- Viewing other people with cynicism
- Lacking concern for conventional morality[32]

Machiavellianism

A behavior pattern that includes using deceit in interpersonal relationships, viewing others cynically, and lacking concern for conventional morality.

People who exhibit this behavior pattern tend to have little trust in others and to say whatever will serve their political purposes. These tendencies enhance the likelihood a person will engage in political behavior.[33]

locus of control

Where individuals place the responsibility for the events that affect them; may be either internal or external.

People are also more likely to engage in political behavior if they have an internal **locus of control.** A locus of control refers to where individuals place the responsibility for the events that affect them. A person who believes he or she is largely responsible for controlling events has an *internal locus of control.* A person who believes that events are the result of outside forces, such as fate or "the powers that be," has an *external locus of control.* People with an internal locus of control believe they have some control over what people do, so they see more purpose to engaging in political behavior. A study comparing the use of political behavior among different kinds of individuals found that those who have an internal locus of control do in fact engage in more political behavior.[34]

Finally, political behavior is most likely among people who are "high self-monitors."[35] Compared with others, these people are more sensitive to social cues, more likely to conform to social norms, and more skilled in political behavior.

Impression Management

impression management

The process by which people seek to control others' perceptions of them.

To enhance individual referent power, as well as people's perceptions that an individual has other sources of power, a person engages in **impression management.** This is the process by which people seek to control others' perceptions of them. In other words, they try to create a good impression of themselves. A whole industry, known as "executive coaching," seeks to help rising managers develop this ability. For example, coach Debra Benton helps executives at companies including Mattel, PepsiCo, and Hewlett-Packard develop what she calls *executive presence*—"the impact you have when you walk into a room, a collection of subtle . . . visual cues; including everything from how your clothes fit to how you walk."[36]

To engage in impression management, people say and do things that make them look smart, nice, agreeable, or whatever will generate approval in a particular situation. For example, name dropping may give the impression a person associates with high-status people and, by extension, is the kind of person that high-status people like. Likewise, flattery is a form of impression management that can help a person seem perceptive and pleasant to be around. (People like to think that the flattery about them is true.) These kinds of behaviors can be helpful when they enable others to appreciate someone's true worth to the organization. Of course, some people engage in such implausible name dropping and insincere flattery that they fail to influence others and instead portray themselves as dishonest.

Steve Harrison used impression management in a positive way when he sold the business he owned, a career services firm. He continues as president of Lee Hecht Harrison, but he was concerned that the new owners would view him, at age 50, as behind the times. So Harrison maintains expert power by keeping up with current issues in management, such as globalization and leadership. He also peppers conversations with references to his "youthful" hobbies of running and collecting electric guitars.[37]

Some studies have tested the effectiveness of impression management by exploring whether it enhances success in job interviews. Research generally suggests that impression management is useful. For example, interviewers in one study rated applicants for a job as customer service representative. Adjusting the results to account for differences in credentials, the researchers found that the interviewers gave superior ratings to the applicants who used impression management techniques. The interviewers also indicated more interest in hiring those applicants.[38] Another study used employment interviews to compare the success of different impression management techniques. This study found that job applicants were more successful when they used a controlling style that focused on themselves—for example, promoting themselves and enhancing their image. Applicants were less successful when they used submissive impression management techniques, such as adopting the interviewer's point of view and offering favors to the interviewer.[39]

Defensive Behaviors

Like a basketball game, organizational behavior involves defensive as well as offensive strategy. Thus, along with impression management, people in organizations engage in various defensive behaviors. These behaviors are designed to protect the person from political damage that arises from taking an unpopular or undesirable action, receiving blame, or undergoing a threatening change. Exhibit 12.7 summarizes basic types of defensive behaviors.

Avoiding Action Sometimes a person's role dictates action, but that person doesn't want to act. For example, two coworkers may be having a dispute, and they want their manager to resolve it. Any solution the manager can think of involves disappointing at least one employee, so the manager may not want to get involved. The manager might use any of a variety of activity-avoiding techniques, such as pretending not to see the problem, putting off a meeting with the employees, or passing the responsibility to

Executive coaching seeks to help rising managers develop the ability to control others' perceptions of them. Although she has never met clients such as Ernst partner Barry Mabry, who works in New Orleans, coach Cynder Niemela provides advice on matters both mundane and strategic, sometimes even from her boat in Sausalito, California. Corporate coaching is one of the most popular aids for today's managers. Workers at all levels of the corporate ladder are enlisting coaches for guidance on how to improve their performance, boost their profits, and make better decisions about everything from personnel to strategy. (Source: © Alex Tehrani)

Behaviors for Avoiding Action

- Pretending not to see a problem or need for action
- Putting off an action in favor of other activities
- Transferring responsibility to someone else
- Invoking rules and policies consistent with inaction

Behaviors for Avoiding Blame

- Blaming someone else
- Justifying personal actions, to put them in the best possible light
- Documenting activities to demonstrate thoroughness and adherence to procedures
- Misrepresenting the truth

Behaviors for Avoiding Change

- Trying to prevent the change
- Focusing on self-protection during change

exhibit | **12.7**
Types of Defensive Behaviors

someone else. Another common way that people in organizations avoid undesirable or risky situations is by invoking organizational rules and policies to protect themselves. For example, they might say, "You know I'm not allowed to handle that," or, "You know we can't process that request because you submitted it after the deadline."

Avoiding Blame   People also use defensive tactics to avoid being blamed for a problem. They might quickly blame someone else—a scapegoat—to deflect attention from their own role in the problem. When a Bell AH-1 Cobra military aircraft crashed shortly after a year's worth of repairs in a Fort Worth, Texas, factory, the manufacturer quickly blamed the U.S. Army, because it is responsible for inspecting Bell's work and requesting modifications to ensure safety. The Army officer in charge of inspecting Bell's work insisted that Bell was responsible for providing safe aircraft: "Bell is the one responsible for wrench turning and for the inspection of all that."[40]

People also use other tactics for avoiding blame. A person might justify his or her actions, so that others will see the person's role in the best possible light, given the circumstances. Another tactic is to carefully document all individual activities, which at least shows a commitment to careful, meticulous work and should bolster any explanations. When the consequences of blame are high, people might even misrepresent the truth in justifying their actions. But remember from Chapter 11 that avoiding blame may be inconsistent with exercising leadership.

Avoiding Change   Defensive behaviors are common when people feel threatened by a change. People may try to prevent the change from occurring, or they may focus on guarding their power during the change. At USA Waste Services, a merger with Waste Management inspired such fear of layoffs that local managers actually helped some employees hide from corporate management. For example, they kept records listing some USA Waste employees who work in the field as being at headquarters. Waste Management CEO John Drury said, "We literally have found 30 to 40 people [at locations] where we were told there were three or four. We've already caught it 10 to 15 times." Apparently, employees hoped that the company couldn't lay them off if it couldn't find them.[41]

Because change is so much a part of life in today's organizations, change avoidance is generally not desirable from the organization's point of view, and managers discourage this type of behavior. For a more detailed discussion on change in organizations, see Chapter 18.

Managing Defensive Behavior   People typically engage in defensive behaviors because they perceive that they have something to lose in a situation. Thus, organizations that prefer employees to collaborate on solutions rather than protect their turf will try to minimize the personal consequences of making a mistake or an unpopular decision. They may do this by empowering employees to share decision-making responsibility and by treating mistakes as an opportunity to add to the organization's knowledge base. Such an organization is more flexible and better positioned to fully utilize its human resources.

apply it

1. In your current (or most recent) job, who do you want to have a favorable impression of you? How do you try to create such an impression? Can you think of any additional impression management strategies you would like to try? If so, which ones?

2. Imagine you are a department supervisor in a store. While you are waiting on a customer, your manager hands you a slip of paper containing a name and phone number and quietly asks you to return a call from an angry customer. Several hours later, your manager asks to hear the outcome of the call, and you realize you completely forgot about making it. How do you think you would handle this situation? How do you think you *should* handle it?

Power and politics should be used ethically

As we have discussed, the use of political behavior can be constructive or destructive for an organization. Political behavior also can be ethical or unethical, depending on whether people use it to help or harm others. Exhibit 12.8 summarizes criteria for determining whether political behavior is ethical

exhibit **12.8**

Criteria for Determining Whether Political Behavior Is Ethical

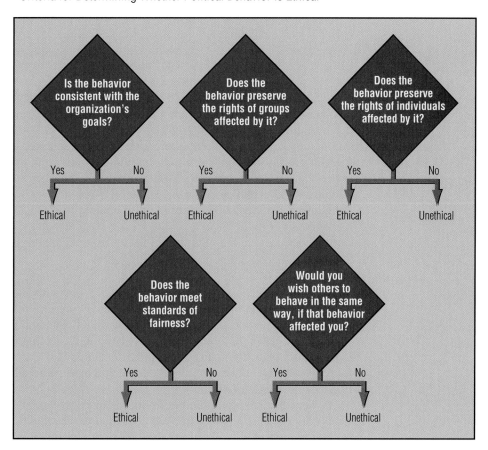

or unethical. In general, political behavior is ethical if it is consistent with the goals of the organization and the rights of groups and individuals. Two important areas in which the use of power involves ethical issues are sexual harassment and conflicts between personal and organizational objectives.

Sexual Harassment

At its core, sexual harassment involves an unethical use of power, because the harasser uses sexual behavior to intimidate, threaten, or embarrass others. In a recent case brought by the Equal Employment Opportunity Commission against Algroup Wheaton, three women claimed that a supervisor had made comments about their physical appearance and had groped two of them. When they complained to another supervisor, they said, they were fired from their jobs at the plastics factory.[42]

The hostile and damaging nature of sexual harassment becomes clearer when we consider the role that power plays in it. In the workplace, employees depend on one another—especially on people at higher levels— for many resources, including knowledge, cooperation, and their very jobs. When access to these resources seems to depend on granting sexual favors, the person who needs the resources can become intimidated and frightened, whether or not the harasser actually withholds the resources. Thus, to understand whether a person's behavior is harassment, it is important to view the situation from the perspective of someone in a dependency position. For instance, an off-color joke is less humorous to a person who perceives it as an effort to take away some of his or her control of a situation.

Sexual harassment is clearly an unethical use of power because of the harm it does to the person being harassed. It also harms the organization. First, it is illegal; organizations that are sued for sexual harassment are subject to embarrassing publicity as well as legal sanctions. In addition, organizations that permit sexual harassment often cannot recruit or retain talented employees and cannot fully benefit from their skills and experience. People in such organizations take power from the harassed employees and thereby prevent them from contributing fully. In addition, the harassers devote energy to power-grabbing behavior that could be better devoted to cooperation and achievement of organizational goals. To prevent such problems, organizations benefit from discouraging sexual harassment, as discussed in Chapter 2.

Personal versus Organizational Objectives

As we have seen, people use power and politics as a resource for meeting objectives. A person will persuade, reward, pressure, and inspire others to behave as the person desires. This behavior is obviously beneficial for the organization when the person uses power to induce others to achieve organizational objectives. In fact, organizations provide position power for just that purpose. But what about situations where personal and organizational objectives conflict?

A person's role as a member of an organization requires him or her to support the organization's objectives. For that reason, it is usually ethical to put the organization's objectives ahead of personal objectives in most situations. For example, a team that has responsibility for scheduling workers should create the schedule based on criteria that benefit the company, such as ensuring the team has the necessary mix of skills and the right number of workers when needed, rather than, say, the most powerful members giving themselves the hours they want.

In some cases, ethical issues are more complex and more difficult to sort through. An individual might determine that an organization's objectives are unrealistic or even unethical. For example, if an organization expects its people to work unreasonably long hours consistently, an individual might use political behavior to resolve this conflict to obtain rest and time with family. A manager who used her position power to take time off while ignoring the plight of her overburdened employees would hardly earn their respect. In contrast, ethical power tactics would address this situation as a problem requiring accommodation of all parties' interests—both employees' and the organization's. A person who wanted to reduce overtime hours could try using rational persuasion and coalitions to explore the problem and also look for alternative methods of staffing. These solutions might benefit the organization by reducing exhaustion, stress, and turnover associated with excessive overtime.

Leaders can influence the kinds of political behavior people use by encouraging or limiting constructive participation. An organization that empowers employees may provide more ways to use power constructively when organizational and personal objectives conflict. In contrast, if an organization discourages employees from participating in problem solving, it can limit employees' options to more selfish political behavior. To learn about strategies for resolving conflict, see Chapter 13.

Handling Destructive Political Behavior

Ideally, organizations help prevent destructive politics by rewarding constructive behavior in their employees. When people do engage in destructive political behavior, the ethical response is to end or repair the damage. As shown in Exhibit 12.9, people in organizations can combat destructive uses of organizational politics by encouraging constructive behavior, recognizing destructive behavior, and ending destructive behavior.

Managers can prevent much political behavior by modeling and rewarding behavior that is ethical and supports cooperation and achievement

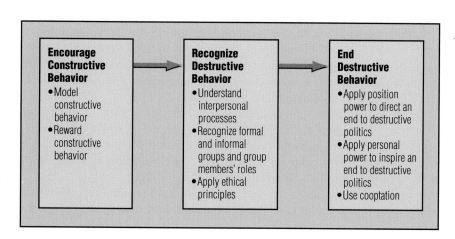

exhibit **12.9**

Ways to Handle Destructive Organizational Politics

of organizational objectives. People at all levels of the organization can try to reward constructive, ethical behavior by using whatever reward power they have. The CEO of Tactics, a technology consulting firm, encourages all of his employees to serve as mentors to new employees. For example, employees may ask any colleague to monitor their work. Establishing the value of sharing knowledge overrides the negative attitude that hoarding knowledge is a way to acquire power.[43] Similarly, the following example describes how the managers at another consulting firm, Viant, support constructive behavior by developing policies that reward cooperation.

❦ Viant Inc.

The key resource and ultimate source of power for a business consultant is knowledge. Consultants may be tempted to hoard their knowledge and use it as a bargaining chip to land the best assignments with the best firms. But from the perspective of a consulting firm, the challenge is to keep talented consultants and encourage them to add value to their knowledge by sharing it with one another.

The executives of Viant, which specializes in Web-based businesses, appreciate these challenges. Their solution is to encourage and reward empowerment, rather than selfish uses of knowledge resources. They do this through policies and procedures that begin when the company interviews candidates for employment. Viant selects employees from a variety of backgrounds who have demonstrated a willingness and ability to share, learn, and collaborate, as opposed to pure intelligence. Each new consultant is then assigned to an "advocate," a more experienced colleague who provides career guidance.

Viant consultants work on teams comprising specialists in e-commerce strategy, technology, and "creative" aspects (advertising, design, and marketing). Company policy dictates that 60 percent of each team's members must have been employed by Viant for at least six months. Together, these criteria for team membership create a work structure in which team members are likely to learn from one another. Further reinforcing collegiality at Viant, company policy dictates that no Viant office will employ more than 125 people; more than that, and employees will not be able to know everyone's name.

Viant's compensation practices reinforce the high value placed on learning and collaboration. The company grants stock options based on employees' contributions to growth, measured not only in terms of billable hours or clients but also in helping to train or mentor coworkers.

These practices may not make Viant the fastest-growing consulting firm, but they inspire commitment and reduce turnover among Viant's carefully chosen consultants. The strategy also positions Viant to be the premium name in its field.[44]

Viant has limited the use of destructive political behavior by carefully developing structures and systems that encourage constructive behavior. When destructive behavior does occur in organizations, damage control first requires someone to be able to recognize the behavior as destructive. To do this, the organization's leaders must understand such interpersonal processes as perception, communication, and conflict management (all topics in this book). They should recognize the informal and formal groups in the organization and be aware of dependency relationships. This knowledge can provide a foundation for recognizing when group or individual goals are ambiguous or conflict with the organization's objectives—a climate in which destructive politics may flourish.

When people recognize destructive politics, they can use their own power to try to stop it. Managers can use position power to discourage such behavior. Even without position power, members of the organization can control negative behavior through referent power and by withholding social rewards from people who behave inappropriately.

In the case of a power struggle that is diverting energy from more beneficial activities, a leader can engage in **cooptation.** The leader diverts the

cooptation

Diverting factions in a power struggle by focusing them on a common goal.

factions in a power struggle by focusing them on a common goal. The formerly opposing parties therefore find themselves on the same side of a new challenge, and the former adversaries may become allies.

apply it

1. Assume you are a supervisor of ten employees. Suggest some practical steps you can take to prevent sexual harassment within your group.

2. How would your suggestions affect your employees' ability to achieve their personal objectives? How would your suggestions affect achievement of your organization's objectives?

summary OF KEY CONCEPTS

- **Power influences what people can do in organizations.** Power is a general ability to influence, in contrast to leadership, which is the ability to influence in a way that supports achieving groups goals. Power may come from a person's position in the organization (legitimate, reward, and coercive power) or from the person him- or herself (expert and referent power). In general, position power can produce compliance or resistance, and personal power can produce commitment. People in organizations are able to exert power because others depend on them for cooperation and a variety of resources. Research suggests that people perceived to have position power have a broad ability to generate obedience.

- **People acquire and share power to meet their objectives.** They add to their power by extending their authority, gaining control over resources, and adding to their status. They may also form coalitions with others, because the coalition controls more resources than any of its members alone. Organizations may redistribute power through empowerment of employees. The objective of empowerment is to allocate power to the people who are best positioned to use it wisely.

- **People acquire and use power through political behavior.** Political behavior usually refers to activities outside a person's formal job responsibilities. It encompasses rational persuasion, inspira-

tional appeal, consultation, ingratiation, exchange, personal appeal, coalition, legitimating, and pressure. People are most likely to use political behavior under conditions that are complex, uncertain, ambiguous, and involve competition for resources. Political behavior is also most likely among people with a strong need for power, a high degree of Machiavellianism, an internal locus of control, and a high degree of self-monitoring behavior. Some political behavior is devoted to impression management (for example, flattery and name-dropping); other political behavior is defensive (for example, blaming others or avoiding responsibility).

- **Power and politics should be used ethically.** An area of unethical political behavior is sexual harassment, which prevents the organization from fully utilizing human resources. Ethical challenges arise when personal and organizational objectives come into conflict. In such situations, individuals behave ethically when they use their power to find a resolution that addresses both organizational and individual needs. Organizations can handle destructive political behavior by enabling their leaders to model and reward behavior that is ethical and supports cooperation and achievement of organizational objectives. Leaders in an organization can use their power to stop destructive behavior. They can also use cooptation to focus people on shared goals.

KEY terms

power, p. 418
legitimate power, p. 419
zone of indifference, p. 419

reward power, p. 420
coercive power, p. 420
compliance, p. 420

resistance, p. 421
expert power, p. 422
referent power, p. 422

commitment, p. 422

coalition, p. 427

networking, p. 427

politics, p. 430

Machiavellianism, p. 433

locus of control, p. 434

impression management, p. 434

cooptation, p. 440

DISCUSSION questions

1. Describe the difference between power and leadership. Then describe briefly someone you know who is a leader and someone else you know who has power. Is each effective in his or her role? Why or why not?

2. Would you rather work for a manager who uses reward power or coercive power? Explain your choice.

3. In a small hospital or health-care facility, what types of expert power might be evident?

4. Might a manager have more power over employees during a time of high unemployment or low unemployment? Why?

5. In what ways do members of an organization acquire and extend their power?

6. List some ways that a restaurant manager could empower her employees.

7. Why do you think the political strategies of rational persuasion, inspirational appeal, and consultation are usually most effective? Can you think of situations in which these strategies might be ineffective or unavailable to a manager?

8. Suppose Jackie, a manager, is aware that a certain employee is leaving work early frequently, taking long lunches, and spending time on the Internet conducting personal business during work hours. Jackie knows she needs to do something about the employee's behavior, but the employee has a lot of expert power in the department and is popular as well. What types of defensive behaviors might Jackie engage in?

9. What types of defensive behaviors might the employee in question 8 engage in, once Jackie confronts the situation? How might Jackie and the employee manage their behaviors?

10. How is sexual harassment related to power? Why is it important for managers and employees to understand what sexual harassment in the workplace is?

11. What steps can managers take to prevent and control destructive political behavior?

SELF-DISCOVERY exercise

How Political Are You?

The Political Behavior Inventory

To determine your political appreciation and tendencies, please answer the following questions. Select the answer that best represents your behavior or belief, even if that particular behavior or belief is not present all the time.

1. You should make others feel important through an open appreciation of their ideas and work.

_____ True   _____ False

2. Because people tend to judge you when they first meet you, always try to make a good first impression.

_____ True   _____ False

3. Try to let others do most of the talking, be sympathetic to their problems, and resist telling people that they are totally wrong.

_____ True   _____ False

4. Praise the good traits of the people you meet and always give people an opportunity to save face if they are wrong or make a mistake.

_____ True   _____ False

5. Spreading false rumors, planting misleading information, and backstabbing are necessary, if somewhat unpleasant, methods to deal with your enemies.

_____ True   _____ False

6. Sometimes it is necessary to make promises that you know you will not or cannot keep.   _____ True   _____ False

7. It is important to get along with everybody, even with those who are generally recognized as windbags, abrasive, or constant complainers.   _____ True   _____ False

8. It is vital to do favors for others so that you can call in these IOUs at times when they will do you the most good.   _____ True   _____ False

9. Be willing to compromise, particularly on issues that are minor to you, but important to others.   _____ True   _____ False

10. On controversial issues, it is important to delay or avoid your involvement if possible.   _____ True   _____ False

Source: From "Connecting Organizational Politics and Conflict Resolution" by Joseph F. Byrnes, *Personnel Administrator,* June 1986, p. 49. Reprinted with the permission of *Personnel Administrator* published by the Society for Human Resource Management, Alexandria, VA. Permission conveyed through Copyright Clearance Center.

ORGANIZATIONAL BEHAVIOR in your life

We all engage in impression management at some point in our lives—during a job or college interview, when asking someone for a date, when engaging in discussion during class. Between now and your next class for this course, keep a log of your own use of impression management to influence others as well as a log of other people's use of impression management in an attempt to influence you. Were any of these efforts effective? Why or why not? Share your findings in class.

ORGANIZATIONAL BEHAVIOR news flash

Coalitions aren't just the domain of individuals seeking power within an organization. In fact, more and more companies today are forming coalitions with other companies to gain more power in the marketplace. That's the case with the European aerospace company Airbus, a network of more than 100 companies that has recently strengthened its relationship with Lockheed Martin Corp. and Mitsubishi Heavy Industries Ltd. Both of which are now becoming Airbus's partners and beginning to collaborate on military and commercial projects. This shift in power could have an impact on American giant Boeing Co. Boeing managers have traditionally viewed Airbus as a weak competitor, but a series of deals like this could change their view substantially. In addition to the Lockheed Martin/Mitsubishi agreement, deals involving Airbus partners Aerospatiale Matra, DaimlerChrysler Aerospace, and British Aerospace should increase Airbus's power in the industry. "Airbus will be the core of a large aerospace group with activities in defense—one of two or three major groups in Europe," predicts Philippe Camus, CEO of the Aerospatiale Matra. Airbus isn't restricting its networking efforts to Europe, however.

Using the news listing on your search engine, such as AP, Reuters, ZDNet News, and the like, look for stories about companies that are creating coalitions such as mergers, joint ventures, or partnerships to increase their influence in the marketplace. When you find a good story, access each company's Web site to learn more about the organizations. Then, write an editorial piece describing ways in which you think the coalition will (or will not) increase the companies' power, considering the following questions:

1. Who are the coalition's competitors, and how much power do they have in the industry?

2. In what ways is dependency involved in the process?

3. What global issues, if any, must the coalition face?

Source: Gail Edmondson, Janet Rae-Dupree, and Kerry Capell, "How Airbus Could Rule the Skies," *Business Week,* August 2, 1999, p. 54.

global diversity EVENTS

@ As more and more American companies expand their business horizons overseas, women face issues of power in the workplace that are complicated by cultural differences. Some women find their gender to be an asset; others find it to be a hindrance in their dealings with international colleagues and customers. Stephanie Nadeau, a partner in Maine-based The Lobster Company, handles the organization's domestic and international sales. Nadeau initially expected to have problems in the male-dominated cultures of Japan and Korea, but she found the opposite to be true. "Being female seems to be an advantage. I've been able to talk to people I need to get on the phone," she reports. Ironically, she says that she has more difficulty with her U.S. customers, who don't seem to trust a woman yet in the traditionally male lobster business. Lynn O'Brien Hallstein, assistant professor of communications at Babson College, traveled to Central Europe and Latin America, where she learned that women were often treated as invisible, but there was also an "odd respect" for women in business that brought them special attention and access to others in power.

Using the news listings in your search engine, look for stories about women in international business or women in power anywhere in the world. Or log on to the Web site www.digital-women.com or www. ivillage.com to see what you can find. When you find an interesting story, consider the following questions:

1. What type of power does the woman (or women) in the story have? In what ways does she (or they) use it?

2. What examples of political power are evident for both men and women in the story?

3. Examine your own views of women in power, whether you are male or female. Are you comfortable with a woman holding a powerful position? Why or why not?

Source: Cynthia E. Griffin, "R-E-S-P-E-C-T," *Entrepreneur,* August 1999, p. 36; Cynthia E. Griffin, "Out of Water Experience," *Entrepreneur,* August 1999, p. 36.

minicase ISSUE

How Can a Small Business Play in a Big Arena?

With the explosion of information technology, large and small companies alike are scrambling to pick up as many pieces of business as they can. To succeed, they need to find ways to gain power; to gain power, they need to practice politics. Sarah Gerdes, founder and CEO of Business Marketing Group Inc. (BMG), is very good at doing both. Gerdes specializes in arranging and building strategic alliances among companies, which is vital in an environment where change is a daily occurrence. "Strategic alliances are an important part of every industry," says Gene Slowinski, director of strategic alliance studies at Rutgers University's Graduate School of Management. How did Gerdes gain the power to develop these relationships? How does she even get her clients in the door at a company like Microsoft?

Politics. Gerdes had to become an expert at engaging in political behavior. With a firm belief that she could influence people's behavior, she ingratiated herself with her first two clients by giving them her services free of charge. As she began to get established, she later persuaded some of her clients to give her a cut of profits. In fact, much of Gerdes's business is based on successful political behavior. "Sarah's taking advantage of a unique confluence of events, building the relationships that start-ups need to grow as fast as they can," notes Kevin Armitage, senior vice president at FAC/Equities at First Albany Corp. "It's a win-win—she builds a thriving business if her clients do." In fact, much of Gerdes's business is based on successful political behavior.

Power. As Gerdes worked her political magic, she began to gain power. She founded her company with her own expert power—knowledge gained at previous jobs before she started BMG. As she developed relationships, her own experience and knowledge grew, and so did her power. "The value of my past experience was primarily in identifying an opportunity, correctly targeting the decision maker, pitching the idea, and then delivering the goods," says Gerdes. To help Full Armor Corp., a 12-person, Boston-based company, gain access to Microsoft, Gerdes used her personal power to guide her client through the maze of departments at the software giant. Gerdes has made many alliances between Microsoft and smaller companies, and in doing so, now has as much or more inside knowledge about the company's strategy than many of its own employees.

In dealing with Microsoft, she uses that knowledge to the advantage of both sides. "When I show up, I don't need to spend time bringing them up to speed," Gerdes explains. "We can move right forward with the tough questions as fast as possible." Here is where her political skills become evident again. "It's a real art to keep things moving without appearing obnoxious," notes Mike Walsh, vice president of worldwide database operations at Navigation Technologies. "But that's really what Sarah does."

Gerdes's personal qualities—her energy and enthusiasm—inspire others to go along with just about anything she proposes. Clients also like her because she avoids high-tech buzzwords and jargon; instead, she focuses on the vocabulary that each corporation uses. For instance, "She knows how they speak at Microsoft," says client Mike Grandinetti. "She knows the words that are most meaningful to them and has a lot of credibility within Microsoft as a result." One could just as easily translate that statement to a single word: *power.*

1. In what ways is Sarah Gerdes's power over clients related to dependency?

2. How important is networking to the success of BMG? Could BMG lose some of its power if small companies formed coalitions to deal with larger companies? Why or why not?

3. You've seen examples of Gerdes's positive use of political behavior. Could there be situations in which the knowledge she could gain about companies results in negative political behaviors? What steps might Gerdes take to avoid this situation?

Source: Christopher Caggiano, "Hotlinks," *Inc.,* October 1999, pp. 72–81.

thirteen
CHAPTER

13

Conflict Management and Negotiation

preview

After studying this chapter, you should be able to:

- Describe instances of conflict in an organization, including sources and stages of the conflict.

- Identify ways to react to a given conflict, recognizing pros and cons of each possible reaction.

- Give an example of a situation in which an organization might want to stimulate conflict.

- Suggest strategies for conflict resolution.

- Apply negotiation strategies to a conflict.

Pentagram Partners Get Along

Many people couldn't understand why James Biber, a successful architect running his own firm, would give up his lucrative business to join a partnership. He seemed to have everything professionally: prestige, steady clients, a good income. But he says that he's got even more now—as a partner in Pentagram, an architectural design firm with offices in London, New York, and San Francisco. It's hard to imagine how 15 artistic egos and their 150 staff members can get along together without stepping on each other's toes. Architects, designers, and other creative businesspeople are notoriously defensive of their turf— their ideas, their office space, and their clients. Putting them all together in one company is bound to create conflict. But Pentagram defies the odds. In fact, several of the company's full partners, like Biber, were actually entrepreneurs working for themselves prior to joining the group. They all seem to prefer being at Pentagram to being on their own.

How does Pentagram manage all these personalities? First, the company has a carefully defined partnership agreement and specific operating principles that offer partners the opportunity to work collaboratively on projects while retaining their artistic identities. "They're more themselves in that partnership than many directors of design businesses are in their own businesses," observes Michael Wolff, a graphic designer at the London firm Fourth Room. The agreement at Pentagram creates a win-win situation, in which neither party gives up significant needs but both gain something, an important component in successful conflict management. Collaboration, another positive approach to potential (or real) conflict, expands the opportunities for each designer to work on a variety of assignments. "You can't have experience on a variety of projects when you're by yourself," says Pentagram partner Lowell Williams, who gave up the graphic design firm he had in Houston for 15 years in order to join Pentagram.

Pentagram's founders based their organization on a few principles that can prevent the kind of conflict that would be destructive to the organization, yet leave room for conflict that can be beneficial. For instance, each full partner runs his or her design practice as a kind of mini-business within the organization, making decisions about which projects to work on, what the fees will be, whom to hire for the project team, and so forth. This way, partners have a free hand to conduct business as they see fit. But to remain in the firm, they must show a profit each month, and they are ranked in the organization by profitability. This promotes competition that ultimately benefits the entire organization. All partners are considered equal—no one has seniority. Every partner receives the same salary, and profits are shared equally. This sharing helps to balance the workload—busy partners are more apt to share work with partners who are less busy at the time so that all are more efficient. In the minds of Pentagram's partners, the benefits of creative freedom and growth outweigh any perceived inequity of compensation.

Pentagram's system allows its partners to collaborate on ideas instead of competing for the organization's resources, a problem that is bound to create conflict. The company pools its resources to create the best of the best—in talent, design innovations, and work environment.[1]

> "They're more themselves in that partnership than many directors of design businesses are in their own businesses."
>
> —**Michael Wolff,** graphic designer, the Fourth Room

conflict

Perceived incompatibility between two or more values, goals, or needs.

Pentagram Partners shows us how preventing negative conflict and making the most of constructive conflict can benefit an organization and its people. But not many organizations plan for or manage conflict as well as Pentagram. When conflict is allowed to fester, it can disrupt the way an organization functions—and even bring the organization down. In general, **conflict** is a perceived incompatibility between two or more values, goals, or needs. Although conflict is often uncomfortable, it is an inevitable part of life in organizations. Therefore, individuals, groups, and organizations benefit from knowing how to handle it constructively.

This chapter explores the nature of conflict in organizations and describes how people manage it. The first section provides an overview of the forms conflict takes, including types of conflict and its sources, levels, and stages. Next, we identify a variety of ways in which people react to conflict. The chapter then explores how organizations and individuals manage conflict by stimulating and resolving it, as well as the ethical issues involved. We conclude the chapter by examining an important tool for conflict management: negotiation.

Conflict is a fact of life in any organization

Conflict is a natural part of being human. From the time we become aware of ourselves and others as children, we realize that our self-interests can collide with others'. Since conflict involves perceived differences in values, goals, or needs, and organizations bring together a variety of individuals who perform a variety of tasks, differences inevitably surface. But although conflict is bound to arise in any organization, its forms and its impact on the organization may vary. Let's look at some of the patterns that conflict may take in organizations.

Types of Conflict

The common picture of conflict is of people fighting. However, this view not only limits our understanding of the many forms conflict can take but also prevents us from identifying conflict in its early stages—before it reaches destructive levels. Viewed more accurately, conflict in organizations varies in terms of the people and behaviors involved, and even whether it is constructive or destructive.

Conflict among Individuals and Groups   To recognize who may be involved in a conflict, consider the possible situations in which values, goals, or needs can be incompatible. As shown in Exhibit 13.1, not only do individuals differ, but so do groups. Furthermore, individuals themselves also try to juggle a variety of conflicts among their own values, goals, and needs.

Conflict among an individual's values, goals, or needs is called **intrapersonal conflict.** Such conflict often takes the form of role conflict, discussed in Chapter 7. For example, the roles of family member and employee impose conflicts concerning the use of time. An employee who wants to work overtime out of commitment to finishing a task may also wish to leave on time because of his love for his wife and children. In a study of hospital workers, Anita Ilta Garey found that many who were mothers chose to work at night so that they could be available to meet their children's needs during the day.[2] Being unavailable for school conferences,

intrapersonal conflict

Conflict among an individual's values, goals, or needs.

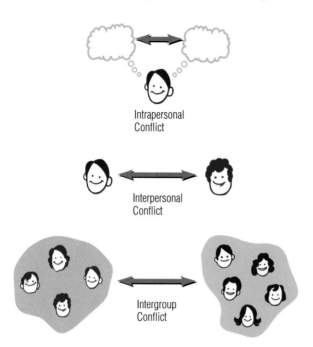

exhibit **13.1**
Parties to a Conflict

Intrapersonal
Conflict

Interpersonal
Conflict

Intergroup
Conflict

sports, and their children's other activities would have conflicted with their perception of a mother's role. Similarly, Andrew Raskin felt intrapersonal conflict over the opportunity to take on the challenging role of chief executive of an Internet start-up called Gazooba—a position that required Raskin to leave his beloved New York City for a new home in Silicon Valley. Raskin complained to his partner, "It's going to be hell out there." His partner replied, "Yes. And you'll love it." Raskin took the job.[3]

Conflict between two or more individuals with perceived differences in values, goals, or needs is **interpersonal conflict.** Values may differ because of differences in culture, personality, or even position in the organization. Conflicts over goals and needs may arise when members of the organization are competing for scarce resources or when they are aiming for different objectives—say, improving quality versus cutting costs, or meeting social needs by chatting with coworkers versus meeting financial needs by serving customers. Conflict arose between partners Jeremiah Shafir and Christopher Nessen when the business they founded, Kettle Cuisine, failed to turn a profit in its first few years. The two blamed one another for the business's problems until Shafir bought Nessen's ownership share, thus ending the partnership. The business has since become profitable.[4]

Remember that conflict involves *perceived* areas of incompatibility. Sometimes conflict occurs because people with different personalities, cultures, or viewpoints interpret a situation in different, incompatible ways. A conflict may also arise because one person believes the

interpersonal conflict

Conflict between two or more individuals with perceived differences in values, goals, or needs.

Japanese women have been educated as equals but have not always found the workplace hospitable. The intrapersonal conflict Japanese women felt between their education and ambition and their role in Japanese business culture is inspiring them to enter a new world of business—the Internet. Some analysts believe women are actually driving Japan's Net economy; they make up just under 40 percent of the country's 22 million Internet users. As Merle Okawara, CEO of eBay Japan states, "Women never had a level playing field in Japanese business. The Internet will change all that." (Source: @ Miao Wang/The Image Bank)

other "just doesn't care." In that case, the other person may in fact care deeply but remain quiet about that concern or handle it in a way that is unfamiliar to the person perceiving a conflict.

Finally, **intergroup conflict** is conflict between two or more groups with perceived differences in values, goals, or needs. The members of each group share perceptions that their group's values, goals, or needs are incompatible with the other group's. A common type of intergroup conflict is **line-staff conflict,** which arises from perceived differences between line employees (those who are directly involved in producing and selling products) and staff employees (those in support functions, such as information systems and human resources). Intergroup conflict may also arise between levels of the organization's hierarchy, between shifts, or among informal groups.

At IBM, intergroup conflict surfaced between employees with different amounts of experience when the company announced a change in its pension plan. IBM originally had a traditional pension plan in which pensions were based mainly on how much employees earned during their last few years on the job. The company switched to a cash balance plan, in which pensions are based on investing a percentage of employees' earnings; employees who leave the company take this investment with them when they go. In general, cash balance plans favor younger employees with less tenure at the company, and traditional plans favor the company's long-term employees. IBM protected its oldest, most experienced employees by giving them the option to continue with the traditional plan. The employees hired too recently to qualify for the protection but too late to benefit from the change were upset, especially if they were close to the cutoff for the traditional plan. A number of them expressed interest in forming a union to protect their interests.[5]

Constructive and Dysfunctional Conflict   Because conflict tends to be uncomfortable, people think of it as bad. However, conflict can also be beneficial. It signals differences that need to be addressed in some fashion. If people address those differences by developing creative solutions, they can move the organization and themselves beyond the status quo to new and possibly better practices. **Constructive conflict** is conflict that contributes to a group's or individual's performance. In the context of group processes, it is the opposite of groupthink (see Chapter 10). It spurs creativity, collaboration, and beneficial change. The collaborative work arrangements at Pentagram Partners, discussed at the beginning of the chapter, allow each partner enough freedom to take responsibility for designs, yet profitability goals promote healthy constructive conflict within the firm.

Research so far suggests that conflict is most likely to be constructive in situations in which groups are handling nonroutine tasks.[6] Groups handling such tasks must innovate in order to succeed, and conflict may help them do so. Pat Means has experienced a good deal of constructive conflict throughout her struggle to make a success of her magazine, *Turning Point,* profiled at the beginning of Chapter 12. The failure rate for new magazines is high; to beat the odds, Means has been forced to continually innovate. The demands of running a start-up magazine have conflicted with personal needs, and Means one day complained to a friend that she was exhausted. Her friend replied, "You don't have the time to be tired. You've got to decide what you want and how to achieve that." The friend's counsel spurred Means to eval-

---

intergroup conflict

Conflict between two or more groups with perceived differences in values, goals, or needs.

line-staff conflict

Intergroup conflict arising from perceived differences between line employees and staff employees.

constructive conflict

Conflict that contributes to a group's or individual's performance.

Thirty-year-old Glen Meakem and top management at General Electric's headquarters in Fairfield, Connecticut, had conflicting ideas. Meakem proposed a bold new business: to make suppliers of industrial parts compete for orders in live, open, electronic auctions. "This idea will transform the global economy," claimed Meakem. Conflict resulted when GE management didn't buy the plan. But the idea stirred Meakem's creativity, so he left his well-paying job at GE and used his visionary passion to form FreeMarkets Inc., a Web auction site that is revolutionizing the $5 trillion market for industrial parts. It is estimated that companies such as General Motors, United Technologies, Raytheon, and Quaker Oats—big, shrewd buyers that thought they were already getting rockbottom prices—have now saved more than 15 percent on average, buying parts, materials, and even services at FreeMarkets auctions. Meakem is now one of America's new Internet megamillionaires, with a net worth of $750 million. (Source: @ Andrew Garn)

uate her goals and resources. She decided to draw on her inner strength, persist with her venture, and learn to accept help whenever it was offered.[7]

In contrast, **dysfunctional conflict** interferes with a group's or individual's performance. On an intrapersonal level, dysfunctional conflict is distracting, exhausting, and confusing. When people express interpersonal or intergroup conflict through insults, evasion, and destructive politics, they generally hurt the organization and some of its members. Valuable employees may leave the organization to escape dysfunctional conflict, and cooperation and sharing of resources often become impossible.

Notice that the difference between constructive and dysfunctional conflict is based on their impact, not necessarily on their intensity or the particular issues involved. So, determining whether a given conflict is constructive or dysfunctional can sometimes be difficult. Diagnosing the conflict requires focusing on its impact, which can pave the way for reducing dysfunctional conflict or making it more beneficial to the organization.

dysfunctional conflict

Conflict that interferes with a group's or individual's performance.

The people involved can shift their focus from personal gain to benefiting the group and the organization. In so doing, they may not eliminate the conflict, but they can work to recast it as a constructive force.

Sources of Conflict

To understand conflict, we need to find its sources. Based on our definition, conflict arises when people perceive a difference in values, goals, or needs. Thus, conflict arises in the source of these differences or in the source of the perception of differences. Exhibit 13.2 summarizes these possible sources of conflict.

As you read about these differences in values, goals, needs, and perceptions, keep in mind that what sometimes seems to be the source of a conflict may actually be only a symptom of the actual cause. In particular, people sometimes experience personality conflicts, where one person is annoyed by another person, and this annoyance aggravates the conflict. To defuse the annoyance and address the conflict, look for the underlying source of conflict. For example, one person may value quiet and gentleness and hence dislike being around a colleague who loudly expresses energy and creativity. Similarly, if an employee thinks, "I value getting the job done, and my boss cares only about punctuality," the employee may have observed a symptom of an underlying difference in values and perceptions. Perhaps the employee is focused on personal task accomplishment, while the supervisor is concerned about the way the employee's work habits affect other employees' motivation. Such differences in style and personality are a necessary—and often beneficial—dimension of workplace diversity, so most people find they must frequently cooperate with people whose company they do not enjoy. At such times, insight into individual and cultural differences, along with a good sense of humor, can be very helpful.

Differences in Values   Value differences may arise from culturally or individually based differences. They can arise even with closely knit organizations such as families. For example, Jean-Emmanuel Renoir, a great-grandson of artist Pierre-Auguste Renoir, recently launched a line of bottled water featuring labels that reproduce his great-grandfather's paintings. Renoir justifies use of the family name for his business by saying, "Art and commerce, they usually tie together," and he predicts that the additional exposure will

exhibit **13.2**

Sources of Conflict in Organizations

Source	Underlying Causes
Differences in values	Cultural differences; individual differences; differences associated with roles
Differences in goals	Personality differences; task or role differences; resource scarcity
Differences in needs	Personality differences; resource scarcity; power imbalance
Differences in perception about values, goals, or needs	Ambiguity about roles, resources, tasks; perceptual distortions

draw people into museums to see the original paintings. In contrast, his cousin Alain Renoir describes the business as cheapening and cashing in on the family name.[8] If such wide differences can exist within families, it is no surprise they can arise in organizations. When organizations bring together a diverse workforce or operate on a global scale, differences in values are especially likely. Such differences also are likely in large groups and where turnover is high. In a high-turnover group, individuals have spent less time learning and adopting the organization's culture.

Differences in Goals Goals may differ when individuals or groups define their objectives in incompatible ways. Before he joined Pentagram, graphic designer Lowell Williams perceived a conflict between his goal of artistic freedom (which he could satisfy by running his own firm) and his desire for professional growth through handling a wide variety of assignments (which a small firm such as his would have difficulty attracting). On an interpersonal level, when Martin Grass became chief executive of Rite Aid Corporation, it quickly became apparent that his goals included building the regional drugstore chain into a national giant. After a failed attempt to buy the Revco pharmacy chain, Rite Aid acquired Thrifty PayLess Holdings. Grass's father, the former Rite Aid CEO, disagreed with that move, on the grounds that Rite Aid lacked the know-how to manage Thrifty's stores, some of which were five times the size of a typical Rite Aid store. The younger Grass persisted, trying to boost the bottom line by requiring pharmacists to work longer hours and even allegedly asking store managers to misreport shrinkage rates (the amount of inventory lost or stolen). Objecting to this single-minded drive for paper profits, pharmacists and managers alike left the company. Rite Aid sales slumped, and the company failed to make payments on its debt. Concerned about lending to a company with apparently poor leadership, the banks persuaded Rite Aid's board of directors to replace Grass with a new CEO, a dramatic resolution to the company's dysfunctional conflict.[9]

In addition to individual objectives, an organization's structure can foster goal incompatibility. If the organization is rigidly divided into functional groups, such as marketing, production, purchasing, and finance, group members are likely to define their objectives in terms of these single functions and not in terms of larger, common goals. Finance may, for example, observe that an ambitious marketing plan is financially risky and thus incompatible with its goals for protecting and growing the organization's capital resources.

Finally, the way the organization and its leaders provide rewards can generate differences in goals. If rewards are allocated so that one person gains at the expense of another, then the reward structure encourages conflict as people compete for these rewards. For example, if the annual bonus goes only to the top producer, salespeople will compete with one another, which may or may not further the organization's goals.

Differences in Needs As we explained in the discussion of motivation sources (Chapter 5), people differ in terms of how they define their needs. In a group of people, it is therefore common for needs to be different and perhaps incompatible. For example, a person with a high need for achievement may be a source of conflict in a group dominated by people who have a high need for affiliation.

Within a person, too, needs may conflict. For example, accepting a promotion may meet financial needs while demanding so much time and energy that a person has difficulty meeting social and self-fulfillment needs.

Organizations can also contribute to need differences. When organizations establish unreasonable requirements, they can conflict with employees' individual needs. Scarce resources intensify conflict related to need fulfillment. In the following example, an organization's attempt to grow in a tight labor market placed heavy demands on managers and stimulated conflict.

edocs Inc.

Internet watchers at the end of the 1990s speculated that consumers would soon pay most of their bills online. This switch to a high-tech system would require a new product: software to replace all the paper invoices and checks used for billing customers and making payments. To capture that software market, a company called edocs quickly raised millions of dollars and lined up customers. But finding money was easy compared with finding talented human resources for a fast-growing high-tech company. A representative from edocs's biggest investor, Sigma Partners, informed CEO Kevin Laracey, "You're now in the hiring business."

Laracey took the message to heart. Sacrificing such personal needs as sleep, exercise, and family time, Laracey began devoting his days to signing up new employees. He set up a recruiting team that outnumbered his sales force and began spending about two-thirds of his work hours trying to close deals with prospective employees. His preoccupation with recruiting forced many responsibilities onto other managers. For example, Jim Moran, an edocs cofounder who serves as the company's executive vice president, shouldered most of the travel duties. On a recent afternoon, he tried in vain to discuss a customer question with Laracey. "I want my CEO back," he later told a *Wall Street Journal* reporter.

Laracey's passion for recruiting is taking a toll on other employees as well. He had the company stage an open house for prospective employees during a September evening. It drew 200 people, almost twice the expected number. Employees were exhausted, but Laracey was thrilled about the turnout. A month later, he proposed another open house, this time with a Halloween theme. His employees responded with snickers and mild sarcasm.

Nevertheless, Laracey has tried to help his employees align the company's needs with their own. For example, edocs pays a $5,000 bonus to employees who refer qualified job candidates who stay with the firm for three months. And, of course, Laracey also hopes that turning a start-up business into an industry leader will provide many more rewards in the years ahead.[10]

Differences in Perception   The differences that create conflict are actually *perceived* differences, so conflict can also arise as a result of perceptual processes. For example, poor communication could create an impression that two departments must compete for resources, even though that is not what management really intended. Or a manager's behavior may convey to employees that he does not care to hear their point of view, even though the manager simply may be quiet and reserved and waiting for employees to initiate communications. Organizations contribute to conflict when policies are unclear or they fail to establish guidelines for managing dependency among individuals or groups. Finally, when employees have expectations that the organization considers unrealistic or inappropriate, conflict results.

In all these instances, conflict results because of differences in perception. Resolving these conflicts can begin when the participants air their points of view. They may discover that they can resolve the conflict simply by correcting misperceptions.

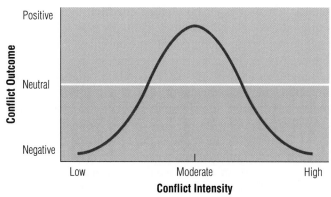

exhibit **13.3**
Levels of Conflict and Associated Outcomes

Source: Based on L. D. Brown, *Managing Conflict of Organizational Interfaces* (Reading, MA: Addison-Wesley, 1986), p. 8.

Desirable Levels of Conflict

Dysfunctional conflict arises not only when people choose to handle conflict in damaging ways but also when the level of conflict is so high that employees cannot cope with it effectively. As shown in Exhibit 13.3, the extent of organizational conflict influences whether it has a positive or negative effect on the organization's performance. A moderate level of conflict can spur creativity and positive change. It thus can have a positive effect on organizational outcomes.

Other levels of conflict are damaging. A high level of conflict distracts employees from their responsibilities and takes energy from creative problem solving. At the other extreme, a near absence of conflict also has a negative influence, because people are apt to accept conditions as they are and miss opportunities for improvement. Such an organization suffers from indecision and apathy.

Stages of Conflict

Some people ignore conflict unless it escalates to high levels—when someone argues with them or overtly refuses to cooperate. This way of managing conflict is not very insightful or even productive, because it postpones action at conflict's early stages, usually the best time for constructive action. In contrast, people have the greatest range of strategies for managing conflict if they consider all its stages, shown in Exhibit 13.4: latent, perceived, felt, and manifest conflict, as well as conflict aftermath.[11]

exhibit **13.4**
Stages of Conflict

Source: Based on Louis R. Pondy. (1967). "Organizational conflict: Concepts and models." *Administrative Science Quarterly* 12: 296–320.

latent conflict

The stage of conflict during which differences in goals, needs, values, or perceptions give someone a suspicion that a conflict may exist.

Latent Conflict   Conflict begins as **latent conflict,** the stage at which differences in goals, needs, values, or perceptions give someone a suspicion that a conflict may exist. Members of a team charged with developing a new product may notice that not everyone seems equally enthusiastic about the same ideas. Sometimes latent conflict is triggered by a change in the organization; the announcement of a new strategy or the hiring of a new manager may cause some members of the organization to wonder whether it will change their status or access to resources.

Members of an organization may ignore conflict at this stage. They may even believe that no conflict actually exists. For example, John Rothschild, a managing partner of an online executive search firm, devoted many, many hours to his business. This created a conflict with his family members, who wanted more of his time as husband and father. However, Rothschild saw himself more as a good breadwinner than as an absent parent.[12]

perceived conflict

The stage of conflict during which the parties perceive that a conflict exists, although they may not yet be able to define it.

Perceived Conflict   During the next stage, **perceived conflict,** the people involved in a conflict perceive that a conflict exists, although they may not yet be able to define it. The members of the product development team mentioned earlier may recognize that team members are not really cooperating with one another. However, they may not understand why.

During this stage, people can choose to act or to ignore the source of the conflict. Taking action during perceived conflict can prevent the conflict from moving to later stages. John Rothschild's children helped him perceive the conflict between his work role and parental role by making it obvious to him. The children presented him with a homemade membership card in their "Family Miles" program. The children explained that family-friendly behavior, such as arriving home in time for dinner, staying home on weekends "without always running to the phone," and spending holidays at home, qualified him to earn points. He could redeem them for such rewards as the children washing the car, raking leaves, or forgoing allowance money.[13]

felt conflict

The stage of conflict during which the parties are aware of the conflict and have an emotional reaction to it.

Felt Conflict   The next stage is **felt conflict.** During this stage, the people involved not only are aware of the conflict but also have an emotional reaction to it, such as being tense, angry, worried, or energized. In the example of the product development team, its members would likely grow angry with one another as the team struggles to accomplish its objectives.

Research suggests that the kinds of emotions experienced affect the way people handle a conflict. Negative emotions have been associated with oversimplifying issues, reducing trust, and interpreting the other party's behavior negatively.[14] Positive emotions have been associated with taking a broad view of a conflict situation, finding potential relationships among its elements, and arriving at more innovative solutions.[15] In John Rothschild's case, he saw the Family Miles program as a creative effort by his children to issue him a wake-up call. This positive perception drove Rothschild to reevaluate his work style and goals. Concluding that he would have a career for many years but only a limited time to watch his children grow up, he began to give higher priority to family activities.

manifest conflict

The stage of conflict during which the parties act out the conflict.

Manifest Conflict   If the conflict continues, it enters the stage of **manifest conflict,** during which the parties act out the conflict. In the case of interpersonal or intergroup conflict, they intentionally frustrate those perceived

what would you do?

RESOLVING INTERGROUP CONFLICT

One summer, several hundred Belgian and French consumers headed to local hospitals with various symptoms that they claimed had appeared after drinking what they thought were tainted cans of Coca-Cola. The European Union swiftly investigated the situation, and just as swiftly came to its official conclusion: it had no idea why the victims had fallen ill.

Immediately, conflict arose. Coke was taken off the grocery shelves in Belgium, France, Luxembourg, and the Netherlands, and a major bottling plant in France was shut down. The European Union accused Coca-Cola of destroying evidence, which the company flatly denied. Then the EU attacked the French and Belgian health agencies, blaming them for confusion and indecisiveness. In turn, the agencies accused Coca-Cola of feeding them misleading or incomplete information. Although outside observers suspected that the victims were suffering from psychosomatic illness, the EU refused to accept this explanation for the events. Coca-Cola claimed that one study showed that nearly half the school children in Belgium who complained of symptoms hadn't drunk Coke at all. Later, the conflict expanded as the Italian government conducted an investigation that concluded Coca-Cola was trying to drive competitors out of the market. Competitors such as Pepsi and Virgin Cola complained to the European Union that Coca-Cola was engaging in anticompetitive tactics, and the EU responded by actually raiding Coca-Cola's European offices looking for evidence.

Coke's problems are an example of intergroup conflict that crosses national and cultural boundaries. To further complicate the situation, the conflict was really based on perceived differences—no one was able to determine whether the drink itself was tainted in the first place, and if so, whether it caused the illness among consumers. Because Coke is a globally recognized brand and Coca-Cola is a huge commercial organization with deep pockets, government officials and consumers alike perceived that the company's only goal was to maintain its image and avoid losing profits. The European Union, anxious not to lose face in the eyes of its own citizens or in the eyes of the world, had to find a way to blame Coca-Cola for the illnesses and later for anticompetitive business practices. Meanwhile, Coca-Cola lost over $100 million in the closing of the French bottling plant, French workers lost jobs, people were ill, and no one knew why.

Imagine that you were called in to help resolve the conflict between Coca-Cola and the European Union. To research the situation further, access Coca-Cola's Web site or news listings on your search engine or review business magazines such as *Adweek, Inc.,* or *Forbes* for stories about similar types of conflicts. Then, outline the steps you might take to find a solution, considering the following questions:

1. What are the differences in goals, values, and needs between the conflicting parties?

2. Could the conflict have been managed more successfully at any point by any of the parties? If so, how and at what point?

3. Identify some similarities between the conflicting parties that you could use to create understanding between the two and formulate some strategies.

Source: Debra Goldman, "Coke in Europe—When a Brand Means Too Much," *Adweek,* August 23, 1999, p. 16.

---

to have incompatible views or goals. They may do this by arguing, engaging in political behavior, or refusing to cooperate. A person experiencing intrapersonal conflict may agonize over a decision, lose sleep, and become angry about related or unrelated matters.

People express manifest conflict in destructive ways, so it is essential to resolve conflict quickly if it reaches this stage. For example, Liza Price and Donn Rappaport were once partners in marriage as well as in business. But eventually the couple, who owned American List Counsel, were divorced. As they worked their way through the divorce proceedings, their differences and conflicts intensified, in spite of both parties' efforts to remain professional. Finally, Price admitted that she was miserable at work whenever her ex-husband was there, that the two were avoiding each other as much as possible, and that the business was suffering as a result. She activated a clause in their partnership agreement that forced Rappaport to either buy her share of the business or sell his share to her. Rappaport decided to buy, and Price left the mailing list firm to start another business.[16]

conflict aftermath

The stage of conflict during which the outcome of the conflict creates conditions that influence future situations.

Conflict Aftermath   The final stage of conflict is **conflict aftermath,** the period during which the outcome of a conflict creates conditions that influence future situations. Resolving a conflict constructively establishes conditions that foster greater cooperation and the achievement of mutual goals. Resolving a conflict in favor of only some participants will likely lead to future conflict. If the people involved dislike the resolution, future conflict may be more dysfunctional. Thus, if the product development team discusses members' viewpoints, it may identify issues that will lead to better decisions than if the team had persisted in ignoring the source of the conflict. However, if some team members' views triumph at the expense of others, the defeated team members may sabotage the implementation of the plan, as conflict among the members continues to escalate in new forms.

Likewise, intrapersonal conflict presents a learning opportunity. A person faced with an ethical dilemma, for example, could address the challenges head on, perhaps discussing them with other managers and members of the department. As a result, the manager can develop decision-making skills that will help when future ethical conflicts arise.

apply it

1. Your friend says, "I just can't get along with my boss. We have a personality conflict." Based on the preceding description of conflict in organizations, list a few questions you could ask to help your friend understand the type and source of this conflict.

2. At what stages of the conflict process do you think your friend could most effectively resolve this conflict? Explain.

People choose how to react to a conflict

When people become aware of a conflict, they have a variety of alternatives to choose from in responding. As Exhibit 13.5 shows, the possibilities vary in terms of the extent to which they are assertive (directed at satisfying the

exhibit **13.5**
Reactions to Conflict

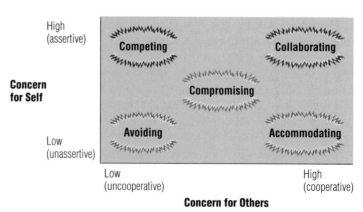

Source: Based on K. W. Thomas, "Conflict and Conflict Management," in M. D. Dunnette (ed.), *Handbook of Industrial Organizational Psychology* (Chicago: Rand McNally, 1976), p. 900.

individual's concerns) and cooperative (directed at satisfying others' concerns).[17] The alternatives range from avoiding, to accommodating, to compromising, to competing, and to collaborating. A person's choice of a response may differ according to the type of conflict, as well as personal and cultural values influencing which choices the person considers appropriate.

Research suggests that individuals are consistent in their type of response to a conflict; they usually prefer the same approach.[18] Thus, one person might avoid most conflicts, whereas another might usually look for ways to collaborate on a solution. However, this tendency need not prevent an individual from experimenting with other approaches that seem more appropriate for a situation.

Avoiding

A person or group may respond to a conflict by **avoiding**—that is, neither seeking to meet personal objectives nor responding to the objectives of the other party. Thus, an avoiding strategy is neither assertive nor cooperative. When people realize there is a conflict but postpone discussing it, they are avoiding the conflict. Similarly, an organization can support an avoiding strategy between two feuding managers by assigning them to different chains of command so that they don't have to communicate directly with one another. On an intrapersonal level, people may adopt an avoiding strategy by busying themselves with other matters or dismissing opportunities to get help with the issue.

Avoiding a conflict does nothing to resolve it, and the dominant U.S. culture tends to place a low value on such a seemingly passive approach. However, even in the context of U.S. culture, there are situations in which avoidance is appropriate. It is practical for handling trivial issues, especially those that may go away on their own. In addition, for a particularly emotional conflict, starting with an avoiding strategy gives the parties time to calm down and prepare for more constructive approaches. People also may adopt an unassertive style when they feel powerless to effect a change. For example, if an employee's values constantly conflict with those of management, the employee may avoid the conflict by leaving the organization. Similarly, Patty Zacks chose to avoid conflict when her ex-husband opened a competing business across the street from her camera store. Already facing the emotional strain of divorce coupled with an unexpected tax bill from the Internal Revenue Service, Zacks decided to focus on differentiating her store. From Zacks's perspective, this strategy enabled personal growth and avoided bitterness.[19]

avoiding
Reacting to a conflict by neither seeking to meet one's own objectives nor responding to the objectives of the other party.

Accommodating

Another unassertive strategy is **accommodating,** in which one person tries to satisfy another person's objectives. This strategy is highly cooperative because it is focused on the other person's concerns. An accommodating strategy would be common when the balance of power is unequal. For example, if a business owner requests a change in a procedure, the employees will probably go along with it, even if they doubt the change will be beneficial.

Eric Silberstein used an accommodating strategy to provide credible leadership for his company, Idiom Technologies, which serves clients that

accommodating
Reacting to a conflict by trying to satisfy the other party's objectives.

have Web sites in more than one language. The company monitors clients' Web pages, and whenever a client makes a change, Idiom automatically supplies translations for the non-English sites. To establish themselves as formidable competitors, Internet firms like Idiom grow as fast as they can, a strategy that depends on access to capital. Potential investors were nervous about Silberstein's inexperience; he founded Idiom when he was in his early twenties. The venture capitalists who offered money made it clear that their confidence came partly from Silberstein's plan to hire a more experienced chief executive. Rather than trying to convince investors he could lead his own company, Silberstein hired Frederick Lizza, who offered the company previous CEO experience and was 20 years older than Silberstein.[20]

An accommodating strategy may be appropriate in a conflict that is significant for one party but not for the other. People may also use accommodating as a political tactic intended to gain someone's goodwill. However, when future conflicts arise, they may expect a favor in return.

Compromising

compromising

Reacting to a conflict by reaching a mutually acceptable solution in which each party meets only part of his or her objectives.

A strategy that is both moderately cooperative and moderately assertive is **compromising.** With this strategy, both parties reach a mutually acceptable solution in which each party meets only part of his or her objectives. The strategy feels fair because each party gets something and each party has to give up something. For example, two managers at budget time may want funding for new projects. The organization has limited funds, so both managers scale back their projects so that each can have a share of the funds. Compromise also may be the model for resolving intrapersonal conflict. The person may look at the conflicting values or needs and identify a solution that satisfies part of each.

Compromising is often easy to rationalize on the grounds of its apparent fairness. However, when people are quick to compromise, the organization and its members may not achieve valid objectives. In the case of the two projects for which managers want funding, the compromise could result in failure of two underfunded projects, robbing the organization of any benefit while squandering money. Furthermore, in cultures that place a high value on individual achievement, a quick effort to compromise may appear to be a sign of weakness.

Compromising is most appropriate for situations in which a speedy resolution to a conflict is more important than finding the best solution. For example, if two nurses are planning a year-end vacation, they might agree that one will work Christmas Day and one will work New Year's Day. Neither gets both holidays off, but both can arrange a vacation, and the hospital can meet its staffing needs.

Competing

competing

Reacting to a conflict by trying to fully attain one's own objectives at the expense of the others involved.

Whereas compromising involves only a moderate level of assertiveness, people may address conflict with a great desire to meet all their objectives. For example, they may engage in **competing,** which is highly assertive but low on cooperation. This strategy involves trying to fully attain one's own objectives at the expense of the others involved. People who handle a conflict in this way view the conflict situation as involving a fixed pool of resources that must be divided among the parties. The competing parties may treat one another with respect, but they focus on expressing their own position and leave it to the others to express theirs.

Since one party loses a competition, it benefits the organization only if the losing party's objectives aren't in the organization's favor. For example, if one party is certainly wrong, the other should prevail. Also, as we saw in the context of decision making (Chapter 10), a fast resolution is sometimes more important than an optimal resolution. Like compromising, competing can bring a conflict to a quick resolution, so it can be appropriate for emergencies. In addition, a person may use competition as a necessary form of self-defense when the other party is using this strategy. Although competition may be appropriate at times, the losing party may resurrect the conflict later in another form. Also, in cultures that value group harmony over individual gain, people may view competition negatively.

Collaborating

The strategy that combines a high degree of assertiveness with a high degree of cooperation is **collaborating,** or working together to achieve the objectives of both parties. In general, collaborating requires creative thinking. The parties try to expand the pool of resources or the definition of values so that they can cover the needs of both sides of the conflict. They define the conflict as a mutual problem to be resolved through common effort.

collaborating

Reacting to a conflict by working with the other party to achieve the objectives of both parties.

Because successful collaboration makes winners of both parties, it generates a high level of commitment to its outcome. Thus, collaboration is appropriate when commitment is important. In addition, because it involves creativity, collaboration is appropriate in situations that call for fresh ideas. However, because collaboration is a group effort requiring time to generate and evaluate new ideas, it is appropriate only when a quick solution is not essential and when the conflict is significant enough to merit the time and energy required.

The ideas for developing creativity in Chapter 10 can improve collaboration in resolving conflicts. People can also bring in experts such as consultants, counselors, and mediators to help them collaborate on conflict resolution or apply collaborative styles of thinking to an intrapersonal conflict. In the following example, two partners used outside experts to help them communicate when interpersonal conflict threatened to split their company.

When Brett Cosor and Jeff Studley formed CPR MultiMedia Solutions, their personality differences seemed to be an asset. Cosor is energetic and full of ideas—a self-described visionary. He came up with the idea for CPR, which produces elaborate displays for trade shows as well as permanent multimedia facilities. Cosor brought in Studley because of his attentiveness to detail and calm, methodical style of decision making.

In the early years of the partnership, the two worked closely, resolving their differences as they went along. Eventually, they built a $10 million company with two divisions. Studley ran the division handling rentals (setups for one-time public events), and Cosor ran the division handling systems (permanent facilities).

CPR MultiMedia Solutions

However, day-to-day conflicts began to escalate, driven by the partners' use of avoidance and competition for resources. Cosor once took three key pieces of equipment to complete an installation when Studley planned to use that equipment just hours later for a client's rental setup. Studley's usual reaction to such crises was stony silence, but he could contain himself no longer and exploded in rage. The two continued to undercut one another until they reached a point at which dissolving the partnership seemed the only solution.

A more constructive suggestion came from Studley's wife, Elaine Studley, who ran the company's information systems. She pushed the two partners to visit Peter Wylie, a psychologist who specializes in counseling business partners, much as a marriage counselor works with troubled spouses. Cosor and Studley spent many sessions just complaining about one another's style. Studley criticized what he perceived as Cosor's blind enthusiasm for new projects at the expense of careful management. Cosor objected to Studley's perceived lack of appreciation for his vision and energy.

Eventually, as they began to listen as well as complain, they saw one another's underlying fears and needs. For example, Studley recognized that Cosor needed to hear affirmation as well as objective analysis of his ideas. With the lines of communication beginning to open, the partners began crafting long-term solutions. They created a board of advisers, established routine financial reporting, and set up regular time for executive retreats, all of which foster information sharing between the two divisions. In addition, they added a layer of management to operate each division, so that the partners can focus on a shared vision for the overall organization. With these changes, the partners applied themselves to the vision they state on their Web site: "The entire CPR organization is committed to a single goal, Effective Communications."[21]

apply it

1. Of the five reactions to conflict described in this section, which do you think you tend to use? Describe a situation in which you reacted with this strategy, either in your work or personal life. What were the consequences?

2. What are some advantages of your preferred strategy? What are some drawbacks?

Organizations can benefit from managing conflict

Since conflict involves a variety of behaviors that can enhance or detract from an organization's performance, the organization can influence its performance by shaping the way people manage conflict. Conflict management includes the ways organizations and individuals stimulate as well as resolve conflict.

Conflict Stimulation

As noted earlier, some conflict in organizations is beneficial. If there is no conflict, an organization can become stagnant and unchallenging. Effective conflict management then stimulates conflict to generate beneficial change and creativity. For example, an organization's managers may stimulate conflict when they want to provoke fresh thinking about a complex problem, such as how to use technology in revamping work processes.

Ways to stimulate conflict include establishing rivalries among groups or individuals, such as a competition for the best new product idea, the highest level of sales, or the suggestion that generates the greatest potential cost savings. Such a competition can be beneficial if it focuses employees on activities consistent with the organization's objectives. However, employees may be so concerned about winning the competition that they neglect more important concerns, such as satisfying customers or sharing information with one another.

Organizations can also stimulate beneficial conflict by forming heterogeneous groups to handle complex issues. Cross-functional teams or work groups that bring together different degrees of experience or different ranks in the organization are more likely to consider and include diverse values and opinions. Working through these differences can generate fresh insights and creative problem solving. Even the arrangement of work spaces can bring together a variety of employees. If employees from various divisions or functions often encounter one another in an open layout, they have more opportunities to work out problems and share ideas.

To bring constructive conflict into the open, the organization may have to establish policies and procedures that encourage communication. Some ways to bring a diversity of viewpoints to group discussions include appointing a devil's advocate and using a technique called multiple advocacy (see Chapter 10). Teams and work groups can also establish ground rules that encourage constructive communication. For instance, they may agree to listen when someone is talking and to criticize only ideas, not personalities.

Conflict Resolution

Except in the conditions when avoiding conflict is more appropriate, conflict should be resolved constructively. Conflict resolution begins with recognizing that there is a conflict and defining the conflict situation. The way the parties define the situation will influence their reactions to the conflict. For example, if you perceive that a ruthless colleague is trying to steal your job, you will handle that conflict much differently than if you perceive that your colleague is new and confused about the nature of his responsibilities. In the first case, you are defining the conflict as a political struggle; in the second, as a need for better ways to integrate new employees into the organization. Therefore, effective conflict resolution begins with probing for the real source of the conflict.

To manage conflict constructively, organizations can help employees learn and use ways to resolve rather than ignore conflict. Managers can initiate the identification and resolution of conflict by communicating about controversial issues, rather than avoiding them. The organization can establish procedures for working out differences. For example, the Hermitage Artists are four practitioners of tramp (rustic) art who live, as well as work, together. In such close quarters, the four men established a climate for success by creating a culture that values sharing of ideas and resources. When one of the men has a problem, the others routinely stop what they are doing and discuss it. When an opportunity to expand the Hermitage Artists came into conflict with the men's desire to live simply, they naturally discussed the situation. Instead of hiring employees to expand production, they opted for simplicity and limited business growth, and they relocated to a farmhouse on 24 acres to reinforce their ideas.[22]

Organizations also can provide access to experts such as coaches and mediators to help with conflict resolution. The following example describes how catalog retailer Damark hired its own expert to help managers resolve conflict.

☙ Damark

Damark, which sells a wide variety of consumer products through its print and online catalogs, has a management position that doesn't even exist in most corporations: director of leadership and team development. Mark Johansson, who fills that job, describes his responsibility as "patching up relationships." Another Damark manager, Kurt Larsen, describes Johansson's role in more colorful terms: "Mark . . . prevents us from killing each other."

Damark executives created Johansson's position at a time when the company was growing rapidly and setting up its Web site. These changes prompted Damark to hire a larger and more diverse group of employees, and management knew that resolving conflict would be a critical skill. Applying his background in psychology, Johansson advises executives in general collaboration skills and helps managers address concerns as they arise. Because he is not part of the normal chain of command, the managers trust him to be impartial.

For example, Michael Delvicio, Damark's vice president of merchandising, has a background in store retailing. He turned to Johansson for advice in learning the language and values of catalog retailing. He credits Johansson for helping him avoid perceptions of conflict: "If not for him, I would have misinterpreted reactions that were neutral or positive as negative." Johansson also helped resolve a dispute between two warring senior managers. He encouraged one of the managers to persist in reaching out to the other, and after several efforts, the other manager finally began to cooperate.[23]

Organizations can help individuals resolve intrapersonal conflict by encouraging communication, mentoring, and knowledge sharing. Some organizations offer employee assistance programs (EAPs), benefits in which employees and their families can obtain a confidential referral to a medical or mental health professional for help with personal problems. EAPs, which are discussed in detail in Chapter 14, are especially common in the United States. Employees in

At Ernst & Young last year, 7,829 of its 34,000 U.S. employees called the company's employee assistance program, EY/Assist. According to EY/Assist director Sandra Turner, employees' most common requests have dealt with legal issues (20 percent), marital problems (10 percent), and financial questions (8 percent). Recently, Ernst & Young employee Glenn Hascher's house in Stamford, Connecticut, burned to the ground, leaving him and his family (photo) with little more than the clothes on their backs. Seeking professional advice on how to handle insurance companies and deal with the trauma his young daughters had experienced, Hascher called EY/Assist. Within days an information packet arrived, explaining how to hire an insurance adjuster, an architect, and a contractor; providing advice on rebuilding; and offering guidelines for handling children's fears after a traumatic event. "It was a comfort," says Hascher's wife Donna. "We've lost our house, but we haven't lost our minds."
(Source: @ Sarah A. Friedman)

Europe are more likely to receive such services through state agencies rather than through an employer. Other resources for handling role conflict include flexible hours and time off for family or personal needs. Aladdin Equipment, a Florida company that makes replacement parts for pools and spas, saw its absenteeism decline by half when it switched to a 4½-day-a-week production schedule. Aladdin's employees were able to take care of personal matters on their Friday afternoons off.[24] Similarly, Deloitte & Touche was concerned about retaining female employees, who often bear the brunt of work-family conflict. The company began offering its employees flexible work arrangements. In follow-up surveys, 89 percent of the employees taking advantage of such arrangements said they would have left the company if the program had not been offered.[25]

Ethical Issues in Conflict Management

As Chapter 1 noted, people encounter ethical issues whenever they are in a position to harm or benefit someone. This certainly describes most conflict situations. Conflict management strategies that define a conflict as a win-lose situation raise the potential to make a loser of one party. According to some views of ethics, exercising this potential can be unethical. Exhibit 13.6 summarizes how the ethical principles introduced in Chapter 1 would apply to conflict resolution.

For example, when evaluated in terms of the Golden Rule, resolving conflict through competition would rarely meet the standard of treating others as you would want to be treated. (An exception would be the person who enjoys competition, even if it results in losses some of the time.) Competitive conflict resolution could also fall short of the utilitarian standard if winning would result in anything but the greatest good for the greatest number. However, pursuing personal interests, on the assumption that others do, too—the standard of enlightened self-interest—would support a high level of assertiveness in conflict management.

In any case, these and other ethical standards assume that a person should handle a conflict with fairness. A focus on fairness preserves a person's long-term interests by maintaining constructive relationships with

View of Ethics	Application to Conflict Resolution
Utilitarian	Identify possible ways of resolving the conflict and the potential harms and benefits of each alternative; identify which outcomes the parties value most; choose the action that results in the greatest good for the most parties.
Golden Rule	Identify possible ways of resolving the conflict and how the other party would feel about that resolution. Resolve the conflict in the way that you would like to be treated if on the other side of the situation.
Kantian/rights	While defining and resolving the conflict, preserve each party's right to privacy, free consent, freedom of speech, freedom of conscience, and due process.
Enlightened self-interest	Use an assertive strategy, considering the potential long-term harm associated with deceit or maliciousness.
Justice approach	Evaluate alternatives in terms of what is fair, equitable, and impartial. Give each party a fair hearing.

exhibit | **13.6**

Applying Ethical Principles to Conflict Resolution

others, and it supports such ethical standards as justice, equal rights, and impartiality. Ways that the parties to a conflict can manage it fairly include being honest, listening to both sides, and focusing on objective measures that all parties can understand and agree on. In addition, conflict management should focus on the issue at hand rather than the persons involved, so that even in a win-lose situation, the loss does not involve unnecessary harm to another person.

Because there is no single, universally accepted standard for ethical behavior, the nature and scope of ethical behavior itself can generate conflict. For instance, a person pursuing a utilitarian approach and trying to define the "greatest good" might seem weak to a person who pursues objectives based on enlightened self-interest. When such differences do exist, a full definition of the conflict should also include the conflict in ethical standards. Differing ethical standards can also complicate conflicts among business partners. Reebok uses Asian suppliers, who typically operate in a different ethical climate. Reebok's solution is to observe suppliers' practices and educate them in what the company expects. It had an Indonesian firm investigate suppliers in that country, and Reebok reported the results frankly. On one matter, the report said, "No workers knew of any sexual harassment incidents. In fact, many did not understand the [Indonesian] term for it." Reebok responded by insisting that an Indonesian organization provide training on the subject. Concern that this action might force the company's own values on someone else was less important to Reebok than ensuring that suppliers understood the consequences of their actions—that Reebok, as the customer, would refuse to accept mistreatment of its suppliers' employees.[26]

Other ethical conflicts involve decisions about which party's goals or needs to meet when they seem to conflict. For example, managers' decisions provide different outcomes for the organization's owners, customers, employees, competitors, and the general public. When the wishes of these groups conflict, managers must decide which group's interests have priority. In a newspaper interview, Unicom Corporation's CEO, John W. Rowe, addressed this type of conflict by saying the CEO's primary responsibility is to the shareholders, but that their needs are ultimately met when customers and the public are satisfied with the company's behavior. Rowe explained, "You can't serve the shareholders in most businesses most of the time by ignoring everybody else."[27] Similarly, management professor David Messick has argued that organizations achieve long-term benefit by making decisions that meet social, economic, and ecological needs, as well as business needs. In this way, they preserve the kind of environment in which they can prosper: "Companies are coming to understand that they flourish in stable, peaceful social environments."[28]

apply it

1. Think of two examples from your life relating to conflicts and their resolution, one in which the conflict was managed *effectively* and the other *ineffectively*. What contributed to the effectiveness of the solutions?

2. Search for a story relating to an ethical conflict. What ethical principles are involved? Do you agree with the resolution? Why or why not?

Skilled negotiators resolve conflict effectively

As we have seen, certain levels of conflict are beneficial in organizations, and organizations can establish a climate in which the levels of conflict their employees experience can be managed and resolved constructively and ethically. An assertive approach to conflict resolution usually involves some use of **negotiation,** which is the process by which the parties to a conflict define what they are willing to give and accept in an exchange. These definitions and the ways people express them differ according to whether the parties view themselves as competing, compromising, or collaborating. The result is a choice to use either distributive or integrative negotiation strategies. Exhibit 13.7 compares these two approaches.

negotiation

The process by which the parties to a conflict define what they are willing to give and accept in an exchange.

Distributive Negotiation

People who are competing or compromising do so through **distributive negotiation,** which is negotiation under zero-sum conditions, meaning that any gain for one party comes at the expense of the other party. Distributive negotiation is also called a *win-lose strategy;* one party tries to win, resulting in a loss for the other. Thus, the parties to distributive negotiation view one another as competitors with opposing interests.

Although distributive negotiation is based on a win-lose motivation, it can result in an outcome that both parties perceive to be acceptable. To arrive at this outcome, each negotiator defines two points along a range: the **target point,** or desired outcome, and the **resistance point,** or the minimum acceptable outcome. These two points define the **aspiration range** for each party. If these ranges overlap, as shown in Exhibit 13.8, the area between the two resistance points defines a range of acceptable settlements.

In general, negotiators use the political tactics described in the preceding chapter, such as rational arguments and emotional appeals, to induce the other side to agree to a settlement near their target point. Usually the

distributive negotiation

Negotiation under the assumption that gains for one party will come at the expense of the other party; a win-lose strategy.

target point

The outcome desired by one party to a negotiation.

resistance point

The minimum acceptable outcome, as defined by one party to a negotiation.

aspiration range

The range of possible negotiated outcomes between the target point and resistance point.

exhibit | **13.7**

Distributive and Integrative Negotiation

Conditions	Distributive Negotiation	Integrative Negotiation
Perception of resources	Fixed amount	Variable amount
Motivations	Win-lose	Win-win
Definition of interests	Opposing one another	Converging or matching
Type of relationships cultivated	Short term	Long term
Key skills required	Use of political tactics, communication, definition of interests	Defining problems broadly, communication, creativity, understanding individual and cultural differences
Applications	When time and other resource constraints do not permit collaboration	When sufficient time and skill are available for reaching a creative solution

Source: The first four conditions are based on R. J. Lewicki and J. A. Litterer, *Negotiation* (Homewood, IL: Irwin, 1985), p. 280.

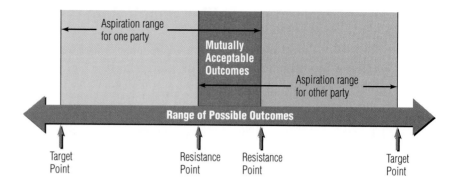

agreed-upon settlement lies somewhere within the settlement range. For example, representatives of Delta Air Lines and the Air Line Pilots Association recently negotiated wages for pilots flying the Boeing 767-400 aircraft. The company originally offered $208 per hour, and the union requested $262 per hour. Eventually, the parties settled on an hourly rate of $230.[29] As in this example, unless one negotiator is much more powerful than the other, the result of distributive bargaining is usually a compromise.

Integrative Negotiation

integrative negotiation

Negotiation that seeks to give both parties what they want; a win-win strategy.

Unlike competing and compromising, collaboration leads to a different negotiating style, **integrative negotiation.** This type of negotiation seeks a *win-win solution*—that is, conflict resolution in which both parties get what they want. Integrative negotiators may have to redefine the options to expand the amount of resources available for resolving the conflict. As they work together, they view the situation as one in which they have a shared interest in finding a mutually beneficial solution. This approach tends to support a positive long-term relationship between the negotiators.

Changes in the business environment have led some labor unions to rely more on integrative negotiation strategies. Throughout most of the 20th century, people viewed union-management relations primarily in distributive terms: either the union wins, or management does. However, this point of view is harder to sustain in a world where employees are often stockholders. In theory at least, benefits to the employer can also benefit the employee-stockholders. In addition, as the business world becomes globalized, not only can businesses take operations overseas, but overseas competitors can cripple a company, especially one weakened by strikes or an inflexible labor force. Not surprisingly, with workers' jobs and pension benefits tied to their employer's competitiveness, unions are modifying their negotiation strategies to encompass integrative approaches. The following example describes such changes at the United Auto Workers union.

❦ United Auto Workers

After General Motors divested Delphi Automotive Systems Corporation, the newly independent company suddenly faced an environment in which some of its competitors were nonunion companies. The change placed Delphi's survival at stake. For the United Auto Workers (UAW) union, which represents Delphi's workers, a win-lose strategy would only make both parties lose, with the company's failure eliminating jobs for workers. Instead, the UAW collaborated with Delphi representatives to help the company stay strong. Together, they identified techniques to improve productivity by restructuring the work environment. The more productive Delphi has since begun to attract customers beyond GM. And now when union members get angry and talk about striking, the president of their local shows them both sides of the issue: "The easy part is getting you guys out on the street. The hard part is getting you back without disruption and losing business."

Similarly, in a recent bargaining session with Ford, UAW negotiators addressed the company's plan to spin off its parts-making division, Visteon Automotive Systems. The union was worried that if the division became independent, wage levels and the number of union jobs would both suffer. The UAW couldn't prevent the corporation's strategic decision, even with a strike, so it worked with Ford to create the best possible situation. The two parties arranged for the existing Visteon employees to remain on Ford's payroll with full wages and benefits. Only the Visteon employees hired after the spinoff would be subject to new (presumably lower) wage levels.

The UAW's more moderate approach not only resolves particular areas of conflict but also is designed to be more palatable to potential members. According to the union's former president, Douglas Fraser, fear of strikes is one of the major reasons that workers resist joining unions. The UAW's current president, Stephen P. Yokich, shares his views: "We don't have to go out there and rattle our swords. We have to be professional about [negotiating]."[30]

Like distributive negotiation, integrative negotiation begins with both parties defining their objectives. However, they share these objectives with one another and try to define them in a noncompetitive way. Thus, instead of saying, "You want a raise, and I want to limit our department's spending growth to 1 percent," a department head might say, "We need to find ways to operate more efficiently so that I can give you and other valued employees a raise while limiting our spending growth to 1 percent a year."

Because integrative negotiation involves finding common solutions, an effective negotiator also prepares by thinking of the other party's needs and possible resolutions. Then, when the parties discuss the conflict, the negotiator can help to maintain a collaborative tone. In the previous example, the department head and the employee seeking a raise might find efficiencies together. As a result, the employee can get a raise, the organization benefits from the greater efficiency, and the department head can present herself as a skilled manager.

Organizations typically benefit when their people use integrative negotiation. Why? It tends to result in creative solutions, enhancing collaboration among individuals and groups in support of an organization's objectives. A laboratory experiment testing this view found that negotiators using an integrative approach produced superior joint outcomes; the distributive negotiators, in contrast, hurt their outcomes by restricting and mismanaging information.[31] In addition, the outcomes of integrative negotiation include skills and relationships that position the organization to handle future conflicts. However, as we noted earlier in the discussion of reactions to conflict, this type of collaboration can be time consuming. It also requires skill in defining problems broadly, as well as interpersonal skills, the desire to collaborate, and a sizable dose of creativity. Therefore, much of the negotiation in organizations tends to be distributive.

Determinants of Successful Negotiation

With smooth functioning and positive employee relations at stake in conflict negotiation, it is important for all members to be skilled in negotiating. The determinants of success for a negotiation vary somewhat according to how we define success. Negotiation is "successful" in the negotiator's eyes if it achieves the negotiator's objectives. But from the organization's perspective, a successful negotiation leads to a conflict aftermath that helps the organization achieve its objectives, usually preservation of long-term working relationships and a positive climate for handling future conflicts.

Careful preparation can enhance the likelihood of success. Negotiators should gather their information ahead of time and clearly know their own position. They should know what they are asking for, why it is feasible, and how it can be accomplished. In addition, a successful negotiator learns about the other parties to the negotiation, including their preferred negotiation style and their likely position. For example, will the other parties engage in a competitive or collaborative style, and are they likely to respond more to rational arguments or an appeal to their emotions?

The parties should also establish ground rules for the negotiation. Everyone should be clear about the time limits, as well as the definition of the conflict. For intergroup conflict, the ground rules also include a definition of who will participate in negotiations. Having clear ground rules can help negotiators stay focused on major concerns and avoid unproductive arguments.

During the negotiation process, successful negotiators communicate effectively, as discussed in Chapter 9. They look for clues to the deeper interests and concerns that underlie every party's negotiating position. Addressing those interests and concerns tends to be more successful than focusing strictly on the formal positions presented by the parties.[32] For example, when Mariam Naficy and Varsha Rao started a business to sell cosmetics and other beauty-related products online, they wanted to call their site "Eve.com," but the site was already registered to Evangeline Rogers, then six years old. Naficy and Rao considered other names, but "Eve" performed best in market tests, so the partners sought an offer that would be attractive to a young girl. (Although Rogers's parents negotiated on her behalf, they left the ultimate decision up to her.) Evangeline Rogers ultimately agreed to sell her rights to the domain name in exchange for $500 worth of toys from eToys, a family trip to Disneyland, a personal computer, and a six-month honorary position on the board of directors, as well as an undisclosed amount of cash.[33] Exhibit 13.9 presents some tips for carrying out an effective negotiation, whether your style is competitive or cooperative. These tips emphasize acknowledging both parties' interests, behaving ethically, and focusing on key objectives rather than getting bogged down in petty details.

At the close of a negotiation, the parties should be certain about the agreements reached. In an informal setting, such as a discussion to resolve a minor dispute, one negotiator may simply state his or her perception of the agreement, to verify that the other person has the same understanding. For more formal negotiations, such as a new work arrangement with a supervisor, revised policies for a team, or union-management bargaining, a written statement of the outcome is very important. Especially when the outcome is complex or must be communicated to a group, a written document provides a record that people can review later to confirm the details of the agreement.

From the organization's standpoint, negotiations should result in outcomes consistent with the organization's objectives. So, as with other as-

exhibit 13.9

Tips for Successful Negotiation

Tactics That Support a Competitive Style

- Try for a resolution in which both sides win something. Even though you want to do your best, remember that the other party matters, too.
- Ask many questions to learn what is important to the other party. Don't just look for an advantage to exploit. Understand the source(s) and type(s) of conflict involved.
- Use objective standards and rational arguments. You can preserve a long-term relationship by relying on reason rather than power plays.
- If possible, have someone skilled in relationship building handle that aspect of the situation.
- Be truthful and reliable. Keep your promises.
- Focus on the major issues; don't haggle over details. Consider granting what the other party considers important in exchange for what is most important to you.
- Treat the other party with respect.

Tactics That Support a Cooperative Style

- Understand the source(s) and type(s) of conflict involved, then focus on your goals and expectations. Set high standards.
- Plan alternatives in case you don't get what you hoped for.
- If the other party is highly competitive, try to bring in someone with a more competitive style to speak on your behalf.
- If getting something for yourself feels selfish, think in terms of advocating for other people or causes. For example, to negotiate a salary, instead of thinking about getting pay for yourself, think about supporting your (current or hypothetical) family.
- Tell someone else about your negotiation, including your goals for it. People tend to be more assertive when they have an audience.
- When the other party makes an implausible offer, reply in a reasonable tone of voice, "You'll have to do better than that because . . . ," and give a truthful reason.

Source: Based on G. Richard Shell, "Negotiator, Know Thyself," *Inc.,* May 1999, pp. 106–107 (excerpting G. Richard Shell, *Bargaining for Advantage: Negotiation Strategies for Reasonable People,* [New York: Viking, 1999]).

pects of organizational behavior, organizations should reward behavior that is consistent with their objectives. When employees are in conflict, managers and other leaders help them define the conflict to include organizational objectives. When practical, the organization should provide the means for integrative negotiation—for example, opportunities to learn the necessary skills, as well as time to negotiate a win-win solution.

Negotiating in the Context of Cultural Differences

Different cultures have established different norms regarding which styles of negotiation are appropriate. For example, Exhibit 13.10 compares acceptable negotiation styles of Japanese, North American, and Latin American cultures. Some of these differences involve the ways people express emotions and rely on rational arguments, as well as the value placed on knowing the participants and on achieving benefits for the good of the group.

Negotiators in a cross-cultural situation can benefit from knowing different cultural viewpoints of the process. North Americans, for example, tend to view negotiation as a means to resolve specific issues; when the issues are resolved, the negotiating ends. Chinese negotiators have a different emphasis. They view negotiation as a means for developing a long-term

exhibit | **13.10**   Negotiation Styles Associated with Three Cultures

Japanese	North American	Latin American
Emotional sensitivity highly valued	Emotional sensitivity not highly valued	Emotional sensitivity valued
Hiding of emotions	Dealing straightforwardly or impersonally	Emotionally passionate
Subtle power plays; conciliation	Litigation not as much as conciliation	Great power plays; use of weakness
Loyalty to employer; employer takes care of its employees	Lack of commitment to employer; breaking of ties by either, if necessary	Loyalty to employer (who is often family)
Group decision-making consensus	Teamwork provides input to a decision maker	Decisions come down from one individual
Face-saving crucial; decisions often made on basis of saving someone from embarrassment	Decisions made on a cost-benefit basis; face-saving does not always matter	Face-saving crucial in decision making to preserve honor, dignity
Decision makers openly influenced by special interests	Decision makers influenced by special interests but often not considered ethical	Execution of special interests of decision maker expected, condoned
Not argumentative; quiet when right	Argumentative when right or wrong, but impersonal	Argumentative when right or wrong; passionate
What is down in writing must be accurate, valid	Great importance given to documentation as evidential proof	Impatient with documentation as obstacle to understanding general principles
Step-by-step approach to decision making	Methodically organized decision making	Impulsive, spontaneous decision making
Good of group is the ultimate aim	Profit motive or good of individual ultimate aim	What is good for group is good for the individual
Cultivate a good emotional-social setting for decision making; get to know decision makers	Decision making impersonal; avoid involvements, conflict of interest	Personalization necessary for good decision making

Source: Nancy J. Adler, *International Dimensions of Organizational Behavior*, 2nd ed. (Boston: PWS-Kent, 1991), pp. 179–217.

working relationship.[34] To the Chinese, the task orientation of a North American negotiator feels abrupt and uncommitted, and this perception can ruin a North American negotiator's chances for success. North Americans may give up in frustration when their Chinese counterparts resume a discussion they thought had ended. However, negotiators who are aware of this difference can cultivate patience and thus strengthen their own position.

Similarly, in a study that compared North American, Arabic, and Russian negotiators, some differences in style could put one culture's negotiator at a disadvantage relative to another. For example, North Americans typically led off a negotiation with small concessions designed to establish a relationship. Arabs, too, made concessions readily. However, the Russian negotiators made few concessions, viewing them as a sign of weakness.[35] Thus, a negotiator preparing to resolve a conflict with Russian negotiators would benefit from crafting a strategy that relied less on making concessions.

These examples are really just an extension of the idea that successful negotiators prepare by learning about the other parties. Of course, cultural descriptions can only be generalizations. For example, further study of Japanese negotiation styles indicates that they vary in different contexts. The description in Exhibit 13.10 applies best to negotiations with "outsiders." Japanese negotiators tend to use a more direct style in the context of long-term relationships.[36] Successful negotiators therefore combine knowledge about cultural differences with what they can learn about the particular situation and the individuals involved. Looking for the sources of conflict, as discussed earlier in this chapter, can help in such an analysis. This diagnostic approach enables negotiators to arrive at outcomes that satisfy both parties—a valuable talent in today's global environment.

The left column is partially cut off:

7. I hold on to n
8. I use "give an
9. I exchange ac
10. I avoid open
11. I accommodat
12. I try to bring ;
    best possible v
13. I propose a m
14. I go along wit
15. I try to keep r
    feelings.

Scoring Key:

Avoidin

Item
6.
10.
15
    Total = _

Competi

Item
1.
5.
7.
    Total = _
Your backup c
(The categor

Your primary c
(The categor

Source: Adapted
dling interperso

ORGANIZ

We all experience ;
in our lives becaus
one role at a time
role of student, so
ployee or employe
and apartment resi
eral days and even

ORGANIZ

Conflict at the
when it invo
seems to make ne

apply it

1. Suppose you are a manager at a company that produces database management systems and the company is preparing to serve markets in Southeast Asia. Your U.S. production leaders are complaining that they can't work with the Asian distribution team members because they are overly critical and demanding. You have decided to bring together representatives from both groups to resolve this conflict. How can you effectively lead the negotiations?

2. In the preceding situation, will you attempt a distributive or an integrative strategy? Why?

summary OF KEY CONCEPTS

- **Conflict is a fact of life in any organization.** Individuals and groups alike can perceive incompatibilities between their values, goals, or needs. Also, intrapersonal conflict can arise between one individual's values, goals, or needs. Depending on conflict's impact, it may be either constructive or dysfunctional. It is most likely to be constructive when it is present at a moderate level. Unresolved conflict progresses through the stages of latent, perceived, felt, and manifest conflict and conflict aftermath.

- **People can choose how to react to a conflict.** They may avoid the conflict, a strategy that is neither assertive nor cooperative. One party to the conflict may try to accommodate the other. The parties may compromise on a solution in which each party meets a portion of his or her objectives. People may be assertive but not cooperative—a competing strategy. Or they may collaborate, working together to achieve the objectives of both parties.

- **Organizations can benefit from managing conflict.** They can stimulate beneficial conflict by forming heterogeneous groups and encourag-

ing open communication to identify and resolve conflicts. They may resolve conflict constructively by helping employees communicate effectively and providing resources such as experts to help with conflict resolution. They can encourage ethical conflict management. Ethical conflict resolution is fair to all parties, preserves the rights of others, and avoids unnecessary harm to others.

- **Skilled negotiators resolve conflict effectively.** Negotiators may use distributive negotiation, a win-lose strategy that generally involves each party establishing a target point and resistance point, then seeking a resolution that falls within both parties' aspiration ranges. An alternative strategy is integrative negotiation, which seeks a win-win solution. Integrative negotiation requires collaboration and creativity. With either negotiation strategy, success is more likely to result from careful preparation, effective communication (including listening), and a focus on key objectives. Negotiation is more complex in the context of cultural differences. In this context, negotiators benefit from understanding how cultural differences shape the way the other party is likely to handle the negotiation.

conflict. Apparently, the two differed in their view of the values, goals, and needs of the organization, as well as in their own values, goals, and needs. Neither was particularly adept at cooperative conflict management, and instead they engaged in more assertive, competitive responses to each other. The conflict was exacerbated by an article appearing in *Fortune* that revealed to the public the problems the two managers were having with each other. Probably perceiving the situation as unresolvable, CEO Sternlicht opted to save his own position in the company and, in a series of maneuvers, engineered company president Nanula's resignation. The impact of the conflict on the organization and its future was huge. John Rohs, an analyst at Schroder Wertheim & Co., noted, "This is a difficult company to manage, with a ways to go in terms of integrating its acquisitions. Barry needs a strong orchestra leader." In the aftermath, although Sternlicht got what he wanted, he still had to face organizational problems at Starwood. Nanula, though ousted, received a $5 million severance package and was free to look for another job.

Using the news listings on your search engine, such as AP, Reuters, ZDNet News and the like, look for stories about interpersonal conflict among top managers at a company or companies and its impact on the company. When you find a good story, access the company's Web site, if possible, to learn more about the organization. Then play the role of a consultant to the company and write a memo to the managers outlining steps you think they could take to resolve their conflict constructively.

Source: Patricia Sellers, "Starwood: Splitsville," *Fortune,* May 24, 1999, p. 52.

global diversity EVENTS

Conflicts in Going Global

Organizations that seek to expand to foreign countries invariably will run into some type of conflict. Often, the key to success in these efforts is skilled negotiation between company managers and government officials or foreign executives. Preventing dysfunctional conflict, making the most of constructive conflict, and an overall strategy for managing conflict can go a long way toward successful global expansion. Executives at General Motors Corp. and Ford Motor Corp. found themselves mired in conflict when they sought to build plants in Brazil. Simply put, the rules changed in the middle of the game. One Brazilian regime approved enormous tax breaks and other incentives for the auto manufacturers to build job-creating plants on Brazilian soil. When the next governor took over, he claimed that Brazil couldn't afford the incentives when its economy was struggling. As part of its negotiation strategy, Ford set a deadline for a resolution of the conflict; GM reported that it would have to delay its plant opening. Meanwhile, Brazilian government officials engaged in their own arguments among each other and with the two companies. One official characterized Ford's stance that the financial incentives were vital to the project as blackmail.

General Motors and Ford are just two companies that have made attempts to make substantial investments in overseas operations and encountered conflicts along the way. Using the news listings on your search engine, look for stories about organizations that are trying to establish a presence overseas and the conflicts they have faced. When you find a good story, access the company's Web site, if possible, to learn more about the organization and the way its managers might approach the conflict situation. Consider the following questions as you write down several strategies for conflict resolution:

1. What are the sources of conflict in this situation?
2. At what level does the conflict appear to be?
3. Would distributive or integrative negotiation strategies be most appropriate in this case?
4. If two or more companies are involved in negotiating with a single government, as in the case of Ford and GM, would they benefit from some sort of collaboration?

Source: Peter Fritsch, "Ford and GM Clash with Brazilian State," *The Wall Street Journal,* April 9, 1999, p. A11.

minicase ISSUE

Turning Conflict into Cooperation

Jerry Strahan manages a motley crew. He is general manager for Lucky Dogs Inc., a $3 million hot dog–vending company that sells its steamed dogs to customers walking equally steamy New Orleans streets. Strahan's crew are like characters in a novel: one man used to live inside the company's elevator shaft and sometimes dresses as a woman; another man has fits of temper; a third is a former aerospace engineer; and one go-getter is immaculately dressed and once sold 3,300 hot dogs during a Super Bowl weekend. Those people are just a few Lucky Dogs employees. Needless to say, the potential for conflict in this group is enormous. Yet Jerry Strahan has been managing it for nearly 30 years.

Varying Needs. The needs of Lucky Dogs employees vary. Sometimes it is the battle between the need to drink alcohol and the need to appear at work. Sometimes it is the battle over vending turf. Intrapersonal and interpersonal conflicts arise every day. Strahan often finds unorthodox ways to negotiate these situations. "[Jerry is] a great mediator," observes Jim Campbell, a Lucky Dogs vendor for over 20 years. "There's a lot of personalities here, and sometimes my personality may not mesh with somebody else's. Then Jerry's got to step in and work out a compromise."

Responding to Conflict. Indeed, personalities range from those who barely show up for work and barely make enough money to get by for a day, to those like vendor James Hudson, who wants Strahan to come up with ideas for improving and expanding the business. Strahan chooses to respond to his employees' different needs and the conflicts that may arise from them in whatever way suits the situation. In the case of Hudson, Strahan simply avoids this conflict, preferring instead to let employees argue over minor issues like who gets which cart for the day. He isn't interested in "improving" the business beyond selling hot dogs. Strahan is also a big proponent of compromise. Whereas managers at more traditional

companies might fire an employee who showed up late for work and drunk or disheveled, Strahan observes, "Here, if you show up for work drunk, at least I've got to give you a C minus because you showed up." Strahan knows that his pool of workers isn't the most highly skilled or educated, so he accommodates them a lot. "The key to being successful in this type of transient business is to have enough dependable people who know how to do enough different things so that there's always someone in control," he explains.

Turning Negative Conflict into Positive Results. Instead of bombarding employees with rules that he knows they will break, Strahan tosses out the rule book. "We have to be flexible," says Strahan. "We make rules I know we're going to bend—I know we're going to break—because of the crew we have." He also believes that there is no benefit to holding a grudge; he needs his workers. "They need work. I need vendors. It's a constant flow," he explains. Finally, Strahan believes in letting conflict go. "Sometimes guys will come in and scream and yell or curse me out because I'm in some sense the figure they rebel against. . . . [But] they don't mean it. And once you realize that what they're saying is not real, then you don't worry about it."

1. Imagine that you could follow Jerry Strahan around for a day. What might you learn about the way he handles conflict that you could apply to your own job or life?

2. If Strahan adopted a more assertive approach to conflict management, how might Lucky Dogs change?

3. Would Strahan be a successful manager at a more traditional company? Why or why not? (Consider his values, needs, and goals in relation to those of the company.)

Source: Leigh Buchanan, "The Taming of the Crew," *Inc.,* August 1999, pp. 29–40.

Stress and Stress Management

preview

After studying this chapter, you should be able to:

- Explain the stress response.

- Discuss how organization changes, job demands, interpersonal relationships, and work-life conflict cause stress.

- Describe the physical and psychological consequences of stress.

- Explain why all individuals do not react the same way to stressful situations.

- Discuss how organizations are changing their culture to manage stress.

- Discuss how organizations are helping employees balance work and life.

- Explain how you can personally manage stress.

Finding the right amount of stress so that work is challenging but not overwhelming can be difficult. Especially in manufacturing jobs, the balance may be hard to find. By using *kaizen,* which is a Japanese manufacturing approach that means "continuous improvement," Westinghouse Air Brake tries to get top performance out of its small Chicago, Illinois, plant. Every two minutes and 27 seconds a buzzer sounds, signaling that a parts conveyor is about to move. Moving quickly between machines, the workers pick up a finished part and set it on the conveyor as it begins to move forward. In traditional assembly lines, workers are assigned to run one machine. But operating in a tight U-shaped work area called a "cell," the Westinghouse worker juggles the operation of three different machines while also making quality checks for defects in finished parts. Workers are not bored—every moment of their ten-hour workday is filled with motion. In addition, they receive continual feedback. Workers are provided with computers that monitor productivity. They know at each moment whether they are meeting production goals. If daily production goals are met, then employees get an additional $1.50 per hour bonus. To receive the bonus, though, everyone in the factory has to work together, since the bonus is rewarded for overall production at the plant.

The intense pace allows employees little time to interact with each other besides during their regular breaks. Although speed is important, it isn't the most important thing. Managers emphasize that the company wants to make pieces only at the speed customers will buy them. That is why the conveyor moves every two minutes and 27 seconds—it's the time needed to produce the right amount of parts to supply the customers. The ideal is for each cell to finish a single part just before it must be put on the conveyor. But most employees keep a buffer of several parts to allow for occasional delays, such as the need to perform minor maintenance on equipment. Managers are constantly looking for such parts hoarding to see whether the process is efficient.

Besides overseeing the conveyors, employees are also supposed to be alert for ways to improve the process. For example, one employee recommended that a welding machine be redesigned because it required too much lifting. Although continuous improvement suggests an openness to change, once an efficient, safe, productive process is established, employees are expected to stick with it. This poses a problem for some employees who like to develop their own personal style of performing work. But in a true *kaizen* plant, employees would be told every detail of their job, including where to stand and how far they should move their arms to perform the job. The system can be stressful: To ensure that employees are following the process, they are often timed with a stopwatch. One employee said, "It [the speed] affects the way that people behave, because they're always stressed out."

Yet, there is a trade-off that makes *kaizen* worthwhile for the employees. Although they are in constant motion, employees find that tasks are usually less physically demanding than in a traditional plant. In this plant, workers are spared the need to move and handle parts as much as they used to under the old assembly system. So the physical demands are reduced. *Kaizen* has an added bonus: Most employees think that the work is more interesting than at a regular plant, where they were stuck at one machine

Westinghouse Workers Trade Boredom for Stress

"It [the speed] affects the way that people behave, because they're always stressed out."
—Westinghouse Air Brake employee

doing the same thing over and over again for the entire day. The fast pace also makes the day seem to move more quickly. More importantly, *kaizen* has helped boost productivity, saving the employees' jobs from moving to overseas plants with lower labor costs.[1]

We have seen the extraordinary amount of change taking place in today's organizations. These changes are necessary for organizations to remain competitive and viable. But, changes in the workplace—whether good or bad—can cause stress. Employees in all types of jobs are affected by stress, but not all stress is harmful. Certain levels are needed to keep jobs interesting, as the opening vignette shows.

The reasons for stress vary. One cause is life events such as divorce, marriage, a new job, or pregnancy. As we will see later in the chapter, the level of stress caused by life events differs depending on the importance of the event. Another common cause is technology. For example, rapid changes in national and international stock markets mean financial advisers are sometimes overrun with calls from anxious clients who can monitor the markets constantly. One adviser complained of a sore neck and ear as a result of having to return more than 40 calls on a Saturday after a Friday market drop.[2] And as we discussed in Chapter 9, employees are more and more tied to their jobs by "electronic leashes" such as beepers and e-mail and barraged with data. One survey found that 40 percent of workers say their duties are interrupted more than six times an hour by intrusive communications![3] Reading about downsizing in the business section of newspapers or hearing about it on television reports, other employees, like Joe Sizemore, want to show managers that they are hardworking and loyal by working between 60 and 70 hours per week. Sizemore often works a 12-hour shift at a Corning Inc. factory in Blacksburg, Virginia.[4] Besides fear and loyalty, many employees work long hours to keep up with increasing job demands or because they like the money. As Sizemore says, "I'm doing a lot better than I ever thought I would do; I don't have any special skill—I'm not a welder or a bricklayer. I didn't finish college." With all these technological and competitive pressures, it is no wonder that U.S. employees put in more hours at work than employees in any other industrialized country.

Regardless of the causes, stress may result in negative consequences. For example, it may place pressure on an employee's family. A study by the Families and Work Institute of 3,000 employees found that nearly one-fourth of all employees felt stressed. Approximately one-fourth reported they had difficulty coping with nonwork demands and did not have the energy to do things with their family or significant others. Barbara Sizemore wishes her husband could spend more time with his two stepdaughters. Many days Joe sees his wife for only a few hours. Sizemore doesn't have time for his hunting and fishing hobbies. The small amount of free time he has is devoted to working on the older house he recently purchased.

Stress can also cause health problems. A recent survey of more than 46,000 employees at several different companies found that employees who reported being under stress are likely to experience significantly higher health care costs than employees who do not experience stress.[5] But all employees do not react to stress in the same way. Sizemore and his colleagues all have different ways of adjusting to the long hours. Some work puzzles in their head. Joe recites skits from *Saturday Night Live* and does impersonations of movie stars to keep himself alert.

As we will see in this chapter, people's responses to stress vary according to their personality, the resources available to help them cope, and the context in which the stress occurs. Thus, a looming deadline will feel different depending on the degree to which you enjoy a challenge, the willingness of your coworkers to team up and help everyone succeed, and family members' understanding of your need to work extra hours, among other factors.

This chapter focuses on stress and stress management. We begin the chapter by defining stress and describing an individual's stress response. Next, we discuss the sources and consequences of stress and what may be responsible for differences in how individuals respond to stress. The chapter concludes with a discussion of what organizations and individuals are doing to manage stress.

Individuals adapt to stress in different ways

Formally defined, **stress** is an individual's physiological and emotional response to stimuli that place physical or psychological demands on the individual and create uncertainty and lack of personal control when important outcomes are at stake.[6] These stimuli, called **stressors,** produce a combination of frustration at the inability to achieve a goal, such as the inability to meet a deadline because of inadequate resources, and anxiety, such as the fear of being disciplined for not meeting deadlines. Stressors are perceived as taxing or exceeding an individual's personal capabilities and resources.

The Stress Response

In biological terms, the stress response follows a pattern known as the General Adaptation Syndrome. The General Adaptation Syndrome (GAS) is a physiological response to a stressor, which begins with an alarm response, continues to resistance, and may end in exhaustion if the stressor continues beyond a person's ability to cope.[7] As shown in Exhibit 14.1, the GAS

stress

An individual's physiological and emotional response to stimuli that place physical or psychological demands on the individual and create uncertainty and lack of personal control when important outcomes are at stake.

stressors

Stimuli that produce some combination of frustration and anxiety.

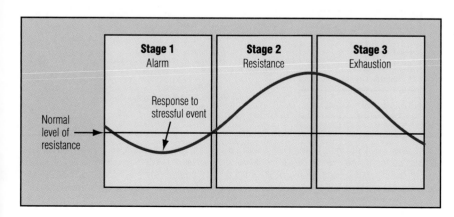

exhibit **14.1**

The Stress Response: General Adaptation Syndrome

begins when an individual first experiences a source of stress (the stressor). The stressor triggers an alarm response; the person may feel panic and helplessness, wondering how to cope with the stressor. Occasionally, people simply give up, but more often they move to the next stage of the stress response, called resistance. At this stage, the person gathers strength and begins to decide how to cope. If exposure to the stressor continues past the person's ability to maintain resistance, the person enters the third stage: exhaustion. Exhaustion results in anxiety, depression, physical illness, dissatisfaction with the job, or other negative consequences.

Sources and Consequences of Stress

Exhibit 14.2 shows a model of the sources and consequences of stress. As the Exhibit shows, there are several different sources or stimuli of stress, including not only a person's job but also changes in the structure or strategy of the organization and even nonwork factors. The individual and organizational consequences of these stressors depend on personality differences, the amount of control a person has over the situation, and support from others. As this model illustrates, an individual's reaction to stress can only be understood by evaluating the causes of stress and considering his or her different responses to stress.[8]

Often we associate stress only with bad things such as dissatisfaction, frustration, or even poor physical conditions such as ulcers. It is important to keep in mind that not all stress is bad. As Exhibit 14.3 shows, if employ-

exhibit | **14.2**

Sources and Consequences of Stress

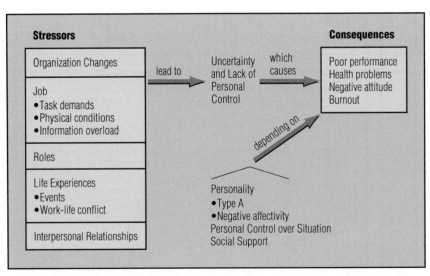

Source: Based on K. Danna and R. Griffin. (1999). "Health and well-being in the workplace: A review and synthesis of the literature." *Journal of Management 25:* 357–384; R. DeFrank and J. Ivancevich. (1998). "Stress on the job: An executive update." *Academy of Management Executive 12:* 55–66; R. Kahn and P. Byosiere, "Stress in Organizations," in M. Dunnette (ed.), *Handbook of Industrial and Organizational Psychology,* 3rd ed. (Palo Alto, CA: Consulting Psychologists Press, 1991).

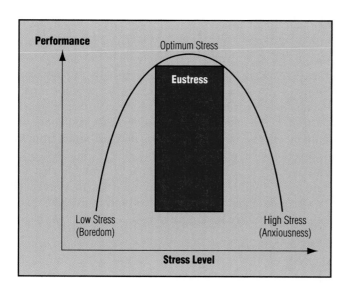

exhibit | **14.3**
Relationship between Stress and Performance

ees are not challenged, they will become bored and demotivated, resulting in low stress and low performance. A moderate level of stress, known as **eustress,** will energize and motivate employees. Consider how the challenge of providing a popular product has caused stress but resulted in satisfaction and success for Mandy Cabot, cofounder of Dansko.

eustress

A moderate level of stress that energizes and motivates employees.

Dansko

Clogs are built for comfort and durability. Over the past five years, they've also carried a U.S. company—Dansko—onto the *Inc.* 500 list. Dansko's annual sales have risen from $1.3 million to $16 million. The demand has been so strong that Dansko, a footwear distributor, has had trouble meeting retailers' demands. "Having shoes that everybody wants and nobody can get is an easier problem to solve than having shoes nobody wants but everybody can get," notes Mandy Cabot, who founded the company with her husband. "Happening on a shoe like a Dansko—you consider yourself lucky if you've done that once in your life."

It was on a trip to her husband's native Denmark in the mid 1980s that Cabot first splurged on a pair of closed-back clogs. "They were terrific for mucking out stalls," recalls Cabot, who then ran a horse-training facility with her husband. Sanita, the Danish manufacturer, had been supplying sturdy wooden clogs to the European market for nearly a century. Sanita signed an exclusive contract with Dansko for American distribution rights in 1990, just in time for a spike in the U.S. comfort-shoe market.

Cabot had mentioned to her father, Louis Wellington Cabot—former CEO of Cabot Corp., the giant specialty chemicals maker—that she'd been selling lots of clogs at horse shows. Louis Cabot arranged for Mandy to meet a friend of his who was CEO of a giant shoe company. In the meeting, Mandy Cabot learned which trade shows to attend, what kind of sales representatives to hire, and what market to focus on. By 1997 Cabot had sold her farm, barn, and animals, and put the profits into a warehouse and office building in West Grove, Pennsylvania. She was moving ahead, but her supplier, Sanita, began slowing down. "It didn't take us long to max out his production capacity," Cabot explains. "We put a moratorium on new accounts and struggled with that for a few years while he geared up another factory." Sanita struggled to handle the variety of new designs that Cabot demanded. Of the 80,000 to 90,000 shoes that Sanita makes monthly, Dansko buys as many as 60 percent, even though Sanita would rather spread out its customer base. To appease retailers, Cabot is broadening her product base. Dansko recently introduced the Solvei line, a more fashionable comfort shoe manufactured in Portugal.[9]

Even though some stress can be beneficial, if employees experience stress over long periods of time (chronic stress) or experience a very stressful event (acute stress), it can harm not only them but also the organization. For example, demands for high performance in a job under extreme physical conditions or constant time pressure can be dysfunctional. Similarly, negative events that occur infrequently but are catastrophic, such as losing a valued customer, can cause anxiety and depression. People who are experiencing the ill effects of too much stress may withdraw from interactions with their coworkers, be absent from work due to illnesses, and seek less stressful jobs elsewhere. They may become so irritable that they cannot work constructively with others; some employees may even explode in tantrums or violence. So, it is important for both individuals and organizations to understand and try to control stress.

apply it

1. Describe a situation in which stress improved your performance in school, work, or another life activity. How did stress improve your performance?

Stress is caused by organization changes and the demands of jobs, roles, life experiences, and interpersonal relations

Most people have a general idea of what a stressful job is like: it is difficult, uncomfortable, exhausting, even frightening. But experiencing stress is different from understanding it; individuals can better cope with their own stress if they can define the conditions that tend to produce work stress. What causes stress? Exhibit 14.2 shows the sources of stress and the individual and organizational consequences of stress. Stressors can be categorized into demands associated with organizational changes, job stressors, roles, life experiences, and interpersonal relationships.

Organization Changes

As we discussed in Chapter 1, organizations are under great pressure to be innovative, creative, and enter new global markets to remain competitive. This pressure has led to new business strategies and organizational restructuring, such as the use of teams and reorganizing by product line instead of function. As a result, employees often must relocate, work with more diverse colleagues from different cultures, take on new assignments, or even face the loss of their jobs. Such radical changes are difficult under the best circumstances, but if the implementation of change is not effectively managed, individuals will experience negative stress, resulting in poor performance and mental or physical health problems. For example, one study found that employees from a supermarket chain who were transferred to new stores experienced more psychological stress compared with employees who were not asked to relocate.[10] We will discuss ways to minimize the stressful consequences of change in Chapter 18.

Job Stressors

Aside from changes in the overall structure and functioning of an organization, an employee's job itself may contribute to stress. Job stressors include task demands, physical conditions, and information overload.

Task Demands **Task demands** are stressors arising from the tasks required of a person holding a particular job. Some kinds of decisions are inherently stressful: those made under time pressure, those that have serious consequences, and those that must be made with incomplete information. For example, emergency room doctors are under tremendous stress as a result of the task demands of their jobs. They regularly have to make quick decisions, based on limited information, that may determine whether a patient lives or dies. Although not as extreme, many other jobs have task demands that lead to stress. Recall from Chapter 10 that managers and employees frequently have to make nonprogrammed decisions—decisions that are characterized by incomplete information and have important consequences for the organization. Managers also experience stress from other factors, such as the responsibility of supervising or disciplining other people. Federal Express found that 10 percent of employees promoted to their first management job left the company within a year or so. The company learned that many didn't realize the difficulty of the task demands facing managers: longer hours, the commitment of representing the company even outside work, and the consequences of having responsibility for others.[11] Similarly, teamwork and giving employees greater decision-making authority (empowering employees) may create stress for employees who have little interest or training in working in teams and decision making, and they may feel overwhelmed by having to accept greater levels of responsibility for their work.

Task demands can require an employee to work long hours and weekends to keep up with the workload and can drive employees to become workaholics. **Workaholism** is working to the exclusion of everything else in life.[12] It causes individuals to become obsessed with work to the point that they are physically and emotionally crippled. Workaholics consistently work long hours, stay late, and work on weekends and holidays, even if they aren't facing deadlines. They constantly think about work. Workaholics sacrifice friends, family, recreation, and all other aspects of their life for work. Individuals may become workaholics to escape problems at home, to be in control, or to ensure their work meets their perfectionistic standards. "Death by overwork," or *karoshi,* was officially recognized as a fatal illness by the Japanese in 1989. But as

task demands

Stressors arising from the tasks required of a person holding a particular job.

workaholism

Working to the exclusion of everything else in life, resulting in obsession with work to the point that employees are physically and emotionally crippled.

At the Chicago Board of Trade, stress levels are high. It is loud, raw, and so physically demanding that some traders lift weights to build stamina. For the last 152 years, the chaos has unfolded every market day. A couple of thousand people, clustered around sunken circular pits, shout themselves hoarse, bidding on contracts on grains, soybeans, and U.S. Treasury securities. The task demands of such a job are inherently stressful.
(Source: © Todd Buchanan)

exhibit **14.4**

- The work environment is fast paced, with little or no time to talk casually with coworkers or peers.
- The environment feels "cold," sterile, and lacking in human interaction.
- The organization thrives on crisis, chaos, and pressure.
- Success depends on working overtime on weekdays, weekends, and holidays.
- Employees are constantly in a hurry or racing against the clock.
- Employees have to juggle many activities and projects at one time to keep up with the job.
- There are short-notice, high-pressure deadlines for employees.
- There is a high incidence of stress-related illnesses among employees.
- Socialization and development of close personal relationships with fellow employees is discouraged.

Source: B. Robinson, *Chained to the Desk* (New York: New York University Press, 1998).

Exhibit 14.4 shows, task demands and the work environment can promote workaholism. Workaholism results in fatigue, sleep deprivation, and loss of physical and mental health, which harm the employee and have the potential to harm others by causing accidents.

Physical Conditions   **Physical demands** are stressors associated with the setting in which an individual works. Some people must cope with work in a poorly designed work setting, such as an office with inadequate lighting or little privacy. Some employees must maneuver in a cramped workspace; some have too little or too much heat for comfort. Some workplaces even present safety and health hazards, from greasy floors to polluted air. Work that involves repetitive movements, such as poultry processing or nonstop computer work, also can lead to injury; thus, this type of work intensifies stress for employees.

Threatening physical conditions may not always be observable. For example, semiconductor manufacturing is usually seen as a "clean" industry—employees wear white jumpsuits in "clean rooms" where the air is filtered. The work environment seems cleaner than a hospital operating room. Unfortunately, these images may hide the actual physical risks associated with working in a semiconductor facility. Making semiconductors requires using many different chemicals including benzene, arsenic, and chromium, which are potential carcinogens (cancer-causing agents). Women employees claim that they breathed dangerous chemical fumes, that monitors to detect chemical leaks were disconnected or did not function correctly, and that they were not warned of the reproductive hazards of chemicals. According to Grace Morrison, a computer-chip employee for 16 years, "We all got a cocktail of gases, acids, and chemicals." Many women who have worked in these facilities are experiencing medical problems including cancer, children with birth defects, and multiple miscarriages.[13]

Information Overload   The explosion of data capabilities due to increased use of e-mail, the World Wide Web, beepers, and cellular phones has bombarded individuals with information in their work and nonwork lives. For example, one statistic states that in the office an average of 60 percent of employees' time is spent processing documents. At home, from 1965 to 1995 the time for the average network television advertisement shrank from 53.1 seconds to 25.4 seconds, but over the same period, the number of ads per network TV minute nearly doubled![14] **Data smog** is the term that refers

physical demands

Stressors associated with the setting in which an individual works, such as inadequate lighting or little privacy.

data smog

Large amounts of data people have to face on a daily basis.

to the large amounts of data people have to face on a daily basis.[15] In the car, on vacation, on planes, in desolate backwoods, and even in the bathroom, we can be interrupted by the expanding reach of media and faced with data demands. Susan Narveson, director of the Phoenix police department forensics laboratory, has a cell phone and laptop computer.[16] She says, "I don't go anywhere without it. It's like a security blanket." She is always "pageable." Narveson says, "There's nowhere to escape anymore. It's sad, but that's the way it is." The inability to escape the relentless blare of data has many employees complaining about being overwhelmed. It can be difficult to concentrate on one thing with constant interruptions from faxes, voice mails, beepers, and e-mails at work.

Having to deal with large amounts of media stimulation and data overload may also be responsible for memory loss. For example, have you ever gone on an errand to a store and, once you entered the store, forgotten why you were there? This happens because memory is stored according to specific cues. Robert Bjork, a memory expert, says, "When many different things get associated with the same situational cues, you're going to have a greater difficulty remembering any one of those things. With information overload, retrieval becomes more difficult."[17]

Roles

Role demands are challenges associated with a role—that is, the set of behaviors expected of a person because of that person's position in the group. Some people encounter *role ambiguity,* meaning they are uncertain about what behaviors are expected of them. For example, one clinical psychologist who specializes in executive stress says that many upper level executives, who grew up at a time when norms were different, do not understand what diversity requires of them—such as what women in the workplace view as appropriate conduct. Consequently, some are fearful of inadvertently doing something that a woman will regard as sexual harassment.[18]

Role ambiguity results in many complications in the workplace, as some employees of Wendy's International experienced personally. Role ambiguity was the norm at Wendy's when the hamburger chain began rapid expansion during the 1970s.

role demands

Challenges associated with a role—that is, the set of behaviors expected of a person because of that person's position in the group.

🐂 Wendy's International

Wendy's top executive, Dave Thomas, says his biggest mistake was not completing high school. Thomas, who knew he wanted to be in the restaurant business, dropped out of school because he thought he could learn more by working. One thing he learned was that quitting school made his business life a lot harder. Thomas found that a lot of people would talk down to him, and he had to work twice as hard to get people to treat him as an equal. Further, when Thomas started building his business, he felt insecure and uncomfortable about his lack of a formal education (he finally returned to school and earned his GED in the 1990s).

Thomas believed that because of his lack of education, he needed to delegate extensively. Unfortunately, Wendy's was growing so fast that Thomas delegated more and more decision-making authority without providing the managers and crew with the training they needed to make good work decisions. The result? People didn't understand what they were supposed to do, didn't know what top management expected from them, felt tremendous stress and anxiety, and eventually became frustrated, some to the point of exhaustion. As soon as Thomas and other top managers realized what was happening, they took immediate action to provide employees with the clear guidelines and training they needed. Today, Wendy's managers work hard to make sure all employees feel empowered—not stressed out.[19]

Although role ambiguity can be stressful, people who experience role conflict can feel as if they are being torn apart by conflicting expectations. *Role conflict* occurs when an individual perceives incompatible demands from others. Managers often feel role conflict because the demands of their superiors conflict with those of the employees in their department. For example, they may be expected to support employees and provide them with opportunities to experiment and be creative, while top executives are demanding a consistent level of output that leaves little time for creativity and experimentation. In a company whose philosophy is "We're one big family," a manager who has to lay off employees would likely feel that this role conflicts with the expectation that she care about employees. These types of role conflict can create a high level of stress. Role conflict may also be experienced when a person's internalized values and beliefs collide with the expectations of others. For example, a manager who believes in being honest and ethical in all his relationships may be told by a superior to "fudge a little" on quality control reports in order to meet an important deadline. This role conflict leaves the manager with the choice of either being disloyal to his superior or acting unethically according to his personal values.[20]

Life Experiences

People do not live and work in a vacuum, and occurrences outside the work environment can intrude and cause conflict and stress. Life experiences that can be stressors include life events and work-life conflict.

exhibit **14.5**

Top 15 Stressful Life Events

Rank	Life Event	Mean Value
1	Death of spouse	100
2	Divorce	73
3	Marital separation	65
4	Jail term	63
5	Death of close family member	63
6	Personal injury or illness	53
7	Marriage	50
8	Fired at work	47
9	Marital reconciliation	45
10	Retirement	45
11	Change in health of family member	44
12	Pregnancy	40
13	Sex difficulties	39
14	Gain of new family member	39
15	Business readjustment	39

Source: Based on T. Holmes and R. Rahe. (1967). " The social readjustment rating scale." *Journal of Psychomatic Research:* 213–218.

Life Events Life events such as death of a spouse, divorce, or a new job can cause stress. Life events cause stress by making individuals adjust their work and personal routines. Exhibit 14.5 shows a ranking of how much personal adjustment is required for different life events. The degree of adjustment required by a life event is also related to a person's health.[21] If a person experiences life events that total over 300 points in one year, that individual is likely to experience a serious health problem.

Work-Life Conflict Stress can also occur from a conflict between work and life roles. Work-life conflict is related to increased health risks, decreased productivity, withdrawal behaviors, and poor mental health.[22] There are three types of work-life conflict.[23] **Time-based conflict** results when work and life events interfere with each other. For example, jobs that demand frequent travel or long hours conflict with personal activities such as exercise, running errands, or even finding time to go to the grocery store. **Strain-based conflict** occurs from the stress of work and nonwork roles. For example, a newborn child deprives parents of sleep, and they cannot concentrate as well on projects at work. **Behavior-based conflict** occurs when an individual's behavior in a work role is inappropriate for his or her behavior in a nonwork role. Managers' work demands that they be logical, analytical, and impartial. However, at the same time, in their nonwork roles, these same managers are expected to be sensitive, open, and emotional with family and friends—behavior at the opposite end of the emotional spectrum.

Interpersonal Demands

Organizational relationships can also cause stress. Interpersonal demands are stressors associated with relationships in the organization. Although in some cases interpersonal relationships can alleviate stress, they also can be a source of stress when a work group puts pressure on an individual or when there are conflicts. Interpersonal conflict occurs when two or more individuals perceive that their attitudes or goals are in opposition. Managers can work to resolve many interpersonal and intergroup conflicts, using techniques discussed in Chapter 13. A particularly challenging stressor is the personality clash. A personality clash occurs when two people simply cannot get along and do not see eye to eye on any issue. This type of conflict can be exceedingly difficult to resolve, and many managers have found that it is best to separate the two people so that they do not have to interact with one another.

time-based conflict

Conflict resulting when work and life events interfere with each other. For example, jobs that demand frequent travel or long hours conflict with personal activities such as exercise or errands.

strain-based conflict

Conflict resulting from the stress of work and nonwork roles. For example, a newborn child deprives parents of sleep, and they cannot concentrate as well on projects at work.

behavior-based conflict

Conflict occurring when an individual's behavior in a work role is inappropriate for his or her behavior in a nonwork role.

When employees at Gould Evans Goodman, a Kansas City architectural firm, experience stress from time-based conflict, they can take a nap in one of the company's three "spent tents" for tired employees. The camping tents are pitched in a corner of the office and equipped with sleeping bags, pillows, alarm clocks, and soothing music.
(Source: © Robert Wright)

apply it

1.   What stressors do you face? Which stressors result in the most negative consequences for you? Why?

The consequences of stress vary depending on an individual's personality and social support

As Exhibit 14.2 shows, whether or not individuals experience negative consequences of stress depends on how they react to the sources of stress. For example, some people find demanding work to be challenging and motivating—a source of positive stress. Others would view the same work to be too demanding, and it would cause them to experience negative consequences (such as headaches). Individuals may be predisposed to react a certain way when they experience stressors because of their behavior, personality, or amount of social support they receive from others.

Type A and Type B Behaviors

Type A behavior

A behavior pattern that includes extreme competitiveness, impatience, aggressiveness, and devotion to work.

Researchers have observed that some people seem to be more vulnerable than others to the ill effects of stress. From studies of stress-related heart disease, they have categorized people as having behavior patterns called Type A and Type B.[24] The **Type A behavior** pattern includes extreme competitiveness, impatience, aggressiveness, and devotion to work. In contrast, people with a Type B behavior pattern exhibit less of these behaviors. They consequently experience less conflict with other people and a more balanced, relaxed lifestyle. Type A people tend to experience more stress-related illness than Type B people.

Americans are especially driven to succeed. If the "I can do it all" attitude is not controlled, negative health and life consequences can result. For example, David L. House, chief executive of Bay Networks, exhibits many Type A characteristics. He proudly told a *Business Week* reporter that on one business trip he led seven meetings in nine hours, handled business on his car phone, and attended a dinner. At his former employer, Intel, coworkers gave him a T-shirt with the message "Captain Adrenaline," reflecting his high-energy, driven style. His drive and discipline carry over to activities outside the workplace. He schedules early morning exercise five days a week, and his aggressive play at racquetball has reportedly caused several opponents to require stitches. House admits that his behavior has consequences; he says his intense schedule is a reason his two marriages ended in divorce.[25]

By pacing themselves and learning control and intelligent use of their natural high-energy tendencies, Type A individuals can be powerful forces for innovation and leadership within their organizations. However, many Type A personalities cause stress-related problems for themselves, and sometimes for those around them. Type B individuals typically live with less stress unless they are in high-stress situations.

Negative Affectivity

Some people may experience more negative stress than others because they tend to focus on the negative aspects of life. **Negative affectivity** represents a person's tendency to focus on shortcomings and the negative aspects of life so that he or she tends to be angry, fearful, and depressed. These people also are very self-evaluative. You might consider persons with high levels of negative affectivity to be "moody." People high in negative affectivity may also complain they are more "stressed out" than persons with low negative affectivity and report that physical and psychological problems are caused by stress.[26]

negative affectivity

A person's tendency to focus on shortcomings and the negative aspects of life so that he or she tends to be angry, fearful, and depressed.

Personal Control

Personal control means that individuals believe their behaviors determine what happens to them. That is, they believe they control their future. Research indicates that individuals who believe they have more personal control are less threatened by stressors and, as a result, experience fewer negative reactions.[27] For example, when faced with having to repair damage caused by flooding, small business owners who believed they had high levels of personal control focused on the task of rebuilding their business by assessing damages and arranging for repairs to be made, while those with less personal control tended to react with anger, anxiety, and hostility.

personal control

Individuals' belief that their behaviors determine what happens to them; they control the future.

Social Support

Social support refers to relationships with other people including peers, friends, and relatives, who listen to problems and are sympathetic and caring. Most people cope with stressors more effectively if they lead balanced lives and are part of a network of people who support and encourage them. Family, relationships, friendships, and memberships in nonwork groups such as community or religious organizations are helpful for stress management, as well as for other benefits.

social support

Relationships with other people, who listen to problems and are sympathetic and caring. These relationships reduce stress levels.

apply it

1. Describe a time in your work or personal life when you experienced stress. Did you have social support? What kind? How did social support help to reduce the potential negative consequences of stress?

Stress can negatively affect performance, attitudes, behavior, and health

One way to think about the consequences of stress is to consider how it affects an individual's well-being. Well-being is a broad concept that considers both positive health and attitudes. **Well-being** refers to positive mental and physical health as well as attitudes related to the job and the organization, such as job satisfaction.[28] Stress can upset this sense of well-being, hindering or destroying a person's resiliency. Its effects can become clear

well-being

Positive mental and physical health as well as attitudes related to the job and the organization, such as job satisfaction.

when people exhibit performance, personal, or health problems. Examples of the negative consequences of stress include poor performance, burnout, physical and mental health problems, negative work attitudes, and counterproductive and withdrawal behaviors.

Poor Performance

When a person is under stress, the daily demands of work and life can become too much to bear. As a result, that person's performance can suffer. On the job, performance can be negatively affected by stress in many ways. A stressed employee might deceive customers, cut corners on quality control, miss appointments, or have interpersonal conflict, errors, and accidents.[29] The consequences of poor performance can be devastating to the organization, resulting in dissatisfied customers, missed opportunities, and ultimately lost competitiveness and lowered revenue.

Burnout

burnout

Emotional exhaustion and a tendency to treat persons as objects and to negatively evaluate work accomplishments.

Burnout is a severe consequence of stress. **Burnout** refers to emotional exhaustion and a tendency to treat persons as objects and to negatively evaluate work accomplishments. Exhibit 14.6 shows the major components of burnout. Burnout has been shown to be related to depression, poor performance, absenteeism, and turnover.[30] Burnout primarily has been shown to affect individuals who work in human service professions such as nursing, counseling, social work, and law enforcement.[31] This type of work requires a high emotional investment, but such professionals are not supposed to demonstrate their feelings outwardly. They can experience much frustration as their clients fail to respond to treatment. Because they may not experience much extrinsic reinforcement day to day for their work, individuals may feel that their work is not important.

Entrepreneurs also are vulnerable to burnout.[32] As entrepreneurs experience a certain amount of financial success, they may feel obligated not to disappoint their employees or change the lifestyle of family members by upsetting or leaving their now successful venture. But one of entrepreneurs' primary joys is the feeling they get from building a new business. Staying with the company primarily to satisfy or please others can quickly lead to burnout.

exhibit | **14.6**
Major Components of Burnout

Burnout

Emotional Exhaustion
Feeling drained, fatigued, unable to cope with job demands

Depersonalization
Having cynical attitudes toward all aspects of work including customers, services, products, and the work environment

Reduced Personal Accomplishment
Downgrading personal accomplishments

Health Problems

Stress has been shown to be related to behavioral, medical, and psychological problems.[33] Behavior changes include abuse of alcohol and drugs, increased cigarette smoking, increased tendency for accidents, and violence. Psychological consequences include family problems, sleeping problems, sexual dysfunction, and depression. Medical problems include ulcers, high blood pressure, and headaches. Because employees who experience these problems are more likely to make use of the health care benefits provided by the organization by visiting doctors and mental health professionals (resulting in more insurance claims), the amount of money that the organization pays for health care coverage for its employees will increase. One estimate is that the total cost of stress to U.S. companies is more than $150 billion per year. [34]

In addition to seeking professional help for health problems, employees may make workers' compensation claims if they believe that stress has been caused on the job. **Workers' compensation claims** include claims for monetary compensation by employees (or their dependents) for job-related injuries or death. The workers' compensation system provides medical and lost wages to employees who are injured on the job. The awards include income, medical care, death benefits, and rehabilitative services. Although the workers' compensation system is administered by the states, organizations pay into the state worker compensation fund (similar to paying taxes). The amount of each organization's "tax" is based on the severity and number of compensation claims made by its employees. This results in an "experience rating" for each organization. Because workers' compensation laws vary from state to state, the type and amount of rewards for injuries or illness differ. For example, the award for the loss of a leg in Pennsylvania is six times the award given to an employee in Colorado. Employees can receive awards for mental stress as well as physical injuries.

The number and costs of workers' compensation claims have increased dramatically. Exhibit 14.7 shows the five most frequent injuries at work. Severe injuries (such as loss of a leg) are less prevalent than minor injuries such as strains and sprains. Lifting injuries are the most prevalent injury, resulting in 31 percent of all injuries and costing an average of $34,000 per claim.[35] According to one study, claims for mental stress now account for 15 percent of all workers' compensation claims.[36] Stress claims result in an

workers' compensation claims

Claims for monetary compensation by employees (or their dependents) for job-related injuries or death.

exhibit | 14.7
Five Most Frequent Nonfatal Injuries in the Workplace

1. Lifting injuries (injuries to back, head, arms, and neck)

2. Contact with objects (machinery, flying objects)

3. Trips and falls

4. Repetitive motion injuries (such as carpal tunnel syndrome from typing)

5. Exposure to harmful substances (chemicals, smoke, etc.)

Source: From Web site www.accidentfund.com (downloaded 1998).

average of 39 weeks of time off, compared with 24 weeks for physical injury claims, and they result in 52 percent higher costs.

Negative Work Attitudes

Stress has been shown to be associated with job dissatisfaction, including both overall dissatisfaction and dissatisfaction with specific aspects of the job, such as the amount of work the individual has been asked to complete.[37]

Counterproductive and Withdrawal Behaviors

As we discussed in Chapter 3, withdrawal behaviors refer to psychological or physical behaviors that individuals use to avoid dissatisfying work. Counterproductive behaviors are behaviors that are detrimental to the organization, such as stealing and sabotage. Stress has been shown to be related to absenteeism, the spread of harmful rumors, drug use, and sabotage.[38]

Thus, stress can have serious consequences for organizations as well as individuals. Consider how the negative consequences of stress affect drivers and companies in the trucking industry.

American Trucking Association

Truck driving is one of the most dangerous jobs. In 1997, deaths of truck drivers accounted for 14 percent of all occupational deaths. Most of them were the result of rollovers, jackknifing, crashes, or other accidents. Drunk driving, a large factor in traffic deaths involving automobiles, has a very small impact on crashes and fatalities involving trucks because of mandatory alcohol testing of truck drivers. Based on accident data collected by the Network of Employers for Traffic Safety, an organization that designs driver safety programs, each crash costs an organization at least $10,000. The costs include lost work time, health insurance, sick leave, property damage, liability insurance, and legal expenses. Organizations also face recruitment and training costs from employees' deaths and long-term disabilities.

A number of factors including fatigue and inattention contribute to crashes and fatalities involving trucks. According to a report by the U.S. Bureau of Labor Statistics, long-distance drivers often drive for long hours through bad weather and heavy traffic and on difficult roads. The drivers face boredom, fatigue, and loneliness.

For the American Trucking Association (ATA), improving safety is a major priority. Truck and bus drivers are now allowed to drive 10 hours straight. They must take a mandatory 8-hour break before driving again. They are also only allowed to drive 60 hours in seven days or 70 hours in eight days. The ATA wants more rest stops, increased enforcement against poor drivers, increased drug testing, and an expanded state and federal roadside inspection program.[39]

apply it

1. Describe a stressful situation that you faced at school, work, or home. How did stress affect your attitudes? Your health? Your behavior?

Stress management is the responsibility of both the organization and the individual

We have seen how stress, left unchecked, can harm both individuals and their organizations. Because of potentially harmful consequences of stress, both organizations and individuals are actively trying to manage it. Stress management involves limiting the amount of stress that individuals experience or improving their ability to cope with stressful situations.

Organizational Strategies

Organizations that want to challenge their employees and stay competitive in a fast-changing environment will never be stress free. But because many consequences of stress are negative, organizations need to participate in stress management for their own sake and for their employees'. They can do so by identifying the major sources of stress, including the task, physical, role, and interpersonal demands of the job and organization. Does the overall level of these demands match an employee's taste for challenge and his or her coping resources? If so, the level of stress may be part of a successful person-job fit. If not, the organization and its employees should look for ways to reduce the stressors and increase employees' coping skills. Organizations can provide training or clearer directions so that employees feel able to handle their responsibilities. They should also provide counseling services so that employees are able to deal with work and life demands that may become overwhelming. They can make the work environment safer and more comfortable, and they can change the culture so that employees are more comfortable in the work environment.

Employee Assistance Programs **Employee assistance programs (EAPs)** are services that help employees with mental health, drug, alcohol, financial, and marital problems. The services usually involve either face-to-face or phone counseling with trained counselors. The counselors help to solve the crisis themselves by providing information or listening to employees' concerns. The counselor may also refer an employee to more in-depth counseling with a clinical psychologist or psychiatrist, if needed. EAPs are usually identified to employees in employee handbooks, other documents, or Web sites provided by the organization. Managers are trained to refer employees to the service if they ask for help with problems. Employees' use of an EAP is usually confidential. For example, Marriott Corporation provides an EAP through phone counseling.[40] Priscilla Johnson, a Marriott employee, faced the problem of having to care for her father, who was diagnosed with cancer. Being single and having no children, Johnson had never taken care of anyone. The resource line helped her. After explaining her situation to the social worker who answered her call, she was sent brochures that provided advice on what questions to ask about her father's treatment. She also received information about how to best use her father's medical benefits. "It was a godsend," says Johnson. "It makes devastating moments in life easier."

Wellness Programs **Wellness programs** focus on changing behaviors that could lead to future health problems. Wellness programs are preventive in nature—they attempt to stop health problems from occurring or detect them while they can be treated at a lower cost to the company and with less physical discomfort for the employee. Wellness programs can involve early detection, education, fitness, and improvements in the work environment to make it more healthy. Prevention programs try to lower employees' risks for heart disease, stroke, and cancer by providing early detection of high blood pressure, breast and prostate cancer, high cholesterol levels, and

employee assistance programs (EAPs)

Services provided by or paid for by organizations that help employees with mental health, drug, alcohol, financial, and marital problems. The services usually involve either face-to-face or phone counseling with trained counselors.

wellness programs

Programs that attempt to stop health problems from occurring by identifying health problems at an early stage (e.g., using mammography to find cancer) or changing negative employee behaviors, such as smoking.

On-site exercise facilities, part of wellness programs, can help employees improve their physical fitness and provide stress relief. At BMC Software in Houston, Texas, recreational facilities include a basketball court, a putting green, beach volleyball, and horseshoe pits. Many BMCers report putting in 10- to 12-hour days, and a trip to the gym is often followed by a long night at the office. "I know this is hard to believe," says Roy Wilson, chief of human resources, "but you do feel like you can get away while you're here. It gives you a balanced life without having to leave."
(Source: © Robert Wright)

obesity. Organizations may also sponsor "stop smoking" programs as part of their wellness programs.

Wellness programs can help employees improve their physical fitness by providing on-site exercise facilities, subsidizing health club memberships, or sponsoring athletic events. Wellness programs also include education programs designed to raise awareness of health issues, such as proper nutrition or ways to stretch your limbs before exercising to avoid injury. The organization may also offer low-fat foods in the cafeteria or unlimited access to fresh fruit during breaks as a way to improve employees' health and prevent disease. For example, employees at Texas Instruments Materials and Controls Group have an on-site fitness facility that is actually a full-service health club.[41] Approximately 1,000 employees actively participate in the wellness program. Employees pay $220 per year to join the facility. There is a complete schedule of fitness and education classes.

Organizations have reported significant reductions in health claims and costs due to wellness programs. For example, Steelcase, a Grand Rapids company that manufactures office equipment, found that three years after a wellness program was started, the number of employees identified as "high risk" based on behavior such as smoking, drinking, and lack of exercise had fallen 50 percent.[42] The annual cost for health claims for employees moving from the high- to low-risk groups also fell by 50 percent. The wellness program provided employees with access to exercise equipment and educational programs.

One problem with wellness programs may be that employees who would most likely benefit from the programs may not participate.[43] As a result, organizations are trying to provide incentives for employees to participate. For example, Quaker Oats gives employees a $140 credit they can use in the company's flexible benefit program if they make a "healthy lifestyle" pledge.[44] Johnson & Johnson employees get $500 discounts on insurance premiums if they agree to have their blood pressure, cholesterol, and body fat checked. Employees determined to be at high risk are asked to join a diet and exercise program. Those who refuse lose the $500 discount. Approximately 96 percent of employees completed the health assessments. Providence General Hospital in Everett, Washington, saved an estimated $1.5 million by offering financial incentives to employees who demonstrated responsibility for their health and fitness.[45] The program resulted in less use of health benefits, lower medical claims, and less absenteeism.

Better Management of Workers' Compensation Claims   There are two things that organizations can do to control workers' compensation claims.[46] One is to eliminate the conditions that caused injury. The second is to get involved in managing the care and treatment of employees who are injured to quicken their return to work. Injury prevention includes educating employees about the costs of injuries and days lost due to injuries. Also, injury prevention involves training employees to deal with the physical demands of their job, such as how to lift properly. Organizations should also provide tools and aids to help reduce the physical demands of jobs. Some examples include lifting belts, brighter and larger computer monitors to reduce eye strain, and portable mechanical lifts to move heavy equipment or patients.

To reduce the chances that employees may fake illness or procrastinate in returning to work, organizations need to periodically contact injured employees to let them know they are valued and needed at work. Employee assistance program counselors can also contact injured employees to help them deal with both the physical and psychological issues associated with their injury. A plan for the employee's return to work should be discussed with the employee. This might involve the employee first performing "light-duty work" (easier work) or working part time or at home until fully recovered.

Helping Employees Cope with Job Loss Because of the increased rate of mergers, acquisitions, and corporate restructuring as a means to gain a competitive advantage, many employees have been downsized. Employees are also downsized due to downturns in business, which force the organization to reduce labor costs. **Downsizing** is a process through which employees lose their jobs. Downsizing causes harmful stress to both the employees who lose their jobs and employees who remain with the company, the **survivors.** To help employees cope with job loss, organizations have two responsibilities. First, the organization is responsible for helping employees who lose their jobs. To prepare employees for downsizing, organizations need to provide outplacement services. Exhibit 14.8 shows the types of services that can be provided. Before employees will be ready to carry out a job campaign, they will need counseling to help them work through the fear, anger, and frustration associated with losing their job.

Second, the organization needs to take actions to ensure that survivors do not experience negative stress, which can result in health problems, counterproductive behaviors, poor performance, and physical and

downsizing

A process through which employees lose their jobs.

survivors

Employees who remain with the company following downsizing.

exhibit | **14.8**

Outplacement Services

- Advanced warning and explanation for layoff
- Psychological, financial, and career counseling
- Skill and interest assessment
- Job campaign services (resume writing, interview training)
- Job postings (newspapers and Web sites)
- Job banks (places where job leads are posted, phones and computers are available, and library of occupation, training, and company information is provided)

Source: Based on S. Quinn. (1988). "Outplacement programs: Separating myth from reality." *Training & Development Journal 42*: 48–49; S. Rosen and C. Paul, "Learn the Inner Workings of Outplacement," *The Wall Street Journal*, July 7, 1997; D. Simon. (1988). "Outplacement: Matching needs, matching services," *Training & Development Journal 42:* 52–57.

psychological withdrawal behaviors (e.g., turnover and absenteeism). Survivors have positive feelings because they have kept their jobs. However, they also experience uncertainty about their future. They may ask themselves whether they will be the next to be downsized. Rather than being concerned about customers, survivors may be preoccupied with talking to each other about rumors regarding who is the next to be downsized and how downsized employees reacted to the news. Survivors do not know how safe their job is and may be unsure of the strategic direction of the company. In addition, survivors' workloads may increase as they are expected to perform their own work and cover the responsibilities of downsized employees.

Survivors experience anxiety, anger toward upper level management, cynicism toward the organization's latest plans, resentment, and resignation.[47] For example, consider the anger of a mid-level manager toward top management in a company experiencing downsizing: "Stop telling us to work smarter. Show us how. . . . Stop blaming us! We've been loyal to the company. We've worked hard and did everything we were told. We've moved for the company, traveled for the company, and we've taken on extra work for the company. And now you say we did wrong. You told us to do it. Management told us to do it! And the company did pretty well while we did it. Stop blaming us!"[48]

Survivors' attitudes and productivity are related to their perceptions of the fairness of the downsizing and changes in working conditions.[49] Downsizing is more likely to be viewed as fair if the factors used to determine who to downsize, such as performance or seniority, are applied equally to management and nonmanagement employees; if advanced warning of the downsizing is provided; and if clear and adequate explanations for the need to downsize employees are communicated. Survivors should be trained to cope with greater workloads and job responsibilities. The organization also needs to give survivors realistic information about their future.

Modifying the Work Environment Organizations are changing the work environment in many different ways to reduce stress. As we discussed in Chapter 5, organizations are using biological approaches to design jobs, changing or replacing equipment so that fewer physical demands are placed on employees. Organizations are also trying to improve the work environment by modifying ventilation systems to improve the flow of fresh air and reduce the number of illnesses and allergic reactions that employees experience from fungus or bacteria.

Many organizations are radically changing the office environment to make it a more relaxing and energizing place to work and to encourage employees to interact.[50] In choosing colors for office space, for example, organizations are relying on research that suggests that colors can influence our moods and behaviors. Colors such as yellow and fire-engine red seem to promote nervousness and anxiety. Blues and greens promote serenity. Also, the shape and size of office space is being manipulated. For example, the Denver headquarters of Tele-Communications Inc is donut shaped, with curving staircases to encourage spontaneous conversations between employees. Doane Pet Care Company's new work space includes wide, curving hallways painted in gold, brown, and green. The office design of

Zagnoli McEvoy Foley, a litigation consulting firm in Chicago, has unusual hallways meeting at odd angles with walls painted purple, red, and yellow. Steelcase, the furniture manufacturer located in Grand Rapids, Michigan, is experimenting with an open office plan with no private offices.[51] The time between eight and nine o'clock is to be used for people to talk to each other. No meetings are permitted to be scheduled. There is a conscious effort to use office furniture and accessories that invite relaxation and a break from routine. For example, a fish tank in the common area is a regular gathering place for employees.

Organizations are also trying to get rid of unnecessary work. For example, the Massachusetts Housing Finance Agency, located in Boston, analyzed the services it provided to the customer to see if they were needed.[52] The agency identified five important roles in the company. Work that was not part of these roles was eliminated.

Changing the Organizational Culture An important element in reducing the negative consequences of stress is that the organizational culture makes stress management an important part of every employee's job, provides programs to help employees cope with stress, and does not punish employees for using programs available to them (such as flexible schedules) to reduce stress. For example, in the chemical industry organizations are teaching employees about unsafe conditions and encouraging them to fix the conditions or report them. Organizations made up of employees in the helping profession are training employees to reduce burnout. These programs involve enabling employees to set more reasonable expectations about what they can do for their customers (patients, students, community members), teaching them to look at their job demands as opportunities for personal growth and challenge rather than barriers, and teaching them relaxation techniques so they can better handle work strains.[53]

Corporations are adopting more permissive work policies as a way to reduce stress. At Text 100, an $18 million international public relations agency, employees get two "duvet days" in addition to vacation and sick time. What does that mean? If employees don't feel like getting out of bed, they simply call in, take a "duvet day," and then sink back under the covers, no questions asked.[54] Other examples include the Netscape Communications "take your pet to work day" and Patagonia's encouraging its staff to use lunch breaks to go mountain biking or surfing.[55]

Organizations are also trying to structure work relationships to facilitate creativity and reduce stress. For example, at Monsanto Corporation, the "two in the box" system pairs a scientist with a marketing or financial specialist in critical management positions.[56] By joining research and development with commercial specialists, Monsanto is hoping to develop breakthrough genetic technologies and reduce the time it takes to bring them to customers. "Box buddies" earn the same pay, bonuses, and benefits. Besides the competitive advantage of "box buddies," the relationships help employees deal with personal demands. The employee knows that work is not going undone because his "box buddy" is attending to it.

A hostile work environment can often be created by "toxic managers." Exhibit 14.9 shows examples of toxic manager behaviors. It is important to recognize that the behaviors shown in Exhibit 14.9 are the opposite of the

exhibit | **14.9**

Examples of Behavior of "Toxic Managers"

Toxic Managers

- Take no responsibility for the impact of their behavior on others.
- Make decisions based on their own convenience.
- Are rigid and controlling.
- Lie to employees.
- Escape through drugs and alcohol.
- Have poor social skills.
- Fixate on one idea or person.
- Act out anger rather than discuss problems.
- Behave differently than they say they will.

Source: Based on L. McClure, *Risky Business* (Haworth Press, 1996).

qualities of charismatic and transformational leaders discussed in Chapter 11. How can toxic managers be identified? Organizations can provide anonymous hotlines for employees to communicate problems with their bosses, use employee attitude surveys, or multisource performance reviews, such as 360-degree feedback. At Spring Engineering in Livonia, Michigan, the company president used 360-degree performance reviews—reviews that were completed by managers, their boss, and their subordinates.[57] The review covered qualities like listening, empathy, and awareness. This type of evaluation identifies managers who are creating a stressful work environment and can be used to identify what types of skills should be the focus of training and performance improvement goals for the manager. If managers are unwilling or unable to change their behaviors, then they should be transferred out of a management position or terminated.

Balancing Work and Life   Organizations use three ways to help employees balance work and life: changing when, where, and who performs work; providing dependent care programs; and training managers to support the use of work-life balance programs.

One way organizations can help employees balance work and life is by considering changes that can reduce or eliminate stress related to when work is performed, where work is performed, and who performs the work.[58] Flexible work schedules include working at home, part-time work, a compressed workweek, or flextime. *Flextime* is a work schedule that requires employees to work a certain number of "core hours" but gives them a choice when to start and end work. A **compressed work schedule** refers to a schedule that compresses the workweek into fewer than five days by increasing the number of hours the employee is required to work each day. For example, employees may be required to work four 10-hour days. Job sharing and work at home are less common options than flextime and part-time work.[59] *Job sharing* refers to having two employees divide the hours, responsibilities, and benefits of a full-time job.

Using employee focus groups and an 800-number hotline, BankAmerica asked its employees how their jobs could be changed to improve their personal and work lives. The company adopted many of the suggestions, including reducing overtime work and cutting unimportant reporting and administrative tasks. Hewlett-Packard was losing talented employees in its computer service group because they were being forced to answer cus-

compressed work schedule

A schedule that compresses the workweek into fewer than five days by increasing the number of hours the employee is required to work each day. For example, employees may be required to work four 10-hour days.

HOW WOULD YOU REDUCE ABSENTEEISM AND TURNOVER?

First Tennessee Bank faced serious problems with employee turnover and absenteeism. One estimate is that the bank lost $132,000 in productivity because employees stayed at home to care for sick children. The absenteeism and turnover problems also caused customer complaints. Customers said they wanted to see familiar faces when they visited the bank branches. They wanted to establish relationships with the employees who cared for their money. First Tennessee Bank does have wellness programs, an employee assistance program, and flexible benefits to help employees deal with work and life stress. The company also has vacation and absenteeism policies, but these policies give employees little flexibility. The company's vacation policy forces employees to take their vacation in two-week blocks. The absenteeism policy is equally strict—missing more than eight days in a 12-month period results in the employee being fired.

First Tennessee used task forces and surveys to help determine the causes of absenteeism and turnover. A task force of employees assigned to see how employees could become more involved in their children's education found that involvement was inhibited by the fact that employees had no say in their work schedules. An anonymous survey of managers found that they often faked being sick so that they could attend a family function. In task force meetings, employees told of leaving sick children at home alone and calling every 15 minutes to ensure they were okay, dissolving aspirin in a baby's bottle to bring down a fever so the child could go to day care, and being afraid to take a child with leukemia to therapy because of fear of losing their job.

1. What recommendations would you give First Tennessee Bank to help reduce the absenteeism and turnover problem?

2. How would you know if your recommendations were successful? That is, how would you determine whether they were effective?

Source: Based on G. Flynn, "First Tennessee National Corp.: Optimas Award Profile," *Workforce,* March 1997, pp. 68–74.

tomer service calls late at night and on weekends. As a result, the company decided to redesign work schedules, allowing employees to volunteer to work either during the week only or also on weekends. As a result, turnover rates decreased and customer response times improved. Deloitte & Touche's Pittsburgh office is using part-time work to help employees balance work and life. Some auditors work part-time schedules, but they are expected to work longer hours when demands for tax preparation increase. In return, they get more time off during less busy periods. Research shows that flextime and compressed workweek schedules have a positive impact on productivity, performance, job satisfaction, and absenteeism.[60]

Shift workers have specific concerns that organizations need to address.[61] Shift workers may work steady afternoon or nighttime hours or rotate shifts. Shift employees are concerned with personal safety when entering and leaving the workplace at night. They may experience problems of alertness because they are working against the body's natural rhythms that make us tired during early morning hours, may feel that they can't get access to training and other programs offered from 8 a.m. to 5 p.m., and may experience digestive problems. Shift work also allows no time for a social life and makes child care or eldercare more difficult to find. Minimizing the use of rotating shift schedules, providing Web-based training that is accessible 24 hours a day, allowing shift workers to take naps, and providing caffeinated drinks and light snacks are some things that organizations are doing to help shift workers cope with the stress of their work schedule.

Another way that organizations help employees balance work and life is by providing programs that are directed at helping them take care of

eldercare

Care for an aging or ill parent.

children or elders. **Eldercare** refers to care for an aging or ill parent. The need for eldercare is expected to grow as the baby boomers (those born between the years 1946 and 1962) reach 65 years old. One estimate is that within the next five years, 37 percent of employees will be more concerned with caring for an elder than for a child. It is estimated that 40 percent of organizations are currently offering assistance with elders.[62]

Eldercare can cause severe stress for employees who are faced with becoming a parent for their parents.[63] Having to care for an elder also forces employees to think about the death of their parents and consider the end of their own lives. Work interruptions for elderly parents are more sudden and can be more catastrophic. Losing a babysitter is different than having to help your parent recover from and cope with a stroke. The most frequent type of eldercare offered by organizations is resource and referral services to identify health care providers, assisted living complexes, and retirement communities. Cendant Mortgage Corporation, located in New Jersey, provides counselors who help employees with everything from infant care to college planning, helping with teens, and finding eldercare.[64] Because Cendant's workforce is young, quality child care is an important employee need. Cendant makes referrals to over a dozen child care centers in the area and is building an on-site child care facility.

Finally, regardless of the work-life balance programs and policies that organizations make available to employees, employees will not use them if they believe their pay or career will be damaged. Organizations need to train managers to understand that employee use of programs to balance work and life should not be punished. Research shows that the more a manager is willing to listen to employees' problems and offer solutions based on the company's work-life balance programs, the less work-family conflict employees experience.[65] Consider the commitment that Eastman Kodak makes to helping employees balance work and life by training and rewarding managers.

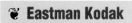

Eastman Kodak

Kodak trains managers to understand all of the work-life balance resources that the company offers. Flexible arrangements can involve working any place, any hours, and on any schedule as long as three conditions are met. First, the flexible arrangement cannot have a negative impact on business operations. Second, the immediate supervisor must approve the plan. Third, if the plan must be reviewed by another level of management, it must be approved.

The managers' training course focuses on how to work with flexible arrangements without having them adversely affect business operations. It is the employee's responsibility to make the business case for the flexible arrangement and to convince the manager that it can be successful. Employees use a booklet provided by Kodak to help create a proposal for a flexible arrangement. The proposal is used by the manager and employee to guide them through a discussion of the pitfalls and advantages of different work arrangements. Kodak's performance measurement system also reinforces its commitment to work-life balance. A part of managers' pay is based on their support for diversity and work life balance. Employees have the opportunity to evaluate how satisfied they are with their managers. One area relates specifically to how helpful the manager is to the employee's understanding of what work-life balance programs are available and how to use them.[66]

Individual Strategies

In addition to organization-sponsored programs, employees can do much themselves to manage stress.

- You need to enjoy what you do and keep it all in perspective.

- I find that taking a couple of days off (alone!) to chill out and just do nothing helps tremendously.

- Start putting more of an emphasis on things that bring you enjoyment and incorporate that at work. How about fresh flowers on your desk? A special Monet print in a gilt frame on your wall? A special note from a loved one stuck up on your computer?

- No matter how good you are, you can only accomplish so much. Set priorities and learn to let the things least important fall through the cracks. You cannot accomplish everything.

- Don't let yourself be the dumping ground for everyone's problems. Make sure that the problems that should be addressed at the supervisory level are being addressed there.

- I find that exercise is very helpful, or even getting outside for half an hour in the middle of the day.

- Don't lose your sense of humor. If that goes, it's time to get out.

exhibit | **14.10**

How to Avoid Stress and Burnout

Source: From L. Grensing-Pophal, "HR, Heal Thyself," *HR Magazine,* March 1999, pp. 82–88.

Exercise, Relaxation, and Meditation A variety of techniques help individuals manage stress. Among the most basic strategies are those that help people stay healthy: exercising regularly, getting plenty of rest, and eating a healthful diet. One study found that employees who used a company-provided health and fitness club reported they felt better both physically and psychologically compared with employees who did not use the facility.[67] Relaxation, meditation, and time off also help people cope with stress and burnout.[68] Exhibit 14.10 provides advice from human resource practitioners regarding how to avoid stress and burnout. Time off is a valuable investment when it allows employees to approach their tasks with renewed energy and a fresh perspective when they return to work.

Nan K. Chase faced a challenge peculiar to business owners: taking time off for herself. Chase, a consultant and freelance writer, loved her work so much that she was neglecting her family life. She found the solution in her Jewish roots: the Sabbath, a weekly day of rest. She began organizing her time so that she could treat each Sabbath day as a mini-vacation, refusing to discuss work even with her husband. As a result, not only did Chase rejuvenate her family relationships, but her more focused work efforts allowed her to double her income within a year.[69]

Telegroup instituted a meditation class to help its employees learn to cope with stress.

❣ Telegroup

Telegroup is an emerging multinational carrier of long-distance telecommunication services. Superior customer service, excellent rates, and state-of-the-art services have helped the company be recognized as one of the fastest growing companies in the United States. Telegroup has a low turnover rate and a drug-free work environment. Chairman Fred Gratzon believes that transcendental meditation (TM) has contributed to a healthier work environment for employees. TM is a type of mantra meditation. Mantra meditation requires the participant to focus on a sound, such as one word or a combination of words (said aloud or repeated to oneself) between 20 and 30 minutes, twice a day. Telegroup started offering classes in transcendental meditation in 1990. Employees hear about the classes as soon as they are hired. They can learn more about TM on the company's intranet. The company pays 80 percent of the $1,000 course fee. Ellen Jones, director of human resources, believes that as a result of TM she has observed better relationships between employees, reduced health care costs, and less absenteeism. Ms. Jones meditates twice a day for 20 minutes. She says, "I can maintain my sense of self and summon the right response spontaneously."[70]

Developing a Social Support System   Individuals need to develop a strong network of work colleagues, friends, and family members who can listen to their problems and provide support and encouragement. Individuals may also want to seek out a **mentor,** a more senior employee in the company who can provide guidance, positive regard, and acceptance.

mentor

A more senior employee in the company who can provide guidance, positive regard, and acceptance.

Time Management   Many employees feel "stressed out" because they have a large amount of work and life demands to meet. Time management involves prioritizing tasks or demands from "must be performed" to "would be nice to do" or optional. The tasks and demands that "must be performed" are completed first before moving on to the less important and optional tasks. Time management helps employees gain more personal control, which helps to buffer or reduce the negative consequences of stressors.

Increasing Personal Control   Individuals can reduce the potentially harmful consequences of stress by taking more control of or responsibility for their lives. One way to do this is to learn to monitor your own stress level. Stress levels can be increased if you are bored or decreased if you feel too tense. For example, if you are not feeling motivated by a task, you need to "psych yourself up." You can do this by focusing on the importance or urgency of the task, setting a challenging goal, using positive suggestion, or performing a job in small parts, drawing satisfaction from completing each part.

Another way to increase personal control is to try to control when important events are scheduled in order to avoid role overload. Consider the readjustment required by adding a new family member. A new birth likely requires one or both family members to take a leave from work, can result in sleep deprivation, and means less freedom for the new parents to spontaneously attend activities such as sporting events, concerts, or restaurants and clubs. Some couples are trying to reduce the adjustment required by childbirth by timing pregnancies around workplace needs.[71] For example, they try to avoid giving birth around big project deadlines or at times when coworkers are on family leave. After finishing a big project, Lisa Yee and her husband, owners of Magic Pencil Studios, a design and advertising concern, headed for Italy to conceive a baby, with the hope of delivering the child before their next project was due.

A third way to increase your personal control over stress is to, whenever possible, observe your environment and ask questions to help you make career and job choices and decisions that create the optimum level of stress for you. For example, Peg Primak challenged the accepted norm that anyone holding a management job has to put in 60 hours per week.[72] She cut back her hours to 40 a week while supervising a seven-person engineering group at GTE Internetworking, located in Burlington, Massachusetts. Then she decided to work only 30 hours a week after her son was born. She says, "While my shorter work hours go against the grain, at least here it's possible to convince people to ask, 'Did she get the job done?' rather than ask, 'How many hours is she working?'"

College students are asking more pointed questions about how people work together and how employees are treated before they accept a job.[73] Kevin Renham, director of recruitment marketing for Johnson & Johnson, says recruits ask, "Is it [the job] going to suck the life out of me?" Students are also skeptical of the answers recruiters give them, so they are using creative means to find out how demanding a job might be. Students at California State University who were interested in working for Intel had observed that the parking lot of the company's Folsom, California, facility was full late into the evening. Some students concluded that long hours must be routine and decided not to interview with Intel because a job with long hours would be too stressful for them. Other savvy college students are asking campus recruiters about how much pressure there is to meet project deadlines and how the company views work-life balance.

apply it

1. What do you do to manage the stress you face in your life? Describe the formal or informal activities or programs that you use to manage stress.

summary OF KEY CONCEPTS

- **Individuals adapt to stress in different ways.** Stress is a response to uncertainty and lack of personal control. Not all stress is bad, and too little stress causes boredom and low performance. A high level of stress can result in health problems, poor attitudes, and poor job performance. A moderate level of stress, known as eustress, energizes and motivates employees. Stress initially causes arousal and excitement (alarm response), which the individual resists. Resistance may be followed by physical and psychological exhaustion if the stress continues.

- **Stress is caused by organization changes and demands of jobs, roles, life experiences, and interpersonal relationships.** Changes in organizational strategy and structure cause stress for individuals by forcing them to relocate, work with more diverse colleagues, handle new types of work, or even lose their jobs. Stress can also be caused by job demands such as physically strenuous work, tight deadlines, information overload, uncertainty as to what tasks are most important (role ambiguity), or competing demands for work time (role conflict). Stress can also be caused by factors outside the job or workplace. Life events such as a death in the family or purchase of a new house can cause stress. Also, work and life can interfere with each other because of conflict, strain, and behavioral demands. Interpersonal relationships may also cause stress when personal goals or personalities clash.

- **The consequences of stress vary depending on an individual's personality and social support.**

Personality differences influence how individuals respond to stress. Individuals who are extremely competitive and aggressive (Type A) tend to be vulnerable to the negative consequences of stress. Individuals who tend to focus on the negative aspects of life, are self-evaluative, and angry and fearful (who have negative affectivity) tend to experience more psychological and physical problems from stress. Individuals who do not believe they can control their work and nonwork lives, that is, who lack personal control, experience more negative consequences of stress. Positive relationships with coworkers and family members result in strong social support, which can provide resistance to the harmful consequences of stress.

- **Stress can negatively affect performance, attitudes, behavior, and health.** Stress can result in poor performance, negative work attitudes, counterproductive and withdrawal behaviors (theft, absenteeism), and health problems such as ulcers, headaches, and high blood pressure. Stress can also cause burnout, characterized by emotional exhaustion, depersonalization, and the belief that accomplishments are unimportant.

- **Stress management is the responsibility of both the organization and the individual.** Organizations use several strategies to manage stress. They may make counseling available to employees through an employee assistance program. Organizations may also try to create a work culture that is more relaxing and appealing to employees by changing the physical work environment and eliminating bad managers. Wellness programs help employees manage stress by promoting healthy eating habits, exercise, education about the causes and consequences of stress, and early detection of physical health problems. Flexible schedules and dependent care assistance can help employees balance work and life. Organizations undergoing downsizing need to provide outplacement for employees who are losing their jobs as well as support for survivors. Individuals can actively manage stress through exercise, relaxation, meditation, and developing a network of friends and family members who can provide social support. Individuals can increase the personal control they have over their lives by making decisions that avoid role overload and create optimum stress levels.

KEY terms

stress, p. 481

stressors, p. 481

eustress, p. 483

task demands, p. 485

workaholism, p. 485

physical demands, p. 486

data smog, p. 486

role demands, p. 487

time-based conflict, p. 489

strain-based conflict, p. 489

behavior-based conflict, p. 489

Type A behavior, p. 490

negative affectivity, p. 491

personal control, p. 491

social support, p. 491

well-being, p. 491

burnout, p. 492

workers' compensation claims, p. 493

employee assistance programs (EAPs), p. 495

wellness programs, p. 495

downsizing, p. 497

survivors, p. 497

compressed work schedule, p. 500

eldercare, p. 502

mentor, p. 504

DISCUSSION questions

1. In what ways can stress have positive consequences?

2. Explain the physiological process through which people respond to stress.

3. What aspects of a person's job can cause stress?

4. What is workaholism? How can an organization unknowingly promote workaholism?

5. How can a manager be a major cause of stress for employees?

6. What is burnout? Explain why entrepreneurs and employees in caring professions such as nursing or mental health might be more susceptible to burnout than employees in other jobs.

7. Suppose an employee comes to you and says, "I am stressed out—do you have any ideas how I can reduce my stress level?" What would you tell her?

8. How does work-life conflict cause stress? What are organizations doing to reduce the stress employees experience trying to balance work and life?

9. What should an organization look at if it is trying to evaluate how its culture might contribute to stress?

10. How do organizations benefit from wellness programs?

SELF-DISCOVERY exercise

Are You a Type A Personality?

Rate the extent to which each of the following statements is typical of you most of the time. There are no right or wrong answers.

3 The statement is typical of me.
2 The statement is somewhat typical of me.
1 The statement is not at all typical of me.

____ 1. My greatest satisfaction comes from doing things better than others.

____ 2. I tend to bring the theme of a conversation around to things I'm interested in.

____ 3. In conversations, I frequently clench my fist, bang on the table, or pound one fist into the palm of the other for emphasis.

___ **4.** I move, walk, and eat rapidly.

___ **5.** I feel as though I can accomplish more than others.

___ **6.** I feel guilty when I relax or do nothing for several hours or days.

___ **7.** It doesn't take much to get me to argue.

___ **8.** I feel impatient with the rate at which most events take place.

___ **9.** Having more than others is important to me.

___ **10.** One aspect of my life (e.g., work, family care, school) dominates all others.

___ **11.** I frequently regret not being able to control my temper.

___ **12.** I hurry the speech of others by saying "Uh huh," "Yes, yes," or by finishing their sentences for them.

___ **13.** People who avoid competition have low self-confidence.

___ **14.** To do something well, you have to concentrate on it alone and screen out all distractions.

___ **15.** I feel others' mistakes and errors cause me needless aggravation.

___ **16.** I find it intolerabble to watch others perform tasks I know I can do faster.

___ **17.** Getting ahead in my job is a major personal goal.

___ **18.** I simply don't have enough time to lead a well-balanced life.

___ **19.** I take out my frustration with my own imperfections on others.

___ **20.** I frequently try to do two or more things simultaneously.

___ **21.** When I encounter a competitive person, I feel a need to challenge him or her.

___ **22.** I tend to fill up my spare time with thoughts and activities related to my work (or school or family care).

___ **23.** I am frequently upset by the unfairness of life.

___ **24.** I find it anguishing to wait in line.

The Type A personality consists of four behavioral tendencies: extreme competitiveness, significant life imbalance (typically coupled with high work involvement), strong feelings of hostility and anger, and an extreme sense of urgency and impatience.

Scores above 12 in each area suggest this is a pronounced tendency.

Research suggests that the hostility aspect of the Type A personality is the most damaging to personal health.

Competitiveness		Life Imbalance (Work Involvement)		Hostility/Anger		Impatience/Urgency	
Item	*Score*	*Item*	*Score*	*Item*	*Score*	*Item*	*Score*
1	_____	2	_____	3	_____	4	_____
5	_____	6	_____	7	_____	8	_____
9	_____	10	_____	11	_____	12	_____
13	_____	14	_____	15	_____	16	_____
17	_____	18	_____	19	_____	20	_____
21	_____	22	_____	23	_____	24	_____
Total	☐	Total	☐	Total	☐	Total	☐

TOTAL SCORE ☐

Source: Based on M. Friedman and R. Rosenman, *Type A Behavior and Your Heart* (New York: Alfred A. Knopf, 1974).

ORGANIZATIONAL BEHAVIOR in your life

Keeping a diary is a good way to find out what causes you stress and what level of stress you prefer. In your "stress diary," note your stress levels and how you feel each day. For each day, note the amount of stress you feel (perhaps using a scale from 1 to 10), how happy you feel, and whether you are enjoying work and school. Identify stressful events that occur each day. Write down each stressful event. When and where did it occur? What factors made the event stressful? How did you handle the event? Keep the diary for two or three days. Review the diary at the end of three days and answer the following questions:

1. What level of stress are you the happiest with?
2. What level of stress allows you to work most effectively?
3. What are the main sources of stress in your life?
4. What strategies do you find most effective for managing stress?

ORGANIZATIONAL BEHAVIOR news flash

Many companies are trying to start programs to help employees balance work and life. Some argue that these programs are not helpful because they don't contribute to the "bottom line" and discriminate against employees who do not have dependents. Using your search engine, find articles that show how work-life programs contribute to the "bottom line." One useful Web site is www.workfamily.com, a clearinghouse of articles about work and family practices.

global diversity EVENTS

There are cultural differences in how people cope with stress. For example, some countries have many more legal holidays than does the United States, allowing employees more time to get away from work stresses. U.S. employees must typically have 25 to 30 years of service before they receive as much paid vacation as all employees receive in some Western European countries. Sweden has a liberal family leave policy for both parents when a new child is born. Some countries, such as France, have laws taxing employers heavily if they lay off employees.

Using the news listings on your search engine, such as Reuters, AP, ZDNet News, or others, look for stories about what organizations in other countries are doing to help reduce the stress employees are experiencing on the job and lower the costs of stress. These stories can deal with government policies on time off and family or medical leave or a non–U.S. organization and its efforts to help employees cope with stress.

minicase ISSUE

Entrepreneurs Need to Manage Stress

Stressed Out. Seph Barnard, founder of Tape Resources, a 13-person company that distributes audiotape and videotape to television stations and production companies, was happy to find a letter in the mail from an investment banking firm stating that a larger corporation was interested in acquiring his company. Barnard knew that selling the company would bring him at least $2 million, which would provide financial security for his family.

At 43 years old, Barnard felt he had reached the breaking point. Years of working long hours and worrying about every detail of the company had left him exhausted. "When you feel fatigued, you don't care anymore," says Barnard. "Just take the company and give me something for it. I could get rid of my worries and end up with money."

Entrepreneurs usually start companies to find a new market. Achieving success, they usually give up managing day-to-day operations to an outsider and concentrate on broader strategic issues or move to their next start-up opportunity. To make that decision, they have to find out which parts of the business are exciting and which parts are draining and stressful. Entrepreneurs who don't know the answers to these questions, such as Barnard, may place their company and themselves in danger when they are forced to deal with an illness or family crisis that their exhaustion and immersion in their company has caused.

Handling Every Detail. For three years, Barnard worked hard to make the company a success, taking charge of the direct marketing efforts to expand the company's customer base. Barnard also wrote each employee's check, examined each invoice, and made every significant decision. He rarely took time away from the business. When he did go on vacation, it was always related to attending a conference. He had isolated himself in the business, and he had no hobbies.

Opening a satellite office in Houston also added to his stress. He commuted back and forth to Houston, but he still could not solve all the problems. He would lie awake at night thinking about the frustrations of running the Houston office. He became more and more dissatisfied with his job, but he wasn't able to keep his mind off work. Eating dinner, he often found himself thinking about work. Too tired to look for new challenges to help solve his problems, he instead focused on minute issues such as how to save money by teaching employees how to tear off an invoice from a printer.

The moment of Truth. Now, struggling over the decision whether to sell the company, Barnard realized that selling would not solve all of his problems. It might eliminate some of his stress, but he would lose the company that he built.

1. Is Barnard experiencing burnout? Explain.

2. What should Barnard do to reduce the stress he is experiencing? Can he change his job demands? What individual stress management strategies might he use?

3. How might having an "entrepreneurial spirit" predispose, or make it easier for, individuals to experience negative stress?

Source: Based on S. Solomon, "Fit to Be Tied," *Inc.,* October 15, 1999.

video CASE

SOUTHWEST AIRLINES—WHERE EVERYONE'S PART OF THE TEAM

With 20,000 employees, Southwest Airlines flies with a full complement of groups, both formal and informal. Yet founder and CEO Herb Kelleher likes to emphasize that everyone who works for Southwest, from pilot to ramp agent, is a member of the same team, equally empowered to make decisions.

Training in group interaction and teamwork is continuous at Southwest. In one session, a trainer gives out a group assignment in which teams of participants are to find a way to protect a raw egg from an eight-foot drop to the ground "wherein there is no cracking, breaking, leaking or spewing of your egg. Your egg must remain sound and intact." Sound silly? Not at all. Team members must work together to complete the task within a seven-minute time frame. They must think quickly and work together, just as they might on the job. At the end of the exercise, the instructor reveals, "It didn't matter if your egg broke or stayed intact. . . . All I'm suggesting is no matter how impossible the task is, if you put your mind to it, and if you put your collective minds to it, you can get it accomplished."

Southwest employees learn that, as part of a group, their role is to do "whatever it takes" to offer the best service to their customers. "Our employees are encouraged to be creative and innovative, to break the rules when they need to in order to provide good service to our customers," explains Libby Sartain, vice-president of people at Southwest. One employee intervened when a young passenger encountered difficulty with the ticketless system and offered to pay the girl's fare. Some experts might argue that these practices could lead to role overload or role ambiguity, in which employees feel either overwhelmed by the scope of expectations or simply unsure of what they are supposed to do. But Southwest workers seem to thrive in their roles as decision makers and leaders.

Since a portion of Southwest's workforce is unionized, these employees are automatically members of two groups: the company and the union. Although this may lead to role conflict at other organizations, Southwest employees enjoy a positive relationship between the two groups. "We don't talk about labor-management relationships at Southwest Airlines," says Kelleher. "We eschew the words 'labor' and 'management' as much as possible because the very utilization of those words, in my estimation, sets up two different groups within the company with two different labels." Southwest has never had layoffs, the annual employee-turnover rate is one of the lowest in the industry, and only one work stoppage has occurred in the company's 25-year history; it lasted a single day.

Herb Kelleher believes that to maintain his organization's success, he needs to shakes things up periodically—break a few eggs, so to speak. He likes to do this in group meetings or forums. "I told some of our people one day . . . 'We're going into this room and I'll tell you what: if somebody doesn't smash something by the time we leave, I'm going to be extremely disappointed, because I want to see passion in the projection of your ideas.'" Kelleher doesn't allow notebooks or calculators in his meetings; he prefers people to "bring their brains and brainstorm. . . . That's a very rejuvenating thing; that's a constant process of refreshment because you're reassessing. And, as a consequence of that, you're doing new things all the time."

Questions

1. Do you think Herb Kelleher's emphasis on teamwork and leadership among his workers creates synergy at Southwest? Why or why not?

2. Describe several norms that might have developed during the training session in which teams were asked to develop protection for their eggs.

Source: Southwest Web site, **www.iflyswa.com;** "Herb Kelleher: Practical Joker Still Flying High," *Financial Times,* **www.ft.com,** accessed May 12, 2000; Steve Salerno, "Laughing All the Way," *Worth Online,* 1999, **www.worth.com;** "1999 Chief Executive of the Year," *Chief Executive,* 1999, **www.chiefexecutive.net,** "Staying Smart," *Fortune,* January 11, 1999, **www.fortune.com.**

video CASE

CENTEX BUILDS ITS REPUTATION ON COMMUNICATION

Building homes is an emotional business. Building office complexes and theme parks is an expensive business. For half a century, Centex has managed to do both, growing to the point where it is now the country's largest and most geographically diverse home builder and the fifth largest general building contractor.

Centex's blueprint for success is surprisingly simple: communication. "I think in any company, the communication philosophy has to come from the top," says Sheila Gallagher, vice-president of corporate communications. True, but the company believes effective communication works both ways. Employees at all levels of the company, members of the supply chain, and customers need to be able to communicate their messages—ideas, questions, frustrations, and satisfactions—to just about anyone within the company.

Centex uses a range of channels for both internal and external formal communication. These channels vary in richness, but each is appropriate for the task. "Many of us spend a lot of time on the phone talking to [outside analysts and the media], keeping them updated on a weekly basis about the company," says Gallagher. As in many organizations, there are plenty of in-person meetings, which allow personal exchange of information. "We have people come in to the office to meet with our executives here and take them on tours of our projects, and really just try to be absolutely accessible," continues Gallagher. Technology has opened new channels, including the Internet. "We are establishing home pages, on the corporate level . . . and for each major division in home building, contracting, and mortgage, so we can reach potential customers that way." In addition, Centex has recently joined forces with several other companies to create an online business exchange called HomebuildersXchange, which will connect homebuilders, trade contractors, distributors, wholesalers, and manufacturers for e-commerce and information exchange.

Centex uses written communication in the form of an annual report to inform stockholders and other interested parties about company activities. The company distributes about 35,000 copies of the annual report, including mailing a copy to each employee at home. Then there's the corporate newsletter called "Sometimes" (because it is published intermittently), which "captures all kinds of information about the company, what's going on financially, new projects we may be building, new markets we may be going into," says Gallagher. Finally, there's the building community brochure that describes the organization's charitable efforts, including Habitat for Humanity. The brochure informs not only company members but also the general public about Centex's charitable projects.

During periods of uncertainty, including changes in healthcare benefits or the acquisition of other companies, informal communication flows freely through the grapevine. To make sure employees received accurate information during one restructuring effort, managers put together a slide show for employees illustrating organizational plans and answering as many questions as possible.

Because Centex is spread across such a wide geographical area, many communication efforts are decentralized. So managers get together regularly at regional and subregional levels to discuss strategies, engage in training, and so forth. "And also, we do have meetings at a national level," says John Lile, vice president of Centex Homes. In addition, every month or so an executive gets together with ten or fifteen employees for a "fishbowl" luncheon, during which employees can ask questions and share ideas. At Centex, communication builds the foundation for trust. It's a tool that works.

Questions

1. Do you think you might encounter filtering at a company like Centex? Why or why not?

2. How might the grapevine actually benefit communication at Centex?

Source: Centex Web site, at **www.centex.com.** accessed May 2000; "U.S. Homebuilders Form Online Business Exchange," Reuters Limited, May 4, 2000; Heather McCune, "Housing Giants," *Professional Builder,* 1999, **www.housingzone.com.**

video CASE

MAKING DECISIONS FOR SUCCESS

Running a successful company involves making many decisions every day. Whether it's deciding to expand globally, to add or delete a product line, where to locate a facility, or what type of computer system to purchase, each decision contributes to the ultimate success of the organization. All of the decisions just mentioned are nonprogrammed decisions; that is, they require more thought in order to reach a conclusion. But workers at organizations also make daily programmed decisions as part of their jobs, such as how much sauce to use when making a large pizza.

Several companies stand out in their industries because of the creativity they apply to the process of decision making. Yahoo! founders David Filo and Jerry Yang acted on intuition when they decided to turn their hobby into an Internet search engine. Drew Pearson Companies suffered the consequences of a poor decision when it decided to sell its athletic wear to a discount market. Paradigm software developers had to solve the problem that its initial product was too complicated and too expensive for customers. And Patrick Esquerré, founder of la Madeleine bakery and restaurants, had to figure out where to put his bakery.

Of course, none of the founders or managers in the companies was operating in a totally certain environment. Each faced degrees of risk and uncertainty, but most entrepreneurs enjoy this sort of challenge. Some had enough information available to make analytic decisions; others, like Jerry Yang and David Filo of Yahoo!, used the availability heuristic and took a chance, because that's all they could do in a completely new industry. In effect, they were pioneers. "We realized that there weren't really any good tools out there to help you find what you were looking for," recalls Filo. "There was no organization of the Web. And so just for ourselves, we started things." Drew Pearson fell prey to the representative heuristic when he and his managers decided to sell some of their sportswear products to convenience stores, undercutting one of their best customers, JCPenney. Doing so, says Steven Bonham, sportswear buyer for Penney, "lowered the value of our inventory." Learning from this mistake, the company chose to diversify its product lines.

Wes Hoffman and David Gatchel found themselves with a frustrating problem: they had developed a terrific new software simulation product, but no one could afford it—the software ran $80,000 and the hardware to run it cost around $300,000. But an opportunity for their company, Paradigm, to design software for Nintendo launched them in a completely new direction. So they reevaluated their original vision and decided to commit themselves completely to the computer game industry. Now they have contracts with Nintendo, Electronic Arts, Infogames, Warner Brothers, and others.

Patrick Esquerré, founder and CEO of La Madeleine French Bakery and Cafes, didn't know a thing about baking or running restaurants when he emigrated form France to Texas. Of course, he wasn't a Texan either—so he didn't know what his new neighbors would think of a French bakery stuck in the middle of Dallas. How did he decide to locate his new bakery on a Dallas street corner? "I sat on the sidewalk of what was going to be my future bakery," he recalls. "There was a supermarket on one side, and a laundry on the other side, and people were walking from one to the other." He simply stopped passersby and described his idea to them, then asked for their ideas on menu and decor. "This was in fact the way La Madeleine was built," he remembers. "We tried to tailor the concept of La Madeleine to the way that our guests told us they wanted it to be."

Questions

1. Do you think that Patrick Esquerré's method of establishing his bakery was an example of good rational decision making? Why or why not?

2. Choose one of the companies described and create a list of programmed decisions that managers in the organization could use to increase the efficiency of decision making.

Source: Company Web sites, www. lamadeleine.com, www.multigen.com (Multigen-Paradigm), www.yahoo.com, all accessed May 2000.

integrative CASE

PART THREE

AOL: BUILDING A GLOBAL MEDIUM THROUGH INDIVIDUAL AND GROUP EFFORT

AMERICA ONLINE AOL is the quintessential group of groups. It operates through a variety of formal groups, informal groups, and teams, from its own business units, like the Interactive Services Group and AOL International; to subsidiaries, like CompuServe; and its numerous strategic alliances with companies like Sun Microsystems. All of these groups and team were formed to focus on its singular mission: "to build a global medium as central to people's lives as the telephone or television . . . and even more valuable."

The team structure is central to AOL. "With one mission and many champions, we offer an incredible environment that is unlike anything. Anywhere," boasts the company Web site. Product development teams work to develop new products and services continually for AOL's 22 million customers. And employees' input and creativity is not only recognized but encouraged. "At America Online, our team structure allows people to shine, to be heard, and to draw strength from their collective intelligence. It's how ideas are sparked and invention comes to life. It's how AOL started. And it's how we continue to build our AOL family of brands," notes the Web site.

Task force teams look for ways to increase the company's involvement in the community, through specific efforts such Read Across America, a project that, in conjunction with such organizations as The National Education Association and First Book, encourages children to read. In addition, groups of AOL volunteers recently joined forces with PowerUp and Youth Service America to help needy children achieve computer literacy and access to the Internet.

The company also fosters the formation of informal groups that may develop through company gatherings such as meetings, picnics, and holiday parties that include employees and their families. This philosophy dovetails with AOL's efforts at stress management through quality of life programs that include stress and time management classes, memberships at health clubs, recreational activities, parenting pro-

grams such as Mother and Me and financial aid toward adoption, and services aimed at helping employees handle dependent care situations.

Despite the organization's emphasis on teamwork, the organization has had its struggles with power and politics, as well as leadership. Though he cofounded AOL, Steve Case has not always had power. In fact, during one of the company's crises, Case was gently ousted by AOL's then-chairman, Jim Kimsey, because, as Kimsey explained, AOL's venture capitalists felt skittish about backing a company run by such a young (age thirty-three) executive. Case had the further disadvantage of a boyish face, which made him look even younger than he was. But even during such a low point, Case displayed the traits of leadership that he is known for: integrity, self-confidence, and intelligence. He stepped aside temporarily for the long-term success of the company. Now Case is back at the helm of AOL not only with maturity and restored power but with a following among employees and investors. His leadership behavior tends to be supportive and participative. "I don't think there's any danger of megalomania with Steve," says Kimsey.

In an environment where technology is changing daily and experts have begun to talk about a "new economy," many of the decisions made by Case and AOL managers involve both risk and uncertainty. Add the company's goal to be as indispensable to consumers worldwide as to those in the United States, and both decision-making conditions are magnified. Decisions about alliances with companies such as Blockbuster, Wal-Mart, and General Motors, along with the development of brands such as AOLMovieFone and iPlanet, which ideally require a thorough, rational process, sometimes have to be made much more quickly, with much less information than is desirable. And the outcomes are equally unclear. Case himself cites industry predictions that never came true: "Six years ago, Time Warner launched Pathfinder, and everybody thought the media companies would emerge as the dominant force, and that really didn't happen. Five years ago Microsoft was gearing up for the launch of MSN, and everybody said they'd kill us, and that didn't quite happen. And four years ago, the Web emerged, and everybody said ISPs [Internet service providers] are the future and AOL was the past, and that didn't really happen. Three years ago everybody said push technology was the next big thing, and that didn't really happen." So AOL continues to push in its own direction, developing relationships with organizations around the world that range from Bertelsmann AG to China.com, with whom AOL has launched a Chinese and English language service in Hong Kong. All decisions within the company lead back to AOL's mission: to build a global medium.

Questions

1. AOL believes that the team structure is valuable to the organization. What might be some of the "costs" of such an emphasis on teams?
2. What steps might AOL managers take to reduce risk and uncertainty in their decision making?
3. Do you think that Steve Case's leadership style is an effective one for AOL? Why or why not?
4. Visit AOL's Web site at www.corp.aol.com and browse throught the "Careers" section and the "Awesome Benefits" link to find out about its benefits programs. Do you think AOL's offering of such wide-ranging benefits to employees creates greater cohesiveness among workers and trust between the employees and the company? Why or why not?

Source: AOL Joins Forces with PowerUP & Youth Service America on Youth Service Day to Bridge the Digital Divide," April 14, 2000, and "Cat in the Hat Comes to Wall Street to Raise Awareness of Nationwide Literacy Campaign," February 29, 2000, company press releases, AOL Web site, www.corp.aol.com; William J. Holstein and Fred Vogelstein, "You've Got a Deal?" *U.S. News & World Report,* January 24, 2000, pp. 34–40; Fred Vogelstein, "The Talented Mr. Case," *U.S. News & World Report,* January 24, 2000, pp. 41–42; Tim Jones and Gary Marx, "Weaned on Crisis, Landing on Top," *Chicago Tribune,* January 16, 2000, sec. 1, p. 1; Jim Hu, "Case: AOL Alive and Well," *CNET News.com,* October 6, 1999, www.cnet.com.

part 4

Impact of Organizations on Behavior

fifteen
CHAPTER

15

Fundamentals of Organization Structure and Design

preview

After studying this chapter, you should be able to:

- Explain the key elements of organizing, including such concepts as work specialization, chain of command, line and staff, and span of management.

- Describe characteristics of functional, divisional, and matrix organization structures.

- Explain the contemporary horizontal and network approaches and why they are being adopted by organizations.

- Identify how structure can be used to achieve strategic goals and meet the needs of the environment.

- Describe how an organization's technology influences structure.

- Explain the difference between organic and mechanistic structures and discuss why organization structures are increasingly organic.

- Identify the impact of advanced electronic technology on organization design.

T he 21st-century organization may not look like anything your grandfather would recognize. Consider Australia's Lend Lease Corporation, a model of the emerging organization without boundaries. If you ask employees about the company's structure, they're likely to scratch their heads and say something like, "Well, it's a mystery."

Lend Lease, Australia's leading real estate company, has been in charge of developing some of the world's most spectacular buildings, including the Bluewater shopping complex in Kent, England, which transformed an industrial wasteland into a spectacular landmark. In addition, Lend Lease is a leader in mutual funds, computer and business services, and other lines of business. Considered the most exciting company to work for in Australia, Lend Lease attracts bright, talented young workers who know they'll be pushed beyond their comfort zones and given a chance to develop skills in many areas. Twenty-eight-year-old Susan MacDonald, for example, has had seven different jobs at Lend Lease. "The basic operating procedure here is that people don't stand on titles," she says. "They don't stand on position, and they don't stand on precedent. It's all about ideas. And it's all about credibility: How do you perform in the heat of a project?"

Lend Lease's organizing principle is project management. A new employee might be assigned a job as project manager on a small residential housing project, a couple of years later be running Australia's largest real estate investment trust, and then be assigned to transform Lend Lease's financial services operations in Indonesia. A project manager for a financial services project will find herself working with architects and engineers as well as actuaries and financial analysts.

There are no functional and hierarchical boundaries at Lend Lease. The first challenge for a project manager is to put together the best possible mix of mind-sets, skills, and experiences, which means including people from different functions and levels of the company, as well as representatives of outside stakeholders. This team, called a Project Control Group (PCG), serves as a sort of "board of directors." The PCG for the Bluewater project in Kent, England, for example, included a revolving collection of architects, engineers, managers, manufacturers, community advocates, planning authorities, construction experts, retail-delivery specialists, financial analysts, and potential customers. The project involved a 250-person development team, 40 contractors, hundreds of subcontractors, and more than 20,000 construction workers, but the PCG—and the project manager—were ultimately responsible for its success or failure.

With each new project, Lend Lease essentially reorganizes. People—including managers—are plucked from one area of expertise and moved to another very quickly. "This is a deliberate strategy," says Peter Scott, who was shifted in an instant from a job running one major project to one that gave him responsibility for *all* projects for the financial services division. "This place is fundamentally different today from what it was five years ago. That's why it's a great place to work."[1]

Australia's Lend Lease: Every Day, It's a New Place

> *"The basic operating procedure here is that people don't stand on titles. They don't stand on position, and they don't stand on precedent. It's all about ideas."*
>
> —**Susan MacDonald,** Lend Lease

Like Lend Lease, most large organizations in the 21st century will no doubt be much more fluid and adaptable than the traditional organizations with which we've become familiar. In turn, the people they employ will have to be much more flexible as well. At Lend Lease, people from wildly different backgrounds come together on a project and start with the question, "How can we do what's never been done before?" Although this new flexibility can be incredibly energizing, it can also be frightening. Many workers may have difficulty adjusting to the new demands and responsibilities created by shifts in organization structure.

In this chapter, we explore the theme of organization structure and design. Every organization faces the question of how to organize to best reflect its strategic direction and meet competitive challenges. Organizations have different structural and design characteristics, and these differences have an impact on employee behavior and attitudes. This chapter examines some basic principles of organizing, presents basic structural options, and reviews contingency factors that influence organization structure and design. In addition, we discuss how recent advances in electronic technology are influencing organization design. The chapter closes with a brief look at the learning organization on both a domestic and global scale.

Organization structure is reflected in the organization chart

organizing

The deployment of organizational resources, including human resources, to achieve strategic goals.

organization structure

The framework in which the organization defines how tasks are assigned to individuals and departments, resources are deployed, and departments are coordinated.

organization chart

The visual representation of a whole set of underlying activities and processes in an organization.

Organizing is the deployment of organizational resources, including human resources, to achieve strategic goals. This process leads to the creation of an organization structure, which defines the division of labor into specific departments and jobs, formal lines of authority, and mechanisms for coordinating diverse tasks. **Organization structure** is defined as (1) the set of formal tasks assigned to individuals and departments; (2) formal reporting relationships, including lines of authority, decision responsibility, number of hierarchical levels, and span of managers' control; and (3) the design of systems to ensure effective coordination of employees across departments.[2]

Organization structure is reflected in the organization chart. It isn't possible to "see" the internal structure of an organization the way we might see its manufacturing tools, offices, or products. Although we may see employees going about their duties, performing different tasks, and working in different locations, the only way to actually see the structure underlying all this activity is through the organization chart.[3] The **organization chart** is the visual representation of a whole set of underlying activities and processes in an organization. Exhibit 15.1 shows a sample organization chart. The organization chart can be quite useful in understanding how a company works. It shows the various parts of an organization, how they are interrelated, and how each position and department fits into the whole.

The concept of an organization chart—showing what positions exist, how they are grouped, and who reports to whom—has been around for centuries. For example, diagrams outlining church hierarchy can be found in medieval churches in Spain. However, the use of the organization chart for business stems largely from the Industrial Revolution and the era of scientific management, discussed in Chapter 1. As work grew more complex and was performed by greater and greater numbers of workers, there was a

exhibit | **15.1**

A Sample Organization Chart for a Soft Drink–Bottling Plant

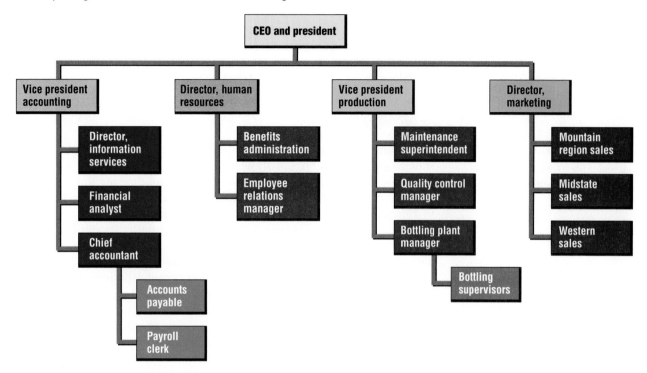

pressing need to develop ways of managing and controlling organizations. The type of organization structure that grew out of these efforts in the late 19th and early 20th centuries was one in which the CEO was placed at the top and everyone else was arranged in layers down below, as illustrated in Exhibit 15.1. The thinking and decision making is done by those at the top, and the physical work is performed by employees who are organized into distinct, functional departments. This structure was quite effective and became entrenched in the business world. For most of the 20th century, the hierarchical, functional structure has predominated. However, over the years, organizations have developed other structural designs, many of them aimed at increasing horizontal coordination and communication and encouraging adaptation to a volatile environment.

apply it

1. Choose an organization with which you're familiar or a department on your campus (for example, the admissions office, food service, or building and grounds department) and draw a simple organization chart showing several positions and lines of authority. You may need to interview a couple of people to determine these elements.

Managers consider several dimensions of organization structure and design

When managers create an organization structure, they consider several basic dimensions of organization design, including chain of command, line and staff positions, span of control, centralization and decentralization, and formalization.

Chain of Command

chain of command

An unbroken line of authority that links all individuals in the organization and specifies who reports to whom.

The **chain of command** is an unbroken line of authority that links all persons in an organization and shows who reports to whom. It is associated with two underlying principles. *Unity of command* means that each employee is held accountable to only one supervisor. The *scalar principle* refers to a clearly defined line of authority in the organization that includes all employees. Authority and responsibility for different tasks should be distinct. Each person in the organization should know to whom he or she reports as well as the successive management levels all the way to the top. In Exhibit 15.1, the payroll clerk reports to the chief accountant, who reports to the vice president of accounting, who in turn reports to the company CEO.

Concepts necessary to an understanding of chain of command include authority, responsibility, accountability, and delegation. The chain of command illustrates the authority structure in the organization. **Authority** is the formal and legitimate right of a manager to make decisions, issue orders, and allocate resources. Managers have authority because of the positions they hold, not because of their personal characteristics. Thus, authority may be distinct from power, as discussed in Chapter 12. Anyone in the same position would have the same authority. Positions at the top of the organizational hierarchy are vested with more formal authority than those at the bottom. In addition, authority flows top down through the organization's hierarchy, and subordinates comply because they believe managers have a legitimate right to issue orders.

authority

The formal and legitimate right of a manager to make decisions, issue orders, and allocate resources.

The *acceptance theory of authority* argues that a manager has authority only if subordinates choose to accept his or her commands. If subordinates refuse to obey because the order is outside their zone of acceptance, a manager's authority disappears.[4] For example, even though Jim Heard and Gregg Trueman founded Buoyant Company and served as CEO and president, respectively, they learned that employees did not accept their authority to make critical decisions. Staff members were aligned with three other managers who had been hired to handle the day-to-day hands-on work of the company. Staffers accepted the authority of these managers because they worked with them on a daily basis; therefore, they supported the managers' decisions over those of the two co-owners.[5]

responsibility

The duty to perform the task or activity an employee has been assigned.

Responsibility is the flip side of authority, meaning it is the duty to perform the task or activity an employee has been assigned. Typically, managers are given authority commensurate with their responsibility level. Accountability is the mechanism through which authority and responsibility are brought into alignment. **Accountability** means that people with authority and responsibility are subject to reporting and justifying task outcomes to those above them in the chain of command.[6] Accountability is

accountability

The fact that people with authority and responsibility are subject to reporting and justifying task outcomes to those above them in the chain of command.

Linda E. McMahon quietly runs the day-to-day operations of the World Wrestling Federation. For much of the past three decades, her responsibilities have included helping to balance the books, "do the deals," and handle the details that go into building a sports entertainment empire. However, her husband, Vince McMahon, as chairman of the WWF, has ultimate authority for the organization, with the formal and legitimate right to make decisions, issue orders, and allocate resources. Says Dusty Anderson, a long-time friend, "Vince is the type to walk in and say he wants an office in Nairobi by Monday. . . . Linda would be the one to put it together." The WWF empire, with its mix of shaved, pierced, and pumped-up-muscle wrestlers, claims over 35 million fans. In the most recent fiscal year, revenues reached $250 million and are projected to soon reach $340 million annually. (Source: © John Abbott)

often built into the organization structure so that people know they will be held accountable for a specific task.

Another concept related to authority is delegation. **Delegation** is the process managers use to transfer authority and responsibility to people in positions below them in the hierarchy. However, even though managers may delegate, they retain ultimate responsibility for the successful completion of the task. The concepts of chain of command and authority are less relevant in today's organizations because of the trend toward pushing power and decision making down to lower organizational levels. Most organizations today encourage managers to delegate authority to the lowest possible level. Recall from Chapter 6 (on motivation) that organizations empower employees by giving them the information, skills, and authority they need to make decisions and act freely. At Johnsonville Foods, for example, a team of employees from the shop floor was delegated the authority and responsibility to formulate the manufacturing budget. Advances in information technology that enable workers to quickly access information that was once available only to managers have enhanced this trend.

delegation

The process managers use to transfer authority and responsibility to people in positions below them in the hierarchy.

Line and Staff Positions

Another important distinction for some organizations is between line and staff positions. *Line departments* perform tasks that reflect the organization's primary goals. In a manufacturing organization, line departments make and sell the product. In Exhibit 15.1, the bottling supervisors and plant manager work in line positions. *Staff departments* include those that provide specialized skills in support of line departments. Staff departments have an advisory relationship with line departments and typically include marketing, labor relations, research, accounting, and human resources. Staff personnel do background research and provide technical advice and recommendations to line managers.

Span of Control

One important question for organizing is, How many employees can a supervisor effectively manage? **Span of control,** sometimes called *span of management,* refers to the number of employees who report to a supervisor. Traditional views of organization design recommended a narrow span of control, with each manager supervising approximately seven subordinates.

span of control

The number of employees who report to a supervisor.

However, many of today's organizations have wide spans of control of as high as 30, 40, or even more subordinates per manager.

The span of control largely determines how many management levels and managers an organization has. A *tall organization structure* has an overall narrow span of control and more hierarchical levels. A *flat organization structure* has a wide span, is horizontally dispersed, and has fewer hierarchical levels. The trend in recent years has been toward wider spans of control as a way to cut costs, increase efficiency, speed up decision making, and increase the delegation of power and authority to lower level workers. Span of control also determines how closely a manager can monitor and direct his or her subordinates. A manager supervising 30 employees cannot be as closely involved in their day-to-day activities as one who supervises only six or seven employees. Many organizations that have cut layers of management and moved toward larger spans of control invest heavily in employee training and information systems so workers have the skills, knowledge, and information they need to perform well without close supervision.

Centralization and Decentralization

centralization

The concentration of decision authority near top organizational levels.

decentralization

The location of decision authority near lower organizational levels.

Centralization and decentralization refer to the hierarchical level at which decisions are made. In some organizations, top managers make all the decisions and lower level workers simply do as they are told. Other organizations go to the opposite extreme and push decision making down to the front lines, to those employees who are closest to the action. Most organizations experiment to find the correct degree of centralization or decentralization. **Centralization** means that decision authority is concentrated near the top of the organizational hierarchy. With **decentralization,** decision authority is pushed downward to lower organizational levels. Decentralization is believed to relieve the burden on top managers, make greater use of employees' skills and abilities, ensure that decisions are made close to the action by well-informed people, and permit a more rapid response to external changes. In addition, employees generally feel a greater sense of involvement and commitment when they have a chance to be involved in making the decisions that affect their work lives.

Over the past few decades, the trend in the United States and Canada has been toward greater decentralization. Johnson & Johnson gives almost complete authority to its 180 operating divisions to develop and market their own products. Decentralization fits the company strategy of empowerment that gets each division close to customers so it can speedily adapt to their changing needs.[7] At Microsoft, Bill Gates and Steve Ballmer have made structural changes to move the company toward greater decentralization.

🐝 Microsoft Corporation

From the outside, Microsoft seemed to be moving at lightning speed, but internally, complaints were growing that things were just too darn slow. With 30,000 employees, more than 180 different products, and at least five layers of management, employees began complaining about the red tape and the snail's pace of decision making. The company even lost a few important staffers because of their frustration with the slow response from overburdened top managers.

So Bill Gates and Steven Ballmer decided to reinvent Microsoft. To be better able to respond to the rapid changes in the industry, they created eight new divisions. The Business and Enterprise Division focuses on bringing software such as Windows 2000 to corporate customers, whereas the Home and Retail Division will handle games, home applications, children's software, and peripherals. A Business Productivity Group targets knowledge workers, developing applications like word processing, while the Sales and Support Group focuses on customer segments such as corporate accounts, Internet service providers, and small business. Other divisions include a Developer Group (creating tools used by corporate programmers), a Consumer and Commerce Group (linking merchants via the company's MSN Web portal), and a Consumer Windows Division, whose goal is to make the PC easier for consumers to use. The final division, Microsoft Research, conducts basic research on everything from speech recognition to advanced networking.

What really makes the new structure revolutionary for Microsoft is that the heads of the eight divisions are given unprecedented freedom and authority to run the businesses and spend their budgets as they see fit, provided they meet revenue and profit goals. Previously, Gates and Ballmer were involved in every decision large and small—from deciding key features in Windows 2000 to reviewing response records for customer support lines. Managers of the divisions are charged up by the new authority and responsibility. One manager said he feels "like I am running my own little company."

"The Internet has changed everything," says Gates, so he recognizes that Microsoft must change as well. He's hoping the new decentralized structure is one step in the right direction.[8] Decentralization may also be important if the company soon has to divide itself into two parts based on a Department of Justice ruling, because managers throughout the company will have gained experience in decision making.

Formalization

Formalization refers to the degree of written documentation, including job descriptions, formal rules and regulations, and explicit policies and procedures, used to direct and control employees. A person working in a formalized job has little leeway in determining how or when to do a task. Formalization helps ensure a level of consistency, but it limits employees' involvement and creativity. Although formalization is intended to be rational and helpful to the organization, it can create "red tape" that causes more problems than it solves. Some U.S. government departments, for example, are notorious for inefficiency caused by extensive policies and procedures. MDP Construction, a small contractor, discovered that winning a contract from the Pentagon meant the company would need to add several staff members just to contend with the load of regulations and mountain of paperwork. However, after MDP's managers invested in sophisticated information technology systems, the company's small administrative staff could easily handle the paperwork.[9] As a practical matter, many organizations are becoming less formalized to be more flexible and to give employees a greater sense of control over their work lives.

formalization

The degree of written documentation, including job descriptions, formal rules and regulations, and explicit policies and procedures, used to direct and control employees.

apply it

1. For the same department or organization you used in the previous Apply It exercise, interview one or two people and answer the following questions: (1) What is the degree of formalization for the department? Are there numerous written procedures, rules, and regulations, or are employees allowed more freedom and opportunities for creativity? (2) Is the department characterized by centralization or decentralization? How is this related to the degree of formalization? Explain.

Organization structures serve important purposes

Besides specifying formal reporting relationships, decision responsibility, span of control, and degree of formalization, organization structures serve other important purposes. One of the most significant is to define how job tasks are assigned, grouped, and coordinated within the organization.

Work Specialization

work specialization

The degree to which organizational tasks are subdivided into different individual jobs; also called *division of labor.*

Organizations perform a tremendous variety of tasks. A fundamental principle developed early in the 20th century is that work can be performed more efficiently if employees are allowed to specialize.[10] **Work specialization,** sometimes called *division of labor,* is the degree to which organizational tasks are subdivided into different individual jobs. In Exhibit 15.1, work specialization is illustrated by the separation of production tasks into bottling, quality control, and maintenance. Employees within each department perform only the tasks relevant to their specialized function. When work specialization is extensive, employees specialize in a single task—each individual does only one small piece of an activity rather than the entire activity. A traditional automobile assembly line provides an example. Each person performs the same task over and over again. With work specialization, jobs tend to be small and routine, but they can be performed efficiently. It would not be efficient, for example, to have a single employee build an entire automobile or an entire jet aircraft. In addition, training workers for specific, repetitive tasks is easier and less expensive for organizations than training them to complete an entire activity.

Despite the apparent advantages of work specialization, many organizations are moving away from this principle, as we learned in the opening vignette about Lend Lease. On its job sites, Lend Lease often cross-trains construction workers, for example, to enable them to perform larger jobs. One project team came up with the idea of a "skills passport," which allows workers to shuttle among different construction jobs throughout Australia, apprenticing in new skills and getting a stamp in their passport for each job. By the end of the project, most workers had been trained in as many as four different trades.[11]

With too much work specialization, employees are isolated and do only a single, tiny, boring job, which can lead to fatigue, stress, lower productivity, increased absenteeism, and higher turnover. Work specialization can reach a point in many jobs where the human costs begin to outweigh the economic advantages.[12] Thus, most managers today recognize that specialization can be carried too far.

Work specialization still exists in many organizations, but many others are finding renewed success by reducing specialization and broadening the scope of employees' jobs. One response is the use of teams, as discussed in Chapter 8. Although some unions in the United States, particularly the United Auto Workers, have challenged the team approach as a ploy by management to reduce the power of unions, many other union leaders support the use of teams as a way to broaden worker skills and provide greater opportunities.[13] Teams can be beneficial to workers as well as organizations. Productivity at Compaq Computer's Scotland and Texas plants increased 51% when the factories switched from assembly lines to four-worker manufacturing teams.[14]

Departmentalization

The next question is how to group jobs and positions into departments so that work can be coordinated. **Departmentalization** is the process by which jobs are grouped into departments and departments into the total organization. Managers make choices about how to group people together to perform their work. There are five approaches to structural design that reflect different uses of the chain of command in departmentalization. The *functional, divisional,* and *matrix* are traditional approaches that rely on the chain of command to define departmental groupings and reporting relationships along the hierarchy. Two contemporary approaches are *horizontal grouping* and the use of *networks*. These newer approaches have emerged to meet new needs of organizations and employees. A brief illustration of the five structural alternatives is shown in Exhibit 15.2. Each approach to departmentalization serves a distinct purpose for the organization and has major consequences for employee goals, attitudes, and behavior. Large organizations may use several different approaches to departmentalization. We will examine each of the five structural designs in more detail in the next section.

departmentalization

The process of grouping jobs into departments and departments into the total organization.

Coordination Mechanisms

Regardless of the type of structure, all organizations need mechanisms for both vertical and horizontal coordination. **Coordination** refers to the quality of collaboration across departments and hierarchical levels. Without coordination, a company's left hand won't know what the right hand is doing, causing problems and conflicts. Coordination is required whether an organization uses a functional, divisional, matrix, horizontal, or network structure.

coordination

The quality of collaboration across departments and hierarchical levels.

The structure should be designed to provide both vertical and horizontal information flow as necessary to achieve the coordination needed to accomplish the organization's overall goal.[15] If the structure doesn't fit the information requirements of the organization, people will either have too little information or spend time processing information that is not vital to their tasks, thus reducing effectiveness. Managers have to find the right balance of vertical and horizontal linkages to fit the organization's needs. *Vertical linkages* are used to coordinate activities between the bottom and top of the organization and include a variety of structural devices, such as the hierarchy or chain of command, the use of rules and plans, and management information and reporting systems. In general, vertical linkages are designed primarily for effective control of the organization. Organizations also need *horizontal linkages,* which are designed primarily for coordination and collaboration across departments.

In general, companies are moving toward greater use of horizontal linkages to break down barriers between departments and ensure stronger horizontal coordination and collaboration. Widely used mechanisms for

exhibit | **15.2**

Five Approaches to Structure

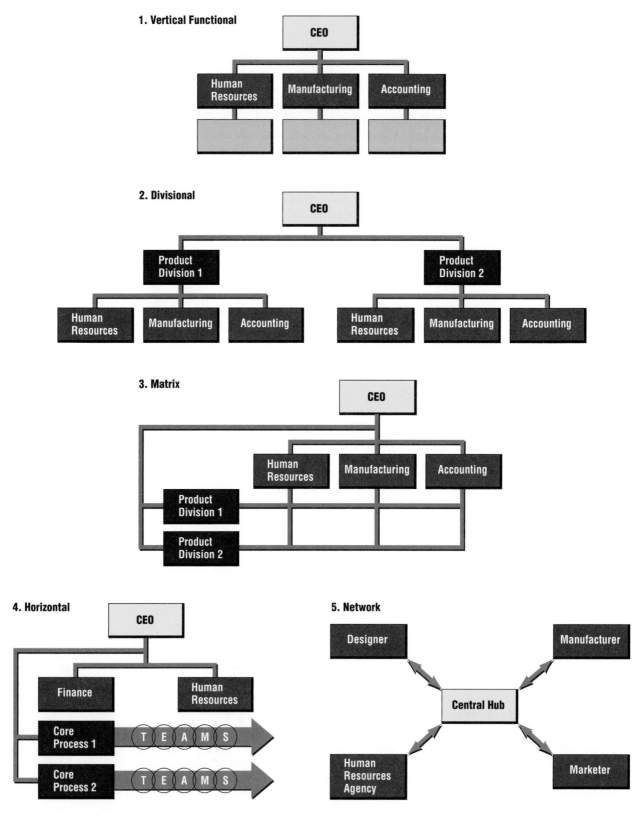

1. Vertical Functional

CEO

- Human Resources
- Manufacturing
- Accounting

2. Divisional

CEO

- Product Division 1
  - Human Resources
  - Manufacturing
  - Accounting
- Product Division 2
  - Human Resources
  - Manufacturing
  - Accounting

3. Matrix

CEO

- Human Resources
- Manufacturing
- Accounting
- Product Division 1
- Product Division 2

4. Horizontal

CEO

- Finance
- Human Resources
- Core Process 1 — T E A M S
- Core Process 2 — T E A M S

5. Network

- Designer
- Manufacturer
- Central Hub
- Human Resources Agency
- Marketer

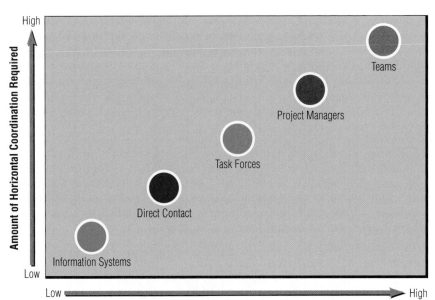

Source: Richard L. Daft, *Organization Theory and Design,* 7th ed. (Cincinnati, OH: South-Western College Publishing, 2001), p. 94.

exhibit | **15.3**

Mechanisms for Horizontal Linkage and Coordination

horizontal linkage, summarized in Exhibit 15.3, include cross-functional information systems, direct contact between managers or employees in different departments, task forces, project managers, and teams. As illustrated in the exhibit, the higher level mechanisms provide greater horizontal information sharing, but the cost to the organization in terms of time and human resources is greater.

Task forces, as defined in Chapter 8, are temporary teams or committees set up to solve a short-term problem involving several departments.[16] Task force members represent the ideas and needs of their various departments and share information that enables coordination. Commercial Casework, a $10 million woodworking and cabinetry shop in Fremont, California, used a task force to research and design the company's bonus plan.

Microsoft's Windows 2000 computer operating system is finished, and project manager Brian Valentine (left), top lieutenant Iain McDonald, and testing director Sanjay Jejurikar are celebrating. Valentine headed a 3,000-strong engineering team, and he even brought 100 customers into the team's development process. Companies such as Texaco and Prudential Insurance tested software on their computing systems. Development of the new software was a long and tedious project, taking roughly four years. The project deadline was met in December 1999. To celebrate, Valentine and the development crew staged a party in a cavernous parking garage. Then it was back to work on another project. (Source: © Rex Rystedt)

A *team* is a group of employees from different departments who meet regularly to solve ongoing problems of common interest. This is similar to a task force except that it works with continuing rather than temporary problems.

A significant way many of today's organizations increase coordination and collaboration is through the use of project managers, similar to those described for Lend Lease Corporation. A **project manager** is a person who is responsible for coordinating the work of several departments and individuals for the completion of a specific project or process, whether it be developing a new multimillion-dollar casino and resort, organizing a campus event, or ensuring that products are manufactured on time. Project managers may also have titles such as *process owner, product manager, brand manager,* or *integrator.* Consider the role of Hugh Hoffman, a project manager at American Standard Companies' chinaware division.

project manager

A person responsible for coordinating the work of several departments and individuals for the completion of a specific project or process.

❦ American Standard Companies

Hugh J. Hoffman began working at American Standard as a ceramic engineer in 1970. Today, he's a key player in the turnaround of American Standard's U.S. chinaware business. Hoffman, whose official title is "process owner, chinaware order fulfillment," coordinates all the activities that ensure that American Standard's factories turn out the products customers order and deliver them on time. Hoffman's job requires that he think about everything that happens between the time an order comes in and the time it gets paid for, including design, manufacturing, painting, sales, shipping and receiving, and numerous other tasks. He even becomes involved in demand forecasting and helping to ensure that factories crank up capacity in the appropriate ways.

Process owners such as Hoffman have to act as if they are running their own business, setting goals and developing strategies for achieving them. It isn't always easy because Hoffman works outside the boundaries and authority structure of traditional departments. His years of expertise and good people skills help him motivate others and coordinate the work of many departments and geographically dispersed factories. "I move behind the scenes," Hoffman says. "I understand the workings of the company and know how to get things done."[17] American Standard encourages managers to move around within the company to broaden their experience and develop the expertise and skills needed to become effective process owners.[18]

Project managers such as those at American Standard are a strong horizontal linkage mechanism because they span the boundaries between departments, and often between the organization and its customers as well. Strong project managers are in hot demand throughout today's corporate world.[19]

apply it

1. Try to recall a time when you or someone you know served as a project manager for a project at work, a student group project, a campus organization project such as a Homecoming activity, or a community activity such as a block party or a church picnic. What tasks were performed to accomplish the goal? What skills were needed to be effective in this role?

Organizations use a variety of structural approaches

Managers' choices about such factors as chain of command, formalization and centralization, work specialization, departmentalization, and coordination mechanisms determine whether the organization will operate on the

what would YOU do?

WILL TEAMWORK SAVE A COMPANY?

Danny Carpenter knew he was facing another sleepless night. He couldn't stop thinking about how he was letting the business his grandfather founded more than 50 years ago go straight down the tubes.

Imperial Industries installs and repairs warehouse doors in a six-county area of California. The company had thrived for years as construction boomed in the region, but in recent years sales had begun to stagnate. In addition, since Danny took over the business after his father died, he knew that costs had been climbing. Now, he was faced with a desperate situation. Several of his workers frequently called in sick, and he knew that one of his best supervisors, Joe Lang, had been spending a lot of time at a local bar after work. Morale in general was low, and the company's reputation for quality service was declining fast. In addition, many of Imperial's customers were turning to other companies that promised faster installation.

Imperial is organized as a traditional functional structure. Extensive work specialization means that each employee handles a specific task, and lately Carpenter noticed workers had been refusing to pitch in and help one another if someone fell behind in his work. Most of Imperial's equipment and workers were bunched at one location near downtown Los Angeles, so workers gathered there each morning before heading out to their work sites. One day, when Carpenter had been to the bank for an early morning meeting about extending his loan, he arrived at 10 a.m. to find Joe Lang's crew still drinking coffee and telling jokes at headquarters. After a good chewing out, the crew headed off—they'd get to the job site around noon. Around 11 a.m., Carpenter got an irate call from the customer threatening to give the job to someone else.

Carpenter thought that perhaps Joe Lang needed more responsibility to make him feel like an important part of the company again. His father had made all the decisions at Imperial, and Danny had carried on that tradition, but lately he was beginning to think morale would improve if workers felt more involved. He had been hearing about "teamwork" and how successfully it had been used at some companies. It might work at Imperial, he thought. After all, some of the workers—like Joe Lang—had been working at Imperial since Carpenter was a child and didn't really need to be told what to do and how to do it. So, when Carpenter found that he would have to be away from the office for about a week, he decided to try an experiment. He asked Lang to handle things at headquarters while he was gone. When he stopped by on his way out of town, Lang's first day as "boss" was going well. The crews had been organized, instructed, and dispatched well before 8 a.m. Danny left on his trip with a relatively easy mind. However, when he returned, he discovered that Lang had fired one of Imperial's best repairman and hired a new secretary—his girlfriend. Although they had previously discussed the need for an additional secretary, no decision had been made to even begin interviewing, much less make a selection.

Now Carpenter was lying awake wondering if he needed to fire Lang to make an impression on the other workers. In addition, he thought he might revise the employee manual and hold some training sessions so workers understood that if they didn't follow the rules, they'd be history. His first step toward getting workers more involved had been a miserable failure. Maybe he needed to take a firmer grip on the company.

1. Do you think Danny Carpenter's plan to fire Joe Lang and "take a firmer grip on the company" will successfully revive Imperial Industries? Why or why not?

2. If you were a consultant to Carpenter, what advice would you give him about his approach to delegation? How could he more effectively begin to decentralize decision making?

3. What other structural changes might you make to help Imperial Industries be more effective?

Source: Inspired by a story in Michael Barrier, "Re-engineering Your Company," *Nation's Business,* February 1994, pp. 16–22.

---

principles of a *mechanistic* or an *organic* system. This relates to the degree of formal structure and control that is imposed on employees. Exhibit 15.4 summarizes the differences between mechanistic and organic systems. An **organic structure** is one that is free flowing and adaptable, has few rules and regulations, encourages teamwork that crosses functional and hierarchical boundaries, and decentralizes authority and responsibility to lower level employees. Job responsibilities are broadly defined and spans of

organic structure

A structure that is flexible and adaptable, has few rules, encourages teamwork that crosses functional and hierarchical boundaries, and decentralizes authority.

exhibit **15.4**

Mechanistic versus Organic
Organization Structures

Mechanistic Structure	Organic Structure
Extensive work specialization	Low degree of specialization, cross-functional teams
Rigidly defined tasks	Adjustable tasks
Strict chain of command	Relaxed chain of command
High formalization, many rules	Low formalization, few rules
Centralized authority and decision making	Decentralized authority and decision making
Typically narrow span of control	Wide span of control

mechanistic structure

A structure characterized by rigidly defined tasks, many rules and regulations, little teamwork, a strict chain of command, and centralized authority.

bureaucracy

A highly mechanistic organization, characterized by routine, highly specialized tasks; extensive formalization through written rules, policies, and procedures; centralization of authority; narrow spans of control; and a strict chain of command.

functional structure

An organization structure in which positions are grouped into departments based on similar skills and common activities, from the bottom to the top of the organization.

control are generally wide. A **mechanistic structure** is just the opposite, characterized by rigidly defined tasks, many rules and regulations (high formalization), little teamwork, and centralized authority. There is a clear chain of command and narrower spans of control.[20]

One type of organization that reflects a strong mechanistic approach is a *bureaucracy.* The systematic study of bureaucracy was launched by Max Weber, a sociologist who studied government organizations and developed a framework of administrative characteristics that would make large organizations rational and efficient.[21] During the 20th century, most large organizations developed bureaucratic characteristics as a way to increase efficiency. A **bureaucracy** is highly mechanistic, characterized by routine, highly specialized tasks; extensive formalization through written rules, policies, and procedures; centralization of authority; and narrow spans of control. Structure is vertically designed, and a strict chain of command is observed. Although bureaucracy carried to an extreme is widely criticized today, it was highly effective for organizations operating in the relatively stable environment of the 1950s and 1960s, and bureaucratic characteristics are still useful to organizations. Bureaucracy provides an effective way to bring order to large numbers of employees and to organize and manage tasks too complex to be understood and handled by a few people.

A highly organic approach is reflected in today's emerging *learning organizations.* The learning organization may be defined as one in which everyone is engaged in identifying and solving problems, enabling the organization to continuously experiment, improve, and increase its capability. Emphasis on learning is associated with shared tasks, few rules and regulations, and informal, decentralized decision making. Structure is horizontal and the chain of command is considerably relaxed.

Few organizations are either entirely organic or entirely mechanistic. We will examine a number of organizational structures that vary between these extremes. An exhibit later in this chapter summarizes the strengths and weaknesses of each type of structure and when each is used.

Functional Structure

With a **functional structure,** activities are grouped together by common function from the bottom to the top of the organization. The organization chart shown earlier, in Exhibit 15.1, is a functional structure. All engineers are located in the engineering department, for example, and the vice president of engineering is responsible for all engineering activities. The same is true for marketing, research and development, and manufacturing. With a functional structure, all human knowledge and skills with respect to specific activities are consolidated, providing a valuable depth of knowledge for the organization. This structure is most effective when in-depth expertise is critical to meeting organizational goals, when the organization needs to be controlled and coordinated through the vertical hierarchy, and when efficiency is important. The structure can be quite effective if there is little need for horizontal coordination. Functional structures are generally mechanistic in that authority is centralized, tasks are narrowly defined, and there is little cross-functional teamwork.[22]

Advantages and Disadvantages One significant advantage of the functional structure is that it promotes economies of scale within functions. That is, all employees are located in the same place and can share facilities and resources. In addition, the functional structure allows in-depth skill development for employees. People are exposed to a range of activities within their functional area. Managers and employees in functional departments share common skills and problems and are compatible because of similar training and experience. Communication and coordination among employees within each department are enhanced. Finally, the functional structure promotes high-quality technical problem solving. Having a pool of well-trained experts motivated toward functional expertise gives the company an important resource.

The primary disadvantage of the functional structure is a slow response to environmental changes that require greater coordination and collaboration across departments. Because people are separated into distinct departments, communication and coordination across functional boundaries are often poor. Thus, innovation to meet changing needs is restricted because innovation and change require the coordinated involvement of several different departments. Another problem is that the vertical hierarchy may become overloaded; decisions pile up and top managers do not respond fast enough. The functional structure also stresses extensive work specialization, which may lead to routine, nonmotivating employee tasks. In addition, employees often have a limited view of overall organizational goals because they are focused on their own functional areas.

Divisional Structure

In contrast to the functional approach, in which people are grouped by common skills and resources, the **divisional structure** occurs when departments are grouped together based on organizational outputs. Functional and divisional structures are illustrated in Exhibit 15.5. In the divisional structure, divisions are created as self-contained units for producing a single product, serving a single geographical region, or serving a particular set of customers. For example, Microsoft's divisional structure, described earlier in the chapter, organizes company activities to serve different customer segments (such as corporate customers, small businesses, and home users). McDonald's divided its U.S. business into five geographic divisions, each with its own president and staff functions.[23] With a divisional structure,

divisional structure

An organization structure in which departments are grouped together based on organizational outputs.

exhibit 15.5
Functional and Divisional Structures

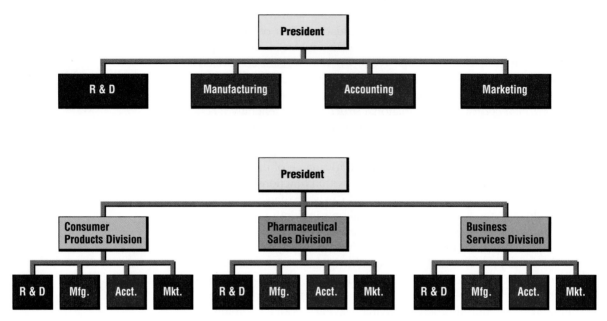

each functional department resource needed to produce the product or serve a geographical region or customer set is assigned to one division. For example, in a functional structure, all engineers are grouped together and work on all products. In a divisional structure, separate engineering departments are established within each division. Thus, departments are duplicated across divisions.

The divisional structure is sometimes called a *product structure, program structure,* or *self-contained unit structure.* Each of these terms means essentially the same thing. Diverse departments are brought together to produce a single organizational output, whether it be a product, a program, or a service for a single set of customers. In very large organizations, a divisional structure is essential. Most large corporations have separate business divisions that perform different tasks, serve different clients, or use different technologies. When a huge organization produces products for different markets, the divisional structure works because each division is an autonomous business.

A major difference between divisional and functional structures is that the chain of command from each function converges at a lower level in the hierarchy. In an organization such as the one in Exhibit 15.5, differences of opinion among research and development, marketing, manufacturing, and accounting would be resolved at the divisional level rather than by the president. Thus, the divisional structure encourages decentralization. Decision making is pushed down at least one level in the hierarchy.

Advantages and Disadvantages Like the functional structure, the divisional structure has distinct advantages and disadvantages. By dividing employees along divisional lines, the organization will be more flexible and responsive to change because each unit is small and tuned in to its environment. Having employees working on a single product line promotes concern for customer needs. Coordination across functional departments is improved because employees are grouped together in a single location and committed to one product line or customer segment. Great coordination exists within divisions. The divisional structure also enables top managers to pinpoint responsibility for performance problems in different product lines. Because each division is a self-contained unit, poor performance can be assigned to the manager of that unit. Finally, employees typically develop a broader goals orientation rather than being focused on their own functional departments.

The major disadvantage of the divisional structure is duplication of resources and the high cost of running separate divisions. Instead of a single research department in which all researchers use a single facility, there may be several. The organization loses efficiency and economies of scale. Also, because departments within each division are small, there may be a lack of technical specialization, expertise, and training. The divisional structure fosters excellent coordination *within* divisions, but coordination *across* divisions may be poor. For example, Johnson & Johnson prides itself on its divisional structure, which gives autonomy to many small divisions. However, problems can arise if these divisions begin to go in opposite directions. As one J & J manager put it, "We have to keep reminding ourselves that we work for the same corporation."[24] Another problem is that divisions may feel themselves in competition with one another, especially for resources from corporate headquarters. This can lead to conflicts and political behavior that is unhealthy for the organization as a whole. Because top management control is somewhat weaker with a divisional structure, top executives have to assert themselves to get divisions to cooperate.

Matrix Structure

The **matrix structure** combines aspects of both functional and divisional chains of command simultaneously in the same part of the organization.[25] The matrix structure evolved as a way to improve horizontal coordination and information sharing. One unique feature of the matrix is that it has dual lines of authority. In Exhibit 15.6, the functional hierarchy of authority runs vertically, and the divisional hierarchy of authority runs horizontally. While the vertical structure provides traditional control within functional departments, the horizontal structure provides coordination across departments. The matrix structure therefore provides a formal chain of command for both functional (vertical) and divisional (horizontal) relationships. As a result of this dual structure, some employees actually report to two bosses simultaneously.

The matrix structure has been used successfully by large, global corporations such as IBM, Ford Motor Company, and Dow Corning. The problem for global companies is to achieve simultaneous coordination of various products within each country or region and for each product line. An example of a global matrix structure is shown in Exhibit 15.7. The two lines of authority are geographic and product. To see how the matrix works, consider that the geographic boss in Germany coordinates all affiliates in Germany, and the plastic products boss coordinates the manufacturing and sale

matrix structure

An organization structure that combines functional and divisional chains of command simultaneously in the same part of the organization.

exhibit **15.6**

Dual Authority Structure in a Matrix Organization

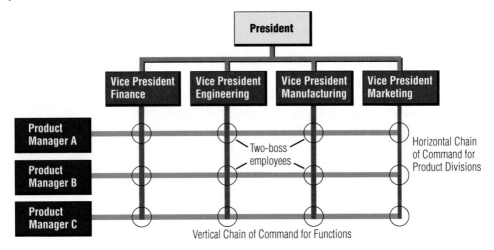

of plastic products around the world. Managers of local affiliate companies in Germany would thus report to two supervisors, both the country boss and the product boss. The dual authority structure violates the unity of command principle described earlier in this chapter but is necessary to give equal balance to both functional and divisional lines of authority.

two-boss employee

An employee who reports to two supervisors simultaneously in a matrix structure.

Two-boss employees, people who must report to two supervisors simultaneously, have to resolve conflicting demands from their bosses. They must be able to confront managers and reach joint decisions. This is a much different role from that of an employee in a functional structure. Two-boss employees need excellent human relations skills with which to confront supervisors and resolve conflicts.

exhibit **15.7**

A Global Matrix Structure

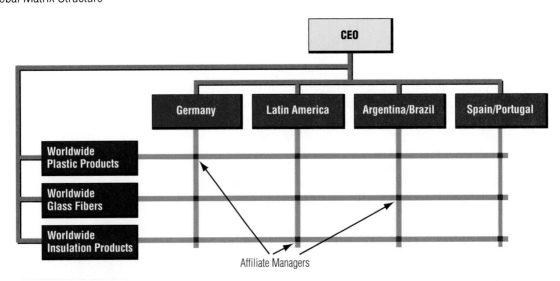

Advantages and Disadvantages   The matrix structure can be highly effective in a complex, changing environment in which the organization needs to be flexible and adaptable.[26] The conflict and frequent meetings generated by the matrix allow new issues to be raised and resolved. The matrix structure also makes efficient use of human resources because specialists can be transferred from one division to another. In addition, employees get training in both specialist and general skills. People within a functional department, for example, have access to in-depth training and specialization. At the same time, they coordinate with other programs and divisions, which helps employees develop a broader perspective. Finally, the matrix engages the participation of employees in team meetings and the achievement of divisional goals. Thus, it challenges and motivates employees, giving them a larger task than would be possible in a functional structure.

The structure also has several disadvantages, however. The major problem is the frustration and confusion caused by the dual chain of command. Employees may have great difficulty with the dual reporting relationships. The matrix structure can also generate high levels of conflict because it pits divisional against functional goals in a domestic structure and product line against country goals in a global matrix. This leads to the third disadvantage: time lost to meetings and discussions devoted to resolving conflicts. To perform well in a matrix structure, employees need human relations training to be able to deal with two bosses, to get by with only "half" of each employee, and to confront and manage conflict. Finally, many organizations find it difficult to maintain the power balance between the functional and divisional sides of the matrix.[27]

Horizontal Structure

A recent approach to organizing is the **horizontal structure,** or *team structure*, which organizes employees around core work processes. All the people who work on a particular process are brought together in teams so that they can easily communicate and coordinate their efforts and provide value directly to customers. This structural approach is largely a response to the profound changes that have occurred in the workplace and the business environment over the past 15 to 20 years. For example, technological advances emphasize computer-based integration and coordination. Customers expect faster and better service. Employees want opportunities to use their minds, learn new skills, and assume greater responsibility. Organizations mired in a vertical, functional mind-set have a hard time meeting these challenges. Thus, numerous organizations have experimented with horizontal mechanisms such as *cross-functional teams* to achieve coordination across departments or *task forces* to accomplish temporary projects. Many companies reorganize into *permanent teams* after a process called reengineering. **Reengineering** is the radical rethinking and redesign of business processes to achieve dramatic improvements in cost, quality, speed, and service. Because the focus is on process rather than function, reengineering often leads to a shift away from vertical structure toward one emphasizing horizontal teamwork.[28]

The horizontal structure takes the team approach to its ultimate level. This is a highly organic organization structure that virtually eliminates both

horizontal structure

An organizational structure that organizes employees around core work processes.

reengineering

The radical rethinking and redesign of business processes to achieve dramatic improvements in cost, quality, speed, and service.

the vertical hierarchy and old departmental boundaries. A horizontal structure is illustrated in Exhibit 15.8 and has the following characteristics:[29]

- Structure is created around cross-functional core processes (for example, new product development or order fulfillment) rather than tasks, functions, or geography. Thus, boundaries between departments are obliterated. Ford Motor Company's Customer Service Division has core process groups for business development, parts supply and logistics, vehicle service and programs, and technical support.
- Self-directed teams, not individuals, are the basis of organizational design and performance.
- Process owners have responsibility for each core process in its entirety. For Ford's parts supply and logistics process, for example, a number of teams may work on jobs such as parts analysis, purchasing, material flow, and distribution, but a process owner is responsible for coordinating the entire process.
- People on the teams are given the skills, tools, motivation, freedom, and authority to think creatively and make decisions central to the team's performance. Team members are cross-trained to learn one another's jobs, and the combined skills are sufficient to perform a major organizational task.

exhibit | **15.8**
The Horizontal Structure

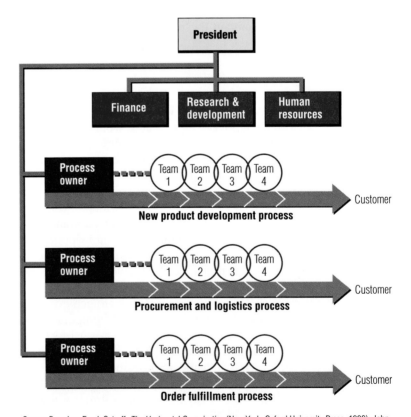

Source: Based on Frank Ostroff, *The Horizontal Organization* (New York: Oxford University Press, 1999); John A. Byrne, "The Horizontal Corporation," *Business Week,* December 20, 1993, pp. 76–81; and Thomas A. Stewart, "The Search for the Organization of Tomorrow," *Fortune,* May 18, 1992, pp. 92–98.

- Effectiveness is measured by end-of-process performance objectives (based on bringing value to the customer), as well as customer satisfaction, employee satisfaction, and financial contribution.

Although experimentation with teams and horizontal organizing often begins at lower levels of the organization, a few companies are structuring practically the entire organization horizontally, with perhaps only a few senior executives in traditional support functions such as human resources or finance. Xerox, for example, still maintains some elements of a vertical design, but below the level of executive vice president, the entire organization is structured horizontally. Xerox's horizontal structure is described later in this chapter.

Advantages and Disadvantages Xerox has achieved impressive results with a horizontal structure but, as with all structures, it has disadvantages as well as advantages. The most significant advantage of the horizontal structure is that it can dramatically increase the company's flexibility and shorten response time to changes in customer needs because of the enhanced coordination. The structure directs everyone's attention toward the customer, which leads to greater customer satisfaction as well as improvements in productivity, speed, and efficiency. In addition, because there are no boundaries between functional departments, employees take a broader view of organizational goals rather than being focused on the goals of a single department. The horizontal structure promotes an emphasis on teamwork and cooperation, and team members share a commitment to meeting common objectives. Finally, the horizontal structure can improve the quality of life for employees by giving them opportunities to share responsibility, make decisions, and contribute significantly to the organization.

A disadvantage of the horizontal structure is that it can harm rather than help organizational performance unless managers carefully determine which core processes are critical for bringing value to customers. Simply defining the processes around which to organize can be difficult and time consuming. AT&T's Network Systems Division eventually counted up 130 processes, then began working to pare them down to fewer than 15 core ones.[30] In addition, shifting to a horizontal structure is time consuming because it requires significant changes in culture, job design, management philosophy, and information and reward systems. Traditional managers may balk when they have to give up power and authority to serve instead as coaches and facilitators of teams. Employees have to be trained to work effectively in a flexible team environment. Finally, because of the cross-functional nature of work, a horizontal structure can limit in-depth knowledge and skill development unless measures are taken to give employees opportunities to maintain and build technical expertise.

Network Structure

A growing trend is for companies to limit themselves to only a few activities that they do extremely well and let outside specialists handle the rest. With a **network organization structure,** a company subcontracts most of its major functions to separate companies and coordinates their activities from a small headquarters organization.[31] The network is a type of horizontal

network organization structure

An organization structure that subcontracts major functions to separate companies and coordinates their activities from a small headquarters organization.

exhibit | **15.9**
The Network Organization Structure

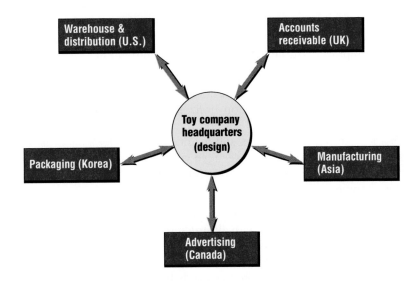

structure, but it represents a totally different approach to structuring the organization. The network may be viewed as a central hub surrounded by a network of outside specialists, as illustrated in Exhibit 15.9.

Rather than being housed under one roof or located within one organization, services such as accounting, manufacturing, packaging, and distribution are outsourced to separate organizations that are connected electronically to the central hub. For example, Monorail Inc., based in Marietta, Georgia, has no factories, no warehouses, no credit department, and no help desks or call centers.

🐾 Monorail Inc.

Monorail's founders believe there are only two things you can't outsource: world-class management expertise and a knack for establishing the right partnerships. Monorail has managed to grow rapidly by using a network structure. The company's core group of employees concentrates on product design and marketing and outsources everything else to other organizations. Founders Doug Johns, David Hocker, and Nicholas Forlenza (all former Compaq Corp. managers) emphasize that relationships with subcontractors are the glue that holds the company together.

Here's how it works: When a retailer such as CompUSA orders a computer from Monorail, the order is transmitted electronically through FedEx Logistics Services to one of Monorail's many contract manufacturing partners, who assembles the PC and ships it directly to the retailer. Meanwhile, FedEx wires an invoice to Sun Trust Bank in Atlanta, whose factoring department handles billing and credit approvals for Monorail. Monorail gets its payment directly from Sun Trust, which assumes the risk of collecting funds from CompUSA. Whenever Monorail customers need technical help, they call a service center that is run by Sykes Enterprises Inc., a call center outsourcing company based in Tampa, Florida. Monorail's success depends on seamless integration with its business partners—particularly FedEx and Sun Trust, which play a central role in operations. For example, Monorail designed its PCs to fit into a standard FedEx box.

By using the network approach, Monorail has been able to keep costs low and grow rapidly. Doug Johns points out that when he left Compaq he was managing six million square feet of warehouse and office space. Now, at Monorail, he and his 50 employees work on a single leased floor of an office building near Atlanta. "We've got the shortest supply lines in the world," he says.[32]

Monorail's network structure replaces the traditional vertical hierarchy with a free-market style. Subcontractors flow into and out of the system as needed to meet changing needs. The speed and ease of electronic communication today make networking a viable option for companies looking to keep costs low but expand activities or market visibility. For example, Rhoda Makoff started R&D Laboratories Inc. to develop specialized vitamin and mineral supplements for dialysis patients. The products are manufactured and packaged by subcontracted pharmaceutical companies, and 200 wholesalers handle warehousing and distribution. Using the network approach enabled quantum leaps in growth for R&D Labs. As soon as the small company has a promising new product, Makoff can ramp up production just by making a few phone calls.[33]

Advantages and Disadvantages A major strategic advantage of network structures is that the organization, no matter how small, can be truly global, drawing on resources worldwide to achieve the best quality and price and then just as easily selling products or services worldwide through subcontractors. In addition, the network structure can allow companies to develop new products and get them to market rapidly without huge investments. The ability to arrange and rearrange resources to meet changing needs and best serve customers gives the network organization greater flexibility and a rapid response time. Managerial and technical talent can be focused on key activities that provide competitive advantage, as at Monorail, while other functions are outsourced.[34] An equally significant advantage is workforce flexibility and challenge. For employees who are a permanent part of the organization, the challenge comes from greater job variety and job satisfaction from working in such a lean organization. The network is the leanest of all organization structures because little supervision is required. Large numbers of staff specialists and administrators are not needed. A network organization may have only two or three levels of hierarchy, compared with ten or more in a traditional functional organization.[35]

One of the major disadvantages of the network structure is lack of hands-on control.[36] Managers don't have all operations under one roof and must rely on contracts, coordination, negotiation, and electronic communication to hold things together. Managers don't have direct control over most employees' work activities because the employees are working in other organizations or as individual subcontractors. There is the potential for significant coordination and negotiation costs to keep the network functioning. A problem of equal importance is the possibility of losing an organizational part. If a subcontractor fails to deliver, goes out of business, or has a plant burn down, the headquarters organization can be put out of business. Uncertainty is high because necessary services are not under one roof and under direct management control. Finally, in this type of organization, employee loyalty can weaken. Employees may feel that they can be replaced by contract workers. Turnover tends to be higher because emotional commitment to the organization is weak. With changing products and markets, the organization may need to reshuffle employees at any time to acquire the correct mix of skills.

apply it

1. Try to identify the basic organization structure of a company you have worked for or that you are familiar with, such as a local dry cleaner, video store, copy center, or auto service center. Does the organization use a primarily organic or a primarily mechanistic structure?

Managers fit organization structure to the company's needs

As we have just learned, every organizational structure has disadvantages as well as advantages. Managers try to select the right structure to fit their company's unique needs. How do managers know whether to design a structure that emphasizes the formal vertical hierarchy and centralizes authority or one that stresses horizontal teamwork and decentralizes decision making to lower level employees? The answer lies in several contingency factors that influence organization structure, including strategic goals, the environment, and the organization's technology. The right structure is designed to fit the contingency factors, as illustrated in Exhibit 15.10.

Strategic Goals

The relationship between structure and strategy has been widely studied. Structure typically reflects organizational strategy, and a change in product or market strategy frequently leads to a change in structure.[37] Managers design the organizational structure to coordinate activities to best achieve the company's strategic goals. Two specific strategies are low-cost leadership and differentiation.[38] With a **low-cost leadership strategy,** the organization aggressively seeks efficient facilities, pursues cost reductions, and uses tight cost controls to produce products more efficiently than competitors. A low-cost strategy means that the company can undercut competitors' prices and still earn a reasonable profit. For example, GoFly Ltd., a start-up airline based in London, England, is using a low-cost strategy to compete successfully against major carriers such as British Airways. CEO Barbara Cassani monitors costs closely so GoFly can keep prices low. For example, the company doesn't use travel agents, requiring that customers book flights directly by phone or on the Web. Rather than serving free food and drinks, GoFly offers travelers a choice of quality refreshments at a fair price.[39] A **differentiation strategy** involves an attempt to distinguish the firm's products or services from others in the industry. The organization strives to produce innovative products that are unique to the market. The differentiation strategy can be profitable because customers are loyal and will pay high prices for the product. Tommy Hilfiger clothing, Maytag appliances, Xerox

low-cost leadership strategy

A competitive strategy in which the organization seeks efficient facilities, cuts costs, and employs tight cost controls to be more efficient than competitors.

differentiation strategy

A competitive strategy in which the organization seeks to distinguish its products or services from those of competitors.

exhibit **15.10**
Contingency Factors Affecting Organization Structure and Design

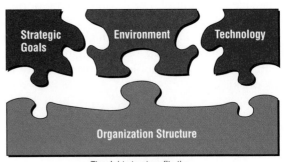

The right structure fits the contingency factors

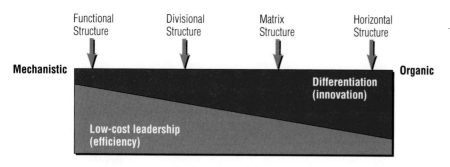

exhibit **15.11**
Relationship of Strategic Goals to Structural Approach

copiers, and Starbucks coffee are examples of products from companies using a differentiation strategy.

The strategies of low-cost leadership and differentiation typically require different structural approaches. With a low-cost leadership strategy, managers generally take a mechanistic approach to organization design, whereas a differentiation strategy calls for an organic approach. Exhibit 15.11 shows a simplified continuum that illustrates how structural approaches are associated with strategic goals. The pure functional structure is appropriate for achieving goals of internal efficiency. The vertical functional structure uses task specialization, centralization, and a strict chain of command to gain efficient use of scarce resources. However, it does not enable the organization to be flexible or innovative. In contrast, a horizontal structure is useful when the primary goal is flexibility, learning, and innovation. Horizontal teams focused directly on providing value to customers enable the organization to differentiate and respond quickly to shifting needs, but at the expense of efficient resource use. Exhibit 15.11 also shows how other forms of structure described in this chapter represent intermediate steps on the continuum.

Xerox Corporation, which uses a differentiation strategy, recently shifted to a horizontal structure to promote learning and innovation.

🍂 **Xerox**

The Xerox 2005 Strategic Intent defines the company's specific goal as "a promise to provide unique value by offering leading-edge products using privileged technology that are of the highest quality and deliver total document solutions quickly and reliably." Xerox's top managers believed the company could achieve this strategic goal only by shifting away from a tight functional structure to a more flexible and adaptable one based on horizontal work flows.

Although the top managerial layers at Xerox remain vertical, responsibility for daily operations, marketing, customer relations, and other activities resides within horizontally aligned groups. For example, Business Groups such as Document Services, Office Document Products, Production Systems, Supplies, and Channels are "mini-businesses." Each group is made up of a number of linked, multi-skilled teams that focus on activities such as business planning, product design and development, manufacturing, marketing, sales, distribution, and customer support. Each set of teams is headed by a core process owner who is responsible for the entire process and for ensuring that performance objectives are met. Teams are accountable for taking an idea through all the stages necessary to produce a marketable product—that is, each set of teams has the information and skills to perform a major task that would once have been divided among separate functional departments.

The new structure at Xerox gives each group greater power to respond more quickly to customer needs, develop innovative solutions, and reach out to new markets. For example, Xerox has launched more than 170 new products in only six years. More subtle, but just as important, are the increases in employee and customer satisfaction that Xerox has realized since implementing its new horizontal structure.[40]

Companies using a differentiation strategy, such as Xerox, benefit from a primarily organic structure, whereas those using a low-cost strategy generally have more mechanistic structures.

Environment

organizational environment

All elements existing outside the organization's boundaries that have the potential to affect the organization's performance and goal achievement.

environmental uncertainty

A condition in which organizational decision makers have a difficult time acquiring good information and predicting external changes that will affect the organization.

The external **organizational environment** includes all elements, forces, and organizations existing outside the boundary of the organization that have a potential to affect the organization's performance and goal achievement. The environment includes such factors as competitors, suppliers, government regulatory agencies, public pressure groups, and customers. An organization's structure is affected by the environment largely because of **environmental uncertainty,** which means that the organization's decision makers have a hard time acquiring good information and predicting external changes that will affect the organization. Uncertainty occurs when the external environment is changing rapidly, such as with rapid technological advances and the growth of Internet commerce in recent years.

An uncertain environment has three major consequences for organizations. First, it leads to increased differences among departments. Each major department—marketing, manufacturing, and so forth—focuses on the aspect of the environment for which it is responsible in order to cope with uncertainty and, hence, differs from other departments in terms of goals, task orientation, and time horizon.[41] Departments work autonomously. This factor can create barriers between different departments. Second, to keep departments working together, the organization needs increased coordination to break down horizontal barriers. Finally, the organization must maintain a flexible and responsive posture to adapt to change in the environment, which also requires greater horizontal coordination.

The relationship between environmental uncertainty and structural approach is illustrated in Exhibit 15.12. When the environment is stable, the organization can succeed with a traditional structure that emphasizes vertical control, specialization, centralized decision making, and a strict chain of command. However, when environmental uncertainty is high, a horizontal structure that emphasizes lateral relationships, decentralized decision mak-

exhibit | **15.12**

Relationship between Environment and Structure

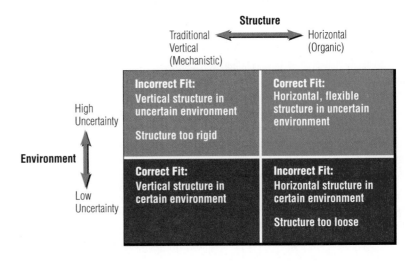

ing, broad tasks, and little formalization is needed. A rigid structure in an uncertain environment prevents the organization from adapting to change.

Technological Factors

The final contingency factor we will consider is the organization's **technology,** which includes the tools, techniques, and activities used to transform organizational inputs (resources) into outputs (products and service). Many studies have looked at the relationship between technology and structure.[42] This relationship can be extremely complex because it involves both manufacturing and service technologies as well as a consideration of organization-level and department-level technology.

One primary dimension that distinguishes technologies is whether they are considered *routine* or *nonroutine.* Charles Perrow developed a framework that classified technologies according to the degree of task *variety* (the frequency of unexpected and novel events that occur) and task *analyzability* (the extent to which work activities can be reduced to mechanical steps allowing employees to follow standard, objective procedures

technology

The tools, techniques, and activities used to transform organizational inputs (resources) into outputs (products and services).

With explosive increases in the use of digital cell phones, pagers, Palm devices, and other wireless Internet appliances, cities are becoming swarms of radio signals that bounce and echo off each other in the same space. This phenomenon limits the number of channels that can be used in one area. To solve this problem, scientists at Lucent Technologies' Bell Labs are using nonroutine technology procedures to figure out how to break the messages into pieces, beam them from multiple antennas into the sea of signals, and reassemble them on the other side. The technology being developed is called BLAST, for Bell Labs Layered Space-Time. In developing the BLAST technology, Gerard Foschini (top right), the Bell Labs researcher who developed the basic principles, and his team perform many nonroutine tasks, such as testing BLAST outdoors in fixed-wireless environments.
(Source: Courtesy Lucent Technologies' Bell Labs)

routine technologies

Technologies that are characterized by little task variety and the use of objective, computational procedures.

nonroutine technologies

Technologies characterized by high task variety, where the conversion process is not analyzable or easily understood.

to complete their work).[43] Studying these two dimensions can determine whether a technology is considered routine or nonroutine. **Routine technologies** are characterized by little task variety and high task analyzability, that is, work can be performed using objective, computational procedures. The tasks are formalized and standardized, as with an automobile assembly line. **Nonroutine technologies,** on the other hand, have high task variety, and the conversion process is not easily analyzable or well understood. With nonroutine technologies, a great deal of human effort goes into analyzing problems and activities, as in a research or strategic planning department. Custom work such as fine furniture making would also be a nonroutine technology. Experience and technical knowledge are needed to solve problems and perform the work.

In general, routine technologies are associated with mechanistic structures. The organization can succeed using a vertical, highly departmentalized structure, such as the traditional functional structure. Extensive formalization, greater centralization, and a strict chain of command are often used with routine technologies. With nonroutine technologies, on the other hand, the organization generally takes an organic approach and uses a more flexible structure, with low formalization, greater decentralization, and extensive horizontal coordination. Exhibit 15.13 summarizes the structural characteristics associated with routine and nonroutine technologies.

Different departments within the same organization may use different technologies and therefore have varied information-processing needs, which require different structural approaches.[44] A manufacturing department might use a routine technology and succeed with a highly mechanistic approach, whereas the research and development department needs a more organic structure to provide the higher level of communication and collaboration needed for nonroutine research activities. This highlights the complexity of organizational structures. Departments that deal with frequent problems and uncertainty require a more flexible approach, even though the organization itself may use a primarily mechanistic structure. For example, in a hospital emergency room such as that depicted on the television series *ER,* highly skilled employees need the authority and freedom to respond on their own initiative and discretion based on the unique problems that arise. Following strict procedures would inhibit emergency room personnel from responding appropriately to unexpected life-or-death problems. However, strict rules and standard procedures are appropriate and even necessary for routine hospital activities such as admissions, accounting, and so forth.

exhibit | **15.13**

Relationship of Technology to Structural Characterisitcs

Routine Technology (Mechanistic Structure)	Nonroutine Technology (Organic Structure)
High formalization	Low formalization
High centralization	Low centralization
High degree of specialization	Low degree of specialization
Wide span of control	Moderate to narrow span of control
Vertical, written communication	Horizontal communications

Source: Based on Richard L. Daft, *Organization Theory and Design*, 6th ed. (Cincinnati, OH: South-Western College Publishing, 1998), Exhibit 4.10, p. 136.

exhibit | **15.14**

Summary of Organization Characteristics Associated with Structure

FUNCTIONAL STRUCTURE:

Strengths: Allows economies of scale within functions; permits in-depth skill development and high-quality technical problem solving; enables organization to efficiently accomplish functional goals.

Weaknesses: Slow response time to environmental changes; communication and coordination across functions are poor; innovation may be restricted; vertical hierarchy may become overloaded.

Fit: Good for use in a stable environment with routine technologies and when strategic goals require internal efficiency and technical quality, as for a low-cost leadership strategy.

DIVISIONAL STRUCTURE:

Strengths: Organization can be more responsive to change; coordination across functional areas within each division is excellent; employees develop a broader goal orientation.

Weaknesses: Eliminates economies of scale within functional departments, so efficiency is reduced; potentially poor coordination across divisions; may limit technical specialization, expertise, and training for employees.

Fit: Used in environments of moderate to high uncertainty and with nonroutine technologies. Strategic goals call for external adaptation, innovation, and customer response, as for a differentiation strategy.

MATRIX STRUCTURE:

Strengths: Allows organization to achieve high coordination needed to meet needs for both innovation and efficiency; employees get training in both specialist and general skills; engages employees actively in team meetings and the achievement of goals.

Weaknesses: Dual chain of command can be frustrating and confusing; may generate high conflict because the matrix pits divisional against functional goals; can be time consuming because of frequent meetings to resolve conflicts; power balance may be difficult to maintain.

Fit: Can be very effective in an uncertain environment and for nonroutine technologies. Strategic goals are for both product innovation and technical specialization.

HORIZONTAL STRUCTURE:

Strengths: Promotes flexibility and rapid response to changes in customer needs; directs attention of everyone toward the customer; gives employees a broad view of overall organizational goals; promotes a focus on teamwork and collaboration.

Weaknesses: Determining core processes is difficult and time consuming; requires changes in culture, job design, management philosophy, and information and reward systems; may threaten established power and authority structures; requires significant training of employees to work effectively in a horizontal team environment; may limit in-depth skill development.

Fit: Used in environments that are both highly complex and rapidly changing; technologies are nonroutine; and strategic goals call for rapid product and service innovations to meet changing customer desires.

NETWORK STRUCTURE:

Strengths: Allows even small organizations to attain global reach and competitiveness; promotes workforce flexibility and greater variety for employees in the core organization; reduced overhead.

Weaknesses: Managers have little or no hands-on control over most work activities; the organization can lose an organizational part if a partner fails to deliver or goes out of business; potential for significant coordination and negotiation costs to keep the network functioning.

Fit: Good for use in rapidly changing, uncertain environments; technologies may be routine or nonroutine; strategic goals call for rapid response to changing customer needs on a global scale.

Summary

Exhibit 15.14 summarizes ideas about the various structures we discussed earlier in the chapter and the organizational characteristics associated with them. Managers design organization structure to fit several contingency factors, including strategic goals, environment, and technology. Structures fall along a continuum from highly mechanistic to highly organic.

apply it

1. Identify examples of both routine and nonroutine technologies at your college or university (or at your workplace).

2. Carnival Cruise Lines (www.carnivalcruising.com) has recently encountered some problems aboard its ships. In fact, over the past few years, the cruise line has had fires aboard its ships *Celebration, Ecstasy,* and *Tropicale.* Search the Web or articles in the library to see what you can find out about how Carnival has responded to these problems. Can you find clues about how the company's organization structure affected its ability to address unexpected events and a changing environment?

Organizational structures are becoming more organic and flexible

Largely because of changes in the environment and advances in technology, many organizations are moving away from traditional vertical hierarchies, extensive formalization, and tight centralized authority toward more flexible, decentralized structures.

Rethinking the Organization

Today's organizations use various combinations of the structures and design elements we have described in this chapter. As we discussed earlier, bureaucratic characteristics such as extensive specialization and formalization are still helpful to organizations, and many large corporations today retain these characteristics to maintain control over the organization. However, in today's rapidly changing environment, managers are recognizing that the machine-like bureaucratic systems of the Industrial Age no longer work so well. Over the past few decades, many organizations have been fighting against increasing formalization and specialization, pushing decision making down to lower levels, widening spans of control, and loosening the chain of command. The emerging learning organization, for example, strives to eliminate both functional and hierarchical boundaries. Status and rank are minimized, and teams include people from all levels of the company. Information is openly shared with everyone throughout the company so people can identify needs and solve problems, and the organization emphasizes the creation and sharing of knowledge. In addition, the learning organization tries to break down barriers between the company and its customers, suppliers, and other organizations. The learning organization strives for a condition that Jack Welch of General Electric has called *boundarylessness.* The free flow of people, ideas, and information that comes from breaking down boundaries both within the organization and with the external environment allows coordinated action to occur in an uncertain and changing environment.

The Impact of Information Technology on Organization Design

One primary factor that is both encouraging and supporting the move toward boundaryless learning organizations is technology for computer networking. *Intranets* or other corporate networks allow people to communicate across geographical, functional, and hierarchical boundaries, share information and knowledge, and collaborate on projects. Networks also enable organizations to keep in close touch with customers and share information with strategic partners, contract manufacturers, or suppliers. This trend toward interorganizational electronic collaboration reaches its ultimate expression in the network organization structure described earlier in this chapter.

Electronic technology is also having other significant implications for organization design, including a trend toward smaller organizations, less hierarchy, decentralized structures, improved coordination, and greater employee participation. For example, the hub of a network organization may be made up of only a few people. In addition, some Internet-based businesses exist almost entirely in cyberspace; there may be no formal "organization" in terms of a building with offices, desks, and so forth. Information technology enables organizations to do the same amount of work with fewer people. Allstate Corp. recently announced the closing of four regional offices and a field support center as the company begins to do more business through electronic commerce and over the Internet.[45] Advanced technology has also enabled organizations to reduce layers of management and decentralize decision making. Information that may have previously been available only to top managers at headquarters can be quickly and easily shared throughout the organization, even across great geographical distances. Technologies that allow people to meet and coordinate online facilitate communication and decision making among distributed, autonomous groups of workers. People and groups no longer have to be located under one roof to collaborate and share information. An organization may be made up of numerous small teams or even individuals who work autonomously but coordinate electronically.

Another important outcome of networking technology is its potential to improve coordination and communication both within the firm and with other organizations. Computer networks can connect people even when their offices, factories, or stores are scattered around the world. For example, General Motors' intranet, dubbed "Socrates" on the basis that the Greek philosopher would be recognizable worldwide, connects some 100,000 staff members around the globe. Employees can use the intranet to communicate with one another and to stay aware of organizational activities and outcomes.[46] This means employees on the front lines can have instant access to pertinent information about their jobs, allowing greater participation and autonomy. It also means employees have to be highly trained and professional to operate and maintain complex computer-based systems. For the most part, unskilled labor is being replaced by technology. The remaining jobs are more interesting, nonroutine, and challenging.

The trend is toward greater decentralization, improved coordination and information sharing, more challenging work, and greater opportunities for participation. However, some organizations use new information technology to reinforce rigid hierarchies and impose even greater control over employees. Organizational culture and management philosophy have a substantial impact on whether information technology is used to decentralize information and authority or to reinforce a centralized authority structure.[47] Culture will be discussed in detail in Chapter 17.

apply it

1. Visit your college career center or library and observe the use of electronic technology by employees and students. How has electronic technology affected the way these departments are designed?

2. Visit a banking or investment e-business on the Internet (for example, wingspan.com, e-loan). What can you learn about the structure of the company from the Web site? In general, what impact do you think electronic technology has had on the structure and design of organizations in the banking industry?

What about today's global organization structures?

Organizations fine-tune the basic structures described in this chapter to meet their particular needs and goals. In addition, these structures may be modified for organizations operating internationally. A company that has only a small amount of international business may start with an export department as part of the domestic functional structure. As international business grows, this usually develops into an international division. Functional structures are rarely used to manage a worldwide business.[48] Some common structures used by international companies are the global product division structure (in which product divisions take responsibility for global operations within their specific product area), the global geographic division structure (which divides the world into regions), and the global matrix structure. An example of a global matrix was illustrated in Exhibit 15.7. The network structure enables even small organizations to be truly global.

In addition, the *transnational model* of organization structure may be used by huge multinational firms with subsidiaries in numerous countries. The **transnational model** of organization structure applies the concept of a boundaryless learning organization to a huge, international corporation. It is useful for large multinational firms that try to exploit both global and local advantages, and perhaps technological superiority, rapid innovation, and global knowledge sharing. While the matrix is effective for handling two issues (such as product and geographic areas), dealing with multiple, interrelated, competitive issues requires a more complex form of organization and structure.

The transnational model operates on a principle of "flexible centralization."[49] It may centralize some functions in one country and some in another, yet decentralize still other functions among its many geographically dispersed divisions. A research and development center may be centralized in Holland and a purchasing center in Sweden, while financial accounting responsibilities are decentralized to operations in many countries. With a transnational model, there is no notion of a single headquarters and no clear top-down corporate level responsibility. Therefore, managers at all levels in any country have authority to develop creative responses and initiate programs that respond to emerging local needs. These ideas may then be dispersed worldwide. Thus, the whole organization is exposed to a broader range of experiences and capabilities, which trigger greater learning and innovation.

transnational model

A model of organization structure and design that applies the concept of a boundaryless learning organization to a huge, global corporation.

Another characteristic of the transnational model is that standard rules, procedures, and close supervision are downplayed. The transnational model is essentially a horizontal structure. It is diverse, extended, and exists in a fluctuating environment, so strict supervision and control are counterproductive. Employees in a transnational structure are not constrained by rigid rules or hierarchies but are instead empowered to think, experiment, develop creative responses, and take action. Leaders in such a structure depend on shared culture, vision, and values to achieve unity and coordination. Similar to the domestic learning organization, the transnational organization strives to break down boundaries between different parts of the organization and with other companies.

Taken together, these characteristics facilitate organizational learning and knowledge sharing on a broad, global scale. Although the transnational model is a truly complex way to conceptualize organization structure, it is becoming increasingly relevant for large, global firms such as Philips Electronics or Unilever that treat the whole world as their playing field and do not have a single country base.

summary OF KEY CONCEPTS

- **Organization structure is reflected in the organization chart.** The organization chart is the visual representation of a whole set of underlying activities and processes in an organization, which make up the organization's structure. Organization structure specifies the set of formal tasks assigned to individuals and departments, the formal reporting relationships that exist within the organization, and the means of coordination across departments.

- **Managers consider several dimensions of organization structure.** Important dimensions of organization structure are chain of command, line and staff, span of management, centralization or decentralization, and formalization. Chain of command is an unbroken line of authority that links all individuals within the organization and specifies who reports to whom. Concepts necessary to an understanding of chain of command are authority, responsibility, accountability, and delegation. An important distinction for some organizations is between line and staff positions. Line departments reflect the organization's primary purpose, whereas staff departments provide specialized skills in support of line departments. Span of control refers to the number of employees who report to a supervisor. A narrow span of control leads to a tall organization structure with more hierarchical levels. A wide span of control means fewer hierarchical levels and a flat structure. Centralization means decision authority is concentrated near the top of the organization; with decentralization, decision authority is pushed downward. Formalization refers to the degree of written documentation, formal rules and procedures, and explicit policies used to direct and control employees.

- **Organization structures serve important purposes.** Organization structures also reflect the degree of work specialization or division of labor within the organization—that is, the degree to which organizational tasks are separated into different jobs. Departmentalization is the process of grouping these different jobs into departments and departments into the total organization. Coordination mechanisms are needed to encourage communication and collaboration across organizational departments and hierarchical levels.

- **Organizations use a variety of structural approaches.** A mechanistic structure is characterized by many rules, extensive work specialization, little teamwork, centralized authority, and a strict chain of command. An organic structure is one that is free flowing and adaptable, has few rules, encourages teamwork that crosses functional and hierarchical boundaries, and decentralizes authority. Organizational structures can be either mechanistic or organic. Some of the most frequently used structures are functional, divisional, matrix, horizontal, and network. Each type of structure has distinct advantages and disadvantages.

- **Managers fit organization structure to the company's needs.** Managers try to design the organization structure to fit the contingency factors of strategy, environment, and technology. An organization using a low-cost leadership strategy can benefit from a vertical, functionally organized structure, whereas an organization with a differentiation strategy needs a flexible, horizontal structure. A flexible, horizontal structure is also associated with environmental uncertainty and a nonroutine technology, whereas a traditional vertical structure is appropriate in a stable environment and for use with routine technologies.

- **Organization structures are becoming more organic and flexible.** Because of changes in the environment and technology, many organizations are moving away from rigid vertical structures, extensive formalization, and tight, central-

ized authority toward more flexible, decentralized, and horizontal structures. The emerging learning organization strives to break down both functional and hierarchical boundaries and achieve a condition of boundarylessness. Technology for electronic networking both encourages and supports this trend. Other significant implications of advanced electronic technology include smaller organizations, less hierarchy, decentralized structures, improved coordination, and greater employee participation.

- **What about today's global organization structures?** Organizations can modify the basic organization structures for international operations. Common structures used by global companies are the global product division structure, the global geographic division structure, and the global matrix structure. In addition, the transnational model applies the concept of the boundaryless learning organization to a huge, global corporation.

KEY terms

organizing, p. 518
organization structure, p. 518
organization chart, p. 518
chain of command, p. 520
authority, p. 520
responsibility, p. 520
accountability, p. 520
delegation, p. 521
span of control, p. 521
centralization, p. 522
decentralization, p. 522
formalization, p. 523

work specialization, p. 524
departmentalization, p. 525
coordination, p. 525
project manager, p. 528
organic structure, p. 529
mechanistic structure, p. 530
bureaucracy, p. 530
functional structure, p. 530
divisional structure, p. 531
matrix structure, p. 533
two-boss employees, p. 534
horizontal structure, p. 535

reengineering, p. 535
network organization structure, p. 537
low-cost leadership strategy, p. 540
differentiation strategy, p. 540
organizational environment, p. 542
environmental uncertainty, p. 542
technology, p. 543
routine technologies, p. 544
nonroutine technologies, p. 544
transnational model, p. 548

DISCUSSION questions

1. Some of today's organizations take pride in the fact that they don't have organization charts. What do you think this says about a company's structure? Discuss.
2. Contrast centralization with span of control. Would you expect these characteristics to affect each other in organizations? Why?
3. What are the primary differences between a hori-

zontal structure and a traditional functional structure? Why do you think many organizations are shifting toward more horizontal structures with the use of teams?

4. Nine million people a week line up to pay two dollars or more for a cup of coffee at Starbucks. The company is constantly innovating and coming up with new coffee drinks or new ideas for mak-

ing a trip to Starbucks "an experience." What would you predict about the structure of a Starbucks Coffee store? Explain.

5. Briefly explain the major differences in the functional and the divisional approaches to structure.

6. Some people argue that a matrix structure should be adopted only as a last resort because the dual chains of command create more problems than they solve. Do you agree or disagree? Why? How would you feel about being a two-boss employee?

7. How does a network organization structure enable an organization to respond rapidly in a shifting, uncertain environment? Is the use of authority and responsibility different in a network compared with other types of structure? Explain.

8. Would you like to work for an organization such as Lend Lease, described in the opening vignette? Why or why not?

9. Why are functional structures rarely used by companies operating on a global scale?

SELF-DISCOVERY *exercise*

Organization Structure and You

This exercise will give you a better understanding of the importance of organization structure. Select one of the following situations to organize:

a. The registration process at your college or university

b. A new fast-food restaurant on or near campus

c. A sports rental business in an ocean resort area, which rents such equipment as jet skis

d. A coffee bar and bakery

Background

Organizing is a way to gain some control in an unreliable environment. The environment provides the organization with inputs, such as raw materials, employees, and financial resources. There is a service or product to produce that involves technology. This output goes to customers, a critically important group. The complexities of the environment and the technology determine the complexity of the organization.

Planning Your Organization

1. Write down the purpose of the organization in a few sentences.

2. What are the specific things to be done to accomplish the purpose?

3. Based on the specifics listed in your answer to question 2, develop an organization chart. Each position in the chart will perform a specific task or be responsible for a certain outcome.

4. Add duties to each job position in your chart. These will be job descriptions.

5. How will you make sure the people in each position will work together?

6. What level of skill and ability is required at each position and level in order to be sure you hire the right individuals?

7. Make a list of the decisions that would have to be made as you develop your organization.

8. Who is responsible for customer satisfaction? How will you know if customers' needs are met?

9. How will information flow within the organization?

Source: This exercise appeared in Richard L. Daft, *Organization Theory and Design,* 6th ed. (Cincinnati, OH: South-Western College Publishing, 1998). Adapted by Dorothy Marcic from "Organizing," in Donald D. White and H. William Vroman, *Action in Organizations,* 2nd ed. (Boston: Allyn and Bacon, 1982), p. 154.

ORGANIZATIONAL BEHAVIOR *in your life*

Organizations are such a common part of our lives that we often take them for granted. Every day, we interact with numerous organizations such as a grocery store, a bank, a doctor's office, a fraternity or sorority, or a college bookstore. Even your family can be thought of as an organization. Choose an organization that you interact with on a fairly frequent basis, such as an athletic team, place of employment, theater group, or social club.

Describe the chain of command, span of control, and degree of work specialization. What kinds of coordinating mechanisms are used? Is there anyone who often acts as a project manager? If you could make changes to the organization's structure to make it function better, what would they be?

ORGANIZATIONAL BEHAVIOR news flash

@ As you learned in the opening vignette for Chapter 1 of this text, Hewlett-Packard has appointed a new president and CEO to replace Lewis Platt, who has led the company since 1992. Before he left the company, Platt initiated a major restructuring and redesign effort, which Carly Fiorina has continued to propel. Go to Hewlett-Packard's Web site (www.hp.com) to learn about the company's organization structure and some of the design changes that are being made. To begin, click on "HP Realignment" on the company's home page. You might also click on "About HP" and "Company Facts" to get information about the structure.

Write a brief description of Hewlett-Packard's structural approach based on what you learn from the Web site. What information can you learn from the Web site about H-P's approach to centralization or decentralization? Search for other news articles about Hewlett-Packard to supplement what you learn.

global diversity EVENTS

@ ABB Asea Brown Boveri AG is one of the most thoroughly global companies around. ABB employs more than 200,000 people worldwide in 5,000 profit centers. Use your search engine to locate two or three business news stories about ABB and answer the following questions.

1. Based on your readings, how would you classify ABB's structure? Why?
2. Describe what it might be like to be a manager in a company such as ABB. Would you enjoy such a job?
3. What skills and abilities do you think you would need to be successful?

minicase ISSUE

The Fairfax County Social Welfare Agency's Need for Restructuring

Background. The Fairfax County Social Welfare Agency was created in 1965 to administer services under six federally funded social service grants:

- The Senior Citizens' Development Grant (SCD)
- The Delinquent Juvenile Act Grant (DJA)
- The Abused Children's Support Grant (ACS)
- The Job Development and Vocational Training Grant (JDVT)
- The Food Stamp Program (Food)
- The Psychological Counseling and Family Therapy Fund (Counseling)

The agency's organizational structure evolved as new grants were received and as new programs were created. Staff members—generally the individuals who had written the original grants—were assigned to coordinate the activities required to implement the programs. All program directors reported to the agency's executive director, Wendy Eckstein, and had a strong commitment to the success and growth of their respective programs. The organizational structure was relatively simple, with a comprehensive administrative department handling client records, financial records, and personnel matters (see the organizational chart on the next page).

Lack of Coordination. The sense of program "ownership" was intense. Program directors jealously guarded their resources and only reluctantly allowed their subordinates to assist on other projects. Consequently, there was a great deal of conflict among program directors and their subordinates.

The executive director of the agency was concerned about increasing client complaints regarding poor service and inattention. Investigating the matter, Eckstein discovered the following:

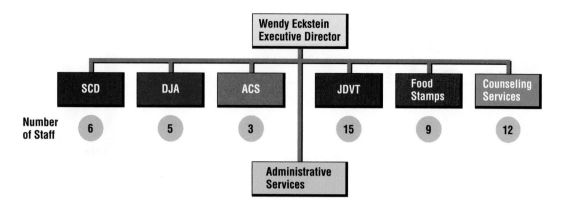

1. Staff members tended to "protect" their clients and not refer them to other programs, even if another program could provide better services.
2. There was a total absence of integration and cooperation among program directors.
3. Programs exhibited a great deal of duplication and redundancy; program directors acquired administrative support for their individual programs.

Eckstein concluded that the present client- or program-based structure no longer met the agency's needs. A major reorganization of this county social welfare agency is being considered.

1. What structural elements might be causing problems for the Fairfax County Social Welfare Agency?
2. What type of structure does the agency use now? If you were Wendy Eckstein, how would you reorganize to increase integration and cooperation?
3. Do you believe a social welfare agency can ever become an organic learning organization? Discuss.

Source: "The Fairfax County Social Welfare Agency," in Fred Maidment (ed.), *1998–99 Annual Editions: Management* (Guilford, CT: Dushkin/McGraw-Hill, 1998), p. 78. Used with permission.

sixteen
CHAPTER
16

Job Design

CONCEPT AND SKILL

preview

After studying this chapter, you should be able to:

- Define and compare job simplification, job rotation, job enlargement, and job enrichment.

- Describe how a specific job could be enriched.

- Discuss why job sharing and flextime are increasingly being used and how these options affect employees.

- Contrast the job characteristics model with the social information processing model of job design.

- Explain why the sociotechnical systems model can increase employee satisfaction and empowerment.

- Describe the potential impact of flexible manufacturing systems and advanced information technology on employees.

- Discuss why organizations are adopting alternative work space design and the effect on employee behavior.

It's a far cry from the assembly line of the past. At General Electric's aircraft engine factory in Durham, North Carolina, no one ever does the same job shift after shift, day after day. Here, nine teams of workers build some of the world's most powerful jet engines, including those that keep *Air Force One* running. The plant manager is the only supervisor in the factory, and teams are given only one directive—the deadline for when their next engine is due to be shipped. The teams themselves make all other decisions. For example, they decide who does what job each day, how to make the manufacturing process more efficient, and what to do about slackers. It is the teams on the shop floor, not bosses in the front office, who write the assembly process, figure out the schedule, order tools and parts, and perform any other jobs necessary, including keeping the plant clean and the machinery and tools in good order.

Each team "owns" an engine from beginning to end. The team is responsible for every step of the process from the time parts are unpacked to the moment a completed engine is loaded on a truck for shipment. Members of the team do the jobs that interest them; no one is required to perform the same task every day. Obviously, to work in such an environment means employees have to be highly skilled. GE/Durham is the only one of the company's engine plants that requires job candidates to be FAA–certified mechanics, for example. Then, everyone learns to assemble different parts of the engine.

Workers at GE/Durham have a high level of responsibility and strive every day to produce perfect jet engines. The philosophy of continuous improvement permeates the plant—employees don't think their job is to make jet engines but to make jet engines *better*. As Bob McEwan, a GE executive, puts it: "Every time I go down there, I'm amazed. They have their washers all sorted into holders, like poker chips sorted into trays. You can easily get the washer you want. It's things like that. They don't ask anybody, they just go and do it."

Some of the factory's workers remember what it was like to work in a place where they were expected to check their minds at the door and perform the same boring, routine task over and over. The difference at GE/Durham is reflected in the words of mechanic Duane Williams, talking about his first six months on the job: "I was never valued that much as an employee in my life. I had never been at the point where I couldn't wait to get to work. But here, I couldn't wait to get to work every day."[1]

GE/Durham's Teams Design Their Own Jobs

> *"I was never valued that much as an employee in my life. . . . I couldn't wait to get to work every day."*
> —**Duane Williams,** GE/Durham mechanic

General Electric's Durham plant is an example of the many companies that have scrapped traditional assembly lines and redesigned manufacturing jobs to give employees greater autonomy, responsibility, and decision-making authority. Although few companies go as far as GE/Durham, many are interweaving individual work with continuous improvement, teamwork and collaboration, trust and openness, shared leadership, employee empowerment and participation, and organizational excellence. In today's environment, where flexibility is a key concern, companies are throwing out traditional job structures and coming up with innovative, customized approaches to getting work done.[2] Many are shifting to team-based work design. Rather than approaching the design of jobs as defining specific tasks and activities that will be performed in isolation, managers look at how teams can be designed to handle complete processes, such as building a jet engine. However, even though organizations are using varied approaches, designing jobs is still a primary concern for managers.

This chapter discusses several ideas related to job design. We begin by looking at the shift to team-based work design and the role of reengineering and total quality management. Then we summarize various approaches to job design and look at new options for scheduling, such as flextime and job sharing. The chapter next considers several concepts and models that can help managers understand work tasks and their relationship to employee satisfaction and productivity. Finally, we summarize the impact of recent technological advances on work design and briefly discuss how employees' physical environment and work space may affect work attitudes and behaviors.

Job design is an important component of organizing

job design

The allocation or alteration of specific tasks and objectives to be attained by employees, including the expected interpersonal and task relationships, to improve productivity and employee satisfaction.

As we learned in the previous chapter, organizing is the deployment of organizational resources to achieve strategic goals. One critical aspect of the job of organizing for managers is to define how the company's human resources can best be assembled and used to accomplish specific tasks and activities. **Job design,** or *job redesign,* refers to the allocation or alteration of specific tasks and objectives to be attained by employees, including the expected interpersonal and task relationships, to improve both employee satisfaction and organizational productivity. For example, job design occurs every time a manager assigns an employee a new task, gives instructions for performing an activity, forms a team, or empowers workers with greater decision-making authority. When managers at Corning's Erwin, New York, plant created production teams and trained all workers to operate and repair the machines, load the kilns, pack and ship the finished product, order parts, and inspect for quality, they were performing job redesign. Each of these tasks had once been assigned to individual workers at the plant, with each employee handling only a small, routine task day after day.[3]

Research findings indicate that effective job design is related to improved organizational profitability and productivity.[4] For example, the Texas Center for the Quality of Work Life found that cross-training workers to perform a variety of jobs and creating job classifications that reflect broad areas of skill (rather than narrow, discrete tasks) helped companies improve their overall performance by 30 to 40 percent.[5]

Early in the 20th century and up until the past several decades, job design was often based on the idea that managers should design jobs to produce maximum economic efficiency. Employees' attitudes about the job were rarely considered. Jobs in general were highly specialized and standardized. Recall from the previous chapter that extensive *work specialization* means that employees specialize in a single task—each individual does only one small piece of an activity rather than the entire activity. Work specialization means that jobs can be performed efficiently, but they tend to be routine and unsatisfying.

More recent approaches suggest that to be effective, job design should consider the human needs of employees as well as the need for efficiency.[6]

These approaches assume that people want more challenge and responsibility at work. Engaging employees more fully helps meet their needs as well as enables the organization to achieve high levels of productivity and customer service. This underlying change in philosophy is partly responsible for the widespread shift toward the use of work teams over the past 15 to 20 years. In addition, the education and skill level of the workforce in the United States and other developed countries has steadily increased over the past several decades, so that employees are increasingly capable of performing expanded jobs rather than narrow, standardized tasks.

Team-Based Work Design

The move toward teams is a significant trend in today's organizations, as described in Chapter 8. Recall from that chapter that organizations are using various types of teams, including problem-solving teams, task forces, cross-functional teams, and self-directed teams. Companies such as General Electric, Motorola, Saturn, AT&T, and Xerox are increasingly using teams in organizing tasks and activities. In the horizontal structure described in Chapter 15, teams are the fundamental unit of work design. These self-directed teams are made up of employees with different skills who rotate jobs to produce an entire product or service, and they often work directly with customers. Teams have the authority to make decisions and improve work processes.

In general, team-based work design broadens the scope of jobs and reduces specialization, as at GE/Durham. Teams can give employees greater involvement in their jobs and a greater sense of identification with the organization. Employees are enthusiastic about their involvement in bigger projects rather than narrow, specialized tasks. Jobs are more interesting and fulfilling. However, team-based work design also has some disadvantages for employees. Whereas people may be energized by their participation in a team, they may also experience new conflicts and greater demands on their time. For example, the need for coordination with others is much greater than when an employee works independently. Teams have to spend time deciding how work will be performed and organizing people and other resources to do it. In addition, today's teams often bring together employees from different countries and cultural backgrounds, who may perceive problems in different ways and have different styles of communication and problem solving. Employees may need training in communication, diversity awareness, and conflict resolution to handle these new demands. In general, the use of teams requires higher level organizational behavior skills for both managers and employees.

Global teams present even greater challenges. **Global teams,** sometimes called *transnational teams,* are made up of members whose activities span multiple countries. For example, Heineken formed a 13-member team representing 13 countries to determine the best reconfiguration for the company's European production facilities.[7] Global teams have to coordinate their work across time, distance, and culture. In some cases, members speak different languages, use different technologies, and have different beliefs about authority, time orientation, decision making, and so forth. Recall the work of Geert Hofstede, discussed in Chapter 2, which found that

global teams

Teams made up of members whose activities span multiple countries.

national culture differences can significantly affect working relationships. Terry Neill, a managing partner at Andersen Consulting's London-based change management practice, uses Hofstede's findings in his work with companies. Based on his experiences with global companies such as Unilever PLC, Shell Oil, and British Petroleum, Neill points out that the Dutch, Irish, Americans, and British are generally quite comfortable with open argument in a team setting. However, Japanese and other Asian employees often feel uneasy with or even threatened by such directness.[8] How these and other cultural differences are handled has a tremendous impact on team members' satisfaction and effectiveness.

For a global team to be effective, all team members have to be willing to deviate somewhat from their own values and norms and establish new norms for the team.[9] The team development steps outlined in Chapter 8—identifying team purpose, selecting members, and training both team members and managers—become even more critical with global teams. For example, when team members are bound by a common, shared purpose, it can serve to bridge culture and distance gaps. Organizations also have to invest the time and resources to adequately educate employees so they can be sensitive to cultural differences among team members. One model for global team effectiveness, called the GRIP model, suggests that organizational leaders focus on developing common understanding among global team members in four critical areas: goals, relationships, information sharing, and work processes.[10]

The Role of Reengineering

The shift to team-based work design sometimes goes hand-in-hand with *reengineering*. Sometimes called *business process reengineering*, this approach involves a complete rethinking and redesign of key work processes and a break from outmoded rules and outdated ways of thinking about job design and task relationships. The primary focus of reengineering is to break down or prevent barriers that separate employees from one another and from customers. Reengineering basically means taking a clean slate approach, pushing aside all notions of how things are done now, and looking at how work can best be designed for optimal performance and customer value. Because reengineering examines work processes that cross functional boundaries, it is frequently associated with a shift toward greater teamwork.

Companies are finding that top-heavy, functionally organized structures, extensive work specialization, and tight centralization can prevent them from meeting rapidly changing customer needs in today's world. Thus, reengineering has been a popular trend in all industries. One poll found that 78 percent of *Fortune* 500 companies and 68 percent of British firms were reengineering one process or another. In response to another recent survey, 44 percent of manufacturing firms, 48 percent of utility companies, and 52 percent of insurance companies indicated that they were involved in reengineering.[11] Such companies as Hoechst Celanese, Union Carbide, DuPont Co., and BellSouth Telecommunications are among dozens of companies that have been involved in major reengineering efforts. At Hallmark, reengineering led to a new approach to greeting card development.

Hallmark used to be organized by functional departments, and employees designed cards in a step-by-step assembly-line process. Artists did their part, then passed designs on to writers, and so forth. Employees rarely got to see how their piece of work fit into the total product. In addition, because of delays, errors, and rework, it sometimes took the company more than two years to create and produce a new greeting card.

After reengineering, Hallmark put employees from every department together in teams and empowered each team to take charge of cards for a particular holiday. Artists, lithographers, writers, designers, and photographers now share ideas, critique their own work, and make decisions without waiting for management approval. Rather than each individual doing only one specific task, the team works together to produce a complete line of cards. Results are impressive: The cycle time for getting new cards to market was halved. For employees, the change brought more responsibility and greater job satisfaction. For a company that lives or dies on new products, reengineering and the shift to team-based work design have led to increased productivity and faster development time, translating into big savings in time and money.[12]

✿ Hallmark Cards

The new process at Hallmark not only helped the company cut costs, but also led to greater employee involvement and satisfaction. However, many reengineering projects have been complete failures. Reengineering is time consuming and expensive and may be best suited to organizations facing serious competitive threats. Reengineering is also usually painful for employees. Some lose their jobs, while those who remain find that their jobs are dramatically different, requiring a broader range of technical and interpersonal skills, the ability to interact with customers, greater challenges, and a higher level of responsibility. Although the changes can lead to greater job satisfaction and employee fulfillment, reengineering can also create high levels of stress for workers who may fear losing their jobs and have difficulty adjusting to new work processes and relationships.

Continuous Improvement and Total Quality Management

Total quality management was described in Chapter 1 as an organization-wide effort to continuously improve the quality of work processes. Implementing TQM in an organization can also have a significant impact on job design. The quality movement emerged in Japan as a result of American influence after World War II. Interestingly, the ideas of W. Edwards Deming, known as the "father of the quality movement," were originally scoffed at in America but were eagerly picked up and modified by the Japanese, who used them to rebuild their industries into world powers. During the 1980s, American companies began putting significant emphasis on total quality management in order to remain competitive. The approach infuses quality values and a customer service orientation throughout every activity within a company, with front-line workers intimately involved in continuously improving all organizational processes. TQM requires companywide participation in quality control, so employees find themselves responsible for constant problem solving. TQM is an ongoing process rather than a specific program that has a beginning and an end.

Many companies use the **Shewhart Cycle** of continuous improvement (sometimes called the PDCA Cycle—Plan, Do, Check, Act Cycle), as illustrated in Exhibit 16.1. Managers first *plan* a test or change in a specific process, then *do* the test or carry out the change, *check* the results, and finally *act* to improve the process based on what they learn. A number of

Shewhart Cycle

A cycle of continuous improvement used in companies that have instituted total quality management; also called PDCA Cycle—Plan, Do, Check, Act Cycle.

exhibit 16.1

exhibit | **16.1**

The Shewhart Cycle of Continuous
Improvement

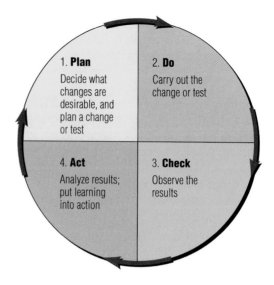

1. **Plan**
Decide what
changes are
desirable, and
plan a change
or test

2. **Do**
Carry out the
change or test

4. **Act**
Analyze results;
put learning
into action

3. **Check**
Observe the
results

cycle reiterations may be needed before satisfactory results are achieved.
The cycle repeats itself continuously, and everyone throughout the organization must be closely involved in planning, solving problems, and learning.[13] Managers look to employees as a source of continuous improvement
ideas not as factors of production and efficiency. One way employees are
involved is through *quality circles,* in which groups of employees meet regularly to discuss and solve problems affecting the quality of their work. This
pushes decision making and problem solving down to the people who do
the job and know it better than anyone else. Team-based work design is
also widely used in organizations that have introduced TQM.

Companies such as Westinghouse, Baltimore Gas & Electric Company,
and Eaton Corporation have successfully used continuous improvement
processes. At South Carolina Baptist Hospital in Columbia, South Carolina,
2,500 employees were trained in continuous improvement techniques.
Managers learn a coaching rather than a controlling role and give employees the authority and responsibility to recognize and act on their ideas for
improvement. Baptist has learned that countless improvements require a
long-term approach to building quality into the very fiber of the organization. Over time, project by project, activity by activity, quality through continuous improvement has become the way all the hospital's employees approach their jobs.[14] However, as with reengineering, TQM programs are not
always successful. In addition, the constant push for quality can create
greater stress and anxiety for some employees.

apply it

1. Think about your current job or your job as a college or university student.
How might you apply the concept of continuous improvement and the Shewhart Cycle to improve your performance and productivity?

Organizations choose among several options for job design

When organizations want to redesign jobs, they have several approaches from which to choose. As a reference point, we begin by describing job simplification, which is based on principles drawn from scientific management (described in Chapter 1) and emphasizes extensive work specialization to achieve efficiency. In general, organizations have moved away from job simplification techniques. Employees are expected to be more actively involved in a broader set of tasks and activities that contribute to problem solving, learning, and continuous improvement. Three widely used options are job rotation, job enlargement, and job enrichment. In addition, we will discuss two recent trends that offer managers additional flexibility for job design: job sharing and flexible scheduling.

Job Simplification

Job simplification pursues task efficiency by reducing the number of tasks one employee must do. Tasks are designed to be simple, repetitive, and standardized, as with a traditional automobile assembly line. The worker has more time to concentrate on doing more of the same routine task, because complexity has been stripped from the job. With job simplification, workers are interchangeable because they need little training or skill and are not expected to use judgment and discretion on the job. Although job simplification enables the organization to attain a high level of efficiency, it has negative consequences as well. People typically dislike routine, boring jobs. Employee satisfaction and morale suffer, and employees may react in a number of negative ways, such as high absenteeism, tardiness, and carelessness on the job. Job simplification is compared with job rotation and job enlargement in Exhibit 16.2.

job simplification

A job design whose purpose is to improve task efficiency by reducing the number of tasks a single employee must perform.

Job Rotation

Job rotation systematically moves employees from one job to another, thereby increasing the number of different tasks they perform without increasing the complexity of any one job. For example, an autoworker might

job rotation

A job design that systematically moves employees from one job to another to provide them with greater variety and stimulation.

exhibit | **16.2**

Types of Job Design

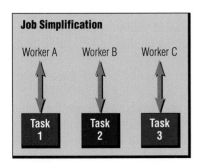
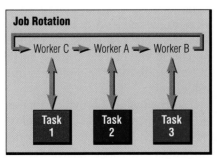
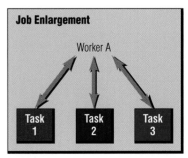

install taillights one week and windshields the next. Job rotation still takes advantage of engineering efficiencies, but it provides a higher level of variety and stimulation for employees. In addition, job rotation gives managers more flexibility in scheduling and hiring. There are some drawbacks, however. Training costs are higher because employees have to be trained to perform more than one single task. Productivity may decrease because an employee has to adjust to the new job and learn to work with others in the new work group. Supervisors may have to spend more time answering questions or guiding employees. Job rotation can also eventually lead to boredom because employees soon master the repetitive work of the new task.

Companies such as Dayton Hudson, Microsoft, and Motorola have expanded the notion of job rotation to train a flexible workforce and enable employees to perform a variety of different jobs. Also called *cross-training,* this approach to job rotation means organizations break away from ossified job categories and descriptions. Employee interest and enthusiasm increase because of the greater variety, and quality often improves because of increased employee skills. In addition, because employees can perform several different jobs, labor costs for the organization may be reduced.

At 800-Flowers, managers knew the order taking and customer service departments required dedicated, enthusiastic employees but found that the routine tasks caused employees to burn out quickly. President Jim McCann began cross-training workers so they could switch to different jobs as organization and employee needs changed. For example, order takers might rotate to a job at one of the company's retail stores or at headquarters for variety. Switching jobs helps keep employee enthusiasm high and revitalizes the business because workers bring fresh perspectives to each job they do.[15]

Technical companies are using cross-training to prevent burnout among help desk staff. According to the Help Desk Institute in San Francisco, the average help desk turnover is 65 percent. Sitting at a phone all day and listening to complaints quickly wears employees down. To combat the routine and repetition, companies such as Sage Software and Autodesk build in job rotation so that help desk employees have the opportunity to work in the lab, handle administrative duties, or work temporarily in other departments.[16]

Job Enlargement

job enlargement

A job design that combines a series of tasks into one new, broader job to give employees variety and challenge.

With **job enlargement,** a series of tasks are combined into one new, broader job. This approach to job design is a response to employee dissatisfaction with oversimplified jobs. Instead of only one task, an employee might be responsible for four or five and have more time to complete them. For example, rather than just changing oil at a location such as Jiffy Lube or Precision Tune, one mechanic changes the oil, greases the car, airs the tires, and checks fluid levels, battery, air filter, and so forth. Then, the same person is responsible for discussing the car's routine maintenance with the customer.

Job enlargement provides greater job variety and challenge for employees. Many manufacturing companies are tearing out the old assembly line and enlarging jobs by training workers to perform several assembly steps rather than one small task. At Sony Corporation's factory in Kohda, Japan, for example, the assembly line for camcorders was dismantled and replaced with small shops where workers walk through a spiral line and assemble an entire camcorder themselves, performing every task from soldering to final testing.[17] Similarly, jobs at Maytag were enlarged when work was redesigned so that employees assembled an entire water pump rather than performing one small, separate task on an assembly line.

The key to effective job enlargement is to ensure that employees are allowed the extra time and support to complete the broader job. One complaint among employees has been that job enlargement simply means that they are doing more work in the same amount of time for the same amount of pay. Some workers view the added demands in a negative way, so managers have to use care when designing enlarged jobs.

Job Enrichment

Rather than just changing the number and frequency of tasks a worker performs, **job enrichment** incorporates high-level motivators—including job responsibility, recognition, and opportunities for learning and personal growth—into the work. Recall our discussion in Chapter 5 of high-level motivators, such as Maslow's need hierarchy and Herzberg's two-factor theory. Whereas job rotation and job enlargement expand jobs *horizontally,* by broadening the tasks performed by employees, job enrichment expands jobs *vertically* as well, by extending the degree of control the worker has over the job. With an enriched job, employees have control over the resources necessary for performing the job, make decisions about how to do the work, and set their own work pace. Exhibit 16.3 compares job enrichment with job simplification for a shirt manufacturing company. With job simplification, employees perform small, routine tasks in a step-by-step fashion. Job enrichment, on the other hand, means that a team of workers coordinates and arranges tasks to complete the entire process. The team has decision-making authority over how to do the job and is accountable for final results.

Many companies enrich jobs by forming workers into teams that perform a complete activity or process. For example, the mechanics at the GE/Durham plant have enriched jobs. They not only perform a complete horizontal process but also have an exceptional degree of control over their own work and immediate feedback regarding how well they are performing. With only one manager in a plant of around 170 workers, teams are responsible for managing themselves. As one employee put it, "I have 15 bosses. All of my teammates are bosses."[18] Another example is Zotefoams, a British foam manufacturer based in Croydon, Surrey. Shop floor employees are organized into teams that perform a wide variety of tasks. In addition, they have responsibility for quality, scheduling, and setting work priorities.[19]

Enriched jobs increase workers' autonomy and allow them to feel a greater sense of responsibility and pride in their work. As with other options, not every employee will respond favorably to increased job responsibility. However, in general, job enrichment leads to increased employee satisfaction and decreased turnover and absenteeism. In a recent survey, for example, empowerment of workers, including increased job responsibility,

job enrichment

A job design that incorporates achievement, recognition, and opportunities for learning and growth into the work.

exhibit **16.3**

Comparing Job Simplification and Job Enrichment

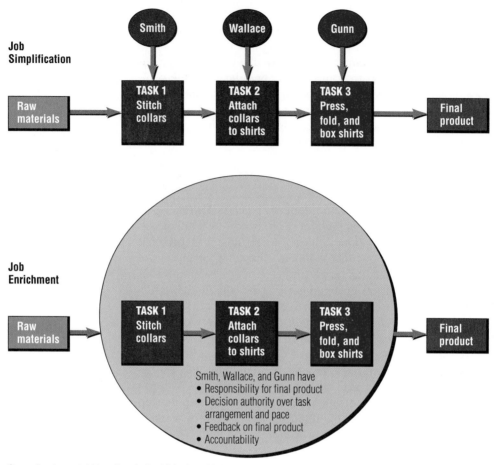

Source: Based on material from *Organizational Behavior and Performance,* 4th ed., by Andrew D. Szilagyi Jr. and Marc J. Wallace Jr. Copyright © 1987 by Scott Foresman and Company.

authority to define their work, and power to make decisions, was found to be the most dramatic indicator of workplace satisfaction.[20]

Here's how Ralcorp, a cereal manufacturing plant in Sparks, Nevada, used ideas about job design to reduce total plant costs and manufacturing expenses while significantly increasing the factory's productivity and yield.

❦ Ralcorp Holdings, Inc.

Managers at Ralston Purina's spin-off cereal manufacturing plant in Sparks, Nevada, knew they needed a new approach to job design to meet the challenges of better customer service, higher quality, and greater efficiency. Consider how a packing line works in a traditional cereal manufacturing plant. The line has at least five different job classifications. Employees operate individual pieces of equipment and perform discrete tasks, with little cross-training or job rotation. As a result, the plant needs large numbers of workers to perform the various tasks, and many workers are idle at certain times during the packing process. In addition, the system can create bottlenecks because some employees have to wait for slower workers to finish their tasks and hand off the work.

Ralcorp decided to take a new approach and build a flexible workforce. It enlarged jobs by combining several packing positions into a single job and trained employees to operate all of the packing line's equipment. Employees were given both the ability and the responsibility to perform all the various functions in their department, not just a single task.

In addition, Ralcorp managers wanted to enrich jobs by giving workers greater autonomy and control over their own work. The employees on the line are responsible for all screening and interviewing of new hires as well as training and advising one another. Employees also manage the production flow to and from their upstream and downstream partners—they understand the entire production process so they can see how their work affects the quality and productivity of employees in other departments. Ralcorp invests heavily in training to be sure employees have the needed operational skills as well as the ability to make decisions, solve problems, manage quality, and contribute to continuous improvement. Although Ralcorp's flexible workforce required a large initial investment, managers believe it has paid off through higher long-term productivity, reduced costs, and happier employees.[21]

Organizations such as Ralcorp, 800-Flowers, and Maytag use ideas about job rotation, job enlargement, and job enrichment to build a flexible workforce. Today's environment demands faster service, higher quality, and better customer relationships, which requires workforce flexibility. In addition, in today's economy there are an increasing number of *knowledge workers,* which also demands a more flexible approach to designing work. For example, Internet-related jobs had increased in number to 2.3 million in the first quarter of 1999, an increase of almost 50 percent from the previous year.[22] These changing business conditions have led to some new approaches to scheduling that allow managers increased flexibility in designing jobs. These options allow employees to work outside the traditional boundaries of time, place, and hierarchy.

Job Sharing

A number of organizations have introduced flexible scheduling options as one way to improve job design for employees, increase productivity, and respond to today's tight labor market. Hundreds of U.S. companies, including Booz, Allen & Hamilton, Xerox, Raytheon Corp., and International Paper Company, are undergoing a major shift in relationships between employer and employee, developing innovative flexibility initiatives to recruit and retain quality employees.[23] For example, after a 1995 employee survey showed that 81 percent of workers wanted greater control in balancing their work and personal lives, Ralston Purina introduced a major initiative that includes job sharing, flextime, and telecommuting options, in addition to sabbaticals and other innovative choices. The company has shifted its perspective from a focus on the *time* employees work to the *results* they produce.[24]

One recent approach is *job sharing,* which allows two or more part-time employees to jointly cover a traditional full-time job. For example, one person might work as a press operator on Mondays and Wednesdays, while another person takes over the same job on Tuesdays, Thursdays, and Fridays. Another option would be for one person to work from 8 a.m to noon, while someone else does the same job from noon to 5 p.m. Job sharing is growing in popularity as an option for employees seeking a better work-life balance, although only about 30 percent of large organizations currently offer job sharing as an option.[25]

One interesting example of job sharing occurs at Hamilton Standard, a United Technologies manufacturing company. Jennifer and Hisham ElShakhs share not only a marriage and a two-year-old son but also a single engineering job. Jennifer works on Monday and Tuesday; Hisham works on Thursday and Friday; and both partners work on Wednesday. United Technologies' alternative work methods include job sharing, flextime, and telecommuting, which will be discussed later in this chapter.[26]

Job sharing increases flexibility for employees who may have young children or elderly relatives to care for, those who have other commitments that prevent them from holding a full-time job, or retirees who want to work only part time. For Jennifer and Hisham ElShakhs, it allows both parents to be closely involved in their son's life and early development, while also continuing the work they both love. Thus, job sharing can be highly beneficial for workers for whom a traditional full-time job is not practical or desirable. For organizations, job sharing means the organization can take advantage of the skills and abilities of workers who might not be available for full-time work. In addition, the different perspectives and talents that are brought to the job can benefit the organization. However, job sharing may increase coordination time and costs for organizations. Work has to be carefully planned and organized, and coordination between the partners sharing a job has to be tight to ensure that the work is performed completely and correctly.

Flextime

flextime

A scheduling option in which employees have some discretion over the hours they work, within certain limits.

A more common approach to flexible scheduling is called **flextime,** which allows employees some discretion over what hours they work. Within certain limits, an employee can decide when to go to work and when to leave. For example, a "morning person" or someone who has a child arriving home from school in the afternoon might choose to arrive at the office at 6:30 a.m. and leave at 3:30 p.m. Someone else might come in at 10:00 a.m. and leave at 7:00 in the evening.

Numerous business and nonprofit organizations offer some type of flextime scheduling. For example, the University of California–Irvine allows employees to stagger their starting and ending times as well as to work four day weeks or other alternate schedules. Mac McCormick, facilities manager for the School of Arts at UCI, works 80 hours spread over a nine-day period and has every other Friday off. He comes in at 7 a.m., which enables him to check buildings for any problems before classes begin. Most companies that allow flextime have certain core hours when all employees are required to be in the office—for example, from 9 a.m to 2 p.m—but employees can adjust their hours around that core time. The two requirements for a flextime program are that all employees must be in the office during core hours and that each employee works the required number of hours per week for which he or she has contracted (for example,

Flextime offers employees some discretion over what hours they work. Lethia Swett Mann, vice president of community development at First Tennessee Bank in Memphis, Tennessee, has a shortened workday, leaving at 3:30 p.m. to meet her two kids at the bus. First Tennessee also provides subsidized child care and was 39th on the list of Fortune *magazine's 100 best companies to work for.*
(Source: © 2000/Tamara Reynolds)

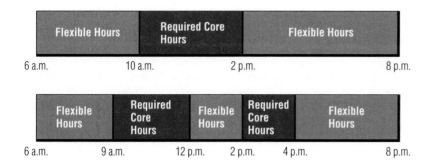

exhibit **16.4**

Examples of Flextime Schedules

40 hours for a full-time job).[27] Two examples of flextime schedules are shown in Exhibit 16.4.

Flextime has become a very popular option for today's organizations and employees. One poll found that 53 percent of companies with more than 1,000 employees offered flextime as an option.[28] Lancaster Laboratories, one of the largest analytical laboratories in the United States, which serves the pharmaceutical, environmental, food, and animal health care industries, has implemented a number of innovative family-friendly policies, including flextime. Lancaster found that these programs resulted in reduced turnover, stronger recruiting, and reduced training costs. Employees report higher morale and job satisfaction, as well as less stress in their work and family lives.[29] Other organizations and research studies support the idea that flextime generally leads to reduced absenteeism and turnover and greater worker productivity.[30] People can schedule their work hours in alignment with their personal and family needs, as well as adjust their schedules so that they are working when they feel most energetic and productive.

Flextime may not be suitable for every job, however. For example, a receptionist's job in a doctor's office demands that the employee be at his or her workplace at a predetermined time every day. Another interesting finding is that employees are sometimes hesitant to take advantage of flexible work opportunities for fear that they will be perceived as underachievers who are willing to compromise their careers for personal concerns. Enlightened companies are working to change corporate cultures that put pressure on employees to be overachievers.[31]

apply it

1. You have been assigned to work with the cafeteria-style food service unit at your college or university to redesign jobs of serving line workers (or you may select any job that you feel could benefit from job redesign). If you choose the cafeteria line, consider the following characteristics: On the line, one worker dishes out entrees, another serves vegetables, someone else keeps bowls of salad available, and so forth. Other jobs include making iced tea and coffee, offering a choice of breads and desserts, and keeping the line stocked. Each person does the same job every day, and they have all become highly efficient even though the line gets extremely hectic at mealtimes. However, tardiness and absenteeism have been increasing, and supervisors want to know if redesigning jobs can help. What approach might you take to redesigning jobs for these workers?

Managers analyze work tasks and processes to determine effective job design

How do managers know how to most effectively design or redesign jobs to meet the needs of employees and the organization? Several models and concepts can help managers analyze work tasks and understand their relationship to organizational productivity as well as to employee performance, motivation, and job satisfaction. These will be briefly discussed in this section.

Understanding Organizational Productivity

organizational productivity

The effective and efficient achievement of an organization's goals.

One of managers' major concerns is organizational productivity, so they try to design jobs to help achieve it. **Organizational productivity** is the effective and efficient achievement of an organization's goals. That is, productivity involves both effectiveness and efficiency. Organizational *effectiveness* is the degree to which the organization achieves its stated goals; it means that the organization accomplishes what it sets out to do. Organizational *efficiency* refers to the amount of resources used to achieve an organizational goal. It is based on how many raw materials and human resources and how much money is used to produce a product or service. Managers want to design jobs that can help attain organizational goals by using resources in an efficient and effective manner. As discussed earlier, managers in earlier years were concerned largely with improving efficiency, at the expense of employee satisfaction and motivation. Today's managers realize that employees' attitudes and needs must be taken into account as well for the organization to achieve high productivity.

Sociotechnical Systems Model

sociotechnical systems model

A model of job design that recognizes the complex interaction of technical and human needs in effective job design, combining the needs of people with the organization's need for technical efficiency.

The **sociotechnical systems model** recognizes the interaction of technical and human needs in effective job design, combining the needs of people with the organization's need for technical efficiency. The *socio* portion of the approach refers to the people and groups who work in organizations and how work is organized and coordinated. The *technical* portion refers to the materials, tools, machines, and processes used to transform organizational inputs into outputs.

The sociotechnical systems model grew out of the work of Eric Trist, a founder of the Tavistock Institute, who studied British coal miners in the mid-1940s.[32] Despite new and expensive mechanization in the industry, productivity had not increased significantly. In addition, labor disputes were common and absenteeism was high, despite improvements in miners'

Why would anyone wear a computer? For organizational productivity, effectiveness, and efficiency, if you're an inspector for a Norwegian company that monitors the safety of large ships. This IBM prototype of a wearable PC features a tiny, headset-mounted display, IBM's Microdrive storage device, and ViaVoice speech-recognition software—all in a belt-mounted package that weighs less than a pound. Productivity is enhanced because the wearable PC allows the inspector, while on the job, to access computer drawings, verbally enter evaluations, and submit digital reports—even while his hands are wearing gloves or toting a wrench. (Source: Courtesy of IBM Corporation)

working conditions. Trist and his associates studied a highly successful experiment that used relatively autonomous work groups that interchanged roles and worked with a minimum of supervision. Their work suggested that the miners had rediscovered a small-group approach to work that had been used successfully before the advent of mechanization. Furthermore, Trist's research suggested that most of the coal industry's problems came about primarily because of significant changes in the technical aspect of production without adequate attention to their appropriateness for the physical environment and their impact on social needs. Trist envisioned a new approach to work that would blend the requirements of both the technical and social aspects of a work system. Since Trist's work, numerous researchers have contributed to the further development of the sociotechnical systems model.

Exhibit 16.5 illustrates the three primary components of the model. The *social system* includes all human elements—such as individual and team behaviors, organizational culture, management practices, and degree of communication openness—that can influence the performance of work. The *technical system* refers to the type of production technology, the level of interdependence among tasks, the complexity of tasks, and so forth.[33] The goal of the sociotechnical systems approach is to design the organization for **joint optimization,** which means that an organization functions best only when the social and technical systems are designed to fit the needs of one another.[34] Designing the organization to meet human needs while ignoring the technical systems or changing technology to improve efficiency while ignoring human needs may inadvertently cause performance problems. The sociotechnical systems approach attempts to find a balance between what workers want and need and the technical requirements of the organization's production system.

One example comes from a museum that installed a closed-circuit TV system. Rather than having several guards patrolling the museum and grounds, the television could easily be monitored by a single guard. Although

joint optimization

A principle that states that the organization functions best when the social and technical systems are designed to fit the needs of one another.

exhibit **16.5**

The Sociotechnical Systems Model

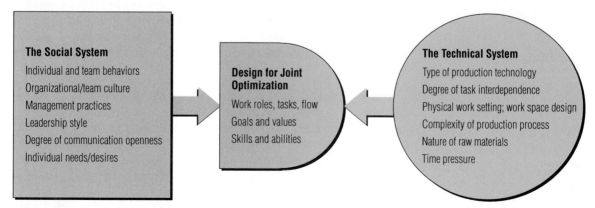

Source: Based on T. Cummings. (1978). "Self-regulating work groups: A socio-technical synthesis." *Academy of Management Review 3:* 625–634; Don Hellriegel, John W. Slocum, and Richard W. Woodman, *Organizational Behavior,* 8th ed. (Cincinnati, OH: South-Western College Publishing, 1998), p. 492; and Gregory B. Northcraft and Margaret A. Neale, *Organizational Behavior: A Management Challenge,* 2nd ed. (Fort Worth, TX: The Dryden Press, 1994), p. 551.

the technology saved money because only one guard was needed per shift, it led to unexpected performance problems. Guards had previously enjoyed the social interaction provided by patrolling; monitoring a closed-circuit television led to alienation and boredom. When a federal agency did an 18-month test of the system, only 5 percent of several thousand experimental covert intrusions were detected by the guard.[35] The system was inadequate because human needs were not taken into account.

Sociotechnical principles first began to be applied to organizations in the 1950s and 1960s, following Trist's work with coal miners in Britain.[36] Since then, organizational change using sociotechnical systems principles has occurred in numerous organizations, including General Motors, Volvo, the Tennessee Valley Authority (TVA), and Procter & Gamble.[37] Although there have been failures, in many of these applications, joint optimization to meet the needs of people as well as achieve technological efficiency improved performance, safety, quality, absenteeism, and employee turnover. Consolidated Diesel's factory in Whitaker, North Carolina, which has always taken a sociotechnical systems approach to work design, considers the widespread sharing of information to be vital to the success of the plant's team-based work system.

🐝 Consolidated Diesel

At Consolidated Diesel's plant, an engine rolls off the assembly line every 72 seconds. The factory has never suffered a major layoff, and average turnover is less than 2 percent. The injury rate at the plant is about one-fifth the national average. The company's managers believe this plant's level of success can be traced to its use of teams based on a sociotechnical systems approach to work.

The company has four principles that guide its approach to work design: fairness, extensive cross-training, giving workers real responsibility and decision-making authority, and open information sharing. Information is considered the lifeblood of Consolidated's team-based system. For one thing, managers listen to employees and involve them closely in solving plant problems. For example, when customer demand became so high that teams were working huge amounts of overtime, managers asked the teams how to handle the problem. They designed new schedules that allowed for greater flexibility, and shifts suddenly decreased from ten hours to eight, with no Saturday work.

To get this kind of involvement, managers must share all information with employees—the bad as well as the good. Managers at the plant spend an hour or two each day just walking around the shop floor, offices, and lab talking informally with workers. They believe it breaks down barriers between workers and management and gives each a chance to learn from the other. In addition, managers hold "state-of-the-plant" meetings each quarter. Small groups of employees meet separately and have a chance to ask any question they want. If managers don't have an answer on the spot, they follow up in the plant's newsletter or closed-circuit television network. "We share the good, the bad, and the ugly," says general manager Jim Lyons. "When good people are given good information, they typically make good decisions."[38]

The factors to be considered in designing jobs based on the sociotechnical systems approach are complex and too detailed for this brief summary. However, one important point illustrated by the Consolidated Diesel example is that managers view employees as valuable resources and provide them with appropriate skills, meaningful work, information, and positive rewards. This principle has become increasingly important in today's world of growing technological complexity.[39] Job design based on achieving maximum technical efficiency, enforcing tight centralized control, and treating workers as mindless and irresponsible is increasingly ineffective.

Job Characteristics Model

One dominant framework that helps managers determine how to best design jobs is the job characteristics model developed by Richard Hackman and Greg Oldham.[40] This model was described in detail in Chapter 5. Hackman and Oldham's research concerned how to alter jobs to increase both the quality of employees' work experience and their productivity. Every job, according to this model, can be defined and described in terms of five key elements or core job dimensions. We now recap these dimensions:

- *Skill variety* means the degree to which a job requires a variety of different tasks and activities, so that an employee must use a variety of personal skills and competencies to carry out the work.
- *Task identity* is the degree to which a job requires completion of a whole and identifiable piece of work, such as completing a water pump at Maytag. The employee completes a process from beginning to end, with an identifiable outcome.
- *Task significance* refers to the degree to which an employee perceives the job as having a substantial impact on the lives or work of others, within or outside of the organization. At Medtronic, which makes medical products such as pacemakers, employees feel that their jobs have great task significance because the products help save lives.
- *Autonomy* is the degree to which a job provides freedom, empowerment, and discretion to the employee in scheduling the work and determining procedures for carrying it out.
- *Feedback* refers to the degree to which carrying out job-related tasks and activities provides the employee with direct and clear information about the effectiveness of his or her performance.

As described in Chapter 5, the model indicates that the more these elements can be designed into a job, the more satisfied, motivated, and productive employees will be. Research in general supports the fact that these elements have a direct and positive impact on employee attitudes and behavior.[41] The job characteristics model contains important insights for managers about job design, and the value of these five core job dimensions is taken into account in new trends toward teamwork, job enrichment, and decentralized decision making.

Social Information Processing Model

The job characteristics model is based on the assumption that employees will perceive the job in the way that managers *intend* for them to perceive it. However, as we learned in the discussion of perception and attribution in Chapter 4, this may not always be the case. Just because a manager gives autonomy to a worker does not necessarily mean the worker will perceive that he or she actually has autonomy.[42]

The **social information processing model** of job design emphasizes the importance of individual perception. An employee's perception of the job may be heavily influenced by social information, including comments, observations, reactions, and other cues provided by people whose opinion

social information processing model

A model of job design that indicates that employees adopt attitudes and behaviors in response to social cues provided by coworkers, managers, and others with whom they come in contact.

the employee values, such as coworkers, managers, customers, family members, or friends.[43] Workers often react to perceptions of their jobs rather than to the objective characteristics of the job. For example, Sarah—a trained financial consultant who left a high-pressure job to gain a better work-life balance—decided to take a job at a warehouse, where she spent her days painting and staining intricate hand-made metal lamps and art pieces. Although the pay was low, Sarah loved the job—she didn't have anyone looking over her shoulder all day, she loved seeing the new pieces and transforming them with colors and stains, and she loved punching out at 4:30 and leaving it all behind, in contrast to her previous job, where she frequently took work home or met clients after hours.

After only a month on the job, however, Sarah's enthusiasm and motivation started to wane, largely because of the social cues she was receiving from coworkers and old friends in the financial services industry. Coworkers consistently bad-mouthed their jobs, said painting metal all day was boring, and complained that having to clock in and out—even for their short lunch break—showed that management didn't trust them. Sarah's old friends often looked embarrassed when she started to talk about her new job and frequently made comments such as "You'll be back in the industry in no time; this is just temporary," or "You know, I could put in a word for you with my boss." The objective characteristics of Sarah's job at the warehouse had not changed, yet Sarah's perception of the job changed because of the social messages she was receiving from others.

Social cues can affect the perception of job characteristics and design in numerous and varied ways. The important point is to be aware that perception plays an important role; managers should pay as much attention to an employee's perceptions of the job as to the actual job characteristics. For example, a manager might spend more time talking with Sarah about how interesting it is to work with pieces of art that will show up in restaurants, homes, and other locations all over the world. Managers should particularly be aware that newly hired employees or those moving into new positions may be more susceptible to social information cues. A positive, open work environment may be as important to work outcomes as characteristics of job design.

apply it

1. Think of a time when your opinions of a job, school activity, or volunteer project were influenced by social information processing. Describe how you felt about the job, activity, or project when you first started and then discuss how your feelings changed over time. What part of the change in your feelings can you attribute to objective factors and what part to the comments and attitudes of others toward your job?

Recent technological advances have had a significant influence on job design

Managers often intentionally change job design to improve productivity or worker motivation. However, managers may also unconsciously influence job design through the introduction of new technologies, which can change how jobs are done and the very nature of jobs.[44] Managers should understand how the introduction of a new technology may affect employees' jobs. In addition, technology offers new options for work scheduling, such as telecommuting, that were not possible before.

Technology and Job Design

The common theme of new automated technologies in the workplace is that they in some way substitute machinery for human labor in transforming inputs into outputs. Automated teller machines (ATMs) have replaced thousands of human bank tellers, for example. IBM has even built a plant in Austin, Texas, that can produce laptop computers without the help of a single worker.[45]

In addition to actually replacing human workers, technology may have several different effects on the jobs that remain. Research has indicated that mass production technologies tend to produce *job simplification,* which means that the variety and difficulty of tasks performed by a single person are reduced. The consequence is boring, repetitive jobs that generally provide little satisfaction. More advanced technology, on the other hand, tends to lead to *job enrichment,* meaning that the job provides greater responsibility, recognition, and opportunities for growth and development. These technologies create a greater need for employee training and education because workers need higher level skills and greater competence to master their tasks. For example, ATMs took most of the routine tasks (deposits and withdrawals) away from bank tellers and left them with the more complex tasks that require higher level skills.

With advanced technology, workers have to keep learning new skills because technology is changing so rapidly. Advances in information technology, for example, are having a significant effect on jobs in the service industry, including doctors' offices and medical clinics, law firms, and libraries. Workers may find that their jobs change almost daily because of new software programs, increased use of the Internet, and other advances in information technology.

Similarly, **flexible manufacturing systems** have significant effects on jobs and employees. These systems integrate computer-aided design, engineering, and manufacturing, enabling factories to produce small batches of custom products at a cost once possible only through mass production. Factories no longer have to turn out thousands of identical products to achieve economies of scale. Computer programs control the assembly process and can produce numerous different products at the same time to meet diverse customer needs. Taken to its ultimate level, flexible manufacturing allows for *mass customization,* which means each separate product can be tailored to customer needs. For example, Deere & Co. can create one-of-a-kind pieces of farm equipment for customers after installing multi-billion-dollar flexible manufacturing systems.

flexible manufacturing systems

The use of computer-integrated systems for design, engineering, and manufacturing to produce small batches of custom products at a cost once possible only through mass production.

The 161-year-old Deere & Co. was the only agricultural machinery manufacturer in the world that survived the farm crisis of the 1980s with its corporate structure intact. After Deere took another pounding in the early 1990s, with a sales slump of 11 percent and a loss of $20 million, top executives began thinking about the need to shed outmoded attitudes and embrace change.

One of the new concepts that is helping Deere compete in an era of declining demand and increasing competition is mass customization. In the past, Deere sold farmers half-million-dollar pieces of

❦ Deere & Co.

equipment and then let small mom-and-pop shops steal new business as they helped farmers customize the equipment to their individual needs. Now, Deere salespeople ask each customer a series of questions, such as how many rows must be planted and how closely spaced they will be. The salesperson electronically sends an order to a Deere factory, and in less than a day a team of Deere workers—in essence, working as a small, custom shop inside the factory—creates a one-of-kind piece of machinery designed specifically for the customer. Deere offers more than six million possible configurations. Farmers who at one time bought Deere equipment only every six to ten years are now regularly buying custom attachments.

The new technology also required that workers be trained to work in teams rather than on mass production assembly lines. Chairman and CEO Hans Becherer wants change and risk taking to become entrenched in the company's culture and a driving force behind everything Deere does. He has created highly autonomous divisions and pushed authority and responsibility to lower levels. In addition, Deere's Business Process Excellence Initiative was created to give workers the freedom and power to reinvent operations. The initiative, which currently has more than 200 cross-functional teams working on about 800 different projects, makes everybody in the company a change agent. Top managers believe new approaches to work design and a willingness to take risks are key to keeping Deere & Co. healthy as it heads toward its third century of doing business.[46]

How does the introduction of flexible manufacturing systems and new computer-based information technology affect front-line workers? In general, studies have found that it produces three noticeable results for employees:

- More opportunities for intellectual mastery and enhanced cognitive skills for workers
- More worker responsibility for results
- Greater interdependence among workers, enabling more social interaction and the development of teamwork and coordination skills[47]

Computer-based technology may also contribute to *job enlargement* and *job enrichment*. Because fewer workers are needed with the new technology, each employee has to be able to perform a greater number and variety of tasks. Workers in factories that use flexible manufacturing systems are often organized into teams, as at John Deere, and given significant levels of authority and responsibility. Work design is changed to support the goal of increased flexibility and greater response to customer needs.

Advanced information and manufacturing technology does not always have a positive effect on employees, but research findings in general are encouraging, suggesting that jobs for workers are enriched rather than simplified, engaging their higher mental capacities, offering opportunities for learning and growth, and providing greater job satisfaction.

Telecommuting

telecommuting

A rapidly growing trend in work scheduling, whereby employees use computers and telecommunications equipment to do work at home or another remote location.

Another result of advances in technology is *telecommuting,* one of the fastest-growing trends in work scheduling. **Telecommuting** means using computers and other telecommunications equipment to do work at home or at another remote location, without going into an office. The U.S. Department of Transportation has predicted that within the next couple of years, the number of telecommuters will increase to at least 15 million workers. Other estimates range as high as 60 million U.S. workers who will be doing some kind of work at home.[48] At PeopleSoft, all 6,000 employees work from home or other remote locations at some time during their employment. Weekly meetings are sometimes held in person and sometimes online. AT&T has about 35,000 telecommuters, who e-mail a list of weekly goals on Monday and follow up on Friday.[49]

Telecommuting allows "virtual" workers to live where they want, untethered by an office location, to avoid time spent commuting, to have almost complete freedom to schedule their own work, and to avoid the interruptions and distractions of an office environment. Many employers believe that telecommuting enhances employee productivity and improves the company's ability to retain valuable workers. A recent survey by Ceridian Employer Services found that 50 percent of employees said the ability to telecommute and work in virtual teams was a highly attractive incentive for joining or staying with a company. Over 90 percent of companies with more than 5,000 employees allow some type of telecommuting,[50] and small companies are also beginning to offer this as an option for some employees. Telecommuting also may offer greater opportunities for organizational diversity. Telecommuting can open doors for workers whose ability to commute to a work site may be limited by family responsibilities, a physical disability, or lack of adequate transportation.

Although many employers and workers have enthusiastically embraced telecommuting, it does have drawbacks. Some employees who telecommute full time feel that they miss out on important meetings or the informal relationships that develop in an office environment. Some people simply don't have the willpower to avoid non-work-related distractions and need the structure of a traditional work environment to be productive.

apply it

1. Think about jobs with which you are familiar. Which parts of these jobs could be done via telecommuting? Group jobs into three categories: jobs with large, medium, or small components that could be performed from a distance. For example, practically the entire job of a medical billings clerk can be performed by telecommuting, whereas that of a university president cannot. What characteristics are common to the jobs within each category? What are the differences between categories?

Employees' jobs and performance are influenced by the physical environment

One final consideration in job design is the physical characteristics of an employee's work space. We all know that it's easier to work or study when we're physically comfortable. If the lighting is poor, the room is too cold, or there's a loud party going on in the next room, it is difficult to concentrate on the task at hand. In recent years, OB researchers have begun to recognize the important impact of factors such as temperature, noise level, and physical work layout on employees' performance and job satisfaction.[51] In general, organizations in developed countries provide employees with comfortable and safe working environments. However, research has found that even minor

Last year, at Silicon Valley law firm Cooley, Godward LLP's office in Menlo Park, California, four young associates fell under the Internet's spell and departed for high-tech ventures with dot-com companies. Three of them—Craig Venable, John Geschke, and Vincent Pangrazîo—have returned to their law firm. Why? Among many issues mentioned, Geschke (center) cited giving up his roomy office space, especially since he shared his new one with 15 other people. He even missed the photocopying and faxing staff. But more than that, he went from being involved daily with top executives from powerful companies to dealing with people who "didn't like the size of their cubicles." With alternative work spaces, employees have a hard time coping with the loss of privacy and the concept of not having a "place of their own."
(Source: © Andy Freeberg)

variations can have a significant effect on employees' performance and feelings about their jobs. Four aspects of the physical environment that have received the most study are temperature, noise level, lighting, and air quality.[52]

One particularly interesting area regarding workers' physical environment today concerns actual work space design. In many organizations in all industries, there is a widespread restructuring of the physical work space to increase communication and collaboration, in alignment with the shift to team-based work design. In the past, a large, private office meant you'd "made it." However, in today's environment, such status symbols are being discarded in favor of work arrangements that break down barriers between departments and between workers and management. At the GE/Durham plant described in the opening vignette, the plant manager has an open cubicle located right on the factory floor. These changes can have both positive and negative results for employees.

Some recent trends include "hoteling," which means multiple workers serially share a single space; "free-address" offices, where employees choose a desk each day on a first-come, first-served basis; and other variations of open, team-oriented work spaces. For example, at Sapient Corporation, an e-business management consulting firm in Cambridge, Massachusetts, each project team has a room that it uses for the duration of the project, which may be a few weeks or more than a year. Although team members can personalize the space any way they choose, the room belongs to them only for the duration of the project. At the Danish company Oticon Holding A/S, all employees have mobile workstations rather than desks or permanent office spaces.[53]

Alternative work spaces have advantages, but organizations often fail to recognize that employees may have difficulty coping with the change. The Alternative Workplace Study found that 27 percent of companies in which employees no longer have their own personal work space reported a decrease in morale.[54] Employees have a hard time coping with the loss of privacy and the concept of not having a "place of their own." In addition, managers should recognize that work space has to be designed to fit the job. For example, hoteling or free-address offices may be appropriate for

what would you do?

IS TELEMARKETING HERE TO STAY?

Wilkinson & Associates is one of the top telemarketing service bureaus in the United States. Its clients include the major long-distance telephone companies and credit card operations, and the company has won several of the industry's awards for quality and integrity. You have recently been hired as a manager in charge of the "production floor," where operators pitch long-distance services to small businesses or push additional services to credit card customers. When you were hired, top managers indicated that they would be willing to consider changes in how work is handled if you can find ways to make things better.

A bank of computers in the control room dials numbers and waits for an answer, hanging up if a machine takes the call. If the computer detects a live voice on the other end of the line, it searches for a salesperson with an open line and routes the call to the production floor. The production floor is a large room with rows of operators sitting a few feet apart, separated by gray partitions. Unless they stand up or peer around the partitions, they can't see or talk to any of their colleagues. There is one narrow window at each end of the long room, allowing for little natural light, although the room is brightly lit with fluorescent bulbs. Each operator reads from a card in front of her (or him, though most of the workers are female), following a script prescribed by management. No deviations are allowed. In addition, the company has a strict dress code so that it presents a professional image to clients who tour the facility. The role of supervisors is to walk the aisles and "motivate" operators to turn calls into sales. They're constantly shouting phrases such as "C'mon folks, we need four more sales; you can do it," and "Let's go! We haven't had a sale this hour!" On average, an operator handles 160 calls and is lucky to make two sales per day. Operators repeat the same spiel over and over and all day long handle rejection after rejection.

You notice that although a few operators project some liveliness and cheer into their calls, most speak monotonously. Many doodle and slouch at their workstations; a few steal a moment here and there to gossip over the dividers, although supervisors frown on such idleness. They recognize that the stress of repetition and rejection is hard on workers but say it's just part of the job. If workers are chatting when a call comes through, they are likely to lose a sale by leaving a caller dangling on the other end of the line. It's the role of the supervisors to spot signs of the blues and help employees cope. However, today, supervisors are having to overcome an added stress on workers. One of them brought in a newspaper article that called telemarketing bureaus the "sweatshop of the '90s," and it has rapidly passed up and down the long rows of operators, leaving even the most cheerful workers feeling a bit down. By the end of the day, three workers have quit and you learn that turnover is around 97 percent annually.

1. How might you redesign the jobs of production floor workers to make their jobs less routine and stressful?
2. What changes might you make in the physical work space to improve employee satisfaction and productivity?
3. Can you think of ways you and your production floor supervisors could use the concept of social information processing to improve jobs for workers?

Source: This case is based on an incident reported in Thomas Petzinger Jr., *The New Pioneers: The Men and Women Who Are Transforming the Workplace and Marketplace* (New York: Simon & Schuster, 1999), pp. 208–211.

some types of workers such as salespeople or consultants who are constantly on the move, but they are not appropriate for all employees.

Some years ago the advertising agency TBWA Chiat/Day designed a free-address office to encourage greater collaboration among workers. Founder Jay Chiat had a vision of a "virtual office" in which employees were constantly on the move, giving them the freedom to be more creative and collaborative. Instead of private work spaces, employees were given laptops and cell phones. Each day, they selected a desk or work space on a first-come, first-served basis. The change drove a lot of people crazy because they were used to working in private offices. In addition, Chiat had failed to consider that employees sometimes *needed* private space for focused work. Today the agency's redesigned headquarters has lots of private space, but is still designed to promote teamwork and creative collaboration.[55] IDEO Product Development has also taken an innovative approach to work space design to break down departmental and hierarchical boundaries.

❧ IDEO Product Development

IDEO, the company that designed products such as Levolor blinds, Crest's Neat Squeeze toothpaste, and cutting-edge laptop computers, depends on creativity and collaboration. The company's work space is multifunctional and devoid of areas such as executive offices and other status symbols that create hierarchical barriers. The open working environment is designed to promote intensive collaboration among industrial designers, engineers, manufacturing specialists, and other experts.

Peter Coughlan, a linguist and behavioral scientist who helped IDEO redesign its physical space, says the company wanted to create an environment that "maximizes the 'surface area,' exposing as much of the work to as much of the internal audience as possible." Common areas and shared work tables are located in high-traffic areas, increasing the chances for individual interactions to occur on a continuous, random basis. Meeting rooms are transparent so people passing by can see who's inside and what's going on. Studio work areas are open so colleagues can "visually eavesdrop" on each other's projects. Employees also have personal cubicles or workstations so they have some degree of privacy when needed for concentration and focus. But their furniture is on wheels, so team members can rapidly reorganize their work area to suit their current project.

To design its space, IDEO first carefully analyzed what employees were already doing—how they interacted with one another and what design elements could support the informal interaction that already existed. Employees were also asked for their opinions about what areas of the office best supported interaction and creative collaboration. Video cameras were positioned to allow office designers to analyze traffic flow and usage patterns. This careful approach helped IDEO design a casual, informal atmosphere that truly works. People have their own space, but they also are constantly running into "corners," those accidental, informal places where employees can share ideas, knowledge, and understanding that might not emerge in any other place.[56]

The trend in work space design is clearly away from personal space toward more open, common areas. Although these environments support team-based work, managers should recognize that most people have a natural desire for privacy and a sense of place. Organizations need to find ways to help employees adjust to new work space designs to prevent a decrease in performance and job satisfaction.

apply it

1. Think of places where you have been most and least productive (at work, school, or elsewhere). Describe the physical environment and work space, and discuss how characteristics such as lighting, temperature, air quality, and noise level, as well as the work space design, affected your satisfaction and productivity.

2. On your next visit to your local bank, observe the layout of the work space. How do you think the work space design either contributes to or detracts from employees' ability to communicate and collaborate with one another? Is there evidence of status, such as executive offices? Does the location of workstations or desks appear to contribute to a feeling of group cohesiveness?

summary OF KEY CONCEPTS

- **Job design is an important component of organizing.** One critical aspect of organizing for managers is to define how the company's human resources can best be assembled and used to accomplish organizational goals. Effective job design is related to improved organizational productivity and profitability. Many companies are shifting to team-based work design to broaden the scope of jobs and give employees increased responsibility and authority. In addition, reengineering of work processes and total quality management have had a significant impact on job design.

- **Organizations choose among several options for designing or redesigning jobs.** Widely used options for job design include job rotation, job enlargement, and job enrichment. Job rotation means systematically moving employees from one job to another. Job enlargement expands jobs horizontally by combining a series of tasks into one new, broader job. Job enrichment also expands the job vertically, by extending the degree of control the worker has over the job. That is, employees have control over the resources necessary for doing the job, make decisions about how to do the work, and set their own work pace. With job enrichment, employees coordinate and arrange tasks and make their own decisions in order to complete an entire process rather than a narrow job.

  Managers use ideas about job rotation, job enlargement, and job enrichment to increase employee satisfaction and productivity and to improve the organization's flexibility in responding to changing customer needs. In addition, two new approaches to scheduling—job sharing and flextime—offer organizations additional flexibility in job design. Job sharing allows two or more workers to cover one full-time job. Flexible scheduling gives employees some discretion over what specific hours they work.

- **To determine effective job design, managers analyze work tasks and processes.** Managers try to design jobs in such a way to achieve organizational productivity, which involves both efficiency and effectiveness. Several models can help managers analyze work tasks and understand their relationship to productivity as well as to employee motivation and job satisfaction. The sociotechnical systems model strives to optimize both the technical and human needs of the organization. The job characteristics model proposes that every job can be defined and described in terms of five core dimensions: skill variety, task identity, task significance, autonomy, and feedback. The social information processing model indicates that an employee's perception of a job may play as significant a role as actual job characteristics. An employee's perception of the job may be heavily influenced by social cues from others.

- **Recent technological advances have had a significant influence on job design.** Managers should understand how the introduction of new technology may change how jobs are done and the nature of jobs. Today's computer-based technology is having a significant effect on job design. Flexible manufacturing systems in general have been found to lead to enriched jobs for workers, providing them with more opportunities for skill development and intellectual mastery and enabling more interaction and teamwork. Similarly, electronic information technology often provides employees with greater responsibility and opportunities for learning and growth. Another result of technology is that it supports telecommuting, in which employees can perform their work from home or another remote location.

- **Employees' jobs and performance are influenced by the physical environment.** OB researchers have begun to pay attention to the important impact of factors such as temperature, noise level, and work space design on employee performance and satisfaction. In many companies, work spaces are being redesigned to support the shift toward collaboration and team-based work design. The trend in work space design is away from personal offices toward more open, common areas. These environments support teamwork but may also lead to problems if they do not provide employees with some degree of privacy and a sense of place.

KEY terms

DISCUSSION questions

1. Why are reengineering and total quality management relevant to a discussion of job design? Explain.

2. How might you determine whether the jobs of retail clerks in the college bookstore need to be redesigned?

3. How does job enlargement differ from job enrichment? Can you see any problems managers might encounter in moving from job enlargement to job enrichment?

4. What do you see as the advantages and disadvantages of job sharing from an employee's perspective? From the organization's perspective? Do you think the trend toward job sharing will continue to grow? Discuss.

5. If you were the manager of a group of warehouse "pickers and packers" who pick books from warehouse shelves and package them for shipment to Amazon.com customers, how might you improve employees' perceptions that their jobs are interesting and important?

6. Describe two jobs with which you are familiar (perhaps at your college or university) that incorporate high levels of the five core dimensions outlined in the job characteristics model. Explain.

7. Would you like to telecommute full time? Why or why not? Why might this be the ideal job for some people and a nightmare for others?

8. To what extent does the development of new manufacturing and information technology simplify and routinize the jobs of employees? How might it also enlarge and enrich jobs?

9. Why might some people in an organization be opposed to taking a sociotechnical systems approach to work? Discuss.

10. The clerical workers in a financial services office have been complaining that they feel isolated from one another and also have little contact with the consultants or clients. In addition, their jobs are highly specialized and routine. How might you design jobs and the work space to improve morale and productivity for these workers?

SELF-DISCOVERY exercise

Is Your Job Design Right for You?

Think about your current job or a part-time or summer job you have held recently, and answer the following questions. Each statement requires two separate responses. In the first column, please mark your response according to the *actual* characteristics of your job. In the second column, mark your response according to *how you would like* the job characteristics to be. Use the following scale to evaluate each statement on the two dimensions.

1 = very little;   2 = little;   3 = a moderate amount;   4 = much;   5 = very much

	Actual	**Desired**
1. To what extent does your job provide the opportunity to perform a number of different activities each day?	_____	_____

1 = very little;   2 = little;   3 = a moderate amount;   4 = much;   5 = very much

	Actual	Desired

2. To what extent do you feel that you are contributing something significant to the organization or society?

3. To what extent do you have the freedom to determine how to do your job?

4. To what extent do you see projects or jobs through to completion, rather than performing only one piece of a job?

5. To what extent does seeing the results of your work give you an idea of how well you are doing in your job?

6. To what extent do you feel that the quality of your work is important to others in the organization?

7. To what extent does the job require you to use a variety of complex skills?

8. To what extent does the job allow you to act and make decisions independently of supervisors?

9. To what extent are you given time and resources to do an entire piece of work from beginning to end?

10. To what extent does doing the work itself provide you with feedback about how well you are performing?

Scoring and Interpretation

Add the scores for the two items that measure each job characteristic according to the job characteristics model:

	Actual	Desired
Skill variety (#1 and #7)		
Task identity (#4 and #9)		
Task significance (#2 and #6)		
Autonomy (#3 and #8)		
Feedback (#10 and #5)		

How well do the actual characteristics of your job match the desired characteristics? How could your job be redesigned to make it right for you?

Source: Adapted from "Job Characteristics Instrument," in Gregory B. Northcraft and Margaret A. Neale, *Organizational Behavior: A Management Challenge,* 2nd ed. (Fort Worth, TX: The Dryden Press, 1994), pp. 455–457; originally appeared in Andrew D. Szilagyi Jr. and Marc J. Wallace Jr., *Organizational Behavior and Performance,* 4th ed. (New York: Scott, Foresman and Company, 1987).

ORGANIZATIONAL BEHAVIOR in your life

Job Design in Action

Visit a McDonald's, Burger King, Taco Bell, or other fast-food restaurant in your community. Find a seat where you can observe employees in action and try to determine the following, based on your observations.

1. Do individuals work alone or in teams?

2. What is the degree of job simplification and routinization?

3. What kinds of skills seem most valuable to employees—technical skills or social skills—and why?

4. How do physical characteristics of the workplace appear to either help or hinder employees in performing their tasks?

Next, visit an office on your campus or in an organization with which you are familiar (for example, admissions, accounting, financial aid, human resources, or purchasing), and answer the same questions. Write a brief summary of the differences you observe between the two organizations. Can you make any recommen-dations for redesigning jobs to improve employee pro-ductivity for either organization?

ORGANIZATIONAL BEHAVIOR news flash

@ Many people agree that the "shape" of work and of the workplace are changing dramatically. A recent exhibit called Future@Work at the Bank of America Tower in downtown Seattle documented the tremendous changes taking place in workplace de-sign, from changes in lighting patterns to alternative work spaces that support telecommuting and virtual collaboration.

One result of the growing interest in the relation-ship between work design and the work environment is the development of companies that promise to im-prove an organization's performance through better workplace design. Visit the Web sites of some compa-nies involved in workplace design (one to start with is Kinetic Workplace Consulting Group, www.kinetic workplace.com.) You may also want to use your search engine to locate news articles related to work-place design. Write a brief summary of "hoteling" and why it is becoming an important approach to work space design in many companies. What job design changes are related to the trend toward hoteling?

Source: For further information about the Future@Work ex-hibit, see Liz Zack, "See the Future@Work," *Fast Company,* December 1999, p. 94.

global diversity EVENTS

@ In the late 19th century, many people toiled in "sweatshops," working for low wages under dif-ficult environmental conditions such as dark, noisy, or cramped work spaces and extreme heat or cold. Today, in the United States and other developed coun-tries, most of us take for granted that companies will provide workers with clean, safe, and comfortable work environments, and many of us even expect meaningful work, a sense of responsibility, and some degree of control over our own jobs and performance. However, sweatshops still exist, particularly in devel-oping areas of the world. Major corporations such as Nike, Levi Strauss, Liz Claiborne, and Wal-Mart have come under attack for business practices that allegedly support the use of sweatshop labor in developing countries.

Use your Web search engine and type in the key word "sweatshops" to search for articles that discuss the history and current state of sweatshops. How do these workplaces compare to a company such as GE/Durham or IDEO, discussed in this chapter? Were you surprised to learn that sweatshops still exist in the United States?

minicase ISSUE

The Power of Workforce Flexibility

The Problem. Several years ago, workers in the tank-house at BHP Copper, Metals, in San Manuel, Arizona, began complaining that the company didn't have enough workers to get the job done. Managers knew there was a problem, but they also knew the company couldn't afford to add more workers. After the union representing tank-house workers filed a grievance with the company, BHP managers began seriously thinking about work redesign as a way to increase productivity without adding to the workforce. "As a result of that action," said Carleton Peltz, tank-house business leader, "we began trying to make the most of the manpower we had."

The Redesign. The company enlisted the help of the union and every tank-house employee in coming up with a new approach to work. By the time it was over, the traditional work structure had been com-pletely discarded. Tank-house workers refine copper using eight key steps, each previously handled by a sin-gle work department. After the redesign, teams of work-ers were cross-trained to handle all eight steps in the re-fining process from beginning to end. Employees became deeply involved in identifying problems with the existing production process and determining how best to organize themselves to get the job done. In addition, tank-house workers now set their own schedules, including determining the specific hours they need to handle their own workloads. "This meant that employees could opt to work for four hours, leave and come back to do the next four," says Peltz. What managers care about now is results, not specific schedules, tasks, or activities. And so far, results have been impressive. Tank-house production increased nearly 20 percent and costs and quality have stayed right in line. In addition, the unit's safety record has dramatically improved. The disabling injury rate fell from 4.19 in April of 1997 to 0.78 in April of 1998.

To support the changes in its work design, BHP developed a pay-for-skills program. Employees rotate through jobs to build their skills and earn a higher pay rate. Pay rates range from entry-level workers to lead operators. Lead operators are those who have demonstrated mastery of all skills, the ability to lead and teach others, and the ability to be self-directed. BHP rewards these employees as models for the new team behavior.

1. Why do you think it would be important to involve employees closely in a work redesign such as that at BHP Copper, Metals?

2. What ideas from this chapter are reflected in the BHP work redesign?

3. Can you think of reasons that shifting to team-based work design would lead to an improved safety record? Discuss.

Source: Based on Glenn L. Dalton, "The Collective Stretch," *Management Review,* December 1998, pp. 54–59.

seventeen
CHAPTER

17

Organizational Culture

preview

After studying this chapter, you should be able to:

- Explain why organizational culture is important and discuss why a strong culture can have either positive or negative outcomes.

- Identify organizational symbols, stories, heroes, slogans, and ceremonies and explain their relationship to corporate culture.

- Describe the different types of cultures that may be found in organizations and give examples from companies with which you are familiar.

- Explain how culture can support a high-performance organization.

- Explain the importance of selection and socialization in maintaining organizational culture.

- Describe how cultural values can encourage ethical behavior in an organization.

Trilogy Software has been called everything from "the cult on the hill" to "the software sweatshop." But that doesn't bother founder and CEO Joe Liemandt—or his corps of young hardworking, hard-playing employees. The average age at the company is 26 (Liemandt himself is barely over 30), and most of Trilogy's 700 employees are overachievers dedicated to accomplishing Liemandt's vision of being the world's next great software company. Those who aren't don't last long. A "just-do-it-now" spirit is instilled throughout the company.

Liemandt has built Trilogy's distinctive culture through one of the most rigorous selection and socialization processes in the business world. The selection process is designed to find people who are "a good technical and cultural fit." Some of Trilogy's top software developers conduct the first-round interviews. Next, Trilogy flies the top candidates—along with their boyfriends, girlfriends, or spouses—to headquarters in Austin, Texas where they are joined by a dozen or more Trilogians for a night on the town. A morning of grueling, highly technical interviews the next day might be followed by an afternoon of mountain biking or roller-blading. The process is time consuming and expensive—around $13,000 per hire—but Trilogy believes it's worth every minute and every penny.

After employees are hired, they spend three exhausting, exhilarating months at Trilogy University (TU), where they bond with one another and learn about the company and the software industry. They work on projects to improve Trilogy's existing products and create entirely new ones. They also get a crash course in Trilogy culture: "how we operate, how we talk, how we party, how we work." Trilogy doesn't have a corporate handbook, but there are a number of unwritten cultural rules. Recruits learn quickly that at Trilogy, you work hard, play hard, practice teamwork, and take risks. A small sign lists TU's business hours as 8 a.m. to midnight Monday through Saturday and noon to 8 p.m. on Sunday. Liemandt makes it clear to his new employees that he will push them to the limit, give them really hard work and lots of responsibility, and then reward them accordingly.

Trilogy's culture has helped it emerge as a flagship company of the new economy. The company is racing to keep up with demand for its front-office products that optimize and streamline complicated sales and marketing processes for big companies like IBM, Whirlpool, and Goodyear Tire & Rubber, which spend millions of dollars on Trilogy technology. Trilogy's hard-charging culture isn't for everyone. However, as Jeff Daniel, the company's director of college recruiting, says, "It's definitely an environment where people who are passionate about what they do can thrive."[1]

Trilogy's Culture Leads to Success

"It's definitely an environment where people who are passionate about what they do can thrive."
—**Jeff Daniel,** director of college recruiting, Trilogy Software

A strong organizational culture such as that at Trilogy Software binds employees into a cohesive whole and provides a set of unwritten guidelines for how things are done in the organization. The nature of a company's culture is highly important because it can affect the organization for better or worse. A *Fortune* magazine survey found that CEOs cite organizational culture as their most important mechanism for attracting, motivating, and retaining talented employees, a capability that may be the single best predictor of overall organizational excellence.[2] The success of such companies as

Southwest Airlines, Johnson & Johnson, and Starbucks has often been attributed to their innovative cultures. On the other hand, culture has also been implicated in problems faced by companies such as Kodak, Kellogg, and Procter & Gamble, where changing the corporate culture is considered a key to remaining competitive.

Today, many organizations are changing their cultures to be more responsive to changes in the environment. Recall from Chapter 1 that organizations are looking for ways to satisfy the needs of diverse employees and customers. Chapters 5 and 6 discussed the ways in which companies attempt to motivate all workers. Chapter 11 examined visionary leadership, which attempts to give people a sense of meaning in their work that goes beyond drawing a paycheck. Many of today's employees are searching for values that they can identify with in their work and their everyday lives. A strong organizational culture can provide people with a grounding that guides their behavior and working relationships.

Throughout this book, we have shown examples of how companies with strong cultures—such as SAS Institute, Microsoft, and General Electric—design work, motivate and lead employees, and manage diversity. This chapter examines the components of organizational culture in detail. The first section describes the nature of corporate culture and its importance to organizations. Then, we examine some different types of cultures, discuss how culture can support a high-performance organization, and discuss cultural characteristics of a learning organization. The chapter also discusses various mechanisms managers use to build, strengthen, and change organizational culture and examines the role of selection and socialization in building a strong culture. Finally, we briefly consider how culture can support ethical values in an organization and how managers translate these ideas about corporate culture to a complex global environment.

Why is organizational culture important?

There's a great deal of talk about corporate culture these days in both the academic and popular literature. However, the concept of organizational culture is fairly recent. Culture became a significant concern in the United States during the 1980s, primarily due to an interest in learning why U.S. companies were not performing as well as their counterparts in Japan. Observers and researchers thought that organizational cultures as well as national cultures could explain differences in performance.[3] Organizational culture and national culture are closely intertwined. Recall Chapter 2's discussion of how national differences affect organizational behavior in different countries. Later in this chapter, we briefly consider how managers apply the ideas about strong corporate cultures in a global environment where employees may hold many varied national cultural values.

Defining Culture

Most organizational leaders recognize that when a company's culture fits the needs of its external environment and company strategy, employees can create a company that is tough to beat.[4] However, culture is elusive and

The "dot.com" businesses are known for their quirky, hard-driving but playful cultures. At CBCi Technologies, a Web marketing firm in New York City, the culture is unique—and open to scrutiny. During working hours, two cameras are trained on the workplace; one captures a wide view of the office and another spotlights a different employee's cubicle each week, following employees as they work. The images are broadcast on the company's Web site for all to see. When interviewing for her job, art director Marta Sant wondered if she would like this unusual feature of the organization's culture. She logged on to the Web site to get a preview. Once on the job, she got used to the idea of being on camera and waved hi to her family in Spain when it was her turn in the spotlight. (Source: © Matthew Salacuse)

often goes unnoticed. Many times, it is only when managers try to implement new strategies or programs that go against basic cultural values that they come face to face with the power of culture. **Culture** can be defined as the set of key values, assumptions, beliefs, understandings, and norms that is shared by members of an organization and taught to new members as correct.[5] At its most basic, culture is a pattern of shared assumptions about how things are done in the organization. This pattern is invented or learned as organizational members cope with internal and external problems and then taught to new members as the correct way to perceive, think, and feel in relation to those problems.[6]

Culture can be thought of as consisting of three levels, as illustrated in Exhibit 17.1, with each level becoming less obvious.[7] At the surface are visible artifacts such as manner of dress, patterns of behavior, physical symbols, organizational ceremonies, and office layout. These include all the things a person can see, hear, and observe by watching members of the organization. For example, at St. Luke's, an advertising agency in London, an open office environment with no personal desks or work spaces is a visible manifestation of a corporate culture that values equality, teamwork, and collaboration. At a deeper level are expressed values and beliefs, which are not observable but can be discerned from how people explain and justify what they do. These are values that members of the organization hold at a conscious level. At 3M, for example, all employees know that innovation is highly valued and rewarded in the company's culture.

Some values become so deeply embedded in a culture that organizational members may no longer be consciously aware of them. These basic, underlying assumptions are the essence of the culture. At 3M, these

culture

The set of key values, assumptions, beliefs, understandings, and norms that members of an organization share.

exhibit **17.1**
Three Levels of Corporate Culture

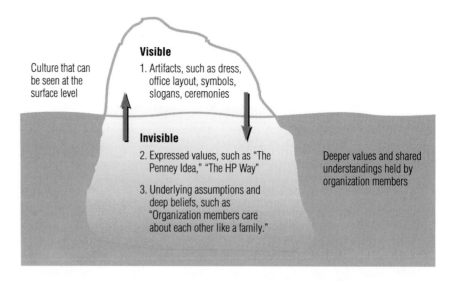

Culture that can be seen at the surface level

Visible
1. Artifacts, such as dress, office layout, symbols, slogans, ceremonies

Invisible
2. Expressed values, such as "The Penney Idea," "The HP Way"

3. Underlying assumptions and deep beliefs, such as "Organization members care about each other like a family."

Deeper values and shared understandings held by organization members

assumptions might include (1) that individual employees are the source of all innovation, (2) that each individual must think and act for him- or herself, even if it means defying supervisors, and (3) that organization members are part of a family and will take care of and support each other in taking risks.[8] Assumptions generally start out as expressed values, but as they stand the test of time, they become more deeply embedded and less open to question—organization members take them for granted and often are not even aware of the deeply held assumptions that guide their behavior, language, and patterns of social interaction.

Emergence and Functions of Culture

Cultures develop among any group of people who interact with one another over a long period of time. When people are successful at what they undertake, the ideas and values that led to success become institutionalized as part of the organization's culture.[9] Though ideas and values that become part of the culture can come from anywhere within the organization, a founder or early leader typically has a significant impact on the company's early culture. A founder may articulate and implement particular ideas and beliefs as a vision, philosophy, or business strategy. When these ideas and beliefs lead to success, an organizational culture begins to develop that reflects the vision of the founder or early leader. For example, the culture at SAS Institute largely reflects the values of president and cofounder Jim Good-

Top-quality day care at software developer SAS Institute reflects the company's focus on the value of humans over profits. SAS's employees who are parents pay only $250 a month for the day-care service. James H. Goodnight, who founded SAS in 1976, states the idea behind his company's culture simply: "If you do right by people, they'll do right by you." To that end, SAS also offers a 35-hour workweek, a free on-site medical clinic, and twelve holidays a year, plus a paid week off between Christmas and New Year's.
(Source: © Gregory Foster)

night, who believes employees should be "treated like adults" and that human relationships should be valued over hard-charging competitiveness and bottom-line profits. In the frantically competitive software industry, SAS is known as a relaxed and calm place where employees are given the freedom to do their work at their own pace and enjoy extraordinary benefits, including a fitness center, free snacks, two day-care centers, and a seven-hour workday. Despite the relaxed pace and tremendous degree of freedom, SAS employees are highly productive.[10]

Culture gives employees a sense of organizational identity and generates a commitment to particular values and ways of doing things. Organizational cultures serve two important functions: (1) to integrate members so that they know how to relate to one another and (2) to help the organization adapt to the external environment.

Internal Integration   Culture helps members develop a collective identity and know how to work together effectively. It is culture that guides day-to-day working relationships and determines how people communicate in the organization, what behavior is acceptable or not acceptable, and how power and status are allocated. Culture can imprint a set of unwritten rules inside employees' minds that can be very powerful in determining behavior, thus affecting organizational performance.[11] Comparative studies of traditional American management practices and Japanese management methods suggest that the relative success of Japanese firms in the 1980s can be partly explained by their strong corporate cultures that emphasized internal integration based on employee participation, open communication, security, and equality.[12]

At Merck, Ray Gilmartin focused on changing the culture for more effective internal integration.

☙ Merck & Co.

When Ray Gilmartin, an outsider to the pharmaceutical industry, first arrived as chairman, president, and CEO of Merck & Co., his primary goal was to halt the exodus of top executives, build morale throughout the company, and change the turf-conscious culture to one focused on teamwork and participation.

Gilmartin started by interviewing each of the top 40 or so managers and asking them how they thought the company's major problems could be resolved. Based on those interviews, he created a broad-based committee that would replace Merck's longstanding leadership by a tiny group of top executives. He then used a series of team-building strategies intended to promote a cooperative spirit and eliminate backstabbing and jockeying for position, which had become hallmarks of Merck's working relationships. Off-site retreats each year break down barriers and build mutual confidence. In addition, Gilmartin has held regular breakfast meetings with staffers to restore morale and foster a new atmosphere of collegiality. At every turn, he pushes employees to air problems and debate issues without regard for hierarchy. He unlocked the doors to the executive suite to show employees they had access to the top management group.

Gilmartin says the way he operates is "to be receptive to other people's ideas and to basically respect what they do. I get a lot in return." At Merck, what he has gotten in return is performance. Sales and income have increased dramatically. Perhaps most importantly, top research and management talent is committed once again. By giving executives autonomy to lead their own domains, Gilmartin has won the loyalty of people often pursued by other firms. Research chief Dr. Edward M. Scolnick, who was a rival for the top job, has stayed with the company. "He's delegated to me . . . and my responsibility is to make sure that I come through for him."[13]

By shifting cultural values related to internal integration from those encouraging backstabbing and power plays to those encouraging cooperation and power sharing, Gilmartin has put Merck back on the path to success and profitablity.

External Adaptation   The second primary function of culture is that it determines how the organization meets goals and deals with outsiders. The right cultural values can help the organization respond rapidly to customer needs or the moves of a competitor. Culture can encourage employee commitment to the core purpose of the organization, its specific goals, and the basic means used to accomplish goals. In comparing 18 companies that have experienced long-term success with 18 similar companies that have not done as well, James Collins and Jerry Porras found one of the determining factors in the successful companies to be a strong culture in which employees "know in their hearts" what is right for the organization.[14]

The culture should embody the values and assumptions needed for the organization to succeed in its environment. If the external environment requires extraordinary customer service, for example, the culture should encourage good service. Nordstrom has built one of the strongest customer service cultures in the retail industry. According to one account, the entire employee manual is a 5 × 8 inch card that reads "Rule #1: Use your good judgment in all situations. There will be no additional rules."[15] However, employees know in no uncertain terms what is expected of them—the company gives them an extraordinary level of responsibility and authority so they can do whatever is needed to best serve the customer.

Strong cultures are important because they bind employees together, making the organization a community rather than just a collection of individuals with no shared values and ways of thinking and acting. However, a strong organizational culture can have either positive or negative outcomes, as we will discuss later in this chapter.

apply it

1. Visit a local company with which you are familiar or an office on your campus. Spend some time observing the office layout, how people dress, work, and interact with one another, and other visible artifacts (the surface level). Based on your observations, do you think the culture leads to effective internal integration? Do you believe it is possible for a casual observer to correctly diagnose an organization's culture? Explain.

2. Interview one or two people and ask them what it is like to work at this company or in this office. Try to elicit their ideas about what the company pays attention to and cares about, then write a brief statement about these "expressed values and beliefs."

Different organizations have different cultures

baseball team culture

A type of organizational culture that emerges in fast-paced, high-risk environments and values and rewards creativity, innovation, and performance.

One way to think about corporate cultures was suggested by Jeffrey Sonnenfeld and includes four types of culture—baseball team, club, academy, and fortress. These four types and their general characteristics are described in Exhibit 17.2. Each culture has a somewhat different potential for supporting a healthy, successful company, and each has a different impact on the satisfaction and careers of employees.[16]

The **baseball team culture** emerges in an environmental situation with high-risk decision making and fast feedback from the environment. Deci-

Type of Culture	Characteristics
Baseball team	Values talent, creativity, and innovation. Rewards high performance and quickly weeds out those who can't keep up. Great opportunities for individual development, but risks are high and job-hopping is common.
Club	Values loyalty, commitment, and conformity. Rewards seniority; promotes from within. Provides stability and long-term job security, but may inhibit innovation and flexibility.
Academy	Values commitment, continuity of service, and functional expertise. Rewards mastery of job skills and expertise in a particular area. Can provide job security but may also limit individual development.
Fortress	Preoccupied with survival. Has difficulty rewarding employees for good performance; may periodically downsize or restructure. Provides little job security or opportunity for professional growth.

exhibit | **17.2**

Types of Organizational Culture

sion makers learn quickly whether their choice was right or wrong. Talent, creativity, innovation, and performance are valued and rewarded. Top performers see themselves as "free agents," and companies scramble for their services. Performers with "low batting averages" are quickly dropped from the lineup. Baseball team cultures are found in fast-paced, high-risk companies involved in areas such as software development, music production, and advertising, where futures are bet on a new product or project. Trilogy Software, described in the opening vignette, might be considered to have a baseball team culture.

The **club culture** is characterized by loyalty, commitment, and fitting into the group. This stable, secure environment values age and experience and rewards seniority. Individual employees generally start young and stay with the company, as in the case of career military personnel. Club cultures promote from within, and members are expected to progress slowly, proving competence at each level. People in club cultures often gain vast experience in a number of organizational functions. For example, top executives in commercial banks often begin as tellers. Strong club cultures can sometimes contribute to the perception of a closed company that is reluctant to change. For example, McDonald's has been criticized in recent years because the top executive ranks and board seats are filled by a group of close-knit insiders who have been with the company for decades. Critics argue that the culture has contributed to a decline in McDonald's ability to recognize and shape popular fast-food trends.[17] However, many club qualities also contribute to flexibility in the organization, and club cultures can be highly successful.

The **academy culture** also hires young recruits interested in a long-term career and a slow, steady climb up the organization. Unlike in the club culture, however, employees rarely cross from one function or division to another. Each person enters a specific career track and gains a high level of expertise in that area. Job and technical mastery are the bases for reward and advancement. Many successful, long-established organizations such as universities, Coca-Cola, Ford, and GM maintain strong academy cultures. Specialization provides job security, but this type of culture may limit broad

club culture

A type of culture that is used in a stable, secure environment and is characterized by loyalty, commitment, and fitting into the group.

academy culture

A type of culture that values long-term commitment and mastery of job skills in a particular area.

individual development and interdepartmental collaboration, which can be detrimental in today's volatile business environment. At Ford, for example, CEO Jacques Nasser has been seeking ways to increase collaboration and make the corporate culture more adaptive to respond quickly to changing consumer needs.[18]

fortress culture

A culture type that may emerge in a survival situation and offers little job security or opportunity for professional growth.

The **fortress culture** may emerge in a "survival" situation. A company in a formerly dominant industry, such as a textile firm, might need to retrench for survival. The fortress culture typically downsizes or restructures periodically. These companies offer little job security or opportunity for growth and professional development. However, they do offer great turn-around opportunities for managers who relish a challenge. Those who succeed, such as Lee Iacocca at Chrysler, William Crouse of Ortho Diagnostic Systems, or Larry Bossidy at Allied Signal, earn recognition nationally as well as within their industry.

apply it

1. From your experiences on campus and with other organizations, try to identify companies, clubs, or offices that appear to have a baseball team, club, or academy culture. Can you think of a company in your community that might be characterized by a fortress culture?

Culture can support a high-performance organization

One common idea is that a strong, well-developed corporate culture is an important element for excellent organizational performance. However, the nature of the organization's cultural values is also important.[19] For an organization to stay healthy and profitable, the culture should reinforce the values the company needs to be effective within its environment. In this section, we discuss several ideas related to culture and high performance in organizations.

Culture Strength and Subcultures

culture strength

The degree of agreement among members of an organization about the importance of specific values and ways of doing things.

One important consideration is the relative strength of the organization's culture. A strong organizational culture can have a powerful impact on employee behavior and company performance. **Culture strength** refers to the degree of agreement among employees about the importance of specific values and ways of doing things. If widespread consensus exists, the culture is strong and cohesive; if little agreement exists, the culture is considered weak.[20] A strong organizational culture can increase employee commitment to the values, goals, and strategies of the organization. In addition, employee turnover is often low in companies with strong cultures because the shared values and understandings build cohesiveness and loyalty. Managers who want to build or maintain strong cultures often pay close attention to selection and socialization of employees. In addition, strong cultures are typically associated with the frequent use of ceremonies, symbols, and rituals, which will be discussed later in this chapter.

We have referred to organizational culture as a pattern of shared values, norms, and assumptions, which implies that all members of the organization subscribe to those values, norms, and assumptions. However, although certain cultural values may be dominant, most organizations actually have more than one culture. Large organizations in particular may have distinctly different subcultures in different parts of the organization. **Subcultures** develop to reflect the common problems, goals, and experiences that members of a team, department, or other unit share. For example, Pitney Bowes, a maker of postage meters and other office equipment, has long thrived with a culture of order and predictability. However, the CEO of Pitney Bowes Credit Corporation began creating a new subculture when he decided his division should be not just a provider of services but also a *creator* of services. Rather than just financing sales of existing products, the division now creates entirely new services for customers to buy. As the nature of the work changed, PBCC began developing a distinctive subculture that emphasizes values of teamwork, risk taking, and creativity.[21] An office, branch, or division of a company that is physically separated from the company's main operations may also take on a distinctive subculture.

subcultures

Minicultures within an organization that develop to reflect the common problems, goals, and experiences members of a team, department, or other unit share.

One expert on corporate culture, Edgar Schein, has suggested that every organization has at least three subcultures: an operating culture (shared by front-line employees), an engineering culture (shared by the organization's technical staff), and an executive culture (shared by middle and upper managers). These three subcultures, he says, stem from the different problems and perspectives of individuals who make up the three groups.[22] Subcultures typically include the basic values of the dominant organizational culture plus additional values unique to members of the subculture. Subcultures are important because they may increase the organization's adaptability—different departments or divisions can respond to the particular needs of their environments. In addition, subcultures can serve as starting points for broad-based culture change when an entire organization faces a need for new values, attitudes, and behaviors to cope with changing circumstances. However, subcultural differences can sometimes lead to conflicts between departments or groups, especially in organizations that do not have strong corporate cultures.

Although most of this chapter focuses on the organization's overall culture, which gives the company its distinctive "personality," it is important to recognize that many organizations also have subcultures that influence the beliefs and behavior of their members.

Adaptive versus Unadaptive Corporate Cultures

Although a strong organizational culture can have a powerful impact, it isn't necessarily always a positive one. Research at Harvard into some 200 corporate cultures found that a strong culture does not ensure success unless it also encourages a healthy adaptation to the external environment.[23] A strong culture that does not encourage adaptation can be more damaging to an organization than a weak culture.

Consider the example of Merry-Go-Round, a once-ubiquitous presence in malls across America. It was *the* place where trendy teens of the 1980s bought their clothes, from knock-offs of the leather jacket featured in Michael Jackson's *Beat It* video to Madonna-style black bustiers. Leonard "Boogie" Weinstein, who founded the chain, created a strong, happy-go-lucky corporate culture, often hiring people in his own image—street-smart kids with a good feel for fashion trends. When a combination of changes in the fashion industry, the shrinking of Merry-Go-Round's target market of 15- to 24-year-olds, and a decline in mall traffic led to a drastic decline in sales, the chain confronted the critical shifts in the market with arrogance and clung to its big-bet mentality of the 1980s. Because of the strong, insular culture, Merry-Go-Round couldn't adapt to the changing environment. Store managers simply weren't able to consider doing things any other way. By the mid-1990s, the nationwide chain was dead.[24]

As illustrated in Exhibit 17.3, adaptive corporate cultures have different values and behavior from unadaptive cultures. In adaptive cultures, managers are concerned about customers and those internal people, processes, and procedures that bring about useful change. Behavior is flexible, and managers initiate change when needed, even if it involves significant risk. In unadaptive cultures, managers are more concerned about themselves or their own special projects, and their values tend to discourage risk taking and change. Thus, a strong culture is not enough, because an unhealthy culture may encourage the organization to march resolutely in the wrong direction. Healthy cultures help companies adapt to the external environment.

Culture Gap

An organization's culture may not always be aligned with the needs of the external environment, or it may not meet the organization's needs for internal integration. The values and ways of doing things may reflect what worked in the past, as at Merry-Go-Round. The difference between desired cultural values and behaviors and actual values and behaviors is called the

---

exhibit **17.3** Adaptive versus Unadaptive Cultures

	Adaptive Corporate Cultures	**Unadaptive Corporate Cultures**
Visible Behavior	Mangers pay close attention to all their constituencies, especially customers, and initiate change when needed to serve their legitimate interests, even if it entails taking some risks.	Managers tend to behave somewhat insularly, politically, and bureaucratically. As a result, they do not change their strategies quickly to adjust to or take advantage of changes in their business environments.
Expressed Values	Managers care deeply about customers, stockholders, and employees. They also strongly value people and processes that can create useful change (e.g., leadership initiatives up and down the management hierarchy).	Managers care mainly about themselves, their immediate work group, or some product (or technology) associated with that work group. They value the orderly and risk-reducing management process much more highly than leadership initiatives.

Source: John P. Kotter and James L. Heskett, *Corporate Culture and Performance* (New York: The Free Press, 1992), p. 51.

culture gap.[25] Organizations can be much more effective when the culture fits the external environment as well as the needs of employees.

Culture gaps can be immense, particularly in the case of mergers. Despite the popularity of mergers and acquisitions as a corporate strategy, many fail. Almost half of all acquired companies are sold within five years, and some experts claim that 90 percent of mergers never live up to expectations.[26]

One reason for this is the difficulty of integrating cultures. When Harty Press acquired Pre-Press Graphics to move its company into the digital age, the two cultures clashed from the beginning. Executives initially focused on integrating the acquired firm's financial systems and production technologies, but their failure to pay attention to culture seriously damaged the company. According to general manager Michael Platt, "I thought all that stuff people said about culture when it came to mergers was a bunch of fluff—until it happened."[27] The merger of Citicorp and Travelers has also suffered from culture clash. John Reed, who recently retired as co-CEO of Citigroup, explained the difficulty and frustration of merging two cultures this way: "I will tell you that it is not simple and it is not easy, and it is not clear to me that it will necessarily be successful. . . . As you put two cultures together, you get all sorts of strange, aberrant behavior, and it's not clear whether each side getting to know the other side helps, or whether having common objectives helps, or whether it is just the passage of time."[28]

Managers should keep in mind that the human systems—in particular, corporate culture—are what make or break any change initiative, especially one as significant as a merger. The problem of integrating cultures increases in scope and complexity with global companies and cross-cultural mergers or acquisitions. Culture gaps may also occur in companies that have not gone through a merger. Many companies that are trying to become learning organizations find that the most important step is changing their culture.

Culture and the Learning Organization

A danger for many successful organizations is that the culture becomes set and the company fails to adapt as the environment changes. Learning organizations strive to create strong, adaptive cultures that encourage continuous experimentation, learning, and change rather than rigidity and stability. The culture of a learning organization generally incorporates the following values:

1. *The whole is more important than the part, and boundaries between parts are minimized.*[29]   In learning organizations, people are aware of the whole system, how everything fits together, and the relationships among various organizational parts. Everyone considers how his or her actions affect other parts and the total organization. This emphasis on the whole reduces boundaries both within the organization and with other companies. Although subcultures may form, everyone's primary attitudes and behaviors reflect the organization's dominant culture. The free flow of people, ideas, and information allows coordinated action and continuous learning. At the Mayo Clinic, founded more than a century ago in Rochester, Minnesota, teamwork permeates the organizational culture. Doctors are expected to consult with doctors in other

culture gap

The difference between an organization's desired culture norms and values and its actual norms and values.

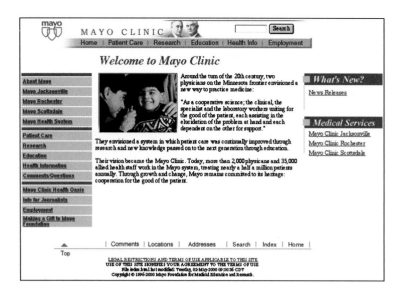

The Mayo Clinic is a learning organization, where employees freely exchange ideas—with each other and with the patients. Boundaries are minimized to provide patients the best care possible. The clinic's Web site states this unique approach to medicine "as a cooperative science; the clinical, the specialist, and the laboratory workers uniting for the good of the patient. . . each dependent on the other for support." Sharing of ideas with colleagues and with patients permeates everything Mayo Clinic does and helps the staff learn and continually progress.
(Source: By permission of Mayo Foundation for Medical Education and Research)

departments, with the patient, and with anyone else inside or outside the clinic who might help with any aspect of a patient's problem. Collaboration is incorporated into everything Mayo does, from diagnosis and surgery to policy making, strategic planning, and leadership.[30]

2. *Equality is a primary value.* The culture of a learning organization creates a sense of community and caring for one another. The organization is a place for creating a web of relationships that allows people to take risks and develop to their full potential. Activities such as assigned parking spaces and executive dining rooms that create status differences are discarded. At Fastenal Co. in Winona, Minnesota, CEO Bob Kierlin has no reserved parking space and often sorts the mail himself. Kierlin treats all his employees the same, whether janitors or vice presidents. The sense of equality and fairness is a core element of Fastenal's culture.[31] The emphasis on treating everyone with care and respect creates a climate of safety and trust that allows experimentation, frequent mistakes, and learning.

3. *The culture encourages risk taking, change, and improvement.* A basic value of a learning organization is to question the status quo. Constant questioning of assumptions opens the gates to creativity and improvement. The culture rewards and celebrates the creators of new ideas, products, and work processes. To symbolize the importance of taking risks, a learning organization culture may also reward those who fail in order to learn and grow.

The culture of a learning organization encourages openness, boundarylessness, equality, continuous improvement, and risk taking. Even though the internal culture is strong, the cultural values encourage a healthy adaptation to a changing external environment. Netscape Communications, recently acquired by America Online, reflects the values of a strong, adaptive organizational culture.

Netscape Communications is viewed by many as a company that is defining the workplace of the future: it's fast, nimble, exciting, and continuously changing. "I'm constantly surprised over the years how at times I thought we were doomed but then things panned out," says Mike McCool, a software engineer who's been with the company almost since the beginning.

The secret to Netscape's survival is its adaptive corporate culture, which encourages creativity, sharing of ideas, change, and learning. Employees are free to come and go as they please and even work at home if they like. Independence, responsibility, and accountability are cultural hallmarks. However, Netscape also rewards teamwork and the sharing of information and ideas, and most employees thrive in its fast-paced environment. Even at 1 a.m. there's usually someone at the company to bounce ideas around and discuss problems or new projects.

To keep employees tuned in to what's going on in other departments, Netscape holds quarterly "all hands" meetings where top managers talk about what's happening in the entire company. Product development groups also hold open weekly meetings to share the status of products or new technologies. These efforts help foster a sense of community so that employees feel involved with the whole company, not just their team or department.

All employees at Netscape are encouraged to participate and have a voice, and equality is a primary value. Everyone works in an open cubicle so that people can see across the dividers and call out to colleagues. Learning is also highly valued. The company offers a full range of training programs, but what employees appreciate most is the opportunity to learn and expand their skills every day on the job. Managers encourage employees to try new things, experiment, take risks, and make mistakes. People are never punished for failures—Netscape's managers realize that some experiments fail, that mistakes are keys to learning. Netscape's adaptive culture has helped the company weather a number of crises, and it played a significant role as the company once again shifted gears after the acquisition by AOL.[32]

🐚 Netscape Communications Corp.

apply it

1. Think of two organizations with which you are familiar—one that seems to be growing and one that seems to be declining. These may be companies you know from personal experience or from your readings. Compare and contrast the two companies in terms of the three characteristics of learning organizations described in this section.

Managers use various mechanisms to build and strengthen organizational culture

It is difficult to "see" organizational culture, so how do managers learn how to build and strengthen an adaptive culture that can lead to a high-performance learning organization? To identify and interpret a company's culture requires making inferences based on observable artifacts, or visible manifestations of the culture. Some of the typical and important observable artifacts of culture include rites and ceremonies, legends and stories, symbols, and language. These may be studied to gain some understanding of the organizational culture. In addition, these artifacts are mechanisms by which cultural values can be developed, strengthened, and transmitted to new members of the organization. Most importantly, managers transmit culture through their daily actions.

Rites and Ceremonies

rites and ceremonies

Organized, planned activities or rituals that make up a special event and often are conducted for the benefit of an audience.

Rites and ceremonies are organized, planned activities or rituals that make up a special event and are often conducted for the benefit of an audience. Company managers can schedule rites or ceremonies to provide dramatic examples of what the company values. These are special occasions that reinforce valued accomplishments, create a bond among people by allowing them to share an important event, and anoint and celebrate heroes.[33]

One example of a rite at Wal-Mart is the Wal-Mart cheer: "Give me a *W!* Give me an *A!* Give me an *L!* Give me a squiggly! (All do a version of the twist.) Give me an *M!* Give me an *A!* Give me an *R!* Give me a *T!* What's that spell? Wal-Mart! What's that spell? Wal-Mart! Who's No. 1? THE CUSTOMER!" This cheer, which is often done when a Wal-Mart executive visits one of the stores, strengthens bonds among employees and reinforces their commitment to the common goal of putting the customer first.[34]

An excellent example of a ceremony is provided by Mary Kay Cosmetics Company. Mary Kay holds elaborate awards ceremonies, presenting gold and diamond pins, furs, and pink Cadillacs to high-achieving sales consultants. The most successful consultants are introduced by film clips like the ones used to present award nominees in the entertainment industry. These ceremonies recognize and celebrate high-performing employees and emphasize the rewards for performance.[35]

Legends and Stories

story

A narrative based on true events that is repeated frequently and shared among organizational employees.

heroes

Figures who exemplify the deeds, character, and attitudes of a strong corporate culture.

legends

Stories about historic events that may be embellished with fictional details.

A **story** is a narrative based on true events that is repeated frequently and shared among organizational employees. Stories are told to new employees to keep the organization's primary values alive. Many stories are about company **heroes** who serve as models or ideals for cultural norms and values. Some stories are considered **legends** because the events are historic and may have been embellished with fictional details. Storytelling has become an increasingly important way for organizations to transmit important values. Telling stories is a powerful way to relay a message because a story evokes both visual imagery and emotion, which helps employees connect with the message and the key values. Companies such as IBM, Coca-Cola, and Royal Dutch/Shell have sent managers to workshops to learn about the advantages of stories as a way to transmit cultural values and promote change.[36]

One often-told story at UPS concerns an employee who, without authority, ordered an extra Boeing 737 to ensure timely delivery of a load of Christmas packages that had been left behind in the holiday rush. As the story goes, rather than punishing the worker, UPS rewarded his initiative. By telling this story, UPS workers communicate that the company stands behind its commitment to worker autonomy and customer service.[37]

Symbols

symbol

An object, act, or event that stands for something else and conveys special meaning to others.

Another important tool for interpreting and transmitting culture is the symbol. A **symbol** is something that stands for something else; it may be an object, act, or event that conveys special meaning to others. In one sense, rites, ceremonies, and stories are also symbols—they symbolize deeper values of the organization.

Other symbols are physical artifacts of the organization. Physical symbols are powerful because they focus attention on a specific item and its meaning. For example, John Thomas, CEO of a mechanical contractor in Andover, Massachusetts, wanted to symbolize the important value of allowing mistakes and risk taking. He pulled a $450 mistake out of the dumpster, mounted it on a plaque, and named it the "No Nuts Award" for the missing parts. The award is presented annually and symbolizes the freedom to make mistakes but not to make the same mistake twice.[38] At Pitney Bowes Credit Corporation, the CEO symbolized the need to break out of conventional ways of thinking by handing out buttons with the phrase "That's the way we've always done it" in a red circle crossed out with a slash.[39] Managers at Mitel Corporation, a high-tech company based outside Ottawa, Canada, have taken symbolism to new heights to instill a culture of change.

Standing just outside Stephen Quesnelle's office at Mitel Corp. is a nearly life-size wooden heifer. Inside, you'll find cow posters, calendars, figurines, and other cow-related items. Quesnelle, who is Mitel's head of quality programs, admits that all this cow business seems a little silly, but the purpose behind it is deadly serious. Quesnelle has been organizing "sacred cow hunts" ever since he came to the struggling organization.

"Sacred cows are the barriers that everybody *knows* about but nobody *talks* about," he says. "They're the policies and procedures that have outlived their usefulness—but that no one dares touch." Quesnelle started using the cow symbolism to create an element of folklore that would get people to start thinking about sacred cows and how to kill them off. Quesnelle and some of his colleagues organized their first sacred cow workshops in 1997, when groups of R&D employees spent three days identifying rules, rituals, and attitudes that were getting in the way of doing things better and faster. In addition to identifying company barriers, each employee had to identify two "personal cows" and devise a plan for attacking them as soon as he or she got back to work on Monday morning. The series of workshops ended with a celebratory barbeque (*beef* barbeque, of course).

Today, signs of change are everywhere at Mitel. The preoccupation with killing off sacred cows has quickly spread from the R&D division to other parts of the company. The intranet features a sacred cow section where people can post questions, identify new cows, and get feedback from others, including top executives. The result of all these change efforts is that Mitel is on the road to renewal, with revenues and stock prices growing and product development time continuing to decrease. "Change is part of the culture now," Quesnelle says. "The attitude is, if you see something that doesn't make sense, get rid of it." And just in case anyone forgets, there's that big heifer standing outside his office.[40]

Specialized Language

Language can also be used to shape and influence organizational values and beliefs. Organizations sometimes use a special slogan or saying to express key corporate values. For example, at Speedy Muffler in Canada, the saying, "At Speedy, You're Somebody" applies to customers and employees alike. Team Tires Plus uses the slogan "Changing the World One Tire at a Time" to reinforce the company's values.

Cultural values may also be expressed and reinforced through written public statements, corporate mission statements, or other formal statements that express core values of the organization. Eaton Corporation developed a philosophy called "Excellence through People," which includes a commitment to encouraging employee involvement in all decisions, regular face-to-face communication between managers and employees, promotion from within, and a focus on the positive behavior of workers.[41]

Changing Culture through Symbolic Leadership

One way managers change norms and values toward what is needed for a high-performance or learning organization is through symbolic leadership. Managers use symbols, stories, slogans, and ceremonies to reinforce or change organizational culture. Cultures can be extremely resistant to change, so managers literally overcommunicate to ensure that employees understand the new cultural values. Most importantly, they signal the new values in actions as well as words.

symbolic leader

A manager who defines and uses signals and symbols to influence organizational culture.

A **symbolic leader** defines and uses signals and symbols to influence organizational culture. Symbolic leaders influence culture by articulating a vision for the organizational culture that generates excitement and that employees can believe in. They define and communicate central values in such a way that employees rally around them. In addition, the symbolic leader heeds the day-to-day activities that reinforce the cultural vision. The leader makes sure ceremonies, symbols, and slogans match the new values. Even more important, actions speak louder than words. Symbolic leaders "walk their talk."[42]

Symbolic leadership works because executives are watched by employees. Employees learn what is valued most in the company by watching what attitudes and behaviors managers pay attention to and reward, how top managers react to organizational crises, and whether managers' own behavior matches the espoused values.[43] Even well-established organizations with strong cultures may implement needed changes through symbolic leadership. Lou Gerstner acted as a symbolic leader to help change an unadaptive culture at IBM. On his first day on the job, Gerstner called a dozen top executives into his office and asked them to write a five-page report answering such questions as "What business are you in?" and "Who are your customers?" He asked for the report in two days. In a company known for lengthy meetings requiring extensive and elaborate preparations and accompanied by massive reports in blue binders, the message was clear: It was no longer business as usual at Big Blue.[44]

Ceremonies, stories, slogans, and symbols are effective only when the daily actions of managers also signal and support important cultural values. At Levi Strauss, for example, managers' bonus pay, which can be up to two-thirds of their total compensation, is tied explicitly to how well they follow the organization's list of "corporate aspirations"—a list of stated core values that includes an emphasis on teamwork, trust, diversity, recognition, ethics, and empowerment. Because managers at Levi Strauss link stated values, training, everyday action, and appraisal and reward systems, employees rely on the aspirations as a standard for their own behavior.

apply it

1. Think about a club, team, or organization to which you belong. Identify and describe at least two observable artifacts (stories, symbols, rituals, cere-

monies, or slogans). Do you know anyone in the organization who acts as a symbolic leader?

Selection and socialization help keep the culture alive

Selection and socialization are particularly important mechanisms for maintaining an organization's cultural values. Many companies are extremely careful about trying to hire people who are a natural fit with the corporate culture. In addition, activities such as training and career development are geared toward transmitting and reinforcing specific values.

Selection

During the **selection** process, companies seek to find and hire people who have the skills and knowledge to perform specific jobs within the organization. However, when several candidates meet the technical job requirements, the final decision often depends on how well the candidates will fit into the organization. Recall the discussion of person-job fit and person-organization fit from Chapter 3. This tendency to seek a "good match" means that organizations generally hire people who have values very similar to those of the organization. In some cases, managers are not even aware of this tendency, but many companies with strong cultures take great care in selecting employees to fit the culture. For example, at Southwest Airlines, prospective employees are subjected to extensive interviewing, sometimes even by Southwest's regular customers, so that only those who fit the culture are hired.

> **selection**
>
> The process of finding and hiring people who have the skills to perform specific jobs and who will fit in with the organization's culture.

The selection process is also a time when the job candidate learns about the organization. If individuals perceive a significant conflict between their own values and those of the company, they may "self-select" themselves out of the pool of candidates. Thus, selection is a two-way process. Organizations want to find talented workers who not only have the necessary skills but also fit in with the organizational culture. Similarly, individuals generally want a job where they feel they "belong" and share at least some of the key cultural values of the organization.

Although selecting candidates who share the company's values can help maintain a strong culture, managers should also keep in mind that it may limit organizational diversity, thus hindering the organization's ability to adapt. Recall from Chapter 2 that diversity can have a positive impact on organizational creativity, problem solving, and the creation of new markets. In addition, it is critical that managers avoid discrimination when selecting candidates who fit the organizational culture.

Socialization

After new employees are selected, they are indoctrinated into the organization's culture. The process by which the organization's core values, beliefs, norms, and expected behaviors are conveyed to employees is called *socialization*. A stronger culture is created when there is a careful and intense socialization process. Through socialization, employees learn the values and norms that make them fully functioning members of the culture.[45]

exhibit | **17.4**

Stages of the Socialization Process

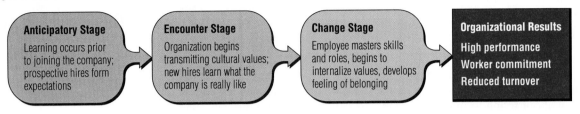

Socialization may be thought of as a three-stage process, as illustrated in Exhibit 17.4. It incorporates the anticipatory stage, the encounter stage, and the change stage.[46] Taken together, these phases impact productivity, the commitment and satisfaction of employees, and the rate of employee turnover. Employees who are effectively socialized into the organization successfully perform their assignments, have a higher level of job involvement and motivation, and are more likely to stay with the organization. Research has found that formal socialization mechanisms have a positive impact on new employees by reducing role ambiguity, role conflict, and stress, thus leading to greater satisfaction and commitment.[47]

Socialization actually begins during the selection process. During the **anticipatory stage** of socialization, prospective organizational members are provided with information that helps them anticipate what it would be like to work in the organization. One aspect of this is the **realistic job preview (RJP),** which gives job applicants all pertinent and realistic information—both positive and negative—about the job and about the overall organization.[48] RJPs help match individuals, jobs, and organizations. Applicants have a better basis on which to determine their suitability to the organization and can self-select into or out of jobs. Anticipatory socialization also goes beyond the specific job to give applicants some feeling about the nature of the organization as a whole. As described in the opening vignette, job applicants at Trilogy Software are interviewed by software developers and programmers, consultants, and salespeople, as well as managers, to give them a broader picture of the organization. In addition, candidates spend a great deal of time socializing with employees during the interview process, thereby learning aspects of the company's culture. The anticipatory stage is highly important because it helps ensure a good match between the individual and the job and organization.

The **encounter stage** of socialization begins after the individual has been hired and first enters the organization. Activities during the encounter stage may include orientation and training programs, formal welcome packages that provide the new employee with useful information, and informal activities designed to transmit an understanding of "how things are done around here." Some companies use on-the-job training, pairing a new hire with an experienced employee. The new organizational member learns not only how to perform job tasks, but also how the organization works, what behaviors are expected, and so forth.

The encounter stage is an extremely important period in the socialization process, but it can also be a difficult period. Sometimes, new employ-

anticipatory stage

The stage of socialization that occurs before a person joins the organization and provides applicants with information that helps them anticipate what it would be like to work there.

realistic job preview (RJP)

A selection technique that gives applicants all pertinent and realistic information about the job and the organization.

encounter stage

The stage of socialization that begins when a person first enters the organization and is designed to transmit information about how things are done within the company.

ees encounter discrepancies between their expectations and the reality of the job. For example, Linda McDermott left a good position with an accounting firm to become an executive vice president of a young management consulting company. She believed the company's culture valued the creativity of its employees and that she would be working closely with top leaders in setting strategic direction and helping the business grow. As it turned out, however, her boss relegated her primarily to routine administrative duties, which left her with little of the entrepreneurial enthusiasm she had felt during the anticipatory socialization stage. McDermott quit after only a few months, causing the company to initiate another lengthy selection process and sidetracking her own career for a year or two.[49]

If the new hire gained a basically accurate understanding of the job and organization during the anticipatory stage, the encounter stage reinforces these perceptions. Even so, the encounter stage may be trying. New employees may have to question their own assumptions and ideas about how things are done to fit in with the organization. At Procter & Gamble, new hires are assigned to minor tasks while they question their old beliefs and behaviors so that they have room to assimilate the values and beliefs of P&G. Through extensive training programs during this encounter stage, new employees constantly hear about the company's values and purpose, about watershed events in the company's history, and about exemplary individuals who represent important cultural values.[50] Starbucks Coffee emphasizes the encounter stage of socialization because the company's managers believe an employee's first days set the tone for his or her entire relationship with the organization.

Starbucks Coffee Co.

Howard Schultz compares a new employee's first days to the early years of childhood. During the early years, parents want to instill in their children good values, high self-esteem, and the confidence to begin making their own decisions. Schultz wants to do the same with his new employees: "I think you have to engage the employee early on by sharing how much you care about what you do. For people joining the company we try to define what Starbucks stands for, what we're trying to achieve, and why that's relevant to them."

Schultz appreciates the importance of a good start because he began as a Starbucks employee in 1982, before he started his own company and bought Starbucks's assets. Today, Schultz tries to replicate the early Starbucks culture—a culture in which people are highly valued and care about one another—in every one of the chain's stores. Schultz himself welcomes each new employee—even part timers (called "partners")—by video. He also tells about the company's history and culture and shares some of his own personal experiences at Starbucks. During the 24 hours of training they receive, new hires are constantly told how much they are valued and appreciated and how they are becoming part of a unique company. An important part of training is also to have employees discuss the Starbucks mission and values and talk about what qualities attracted them to the company.

Schultz believes businesspeople should heed the old cliché that "you never get a second chance to make a first impression" and recognize that an employee's first two weeks with the company may well be the most important.[51]

Another company that recognizes the importance of an employee's first days is Nike, which holds a two-day orientation period during which new hires learn the story of how and why the company was founded and begin their indoctrination into the Nike culture. Nike also uses corporate storytelling throughout an employee's tenure to help connect what's going on today with Nike's heritage.[52]

change stage

The stage of socialization that begins when a new employee works out any value conflicts and begins to feel like an "insider."

The **change stage** of socialization is when a new organizational member works out any problems or conflicts discovered during the encounter stage and begins to feel comfortable in the organization. Those individuals who don't successfully make the transition to this stage often leave the organization voluntarily or are dismissed. During the change stage, special attention is given to evaluating the employee's performance, providing feedback, and rewarding the new employee for exhibiting attitudes and behaviors that fit the organizational culture. In addition, some organizations, such as Starbucks, pair each new employee with a mentor to help him or her accomplish the change stage. Mentoring can be valuable at this time because this is the stage in which the employee begins to internalize the organization's values, norms, and expected behaviors. The change stage is complete when the individual feels like "an insider" and is confident that he or she can perform the job, understands how the organization works, and knows what is expected.

These three stages complete the employee's early socialization. However, socialization is actually an ongoing process. Organizations continue to socialize employees throughout their careers with the company, although the process may not be formalized or explicit. This continuous socialization helps to strengthen and reaffirm the organizational culture.

The Role of Mentoring

mentoring

The process by which a senior employee sponsors and supports a junior or less experienced employee.

Among socialization mechanisms, mentoring deserves special mention because of the powerful impact it can have. **Mentoring** is the process by which a senior employee sponsors and supports a less experienced employee.[53] Four stages of the mentoring process have been identified and are described in Exhibit 17.5.[54] Keep in mind that the time frame of mentoring relationships may vary widely.

Many organizations establish formal mentoring programs, which are particularly important for minorities and women. Research indicates that these groups are less likely than men to develop mentoring relationships on their own.[55] To gain the benefits of mentoring, organizations can institutionalize cultural values that encourage upper level executives to actively help steer female and minority protégés into pivotal positions that can further their development and progress within the organization.

Mentoring helps to transmit cultural values and provides new or less experienced workers with a sense of belonging. The mentor can provide information about and a historical context for organizational values, norms, and activities. In addition, these relationships prove to be valuable throughout an employee's tenure with the organization. Research suggests that individuals who have mentors early in their careers are more satisfied and progress faster in the organization than those who do not.[56] Mentoring also provides benefits for the organization. In addition to socializing new employees, mentoring promotes ongoing employee development and improves communication across hierarchical levels.

Corporate Culture in a Global Environment

How do managers translate ideas for developing and maintaining strong corporate cultures to a complex global environment? As business increasingly crosses geographical and cultural boundaries, the need to be aware of

exhibit | **17.5** The Mentoring Process

Phase	Definition	Turning Points*
Initiation	A period of six months to a year during which time the relationship gets started and begins to have importance for both managers.	Fantasies become concrete expectations.
		Expectations are met; senior manager provides coaching, challenging work, visibility; junior manager provides technical assistance, respect,and desire to be coached.
		There are opportunities for interaction around work tasks.
Cultivation	A period of two to five years during which time the range of career and psychosocial functions provided expands to a maximum.	Both individuals continue to benefit from the relationship. Opportunities for meaningful and more frequent interaction increase.
		Emotional bond deepens and intimacy increases.
Separation	A period of six months to two years after a significant change in the structural role relationship and/or in the emotional experience of the relationship.	Junior manager no longer wants guidance but rather the opportunity to work more autonomously. Senior manager faces midlife crisis and is less available to provide mentoring functions.
		Job rotation or promotion limits opportunitites for continued interaction; career and psychosocial functions can no longer be provided.
		Blocked opportunity creates resentment and hostility that disrupts positive interaction.
Redefinition	An indefinite period after the separation phase, during which time the relationship is ended or takes on significantly different characteristics, making it a more peerlike friendship.	Stresses of separation diminish, and new relationships are formed.
		The mentor relationship is no longer needed in its previous form. Resentment and anger diminish; gratitude and appreciation increase.
		Peer status is achieved.

*Examples of the most frequently observed psychological and organizational factors that cause movement into the current relationship phase.

Source: Republished by permission of the Academy of Management from K. E. Kram, "Phases of the Mentor Relationship," *Academy of Management Journal,* December 1983, p. 622, copyright 1983 Academy of Management. Permission conveyed through Copyright Clearance Center.

and sensitive to other cultures—as well as to understand the impact of national culture on the organization—becomes paramount. About 75 percent of companies believe they have had alliances that failed because of an incompatibility between the national and the corporate culture.[57] Corporate culture and national culture are intertwined, and the global diversity of many of today's companies presents a challenge to managers trying to build a strong organizational culture. Employees who come from different countries often have varied attitudes and beliefs that make it difficult to establish a sense of community and cohesiveness based on the corporate culture. In fact, research has indicated that national culture has a greater impact on employees than does corporate culture.[58]

However, in this multicultural environment some companies are developing a broad, global perspective that permeates the entire organizational culture. One such organization is Omron, a global company with headquarters in Kyoto, Japan. Even though Omron has long had offices on each continent, until a few years ago executives had always assigned Japanese managers to head them. Today, Omron relies on local expertise in each geographical area and blends the insights and perspectives of local managers into a global whole. Global planning meetings are held in offices around the world. In addition, the company established a global database and standardized its software to ensure a smooth exchange of information among its offices worldwide. It takes time to develop a broad cultural mind-set and spread it throughout the company, but firms such as Omron manage to bring a multicultural approach to every business issue.

Vijay Govindarajan, a professor of international business and director of the "Global Leadership 2020" management program at Dartmouth College, offers some guidance for managers trying to build a global culture. His research indicates that, even though organizational cultures may vary widely, specific components characterize a global business culture. Companies with **global business cultures** emphasize multicultural rather than national values and are open to new ideas from other countries and cultures. In addition, these companies exhibit excitement rather than trepidation when entering new cultural environments, and managers are trained to be sensitive to cultural differences without being limited by them. An important aspect of supporting a global culture is that the organization bases status and rewards on merit rather than nationality.[59] In the 21st century, organizations will continue to evolve in their ability to work with varied cultures, blend them into a cohesive whole, and cope with the conflicts that may arise in a multicultural environment.

global business culture

An organizational culture that emphasizes multicultural rather than national values and is open to new ideas from other countries and cultures.

apply it

1. Describe the socialization process you went through when you began your current job or when you first came to your college or university. Can you identify the anticipatory, encounter, and change stages?
2. Have you or anyone you know ever had a mentor, perhaps a teacher or older student? If so, describe the relationship and how it changed over time.

Cultural values can encourage ethical behavior

Of the values that make up an organization's culture, ethical values are now considered among the most important. Ethical standards are becoming part of the formal policies and informal cultures of many organizations. Some organizations place a significant emphasis on ethics. Dollar General Corp., for example, emphasizes ethics in its business conduct. The company is infused with the traditional small-town values of CEO Cal Turner and distributes wallet-sized cards to all employees that tell them about Dollar General's commitment to hard work and moral integrity. Company leaders uphold the ethical values in their words and deeds. After an experimental learning center and store the company built in a public housing development in Nashville was looted and burned following a police shooting of a black suspect, Dollar General immediately began reinvesting time and

what would you do?

WHEN A "ROCK-SOLID" CULTURE STARTS TO ERODE

Randy Patterson started his catalog clothing company with $500 in savings and a $20,000 loan from his family. With Randy's keen eye for unique yet inexpensive clothing designs and his wife Samantha's flair for writing artistic copy that tapped into the longing of buyers for novelty, adventure, and romance, the new company gained rapid success. Sam & Randy's went from two employees to 15 within the first six months, and a year later the number of employees had jumped to 65. The Pattersons found themselves needing to hire people quickly, and they often had to pay them higher salaries than the company's long-term employees earned to match what they were making elsewhere.

The Pattersons didn't have any trouble finding people who wanted to work at the company. It was well known that the corporate culture at Sam & Randy's was one that respected people; valued equality, creativity, and innovation; and allowed employees a great deal of freedom. Patterson believed his firm's culture was rock solid and that it was one of the company's greatest strengths. As rapid growth continued, however, the culture began to erode. New employees who came to Sam & Randy's from other companies that had more rigid, authoritarian cultures began to slip into their old cultural habits. Soon, people were bickering over job responsibilities, salaries, and numerous other issues. The previously open and egalitarian culture was being replaced by one that set up boundaries between people, hierarchical levels, and departments.

Patterson recalled that in the years before he got so busy, he would have breakfast each Friday with a different group of employees randomly selected from all levels and areas of the company. The breakfast meetings had been excellent for helping people get to know one another and develop trusting relationships among themselves and with top management. The friendly culture had gelled quickly, thanks largely to those weekly meetings, but now that Randy was traveling so much, he felt he didn't have time for regular breakfast meetings. In addition, costs have recently been going up and sales have been declining, and Randy knows those issues need his urgent attention. He began thinking about how he could get the culture back on track without investing too much of his time. Randy and Samantha have approached your consulting company for ideas.

1. What do you think is the primary problem with the culture at Sam & Randy's?

2. What advice would you give the Pattersons regarding selection and socialization of employees?

3. How would you suggest Randy go about getting the culture back on track?

Source: This story is based on information in John Peterman, "The Rise and Fall of the J. Peterman Company," *Harvard Business Review,* September-October 1999, pp. 59–66.

---

money in rebuilding the center, despite warnings from observers that the same thing could happen again. The company believes the center, which provides GED training and job skills to low-income residents, offers people a way out of poverty.[60]

Ethics is difficult to define in a precise way. In general, **ethics** is the code of moral principles and values that governs the behavior of a person or group with respect to what is right or wrong. Ethics sets standards as to what is good or bad in conduct and decision making.[61] Many people believe that if you are not breaking the law, you are behaving in an ethical manner, but ethics often go far beyond the law.[62] The relationship between ethical standards and legal requirements is illustrated in Exhibit 17.6. The law arises from a set of codified principles and regulations that are generally accepted in society and are enforceable in the courts. Ethical standards for the most part apply to behavior not covered by law, and the law covers many areas not covered by ethical standards. Although current laws often reflect combined moral standards, not all moral standards are codified into law. The morality of aiding a drowning person, for example, is not specified by law, and driving on the right-hand side of the road has no moral

ethics

The code of moral principles and values that governs the behavior of a person or group with respect to what is right or wrong.

607

exhibit | **17.6**

Relationship betweeen Ethical
Standards and Legal Requirements

Source: Based on LaRue Tone Hosmer, *The Ethics of Management,* 2nd ed. (Homewood, II: Irwin, 1991).

basis; but in areas such as robbery or murder, law and ethical standards overlap.

The organizational standards for ethical conduct are embodied within each employee as well as within the organization itself. In a recent survey about unethical conduct in the workplace, more than half of the respondents cited poor leadership as a factor.[63] Top executives can create and sustain a cultural climate that emphasizes the importance of ethical behavior for all employees.

Values-Based Leadership

values-based leadership

A relationship between leaders and followers that is based on shared, strongly internalized values that are advocated and acted upon by the leader.

Ethical values in organizations are developed and strengthened primarily through **values-based leadership,** a relationship between leaders and followers that is based on shared, strongly internalized values that are advocated and acted upon by the leader.[64] Managers influence ethical values through their personal behavior as well as through the organization's systems and policies. Employees learn about values from watching managers. Managers who act as values-based leaders generate a high level of trust and respect from employees based not just on stated values but on the courage, determination, and self-sacrifice they demonstrate in upholding those values. When managers are willing to make personal sacrifices for the sake of values, employees become more willing to do so. At Eastman Kodak, for example, CEO George Fisher has emphasized a commitment to corporate social responsibility by linking a portion of his own pay to social factors.[65]

For organizations to be ethical, top managers need to be openly and strongly committed to ethical conduct, and they should develop policies, procedures, and reward systems that encourage others to act in an ethical manner. Consider how Peter Holt has made ethical values a core part of his organization's culture.

Holt Companies

At the Holt Companies, every meeting opens with "Values in Action" stories that highlight recent values-relevant events, how they were handled, and how the company can learn from them. Everyone in the firm—especially the CEO, Peter Holt—is expected to be responsible for upholding the organization's ethics. Ethical values are woven into the organizational culture, and Holt continually works to renew the values and signal his total commitment to them.

Holt began developing his approach to ethics in the mid-1980s after joining the company founded by his great-grandfather a century ago. The Holt Companies have more than 1,200 employees in 14 Texas and Ohio locations. To develop his Values-Based Leadership (VBL) process, Holt first involved the entire workforce in determining a set of core values that would guide everything the company did. The final list puts ethical values—being honest, showing integrity, being consistent, and providing fair treatment—at the top, followed in order by values of attaining success through meeting goals, achieving continuous improvement, being commited to the long-term health of the company, and pursuing new strategic opportunities through creativity and change.

All new employees attend a two-day training program, where they learn about the values and discuss values-related cases and dilemmas. In addition, the Holt Companies presents a two-day ethics awareness course for all managers and supervisors. Peter Holt visits each of the firm's locations twice a year to conduct two-hour meetings with employees, where he discloses financial information, answers questions, and talks about the importance of each employee upholding Holt's core values every day in every action. The close involvement of the CEO and other top leaders has contributed to an environment of candor and respect between management and workers. Importantly, Holt's evaluation and reward systems are also tied to the values-based leadership process.[66]

By integrating ethics throughout the organization, companies like Holt make personal and organizational integrity a part of day-to-day business. Holt's system was not an overnight success. It took several years to develop the system and the level of trust needed to make it work. Only when employees are convinced that ethical values play a key role in all management decisions and actions can they become committed to making them a part of their everyday behavior.

Managers set the ethical tone for the organization through their own actions. Several factors contribute to an individual's ethical stance. Every individual brings a set of personal beliefs, values, personality characteristics, and behavior traits to the job. The family backgrounds and spiritual beliefs of managers often provide principles by which they conduct business. Personality characteristics such as ego strength, self-confidence, and a strong sense of independence may enable managers to make ethical decisions even if those decisions might be unpopular. One important personal factor is the stage of moral development, which affects an individual's ability to translate values into behavior.[67]

Three stages of personal moral development are illustrated in Exhibit 17.7. For example, young children have a low level of moral development, making decisions and acting to obtain rewards and avoid punishment. As they mature, most people learn to conform to expectations of good behavior as defined by society. This means willingly upholding the law and

Level 1: Preconventional

Follows rules to avoid punishment. Acts in own interest. Obedience for its own sake.

Level 2: Conventional

Lives up to expectations of others. Fulfills duties and obligations of social system. Upholds laws.

Level 3: Postconventional

Follows self-chosen principles of justice and right. Aware that people hold different values and seeks creative solutions to ethical dilemmas. Balances concern for individual with concern for common good.

exhibit | **17.7**

Three Levels of Personal Moral Development

Source: Based on L. Kohlberg, " Moral Stages and Moralization: The Cognitive-Development Approach," in T. Lickona (ed.), *Moral Development and Behavior: Theory, Research, and Social Issues* (New York: Holt, Rinehart, and Winston, 1976), pp. 31–53; and Jill W. Graham. (1995, January). "Leadership, moral development and citizenship behavior." *Business Ethics Quarterly 5* (1): 43–54.

responding to the expectations of others. At the highest level of moral development are people who are guided by an internalized set of standards universally recognized as right or wrong. People at this stage of moral development may even break laws if necessary to uphold their moral principles. Values-based leaders strive to develop higher moral reasoning, so that their daily actions reflect important ethical values. When faced with difficult decisions, values-based leaders know what they stand for and have the courage to act on their principles.

Organizational Structure and Systems

Ethical values and behavior are also influenced through formal systems, programs, and policies. Some that have effectively influenced organizational ethics in recent years are codes of ethics, ethical structures, training programs, and disclosure mechanisms.

code of ethics

A formal statement of the company's ethical values, stating the behaviors that are expected and those that will not be tolerated.

Codes of Ethics   A **code of ethics** is a formal statement of the company's ethical values. It communicates to employees what the company stands for. Codes of ethics state the values and behavior that are expected and those that will not be tolerated. A study by the Center for Business Ethics found that 90 percent of *Fortune* 500 companies and almost half of all other companies now have codes of ethics.[68] When leaders support and enforce these codes, they can uplift a company's ethical climate.

Some companies include ethics as a part of broader statements that also define their mission. These statements generally define ethical values as well as corporate culture and contain language about company responsibility, quality of product, and treatment of employees. For example, Northern Telecom's *Code of Business Conduct,* which is provided to all employees and is also available on the Internet, is a set of guidelines and standards that illustrate how the company's mission and core values translate into ethical business practices.

ethics committee

A group of employees, usually top managers, appointed to oversee a company's ethics.

Ethical Structures   Ethical structures represent the various positions or programs an organization uses to encourage ethical behavior. One example is an **ethics committee,** a group of employees—usually top managers—appointed to oversee a company's ethics. The committee provides rulings on questionable ethical issues. An ethics ombudsperson is a single person given the responsibility of being the corporate conscience who hears and investigates complaints and points out potential ethics failures to top leaders.

Many organizations today are setting up ethics departments with full-time staff. These offices, such as the one at Northrup Grumman, work as counseling centers more than police departments. They are charged with helping employees deal with day-to-day ethical problems or questions. The offices also provide training based on the organization's code of ethics so that employees can translate the values into daily behavior.[69]

In addition to structural components such as these, it is important that the organization tie its evaluation and reward systems to ethical concerns so that employees know ethical behavior is valued and rewarded. Companies may have model ethics programs, but if managers emphasize profits over ethics and reward employees who attain goals through any means necessary—even unethical ones—the programs are of little value. For a company to be ethical, all organizational systems should support and encourage ethical behavior, as in the case of the Holt Companies described earlier.

Training Programs   To make sure ethical issues are considered in daily actions, leaders often implement training programs to supplement a written code of ethics. Texas Instruments developed an eight-hour ethics training course for all employees. In addition, the company incorporates ethics into every course it offers. For example, a course on how to use Windows 98 included information on the ethical issues of copying and distributing software.

Companies like Texas Instruments with a strong commitment to ethical values make ethical issues a part of all training. Starbucks Coffee uses new employee training to begin instilling values such as taking personal responsibility, treating everyone with respect, and doing the right thing even if others disagree with you.[70] Levi Strauss also includes ethics in its training programs, and the leadership training course in particular stresses the importance of honesty, fairness, and personal integrity.

Disclosure Mechanisms   Finally, organizational managers can develop mechanisms to support employees who do the right thing and voice their concerns about ethical practices. One important step is to develop policies about whistle-blowing. **Whistle-blowing** is employee disclosure of illegal, unethical, or immoral practices on the part of the organization. It can be risky for employees to blow the whistle—they can lose their jobs, be transferred to lower-level positions, or be ostracized by coworkers.

Top managers set the standard for how whistle-blowers are treated. If the organization genuinely wants to maintain ethical standards, whistle-blowers are valued, and managers make dedicated efforts to protect them.[71] To begin with, managers create a climate where people feel free to point out problems without fear of punishment. In addition, they may set up hot lines or other mechanisms to give employees a confidential way to report problems, then make sure action is taken to investigate reported concerns.

In summary, managers create an ethical climate for the organization through systems and programs such as codes of ethics, ethical structures, training programs, and mechanisms to protect whistle-blowers. However, top managers instill and encourage ethical values most clearly through their own personal actions and by working to ingrain ethics into the organizational culture.

While culture is not the only aspect of an organization that influences ethics, it is a major force because it defines the company's values. Exhibit 17.8 presents questions that can be asked to understand the organizational culture's impact on ethical standards.

whistle-blowing

Employee disclosure of illegal, unethical, or immoral practices on the part of the organization.

apply it

1.   Imagine yourself in a situation where you are being encouraged to inflate your expense account. Do you think your choice would be most affected by your individual moral development or by the cultural values of the company?

exhibit | **17.8**

Analyzing an Organization's Cultural
Impact on Ethics

The following questions can help determine the corporate culture's impact on organizational ethics:

1. Identify the organization's heroes. What values do they represent? Given an ambiguous ethical situation, what decisions would they make and why?

2. What are some important organizational rituals? How do they encourage or discourage ethical behavior? Who gets the awards—people of integrity or individuals who use unethical methods to attain success?

3. What are the ethical messages sent to new members of the organization? Must they obey authority at all costs, or is questioning authority acceptable or even desirable?

4. Does analysis of organizational stories and myths reveal individuals who stand up for what's right, or is conformity the valued characteristic? Do people get fired or promoted in these stories?

5. Does language exist for discussing ethical concerns? Is this language routinely incorporated and encouraged in business decision making?

6. What formal and informal socialization processes exist, and what norms for ethical/unethical behavior do they promote?

Source: Based on Linda Klebe Trevino, "A Cultural Perspective on Changing and Developing Organizational Ethics," in R. Woodman and W. Pasmore (eds.), *Research in Organizational Change and Development* (Greenwich, CT: JAI Press, 1990), p. 4.

Now, think about your role as a student and recall instances where you have faced an ethical decision, such as whether to help a friend cheat on a test. What influenced your decision?

2. Review a copy of the code of ethics for an organization with which you are familiar (perhaps your college or university). Do you believe leaders uphold and enforce the code?

summary OF KEY CONCEPTS

- **Why is culture important?** Culture is the set of key values, assumptions, beliefs, understandings, and norms shared by members of an organization and taught to new members as correct. It can be thought of as consisting of three levels: visible artifacts, expressed values and beliefs, and deeply embedded assumptions. Culture serves two important functions. First, it facilitates internal integration. Culture guides day-to-day working relationships and helps organization members know how to communicate and relate to one another, what behavior is acceptable or unacceptable, and how power and status are allocated. The second primary function is external adaption. Culture determines how the organization meets goals and deals with outsiders. A strong culture can encourage employee commitment to the core purpose of the organization, its specific goals, and the basic means used to accomplish goals.

- **Different organizations have different types of culture.** Four types of cultures found in organizations are the baseball team culture, club culture, academy culture, and fortress culture. Each type has somewhat different potential for supporting a successful company, and each has a different impact on the satisfaction and careers of employees.

- **Culture can support a high-performance organization.** Almost all organizations have subcultures that reflect the common problems, goals, and experiences of different groups within the company. Subcultures can help companies be more adaptive, but they may also lead to conflicts, particularly in organizations that do not have strong overall corporate cultures. A strong culture has a powerful impact on a company, but research has found that it may not always be positive. The nature of the cultural values should encourage a healthy adaptation to the external environment. Adaptive and unadaptive cultures have different values and behaviors. When a culture's values are out of alignment with the needs of the environment, a culture gap exists. Many companies trying to shift to a learning organization find that an important step is changing the culture to embody the values of boundarylessness, equality, risk taking, and continuous improvement.

- **Managers use various mechanisms to build and strengthen organizational culture.** Mechanisms that managers can use to build, strengthen, or change culture include rites and ceremonies, stories and legends, symbols, and specialized language. Most importantly, managers reinforce or change culture through symbolic leadership. Symbolic leaders use stories, symbols, slogans, and ceremonies to emphasize the desired cultural values. In addition, leaders make sure their daily actions signal and support the values. Employees learn what is valued most in a company by watching how managers behave.

- **Selection and socialization help keep the culture alive.** Selection and socialization are particularly important mechanisms for maintaining strong cultural values. Organizations try to select people who will "fit into" the organization. This tendency to find a good match means that companies often hire people who have values very similar to those of the organization. After new em-

ployees are selected, they are indoctrinated into the organizational culture through a socialization process. Three phases of socialization are the anticipatory stage, the encounter stage, and the change stage. Mentoring is a particularly strong socialization technique. Building and maintaining strong cultural values with which all employees can identify and agree is particularly difficult in a global environment. Companies with a global culture emphasize multicultural values, base status on merit rather than nationality, are excited about new cultural environments, remain open to ideas from other cultures, and are sensitive to different cultural values without being limited by them.

- **Cultural values can encourage ethical behavior.** Of the values that make up a corporate culture, ethical values are considered highly important. The organizational standards for ethical conduct are embodied within each person as well as within the organizational culture. Ethical values are developed and strengthened through values-based leadership. For organizations to be ethical, top leaders must be firmly and openly committed to ethical conduct. One consideration for leaders and other individuals is their level of personal moral development. Ethical values are also influenced through formal organizational programs, including codes of ethics, ethics committees or ethics departments, training programs, and policies to support whistle-blowing.

KEY terms

culture, p. 587	story, p. 598	change stage, p. 604
baseball team culture, p. 590	heroes, p. 598	mentoring, p. 604
club culture, p. 591	legends, p. 598	global business culture, p. 606
academy culture, p. 591	symbol, p. 598	ethics, p. 607
fortress culture, p. 592	symbolic leader, p. 600	values-based leadership, p. 608
culture strength, p. 592	selection, p. 601	code of ethics, p. 610
subcultures, p. 593	anticipatory stage, p. 602	ethics committee, p. 610
culture gap, p. 595	realistic job preview (RJP), p. 602	whistle-blowing, p. 611
rites and ceremonies, p. 598	encounter stage, p. 602	

DISCUSSION questions

1. Define *corporate culture* and discuss its importance in organizations.

2. Describe the cultural values of a company for which you have worked. Did the values fit the needs of the external environment? Of the company's employees? Discuss.

3. What is a culture gap? What are some of the techniques managers might use to change cultural values when necessary?

4. Discuss how a strong culture could have either positive or negative consequences for an organization. Do you think there is ever a situation in which an organization might want to maintain a weak culture? Discuss.

5. What is meant by the statement that culture helps a group or organization solve the problem of internal integration?

6. The selection and socialization process in organizations has taken on increasing importance in the last decade. What factors do you think might account for this?

7. Why is values-based leadership important for influencing ethical values in an organization?

8. What might be some of the advantages of having a variety of subcultures in an organization? The disadvantages?

9. Why do you think equality is an important value in the culture of a learning organization?

10. Which do you think communicates more about a company's values, a symbolic act or an explicit statement? Discuss.

11. In what type of environment is a baseball team culture most effective? What do you think it would be like to work in a baseball team culture? An academy culture?

SELF-DISCOVERY *exercise*

What Are Your Values?

Following is a list of 18 values that have been found to be more or less universal. Individuals and organizations differ from one another in how they prioritize these values. In column 1, rank the values from your most preferred to least preferred. For example, the value that is most important to you would be ranked 1; the value that is least important would be ranked 18. Next, in column 2, rank the values of the organization where you work or of a group to which you belong.

Note: The values are listed in alphabetical order.

Value	Your Ranking	Organization Ranking
Ambition *(being hardworking and aspiring)*	_____	_____
Broad-mindedness *(being open-minded; diversified)*	_____	_____
Capability *(being competent; effective)*	_____	_____
Cheerfulness *(being light-hearted; joyful)*	_____	_____
Cleanliness *(being neat and tidy)*	_____	_____
Courage *(standing up for your beliefs)*	_____	_____
Forgiveness *(being willing to pardon others)*	_____	_____
Helpfulness *(working for the welfare of others; showing caring and compassion)*	_____	_____

Value	Your Ranking	Organization Ranking
Honesty (being sincere and truthful; showing trustworthiness)	_____	_____
Imagination (being daring and creative)	_____	_____
Intellectualism (being self-reliant; self-sufficient)	_____	_____
Logic (being consistent; rational)	_____	_____
Ability to love (being faithful to friends or the group; respectful)	_____	_____
Loyalty (being faithful to friends)	_____	_____
Obedience (being dutiful)	_____	_____
Politeness (being courteous and well-mannered; respectful)	_____	_____
Responsibility (being dependable and reliable)	_____	_____
Self-control (being restrained; self-disciplined)	_____	_____

How closely do your values match those of the organization or group? Based on current literature, today's successful organizations try to incorporate the following values into their corporate cultures: honesty, logic, responsibility, helpfulness, broad-mindedness, capability, and ambition. Why do you think each of these values would be important to an organization?

Source: Robert C. Benfari, *Understanding and Changing Your Management Style* (San Francisco: Jossey-Bass, 1999), pp. 178–183; and M. Rokeach, *Understanding Human Values* (New York: The Free Press, 1979).

ORGANIZATIONAL BEHAVIOR in your life

Are Ethics on the Decline?

Read and think about the following paragraph:

Today's younger generation has views somewhat like those of the young student named Raskolnikov in Dostoevski's classic novel, *Crime and Punishment,* who believed that the "end justified the means." As long as Raskolnikov achieved his goals, he believed it mattered little what he did in pursuing them. Many of America's contemporary youth have been equated with the student. They are considered by some observers as "the least morally anchored generation ever." Young people today tend to believe that the only important consideration is winning and "looking out for *numero uno.*" As with Raskolnikov, they are willing to do whatever it takes to accomplish their own personal goals.

Show the paragraph to at least five people under 25 years old. Ask them an open question, such as, "What is your reaction to the comments?" Did the people you interviewed agree or disagree with the views presented? If they disagreed, what were their reasons for disagreeing? What did your informal survey tell you about the current values of some young people? How do you personally feel about their responses?

Source: Stan Kossen, *The Human Side of Organizations,* 5th ed. (New York: HarperCollins Publishers, 1991), p. 502.

ORGANIZATIONAL BEHAVIOR news flash

What Texas-based organization is considered the best airline in the United States, famous for excellent customer service; happy employees; and a strong, adaptive corporate culture? For years, the quick answer was Southwest Airlines. But Gordon Bethune, a former Navy mechanic, is changing that as CEO of Continental. Robert Levering, co-author of a series of *Fortune* magazine studies called "The 100 Best Places to Work For in America," says about Bethune's impact at Continental: "I've been doing this for 20 years, and I've never seen a turnaround of the workplace culture as dramatic as this one."

Find at least two articles (in addition to the one listed below from *Fortune*) that deal with the turnaround at Continental Airlines. To find them, check news listings on your Internet search engine or check sources such as *The Wall Street Journal*

and *Business Week*. Then answer the following questions:

1. How would you describe the culture of Continental Airlines before Gordon Bethune became CEO? What do you think contributed most to creating this culture?
2. Describe the culture and important cultural values at Continental today and discuss how Bethune orchestrated such a significant cultural turnaround. How have Bethune or other top managers acted as symbolic leaders at Continental?
3. Try to find at least two examples of how the processes of selection and socialization are keeping the new culture alive.

Source: Brian O'Reilly, "The Mechanic Who Fixed Continental," *Fortune,* December 20, 1999, pp. 176–186.

global diversity EVENTS

An area of growing concern for companies doing business internationally is developing codes of ethics that focus on the issue of human rights in developing countries. A New York–based nonprofit organization and a number of influential companies have joined together to propose a set of global labor standards to deal with issues such as child labor, low wages, and unsafe working conditions. The group has come up with a scheme called Social Accountability 8000, or SA 8000, the first auditable social standard in

the world. Many companies, including Avon and Toys 'R' Us, are certifying their factories and requiring their suppliers to do likewise. Using your Internet search engine, look up information about "SA 8000" or "Social Accountability 8000" and write a brief report about these standards, including some of the other companies that have become involved. Do you believe it is possible to develop a set of ethical standards that can be accepted and effective on a global basis? Why or why not?

minicase ISSUE

Merging Conflicting Cultures—Acme and Omega

Background. Acme Electronics and Omega Electronics both manufacture integrated circuits and other electronic components as subcontractors for large manufacturers. Both Acme and Omega are located in Ohio and often bid on contracts as competitors. As subcontractors, both firms benefited from the electronics boom of recent years, and both looked forward to growth and expansion. Acme has annual sales of $100 million and employs 950 people. Omega has annual sales of $80 million and employs about 800 people. Acme typically reports greater net profits than Omega.

Acme's culture. The president of Acme, John Tyler, believed that Acme was the far superior company. Tyler credited his firm's greater effectiveness to his managers' abilities to run a "tight ship." Acme had detailed organization charts and job descriptions. Tyler believed that everyone should have clear responsibilities and narrowly defined jobs, which would generate efficient performance and high company profits. Employees were generally satisfied with their jobs at Acme, although some managers wished for more autonomy and empowerment opportunities.

Omega's culture. Omega's president, Jim Rawls, did not believe in organization charts. He believed organization charts just put artificial barriers between specialists who should be working together. He encouraged people to communicate face to face rather than with written memos. The head of mechanical engineering said, "Jim spends too much time making sure everyone understands what we're doing and listening to suggestions." Rawls was concerned with employee satisfaction and wanted everyone to feel part of the organization. Employees were often rotated among departments so they would be familiar with activities throughout the organization. Although Omega wasn't as profitable as Acme, it was able to bring new products onstream more quickly, work out bugs in new designs more accurately, and achieve higher quality because of superb employee commitment and collaboration.

Culture clash. It is the end of May, and John Tyler, president of Acme, has just announced the acquisition of Omega Electronics. Both management teams are proud of their cultures and have unflattering opinions of the other's. Each company's customers are rather loyal, and their technologies are compatible, so Tyler believes a combined company will be more effective, particularly in a time of rapid change in both technology and products.

The Omega managers resisted the acquisition, but the Acme president is determined to unify the two companies quickly, increase the new firm's marketing position, and revitalize product lines—all by the end of the year.

1. How would you characterize the two different cultures at Acme and Omega? What are the dominant cultural values?

2. Is there a culture gap at the company following the acquisition? What cultural values would you consider most important for the new company?

3. If you were John Tyler, what techniques would you use to integrate and shape the culture to overcome the culture gap?

Source: Adapted from John F. Veiga, "The Paradoxical Twins: Acme and Omega Electronics," in John F. Veiga and John N. Yanouzas, *The Dynamics of Organization Theory* (St. Paul, MN: West Publishing Company, 1984), pp. 132–138; and "Alpha and Omega," Harvard Business School Case 9-488-003, published by the President and Fellows of Harvard College, 1988.

eighteen
CHAPTER

18

Organizational Learning and Change

preview

After studying this chapter, you should be able to:

- Discuss why coping with change is a major challenge for today's companies and explain the forces that create a need for change.

- Give examples of the types of planned change in organizations.

- Cite individual and organizational sources of resistance to change and explain how to overcome resistance.

- Describe Lewin's three-stage change model and Kotter's eight steps for leading organizational change.

- Explain the primary characteristics of the organizational development (OD) approach to change and describe major OD interventions.

- Apply the adaptive learning cycle used by learning organizations.

- Describe how to build a learning organization through changes in structure, tasks, information sharing, strategy, and culture.

A Community Hospital Transforms to Survive in a Chaotic Industry

As you pull into the parking lot at Griffin Hospital in Derby, Connecticut, you're greeted by classical music piped through loudspeakers. Step inside the lobby and, rather than a crowded, noisy, and confusing jumble, you are met by cheerful volunteers who personally take you wherever you need to go. Hallways and rooms are clean, orderly, and comforting. Handrails are warm wood, not cold stainless steel, and fluorescent bulbs have been banned in favor of soft, indirect lighting. The feeling is more of being in a luxury hotel than a hospital. No room is more than 100 feet from a cozy, home-style kitchen where families can gather with a pot of coffee or a patient can bake a batch of banana muffins. Well-groomed, white-coated therapy dogs rest their muzzles on the edge of patients' beds for some gentle petting.

Without a doubt, it's not your average hospital. The striking transformation at Griffin began after the community hospital began losing patients to larger competitors at an alarming rate. In addition, changes in the hospital industry began sucking per patient revenues down a black hole. For a while, it looked as if Griffin might close its doors for good. But that was before Griffin Hospital started asking patients what they wanted and decided to give it to them.

As extreme as the changes in the hospital environment seem, the changes in patient care are even more radical. Every patient takes part in a detailed "case conference" on the day after admission, in which doctors and nurses discuss what they plan to do, explain why, answer any questions, and describe what they expect over the next weeks, months, or even years. Patients are encouraged to look at their medical charts and are given detailed literature about their condition. A large health-resource center, open to the public, has medical books geared toward laypeople and computers linked to health related Web sites. Patients and visitors also have open access to the medical library where doctors and nurses do their own research.

Griffin managers report that changing behavior—"the very nature of nursing and doctoring"—was the most difficult aspect of the transformation at Griffin. Many doctors and nurses were fiercely protective of their established routines and resisted the changes. However, because the changes were implemented gradually, most employees eventually adjusted and even grew to love the greater sense of responsibility and autonomy that came with a new philosophy of putting the patient first. Griffin's Lynn Werdal recalled a patient who was due in the lab for an echocardiogram but wasn't feeling well enough to be moved. "The nurse in the lab just decided to wheel the machine down to his room and do it there, even though no one had ever done that before," she says. "She didn't feel she had to ask my or anyone's permission, and I like that." Today, the entire culture at Griffin has been shifted toward pleasing patients—not hospital administrators. In addition, Griffin's top managers continue to relentlessly drive change through every aspect of Griffin's operations. They believe that in today's environment, you either embrace change and never stop pushing the envelope, or you fail.[1]

> *"The nurse in the lab just decided to wheel the machine down to his room and do it there, even though no one had ever done that before. She didn't feel she had to ask my or anyone's permission, and I like that."*
> —**Lynn Werdal,** Griffin Hospital

Griffin Hospital isn't the only organization that has had to reconceptualize almost every aspect of how it does business to remain competitive. Apple Computer, considered dead only a few years ago, has been revived by the dramatic changes initiated by Steven Jobs. Gateway Computer recently replaced most of its top management team, moved the company headquarters from North Sioux City, South Dakota, to San Diego, California, and instituted a rigorous evaluation process to ensure that employees are performing up to the standards needed to keep Gateway growing. Yun Jong Yong, CEO of Samsung Electronics, cut one-third of the payroll, replaced half of his senior managers, sold off $1.9 billion in assets, and introduced a slew of new cutting-edge products to bring the Asian company back from the brink to earnings of around $2 billion in 1999. Even the General Services Administration (a U.S. government agency) has undergone a spectacular transformation to become more customer oriented and shed its reputation as an old-fashioned, bloated, and irrelevant bureaucracy.[2] The pressing need for change management is reflected in the fact that an increasing number of companies are appointing "transformation officers," who are either high-ranking company executives or highly skilled outside consultants charged with radically rethinking and remaking either the entire corporation or major pieces of it.[3]

organizational change

The adoption of a new idea or behavior by an organization.

In this chapter, we look at the process of **organizational change,** which is defined as the adoption of a new idea or behavior by an organization. We examine some of the basic forces for change in organizations, look at the types of planned change, and consider how managers can overcome resistance to change. The chapter also presents several models and techniques that can help managers smoothly implement major change. The chapter concludes by looking at how managers can change their companies to become learning organizations that are poised for constant learning, change, and adaptation.

Managers can recognize and interpret the forces that call for organizational change

Every organization goes through periods of change. Sometimes, change is brought about because of forces outside the organization. At other times, managers within the company want to initiate major change or spur innovation, but they may not know how. To remain successful, organizations must embrace many types of change. Organizations that invest most of their time and resources in maintaining the status quo are unlikely to prosper in today's environment of uncertainty and chaos.[4] Today's organizations are buffeted from all sides by pressures that call for changes in structure, job design, management policies, culture, or entire ways of doing business.

For much of the 20th century, organizations and the business environment remained relatively stable, so managers rarely had to cope with major change. However, the challenge for managers and organizations in most countries today is not just to cope with change but to embrace and even create it. The structures and patterns of behavior that were once successful no longer work, yet new patterns are just emerging. Most employees are struggling just to keep pace. Whereas change efforts such as corporate restructurings, introduction of new technologies, and development of new products took years to accomplish in the past, they now must be done in months. Managers want to develop clear and logical plans to help their organizations move into the future, and yet they find that real-life change is often a complex, messy, trial-and-error process.[5] One important ability for managers is to know where to look for the forces of change as they emerge and develop. In this section, we will discuss several forces that create and require organizational change.

Globalization

Perhaps the greatest force for change in recent years is globalization. The cliché that the world is getting smaller is dramatically true for today's organizations. With rapid advances in technology and communications, the time it takes to exert influence around the world from even the most remote locations has been reduced from years to only seconds. Business is becoming a unified global field as trade barriers fall, communication becomes faster and cheaper, and consumer tastes in everything from clothing to cellular phones converge.

Thomas Middelhoff of Germany's Bertelsmann AG, which bought the U.S. publisher Random House, captured the nature of today's global business world when he said, "There are no German and American companies. There are only successful and unsuccessful companies."[6] In the 21st century, successful organizations will feel at home anywhere in the world. For example, so-called American companies such as General Motors and Coca-Cola rely on international business for a substantial portion of their sales and profits. Whirlpool Corporation's Brazilian affiliates contributed $78 million to 1997 earnings, compared with only an $11 million operating profit for the parent company, based in Benton Harbor, Michigan.[7]

No company today is isolated from global influence. Countries such as Korea, Taiwan, and Spain are fast growing and rapidly becoming industrialized. Their companies produce low-cost, high-quality commodities and are moving into high-value items such as automobiles and high-technology electronic goods. The shift toward market economies in China, India, Eastern Europe, and the former Soviet republics is producing more sources of goods, new markets and competitors, and, to some extent, uncertainty about how these countries will affect the global economy.[8] U.S. companies have had to slash prices, keep wages down, and increase productivity to earn a profit in the face of this new competition. Even more uncertainty is being created by international trading blocs such as the North American Free Trade Agreement (NAFTA), the Association of Southeast Asian Nations (ASEAN), and the European Union, which have significantly reduced tariffs and barriers to trade. These power blocs will continue to reshape the world economy and will likely mean the end of U.S. domination of international trade policy.

Globalization presents many advantages for organizations, but it also means that the business environment is becoming extremely complex and competitive. Today's managers have to keep an eye on the global economic environment and world politics, not just the events happening in their own backyard. Worldwide events that change rapidly and unpredictably are forcing companies in all industries to rethink their approach to business and initiate change.[9] Large companies such as IBM and Ford are globalizing their management structures to remain competitive internationally, while even the smallest companies are searching for ways to reap the advantages of global interdependence and minimize the disadvantages. One way companies are being more competitive globally is through e-commerce. The Internet and other e-commerce technology enables even the smallest organization to conduct international business quickly and easily.

Technological Advances

Many of the changes in today's world are being driven by advances in computer technology. Both manufacturing and service organizations are using new technology to improve productivity, customer service, and competitiveness. Mass production and distribution techniques are being replaced by new computer-aided systems that can produce one-of-a-kind variations at a cost previously unimagined.

Only four years ago at a CEO Forum in San Francisco, General Electric CEO Jack Welch (left) said, "I don't have a computer in my office, and I don't need a computer." However, by the beginning of 1999 Welch had declared that e-business would be a major GE initiative. Within days, things started happening at all of GE's 20 key businesses. Its plastics distribution business, Polymerland, didn't have an e-commerce team. But today its team is 30 members, and they do $2 million of business a day on-line, with that amount expected to double soon. Such technological changes encourage new alliances between leaders of the old economy and the new economy. As part of his initiative to make GE Net savvy, Welch invited Sun Microsystems CEO Scott McNealy (right) to join GE's board of directors. Now the two CEOs are friends and give each other advice. (Source: © Michael O'Neill/Corbis Outline)

Companies find that because technology changes so rapidly, they must constantly evaluate and upgrade systems, examine new technological developments, adopt new ways of doing business, and train employees in new skills. Thanks to advanced technology, products can be made and sold anywhere in the world, communications are instant, and product development and life cycles are shorter than ever before. In addition, the financial basis of today's economy is becoming *information* rather than such tangible assets as land, buildings, and capital. This means that the primary factor of production has become human knowledge rather than machines, increasing the power of employees and the importance of organizational behavior.

One significant area of technological change for organizations is the Internet and e-commerce. The idea of communicating instantly with people around the world via the Internet was unimaginable as recently as a decade ago. Within just a few years, the Internet has been transformed from a small, specialized network used by a few computer experts to a broad communications and trade center where more than 90 million people exchange information or close deals around the world.[10] Most managers know that the Internet could change almost everything in every industry, but many of them are struggling to transform their organizations to fit into this new world. Companies embracing the new world of e-commerce, whether to sell products, streamline operations, or improve communications with customers and partners, are thriving. Those that ignore the trend do so at their own peril. The significance of the Internet and its effect on the rate of change are illustrated by the results of a study by Opinion Research Corporation International of Princeton, New Jersey. The study found that a handful of Internet companies, including Amazon, Yahoo!, and America Online, became household names (meaning that more than 50 million Americans recognize them by name) within only a few years, whereas it took powerhouse companies such as Coca-Cola and McDonald's decades longer to achieve the same status.[11]

Technology also plays a key role in the trend toward knowledge management and the sharing of information within and between organizations.

Recognizing that intellectual capital—what employees know—matters more than any other asset today, companies seek to manage knowledge just as they manage cash flow or raw materials. New positions such as chief information officer, chief knowledge officer, director of knowledge management, and chief learning officer reflect the importance of information and knowledge in today's organizations. Daniel Holtshouse, director of knowledge initiatives at Xerox, estimates that about a fifth of *Fortune* 500 companies have someone who serves in the capacity of a chief knowledge officer, and the number is growing.[12]

Changes in Society and the Workforce

Another force for change that managers should pay close attention to is people both within and outside the organization. One consideration is the changing nature of the workforce—specifically, the need to adjust to greater diversity, as discussed in Chapter 2. Due to the aging of the U.S. population, the average worker is older now, but a tightening labor market has led to more companies filling key positions with younger employees. This means that people working together on a team may have the same rank and status but be 30 or 40 years apart in age. This fundamental shift has begun to affect companies only in the past five years, but it will likely continue as a significant force for organizational change.[13] In addition, many more women, people of color, and immigrants are entering the workforce. Organizations have to make changes in their human resource practices to attract and retain diverse employees, as well as to meet the changing needs of highly skilled knowledge workers.

Organizations must also pay close attention to shifting societal expectations and the changing desires of customers. For example, in today's fast-paced world, customers expect new products and services developed more often and delivered more rapidly—and they often want them customized to their exact needs. Banks are setting up online banking and bill-paying services, manufacturers are retooling people and processes to provide customized products, and practically every organization has set up an e-commerce department. Many restaurants introduced reduced fat items to respond to consumers' interest in healthier food; for example, Kentucky Fried Chicken changed its name to KFC when it began selling non-fried chicken products. And almost every U.S. organization has instituted some kind of no smoking policy in response to antismoking sentiments and concerns about second-hand smoke. As mentioned earlier in this chapter, U.S. government agencies such as the General Services Administration have also gone through dramatic transformations in response to shifting societal expectations.

General Services Administration

The U.S. public has grown increasingly tired of seeing tax dollars squandered by inefficient, overstaffed government agencies. The General Services Administration (GSA), created in 1949, was considered one of the most old-fashioned, change-averse agencies in the U.S. government as recently as 1996. That's when Dave Barram came in with a mandate to transform the GSA from a bloated bureaucracy into a nimble, customer-oriented organization that behaves like a private-sector business.

Barram used what he had learned working at companies such as Hewlett-Packard and Apple Computer to instill major changes, focused specifically on providing better customer service, fixing the GSA's

poor reputation, and improving the lives of employees. The GSA provides more than $50 billion worth of office space, products, and services to other federal agencies. As chief of staff Martha Johnson describes it, GSA is Office Depot, Home Depot, an airline, and a real estate agency rolled into one. In the past, federal agencies were required to purchase from GSA, even if prices were outrageous compared with the private sector. No more. As Barram puts it, "We should exist only if we provide services for our customers at the best value." Today, agencies are free to buy their supplies from other companies. The thought that GSA could actually cease to exist spurred employees to find ways to cut costs, lower prices, and provide excellent customer service.

Barram used several approaches to encourage employee involvement in the change process. For example, a program called Changemasters allowed administrative-level workers to participate in six months of training sessions where they talked with architects, educators, and businesspeople about ways to improve service and encourage employee creativity and risk taking. Another step Barram took to promote a new way of working was to set up a Web-based chat line where employees can freely exchange uncensored thoughts and ideas.

Barram knows the recent changes at GSA are only a beginning point, not an end. In today's world, he believes, "any organization has to be in a constant state of reinvention, or it's all over."[14]

Other Forces

A number of other factors may require an organization to change. For example, new government regulations, rapid company growth, the moves of a competitor, the default of a supplier, or general economic conditions may all create a need for change. Managers should be aware that forces for change may arise both within and outside the organization. Exhibit 18.1 illustrates aspects of the organization's internal and external environment that may generate forces for change.

exhibit **18.1**
Internal and External Forces for Change

apply it

1. What are some of the forces for change that have affected your life? What forces are affecting your place of employment or college/university? Try to think of an example in each category: globalization, technology, and society.

Organizations experience several types of planned change

Now that we have explored some forces for change, let's look at the various types of change that occur in organizations. We examine changes in three broad categories illustrated in Exhibit 18.2: strategy and structure, internal work processes and the work environment, and organizational culture. Organizations may innovate in one or more areas, depending on their needs and the forces for change.

In the exhibit, the arrows indicate that a change in one area may affect other areas. For example, a change in structure may require changes in the work environment or work processes, or a new strategy may call for a change in organizational culture.

The **systems model of change** recognizes that the organization is made up of many highly interdependent parts. Any change, no matter how small, in one part will have an impact on other parts of the organization. For example, when a Levi Strauss plant near Knoxville, Tennessee, instituted work teams, managers found that compensation and evaluation systems had to be revised to suit the new structure. When Procter & Gamble shifted its strategic focus from internal cost cutting and efficiency toward innovation and rapid response to customers, the organization also needed to make changes in structure, work processes, and culture to support the new strategy.[15] Managers should recognize that organizations are interrelated systems and be aware that making a change in one part of the organization will likely require changes in other areas as well.

systems model of change

An approach that recognizes that change in one part of the organization will have an impact on other parts of the organization and may require changes there as well.

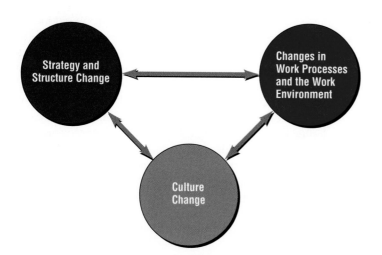

exhibit | **18.2**

Three Categories of Organizational Change

Changes in Strategy and Structure

strategy and structure changes

Changes in the administrative domain of an organization, which involves supervision and management; may include changes in reward systems, policies, coordination devices, control systems, and so forth, as well as changes in organizational structure or strategic focus.

Strategy and structure changes pertain to the administrative domain of an organization, which involves supervision and management. These may include changes in reward systems, policies, coordination devices, control systems, and so forth, in addition to changes in the organization's structural characteristics or strategic focus. One example is when top managers at Orchids Paper Products reoriented to a low-cost strategy, implemented enterprise resource planning (ERP) and computerized accounting systems for improved coordination and control, and relocated headquarters to Oklahoma to save on utility costs.[16] Changes in strategy and structure are almost always implemented through a top-down change process because the expertise for administrative improvements originates at the middle and upper levels of the organization. For successful change to occur, however, it is important that lower level employees be educated about the changes and allowed to participate. Otherwise, they may resist or even sabotage the change. Later in this chapter, we talk about resistance to change and how organizations can effectively manage change to overcome resistance.

In Chapter 15, we discussed a number of structural characteristics, including chain of command, centralization, division of labor, and formalization. Managers may make modifications in any of these areas to meet changing environmental conditions. For example, at Procter & Gamble, top executives might choose to increase decentralization and loosen the chain of command in order to encourage innovation and speed up the decision-making process. Managers may also make major changes in the organization's overall structural design, such as shifting from a vertical functional structure to a horizontal structure with self-directed teams. Today, many organizations are exploring options such as outsourcing, networks, and virtual organizations; participating in alliances, joint ventures, and consortia; and experimenting with self-organizing teams and work units. Some observers have suggested that 21st century organizations may come to resemble amoebas—collections of workers that subdivide into ever-changing teams to meet current needs and goals.[17]

Changes in Internal Work Processes and the Work Environment

Changes in internal work processes and the work environment include modifications in how people do their work. These changes pertain to the technical level of the organization and may include the implementation of quality circles or quality of work life programs; changes in job design, communication processes, or degree of empowerment; the introduction of new technology; and changes in the physical work environment. Although these changes are sometimes initiated at the top of the company, the impetus for change often comes from lower levels of the organization. For example, managers may have to make changes in response to demands from workers for better working conditions. **Quality of work life (QWL) programs** may be introduced to improve conditions that affect an employee's experience with the organization.[18] These programs might focus on worker safety, protection from unfair treatment, and job security or on higher level concerns such as opportunities for meaningful work and participation in decision making.

quality of work life (QWL) programs

Activities undertaken by an organization to improve conditions that affect an employee's experience with the organization.

quality circle

A group of volunteer employees who meet regularly to discuss and solve problems affecting their work.

One QWL mechanism is quality circles, a part of total quality management programs, introduced in Chapter 16. A **quality circle** is a group of six to twelve volunteer employees who meet regularly to discuss and solve problems affecting their work.[19] As a component of quality of work life programs, quality circles may be used to improve working conditions, increase employee participation and commitment, and give employees opportunities for professional development. Although management retains some control over the activities of employees, quality circle participants are given the freedom to collect information, analyze problems, and recommend solutions.

Changes in the physical work environment or job design may also be implemented in response to the concerns of lower level workers. At Lipschultz, Levin & Gray, Certified Public Accountants, manager Steve Siegel said his "door was always open," but he learned that staff members perceived that his door was closed about 95 percent of the time. Siegel took down the door—and a wall as well—to encourage more openness. Eventually, LLG shifted to a completely open office environment, with no walls, offices, or even cubicles to hinder communication and creativity.[20]

Other important changes in this category relate to production technology. These changes are frequently bottom-up, meaning that ideas are initiated at lower levels and channeled upward for approval. Employees at the technical level of the organization understand how to best do the job and can propose ideas for technology changes. For example, at Dana Corp.'s Elizabethtown, Kentucky, plant, technical workers came up with an idea for automatically loading steel sheets into a forming press, a change that now saves the auto parts maker $250,000 a year.[21] A top-down approach to technology change often does not work.[22] Top managers are not close to the production process and lack expertise in technological developments. The spark for a creative new idea often comes from the people closest to the job.

Changes in Culture

Culture change refers to a change in employees' values, norms, attitudes, beliefs, and behavior. Changes in culture pertain to how employees think; these are changes in mind-set rather than in work processes, technology, or structural characteristics. Significant changes in any area of the organization almost always involve some degree of culture change as well, because all change requires altering people's attitudes and behaviors.

culture change

A change in employees' values, norms, attitudes, and behavior.

Because change is ubiquitous in today's organizations, top managers are paying increasing attention to corporate culture. In a recent survey, CEOs reported spending as much time reshaping culture and behavior as monitoring corporate financial performance.[23] In the last couple of decades, numerous large corporations, including Kodak, IBM,

The announcement on January 10, 2000, of America Online's $183 billion agreement to purchase Time Warner—the biggest merger ever—signals the profound change occurring in the business world today. AOL had just one fifth the revenue and 15 percent of the workforce of Time Warner, but investors valued AOL's new economy outlook more than the traditional media giant's. If the merger succeeds, it will give birth to a new global powerhouse—with a foot in both the digital and media worlds and capable of drawing on each other's strengths.
(Source: © Peter Blakely/SABA)

Ford Motor Company, and Procter & Gamble, have undertaken some type of culture change initiative to reinforce and support other significant changes, such as changes in structure and strategy.

Changing a corporate culture fundamentally changes the organization and generally leads to a renewed commitment and empowerment of employees and a stronger bond between the organization, its workers, and its customers.[24] Changing the culture is often essential to an organization's success, but culture change can be extremely difficult. As we learned in the previous chapter, simply interpreting the culture accurately is a challenge. In addition, deeply held values are highly resistant to change. Nevertheless, organizations find ways to meet these challenges.

A major approach to changing people and culture is *organizational development,* which will be discussed later in this chapter. The example of Rowe Furniture illustrates how the areas of change—culture, strategy and structure, and work processes—are interrelated.

❦ Rowe Furniture Corporation

The Rowe Furniture Company of Salem, Virginia, has been cranking out sofas, loveseats, and easy chairs for over half a century. For most of that time, workers have punched their time cards, turned off their brains, and done exactly what the boss told them to do. When Charlene Pedrolie came to Rowe as the plant's new manufacturing chief, she knew things needed to change to keep pace with shifts in the marketplace. Customers were demanding custom-designed pieces, but they would no longer tolerate the traditionally long lead times, which could be up to six months. Rowe's top leaders wanted to promise delivery in 30 days, which meant redesigning the entire assembly process to be hyperefficient.

Pedrolie recognized that the people on the shop floor—not the managers—were the ones who knew how to redesign technology and jobs to accomplish the ambitious goal of 30-day delivery. But getting people to work together for change required a big shift in attitudes and behavior. What Rowe needed was a new culture of empowerment, speed, and innovation. As a start toward a new, more flexible culture, Pedrolie began giving employees more authority and responsibility, as well as open access to information. She also changed the structure, eliminating most supervisory positions and asking front-line workers to form themselves into horizontal clusters, or "cells," and to design the new production system. Each group selected its own members from the various functional areas then created the processes, schedules, and routines for a particular product line. Employees who had once completed only a small, narrow task were cross-trained to perform all the various jobs required to build a piece of furniture.

When the time came to put the new plans into action, the assembly line was a thing of the past. Five hundred workers who had been accustomed to standing in one place and having the furniture come to them were suddenly wandering from one partially assembled piece to another, performing a variety of jobs. Before long, the factory was delivering custom-made pieces within 30 days. Only a few months later, that lead time had decreased to a mere 10 days.

A key to Rowe's new system is open information. Every member of every team has instant access to up-to-date information about order flows, output, productivity, and quality. The sense of personal control and responsibility has led to a dramatic change in worker attitudes. Employees often hold impromptu meetings to discuss problems, check each other's progress, or talk about new ideas and better ways of doing things. Change has become part of the culture at Rowe, where workers are constantly learning and solving problems.[25]

apply it

1. From your personal experience and your readings, think of companies that have experienced significant change in the three areas described in this section (at least one company for each area of change). What precipitated the change? What facilitated change or made it more difficult in each organization?

Managers can anticipate and handle resistance to change

Most of us are creatures of habit. We find a good way of doing something, and we stick with it. The problem for organizations is that the old ways of doing things often become detrimental, but the natural human tendency to resist change gets in the way of adopting new methods. It is often frustrating for managers that employees seem to resist change for no apparent reason. To effectively implement change, managers can learn to anticipate employee resistance and understand the reasons for it. There are many barriers to change on both the individual and organizational level, but there are techniques managers can use to overcome resistance. Exhibit 18.3 summarizes the sources of resistance to change. Although for clarity we have categorized them as either individual or organizational sources, they often overlap in the real world.

Individual Sources of Resistance

Habit and Personality Unless individuals perceive a dramatic need to change, they will generally continue to respond to stimuli in their usual ways. Most people find habits comforting; they provide a way to cope with a complex world. However, when confronted with change, the tendency to rely on habitual ways of behaving can become a source of resistance. In addition, some individuals are naturally more predisposed to resist change than others. Sometimes, deeply ingrained personality characteristics may cause people to resist change.

Fear of the Unknown Employees often do not understand how a proposed change may affect them. This uncertainty, or lack of complete information about future events, may cause them to resist the change even if they recognize that some kind of change is needed. In addition, employees may doubt their ability to meet the demands of a new task, procedure, or technology.

Fear of Personal Loss Employees typically resist a change they believe will take away something of value. Changes in job design, structure, or technology may cause employees to fear the loss of power, status, pay, benefits, or even their jobs. Fear of personal loss may be the biggest obstacle to organizational change.[26] Any change can produce both positive and negative results. Education may be needed to help managers and employees perceive more positive than negative aspects of change.

Individual Sources of Resistance	Organizational Sources of Resistance
Habit and personality	Limited focus of change
Fear of the unknown	Lack of coordination and cooperation
Fear of personal loss	Different assessments and goals
Lack of understanding and trust	Established power relationships

exhibit **18.3**

Sources of Resistance to Change

Lack of Understanding and Trust   Employees often distrust the intentions behind a change or do not understand its intended purpose. If previous working relationships with the change agents have been negative, employees may resist. One manager had a habit of initiating a change in the financial reporting system about once a year but then losing interest and not following through. After the third time this occurred, employees no longer went along with the change because they didn't trust the manager's intention to follow through to their benefit.

Organizational Sources of Resistance

Limited Focus of Change   Sometimes managers fail to recognize that making a change in one area usually means changes will be needed in other areas as well. They may underestimate the human and social consequences of technical changes, which can lead to resistance from employees. For example, if managers change technological processes but fail to revise the organization structure, job design, or compensation system to match, the change is likely to be resisted. Another problem occurs when the organization's management has the mind-set that costs are all-important and fails to appreciate changes not focused specifically on costs. This may lead some managers to unintentionally sabotage changes, such as those designed to improve employee motivation or increase customer satisfaction.

Lack of Coordination and Cooperation   Organizational fragmentation and conflict often result from a lack of coordination for change implementation. Recall that the different parts of an organization are interdependent, and changing one part will necessarily bring about changes in other parts as well. Therefore, coordination and cooperation between various units or departments is critical to the success of a change effort.

Different Assessments and Goals   Another reason for resistance to change is that the people who will be affected by the change may assess the situation differently than do managers or other change agents. Managers in each department pursue different goals, and a change may hurt the performance of some departments. For example, if marketing gets the new product it wants for customers, the cost of manufacturing may increase, and the manufacturing supervisor may resist.

Established Power Relationships   Some changes may threaten long-established power relationships within the organization and will thus be resisted. In particular, the introduction of self-directed work teams, empowerment programs, or participative management may be perceived as threatening to the power of lower and middle managers, and these managers may not go along with the changes or help employees understand and support them.

Overcoming Resistance to Change

One of the most important means of overcoming resistance to change is to have the strong, visible support of top management for the proposed change. Top management support symbolizes to all employees that the change is important for the organization. In addition, top management support is crucial when a change involves several departments or when resources are being reallocated. Without strong support at the top, change efforts may get bogged down in squabbling among departments. Change managers at all levels can also use specific tactics to help overcome employee resistance to change. Four tactics, summarized in Exhibit 18.4, have proven particularly helpful in reducing or quelling resistance.

Communication and Education   Managers can reduce resistance by communicating to employees full information about the proposed change and its possible consequences. Communication helps to build trust, prevent false rumors and misunderstandings, and avoid resentment. One study of change efforts found that the most commonly cited reason for failure was that employees learned of the change from outsiders rather than from organizational leaders.[27] Top managers concentrated on communicating with the public but failed to communicate with the people who would be most affected by the changes—their own employees. Education is also needed to help employees acquire the new skills needed for their role in the change process and for their new responsibilities. When Canadian Airlines International wanted to change its entire reservations, airport, cargo, and financial systems, the company first involved 12,000 employees around the world in a comprehensive communication and education program to ensure smooth implementation of the changes.[28]

Employee Participation   Participation involves employees in helping to design the proposed change. Although this approach is time consuming, it pays off by helping people understand the change and gain a sense of control. Involving employees also helps managers determine potential problems and understand the differences in perceptions of change among employees.[29] One study of the implementation of new computer technology systems at two companies, for example, found that implementation was much smoother at the organization that introduced the change using a participatory approach.[30]

Negotiation   Negotiation is a more formal means of achieving participation and cooperation. With negotiation, change agents attempt to provide something of value to resisters to gain their cooperation and acceptance of a desired change. Negotiation is frequently necessary when resistance comes from a powerful source, such as a union. Companies with strong unions,

Approach	When to Use
Communication and education	Change is technical and employees need new skills.
	Employees need accurate information to understand change.
Employee participation	Employees need to feel involved.
	Design and implementation of change requires information from others.
Negotiation	Group, such as a union, has power over implementation.
	Group may lose out in the change.
Coercion	A crisis exists and a rapid response is needed.
	Other implementation tactics have failed.

exhibit | **18.4**

Tactics for Overcoming Resistance to Change

such as General Motors, frequently must formally negotiate change with the unions. The change may become part of a contract, reflecting the agreement of both parties.

Coercion   As a last resort, managers use formal power to overcome resistance. Employees are told to accept the change or risk losing rewards, promotions, or even their jobs. Coercion may sometimes be necessary in crises, when a rapid response is needed. For example, after Con Edison was fined $14 million for dumping oil and other pollutants into New York City waterways, the company embarked on a major transformation project aimed at making the company an environmental leader. Because of the urgency of the situation, managers and other employees who resisted the changes were threatened with disciplinary action, including suspension or the loss of their jobs.[31] Coercion may also be needed for some administrative changes that flow from the top down. However, as a general rule, this approach should not be used because employees feel like victims, are angry at change managers, and may even sabotage the changes. Consider how coercion as a change tactic backfired at Hire Quality, Inc.

🐝 Hire Quality, Inc.

When Dan Caulfield installed an expensive information technology system at his job placement firm, Hire Quality, Inc., he believed employees would jump at the chance to get rid of the stacks of paper that were overwhelming the office and its small staff. But such was not the case.

A former lieutenant in the U.S. Marine Corps, Caulfield started his firm to place honorably discharged veterans in mostly blue-collar and service technician jobs. The company was soon screening about 35,000 candidates and sending out at least 3,000 resumes a month. Caulfield knew there was no way the company could afford the number of staff it would take to handle everything on a paper-only basis, so he began exploring the idea of a paperless office.

Caulfield was proud of the new computerized system, which consisted of a massive database that could store information on up to 200,000 job candidates and be searched by more than 150 possible fields, making it much easier to match candidates with potential jobs. Candidates could register electronically, and clients could send job descriptions online. Almost every employee's desk had a scanner so that any paper that came into the office could automatically be converted to an electronic file. But, to Caulfield's dismay, employees continued to rely on the old, familiar way of doing things—desks were still cluttered with stacks of resumes and spreadsheets, yellow Post-it notes, and bound reports. Employees were drowning in paper, but they simply weren't using the new system. Caulfield's response was to storm through the office one morning with a large trash barrel, snatching every piece of paper in sight, and to set the whole thing ablaze. Employees could start using the computerized systems or risk watching even more of their work go up in flames. As "incentive," Caulfield instituted a penalty system, enacting a fine of $1 for using the fax machine and 25¢ per page for printing any resume.

Caulfield soon found that resistance to the new system grew *stronger* rather than weaker. Employees seemed to spend most of their time looking for ways to rebel. Eventually, Caulfield realized that his brutal tactics were counterproductive. He still believes his goal of a totally paperless office is a wise one, but he is now working to communicate and educate employees and allow them to be involved in making a more gradual transition.[32]

apply it

1.   Think of a time when you were required to make a change that was difficult for you at home, school, or work. Honestly examine why the change was difficult for you and try to determine the sources of resistance. What

could your parents, teachers, or supervisors have done to make the change easier?

2. Assume that your university has previously had three student representatives on the student activities council, which also includes three university administrators. Thanks to lobbying by students, the school has recently hired a student activities coordinator—a new position. However, administrators have asked that the number of student representatives be cut to two, since the coordinator's primary responsibility is to be an advocate for the students. You have been asked to help implement this change. What resistance might you anticipate and why? How would you overcome it?

Organizations use various approaches to smoothly implement change

Organizations today initiate many dramatic changes, but they are not always successful. For example, many organizations have responded to global forces by reengineering business processes (as described in Chapter 16), yet by one estimate, nearly 70 percent of reengineering projects fail. The past few decades have seen the greatest wave of mergers and acquisitions in American history, including the purchase of McDonnell-Douglas by Boeing and the proposed merger of AOL and Time Warner. In one recent year alone, more than 10,000 mergers took place, with more than $600 billion changing hands. Although many of these "marriages" have the potential to be enormously successful, more than half will be disappointing failures.[33]

Even though change is risky, many organizations today face serious threats, and managers must lead the way through needed change. We have just discussed some tactics managers or other change agents use to overcome resistance to change in organizations. In this section, we examine three approaches that can help managers smoothly implement organizational change.

Lewin's Three-Stage Change Model

Social psychologist Kurt Lewin developed a three-stage model of planned change that explains how to initiate, manage, and stabilize the change process.[34] Most recent theories of change are based partly on Lewin's classic model. According to Lewin's model, the change process involves unlearning old attitudes and habits as well as learning something new. In addition, to be effective, new attitudes and behaviors must be reinforced to become a part of the normal way of doing things.

Unfreezing In the first stage, **unfreezing,** employees are made aware of the problems and the need for change. This stage creates the motivation for people to modify their attitudes and behavior. Unfreezing is often begun by providing employees with information that shows discrepancies between desired behaviors or performance and the current state of affairs.

unfreezing

A step in the change process that makes employees aware of the problems and the need for change.

Changing The second stage of Lewin's model, **changing,** shifts attitudes and behavior toward the new, desired state. This is the learning part of the change process and involves providing employees with new information, new models of behavior, and new ways of thinking. This stage may involve

changing

A step in Lewin's change model that involves shifting attitudes and behavior toward what is desirable.

a specific plan for training managers and employees in the new way of doing things. In addition, employees experiment with new ideas and behaviors and may modify them during the learning process.

refreezing

Stabilizing a change by reinforcing it and rewarding employees who support the new behaviors.

Refreezing   During the **refreezing** stage, change is stabilized. Employees integrate the new attitudes, skills, and behaviors and are rewarded by the organization for doing so. The impact of new behaviors is evaluated and reinforced. Change managers may present analyses that show positive results of the change, and top executives provide positive reinforcement to support new behaviors. In addition, employees participate in refresher courses or additional training to maintain the desired skills and behaviors.

Lewin proposes that change is a result of the competition between *driving forces* and *restraining forces*.[35] When a change is introduced, some forces drive it and other forces resist it. Managers analyze the change forces to unfreeze participants and enable change to occur. Selectively removing or reducing forces that restrain change will strengthen the driving forces enough to enable implementation, as illustrated by the move from A to B in Exhibit 18.5.

Just-in-time (JIT) inventory control systems are designed to schedule materials to arrive just as they are needed on the production line. In one manufacturing company, managers' analysis found that the driving forces associated with implementing JIT were (1) the large cost savings from reduced inventories, (2) savings from needing fewer workers to handle the inventory, and (3) a quicker, more competitive market response. Restraining forces were (1) a freight system too slow to deliver inventory on time, (2) a facility layout that emphasized inventory maintenance over new deliveries, (3) inadequate worker skills for handling rapid inventory deployment, and (4) union resistance to loss of jobs. The driving forces were not sufficient to overcome the restraining forces.

To shift behavior to a JIT system, managers attacked the restraining forces. First, they shifted to delivery by truck, which provided the flexibility and quickness needed to schedule inventory delivery at a specific time each day. The addition of four new loading docks solved the problem with facility layout. Inadequate worker skills were attacked with training in JIT

exhibit | **18.5**

Changing from a Traditional to Just-in-Time Inventory Style

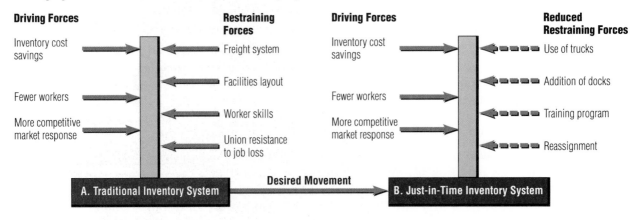

methods and in assembling products with uninspected parts. To overcome union resistance, the company agreed to reassign workers no longer needed for maintaining inventory to jobs in another plant. With the restraining forces reduced, the driving forces were sufficient to allow the JIT system to be successfully implemented.

Kotter's Eight Steps for Leading Change

Exhibit 18.6 presents a model of planned change developed by John Kotter at Harvard University.[36] Kotter's model expands the stages of unfreezing, changing, and refreezing to eight clearly defined steps. Although in reality the steps often overlap, the breakdown enables managers to pay careful attention to each element required to successfully implement major change.

Step 1: Establish a Sense of Urgency   The first step is for managers to establish a sense of urgency that change is really needed. In some cases, a crisis provides an undoubted sense of urgency for employees. For example, Midwest Contract Furnishings lost 80 percent of its revenues practically overnight when its major customer, Renaissance Hotels, was sold to a company that handled interior design and furnishing in-house. Employees easily recognized that change was necessary for the company to survive.[37] In many cases, however, there is no immediate crisis, and managers have to make others aware of the need for change. Managers carefully scan the external and internal environments, looking at competitive conditions; market position; social, technological, and demographic trends; financial performance; operations; and other factors. After identifying potential crises or major opportunities, they find ways to communicate the information broadly and dramatically to create a sense of urgency for change.

Step 2: Build a Coalition   Next, the organization must build a coalition with enough power to guide the change process and then create a sense of

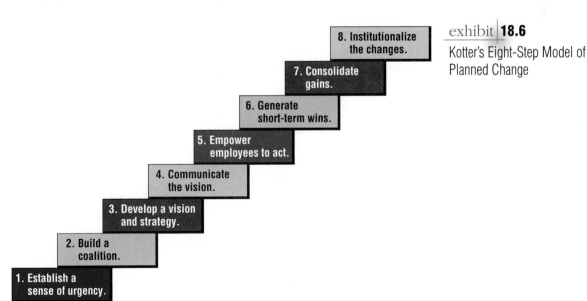

exhibit | **18.6**

Kotter's Eight-Step Model of Planned Change

Source: Based on John P. Kotter, *Leading Change* (Boston: Harvard Business School Press, 1996), p. 21.

what would you do?

A COMPANY'S CULTURE KEEPS IT IN THE DANGER ZONE

Forest International operates in one of the most dangerous industries around. Paper mills, sawmills, and plywood factories are filled with constant noise, giant razor-toothed saw blades, caustic chemicals, and chutes loaded with tons of lumber. Even in this notoriously hazardous industry, Forest's safety record is rock bottom. Within a four-year period, 27 workers have been killed on the job. There are an average of nine serious injuries per 100 employees each year. In addition, productivity has been declining in recent years, and Forest's competitors are gaining market share. As the director of workers' compensation, you have just been asked by Forest International's new CEO for advice on how to improve the company's safety record and increase productivity.

Forest International, based outside Atlanta, Georgia, has around $11 billion in annual revenues and employs 45,000 people. Many employees' parents and grandparents also worked in Forest's mills and factories. Among many of the workers, missing a finger or two is considered a badge of honor. Taking chances is a way of proving that you're a true "Forest man" (the term persists even though the company now has a good percentage of female workers). During lunch or break, groups of workers routinely brag about their "close calls" and share stories about parents' or grandparents' dangerous encounters with saw blades or lumber chutes. In addition to worker attitudes, you think management attitudes are part of the problem as well. Staff meetings emphasize the importance of keeping the line moving, getting the product out no matter what. Rather than finding a supervisor and asking that the production line be shut down, most employees take chances and stick their hands into moving equipment whenever there is a minor problem.

As you talk with workers, you learn that most of them believe managers care more about productivity and profits than they do about the well-being of people in the plant. In fact, most Forest employees don't feel that they're valued at all by the company. One saw operator who has made several suggestions for improving productivity and safety on his line has been routinely ignored by management. "They never listen to us; they just expect us to do what we're told," he says. This same employee was one of the most vocal in opposing some recent safety changes requiring that all workers wear safety gear anytime they're on the production floor, not just when they are on the line. "They don't really care about our safety," he boomed. "They just want another way to push us around." Many of the other workers also oppose the new rules, saying that "managers walk around the production floor all the time without goggles and ear plugs, so why shouldn't we?"

You have a meeting with Philip Thomas, Forest's new CEO, in the morning to offer your recommendations for change.

1. What areas of change will you suggest most critically need attention at Forest International?

2. Describe how you would enact Lewin's stages of unfreezing, changing, and refreezing.

3. Why do you think workers have resisted the initial safety changes? What techniques would you use to overcome resistance?

Source: Based in part on information in Anne Fisher, "Danger Zone," *Fortune*, September 8, 1997, pp. 165–167.

---

teamwork among the group. For the change process to succeed, there should be a shared commitment to the need and possibilities for transformation. Top managers form the core of the coalition; however, it is essential that lower level managers also become involved. Mechanisms such as off-site retreats can be used to get people together and help them develop a shared assessment of problems and how to approach them. At Master-Brand Industries, the change process began with an off-site meeting of key managers who examined the need for change and discussed ways to remake MasterBrand into a team-based organization.[38]

Step 3: Develop a Vision and Strategy In this step, managers formulate and articulate a compelling vision that will guide the change effort and then develop strategies for achieving it. At Whirlpool, managers developed a vision that involved changing the company from a conservative operation with limited marketing skills into a strong marketing organization with secondary manufacturing and engineering skills, thus making it stronger in the face of new competition.[39]

Step 4: Communicate the Vision   Once a vision has been formed, managers use every means possible to widely communicate the vision and strategy. At this stage, the coalition of change agents should set an example by modeling the new behaviors needed from employees. Major change is impossible unless a majority of people in the organization are willing to help, often to the point of making personal sacrifices.

Step 5: Empower Employees to Act   Employees throughout the organization must then be empowered to act on the vision. This means getting rid of obstacles to change, which may require revising systems, structures, or procedures that hinder or undermine the change effort. For example, with the survival of the company at stake, labor and management at Rolls-Royce Motor Company revised narrow job categories that were undermining a major change effort. Whereas Rolls-Royce once had hundreds of precise job descriptions, the new contract specified that all employees would do anything within their capabilities as needed.[40] At this stage, managers also encourage and reward risk taking and nontraditional ideas and actions.

Step 6: Generate Short-Term Wins   So that employees can see results of their efforts and the change effort does not lose momentum, it is critical that they experience short-term wins. Change agents plan for visible performance improvements, make them happen, and reward employees who were involved in the improvements. At one U.S. manufacturing company, the guiding coalition worked to produce a highly visible and successful new product introduction about 20 months after the start of its transformation efforts. This success boosted the credibility of the renewal process and renewed the commitment and enthusiasm of employees.[41]

Step 7: Consolidate Gains   Building on the credibility achieved by short-term wins, the next step consolidates improvements, tackles bigger problems, and creates greater change. Managers change systems, structures, and policies that don't fit the vision and haven't yet been confronted. They hire, promote, and develop employees who can implement the change vision. In addition, managers revitalize the process with new projects, themes, or change agents as needed.

Step 8: Institutionalize the Changes   Once the changes have been implemented, it is important to institutionalize the new approaches in the organizational culture. This is the follow-through stage that makes the changes stick. Managers articulate the connection between new behaviors and organizational success. New values and beliefs are instilled in the culture so that employees view the change as a normal and integral part of how the organization operates. In addition, appraisal and reward systems are modified to support and reinforce the new behaviors.

Organizational Development

Organizational development is a set of techniques and interventions that may be applied using either of the change models just discussed. Organizational development has been particularly useful for changing people and

organizational development

A planned, systematic process of change that uses behavioral science knowledge and techniques to improve an organization's health and effectiveness by improving internal relationships and increasing learning and problem-solving capabilities.

culture. All successful change requires a shift in people's attitudes and behaviors, and organizational development encompasses a number of people-changing interventions, which we discuss in this section.

Organizational development (OD) is a planned, systematic process of change that uses behavioral science knowledge and techniques to improve an organization's health and effectiveness through its ability to adapt to the environment, improve internal relationships, and increase learning and problem-solving capabilities.[42] OD focuses on the human and social aspects of the organization and emphasizes the values of human development, fairness, openness, freedom from coercion, and individual autonomy.[43] Although the field of OD evolved in the 1970s as a way to achieve organizational excellence, the concept has been enlarged to examine how people and groups can change to a learning organization culture in today's complex and turbulent environment. Organizational development is not a step-by-step procedure to solve a specific problem but rather a process of fundamental change in the human and social systems of the organization, including organizational culture.[44]

Although organizational development is directed from the top, it places a strong emphasis on participation and collaboration. OD uses knowledge and techniques from the behavioral sciences to create a learning environment through increased trust, open confrontation of problems, employee empowerment and participation, knowledge sharing, the design of meaningful work, cooperation between groups, and the full use of human potential. A number of OD interventions have been used successfully to bring about change in organizations. Some of the most popular and effective are survey feedback, process consultation, team building, and intergroup activities. In addition, large group intervention is a more recent application that has proven highly effective for large-scale change in organizations.

Survey Feedback   One useful technique for analyzing employee attitudes, identifying problems or discrepancies, and involving organization members in finding solutions is *survey feedback*.[45] Survey feedback begins with the collection of information from employees, usually via a written questionnaire. Employees may be surveyed about their attitudes and perceptions concerning a broad range of issues, such as job satisfaction, work group performance, group cohesion, leader behavior, quality of work relationships, decision-making practices, and communication effectiveness. OD specialists then tabulate and analyze the collected data and organize it into an understandable format. A consultant feeds back the data to the employees who provided it as a way to stimulate discussion or identify specific problems and ideas for solving them. In addition to a goal of identifying issues, survey feedback aims to improve relationships among the members of a work group or department through the discussion of shared problems. It is hoped that open and honest discussion will lead to the development of agreed-upon ideas for action.

process consultation

An OD technique whereby a consultant works with managers and other employees to help them identify processes that need change; emphasizes involvement and improving interpersonal relationships but is also task directed.

Process Consultation   **Process consultation** is a technique whereby an OD consultant works with managers or other members of an organization to help them perceive, understand, and take action to improve specific events that occur in the work environment.[46] These events may include work flow, formal or informal relationships among employees in the work group, or other work-related behaviors. Process consultation focuses on how employees work together to perform their interrelated tasks. The consultant works with the group to jointly diagnose what processes need improving. Process consultation is often used to address communication problems, leadership conflicts, poor decision-making processes, or role conflicts.

Team Building   **Team building** encompasses various activities designed to enhance the trust, cohesiveness, and success of organizational teams or work groups. Team-building activities are used in many companies to train task forces, committees, and new product development groups. An organization might plan a series of OD activities to help members of a cross-functional team working on a new product or project function more effectively, communicate and collaborate better, and be more cohesive. Activities typically include setting common goals, developing interpersonal relationships, clarifying roles and responsibilities, and analyzing work processes.

team building

An OD intervention that enhances the trust cohesiveness, and success of organizational teams or work groups.

Intergroup Activities   Whereas team building is designed to improve relationships within a group or team, **intergroup activities** aim to improve relationships between different groups, teams, or departments. These activities seek to change the attitudes and stereotypes different groups have about each other. Representatives from various departments are brought together in a neutral location to uncover conflict, diagnose its causes, and plan improvements in communication and coordination. Intergroup interventions have been applied to union-management conflict, headquarters–field office conflict, interdepartmental conflict, and conflict brought about by mergers.[47] One technique involves having the two groups meet separately to list perceptions of themselves and of the other group. Each group also develops a list of how it *believes* the other group perceives it. The groups then meet to discuss similarities and differences in perception and how stereotypes or misperceptions have developed. These discussions can clarify the nature of intergroup conflict and move the groups toward solutions.

intergroup activities

OD activities designed to improve the relationships between groups by examining and changing the attitudes, perceptions, and stereotypes they have about each other.

Large-Group Intervention   Most early OD activities involved small groups and focused on incremental change. However, in recent years, there has been growing interest in the application of OD techniques to large-group settings, which are more attuned to bringing about radical or transformational change in organizations operating in complex environments.[48] The **large-group intervention** approach brings together participants from all parts of the organization—and often key stakeholders from outside the organization as well—in an off-site setting to discuss problems or opportunities and plan for change.[49] A large-group intervention might involve 50 to 500 people and last for several days. The off-site setting limits interference and distractions, enabling participants to focus on new ways of doing things.

large-group intervention

An approach that brings together participants from all parts of the organization, often including outside stakeholders, in an off-site setting to discuss problems or opportunities and plan for change.

General Electric's "Work Out" program, an ongoing process of solving problems, learning, and improving, began with large-scale, off-site meetings that grew out of Jack Welch's desire to create a "culture of boundarylessness" he felt was critical to learning and growth.

General Electric's Work Out Program

One of the mechanisms Jack Welch has used to reshape General Electric for renewed productivity and growth is the Work Out program. The program grew out of Welch's desire to reach and motivate 300,000 worldwide employees. He insisted that the people on the front lines, where change has to happen, be empowered to create that change rather than having it imposed on them by top managers.

GE's Work Out began in large-scale, off-site meetings facilitated by a combination of top managers, outside OD consultants, and human resource specialists. In each business unit, the basic pattern was the same. Hourly and salaried workers from many different parts of the organization met jointly in an informal three-day meeting to discuss and solve problems. Gradually, the Work Out events began to include external stakeholders such as suppliers and customers as well as employees. Today, Work Out is not an event, but a process of how work is done and problems are solved at GE.

The format for Work Out includes seven steps:

1. Choose a work process or problem for discussion.
2. Select an appropriate cross-functional team, to include external stakeholders.
3. Assign a "champion" to follow through on recommendations.
4. Meet for several days and come up with recommendations to improve processes or solve problems.
5. Meet with top managers, who are required to respond to recommendations on the spot.
6. Hold additional meetings as needed to pursue the recommendations.
7. Start the process all over again with a new process or problem.

GE's Work Out process not only solves problems and improves productivity for the company but also gives employees the experience of openly and honestly interacting with one another without regard to vertical or horizontal boundaries.[50]

Large-group interventions, such as GE's Work Out, reflect a significant shift in the approach to organizational change from earlier OD approaches. Exhibit 18.7 lists the primary differences between the traditional OD model and the large-group intervention model of organizational change.[51] In the newer approach, the focus is on the entire system, which accounts for the organization's interaction with its environment. The source of information for discussion is expanded to include customers, suppliers, community members—even competitors—and this information is shared

exhibit 18.7

OD Approaches to Change

	Traditional Organizational Development Model	Large-Group Intervention Model
Focus for action:	Specific problem or group	Entire system
Information Source:	Organization	Organization and environment
Distribution:	Limited	Widely shared
Time frame:	Gradual	Fast
Learning:	Individual, small group	Whole organization
Change process:	Incremental change	Rapid transformation

Source: Adapted from Barbara Benedict Bunker and Billie T. Alban. (1992, December). "Conclusion: What makes large group interventions effective." *The Journal of Applied Behavioral Science 28* (4): 579–591.

widely so that everyone has the same picture of the organization and its environment.

The acceleration of change when the entire system is involved can be remarkable. In addition, learning occurs across all parts of the organization or division simultaneously, rather than in individuals or small groups. The end result is that the large-group approach offers greater possibilities for fundamental, radical transformation of the entire culture, whereas the traditional approach creates incremental change in a few individuals or small groups at a time.

Large-group intervention reflects an increasing awareness of the importance of dealing with the entire system—including external stakeholders—in any significant change effort. The approach can be particularly beneficial for companies wanting to shift to a learning organization culture, because the transformation requires major changes in all parts of the company.

apply it

1. Recall a time when you went through a major change in attitudes and behavior. Describe the process using Lewin's three-stage model of unfreezing, changing, and refreezing.

The learning organization is constantly changing

As we have discussed, today's organizations face a need for almost continuous change. Some management experts suggest that to survive the upheaval of the early 21st century, managers must turn their organizations into "change leaders" by using the present to create the future—breaking industry rules, creating new market space, and routinely abandoning outmoded products, services, and processes to free up resources to build the future.[52] The current trend in efforts to create a company that can continually adapt to new situations is toward the learning organization. A *learning organization,* which engages everyone in problem solving and continuous improvement based on the lessons of experience, is the epitome of continuous organizational change and growth. In this section, we discuss how organizations learn and briefly examine the qualities of a learning organization.

The Adaptive Learning Cycle

Organizations look for ways to build and enhance their learning capabilities. Organizations may participate in either single-loop learning or double-loop learning. With **single-loop learning,** the organization detects problems or mistakes and then relies on previous solutions and routines or on present policies and procedures to correct them. In contrast, **double-loop learning** corrects errors and solves problems by changing the organization's policies and standard routines. This type of learning challenges old assumptions and norms to provide the opportunity for radically different solutions.[53]

Learning organizations go a step further. Rather than simply solving problems and correcting errors, these companies learn, change, and evolve continuously. Exhibit 18.8 illustrates the **adaptive learning cycle** used by

single-loop learning

Learning that occurs when the organization corrects errors or solves problems using past routines or present policies and procedures.

double-loop learning

Learning that occurs when the organization corrects errors and solves problems by changing policies, procedures, or standard routines; provides an opportunity for radical change.

adaptive learning cycle

The cycle of action, feedback, and synthesis used by learning organizations, in which employees sense the environment, try something, and make changes based on feedback.

Harper's Bazaar, *one of the best-known fashion magazines in the world since 1867, stumbled badly in recent years and needed dramatic change. "It's gotten stodgy," said magazine consultants, a death sentence for fashion magazines, whose advertisers seek the young and willing to spend. Using the double-loop form of learning to challenge old assumptions, the company hired Kate Betts, fashion news director at* Vogue, *as editor-in-chief. Within months, nearly half the staff was replaced, and the magazine's 133-year-old logo was changed. Betts's challenge is to bring* Harper's *into the 21st century to capture that all-important next generation of consumers. So far, Betts is succeeding. A recent issue had 70 percent more ad revenues than those of a year before.*

(Source: © Marc Baptiste)

learning organizations.[54] The cycle of *action, feedback,* and *synthesis* is based on the natural adaptive process that all living organisms share. Every living thing survives by sensing the environment around it, responding with action, and correcting itself if feedback and synthesis indicate that previous actions were inappropriate. When feedback causes a plant, animal, person, or organization to change its behavior, learning takes place. For example, a child might learn not to touch a hot stove by being burned after touching one. Learning organizations "live" the adaptive learning cycle every day. They are constantly experimenting, taking risks, making mistakes, and changing.

Adaptive learning can lead to new products, services, and ways of doing business that would never emerge in companies that rely on traditional approaches. For example, Kinko's encourages continuous experimentation and shares the learning throughout the company. A copy machine operator at one store used Kinko's color copying technology to make custom calendars from his customers' photographs. When the idea turned out to be successful, he shared it with Kinko's founder and chairman Paul Orfalea, who spread the word throughout the franchise. Now, custom calendars are a hot item in all 800 Kinko's stores around the world. Great Harvest Bread Company also uses adaptive learning. The company doesn't have standardized operating procedures or top-down rules and regulations. The mission statement begins with a call to "Be loose and have fun." Franchise owners are encouraged to experiment and share what they learn with others on the company's intranet.[55]

Arie de Geus, who studied companies that have survived for more than a century, found that adaptive learning is a key to long-term organizational survival. De Geus argues that the reason the average lifespan of *Fortune* 500 companies is only about 50 years is because they focus so strongly on turning a profit that they shut down the feedback mechanisms that encourage learning and change.[56] Learning organizations keep feedback mechanisms open so they can evolve, adapt, learn, and grow over time in response to changes in the environment.

Qualities of a Learning Organization

How does a company become a learning organization? The learning organization is a model or ideal of what an organization can become when people put aside their habitual ways of thinking and remain open to new ideas

exhibit | **18.8**

The Adaptive Learning Cycle

Source: Based on "The Adaptive Loop," Exhibit 5.1, in Stephan H. Haeckel, *Adaptive Enterprise: Creating and Leading Sense-and-Respond Organizations* (Boston: Harvard Business School Press, 1999), p. 76.

exhibit 18.9

Changing to a Learning Organization

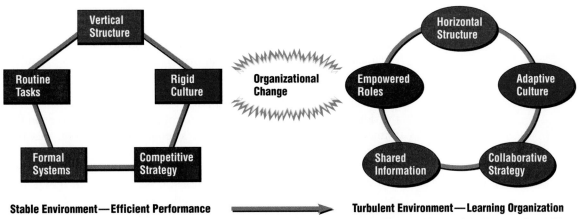

Source: Adapted from David K. Hurst, *Crisis and Renewal: Meeting the Challenge of Organizational Change* (Boston: Harvard Business School Press, 1995) p. 54. This exhibit appeared in Richard L. Daft, *Organization Theory and Design,* 7th ed. (Cincinnati, OH: South-Western College Publishing, 2001), p. 26.

and methods. Managers can make changes in specific characteristics of the company that help turn it into a learning organization. The learning organization is based on equality, open information, little hierarchy, and a strong culture that encourages adaptability and enables the organization to seize opportunities and handle crises. In a learning organization, managers emphasize employee empowerment and encourage collaboration across departments and with other organizations. Essential values are problem solving and continuous learning, in contrast to the traditional organization's values of stability and efficient performance.

Exhibit 18.9 compares organizations designed for efficiency with those designed for continuous learning by looking at five elements: structure, tasks, systems, culture, and strategy.

From Vertical to Horizontal Structure As described in Chapter 15, the traditional organizational structure groups common activities together from the bottom of the organization to the top. Generally, little collaboration occurs across functional departments, and the whole organization is coordinated and controlled through the vertical hierarchy, with decision-making authority residing with upper level managers. This structure promotes efficient production and in-depth skill development for employees, and the hierarchy of authority provides a sensible mechanism for supervision and control in large organizations. However, in a rapidly changing environment, top executives are not able to respond rapidly enough to problems or opportunities. Also, lower level workers have little motivation to solve problems.

In the learning organization, the vertical structure that creates distance between managers at the top of the organization and workers on the front lines is disbanded. Structure is created around horizontal workflows or processes rather than departmental functions. The vertical hierarchy is dramatically flattened, with perhaps only a few senior executives in traditional support functions such as finance or human resources. Self-directed teams are the fundamental work unit in the learning organization. Boundaries between functions are practically eliminated because teams include members from several functional areas. In some cases, organizations do away with departments altogether. For example, at Oticon Holding A/S, a Danish company that introduced the world's first digital hearing aid, there are no organization charts, no departments, no functions, and no titles. All vestiges of an organizational hierarchy have disappeared. Employees are constantly forming and reforming into self-directed teams that work on specific projects.[57]

From Routine Tasks to Empowered Roles   Another significant shift relates to the degree of formal structure and control placed on employees in the performance of their work. Recall that scientific management, described in Chapters 1 and 15, advocated precisely defining each job and the way it should be performed. A **task** is a narrowly defined piece of work assigned to a person. In traditional organizations, tasks are broken down into specialized, separate parts. Knowledge and control of tasks are centralized at the top of the organization, and employees are expected to do as they are told. A *role*, in contrast, is a part in a dynamic social system. A role offers responsibility, allowing the person to use his or her discretion and ability to meet a goal. In learning organizations, employees play a role in the team or department, and roles may be constantly redefined or adjusted. There are few rules or procedures, and knowledge and control of tasks are concentrated among employees rather than supervisors or top executives. Employees are encouraged to take care of problems by working with one another and with customers.

From Formal Control Systems to Shared Information   In young, entrepreneurial companies, communication is generally informal and face to face. There are few formal control and information systems because the top leaders of the company usually work directly with employees in the day-to-day operation of the business. However, when organizations grow large and complex, the distance between top managers and employees on the front lines increases. Formal systems are often implemented to manage the growing amount of complex information and to detect deviations from established standards and goals.[58]

In learning organizations, information serves a very different purpose. The widespread sharing of information keeps the organization functioning at an optimum level. The learning organization strives to return to the condition of a small, entrepreneurial firm in which all employees have complete information about the company so they can act quickly. Ideas and information are shared throughout the company. Rather than using information to control employees, managers try to find ways to open channels of communication so that ideas flow in all directions. In addition, learning organizations maintain open lines of communication with customers, suppliers, and even competitors to enhance learning capability.

From Competitive to Collaborative Strategy   In traditional organizations designed for efficient performance, strategy is formulated by top managers and imposed on the organization. Top executives think about how the organization can best respond to competition, efficiently use resources, and cope with environmental changes. In contrast, in the learning organization,

task

A narrowly defined piece of work assigned to a person.

the accumulated actions of an informed and empowered workforce contribute to strategy development. Since all employees are in touch with customers, suppliers, and new technology, they help identify needs and solutions and participate in strategy making. In addition, strategy emerges from partnerships with suppliers, customers, and even competitors. Organizations become collaborators as well as competitors, experimenting to find the best way to learn and adapt. Johan Liedgren, the 34-year-old CEO of Honkworm International, an online entertainment agency, sits on the board of seven other Internet commerce companies, some of whose CEOs, in turn, sit on his board of directors. They know one another's forecasts, marketing plans, and new product launches and even share one another's financial information.

From Rigid to Adaptive Culture   For an organization to remain healthy, its culture should encourage adaptation to the external environment, as discussed in Chapter 17. In many organizations, however, the culture becomes fixed, as if set in concrete, and the firm has difficulty adapting if the environment changes rapidly or dramatically. The culture of a learning organization encourages openness, boundarylessness, equality, risk taking, continuous improvement, and change.

No company represents a perfect example of a learning organization, although many of today's most competitive organizations have shifted toward ideas and forms based on these concepts. One company that illustrates many characteristics of a learning organization is Cisco Systems, which has been called "the corporation of the future."

Cisco Systems

John Chambers, CEO of Cisco Systems, got a firsthand look at how the reluctance to change can damage a company when he worked at IBM and Wang Laboratories. He believes the new rules of business competition demand new organizational forms: ones based on change rather than stability, organized around networks rather than rigid hierarchies, and based on interdependencies with organizational partners.

Not surprisingly, Cisco—the leading maker of routers, switches, software, and other gear that keeps the Internet running—uses the Internet in virtually every aspect of its business, from sales and marketing to recruiting. Not only does Cisco's network keep more than 17,000 employees in 50 countries intimately connected, but it also keeps the company in close touch with customers and swiftly connects Cisco with its web of partners, making the constellation of suppliers, contract manufacturers, and assemblers look and act like one seamless company.

It isn't just technology that sets Cisco apart from the crowd, however. Just as important is the company's culture and mind-set. Chambers works hard to encourage open and direct communication among all employees and with Cisco's leaders. He holds quarterly meetings with employees and invites all employees in the month of their birthday to one of his "birthday breakfasts," where they can talk about anything they want. In addition, Chambers spends up to 55 percent of his time with customers. Customers, not executives, drive the business at Cisco. Strategy is not something that is formulated in the executive suite; rather, it emerges from the network of employees, customers, and partners.

Chambers believes an egalitarian culture is central to the success of Cisco because it builds teamwork and employee morale. "You never ask your team to do something you wouldn't do yourself," he says. Chambers, for example, always flies coach rather than first class, and he has to fight for a parking place at Cisco's headquarters just like everyone else. Cisco's top managers work hard to include all employees in decision making, helping them to feel like true partners in the business. Managers spend tremendous amounts of face-to-face time coaching, mentoring, and communicating with workers. The result is an energized, motivated workforce that agrees with Chambers's conviction that his people and his organization are "in the sweet spot"—where technology and the future meet to transform business and everyday life.[59]

apply it

1. Just like organizations, individuals participate in different types of learning. Recall a problem that you have faced, whether in your personal life, in your job, or as a student. How did you solve the problem and what did you learn from it? Do you believe you engaged in single-loop or double-loop learning? Can you identify instances where you have engaged in adaptive learning?

2. Describe an organization with which you are familiar and compare it to the description of the adaptive learning organization. How do you think the company could be more like a learning organization?

summary OF KEY CONCEPTS

- **Managers can recognize and interpret the forces that call for organizational change.** Pressures for change exist both within the organization and in the external environment. Some of the primary forces for change are globalization, technological advancements, and changes in society and the workforce. Managers keep a close watch on both the internal and external organizational environment to detect factors that may require the company to change.

- **Organizations experience several types of planned change.** Three broad areas of change are strategy and structure changes, changes in internal work processes and the work environment, and culture changes. Depending on the forces for change, managers may innovate in one or more areas. In addition, changes in one area will impact other areas, requiring additional changes.

- **Managers can anticipate and handle resistance to change.** There are many barriers to change on both the individual and organizational level. Individual sources of resistance include habit and personality, fear of the unknown, fear of personal loss, and lack of understanding and trust. Organizational sources include a limited focus of change, lack of coordination and cooperation, varied assessments and goals, and established power relationships. Techniques managers use to overcome resistance to change are communication and education, employee involvement, negotiation, and coercion.

- **Organizations use various approaches to smoothly implement change.** Change is difficult and not always successful. However, managers are responsible for leading their organizations through needed changes. Researchers have developed models that can help smooth the process. Lewin's model follows the three stages of (1) *unfreezing,* in which employees are made aware of the need for change; (2) *changing,* during which attitudes and behaviors are shifted toward what is desirable; and (3) *refreezing,* in which employees integrate the new attitudes and behaviors into their normal way of doing things. Kotter expands the three-stage model to eight clearly defined steps that help managers focus on the various elements needed to successfully implement major change. Organizational development is a set of techniques and interventions that is particularly useful for changing people and culture. OD change interventions include survey feedback, process consultation, team building, intergroup activities, and large-group intervention.

- **The learning organization is constantly changing.** Learning organizations use an adaptive learning cycle of action, feedback, and synthesis to continuously adapt to changes in the environment. These companies are constantly experimenting, taking risks, making mistakes, and changing. Managers can help transform their companies into learning organizations by making changes in structure, job tasks, information sharing, strategy, and culture.

KEY terms

organizational change, p. 620

systems model of change, p. 625

strategy and structure changes, p.626

quality of work life (QWL) programs, p. 626

quality circle, p. 626

culture change, p. 627

unfreezing, p. 633

changing, p. 633

refreezing, p. 634

organizational development, p. 638

process consultation, p. 638

team building, p. 639

intergroup activities, p. 639

large-group intervention, p. 639

single-loop learning, p. 641

double-loop learning, p. 641

adaptive learning cycle, p. 641

task, p. 644

DISCUSSION questions

1. Discuss some of the ways changes in the workforce over the past ten years might have affected human resource policies and management practices at your college or university.

2. Which of the forces for change discussed in this chapter do you think will be most significant for organizations over the next decade? Explain.

3. Carefully planned change is often assumed to be effective. Do you think unplanned change can sometimes be beneficial to an organization? Discuss.

4. To what extent do changes in strategy and structure affect organizational culture? Explain.

5. Why are changes in technology frequently bottom-up whereas changes in structure are usually top-down?

6. Why do organizations experience resistance to change? How do Lewin's three-stage model and Kotter's eight-step model handle the issue of resistance?

7. Is coercion an appropriate method for implementing top-down changes such as changes in structure and strategy? Discuss.

8. Explain the underlying values of the organizational development approach to change. Why do these values make OD particularly useful for changing culture?

9. Why would employee participation and involvement be considered important for overcoming resistance to change?

10. Throughout this chapter, we have talked about the need for organizations to be constantly changing. Do you think there are some aspects of organizations that should not be open to constant questioning and change? Discuss.

11. How does the adaptive learning cycle differ from double-loop learning? Which area of change (strategy and structure, work processes, culture) do you think would be most directly affected when a company uses adaptive learning?

12. Discuss how the qualities of a learning organization—horizontal structure, empowered roles, shared information, collaborative strategy, and a flexible culture—enable and support the adaptive learning cycle.

SELF-DISCOVERY exercise

How Resilient Are You?

In a world that is changing faster than ever, one of the most important qualities a person or organization can have is *resilience*—the ability to bounce back, to thrive in the face of constant chaos and uncertainty. Some companies offer their employees resilience training. Resilience is an important characteristic for people working in learning organizations because they have to become comfortable with constant questioning and change. The following exercise will help you rate your resilience skills. From 1 to 5, rate how much each statement applies to you, with 1 being very little and 5 being very much.

	Very Little Like Me				Very Much Like Me
1. I am curious, ask questions, want to know how things work, experiment.	1	2	3	4	5
2. I constantly learn from my experience and the experiences of others.	1	2	3	4	5

	Very Little Like Me				Very Much Like Me
3. I need and expect to have things work well for myself and others. I take good care of myself.	1	2	3	4	5
4. I play with new developments, find the humor, laugh at myself, chuckle.	1	2	3	4	5
5. I adapt quickly to change, am highly flexible.	1	2	3	4	5
6. I feel comfortable with paradoxical qualities.	1	2	3	4	5
7. I anticipate problems and avoid difficulties.	1	2	3	4	5
8. I develop better self-esteem and self-confidence every year. I develop a conscious self-concept of professionalism.	1	2	3	4	5
9. I listen well. I read others, including difficult people, with empathy.	1	2	3	4	5
10. I think up creative solutions to challenges, invent ways to solve problems. I trust my intuition and hunches.	1	2	3	4	5
11. I manage the emotional side of recovery. I grieve, honor, and let go of the past.	1	2	3	4	5
12. I expect tough situations to work out well; I keep on going. I help others, bring stability to times of uncertainty and turmoil.	1	2	3	4	5
13. I find the gift in accidents and bad experiences.	1	2	3	4	5
14. I convert misfortune into good fortune.	1	2	3	4	5

Scoring and Interpretation: Add up your scores. If you scored 60–70, you are highly resilient; 50–60, you're better than average; 40–50, adequate; 30–40, struggling to cope; and less than 30, lost—seek help. You can improve your resilience by practicing the qualities described in this list.

Source: Monika Guttman, "Find Out How Resilient You Are," *USA Weekend,* March 5–7, 1999, pp. 4–6, adapted from Al Siebert, *The Survivor Personality.* Used with permission.

ORGANIZATIONAL BEHAVIOR in your life

Open Up!

Change is difficult and sometimes painful. Because we have a natural tendency to resist change, many of us miss opportunities for learning and improving our lives. The following simple steps can help you "open up" and learn to handle new ideas and challenges without triggering your change-avoidance impulses. Try them for at least a couple of weeks—they might also lead to opportunities you'd otherwise miss.

1. For lunch or dinner tomorrow, eat a food that you've never tasted.

2. Walk or drive a different route to school or work at least one day this week.
3. Seek out a student or colleague you don't know well who is from a different culture than your own and invite him or her to lunch. Then *talk.*
4. Attend a student activity you never participate in—a sporting event if you don't like sports; a play or poetry reading if you usually avoid them.
5. Change the layout of your home office/study or your dorm room (to the extent possible).
6. Listen to a CD from a musical genre that you don't like (for example, if you hate opera, try it; if you can't stand jazz, listen to that). Listen to *all* of it.

7. Visit a department or building on campus that you've never been to.

8. Once a week, read a magazine or newspaper you've never read.

Source: Based on Seth Godin, "Change Agent: 'Why Is It That the Really Obvious Chances to Improve Our Businesses and Careers Almost Always Pass Us By?' " *Fast Company,* November 1999, pp. 354–359.

ORGANIZATIONAL BEHAVIOR news flash

@ It's a Topsy-Turvy High-Tech World

High-tech companies are constantly in the news these days because the industry is changing so rapidly. One of the hottest recent stories is the merger of AOL and Time Warner, in which AOL plans to buy the media giant for stock valued at around $165 billion, the biggest merger ever. In discussing the merger, Steve Case of AOL said, "This company is perfectly positioned at the epicenter of change. . . . There is probably going to be more confusion in the business world in the next decade than there has been in any decade, maybe, in history. I can't think of any that brought the kind of topsy-turvy change that's starting to happen now, and the pace is only going to accelerate." Case sees the degree of dislocation and confusion not as a threat, but as an amazing opportunity. Not everyone, though, is as comfortable with topsy-turvy change as Steve Case. Undoubtedly, the merger of these two companies will bring many difficult changes for employees in both AOL and Time Warner.

Using the news listings on your search engine, such as AP, Reuters, or ZDNet News, look for stories about companies that are merging—preferably within a high-tech industry. When you find a couple of stories that interest you, download them and study them for information about changes that are affecting or will affect employees. Do the changes seem positive or negative? Do your articles include any evidence of resistance to change within the companies? How are leaders helping employees deal with this major change?

Source: Quote by Steve Case is from Marc Gunther, "These Guys Want It All," *Fortune,* February 7, 2000, pp. 71–78.

global diversity EVENTS

@ As described in the chapter, globalization has been a significant force for change in recent years. Each day for a week, read a large, national newspaper (or the News of the Day on your favorite search engine) and keep a list of some global events that will likely affect organizations in your hometown or the town where you now live. For example, one such event during early 2000 was when the price of a barrel of oil tripled due to decreased production and growing demand. Describe briefly how and why each event you list may impact local businesses.

minicase ISSUE

Creating a Learning Organization at SuperJuice

The New CEO. Luisa de la Cruz sat in her new office thinking about her company's future. After working her way up the corporate ladder for 15 years, she had just been appointed CEO of SuperJuice, a Florida-based company that makes juice drinks that are marketed to high schools and restaurants throughout the Southeast. For nearly two decades, SuperJuice has been the most successful juice drink maker in the region. However, profits haven't risen for four straight years, and several new competitors continue to steal market share. In fact, one of the new companies was started by two former SuperJuice employees who left after top management continually rejected their ideas for new exotic drink mixes and new approaches to marketing. Luisa cringed at the thought that the hottest-selling drink flavors in Florida and several other states had been invented in SuperJuice's own labs but were now being made and sold by a competitor. Competitors were setting up drink carts at outdoor festivals and advertising with jingles and slogans that caught the imaginations of the region's youth. Even Luisa's own 17-year-old son often purchased her competitors' products, saying that "SuperJuice is for kids."

SuperJuice management has always prided itself on the company's efficient set of systems, both in the factory and at headquarters. Managers concentrated on making a high-quality product as inexpensively as possible. "SuperJuice is like a well-oiled machine," Luisa told herself with some pride. Most of the company's 200 employees had joined SuperJuice right out of high school or college and liked the way the company operated. They showed up for work on time, performed their jobs efficiently, and rarely complained. The long-standing rules and procedures, combined with an organizational culture that reflected the traditional, family-oriented background of SuperJuice's Cuban-born founder, contributed to a level of politeness and civility in the company that sometimes seemed like a throwback to the 1950s. SuperJuice was a calm and civilized place to work in the midst of a rapidly changing, chaotic world, Luisa reflected with pleasure.

The Need for Change. But Luisa's pleasure evaporated as she realized that the company could collapse beneath her if it didn't somehow respond to the changes in the environment. She remembered the scandal that had erupted several years ago when two new employees started "breaking the rules" and pushing for changes in the company. The two worked odd hours, played rock music, and decorated their offices with brightly colored posters, unique photographs, and fanciful "dream catchers" hung from the ceiling. Occasionally, one would tape a note to his door that read, "Gone to the movies to get my creative juices flowing!" Although both workers were highly productive, top management quickly took action to try to bring the two back in line. They worried that this kind

of attitude would have a negative impact on the productivity of other employees, who were accustomed to coming to work and putting in their solid eight hours. The CEO really blew his stack when the two presented four new drink flavors they had concocted on the sly. He was so angry about the unauthorized use of lab time that he nearly fired both employees on the spot. Luisa remembered finding one of the employees in the lab dejectedly pouring the prototypes down the drain. "You know you can't do anything new in this company," Luisa told her at that time. "It's just not the SuperJuice way." Since that time, SuperJuice has lost a few other young, ambitious employees who have chafed under the tight management control.

Luisa knew she was promoted because she had always followed the rules. But she also realized that continuing to follow the rules could take this company she loved right into bankruptcy. She knew the company had a lot of potential, starting with its loyal, committed workforce. But where should she begin? Can SuperJuice really change itself into a forward-thinking, creative company?

1.   What are some of the forces for change affecting SuperJuice and calling for a new approach to management?

2.   What do you think Luisa needs to do first to begin a transformation at the company?

3.   How would you suggest she turn SuperJuice into a learning organization? Think about specific changes she can make to get all employees thinking of new and exciting ways to revitalize the SuperJuice product line and way of doing business.

Source: Based on Suzy Wetlaufer, "What's Stifling Creativity at CoolBurst?" *Harvard Business Review,* September-October 1997, pp. 36–40.

video CASE

HARD CANDY IS SWEET ON STRUCTURE

Twenty-two-year-old Dineh Mohajer didn't have the color nail polish she wanted, so one weekend she made her own: sky blue. While Dineh and her sister Pooneh were shopping in southern California, several people noticed Dineh's painted toenails and complimented her on them. With this instant on-the-street interest, the two young women thought, "Let's go into business." They mixed up a batch of sky blue enamel and took it to an upscale shop in Beverly Hills called Fred Segal. Segal bought the whole batch, and Hard Candy was born.

That's how the Hard Candy organization was formed. The story is similar to those of many entrepreneurs, whose efforts focus first on the core idea and hardly pay attention to issues of organizational structure and job design. What Dineh, Pooneh, and Dineh's boyfriend, Ben Einstein, didn't count on was how successful their products would be. The first few colors—sky blue, violet, sunshine, bubblegum, and mint—sold out at $17 per bottle as fast as the young partners could fill the bottles. They continued to accept orders from several upscale stores but they fell behind.

Dineh explains that they had a window of opportunity—before the big cosmetics companies began to copy them—to establish themselves as a company. "It came to a point where if there's no formal structure implemented into this organization there's no way that this company can get to the next level," says Dineh. So the trio accepted a loan from the sisters' parents, found a high-quality manufacturer, and set up headquarters in Beverly Hills. In doing so, they began to create jobs, for themselves and employees. They also needed to delegate, even at the highest level. "We decided that the company needed a seasoned businessperson to come in and help lead the growth," says Pooneh. They called Ernst & Young to assist them in some accounting problems, and that firm ultimately helped them find managers and a temporary CEO.

Today, Hard Candy has an organizational chart that looks a bit more conventional, although the three co-founders would be quick to point out some major differences. "There's a core team that drives the growth of the company," says Dineh. "Then we have an executive vice-president of sales and marketing.

And we have a head of PR [public relations], and we have a director of operations." Dineh wants people to know that, although Hard Candy now fills some traditional department positions, "It is not the typical corporate environment . . . it is very free flowing."

Ben Einstein points out that "everyone in this company wears a lot of hats." Everyone has varied responsibilities, and everyone is accountable. Delegation is an important part of Hard Candy's culture. "The environment that I create is open, exciting," remarks Dineh. "You're only as good as the people you've delegated responsibility to on your behalf. . . . If you have good people who know what needs to be done and they're experts, you don't need to hold their hand." Einstein notes that although delegation—and empowerment of employees—is an integral part of Hard Candy's structure, managers must still be accountable.

Hard Candy is now a multimillion-dollar organization with forty employees and several product lines, including nail enamel, lipstick, and eye color. The company was recently sold to a French fashion company, which has agreed to leave Mohajer in charge. For now, things will stay the same. "I don't think we've grown large enough yet to . . . feel restricted by the . . . corporate grind, or whatever," says Ben, "but we are more regular about having meetings and how we conduct the meetings." With the right team of managers and employees assembled, the three co-founders now have time to devote to their individual strengths within the organization.

Questions

1. Write a brief paragraph for Hard Candy's employee handbook, describing how the concept of authority is viewed at the company.

2. Can you envision a scenario in which Hard Candy could develop a network organization structure? Why or why not?

Source: "Turning a Fluke into a Fortune," **CPNET.com,** October 18, 1999, **www.cpnet.com;** Eric Schine, "Such Polish for One So Young," *Business Week Online,* March 3, 1997, **www.businessweek.com;** "The Name Game," *PBS Online,* **www.pbs.org,** accessed May 16, 2000; Silvia Sansoni, "Fashion Renegade," *Forbes,* March 10, 1997, **www.forbes.com.**

video CASE

MULTIGEN-PARADIGM CHANGES THE GAME

A decade ago, the 3-D computer simulation industry was creating products that hardly anyone understood and even fewer people could afford. "Before Paradigm came along, 3-D simulation wasn't accessible to anybody," explains Wes Hoffman, one of Paradigm Simulation's founders. "It was too expensive. Software products were selling for $70,000 to $80,000, and the hardware was $300,000." Hoffman and David Gatchel figured that if they could drop the price to around $5,000, they could sell a lot more product. Then along came a contract with Nintendo, and a game called Pilot 64, which quickly sold 1 million copies. Then things began to change for the young organization.

First was a re-evaluation of mission, strategy, and culture, resulting in a spin-off from Paradigm Simulation called Paradigm Entertainment, which focused entirely on producing various games.The atmosphere naturally lent itself to a baseball culture, in which talent, creativity, innovation, and performance were highly valued. The industry was young, fast-paced, and risky, perfectly suited to that type of culture—and to the young employees who came on board. From the beginning, Gatchel acknowledged the importance of the environment in which Paradigm employees worked. "In our business really the value of our company is in the employee base and maintaining good relationships with them," he notes. "We're in a very young industry. Most of our employees, I would say, are in their mid to upper twenties. We're in an industry where, although we have a lot of fun, we're under a lot of pressure to get product out."

As the organization matured, more structure was necessary. "We've gone to great lengths to try to present a real professional structured environment," says Gatchel. The young baseball culture began to shift a bit toward a club culture that included employees with more experience. "We have a real balance of not only the young artistic creative types, but some more seasoned veterans that understand what schedules are and program management and those kinds of issues," remarks Gatchel. Still, says Gatchel, "The culture that we've tried to create at Paradigm Entertainment is a very informal and casual atmosphere."

Part of the culture has been built by QWLs, or quality-of-worklife programs, which include everything from flextime to on-site foosball games. "People can relax as far as their dress," notes Gatchel. "The hours are flexible. We provide free soft drinks and snacks, and distractions for people when they want to take a break—foosball or pool or basketball—activities where the employees can relax a little bit, forget about a problem they're working on for a few minutes, and take a little bit of time off, and then refocus and get back to it."

In 1998, Paradigm underwent another significant change—a merger with MultiGen Inc., to become MultiGen-Paradigm. "With complementary expertise and products, MultiGen and Paradigm Simulation will combine their professional services organizations to create a major growth engine for the company," touted a press release. Meanwhile, two organizational cultures had to merge, a situation that often creates fear and resistance to change. However, the merger was completed successfully, and the company is now a leader in real-time 3-D solutions for visual simulation, entertainment, urban simulation, and simulation-based training applications. The new organization still values workers with initiative and creativity. Despite major changes, it's very likely that anyone wandering the halls of the new organization could call out, "Foosball, anyone?" and get a positive response.

Questions

1. Is it likely that the new organization still maintains a strong baseball culture? Why or why not? If not, what type of culture might best describe the new organization?

2. What fears might employees of both organizations have had before the merger? What steps might managers have taken to overcome those fears and any resulting resistance to change?

Source: MultiGen-Paradigm Web site, **www.multigen-paradigm.com;** "MultiGen Inc. and Paradigm Simulation Inc. Sign Definitive Merger Agreement," press release, September 3,1998, **www.paradigmsim.com.**

integrative CASE

PART FOUR

AOL: UNLIKE ANY ORGANIZATION—ANYWHERE

AMERICA ONLINE

"AOL. Unlike Anything. Anywhere." Specialized language is a key component to any organization's culture, and AOL is no exception. Visitors to the Web site see the slogan almost everywhere they look, and much of the language used on the site works back to this slogan. For instance, "AOL Anywhere" is the company's service-marked strategy to make AOL's interactive brands, services, and features available to all consumers, across a variety of products and devices. The language of AOL is intended to convey the idea that AOL is unique—and is everywhere.

AOL's culture reflects its organization—and vice versa, although both must continuously evolve if the company is to maintain a competitive edge far into the twenty-first century. In the beginning, the fledgling company maintained an organic structure as its entre-preneurial founders went from project to project, and sometimes crisis to crisis. As the company grew, AOL's structure necessarily evolved into something that combines both horizontal and network organization, with an emphasis on teams. Company growth came partly through the creation of its own divisions such as the Interactive Services Group (which operates AOL and CompuServe), partly through alliances with other organizations (which bring in brands such as iPlanet), and partly through the acquisition of other organizations such as Netscape.

In an environment that includes a rapidly changing economy and ever-advancing technology, AOL's culture must find a way to complement its growing size without sacrificing speed in decision making. "The world moves fast at AOL," notes the Web site. "As the first multibillion, multibrand new media company, we're committed to continued growth through the recruitment of talented people who know how to invent and reinvent themselves." To keep pace with the constantly changing environment, AOL looks for flexible workers who can "think outside the box"—who are talented, creative, and innovative. Since the company relies on its knowledge workers, it also wants to keep them happy—and at AOL. The company emphasizes QWLs—quality of work life pro-

grams designed to entice and keep the best employees. Flexible work hours, inside and outside education and training programs, dependent care and parenting programs, as well as stress and time management classes and access to fitness facilities are all part of the overall organizational belief that work and quality of life are intertwined. "Because we believe in what we do, we work hard and have fun doing it," boasts the Web site. AOL's quality of work life programs also foster socialization of its workers—employees can work out together, take classes together, engage in parenting programs together, attend company picnics and functions together.

If AOL has a hero, most insiders—and outsiders—would say it is Steve Case, not just because of his role in founding the company, or because of his role at the helm, or even because of his ability to create a vision for his company. But when AOL was faced with a major change during the early 1990s, he was willing to step aside for the good of the company. "Some guys would have . . . tried to sabotage the process," recalls Jim Kimsey, who was AOL's chairman at the time, and charged with the task of removing Case. "He obviously didn't agree with me, but he had his eye on the greater good and the longer term. Not a lot of guys would do that." AOL was poised to go public, and Kimsey was worried that venture capitalists would balk at the idea of a boyish-faced thirty-three-year-old heading the company they were preparing to back. A decade later, Case is back in charge. Both he and his company had a few more years of experience, and investors weren't shy, perhaps because they had become more accustomed to the workings of the new economy and saw that Case and AOL had staying power. Still only in his early forties, Case was ready to lead the world's largest media company into the new millennium. What does the man who had the awkward task of replacing Case ten years ago now say about the company's more mature leader? "He is probably the most focused individual I've ever seen," notes Kimsey. "He will be the strategic beacon of this company." It might be said that Case is unlike anyone. Anywhere.

Questions

1. Based on what you have read in the four AOL cases, sketch out an organizational chart for the company. Don't worry about whether your chart matches the real one exactly; instead, concentrate on what you know about the company.

2. Does AOL's organizational culture reflect a baseball team, a club, an academy, or a fortress? Explain your answer.

3. Would you describe AOL as a learning organization? Why or why not?

4. Visit AOL's Web site and browse through a variety of sections to get a good review of the company's products and services, career opportunities, people, and the like. Then write a brief memo describing what you see as possible forces for change for the company over the next five years—environment, society, technology, and so forth. How well do you think the company is equipped to meet these challenges?

Source: AOL Web site, www.corp.aol.com, accessed April 2000; William J. Holstein, "You've Got a Deal!" *U.S. News & World Report,* January 24, 2000, pp. 34–40; Fred Vogelstein, "The Talented Mr. Case," *U.S. News & World Report,* January 24, 2000, pp. 41–42; Tim Jones and Gary Marx, "Weaned on Crisis, Landing on Top," *Chicago Tribune,* January 16, 2000, sec. 1, p. 1.

APPENDIX

Methods for Researching Organizational Behavior

Benjamin Franklin, that master of commonsense principles, wrote in *Poor Richard's Almanac,* "Experience keeps a dear school, yet fools will learn in no other." To put his 18th century prose into modern language, we might say that to learn only through your own experiences is risky and often costly. A wise person benefits from applying the principles that others have learned and are willing to share.

For employees and managers alike, success requires understanding human behavior in the context of organizations. Many people are satisfied to develop that understanding through observing their own and their coworkers' behavior, then drawing conclusions about what works. However, the management discipline of organizational behavior provides valuable resources in the form of scientific research. To use those resources effectively, you must be able to understand the scope and nature of scientific research so that you can evaluate the results of studies you read about. This appendix summarizes the methods of researching organizational behavior, including the nature of scientific research, basic research designs and methods of data collection, principles for evaluating research, and ethical issues related to research.

The Scientific Approach to Research

Scientific research tests ideas by gathering and studying data in a systematic way. The objective of this process is to find patterns that occur consistently and use them to develop and test theories. For example, research into leadership has tested the idea that certain individual characteristics and types of behavior consistently make a person an effective leader. Chapter 11 summarizes the outcome of such efforts so far.

Research involves studying data about variables. A **variable** is a characteristic that can be measured over time or among research subjects. One variable mentioned in several chapters is job satisfaction. Researchers can develop ways to measure a person's level of job satisfaction, then use those measures to compare satisfaction among different employees or over time. Researchers might measure whether the level of satisfaction differs in jobs with different characteristics, or they might measure whether people's satisfaction levels change as something in the organization changes.

variable

A characteristic that can be measured over time or among research subjects.

Researchers use the data they gather about variables to test and refine hypotheses. A **hypothesis** is a statement that tries to explain the relationship between two or more variables. For example, a study might test the hypothesis "Employees are more satisfied when their supervisor discusses their accomplishments with them at the end of each week." The variables are job satisfaction and weekly meetings to discuss accomplishments. The relationship to be tested is that the meetings possibly cause greater job satisfaction. In this hypothesis, the meetings are a type of variable called an **independent variable**—a variable that is presumed to affect the size or intensity of another variable. The variable that changes—the one the researcher is trying to explain—is called a **dependent variable.** In the example given in this paragraph, the dependent variable is job satisfaction.

hypothesis

A statement that tries to explain the relationship between two or more variables.

independent variable

A variable presumed to affect the size or intensity of another variable.

dependent variable

A variable that a hypothesis attempts to explain; the variable that presumably changes in response to the independent variable.

The same measure could be either a dependent or independent variable, depending on the hypothesis. Thus, in another study, job satisfaction could be the independent variable. A researcher might test whether the quantity of output increases when job satisfaction is great. In that case, the hypothesis says job satisfaction (the independent variable) somehow predicts increased output (the dependent variable).

A more complex hypothesis might include moderating and intervening variables. A **moderating variable** affects the relationship between an independent variable and the dependent variable. Consider again the hypothesis that weekly meetings to discuss accomplishments are associated with higher job satisfaction. Research to test this hypothesis might generate mixed results. If researchers investigate further, they might find that the outcome is influenced by whether employees accomplished a lot during the week. If employees have had a productive week, they like to discuss their accomplishments with their supervisor, and their satisfaction increases. In this case, the employee's level of accomplishment may be a moderating variable.

moderating variable

A variable that affects the relationship between an independent variable and the dependent variable.

An **intervening variable** acts as the mechanism by which the independent variable affects the dependent variable. It answers the question, How does the independent variable work? In the example of weekly meetings and job satisfaction, further research might find that the meetings give employees a clearer understanding of what the supervisor expects, as well as an opportunity for the supervisor to deliver praise. The clearer understanding and the praise are intervening variables that help to explain the link between the weekly meetings and the employees' job satisfaction.

intervening variable

A variable that acts as the mechanism by which an independent variable affects a dependent variable.

Of course, there may be other ways to explain these relationships. This example is invented and simplified, to show various relationships among variables in a hypothesis. To demonstrate such relationships scientifically requires a good research design.

Research Designs

The methods for designing a research project can be very complex, and entire courses are devoted to the subject of research methodology. However, these methods usually fall into a few basic groups: case studies, field surveys, laboratory experiments, and field experiments. In addition, most researchers begin their work with **secondary research**—reviewing existing data and research reports to see what is already known in a subject area.

secondary research

Research that consists of reviewing existing data and research reports to see what is already known in a subject area.

Case Studies   A **case study** is an in-depth investigation of one person's, group's, or organization's experiences. It is a descriptive report, often including historical background, a statement of one or more problems and accomplishments, and a summary of some resources available for solving the problem or used to produce the accomplishments. Case studies typically include many details, such as an organization's financial reports or an individual's career history. Researchers usually prepare case studies by observing organizations, requesting documents, and interviewing individuals.

case study

An in-depth investigation of one person's, group's, or organization's experiences.

Case studies are useful teaching tools. This textbook contains simple case studies at the beginning and end of each chapter. Cases are often interesting and provide an opportunity to identify principles that may be at work in real organizations. Researchers sometimes use them to help in developing hypotheses to test with other research designs. However, case studies are subjective. The person who prepares them typically has a point of view that may influence what is included, and the people who provide information also may be biased. In addition, what works for the people or organization in a case study may not apply to other situations, where circumstances are different.

Field Surveys   A **field survey** involves identifying a group that the researcher is interested in studying and then gathering data by asking some members of the group a set of questions. Such a research design might involve mailing questionnaires to sales managers, telephoning secretaries, or visiting companies to interview selected members of work teams.

field survey

A research design that involves identifying a group that the researcher is interested in studying, then gathering data by asking members of the group a set of questions.

With field surveys, the researcher obtains a more limited set of data than with a case study, but the data come from a wide range of subjects and are easy to quantify for analysis. This type of research design also tends to be the most efficient and least expensive of the options available. Field surveys do, however, pose a variety of limitations, most of which involve getting responses from a group of people who truly represent the whole group being studied. For example, if the researcher mails out a questionnaire to chief executives, many of them will throw it away without answering it. The executives who do respond may not be typical of the whole group, but may be, for example, the least busy. Unless the researcher particularly wanted to learn about chief executives who are not very busy, the quality of the results will suffer.

Laboratory Experiments   A more complicated type of research is the **laboratory experiment.** This method involves setting up an artificial environment in which the researcher controls the independent variable(s), then measures the dependent variable(s). The researcher then evaluates the resulting data to see whether there is a relationship between these variables.

laboratory experiment

A research design that involves setting up an artificial environment in which the researcher controls the independent variable(s), then measures the dependent variable(s).

The most scientific approach to a laboratory experiment is to randomly assign subjects to either an experimental or a control group. The

experimental group

The group of subjects in an experiment who are exposed to the independent variable.

control group

The group of subjects in an experiment who are not exposed to the independent variable.

experimental group is exposed to the independent variable, and the **control group** is not exposed to the independent variable. Then the experimenter compares whether the results are different for the two groups. Assuming that subjects are randomly assigned to the groups, a difference would suggest that the independent variable has an effect on the dependent variable.

An experiment has some advantages as a research design. The researcher can watch what people actually do, as opposed to asking them to say what they will do. (People don't always do as they say they will.) The researcher can control which variables the subjects are exposed to. Thus, the results are a good description of how people respond to the independent variable *in the laboratory setting*. However, a laboratory experiment may not explain what people will do in the real world, where they are exposed to many other influences along with the independent variable. Also, laboratory experiments tend to be expensive, and it may be difficult to recruit subjects from the population the researcher is interested in. For example, if you wanted to study successful leaders, you might have trouble convincing successful people to spend time in your laboratory. Therefore, laboratory experiments often use college students, who are close at hand to many researchers. The ways college students behave may or may not describe the ways other people behave.

Field Experiments   To avoid some of the limitations of a laboratory experiment, researchers may test their hypotheses with field experiments. A **field experiment** is an experiment conducted outside a laboratory setting; in the case of organizational behavior research, field experiments would take place in existing organizations. For example, a company might be willing to test the effectiveness of different organizational structures or work designs by setting up different structures or designs in its facilities in different cities. It could compare performance at the facilities, then draw conclusions about which structure or design is associated with the best outcomes.

Clearly, this approach has some drawbacks. Most notably, researchers cannot control all the variables in a field experiment. In the example, there would necessarily be differences among the organization's facilities beyond the differences in organizational structure or work design. Researchers can try to control for these differences in their data analysis, but they can only control for differences they identify. Other drawbacks are that field research tends to be expensive and time consuming, and it requires the researcher to convince the organization to participate. On the positive side, field experiments show what people do in real organizations. Thus, a good field experiment can be extremely valuable in advancing knowledge of organizational behavior.

field experiment

An experiment conducted outside a laboratory setting (for example, in an existing organization).

Data Collection

For any of these research methods, researchers have some choice in how they collect data. The basic alternatives involve some combination of questionnaires, interviews, observation, and nonreactive measures.

questionnaire

A set of questions with a predetermined set of answer choices.

Questionnaires   Perhaps the most widely known method of data collection is the use of questionnaires. A **questionnaire,** as the name implies, is a set of questions presented to subjects. Typically, it offers a predetermined set of answer choices. Subjects may independently answer questions on a printed questionnaire or online survey, or they may select from among answer choices read by a researcher over the phone or in person. Questionnaires are the basic method for conducting field surveys. Researchers also may use them to gather data about attitudes or opinions of subjects in experiments or case studies.

An advantage of using questionnaires is that they provide a way to get the same categories of information from each subject. Questionnaires are also especially useful when researchers want to learn about attitudes, opinions, and feelings. They are not as useful for measuring behavior or for gathering data that subjects may not want to disclose or do not know. For example, if a researcher asked, "Would you work harder if you took a nap each afternoon?" a subject really could only guess at the answer. Similarly, if the researcher asked, "Do you ever nap on the job?" subjects might think they will look bad if they say they do.

Interviews   Another way to gather data verbally is to conduct interviews. An **interview** involves gathering data through an open-ended discussion, in contrast to the preestablished answer choices of a questionnaire. Although the interview is based on a set of predetermined questions, interviewers can encourage subjects to offer ideas or elaborate on answers. As mentioned earlier, interviews are an important part of data collection for case studies. Researchers also use interviews to explore the attitudes behind behaviors they observe in experimental settings. For example, following an experiment, researchers might supplement their observations by conducting follow-up interviews with some of the subjects.

interview

A method of gathering data through open-ended questions asked by an interviewer.

As with questionnaires, interviews are useful as a way to learn opinions, beliefs, and emotions. In contrast to questionnaires, they allow the researcher to pursue ideas that the subject raises and the interviewer had not thought of. This makes interviews helpful for refining hypotheses and generating new hypotheses.

Observation   As the term suggests, **observation** involves watching and recording behavior. Researchers may observe subjects in the field or watch how they behave in a laboratory experiment. They may be in view of the subjects, observe from behind a one-way mirror, or watch videotaped interactions. They also may set up the experiment to generate data such as changes in subjects' physiology (for example, heart rate) or speed or accuracy in performing a task.

observation

A method of gathering data by watching and recording behavior.

Observation has the major advantage that it measures what subjects really do, as opposed to what they say they will do. However, when researchers record their observations—for example, noting who speaks at a meeting—they may introduce biases into the results. Likewise, the experience of being watched may affect how subjects behave. Observation also tends to be expensive, because researchers need to watch every subject.

Nonreactive Measures   The use of **nonreactive measures** means collecting data through means that do not directly involve the subjects, so that presumably they are not affected by the data collection. A nonreactive measure mentioned with regard to case studies is the study of an organization's existing records, such as financial reports, sales reports, or personnel

nonreactive measures

A method of collecting data through means that do not directly involve the subjects, so they are unaffected by data collection.

records. Researchers might also gather other types of physical evidence—for example, they might visit an organization's office after hours to count the number of computers that are running or to record which offices have cartoons hanging on the wall.

Nonreactive measures can provide more objective data than if subjects are aware they are being watched. Also, the use of existing reports is a very economical way to gather a great deal of information. However, researchers must be careful to avoid drawing inferences that are not really warranted. In the case of counting cartoons on the walls, the measure might not say what researchers think it does about employees' attitudes—not even their sense of humor. Such a measure would have to be supplemented with other types of data collection, if it is used at all.

Evaluation of Research

When you read a research report, you should consider the quality of the study. Identify the type of research design and data collection methods, taking into account their advantages and limitations. Consider whether the research has the following qualities:

generalizable

Able to describe a larger population, not just the actual subjects of the study.

- Are the results **generalizable?** This means the results describe a larger population, not just the subjects of the study. In contrast, case studies describe the unique conditions facing individual companies. A management technique that worked well at Dell Computer or Amazon.com might not succeed as well at Sears or a neighborhood tire store. Similarly, the results of a field survey of human resource managers may not be generalizable to sales manager.

reliable

Able to generate the same results, if the study were repeated.

- Are the results **reliable?** This means that if researchers were to keep repeating the same research design, they would get the same results. If an experiment measured the impact of weekly meetings with supervisors and found that employees' performance improved, researchers could test the reliability of the study by trying it on various groups of employees at various times to see whether the relationship between the variables was always the same.

valid

Actually having the same meaning as the researcher infers.

- Are the results **valid?** In other words, do they really mean what the researcher interprets them to mean? For example, a study that measures employee satisfaction may not be valid for predicting organizational success. Most organizations do not define success solely in terms of employee satisfaction.

Research that is generalizable, reliable, and valid is most likely to produce results that advance our knowledge of organizational behavior.

causality

The condition in which an independent variable actually produces the change observed in a dependent variable.

Often, research results are described as if they indicate **causality.** In other words, the independent variable causes the dependent variable to change in one direction or the other. An example is a report that says a particular style of leadership causes a lower rate of employee turnover. Sometimes, however, people assume causality when two variables actually have some other relationship. The true influence might move in the opposite direction; in the example, people might tend to use a certain type of leadership in a low-turnover group. Or perhaps the two variables tend to occur together because of some third, unknown factor. Perhaps a particular culture values employee loyalty and the leadership style being studied. The two variables occur together because they are both part of the culture, not because one causes the other. Therefore, if you encounter a statement that one variable causes another, question whether all other kinds of relationships between the variables have been carefully ruled out.

Ethics in Research

As in any other endeavor, conducting research gives rise to ethical issues. In particular, the researcher should consider the study's effect on participants, the need for honesty in compiling and reporting results, and the researcher's role as a member of the organization. Researchers can find guidance in handling such issues from the codes of ethics of the American Psychological Association, the Academy of Management, and other professional organizations.

Effect on Participants   Participating in research can change subjects' perceptions and experiences. Setting up an experiment may require creating uncomfortable or undesirable situations for some participants, or the researcher may deny the control group possibly beneficial conditions being offered to the experimental group. In questionnaires and interviews, the researcher may ask questions that cause subjects to view their work situation differently and become dissatisfied. Other questions might invade the privacy of participants. The basic ethical issue underlying all these situations is whether it is right to treat subjects in any of these ways.

Many researchers believe that the ethical course is to ensure that subjects give "informed consent." This means the subjects understand what the possible costs and benefits of the research will be to themselves and others, then freely agree to participate. Informed consent is not an easy solution. It can be difficult for researchers to identify all the consequences of participating in a study and to communicate them clearly. In addition, some experiments are not as valid if subjects understand what the researcher is trying to do. Finally, for research conducted within an organization, subjects may feel that they will make a poor impression on management if they decline to participate, so their consent may not really be voluntary.

Honesty about Results   Researchers may care whether their results support their hypothesis—that is, they may have a stake in the outcome. They may belong to a department or an organization that will benefit if the results support a particular point of view, or their next project may be easier or more interesting if the results support a particular hypothesis. Especially under such conditions, it can be tempting to slant the results so that they support a particular interpretation. Maybe changing just a couple of test results feels trivial in support of a larger goal. Of course, such dishonesty compromises the value of the research and, if discovered, the credibility of the researcher. Scientific research requires complete honesty.

The Researcher as Organization Member   Ethical issues often arise out of the researcher's role as a member of an organization. For example, the role of objective, scientific researcher may conflict with the role of finding support for the organization's mission. The researcher is subject to the power of others in the organization, who may want work done quickly and inexpensively, even if the result may not be valid or generalizable. In turn, the researcher will benefit from acquiring power to be able to resist influence attempts that may compromise the research quality. Thus, researchers, like others in the organization, often engage in political behavior. The challenges of leading organizations so that people use power constructively apply as much to researchers as to others in the organization. Effective leadership is important for creating an organizational culture that favors ethical research.

The researcher especially has a key role to play in a learning organization. In an environment that fosters learning and positive change, the researcher can help the organization develop. Similarly, members of such an organization can contribute much by learning to apply the results of research done inside as well as outside the organization.

notes

CHAPTER 1

1. Peter Burrows and Peter Elstrom, "The Boss," *Business Week,* August 2, 1999, pp. 76–84.
2. Frederick W. Taylor, *Principles of Scientific Management* (New York: Harper and Brothers, 1911).
3. Henri Fayol, *Industrial and General Administration* (Paris: Dunod, 1916).
4. Mary Parker Follett, *The New State: Group Organization in the Solution of Popular Government* (London: Longmans, Green and Co, 1918).
5. Chester Barnard, *The Functions of the Executive* (Cambridge, MA: Harvard University Press, 1938).
6. Christopher Caggiano, "The New Urban Chic," *Inc.,* May 1999, pp. 60–61.
7. D. Katz and R. L. Kahn, *The Social Psychology of Organizations* (New York: John Wiley & Sons, 1966).
8. David Mendell and Rogers Worthington, "Questions and Mystery Dog O'Hare Evacuation," *Chicago Tribune,* August 28, 1999, sec. 1, pp. 1, 10; John Schmeltzer, "United Assessing Its Damage from O'Hare Security Breach," *Chicago Tribune,* August 28, 1999, sec. 1, p. 10; James Janega and Rogers Worthington, "Going Nowhere at O'Hare," *Chicago Tribune,* August 27, 1999, sec. 1, pp. 1, 23; United Airlines, untitled press release, August 26, 1999, downloaded from United Airlines Web site, www.ual.com, August 30, 1999; Eric Zorn, "O'Hare's Reaction Just Doesn't Fly in the Real World," *Chicago Tribune,* August 30, 1999, sec. 2, p. 1.
9. Jay Barney, "Firm Resources and Sustained Competitive Advantage," *Journal of Management* 17(1) (1991): 99–120.
10. Jeffrey Pfeffer, *Competitive Advantage through People: Unleashing the Power of the Work Force* (Boston: Harvard Business School Press, 1994).
11. Shelly Branch, "The 100 Best Companies to Work for in America," *Fortune,* January 11, 1999, pp. 118–122+.
12. Peter F. Drucker, *Management Challenges for the 21st Century* (New York: HarperBusiness, 1999), pp. 135–159.
13. Debra Phillips, G. David Doran, Elaine W. Teague, and Laura Tiffany, "Young Millionaires," *Entrepreneur,* November 1998, pp. 118–126.
14. Marc Ballon, "Scoring on the Rebound," *Inc.,* October 20, 1998 (*Inc.* 500 special issue), pp. 31–32; SurfSoft Web site, www.surfsoft.com, downloaded September 7, 1999.
15. Robert L. Katz, "Skills of an Effective Administrator," *Harvard Business Review* 52 (September–October 1974): 90–102.
16. George Donnelly, "Acquiring Minds," *CFO,* September 1999, pp. 54–59.
17. Kathleen Melka, "Sky King," *Computerworld,* September 28, 1998, accessed at www.computerworld.com, September 27, 1999.
18. David Barber, "Star Techs," *Inc Technology,* no. 3, September 15, 1999, pp. 46, 52.
19. Hope Katz Gibbs, "The ET List: 20 Top US. States," *Export Today,* April 1999, pp. 40–46.
20. Stephen Franklin, "Help Wanted . . . Really Wanted," *Chicago Tribune,* June 6, 1999, sec. 5, pp. 1, 14.
21. Jeremy Kahn, "Wal-Mart Goes Shopping in Europe," *Fortune,* June 7, 1999, pp. 105–106+.
22. Jennifer Cheeseman Day, *Population Projections of the United States by Age, Sex, Race, and Hispanic Origin: 1995 to 2050,* U.S. Bureau of the Census, Current Population Reports, P25-1130 (Washington, D.C.: U.S. Government Printing Office, 1996), p. 1.
23. *Ibid.*
24. *Ibid.*
25. Phillip J. Longman, "How Global Aging Will Challenge the World's Economic Well-Being," *U.S. News & World Report,* March 1, 1999, pp. 30–35, 38–39.
26. Drucker, *Management Challenges for the 21st Century,* p. 45.
27. William C. Byham, "Grooming Next-Millennium Leaders," *HR Magazine,* February 1999 (downloaded from the Society for Human Resource Management Web site, www.shrm.org, May 25, 1999).
28. Robert J. Grossman, "Heirs Unapparent," *HR Magazine,* February 1999 (downloaded from the Society for Human Resource Management Web site, www.shrm.org, May 25, 1999).
29. Drucker, *Management Challenges for the 21st Century,* pp. 17–21.
30. "CIO Panel: Knowledge-Sharing Roundtable," *Information-Week Online,* News in Review, April 26, 1999 (downloaded from *InformationWeek* Web site, www.informationweek.com, April 30, 1999); Buckman Laboratories Web site, www.buckman.com, downloaded September 7, 1999.
31. Jenny C. McCune, "The Change Makers," *Management Review* (downloaded from the American Management Association Web site, www.amanet.org, May 4, 1999).
32. Geoffrey Colvin, "How to Be a Great e-CEO," *Fortune,* May 24, 1999, pp. 104–110.
33. Drucker, *Management Challenges for the 21st Century,* pp. 73–93.
34. Drucker, *Management Challenges for the 21st Century,* p. 142.
35. See, for example, Peter Senge, *The Fifth Discipline: The Art and Practice of Learning Organizations* (New York: Doubleday/Currency, 1990); John A. Byrne, "Paradigms for Postmodern Managers," *Business Week,* Reinventing America special issue 1992, pp. 62–63; George Land and Beth Jarman, *Breakpoint and Beyond* (New York: Harper Business, 1992); Robert Barner, "Seven Changes That Will Challenge Managers—and Workers," *The Futurist,* March/April 1996, pp. 33–42; and Lawrence Chimerine, "The New Realities in Business," *Management Review,* January 1997, pp. 12–17.

CHAPTER 2

1. Laabs, "Molex Makes Global HR Look Easy," *Workforce,* March 1999, pp. 42–46. To learn more about Molex's history, products, markets, and culture, visit www.molex.com.
2. "A Challenge for the 1990s—Managing the Diverse Workplace," *The Challenge of Diversity: Equal Opportunity and Managing Differences in the 1990s* (Rockville, MD: BNA Communications, Inc.) pp. 5–7; E. Kossek and Sharon Lobel, "Introduction: Transforming Human Resource Systems to Manage Diversity—an Introduction and Orienting Framework," in E. Kossek and S. Lobel (eds.), *Managing Diversity* (Cambridge, MA: Blackwell Publishers, 1996) pp. 1–20.
3. C. Hill, *International Business* (Burr Ridge, IL: Irwin McGraw-Hill, 1997).
4. R. Narisetti and J. Friedland, "Diaper Wars of P&G and Kimberly-Clark Now Heat Up in Brazil," *The Wall Street Journal,* June 4, 1997; S. Baker, "The Bridges Steel Is Building," *Business Week,* June 2, 1997, p. 39.
5. J. Lee-Young, "Starbucks Expansion in China is Slated," *The Wall Street Journal,* October 5, 1998, p. B13c.
6. Bureau of Labor Statistics, "BLS Releases New 1996–2006 Employment Projections," www.bls.gov/new.release/ecopro.nws.htm.

7. Richard W. Judy and Carol D'Amico, *Workforce 2020: Work and Workers in the 21st Century* (Indianapolis, IN: Hudson Institute, 1997).
8. N. Copeland, "Valuing Diversity, Part I: Making the Most of Cultural Differences at the Workplace"; and Judy and D'Amico, *Workforce 2020.*
9. S. Hutchins, Jr. (1989). "Preparing for diversity: The year 2000." *Quality Process 22,* no. 10: 66–68.
10. "Employee Dissatisfaction on Rise in Last 10 Years, New Report Says," *Employee Relations Weekly* (Washington, DC: Bureau of National Affairs, 1986).
11. D. T. Hall and J. Richter. (1990). "Career gridlock: Baby boomers hit the wall." *The Executive 4:* 7–22.
12. Michael L. Wheeler, "Global Diversity: Reality, Opportunity, and Challenge," *Business Week,* December 1, 1997, special advertising section. Also, see the company's Web site at www.hp.com.
13. Marilyn Loden and Judy B. Rosener, *Workforce America!* (Homewood, IL: Business One Irwin, 1991); Marilyn Loden, *Implementing Diversity* (Homewood, IL: Irwin, 1996); P. Digh, "Coming to terms with diversity," *HR Magazine* (November 1998): 117–120.
14. Frances J. Milliken and Luis I. Martins. (1996). "Searching for common threads: Understanding the multiple effects of diversity in organizational groups." *Academy of Management Review 21,* no. 2: 402–433.
15. J. Useem, "Welcome to the New Company Town," *Fortune,* January 10, 2000, pp. 62–70.
16. E. H. Schein, *Organizational Culture and Leadership* (San Francisco: Jossey-Bass 1992).
17. B. P. Sunco, "How fun flies at Southwest Airlines," *Personnel Journal* (June 1995): 62–73; K. Henderson and J. C. Quick. (1992). "Crafting an organizational culture: Herb's hand at Southwest." *Organizational Dynamics 21:* 45–56; S. Gruner, "Have Fun Make Money," *Inc.,* May 1998, p. 123.
18. G. Haight. (1990). "Managing diversity." *Across the Board 27,* no. 3: 22–29.
19. Songer, "Workforce Diversity," *B&E Review* (April–June 1991): 3–6.
20. Robert Doktor, Rosalie Tung, and Mary Ann von Glinow. (1991). "Future directions for management theory development." *Academy of Management Review 16:* 362–365; and Mary Munter, "Cross-Cultural Communication for Managers," *Business Horizons* (May–June 1993): 69–78.
21. Renee Blank and Sandra Slipp, "The White Male: An Endangered Species?" *Management Review* (September 1994): 27–32; Michael S. Kimmel, "What Do Men Want?" *Harvard Business Review* (November–December 1993): 50–63; and Sharon Nelton, "Nurturing Diversity," *Nation's Business,* June 1995, pp. 25–27.
22. S. Shellenbarger, "Family-friendly CEOs are changing cultures at more workplaces," *The Wall Street Journal,* September 15, 1999, p. B1.
23. M. Bennett. (1986). "A developmental approach to training for intercultural sensitivity." *International Journal of Intercultural Relations 10:* 179–196.
24. Jenny C. McCune, "Diversity Training: A Competitive Weapon," *Management Review* (June 1996): 25–28.
25. Judy and D'Amico, *Workforce 2020.*
26. Madeline E. Heilman, Caryn J. Block, and Peter Stathatos. (1997). "The affirmative action stigma of incompetence: Effects of performance information ambiguity." *Academy of Management Journal 40,* no. 1: 603–625.
27. S. Hutchins, Jr. (1989). "Preparing for diversity: The year 2000." *Quality Process 22,* no. 10: 66–68.
28. Arthur P. Brief, Robert T. Buttram, Robin M. Reizenstein, S. Douglas Pugh, Jodi D. Callahan, Richard L. McCline, and Joel B. Vaslow. (1997). "Beyond good intentions: The next steps toward racial equality in the American workplace." *Academy of Management Executive 11:* 59–72.
29. B. Geber. (1990). "Managing diversity." *Training 27,* no. 7: 23–30.
30. Julie Amparano Lopez, "Study Says Women Face Glass Walls as Well as Ceilings," *The Wall Street Journal,* March 3, 1992, pp. B1, B2; and Ida L. Castro, "Q: Should Women Be Worried about the Glass Ceiling in the Workplace?" *Insight,* February 10, 1997, pp. 24–27.
31. Nelton, "Nurturing Diversity."
32. C. Soloman. (1990). "Careers under glass." *Personnel Journal 69,* no. 4: 96–105.
33. U.S. Census Bureau, "Comparison of Summary Measures of Income by Selected Characteristics: 1989, 1997, 1998," *Current Population Survey,* March 1999, from U.S. Census Bureau Web site, www.census.gov/hhes/www.income98.html.
34. Deborah L. Jacobs, "Back from the Mommy Track," *The New York Times,* October 9, 1994, pp. F1, F6.
35. Barbara Presley Noble, "A Quiet Liberation for Gay and Lesbian Employees," *The New York Times,* June 13, 1993, p. F4.
36. Soloman, "Careers under glass."
37. Belle Rose Ragins, Bickley Townsend, and Mary Mattis. (1998). "Gender gap in the executive suite: CEOs and female executives report on breaking the glass ceiling." *Academy of Management Executive 12,* no. 1: 28–42.
38. P. Sellers, "These women rule," *Fortune,* October 25, 1999, pp. 94–126.
39. E. G. Collins, "Managers and Lovers," *Harvard Business Review* 61 (1983): 142–153.
40. Sharon A. Lobel, Robert E. Quinn, Lynda St. Clair, and Andrea Warfield, "Love without Sex: The Impact of Psychological Intimacy between Men and Women at Work," *Organizational Dynamics* (Summer 1994): 5–16.
41. Carol Hymowitz, "Drawing the Line on Budding Romances in Your Workplace," *The Wall Street Journal* ("Managing Your Career" column), November 18, 1997, p. B1.
42. William C. Symonds with Steve Hamm and Gail DeGeorge, "Sex on the Job," *Business Week,* February 16, 1998, pp. 30–31.
43. Carol Hymowitz and Ellen Joan Pollock, "The One Clear Line in Interoffice Romance Has Become Blurred," *The Wall Street Journal,* February 4, 1998, pp. A1, A8.
44. Section 1604.11 of the "Guidelines on Discrimination Because of Sex," Civil Rights Act of 1991. From Web site for the Equal Employment Opportunity Commission, www.eeoc.gov.
45. Jack Corcoran, "Of Nice and Men," *Success,* June 1998, pp. 65–67.
46. De'Ann Weimer with Emily Thornton, "Slow Healing at Mitsubishi," *Business Week,* September 22, 1997, p. 74.
47. Corcoran, "Of Nice and Men."
48. Barbara Carton, "At Jenny Craig, Men Are Ones Who Claim Sex Discrimination," *The Wall Street Journal,* November 29, 1994, pp. A1, A11.
49. Jennifer J. Laabs, "Sexual Harassment: HR Puts Its Questions on the Line," *Personnel Journal* (February 1995): 35–45; Sharon Nelton, "Sexual Harassment: Reducing the Risks," *Nation's Business,* March 1995, pp. 24–26; and Gary Baseman, "Sexual Harassment: The Inside Story," *Working Woman,* June 1992, pp. 47–51, 78.
50. Copeland, "Learning to Manage a Multicultural Workforce."
51. G. Flynn, "Do you have the right approach to diversity?" *Personnel Journal* (October 1995): 68–72; M. Galen and A. T. Palmer, "Diversity: Beyond the numbers game," *Business Week,* August 14, 1995, pp. 60–61.
52. L. E. Wynter, "Allstate rates managers on handling diversity," *The Wall Street Journal,* November 1, 1997; p. B1.
53. Loden and Rosener, *Workforce America!;* and Genevieve Capowski, "Ageism: The New Diversity Issue," *Management Review* (October 1994): 10–15.
54. B. Ragins. (1989). Barriers to mentoring: The female manager's dilemma." *Human Relations 42,* no. 1: 1–22; and Ragins *et al.,* "Gender Gap in the Executive Suite."
55. Mary Zey, "A Mentor for All," *Personnel Journal* (January 1988): 46–51.
56. J. Black and M. Mendenhall. (1990). "Cross-Cultural Training Effectiveness: A Review and a Theoretical Framework for Fu-

ture Research." *Academy of Management Review* 15: 113–136.

57. Hanna Rosin, "Cultural Revolution at Texaco," *The New Republic,* February 2, 1998, pp. 15–18; K. Labich, "No more crude at Texaco," *Fortune,* September 6, 1999, pp. 205–212.

58. Deogen, N. "Coke was told in '95 of need for diversity," *The Wall Street Journal,* May 20, 1999, pp. A3, A4.

59. G. Hostede. (1985). "The interaction between national and organizational value systems." *Journal of Management Studies* 22: 347–357; G. Hofstede. (1984). "The cultural relativity of the quality of life concept." *Academy of Management Review 9:* 389–398.

60. I. Johnson, "The longest leap," *The Wall Street Journal,* September 27, 1999, p. R21.

61. Valerie Frazee, "Keeping Up on Chinese Culture," *Global Workforce,* October 1996, pp. 16–17.

62. Fons Trompenaars, *Riding the Waves of Culture: Understanding Diversity in Global Business* (Burr Ridge, IL: Irwin, 1994).

63. Randall S. Schuler, Susan E. Jackson, Ellen Jackofsky, and John W. Slocum, Jr., "Managing Human Resources in Mexico: A Cultural Understanding," *Business Horizons,* May–June 1996, pp. 55–61.

64. R. Frank and T. Burton, "Culture clash causes anxiety for Pharmacia and UpJohn, Inc.," *The Wall Street Journal,* February 4, 1997, pp. A1 and A12.

65. S. Caudron, "Lessons from HR Overseas."

66. Brenton R. Schlender, "Matsushita Shows How to Go Global," *Fortune,* July 11, 1994, pp. 159–166.

67. Moran and Riesenberger, *The Global Challenge,* p. 255; and Caudron, "Lessons from HR Overseas."

68. Alex Markels, "Power to the People," *Fast Company,* February–March 1998, pp. 155–165.

69. J. Ledvinka and V. Scarpello, *Federal Employment Regulation in Human Resource Management* (Boston: PWS-Kent, 1991).

70. L. Kraar, "China's car guy," *Fortune,* October 11, 1999, pp. 238–246.

71. G. P. Zachary and S. Marshall, "Nike tries to quell exploitation charges," *The Wall Street Journal,* June 25, 1997, p. A16; A. Bernstein, "Nike finally does it," *Business Week,* May 25, 1998, p. 46; A. Bernstein, "A Floor under foreign factories," *Business Week,* November 2, 1998, pp. 126–127.

72. S. Snell and J. Dean. (1992). "Integrated manufacturing and human resource management: A human capital perspective." *Academy of Management Journal 35:* 467–504.

73. B. O'Reilly, "Your new global workforce," *Fortune,* December 14, 1992, pp. 52–66.

74. N. Adler and S. Bartholomew. (1992). "Managing globally competent people." *The Executive 6:* 52–65.

75. R. Grossman, "HR in Asia," *HRMagazine 42* (July 1997): 105–110.

76. "America vs. the New Europe: By the numbers," *Fortune,* December 21, 1998, p. 149.

77. G. Steinmetz, "U.S. firms, honed in huge home market, are poised to pounce in the new Europe," *The Wall Street Journal,* 1999, pp. A1 and A7.

78. Czinkota *et al., Global Business,* (Fort Worth, TX: The Dryden Press, 1995) p. 151; and Robert D. Gatewood, Robert R. Taylor, and O. C. Ferrell, *Management* (Burr Ridge, IL: Irwin, 1995), pp. 131–132.

79. "For Richer, for Poorer," *The Economist,* December 1993, p. 66; Richard Harmsen, "The Uruguay Round: A Boon for the World Economy," *Finance & Development,* March 1995, pp. 24–26; Salil S. Pitroda, "From GATT to WTO: The Institutionalization of World Trade," *Harvard International Review* (Spring 1995): 46–47 and 66–67; and David H. Holt, *International Management: Text and Cases* (Fort Worth: Dryden, 1998).

80. L. Turnbull, "Activists on the Road, Protesting Price of Free Trade," *The Columbus Dispatch,* November 5, 1999, p. B2.

81. Mark M. Nelson, "Extra Accommodations," *The Wall Street Journal,* September 30, 1994, pp. R13, R14.

82. Thane Peterson, "The Euro," *Business Week,* April 27, 1998, pp. 90–94.

83. Lynda Radosevich, "New Money," *CIO Enterprise,* sec. 2, April 15, 1998, pp. 54–58.

84. G. Steinmetz, "U.S. firms, honed in huge home market."

85. Barbara Rudolph, "Megamarket," *Time,* August 10, 1992, pp. 43–44.

86. Amy Barrett, "It's a Small (Business) World," *Business Week,* April 17, 1995, pp. 96–101.

87. Robert S. Greenberger, "As U.S. Exports Rise, More Workers Benefit and Favor Free Trade," *The Wall Street Journal,* September 10, 1997, pp. A1, A10.

88. Amy Borrus, "A Free-Trade Milestone, with Many More Miles to Go," *Business Week,* August 24, 1992, pp. 30–31.

89. B. Palmer, "What Chinese want," *Fortune,* October 11, 1999, pp. 229–234.

90. N. Adler, *International Dimensions of Organizational Behavior,* 2nd ed. (Boston: PWS-Kent, 1991).

91. T. Aeppel, "A 3Com factory hires a lot of immigrants, gets mix of languages," *The Wall Street Journal,* March 30, 1998, p. A1; L. Uchitelle, "The new faces of U.S. manufacturing," *The New York Times,* July 3, 1994, section 3, pp. 1, 6.

92. G. Brewer, "New world orders," *Sales and Marketing Management,* January 1994, pp. 59–63.

93. J. S. Lublin, "Expatriates go the extra mile," *The Wall Street Journal,* pp. B1 and B6.

94. Adler, *International Dimensions of Organizational Behavior,* pp. 7–8; William Holstein *et al.,* "The Stateless Corporation," *Business Week,* May 14, 1990, pp. 98–105; and Richard Daft, *Organization Theory and Design* (St. Paul, MN: West, 1992).

95. J. Millman, "Mexico builds a home-appliance bonanza," *The Wall Street Journal,* August 23, 1999, p. A12.

96. E. Dunbar and A. Katcher, "Preparing managers for foreign assignments," *Training and Development Journal* (September 1990): 45–47.

97. J. S. Black and M. Mendenhall, "A practical but theory-based framework for selecting cross-cultural training methods," in *Readings and Cases in International Human Resource Management,"* M. Mendenhall and G. Oddou (eds.) (Boston: PWS-Kent, 1991), pp. 177–204.

98. J. S. Black and J. K. Stephens. (1989). "The influence of the spouse on American expatriate adjustment and intent to stay in Pacific Rim overseas assignments," *Journal of Management 15:* 529–544; W. Arthur and W. Bennett. (1995). "The international assignee: The relative importance of factors perceived to contribute to success." *Personnel Psychology 48:* 99–114; M. A. Shaffer and D. A. Harrison. (1998). "Expatriates' psychological withdrawl from international assignments: Work, nonwork, and family influences." *Personnel Psychology 51:* 87–118.

99. Gilbert Fuchsberg, "As Costs of Overseas Assignments Climb, Firms Select Expatriates More Carefully," *The Wall Street Journal,* January 9, 1992, pp. B3, B4.

100. P. R. Harris and R. T. Moran, *Managing Cultural Differences* (Houston: Gulf Publishing, 1991).

101. *Ibid.*

102. H. Lancaster, "Before going overseas smart managers plan their homecoming," *The Wall Street Journal,* September 28, 1999, p. B1.

103. C. M. Solomon, "Repatriation: Up, down, or out," *Personnel Journal* (January 1995): 28–37; D. R. Briscoe, *International Human Resource Management* (Englewood Cliffs, NJ: Prentice-Hall, 1994).

CHAPTER 3

1. "Gates Ready to Lead Microsoft in New Direction as Innovator," *Columbus Dispatch,* January 15, 2000, p. 8F; David Bank, "Gates Steps Aside as Microsoft's CEO; Ballmer to Take over Daily Operations," *The Wall Street Journal,* January 14, 2000, pp. A3, A6; A. Fisher, "The World's Most Admired Companies," *Fortune,* October 27, 1997, pp. 230–232; R. E. Stross, "Mi-

crosoft's advantage—Hiring only the Supersmart," *Fortune,* November 25, 1996, pp. 159–162; D. Seligman, "Brains in the office," *Fortune,* January 13, 1997.

2. D. M. Rousseau. (1989). "Psychological and implied contracts in organizations." *Employee Rights and Responsibilities Journal 2:*121–129.

3. National Public Radio, "Employees Make Success Story of Running Steel Plant," *Morning Edition,* March 23, 1994.

4. S. L. Robinson and D. Rousseau. (1994). "Violating the psychological contract: Not the exception but the norm." *Journal of Organizational Behavior 15:*245–259; M. A. Cavanaugh and R. A. Noe. (1999). "Antecedents and consequences of relational components of the new psychological contract." *Journal of Organizational Behavior 20:*323–340.

5. D. Rousseau. (1996). "Changing the deal while keeping the people." *Academy of Management Executive 11:*50–61.

6. R. H. Waterman, J. A. Waterman, and B. A. Collard. (1994, July–August). "Toward a career-resilient workforce." *Harvard Business Review,* 87–95.

7. Ford Motor Company brochure, "Personal Development Roadmap," 1998. Courtesy of Ford Motor Company.

8. B. W. Altman and J. E. Post, "Beyond the social contract: An analysis of the executive view at twenty-five larger companies." In D. T. Hall (ed.), *The Career Is Dead—Long Live the Career* (San Francisco: Jossey-Bass, 1996), pp. 46–71.

9. A. S. Tsui, J. L. Pearce, L. W. Porter, and A. M. Tripoli. (1997). "Alternative approaches to the employee-organization relationship: Does investment in employees pay off?" *Academy of Management Journal 40:*1089–1121.

10. Charles A. O'Reilly III, Jennifer Chatman, and David F. Caldwell. (1991). "People and organizational culture: A profile comparison approach to assessing person-organization fit." *Academy of Management Journal 34*(3):487–516.

11. Mike Hofman, "The Leader Within," *Inc.,* September 1998, p. 127.

12. D. Bowen, G. Ledford, and B. Nathan. (1991). "Hiring for the organization, not the job." *Academy of Management Executive 5:*35–51.

13. S. Wetlaufer, "Organizing for empowerment: An interview with AES's Roger Sant and Dennis Bakke." *Harvard Business Review,* January–February 1999, pp. 111–123.

14. J. R. Hollenbeck and E. M. Whitener. (1988). "Reclaiming personality traits for personnel selection: Self-esteem as an illustrative case." *Journal of Management 14:*81–91; P. M. Wright, K. Kacmar, G. C. McMahan, and K. Deleeuw, "P = F (MXA): Cognitive ability as a moderator of the relationship between personality and job performance." *Journal of Management:* J. P. Campbell, R. A. McCloy, S. H. Oppler, and C. E. Sager, "A Theory of Performance." In N. Schmitt and W. C. Borman (eds.), *Personnel Selection in Organizations* (San Francisco: Jossey-Bass, 1993), pp. 35–70.

15. J. Hogan. (1991). "Structure of physical performance in occupational tasks." *Journal of Applied Psychology 76:*495–507.

16. J. Hollenbeck, D. Ilgen, and S. Crampton. (1992). "Lower-back disability in occupational settings: A human resource management view." *Personnel Psychology 42:*247–278.

17. *Americans with Disabilities Act of 1990.* S. 933, U.S. Public Law 101-336, 1990.

18. R. Kanfer and P. Ackerman. (1989). "Motivation and cognitive abilities: An integrative/aptitude-treatment interaction approach to skill acquisition." *Journal of Applied Psychology 74:*657–690.

19. M. Ree, J. Earles, and M. Teachout. (1994). "Predicting job performance: Not much more than g." *Journal of Applied Psychology 79:*518–524.

20. Y. Ganzach. (1998). "Intelligence and job satisfaction." *Academy of Management Journal 41:*526–539.

21. A. P. Carnevale, "Enhancing Skills in the New Economy." In A. Howard (ed.), *The Changing Nature of Work* (San Francisco: Jossey-Bass, 1995) pp. 238–251.

22. S. Hays, "The ABCs of workplace literacy," *Workforce,* April 1999, pp. 70–74.

23. See J. M. Digman. (1990). "Personality structure: Emergence of the Five-Factor Model." *Annual Review of Psychology 41:*417–440; M. R. Barrick and M. K. Mount. (1993, February). "Autonomy as a moderator of the relationships between the Big Five personality dimensions and job performance." *Journal of Applied Psychology,* 111–118; and J. S. Wiggins and A. L. Pincus. (1992). "Personality: Structure and assessment." *Annual Review of Psychology 43:*473–504.

24. W. Dunn, M. Mount, M. Barrick, and D. Ones. (1995). "Relative importance of personality and general mental ability on managers' judgments of applicant qualifications." *Journal of Applied Psychology 80:*500–509.

25. M. Mount, M. Barrick, and J. Strauss. (1994). "Validity of observer ratings of the Big Five personality factors." *Journal of Applied Psychology 79:*272–280.

26. Alex Tresniowski and Ron Arias, "Misters Bean," *People,* November 9, 1998, pp. 69–70.

27. Debra Phillips, G. David Doran, Elaine W. Teague, and Laura Tiffany, "Young Millionaires," *Entrepreneur,* November 1998, pp. 118–126.

28. S. K. Hirsch, *MBTI Team Member's Guide* (Palo Alto, CA: Consulting Psychologists Press, 1992); A. L. Hammer, *Introduction to Type and Career* (Palo Alto, CA: Consulting Psychologists Press).

29. D. Goleman, "What makes a leader?" *Harvard Business Review,* November-December 1998, pp. 93–102.

30. J. Mayer and D. Sluyter (eds.), *Emotional Development and Emotional Intelligence* (Basic Books: 1997).

31. L. M. Spencer and S. Spencer, *Competence at Work: Models for Superior Performance* (New York: John Wiley and Sons, 1993); L. M. Spencer, D. C. McClelland, and S. Kelner, *Competency Assessment Methods: History and State of the Art* (Boston: Hay/McBer, 1997). Also, see C. Cherniss. "The business case for emotional intelligence" at the Web site www.eiconsortium.org/business.htm.

32. J. Laabs, "Emotional Intelligence at Work," *Workforce,* July 1999, pp. 68–71.

33. David A. Kolb. (1996, Spring). "Management and the learning process." *California Management Review 18,* 3:21–31.

34. De' Ann Weimer, "The Houdini of Consumer Electronics," *Business Week,* June 22, 1998, pp. 88, 92.

35. See David A. Kolb, I. M. Rubin, and J. M. McIntyre, *Organizational Psychology: An Experimental Approach,* 3rd ed. (Englewood Cliffs, NJ: Prentice-Hall, 1984), pp. 27–54.

36. Steve Hamm, "Bill's Co-Pilot," *Business Week,* September 14, 1998, pp. 76–78+.

37. D. Leonard and S. Straus, "Putting your company's whole brain to work," *Harvard Business Review,* July–August 1997, pp. 111–121.

38. Chuck Salter, "This is brain surgery," *Fast Company,* February/March 1998, pp. 147–150.

39. D. H. Pink, "Hey, your CEO wears combat boots!" *Fast Company,* June-July 1997, pp. 46, 48.

40. Leonard and Straus. "Putting your company's whole brain to work."

41. E. C. Ravlin and B. M. Meglino. (1987). "Effects of values on perception and decision-making: A study of alternative work values measures." *Journal of Applied Psychology 72:* 666–673.

42. M. Rokeach, *The Nature of Human Values* (New York: Free Press, 1973); M. Rokeach and S. Ball-Rokeach. (1989, May). "Stability and change in American value priorities, 1968–1981." *American Psychologist,* 775–784.

43. E. Shapiro, "Time Warner defines, defends, system of values," *The Wall Street Journal,* April 9, 1999, pp. B1 and B4.

44. T. Judge and R. Bretz. (1992). "Effects of work values on job choice decisions." *Journal of Applied Psychology 77:*261–271; B. Meglino, E. Ravlin, and C. Adkins. (1989). "A work values approach to corporate culture: A field test of the value congruence process and its relationship to individual outcomes." *Journal of Applied Psychology 74:*424–432.

45. S. Ratan, "Generational tension in the office: Why busters hate boomers," *Fortune,* October 4, 1993, pp. 56–70; B. Filipczak, "It's just a job: Generation X at work," *Training,* 1994, pp. 21–27.

46. L. K. Gundry, J. R. Kickul, and C. W. Prather. (1994, Spring). "Building the creative organization." *Organizational Dynamics,* 25–28; J. S. Chatzky, "Changing the world," *Forbes,* March 2, 1992, pp. 83–84.

47. S. J. Breckler. (1984, May). "Empirical validation of affect, behavior, and cognition as distinct components of attitude." *Journal of Personality and Social Psychology,* 1191–1205; and J. M. Olson and M. P. Zanna. (1993). "Attitudes and attitude change." *Annual Review of Psychology 44*:117–154.

48. For a discussion of cognitive dissonance theory, see Leon A. Festinger, *Theory of Cognitive Dissonance* (Stanford, CA: Stanford University Press, 1957).

49. John A. Byrne, "Virtual Management," *Business Week,* September 21, 1998, pp. 80–82.

50. E. R. Kemery, A. Bedeian, and S. Zacur. (1996). "Expectancy-based job cognitions and job affect as predictors of organizational citizenship behaviors." *Journal of Applied Social Psychology 26*:635–651.

51. M. T. Iaffaldano and P. M. Muchinsky. "Job satisfaction and job performance: A meta-analysis." *Psychological Bulletin,* March 1985, pp. 251–273; C. Ostroff. (1992, December). "The relationship between satisfaction, attitudes, and performance: An organizational level analysis." *Journal of Applied Psychology,* 963–974; and M. M. Petty, G. W. McGee, and J. W. Cavender. (1984, October). "A meta-analysis of the relationship between individual job satisfaction and individual performance." *Academy of Management Review,* 712–721.

52. William C. Symonds, "Where Paternalism Equals Good Business," *Business Week,* July 20, 1998, pp. 16E4, 16E6.

53. Aaron Bernstein, "We Want You to Stay, Really," *Business Week,* June 22, 1998, pp. 67–68+.

54. G. Dessler. (1999). "How to earn your employees' commitment." *Academy of Management Executive 13*:58–67.

55. A. Rucci, S. Kirn, and R. Quinn, "The employee-customer-profit chain at Sears," *Harvard Business Review,* January–February 1998, pp. 82–97.

56. See "The 100 Best Companies to Work for in America," *Fortune,* January 11, 1999.

57. "The 90-day checkup," *Inc.,* March 1999, pp. 111–112.

58. C. Ostroff. (1992). "The relationship between satisfaction, attitudes, and performance: An organization level analysis." *Journal of Applied Psychology 77*:963–974; J. P. Meyer, S. Paunonen, I. Gellatly, R. Goffin, and D. Jackson. (1974). "Organizational commitment and job performance: It's the nature of the commitment that counts." *Journal of Applied Psychology,* 152–156.

59. W. Watson, K. Kumar, and L. Michaelsen. (1993). "Cultural diversity's impact on interaction process and performance: Comparing homogeneous and diverse task groups." *Academy of Management Journal 36*:590–602.

60. R. Muller, "Training for a change," *Canadian Business Review,* Spring 1995, pp. 16–19.

61. G. Vessels. (1982). "The creative process: An open-systems conceptualization." *Journal of Creative Behavior 16*:185–196.

62. C. Browne, "Jest for success," *Moonbeams,* August 1989, pp. 3–5; R. Kanter, *The Change Masters* (New York: Simon and Schuster, 1983).

63. "Hands on: A manager's notebook," *Inc.,* January 1989, p. 106.

64. E. Nelson, "Creatologist on creativity," *The Boston Globe,* July 19, 1994, pp. 41–43.

65. J. P. Campbell, "The definition and measurement of performance in the new age." In D. Ilgen and E. Pulakos (eds.), *The Changing Nature of Performance* (San Francisco: Jossey-Bass, 1999), pp. 399–432.

66. B. Blakley, M. Quinones, and I. Jago. "The validity of isometric strength tests: Results of five studies." *Personnel Psychology 44*:1–25.

67. M. Barrick and M. Mount. (1991). "The Big Five personality dimensions and job performance: A meta-analysis." *Personnel Psychology 44*:1–25.

68. M. D. Newcomb, *Drug use in the workplace: Risk factors for disruptive substance abuse in the workplace* (Dover, MD: Auburn House, 1988).

69. E. Lasson and A. Bass. (1997). "Integrity testing and deviance: Construct validity issues and the role of situational factors." *Journal of Business and Psychology 12*:121–146.

70. D. Skarlicki, R. Folger, and P. Tesluk. (1999). "Personality as a moderator in the relationship between fairness and retaliation." *Academy of Management Journal 42*:100–108.

71. P. Heaven. (1996). "Personality and self-reported delinquency: Analysis of the Big Five personality dimensions." *Personality and Individual Differences 20*:47–54.

72. National Institute for Occupational Safety and Health, "Violence in the workplace," *Central Intelligence Bulletin 57* (June 1996), Washington, DC: U.S. Department of Health and Human Services.

73. M. Elias, "Making jobs safe," *USA Today,* August 8, 1996, p. D1.

74. D. Bencivenga, "Dealing with the dark side," *HRMagazine,* January 1999, pp. 50–58.

75. J. Rosse and T. Noel, "Leaving the organization." In K. Murphy (ed.), *Individual Differences and Behavior in Organizations* (San Francisco: Jossey-Bass, 1996), pp. 451–504.

76. P. W. Hom and R. Griffeth, *Employee Turnover* (Cincinnati: Southwestern, 1995).

77. S. Rhodes and R. Steers, *Managing Employee Absenteeism* (Reading, MA: Addison-Wesley, 1990).

78. A. Elkin and P. Roach. (1990). "Promoting mental health at the workplace: The prevention side of stress management." *Occupational Medicine: State-of-the-Art Review 5*:739–754.

79. T. Judge, J. Martocchio, and C. Thoresen. (1997). "Five-factor model of personality and employee absence." *Journal of Applied Psychology 82*:745–755.

80. D. Dalton, W. Tudor, and D. Krackhardt. (1982). "Turnover overstated: A functional taxonomy." *Academy of Management Review 7*:225–235.

81. D. Machalaba, "Trucking firms find it is a struggle to hire and retain drivers," *The Wall Street Journal,* December 28, 1993, pp. A1 and A5.

82. J. Shaw, J. Delery, G. Jenkins, Jr., and N. Gupta. (1998). "An organization-level analysis of voluntary and involuntary turnover." *Academy of Management Journal 41*:511–525.

83. B. O'Reilly and A. Moore, "On the road," *Fortune,* April 27, 1998, pp. 183–195.

84. D. W. Organ, *Organizational Citizenship Behavior: The Good Soldier Syndrome* (Lexington, MA: Lexington Books, 1988).

85. L. Van Dyne and S. Ang. (1998). "Organizational citizenship behavior of contingent workers in Singapore." *Academy of Management Journal 41*:692–703; L. Van Dyne, J. Graham, R. Dienesch. (1994). "Organizational citizenship behavior: Construct redefinition, operationalization, and validation." *Academy of Management Journal 38*:765–802.

CHAPTER 4

1. Amy Barrett, Steve Hamm, and Ronald Grover, "Like Father, Like Son at Comcast," *Business Week,* September 21, 1998, pp. 75–78.

2. Christopher Caggiano, "Insider Training," *Inc.,* May 1999, pp. 63–64.

3. David S. Bernstein, "Starting from Scratch," *Inside Technology Training,* June 1999, pp. 24–26; The Limited Web site, www.limited.com, downloaded September 16, 1999.

4. Patricia Digh, "Coming to Terms with Diversity," *HR Magazine,* November 1998 (downloaded from the Society for Human Resource Management Web site, wwwshrm.org, May 25, 1999).

5. Kenneth Labich, "Fasten Your Seat Belts," *Fortune,* May 10, 1999, pp. 114–118.

6. Malcolm Ritter, "Are Faster Lanes an Illusion?" Yahoo! News, September 1, 1999 (downloaded from the Yahoo! Web site, www.yahoo.com, September 2, 1999); University of Toronto, "Study Finds Highway Traffic Speed to Be an Illusion," news release, September 1, 1999 (downloaded from the University of Toronto Web site, www.library.utoronto.ca, September 2, 1999).

7. Elaine N. Aron, *The Highly Sensitive Person* (New York: Birch Lane Press, 1996).

8. See A. Varma, A. S. DeNisi, and L. H. Peters, "Interpersonal Affect and Performance Appraisal: A Field Study," *Personnel Psychology,* Summer 1996, pp. 341–360; J. P. Forgas, "Mood and Judgment: The Affect Infusion Model (AIM)," *Psychological Bulletin,* January 1995, pp. 39–66.

9. See D. B. Burt, M. J. Zembar, and G. Niederehe, "Depression and Memory Impairment: A Meta-Analysis of the Association, Its Pattern, and Specificity," *Psychological Bulletin,* March 1995, pp. 285–305.

10. See A. J. Kinicki, P. W. Hom, M. R. Trost, and K. J. Wade. (1995, June). "Effects of category prototypes on performance-rating accuracy." *Journal of Applied Psychology:* 354–370; J. A. Bargh, M. Chen, and L. Burrows. (1996, August). "Automaticity of social behavior: Direct effects of trait construct and stereotype activation on action." *Journal of Personality and Social Psychology:* 230–244.

11. D. C. McClelland and J. W. Atkinson. (1948). "The projective expression of needs: The effect of different intensities of the hunger drive on perception." *Journal of Psychology 25:* 205–222.

12. S. T. Fiske and S. E. Taylor, *Social Cognition,* 2nd ed. (Reading, MA: Addison-Wesley, 1991), pp. 247–250.

13. Jennifer Lawton, "Women Entrepreneurs. Managing Perception, Managing Guilt," originally published by *EntreWorld.org,* February 1, 1998; accessed at "Small Business Planning and Advice," *inc.com,* February 21, 2000.

14. Bill Saporito, "Taking a Look Inside Nike's Factories," *Time,* March 30, 1998 (downloaded from http://cgipathfinder.com, May 4, 1999); Aurelio Rojas, "Nike Faces Suit over Factory Conditions: Firm Accused of Lying about Asian Workers," *San Francisco Chronicle,* April 21, 1998 (downloaded from www.sfgate.com, May 4, 1999); "Nike CEO: 'I Can' Change," CNN Financial Network, May 12, 1998 (downloaded from http://cnnfn.com, May 4, 1999); "Nike Raising Overseas Wages," CNN Financial Network, March 23, 1999 (downloaded from http://cnnfn.com, May 4, 1999).

15. J. S. Phillips and R. G. Lord. (1982). "Schematic information processing and perceptions of leaders in problem-solving groups." *Journal of Applied Psychology 67:* 486–492.

16. M. C. Rush and L. L. Beauvais. (1981). "A critical analysis of format induced versus subject imposed bias in leadership ratings." *Journal of Applied Psychology 66:* 722–727.

17. M. Bazerman, R. Beekun, and F. Schoorman. (1982). "Performance evaluation in a dynamic context: A laboratory study of the impact of prior commitment to the ratee." *Journal of Applied Psychology 67:* 873–876.

18. See R. Rosenthal and L. Jacobson, *Pygmalion in the Classroom: Teacher Expectations and Pupils' Intellectual Development* (New York: Holt, Rinehart & Winston, 1968).

19. See D. Eden, *Pygmalion in Management: Productivity as a Self-Fulfilling Prophecy* (Lexington, MA: Lexington Books, 1990), chap. 2; D. Eden and Y. Zuk. (1995, October). "Seasickness as a self-fulfilling prophecy: Raising self-efficacy to boost performance at sea." *Journal of Applied Psychology:* 628–635.

20. D. Eden and A. B. Shani. (1982, April). "Pygmalion goes to boot camp: Expectancy, leadership, and trainee performance." *Journal of Applied Psychology:* 194–199.

21. T. Dvir, D. Eden, M. L. Banjo. (1995, April). "Self-fulfilling prophecy and gender: Can women be Pygmalion and Galatea?" *Journal of Applied Psychology:* 253–270.

22. H. H. Kelley and J. L. Michela. (1980). "Attribution theory and research." *Annual Review of Psychology 12:*457–501; H. H. Kelley, "Attribution in Social Interaction," in *Attribution: Perceiving the Causes of Behavior* E. E. Jones, D. E. Kanouse, H. H. Kelley, R. E. Nesbitt, S. Valins, and B. Weiner (eds.) (Morristown, NJ: General Learning Press, 1971), p. 71.

23. Christopher Caggiano, "Seller, Beware!" *Inc.,* May 1999, pp. 99–100.

24. P. J. Corr and J. A. Gray. (1996, March). "Attributional style as a personality factor in insurance sales performance in the UK." *Journal of Occupational Psychology:* 83–87.

25. J. Greenberg. (1996, May). "Forgive me, I'm new: Three experimental demonstrations of the effects of attempts to excuse poor performance." *Organizational Behavior and Human Decision Processes:* 165–178; W. S. Silver, T. R. Mitchell, and M. E. Gist. (1995, June). "Responses to successful and unsuccessful performance: The moderating effect of self-efficacy on the relationship between performance and attributions." *Organizational Behavior and Human Decision Processes:* 286–299; G. E. Prussia, A. J. Kinicki, and J. S. Bracker. (1993, June). "Psychological and behavioral consequences of job loss: A covariance structure analysis using Weiner's (1985) attribution model." *Journal of Applied Psychology:* 382–394.

26. Marc Gunther, "Eisner's Mouse Trap," *Fortune,* September 6, 1999, pp. 107–108+.

27. S. Nam. *Cultural and managerial attributions for group performance.* Unpublished doctoral dissertation, University of Oregon. Cited in R. M. Steers, S. J. Bischoff, and L. H. Higgins. (1992, December). "Cross-cultural management research." *Journal of Management Inquiry:* 325–326.

28. Brendan I. Koerner, "The Boys' Club Persists," *U.S. News & World Report,* April 5, 1999, pp. 56–57.

29. Denise Power, "Hy-Vee Shifts Mind-Set, Cuts Turnover," *Executive Technology,* June 1999, p. 27.

30. Peter F. Drucker, *Management Challenges for the 21st Century* (New York: HarperBusiness, 1999), p. 77.

CHAPTER 5

1. T. D. Schellhardt, "An idyllic workplace under a tycoon's thumb," *The Wall Street Journal,* November 23, 1998, pp. B1 and B4.

2. David Silburt, "Secrets of the Super Sellers," *Canadian Business,* January 1987, pp. 54–59; "Meet Today's Young American Worker," *Fortune,* November 11, 1985, pp. 90–98; and Tom Richman, "Meet the Masters. They Could Sell You Anything . . .," *Inc.,* March 1985, pp. 79–86.

3. R. M. Steers and L. W. Porter (eds.), *Motivation and Work Behavior* (New York: McGraw-Hill, 1975).

4. Linda Grant, "Happy Workers, High Returns," *Fortune,* January 12, 1998, p. 81.

5. Anne Fisher, "The 100 Best Companies to Work for in America," *Fortune,* January 12, 1998, pp. 69–70.

6. J. Pfeffer *Academy of Management Executive.*

7. Richard M. Steers and Lyman W. Porter (eds.), *Motivation and Work Behavior,* 3rd ed. (New York: McGraw-Hill, 1983).

8. J. F. Rothlisberger and W. J. Dickson, *Management and the Worker* (Cambridge, MA.: Harvard University Press, 1939).

9. Abraham F. Maslow. (1943). "A Theory of Human Motivation." *Psychological Review 50:* 370–396.

10. Roberta Maynard, "How to Motivate Low-Wage Workers," *Nation's Business,* May 1997, pp. 35–39.

11. Clayton Alderfer, *Existence, Relatedness and Growth* (New York: Free Press, 1972).

12. Maynard, "How to Motivate Low-Wage Workers,"

13. Nina Munk, "The New Organization Man," *Fortune,* March 16, 1998, pp. 62–74.

14. Based on C. J. Bachler, "Workers take leave of job stress," *Personnel Journal,* January 1995, pp. 38–48.

15. David C. McClelland, *Human Motivation* (Glenview, IL.: Scott, Foresman, 1985).

16. David C. McClelland, "The Two Faces of Power," in D. A. Colb, I. M. Rubin, and J. M. McIntyre (eds.), *Organizational Psychology* (Englewood Cliffs, NJ: Prentice-Hall, 1971), pp. 73–86.

17. E. L. Deci. (1971). "Effects of externally mediated rewards on intrinsic motivation." *Journal of Personality and Social Psychology 18:*105–115.

18. E. L. Deci and R. M. Ryan, "The Empirical Exploration of Intrinsic Motivational Processes," in L. Berkowitz (ed.), *Advances in Experimental Social Psychology* (New York: Academic Press, 1980), pp. 39–80.

19. Q. Hardy, "Aloft in a career without fretters," *The Wall Street Journal,* September 29, 1998, p. B1.

20. See summary of research on cognitive evaluation theory in R. Kanfer, "Motivation Theory in Industrial and Organizational Psychology," in M. D. Dunnette and L. M. Hough (eds.), *Handbook of Industrial Organizational Psychology,* 2nd ed. (Palo Alto, CA: Consulting Psychologists Press, 1990), pp. 75–170; M. L. Ambrose and C. T. Kulik. (1999). "Old friends, new faces: Motivation research in the 1990s." *Journal of Management 25:* 231–292.

21. Frederick Herzberg, "One More Time: How Do You Motivate Employees?" *Harvard Business Review,* January–February 1968, pp. 53–62.

22. J. Phillipchuk and J. Whittaker. (1996). "An inquiry into the continuing relevance of Herzberg's motivation theory." *Engineering Management 8:* 15–20; R. J. House and L. A. Wigdor. (1967). "Herzberg's dual-factor theory of job satisfaction and motivation: A review of the empirical evidence and a criticism." *Personnel Psychology 20:* 369–389.

23. Jay Finegan, "Unconventional Wisdom," *Inc.,* December 1994, pp. 44–58.

24. M. Campion and P. Thayer. (1958). "Development and field evaluation of an intradisciplinary measure of job design." *Journal of Applied Psychology 70:* 29–34.

25. J. Richard Hackman and Greg R. Oldham, *Work Redesign* (Reading, MA.: Addison-Wesley, 1980); and J. Richard Hackman and Greg Oldham. (1976). "Motivation through the design of work: Test of a theory." *Organizational Behavior and Human Performance 16:* 250–279.

26. Ambrose and Kulik, "Old friends, new faces."

27. "City of Portland Wins 1999 Outstanding Office Ergonomics Award Honorable Mentions." From Web site www.cot.org, Center for Office Technology, Alexandria, Virginia.

28. D. May and C. Schwoerer. (1994). "Employee health by design: Using job involvement teams in ergononomic job redesign." *Personnel Psychology 47:* 861–886.

29. K. Tolbert, "Nuclear spill may be worse than reported," *Washington Post Foreign Service,* October 8, 1999, p. A21.

30. M. Campion and C. McClelland. (1991). "Interdisciplinary examination of the costs and benefits of enlarged jobs: A job-design quasi-experiment." *Journal of Applied Psychology 76:* 186–198.

31. T. Horwitz, "These six growth jobs are dull, dead-end and sometimes dangerous," *The Wall Street Journal,* December 1, 1994, pp. A1, A8, and A9.

32. Barbara Ettorre, "Retooling People and Processes," *Management Review,* June 1995, pp. 19–23.

33. R. Noe, J. Hollenbeck, B. Gerhart, and P. Wright, *Human Resource Management,* 3rd ed. (Burr Ridge, IL: Irwin-McGraw-Hill, 2000).

34. S. Caudron, "Andersen is at employees' service," *Personnel Journal,* September 1995, pp. 88–96.

35. E. E. Kossek, B. J. DeMarr, K. Backman, and M. Kollar. (1993). "Assessing employees' emerging elder care needs and reactions to dependent care benefits." *Public Personnel Management 22:* 617–637.

36. G. Flynn, "Making a business case for balance," *Workforce,* March 1997, pp. 68–74.

37. L. Faught, "At Eddie Bauer you can have work and a life," *Workforce,* April 1997, pp. 83–90.

38. A. E. Barber, R. B. Dunham, and R. A. Formisano. (1992). "The impact of employee benefits on employee satisfaction: A field study." *Personnel Psychology 45:* 55–75; Noe *et al., Human Resource Management.*

39. L. Asinof, "Click and shift: Workers control their benefits online," *The Wall Street Journal,* November 21, 1997, pp. C1, C17.

40. Keith H. Hammonds with Gabrielle Saveri, "Accountants Have

Lives, Too, You Know," *Business Week,* February 23, 1998, pp. 88, 90.

41. M. A. Gephart, V. J. Marsick, M. E. Van Buren, and M. S. Shapiro. (1996). "Learning organizations come alive." *Training and Development Journal 50:* 35–45.

42. C. D. McCauley, M. N. Ruderman, P. J. Ohlott, and J. E. Morrow. (1994). "Assessing the developmental components of managerial jobs." *Journal of Applied Psychology 79:* 544–560.

43. D. Dotlich and J. L. Noel, *Action Learning* (San Francisco: Jossey-Bass, 1998), pp. 84–87.

44. K. Dobbs, "Winning the retention game," *Training,* September 1999, pp. 51–56.

45. T. D. Wall, M. Corbett, R. Martin, C. W. Clegg, and P. R. Jackson. (1990). "Advanced manufacturing technology, work design, and performance: A change study." *Journal of Applied Psychology 75:* 691–697.

46. S. A. Mohrman and S. G. Cohen, "When People Get Out of the Box: New Relationships, New Systems," in A. Howard (ed.) *The Changing Nature of Work* (San Francisco: Jossey-Bass), pp. 365–410.

47. For example, see A. M. Townsend, S. M. DeMarie, and A. R. Hendrickson. (1998). "Virtual teams: Technology and the workplace of the future." *Academy of Management Executive 12:* 17–29.

48. J. Gordon, "Intellectual capital and you," *Training,* September 1999, pp. 30–38.

49. M. Martinez, "The collective power of employee knowledge," *HR Magazine,* February 1998, pp. 89–94.

CHAPTER 6

1. C. Hymowitz and M. Murray, "Raises and praise or out the door," *The Wall Street Journal,* June 21, 1999, pp. B1 and B4.

2. J. Stacy Adams, "Injustice in Social Exchange," in *Advances in Experimental Social Psychology,* 2nd ed., L. Berkowitz (ed.) (New York: Academic Press, 1965); and J. Stacy Adams. (1963, November). "Toward an understanding of inequity." *Journal of Abnormal and Social Psychology:* 422–436.

3. Ray V. Montagno. (1985). "The effects of comparison to others and primary experience on responses to task design." *Academy of Management Journal 28:* 491–498; and Robert P. Vecchio. (1982). "Predicting worker performance in inequitable settings." *Academy of Management Review 7:* 103–110.

4. T. D. Schellhardt, "Rookie gains in pay wars rile veterans," *The Wall Street Journal,* June 4, 1998, pp. B1 and B7.

5. J. Greenberg. (1990). "Organizational justice: Yesterday, today, and tomorrow." *Journal of Management 16:* 399–432.

6. For a review of literature on the relationship between justice and organizational outcomes, see: M. L. Ambrose and C. T. Kulik. "Old friends, new faces: Motivation research in the 1990s." *Journal of Management 25:* 231–292; R. Kanfer, "Motivational Theory and Industrial Organizational Psychology," in *Handbook of Industrial and Organizational Psychology* (Palo Alto, CA: Consulting Psychologists Press); N. D. Cole and G. P. Latham. (1997). "Effects of training in procedural justice on perceptions of fairness by unionized employees and disciplinary subject matter experts." *Journal of Applied Psychology 82:* 699–705.

7. J. Greenberg. (1990). "Employee theft as a reaction to underpayment inequity: The hidden costs of pay cuts." *Journal of Applied Psychology 75:* 561–568.

8. W. C. Kim and R. Mauborgne, "Fair process: Managing in the knowledge economy," *Harvard Business Review,* July-August 1997, pp. 65–75.

9. M. N. Martinez, "Rewards given the right way," *HR Magazine,* May 1997, pp. 109–116.

10. Victor H. Vroom, *Work and Motivation* (New York: Wiley, 1964); B. S. Gorgopoulos, G. M. Mahoney, and N. Jones. (1957). "A path-goal approach to productivity." *Journal of Applied Psychology 41:* 345–353; and E. E. Lawler III, *Pay and Organizational Effectiveness: A Psychological View* (New York: McGraw-Hill, 1981).

11. Richard L. Daft and Richard M. Steers, *Organizations: A Micro/Macro Approach* (Glenview, IL.: Scott, Foresman, 1986).

12. J. Laabs, "Trident Precision Manufacturing Inc.: Optimas Award Profile," *Workforce,* February 1998, pp. 44–49.

13. W. Van Eerde and H. Thierry. (1996). "Vroom's expectancy model and work-related criteria: A meta-analysis." *Journal of Applied Psychology 81:* 575–586; T. R. Mitchell. (1974). "Expectancy models of job satisfaction, occupational preference and effort: A theoretical, methodological, and empirical appraisal." *Psychological bulletin 81:*1053–1077; Ambrose and Kulik, "Old friends, new faces."

14. Alexander D. Stajkovic and Fred Luthans. (1997, October). "A meta-analysis of the effects of organizational behavior modification on task performance, 1975–95." *Academy of Management Journal 40:*1122–1149; H. Richlin, *Modern Behaviorism* (San Francisco: Freeman, 1970); and B. F. Skinner, *Science and Human Behavior* (New York: Macmillan, 1953).

15. Fred Goodman, "Suite Smarts," *Success,* January 1998, p. 11.

16. Stajkovic and Luthans, "A meta-analysis of the effects of organizational behavior modification on task performance, 1975–95."

17. H. Lancaster, "Given a second chance, a boss learns to favor carrots over sticks," *The Wall Street Journal,* November 30, 1999, p. B1.

18. Kenneth D. Butterfield and Linda Klebe Trevino. (1996, December). "Punishment from the manager's perspective: A grounded investigation and inductive model." *Academy of Management Journal 39*(6): 1479–1512; and Andrea Casey (1997). "Voices from the firing line: Managers discuss punishment in the workplace." *Academy of Management Executive 11* (3): 93–94.

19. Tom Peters and Nancy Austin, *A Passion for Excellence: The Leadership Difference* (New York: Random House, 1985), p. 267.

20. Roberta Maynard, "How to Motivate Low-Wage Workers," *Nation's Business,* May 1997, p. 35–39.

21. M. Somerson, "New Aneurysm Procedure Speeds Recovery for Patients," *Columbus Dispatch,* January 4, 2000, pp. 1A and 2A.

22. L. M. Sarri and G. P. Latham. (1982). "Employee reaction to continuous and variable ratio reinforcement schedules involving a monetary incentive." *Journal of Applied Psychology 67:* 506–508; and R. D. Pritchard, J. Hollenback, and P. J. DeLeo. (1980). "The effects of continuous and partial schedules of reinforcement on effort, performance, and satisfaction." *Organizational Behavior and Human Performace 25:*336–353.

23. "Creating Incentives for Hourly Workers," *Inc.,* July 1986, pp. 89–90.

24. A. Bandura, *Social Learning Theory* (Englewood Cliffs, NJ: Prentice Hall, 1977).

25. See, for example, M. E. Gist, C. Schwoerer, and B. Rosen. (1989). "Effects of alternative training methods on self-efficacy and performance in computer software training." *Journal of Applied Psychology 74:*884–891; M. E. Gist and T. R. Mitchell. (1992). "Self-efficacy: A theoretical analysis of its determinants and malleability." *Academy of Management Review 17:* 183–211.

26. E. A. Locke and G. P. Latham, *A Theory of Goal Setting and Task Performance* (Englewood Cliffs, NJ: Prentice Hall, 1990); G. P. Latham and E. A. Locke. (1991). "Self-regulation through goal setting." *Organizational Behavior and Human Decision Processes 50:*212–247.

27. Mark Fischetti, "Team Doctors, Report to ER!" *Fast Company,* February/Match 1998, pp. 170–177.

28. Gina Imperato, "Dirty Business, Bright Ideas," *Fast Company,* February/March 1997, pp. 80–93.

29. John O. Alexander, "Toward Real Performance: The Circuit-Breaker Technique," *Supervisory Management,* April 1989, pp. 5–12.

30. Cathy Lazere, "All Together Now," *CFO,* February 1998, pp. 29–36.

31. Joy Riggs, "Empowering Workers by Setting Goals," *Nation's Business,* January 1995, p. 6.

32. A. J. Vogl, "Noble Survivors," *Across the Board,* June 1994, pp. 25–30; and Rahul Jacob, "Corporate Reputations," *Fortune,* March 6, 1995, pp. 54–67.

33. Edwin A. Locke, Garp P. Latham, and Miriam Erez. (1988). "The determinants of goal commitment." *Academy of Management Review 13:* 23–29.

34. V. B. Hinsz, L. R. Kalnbach, and N. R. Lorentz. (1997). "Using judgmental anchors to establish challenging self-set goals without jeopardizing commitment." *Organizational Behavior and Human Decision Processes 71:*287–308.

35. Ambrose and Kulik, "Old friends, new faces: Motivation research in the 1990s."

36. E. Matson, "The Discipline of High-Tech Leaders," *Fast Company,* April/May 1997, pp. 34–36.

37. R. A. Noe, J. H. Hollenbeck, B. Gerhart, and P. Wright, *Human Resource Management,* 3rd ed. (Burr Ridge, IL: Irwin-McGraw-Hill, 1999).

38. M. S. Taylor, K. B. Tracy, M. K. Renard, J. K. Harrison, and S. J. Carroll. (1995). "Due process in performance appraisal: A quasi-experiment in procedural justice." *Administrative Science Quarterly 40:*495–523; J. M. Werner and M. C. Bolino. (1997). "Explaining U.S. court of appeals decisions involving performance appraisal: Accuracy, fairness, and validation." *Personnel Psychology 50:*1–24.

39. S. W. Gilliland and J. C. Langdon, "Creating Performance Management Systems That Promote Perceptions of Fairness," in J. M. Smither (ed.), *Performance Appraisal: State of the Art in Practice* (San Francisco: Jossey-Bass, 1998), pp. 209–243; R. Folger and M. A. Konovsky. (1989). "Effects of procedural and distributive justice on reactions to pay raise decisions." *Academy of Management Journal 32:*115–130.

40. F. Luthans and A. D. Stajkovic. (1999, May). "Reinforce for performance: The need to go beyond pay and even rewards." *Academy of Management Executive 13:*49–57; F. Luthans and R. Kreitner, *Organizational Behavior Modification* (Glenview, IL: Scott-Foresman, 1985).

41. J. Komaki, K. D. Bardwick, and L. R. Scott. (1978). "Pinpointing and reinforcing safe performance in a food manufacturing plant." *Journal of Applied Psychology 63:*434–445.

42. Stajkovic and Luthans. "A meta-analysis of the effects of organizational behavior modification on task performance, 1975-95."

43. George S. Odiorne. (1978, October). "MBO: A backward glance." *Business Horizons 21:*14–24.

44. Jan P. Muczyk and Bernard C. Reimann. (1989). "MBO as a complement to effective leadership." *The Academy of Management Executive 3:*131–138; and W. Giegold, *Objective Setting and the MBO Process,* vol. 2 (New York: McGraw-Hill, 1978).

45. "Delegation," *Small Business Reports,* July 1986, pp. 71–75; and R. Henry Migliore, Constance A. Pogue, and Jeffrey S. Horvath, "Planning for the Future," *Small Business Reports,* July 1991, pp. 53–63.

46. John Ivancevich, J. Timothy McMahon, J. William Streidl, and Andrew D. Szilagyi. (1978, Winter). "Goal setting: The Tenneco approach to personnel development and management effectiveness." *Organizational Dynamics:*48–80.

47. R. Eisenberger and J. Cameron. (1996). "Detrimental effects of reward: Reality or myth?" *American Psychologist 51:*1157.

48. G. Jenkins, A. Mitra, N. Gupta, and J. Shaw. (1998). "Are financial incentives related to performance? A meta-analytic review of empirical research." *Journal of Applied Psychology 83:* 777–787.

49. Geoffrey Colvin, "What Money Makes You Do," *Fortune,* August 17, 1998, pp. 213–214; R. Ganzel, "What's wrong with pay for performance?" *Training,* December 1998, pp. 35–40

50. Alfie Kohn, "Incentives Can Be Bad for Business," *Inc.,* January 1998, pp. 93–94; A. J. Vogl, "Carrots, Sticks, and Self-Deception" (an interview with Alfie Kohn), *Across the Board,* January 1994, pp. 39–44.

51. Edwin P. Hollander and Lynn R. Offermann. (1990, February). "Power and leadership in organizations." *American Psychologist 45*:179–189.

52. Jay A. Conger and Rabindra N. Kanungo. (1988). "The empowerment process: Integrating theory and practice." *Academy of Management Review 13:* 471–482.

53. Thomas A. Stewart, "New Ways to Exercise Power," *Fortune,* November 1989, pp. 52–64.

54. David E. Bowen and Edward E. Lawler III. (1992, Spring). "The empowerment of service workers: What, why, how, and when." *Sloan Management Review:* 31–39; and Ray W. Coye and James A. Belohav. (1995, March). "An exploratory analysis of employee participation." *Group and Organization Management 20* (1): 4–17.

55. John Holusha, "Grace Pastiak's 'Web of Inclusion,'" *The New York Times,* May 5, 1991, pp. F1, F6.

56. Arno Penzias, "New Paths to Success," *Fortune,* June 12, 1995, pp. 90–94.

57. Ralph Stayer, "How I Learned to Let My Workers Lead," *Harvard Business Review,* November–December 1990, pp. 66–83.

58. This discussion is based on Robert C. Ford and Myron D. Fottler. (1995). "Empowerment: A matter of degree." *Academy of Management Executive 9*(3):21–31.

59. Jay A. Cougar and Rabindra N. Kanungo. (1998). "The empowerment process: Integrating theory and practice." *Academy of Management Review 13:*471–482.

60. Oren Harari, "Good News/Bad News about Strategy," *Management & Review,* July 1995, pp. 29–31.

61. Gerald E. Ledford, Jr., Jon R. Wendenhof, and James T. Strahley. (1995, Winter)."Realizing a corporate philosophy." *Organizational Dynamics:*5–18.

62. James C. Collins, "Building Companies to Last," *The State of Small Business,* 1995, pp. 83–86; James C. Collins and Jerry I. Porras. (1995, Winter). "Building a visionary company." *California Management Review 37:*80–100; James C. Collins and Jerry I. Porras, "The Ultimate Vision," *Across the Board,* January 1995, pp. 19–23; and B. O'Reilly, "J&J Is on a Roll," *Fortune,* December 26, 1994, pp. 178–191.

63. See Kenneth R. Thompson, Wayne A. Hockwarter, and Nicholas J. Mathys. (1997, August). "Stretch targets: What makes them effective?" *Academy of Management Executive 11*(3):48.

64. Edward O. Welles, "Bootstrapping for Billions," *Inc.,* September 1994, pp. 78–83; also see Kenneth E. Iverson with Tom Varian, *Plain Talk: Lessons from a Business Maverick* (New York: John Wiley & Sons, 1997).

65. Henry Mintzberg, "The Fall and Rise of Strategic Planning," *Harvard Business Review,* January–February 1994, pp. 107–114.

66. Jay Finegan, "Everything According to Plan," *Inc.,* March 1995, pp. 78–85.

67. F. Jossi, "From Welfare to Work," *Training,* April 1997, pp. 45–50; D. Milbank, "Hiring welfare people, hotel chain finds is tough but rewarding," *The Wall Steet Journal,* October 31, 1996, pp. A1 and A14.

68. A. Bandura, *Social Foundations of Thought and Action: A Social Cognitive Theory* (Englewood Cliffs, NJ: Prentice-Hall, 1986).

69. Ambrose and Kulik, "Old friends, new faces: Motivation research in the 1990s."

70. A. J. Dubinsky, M. Kotabe, C. Lim, and R. E. Michaels. (1994). "Differences in motivational perceptions among U.S., Japanese, and Korean sales personnel." *Journal of Business Research 30:*175–185.

71. J. Pennings. (1993). "Executive reward systems: A cross-national comparison." *Journal of Management Studies 30:* 261–280.

72. K. Delaney and D. Wessel, "Suppose stock options involved more pain than financial gain," *The Wall Street Journal,* December 21, 1999, pp. A1 and A10.

CHAPTER 7

1. Emily Barker, "The Old Neighborhood," *Inc.,* May 1999, p. 65.

2. Carla Joinson, "Teams at Work," *HR Magazine,* May 1999, downloaded from the Society for Human Resource Management Web site, www.shrm.org, May 25, 1999.

3. E. H. Schein, *Organizational Psychology,* 3rd ed. (Englewood Cliffs, NJ: Prentice-Hall, 1980), p. 145.

4. Jill Hecht, "Fourteen Heads—and Budgets—Are Better than One," *Inside Technology Training,* March 1999, p. 37.

5. Small but Mighty," *Chicago Tribune,* January 16, 2000, sec. 6, pp. 1, 7.

6. Robert McGarvey, "Fun and Games," *Entrepreneur,* April 1999, pp. 82–84; digitalNATION Web site, www.dn.com, downloaded October 13, 1999.

7. Cécile Daurat, "Mixing Work and Play," *Forbes,* November 16, 1998, downloaded from the *Forbes* Web site, wwwforbes.com, November 6, 1998.

8. "For California Winemakers, the Business Is about Family," *Chicago Tribune,* June 20, 1999, sec. 5, p. 8.

9. See, for example, J. P. Wanous, A. E. Reichers, and S. D. Malik. (1984, October). "Organizational socialization and group development: Toward an integrative perspective." *Academy of Management Review:* 670–683.

10. B. W. Tuckman, "Developmental Sequences in Small Groups," *Psychological Bulletin,* June 1965, pp. 384–399; and B. W. Tuckman and M. A. C. Jensen, "Stages of Small-Group Development Revisited," *Group and Organization Studies,* December 1977, pp. 419–427.

11. Joinson, "Teams at Work," p. 4.

12. I*bid.,* pp. 4–5.

13. Linda N. Jewell and H. Joseph Reitz, *Group Effectiveness in Organizations* (Glenview, IL.: Scott, Foresman and Co., 1981), p. 22.

14. P. G. Zimbardo, C. Haney, W. C. Banks, and D. Jaffe, "The Mind Is a Formidable Jailer: A Pirandellian Prison," *The New York Times,* April 8, 1973, pp. 38–60.

15. Paul Orfalea, "My Biggest Mistake," *Inc.,* March 1999, p. 88.

16. R. C. Ginnett, "The Airline Cockpit Crew," in J. R. Hackman (ed.), *Groups That Work (and Those That Don't)* (San Francisco: Jossey-Bass, 1990).

17. Michael Krantz, "Steve Jobs at 44," *Time.com,* October 18, 1999, www.pathfinder.com.

18. Joinson, "Teams at Work."

19. Donna Fenn, "Domestic Policy," *Inc.,* November 1999, pp. 38–45.

20. *Ibid.*

21. Patricia Schiff Estess, "Inside Jobs," *Entrepreneur,* May 1999, pp. 88–89+.

22. "Wanted: CEO," *Entrepreneur,* April 1999, p. 90.

23. McGarvey, "Fun and Games," p. 82.

24. Erika Rasmusson, "Brief Case: Wild Ideas at Work," *Sales & Marketing Management,* July 1999, pp. 22–23.

25. O. J. Harvey and C. Consalvi. (1960, Spring). "Status and conformity to pressures in informal groups." *Journal of Abnormal and Social Psychology:*182–187.

26. See J. R. Hackman, "Group Influences on Individuals in Organizations," in M. D. Dunnette and L. M. Hough (eds.), *Handbook of Industrial and Organizational Psychology,* 2nd ed., vol. 3 (Palo Alto, CA.: Consulting Psychologists Press, 1992), p. 236.

27. J. A. Wiggins, F. Dill, and R. D. Schwartz, "On 'Status-Liability,'" *Sociometry,* April-May 1965, pp. 197–209.

28. George C. Homans, *The Human Group* (New York: Harcourt Brace, 1950).

29. Hope Katz Gibbs, "The ET List: 20 Top U.S. States," *Export Today,* April 1999, pp. 40–46; California Office of Foreign Investment Web site, www.commerce.ca.gov/international/ofi, downloaded October 13, 1999.

30. Gladys Montgomery Jones, "Fast-Track Partners," *Continental,* April 1998, pp. 27–29; David Stipp, "Why Pfizer Is So Hot,"

Fortune, May 11, 1998, downloaded from the Pfizer Web site, www.pfizer.com, October 13, 1999; Pfizer, "Pfizer Never Stronger as Company Celebrates 150th Anniversary, Steere Tells Shareholders at Annual Meeting," press release, April 22, 1999, downloaded from Pfizer Web site, www.pfizer.com, October 13, 1999; Warner-Lambert, "Warner-Lambert and Pfizer Agree to Continue and Expand Highly Successful Marketing Alliance," press release, June 16, 1999, downloaded from Warner-Lambert Web site, www.warner-lambert.com, October 13, 1999; "Warner-Lambert Facts 1999," downloaded from Warner-Lambert Web site, www.warner-lambert.com, October 13, 1999; Warner-Lambert, "Pfizer and Warner-Lambert Agree to $90 Billion Merger Creating the World's Fastest-Growing Major Pharmaceutical Company," news release, February 7, 2000, downloaded from Warner-Lambert Web site, www.warner-lambert.com, March 16, 2000.

31. Gibbs, "The ET List," p. 41.

32. C. F. Bond, Jr., and L. J. Titus, "Social Facilitation: A Meta-Analysis of 241 Studies," *Psychological Bulletin,* September 1983, pp. 265–292.

33. S. J. Zaccaro, "Social Loafing: The Role of Task Attractiveness," *Personality and Social Psychology Bulletin,* March 1984, pp. 99–106; J. M. Jackson and K. D. Williams. (1985, October). "Social loafing on difficult tasks: Working collectively can improve performance." *Journal of Personality and Social Psychology:* 937–943; and J. M. George. (1992, March). "Extrinsic and intrinsic origins of perceived social loafing in organizations." *Academy of Management Journal:*191–202.

34. K. Williams, S. Harkins, and B. Latane. (1981, February). "Identifiability as a deterrent to social loafing: Two cheering experiments." *Journal of Personality and Social Psychology:*303–311.

35. J. M. Jackson and S. G. Harkins. (1985, November). "Equity in effort: An explanation of the social loafing effect." *Journal of Personality and Social Psychology:*1199–1206.

36. S. G. Harkins and K. Szymanski. (1989, June). "Social loafing and group evaluation." *Journal of Personality and Social Psychology:*934–941.

37. J. A. Wagner III. (1995, February). "Studies of individualism-collectivism: Effects on cooperation in groups." *Academy of Management Journal:*152–172.

38. See P. C. Earley, "Social Loafing and Collectivism: A Comparison of the United States and the People's Republic of China," *Administrative Science Quarterly,* December 1989, pp. 565–581; and P. C. Earley. (1993, April). "East meets West meets Mideast: Further explorations of collectivistic and individualistic work groups." *Academy of Management Journal:*319–348.

39. Philip Yetton and Preston Bottger, "The Relationships among Group Size, Member Ability, Social Decision Schemes, and Performance," *Organizational Behavior and Human Performance,* October 1983, pp. 145–159.

40. E. J. Thomas and C. F. Fink, "Effects of Group Size," *Psychological Bulletin,* July 1963, pp. 371–384; A. P. Hare, *Handbook of Small Group Research* (New York: Free Press, 1976); and M. E. Shaw, *Group Dynamics: The Psychology of Small Group Behavior,* 3rd ed. (New York: McGraw-Hill, 1981).

41. M. E. Shaw, *Contemporary Topics in Social Psychology* (Morristown, NJ: General Learning Press, 1976), pp. 350–351.

42. See P. S. Goodman, E. C. Ravlin, and L. Argote, "Current Thinking about Groups: Setting the Stage for New Ideas," in P. S. Goodman *et al., Designing Effective Work Groups* (San Francisco: Jossey-Bass, 1986), pp. 15–16; R. A. Guzzo and G. P. Shea, "Group Performance and Intergroup Relations in Organizations," in M. D. Dunnette and L. M. Hough (eds.), *Handbook of Industrial and Organizational Psychology,* 2nd ed., vol. 3 (Palo Alto, CA.: Consulting Psychologists Press, 1992), pp. 288–290; and Shaw, *Contemporary Topics in Social Psychology,* p. 356.

43. Warren E. Watson, Kamalesh Kumar, and Larry K. Michaelsen. (1993, June). "Cultural diversity's impact on interaction process and performance: Comparing homogeneous and diverse task groups." *Academy of Management Journal 36*(3):590–602.

44. M. Hill, "Group versus Individual Performance: Are $N + 1$ Heads Better than One?" *Psychological Reports,* April 1982, pp. 517–539; and A. Tziner and D. Eden. (1985, February). "Effects of crew composition on crew performance: Does the whole equal the sum of its parts?" *Journal of Applied Psychology:*85–93.

45. See P. S. Goodman, E. Ravlin, and M. Schminke, "Understanding Groups in Organizations," in L. L. Cummings and B. M. Staw (eds.), *Research in Organizational Behavior,* vol. 9 (Greenwich, CT.:" JAI Press, 1987), pp. 124–128.

46. National Public Radio, *Morning Edition,* May 28, 1999.

47. Samuel Fromartz, "Rare Commodity," *Inc.,* October 19, 1999 (*Inc.* 500 special issue), pp. 169–170, 173–178.

48. Daniel Roth, "Meg Muscles eBay Uptown," *Fortune,* July 5, 1999, pp. 81–84+; Ann Grimes, "Hoaxes on eBay Raise Questions on Safeguards," *The Wall Street Journal,* January 7, 2000, p. B6.

49. Carla Joinson, "Don't Forget Your Shift Workers," *HR Magazine,* February 1999, downloaded from Society for Human Resource Management Web site, www.shrm.org, October 18, 1999.

50. *Ibid.*

51. See Rensis Likert, *New Patterns of Management* (New York: McGraw-Hill, 1961).

52. Malcolm Campbell, "The Best Manager in America," *Selling Power,* January/February 1999, pp. 51–56, 58; John Hogan, "Generating a Boundaryless Corporation," *Sam's Club Source,* June 1999, pp. 16–17, 19; "Web Exclusive: Jack Welch and Herbert Kelleher—Create Great Companies and Keep Them That Way," transcript of Fortune.com satellite broadcast, January 11, 1999, downloaded from Pathfinder Web site, http://cgi.pathfinder.com, March 26, 1999.

CHAPTER 8

1. N. Munk, "How Levi's Trashed a Great American Brand," *Fortune,* April 12, 1999, pp. 83–90; R. King, "Levi's Factory Workers Are Assigned to Teams, and Morale Takes a Hit," *The Wall Street Journal,* May 20, 1998, pp. A1 and A6.

2. Susan G. Cohen, Gerald E. Ledford, Jr., and Gretchen M. Spreitzer. (1996). "A predictive model of self-managing work team effectiveness." *Human Relations 49*(5):643–676: "Training in the 1990s," *The Wall Street Journal,* March 1, 1990, p. B1; and Patricia Booth, "Embracing the Team Concept," *Canadian Business Review,* Autumn 1994, pp. 10–13.

3. Rajiv D. Banker, Joy M. Field, Roger G. Schroeder, and Kingshuk K. Sinha. (1996). "Impact of work teams on manufacturing performance: A longitudinal field study." *Academy of Management Journal 39*(4):867–890.

4. Eric Schine, "Mattel's Wild Race to Market," *Business Week,* February 21, 1994, pp. 62–63; Frank V. Cespedes, Stephen X. Dole, and Robert J. Freedman, "Teamwork for Today's Selling," *Harvard Business Review,* March–April 1989, pp. 44–55; Victoria J. Marsick, Ernie Turner, and Lars Cederholm, "International Managers as Team Leaders," *Management Review,* March 1989, pp. 46–49; and "Team Goal-Setting," *Small Business Report,* January 1988, pp. 76–77.

5. Carl E. Larson and Frank M. J. LaFasto, *TeamWork* (Newbury Park, CA.: Sage, 1989).

6. C. Hymowitz, "How to Avoid Hiring the Prima Donnas Who Hate Team Work," *The Wall Street Journal,* February 15, 2000, p. B1.

7. Eric Sundstrom, Kenneth P. De Meuse, and David Futrell. (1990, February). "Work teams," *American Psychologist 45:* 120–133.

8. Deborah L. Gladstein. (1984). "Groups in context: A model of task group effectiveness." *Administrative Science Quarterly 29:*499–517.

9. Dora C. Lau and J. Keith Murnighan. (1998). "Demographic diversity and faultlines: The compositional dynamics of organizational groups." *Academy of Management Review* 23(2): 325–340.

10. Chuck Salter, "Roberts Rules of the Road," *Fast Company,* September 1998, pp. 114–128.

11. Gary Jacobson, "A Teamwork Ultimatum Puts Kimberly-Clark's Mill Back on the Map," *Management Review,* July 1989, pp. 28–31; "The 1999 *Fortune* 500 List," accessed December 13, 1999, at cgi.pathfinder.com; "America's Most Admired Companies: Kimberly-Clark Survey Results," accessed December 13, 1999, at cgi.pathfinder.com.

12. R. B. Zajonc. (1965). Social facilitation." *Science* 149:269–274; and Erez and Somech, "Is Group Productivity Loss the Rule or the Exception?"

13. "The Culture: K-C Work Environment," Kimberly-Clark Web site, accessed December 13, 1999, at www.kc-careers.com/culture.htm.

14. S. Caudron, "Diversity Ignites Effective Work Teams," *Personnel Journal,* September 1994, pp. 54–63.

15. Aaron Bernstein, "Detroit vs. the UAW: At Odds over Teamwork," *Business Week,* August 24, 1987, pp. 54–55.

16. Robert Albanese and David D. Van Fleet. (1985). "Rational behavior in groups: The free-riding tendency." *Academy of Management Review* 10:244–255.

17. Baron, Behavior in Organizations.

18. Harvey J. Brightman, *Group Problem Solving: An Improved Managerial Approach* (Atlanta: Georgia State University, 1988).

19. A. Bernstein, "Putting a Damper on That Old Team Spirit," *Business Week,* May 4, 1992, p. 60.

20. *Ibid.;* and Hoerr, "Is Teamwork a Management Plot? Mostly Not," 70.

21. Sundstrom, DeMeuse, and Futrell, "Work teams."

22. Susan Carey, "US Air Team Pilots Start-Up of Low-Fare Airline," *The Wall Street Journal,* March 24, 1998, p. B1.

23. "Participation Teams," *Small Business Report,* September 1987, pp. 38–41.

24. Gregory L. Miles, "Suddenly, USX Is Playing Mr. Nice Guy," *Business Week,* June 26, 1989, pp. 151–152.

25. Larson and LaFasto, *TeamWork.*

26. B. Fryer, "The ROI Challenge," *CFO,* September 1999, pp. 85–90.

27. James H. Shonk, *Team-Based Organizations* (Homewood, IL.: Business One Irwin, 1992); and John Hoerr, "The Payoff from Teamwork," *Business Week,* July 10, 1989, pp. 56–62.

28. Jeanne M. Wilson, Jill George, and Richard S. Wellings, with William C. Byham, *Leadership Trapeze: Strategies for Leadership in Team-Based Organizations* (San Francisco: Jossey-Bass, 1994).

29. Ruth Wageman, "Critical Success Factors for Creating Superb Self-Managing Teams," *Organizational Dynamics,* Summer 1997, pp. 49–61.

30. Thomas Owens, "The Self-Managing Work Team," *Small Business Report,* February 1991, pp. 53–65.

31. Mary Cianni and Donna Wnuck. (1997). "Individual growth and team enhancement: Moving toward a new model of career development." *Academy of Management Executive* 11(1): 105–115.

32. Brian Dumaine, "The Trouble with Teams," *Fortune,* September 5, 1994, pp. 86–92; and Brian Dumaine, "Who Needs a Boss?" *Fortune,* May 7, 1990. pp. 52–60.

33. A Townsend, S. DeMarie, and A. Hendrickson. (1998). "Virtual teams: Technology and the workplace of the future." *Academy of Management Executive* 12:17–29.

34. Dumaine, "The Trouble with Teams"; and Beverly Geber, "Virtual Teams," *Training,* April 1995, pp. 36–40.

35. K. Kiser, "Working on World Time," *Training,* March 1999, pp. 28–34.

36. William R. Pape, "Group Insurance," *Inc. Technology* 1997, no. 2, pp. 29, 31.

37. For research findings on group size, see M. E. Shaw, *Group Dynamics,* 3rd ed. (New York: McGraw-Hill, 1981); and G.

Manners. (1975). Another look at group size, group problem-solving and member consensus." *Academy of Management Journal* 18:715–724.

38. Shaw, *Group Dynamics.*

39. Daniel C. Feldman and Hugh J. Arnold, *Managing Individual and Group Behavior in Organizations* (New York: McGraw-Hill, 1983).

40. C. Joinson, "Teams at Work," *HR Magazine,* May 1999, pp. 30–36.

41. H. Campbell, "Evart Glass: Adventures in Teamland," *Personnel Journal,* May 1996, pp. 56–62.

42. Ricky W. Griffin, *Management* (Boston: Houghton Mifflin, 1990).

43. Dumaine, "Who Needs a Boss?"

44. Based on Kathleen M. Eisenhardt, Jean L. Kahwajy, and L. J. Bourgeois III, "How Management Teams Can Have a Good Fight," *Harvard Business Review,* July–August 1997, pp. 77–85.

45. J. Richard Hackman, "Group Influences on Individuals," in M. Dunnette (ed.), *Handbook of Industrial and Organizational Psychology* (Chicago: Rand McNally, 1976).

46. The following discussion is based on Daniel C. Feldman. (1984). "The development and enforcement of group norms." *Academy of Management Review* 9:47–53.

47. G. Flynn, "Grace Cocoa Associates: Optimas Award Profile," *Workforce,* June 1997, pp. 52–60.

48. Wilson *et al., Leadership Trapeze,* p. 12.

49. D. Anfuso, "City of Hampton, Virginia: Optimas Award Profile," *Personnel Journal,* December 1995, pp. 38–46.

50. S. Caudron, "Diversity Ignites Effective Work Teams," *Personnel Journal,* September 1994, pp. 54–63.

51. George Prince, "Recognizing Genuine Teamwork," *Supervisory Management,* April 1989, pp. 25–36; K. D. Benne and P. Sheats. (1948). "Functional roles of group members." *Journal of Social Issues* 4:41–49; and R. F. Bales, *SYMOLOG Case Study Kit* (New York: Free Press, 1980).

52. Robert A. Baron, *Behavior in Organizations,* 2nd ed. (Boston: Allyn & Bacon, 1986).

53. *Ibid.*

54. R. Banker, J. Filed, R. Schroeder, and K. Sinha. (1997). "Impact of work teams on manufacturing performance: A longitudinal study." *Academy of Management Journal* 39:867–890.

55. S. Caudron, "Strength in Numbers: Part Two," *Controller Magazine,* March 1996, p. 31.

56. Caudron, "Diversity Ignites Effective Work Teams."

57. M. Barrick, G. Stewart, M. Neubert, and M. Mount. (1998). "Relating member ability and personality to work-team processes and team effectiveness." *Journal of Applied Psychology* 83:377–391; G. Neuman and J. Wright. (1999). "Team effectiveness: Beyond skills and abilities." *Journal of Applied Psychology* 84:376–389; M. Stevens and M. Campion. (1999). "Staffing work teams: Development and validation of a selection test for teamwork settings." *Journal of Management* 25:207–228.

58. S. Overman, "No-frills HR at Nucor," *HR Magazine,* July 1994, pp. 56–60.

59. A Nurick. (1993, Winter). "Facilitating effective teams." *SAM Advanced Management Journal* 58:22–27.

60. D. Fenn, "Teams: A Formula for Success," *Inc.,* May 1, 1996.

61. Joinson, "Teams at Work."

62. E. Salas and J. Cannon-Bowers, "Strategies for Team Training," in M. Quinons and A. Dutta (eds.), *Training for 21st Century Technology: Applications for Psychological Research* (Washington, DC: American Psychological Association, 1997).

63. R. Oser, A. McCallum, E. Salas, and B. Morgan, "Toward a Definition of Teamwork: An Analysis of Critical Team Behaviors," technical report 89-004 (Orlando, FL: Naval Research Center, 1989); J. Hollenbeck, D. Ilgen, J. Colquitt, and J. Hedlund. (1998). "Extending the multilevel theory of team decision-making: Effects of feedback and experience in hierarchical teams." *Academy of Management Journal* 41:269–282.

64. B. Filipczak, "Concurrent Engineering," *Training,* August 1996, pp. 54–59.

65. D. Jaffe and C. Scott, "How to Link Personal Values with Team Values," *Training & Development,* March 1998, pp. 24–30.

66. Joinson, "Teams at Work."

67 *Ibid.*

68. B. Kirkman and B. Rosen. (1999). "Beyond self-management: Antecedents and consequences of team empowerment." *Academy of Management Journal 42:*58–74; B. Janz, J. Colquitt, and R. Noe. (1997). "Knowledge worker team effectiveness: The role of autonomy, interdependence, team development, and contextual support variables." *Personnel Psychology 50:*877–904; M. Campion, E. Papper, and G. Medsker. (1996). "Relations between work team characteristics and effectiveness: A replication and extension." *Personnel Psychology 49:*429–452.

69. Joinson, "Teams at Work."

70. Charles Fishman, "Whole Foods Is All Teams," *Fast Company,* April–May 1996, pp. 102–109.

CHAPTER 9

1. "Canon: Where Communication Is King," *Fortune,* August 2, 1999, p. S-4.

2. William J. Holstein, "Rage on the Runway," *U.S. News & World Report,* March 15, 1999, pp. 45–48.

3. John Grossmann, "We've Got to Start Meeting Like This," *Inc.,* April 1998, pp. 70–72, 74.

4. Jenny C. McCune, "The Change Makers," *Management Review* (downloaded from the American Management Association Web site, www.amanet.org, May 4, 1999).

5. Donna Fenn, "Redesign Work," *Inc.,* June 1999, pp. 75–76+.

6. Terry Higgins, "Communication Skills Valued by Employers," *Milwaukee Journal Sentinel,* January 20, 1999 (downloaded from the Dow Jones Interactive Publications Library, http://nrstglp.djnr.com, March 21, 2000).

7. Jerry Langdon, "Workplace Briefs," Gannett News Service, October 15, 1999 (downloaded from the Dow Jones Interactive Publications Library, http://nrstglp.djnr.com, March 21, 2000).

8. R. L. Daft, R. H. Lengel, and L. K. Trevino, "Message Equivocality, Media Selection, and Manager Performance: Implications for Information Systems," *MIS Quarterly,* September 1987, pp. 355–368.

9. Dana Ray, "Re: Think It Over," *Selling Power,* January/February 1999, pp. 28–30.

10. Robert Lee Hotz, "'Dumb' Math Error Blamed for Death of Martian Probe," *San Jose Mercury News,* October 1, 1999 (downloaded from the NewsLibrary Web site, www.newslibrary.com, November 4, 1999).

11. Norm Brodsky, "Parting Company," *Inc.,* March 1999, pp. 27–28.

12. See, for example, Deborah Tannen, *Talking from 9 to 5* (New York: William Morrow and Co., 1994), pp. 283–285.

13. Bill Spindle, "Nomura Restructuring Falters; Can Mr. Ujiie Still Remake the Firm?" *The Wall Street Journal,* September 3, 1999, pp. A1–A2.

14. "Web Exclusive: Jack Welch and Herbert Kelleher—Create Great Companies and Keep Them That Way," online interview with John Huey and Geoffrey Colvin, January 1, 1999 (transcript downloaded from Fortune.com at http://cgi.pathfinder.com, March 26, 1999).

15. See Robert H. Lengel and Richard L. Daft. (1988, August). "The selection of communication media as an executive skill." *Academy of Management Executive 2:*225–232; and Richard L. Daft and Robert H. Lengel. (1986, May). "Organizational information requirements, media richness, and structural design." *Managerial Science 32:*554–572.

16. Lauren Goldstein, "A Career Coach Tries to Make a Leader Out of Me," *Fortune,* September 6, 1999, pp. 290, 292.

17. Albert Mehrabian, *Silent Messages* (Belmont, CA.: Wadsworth, 1971); and Albert Mehrabian, "Communicating without Words," *Psychology Today,* September 1968, pp. 53–55.

18. Nancy J. Lyons, "The 90-Day Checkup," *Inc.,* March 1999, pp. 111–112.

19. R. C. Longworth, "Sarah Lee Silence about Departure Leaves Bitter Taste in Iowa Town," *Chicago Tribune,* June 27, 1999, sec. 5, pp. 1, 10.

20. Ken Anderson, "By the (Open) Book," *Inc. Technology,* September 15, 1999, pp. 33–34.

21. Robert L. Simison, "Ford's Heir-Apparent Is a Maverick," *The Wall Street Journal,* February 13, 1998 (reprinted in *Continental,* April 1998, pp. 57–59); Kathleen Kerwin, "Nasser: Ford Be Nimble," *Business Week,* September 27, 1999 (downloaded from the Dow Jones Publications Library, www.dowjones.com, November 4, 1999); Kathleen Kerwin, "Remaking Ford," *Business Week,* October 11, 1999 (downloaded from the Dow Jones Publications Library, www.dowjones.com, November 4, 1999); and Eryn Brown, "9 Ways to Win on the Web," *Fortune,* May 24, 1999 (downloaded from Fortune.com at http://cgi.pathfinder.com, May 4, 1999).

22. Barbara Ettorre, "Hellooo, Anybody Listening?" *Management Review,* November 1997, p. 9.

23. S. J. Modic, "Grapevine Rated Most Believable," *Industry Week,* May 15, 1989, pp. 11, 14.

24. See L. Hirschhorn, "Managing Rumors," in L. Hirschhorn (ed.), *Cutting Back* (San Francisco: Jossey-Bass, 1983), pp. 49–52.

25. Gerald M. Goldhaber, *Organizational Communication,* 4th ed. (Dubuque, IA: William C. Brown, 1980); and Philip V. Louis, *Organizational Communication,* 3rd ed. (New York: Wiley, 1987).

26. Donald B. Simmons, "The Nature of the Organizational Grapevine," *Supervisory Management,* November 1985, pp. 39–42; "Spread the Word: Gossip Is Good," *The Wall Street Journal,* October 4, 1988, p. B1.

27. A. Bavelas and D. Barrett. (1951). "An experimental approach to organization communication." *Personnel 27:*366–371; and M. E. Shaw, *Group Dynamics: The Psychology of Small Group Behavior* (New York: McGraw-Hill, 1976).

28. James Coates and Jon Van, "CEOs Connect with the Web," *Chicago Tribune,* May 3, 1999, sec. 4, pp. 1, 9.

29. Jill Amadio, "Upward Mobility," *Entrepreneur,* pp. 52, 54–55.

30. Emily Kay, "The Next Small Thing," *Inside Technology Training,* March 1999, pp. 24–26.

31. Gene Koprowski, "Directing Traffic," *Entrepreneur,* April 1999, p. 32.

32 Jill Amadio, "In Your Face," *Entrepreneur,* April 1999, p. 64.

33. Jon Van, "Sprint PCS to Offer Wireless Internet Service," *Chicago Tribune,* August 12, 1999. sec. 3, p. 3.

34. Stephen Franklin, "Longer Days Not Always Time Well Spent," *Chicago Tribune,* June 27, 1999, sec. 5, p. 1.

35. Laura Pincus Hartman, "The Rights and Wrongs of Workplace Snooping," *Journal of Business Strategy,* May–June 1998 (downloaded from the Northern Light Web site, http://library.northernlight.com, November 8, 1999).

36. Tom Diederich, "Report Shows Monitoring of Employees on the Rise," *Computerworld,* April 26, 1999 (downloaded from the Northern Light Web site, http://library.northernlight.com, November 8, 1999).

37. Michael J. McCarthy, "Web Surfers Beware: The Company Tech May Be a Secret Agent," *The Wall Street Journal,* January 10, 2000, pp. A1, A12.

38. National Public Radio, *Morning Edition,* October 21, 1999 (audio recording downloaded from the NPR Web site, www.npr.org, November 8, 1999).

39. Hartman, "The Rights and Wrongs of Workplace Snooping."

40. *Ibid.;* and Edward Cone, "Privacy Rights and Wrongs," *Windows Magazine,* July 1999 (downloaded from the Northern Light Web site, http://northernlight.com, November 8, 1999).

41. McCarthy, "Web Surfers Beware," p. A12.

42. Cone, "Privacy Rights and Wrongs."

43. McCune, "The Change Makers."

44. "CIO Panel: Knowledge-Sharing Roundtable," *Information*

Week, April 26, 1999 (downloaded from the Information Week Web site, www.informationweek.com, April 30, 1999).

45. Mary G. Gotschall, "Bankers Trust Invests in Knowledge Management" (downloaded from http://webcom.com, April 28, 1999); "Acquisition of Bankers Trust Successfully Closed," press release, June 4, 1999 (downloaded from the Deutsche Bank Web site, www.deutsche-bank.com, November 8, 1999).

46. Peter F. Drucker, *Management Challenges for the 21st Century* (New York: HarperBusiness, 1999), pp. 123–125.

47. David Barber, "Star Techs," *Inc. Technology,* September 15, 1999, pp. 42–44+.

48. Richard L. Daft and Robert H. Lengel, "Information Richness: A New Approach to Managerial Behavior and Organizational Design," in B. Staw and L. Cummings (eds.), *Research in Organizational Behavior 6* (Greenwich, CT.: JAI Press, 1984), pp. 191–233; and Lengel and Daft, "The Selection of Communication Media as an Executive Skill."

49. Jill Andresky Fraser, "Money Talk," *Inc.,* September 1999, pp. 109–110, 112.

50. Leigh Buchanan, "Sticks, Stones . . . and a Challenge," *Inc. Technology,* September 15, 1999, p. 18.

51. Goldhaber, *Organizational Communication,* p. 189.

52. Ilan Mochari, "How Motley Fools Talk Back," *Inc.,* June 1999, p. 108.

53. Dale K. DuPont, "Tools for Encouraging Employee Suggestions," *HR Magazine,* September 1999 (downloaded from the Society for Human Resource Management Web site, www.shrm.org, October 18, 1999).

54. Grossmann, "We've Got to Start Meeting Like This," p. 72.

55. "Web Exclusive."

56. Tyler Maroney, "Quantum Design: A Cube with a View," *Fortune,* August 2, 1999, p. 242; and Quantum Web site, www.quantum.com (downloaded November 8, 1999).

57. Jeffrey Zygmont, "Parting a Sea of E-Mail," *Inc. Technology,* June 15, 1999, pp. 106, 108–109.

58. "CIO Panel."

CHAPTER 10

1. John J. Byczkowski, "Over the Digital Rhine," *The Cincinnati Enquirer,* October 24, 1999, pp. A1, A19; home page for Synchrony Communications Web site (accessed December 9, 1999).

2. Ronald A. Howard. (1988). "Decision analysis: Practice and promise." *Management Science 34:*679–695.

3. Norm Brodsky, "A Moving Experience," *Inc.,* May 1999, pp. 25–26.

4. See E. F. Harrison, *The Managerial Decision-Making Process,* 4th ed. (Boston: Houghton Mifflin, 1995), pp. 75–85; H. A. Simon. (1986, October). "Rationality in psychology and economics." *Journal of Business:*209–224; and A. Langley. (1989, December). "In search of rationality: The purposes behind the use of formal analysis in organizations." *Administrative Science Quarterly:*598–631.

5. For a discussion of the assumptions of the rational decision-making model, see J. G. March, *A Primer on Decision Making* (New York: Free Press, 1994), pp. 2–7.

6. Larry Armstrong, "E-tailers Keep Giving Away the Store," *Business Week,* January 10, 2000, p. 44.

7. Thomas Petzinger Jr., "A Humanist Executive Leads by Thinking in Broader Terms," *The Wall Street Journal,* April 16, 1999, p. B1.

8. Lillian Vernon, "My Biggest Mistake," *Inc.,* August 1999, p. 109.

9. James G. March and Herbert A. Simon, *Organizations* (New York: Wiley, 1958); Herbert A. Simon, *Administrative Behavior,* 2nd ed. (New York: Free Press, 1957); and Herbert A. Simon, "Altruism and Economics," *American Economic Review,* May 1993, pp. 156–161.

10. Lauran Neergaard, "Report Cites Deadly Medical Errors," Associated Press (downloaded from America Online, www.

aol.com, December 1, 1999); Institute of Medicine, "Preventing Death and Injury from Medical Errors Requires Dramatic, System-wide Changes," press release, November 29, 1999 (downloaded from the National Academies Web site, www.nationalacademies.org, December 1, 1999); National Public Radio, *All Things Considered,* November 30, 1999 (downloaded from the NPR Web site, www.npr.org, December 1, 1999).

11. Herbert A. Simon, *Models of Man* (New York: Wiley, 1957), pp. 196–205; and Simon, *Administrative Behavior.*

12. Owen Ullmann. "Treasury and the Fed Were Never This Close," *Business Week,* May 31, 1999, p. 41.

13. C. E. Lindholm, "The Science of 'Muddling Through,'" *Public Administration Review,* Spring 1959, pp. 79–88.

14. James W. Fredrickson. (1985). "Effects of decision motive and organizational performance level on strategic decision processes." *Academy of Management Journal 28:*821–843; James W. Fredrickson. (1984). "The comprehensiveness of strategic decision processes: Extension, observations, future directions." *Academy of Management Journal 27:*445–466; James W. Dean Jr. and Mark P. Sharfman. (1993, July). "Procedural rationality in the strategic decision-making process." *Journal of Management Studies 30*(4):587–610; Nandini Rajagopalan, Abdul M. A. Rasheed, and Deepak K. Datta. (1993). "Strategic decision processes: Critical review and future directions." *Journal of Management 19*(2):349–384; and Paul J. H. Schoemaker. (1993, January). "Strategic decisions in organizations: Rational and behavioral views." *Journal of Management Studies 30*(1):107–129.

15. D. L. Rados. (1972, June). "Selection and evaluation of alternatives in repetitive decision making." *Administrative Science Quarterly:*196–206.

16. "Fast Track," *Entrepreneur,* October 1999, p. 52.

17. Karen Dillon, "The Perfect Decision," *Inc.,* October 1998, pp. 74–76, 78 (interview with Howard Raiffa, John S. Hammond, and Ralph L. Keeney).

18. Mark Henricks, "Beneath the Surface," *Entrepreneur,* October 1999, pp. 108, 110, 113.

19. Lee H. Smith, "If You Come . . . They Will Build It," *Inc.,* November 1999, pp. 94–96+.

20. Brad Stone, "Amazon's Pet Projects," *Newsweek,* June 21, 1999, p. 56.

21. Darren McDermott, "For Bankers, a Job Lost Is Often an Opportunity Gained," *The Wall Street Journal,* April 13, 1999, pp. B1, B14.

22. N. Harvey. (1995, September). "Why are judgments less consistent in less predictable task situations?" *Organizational Behavior and Human Decision Processes:*247–263; J. W. Dean Jr. and M. P. Sharfman. (1996, April). "Does decision process matter? A study of strategic decision-making effectiveness." *Academy of Management Journal:*368–396; S. W. Gilliland, N. Schmitt, and L. Wood. (1993, November). "Cost-benefit determinants of decision process and accuracy." *Organizational Behavior and Human Decision Processes:*308–330.

23. Ilan Mochari, "Too Much, Too Soon," *Inc.,* November 1999, p. 119.

24. Joshua Macht, "By the Numbers," *Inc.,* May 1999, p. 53; Archives management Web site (www.archivesmanagement.com, downloaded December 2, 1999); Joe Coombs, "Company Delivers Documents That It Stores," *Waterbury Republican-American,* September 5, 1999 (downloaded from the Archives Management Web site, December 2, 1999).

25. Stanley Marcus, "My Biggest Mistake," *Inc.,* July 1999, p. 95.

26. Lee Roy Beach and Terence R. Mitchell. (1978, July). "A contingency model for the selection of decision strategies." *Academy of Management Review:*439–444.

27. James Coates and Darnell Little, "Thirst for Knowledge Drowns Site," *Chicago Tribune,* October 27, 1999, sec. 3, pp. 1, 3.

28. Robert McGarvey, "Take a Load Off!" *Entrepreneur,* August 1999, pp. 78–79.

29. Lambeth Hochwald, "Caution: Global Selling Can Be Hazardous to Your Company's Health," *Sales & Marketing Management,* July 1999, pp. 80–86.

30. Ron MacLean, "Big Manager on Campus," *Inc.,* October 19, 1999 (*Inc.* 500 issue), pp. 62–64, 66.

31. Robert Block, "How Big Mac Kept from Becoming a Serb Archenemy," *The Wall Street Journal,* September 3, 1999, pp. B2–B3.

32. Hal Lancaster, "An Ex-CEO Reflects: H-P's Platt Regrets He Wasn't a Rebel," *The Wall Street Journal,* November 16, 1999, p. B1 (interview with Lewis Platt).

33. Carol Gentry, "New Rules Hurt HMOs Caring for Ill at Home," *The Wall Street Journal,* November 16, 1999, pp. B1, B4.

34. Scott S. Smith. "Dell on . . . ." *Entrepreneur,* April 1999, pp. 121–123.

35. Jeffrey L. Seglin, "ROM Service," *Inc. Technology,* September 15, 1998, pp. 103–105.

36. Herbert A. Simon, *The New Science of Management Decision* (New York: Harper & Row, 1960), pp. 5–6.

37. Ilan Mochari, "The Screen Machine," *Inc.,* October 19, 1999 (*Inc.* 500 issue), pp. 198, 201.

38. Tim Larimer, "The Japan Syndrome," *Time,* October 11, 1999, pp. 50–51.

39. Barry Newman, "The 'National Interest' Causes INS to Wander Down Peculiar Paths," *The Wall Street Journal,* August 20, 1998, pp. A1, A6.

40. Susan Chandler, "Lands' End Ad Aimed at German Ruling," *Chicago Tribune,* September 25, 1999, sec. 2, p. 2.

41. Herbert A. Simon, *The New Science of Management* (Englewood Cliffs, NJ: Prentice-Hall, 1977), p. 47.

42. Ann Winblad, "My Biggest Mistake," *Inc.,* December 1999, p. 115 (from an interview with Mike Hofmann).

43. Donald E. Conlon and Howard Garland. (1993). "The role of project completion information in resource allocation decision." *Academy of Management Journal* 36(2):402–413.

44. Alex Taylor II, "Kellogg Cranks Up Its Idea Machine," *Fortune,* pp. 181–182; Lisa Singhania, "Kellogg to Unveil 5 New Cereals," Associated Press, November 30, 1999 (downloaded from Yahoo! Finance, http://biz.yahoo.com, December 2, 1999); Emily Kaiser, "Kellogg Says Turnaround on Track," Reuters, November 30, 1999 (downloaded from Yahoo! News, http://dailynews.yahoo.com, December 2, 1999).

45. Andre L. Delbecq, Andrew H. Van de Ven, and David H. Gustafson, *Group Techniques for Program Planning* (Glenview, IL: Scott, Foresman, 1975).

46. Emily Barker, "The Pentagram Papers," *Inc.,* September 1999, pp. 58–64.

47. Ilan Mochari, "By the Numbers," *Inc.,* November 1999, p. 123.

48. Richard A. Guzzo and James A. Waters. (1982, February). "The expression of affect and the performance of decision making groups." *Journal of Applied Psychology:*67–74; Dean Tjosvold and R. H. G. Field. (1983, September). "Effects of social context on consensus and majority vote decision making." *Academy of Management Journal:*500–506; Fredrick C. Miner Jr. (1984, Winter). "Group versus individual decision making: An investigation of performance measures, decision strategies, and process losses/gains." *Organizational Behavior and Human Decision Processes:*112–124.

49. Diane M. Mackie, M. Cecilia Gastardo-Conaco, and John J. Skelly, (1992, April). "Knowledge of the advocated position and the processing of in-group and out-group persuasive messages." *Personality and Social Psychology Bulletin:*145–151.

50. Leonard Pitts Jr., "My Morbid Imagination Takes Me on an Awful Flight," *Chicago Tribune,* November 30, 1999, sec. 1, p. 25.

51. Irving L. Janis, *Group Think,* 2nd ed. (Boston: Houghton Mifflin, 1982), p. 9; Glen Whyte. (1989). "Groupthink reconsidered." *Academy of Management Review* 14:40–56; and Brian Mullen, Tara Anthony, Eduardo Salas, and James E. Driskell. (1994, May). "Group cohesiveness and quality of decision

52. Victor H. Vroom and Philip W. Yetton, *Leadership and Decision Making* (Pittsburgh, PA.: University of Pittsburgh Press, 1973); and Victor H. Vroom and Arthur G. Jago, *The New Leadership: Managing Participation in Organizations* (Englewood Cliffs, NJ: Prentice-Hall, 1988).

53. R. H. G. Field and R. J. House. (1990, June). "A test of the Vroom-Yetton model using manager and subordinate reports." *Journal of Applied Psychology:*362–366; R. J. Paul and Y. M. Ebadi. (1989, September). "Leadership decision making in a service organization: A field test of the Vroom-Yetton model." *Journal of Occupational Psychology:*201–211; Jennifer T. Ettling and Arthur G. Jago. (1988). "Participation under conditions of conflict: More on the validity of the Vroom-Yetton model." *Journal of Management Studies* 25:73–83; A. Crouch and P. Yetton. (1987, June). "Manager behavior, leadership style, and subordinate performance: An empirical extension of the Vroom-Yetton conflict rule." *Organizational Behavior and Human Decision Processes:*384–396; Madeline E. Heilman, Harvey A. Hornstein, Jack H. Cage, and Judith K. Herschlag. (1984, February). "Reactions to prescribed leader behavior as a function of role perspective: The case of the Vroom-Yetton model." *Journal of Applied Psychology:*50–60; and Arthur G. Jago and Victor H. Vroom. (1982, December). "Some differences in the incidence and evaluation of participative leader behavior." *Journal of Applied Psychology:*776–783.

54. David M. Schweiger and William R. Sandberg. (1989). "The utilization of individual capabilities in group approaches to strategic decision-making." *Strategic Management Journal* 10:31–43; and "The Devil's Advocate," *Small Business Report,* December 1987, pp. 38–41.

55. Norman Dalkey, *The Delphi Method: An Experimental Study of Group Opinion* (Santa Monica, CA: Rand Corp., 1969).

56. Susan Greco, "Where Great Ideas Come From," *Inc.,* April 1998, pp. 76–77+.

57. Richard W. Woodman, John E. Sawyer, and Ricky W. Griffin. (1993). "Toward a theory of organizational creativity." *Academy of Management Review* 18(2):293–321.

58. Greco, "Where Great Ideas Come From," p. 85.

59. Christopher Caggiano, "Photo Opportunities," *Inc.,* May 1999, pp. 104–105 (interview with Nick Graham); Joe Boxer Web site (www.joeboxer.com, downloaded November 2, 1999).

60. Lisa K. Gundry, Jill R. Kickul, and Charles W. Prather. (1994, Spring). "Building the creative organization." *Organizational Dynamics:*22–37.

61. C. G. Morris, *Psychology: An Introduction,* 9th ed. (Upper Saddle River, NJ: Prentice Hall, 1996), p. 344.

62. M. A. Colgrove. (1968). "Stimulating creative problem solving: Innovative set." *Psychological Reports* 22:1205–1211.

63. Mark Henricks, "Daydream Believers," *Entrepreneur,* May 1999, pp. 78, 80–81.

64. David H. Freedman, "Got Guts?" *Inc.,* March 1999, pp. 50–52+ (interview with Robert Lutz).

65. Jeff Borden, "A Collision of Media," *Crain's Chicago Business,* June 7, 1999, "2000 & Beyond" sec., pp. E35–E36.

66. See P. B. Paulus, T. S. Larey, and A. H. Ortega. (1995, August). "Performance and perceptions of brainstormers in an organizational setting." *Basic and Applied Social Psychology:*249–265; and R. Zemke, "In Search of . . . : Are Your Quality Teams Getting Tired of Using Traditional Brainstorming to Solve Problems? It's Not the Only Way to Generate Solutions," *Training,* January 1993, pp. 46–52.

67. Donna Fenn, "Niche Picking," *Inc.,* October 1999, pp. 97–98.

68. Leigh Buchanan, "Accentuate the Negative," *Inc. Technology,* September 15, 1999, p. 15.

69. Fenn, "Niche Picking," p. 98.

70. Dillon, "The Perfect Decision," p. 75 (quoting John S. Hammond).

71. Phaedra Hise, "Avoid the Stuff That Sucks," *Inc.,* October 19, 1999 (*Inc.* 500 issue), pp. 195–196.

72. Jack Stack, "The Training Myth," *Inc.,* August 1998, pp. 41–42.

73. Rob Kaiser, "Brunswick to Follow Bike Path to China," *Chicago Tribune,* January 14, 2000, sec. 3, pp. 1–2.

74. Ann Marie Kerwin, "ASME Maps Out 'Uncharted Water' in New Guidelines," *Advertising Age,* April 19, 1999, p. 4.

75. Cathy Booth, "Worst of Times," *Time,* November 15, 1999, pp. 79–80.

76. N. J. Adler, *International Dimensions of Organizational Behavior,* 2nd ed. (Boston: Kent Publishing, 1991), pp. 160–168.

77. "The Kremlin's Housekeeper," *The Economist,* September 18, 1999, p. 76.

78. Amy Barrett, "Marty Wygod Rides Again," *Business Week,* August 2, 1999, pp. 89–90.

79. Michael Schrage, "Do You Strive to Be Tough, Yet Fair? Leadership by the Numbers," *Fortune,* September 6, 1999, p. 294.

80. Michael Krantz, "The Next E-volution," *Time,* July 12, 1999, p. 47.

81. Leigh Buchanan, "Invention Machine Builds Software Bridges across Engineers' Knowledge Gaps," *Inc.,* November 1999, p. 100.

82. Jean Thilmany, "OfficeMax: Balanced Staffing Levels Lift Sales," *Executive Technology,* June 1999, p. 28.

CHAPTER 11

1. "Coach Bio: Phil Jackson," http://www.nba.com/lakers/bios/coach.html, accessed May 19, 2000; Paul Buker, "The Man with the Jewelry," *OregonLive,* Monday, May 22, 2000, http://www.oregonlive.com, accessed May 22, 2000; Brian S. Moskal, "Running with the Bulls," *IW,* January 8, 1996, pp. 26–34; Charley Rosen, "No More Bull," *Cigar Aficionado,* September–October 1998, http://www.cigaraficionado.com/Cigar/Aficionado/people/fe1098.html; "The NBA at 50: Phil Jackson," http://nba.com/history/jackson_50.html; and Review of *Scared Hoops,* from *Booklist,* September 1, 1995, accessed online at http://liss.hypermart.net/basketball/books/people/jackson_phil/sacred_h.../sacred_hoops_.ht.

2. Kenneth Labich, "Fasten Your Seat Belts," *Fortune,* May 10, 1999, pp. 114–118.

3. Charles Pappas, "The Top 20 Best-Paid Women in Corporate America," *Working Woman,* February 1998, pp. 26–39; Sharon Nelton, "Men, Women, and Leadership," *Nation's Business,* May 1991, pp. 16–22; B. Dumaine, "America's Toughest Bosses," *Fortune,* October 18, 1993, pp. 39–50; "Chief Linda Wachner Got About $9.8 Million for Year," *The Wall Street Journal,* April 11, 1996, p. B10; and Esther Wachs Book, "Leadership for the Millenium," *Working Woman,* March 1998, pp. 29–34.

4. Warren Bennis and Burt Nanus, *Leaders: The Strategies for Taking Charge* (New York: Harper & Row, 1985), p. 4; James MacGregor Burns, *Leadership* (New York: Harper & Row, 1978), p. 2.

5. J. Meindl, S. Ehrlich, and J. Dukerich. (1985). "The romance of leadership." *Administrative Science Quarterly 30:* 78–102.

6. "By the Numbers: Director's Set," in *Success,* August 1998, p. 14.

7. Joseph C. Rost, *Leadership for the Twenty-First Century* (Westport, CT: Praeger, 1993), p. 102.

8. Robert E. Kelley, "In Praise of Followers," *Harvard Business Review,* November-December 1988, pp. 142–148.

9. Mary Parker Follett, quoted in "A Guru Ahead of Her Time," *Nation's Business,* May 1997, p. 24.

10. Patricia Sellers, "These Women Rule," *Fortune,* October 25, 1999, pp. 94–126.

11. Kelley, "In Praise of Followers"; Ira Chaleff, *The Courageous Follower: Standing Up To and For Our Leaders* (San Francisco, CA: Berrett-Koehler, 1995).

12. Kelly, "In Praise of Followers."

13. Chaleff, *The Courageous Follower.*

14. D. E. Whiteside, *Command Excellence: What It Takes to Be the Best!* (Washington, DC: Department of the Navy, Naval Military Personnel Command, 1985).

15. Based on Kelley, "In Praise of Followers," and Richard L. Daft, *Leadership: Theory and Practice* (Fort Worth, TX: The Dryden Press, 1997), pp. 397–410.

16. Gary A. Yukl, *Leadership in Organizations* (Englewood Cliffs, NJ: Prentice-Hall, 1994), pp. 254–255; and S. C. Kohs and K. W. Irle. (1920). "Prophesying Army promotion." *Journal of Applied Psychology 4:* 73–87.

17. Thomas A. Stewart, "Leaders of the Future: Have You Got What It Takes?" *Fortune,* October 11, 1999, pp. 318–322.

18. Kurt Lewin. (1939). "Field theory and experiment in social psychology: Concepts and methods." *American Journal of Sociology 44:* 868–896; K. Lewin and R. Lippett. (1938). "An experimental approach to the study of autocracy and democracy: A preliminary note." *Sociometry 1:* 292–300; and K. Lewin, R. Lippett, and R. K. White. (1939). "Patterns of aggressive behavior in experimentally created social climates." *Journal of Social Psychology 10:* 271–301.

19. R. Tannenbaum and W. H. Schmidt. (1958). "How To choose a leadership pattern." *Harvard Business Review 36:* 95–101.

20. F. A. Heller and G. A. Yukl. (1969). "Participation, managerial decision making, and situational variables." *Organizational Behavior and Human Performance 4:* 227–241.

21. John Peterman, "The Rise and Fall of the J. Peterman Company," *Harvard Business Review,* September-October 1999, pp. 59–66.

22. C. A. Schriesheim and B. J. Bird. (1979). "Contributions of the Ohio State studies to the field of leadership." *Journal of Management 5:* 135–145; and C. L. Shartle. (1979). "Early years of the Ohio State leadership studies." *Journal of Management 5:* 126–134.

23. P. C. Nystrom. (1978). "Managers and the high-high leader myth." *Academy of Management Journal 21:* 325–331; and L. L. Larson, J. G. Hunt, and Richard N. Osborn. (1976). "The great high-high leader behavior myth: A lesson form Occam's razor." *Academy of Management Journal 19:* 628–641.

24. Renisis Likert. (1979). "From production- and employee-centeredness to systems 1–4." *Journal of Management 5:* 147–156.

25. Robert Blake and Jane S. Mouton, *The Managerial Grid III* (Houston, TX: Gulf, 1985).

26. William C. Symonds, "The Power of the Paycheck," *Business Week,* May 24, 1999, pp. 71–72; and Katharine Mieszkowski, "Changing Tires, Changing the World," *Fast Company,* October 1999, pp. 58–60.

27. Fred E. Fiedler. (1954). "Assumed similarity measures as predictors of team effectiveness." *Journal of Abnormal and Social Psychology 49:* 381–388; Fred E. Fiedler, *Leader Attributes and Group Effectiveness* (Urbana, IL: University of Illinois Press, 1958); and Fred E. Fiedler, *A Theory of Leadership Effectiveness* (New York: McGraw-Hill, 1967).

28. Fred. E. Fiedler and M. M. Chemers, *Leadership and Effective Management* (Glenview, IL: Scott, Foresman, 1974).

29. Fred E. Fiedler. (1965). "Engineer the job to fit the manager." *Harvard Business Review 43:* 115–122; and F. E. Fiedler, M. M. Chemers, and L. Mahar, *Improving Leadership Effectiveness: The Leader Match Concept* (New York: Wiley, 1976).

30. Carl Quintanilla, "Maytag's Top Officer, Expected to Do Little, Surprises His Board," *The Wall Street Journal,* June 23, 1998, pp. A1, A8.

31. R. Singh. (1983). "Leadership style and reward allocation: Does least preferred coworker scale measure tasks and relation orientation?" *Organizational Behavior and Human Performance 27:* 178–197; and D. Hosking. (1981). "A critical evaluation of Fiedler's contingency hypotheses." *Progress in Applied Psychology 1:* 103–154.

32. Paul Hersey and Kenneth H. Blanchard, *Management of Organizational Behavior: Utilizing Human Resources,* 4th ed. (En-

glewood Cliffs, NJ: Prentice-Hall, 1982); and Kenneth H. Blanchard, Drea Zigarmi, and Robert B. Nelson. (1993). "Situational leadership after 25 years: A retrospective." *The Journal of Leadership Studies 1*(1): 22–36.

33. Michael Barrier, "Leadership Skills Employees Respect," *Nation's Business,* January 1999.

34. M. G. Evans. (1970). "The effects of supervisory behavior on the path-goal relationship." *Organizational Behavior and Human Performance 5:* 227–298; M. G. Evans, (1970). "Leadership and motivation: A core concept." *Academy of Management Journal 13:* 91–102; and B. S. Georgopoulos, G. M. Mahoney, and N. W. Jones. (1957). "A path-goal approach to productivity." *Journal of Applied Psychology 41:* 343–353.

35. Robert J. House. (1971). "A path-goal theory of leader effectiveness." *Administrative Science Quarterly 16:* 321–338.

36. M. G. Evans, "Leadership," in S. Kerr (ed.) *Organizational Behavior* (Columbus, OH: Grid, 1974), pp. 230–233.

37. Robert J. House and Terrence R. Mitchell. (1974, Autumn). "Path-goal theory of leadership." *Journal of Contemporary Business:* 81–97.

38. James O'Toole, *Leading Change: The Argument for Values-Based Leadership* (San Francisco: Jossey-Bass, 1995).

39. Mike Hofman, "Everyone's a Cost-Cutter," *Inc.,* July 1998, p. 117; and Abby Livingston, "Gain-Sharing Encourages Productivity," *Nation's Business,* January 1998, pp. 21–22.

40. R. T. Keller. (1989, April). "A test of the path-goal theory of leadership with need for clarity as a moderator in research and development organizations." *Journal of Applied Psychology:* 208–212; J. C. Wofford and L. Z. Liska. (1993, Winter). "Path-goal theories of leadership: A meta-analysis." *Journal of Management:* 857–876; Charles Greene. (1979, March). "Questions of causation in the path-goal theory of leadership." *Academy of Management Journal 22:* 22–41; and C. A. Schriesheim and Mary Ann von Glinow. (1977). "The path-goal theory of leadership: A theoretical and empirical analysis." *Academy of Management Journal 20:* 398–405.

41. S. Kerr and J. M. Jermier. (1978, December). "Substitutes for leadership: Their meaning and measurement." *Organizational Behavior and Human Performance 22:* 375–403; Jon P. Howell and Peter W. Dorfman. (1986). "Leadership and substitutes for leadership among professional and nonprofessional workers." *Journal of Applied Behavioral Science 22:* 29–46; P. M. Podsakoff, S. B. MacKenzie, and W. H. Bommer. (1996, August). "Meta-analysis of the relationships between Kerr and Jermier's substitutes for leadership and employee attitudes, role perceptions, and performance." *Journal of Applied Psychology:* 380–399.

42. This section is based on George B. Graen and Mary Uhl-Bien. (1995). "Relationship-based approach to leadership: Development of leader member exchange (LMX) theory of leadership over 25 years—Applying a multi-level multi-domain approach." *Leadership Quarterly 6*(2): 219–247; and Fred Danereau. (1995). "A dyadic approach to leadership: Creating and nurturing this approach under fire." *Leadership Quarterly 6,*(4): 479–490.

43. See A. J. Kinicki and R. P. Vecchio. (1994, January). "Influences on the quality of supervisor-subordinate relations: The role of time pressure, organizational commitment, and locus of control." *Journal of Organizational Behavior:* 75–82; and R. C. Liden, S. J. Wayne, and D. Stilwell. (1993, August). "A longitudinal study on the early development of leader-member exchanges." *Journal of Applied Psychology:* 662–674.

44. R. Z. Gooding and A. J. Kinicki. (1995). "Interpreting event causes: The complementary role of categorization and attribution process." *The Journal of Management Studies 32:* 1–23; N. M. Ashkanasy and C. Gallois. (1994). "Leader attributions and evaluations: Effects of locus of control, supervisory control, and task control." *Organizational Behavior and Human Decision Processes 59:* 24–51.

45. Jeffrey Zaslow, "Straight Talk: Joe Montana," *USA Weekend,* January 30–February 1, 1998, p. 14.

46. Don Hellriegel, John W. Slocum, Jr., and Richard W. Woodman, *Organizational Behavior,* 8th ed. (Cincinnati, OH: South-Western College Publishing, 1998), pp. 339–340.

47. Katherine J. Klein and Robert J. House. (1995). "On fire: Charismatic leadership and levels of analysis." *Leadership Quarterly 6,*(2): 183–198.

48. Patricia Sellers, "What Exactly Is Charisma?" *Fortune,* January 15, 1996, pp. 68–75; and Charles A. Jaffe, "Moving Fast by Standing Still," *Nation's Business,* October 1991, pp. 57–59.

49. Jennifer O'Connor, Michael D. Mumford, Timothy C. Clifton, Theodore L. Gessner, and Mary Shane Connelly. (1995). "Charismatic leaders and destructiveness: An historiometric study." *Leadership Quarterly 6,*(4): 529–555; and Robert J. House and Jane M. Howell. (1992). "Personality and charismatic leadership." *Leadership Quarterly 3*(2): 81–108.

50. The terms *transactional* and *transformational leadership* are from James MacGregor Burns, *Leadership* (New York: Harper & Row, 1978), and Bernard M. Bass. (1985, Winter). "Leadership: Good, better, best." *Organizational Dynamics 13:* 26–40.

51. Based on Bernard M. Bass. (1995, Winter). "Theory of transformational leadership redux." *Leadership Quarterly 6*(4): 463–478; "From transactional to transformational leadership: Learning to share the vision." *Organizational Dynamics 18,* (4): 19–31; and Francis J. Yammarino, William D. Spangler, and Bernard M. Bass. (1993, Spring). "Transformational leadership and performance: A longitudinal investigation." *Leadership Quarterly 4,*(1): 81–102.

52. Noel M. Tichy and Mary Anne Devanna, *The Transformational Leader* (New York: John Wiley & Sons, 1986), pp. 265–266.

53. Bethany McLean, "Is This Guy the Best Banker in America?" *Fortune,* July 6, 1998, pp. 126–128.

54. Based on Marshall Sashkin, "The Visionary Leader," in J. A. Conger and R. N. Kanungo and Associates, *Charismatic Leadership* (San Francisco: Jossey-Bass, 1988), pp. 124–125; and Burt Nanus, *Visionary Leadership* (New York: The Free Press, 1992), p. 8.

55. This section is based on Nanus, *Visionary Leadership,* pp. 16–18; and Richard L. Daft and Robert H. Lengel, *Fusion Leadership: Unlocking the Subtle Forces That Change People and Organizations* (San Francisco: Berrett-Koehler, 1998).

56. Oren Harari, "Looking Beyond the Vision Thing," *Management Review,* June 1997, pp. 26–29; and William D. Hitt, *The Leader-Manager: Guidelines for Action* (Columbus, OH: Battelle Press, 1988), p. 54.

57. Nanus, *Visionary Leadership,* p. 16.

58. James M. Kouzes and Barry Z. Posner, *The Leadership Challenge: How to Get Extraordinary Things Done in Organizations* (San Francisco: Jossey-Bass, 1988), p. 98.

59. Keith H. Hammonds, "The Monroe Doctrine," *Fast Company,* October 1999, pp. 230–236; and Lorraine Monroe, *Nothing's Impossible: Leadership Lessons from Inside and Outside the Classroom* (New York: Times Books, 1997).

60. Peter M. Senge, "The Leader's New Work: Building Learning Organizations," *Sloan Management Review,* Fall 1990, pp. 7–22.

61. Based on Robert K. Greenleaf, *Servant Leadership* (Mahwah, N.J.: Paulist Press, (1977); and Walter Kiechel III, "The Leader as Servant," *Fortune,* May 4, 1992, pp. 121–122.

62. Parker J. Palmer, *Leading from Within: Reflections on Spirituality and Leadership* (Indianapolis: Indiana Office for Campus Ministries, October 1990), p. 2.

63. Sharon Cohen, "Boss Treats His Workers Like a Million Bucks—By Giving It To Them," *Johnson City Press,* September 12, 1999.

64. LaRue Tone Hosmer. (1995, April). "Trust: The connecting link between organizational theory and philosophical effects." *Academy of Management Review 20,*(2): 379–403.

65. Based on C. C. Manz and H. P. Sims Jr., (1987, March). "Leading workers to lead themselves: The external leadership of self-managed work teams." *Administrative Science Quarterly:* 106–129; W. W. Burke, "Leadership as Empowering Others," in

S. Srivastva and Associates, *Executive Power* (San Francisco: Jossey-Bass, 1986); and Robert Kreitner and Angelo Kinicki, *Organizational Behavior,* 4th ed. (Burr Ridge, IL: Irwin Mc-Graw-Hill, 1998), pp. 413–415, 515–516.

66. Robert C. Ford and Myron D. Fottler. (1995). "Empowerment: A matter of degree." *Academy of Management Executive 9:* 21–31.

67. Jeanne M. Wilson, Jill George, and Richard S. Wellins, with William C. Byham, *Leadership Trapeze: Strategies for Leadership in Team-Based Organizations,* (San Francisco: Jossey-Bass 1994), p. 14.

68. Based on Mark Sanborn, *TeamBuilt: Making Teamwork Pay* (New York: MasterMedia Limited, 1992), pp. 99–101.

69. Lawrence Holpp, "New Roles for Leaders: An HRD Reporter's Inquiry," *Training & Development,* March 1995, pp. 46–50.

70. J. Thomas Buck, "The Rocky Road to Team-Based Management," *Training & Development,* April 1995, pp. 35–38; Wilson *et. al., Leadership Trapeze,* pp. 15–16.

71. Lee G. Bolman and Terrence E. Deal, "What Makes a Team Work?" *Organizational Dynamics,* Autumn 1992, pp. 34–44; Stratford Sherman, "Secrets of HP's 'Muddled' Team," *Fortune,* March 18, 1996, pp. 116–120.

72. Based on Bolman and Deal, "What Makes a Team Work?"

73. David Climer, "Vols Really Know How to Raise Cane," *The Tennessean,* January 6, 1999, p. 1C.

CHAPTER 12

1. Geoff Williams, "Making Headlines," *Entrepreneur,* September 1999, pp. 114–117.

2. John R. P. French Jr. and Bertram Raven, "The Bases of Social Power," in D. Cartwright and Alvin F. Zander (eds.), *Group Dynamics* (Evanston, IL: Row, Peterson, 1960), pp. 607–623.

3. C. I. Barnard, *The Functions of the Executive* (Cambridge, MA: Harvard University Press, 1938); M. Zelditch and H. A. Walker, "Legitimacy and the Stability of Authority," in S. B. Bacharach and E. J. Lawler (eds.), *Advances in Group Processes,* vol. 1 (Greenwich, CT: JAI Press, 1984), pp. 1–25.

4. "Recruiting Strategies: Motivation," *Inc.* online, October 15, 1999, *Inc.* 500 (accessed at www.inc.com).

5. Gary A. Yukl and T. Taber, "The Effective Use of Managerial Power," *Personnel,* March-April 1983, pp. 37–44.

6. Nancy K. Austin, "First Aide," *Inc.,* September 1999, pp. 68–72+.

7. See Walter Kiechel III, "A Manager's Career in the New Economy," *Fortune,* April 4, 1994, pp. 68–72.

8. Stephanie Armour, "Blue Collar Can Mean Big Pay," *USA Today,* September 3, 1999, pp. 1B–2B.

9. Yukl and Taber, "The Effective Use of Managerial Power."

10. R. E. Emerson. (1962). "Power-dependence relations," *American Sociological Review 27:* 31–41.

11. Robert Johnson, "There's No Place Like It," *The Wall Street Journal,* May 24, 1999, pp. R23.

12. H. Mintzberg, *Power in and around Organizations* (Englewood Cliffs, NJ: Prentice-Hall, 1963).

13. Hal Lancaster, "Cleaning Up on Dirty Jobs," *The Asian Wall Street Journal,* December 10-11, 1999, p. P4; "Senior Management," "Web Speed for e-Business," and "Company Milestones" pages, (Alteon WebSystems Web site, downloaded March 27, 2000).

14. Susan Chandler, "Shake-up Mars Sears' State St. Homecoming," *Chicago Tribune,* September 3, 1999, sec. 1, pp. 1, 12; Sears, Roebuck and Co., "Sears Accelerates Succession Planning Process," news release, March 15, 2000 (downloaded from the Sears Web site, www.sears.com, March 27, 2000).

15. Stanley Milgram, "Behavioral Study of Obedience," in Dennis W. Organ (ed.), *The Applied Psychology of Work Behavior* (Dallas: Business Publications, Inc., 1978), pp. 384–398; Stanley Milgram. (1963). "Behavioral study of obedience." *Journal of Abnormal and Social Psychology 67:* 371–378; Stanley Milgram, *Obedience to Authority* (New York: Harper and Row, 1974).

16. See, for example, Stephen C. Schoonover, "HR Competencies

for the Year 2000: The Wake-Up Call!" SHRM Foundation page of the Society for Human Resource Management Web site (www.shrm.org, downloaded April 28, 1999).

17. Joshua Harris Prager, "An Evening in the Hatchery of High-Tech Start-ups," *The Wall Street Journal,* October 20, 1999, pp. B1, B4.

18. Mike Hofman, "Local Area Network," *Inc.,* May 1999, pp. 71–72.

19. Bruce Japsen, "AMA Sets Debate on Union Step," *Chicago Tribune,* June 20, 1999, sec. 5, pp. 1, 6–7.

20. J. Pfeffer, *Managing with Power* (Boston: Harvard Business School Press, 1992), pp. 155–157.

21. Jane L. Lee, "Korean Union Gears Up for Strike Despite Fears in the Rank and File," *The Wall Street Journal,* April 14, 1999, p. A23.

22. "CIO Panel: Knowledge-Sharing Roundtable," Information-Week Online, April 26, 1999 (downloaded from the InformationWeek Web site, www.informationweek.com, April 30, 1999).

23. "Many Close Calls for Jets on Runways Raise Concern," *Sacramento Bee,* December 19, 1999, p. A9.

24. Gary Yukl, P. J. Guinan, and D. Sottolano. (1995). "Influence tactics used for different objectives with subordinates, peers, and superiors." *Group & Organization Management 20:* 275.

25. C. M. Falbe and G. Yukl. (1992). "Consequences of managers using single influence tactics and combinations of tactics." *Academy of Management Journal 35:* 638–652; G. Yukl, C. M. Falbe, and J.Y. Youn. (1993). "Patterns of influence behavior for managers," *Group & Organization Management 18:* 5–28; G. Yukl, P. J. Guinan, and D. Sottolano. (1995). "Influence tactics used for different objectives with subordinates, peers, and superiors." *Group & Organization Management 20:* 272–296; G. Yukl and J. B. Tracey. (1992). "Consequences of influence tactics used with subordinates, peers, and the boss." *Journal of Applied Psychology 77:* 525–535.

26. James R. Hagerty, "Pat Farrah Named Top Merchandiser at Home Depot," *The Wall Street Journal,* September 8, 1999, p. A10.

27. Mel Duvall, "Oracle Sings a New Tune," *Inter @ctive Week,* November 29, 1999 (downloaded from ZDNet, www.zdnet.com, December 15, 1999); Brent Schlender, "Larry Ellison: Oracle at Web Speed," *Fortune,* May 24, 1999, pp. 128–133.

28. G. Yukl, H. Him, and C. M. Falbe. (1996, June). "Antecedents of influence outcomes." *Journal of Applied Psychology:* 309–317.

29. For a discussion of these issues, see P. Rosenfeld, S. Booth-Kewley, J. E. Edwards, and D.L. Alderton, "Linking Diversity and Impression Management: A Study of Hispanic, Black, and White Navy Recruits," *American Behavioral Scientist,* March 1994, pp. 672–681; and K. F. Dunn and G. Cowan, "Social Influence Strategies among Japanese and American College Women," *Psychology of Women Quarterly,* March 1993, pp. 39–52.

30. William O. Beeman, *Language, Status, and Power in Iran* (Bloomington, IN: Indiana University Press, 1986).

31. "Employee Options," *Export Today,* April 1999, p. 27.

32. R. Christie and F. L. Geis, *Studies in Machiavellianism* (New York: Academic Press, 1970); D. S. Wilson, D. Near, and R. R. Miller. (1996). "Machiavellianism: A synthesis of the evolutionary and psychological literatures," *Psychological Bulletin 119:* 285–299.

33. R. W. Woodman, S. J. Wayne, and D. Rubinstein, "Personality Correlates of a Propensity to Engage in Political Behavior in Organizations," *Proceedings of the Southwest Academy of Management,* 1985, pp. 131–135.

34. Ibid.

35. G. Biberman, "Personality and Characteristic Work Attitudes of Persons with High, Moderate, and Low Political Tendencies," *Psychological Reports,* October 1985, pp. 1303–1310; and G. R. Ferris, G. S. Russ, and P. M. Fandt, "Politics in Organizations," in R. A. Giacalone and P. Rosenfeld (eds.), *Impression Management in the Organization* (Hillsdale, NJ: Lawrence Erlbaum Associates, 1989), pp. 155–156.

36. Anne Fisher, "Ask Annie: Studying in Charm School, and Meeting Laggards," *Fortune,* June 7, 1999, p. 226.

37. Hal Lancaster, "For Some Managers, Hitting Middle Age Brings Uncertainties," *The Wall Street Journal,* April 20, 1999, p. B1.

38. D. C. Gilmore and G. R. Ferris. (1989, December). "The effects of applicant impression management tactics on interviewer judgments." *Journal of Management:* 557–564.

39. K. M. Kacmar, J. E. Kelery, and G. R. Ferris. (1992, August 16–31). "Differential effectiveness of applicant IM tactics on employment interview decisions." *Journal of Applied Social Psychology:* 1250–1272.

40. Mark Thompson, "A Crash and a Collusion?" *Time,* September 20, 1999, pp. 40–41.

41. Jeff Bailey, "Facing a Downsizing? You Can't Be Fired if You Can't Be Found," *The Wall Street Journal,* August 20, 1998, p. B1.

42. Teresa Puente, "Workers, EEOC Target Two Firms," *Chicago Tribune,* December 21, 1999, sec. 3, pp. 1–2.

43. Ilan Mochari, "Roll Out the Welcome Mat," *Inc.,* May 1999, p. 101.

44. Edward O. Welles, "Mind Gains," *Inc.,* December 1999, pp. 112–117+.

CHAPTER 13

1. Emily Barker, "The Pentagram Papers," *Inc.,* September 1999, pp. 58–64.

2. Sue Shellenbarger, "Six Trends to Watch for Harried Workers," *The Wall Street Journal,* December 29, 1999 (downloaded from the Wall Street Journal Interactive Edition, http://interactive. wsj.com, December 29, 1999).

3. Andrew Raskin, "Episode I: A New Beginning," *Inc.,* January 2000, pp. 31–32.

4. Jeffrey A. Tannenbaum, "After 8 Long Years, Harvard M.B.A. Brings Soup Business to a Boil," *The Wall Street Journal,* April 16, 1999, pp. A1, A6.

5. Stephen Franklin, "A Corporate Pension Headache," *Chicago Tribune,* August 29, 1999, sec. 5, pp. 1, 7.

6. K. Jehn. (1995, June). "A multimethod examination of the benefits and detriments of intragroup conflict." *Administrative Science Quarterly:* 256–282.

7. Geoff Williams, "Making Headlines," *Entrepreneur,* September 1999, pp. 114, 116–117.

8. Kruti Trivedi, "The Selling of Renoir," *The Wall Street Journal,* September 2, 1999, pp. B1, B4.

9. Robert Berner and Mark Maremont, "As Rite Aid Grew, CEO Seemed Unable to Manage His Empire," *The Wall Street Journal,* October 20, 1999, pp. A1, A12.

10. Joann S. Lublin, "An E-Company CEO Is Also the Recruiter-in-Chief," *The Wall Street Journal,* November 9, 1999, pp. B1, B20.

11. Louis R. Pondy. (1967). "Organizational conflict: Concepts and models." *Administrative Science Quarterly 12:* 296–320.

12. Sue Shellenbarger, "Three Harried Workers Make Some Big Changes," *The Wall Street Journal,* December 15, 1999 (downloaded from the Wall Street Journal Interactive Edition, http://interactive.wsj.com, December 16, 1999).

13. *Ibid.*

14. R. Kumar, "Affect, Cognition and Decision Making in Negotiations: A Conceptual Integration," in M. A. Rahim (ed.), *Managing Conflict: An Integrative Approach* (New York: Praeger, 1989), pp. 185–194.

15. P. J. D. Carnevale and A. M. Isen. (1986, February). "The influence of positive affect and visual access on the discovery of integrative solutions in bilateral negotiations." *Organizational Behavior and Human Decision Processes:* 1–13.

16. Stephanie Gruner, "Irreconcilable Differences," *Inc.,* September 1998, pp. 74–76+.

17. K. Thomas, "Conflict and Conflict Management," in M. D. Dunnette (ed.), *Handbook of Industrial and Organizational Psychology,* (Santa Monica, CA: Goodyear Publishing Company, 1976), p. 900.

18. See R. J. Sternberg and L. J. Soriano. (1984, July). "Styles of conflict resolution." *Journal of Personality and Social Psychology:* 115–126; R. A. Baron. (1989, October). "Personality and organizational conflict: Effects of the Type A behavior pattern and self-monitoring." *Organizational Behavior and Human Decision Processes:* 281–296; and R. J. Volkema and T. J. Bergmann. (1995, February). "Conflict styles as indicators of behavioral patterns in interpersonal conflicts." *Journal of Social Psychology:* 5–15.

19. Elaine W. Teague, "Pulse: My Ex-Husband Opened a Competing Store across the Street," *Entrepreneur,* August 1999, p. 13.

20. David H. Freedman, "Help Wanted: An Adult," *Inc.,* November 1999, pp. 48–50+; Ilan Mochari, "Found: An Adult," *Inc.,* January 2000, p. 16.

21. Jerry Useem, "Partners on the Edge," *Inc.,* August 1998, pp. 52–57+; and CPR MultiMedia Solutions Web site (downloaded December 31, 1999).

22. Arthur Lubow, "Redemption," *Inc.,* November 1999, pp. 85–88, 92.

23. Carol Hymowitz, "Damark's Unique Post: A Manager Who Helps Work on Relationships," *The Wall Street Journal,* September 7, 1999, p. B1.

24. Shellenbarger, "Six Trends to Watch for Harried Workers."

25. George Donnelly, "Networking and the Net," *CFO,* August 1999, pp. 93–95.

26. "Best Foot Forward at Reebok," *The Economist,* October 23, 1999, p. 74.

27. "CEO Outlook: Fewer Buccaneers, More Coaches," *Crain's Chicago Business,* 2000 & Beyond special section, June 7, 1999, p. E68.

28. "New Directions: Biz Must Adjust Its Moral Compass," *Crain's Chicago Business,* 2000 & Beyond special section, June 7, 1999, p. E71.

29. "Delta Makes Offer to Pilots Set to Fly New Boeing Model," *The Wall Street Journal,* September 1, 1999, p. A12; and UPI, "Delta, Pilots Reach Jet Agreement," news wire (downloaded September 23, 1999 from Northern Light Web site, http: //library.northernlight.com, January 5, 2000).

30. Jeffrey Ball, Glenn Burkins, and Gregory L. White, "The Global High-Tech Economy Makes Striking Riskier for Unions," *The Wall Street Journal,* December 16, 1999 (downloaded from the Wall Street Journal Interactive Edition, http://interactive. wsj.com, December 16, 1999).

31. R. L. Pinkley, T. L. Griffith, and G. B. Northcraft. (1995, April). "Fixed pie à la mode: Information availability, information processing, and the negotiation of suboptimal agreements." *Organizational Behavior and Human Decision Processes:* 101–112.

32. R. Fisher and W. Ury, *Getting to Yes: Negotiating Agreement without Giving In* (New York: Penguin Books, 1981); B. Benedict Bunker, J. Z. Rubin *et al., Conflict, Cooperation and Justice* (San Francisco: Jossey-Bass, 1995).

33. Mike Hofman, "You Are Your URL," *Inc.,* November 1999, pp. 120, 124.

34. S. Lubman, "Round and Round," *The Wall Street Journal,* December 10, 1993, p. R3.

35. E. S. Glenn, D. Witmeyer, and K. A. Stevenson. (1977, Fall). "Cultural styles of persuasion." *Journal of Intercultural Relations:* 52–66.

36. J. S. Black and M. Mendenhall, "Resolving Conflicts with the Japanese: Mission Impossible," *Sloan Management Review,* Spring 1993, pp. 49–59.

CHAPTER 14

1. T. Aeppel, "Rust Belt Factory Lifts Productivity , and Staff Finds It's No Picnic," *The Wall Street Journal,* May 18, 1999, pp. A1 and A10.

2. E. Pollock, "It's Getting Stressful! On the Job," *The Wall Street Journal,* November 10, 1998, pp. B1 and B24.

3. Results of Pitney Bowes's "Workplace Communications in the 21st Century" study as reported in "Data Data," *Inc.,* January 1, 1999.

4. T. Aeppel, "Living Overtime: A Factory Workaholic," *The Wall Street Journal,* November 13, 1998, pp. B1 and B18.

5. R. Winslow, "Big Study Shows Workers under Stress Likely to Have Higher Health-Care Costs," *The Wall Street Journal,* October 16, 1998, p. B5.

6. T. A. Beehr and R. S. Bhagat, *Human Stress and Cognition in Organizations: An Integrated Perspective* (New York: Wiley, 1985).

7. Hans Selye, *The Stress of Life* (New York: McGraw-Hill, 1976).

8. R. Lazarus. (1993). "From psychological stress to the emotions: A history of changing outlooks." *Annual Review of Psychology 44:* 1–21.

9. P. Hise, "Solemates," *Inc.,* October 15, 1999.

10. P. Moyle and K. Parkes. (1999). "The effects of transition stress: A relocation study." *Journal of Organizational Behavior 20:* 625–646.

11. Heath Row, "Is Management for Me? That Is the Question," *Fast Company,* February/March 1998, pp. 50, 52.

12. K. Tyler, "Spinning Wheels," *HR Magazine,* September 1999, pp. 34–40.

13. B. Richards, "Computer-Chip Plants Aren't as Safe and Clean as Billed, Some Say," *The Wall Street Journal,* October 10, 1998, pp. A1 and A13.

14. D. Shenk, *Data Smog: Surviving the Information Glut* (New York: HarperCollins, 1997).

15. *Ibid.*

16. N. Thompson, "Workplace Can Be Anywhere, Thanks to Nifty Gadgets," *The Columbus Dispatch,* March 8, 2000, p. 6E.

17. *Ibid.*

18. Anne Fisher, "Why Are You So Paranoid?" *Fortune,* September 8, 1997, pp. 171–172.

19. Dave Thomas, "My Biggest Mistake," *Inc.,* September 1998, p. 129.

20. Robert Kreitner and Angelo Kinicki, *Organizational Behavior,* 4th ed. (Boston: Irwin/McGraw-Hill, 1998), p. 293.

21. Based on T. Holmes and R. Rahe. (1967). "The social readjustment rating scale." *Journal of Psychomatic Research 11:* 213–218.

22. E. Kossek and C. Ozeki. (1998) "Work-family conflict, policies, and the job-life satisfaction relationship: A review and directions for OB/HR research." *Journal of Applied Psychology 83:* 139–149; and J. Boles, M. Johnston, J. Hair. (1997). "Role stress, family conflict, and emotional exhaustion: Inter-relationships and effects of some work-related consequences." *Journal of Personal Selling and Sales Management 17:* 17–28.

23. J. Greenhaus and N. Beutell. (1985). "Sources of conflict between work and family roles." *Academy of Management Review 10:* 76–88; and J. Greenhaus. (1988). "The intersection of work and family roles: Individual, interpersonal, and organizational issues." *Journal of Social Behavior and Personality 3:* 23–44.

24. M. Friedman and R. Rosenman, *Type A Behavior and Your Heart* (New York: Knopf, 1974).

25. Andy Reinhardt, "Mr. House Finds His Fixer-Upper," *Business Week,* February 2, 1998, pp. 66–68.

26. D. Watson and J. Pennebaker. (1989). "Health complaints, stress, and distress: Exploring the central role of negative affectivity." *Psychological Review 96:* 234–254.

27. J, Quick and J. Quick, *Organizational Stress and Preventative Management* (New York: McGraw-Hill, 1984); C. Anderson. (1977). "Locus of control, coping behavior, and performance in a stress setting: A longitudinal study." *Journal of Applied Psychology 62:* 446–451.

28. K. Danna and R. Griffin. (1999). "Health and well-being in the workplace: A review and synthesis of the literature." *Journal of Management 25:*357–384.

29. For example, see A. Boyd. (1997). "Employee traps—corruption in the workplace." *Management Review 86:* 9.

30. C. Cordes and T. Dougherty. (1993). "A review and integration of research on job burnout." *Academy of Management Review 18:* 621–656.

31. W. Schaufeli, C. Maslach, and T. Marek, *Professional Burnout: Recent Developments in Theory and Research* (Washington, DC: Taylor and Francis, 1993).

32. S. Berglas "The Big Lie", *Inc.* March 1, 1996, available at www.inc.com.

33. J. Quick, R. Horn, and J. Quick. (1986). "Health consequences of stress." *Journal of Organizational Behavior Management 8:* 19–36.

34. Danna and Griffin, "Health and well-being in the workplace: A review and synthesis of the literature," *Journal of Management 25:* pp. 357–384.

35. From Web site www. accidentfund.com (downloaded 1998).

36. As reported in R. Yandrick, "Speed Your Disabled Worker's Return," *HR Magazine,* June 1997, pp. 154–157.

37. R. Kahn and P. Byosiere, "Stress in Organizations," In M. Dunnette and L. Hough (eds.), *Handbook of Industrial and Organizational Psychology,* 2nd ed. (Palo Alto, CA: Consulting Psychologists Press, 1992) pp. 571–650.

38. For example, see M. Matteson and J. Ivancevich, *Controlling Work Stress* (San Francisco: Jossey-Bass, 1987) and B. Mangione and R. Quinn. (1975). "Job satisfaction, counterproductive behavior, and drug use at work." *Journal of Applied Psychology 63:* 114–116.

39. C. Hirschman, "Take Control of the Wheel," *HR Magazine,* June 1999, pp. 90–97.

40. D. Anfuso, "It Makes Devastating Moments in Life Easier," *Workforce,* March 1999, p. 112.

41. H. Luthar, "Learning Meditation Training," *Workforce,* February 1999, pp. 10–11.

42. R. Kotulak, "Firm Cuts Costs by Boosting Worker Health," *Chicago Tribune,* January 13, 1994, pp. 1, 26.

43. D. Harrison and L. Liska. (1994). "Promoting regular exercise in organizational fitness programs: Health-related differences in motivational building blocks." *Personnel Psychology 47:* 47–71.

44. N. Jeffrey, "Wellness Plans Try to Target the Not-So-Well," *The Wall Street Journal,* June 20, 1996, pp. B1 and B9.

45. B. Sunoo, "Wellness Pays Off," *Workforce,* December 1997, p. 52.

46. Yandrick, "Speed Your Disabled Worker's Return."

47. H. O'Neill and D. Lenn. (1995). "Voices of survivors: Words that downsizing CEOs should hear." *Academy of Management Executive 9:* 23–34.

48. *Ibid.*

49. J. Brockner. (1992, Winter). "Managing the effects of layoffs on survivors." *California Management Review:* 9–28; and J. Brockner, M. Konovsky, R. Cooper-Schneider, R. Folger, C. Martin, and R. Bries. (1994). "Interactive effects of procedural justice and outcome negativity on victims and survivors of job loss." *Academy of Management Journal 37:* 397–409.

50. S. Kravetz, "Curves Ahead," *The Wall Street Journal,* March 10, 1999, pp. B1 and B10.

51. J. Laabs, "Overload: What's Causing It and How to Solve It," *Workforce,* January 1999, pp. 30–37.

52. *Ibid.*

53. See, for example, D. Dierendonck, W. Schaufeli, and B. Buunk. (1998). "The evaluation of an individual burnout intervention program: The role of inequity and social support." *Journal of Applied Psychology 83:* 392–407.

54. S. Gruner, "Hot Tip: Employee Stress," *Inc.,* November 1, 1998, pp.

55. C. Solomon, "Stressed to the Limit," *Workforce,* September 1999, pp. 48–54.

56. T. Schellhardt, "Monsanto Bets on 'Box Buddies'," *The Wall Street Journal,* February 23, 1999, pp. B1 and B10.

57. G. Flynn, "Stop Toxic Managers before They Stop You!" *Workforce,* August 1999, pp. 40–44.

58. S. Shellenbarger, "Are Saner Workloads Key to More Productivity?" *The Wall Street Journal,* March 10, 1999, p. B1.

59. J. Bond, E. Galinsky, and J. Swanberg. (1998). "The 1997 National Study of the Changing Workforce." Available at www. familiesandworkinstitute.org.

60. B. Bates, T. Briggs, J. Huff, J. Wright, G. Neuman. (1999). "Flexible and compressed workweek schedules: A meta-analysis of their effects on work-related criteria." *Journal of Applied Psychology 84:* 496–513.

61. C. Johnson, "Don't Forget Your Shift Workers," *HR Magazine,* February 1999, pp. 80–84.

62. "Work-Life Benefits on the Rise," *Training & Development,* October 1999, p. 12.

63. C. Solomon, "Eldercare Issues Shake the Workplace," *Workforce,* October 1999, pp. 58–67.

64. I. Singer, "Work-Life Benefits Can Lighten the Load," *Business and Health,* October 1999, pp. 25–31.

65. S. Goff, M. Mount, and R. Jamison. (1990). "Employer supported child care, work/family conflict, and absenteeism: A field study." *Personnel Psychology 43:* 793–809.

66. C. Solomon, "Workers Want a Life! Do Managers Care?" *Workforce,* August 1999, pp. 54–58.

67. A. Daley and G. Parfitt. (1996). "Good health: Is it worth it? Mood states, physical well-being, job satisfaction and absenteeism in members and non-members of British corporate health and fitness clubs." *Journal of Occupational and Organizational Psychology 69:* 121–134.

68. H. Luthar, "Learning Meditation Training," *Workforce Extra,* February 1999, pp. 10–11.

69. Nan K. Chase, "The One-Day Rest Cure," *Inc.,* August 1998, p. 106.

70. Luthar, "Learning meditation training," *Workforce* (February 1999), pp. 10–11.

71. S. Shellenbarger, "More Couples Try to Time Childbirth to Accommodate Jobs." *The Wall Street Journal,* October 27, 1999, p. B1.

72. S. Shellenbarger, "The American Way of Work (More!) May Be Easing Up," *The Wall Street Journal,* January 19, 2000, p. B1.

73. S. Shellenbarger, "What Job Candidates Really Want to Know: Will I Have a Life?" *The Wall Street Journal,* November 17, 1999, p. B1.

CHAPTER 15

1. Polly LaBarre, "The Company without Limits," *Fast Company,* September 1999, pp. 160–186.

2. John Child, *Organization: A Guide to Problems and Practice,* 2nd ed. (London: Harper & Row, 1984).

3. This section is based on Frank Ostroff, *The Horizontal Organization: What the Organization of the Future Looks Like and How It Delivers Value to Customers* (New York: Oxford University Press, 1999).

4. Chester I. Barnard, *The Functions of the Executive* (Cambridge, MA: Harvard University Press, 1938).

5. Russ Baker, "Edged Out," *Inc.,* August 1998, pp. 69–77.

6. Michael G. O'Loughlin. (1990, November). "What is bureaucratic accountability and how can we measure it?" *Administration and Society 22* (3): 275–302.

7. Brian O'Reilly, "J & J is On a Roll," *Fortune,* December 26, 1994, pp. 178–191; and Joseph Weber, "A Big Company That Works," *Business Week,* May 4, 1992, pp. 124–132.

8. Michael Moeller, with Steve Hamm and Timothy J. Mullaney, "Remaking Microsoft," *Business Week,* May 17, 1999, pp. 106–114.

9. Christopher Caggiano, "Thriving on Bureaucracy," *Inc. Technology,* 1997, no. 1, pp. 63–66.

10. Adam Smith, *The Wealth of Nations* (New York: Modern Library, 1937).

11. LaBarre, "The Company without Limits."

12. Stephen P. Robbins, *Organizational Behavior,* 8th ed. (Upper Saddle River, NJ: Prentice-Hall, 1998), pp. 479–480.

13. Aaron Bernstein, "Putting a Damper on That Old Team Spirit," *Business Week,* May 4, 1992, p. 60; Wendy Zeller, "The UAW Rebels Teaming Up Against Teamwork," *Business Week,* March 27, 1989, pp. 110–114; and John Hoerr, "Is Teamwork a Man-

agement Plot? Mostly Not," *Business Week,* February 20, 1989, p. 70.

14. Michael Williams, "Some Plants Tear Out Long Assembly Lines, Switch to Craft Work," *The Wall Street Journal,* October 24, 1994, pp. A1, A6.

15. David Nadler and Michael Tushman, *Strategic Organization Design* (Glenview, IL: Scott, Foresman, 1988).

16. William J. Altier, "Task Forces: An Effective Management Tool," *Management Review,* February 1987, pp. 52–57.

17. Jeffrey A. Tannenbaum, "Why Are Companies Paying Close Attention to This Toilet Maker?" *The Wall Street Journal,* August 20, 1999, p. B1.

18. Based on Tannenbaum, "Why Are Companies Paying Close Attention to This Toilet Maker?" and American Standard Companies 1998 Annual Report, www.americanstandard.com/annual98/ (accessed on September 3, 1999).

19. "Middle Managers Are Back—But Now They're High-Impact Players," *The Wall Street Journal,* April 14, 1998, p. B1.

20. Tom Burns and G. M. Stalker, *The Management of Innovation* (London: Tavistock, 1961); and John A. Courtright, Gail T. Fairhurst, and L. Edna Rogers. (1989). "Interaction patterns in organic and mechanistic systems." *Academy of Management Journal 32:* 773–802.

21. Max Weber, *The Theory of Social and Economic Organizations,* translated by A. M. Henderson and T. Parsons (New York: The Free Press, 1947).

22. The discussion of functional and divisional structures is based on Robert Duncan (1979, Winter). "What is the right organization structure? Decision-tree analysis provides the answer," *Organizational Dynamics:* pp. 59–80.

23. Shelly Branch, "What's Eating McDonald's?" *Fortune,* October 13, 1997, pp. 122–125.

24. Weber, "A Big Company That Works."

25. Lawton R. Burns. (1989). "Matrix management in hospitals: Testing theories of matrix structure and development." *Administrative Science Quarterly 34:* 349–368; and Stanley M. Davis and Paul R. Lawrence, *Matrix* (Reading, MA: Addison-Wesley, 1977).

26. Robert C. Ford and W. Alan Randolph. (1992). "Cross-functional structures: A review and integration of matrix organization and project management." *Journal of Management 19*(2): 267–294.

27. Eric W. Larson and David H. Gobeli. (1987, Summer). "Matrix management: Contradictions and insight." *California Management Review 29:* 126–138.

28. Michael Hammer with Steven Stanton, "The Art of Change," *Success,* April 1995, pp. 44A–44H; and Michael Hammer, *Beyond Reengineering* (New York: HarperBusiness, 1996).

29. Based on Ostroff, *The Horizontal Organization,* and Richard L. Daft, *Organization Theory and Design,* 6th ed. (Cincinnati OH: South-Western College Publishing, 1998), pp. 250–253.

30. John A. Byrne, "The Horizontal Corporation," *Business Week,* December 20, 1993, pp. 76–81.

31. Raymond E. Miles and Charles C. Snow. (1995, Spring). "The new network firm: A spherical structure built on a human investment philosophy." *Organizational Dynamics:* 5–18; and Raymond E. Miles, Charles C. Snow, John A. Matthews, Grant Miles, and Henry J. Coleman, Jr. (1997). "Organizing in the Knowledge Age: Anticipating the cellular form." *Academy of Management Executive 11*(4): 7–224.

32. Heath Row, "This 'Virtual' Company is for Real," *Fast Company,* December-January 1998, pp. 48–50; and Evan Ramstad, "A PC Maker's Low-Tech Formula: Start with the Box," *The Wall Street Journal,* December 29, 1997, pp. B1, B8.

33. John Case, "The Age of the Specialist," *Inc.,* August 1995, pp. 15–16.

34. Miles and Snow, "The new network firm"; and Gregory G. Dess, Abdul M. A. Rasheed, Kevin J. McLaughlin, and Richard L. Priem. (1995). "The new corporate architecture." *Academy of Management Executive 9*(2): 7–20.

35. Raymond E. Miles. (1989, Winter). "Adapting to technology and competition: A new industrial relation system for the twenty-first century." *California Management Review*: 9–28; and Miles and Snow, "The new network firm."

36. Dess *et al.*, "The new corporate architecture."

37. See Jay R. Galbraith, *Competing with Flexible Lateral Organizations,* 2nd ed. (Reading, MA: Addison-Wesley, 1994), ch. 2; Terry L. Amburgey and Tina Dacin. (1994). "As the left foot follows the right? The dynamics of strategic and structural change." *Academy of Management Journal* 37(6): 427–452; and Raymond E. Miles and W. E. Douglas Creed. (1995). "Organizational forms and managerial philosophies: A descriptive and analytical review." *Research in Organizational Behavior* 17: 333–372.

38. Michael E. Porter, *Competitive Strategy* (New York: The Free Press, 1980), pp. 36–46.

39. Lucy McCauley (ed.), "Unit of One: Measure What Matters," *Fast Company,* May 1999, pp. 97+.

40. Ostroff, *The Horizontal Organization,* pp. 130–143.

41. Paul R. Lawrence and Jay W. Lorsch, *Organization and Environment* (Homewood, IL: Irwin, 1969).

42. See Joan Woodward, *Industrial Organization: Theory and Practice* (London: Oxford University Press, 1965); Charles Perrow. (1967, April). "A framework for the comparative analysis of organizations." *American Sociological Review* 32: 194–208; Denise M. Rousseau and Robert A. Cooke. (1984). "Technology and structure: The concrete, abstract, and activity systems of organizations." *Journal of Management 10*: 345–361.

43. Perrow, "A framework for the comparative analysis of organizations"; and Charles Perrow, *Organizational Analysis: A Sociological Approach* (Belmont, CA: Wadsworth, 1970).

44. Peggy Leatt and Rodney Schneck. (1984). "Criteria for grouping nursing subunits in hospitals." *Academy of Management Journal 27*:150–165; and Robert T. Keller. (1994). "Technology-information processing." *Academy of Management Journal* 37(1): 167–179.

45. Herbert G. McCann, "Allstate Announces Plan to Cut 4,000 Jobs," *Johnson City Press,* November 11, 1999, p. 8.

46. Sari Kalin, "Overdrive," *CIO Web Business,* sec. 2, July 1, 1999, pp. 36–40.

47. Siobhan O'Mahony and Stephen R. Barley. (1999). "Do digital telecommunications affect work and organization? The state of our knowledge." *Research in Organizational Behavior* 21:125–161.

48. John D. Daniels, Robert A. Pitts, and Marietta J. Tretter. (1984). "Strategy and structure of U. S. multinationals: An exploratory study." *Academy of Management Journal 27*: 292–307.

49. For a complete description of the transnational model, see Christopher A. Bartlett and Sumantra Ghoshal, *Managing Across Borders: The Transnational Solution* (Boston: Harvard Business School Press, 1998).

CHAPTER 16

1. Charles Fishman, "Engines of Democracy," *Fast Company,* October 1999, pp. 174–202.

2. Glenn L. Dalton, "The Collective Stretch," *Management Review,* December 1998, pp. 54–59.

3. Jaclyn Fierman, "Blue-Collar Blues," *Fortune,* April 22, 1991, pp. 209–218.

4. Michael West and Malcolm Patterson, "Profitable Personnel," *People Management,* January 8, 1998, pp. 28–31.

5. Cited in Dalton, "The Collective Stretch."

6. S. A. Mohrman, S. G. Cohen, and A. M. Mohrman Jr., *Designing Team-Based Organizations: New Forms for Knowledge Work* (San Francisco: Jossey-Bass, 1995).

7. Mary O'Hara Devereaux and Robert Johansen, *Globalwork: Bridging Distance, Culture, and Time* (San Francisco: Jossey-Bass, 1994); Charles C. Snow, Scott A. Snell, Sue Canney Davision, and Donald C. Hambrick. (1996, Spring). "Use transna-

tional teams to globalize your company." *Organizational Dynamics 24*(4): 50–67.

8. Debby Young, "Team Heat" *CIO,* sec. 1, September 1, 1998, pp. 43–51.

9. Sylvia Odenwald, "Global Work Teams," *Training and Development,* February 1996, pp. 54–57; and Young, "Heat."

10. O'Hara-Devereaux and Johansen, *Globalwork,* pp. 227–228.

11. S. L. Mintz, "The Reengineers: A Guide for the Perplexed," *CFO,* Ocotber 1994, pp. 422–454, and "The Bigger Picture: Reorganizing Work," *Industry Week,* August 2, 1993, p. 24.

12. John Hillkirk, "Challenging Status Quo Now in Vogue," *USA Today,* November 9, 1993; and Thomas A. Stewart, "The Search for the Organization of Tomorrow," *Fortune,* May 18, 1992, pp. 92–98.

13. Richard A. Luecke, *Scuttle Your Ships before Advancing* (New York: Oxford University Press, 1994), pp. 64–68; Thomas F. Rienzo. (1993, May–June). "Planning Deming management for service organizations." *Business Horizons 36*(3): 19–29; and Gregory M. Bounds, Gregory H. Dobbins, and Oscar S. Fowler, *Management: A Total Quality Perspective* (Cincinnati: South-Western College Publishing, 1995), pp. 219–220.

14. Robert W. Haney and Charles D. Beaman Jr., "Management Leadership Critical to CQI Success," *Hospitals,* July 20, 1992, p. 64.

15. Jenny C. McCune, "On the Train Gang," *Management Review,* October 1994, pp. 57–60.

16. John P. Mello, "Good Help Is Hard to Keep," *Inside Technology Training,* November 1998, pp. 20–24.

17. Michael Williams, "Some Plants Tear Out Long Assembly Lines, Switch to Craft Work," *The Wall Street Journal,* October 24, 1994, pp. A1, A6.

18. Fishman, "Engines of Democracy."

19. Wendy Zellner, "Team Player: No More Same-ol'-Same-ol'," *Business Week,* October 17, 1994, pp. 95–96; West and Patterson, "Profitable Personnel."

20. "Great Expectations?" *Fast Company,* November 1999, pp. 212–224.

21. Dalton, "The Collective Stretch."

22. Bethany McLean, "More Than Just Dot-Coms," *Fortune,* December 6, 1999, pp. 130–138.

23. Aaron Bernstein, "We Want You to Stay. Really," *Business Week,* June 22, 1998, pp. 67–72.

24. Edward L. Gubman, *The Talent Solution: Aligning Strategy and People to Achieve Extraordinary Results* (New York: McGraw-Hill, 1998), p. 221.

25. C. M. Solomon, "Job Sharing: One Job, Double Headache?" *Personnel Journal,* September 1994, p. 90.

26. "Wherever, whenever," www.utc.com/ARCHIVE/op080698.htm (accessed on November 30, 1999).

27. "UCI Gets Creative with Work Schedules," www.communications.uci.edu/99news/990414d.html, and "Flexible Work Schedules," www.doi.gov/hrm/pmanager/er8c1.html (accessed on November 30, 1999).

28. Solomon, "Job Sharing: One Job, Double Headache?"

29. "Lab Wins Family-Friendly Employer Award," www.lancaster-labs.com/pg0616.html (accessed on November 30, 1999).

30. See D. A. Ralston, W. P. Anthony, and D. J. Gustafson. (1985, May). "Employees may love flextime, but what does it do to the organization's productivity?" *Journal of Applied Psychology*: 206–217; D. R. Dalton and D. J. Mesch. (1990, June). "The impact of flexible work scheduling on employee attendance and turnover." *Administrative Science Quarterly*: 370–387.

31. Keith H. Hammonds with Ann Therese Palmer, "The Daddy Trap," *Business Week,* September 21, 1998, pp. 56–64.

32. This brief historical summary is based on William M. Fox. (1995, March). "Sociotechnical system principles and guidelines: Past and present." *Journal of Applied Behavioral Science* 31(1): 91–105.

33. *Ibid.*

34. F. Emery, "Characteristics of Sociotechnical Systems," Tavistock

Institute of Human Relations, document 527, 1959; William A. Passmore. (1995). "Social science transformed: The sociotechnical perspective." *Human Relations 48*(1): 1–21.

35. W. S. Cascio, *Managing Human Resources* (New York: McGraw-Hill, 1986), p. 19.

36. Derek S. Pugh and David J. Hickson, "Eric Trist and the Work of the Tavistock Institute," in *Writers on Organizations,* 5th ed. (Thousand Oaks, CA: Sage Publications, 1996), pp. 158–164; Eric Trist and Hugh Murray (eds.), *The Social Engagement of Social Science: A Tavistock Anthology,* vol. 11 (Philadelphia: University of Pennsylvania Press, 1993); and Pasmore, "Social science transformed."

37. R. E. Walton. (1985). "From control to commitment in the workplace." *Harvard Business Review 63*(2): 76–84; E. W. Lawler III, *High Involvement Management* (London: Jossey-Bass, 1986), p. 84; and Don Hellriegel, John W. Slocum Jr., and Richard W. Woodman, *Organizational Behavior,* p 491.

38. Curtis Sittenfeld, "Powered by the People," *Fast Company,* July/August 1999, pp. 178–189.

39. Pasmore, "Social science transformed," pp. 74–84.

40. J. Richard Hackman and Greg R. Oldham, *Work Redesign* (Reading, MA: Addison-Wesley, 1980); and J. Richard Hackman and Greg R. Oldham. (1976). "Motivation through the design of work: Test of a theory." *Organizational Behavior and Human Performance 16*: 250–279.

41. M. L. Ambrose and C. T. Kulik. (1999). "Old friends, new faces: Motivation research in the 1990s." *Journal of Mangement 25*: 231–292.

42. This discussion is based on Gregory B. Northcraft and Margaret A. Neal, *Organizational Behavior: A Management Challenge* (Fort Worth, TX: The Dryden Press, 1994), pp. 447–448.

43. J. G. Thomas and R. W. Griffin. (1989, Winter). "The power of social information in the workplace." *Organizational Dynamics*: 63–75; and M. D. Zalesny and J. K. Ford. (1990, December). "Extending the social information processing perspective: New links to attitudes, behaviors, and perceptions." *Organizational Behavior and Human Decision Processes*: 205–246.

44. Michele Liu, Héléné Denis, Harvey Kolodny, and Benjt Stymne. (1990, January). "Organization and design for technological change." *Human Relations 43*: 7–22.

45. Stephen P. Robbins, *Organizational Behavior* (Upper Saddle River, NJ: Prentice-Hall, 1998), p. 521.

46. Anita Lienert, "Plowing Ahead in Uncertain Times," *Management Review,* December 1998, pp. 16–21.

47. Gerald I. Susman and Richard B. Chase. (1986). "A sociotechnical analysis of the integrated factory." *Journal of Applied Behavioral Science 22*: 257–270; and Paul Adler. (1986, Fall). "New technologies, new skills." *California Management Review 29*: 9–28.

48. Richard W. Judy and Carol D'Amico, *Workforce 2020: Work and Workers in the 21st Century* (Indianapolis: The Hudson Institute, 1997); M. Hequet, "Virtually Working," *Training,* August 1996, pp. 29–35. For further information on telecommuting and its impact, see Mahlon Apgar IV, "The Alternative Workplace: Changing Where and How People Work," *Harvard Business Review,* May-June 1998, pp. 121–133; and Jenny C. McCune, "Telecommuting Revisited," *Management Review,* February 1998, pp. 10–16.

49. Carol A. Dannhauser, "The Invisible Worker," *Working Woman,* November 1998, p. 38.

50. Cited in Eleena De Lisser, "Companies with Virtual Environments Find Success in Retaining Workers," *The Wall Street Journal Interactive Edition,* October 5, 1999, www.wsj.com (accessed on December 7, 1999).

51. See R. A. Baron, "The Physical Environment of Work Settings: Effects on Task Performance, Interpersonal Relations, and Job Satisfaction," in *Research in Organizational Behavior,* vol. 16, B. M. Staw and L. L. Cummings (eds.) (Greenwich, CT: JAI Press, 1994), pp. 1–46.

52. Stephen P. Robbins, *Organizational Behavior,* 8th ed. (Cincinnati, OH: South-Western College Publishing, 1998), pp. 528–529.

53. Polly LaBarre, "This Organization Is Disorganization," *Fast Company,* June-July 1996, p. 77.

54. Daintry Duffy, "Cube Stakes," *CIO Enterprise,* sec. 2, April 15, 1999, pp. 67–72.

55. *Ibid.;* and Eric Ransdell, "Work Different," *Fast Company,* June 1999, pp. 143–149.

56. Paul Roberts, "Live! From Your Office! It's . . .," *Fast Company,* October 1999, pp. 150–170; and David M. Kelley, "Performing Rapid Innovation Magic: Ten Secrets of a Modern Merlin," in *Straight from the CEO: The World's Top Business Leaders Reveal Ideas That Every Manager Can Use,* G. William Dauphinais and Colin Price, Price Waterhouse (eds.) (New York: Simon & Schuster, 1998), pp. 271–281.

CHAPTER 17

1. Chuck Salter, "Insanity Inc.," *Fast Company,* January 1999, pp. 100–108.

2. Jeremy Kahn, "What Makes a Company Great?" *Fortune,* October 26, 1998, p. 218; James C. Collins and Jerry I. Porras, *Built to Last: Successful Habits of Visionary Companies* (New York: HarperCollins, 1994); and James C. Collins, "Change is Good—But First Know What Should Never Change," *Fortune,* May 29, 1995, p. 141.

3. Edgar H. Schein. (1990, February). "Organizational culture." *American Psychologist 45* (2): 109–119.

4. Yoash Wiener. (1988). "Forms of value systems: A focus on organizational effectiveness and culture change and maintenance." *Academy of Management Review 13*: 534–545; V. Lynne Meek. (1988). "Organizational culture: Origins and weaknesses." *Organizational Studies 9*:453–473; and John J. Sherwood. (1988, Winter). "Creating work cultures with competitive advantage." *Organizational Dynamics*:5–27.

5. W. Jack Duncan. (1989). "Organizational culture: Getting a 'fix' on an elusive concept." *Academy of Management Executive 3*: 229–236; Linda Smircich. (1983). "Concepts of culture and organizational analysis." *Administrative Science Quarterly 28*: 339–358; and Andrew D. Brown and Ken Starkey. (1994, November). "The effect of organizational culture on communication and information." *Journal of Management Studies 31*(6): 807–828.

6. Schein, "Organizational culture."

7. This discussion of the levels of culture is based on Edgar H. Schein, *Organizational Culture and Leadership,* 2nd ed. (San Francisco: Jossey-Bass, 1992), pp. 3–27.

8. Schein, "Organizational culture," p. 113.

9. John P. Kotter and James L. Heskett, *Corporate Culture and Performance* (New York: The Free Press, 1992), p. 6.

10. Sharon Overton, "And to All a Goodnight," *Sky,* October 1996, pp. 37–40; and Charles Fishman, "Sanity Inc.," *Fast Company,* January 1999, pp. 85–96.

11. W. Mathew Juechter, Caroline Fisher, and Randall J. Alford, "Five Conditions for High-Performance Cultures," *Training and Development,* May 1998, pp. 63–67.

12. William Ouchi, *Theory Z: How American Business Can Meet the Japanese Challenge* (Reading, MA: Addison-Wesley, 1979); and R. Pascale and A. Athos, *The Art of Japanese Management* (New York: Simon & Schuster, 1981).

13. Joseph Weber, "Mr. Nice Guy With a Mission," *Business Week,* November 25, 1996, pp. 132–142.

14. Collins, "Change is Good—But First Know What Should Never Change."

15. Robert Specter, "The Nordstrom Way," *Corporate University Review,* May/June 1997, pp. 24–25, 66.

16. Jeffrey Sonnenfeld, *The Hero's Farewell: What Happens When CEOs Retire* (New York: Oxford University Press, 1988).

17. David Leonhardt, "McDonald's: Can It Regain Its Golden Touch?" *Business Week,* March 9, 1998, pp. 70–77.

18. Robert L. Simison, "Ford Rolls Out New Model of Corporate Culture," *The Wall Street Journal,* January 13, 1999, pp. B1, B4.
19. Juechter, Fisher, and Alford, "Five Conditions for High-Performance Cultures."
20. Bernard Arogyaswamy and Charles M. Byles. (1987). "Organizational culture: Internal and external fits." *Journal of Management 13*: 647–659.
21. Scott Kirsner, "Designed for Innovation," *Fast Company,* November 1998, pp. 54, 56.
22. Edgar H. Schein, "Three Cultures of Management: The Key to Organizational Learning," *Sloan Management Review,* Fall 1996, pp. 9–20.
23. Kotter and Heskett, *Corporate Culture and Performance.*
24. Justin Martin, "The Man Who Boogied Away a Billion," *Fortune,* December 23, 1996, pp. 89–100.
25. Ralph H. Kilmann, Mary J. Saxton, Roy Serpa, and Associates, *Gaining Control of the Corporate Culture* (San Francisco: Jossey-Bass, 1985).
26. Oren Harari, "Curing the M&A Madness," *Management Review,* July/August 1997, pp. 53–56; Morty Lefkoe, "Why So Many Mergers Fail," *Fortune,* June 20, 1987, pp. 113–114.
27. Edward O. Welles, "Mis-Match," *Inc.,* June 1994, pp. 70–79; Thomas A. Stewart, "Rate Your Readiness to Change," *Fortune,* February 7, 1994, pp. 106–110.
28. "Reed: Reflections on a Culture Clash," box in Patricia Sellers, "Behind the Shootout at Citigroup," *Fortune,* March 20, 2000, pp. 27–32.
29. Mary Anne DeVanna and Noel Tichy. (1990, Winter). "Creating the competitive organization of the twenty-first century: The boundaryless corporation." *Human Resource Management 29*: 455–471; and Fred Kofman and Peter M. Senge. (1993, Autumn). "Communities of commitment: The heart of learning organizations." *Organizational Dynamics 22*(2): 4–23.
30. Paul Roberts, "The Best Interest of the Patient is the Only Interest to be Considered," *Fast Company,* April 1999, pp. 149–162.
31. Marc Ballon, "The Cheapest CEO in America," *Inc.,* October 1997, pp. 53–61.
32. Polly Schneider, "The Renaissance Company," *CIO,* December 15, 1998–January 1, 1999, pp. 66–76.
33. Harrison M. Trice and Janice M. Beyer. (1984). "Studying organizational cultures through rites and ceremonials." *Academy of Management Review 9*: 653–669.
34. Don Hellriegle and John W. Slocum Jr., *Management,* 7th ed. (Cincinnati, OH: South-Western College Publishing, 1996), p. 537.
35. Alan Farnham, "Mary Kay's Lessons in Leadership," *Fortune,* September 20, 1993, pp. 68–77.
36. Robert F. Dennehy, "The Executive as Storyteller," *Management Review,* March 1999, pp. 40–43; and Elizabeth Weil, "Every Leader Tells a Story," *Fast Company,* June-July 1998, pp. 38–39.
37. Robert E. Quinn and Gretchen M. Spreitzer, "The Road to Empowerment: Seven Questions Every Leader Should Consider," *Organizational Dynamics,* Autumn 1997, pp. 37–49.
38. "Make No Mistake," *Inc.,* June 1989, p. 115.
39. Kirsner, "Designed for Innovation."
40. David Beardsley, "This Company Doesn't Brake for (Sacred) Cows," *Fast Company,* August 1998, pp. 66–68.
41. Gerald E. Ledford Jr., Jon R. Wendenhof, and James T. Strahley. (1995, Winter). "Realizing a corporate philosophy." *Organizational Dynamics 23*(3): 5–19.
42. Thomas J. Peters and Robert H. Waterman Jr., *In Search of Excellence* (New York: Warner Books, 1988).
43. Deanne N. Den Hartog, Jaap J. Van Muijen, and Paul L. Koopman. (1996). "Linking transformational leadership and organizational culture." *The Journal of Leadership Studies 3*(4): 68–83; and Schein, "Organizational culture."
44. Steve Lohr, "On the Road with Chairman Lou," *The New York Times,* June 26, 1994, secs. 1, 3.
45. E. A. Schein and J. Van Maanen, "Toward a Theory of Organizational Socialization," in B. M. Staw (ed.), *Research in Organizational Behavior* (Greenwich, CT: JAI Press, 1979); J. Van Maanen, "Breaking In: Socialization to Work," in R. Dubin (ed.), *Handbook of Work: Organization and Society* (Chicago: Rand McNally, 1976); and G. T. Chao, A. M. O'Leary-Kelly, S. Wolf, H. J. Klein, and P. D. Gardner. (1994, October). "Organizational socialization: Its content and consequences." *Journal of Applied Psychology*: 730–743.
46. Daniel C. Feldman. (1981, April). "The multiple socialization of organization members." *Academy of Management Review*: 309–318.
47. B. E. Ashforth and A. M. Saks. (1996, February). "Socialization tactics: Longitudinal effects on newcomer adjustment." *Academy of Management Journal*:149–178; and R. H. Heck, "Organizational and Professional Socialization: Its Impact on the Performance of New Administrators," *The Urban Review,* March 1995, pp. 31–49.
48. J. P. Wanous, *Organizational Entry* (Reading, MA: Addison-Wesley, 1980).
49. Larry Reibstein, "Crushed Hopes: When a New Job Proves to Be Something Different," *The Wall Street Journal,* June 10, 1987.
50. Richard Pascale, "Fitting New Employees into the Company Culture," *Fortune,* May 28, 1984, pp. 28–39; and Richard Pascale. (1985, Winter). "The paradox of 'corporate culture': Reconciling ourselves to socialization." *California Management Review 29*: 26–41.
51. Stephanie Gruner, "Lasting Impressions," *Inc.,* July 1998, p. 126.
52. Eric Ransdell, "The Nike Story? Just Tell It!" *Fast Company,* January-February 2000, pp. 44–46.
53. Kathy E. Kram, *Mentoring at Work: Developmental Relationships in Organizational Life* (Glenview, IL: Scott Foresman, 1985).
54. K. E. Kram. (1983). "Phases of the mentor relationship." *Academy of Management Journal 26*: 608–625.
55. Mary Zey, "A Mentor for All," *Personnel Journal,* January 1988, pp. 46–51.
56. W. Whitely, T. Dougherty, and G. Dreher. (1991). "Relationship of career mentoring and socioeconomic origins to managers' and professionals' early career progress." *Academy of Management Journal 34*: 331–351; and E. Fagenson (1989). "The mentor advantage: Perceived career/job experiences of proteges and nonproteges." *Journal of Organizational Studies 10*: 309–320.
57. Gail Dutton, "Building a Global Brain," *Management Review,* May 1999, pp. 34–38.
58. S. C. Schneider, "National vs. Corporate Culture: Implications for Human Resource Management," *Human Resource Management,* Summer 1988, p. 239.
59. Dutton, "Building a Global Brain."
60. Michael Davis, "Dollar General Jobs Offer 'A Way Out', " *The Tennessean,* June 15, 1996, p. 1E; Lisa Benavides, "Workplace Ethics a Way of Life for Christians," *The Tennessean,* October 19, 1997, p. 1E; and Candy McCampbell, "Dollar General Wins Award," *The Tennessean,* April 19, 1997, p. 1E.
61. Gordon F. Shea, *Practical Ethics* (New York: American Management Association, 1988); and Linda Klebe Trevino. (1986). "Ethical decision making in organizations: A person-situation interactionist model." *Academy of Management Review 11*: 601–617.
62. Dawn-Marie Driscoll, "Don't Confuse Legal and Ethical Standards," *Business Ethics,* July/August 1996, p. 44.
63. Alison Boyd, "Employee Traps—Corruption in the Workplace," *Management Review,* September 1997, p. 9.
64. Robert J. House, Andre Delbecq, and Toon W. Taris, "Value Based Leadership: An Integrated Theory and an Empirical Test," working paper.
65. "Best Moves of 1995," *Business Ethics,* January/February 1996, p. 23.

66. Linda Klebe Treviño and Katherine A. Nelson, *Managing Business Ethics: Straight Talk about How to Do It Right,* 2nd ed. (New York: John Wiley & Sons Inc., 1999) pp. 274–283.

67. L. Kohlberg, "Moral Stages and Moralization: The Cognitive-Developmental Approach," in T. Likona (ed.), *Moral Development and Behavior: Theory, Research, and Social Issues* (New York: Holt, Rinehart & Winston, 1976); and Jill W. Graham. (1995, January). "Leadership, moral development, and citizenship behavior." *Business Ethics Quarterly 5* (1): 43–54.

68. Carolyn Wiley, "The ABCs of Business Ethics: Definitions, Philosophies, and Implementation," *IM,* January-February 1995, pp. 2–27.

69. Beverly Geber, "The Right and Wrong of Ethics Offices," *Training,* October 1995, pp. 102–118.

70. Jennifer Reese, "Starbucks: Inside the Coffee Cult," *Fortune,* December 9, 1996, pp. 190–200.

71. Eugene Garaventa. (1994, December). *"An Enemy of the People* by Henrik Ibsen: The politics of whistle-blowing." *Journal of Management Inquiry 3*(4): 369–374; and Marcia P. Miceli and Janet P. Near. (1994). "Whistleblowing: Reaping the benefits." *Academy of Management Executive 8*(3): 65–74.

CHAPTER 18

1. David H. Freedman, "Intensive Care," *Inc.,* February 1999, pp. 72–80.

2. Brent Schlender, "Steve Jobs' Apple Gets Way Cooler," *Fortune,* January 24, 2000, pp. 66–71; Geoffrey Colvin, "The Truth Can Hurt—Get Used To It," *Fortune,* February 7, 2000, pp. 52–53; Louis Kraar, "The Man Who Shook Up Samsung," *Fortune,* January 24, 2000, p. 28; and Curtis Sittenfeld, "Here's How GSA Changed Its Ways," *Fast Company,* June 1999, pp. 86–88.

3. Marlene Piturro, "The Transformation Officer," *Management Review,* February 2000, pp. 21–25.

4. Peter F. Drucker, *Management Challenges for the 21st Century* (New York: HarperBusiness, 1999).

5. Barbara Ettorre, "Change Management," *Management Review,* May 1999, p. 8.

6. Joseph B. White, "There Are No German or U.S. Companies, Only Successful Ones," *The Wall Street Journal,* May 7, 1998, p. A1.

7. Ian Katz, "Whirlpool: In the Wringer," *Business Week,* December 14, 1998, pp. 83–85.

8. Cesare R. Mainardi, Martin Salia, and Muir Sanderson, "Label of Origin: Made on Earth," *Strategy & Business,* Issue 15, Second Quarter 1999, pp. 42–53.

9. R. Duane Ireland and Michael A. Hitt. (1999). "Achieving and maintaining strategic competitiveness in the 21st century: The role of strategic leadership." *Academy of Management Executive 13* (1): 43–57.

10. Robert D. Hof with Gary McWilliams and Gabrielle Saveri, "The 'Click Here' Economy," *Business Week,* June 22, 1998, pp. 122–128.

11. Megan Santosus, "The Organic Root System," *CIO,* December 15, 1998–January 1, 1999, pp. 38–45.

12. Thomas A. Stewart, "Is This Job Really Necessary?" *Fortune,* January 12, 1998, pp. 154–155.

13. Barbara Ettorre, "It's In the Mix," *Management Review,* February 2000, p. 9. Also see Claire Raines, Ron Zemke, and Bob Filipczak, *Generations at Work: Managing the Clash of Veterans, Boomers, Xers, and Nexters in Your Workplace* (New York: AMACOM, 1999).

14. Sittenfeld, "Here's How GSA Changed Its Ways."

15. Peter Galuszka and Ellen Neuborne, with Wendy Zellner, "P & G's Hottest New Product: P & G," *Business Week,* October 5, 1998, pp. 92, 96; and Katrina Brooker, "Can Procter & Gamble Change Its Culture, Protect Its Market Share, and Find the Next Tide?" *Fortune,* April 26, 1999, pp. 146–152.

16. Gary Abramson, "From the Ashes," *CIO,* December 15, 1998–January 1, 1999, pp. 57–64.

17. Ireland and Hitt, "Achieving and maintaining strategic competitiveness in the 21st century."

18. Based on Don Hellriegel, John W. Slocum Jr., and Richard W. Woodman, *Organizational Behavior,* 8th ed. (Cincinnati, OH: South-Western College Publishing, 1998), p. 595.

19. Edward E. Lawler III and Susan A. Mohrman, "Quality Circles after the Fad," *Harvard Business Review,* January-February 1985, pp. 65–71; and N. S. Bruning and P. R. Liverpool. (1993). "Membership in quality circles and participation in decision making." *Journal of Applied Behavioral Science 29*: 76–95.

20. Nancy K. Austin, "Tear Down the Walls," *Inc.,* April 1999, pp. 66–76.

21. Richard Teitelbaum, "How to Harness Gray Matter," *Fortune,* June 9, 1997, p. 168.

22. Richard L. Daft. (1978). "A dual-core model of organizational innovation." *Academy of Management Journal 21*: 193–210; and Rosabeth Moss Kanter, *The Change Masters* (New York: Simon & Schuster, 1983).

23. G. William Dauphinais and Colin Price, "The CEO as Psychologist," *Management Review,* September 1998, pp. 10–15.

24. Benson L. Porter and Warrington S. Parker Jr. (1992, Spring-Summer). "Culture change." *Human Resource Management 31*: 45–67.

25. Thomas Petziner Jr., *The New Pioneers: The Men and Women Who Are Transforming the Workplace and Marketplace* (New York: Simon & Schuster, 1999), pp. 27–32.

26. John P. Kotter and Leonard A. Schlesinger, "Choosing Strategies for Change," *Harvard Business Review,* March-April 1979, pp. 106–114; and Paul Stebel, "Why Do Employees Resist Change?" *Harvard Business Review,* May-June 1996, pp. 86–92.

27. Peter Richardson and D. Keith Denton. (1996, Summer). "Communication change." *Human Resource Management 35*(2): 203–216; and T. J. Larkin and S. Larkin, "Reaching and Changing Front Line Employees," *Harvard Business Review,* May-June 1996, pp. 95–104.

28. Rob Muller, "Training for Change," *Canadian Business Review,* Spring 1995, pp. 16–19.

29. Taggard F. Frost, "Creating a Teamwork-Based Culture within a Manufacturing Setting," *IM,* May-June 1994, pp. 17–20.

30. Phillip H. Mirvis, Amy L. Sales, and Edward J. Hackett. (1991, Spring). "The implementation and adoption of new technology in organizations: The impact of work, people, and culture." *Human Resource Management 30*: 113–139.

31. Minda Zetlin, "Clean Slate," *Management Review,* February 2000, pp. 26–31.

32. Joshua Macht, "Pulp Addiction," *Inc. Technology* (1), 1997, pp. 43–46.

33. David M. Schneider and Charles Goldwasser, "Be a Model Leader of Change," *Management Review,* March 1998, pp. 41–45; David Whitford, "Sale of the Century," *Fortune,* February 17, 1997, pp. 92–100; and Bill Trahant, W. Warner Burke, and Richard Koonce, "12 Principles of Organizational Transformation," *Management Review,* September 1997, pp. 17–21.

34. Kurt Lewin, *Field Theory in Social Science* (New York: Harper & Row, 1951).

35. *Ibid.*

36. This discussion is based on John P. Kotter, *Leading Change* (Boston: Harvard Business School Press, 1996), pp. 20–25; and John P. Kotter, "Leading Change: Why Transformation Efforts Fail," *Harvard Business Review,* March-April 1995, pp. 59–67.

37. Michael Barrier, "Managing Workers in Times of Change," *Nation's Business,* May 1998, pp. 31, 34.

38. Patrick Flanagan, "The ABCs of Changing Corporate Culture," *Management Review,* July 1995, pp. 57–61.

39. Noel M. Tichy and Mary Anne Devanna, *The Transformational Leader* (New York: John Wiley & Sons, 1986), pp. 122, 124.

40. Charles Matthews, "How We Changed Gear to Ride the Winds of Change," *Professional Manager,* January 1995, pp. 6–8.

41. Kotter, "Leading Change: Why Transformation Efforts Fail," p. 65.

42. M. Sashkin and W. W. Burke. (1987). "Organizational development in the 1980s." *General Management 13*:393–417; and Richard Beckhard, "What Is Organization Development?" in Wendell L. French, Cecil H. Bell Jr., and Robert A. Zawacki (eds), *Organization Development and Transformation: Managing Effective Change* (Burr Ridge, IL: Irwin McGraw Hill, 2000), pp. 16–19.

43. W. Warner Burke, "The New Agenda for Organization Development," in French, Bell, and Zawacki, *Organization Development and Transformation,* pp. 523–535.

44. Wendell L. French and Cecil H. Bell Jr., "A History of Organizational Development," in French, Bell, and Zawacki, *Organization Development and Transformation,* pp. 20–42.

45. Survey feedback is discussed in Wendell L. French and Cecil H. Bell, *Organization Development: Behavioral Science Interventions for Organization Improvement,* 4th ed. (Englewood Cliffs, NJ: Prentice-Hall, 1990), pp. 169–172; and David A. Nadler, *Feedback and Organizational Development: Using Data-Based Methods* (Reading, MA: Addision-Wesley, 1977), pp. 5–8.

46. Edgar H. Schein, *Process Consultation: Its Role in Organization Development,* 2nd ed. (Reading, MA: Addison-Wesley, 1988), p. 11.

47. Paul F. Buller, "For Successful Strategic Change: Blend OD Practices with Strategic Management," *Organizational Dynamics,* Winter 1988, pp. 42–55.

48. French and Bell, "A History of Organizational Development."

49. The information on large-group intervention is based on Kathleen D. Dannemiller and Robert W. Jacobs. (1992, December). "Changing the way organizations change: A revolution of common sense." *The Journal of Applied Behavioral Science 28*(4): 48–49; and Barbara B. Bunker and Billie T. Alban. (1992, December). "Conclusion: What makes large group interventions effective?" *The Journal of Applied Behavioral Science 28*: 570–591; and Marvin R. Weisbord, "Inventing the Future: Search Strategies for Whole System Improvements," in French, Bell, and Zawacki, *Organization Development and Transformation,* pp. 242–250.

50. Judy Quinn "What a Work-Out!" *Performance,* November 1994, pp. 58–63; and Bunker and Alban, "Conclusion: What makes large group interventions effective?"

51. Bunker and Alban, "What makes large group interventions effective?"

52. Drucker, *Management Challenges for the 21st Century;* Michael L. Tushman and Charles A. O'Reilly III. (1996, Summer). "Ambidextrous Organizations: Managing evolutionary and revolutionary change." *California Management Review 38* (4): 8–30; Gary Hamel and C. K. Prahalad, "Seeing the Future First," *Fortune,* September 4, 1994, pp. 64–70; and Linda Yates and Peter Skarzynski, "How Do Companies Get to the Future First?" *Management Review,* January 1999, pp. 16–22.

53. Chris Argyris and D. A. Schon, *Organizational Learning* (Reading, MA: Addison-Wesley, 1978); and Stephen P. Robbins, *Organizational Behavior,* 8th ed. (Upper Saddle River, NJ: Prentice-Hall, 1998), p. 649.

54. This discussion is based on Stephan H. Haeckel, *Adaptive Enterprise: Creating and Leading Sense-and-Respond Organizations* (Boston: Harvard Business School Press, 1999), pp. 75–92; and Petzinger, *The New Pioneers,* pp. 34–42.

55. Santosus, "The Organic Root System"; and Heath Row, "Great Harvest's Recipe for Growth," *Fast Company,* December 1998, pp. 46–48.

56. Arie de Geus, *The Living Company* (Boston: Harvard Business School Press, 1997).

57. Polly LaBarre, "This Organization Is Disorganization," *Fast Company,* June-July 1996, pp. 77+.

58. David K. Hurst, *Crisis and Renewal: Meeting the Challenge of Organizational Change* (Boston: Harvard Business School Press, 1995), pp. 32–52.

59. John A. Byrne, "The Corporation of the Future," *Business Week,* August 31, 1998, pp. 102–106; and "And the Winner Is . . . Cisco Systems," in "In Depth: Business 2.0 100," compiled by Walid Mougayar, project head; Michael Mattis, Kate McKinley, and Nissa Crawford, *Business 2.0,* May 1999, pp. 58–94.

glossary

ability What individuals know and can do if they choose.

academy culture A type of culture that values long-term commitment and mastery of job skills in a particular area.

accommodating Reacting to a conflict by trying to satisfy the other party's objectives.

Accommodators A learning style in which persons' strengths include leadership, taking risks, getting things done, and adapting to new experiences. They are often drawn to occupations such as sales and marketing.

accountability The fact that people with authority and responsibility are subject to reporting and justifying task outcomes to those above them in the chain of command.

acquired needs theory A need theory that proposes that certain types of needs are acquired during an individual's lifetime.

action or negotiation team A team of experts who often perform in specialized facilities or need special equipment. The team performance is usually synchronized with that of other units in the organization.

adaptive learning cycle The cycle of action, feedback, and synthesis used by learning organizations, in which employees sense the environment, try something, and make changes based on feedback.

adventure learning Team training in which members participate in physically challenging, structured outdoor activities.

advice or involvement team A team that provides decisions, suggestions, proposals, and recommendations. Its work cycle may be brief and may not be repeated. It usually includes members with diverse skills who may come from different parts of the organization.

ambiguity A condition in which the decision maker lacks information about possible alternatives and outcomes, and there is no clearly defined goal.

anchoring and adjustment effect A perceptual error that involves making an insufficient adjustment from the anchor (reference point) used.

anticipatory stage The stage of socialization that occurs before a person joins the organization and provides applicants with information that helps them anticipate what it would be like to work there.

aptitude An individual's natural tendency to learn or understand.

aspiration range The range of possible negotiated outcomes between the target point and resistance point.

assimilation effect The tendency to bias future judgments in the direction of past judgments.

Assimilators A learning style in which persons are strong in planning, creating models, and developing theories. Assimilators are in occupations that emphasize ideas and abstract concepts, such as strategic planning or research.

attention The stage in the perception process that involves noticing some of the information available and filtering out the rest.

attitude An evaluation that predisposes a person to act in a certain way and includes a cognitive, affective, and behavioral component.

attribution Using observations and inferences to explain people's behavior.

attribution theory of leadership A theory suggesting that the leader's judgment about and behavior toward subordinates is influenced by his or her interpretation of what causes an employee's behavior and performance.

authority The formal and legitimate right of a manager to make decisions, issue orders, and allocate resources.

authority structure A formal hierarchy of reporting relationships.

autocratic leader A leader who tends to centralize authority and rely on formal position, use of rewards, and coercion to influence subordinates.

autonomy The degree to which the worker has freedom, discretion, and self-determination in planning and carrying out tasks.

availability heuristic The tendency to base judgments primarily on readily available information.

avoidance learning The removal of an unpleasant consequence following a desired behavior.

avoiding Reacting to a conflict by neither seeking to meet one's own objectives nor responding to the objectives of the other party.

baseball team culture A type of organizational culture that emerges in fast-paced, high-risk environments and values and rewards creativity, innovation, and performance.

behavioral model A model of decision making that describes how people actually behave throughout the decision-making process.

behavioral theories of leadership A group of theories that suggest it is the behavior of the leader that determines leadership effectiveness.

behavior-based conflict Conflict occurring when an individual's behavior in a work role is inappropriate for his or her behavior in a nonwork role.

benefits Social insurance (Social Security), private group insurance (medical and disability), retirement plans, pay for time not worked (vacations and holidays), and family-friendly policies (such as child care) are examples of benefits. They are usually provided to employees as part of their compensation.

Big Five personality factors An individual's extroversion, agreeableness, conscientiousness, emotional stability, and openness to experience.

biological approach A job-design approach that focuses on individuals' physical capabilities and limitations. The goal is to minimize the physical strain on the employee by structuring the work environment around the way the human body naturally moves. The biological approach emphasizes the design of technology and equipment.

bounded rationality The practice of setting limits on how rational to be.

brainstorming Decision-making technique that brings together group members to generate ideas freely and spontaneously, without criticism.

bureaucracy A highly mechanistic organization, characterized by routine, highly specialized tasks; extensive formalization through written rules, policies, and procedures; centralization of authority; narrow spans of control; and a strict chain of command.

burnout Emotional exhaustion and a tendency to treat persons as objects and to negatively evaluate work accomplishments.

case study An in-depth investigation of one person's, group's, or organization's experiences.

causality The condition in which an independent variable actually produces the change observed in a dependent variable.

centralization The concentration of decision authority near top organizational levels.

centralized network A communication network in which most communications pass through a single individual.

certainty A condition in which the decision maker has full knowledge of all the relevant information.

chain of command An unbroken line of authority that links all individuals in the organization and specifies who reports to whom.

change stage The stage of socialization that begins when a new employee works out any value conflicts and begins to feel like an "insider."

changing A step in Lewin's change model that involves shifting attitudes and behavior toward what is desirable.

channel The carrier of a message.

channel richness The amount of information that a channel can transmit in one message.

charismatic leader A leader who has the ability to inspire and motivate followers to transcend their expected performance.

club culture A type of culture that is used in a stable, secure environment and is characterized by loyalty, commitment, and fitting into the group.

cluster chain A pattern of grapevine communication in which a few people convey a message to many other people; one person tells several others, then one of those people tells a few others, and so on.

coalition A group formed to achieve political objectives.

code of ethics A formal statement of the company's ethical values, stating the behaviors that are expected and those that will not be tolerated.

coercive power Power that arises from the ability to punish behavior.

cognitive abilities Individuals' mental capacity to think and analyze information.

cognitive dissonance A theory that people want to behave in accordance with their attitudes and usually will take corrective action to alleviate dissonance and achieve balance.

cognitive evaluation theory The theory that there are two motivational systems—an intrinsic system and an extrinsic system. One of its major assumptions is that providing extrinsic rewards for behaviors that previously had been intrinsically rewarding tends to decrease motivation.

cognitive styles The different ways individuals perceive and process information.

collaborating Reacting to a conflict by working with the other party to achieve the objectives of both parties.

collectivism A preference for a tightly knit social framework in which individuals look after one another and organizations protect their members' interests.

command group A formal group that consists of a manager and the employees who report to that manager.

commitment Adopting a viewpoint and enthusiastically following directions.

committee A long-lasting, sometimes permanent team in the organization structure created to deal with tasks that recur regularly.

communication The process by which two or more people exchange information using a shared set of symbols.

communication network A pattern of organizational communication describing who people communicate with.

competing Reacting to a conflict by trying to fully attain one's own objectives at the expense of the others involved.

competitive group rewards Rewards allocated to individual group members according to their successful performance within the group.

compliance Following the directions of a person with power, even if you do not agree with the directions.

compressed work schedule A schedule that compresses the workweek into fewer than five days by increasing the number of hours the employee is required to work each day. For example, employees may be required to work four 10-hour days.

compromising Reacting to a conflict by reaching a mutually acceptable solution in which each party meets only part of his or her objectives.

conceptual skills The ability to see the organization as a whole and to see how its parts are related.

confirmation bias The tendency to give heavy weight to information that reaffirms past judgments and to discount information that would contradict past judgments.

conflict Perceived incompatibility between two or more values, goals, or needs.

conflict aftermath The stage of conflict during which the outcome of the conflict creates conditions that influence future situations.

consensus The extent to which people engage in the same behavior or experience the same outcome.

consideration A type of leader behavior that describes the extent to which a leader is sensitive to subordinates, respects their ideas and feelings, and establishes mutual trust.

consistency The degree to which a person being observed behaves in the same way or obtains the same outcome at different times.

constructive conflict Conflict that contributes to a group's or individual's performance.

content theories Motivation theories that emphasize the needs that motivate people.

context satisfaction An employee's satisfaction with work conditions such as pay, supervision, coworkers, and job security.

contingency approaches Leadership models that describe the relationship between leader styles and specific organizational situations.

continuous learning Looking for opportunities to learn from classes, reading, and talking to others, as well as looking for the lessons in life's experiences. Organizations promote continuous learning through processes and systems that enable employees to learn, share their growing knowledge, and apply it to their work.

continuous reinforcement schedule   A schedule in which every occurrence of the desired behavior is reinforced.

contrast effect   A perceptual error that involves perceiving something as larger or smaller than it really is because it differs significantly from the reference point used to interpret it.

control group   The group of subjects in an experiment who are not exposed to the independent variable.

controlling   The management function of measuring performance, comparing it with objectives, and making any adjustments necessary for keeping the organization on track toward its goals.

Convergers   A learning style in which persons are good at making decisions, defining and solving problems, and applying ideas. Convergers are in occupations that involve technical problems, such as engineering or production.

cooperative group rewards   Rewards based on the overall performance of a group.

cooptation   Diverting factions in a power struggle by focusing them on a common goal.

coordination   The quality of collaboration across departments and hierarchical levels.

coordination costs   The time and energy needed to coordinate the activities of a group to enable it to perform its task.

counterproductive behavior   Activities that damage the organization, such as drug use, theft, or violence.

creativity   The ability to combine or associate information in ways that generate new ideas.

critical psychological states   Psychological states influenced by job characteristics including meaningfulness of the work, responsibility, and knowledge of results.

cross-cultural preparation   Activities for the employee and his or her family (or significant other) prior to departure, on-site, and in preparation for returning home (known as *repatriation*).

cross-training   Training in which team members gain an understanding of and practice each other's skills.

culture   The set of key values, assumptions, beliefs, understandings, and norms that members of an organization share.

culture change   A change in employees' values, norms, attitudes, and behavior.

culture gap   The difference between an organization's desired culture norms and values and its actual norms and values.

culture strength   The degree of agreement among members of an organization about the importance of specific values and ways of doing things.

data smog   Large amounts of data people have to face on a daily basis.

decentralization   The location of decision authority near lower organizational levels.

decentralized network   A communication network in which individuals share information equally.

decision   A choice made from available alternatives.

decision making   The process of identifying problems and opportunities, then resolving them.

decision support system   Computerized information system that uses decision models to analyze alternatives and recommend the alternative that will provide the optimal outcome, based on the user's information about the situation and goals.

decoding   Translating the symbols of a message in order to interpret its meaning.

delegation   The process managers use to transfer authority and responsibility to people in positions below them in the hierarchy.

Delphi method   Group decision-making technique in which the group uses questionnaires to gather anonymous judgments on an issue, then provides written feedback for comparing and refining judgments until the group reaches a consensus.

democratic leader   A leader who delegates authority to others, encourages participation, relies on subordinates' knowledge for completion of tasks, and depends on subordinate appreciation and respect for influence.

departmentalization   The process of grouping jobs into departments and departments into the total organization.

dependent variable   A variable that a hypothesis attempts to explain; the variable that presumably changes in response to the independent variable.

descriptive   Specifying what people do, not necessarily what they should do.

devil's advocate   Group role that involves challenging the statements and assumptions of the other group members.

differentiation strategy   A competitive strategy in which the organization seeks to distinguish its products or services from those of competitors.

distinctiveness   The extent to which a person being perceived achieves the same results on tasks that are much different.

distributive justice   Part of equity theory that focuses on the *amount and allocation* of rewards among individuals.

distributive negotiation   Negotiation under the assumption that gains for one party will come at the expense of the other party; a win-lose strategy.

Divergers   A learning style in which persons are particularly effective at generating ideas, seeing a situation from multiple perspectives, and being sensitive to other people's values. They tend to be in occupations that emphasize solving people problems, such as human resource management or counseling.

diversity   Differences among people based on their identification with various groups.

diversity awareness training   Special training designed to make people aware of their own prejudices and stereotypes so they can learn to work and live together.

divisional structure   An organization structure in which departments are grouped together based on organizational outputs.

domestic organization   An organization that operates within a single country.

double-loop learning   Learning that occurs when the organization corrects errors and solves problems by changing policies, procedures, or standard routines; provides an opportunity for radical change.

downsizing   A process through which employees lose their jobs.

downward communication   Organizational communication from a sender to a receiver at a lower level of the organization's hierarchy.

dual role   A role in which the individual both contributes to the team's task and supports members' emotional needs.

dysfunctional conflict   Conflict that interferes with a group's or individual's performance.

E → P expectancy   A judgment as to whether putting effort into a given task will lead to high performance.

effective follower   A person who thinks independently, is capable of self-management, and plays an active role in the organization.

effectiveness   Accomplishment of the desired goal.

efficiency   The achievement of maximum results with minimal resources.

eldercare   Care for aging or ill parent.

emergent behaviors   Activities that group members perform instead of or in addition to required behaviors.

emotional intelligence   The ability to accurately perceive, evaluate, express, and regulate emotions and feelings.

employee assistance programs (EAPs)   Services provided by or paid for by organizations that help employees with mental health, drug, alcohol, financial, and marital problems. The services usually involve either face-to-face or phone counseling with trained counselors.

employee-centered leader   A leader who focuses on the human needs of followers in order to build effective work groups and help them meet high performance goals.

empowerment   The delegation of power or authority to subordinates in an organization.

encoding   Selecting symbols, such as words or facial expressions, to create a message.

encounter stage   The stage of socialization that begins when a person first enters the organization and is designed to transmit information about how things are done within the company.

environmental uncertainty   A condition in which organizational decision makers have a difficult time acquiring good information and predicting external changes that will affect the organization.

equity theory   A process theory of motivation that focuses on individuals' perceptions of how fairly they are treated compared with others.

ERG theory   A need theory that identifies three categories of needs: existence needs (needs for physical well-being), relatedness needs (needs for satisfactory relationships with others), and growth needs (needs for development of human potential and the desire for personal growth and increased competence).

ergonomics   The science concerned with the relationship between an individual's physiological characteristics and the physical work environment.

escalation of commitment   An increased commitment to a previous decision in spite of evidence that it was wrong.

ethics   Principles and values defining what conduct is morally acceptable. The code of moral principles and values that governs the behavior of a person or group with respect to what is right or wrong.

ethics committee   A group of employees, usually top managers, appointed to oversee a company's ethics.

ethnocentrism   The belief that one's own group or subculture is inherently superior to other groups or cultures.

ethnorelativism   The belief that groups and subcultures are inherently equal.

euro   The single European currency that will replace up to 15 national currencies.

eustress   A moderate level of stress that energizes and motivates employees.

expatriates   Employees sent by a company in one country to work in operations in a different country.

expectancy theory   A process theory of motivation that proposes that motivation depends on individuals' expectations about their ability to perform tasks and receive desired rewards.

expectations   Beliefs about future events.

experimental group   The group of subjects in an experiment who are exposed to the independent variable.

expert power   Power that arises from important knowledge or skill.

extinction   The withdrawal of a positive reward, meaning that behavior is no longer reinforced and hence is less likely to occur in the future.

extrinsic rewards   Rewards given by another person as a result of a particular action, such as completion of a task, good performance, or positive behavior. Examples include promotions and pay increases.

feedback   A response from the receiver of a message to the original sender.

felt conflict   The stage of conflict during which the parties are aware of the conflict and have an emotional reaction to it.

femininity   A cultural preference for cooperation, group decision making, and a desirable quality of life.

field experiment   An experiment conducted outside a laboratory setting (for example, in an existing organization).

field survey   A research design that involves identifying a group that the researcher is interested in studying, then gathering data by asking members of the group a set of questions.

filtering   Manipulating information being communicated so that it appears more favorable.

fixed-interval schedule   A reinforcement schedule that rewards employees at specified time intervals.

fixed-ratio schedule   A reinforcement schedule in which reinforcement occurs after a specified number of desired responses, say, after every fifth.

flexible benefit plans   Also known as cafeteria-style plans, benefit plans that permit employees to choose the types and amounts of benefits that best meet their needs.

flexible manufacturing systems   The use of computer-integrated systems for design, engineering, and manufacturing to produce small batches of custom products at a cost once possible only through mass production.

flextime   A scheduling option in which employees have some discretion over the hours they work, within certain limits.

formal communication   Organizational communication along lines of responsibility and authority.

formal group   A group formed by the organization to contribute toward attaining organizational goals.

formalization   The degree of written documentation, including job descriptions, formal rules and regulations, and explicit policies and procedures, used to direct and control employees.

fortress culture   A culture type that may emerge in a survival situation and offers little job security or opportunity for professional growth.

free rider A person who benefits from team membership but does not make a proportionate contribution to the team's work.

functional structure An organization structure in which positions are grouped into departments based on similar skills and common activities, from the bottom to the top of the organization.

fundamental attribution error The tendency to overestimate the impact of internal factors and underestimate the impact of external factors on other people's behavior.

general cognitive ability An individual's capacity to acquire, store, retrieve, manipulate, and use information.

generalizable Able to describe a larger population, not just the actual subjects of the study.

glass ceiling Invisible barrier that separates women and minorities from top management positions.

global business culture An organizational culture that emphasizes multicultural rather than national values and is open to new ideas from other countries and cultures.

global organization An organization with multiple headquarters spread across the world that relies on flexibility and customization of products and services to meet the needs of each global market.

global teams Teams made up of members whose activities span multiple countries.

goal A desired future state.

goal-setting theory A theory that suggests that employee behavior is influenced by a future state that the employee desires to reach.

gossip chain A pattern of grapevine communication in which one person conveys a message to many other people.

grapevine An unofficial network of employees who share information with one another.

group Two or more members of an organization who interact, share norms and goals, influence one another, and identify themselves as a group.

group cohesiveness Mutual attraction among group members and desire to remain part of the group.

groupthink Reluctance of group members to express opinions contrary to the group consensus.

growth-need strength The need for growth and development.

halo error A perceptual bias in which the perceiver has an overall opinion of someone, and that opinion shapes the perceiver's ratings of specific behaviors or characteristics.

heroes Figures who exemplify the deeds, character, and attitudes of a strong corporate culture.

heuristics Shortcuts for making judgments about the alternatives identified.

hierarchy of needs Motivation theories that propose that humans are motivated by multiple needs and that these needs vary in importance.

horizontal communication Organizational communication transmitted across a single level of the organization's hierarchy.

horizontal structure An organizational structure that organizes employees around core work processes.

host country The foreign country in which a parent-country organization is operating.

host-country nationals Employees who were born and raised in the host country.

human capital The knowledge, skills, and experiences of individuals, which have economic value.

human relations school A school of management that explores ways managers can influence productivity by establishing positive relationships with employees.

human skills The ability to work with and through other people and to work effectively as a group member.

hygiene factors The presence or absence of job dissatisfiers, such as working conditions, pay, company policies, and interpersonal relationships. When hygiene factors are poor, work is dissatisfying.

hypothesis A statement that tries to explain the relationship between two or more variables.

impression management The process by which people seek to control others' perceptions of them.

incentive compensation The use of such rewards as stock or cash when employees meet individual, team, department, or organizational goals.

independent variable A variable presumed to affect the size or intensity of another variable.

individual differences Characteristics that vary from one person to another.

individualism A preference for a loosely knit social framework in which individuals are expected to take care of themselves.

informal communication Organizational communication that is not strictly work related and may not follow lines of responsibility or authority.

informal group A group formed to meet personal needs; membership does not correspond to lines on an organizational chart.

initiating structure A leader behavior that describes the extent to which a leader is task oriented and directs subordinates' work toward goal achievement.

instrumental values Beliefs about the types of behavior that are appropriate for reaching goals. Examples are ambition, imagination, and politeness.

integrative negotiation Negotiation that seeks to give both parties what they want; a win-win strategy.

intergroup activities OD activities designed to improve the relationships between groups by examining and changing the attitudes, perceptions, and stereotypes they have about each other.

intergroup conflict Conflict between two or more groups with perceived differences in values, goals, or needs.

international organization An organization that has one or a few facilities in another country.

interpersonal conflict Conflict between two or more individuals with perceived differences in values, goals, or needs.

interpretation The stage in the perception process that involves looking for explanations for stimuli that have been observed.

intervening variable A variable that acts as the mechanism by which an independent variable affects a dependent variable.

interview A method of gathering data through open-ended questions asked by an interviewer.

intrapersonal conflict Conflict among an individual's values, goals, or needs.

intrinsic rewards The satisfaction a person receives while performing a particular action. Examples include feelings of accomplishment and challenge.

job characteristics model A model for designing motivating work consisting of three major parts: core job dimensions, critical psychological states, and employee growth-need strength.

job design The allocation or alteration of specific tasks and objectives to be attained by employees, including the expected interpersonal and task relationships, to improve productivity and employee satisfaction.

job enlargement A job design that combines a series of tasks into one new, broader job to give employees variety and challenge.

job enrichment A job design that incorporates achievement, recognition, and opportunities for learning and growth into the work.

job experiences Relationships, problems, tasks, or other features that employees face in their jobs. Motivation can be enhanced by providing employees with challenging job experiences.

job performance The measurement of how an individual's behavior or actions contribute to an organization's goals.

job rotation A job design that systematically moves employees from one job to another to provide them with greater variety and stimulation.

job satisfaction A person's positive attitude toward his or her job.

job simplification A job design whose purpose is to improve task efficiency by reducing the number of tasks a single employee must perform.

job-centered leader A leader who focuses on the technical and task aspects of the job and directs followers' activities toward efficiency, cost cutting, and scheduling.

joint optimization A principle that states that the organization functions best when the social and technical systems are designed to fit the needs of one another.

judgment The stage of the perception process that involves aggregating and weighting information to arrive at an overall conclusion.

laboratory experiment A research design that involves setting up an artificial environment in which the researcher controls the independent variable(s), then measures the dependent variable(s).

large-group intervention An approach that brings together participants from all parts of the organization, often including outside stakeholders, in an off-site setting to discuss problems or opportunities and plan for change.

latent conflict The stage of conflict during which differences in goals, needs, values, or perceptions give someone a suspicion that a conflict may exist.

leader-member exchange (LMX) model A leadership model that suggests that leaders develop unique one-on-one relationships with each subordinate, and that subordinates may exist in either an in-group or an out-group.

leadership An influence relationship among leaders and followers who intend real changes that reflect their shared purposes.

leadership grid A two-dimensional leadership theory that measures a leader's concern for people and concern for production.

leading The management function of using influence to inspire and empower others to work toward the organization's goals.

learning A change in behavior or performance that occurs as the result of experience.

learning organization An organization that embraces a culture of lifelong learning, enabling its groups and individuals to continually acquire and share knowledge.

legends Stories about historic events that may be embellished with fictional details.

legitimate power Power that arises from the authority associated with a position in an organization.

line-staff conflict Intergroup conflict arising from perceived differences between line employees and staff employees.

listening The process of hearing and interpreting the meaning of a spoken message.

locus of control Where individuals place the responsibility for the events that affect them; may be either internal or external.

long-term orientation Focus on the values of savings and persistence, which have future rather than present benefits.

low-cost leadership strategy A competitive strategy in which the organization seeks efficient facilities, cuts costs, and employs tight cost controls to be more efficient than competitors.

LPC scale A questionnaire designed to measure relationship-oriented versus task-oriented leadership style according to the leader's choice of adjectives for describing the "least preferred coworker."

Machiavellianism A behavior pattern that includes using deceit in interpersonal relationships, viewing others cynically, and lacking concern for conventional morality.

maintenance roles Roles that involve building and sustaining positive relationships among group members.

management by objectives (MBO) A method of management whereby managers and employees define goals for every department, project, and person and use them to monitor subsequent performance.

management by wandering around (MBWA) The practice of gathering information by visiting the workplace to observe and talk with employees.

management science school A school of management that applies the scientific method of research and sophisticated mathematical techniques to management problems.

manager A person whose responsibility is to achieve goals by enabling and directing the activities of others in the organization.

manifest conflict The stage of conflict during which the parties act out the conflict.

masculinity A cultural preference for achievement, heroism, assertiveness, work centrality, and material success.

matrix structure An organization structure that combines functional and divisional chains of command simultaneously in the same part of the organization.

mechanistic approach A job-design approach that emphasizes identifying the simplest way to perform a job to maximize efficiency.

mechanistic structure A structure characterized by rigidly defined tasks, many rules and regulations, little teamwork, a strict chain of command, and centralized authority.

mentor A more senior employee in the company who can provide guidance, positive regard, and acceptance.

mentoring The process by which a senior employee sponsors and supports a junior or less experienced employee.

message A tangible representation of the idea or other information to be sent in a communication.

moderating variable A variable that affects the relationship between an independent variable and the dependent variable.

monoculture A culture that accepts only one way of doing things and one set of values and beliefs.

motivation The forces either within or external to a person that energize, direct, and maintain behavior.

motivators Factors related to high-level needs, such as achievement, recognition, responsibility, and opportunity for growth. When motivators are present, work is satisfying.

multinational organization An organization with facilities in several different countries and a substantial proportion of sales in foreign countries.

multiple advocacy Group decision-making technique in which the group assigns different points of view to different group members, who must argue their assigned point of view.

national culture Shared knowledge, beliefs, and values, as well as the common modes of behavior and ways of thinking, among members of a society.

need for achievement The desire to accomplish something difficult, attain a high standard of success, master complex tasks, and surpass others.

need for affiliation The desire to form close personal relationships, avoid conflict, and establish warm friendships.

need for power The desire to influence or control others, be responsible for others, and have authority over others.

negative affectivity A person's tendency to focus on shortcomings and the negative aspects of life so that he or she tends to be angry, fearful, and depressed.

negotiation The process by which the parties to a conflict define what they are willing to give and accept in an exchange.

network organization structure An organization structure that subcontracts major functions to separate companies and coordinates their activities from a small headquarters organization.

networking Cultivating a range of relationships with people interested in trading favors.

neutralizer A situational variable that counteracts a leadership style and prevents the leader from displaying certain behaviors.

noise Anything that distorts a message.

nominal group technique Group decision-making technique using a structured meeting with three phases: (1) writing ideas individually; (2) discussing the ideas together; and (3) voting on the ideas by secret ballot.

nonparticipator role A role in which the individual contributes little to either the task or members' socioemotional needs.

nonprogrammed decision Decision for which there are no predetermined decision rules.

nonreactive measures A method of collecting data through means that do not directly involve the subjects, so they are unaffected by data collection.

nonroutine technologies Technologies characterized by high task variety, where the conversion process is not analyzable or easily understood.

nonverbal communication Conveying messages without words; communication through channels such as body posture and facial expressions.

normative Telling what people should do, not necessarily how they actually behave.

norms Shared standards of behavior that define what kinds of behavior are acceptable and desirable.

observation A method of gathering data by watching and recording behavior.

on-site preparation Orientation to the host country and its customs and culture through training programs or a mentoring relationship.

open communication Communication that involves sharing all types of information among all members of the organization.

open systems school A school of management that describes organizations as systems that interact with their environment, transforming inputs into outputs.

optimizing Reaching the best possible decision.

oral communication All forms of communication using spoken words.

organic structure A structure that is flexible and adaptable, has few rules, encourages teamwork that crosses functional and hierarchical boundaries, and decentralizes authority.

organization A social entity that is goal directed and deliberately structured.

organization chart The visual representation of a whole set of underlying activities and processes in an organization.

organization structure The framework in which the organization defines how tasks are assigned to individuals and departments, resources are deployed, and departments are coordinated.

organizational behavior (OB) The actions and interactions of individuals and groups in organizations.

organizational behavior modification (OB mod) The set of techniques by which organizations use reinforcement theory to modify human behavior.

organizational change The adoption of a new idea or behavior by an organization.

organizational citizenship behaviors (OCBs) Behaviors that individuals are not expected to perform as part of their jobs. Examples of OCBs include encouraging others to speak up at meetings or helping orient new employees even though it is not required.

organizational commitment A person's loyalty to and heavy involvement in the organization.

organizational culture System of shared meaning held by employees that distinguishes the organization from other organizations.

organizational development A planned, systematic process of change that uses behavioral science knowledge and techniques to improve an organization's health and effectiveness by improving internal relationships and increasing learning and problem-solving capabilities.

organizational environment All elements existing outside the organization's boundaries that have the potential to affect the organization's performance and goal achievement.

organizational productivity The effective and efficient achievement of an organization's goals.

organizing The management function of assigning tasks to departments, delegating responsibility, and allocating resources. The deployment of organizational resources, including human resources, to achieve strategic goals.

P → O expectancy Involves whether successful performance of a task will lead to the desired outcome.

parent country The country in which a company's corporate headquarters is located.

parent-country nationals Employees who were born and raised in the parent country.

partial reinforcement schedule A schedule in which only some occurrences of the desired behavior are reinforced.

path-goal theory A contingency approach specifying that the leader's responsibility is to increase followers' motivation to attain organizational goals.

perceived conflict The stage of conflict during which the parties perceive that a conflict exists, although they may not yet be able to define it.

perception The process by which people notice and make sense of information from the environment.

perceptual defense The tendency to protect ourselves from ideas, objects, and people that are threatening by selecting which stimuli to perceive and which to disregard.

perceptual-motor approach A job design approach that focuses on an individual's mental capabilities and limitations. In this approach, jobs are designed so that they do not exceed humans' mental capabilities. The focus is on making sure that an individual's information-processing capabilities are not overloaded.

performance The attainment of organizational goals by using resources effectively and efficiently.

performance cues Information from an external source that biases what people recall.

performance management The process through which managers ensure that employees' activities are meeting organizational goals.

person-job fit The extent to which a person's ability and personality match the requirements of a job.

person-organization fit The match between the individual's personality, goals, and values and the organizational culture.

personal control Individuals' belief that their behaviors determine what happens to them; they control the future.

personality The set of characteristics that underlie a relatively stable pattern of behavior in response to ideas, objects, or people in the environment.

physical abilities Strength, endurance, flexibility, coordination, and balance.

physical demands Stressors associated with the setting in which an individual works, such as inadequate lighting or little privacy.

physical withdrawal Employee turnover, lateness, and absence from work.

planning The management function of defining goals and determining how to achieve them.

pluralism An organization's accommodation of several subcultures, including employees who would otherwise feel isolated and ignored.

politics The activities through which people acquire and use power.

positive reinforcement The administration of a pleasant and rewarding consequence following a desired behavior.

power A person's potential to influence other people's behavior or to resist the influence of others.

power distance The degree to which people accept inequality in power among institutions, organizations, and people.

predeparture activities Careful screening, selection, and training of employees to serve overseas.

priming Asking people to recall a set of events before asking them to make a judgment that may be related to those events.

problem Difference between a desired state and an actual state.

problem-solving team Typically 5 to 12 hourly employees from the same department who meet to discuss ways of improving quality, efficiency, and the work environment.

procedural justice Perceptions of the *process used* to determine how rewards should be distributed.

process consultation An OD technique whereby a consultant works with managers and other employees to help them identify processes that need change; emphasizes involvement and improving interpersonal relationships but is also task directed.

process theories A group of theories that explain how employees select behaviors with which to meet their needs and determine whether their choices were successful.

production or service team A team directly involved in providing a product or service to customers, such as sales, food, chemicals, or repairs. Its work cycle is typically repeated many times, and it is integrated with customers and external suppliers.

programmed decision Routine decision made according to rules established for a particular situation.

project manager A person responsible for coordinating the work of several departments and individuals for the completion of a specific project or process.

project or development team A team that provides plans, designs, or prototypes of products or services. Its members may be specialists who are experts in their fields. Its work cycle differs for each project.

projection Assigning one's own thoughts and feelings to a person being perceived.

prototype A schema that summarizes a category of people or objects.

psychological contract What an employee expects to contribute and what the organization will provide to the employee for these contributions.

psychological withdrawal Wasting time, daydreaming, and goofing off at work.

psychomotor abilities Muscle control and precise manipulations of fingers and limbs.

punishment The imposition of unpleasant outcomes on an employee. Punishment typically occurs following undesirable behavior.

quality circle A group of volunteer employees who meet regularly to discuss and solve problems affecting their work.

quality of work life (QWL) programs Activities undertaken by an organization to improve conditions that affect an employee's experience with the organization.

quantitative ability An individual's speed and accuracy in solving math problems.

questionnaire A set of questions with a predetermined set of answer choices.

rational model A model of decision making that applies principles of logic and economics to describe how a person would arrive at an optimal solution.

realistic job preview (RJP) A selection technique that gives applicants all pertinent and realistic information about the job and the organization.

reasoning ability An individual's capacity to solve different types of problems.

reengineering The radical rethinking and redesign of business processes to achieve dramatic improvements in cost, quality, speed, and service.

reference group A group that people use as a source of examples to imitate (or avoid imitating).

referent power Power that arises from personality characteristics that command admiration, respect, and identification.

refreezing Stabilizing a change by reinforcing it and rewarding employees who support the new behaviors.

reinforcement theory A motivation theory based on the relationship between a given behavior and its consequences.

reliable Able to generate the same results, if the study were repeated.

repatriation Preparing employees to return to the parent company and country from the global assignment.

representativeness heuristic The tendency to base the assessment of an event's likelihood on false analogies.

required behaviors Activities that the organization defines as necessary conditions of group membership.

resistance Attempts to avoid following instructions.

resistance point The minimum acceptable outcome, as defined by one party to a negotiation.

responsibility The duty to perform the task or activity an employee has been assigned.

retrieval The stage of the perception process that involves recalling information about past events.

reward power Power that arises from the ability to grant rewards to others.

risk A condition in which the decision maker has defined goals and knows possible outcomes, but the outcomes are subject to chance, which the decision maker can estimate.

risk propensity The degree of willingness to assume risk in exchange for the opportunity of a possible return.

rites and ceremonies Organized, planned activities or rituals that make up a special event and often are conducted for the benefit of an audience.

role A set of behaviors that group members expect of someone in a certain position.

role ambiguity The condition of lacking information needed for defining how to perform a role.

role conflict Inconsistencies in the expectations associated with a person's role.

role demands Challenges associated with a role—that is, the set of behaviors expected of a person because of that person's position in the group.

role expectations Group members' definitions of how a person with a given role should act in a particular situation.

role identity The attitudes and behaviors defined as being consistent with a role.

role overload The experience of having the demands of a role exceed a person's abilities.

routine technologies Technologies that are characterized by little task variety and the use of objective, computational procedures.

satisficing Choosing the first alternative that meets minimal decision criteria.

schedule of reinforcement The frequency with which and intervals over which reinforcement occurs.

schemas Cognitive (mental) structures in which related items of information are grouped together.

scientific management A school of management that involves developing a standard method for performing each job, training workers in the method, eliminating interruptions, and offering wage incentives.

script A schema that describes a sequence of actions.

secondary research Research that consists of reviewing existing data and research reports to see what is already known in a subject area.

selection The process of finding and hiring people who have the skills to perform specific jobs and who will fit in with the organization's culture.

self-directed team A team of 5 to 20 multiskilled workers who rotate jobs to produce an entire product or service, often supervised by an elected member.

self-efficacy A person's judgment about whether he or she can successfully behave in a certain way.

self-fulfilling prophecy The effort to keep perceptions in line with expectations, resulting in high performance when expectations are high and low performance when expectations are low.

self-management leadership A leadership style that relies on the empowerment of employees and helps followers lead themselves; sometimes called *participative leadership*.

self-serving bias The tendency to attribute our successes to internal causes and our failures to external causes.

servant leader A leader who transcends self-interest to serve the needs of followers and help them learn and grow while also achieving the organization's larger purpose.

Shewhart Cycle A cycle of continuous improvement used in companies that have instituted total quality management; also called PDCA Cycle—Plan, Do, Check, Act Cycle.

short-term orientation Emphasis on respect for tradition, meeting social obligations, and present rather than future benefits.

single-loop learning Learning that occurs when the organization corrects errors or solves problems using past routines or present policies and procedures.

situational theory A contingency approach that links the leader's behavioral style with the task readiness of subordinates.

skill variety The number of diverse activities that compose a job and the number of skills used to perform it.

social facilitation The process by which the presence of a group causes performance to improve or decline.

social information processing model A model of job design that indicates that employees adopt attitudes and behaviors in response to social cues provided by coworkers, managers, and others with whom they come in contact.

social learning theory A learning and motivation theory that proposes that individuals learn to behave by observing others, or models.

social loafing The tendency of group members to reduce their effort as the size of the group increases.

social support Relationships with other people, who listen to problems and are sympathetic and caring. These relationships reduce stress levels.

socialization A process by which team members get acquainted with one another and are encouraged to engage in informal social discussions.

socioemotional role A role in which the individual provides support for team members' emotional needs and helps strengthen the social entity.

sociotechnical systems model A model of job design that recognizes the complex interaction of technical and human needs in effective job design, combining the needs of people with the organization's need for technical efficiency.

span of control The number of employees who report to a supervisor.

status An agreed-upon rank that people give to groups or individuals within groups.

stereotype A rigid, widely held prototype about the general characteristics of a group of people.

story A narrative based on true events that is repeated frequently and shared among organizational employees.

strain-based conflict Conflict resulting from the stress of work and nonwork roles. For example, a newborn child deprives parents of sleep, and they cannot concentrate as well on projects at work.

strategy and structure changes Changes in the administrative domain of an organization, which involves supervision and management; may include changes in reward systems, policies, coordination devices, control systems, and so forth, as well as changes in organizational structure or strategic focus.

stress An individual's physiological and emotional response to stimuli that place physical or psychological demands on the individual and create uncertainty and lack of personal control when important outcomes are at stake.

stressors Stimuli that produce some combination of frustration and anxiety.

subcultures Minicultures within an organization that develop to reflect the common problems, goals, and experiences members of a team, department, or other unit share.

substitute A situational variable that makes a leadership style redundant or unnecessary.

survey-feedback process An ongoing process of measuring employee attitudes, presenting the results to employees, setting goals, making changes, and measuring goal attainment.

survivors Employees who remain with the company following downsizing.

sustained competitive advantage A means by which an organization can create value better than current and potential competitors over the long term.

symbol An object, act, or event that stands for something else and conveys special meaning to others.

symbolic leader A manager who defines and uses signals and symbols to influence organizational culture.

synergy Creation of total output that is greater than the sum of its parts.

systems model of change An approach that recognizes that change in one part of the organization will have an impact on other parts of the organization and may require changes there as well.

target point The outcome desired by one party to a negotiation.

task A narrowly defined piece of work assigned to a person.

task demands Stressors arising from the tasks required of a person holding a particular job.

task force A group of employees from different departments formed to deal with a specific activity; it exists only until the task is completed.

task group A formal group that brings together employees to work on a particular project or task.

task identity The degree to which an employee performs a complete job with a recognizable beginning and ending.

task roles Roles that allow the group to define and pursue a group objective.

task significance The degree to which the job is perceived as important and having impact on the company or consumers.

task specialist role A role in which an individual devotes personal time and energy to helping the team accomplish its task.

team A unit of two or more people who interact and coordinate their work to accomplish a specific goal.

team building An OD intervention that enhances the trust cohesiveness, and success of organizational teams or work groups.

team training Coordination of the performance of individuals who work together to achieve a common goal. The three components of team training are knowledge, attitudes, and behavior.

technical skills The ability to understand specific tasks and to perform them well.

technology The tools, techniques, and activities used to transform organizational inputs (resources) into outputs (products and services).

telecommuting A rapidly growing trend in work scheduling, whereby employees use computers and telecommunications equipment to do work at home or another remote location.

terminal values Beliefs about what outcomes are worth trying to achieve. Examples are family security, social recognition, and achievement.

third country A country other than the host country or parent country; a company may or may not have a facility there.

third-country nationals Employees born in a country other than the parent country or the host country but who work in the host country.

time orientation The emphasis a culture places on the future versus the present and past.

time-based conflict Conflict resulting when work and life events interfere with each other. For example, jobs that demand frequent travel or long hours conflict with personal activities such as exercise or errands.

total quality management (TQM) An organizationwide effort to continuously improve the quality of work processes.

traits The distinguishing personal characteristics of a leader, such as intelligence, self-confidence, and appearance.

transactional leader A leader who clarifies role and task requirements and indicates how subordinates' needs will be satisfied in exchange for the accomplishment of established goals.

transformational leader A leader who motivates followers to bring about change by focusing on a vision, shared values, and ideas.

transnational model A model of organization structure and design that applies the concept of a boundaryless learning organization to a huge, global corporation.

two-boss employee An employee who reports to two supervisors simultaneously in a matrix structure.

two-factor theory The theory that two factors influence motivation. The work characteristics associated with dissatisfaction (hygiene factors) are quite different from those pertaining to satisfaction (motivators).

Type A behavior A behavior pattern that includes extreme competitiveness, impatience, aggressiveness, and devotion to work.

uncertainty A condition in which the decision maker knows the goal of the decision but has too little information to estimate the likelihood of the possible outcomes.

uncertainty avoidance A value characterized by people's intolerance for uncertainty and ambiguity and resulting support for beliefs that promise certainty and conformity.

unfreezing A step in the change process that makes employees aware of the problems and the need for change.

upward communication Organizational communication from a sender to a receiver at a higher level of the organization's hierarchy.

valence The value an individual places on an outcome.

valid Actually having the same meaning as the researcher infers.

values Beliefs that meet three criteria: they are stable, identify what a person considers important, and influence behavior.

values-based leadership A relationship between leaders and followers that is based on shared, strongly internalized values that are advocated and acted upon by the leader.

variable A characteristic that can be measured over time or among research subjects.

variable-interval schedule A reinforcement schedule in which reinforcement is administered at random times that cannot be predicted by the employee.

variable-ratio schedule A reinforcement schedule based on a random number of desired behaviors rather than on variable time periods.

verbal comprehension An individual's capacity to understand and use written and spoken language.

virtual team A team that uses telecommunications and information technology so that geographically distant members can collaborate on projects and reach common goals.

vision An attractive, ideal future for the organization that is credible yet not readily attainable.

visionary leader A leader who sees beyond current realities, creates a compelling vision of the future, and energizes followers to help achieve the vision.

well-being Positive mental and physical health as well as attitudes related to the job and the organization, such as job satisfaction.

wellness programs Programs that attempt to stop health problems from occurring by identifying health problems at an early stage (e.g., using mammography to find cancer) or changing negative employee behaviors, such as smoking.

whistle-blowing Employee disclosure of illegal, unethical, or immoral practices on the part of the organization.

withdrawal behaviors Psychological or physical behaviors that individuals use to avoid dissatisfying work.

work redesign Altering jobs to increase both the quality of employees' work experience and their productivity.

work specialization The degree to which organizational tasks are subdivided into different individual jobs; also called *division of labor*.

workaholism Working to the exclusion of everything else in life, resulting in obsession with work to the point that employees are physically and emotionally crippled.

workers' compensation claims Claims for monetary compensation by employees (or their dependents) for job-related injuries or death.

workplace violence Physical assaults and threats of assault directed toward people at work.

written communication Any communication whose message is encoded in writing.

zone of indifference The range of activities within which employees readily accept a person's use of legitimate power.

name index

company index

subject index

Causal attribution
  locus of causality and, 146
  models of, 146–148
  stability of cause and, 146
Causality in research, **660**
Cellular phones, 317, 318
Centralization, 522
Centralized network, 316
CEOs, 4
Certainty, 349
Chain of command, 520
Change. *See also* Organizational change
  avoiding, 435, 436
  stress and, 484
Change stage, of socialization, 602, **604**
Changing stage of Lewin's model,
  633–634
Channel (communication), 308, **310**
  appropriate, 327
  at Centex Homes, 511
  encoding and, 308
  in face-to-face communication, 313
  improving, 326
  information richness of, 311
  personal communication and, 324–325
Channel richness, 311
Charismatic leader, 402
Child care, 502
  benefits for, 180
China, 69
  joint ventures in, 40, 65
  market in, 40
Choice
  aided and unaided, 345–346
  in decision making, 344–347
Civil Rights Act (1964), 48
Civil Rights Act (1991), mentoring programs
  and, 56
Closure, in organizing stimuli, 130
Club culture, 591
Cluster chain, 315
Coaching, corporate, 435
Coalition, 427–429, 443
  for change, 635–636
Code of ethics, 610, 616
Coercion, overcoming resistance to change
  and, 631–632
Coercive power, 420
  as power source, 427
Cognitive abilities, 97–98
Cognitive dissonance, 112
Cognitive evaluation theory, 168–169
Cognitive styles, 101–102
Cohesiveness, in team, 283–286
Collaborating, 461–462
Collaborative work software, 184
Collective bargaining, power and, 428
Collectivism, 61
Collectivist culture, social loafing and, 251
Command group, 236
Commitment, 116, 422
  escalation of, 353–354
  organizational, 113–114
  in Vroom-Jago decision-making model,
  357
Committee, 278
Common sense, 5–6
Communication, 304. *See also* Channel
  (communication); Communication
  skills

barriers to, 326–328
at Centex Homes, 511
cross-cultural, 321–322
culture and, 63
directions of, 313–314
distortion in, 307–310
downward, 313
by entrepreneur, 333–334
face-to-face, 313
feedback in, 306–307
formal, 314–315
horizontal, 314
improving, 323–329
informal, 315, 316
by leaders, 410
in learning organization, 322–323
message in, 306
mobile office and, 368
during negotiation, 470
networking technology and, 547
nonverbal, 312–313
oral, 312
organizational change and, 622
overcoming resistance to change and,
  631
patterns of, 310–317
process of, 306–307
purposes of, 304–306
technology in, 317–321
upward, 314
of vision, 637
written, 310–311
Communication networks, 315–317, **316**
Communication skills, personal, 324–325
Compensation
  culture and, 221
  incentive, 213–216
Competing, 460–461
Competitive advantage
  diversity management and, 44
  of Microsoft, 89
Competitive advantage school, 12–13
Competitive group rewards, 258
Competitive position, maintaining, 3–4
Competitive style, of negotiation, 471
Compliance, 420–421
Composition, of group, 253–254
Comprehension, verbal, 98
Compressed work schedule, 500
Compromising, 460
Computer companies, competitive position
  of, 3–4
Computer networks, 547
Computers. *See also* Technology;
  Telemarketing
  in job design, 574
  and organizational effectiveness, 568
Conceptual skills, 18
Concierge service, as benefit, 180
Confidence, self-fulfilling prophecy and,
  127
Confirmation bias, 143
Conflict, 448
  accommodating, 459–460
  avoiding, 459
  competing and, 460–461
  compromise and, 460
  constructive, 450–451
  cooperation and, 477
  dysfunctional, 451–452

ethical issues in managing, 465–466
felt, 456
in going global, 476
intergroup, 450, 457
interpersonal, 449–450, 475–476
intrapersonal, 448–449
latent, 456
levels of, 455
line-staff, 450
managing, 462–466
manifest, 456–458
negotiation and, 467–473
parties to, 449
perceived, 456
reactions to, 458–462
reducing, 8
resolution of, 463–465
role, 243–245
sources of, 452–454
stages of, 455–458
stimulation of beneficial, 462–463
in storming stage, 285–286
types of, 448–452
Conflict aftermath, 458
Conflict management, among partners, 447
Conscientiousness, 99
Consensus, 147
Consideration, 386–387
Consistency, 147–148
Constraints, in decision making, 350–351
Constructive conflict, 450–451
Consultants, in decision making, 345
Contemporary approaches, to motivation,
  163
Content theories, 161
Context, high- and low-, 63
Context satisfaction, 175
Contingency approaches to leadership,
  389–399
  Fiedler's contingency theory, 389–392
  Hersey and Blanchard's situational
  theory, 393–394
  path-goal theory, 394–398
  substitutes for leadership, 398–399
Contingency factors, choice of organization
  structure and, 540–545
Continuity, in organizing stimuli, 130
Continuous improvement, 220
  at GE/Durham, 555
  Shewhart Cycle of, 559–560
Continuous learning, 106–108
**Continuous reinforcement schedule,
  202,** 203
Contrast, of stimuli, 137
Contrast effect, 141–142
Control
  culture and, 63
  formal vs. shared information, 644
  in network organization structure, 539
Control group, 658
Controlling, 21
  in chaotic environment, 35–36
Convergers, 105, **106**
Cooperation, conflict and, 477
Cooperative group rewards, 258
Cooperative style, of negotiation, 471
Cooptation, 440–441
Coordination, 525–528
  networking technology and, 547
  restructuring and, 552–553